BOYD'S BIBLE HANDBOOK

BY

ROBERT T. BOYD

HARVEST HOUSE PUBLISHERS
Eugene, Oregon 97402

BOYD'S BIBLE HANDBOOK

Copyright©1983 by Harvest House Publishers
Eugene, Oregon 97402

Library of Congress Catalog Card Number 82-81088
ISBN 0-89081-352-3

Printed in the United States of America.

Affectionately Dedicated

To my wife,
Peggy,

whose inspiration, encouragement,
and patience have been a constant
help in my ministry of writing.

Acknowledgements

The author wishes to express his appreciation to Dr. George B. Fletcher, whose research in many areas helped make this volume possible. Also, to Debbie Ann Uhler and Judy Hopkins for their help in typing, to my brother Ernest and my sister Helen McConnell, for their encouragement, and to my wife, Peggy, who labored many long hours in proofreading and checking Bible references and cross-references, and to George Mundell for his inspiration.

Material contained in this book is inexhaustible and the reader is to enlarge upon its contents. It has been gleaned from many sources, some of which are listed in the Bibliography, and excerpts given credit where permission has been granted and where the source could be recalled.

The King James Version is used throughout unless otherwise noted.

The Trustworthiness of the Scriptures

One of the greatest and most respected scholars of Oriental studies was William F. Albright. The list of his earned doctorate degrees would remind us of our government's alphabetical organizations we have today. He wrote the following concerning the Bible and historical findings—

> *"The reader may rest assured that nothing has been found [by archaeologists] to disturb a reasonable faith, and nothing has been discovered which can disprove a single theological doctrine. We no longer trouble ourselves with attempts to 'harmonize' religion and science, or to 'prove' the Bible. The Bible can stand for itself."*

Probably the most qualified Old Testament linguist of all time was Robert Dick Wilson. His skill as a linguist is phenomenal, unsurpassed. Born in 1856, he took his undergraduate work at Princeton University. He then completed both the M.A. and Ph.D., and completed further postgraduate studies in Berlin, Germany. He taught Old Testament courses at Western Theological Seminary in Pittsburgh, Pennsylvania, and returned to Princeton where he received international fame as a Hebrew scholar without peer. He was at home in over forty ancient Semitic languages! Dr. Wilson wrote the following about himself—

> *"If a man is called an expert, the first thing to be done is to establish the fact that he is such. One expert may be worth more than a million other witnesses that are not experts. Before a man has the right to speak about the history and the language of the Old Testament, the Christian Church has the right to demand that a man should establish his ability to do so. For forty-five years continuously, since I left college, I have devoted myself to the one great study of the Old Testament, in all its languages, in all its archaeology, in all its translations, and as far as possible in everything bearing upon its text and history. I tell you this so that you may see why I can and do speak as an expert. I may add that the result of my forty-five years of study of the Bible has led me all the time to a firmer faith that in the Old Testament we have a true historical account of the Israelite people; and I have a right to commend this to some of those bright men and women who think they can laugh at the old-time Christian and believer in the Word of God.*
>
> *"I have claimed to be an expert. Have I the right to do so? Well, when I was in Seminary, I used to read my New Testament in nine different languages. I learned my Hebrew by heart, so that I could recite it without the intermission of a syllable. As soon as I graduated from the Seminary, I became a teacher of Hebrew for a year and then went to Heidelburg, Germany. There I made a decision, and I did it with prayer—to dedicate my life to the study of the Old Testament. The first fifteen years I devoted myself to the study of the language necessary. The second fifteen years I devoted myself to the study of the text of the Old Testament, and I reserved the last fifteen years for the work of writing the results of my previous studies and investigations, so as to give them to the world. The Lord has enabled me to carry out this plan."* Thus did Dr. Robert Dick Wilson testify.

One of the stirring moments with his students occurred when, after a dissertation on the complete trustworthiness of the Scriptures, the renowned scholar said with tears in his eyes: *"Young men, there are many mysteries in this life I do not pretend to understand, many things hard to explain. But I can tell you today with the fullest assurance that—*

> *'Jesus loves me, this I know*
> *For the Bible tells me so.' "*

Contents

Illustrations & Maps

MAPS

Introduction

Dr. James M. Grey, a spiritual giant well versed in the Scriptures and a former president of the Moody Bible Institute, made this statement just before he went home to be with the Lord. ''I haven't even begun to scratch the surface of God's Word.'' To be sure, no one has ever been able to fathom the unsearchable riches of the Bible, yet God's people are without excuse if His Word is not pursued to find out how Christ is seen from Genesis to Revelation—they are without excuse if they do not have a working knowledge of enough verses to carry on an intelligent conversation about spiritual matters—if they cannot use several verses to help the lost to see their need of Christ, and if they are not knowledgeable as to what the Bible has to say about future events.

Within the pages of this Handbook one will find those things with which every believer should be familiar, viz., a condensed analysis (or survey) of the sixty-six Books of the Bible, its divisions, and what each Book is about (subject, purpose, etc.). There are a variety of subjects which illuminate many passages of Scripture, an in-depth study of the life of Christ, and over 1000 Bible Studies and Sermon Outlines.

There are 131 pictures, 12 maps, over 200 archaeological tid-bits relating to the Scriptures, types and character studies, over 140 prophecies listed, stating when they were made and when and how fulfilled, over 150 Bible customs explained, purposes of all miracles given, 100 scientific facts explained, over 100 illustrations, an encyclopedia of numerous Bible subjects with spiritual applications, a dictionary of symbolical language, figures of speech, Bible names and numbers, idols and gods, and separate indexes for prophecies, Bible customs, scientific facts, illustrations, archaeological tid-bits, sermon outlines, and a general index.

The main feature of this work is that it is a ''cross-reference'' handbook, which enables the reader and student to check the same subject in a number of other books of the Bible.

The desire of the author is that from these pages one might be challenged to have a greater desire to study the Word of God, and hopefully be helped by any information contained in this Handbook.

Robert T. Boyd

THE

BIBLE

❧

GOD'S

HOLY WORD

There is a Golden Key that will unlock for you the mysteries of the Sacred Scriptures. It will open the vault of God's exhaustless treasure of Truth. It will make the bells of gladness ring within your heart. The Lord Jesus Christ is the Golden Key. He makes the Bible an open Book.

Colossians 2:2,3

The Bible Palace

With the Holy Spirit as my Guide, I entered this wonderful Temple called the Bible. I entered the portico of Genesis, walked down through the Old Testament art gallery, where pictures of Noah, Abraham, Moses, Joseph, Isaac, Jacob, and Daniel hung upon the wall. I passed into the music room of Psalms, where the Spirit swept the keyboard of nature and brought forth a dirgelike wail of the weeping prophet Jeremiah to the grand, impassioned strain of Isaiah, until it seemed that every reed and pipe in God's great organ of nature responded to the tuneful harp of David, the sweet singer of Israel. I entered the beautiful chapel of Ecclesiastes, where the preacher's voice was heard, and into the conservatory room of Sharon, and the Lily of the Valley's sweet scented spices filled and perfumed my life. I entered the business office of Proverbs, then into the observatory room of the Prophets, where I saw telescopes of various sizes, some pointed to far-off events, but all concentrated upon the Bright and Morning Star which was to rise above all the moonlit hills of Judea for our salvation.

I entered the audience-room of the King of kings, and caught a vision of His glory from Matthew, Mark, Luke, and John; passing on into the Acts of the Apostles, where the Holy Spirit was performing His work in forming the infant church. Then into the correspondence room, where sat Saints Paul, Peter, James, John, and Jude penning their letters. I stepped into the throne room of Revelation, where all towered in glittering peaks and I got a vision of the King sitting upon His throne in all His glory, and I cried:[1]

> *All hail the power of Jesus' name!*
> *Let angels prostrate fall;*
> *Bring forth the royal diadem,*
> *And crown Him Lord of all.*

"This Book, which we call the Bible, contains the mind of God, the state of man, the way of salvation, the doom of sinners, and the happiness of believers. Its doctrines are holy, its precepts are binding, its histories are true, and its decisions are immutable. Read it to be wise, believe it to be safe, practice it to be holy. It contains light to direct you, food to support you, and comfort to cheer you. It is the traveler's map, the pilgrim's staff, the pilot's compass, the soldier's sword, and the Christian's charter. Here paradise is restored, heaven opened and the gates of hell disclosed. Christ is its grand subject, our good its design, and the glory of God its end. It should fill the memory, rule the heart, and guide the feet. It is a mine of wealth, a paradise of glory, and a river of pleasure. It is given you in life, will be opened at the judgment, and will be remembered forever. It involves the highest responsibilities, rewards the greatest labors, and condemns all who trifle with its contents." It *is* the Word of the living God, and is—

1. Indestructible: Matthew 24:35
2. Incorruptible: I Peter 1:23-25
3. Indispensable: Deuteronomy 8:3; Matthew 4:4; Job 23:12
4. Infallible: Matthew 5:18
5. Inexhaustible: Psalm 92:5

Subject of the Bible: Redemption: Ephesians 1:3-14.

1. Purposed and planned by the Father: I John 4:9,10
2. Accomplished by the Son: Matthew 20:28; I Corinthians 15:3,4
3. Revealed by the Spirit: John 16:7-9,13,14

"God thought it, Christ wrought it, the Holy Spirit brought it, the devil fought it, but I got it!"

Purpose of the Bible:

1. To provide a foundation for our faith: Romans 10:17
2. To make us wise unto salvation: II Timothy 3:15

    3. "For doctrine, for reproof, for correction, for instruction in righteousness, that the man of God may be perfect, thoroughly furnished unto all good works:" II Timothy 3:16,17

The Scriptures Were Designed by God to:

1. Testify of Christ: John 5:39
2. Search the heart: Hebrews 4:12
3. Illuminate: Psalm 119:105,130
4. Hear and apply: James 1:22; Luke 11:28
5. Make one wise unto salvation: II Timothy 3:15
6. Produce faith: Romans 10:17; John 20:31
7. Quicken: Psalm 119:50,93; Hebrews 4:12
8. Regenerate: James 1:18; I Peter 1:23; Psalm 19:7a
9. Cleanse the heart and our ways: John 15:3; Psalm 119:9
10. Make wise the simple: Psalm 19:7b
11. Promote growth: I Peter 2:2; Matthew 4:4; Hebrews 5:12-14
12. Build up the faith: Acts 20:32; Jude 20a
13. Admonish: Psalm 19:9-11; I Corinthians 10:11; II Timothy 3:16
14. Produce obedience: Deuteronomy 17:19,20
15. Keep from destructive ways: Psalm 17:4
16. Support life: Deuteronomy 8:3; Jeremiah 15:16
17. Sanctify (set apart): John 17:17; Ephesians 5:26
18. Work effectively in the believer: I Thessalonians 2:13; Colossians 3:16
19. Produce hope: Psalm 119:49; Romans 15:4
20. Comfort: Psalm 119:82
21. Rejoice the heart: Psalm 19:8; 119:111
22. Study daily and meditate upon: Psalm 1:2; Acts 17:11; II Timothy 2:15
23. Keep us straight doctrinally: II Timothy 3:16
24. Keep the believer from sinning: Psalm 119:11; I John 2:1
25. Try everything by them: Isaiah 8:19,20; Acts 17:11
26. Win souls: Psalm 126:6 with Luke 8:11-15
27. Bear fruit: John 15:3,5,7
28. Perfect the man of God: II Timothy 3:17; Colossians 3:16
29. Give victory over Satan: Matthew 4:1-10; Ephesians 6:11,17
30. Accomplish its purpose: Isaiah 55:11
31. Be judged by: John 12:48
32. Give assurance of heaven: John 14:1-3
33. Endure forever: Psalm 119:89; Matthew 24:35; I Peter 1:25

To Whom Was the Bible Written? It was written to the Jews (Romans 3:1,2; 9:4,5), and to the believer (I Corinthians 10:11; II Timothy 3:16,17). In other words, the Bible was written to everyone, especially *me* (Romans 15:4).

How to Read the Bible: Read the Bible *daily,* not as a newspaper, but as a letter from your heavenly Father—as a letter from home.[2]

1. When a cluster of heavenly fruit hangs within your reach, gather it
2. When a promise lies upon its pages as a blank check, cash it
3. When a prayer is recorded, appropriate it and launch it as a feathered arrow from the bow of your heart's desire
4. When an example of holiness gleams before your eyes, ask God to do as much for you
5. When the truth of Christ is revealed in all its intrinsic splendor, entreat that His glory and beauty may irradiate the hemisphere of your life
6. If a portion is difficult to understand, don't despair. Ask the Holy Spirit to either give understanding then, or be patient to wait

    The Bible can be read through completely in seventy hours and forty minutes at the tempo usually read in public services. The Old Testament can be read in fifty-two hours and twenty minutes, and the New Testament in eighteen hours and twenty minutes. To read all the Psalms will take better than four hours. To read the gospel account of Luke will take about three hours. And yet, there is such widespread ignorance of this Book! Everybody agrees it is the world's best seller, and yet many know nothing about it. If one is to show himself approved unto God, he must not only read this Book but *study* it as well, rightly dividing its truths, arriving not only at comprehension, but also at appropriation.

Views of Inspiration of the Scriptures:[3] Where there are groups of believers who give a statement of their views on the Scriptures, it will usually read something like this: "We believe in the Scriptures, both the Old and the New Testaments, as verbally inspired by God and inerrent in the original writings. . . ." Very seldom does one see a statement by those who hold views other than the above mentioned.

The fate of the Bible is the fate of Christianity. In every generation Christians have had their own battle to uphold the truthfulness of Scripture, and ours is no exception. The author of this book stands unashamedly for Bible inerrancy. But there are others who do not, and it is well to consider their views. When we encounter a modern-day view of the Bible we are thus encountering more than *a* view of Scripture. One's view of the Bible is so foundational that it will also be bound up with a total theology concerning God and man. What are some of the views which are current in our day?

1. The *Liberal* view, which regards the Bible merely as a collection of human writings containing fallible human insights which under the scrutiny of reason and experience are subject to revision and even reversal as human understanding advances. In this view the Bible is error-ridden, but nevertheless still bears human witness to God's activities and inner illuminations to people in past days. While this view (and variations of it) enjoys considerable acceptance today (tragically in many institutions which were founded to preserve truth), it nevertheless has led to a widespread loss of confidence in the authority of the Bible and has produced a liberal perspective and a labyrinth of modern theologies which are mere echoes of modern culture. This view would "de-sex" the Bible, making it to read that males would not feel superior to the female. "Our Father, which art in heaven," would read, "Our Parent . . ." "Son of God" would be changed to "this Unique Being." Instead of crying "Abba Father!" we would have to say "My loving Parent." Jesus would no longer be Lord, He would be mere "Teacher." Such terms which designate God as Father, Lord, King, or "He" are "accidents" to the modernists and liberals who say such terms have resulted from "limitations of human language." To them, it is a matter of "believe what you want, reject all else."

2. The *Existentialist* or *Neo-Orthodox* view, which identifies the Word of God not with biblical writings as such, but solely with Jesus Christ who is encountered existentially through the *errant* Scriptures. There is recognition of Christ as the revelation of God (Christ's existence to reveal God), yet what has been written about Him was done by fallible human witnesses (not witnesses who were moved by the Spirit of God). Such a belief would deny the bodily resurrection of Christ, His deity, or the personal and triune nature of God. This view lacks any objective, informative, Divine word of truth from which to derive a sure foundation for its theology and living.

3. *The Historic and Evangelical View,* simply stated, affirms that God has not only acted redemptively in history to reveal Himself, but He has also declared the meaning of His acts and life itself through the prophets and apostles. Thus the Bible is both the inspired human witness of God's revelation in the past as well as written revelation. Therefore, what the Bible teaches or affirms is the divinely authoritative Word of truth. Since the Bible teaches us only truth from God, it is totally trustworthy (reliable, valid, or inerrant). Furthermore, in the Scriptures God has revealed Himself, as well as objective truth or knowledge about Himself (though man subjectively responds to God through the truth of Scripture). Therefore, man has, in the Bible, true

information about God, Christ, man, the world, Satan, life, ethics, death, salvation, and the future, all of which are derived directly from God Himself.

4. The *Neo-Evangelical* view, which uses the language of Scripture to give the impression of a true belief in the inerrancy of Scripture, but stresses a "love for everybody, offend none regardless of their beliefs." It is not necessary to believe in the virgin birth of Christ, hell could be a figurative term, etc., etc. Doctrine is relatively unimportant. Fellowship with all is accepted, so long as they have a "biblical language." This is a permissive age—no room for narrow-mindedness. No room for separation. If the Bible doesn't spell something out in "black and white," then do it, regardless of example. The Bible is to be interpreted to suit one's fancy, not to be obeyed necessarily if others take offense. Error is not vigorously opposed. There is no separation from apostasy. Ecumenical evangelism is accepted. Always be positive, never negative. Overemphasize love. Local churches are not important. Theistic evolution is readily accepted. The end justifies the means. In other words, this view says the Bible doesn't really mean what it says, although they claim to be Christians.

Some Reasons for Believing in Its Divine Inspiration:[4]

1. The testimony of the Bible itself—by its unique representations:
   a. In relation to God: infinite, sovereign, holy, loving: Isaiah 6:1-3; Hebrews 1:8-12; I John 4:7-10
   b. In relation to man: condemned as debased in character and sinful in conduct: Romans 3:10-12,23; Genesis 5:6; Psalms 51:5; Jeremiah 17:9
   c. In relation to the world: evil, opposed to God: I John 2:15-17
   d. In relation to sin and its punishments: separated from God, death: Isaiah 59:2; Ezekiel 18:4; Romans 6:23b; James 1:15
   e. In relation to salvation from sin: saved by grace through faith, apart from human merit: Romans 3:20,24; 4:3-5; Ephesians 2:8,9; Titus 3:5
   f. In relation to Christ Himself:
   —His works: Matthew 11:4,5; John 14:11
   —His words: Luke 24:44,45; John 10:35; Matthew 5:18
   —His resurrection: Acts 17:31; Romans 1:4

The entire life and ministry of Jesus, together with His resurrection, set their seal to the Divine Inspiration and Authority of the Scriptures. In the resurrection of Christ we have the outstanding miracle of the New Testament, and its evidential value is most marked. It furnishes positive proof that Jesus Christ was all He claimed to be.

   g. In relation to Prophecy—fulfilled and unfulfilled: Deuteronomy 18:22; Isaiah 46:9-11; John 14:29
   —Regarding the Jew: II Kings 21:11-15; Matthew 23:37—24:35
   —Regarding the Gentiles (Nations): Daniel 2; Joel 3:12; Matthew 25:31,32
   —Regarding Christ. The Old Testament is full of Jesus

It was all that Paul had and used to preach the gospel (I Corinthians 15:3,4). It was what Phillip used to lead the Ethiopian Eunuch to Christ (Acts 8:26-39). All prophecy has Him as its theme. Therein we find the line of Messiah's descent, from the seed of the woman, of the race of Shem, of the line of Abraham through Isaac and Jacob, not through Ishmael and Esau, and of the tribe of Judah and the family of David. We also find predicted His entire life and ministry. His birthplace, His miraculous virgin birth, sojourn into Egypt, His forerunner, the character of His ministry, riding into Jerusalem upon an ass, His betrayal, trial, crucifixion, death, burial, resurrection and ascension, His second coming and personal reign—all these are predicted in unmistakable terms from Genesis through Malachi. In the New Testament we have many of these prophecies fulfilled (see PROPHECIES Fulfilled in Christ in Index).

No one but God can foretell the future with certainty; therefore, if it can be shown that the Bible contains numerous predictions that have been literally fulfilled, we at least cannot doubt that the Book came from God. The Bible *has* shown this. See PROPHECIES in each Book.

2. Unity of the text. There are sixty-six separate books bound in this one volume called the Bible. These books were written by forty writers over a period of almost 1600 years, separated by a distance of some 1500 miles. The writers were of different classes, from the king upon his throne to the humble fisherman with hard, horny hands. Portions were written in Babylon, the capital of the Chaldean monarchy. Some were written in Jerusalem, the capital of Israel's kingdom. Other parts were written in the wilderness where Israel wandered, in Rome, in Asia Minor, in prison, and in scattered parts of Palestine.

Though the Bible was written by forty writers, over a period of sixteen centuries, and in many places, it is ONE Book. It bears witness to ONE God, it tells ONE continuous story, it is ONE progressive unfolding of Truth, it speaks of ONE redemption, and has ONE theme—the Person and the work of Jesus Christ. There is perfect harmony of the writers who wrote during this period of many centuries. How can we account for such unity? The answer—"Holy men of God spake as they were moved by the Holy Ghost" (II Peter 1:21).

3. Universal appeal. Other "so-called" sacred writings of various religions appeal only to the cultural backgrounds of their founders, and are designed primarily to meet social needs. Hence, an oriental religion would have very little meaning for one, say, in the West. But the Bible meets the need of the individual heart, no matter who the individual might be or where he might live (see points a-e of point 1).

4. Miraculous preservation—its complete triumph over enemies who down through the centuries have sought to destroy it. Only God could preserve such a Book, and this He has done and is doing in fulfillment of His Word (Matthew 24:35).

5. The integrity of copies (translations) in various languages through human hands. Though there have been differences in the spelling of some words due largely to language barriers, its cardinal truths still stand, as shown by such discoveries as the book of Isaiah of the Dead Sea Scrolls and other ancient manuscripts (see SCROLLS in Index). "The exact transmission of the text of the Word by copyists through the many centuries is a phenomenon unequalled in the history of literature."

6. Perennial freshness. Though the story is old, its message is new, and for centuries its promises have given spirit and life to those who have sought and still seek the deep thoughts of God (John 6:63; Psalm 92:5). God's mercies are new every morning, and daily through His Word He loads His benefits upon those who have experienced His "so great salvation" (Lamentations 3:23; Psalm 68:19).

7. Scientific accuracy. The question is often raised as to the scientific accuracy of the Bible, and it is sometimes disposed of by saying that the Word of God is not a scientific textbook. It is not, but it does make some scientific statements. When rightly interpreted, these statements harmonize with all the known facts relating to the physical constitution of the earth, planetary and stellar worlds, man and his complex nature, lower animals, plants and vegetable life. There is *no* discrepency between *true* Science and the Scriptures. In Science nothing is a *fact* while it is in the *theory* stage. Many illustrations of Scientific fact will be borne out under the heading SCIENTIFICALLY SPEAKING Index.

8. Archaeology. Discoveries have confirmed the historical accuracy of the Bible, and have been helpful in illuminating many customs of antiquity (see CUSTOMS in Index). To date, no archaeological discovery which relates to biblical records has ever repudiated the the Word of God! The testimony of archaeology to the truthfulness or credibility of the Scriptures may be regarded as confirming evidence of their inspiration. See illustrations under ARCHAEOLOGICAL Index.

9. Reaction of the unregenerate to the preaching of the Word. They oppose and reject the things of God; they are foolishness unto them (I Corinthians 2:14). Only the redeemed receive and understand them (I Corinthians 2:9-13).

10. The manner in which the Bible comes to the aid of those troubled in mind and spirit as no other Book. The Bible is *"God's First Aid Kit."*

    a. If sudden trouble comes, one can instantly apply Hebrews 12:5-11

    b. If loneliness and fear steal over one's heart, a good stimulant can be found in Psalm 91

    c. If one is suffering from loss of memory and cannot remember the goodness of God, he can take a good dose of Psalm 103

    d. In times of failing strength and courage, one can try two or three applications of Philippians 4:12,13,19

    e. If one finds a bitter taste in the mouth and cannot speak lovingly of others, I Corinthians 13 is a good pill to swallow

    f. If the "thorn" in one's flesh persists and complications seem to arise, one can rely on a tried remedy—God's grace: II Corinthians 12:7-9

Men keep trying with their own prescriptions to cure man's inner needs, but failure awaits every case. But God's simple remedies, found only in the Bible, have never failed. "O taste and see that the Lord is good: blessed is the man who trusteth in Him" (Psalm 34:8).

11. The testimony of transformed lives—the influence of the Bible upon character and conduct. The purpose of God in redemption as revealed in the Scriptures is to restore fallen, sinful man to God from Whom he became estranged through sin; "to redeem them from all iniquity and purify unto Himself a peculiar people, zealous of good works" (Titus 2:14). Has this been done? The history of the Christian church replies in the affirmative! Saul, the persecutor of the church, became Paul the establisher of the church. The early New Testament saints, John Bunyan, Martin Luther, the Wesley boys, Spurgeon, Moody, Billy Sunday, Jerry McCauley, and yes, even this author, all have been transformed by grace divine, and attest to the avowed purpose of the Scriptures.

A mechanic was ridiculed by an engineer for reading his well-worn Bible during the lunch hours. Because he could not "prove" who wrote each book, the engineer sought to discredit God's Word. Finally the mechanic asked the engineer who wrote the multiplication table. "I don't know," replied the critic. Asked if he used it, he had to admit that he did. Asked why he relied upon something whose author was unknown to him, he heatedly replied, "It works in my profession." And so the mechanic said, "For that same reason I believe the Bible—it works out all right in my life."

Dispensations of the Bible: The entire period of Scripture from the creation of Adam to the "new heaven and new earth" of Revelation 21:1 is divided into several "ages" or "dispensations" of time. These periods are marked off in Scripture by some change in God's method of dealing with all men, with respect to man's sin and his responsibility. Strictly speaking, between eternity past and eternity future, there are three basic dispensations:

    1. Man innocent

    2. Man with types and shadows looking forward to the Cross

3. Man looking back to Christ's finished work on the cross

The Cross is the *center* of God's plan and purpose, with man on either side of it looking to the Lamb of God as the *only* means of his salvation (Revelation 13:8; Romans 4:3; Acts 19:4; 16:31; Revelation 6:9-14). Included in these three dispensations we have the different methods used by God in His dealings with man, such as:

1. Man in innocency
2. Man under conscience
3. Human government (man in authority)
4. Man under promise
5. Man under law
6. Man under grace
7. Man in the tribulation period
8. Man under the reign of Christ

Since Adam is the federal head of the human family (Genesis 5:3; Romans 5:12; Psalm 51:5), we have represented in him all these dispensations—

1. Innocency—
   a. Reign: Genesis 1:28
   b. Human government: Genesis 2:15
   c. Law and Grace: Genesis 2:16,17
2. Before expulsion from Eden—
   a. Conscience: Genesis 3:6,7
   b. Promise: Genesis 3:15
3. During and after expulsion from Eden—
   a Grace:
   —Ground cursed for Adam's sake: Genesis 3:17
   —Clothed with "coats of skin": Genesis 3:21
   —Entrance to Eden closed: Genesis 3:24

The Holy Spirit has been active since the creation of the earth. Note His activity before and after the Cross—

1. In creation: Genesis 1:2b
2. In man's creation (let "Us"): Genesis 1:26,27
3. In convicting of sin: Genesis 6:3; Acts 7:51; John 16:7-9
4. "*In*" and "*within*" the prophets to testify: Nehemiah 9:30; Isaiah 63:10,11
5. In instructing God's people: Nehemiah 9:20; John 16:13

The gospel, God's good news of man's deliverance from sin, is the theme of the Bible in any dispensation. Notice the "gospel" and "Christ," especially before the Cross—

1. Coats of skin—sacrifice; Adam's deliverance: Genesis 3:21
2. The gospel preached: Galatians 3:8; John 8:56
3. Faith counted for righteousness: Romans 4:3
4. The reproach of Christ: Hebrews 11:26
5. Christ in the wilderness: I Corinthians 10:4,9
6. The "Spirit of Christ" *in* the prophets: I Peter 1:10,11

Though man is still under conscience, human government, promise, law, and grace, he has lost his right to reign, except "in the heavenlies in Christ Jesus" (Ephesians 2:6). There is yet the "Blessed Hope" (rapture: Titus 2:13; I Thessalonians 4:16,17), and the coming of Christ in glory (II Thessalonians 1:7-10), when the believer shall rule and reign with Christ on earth (Revelation 5:10; 20:6).

The consummation of the ages is when Satan is "loosed for a little season" to make war against the saints of God (See SATAN, Why Loosed, in Index). He and his army are defeated with fire from heaven being poured out upon them. Then follows the "Great White Throne" judgment, and the ushering in of a "new heaven and a new earth" (Revelation 21,21; II Peter 3:13,14).

The Bible is primarily a history of man's redemption, not a history of man. It opens with man under probation, disobedient, paradise lost, and salvation instituted with the promise of the "seed of the woman" (Genesis 3:15). The Bible closes with the promise of man redeemed, and paradise regained (Revelation 21,22).

Divisions of the Bible: The division into chapters and verses as we find the arrangement today was made about the year 1550 by Robert Stephens, a printer of Paris. We do not find these divisions in the original. The King James version of the Bible contains 66 books—39 in the Old Testament and 27 in the New. There are 31,173 verses, 774,746 words, and 3,566,480 letters in the entire Bible. The longest chapter is Psalm 119, and the shortest, and middle, is Psalm 117. The longest verse is Esther 8:9, and the shortest is John 11:35. The middle verse in Scripture is Psalm 118:8, and contains a message for all: "It is better to trust in the Lord than to put confidence in man."

Titles of the Bible: The word "Bible" is taken from the Greek word *Biblos,* which signifies *book.* Christ and His followers referred to the Old Testament books as "the Scriptures" (Matthew 21:42; Luke 24:27; John 5:39; Acts 18:24; Romans 15:4). While teaching and preaching Christ also designated them as those things "which were written in the law of Moses, and in the prophets, and in Psalms" (Luke 24:44,45), and "the law and the prophets" (Matthew 5:17; 11:13). Paul referred to them as "the holy Scriptures" as well as "the oracles of God" (Romans 1:2; 3:2). The two parts of the Bible are called the Old and New Testaments, or covenants (II Corinthians 3:6,14). The earliest of Paul's Epistles in the New Testament are referred to as "Scriptures" (II Peter 3:16). The Old Testament is the New concealed, and the New Testament is the Old revealed.

PREACH THE BIBLE[5]

I am greatly disappointed with some preachers of today,
With their logic and their ethics, their aristocratic way;
With their science and their theories and their new theology,
Full of everything but Jesus and His love for you and me.

There is plenty in the Bible for preachers of today
If they will but search its pages and for help Divine would pray;
For God's Word is everlasting—it never will grow old,
'Tis indeed a priceless treasure—far more precious than gold.

If the preachers in our churches would preach Jesus crucified,
How through love for us He suffered and through love for us He died,
Then our lives would not be empty as so many are today,
But be filled to overflowing in a Pentecostal way!

What we need is just plain gospel, in the good old-fashioned way,
Place of Emerson and Shakespeare, or topics of the day.
What care we for all their sayings, or teachings true and tried?
We want the dear old story of the Savior crucified!

What we need is consecration in a good true man of God,
With a Bible education, and a love for God's dear Word;
Who can lead us and direct us to the Truth, the Life, the Way,
Who brings peace to soul and body through the burdens of the day.

This alone can save the sinner, this alone can set men free,
  Just the precious dear old story of God's love for you and me;
That is what the people's needing, that is where the crowds'll be,
  Where they bear the same old story that they beard at mother's knee.

Part One
THE OLD TESTAMENT

Subject: Redemption as set forth in type, promise, prophecy, and Psalm: Luke 24:25-27, 44-47.

Purpose: To reveal the Person and work of the coming Redeemer: Hebrews 1:1-3; 9:6-14.

The Old Testament has
39 Books
929 Chapters
23,214 Verses
592,493 Words
2,728,100 Letters

Books of the Old Testament
DIVISION I
Law, or Pentateuch

In this division we note the following—

1. God speaking His word to reveal Truth
2. Supernatural intervention to promote faith and confidence
3. Institution of moral and civil laws to preserve society
4. The Tabernacle, for God to dwell among His people
5. The Priesthood and Sacrifices to promote obedience and separation
6. Memorial feasts to remind of the past, present, and future
7. Capable leaders to guide in His way

Subject: God's way in redemption as revealed in the beginning of His work: Psalm 103:7.

Purpose: To teach us the end of God's purpose in all His ways in redemption: Acts 15:18; Isaiah 46:9,10.

Genesis
Exodus
Leviticus
Numbers
Deuteronomy

Genesis—The Book of Beginnings

Name: This book is called "In the Beginning" by the Jews. The Septuagint labels it "Genesis" because it recounts the beginning of the world and mankind.

Contents: "Genesis gives to us a divinely inspired account of *direct* creation; Adam's sin and disobedience; the means of recovery through sacrifice and of the promised Seed—Messiah; and an account of the state of the spiritual seed of faith in the time of the patriarchs, both before and after the flood to the time of Joseph in Egypt. This Book starts with life (1:20-28) and ends with a coffin (50:26)."[1] It has 50 chapters, 1533 verses, and 38,267 words. See KEY THOUGHT.

Genesis shows that God first came down to create, then to do a work of redemption. To create He had only to speak. To redeem His fallen creature, He had to suffer. He made man by His own breath; He saves him by His own blood. When all around was life God spoke of death. Now when all is death, He speaks of life.

Character: Historical.

Subject: God's works and ways in restoring a ruined earth and His ways with seven men: Adam, Abel, Noah, Abraham, Isaac, Jacob, and Joseph.

Purpose: To introduce to us (typically) God's purpose and plan in redemption: 3:15,21; 22:8 with Galatians 4:4,5; John 1:29; Matthew 20:28.

Outline: The first eleven chapters cover well over 2000 years in telling of the origin of the universe and the race of man. From Genesis 12 through the remainder of the Old Testament is a period of approximately 2000 years, dealing with Abraham and his family. To God, Abraham and man in general are more important than the universe (Psalm 8:3-9).

I. The Beginning of the World: 1—11
   A. Account of Creation: 1:1—2:25
      1. Heaven: 1:1a
      2. Earth and the solar system: 1:1b-19
      3. Creatures: 1:20-25
      4. Man: 1:26—2:25. Some say that Genesis 2:4-25 is a second account of man's creation, differing from the account given in Genesis 1:26-2:3. The second chapter gives details of man's origin without repeating the story of creation as recorded in chapter one. Chapter two is referred to as the *Law of Recurrence or Recapitulation*. See RECURRENCE, Law of, in Index.

   B. Fall of man: 3—5
      1. Sin's entrance: 3
      2. Sin's development: 4
      3. Sin's result: Death: 5
   C. Flood: 6—9
      1. Corruption of man: 6
      2. Judgment: The Flood: 7,8
      3. New beginning: 9
   D. Nations: 10—11. See MAP (end of Genesis).
      1. Their origin: 10
      2. Their rebellion: 11:1-9
      3. Origin of the chosen Nation: 11:10-32

II. The Beginning of the Nation Israel: 12—50
   A. Abraham: 12—23
      1. God's call and Abraham's obedience: 12—14
      2. Covenant made and received: 15,16
      3. Covenant sealed by circumcision: 17—21
      4. Covenant confirmed by God's oath: 22,23
   B. Isaac: 21—27
      1. Miraculous birth: 21:1-3 (see 17:15-19)
      2. Offered by his father: 22:1-18
      3. Marriage and his family: 24—27
   C. Jacob: 27—36
      1. Vision at Bethel: 28
      2. Discipline at Haran: 29,30

3. Return to Bethel: 31—36
D. Joseph: 37—50
   1. Exhaltation in Egypt: 37-41
   2. Israel's settlement in Egypt: 42—47
   3. Last days in Egypt: 48—50

Scope: Period related to man covers more than 2,000 years.

Writer: Moses. See AUTHOR, p. 104.

To Whom Written: Israel in particular; mankind in general: Romans 15:4; I Corinthians 10:11; II Timothy 3:16,17.

Key Chapters: 1, Creation; 12, Abraham's Call.

Key Verse: 1:1. "In the beginning God created the heaven and the earth." When one *really* believes this verse, he will have little difficulty believing all the rest of God's Word. "This single verse refutes all the various false theories about origins that men have invented. Thus: *Atheism* is false because God *is* [a fact—a reality]. *Materialism* is false because matter had a *beginning. Pantheism* is false because God was *outside* His creation. *Polytheism* is false because there was only *one* God creating. *Evolution* is false because heaven and earth were *created.*

"Actually, all of these false philosophies are essentially the same. All theories or origins—other than the true account in the Bible—teach that the present 'cosmos' came into existence by the operation of the 'gods' or the forces of nature or some mystical principle acting upon the previously existing material 'stuff' of the earlier 'chaos.' Thus, all other of the explanations of origins, whether religious or philosophical or scientific [so-called], are basically only different forms of the concept of evolution."[2] It really takes more faith to believe in the theory of evolution than it does to believe the Word of God!

Key Word: Beginning.

Key Phrase: In the beginning.

Key Thought: The Book of Beginnings. In Genesis we have the beginning of everything but God Himself. Statements about creation—the beginning of heaven and earth, light, vegetation, and life (especially as it relates to man), are offered. Questions concerning creation, sin, prophecy, judgment, redemption, work, a day of rest, marriage and the family, childbearing, death, sacrifice, faith and obedience, races and nations, language, science and arts, and the Jew, are answered in a simple and rational way in the first Book of the Bible.

Spiritual Thought: Begin with God. With Him all things are possible (Luke 1:37). Without Him we can do nothing (John 15:5b).

Christ Is Seen As:
   1. Seed of the woman: 3:15 with Matthew 1:18-25; Galatians 4:4. *From* Him we receive a *New Birth*
   2. The Seed of Abraham: 12:1,2 with Galatians 3:29. *Through* Him we enter into a *New Family*
   3. Shiloh, our Peace: 49:10 with John 16:33; Romans 5:1. *By* Him we have a *New Relationship*
   4. The Shepherd—the Stone of Israel: 49:24 with John 10:11. *With* Him we have a *New Leader*

Covenants in Genesis: See COVENANTS in Index.
   1. Edenic—the Creative Covenant: 1:26-28
   2. Adamic—the Discipline Covenant: 3:14-19
   3. Noahic—the Human Government Covenant: 8:20—9:6
   4. Abrahamic—the Promise Covenant: 12:1-3
   5. Palestinian—the Land (territory) Covenant: 15:18-21

Names and Titles of God: See NAME in Dictionary of Names.

1. Elohim—Deity's relationship to man: 1:1
   a. As Creator: 2:7-15
   b. In authority over man: 2:16-24; 3:16-19,22-24
   c. In redeeming mankind: 3:8-15,21
2. Lord God—self-existent One, the ever-living, never-dying God: 2:4
   —Lord God—Creature relationship established with Creator: 2:7
3. Most High God—possessor of heaven and earth: 14:18
4. Lord God—Master: 15:2
5. Lord—the God who sees me: 16:13
6. Almighty God—the strong One, the all-sufficient One, the comforting, satisfying, nourishing, enriching One: 17:1; 48:3
7. Judge of all the earth: 18:25
8. Everlasting God—forever existent One, the God over everlasting things: 21:33
9. Jehovah-jireh—the Lord will provide: 22:13,14; Psalm 23:1; Philippians 4:19

Names and Titles of the Holy Spirit: The Spirit of God: 1:2. See NAMES in Dictionary.

1. Seed of the woman: 3:15 with Galatians 4:4,5. *Stated:* before 4,000 B.C. *Fulfilled:* Birth of Christ.
2. Covenant with Abraham's Seed—physical and spiritual (Isaac, Jacob, Christ, and believers in Christ): 12:1-3; 21:12; 22:18 with Galatians 3:16,29; Hebrews 11:17-19. *Stated:* 2,000-1,900 B.C. *Fulfilled:* 1,900 B.C.—through present.
3. Israel in Egypt: 15:13,14 with 42—46; Exodus 1:7—12:36. *Stated:* ca. 2,000 B.C. *Fulfilled:* ca 1850—1450 B.C.
4. Palestinian Covenant—the Land: 15:18-21; 17:6-8 with Joshua 1—11; 21:43-45. *Stated:* ca. 1925 B.C. *Fulfilled:* ca. 1450—1400 B.C.
5. Scepter not depart from Judah till Shiloh come: 49:10 with Luke 2:7,11. *Stated:* ca. 1700 B.C. *Fulfilled:* Birth of Christ.

Types of Christ:

1. Adam, head of the human race—Christ, Head of the new creation: Romans 5:12-14; I Corinthians 15:21,22,45; Galatians 3:22,26; Ephesians 1:22,23. There are at least eight things that came as a result of Adam's sin which have their compliment in Christ—

   a. Servitude: 3:16 with Philippians 2:7
   b. Pain: 3:16 with Acts 2:24
   c. Curse: 3:17 with Galatians 3:13
   d. Sorrow: 3:17 with Isaiah 53:3
   e. Thorns: 3:18 with Mark 15:17
   f. Sweat: 3:19 with Luke 22:44
   g. Separation: 3:8 with Mark 15:34
   h. Death: 3:19 with Philippians 2:8
2. Adam and Eve—Christ and His Church: 2:23,24 with Ephesians 5:31,32
3. Coats of skin—an acceptable covering of the righteousness of Christ: 3:21 with I Corinthians 1:30; I John 2:2; Revelation 19:8
4. The Tree of Life: 2:9 with John 1:4; Revelation 2:7
5. Abel, who offered a more excellent sacrifice: 4:4 with Hebrews 11:4; 10:12
6. Firstling of Abel's flock—sacrifice accepted: 4:4 with John 1:19

7. Noah:
   a. Pleased God: 6:8,9 with Matthew 3:17; John 8:29
   b. God's will revealed to him: 6:13-22 with John 17:4,8
   c. Prepared the way of salvation (ark): 6:14 with Hebrews 11:7; 10:19,20; Romans 5:6,8; John 14:6
   d. Finished God's work: 6:22 with John 17:4; 19:30
8. Noah's Art, an Ark of Safety: 7:1,7,16 with I Peter 3:20,21
   a. One Ark: 6:14a with:
      —One offering of Christ: I Peter 3:18; Hebrews 10:12
      —One gospel: I Corinthians 15:1-4; Galatians 1:8
      —One Way: John 14:6
      —One Name: Acts 4:12
   b. One Window—for light: 6:16a with John 8:12; II Corinthians 4:6
   c. One Door—for entrance: 6:16b with John 10:9
9. The Rainbow—God's promise and assurance after the offering: 9:11-17 with II Corinthians 1:20 (see RAINBOWS in Index). The rainbow reveals—
   a. God's mercy: 9:11 with I Corinthians 15:17-20
   b. God's fullness: 9:12 with Colossians 2:9
   c. God's faithfulness: 9:13 with Hebrews 1:3; 7:25; 8:13
10. Melchizedek, the Priest-King: 14:18-20 with Hebrews 6:20; 7:1-17,24,25

11. Tithing and Communion (the Lord's Supper): 14:17-20. It is interesting to note that when Abraham met Melchizedek after his return from rescuing Lot, Melchizedek brought forth bread and wine and Abraham gave Melchizedek tithes of all. Since Melchizedek is a type of Christ, the bread and wine could be a type of the body and blood of Christ. This probably is another instance when Abraham saw Christ's day and rejoiced (John 8:56). "Tithes of all" represent Abraham's gift of all to Christ who gave His all. See TITHING in Index.

12. Abraham:
   a. Left home to begin a new people: 12:1-3 with Ephesians 5:25; Philippians 2:5-8; II Corinthians 5:17a
   b. Head of many nations: 17:5 with Galatians 3:6-9; Ephesians 3:14,15
13. Isaac:
   a. Birth predicted: 17:16 with Isaiah 7:14; Matthew 1:23
   b. Supernatural birth: 17:17 with Matthew 1:18-25
   c. Named before birth: 17:19a with Matthew 1:21
   d. Only son of promise: 17:19b; 22:2 with John 3:16
   e. Offered by his father: 22:1-14 with Hebrews 11:17-19
   f. Willingly submitted: 22:6-8 with Philippians 2:5-8; Hebrews 10:5-17
   g. His deliverance: 22:10-14 with Christ's resurrection: Matthew 28:6
   h. His bride selected by his father: 24:2-4 with John 6:37,44
   i. Rebekah's going to meet Isaac, sight unseen: 24:58-61 with our being caught up to meet Christ, "Whom having not seen, we love"; I Peter 1:8
   j. Isaac's going to meet Rebekah: 24:62-67 with Christ's coming for His bride: I Thessalonians 4:16-18
   k. His marriage to Rebekah: 24:67 with Christ's marriage to the church: II Corinthians 11:2; Ephesians 5:25-32; Revelation 19:7-10
14. Ram Caught in a Thicket—a substitute: 22:13 with Hebrews 10:5-10. See ISAAC in Index.
15. Jacob's Ladder to Heaven: 28:12 with John 1:51; 14:6
16. Jacob, a Man of Prayer: 32:28 with John 11:41,42; 17:1-26
17. Drink Offering ("poured out"—never drunk): 35:14 with Psalm 22:14; Isaiah 53:12
18. Joseph: 37—50.
   a. Loved by his father: 37:3 with Matthew 3:17; John 3:35

  b. A shepherd: 37:2 with John 10:11-14; I Peter 2:21-25
  c. Sent by his father to his brethren: 37:13,14 with John 1:11; Luke 20:13; Hebrews 10:7
  d. Hated by his brethren: 37:4,5,8 with John 15:25
  e. Superior claims rejected by his brethren: 37:8 with Matthew 21:37-39; John 15:24,25
  f. Life plotted against by his brethren: 37:18-24 with Matthew 26:3,4; John 11:53
  g. Stripped of his coat (robe): 37:23 with John 19:23,24
  h. Cast into a pit: 37:24 with Psalm 88:4,6; I Peter 3:18-22
  i. Sold for the price of a slave: 37:28a with Matthew 26:15
  j. Taken to Egypt: 37:28b with Matthew 2:14,15
  k. Suffered because of his brethren: 39:1—40:13 with Matthew 27:33-50
  l. Was tempted: 39:7 with Matthew 4:1-11
  m. Was falsely accused: 39:16-18 with Matthew 26:59,60
  n. Was bound: 39:20 with Matthew 27:2
  o. Offered no defense: 39:20 with Isaiah 53:7
  p. Experienced God's presence: 39:21,23; John 11:32
  q. Respected his jailer: 39:21 with Luke 23:47
  r. Placed with two prisoners—one of which was later lost—the other saved: 40:2,3,21,23 with Luke 23:32,33,39-43
  s. Was thirty years old when he began his ministry: 41:46 with Luke 3:23
  t. Elevated to a place of glory after suffering: 41:14,41 with Luke 24:13-27; Philippians 2:9-11
  u. Took a Gentile bride: 41:45 with Ephesians 3:1-12
  v. Became a blessing to Gentile Nations: 45:46-57 with John 1:12; Acts 15:14
  w. Lost to their brothers for awhile: 42:7,8 with Romans 10:1-3; 11:7,8
  x. Forgave and restored their repentant brethren: 45:1-15; Micah 7:18,19; Zechariah 12:10-12; Revelation 1:7
  y. Was visited and honored by all earthly nations: 41:57 with Isaiah 2:2,3; 49:6

Joseph and his brethren depict the rejection of Christ by the Jews (John 1:11). Later, their acceptance of Him depicts the Jews receiving Christ when they look upon Him whom they have pierced (Revelation 1:7).

Types of God the Father:

1. Abraham, who spared not his own son: 22:9 with Romans 8:32

Types of the Holy Spirit:

1. The servant of Abraham, Eliezer, sent to seek out and bring back a bride to Isaac: 24:2-67 with John 16:13,14
  a. Did not go unsent: vss. 2-9
  b. Went where sent: vss. 4,10
  c. Was wise to win: vss. 17,18,21
  d. Spoke not of himself: vss. 22,34,36
  e. Required a clear decision: vs. 49
  f. Led the bride to the groom: vss. 61-67

Types of the Believer's Experiences:

1. The Six Days of Creation and Rest: 1:2—2:3[3].
  a. First Day—First work of God *in* us: 1:2—4

Earth		*Man*
Genesis 1:2a	*Dead State*	Ephesians 2:1b, 5a
Genesis 1:2b	*Holy Spirit Sent*	John 16:7-9
Genesis 1:3,4	*Light*	John 8:12
Key Word:		*Key Verse:*
Light		II Corinthians 4:6

  b. Second Day—A Day of Division: 1:6,7

Key Word:	*Key Verses:*
Separation	II Corinthians
	6:16,17

c. Third Day—Fruitbearing: 1:9-12. When the earth became separated from the water, it bore fruit. It is only when we become separated from the world, the flesh, and the devil that we bear fruit (I John 2:15-17)

Key Word:	*Key Verses:*
Fruitfulness	John 15:5,16

d. Fourth Day—Letting Our Light Shine: 1:14-19
—The sun—Christ, our Light, the "Sun" of Righteousness with healing in His wings (John 9:5; Malachai 4:2)
—The Moon, in reflecting the light of the sun—the Church, who gets her light from Christ. When the world passes between the sun and the moon, there is an eclipse of the moon. When the world gets between Christ and the Church, her light is obscured.
—The individual stars—individual believers who let their light shine for the glory of God (Matthew 5:16)

Key Word:	*Key Verse:*
Lightened	Psalm 34:5

e. Fifth Day—Victory and Progress: 1:20-23. This day includes *moving* creatures in the waters, in the air, and on the earth. It suggests that we, as new creatures in Christ, should be on the move for God (Philippians 3:8-14; I Corinthians 9:24-27)

Key Word:	*Key Verses:*
Self-discipline	Romans 6:11;
	12:1,2

f. Sixth Day—Purpose of Man's Creation: 1:24-31
—Companionship with God: 1:26 with I John 1:7
—Co-laborers with God: 1:28 with I Corinthians 3:9
—Co-rulers with God: 1:26-28 with Revelation 1:5,6; 5:10

Key Word:	*Key Verse:*
Dominion	I Peter 2:5

g. Seventh Day—Rest: 2:1-3. The believer has three rests—
—The rest of Salvation—given: Matthew 11:28
—The rest of yieldedness—found: Matthew 11:29
—The rest of heaven—remaining: Hebrews 4:9,10

2. Security in Christ—the One Ark of safety, sealed with pitch, within and without: 6:14c with John 10:27-29

3. Discipleship: See DISCIPLESHIP in Index.
   a. Abel and Noah—obedience: 4:4; 6:22 with Acts 5:29
   b. Enoch—walking with God: 5:24 with I John 1:7
   c. Abraham—faith: 15:6; Romans 4:19-22 with Romans 1:17; Hebrews 11:6
   d. Jacob—service: 28:1—35:15 with Romans 7:6; Colossians 3:24
   e. Joseph—suffering and glory: 37:1—41:57 with II Timothy 2:12a

Types of the Sinner:

1. Cain, who rejected God's way and was rejected by God: 4:3,5,16 with Jude 11a; Matthew 7:21-23. Grace does not run in the blood of one's family, so the "way of Cain" is spoken of as opposed to God's way. Cain's is the "broad way that leads to destruction"—Christ's is the "narrow way that leads to eternal life." Cain's way is a way of—
   a. Human opinion, offering "his" offering, the best he had, the "works" of his hands: vs. 3 with Titus 3:5
   b. Willful refusal to do right, though he knew of the "coats of skin" (probably told by Adam). The fact that Abel came the "right" way with the "right" offering shows Cain knew what to offer

    c. Utter rejection: vs. 5. The offering and offerer stand or fall together. In Cain's case, he and his offering were wrong. It is possible to have the right offering and still be wrong: Isaiah 1:10-20; Matthew 7:21-23

    d. Unyielding pride: vs. 5. See PRIDE in Index.

    e. Anger: vss. 6,8. See ANGER in Index.

    f. Excuses, not admitting to guilt as a sinner: vs. 9

    g. Being past feeling, God's Spirit no longer striving: vs. 10 with Ephesians 4:19; Genesis 6:3a

    h. Condemnation: vs. 11 with John 3:18

    i. No return: vs. 16. One of the saddest verses in the Bible

Cain's way might have seemed right (Proverbs 14:12), but it was a "hard" way (Proverbs 13:15) and there was no remedy for him once he refused God's offer to come again with an acceptable offering (vs. 4:a with Proverbs 29:1). One cannot blame God for His actions with Cain, for grace was offered to him before punishment was meted out (vs. 7). "Today, if ye hear His voice, harden not your heart as [Israel did in provoking the Lord]" (Hebrews 3:15 with Numbers 14:11).

    2. Abel, who accepted God's way and was accepted by God: 4:4 with Hebrews 11:4

    3. Building of the Tower of Babel, which typifies the uselessness on the part of any who try to reach heaven by their own works: 11:1-9 with Ephesians 2:8,9; Titus 3:5; John 14:6; Acts 4:12; Romans 10:9,10

    4. Isaac: 22:1-17. Previously, Isaac was seen as a type of Christ (see ISAAC in Index), but here he cannot be a type of Christ. About to be slain upon the altar of sacrifice, a substitute takes his place—the ram caught in the thicket (vs. 13). When Isaac asked, "Where is the lamb for a burnt offering?": (vs. 7), Abraham replied, "My son, God will provide HIMSELF [not *for* Himself, but *Himself*] a lamb. . . ." (vs. 8). Just before death struck Isaac, a substitute was found. As God's creatures, we deserved death—the penalty for our sin, but God provided HIMSELF the Lamb—our substitute—the Just for the unjust; 2:24 with John 1:29; I Peter 3:18; II Corinthians 5:21.

Types of Law and Grace: See ALLEGORY in Index.

    1. Hagar, the bondwoman—a type of the Law "which gendereth to bondage": 21:10 with Galatians 4:22-25

    2. Sarah, the free woman—a type of grace: 17:15-19 with Galatians 4:22-31

Types of the Flesh and the Spirit: (Romans 7:15-25).

    1. Ishmael—son of the flesh: 16:1-16 with Galatians 4:22,23,30

    2. Isaac—son of promise, born of the Spirit: 17:15-21; 21:2 with Galatians 4:22,23,28,31; Romans 9:4-9; John 3:3,5,7

    1. God's acts of direct creation—to reveal Himself: 1:1-27; Psalms 8; 19:1

    2. Birth of Seth—to replace Abel and to preserve a spiritual seed: 4:25,26

    3. Translation of Enoch—to reward for fellowship and communion: 5:24

    4. Noah building the ark—to save seed for a new beginning: 6:8—9:17

    5. The Flood—to destroy wicked men: 6:5-17; 7:11,12,34

    6. Severe punishment upon Noah's son, Ham (Canaan)—to show that God, even with a new beginning after the flood, will not tolerate sin: 9:20-27

    7. Building of the Tower of Babel—to defy God: 11:1-4

    8. Destruction of Tower of Babel and confusion of tongues (beginning of Nations)—to defeat wrong desires and ambitions: 11:5-9

9. Choosing of Abraham—to preserve a lineage through which Messiah would come: 12:1-3 with Genesis 3:15 and Galatians 4:4,5

10. Natural birth of Ishmael—to constantly remind man of the deeds of the flesh: 16. Constant division between Arabs and Israel today is a result

11. Supernatural birth of Isaac—to fulfill God's promise and to show His power over nature; also to show us that it pays to wait upon the Lord and do things His way: 17:15-19; 21:1-3

12. Sodomites smitten with blindness—punishment for immoral intent: 19:11

13. Destruction of Sodom and Gomorrah—for great wickedness: 19:24,25

14. Lot's wife turned into a pillar of salt—for disobedience: 19:26

15. Ram caught in a thicket—substitute for Isaac: 22:13

16. Joseph's interpretation of Pharaoh's dream—to reveal God's Spirit to an idolatrous king: 41:14-44

17. Worldwide famine—to cause Joseph to be reunited with his family and Israel's settlement in Egypt: 41:47; 45:4-11

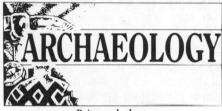

1. Creation: 1,2. Clay tablets have preserved for us at least three accounts of creation—"The Creation Epic," the "Babylonian Creation" record, and a recent find at Ebla in northern Syria. While they preserve for us a perverted polytheistic version, they have much in common with the Word of God:

a. Primeval chaos
b. Beginning of light
c. Creation of the firmament
d. Appearance of dry land
e. Creation of luminaries
f. Creation of man
g. Deity rests

Other clay tablets supply further information:

a. The gods creating the heaven and the earth
b. Man's origin by the handiwork of god(s), made in his god's likeness
c. A special day having been set aside after creation
d. Man civilized at his beginning, intelligent and reverent in his ways, without disease and sin, living in a garden appointed by his god(s)
e. Trees in the garden for food
f. Peace among the animals in the garden
g. Man offending his god(s), resulting in his expulsion from this garden and followed by sin, sickness, misery, and sorrow
h. Re-entrance into the garden prohibited by sacred images (similar to the cherubim)

In records which relate to creation, both biblical and archaeological, none mentions or even hints at a theory of evolution. No nations yet have been found with a tradition or a record to the effect that man descended from any of the lower forms of life!

2. Temptation Seal: 3:1-7. A clay impression from this seal shows two figures seated beside a sacred tree, plucking fruit. A serpent stands behind the woman, erect, as though whispering to her. This seal shows that the main features of the biblical story were a part of the accepted beliefs of early man.

3. Garden of Eden Seal: 3:22-24. This seal shows a man and a woman walking in a downcast position, and strongly suggests the story of Adam and Eve being driven from Eden.

4. Pre-Flood Longevity: 5:1-32. The "Sumerian Prism," written over 100 years before Abraham, lists eight kings who reigned before the flood. At the end of this list there is a sum

Temptation Seal

mary: "Then the Flood swept over the earth." There is a line drawn which divides the account of the pre-flood and post-flood events, and then follows a list of seventy-eight post-flood rulers. This prism gives an exaggerated life-span for the pre-flood kings, but their "ageless" life-span is akin to the longevity of the patriarchs who lived in the same era. The age-span of the post-flood monarchs decreased, which corresponds to the biblical record (Abraham, 175; Moses, 120; and subsequently 70 years became the norm—Psalm 90:10).

5. Size of Noah's Ark: 6:15. The discovery of Hezekiah's Conduit (see CONDUIT in Index) has made it possible to know the length of the cubit. If the cubit was the same size in Noah's day, his ark was 450′ long, 75′ wide, and 45′ high. These dimensions are not out of reason when we consider that legendary tales about the ark made it much larger. One clay tablet tells of a six-story ark with nine compartments in each story. A Grecian account makes the ark 3,000 feet long and 12,000 feet wide! The scientific accuracy of Noah's ark is attested to by ships which are built in our present day—six times as long as they are wide.

On the basis of the dimensions of the cubit given, Noah's ark would have had a displacement of 43,000 cubic feet, giving a capacity to store 522 standard railroad stock cars. A stock car holds 240 sheep—or a total of 125,280. There are approximately 17,600 species of animals today. By taking two each and seven pairs of clean animals (as Noah did), this would total 45,000 animals. Some animals are larger than sheep; most are smaller. Only one-third of the ship's capacity would be needed to hold 45,000 sheep-sized animals—leaving the remaining two-thirds for food, storage, and Noah's family.

6. The Flood: 6—8. There are no less than thirty-three separate racial records of a great deluge among people and races living today. Of this number, only the Egyptian and Scandinavian records fail to coincide absolutely with Moses' account. Some appear weird and distorted, but they testify to at least four biblical truths: (1) God was offended by man's wickedness; (2) there was an earth-covering flood; (3) there was an ark which saved an obedient man and his family; and (4) there was a new beginning for man.

7. The Tower of Babel: 11:1-9. Throughout ancient Mesopotamia numerous towers, called "ziggurats," have been discovered. The word "ziggurat" means "hill of heaven," which is in line with the Bible's thought of a tower "whose top may reach to heaven." A clay tablet was unearthed which gives the following account of a ziggurat: "The erection [building] of this tower [temple] highly offended all the gods. In a night they threw down what man had built, and impeded their progress. They were scattered abroad, and their speech was strange."[4]

8. Ur of the Chaldees: 11:31—12:3. In the Ur of Abraham's day, man was stooping to low levels of sin—worshiping fire, heavenly bodies, the forces of nature, sex, wine, and so forth. Towers were built to honor gods. Kings were deified and images were made of them for their subjects to worship. Passionate sex-acts, "sacred" prostitution, sodomy, and many licentious, disgraceful ceremonies between priestesses and male worshipers were the order of Abraham's

day. Even Abraham's father served "other gods" (Joshua 24:2). His cultural background might lead one logically to assume that his "religion" was the same as the people of Ur, but God's call to him indicates otherwise.

9. Sarah's Beauty: 12:11,14. A scroll found in a cave near the Dead Sea in 1947 describes Sarah as follows: "How fine is the hair of her head, how fair indeed, and her eyes, and how pleasing her nose and all the radiance of her face, how lovely all her whiteness. Her arms goodly to look upon and how perfect her hands. How fair her palms and how long and fine all the fingers of her hands. Her legs how beautiful and without blemish her thighs. All the maidens, and all the brides that go beneath the wedding canopy are not more fair than she. Above all women she is lovely, and higher is her beauty than that of them all, and with her beauty there is much wisdom in her. . . ." The account goes on to give Abraham's version of how the Egyptian king, Pharaoh Zoan, upon hearing of the beauty of Sarah, "desired her exceedingly, and he sent at once to bring her to him. He looked upon her and marvelled at all her loveliness, and took her to him to wife."

10. Abraham and the five Mesopotamian Kings: 14. These kings invaded Canaan and kidnapped Lot as they returned home. Abraham pursued them and rescued his nephew. Critics of Bible history said that the names of these kings were fictional, that extensive travel in Abraham's day (such as indicated by this military exploit) was unknown, and that there was no route east of Palestine. Evidence now shows that the ancient archaic names of these kings are not fictional as claimed, but are linked with other Babylonian names. A clay tablet from ancient Mesopotamia reveals a contract for a rented vehicle, directing the renter not to drive the wagon as far as the Mediterranean Sea. Further archaeological evidence shows that there was a route from Babylon to Canaan, later known as the "King's Highway."

11. The Hittites: 15:18-21. Among the nations mentioned by God to Abraham was the Hittite kingdom. The people of this nation are mentioned forty-six times in Scripture, yet critics declared that they never existed, simply because of the absence of any reference to them in ancient literature. Discovery of ruins in Boghazkoy (in central Turkey) reveals evidence of a Hittite empire that flourished even before Abraham's day. The kingdom extended from north of the River Euphrates, and west to the Black Sea in Asia Minor. It formed a worthy third with two other empires of importance—Babylonia-Assyria and Egypt.

Hittite Divinities

12. Mrs. Lot—a Pillar of Salt: 19:26. To get the proper setting for this event, read verses 1 through 28. God pronounced judgment upon the inhabitants of Sodom and Gomorrah because of their wickedness, warning Lot and his family to flee—escape for thy life—"look not behind thee." But as God was pouring down fire and brimstone from heaven, Mrs. Lot looked "back from behind," and became a pillar of salt (vss. 15,17,24,26). Archaeological excavations in

Pompeii, Italy, shed some light on this subject. Pompeii, like Sodom and Gomorrah, shows mute evidence of vast volcanic deposits. When Mt. Vesuvius erupted in A.D. 79, poisonous volcanic gas asphyxiated many of Pompeii's citizens in their sleep, and then covered the city with volcanic ash to a depth of about twenty feet. There they "slept" until the archaeologists went to work. The pickmen noticed that their picks struck hollow places in the ashes, and the director gave instructions to the pickmen to open another hole near the first one to act as an air vent. He then pumped in plaster of Paris into the "hollow place" and allowed it to dry. After breaking away the brittle ashes from the hardened cast, they were amazed to gaze upon perfectly "preserved" forms of sleeping women, children, men, and even animals.

What happened to cause humans and animals to retain their physical form? The late Dr. Harry Rimmer had this to say: "Volcanic ash is heavily impregnated with chemicals, which are water soluble. As time went on, the ash later metamorphosed into a soft stone, somewhat similar to pumice stone. Being porous, water penetrated it freely. The chemical content of the ash worked quickly on the forms of the deceased, and wrought a chemical change which turned their bodies into some chemical, crystalline substance of sufficient hardness to permit the surrounding ash to retain a perfect cast of the buried bodies as it slowly formed into a soft stone. Under the action of water, leaking through the porous rock, the concentration of chemicals which had been a physical form melted, and then disappeared. But the ash-stone retained the shape and features—even their expressions! After a score of centuries, we are able to look upon the countenances of the people of Pompeii once again.

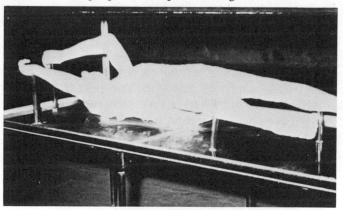

Citizen of Pomeii

"In plain and simple language the recovered 'dead' of Pompeii must have been changed 'into a pillar of salt' of some variety. We use the word 'salt' in its true chemical sense. The term 'pillar of salt' cannot be restricted in its meaning to sodium chloride—common 'table salt,' but must be understood in its broader and fuller sense as a chemical substance. The term 'salt' can be applied to any mineral salt, an iron salt, saltpeter, etc. How long it would take to change a body into any 'salt' is a question whose answer depends upon so many factors we cannot even hazard a guess. It would depend upon the nature of the chemicals present, the amount of heat involved, the degree of pressure applied, and the strength of the solution involved. We can only say that we have at Pompeii the exact conditions which prevailed at Sodom, and clear evidence of the same effect."[5]

Excavations in 1928 in the region of Sodom reveal a stratum of salt 150′ thick. Over this were large quantities of sulphur, or brimstone. The place was a burned-out region of oil and asphalt, where a great rupture in the strata took place centuries ago. Formerly there had been a subterranean lake of oil and gas beneath Sodom. It had been ignited in some mysterious way. A tremendous explosion took place, which carried burning sulphur oil and asphalt into the air above the cities. Mingled with salt, this burning brimstone and fire rained down from heaven upon the whole plain—just like the Bible says (Genesis 19:24,25).

The reference concerning Mrs. Lot becoming a pillar of salt is very interesting. It is stated that she "looked back from behind." She did more than stop to see what was taking place. Having left the city with her husband and daughters, she literally lingered behind—straggled behind the rest. It is quite clear that "back from behind" means that she had deserted the group. Lot had moved so swiftly that he was already in the city of Zoar when the fire and brimstone fell upon Sodom and Gomorrah. Because Mrs. Lot had lingered behind, she evidently was caught in clouds of volcanic gas, and was buried beneath volcanic ashes, just like those at Pompeii. The word "became" is also important. It allows this thought: "In due process of time she became a pillar of salt," or "after a chain of events she eventually was turned, or formed, into a pillar of salt." Regardless of the "how" of her being turned into a pillar of salt, Christ has warned us against disobedience by simply saying—"remember Lot's wife" (Luke 17:28-32).

13. Wells of Abraham: 21:22-34; 26:17-19. In the forbidding Negev desert region south of Beer-sheba, no settlement had existed since about A.D. 600. These references in Genesis imply that Abraham had great herds in this region, and that Isaac had dug wells. Archaeologists took a close look at these hills, even searching out the smallest gullies. There they found the remains of dikes, all woven into an intricate drainage system which conserved every drop of rain water. They discovered many stopped-up wells dating back to Abraham's day, which are now utilized, and rebuilt irrigation ditches. Today the Jews are making the "desert blossom as the rose," just like Abraham had done centuries before Christ. See DESERT BLOSSOM in Index.

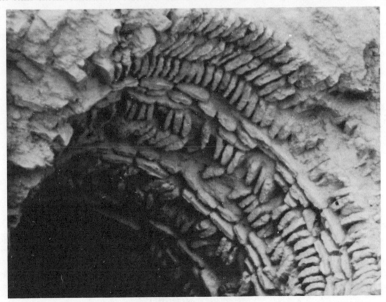

Well of Abraham's Day

14. The City of Ebla.[6] In the early 1960s a farmer in Northern Syria at Tell Mardikh ploughed upon a large stone object which, when dug around, proved to be a storage bin dating back to about 1800 B.C. An Italian student in Near Eastern Studies became interested in the site, and since 1964 he and his team of archaeologists have uncovered the remains of a city whose unearthed objects go back to about 2300 B.C. The excavated city was identified as "Ebla" from a 26-line inscription. Over 17,000 clay tablets have been found. One text states that the city had a population of 260,000. The tablets appear to date the last two generations of the city to about

2300 B.C., possibly 200 years earlier. The tablets are in two languages, which make it easier for the scholars to decipher. There are such subjects as tariffs, tributes, treaties, judicial proceedings and, of course, religion. Of significance to the Christian, a creation account was discovered, which closely parallels our biblical account. A ''flood'' account was also found. One tablet mentions the cities of Sodom and Gomorrah—the first discovery of these named cities mentioned outside the Bible. Of special interest is the name ''Urusalima'' (Jerusalem), this being the earliest known reference to this city. Other cities whose existence was denied just because the only source was the Bible, are also mentioned, thus showing that the authors of the Scriptures knew exactly what they were talking about. Reference to a god whose name has the same root as the Yahweh of the Old Testament is significant, showing that early man was monotheistic (at least some were). Names like Eber of Genesis 10 (Abraham's ancestor), Adam, Israel, Saul, and David appear in a millenium before such names were written down in Scripture. *Time* magazine (Oct. 18, 1976), quoted University Professor David Noel Freedman regarding these discoveries at Ebla: ''We always thought of ancestors like Eber [and others mentioned] as symbolic. Nobody ever regarded them as historic, at least not until these tablets were found [he means liberals and modernists]. Fundamentalists could have a field day with this one.'' (I'll say ''Amen'' to that!) It is at least thought-provoking that findings such as those at Ebla consistently support the Bible as a thoroughly accepted record. And there's more to come as tablets are deciphered.

15. Joseph's Granaries: 41:25-57. Ruins of ancient granaries are located on the west bank of the Nile River in the Valley of Kings (opposite Luxor), which are typical of granaries of Joseph's time.

Joseph's Granaries

LIGHT FROM
BIBLICAL
CUSTOMS

[7] 1. Hagar and Ishmael: 16:1-4; 21:9-14. Sarah was only following a custom of her day when she gave Hagar to Abraham to bear a child. An inscribed contract from ancient Mesopotamia states that if a wife was childless she shall give a slave girl as a wife to her husband. If the wife were to bear a son later, the son of the slave-wife could not be driven away. This could explain why Abraham was so reluctant to

drive both Hagar and Ishmael out of sight when commanded to do so by God.

2. Stones for pillows: 28:11. See BEDS in Index.

3. Family gods: 31:19,34. After twenty years in Haran, Jacob and his family left to go back to Bethel. Rachel stole her father's household gods ("teraphim") and hid them in her camel's furniture (saddle). Ancient Nuzi tablets reveal a law which states such images belonged to the head of the family, and served as a title-deed to all his possessions. With Rachel now in possession, she could declare Jacob to be the head of all Laban's goods, and could explain why Laban was so anxious to overtake Jacob and recover his "teraphim" (31:11-55). He never did recover them because Rachel refused to get off her camel.

Why did Rachel steal them? Possibly to get even with her father for making Jacob work fourteen years for her, and possibly because Laban had always taken the best of livestock and had given her husband the bad ones. With one stroke, in taking these family gods, Jacob could have become the sole possessor of all Laban's houses, lands, livestock, and servants, and no doubt, become Laban's employer. Later, before Jacob and his family arrived at Bethel, he buried these "strange gods," turning his back on earthly fortune just to be in the place of God's choicest blessings (35:1-4).

"Teraphim"—Family Gods

4. In childbearing . . . fear not: 35:17,18. When a son is born in the East, there is cause for rejoicing. If a daughter is born, there is no such blessing. Even in our day kings in Bible lands will seek a divorce if no son is born to inherit the throne. For this reason the wife in hard labor will fear greatly. Such mental anguish is the cause of many deaths in childbirth. Rachel's plight was such, although she was encouraged by the midwife saying, "Fear not, thou shalt have this *son* also." Jesus also remarked concerning the anguish of childbirth: "A woman when she is in travail hath sorrow, but as soon as she is delivered, she remembereth no more the anguish, for joy that a *man* is born" (John 16:21).

During the time of the wife's labor, a vigil is kept by friends of the family. If a son is born, the midwife makes the announcement by striking the ceiling three times. Then the friends break into song: "Unto Jacob (the name of the father) a child is born, unto Jacob a son is given." This same type song is found in Isaiah's prophecy (9:6) in regard to Christ's birth: "Unto *us* a child is born, unto us a son is given [to inherit His Father's throne]."

5. Joseph's coat of many colors: 37:3,4. This actually was a "long-sleeved" robe. Only two people in a tribe were allowed the privilege of wearing such a robe—the head of the tribe

and the one chosen as the heir. The oldest son, according to tradition, was the heir apparent, but Jacob chose rather a younger son by Rachel (Joseph) to be the heir. He symbolized it by giving him the long-sleeved robe, or the "coat of many colors."

6. Mummification: 50:2,3. Upon the death of Jacob, "Joseph commanded his servants the physicians to embalm his father . . . and forty days are fulfilled . . . of those which are embalmed. . . ." Egypt's method of embalming was "mummification," a forty-day (sometimes 70-day) process which preserved (petrified) the body. An iron hook was used to draw out part of the brains through the nostrils, and the rest by infusion of drugs. Cutting open the abdomen, the internal organs were removed. Having rinsed the abdomen with palm wine, it was then filled with oils, spices, and perfumes. The physicians then sewed up the body, and steeped it in natrum for the prescribed number of days. Afterward the body was washed and wrapped in a flaxen cloth, and placed in a coffin.

We understand now how Joseph could make the long journey to Canaan with his father's body (50:4-13). Just before Joseph died, he gave instructions for his "bones" (body) to be taken to the "Promised Land" when Israel left Egypt. When he died, he was "embalmed," placed in a coffin, and "stayed put" until Moses later carried out his wishes (50:24-26; Exodus 13:19; Joshua 24:32).

1. Earth rotating on axis—giving night and day: 1:4,5,18,19 with Amos 5:8b—"turning the shadow of death [darkness of night] into morning, and maketh the day dark with night."

2. Oceans: 1:9,10. Science today acknowledges that since 70-71 percent of the earth's surface is covered with water, there is just *one* mass of water, which they call "world ocean." This same thought is seen in our verse: "And God said Let the waters under the heavens be gathered together into one place, and let the dry land appear. And God called the dry land Earth; and the gathering together of the waters He called Seas." He divided the water of the earth into four main divisions—Atlantic, Pacific, Indian, and Arctic Oceans. Though Genesis 1:9 states the waters are gathered together into one place, they are called "Seas." See OCEANS in Index.

3. Our Planet Earth is a water planet: 1:9. It is interesting that recent flights to other planets reveal a lack of water. It is singular in our solar system due to a temperature that keeps water in a liquid state, and the properties of water—liquid, vapor (gas), and solid—make the earth unique for vegetation and habitat for animal and human beings (1:9-31).

4. Herb-yielding and living creatures producing "after their kind:" 1:11,12,20-25. *No room here for the evolutionary process!*

5. Lights in the heavens as signs: 1:14. See ORDINANCE OF HEAVEN in Index.

6. Greater light (sun) ruling the day, the lesser light (moon) to rule the night: 1:16. There are numerous stars far bigger than our sun, and Moses was careful not to say the "greatest light to rule the day."

7. Man's dominion over animals: 1:28. Evolutionists claim that most of the great fossil beds were deposited hundreds of millions of years ago, with "simple" forms below and more "complex" forms above them. But fossil footprints of human beings have been found with the tracks of huge dinosaurs in the Paluxy River bed of Texas near Glen Rose. This fits the biblical picture of man being contemporary with *all* the kinds of animals, for he was given dominion over them *all*.

8. Man formed from dust: 2:7; 3:19; Psalm 103:14. The same sixteen or seventeen elements found in the dust of earth's surface are the very same elements out of which man's body is formed. When God breathed into man's nostrils the breath of life, man became a living

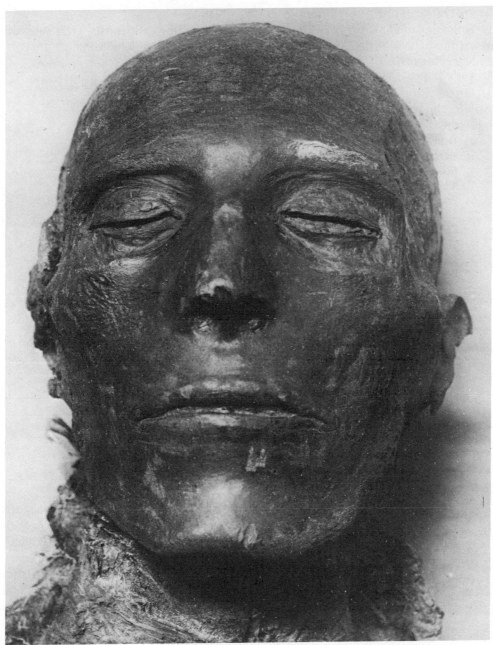

Mummified Head

soul (being): 2:7. Death is defined as cessation or withdrawal—recalling of this God-breathed breath (Psalm 104:29). God has so wonderfully made us (Psalm 139:14), that even in death "nature" takes over with "minute undertakers," whose function it is to start immediate decomposition (even in spite of embalming). "The worm shall feed swiftly on him" (Job 24:20), and soon "the dust is returned to the earth as it was" (Ecclesiastes 12:7).

9. Sir James Simpson who, in 1847, discovered the value of chloroform as an anesthetic, gave Genesis 2:21 as the basis for his discovery. We read here that God caused "a deep sleep" to fall on Adam in the first recorded surgical operation in history.

10. Size of Noah's Ark. See ARK in Index.

11. Fountains of the Great Deep: 7:11. There are, according to scientists, great submarine springs at the bottom of the ocean which empty into the seas. See Job 38:16a.

12. Stars Numberless: 15:5. See STARS in Index.

13. Lot's Wife—a Pillar of Salt: 19:26. See ARCHAEOLOGY in Genesis, point 12.

14. Circumcision: 21:4. See CIRCUMCISION in Index.

Genesis in the New Testament:

1. Creation: 1:1 with John 1:3; Hebrews 11:3
2. Genealogy of Christ: 1—38; with Matthew 1:1-3; Luke 3:34-38
3. Marriage and divorce: 1:27; 2:23,24 with Matthew 19:4,5
4. Eve beguiled: 3:4 with II Corinthians 11:3
5. Adam's disobedience: 3:6 with I Timothy 2:14
6. Promised Messiah: 3:15 with Galatians 4:4,5
7. Abel's accepted offering: 4:4 with Hebrews 11:4
8. Cain's way: 4:3-16 with Jude 11a
9. The first murderer: 4:8 with I John 3:12
10. Translation of Enoch: 5:24 with Hebrews 11:5
11. Deliverance of Noah: 6:8-13 with I Peter 3:20
12. Noah prepares an ark: 6:14 with Hebrews 11:7
13. The flood: 7:4 with Matthew 24:37-39
14. Abraham's call: 12:1 with Hebrews 11:8
15. Melchizedek's priesthood: 14:18 with Hebrews 7:1
16. Abraham's faith counted for righteousness: 15:6 with Romans 4:4; James 2:23
17. Hagar and Ishmael: 16:15 with Galatians 4:22
18. Abraham's lordship: 18:12 with I Peter 3:6
19. Days of Lot: 19:1-29 with Luke 17:28,29
20. Destruction of Sodom and Gomorrah: 19:25 with Matthew 10:15; 11:23,24
21. Remember Lot's wife: 19:26 with Luke 17:32
22. Offering of Isaac: 22:1-10 with Hebrews 11:17; James 2:21
23. Esau sells his birthright: 25:33 with Hebrews 12:16
24. Jacob blesses Joseph's sons: 48:15 with Hebrews 11:21
25. Christ the King: 49:10 with Matthew 2:6; Luke 1:32,33
26. Joseph's dying request: 50:24,25 with Hebrews 11:22

1. The probability of life originating from accident is comparable to the probability of the unabridged dictionary resulting from an explosion in a printing shop!

2. The "Creator-God" (1:1; John 1:1) became "Savior (Redeemer) God:" 22:8; John 1:14; II Corinthians 5:21

3. Woman was taken, not from man's head that he might *rule* over her, nor from his foot that he might keep her in *submission,* but from his side, near his heart, that he might *love* her: 2:21-23; Ephesians 5:25-33

4. The *TEMPTATION* that caused Lucifer (Satan) to be cast out of heaven is a threefold pattern: Isaiah 14:12-17

    a. *Saw* the glory of God and the honor He received
    b. *Desired* in his heart to be above God
    c. Sought to *take* God's place

Eve *saw* the fruit, *desired* it, then *took* it: 3;6. Lot *saw* the fertile plains of Jordan, *desired* to have them, and *settled* (took) there: 13:10,11. Achan's sin was the same—"when I *saw* . . . then I *coveted* . . . and *took* them:" Joshua 7:21. So was David's sin with Bathsheba—he *saw* her nakedness, *desired* to have her, and then *took* her: II Samuel 11:2-4. Christ's temptation followed the same pattern—a *look* at all the kingdoms, a *desire* to eat, and to *take* His life in His own hands in casting Himself from the pinnacle of the Temple: Matthew 4:1-11. It is the same pattern described by John (I John 2:16): lust of the eyes—*seeing*; lust of the flesh—*desiring*; and pride of life—*taking* to have for self.

The Word of God offers a three-fold pattern to overcome temptation:

    a. Use the Scriptures: Matthew 4:4,7,10; Psalm 119:11; I John 2:1a

    b. Watch and pray: Matthew 26:41. If the devil could get Adam to yield to temptation when he was in an innocent state, how much more can he tempt us in our sinful state. See SATAN in Index.

    c. Rely on God's faithfulness, which will provide an "exit" for us: I Corinthians 10:13

5. Adam's Fall: 2:15-17; 3:1-6

    a. Commandment *given*—"thou shalt not eat of it": 2:17

    b. Commandment *questioned*—"hath God said . . . ?" 3:1

    c. Commandment *added to*—"neither shall ye touch it": 3:3

    d. Commandment *denied*—"ye shall not surely die": 3:4

    e. Commandment *disobeyed*—"and he did eat": 3:6

6. What Eve Learned: Ch. 3. In "beguiling" (leading astray) Eve, Satan planted a seed of doubt in her mind. She was so deluded that she not only questioned the Word of God but added to it. When she finally yielded, thinking she would not die but would become a "god" unto herself, she learned the following from her encounter with Satan:

    a. That sin left her without a covering before God: vs. 7

    b. That she was guilty and ashamed before God: vs. 8

    c. That when guilty, one blames another: vs. 13

    d. That the pleasures of sin are short-lived: vss. 6,7 with Hebrews 11:25,26. "All the devil's apples have worms."

    e. That the devil is a liar: vss. 1-5 with John 8:44

    f. That she is going to suffer and die: vss. 16-19 with Proverbs 13:15

    g. That disobedience robs one of God's best: vss. 22-24

    h. That the blood of another must be shed before one can have standing again before God: vs. 21

7. The First Messianic Promise: 3:15. When we examine this statement in its context, it turns out to be an *ultimatum* to "that old serpent, the devil." Fellowship between God and His creatures had been broken when Adam disobeyed. In seeking to strike at the *cause* of sin, or this broken fellowship, God used a method of interrogation with Adam and Eve. When God questioned Adam, he "passed the buck" to Eve (3:8-12). God abruptly broke off conversation with Adam and turned to Eve, who also "passed the buck" to the serpent (3:13). God immediately turned to the serpent, and instead of questioning, boldly stated, "because *thou* hast done this." Judgment was meted out (vs. 14), and then the *ultimatum* to the devil—vs. 15. This was fulfilled when Christ came and died on the cross (Galatians 4:4,5). God first strikes at the *cause* of sin, then turns to fallen man to redeem (3:14-21). This truth is seen when Christ was crucified, buried, and was resurrected. The "prince of the world was judged" (John 12:31; 16:11), principalities and powers were spoiled (Colossians 2:15), and Christ came forth from the grave with the "keys of hell and of death" (Revelation 1:18). As a result of this victory over the enemy of our souls, our sins and the handwriting of ordinances against us were nailed to the cross, and redemption is possible for all who have disobeyed the Lord (Colossians 2:14). Remember, it wasn't until God judged the serpent that He was able to judge and offer to Adam and Eve "coats of skin" for an acceptable covering for them. When Christ defeated the devil at Calvary, He was then able to offer us a complete, victorious salvation. He could have shed His blood and saved lost sinners, but without defeating the devil first, we would not have had victory to "withstand all the firey darts of the evil one," we wouldn't be able to "resist the devil that he flee from us," nor could we say with Paul, "I am more than a conqueror through

Christ who loves me" (Ephesians 6:16; James 4:7; I Peter 5:8,9; Romans 8:37). Somebody has said it wasn't the "apple" in the tree that caused all the trouble, it was the "pair" on the ground!

8. Mountaintop Experiences. See MOUNTAINS in Index.

—*Ararat*—new beginning, the patriarch of mountains, smoked with the first sacrifice in therestored world: 8:4 with Romans 12:1,2

—*Moriah*—the mount of testing, the victory of faith, where Jehovah-jirah supplies every need: 22:2-14 with I Peter 4:12-14; Philippians 4:19. Moriah is also the Mount of the Temple—the place of God's presence: II Chronicles 3:1; 8:16; I Kings 8:6-11. (See Mount Zion)

—*Gilead*—mount of disunity—anger and grudge—between brethren: Genesis 31:25,42-52. This incident (vs. 49) is often called a "benediction," but it is a malediction between two who were at odds. Solomon later referred to Mount Gilead as "beauty" (Songs of Solomon 4:1)

—*Seir*—opposition—mountain of an unforgiving spirit: 36:8,9 with Numbers 20:14-21. Esau and his descendants never forgave Jacob and his descendants for Jacob's inheriting Esau's birthright

—*Horeb*—the mount of refreshing water—an abundant, overflowing, strengthened life, walking and living on holy ground: Exodus 3:1-5; 17:6; I Kings 19:8 with John 7:37,38

—*Sinai*—Law (Ten Commandments) and Grace (pattern of the Tabernacle), the Law being the Schoolmaster which leads to Christ: Exodus 19:20; 20:1-17; 24:15—25:9 with Galatians 3:24

—*Hor*—unbelief and rebellion against God—death: Numbers 20:7-29. In Aaron's case, his could have been a "sin unto death," a premature death (I John 5:16).

—*Gerizim*—the mount of blessing for obedience: Deuteronomy 11:29; 27:12 with Ephesians 1:3

—*Ebal*—barren—the mount of judgment for disobedience: Deuteronomy 11:29; 27:13 with I Corinthians 11:31,32

—*Nebo*—Pisgah—the mount of vision, to behold the milk and honey of God's promises: Deuteronomy 34:1-4 with II Peter 1:4; Proverbs 29:18a

—*Caleb's mountain*—the mount of yieldedness and conquest, possessing one's possessions. Joshua 14:6-14 with I John 5:4

—*Ephraim*—rest: Joshua 24:33

—*Lebanon*—goodly—the mount of spiritual growth: Judges 3:3; Psalm 92:12 with I Peter 2:2; II Peter 3:18

—*Tabor*—victory—the strength of the Lord in fighting our battles: Judges 4:12-16 with Psalm 18:2

—*Moreh*—teacher: Judges 7:1-8 with John 14:26; 16:13

—*Bethel*—house of God—meeting place with God: I Samuel 13:2 with Genesis 28:11-22.

—*Hachilah*—hiding—darkness: I Samuel 23:19 with John 3:19

—*Gilboa*—the mount of defeat: I Samuel 31:8. Had Saul slain all the Amalekites as Samuel commanded (I Samuel 15), an Amalekite would not have been around to kill him (II Samuel 1:1-16). If we don't slay sin, sin will slay us. The Bible will keep me from sin, or sin will keep me from the Bible

—*Zion*—the mount of God's glory—zeal—His stronghold to deliver and bless—our future heavenly Jerusalem: II Samuel 5:7; II Kings 19:31; Psalm 133:3 with Romans 11:26; Hebrews 12:22. With the Tabernacle having been erected on Zion, and all the Temple worship arranged by David, and many Psalms composed during his forty years' reign, which were used in worship, "Zion" had become incorporated into the devotional books and language of the Israelites. So, after the erection of Solomon's Temple, the name "Zion" passed over to it with the Tabernacle and the service. "Moriah" dropped out of the phraseology, and the two hills became one in name—Zion (Psalms 76:1,2)

—*Carmel*—the mount of decision: I Kings 18:19-21 with Joshua 24:24; I John 1:7; 2:15-17

—*Mizar*—little mountain—babe in Christ: Psalm 42:6 with I Peter 2:2

—*Bashan*—high hill—new heights: Psalm 68:15 with Ephesians 2:5,6

—*Hermon*—the lofty mount of Dew—separation from worldliness: Psalm 89:13; 133:3 with Colossians 1:13; Lamentations 3:22,23; I John 2:15-17

—*Samaria*—false trust: Amos 6:1 with Revelation 3:14-19

—*"The"* mountain—"up" where the Word of God is taught: Matthew 5—7 with II Timothy 2:15

—*"A"* mountain—for prayer: Matthew 14:23; Luke 6:12 with Philippians 4:6

—*Transfiguration*—the mount where the eyes of our understanding are enlightened to spiritual things: Matthew 17:1-8 with Ephesians 1:18; Colossians 1:9

—*Olives*—illuminating—the mount of intimate relationship with Christ: Matthew 24:3 with Acts 1:4,12; Zechariah 14:4

—*Calvary*—Golgotha—the place of the skull—the mount where our sins were blotted out, the mount of victory over Satan: Luke 23:33; John 19:16-18; I John 3:8 with II Corinthians 4:6-11; Romans 8:37; Colossians 2:14,15

9. Church Members Seen in the Twelve Tribes: 49:1-27
   a. Unstable Reubens: vss. 3,4
   b. Hurtful Simeons and Levis: vss. 5-7
   c. Praiseworthy Judahs: vs. 8
   d. Sympathetic Zebuluns: vs. 13
   e. Burden-bearing and Serving Issachars: vss. 14,15
   f. Shrewd, crafty and backbiting Dans: vss. 16,17

It should be noted here that the tribe of Dan is not mentioned with the 144,000 of the Twelve Tribes mentioned in Revelation 7:4-8. We note that Dan was to be a "serpent that biteth the heels of the horse so that the rider shall fall backward" (vs. 17). In the book of Judges it reveals that Dan, less than forty years after the death of Joshua, divided the religious unity of the nation of Israel—they became the first Tribe to openly set up images for idolatry, and this led to Israel, a nation that rideth upon a horse (see Exodus 15:1 with Deuteronomy 32:13; Isaiah 58:14), becoming divided and later dispersed. When the kingdom was divided, Jeroboam established the Northern Kingdom of Israel, setting up two golden calves to be worshiped, one in Bethel and the other in the territory of Dan (I Kings 12:25-30). Dan's role in the nation's destruction is possibly one reason why this tribe is omitted from the list of Tribes in Revelation seven.

   g. Overcoming Gads: vs. 19
   h. Nurturing Ashars: vs. 20
   i. Counseling Naphtalis: vs.21
   j. Fruitful and Separated Josephs: vss. 22-26
   k. Destructive Benjamins: vs. 27

10. Types of Families. Although God told Abraham that in him all the families of the earth would be blessed (12:3), Augustine said he did not know but that some of his family might turn out bad, for in the family of—
    a. Adam, there was a murderous Cain: 4:8
    b. Noah, there was an immoral Ham: 9:2-25
    c. Abraham, there was a persecuting Ishmael: Galatians 4:22-29
    d. Lot, there were adulterous daughters: 19:32
    e. Isaac, there was a profane Esau: Hebrews 12:16
    f. Jacob, there were treacherous sons: 37:11-33
    g. Eli, there were ungodly sons: I Samuel 2:12,22-24
    h. David, there was rebellious Absalom: II Samuel 15:6
    i. Ahab, there was an ungodly wife: I Kings 16:29-33; 21:1-16
    j. Hezekiah, there was an idolatrous Manasseh: II Kings 21:1-16

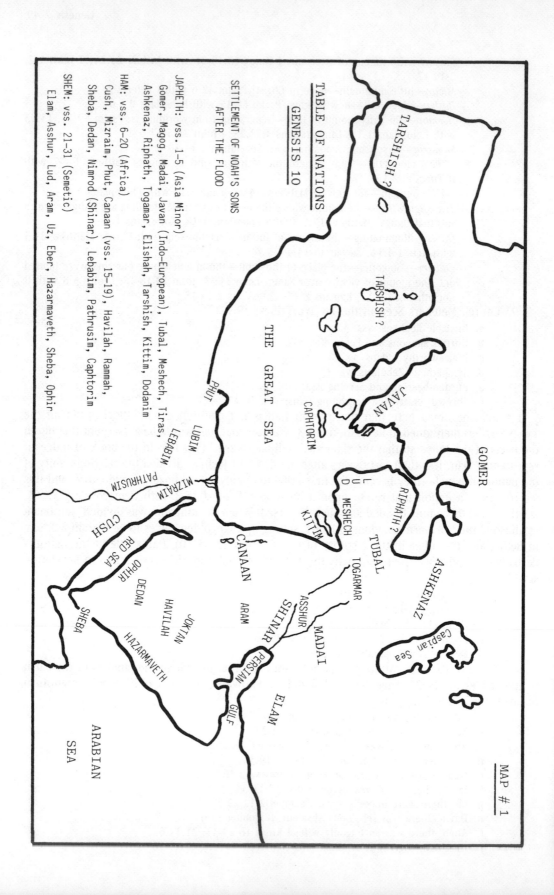

TABLE OF NATIONS

GENESIS 10

SETTLEMENT OF NOAH'S SONS
AFTER THE FLOOD

JAPHETH: vss. 1-5 (Asia Minor)
Gomer, Magog, Madai, Javan (Indo-European), Tubal, Meshech, Tiras,
Ashkenaz, Riphath, Togamar, Elishah, Tarshish, Kittim, Dodanim

HAM: vss. 6-20 (Africa)
Cush, Mizraim, Phut, Canaan (vss. 15-19), Havilah, Ramnah,
Sheba, Dedan, Nimrod (Shinar), Lebabim, Pathrusim, Caphtorim

SHEM: vss. 21-31 (Semetic)
Elam, Asshur, Lud, Aram, Uz, Eber, Hazarmaveth, Sheba, Ophir

MAP # 1

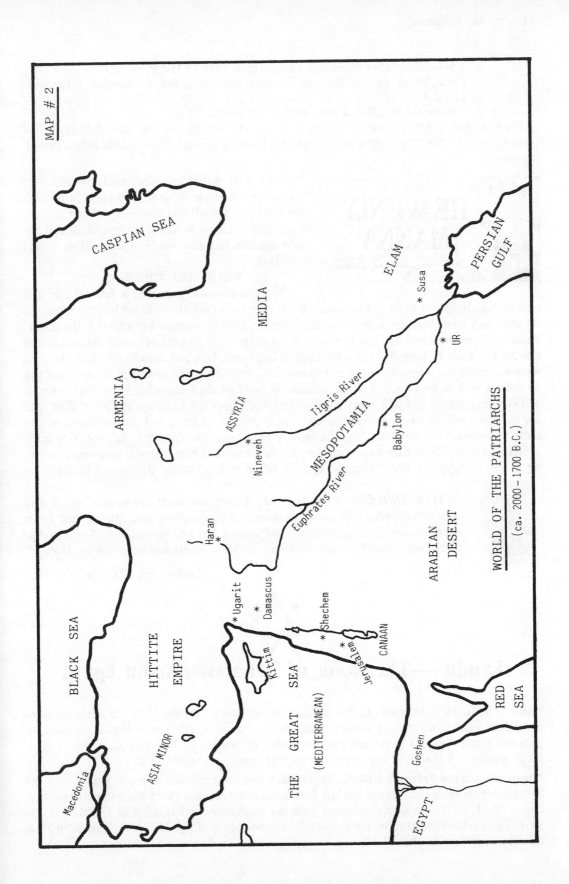

MAP # 2

CASPIAN SEA

ARMENIA

MEDIA

ELAM

PERSIAN
GULF

* Susa

* UR

ASSYRIA

Tigris River

* Nineveh

MESOPOTAMIA

Babylon

Euphrates River

ARABIAN
DESERT

* Haran

BLACK SEA

HITTITE
EMPIRE

ASIA MINOR

Macedonia

* Ugarit

* Damascus

Kittim

* Shechem

* Jerusalem

CANAAN

THE GREAT SEA
(MEDITERRANEAN)

Goshen

EGYPT

RED
SEA

WORLD OF THE PATRIARCHS
(ca. 2000 – 1700 B.C.)

    k. A benevolent father, there was a black sheep: Luke 15:11-24

    l. Christ, there were unbelieving relatives (John 7:5) and a traitorous Judas: Luke 22:1-6,47,48

    m. Ananias and Sapphira, a lying couple: Acts 5:1-10

Someone has said that it doesn't pay to look up your "family tree" because they might find themselves to be the "sap"! How true—"Many a *budding* genius has turned out to be a *blooming* idiot!"

A BIT OF **HEAVENLY MANNA**

As we have noted, the "Spiritual Thought" for Genesis is *"Begin with God."* To begin with God, one must ask himself this question: "Where am I?" When this question is answered truthfully and the right decision has been made, one can then "begin with God."

WHERE ART THOU?—3:9[8]

"This question was proposed to fallen Adam, and may well be proposed to us. All by nature try to hide from God, they cannot bear the glance in His eye: they tremble at His justice, hate His holiness, and are too proud to appeal to His mercy. Reader, Where art thou? Are you in your natural state? Then you are at enmity with God, and may at any hour be banished from the land of hope into dark and hopeless despair. Are you wrapped up in the garments of self-righteousness? Then you are in imminent danger, and you do not see it. You are rejecting Christ, refusing to build on the foundation which God has laid, and will be required to fulfill every command of God's holy law. Are you in Christ? If so, you are truly blessed; for every sin is pardoned, every promise of grace and glory is yours, to you there is no condemnation, and from Christ you shall never be separated. Beloved, God asks, 'Where art thou?' No matter where you are, if you are not in Christ, there is no place of safety, no source of supply, no title to glory. O to be found in Him, living, dying, and forever!"

PRAYER THOUGHT: "Eternal God, deliver me from coldness of heart and wandering mind. Help me to be rekindled by fire from Thy altar, to cast down every imagination that exalteth itself against Thy knowledge, and bring into captivity every thought to the obedience of Christ. In His dear name I pray. Amen."[9]

Genesis 6:5; II Corinthians 10:5

Exodus—The Book of Departure from Egypt

Name: The Greek translators call this second book of Moses "Exodus." By this name the Gentile world has known it ever since. Exodus means "departure." The writer of the book of Hebrews recognizes this in referring to the exodus of Israel: "By faith Joseph, when he died, made mention of the departing of the children of Israel" (Hebrews 11:22).

Connection with Preceding Book: Exodus assumes the existence of a previous record. Its first six verses are a summary of the last five chapters in Genesis. There are references to creation—20:11; 31:17; to God's covenant with the patriarchs—2:24; 6:3,4,8; 13:5,11; 32:13; 33:1. The twelve sons of Jacob are frequently spoken of (e.g., 6:14-25; 24:4). Genesis 50:25 is directly quoted in Exodus 13:19.

Genesis 15:13 says that the seed of Abraham would spend 400 years in Egypt. Exodus 12:40 lists 430 years, and is confirmed by Paul (Galatians 3:16,17). The expression 400 years is general, meaning at least 400 years elapsing between the promise of Canaan as an inheritance and entrance into the land by his seed. The reference of 430 years is to the covenant renewed to Jacob when he went down into Egypt (Genesis 35:9; 46:1-3) to the actual exodus. The exodus took place ca. 1440 B.C.

Contents: "The principal things contained in Exodus are the accomplishments of God's promises made to Abraham concerning the increase of his seed; the rigorous treatment of the Israelites and their suffering in Egypt; the Lord's emancipating them from bondage; and the ordinances of Tabernacle worship appointed in the wilderness. Throughout the whole, there is a figure and representation of the passage of the people of God out of spiritual Egypt through the wilderness of this world to victorious Canaan, and of the various things which they must meet in their journey."[1] There are many types in this Book, particularly of Christ, His Person, office and grace. Exodus has 40 chapters, 1213 verses, and 32,692 words. See MAP, p. 100, and WILDERNESS, points 1-10, p. 101.

Character: Law: Luke 24:44.

Subject: Israel's bondage, deliverance, and their relation to God: 6:6-8; 19:4-8; 24:1-7; 25:8.

Purpose: To teach us the necessity, method, and the result of God's purpose in redemption (Ephesians 2:1-10).

Outline:

    I. Israel's Deliverance from Egypt: 1—18
        A. Bondage—Egyptians Oppress Israel: 1
        B. The Preparation from Deliverance: 2—6
            1. Birth and Training of Moses: 2
            2. Call of Moses: 3,4
            3. Mission to Pharaoh: 5,6
        C. Conflict with Pharaoh: 7—12
            1. The Ten Plagues: 7—11. See PLAGUES in Index.
            2. The Passover: 12:1-36. See PASSOVER in Index.
        D. March to Sinai: 12:37—18:27
            1. Departure from Egypt: 12:37—14:31
            2. Stages of the March: 15—17
            3. Organization of the People: 18

   II. Israel's Separation to God: 19—40
        A. Giving of the Law: 19—24. See LAW Added in Index.
            1. Manifestation of God: 19
            2. Ten Commandments: 20. (Under the Law they labored first, then rested: 20:8-11. Under Grace we first find rest in Christ, then work: Matthew 11:28; Ephesians 2:8-10). See COMMANDMENT in Index.
            3. Civil Law: 21—23
            4. Covenant of the Law: 24
        B. Instructions for the Tabernacle: 25—31. See TABERNACLE in Index.
            1. Vessels and Structure: 25—27
            2. Garments and Consecration of the Priests: 28:1—29:37
            3. Service of the Tabernacle: 29:38—31:18
        C. Israel's Sin and Restoration: 32—34
            1. Sin of the People: 32:1-29
            2. Intercession of Moses: 32:30—33:23
            3. Renewal of the Covenant: 34
        D. Construction of the Tabernacle: 35—40

      1. Offering of the People: 35:1—36:7
      2. Making of the Parts and Priests' Garments: 36:8—39:43
      3. Setting up of the Tabernacle: 40

Scope: The Exodus events cover a period of approximately 145 years.

Writer: Moses. See AUTHOR, p. 104.

To Whom Written: Israel; to the believer: Romans 15:4.

When Written: Approximately 1500 B.C.

Where Written: In the wilderness: Acts 7:37,38.

Key Chapter: 12. The Passover.

Key Verse: 12:23.

Key Word: Redemption. Broadly, Exodus teaches that redemption is essential to every relationship with a holy God; and that a redeemed people cannot have fellowship with Him unless they are constantly cleansed from all defilement.

Key Phrase: Pass over you: 12:13.

Key Thought:[2] "The making of a Nation. It is important that we should understand the meaning of the creation of this Nation. It cannot be too often emphasized that it *was not* the election of a nation from among others in order that upon that nation God might lavish His love while He abandoned the others.

"The purpose of God was far wider than that of the creation of this nation. It was that of the creation of a testimony through this nation for the sake of the others. The Divine intention was the creation of a people who, under His covenant and government, should reveal in the world the breadth and beauty and beneficence of that government; a people who, gathered in their national life about His throne and His altar, obeying His commands and worshiping him, should reveal to outside nations the meaning of the Kingship of God. *It was not the selection of a pet but the creation of a pattern.*

"This nation's Ruler was to be Jehovah, its constitution was the Law given on Mount Sinai; its central national Shrine was the Tabernacle; its bond of unity was the spiritual worship of the One True God; and its national hope was the 'prophet like unto Moses' whose blood would be shed for the spiritual emancipation of the nation, as was the Passover Lamb, and whose bones, like the lamb's, should not be broken, who would come down from heaven to be the world's Bread of Life as the manna was the heaven-sent sustenance of Israel during its forty years of wandering in the wilderness of Sin."

Spiritual Thought: Come out for God.

Christ Is Seen as:
      1. God—"I AM THAT I AM": 3:14 with John 8:58
      2. Our Passover: 12:5 with I Corinthians 5:7b
      3. Manna: 16:14-22 with John 6:35
      4. Rock: 17:1-7 with I Corinthians 10:5
      5. Veil: 26:31-35 with Hebrews 10:19,20

Names and Titles of God. See NAME in Dictionary.
      1. El-Shaddai—I AM: 3:14,15
      2. Jehovah: 6:3. See JEHOVAH in Dictionary
      3. Jehovah-rophe—the Lord that healeth: 15:22-26
      4. Jehovah-nissi—the Lord our Banner: 17:8-15

Covenants in Exodus: See COVENANTS in Index.
      The Mosaic or Legal Covenant: 20:1—31:18

1. Israel's first Exodus: 12:29—15:22 with Genesis 15:13,14 (see EXODUS in Index).
Stated: ca. 2,000 B.C. *Fulfilled:* ca. 1,440 B.C.

2. No bones broken when Christ was on the cross: 12:46 with Psalm 34:20; John 19:36
Stated: ca. 1,480 B.C. *Fulfilled:* Christ's crucifixion.

Types of Christ:

1. The Passover: 12 with I Corinthians 5:7b. See PASSOVER in Index.
2. The Passover (paschal) Lamb: 12:3-6,46.
   The Lamb was—
   a. Appointed by God: 12:3 with John 1:29; Revelation 13:8
   b. Subjected to a time of testing: 12:5,6 with Luke 4:1-30
   c. Without blemish: 12:5 with I Peter 1:18,19
   d. Slain: 12:6 with Luke 24:26
   e. To have no broken bones: 12:46 with John 19:36
   f. To have its blood sprinkled: 12:7 with Hebrews 9:21-23
   g. To be roasted with fire, then eaten: 12:8 with John 6:53,54; Acts 2:23. It is Christ Himself crucified who satisfies. In Communion or the Lord's Supper we eat the elements, which are symbolic of His body and blood.
3. Manna: 16:11-35 with John 6:32-35
   a. Of divine origin: vs. 4 with John 1:1,2; 17:5
   b. Undeserved: vs. 12 with Romans 5:6,8
   c. Essential: vs. 15 with John 6:35; 15:5
   d. Suitable: vss. 16-18 with 6:48
   e. Adequate: vs. 18 with Philippians 4:19
   f. Satisfying: vs. 35 with John 6:35; Psalm 34:8a
   g. Gift of God: vs. 15 with Romans 6:23b; II Corinthians 9:15
4. Rock of Horeb: 17:1-7 with I Corinthians 10:4
   a. Chosen of God: vs. 6 with Matthew 3:17
   b. In a wilderness—Christ a Rock in a weary land: Isaiah 32:2
   c. Was smitten: vs. 6 with Isaiah 53:5,10; Zechariah 13:7. God instructed Moses to *speak* to the rock at Meribah (Numbers 20:8). Instead, Moses *smote* the rock twice. In disobeying God, he forfeited his privilege of entering the Promised Land. The rock, once smitten at Horeb, and representing the crucifixion of Christ, needed not to be smitten again. Moses' act of striking the rock implied that the one sacrifice of Christ was not sufficient (Hebrews 9:25-28). The water gushing out from the rock, in spite of disobedience, reveals the grace of God to a needy people (Numbers 20:10-12).
   d. A merciful provision: vs. 6: Psalms 78:15-20 with John 4:10,14
   e. Was free: vs. 6; Isaiah 55:1 with Revelation 22:17
   f. The Rock followed them—a continual supply—full of unseen blessings: I Corinthians 10:4; Philippians 4:19; Ephesians 1:3; Colossians 1:19
5. Moses—opened a new dispensation: 20:1—17 with John 1:17. See MOSES as Type in Index.
6. First fruits: 22:29 with I Corinthians 15:20
7. Aaron: 28:1 with Hebrews 5:4,5. While Christ is a priest after the order of Melchizedec,

THE TABERNACLE IN THE MIDST OF ISRAEL

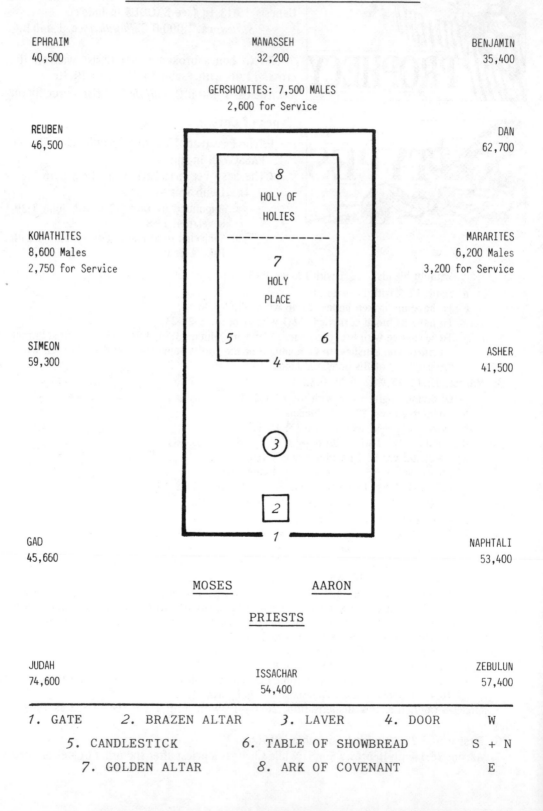

EPHRAIM
40,500

MANASSEH
32,200

BENJAMIN
35,400

GERSHONITES: 7,500 MALES
2,600 for Service

REUBEN
46,500

DAN
62,700

8

HOLY OF

HOLIES

KOHATHITES
8,600 Males
2,750 for Service

MARARITES
6,200 Males
3,200 for Service

7

HOLY

PLACE

5   6

SIMEON
59,300

ASHER
41,500

4

3

2

1

GAD
45,660

NAPHTALI
53,400

MOSES   AARON

PRIESTS

JUDAH
74,600

ISSACHAR
54,400

ZEBULUN
57,400

---

1. GATE   *2.* BRAZEN ALTAR   *3.* LAVER   *4.* DOOR   W

5. CANDLESTICK   *6.* TABLE OF SHOWBREAD   S + N

7. GOLDEN ALTAR   *8.* ARK OF COVENANT   E

He executes His priestly office after the pattern of Aaron. Hebrews 7 gives the *order;* Hebrews 9 gives the *pattern.*

    8. The Tabernacle: 25-40 [3]

        a. The PURPOSE of the Tabernacle: "Let them make Me a sanctuary; that I may dwell among them": 25:8

        b. The KEY VERSE which opens up to us the typical meaning of the Tabernacle is Hebrews 9:24: "For Christ is not entered into the holy places made with hands, which are the figures of the true; but into heaven itself, now to appear in the presence of God for us."

For Israel, the Tabernacle was instituted for the purpose of revealing through object lessons God's plan of redemption for every believing Israelite. Every part of the Tabernacle and all its appointed ministries were to Israel a symbol, a testimony of the coming Messiah and His blessed work of redemption. In the Tabernacle "they saw Him who is invisible" (Acts 7:44; Hebrews 11:27).

For us, the Holy Spirit has recorded the things concerning the Tabernacle to illustrate the work of redemption which has been accomplished by our Lord Jesus. To us these things are types or figures of the person and work of Christ. Without a knowledge of the Tabernacle and its typical meaning, very much of what the New Testament tells us of Christ and His ministry is but little understood.

        c. The Tabernacle as a Whole: 25—31. Jehovah designed His own sanctuary and set it up in the midst of Israel's camp as His dwelling place, meeting place, and revealing place. With unsearchable wisdom and marvelous grace the Lord grouped His people about Himself as worshipers, workers, and warriors. The worshipers, the priests, the Levites, and the workers were encamped close about the Tabernacle to minister in and care for Jehovah's tent. The camps of the warriors were outside the camps to guard the worshipers and workers. The outer court measured 150 feet by 75 feet

The Tabernacle was for Jehovah a sanctuary, a place "set apart," a holy place, the dwelling place of Him who is absolutely and eternally holy. As the Leader of His people, the Tabernacle was Jehovah's pavilion, in which His redeemed ones might hide in the day of trouble (Psalm 27:5; Colossians 3:3). As the King of Israel, Jehovah was enthroned in the Tabernacle as His Palace. As the Father of His people, the Tabernacle was the House of the Lord, in which His children might enjoy fellowship with Him. In the Tabernacle Jehovah dwelt in the midst of His people whom He had redeemed and brought near to Himself. His presence, manifested in the cloud by day and the pillar of fire by night, guided and protected them, and illuminated their pathway all through their wilderness journey (Nehemiah 9:18,19).

    1. The Foundation—Atonement Money: 30:11-16. This money, given by the people as an "atonement for their souls," went to form the foundation of the Tabernacle, so that the Tabernacle, as the House of God, literally stood upon the price of souls—Redemption. The Church of God today has no other standing. This "half shekel" is a figure of the precious blood of Christ, by which we have been ransomed for God (I Peter 1:18,19).[4]

        —All needed a ransom—"every man": vs. 12 with Romans 3:23

        —Ransom price divinely fixed: "half a shekel": vs. 13 with I Corinthians 6:19,20; I Peter 1:18,19

        —Ransom alike for all—"rich give no more, poor give no less": vs. 15 with I Timothy 2:6; Ephesians 2:8,9; Titus 3:5

        —Ransom presented personally: vs. 14 with "none of them can by any means redeem his brother, nor give God a ransom for him" (Psalm 49:7). It is "What must *I* do to be saved?" (Acts 16:30,31)

        —Ransom only ground of acceptance—"An half shekel *shall* be the offering:" vs. 13 with John 3:18,19

        —Those ransomed expected to serve: Numbers 1:45; Psalm 106:8 with Luke 1:74,75; Acts 27:23; Psalm 107:2

2. The Hangings of the Court: 27:9-19. The Court, or open space about the Tabernacle, measured 150 feet by 75 feet, and was enclosed by hangings of fine twined linen supported by pillars of brass (copper) which rested upon sockets of brass. These pillars were ornamented on top with chapiters of silver, under which were the hooks and fillets of silver which held up the hangings of linen. The fine twined linen to us is typical of the righteousness of God. The brass pillars and brass sockets which held up the hangings of linen speak to us typically of judgment (Revelation 1:15 RV). The silver chapiters, hooks and fillets, which helped to hold the linen, were made of the silver atonement money obtained from the men of war in Israel. This silver is typical of the precious blood of Christ by which we have been redeemed (I Peter 1:18,19). For us, the meaning of the linen hangings of the court, supported by the silver and brass pillars and sockets and hooks, is that God's righteousness was fully revealed on Calvary when God judged the sins of all the world through the atoning work of His Son (Romans 3:21,22; Hebrews 9:26).

3. The Gate: 27:16 (#1 in diagram). The Gate was the only opening through the hangings of the Court of the Tabernacle. It was made of blue, purple, scarlet, and fine twined linen, which hung at the east end of the Court. Under this Gate any or all the people of Israel might approach into the Court of Jehovah, Who dwelt in their midst. For us, the Gate is a type of Christ as the Way, the *only* way opened for man to come to the Father (John 14:6). The Gate was made of four colors:

—Blue—the color of the atmospheric heavens encircling the earth, is typical of Christ the heavenly One, the Son of God, as revealed in John's account of the gospel.

—Purple—the color of royalty, the color of a king's garment, is typical of Christ as the royal One, the King of Israel, as revealed in Matthew's account of the gospel.

—Scarlet—the color of blood, typifies the suffering, sorrowing, sympathizing Savior seeking and saving the lost, as revealed in Luke's account of the gospel.

Fine Linen—a type of the righteousness of Christ as the righteous, faithful Servant of God, as revealed in Mark's account of the gospel. See GOSPEL, Why Four, in Index.

4. The Brazen Altar: 27:1-8 (#2 in diagram). The Brazen Altar, or burnt offering altar, was made of heavy boards of shittim or acacia wood, overlaid with heavy plates of brass. Upon the Brazen Altar the Lord consumed the whole burnt offering. The only ground for forgiveness and acceptance for Israel before God was acceptable offerings. The five kinds of offerings (Leviticus 1—7) all pointed typically to Christ, the sum and fulfillment of them all (Hebrews 10:1-17). He is the offering which God provided, by and through whom sinful man is forgiven and accepted in the Father's holy presence (John 1:29; 14:6). The five offerings typical of Christ are:

—The Burnt Offering (Leviticus 1). Willingly and wholly offered unto God, it is typical of Christ Who so delighted in doing God's will that He obeyed the Father perfectly, pleasing Him in all things in His life, and then becoming obedient unto death (John 8:29; Galatians 1:4; Philippians 2:8). Christ's perfect obedience, and therefore perfect holiness, is the basis for God's acceptance of His death for us, and thus our acceptance in Him. The acceptance of all other sacrifices depend upon the acceptance of the whole burnt offering. The ascending smoke of the consumed burnt offering was the testimony that God accepted the offering. So the resurrection and ascension of Christ is the eternal proof of God's acceptance of Him, and of every believer in Him (Ephesians 1:6; 2:6).

—The Meat Offering (Leviticus 2). Of fine flour, ground between the upper and nether millstones, it was the food of the priests and their families, after a handful, anointed with oil, had been offered unto God. It typifies Christ anointed with the Spirit, living, loving, and dying for man by the hand of the lawless, yet in accordance with the determined counsel and foreknowledge of God (Acts 2:23; 10:38; Ephesians 5:25,26). Christ as the meat offering meets the demand of God against man because of man's lack of love toward Him and his fellowman, and becomes also the One to supply that need in the believer's heart by filling us with His love for others (II Corinthians 5:14a).

—The Peace Offering (Leviticus 3). It was eaten by the Levites after the fat, the food of the offering for God, had been burned on the altar with the burnt offering. This offering is a type of Christ as the One Who reconciled us to God by giving that which satisfies and delights Him, and which satisfies Christ, our great High Priest, and thus satisfying us in Him. The peace offering depended upon the whole burnt offering for its acceptance, and the crowning result of Christ satisfying God's claim against us was not only His bearing our sins but being made sin for us as well (I Peter 2:24; II Corinthians 5:18,19; Colossians 1:20).

—The Sin Offering (Leviticus 4). It was a sacrifice atoning for the sins committed ignorantly, and is typical of Christ's bearing the judgment of God against man's sinful nature (Ephesians 2:3). The sinful nature inherited from the first Adam was judged in the death of the second Adam, as the Head of a new race, of which every believer is a member (I Corinthians 15:45-47; II Corinthians 5:17; Romans 5:12—8:38). But He Who was made sin for us was made unto us sanctification and redemption also; for in Him not only was our sinful nature judged, thus delivering us from the power of sin, but His own divine nature is imparted to every believer, and thus power to please God realized in the fullness of the Holy Spirit (I Corinthians 1:30; II Peter 1:4; Romans 8:13).

—The Trespass Offering (Leviticus 5:1—6:7). It was a sacrifice of atoning for known sins, and is typical of Christ as the One Who bore in His own body the penalty of man's sinful acts, words, deeds, and thoughts (Romans 5:6; I Peter 2:24; I Corinthians 15:3,4). By His act of faith in laying down His life for us, He made it possible for God to manifest His righteousness in dealing with man's sins in such a way that He maintained His holy character and government, and at the same time justifies every sinner who believes that Christ died for his sins. Oh, what holiness and love, what truth and grace, when righteousness and peace kissed each other at the cross, and all for me (Psalm 85:10).

The position of the Altar was within the Gate of the Court before the Door of the Tabernacle (40:6). At this Altar the Lord met the people as they came under the Gate, and judged them and their sins. As a holy God He dealt with them according to His law, not on the ground of the law, but on the ground of grace, for His love provided for that sinning Israelite a substitute to be judged. Had Jehovah dealt with them on the ground of the law, no innocent lamb without blemish would have received the stroke of God's wrath, but the guilty sinner himself would have paid the penalty for his own sin. When an Israelite came to the Altar with a trespass or sin offering, according to the word of His grace, the death of the offering answered for the death of the guilty Israelite, and the acceptance of the offering meant the acceptance and forgiveness of the one for whom the sacrifice was offered (Leviticus 4—5). Jehovah manifested His acceptance of a sin offering or trespass offering by consuming the fat on the Altar with the burnt offering. The sinner who believed the testimony of the ascending smoke was filled with peace and joy in the assurance that he was delivered from the penalty and guilt of his sins (Romans 5:1).

This Altar with all its appointed ministry speaks to us of Christ's finished work upon the cross. The Altar itself was so built that it could endure the devouring fire of God's wrath. As such it is a type of Christ as the only One Who was humbly and divinely able to bear the wrath of God against sin and the sinner. On Calvary God met us and righteously judged all of our sins and reconciled us unto Himself, having made peace by the blood of the cross, so that every believer may come acceptably into His holy presence. The result of God's work for every believer is peace and righteousness, and the effect of righteousness—quietness and assurance forever (Isaiah 32:17; Colossians 1:20).

5. The Laver: 30:17:21; 38:8 (#3 in diagram). As a polished brass vessel, its use was to reveal uncleanness, as a mirror, and to hold water for cleansing. Here the high priest and priests washed their hands and feet often every day, that their ministry at the Altar and in the holy place might be acceptable to the Lord (29:4). Any omission of this washing at the Laver meant death (30:20,21). For us the typical meaning of the Laver is "Christ loved the Church

and gave Himself for it, that the Church might be made holy, purified in the bath with the water of His Word'' (Ephesians 5:25,26—Fenton). ''Bath'' or ''washing'' is the Greek word for ''laver.'' Here we learn that the Laver is a type of the Word of God whereby we are sanctified, or cleansed (John 15:3; 17:17). The daily washing of the hands and feet of the priests foreshadowed the sanctification or cleansing of believers as to their service (hands) and their walk (feet) by His Word and His Spirit. This washing is necessary, for Jesus answered, ''If I wash thee not, thou hast no part with Me'' (John 13:8). As the priests were cleansed daily and entered into the presence of the Lord to live for others a life of service, so it is our privilege, as priests, to live wholly unto the Lord for Him and for others in a life of service and walk (I Peter 2:5; Revelation 1:5,6).

6. The Door: 26:36,37 (#4 in diagram). The Door was the entrance to the Tabernacle proper. The Tabernacle measured 45 feet long and 45 feet wide. The Holy Place of the Tabernacle measured 15 feet wide and 30 feet long, and the Holy of Holies of the Tabernacle measured 15 feet by 15 feet. This Door hung at the east entrance or end of the Tabernacle. The Gate, leading into the Court of the Tabernacle, represents the historical Christ as revealed in the four gospels; but the Door, upheld by five pillars, is typical of the risen and glorified Christ as represented or revealed through the five writers of the Epistles. For us, the Door is clearly a shadow of Him who said, ''I am the Door'' (John 10:7). Christ as the Door is the One through whom we have ''access by faith into this grace wherein we stand'' (Romans 5:2; Ephesians 2:18). As the Gate, Christ opened the Way for us to come unto the Father. As the Door, having come through the Gate, we find Christ leading us in paths of righteousness, in and out, finding green pastures and rest to our souls (John 10:9; Matthew 11:28,29).

7. The Veil: 26:31-35. The Veil was a hanging of blue, purple, scarlet, and fine twined linen, with the figures of cherubim embroidered upon it. See GOSPEL, Why Four, in Index. The veil separated the most holy place from the holy place, shutting the priests out from the presence of Jehovah, and shutting in His glory, which was revealed alone to the high priest once a year. The Veil of the Temple was rent in twain from top to bottom when Christ died on the cross. For us the Veil is typical of the ''flesh'' of Christ (Hebrews 10:19,20). The body of flesh in which Jesus dwelt was the Veil which shut in His glory as the only begotten Son of God (John 1:14). When the flesh of Christ was rent on Calvary, the Veil of the Temple was rent, so that now, as priests, we may come boldly into the presence of our Father, into the most holy place, and there behold the glory of God in the face of Jesus Christ (Hebrews 4:16; II Corinthians 4:6). See VEIL in Index.

8. The Boards: 26:15-30. Forty-eight boards of shittim wood ''standing up'' made the walls of the Tabernacle. The boards resting on and fixed in the foundation typify the believers' relationship to Christ and to one another (see BOARDS, p. 69).

> —Cut down. Saul (Paul) had this experience while on his way to Damascus and was severed from his old ways and works (Acts 9:1-20)
> —Dried up. The old sap of selfishness and carnality must be dried up before work can be done in us and by us
> —Cleansed. It is not enough to be cut off from the old life; everything about us that would hinder us from filling a place in God's service must be cleansed (John 15:3)
> —Clothed. These boards were not only cleansed but covered with gold. A new beauty was put upon them. When the sinner is cleansed, he is clothed with the beauty of the Lord (Psalm 149:4). See BOARDS in Index.
> —Fitly framed together. When planted in the foundation they were closely joined one to another. On the foundation alone could they be joined together. True spiritual union only comes through our being joined together in Christ. Every board resting on the sockets of atonement had a point of contact and fellowship with the foundation. We too, upon our Foundation (Christ Jesus), have a point of contact with Him and with one another (Ephesians 2:19-22; 4:16) [4]

9. The Coverings: 26:7-14. A tent made of curtains covered the Tabernacle. Ten curtains of fine twined linen (blue, purple, and scarlet, with cherubim) made the Tabernacle proper (26:1-6). The holy place, God's dwelling place, was made by hanging these ten curtains, fastened together, over the boards. Eleven curtains of goats' hair covered the Tabernacle. A covering of rams' skins dyed red was placed over the goats' hair covering, and above and over all was the covering of badgers' skins.

The four coverings—linen, goats' hair, rams' skin, and badgers' skins, represent the different divisions in connection with the Tabernacle. Each teaches us an experience in Christ.

> —The wilderness without—by the badgers' skins. In our natural state we could only see the blessed Redeemer as the "badger skin" covering—no beauty, no attractiveness—because we had no sense of our guilt or need.
> —The Court of Sacrifice—by the rams' skins dyed red. In the "rams' skins dyed red" we have been cleansed and changed by the power of His atoning blood through faith.
> —The Holy Place—by the pure goats' hair. In the "goats' hair" covering we experience what it is to be made clean, delivered from the power of sin, hid in God, and kept by His mighty, overshadowing power
> —The Holy of Holies—by the fine twined linen. In the innermost curtain of "fine twined linen" we are walking in the light as He is in the light, beholding His glory, and filled with all the fullness of God [5]

10. The Candlestick: 25:31-40 (#5 in diagram). The first need for the priestly ministry in the holy place was light, for all natural light was shut out of this sacred place. To give light, a one-piece, six-branch Candlestick was beaten out of pure gold. Pure olive oil was burned in the lamps continually (27:20,21). For us, the Candlestick is a dim shadow of our glorious Lord, who is the Light and Glory of heaven, as well as the Light of the world (John 8:12; Revelation 21:22,23). The beating of the gold suggests to us the suffering which preceded the glory, for the "Lamb is the light thereof" (Revelation 21:23). The Candlestick, with its main stem and six branches, typifies Christ and His Church, for the lamps which reveal the beauty of the Candlestick pre-figured those who "show forth the praises of Him who hath called us out of darkness into His marvelous light" (I Peter 2:9). The oil for the lamp is always a type of the Holy Spirit, the great Illuminator, who reveals Christ to us and empowers us for service that Christ might be revealed in us: I Samuel 16:13; John 16:14; Acts 1:8; I John 2:27. See CANDLESTICK in picture, p. 384.

11. The Table of Showbread: 25:23-30 (#6 in diagram). Food, as well as light, was needed by the priests who ministered in Jehovah's presence; therefore, He set a Table for them in His sanctuary. Twelve loaves of showbread, baked out of fine flour, were placed fresh upon the Table every Sabbath day, and the other loaves were eaten by the high priest and priests in the holy place (Leviticus 24:5-9). The Table and bread foreshadow the provision our Father's love has made to nourish His priests in His presence today. The loaves are typical of Christ presenting Himself to God as food for man. The eating of the showbread by the priests in the holy place is typical of the experience which we enjoy, as we live in fellowship with the Lord, and realize in the full assurance of faith the blessed way we are upheld in and by Him before our Father.

12. The Golden Altar: 30:1-10, 34-38 (#7 in diagram). That His priests might work and worship acceptably, Jehovah commands Moses to make an Altar upon which to burn incense. A crown of gold and four horns adorned its top. Upon the horns, once a year, the high priest sprinkled blood for the sin offering. The position of the Altar before the veil places it before the Ark, or the throne of God. Perpetual incense was burned upon the Golden Altar by the high priest. How simple, yet how necessary was every piece of furniture in the Tabernacle! A Candlestick for light, a Table for food, and an Altar for worship. For us, the Altar overlaid with gold and crowned with gold is clearly a type of our blessed Lord, now crowned with glory and honor (Hebrews 2:9). The Altar represents the glorious Person of Christ, and the offering of the perpetual incense by the high priest typifies His ever-living intercession in our behalf, as our

High Priest (Hebrews 7:25-28). As a cloud of incense must cover the Mercy Seat, so Christ, our High Priest, entered with His own blood into the presence of God for us, covering the Mercy Seat with the cloud of incense—His intercessory prayer of John 17.

13. The Ark: 25:10-22 (#8 in diagram). The Ark was the only piece of furniture in the most holy place, unless it was the Golden Censer (Hebrews 9:3,4). It was used as a chest in which to keep the second tablets or tables of the Law. The first set of the tables of the Law were broken by Moses (32:19). Then the Lord gave him a special command to make an Ark in which to keep the second set of tables (Deuteronomy 10:1-5). For us, the vessel in which the Law was kept is a type of Christ in Whose heart the law of God was written and Who kept it perfectly in letter and in spirit (Psalm 40:8; Matthew 5:17).

Ark of the Covenant

14. The Mercy Seat: 25:17,21,22. The Mercy Seat was a lid of pure gold made to cover the Ark, and thus to cover the Law within (26:34; 30:6; Leviticus 16:13). The blood of the bullock and goat was sprinkled upon the Mercy Seat by the high priest, once a year, on the great day of atonement. Above the Mercy Seat, between the Cherubim, Jehovah manifested His presence in the most holy place. The Mercy Seat was thus His throne, "the throne of grace" (Hebrews

4:16). The Holy Spirit has given the key to the typical meaning of the Mercy Seat in Hebrews 9:5 and Romans 3:25. The same Greek word translated "mercy seat" in Hebrews 9:5 is translated "propitiation" in Romans 3:25. Therefore, Christ is the One Whom God has set forth as a Mercy Seat. Christ, as the Mercy Seat, is the One Who has covered the Law, or satisfied all the claims of the Law as a man under the Law, by perfectly obeying it (Galatians 4:4,5). Second, the blood on the Mercy Seat tells us that Christ by His death satisfied the demand of the Law against every sinner who will believe in God's Word (Ezekiel 18:4; Romans 6:23; 5:6).

15. The Cherubim: 25:18-22. The two Cherubim, on the two ends of the Mercy Seat, were beaten work of one piece of gold with the Mercy Seat. The oneness of the Cherubim with the Mercy Seat typifies our oneness with Christ in the glory which is now His at the right hand of the Majesty on high. The Scripture indicates that the living creatures and the Cherubim are the same, and typically, they represent the redeemed, blood-bought believers in glory (Ezekiel 1—10; Revelation 4,5). The pictured ivory fragment could well depict the Tabernacle Cherubim. This oneness with Him, made possible by our acceptance of Him by faith, sets forth our marvelous standing with Him.

Cherubim

—Beaten out of the same piece of gold, one with Him in suffering, as well as one with Him in glory: Romans 8:17

—One with Him in death, and one with Him in life: Romans 6:8

—One with Him in weakness, and one with Him in power: 12:9,10; II Corinthians 13:4

—One with Him in poverty, and one with Him in riches: II Corinthians 8:9; Ephesians 3:8; Romans 8:17

The facing of the Cherubim "toward the Mercy Seat" suggests that our hearts and minds will be occupied with our Lord above all else. His will, His pleasure, His glory is to be the supreme ambition of our whole being; II Corinthians 5:9; Colossians 1:10,18. Enthroned between the Cherubim was the One Who said, "Let them make Me a sanctuary that I may dwell among them." From thence He communed with the high priest, and from thence He ruled over Israel by revealing His will to the high priest. "He that dwelleth in the secret place of the Most High shall abide under the shadow of the Almighty" (Psalm 91:1). This secret place, in the presence of the Most Holy One, is the place where the Father covers us with His pinions, where He guards us from all evil, where He gives us victory of the enemy, where He answers our prayers, where He honors us, where He satisfies us, and where He shows to us our salvation.

Types of the Believer's Experiences:

1. The Egyptian bondage: 1:7-14; 5:1-14—a type of our bondage to sin: Ephesians 2:1-3
2. The Exodus from Egypt—a type of abandonment of the sinful life
3. Pharaoh's pursuit of Israel: 14:9,10—a type of the evil forces pursuing believers
4. The Cloud by day and the Pillar of fire by night: 14:19,20—a type of God's divine

presence with His protection for us: Hebrews 13:5b; Matthew 28:20b. See CLOUD in Index.

5. Opening of the Red Sea: 14:26-31—a type of hindrance removed

6. Closing the Red Sea after crossing: 14:28—a type of separation from the world: Romans. 12:1,2; II Corinthians 6:13-18

7. The Wilderness Journey—a type of our going around in circles of doubt, perplexity, fear, and anxiety. When the Israelites had crossed the Sea and had received the Law at Sinai, they soon reached the border of Canaan. Fear of the inhabitants of the land and distrust of God's greatness caused them to turn toward the wilderness. We do nothing but go around in circles when we are out of the will of God.

8. Marah and Elim: 15:23-27—a type of bitter and sweet experiences of the Christian life: Romans 8:28

9. The Flesh Pots: 16:3—a type of the sensual desires and pleasures of the old self-life.

10. The Mixed Multitude: 12:38—a type of the worldly element in the church: Matthew 13:24-30

11. Upholding the hands of Moses: 17:12—a type of cooperation with God's leaders and working together in the unity of the Spirit: Ephesians 4:11-16; Hebrews 13:17

12. The Tabernacle.[6] From the wilderness without to the presence of God within the Holy of Holies, there were seven steps or experiences:

   a. Decision at the Gate
   b. Acceptance at the Altar
   c. Cleansing at the Laver
   d. Intercession at the Altar of Incense
   e. Fellowship at the Table
   f. Testimony at the Candlestick
   g. Faith turned into sight within the Veil

Types of Law and Grace:

Mount Sinai. Moses not only received the Law from God on Sinai, but also the pattern for the Tabernacle, which is a type of Christ. The Law, as the schoolmaster, leads to Christ (Galatians 3:24,25). See ALLEGORY in Index.

1. Burning bush, but not consumed—to attract Moses, and to remind him that he was on holy ground and in the presence of a holy God: 3:2

2. Moses' Rod turned into a serpent and back into a rod—to confirm his faith: 4:2-5

3. Moses' hand made leprous and healed—to increase his faith: 4:6,7

4. Aaron's rod turned into a serpent—to convince Pharaoh that his and Moses' mission was of God: 7:10-12

5. Aaron's rod swallowed up the rods of the magicians—to show the magicians that Aaron's God could overcome their power: 7:10-13

6. The Ten Plagues: 7:20-12:30.[7] Each time Moses sought permission from Pharaoh for Israel to leave Egypt, he was refused. For each refusal, God sent a plague. Not only were these plagues a great annoyance and a heavy burden to the Egyptians, they revealed the helplessness and powerlessness of their gods before the one true God of Israel. It is repeated over and over that by these plagues Israel and Egypt both would come to "know that Jehovah is God" (6:7; 7:5,17; 8:22; 10:2; 14:4,18). Archaeological findings show that each plague was either a direct or an indirect "strike" at one or more of Egypt's deities.

   a. Turning of the Nile river into blood: 7:20-25. The priests of Egypt held blood in abhorrence, yet they cruelly sported with the blood of the captive Israelites whose children they caused to be cast into the river. The Egyptians worshiped the river Nile, but its waters being turned into blood must have excited their loathing and detestation, while the calamity would cover them with confusion and shame of their deity being degraded.

b. The plague of frogs: 8:5-14. Frogs were consecrated to the Egyptian deity Osiris and were the symbol of inspiration. Egypt's gross superstition was suitably punished when their sacred river was polluted with swarms of these creatures, filling the land, entering their houses, their beds, the vessels of their food—making the whole country offensive.

c. The plague of lice: 8:16-18. The idolatries of Egypt were accompanied with rites, the most unclean, foul, and abominable, but were performed under the appearance of scrupulous external cleanliness, especially in respect to the priests. They were excessively cautious lest any lice should be found on their garments; so that by this plague their superstitious prejudices must have been distressingly shocked and the people with the priests overwhelmed with a common disgrace.

d. The plague of flies: 8:20-24. The Egyptians worshiped several deities, whose province it was to drive away flies. In many places they even offered an ox in sacrifice to these despicable insects. Beelzebub, or Baalzebul, the god of Ekron, was a fly deity of this people (II Kings 1:2). The plague of flies, therefore, was the more grievous to them, as it so utterly degraded this revered divinity.

e. The Murrain of the cattle: 9:3-6. The Egyptians held many beasts in idolatrous veneration. The lion, wolf, dog, cat, ape, and goat were held sacred by them; but especially the ox, heifer, and ram. The soul of their god Osiris was believed to reside in the body of the bull Apis, yet neither Osiris nor all the rest could save the beasts of Egypt from the fatal disease which fell upon them at the command of Moses.

f. The plague of boils: 9:8-11. The Egyptians had several medical divinities, to whom, on special occasions, they sacrificed human beings. They were burnt alive on a high altar, and their ashes were cast into the air, that with every scattered ash a blessing might descend. Moses took ashes from the furnace and cast them into the air. Scattered by the wind—overspreading the land, they descended upon priests, people, and beasts as tormenting boils, and shamed their honored, medical deities.

g. The plague of hail: 9:22-26. Egypt's gods of Nature were helpless when Israel's God, through an act of nature, spoiled much of the land's food.

h. The plague of locusts: 10:12-19. As though to add insult to injury, swarms of locusts went up over all the land of Egypt and devoured every herb of the land and fruit of the trees which the hail had left

i. The plague of darkness: 10:21-23. The Egyptians worshiped darkness as the origin of their gods. Orpheus, the most ancient pagan writer, said in one of his hymns: "I will sing of night, the parent of the gods and men—night, the origin of all things." Egypt was plagued with a terrible darkness—the blackness of darkness which is felt, and which their gods had no power to prevent or alleviate, while the Israelites enjoyed light in all their dwellings, truly a miracle that only the living God could perform! Imagine being in a living room with a lighted bulb and one-half of the room had light (Israel) and the other half (Egypt) was in total darkness. Impossible, but not with God (Luke 1:37).

j. The death of the firstborn: 12:29,30. There were at least two reasons for this plague—(1) Pharaoh himself was considered a god, and his first-born son, in succeeding him upon the throne, also succeeded him as deity. Because of this plague, one of Egypt's gods actually died. (2) This plague was to avenge their unlamented cruelties upon the people of Israel. Egypt had enslaved Israel and had murdered their male children, but now the awful vengeance of God overtook them in righteous retribution visiting every house.

The miracle of the plagues takes on greater weight when we consider:

a. That some were predicted—"tomorrow"—flies, 8:23,24; murrain, 9:5,6; hail, 9:18; locust, 10:4. The removal time was also made known: frogs, 8:10,11; and hail, 9:29.

b. That a division was drawn between Israel and Egypt. Where Israel resided in Goshen there were no flies, 8:22; no Murrain, 9:4; no hail, 9:26; no darkness, 10:21-23, etc.

7. Cloud by day and Pillar of fire by night—to baffle the Egyptians and for Israel's guidance and protection: 13:20,21: Numbers 9:15-23. It gave them comfort from the heat of the noon-day desert sun and warmth in the extreme coldness of the desert land at night; also, as long as the surrounding nations saw the cloud, they dared not touch God's people. See CLOUDS in Index.

8. The Red Sea divided—an avenue of escape for Israel from Pharaoh's army and to destroy the Egyptians: 14:21,30,31. See DELIVERANCE in Index. Pictured is a swift chariot that dates back to Israel's exodus from Egypt, a type used by Pharaoh in pursuit of the children of Israel.

9. Waters of Marah made sweet, water from the rock of Horeb, and manna sent daily, the Sabbath excepted—to supply Israel's need in a weary land: 15:23:25; 16:14-35; 17:5-7

10. Victory over the Amelekites—to show Israel that God would fight their battles: 17:8-16

11. The Tablets of Stone (Ten Commandments), written with the finger of God—to show that God's laws are of Divine origin, apart from man's wisdom: 31:18; 32:16-18. Why written on stone? Someone has said that the Law was given to be kept—stone cannot be bent or twisted or stretched—it is either kept or broken. The Law can only be kept or broken. It, too, cannot be bent or twisted or stretched.

1. Straw in brickmaking: 1:11-14; 5:7,12. When the Israelites were placed in bondage, they were required to build treasure cities (or store cities), and their lives were made hard with bondage "in mortar and brick." Their labor was made even more difficult under the taskmasters when Pharaoh withheld straw for brickmaking. The Israelites first had to gather straw for themselves and finally had to resort to collecting stubble. An ancient Egyptian document, the Papyrus Anastasi, contains a complaint of an officer in charge of erecting buildings. "I am without equipment. There are no people to make bricks, and there is no straw in the district." When a site in the delta of Egypt, called Tell el Maskhuta, was excavated, inscriptions were found containing the word "Pi Tum." This caused archaeologists to identify this site with the treasury city of Pithom, built by the Israelites. Some bricks found there were actually made without straw. There is a monument of Raamses in the University Museum (Philadelphia, Pa.) which makes mention of the cities of Raamses and Pithom having been built by Semetic slaves. Although the picture on the following page is of a Pharaoh, it is a good likeness of a "taskmaster." Note the "straw" in these ancient Egyptian bricks.

2. Egypt's Wisdom and Riches: 2:1-11a; Acts 7:18-23; Hebrews 11:23-27. Moses, reared as the son of an Egyptian princess, required a princely education, and was schooled in all the wisdom (sciences) of the Egyptians, who were unsurpassed in those days in civilization by any people in the world. This, coupled with the fact that Moses lived in the palace for forty years, would fit him for any office in the government, even the throne. He became familiar with court life, with the military, with their sciences and law, their literature, their architecture, and the pomp of their religious life, and acquired a general acquaintance with the arts of his day (see SCIENTIFICALLY SPEAKING in Acts). He also enjoyed the riches possessed by Egyptian royalty.

The huge buildings, temples, pyramids, obelisks, etc., left by the ancient Pharaohs, reveal wisdom par excellence. When archaeologists opened the tomb of Tutankhamen (King "Tut" to us) in 1922, their eyes gazed upon an untold wealth of personal belongings for his future life. His solid gold coffin has a current value of $2,750,000. The jewelry is priceless and his throne and furniture were overlaid with gold. Such "burial" wealth gives us an idea of the personal wealth of a single Pharaoh.

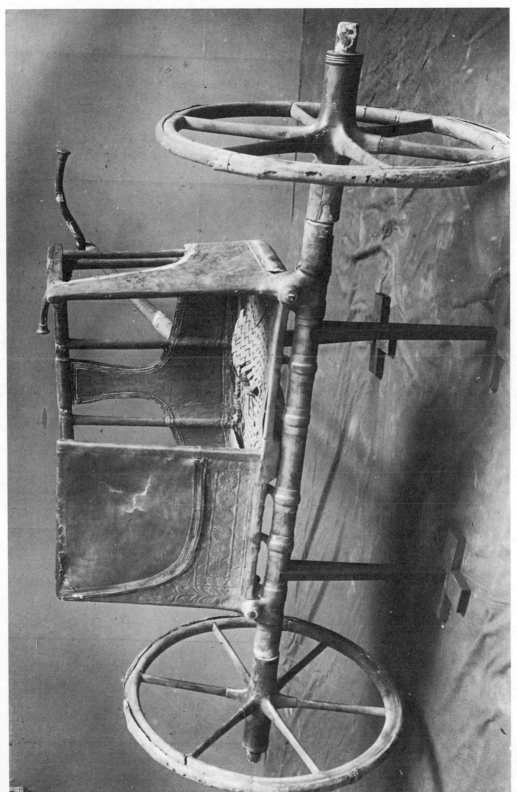

Egyptian Chariot

Egyptian "Taskmaster"

Straw in Bricks

Moses was instructed in all Egypt's wisdom, mighty in words and in deeds. Josephus, the noted Jewish historian of the first century A.D., informs us that Moses was mighty in military deeds as an Egyptian officer, which, no doubt, prepared him for leading Israel in the wilderness. As the "son" of a princess he might have become a Pharaoh and a "god," plus being a multi-millionaire as a member of the royal family. Yet he "refused to be called the son of

Pharaoh's daughter, . . . esteeming the reproach of Christ greater riches than the treasures in Egypt.'' What a tremendous help the archaeologist has been to us in revealing what Moses forsook in casting his lot with God and Christ.

3. The Ten Plagues. See PLAGUES in Index.

4. The Passover and Tabernacle Worship: 12, 25—40. Archaeological evidence shows there is no comparison between the Canaanite's religion and the feasts revealed by God to Israel. The Ras Shamra tablets, found in 1929 in northern Syria, reveal a vulgar, immoral paganism, as illustrated in the description of the chief god, El, and his son Baal. "Every fresh publication of Canaanite mythological texts makes the gulf between the religions of Canaan and of Israel increasingly clear."[8] "The critical idea that the feasts of Israel are to be connected with the pagan Canaanite religion is completely different from that of Israel, as shown by the Ras Shamra tablets."[9] See BAAL in Index.

5. Hornets sent before Israel: 23:28; Deuteronomy 7:20; Joshua 24;12. See HORNETS in Index.

6. Boards for the Holy of Holies: 26:15-25. When King Tut-ankh-amun's tomb was discovered in Egypt in 1922, his solid gold coffin was inside two wooden cases overlaid with gold, a rose-granite sarcophagus (stone vault), and four shrines (or chapels), the outer one 17 feet long, 11 feet wide, 9 feet high, made of gold overlaid boards, and portable. A linen covering which draped over the framework of the outer chapel was folded and placed on a stool. This portable chapel with the linen covering could be an example of the "Holy of Holies" and the linen curtains of the Tabernacle made by Moses and transported by Israel in the wilderness.

7. Lookingglasses: 35:22-29; 38:8. When Moses asked Israel for gifts to be presented for the construction of the Tabernacle, the women gave rings, bracelets, and the "lookingglasses." This reference is most puzzling since there is no mention of "glass" being used. Archaeologists give us the answer—"lookingglasses" in our King James translation were "molten looking glasses"—made of copper and finely polished to give a good reflection (Job 37:18). Such bronze or copper mirrors were especially common during the time of bondage, exodus, and later years (1,500—1,200 B.C.).

[10] 1. Loins girded: 12:11. An important part of the Eastern custom is the girdle—a long piece of cloth like a shawl, folded around the waist or loins. It is useful in keeping in order the long loose robes. Paul, in listing what a well-dressed Christian wears, says to "stand therefore, having your loins girt about with truth" (Ephesians 6:14). "Loins girded" implies being ready, waiting on the Lord, not sitting in idleness with loose and disorderly garments, which could easily trip us, causing us to stumble, fall—becoming a reproach to Christ.

2. Garment not to be taken in pledge: 22:26,27. "If thou at all take thy neighbor's raiment to pledge, . . . wherein shall he sleep?" Articles were given as a pledge of security, such as a shoe (see SHOE in Index). It was most unkind to take and keep a coat or cloak for a pledge, since it might deprive the owner of his nightly covering.

Scientifically Speaking: See SCIENTIFICALLY SPEAKING in Acts for enlightenment of paintings on many ancient Egyptian buildings.

Exodus in the New Testament:
1. Birth of Moses: 2:2 with Hebrews 11:23
2. Moses' smiting a Hebrew: 2:11,12 with Acts 7:24
3. Burning bush: 3:2 with Acts 7:30
4. Sprinkled blood: 12:7 with Hebrews 12:24

Copper Mirrors

5. Crossing the Red Sea: 14:22 with I Corinthians 10:2; Hebrews 11:29
6. Manna: 16:15 with John 6:31-51
7. Rock in Horeb: 17:6 with I Corinthians 10:4
8. Setting bounds around Mt. Sinai: 19:12 with Hebrews 12:18-20
9. The Ten Commandments: 20:1-17
   a. First—no other gods: vs. 3 with Mark 12:29,30.
   b. Second—no graven images: vss. 4-6 with I Corinthians 10:14; I John 5:21
   c. Third—honor God's name: vs. 7 with Matthew 5:33-37; Philippians 2:9-11
   d. Fourth—keeping the Sabbath: vss. 8-11 with Luke 23:56
   e. Fifth—honoring parents: vs. 12 with Matthew 15:4a; Ephesians 6:2,3.
   f. Sixth—committing no murder: vs. 13 with Matthew 5:21,22
   g. Seventh—committing no adultery: vs. 14 with Matthew 5:27,28
   h. Eighth—committing no robbery: vs. 15 with Romans 13:9
   i. Ninth—not bearing false witness: vs. 16 with Romans 13:9
   j. Tenth—not coveting: vs. 17 with Mark 12:31; Romans 7:7

It is interesting to note that all the Ten Commandments are repeated in the New Testament—to be kept—*except the fourth*. This commandment was to be a *sign between God and Israel* throughout all her generations—forever (31:12-18). It is not repeated in the New Testament as a commandment for this dispensation. See SABBATHS in Index.

10. Blood of the Covenant: 24:6,8 with Hebrews 9:19-22
11. Tabernacle furniture: 26:35 with Hebrews 9:2
12. Israel's folly: 32:6b with I Corinthians 10:7
13. Veil over Moses' face: 34:33 with II Corinthians 3:13
14. A large portion of Stephen's address before the Sanhedrin is a recalling of events in Exodus: babies killed, bondage, Moses' education, burning bush, Moses before Pharaoh, the Exodus, Red Sea crossing, giving of the Law, Israel's "golden calf," making of the Tabernacle, etc. (Acts 7:17-44).
15. Companion references:
    a. Kingdom of priests: 19:6a with I Peter 2:5,9
    b. Holy Nation: 19:6b with I Peter 2:9

SEED THOUGHTS

1. Excuses of Moses: 3:1—4:16.
   a. The excuse of *proud humility*—"Who am I that I should go ...": 3:11. God's answer: 3:12
   b. The excuse of *educated ignorance*—"What is His name? What shall I say . . . ": 3:13. God's answer: 3:14-22

c. The excuse of *doubting faith*—"They will not believe me, nor hearken unto my voice . . .": 4:1. God's answer: 4:2-9

      d. The excuse of *speaker's fright*—"I am not eloquent . . . ": 4:10. God's answer: 4:11-13

      e. The result of arguing with God: someone else shares in the blessing that could have been ours if we had only said "yes" and not "but" like Moses: 4:14-16. See POEM, "But," in Index.

2. We are not called upon by God to be successful, but to be *obedient*. It is the work of the Holy Spirit to make men believe—it is ours to answer God's call and trust Him with the results: 4:1 with I Corinthians 4:2; 3:7.

3. The "I Wills" of God: 6:1-8. See "I WILLS" in Index.

      a. I will defeat Pharaoh (the *cause* of their bondage): vs. 1 with Hebrews 2:14; I John 3:8

      b. I will lift your burdens: vs. 6a with Matthew 11:28

      c. I will rid you of bondage: vs. 6b with John 8:32,36

      d. I will redeem you: vs. 6c with Galatians 3:13a; I Peter 1:18,19.

NOTE: Redemption could not come until the *cause* of bondage was dealt with. Jesus *first* judged the prince of this world and spoiled principalities and powers before a victorious redemption could become effective (John 12:31; Colossians 2:15). What good would redemption be if our foe were not defeated? We could never "resist the devil that he flee from us," have the "whole armor of God" to quench all his fiery darts, or be "more than conquerors" (James 4:7; Ephesians 6:11-17; Romans 8:37). God did not provide "coats of skins" for Adam and Eve until He first pronounced judgment upon that old serpent, Satan (Genesis 3:9-21). The Passover (redemption) was not instituted until after the judgments of the plagues against Pharaoh (Exodus 7:1—12:33). Our redemption was established when Christ defeated Satan and came forth from the grave with "the keys of hell and of death" (Revelation 1:18).

      e. I will make you a people: vs. 7a with John 1:12; I Peter 2:10

      f. I will be your God: vs. 7b with II Corinthians 6:16,18. NOTE: No room here for the "Fatherhood of God and the Brotherhood of man" doctrine! One does not become a part of God's people, nor He their God, until first redemption takes effect in the individual heart.

      g. I will bring you into the land (rest): vs. 8a with Matthew 11:29,30; Hebrews 4:9

      h. I will give you a heritage: vs. 8b with I Peter 1:3,4

4. Man has nothing about which to rejoice (sing) until he accepts God's redemption. Israel in Egyptian bondage had no song. God provided redemption (the Passover) in chapter 12, and Israel sang in chapter 15. There was no song during the 400 silent years from Malachi to the birth of Christ. With His coming, we have the "Magnificat" of Mary, the heavenly chorus in the shepherd's field, and the rejoicing of Simeon and Anna when they "saw" God's redemption (Luke 1:46-55; 2:8-13, 25-28).

5. Deliverance at the Red Sea; 14. In Israel's exodus from Egypt, she had advanced to the shores of the Red Sea. *Behind* them was Pharaoh's army, *before* them was the sea, and *around* them was the shore line. There was no avenue of escape and the people complained bitterly that Moses had brought them out to die in the wilderness. The "pillar of the cloud," which had gone before them (13:21,22), moved to the rear and settled between Israel and the Egyptians (14:19). When Moses looked up and lifted up his rod, God revealed His salvation (deliverance) in parting the waters of the Red Sea and Israel walked over dry shod. God was—

      a. For them: Romans 8:31

      b. With them: Genesis 28:15; Isaiah 41:10-13

      c. Before them: 13:21

      d. Behind them: 14:19; Isaiah 30:21

      e. Above them: Joshua 2:11; Psalms 18:16; 144:7

      f. Underneath them: Deuteronomy 33:27

      g. Around them: Psalm 125:2

      h. Over them: Song of Solomon 2:4

6. Israel Set to Mischief: 32:22. Her "mischief" is seen in her complaints about:

      a. Leaders: 15:24; 16:8; Numbers 16:3; 21:5

    b. Water: 15:24; Numbers 20:2-11
    c. Moses' absence, which resulted in making the golden calf: 32:1
    d. The desert: 16:1,2; Numbers 20:2-5
    e. Food and meat: 16:2,3; Numbers 11:4-6,18-20,31-33; 21:5
    f. Inhabitants of other Nations: Numbers 13:31; 14:2
    g. God's judgment: Numbers 16:41
    h. Having to encompass the land: Numbers 21:4

It is no wonder that Moses called the children of Israel "rebels" (Deuteronomy 9:24; Numbers 20:10).

    7. At the proclamation of the law, three thousand lost their lives. At the first preaching of the gospel after Christ's ascension, three thousand received everlasting life: 32:15-28 with Acts 2:41.

    8. When a judge in Greensboro, North Carolina, administered the oath of citizenship to fifty persons, he advised them to obey the Ten Commandments. If they did, he said, they need not worry about keeping over 35,000,000 laws which have been enacted in their new country!

The *Spiritual Thought* for Exodus is "Come out for God." That is what God wanted Moses to do but his excuse-making irritated God to the point where He had to deal frankly with a thunderous "I AM THAT I AM." Moses saw that to "come out for God" meant to have God's presence with him. The New Testament way of saying "I AM THAT I AM" is "Jesus Christ the same yesterday, today, and forever" (Hebrews 13:8).

I AM THAT I AM—3:14[11]

    "Immutability is the peculiar prerogative of Jehovah. Everything out of the Divine nature is changeable. Angels in heaven changed and became demons. Man, who was created in the image and likeness of his Maker, sinned, and was changed to a sinful creature. Saints renewed by grace often change; they backslide, and are restored. Now they are happy, then dejected. Now they are active, then dull and lifeless. But Jehovah is the same. He is what He was, and what He is He ever will be. There can be no addition to His wisdom, for it is perfect; to His power, for it is omnipotent; or to His love, for it is infinite. There can be no diminution of His justice, His holiness, or His veracity, for He would cease to be God if He were less just, holy, or true. He never did injure one of His creatures by any purpose He formed or by any work He ever wrought, nor will He ever. He is holy in all His ways, and His Word is true from the beginning. This should comfort His people. He is now what He was when He entered into covenant, when He made His promises, and when He gave His only begotten Son. Friends may change, but God is the same."

PRAYER THOUGHT: "O Father, plant within my heart such holy fear that I may ever realize the sacredness of Thy holy name and Thy presence. Guard the door of my mind and keep me from irreverent thoughts and unholy actions. In Jesus' name I pray. Amen."[12]

Exodus 20:7; Philippians 2:9-11; 4:8

Leviticus—The Book of Atonement

Name: The Hebrew name given this third book of Moses is titled "The Lord Called." Greek translators gave it the name "Leviticus" because it deals principally with the Levitical Priesthood, the services of the priests, and the law of sacrifice.

Connection with Preceding Book: Leviticus is related to Exodus the same as the Epistles are to the four gospels. Exodus is the record of redemption, and lays the foundation for cleansing, worship, and service of a redeemed people to their God. The Israelites built upon this foundation in Leviticus. In Exodus God speaks out from the mount to which approach was forbidden. In Leviticus He speaks out from the Tabernacle, in which He dwells, to His people as they approach Him.

Contents: "The contents are purely legislative and the laws enacted are civil, ceremonial, moral, religious, and sanitary. Those which receive the most attention are religious and ceremonial. The various sacrifices, feasts, rites, and ceremonies made mention of in Leviticus are typical of Christ and are shadows of good things to come."[1] The Epistle to Hebrews is said to be a commentary on this book. The two should be read together. Leviticus has 27 chapters, 859 verses, and 24,546 words.

Character: Law: Luke 24:44.

Subject: The acceptable way of approach unto a holy God for Israel and the holy walk becoming them as an accepted people.

Purpose: To teach us the only acceptable way of approach unto a holy God, and the holy walk becoming us as an accepted people (Ephesians 1:7; Hebrews 10:19-22).

Outline:

    I. The Way to God by Sacrifice: 1—10
        A. The Law of the Offering: 1-7
        B. The Law of the Priesthood: 8—10
            1. Consecration of Aaron and his Sons: 8
            2. Inauguration of Tabernacle Services: 9
            3. The Sin and Punishment of Nadab and Abihu: 10
    II. The Walk with God by Sanctification: 11—27.
        A. The Law of Purity: 11—16
            1. Pure Food: 11
            2. Pure Body: 12
            3. Pure Garments: 13
            4. Pure House: 14,15
            5. Pure Nation: 16
        B. The Law of Holiness: 17—24
            1. Holiness in Personal Life: 17
            2. Holiness in Family Life: 18
            3. Holiness in Social Relations: 19,20
            4. Holiness in Priesthood: 21,22
            5. Holiness in Feasts: 23
            6. Relative Holiness: 24
        C. Other Laws: 25—27
            1. Law of the Sabbatical Year and Year of Jubilee: 25
                a. The Land of the Seventh Year: 25:1-7
                b. The Land of the Fiftieth Year: 25:8-24
                c. The Land of the Poor: 25:25-55
            2. Law of Obedience and Disobedience: 26

       a. Conditional Prosperity: 26:1-13
       b. Conditional Punishments: 26:14-46
    3. Law of Vows and Tithes: 27
       a. The Liberty of Vows: 27:1,2
       b. The Law of Vows: 27:3-25
       c. The Limit of Vows: 27:26-34

Writer: Moses. See AUTHOR, p. 104.

To Whom Written: Israel in general; the Levites in particular.

When and Where Written: About 1500 B.C.,in the wilderness: Acts 7:37,38.

Key Chapter: 16. Day of Atonement.

Key Verse: 19:2.

Key Words:
    1. Holiness, found 87 times
    2. Holy, found 65 times

Key Phrase: "Be ye holy, for I am holy": 11:44 with I Peter 1:16.

Key Thought: The Laws of the Nation.

Spiritual Thought: Get right with God.

Christ Is Seen As: Our Great High Priest: Hebrews 4:14.

Names and Titles of God: See NAME in Dictionary.
    1. Lord, the Annointed One: 10:7
    2. Jehovah-M'Kaddesh—the Lord who sanctifieth: 20:7,8

Israel's Captivity—to show the need to keep all God's laws, even though we may categorize some as secondary: 26:27-35 with II Chronicles 36:14-21. Israel was instructed in chapter 25:1-24 to till the soil for 6 years and let the land rest the seventh. Failure to do this over a period of 490 years brought about the seventy years' captivity.

Stated: ca. 1,450 B.C. *Fulfilled:* ca. 1,400—586 B.C.

Types of Christ:

    1. Aaron, as high priest, making proper sacrifice for sin: 16:11,15 with Hebrews 9:7,11-14,24-28; 12:24

       a. Called of God: Hebrews 5:4; 8:3 with I Timothy 2:5
       b. Clothed: 8:7 with the robe of righteousness: I Corinthians 1:30; Revelation 19:8
    c. Crowned: 8:9; Zechariah 3:1-5. The mediator between God and man wears a crown of holiness
    d. Anointed: 8:12 with Acts 10:38. Christ is the Lord's Anointed
    e. Consecrated: 8:23-27. "And Moses took the blood of it, and put it upon the tip of Aaron's right ear, and upon the thumb of his right hand, and upon the toe of his right foot" (vs. 23). Hearing, studying, and meditating upon the Word of God applied to his ear (Romans 10:17; II Timothy 2:15; Psalm 1:2); acts of obedience and working for the Lord applied to his hand (Ecclesiastes 9:10); a holy walk before the Lord applied to his foot (Psalm 121:3). Aaron was claimed and filled for the Lord, truly consecrated. The Lord Jesus Christ was both claimed and filled. The voice from heaven said, "This is my

beloved Son''—*claimed* (Matthew 3:17). ''God giveth not the Spirit by measure unto Him''—*filled* (John 3:34b)

    f. Blameless: Hebrews 7:26

2. Sacrificial Offering: 1—7. See ALTAR, Brazen, in Index.

3. The Two Birds—one slain, one left alive—death and resurrection of Christ; the one slain—delivered for our offenses; the one alive—raised for our justification: 14:49-53; Romans 4:25; I Corinthians 15:3,4. See LEPER below.

4. Scapegoat bearing away sins of Israel—Christ bore our sins in His own body: 16:20-22 with Isaiah 53:6,12; I Peter 2:24; Hebrews 9:26,28

Types of the Believer's Experiences:

1. Aaron's Sons

    a. Their names were closely associated with the high priest. So are ours, because we are sons by birth: John 1:12,13

    b. Same calling—called to be priests: 8:1,2; Exodus 28:1,41 with I Peter, 2:5,9; Revelation 1:5,6

    c. Same clothing: 8:13 with believer clothed in the righteousness of Christ: Revelation 3:5; 19:7,8

    d. Hands filled for service: 8:24-27 with talents given: Matthew 25:14-30

    e. Same anointing: 8:30 with I John 2:27

    f. Under the same authority: 8:33-36 with John 20:21

2. The Cleansed Leper: 14:1-7

    a. Leprosy is a type of the terrible nature of sin. Sin, like leprosy, afflicts the person himself, and those whom he contacts. It—

    —Makes unclean: 13:44 with Romans 3:10; Isaiah 64:6

    —Brings judgment: 13:44 with ''he that believeth not is condemned already'': John 3:18

    —Must be admitted: 13:45

        —Clothes rent, indicating wretchedness

        —Head bare, indicating impotency

        —Lips covered, indication of defiled breath

        —Cry was ''unclean,'' admission of true condition

    —We too must confess our condition: Romans 3:23; Luke 18:13

    —Brings separation: 13:46 with Ephesians 2:12; Matthew 7:23

    b. As leprosy reveals sin, so its cleansing shows God's method of salvation

    —The leper does nothing: 14:2 with Romans 4:4,5

    —The priest seeks the leper, not the leper the priest: 14:3 with Luke 19:10

    —An offering is made: 14:4-6 with Hebrews 9:26,28

    —Blood is applied: 14:7 with I Peter 1:18,19

    —Personal cleansing: 14:8 with Colossians 2:20-23

    —Priest speaks the word, pronouncing the leper and his house clean: 14:11,48 with John 15:3

    —Restoration after cleansing: 14:8 with John 10:9

    —Consecration: 14:14-18 with Romans 12:1,2

When the priest seeks the leper, this is a type of Christ seeking the sinner. Since the leper can do nothing about his condition, he must be sought (vs. 3 with Luke 19:10). A leper has absolutely nothing with which to purchase an animal for sacrifice, but he can, without money and without price, catch two birds in the field. The priest takes the two birds, along with a piece of cedar wood, a piece of scarlet thread, and some shrub called ''hyssop'' (vs. 4). The scarlet thread is a type of Christ's blood (see SCARLET THREAD in Index); hyssop is a symbol of cleansing; and the cedar wood is a type of righteousness (see CEDAR in Index). One bird is killed in an earthen vessel, with running water mixed with the blood. This is a type of Christ's death. The priest then takes the live bird, along with the hyssop tied to the cedar wood with the scarlet thread, and dips them both in the blood of the bird that was killed. The live bird is then let loose (vss. 5,6), a type of the resurrection of Christ. With this "finished work" the priest sprinkles the leper seven times for cleansing. The water mixed with the blood is a symbol of the Word of God—blood to forgive, and the Word to cleanse (Ephesians 1:7; 5:26; John 15:3).

When David made his great confession of sin with Bathsheba (II Samuel 11), he asked the Lord to "purge me with hyssop" (Psalm 51:7). This was David's way of seeing sin as God saw sin—hopelessly and helplessly undone before God, and a willingness to take the lowest place of any sinner, that of a leper crying "unclean, unclean" (Leviticus 13:45). He knew he deserved death for his adultery (Leviticus 20:10), but he asked the Lord to "have mercy upon me" (Psalm 51:1). Mercy is God's withholding from us what we rightly deserve. See DAVID'S DOWNFALL in Index.

3. The Seven Feasts: 23. See FESTIVALS in Index.
   a. The Passover—Christ our Passover bearing God's judgment against us: vss. 4,5 with I Corinthians 5:7b
   b. Unleavened Bread—practical holiness becoming His redeemed ones: vss. 6-8 with I Thessalonians 4:3-7
   c. First fruits—resurrection of Christ—accepted by God: vss. 9-14 with I Corinthians 15:20
   d. Pentecost—descent of the Holy Spirit: vss. 15-22 with Acts 2:1-4
   e. Trumpets—to herald the good news of the feast of Atonement which is to follow shortly: vss. 23-25
   f. Atonement—mourning for and deliverance from sin: vss. 26-32 with II Corinthians 7:10. "Atonement" is the Hebrew for plural, having to do with atonement or deliverance from (1) the penalty of sin; (2) from the power of sin; and (3) atonement or redemption of the body—deliverance from the very presence of sin: II Corinthians 1:9,10; Philippians 3:21; I John 3:2
   g. Tabernacles—a reminder of redemption out of Egypt: vss. 33,34 with Colossians 1:13,14

1. Aaron's sons consumed by fire for the offering of strange fire before the Lord—showing that "will worship," even in doing a right thing, is not accepted by God: 10:1,2 with Colossians 2:23; Psalm 66:18.

2. The Year of Jubilee: 25:8-16. Once every 50 years the slaves were liberated, debtors were freed, and a general restitution took place. See JUBILEE in Index.

1. Pure Food and Water: 1. The meat diet of Moses' day roughly corresponds to that of our own scientific age, except that we eat pork and rabbit, both of which are susceptible to infectious parasites, and even though cleanly fed and well cooked, they can still be a source of disease, especially fresh pork. Israel was forbidden to eat pork because God knew that lack of refrigeration and roasting pork over an open flame are not sufficient to destroy these parasites. Israel was told not to touch the dead bodies of swine because these parasites can be communicated simply by handling pork. This is a scientific fact in our day, in spite of all the equipment and gadgets we have for sterile cooking.

Eating an animal that died by itself was forbidden by God (Deuteronomy 14:21). Today we know that the bodies of dead animals crawl with fleas, lice, and flies—all of which are carriers of disease, some even fatal.

The need for pure water is stressed by Moses: vs. 36. It has only been a little over eighty years since it was learned that typhoid fever in our country, cholera in Egypt and India, and other diseases were spread by contaminated water.

2. Circumcision: 12:2,3. God gave Moses this command for all Israelite male infants. Today, this is an up-to-date hygiene measure. However, it has only been "standard" practice for doctors to circumcise *all* males since about 1940. They do it soon after birth as a matter of convenience before the mother and baby are discharged from the hospital. But the Bible says "and in the eighth day the flesh . . . shall be circumcised." It is a matter of modern medical record that this *is* the best time to do it.

A baby's blood is saturated with antitoxins or disease-fighting elements which it receives from its mother before birth. For the first week of life the infant is protected against infection. Also in the blood is a "blood-clotting ability" which increases rapidly the first week and reaches its normal concentration about the beginning of the second week of life. "Now note carefully. Since the disease-fighting antibodies begin to decrease after the first week, operations *after* that time are attended with infection. But since the coagulating properties of the infant's blood (the clotting ability) do not reach their normal number until the end of the first week, operations *before* that time are attended with the danger of hemorrhage. Hence the safest time for surgery is at the very point where both the disease-fighting qualities and the blood-clotting ability are at their highest point—the eighth day."[2] God gave this same information to Moses almost 1500 years before Christ.

3. Lip covering (mask): 13:45. Today, surgeons would not dare operate without such a mask. They regard such a sanitary precaution in Moses' day as almost unbelievable, especially since he gave these instructions about 3,375 years before Pasteur "discovered" the same thing!

4. Quarantining contagious diseases: 13:45,46. The Bible is the only ancient book in all the world that insists on this practice.

5. Body cleanliness and sewage disposal: 15:8,9. The Israelites stressed the need to wash or bathe—an important factor to public health—past, present, or future. Body wastes were to be buried with a shovel or paddle (Deuteronomy 23:13). The practice of this order would go far toward eliminating typhoid fever. This is a well-known "scientific" truth today.

6. Rules for disinfection: 15. A surgeon preparing for an operation will scrub his hands for about fifteen minutes under a faucet. Unless this continuous washing is done beforehand, germs which hide under the scales of his skin will be carried to the body of the patient. If the hands were washed in a basin of water, no matter how long he would wash in that water, he would never be rid of germs because of the contaminated water. Running water carries away the germs until the hands are surgically clean. Moses knew this long before Pasteur knew what a germ was (15:13).

7. Circulation of the blood: 17:11,14. William Harvey, an Englishman physician, proved that blood circulated from the heart through the arteries and back to the heart through the veins. He also knew there were small vessels that united the arteries and veins, but was unable to prove it. Soon afterwards, an Italian physician discovered these small vessels, calling them "capillaries." All this took place just before the mid-1600s. These men discovered the circulation of the blood and ascertained that the life of the flesh is in the blood. Moses said the same thing over 3,100 years before. It is only as men make these discoveries that we appreciate what an up-to-date book the Bible really is.

Blood is also essential for bone growth. Job (21:23,24) states "his bones are moistened with marrow." Bones *are* moistened with blood tissue fluids. Job made his statement possibly 2200

B.C., 700 years before Moses' day. Speaking of bone (cells) and marrow, and how closely knit they are, God implies that His Word can pierce or even divide asunder such closeness when it comes to revealing sin in an individual (Hebrews 4:12).

8. Purebred Stock: "Thou shalt not let thy cattle gender with a diverse kind": 19:19a. This was God's instruction over 3,400 years ago for the improvement of stock by scientific selective breeding! Science has found that breeding the select and the strong with the select and the strong will produce a pure strain of superior stock. See CONGREGATIONS in Index.

9. Cross-pollination. Only recently have men found that the secret of producing better grain and produce is by avoiding cross-pollination. Yet God told Moses 1500 B.C., "thou shalt not sow thy field with mingled seed:" 19:19b; Deuteronomy 22:9. If citron and squash are planted too near watermelon, the melons will taste like citron.

10. Pest Control. A sure-fire remedy for control of pests was given centuries ago, and yet we are plagued today with insects, oftimes with no remedy. Moses commanded Israel to set aside one year in seven when no crops were raised: 25:1-24. God promised sufficient harvest in the sixth year to provide for this period. Following this plan, here's what would happen—insects winter in the stalks of last year's harvest, hatch in the spring, and are perpetuated by laying eggs in the new crop. Now, if one year in seven no crop were raised, there is nothing for the insects to subsist upon and the pests are controlled by this method. Man's method today is crop rotations, but we're still pestered with insects. This method will never approach God's method. "Then there was the Year of Jubilee after every seven Sabbatical years, which would serve to eliminate the insects which had a cycle of seven years or more or less and which were not affected by the one year in seven."[3]

Leviticus in the New Testament:
1. Sacrificed animals burned without the camp: 4:21,22 with Hebrews 13:11
2. "Be ye holy for I am holy": 11:44 with I Peter 1:16
3. Sin-offering: 12:6 with Luke 2:21-24
4. Cleansing the leper: 14:2-20 with Matthew 8:1-4
5. Blood of bullock: 16:14-16 with Hebrews 9:13
6. Righteousness of the Law: 18:5 with Romans 10:4,5
7. No respect of persons: 19:15 with James 2:1
8. Hate not in the heart: 19:17 with I John 2:9,11; 3:15; 4:20
9. Love thy neighbor: 19:18 with Gal. 5:14
10. Death penalty for adultery: 20:10 with John 8:1-5
11. Feast of Tabernacles: 23:34-36 with John 7:2-37
12. Personal relationship with God: 26:12 with II Corinthians 6:16
13. Companion references:
   The priest's office: 16:17 with Luke 1:8-10

SEED THOUGHTS

1. It is said fifty times of Moses that he "did as the Lord commanded him": 8:4
2. "Be ye holy for I am holy": 11:44
   a. Holy in our calling: II Timothy 1:9
   b. Holy in heart: I Thessalonians 3:13
   c. Holy in our bodies: Romans 12:1
   d. Holy in conversation and godliness: II Peter 3:11
   e. Holy in worship—a holy priesthood: I Peter 2:5

3. "Thou shalt love thy neighbor as thyself": 19:18. "This was one of the highlights of Mosaic law. Great consideration was shown to the poor. Wages were to be paid day by day. No usury was to be taken. Loans and gifts were to be made to the needy. Gleanings were to be left

in the harvest fields for the poor. Although the Bible nowhere gives encouragement to laziness, unceasing emphasis is placed on kindness to widows, orphans, and strangers."[4] See James 1:27.

4. Many congregations today are looking for a pastor who is a "good mixer"— someone who is versatile, adept, can lead singing, direct the choir, work with young people, be a good counselor, make visits, who can adapt to any situation, be a good executive, etc., etc., but God is looking for a man who will adhere to sound doctrine, who will study and pray, who will set a good example—not by being a "good mixer" but by being a "good separator" in godly living (II Corinthians 6:14-18). The Scriptures teach—

 a. Do not *mix* your full-bred cattle with any half-breeds: 19:19a. This tends to produce inferior stock. When believers tend to mix with lukewarm, cold and indifferent people, apathy and apostasy soon follow. Many Israelites fell in the wilderness because of a "mixed multitude" (Exodus 12:38a; Numbers 11:4a; Hebrews 3:7-19). The Word (Law) must keep us separated from such mixtures (Nehemiah 13:3)

 b. Do not *mix* seed in planting: 19:19b. This tends to take away the true value and taste of the grain or fruit and results in a weakness of strength by those whose life is dependent upon it. The Word of God, which is the Seed for the promotion of life and growth, cannot be mixed with human wisdom (Luke 8:11; I Corinthians 2:4,5). Only as the pure Seed of God's Word is planted and men "taste and see that the Lord is good" can there be an excellent production of fruit in the lives of believers (Psalm 34:8; John 15:7,8)

 c. Do not *mix* material in clothing: 19:19c. Mixed fabrics soon fill with creases and folds due to uneven shrinkage, and the garment wears out in the uneven places. We are not to mix the fine linen of Christ's righteousness with the wool of the world. "Love not the world. . ." A fountain *cannot* send forth at the same place "sweet water and bitter—salt water and fresh" (I John 2:15-17; James 3:10-12)

 d. Do not *mix* clean and unclean animals in service together: Deuteronomy 22:10. See PLOW in Index.

5. Capital Punishment. Offenses punishable with death were:

 a. Idolatry: 20:1-5; Deuteronomy 13:1-18
  —Prophesying falsely: Deuteronomy 13:1-5
  —Worshiping heavenly bodies: Deuteronomy 17:2-5
 b. Smiting or cursing a parent: 20:9; Deuteronomy 21:18-21
 c. Incestuous marriages: 20:11,12,14
 d. Sodomy (homosexuality; lesbianism): 20:13
 e. Bestiality: 20:15,16
 f. Adultery: 21:10; Deuteronomy 22:22
 g. Blasphemy: 24:15,26
 h. Murder: Genesis 9:6; Exodus 21:12; Deuteronomy 19:11-13
 i. Kidnapping: Exodus 21:16; Deuteronomy 24:7
 j. Death by negligence: Exodus 21:28,29
 k. Sorcery: Exodus 22:18; Leviticus 20:6
 l. Sabbath profaning: Exodus 31:14
 m. False prophecy: Deuteronomy 18:10,11,20
 n. Pre-marriage immorality: Deuteronomy 22:13-21
 o. Rape: Deuteronomy 22:23-27

6. The Path of Obedience: 26:1-13. Two paths are opened for us in this portion—one of obedience and blessing, the other of disobedience and failure: Matthew 7:13,14

 a. Characteristics of the obedient. They—
  —Have no idols: vs. 1
  —Reverence the appointments of God: vs. 2
  —Are guided by His Word: vs. 3a
  —Delight to do His will: vs. 3b

b. Blessings that accompany obedience—
 —Fruitfulness: vs. 4
 —Peace and rest: vs. 6a
 —Deliverance from evil things: vs. 6b
 —Power to overcome: vs. 7,8
 —God's favor: vs. 9
 —Abundant provision: vs. 10
 —God's fellowship: vs. 12

The path of disobedience ends in misery and woe, reaping sins sevenfold: vs. 14-39. These verses list numerous punishments. Look them up.

7. Cycles of Sevens (see SEVENS in Index). The Levitical system of feasts and seasons was erected on a cycle of sevens:

 —Every seventh day a Sabbath
 —Every seventh year a Sabbatical year
 —Every seventh Sabbatical followed by Year of Jubilee
 —Every seven months had three feasts
 —Seven weeks before Passover and Pentecost
 —Feast of Passover seven days
 —Feast of Tabernacles seven days
 —Fourteen lambs (twice 7) offered daily at Passover
 —Fourteen lambs (twice 7) offered daily at Tabernacle
 —Seven lambs offered at Pentecost

The Bible begins with seven days of creation and rest and ends with a book of Sevens (Revelation), which carries us on to the final destiny of a new heaven and a new earth.

Because of the prominence of the Priesthood in Leviticus and the fact that Christ is seen as "Our great High Priest," Aaron, who is a type of Christ, wears an ephod as part of his priestly apparel, which points to a great spiritual truth. On this ephod Aaron bore the names of the Twelve Tribes before the Lord. See BREASTPLATE in Index.

AARON SHALL BEAR THEIR NAMES—8:7 WITH EXODUS 28:12[5]

"Aaron was a type of Christ as the Great High Priest of our profession. What Aaron was to Israel, Jesus is to us. What Aaron did for Israel, Jesus does for us. The names of the Twelve Tribes were engraved and placed on Aaron's breast, and whenever he appeared before God in the holiest of all, the light of the Shekinah rested upon them, and God read them in His own light. Nothing was allowed to come between the names and the mercy seat but the blood as he sprinkled it; or the smoke of the incense as he waved it before the Lord. O beloved, Jesus has our names on His breast! The light of the Father's countenance rests upon them. There is nothing between them and God but the blood that atoned for our sins and the smoke of incense which perfumes our prayers. Jesus constantly presents us to God, for he has entered into heaven now to appear in the presence of God for us. Sweet thought—my name is on my Savior's heart, my cause is in His hands, and He ever takes the deepest interest in my welfare! O that I would only love Him more!"

PRAYER THOUGHT: "Blessed Savior, because Thou hast redeemed me and set me free from sin, help me to have no other desire than to walk uprightly before Thee and to stand for the hard right against the easy wrong, even if it means being one with a small minority. In Thy name I ask this. Amen."[6]

Leviticus 26:12,13; I Corinthians 16:13

Numbers—The Book of Pilgrimage

Name: This book gets its name "Numbers" from the Septuagint, and is so called from the two numberings of the people: one at Mt. Sinai (ch. 1), and the other in the plains of Moab about 39 years later (ch. 26).

Contents: Historically, Numbers continues where Exodus leaves off. It is the story of the wilderness wanderings of a redeemed people who failed to enter the promised land at Kadesh-barnea. Typically, Numbers completes, with the preceding books, a picture of the believer's experience. *Genesis,* the book of creation and fall; *Exodus,* of redemption; *Leviticus,* of worship and fellowship; and *Numbers,* of that which should follow—service and walk. This book has 36 chapters, 1,288 verses, and 32,902 words.

Character: Historical.

Subject: Israel's preparation for their wilderness journey and for entrance into the Promised Land.

Purpose: To teach us how God would lead us through the place of testing into the place of blessing, by belief and trust in Him.

Outline:[1]
  I. The Encampment at Mt. Sinai: 1—10
  A. The Organization of the Camp: 1—4
  B. The Purity of the Camp: 5,6
  C. The Consecration of the Camp: 7:1—9:14
  D. The Movement of the Camp: 9:15—10:36
  II. The March in the Wilderness: 11—21
  A. From Sinai to Kadesh: 11—14
  B. In and Around Kadesh: 15—19
  C. From Kadesh to Plains of Moab: 20,21
  III. The Encampment of the Plains of Moab: 22—36
  A. Attempts to Destroy Israel: 22—25
  B. The New Beginning: 26—30
  C. Conquest and Settlement East of Jordan: 31,32
  D. Retrospect and Prospect: 33—36

Scope: The events recorded in Numbers cover a period of about forty years: 32:13. See MAP, p. 100, and points 11-27, p. 101.

Writer: Moses. See AUTHOR, p. 104.

When and Where Written: About 1451 B.C., after the Israelites had reached the plains of Moab.

Key Chapter: 14. Unbelief at Kadesh-barnea.

Key Verse: 33:1.

Key Word: Sojourn.

Key Phrase: These are the journeys: 33:1.

Key Thought: The training of the nation Israel. Review the "Key Thought" of Exodus ("The Making of a Nation"), and the "Laws" for Israel from the OUTLINE of Leviticus.

In *Genesis* God's covenant had been made with Abraham and his seed; in *Exodus* the Law had been proclaimed and the Tabernacle built and set up; in *Leviticus* the priests had been consecrated; and now in *Numbers* the Nation is trained in the laws and ceremonies of its religion and life. Refusing to go on into the Promised Land at Kadesh-barnea because of unbelief, the wilderness wandering is declared—one year for each day they took to spy out the land

(13:1,2,5; 14:34). This training was necessary because all who left Egypt except Joshua, Caleb, and those under twenty years died in the wilderness (14:22-34), and was particularly necessary for the new generation who was to have the national responsibility in the conquest and settlement of Canaan. All during their wilderness wandering after Kadesh-barnea, *Israel went around in circles.* And to think, only an eleven-day journey from Horeb to Kadesh-barnea (Deuteronomy 1:2), and a few more days into the Promised Land!

Spiritual Thought: Get somewhere by the grace of God.

Christ Is Seen As:
1. The Rock: 20:11 with I Corinthians 10:4
2. The Star—Prince: 24:17a with Revelation 22:16
3. The Scepter—Ruler or King: 24:17b with I Timothy 6:14,15

1. Of Christ—a Star out of Jacob, a Scepter out of Israel: 24:17-19

Stated: ca. 1,450 B.C. *Fulfilled:* birth of Christ

2. An "indirect" prophecy is made in the form of judgment if Israel failed to drive out the inhabitants of Canaan: 33:51,56. Israel was to be God's instrument of judgment upon the wicked Canaanites after entering the Land. If she failed, then Canaan would become God's instrument of judgment upon them. She did fail, and the Canaanites became "pricks in their eyes and thorns [snares] in their sides" (Judges 2:3; 3:5-8; Psalm 106:34-36). We do indeed reap what we sow (Galatians 6:7).

Stated: ca. 1,450 B.C. *Fulfilled:* ca. 1,400—586 B.C.

Types of Christ:
1. The Cloud by Day and the Pillar of Fire by Night: 9:15-23. Though Israel turned back into the wilderness at Kadesh-barnea, the Lord did not leave them nor forsake them. The cloud by day and the pillar of fire by night was both a standing and a moving miracle and a witness of the presence of God in the midst of His people. See CLOUD in Index.

a. Its origin. We have no account of how this cloud was formed. The fact is that it appeared and to Israel it was the visible manifestation of the invisible God. So Christ is to us. "Great is the mystery of godliness, God was manifested in the flesh" (I Timothy 3:16)

b. Its appearance: vss. 15a,16. When the Tabernacle was set in order, the cloud appeared. When we present our bodies as living sacrifices (our bodies now God's tabernacle or temple—I Corinthians 3:16,17), having set things in order, His presence is manifested in our midst (Romans 12:1,2; II Corinthians 6:16-18)

c. Its purpose:
—Testimony—God's presence with them: vs. 15b; Deuteronomy 31:6
—Protection—by day and by night
—Leadership: vss. 18-23

2. Moses—faithful servant: 12:7 Hebrews 3:1-6. See MOSES as Type in Index.
3. Aaron, a Representative of Christ: 18:1-20. See AARON in Index.
   a. A revealer of God, with John 8:12. His name means "Enlightener."
   b. Holy things entrusted to his care: vs. 8 with Hebrews 8:1,2
   c. Was anointed for his ministry: vs. 8 with Acts 10:38
   d. Had a ministry of redemption: vs. 15 with Galatians 3:13; Ephesians 1:7
   e. His seed was also blessed: vs. 19 with Ephesians 1:3; Colossians 2:10; Romans 8:32

4. The Offering of the Red Heifer: 19. This offering was appointed by God and is symbolic of salvation in and through the offering of Christ. The Israelites could not question God's method in this offering any more than we can question the sacrifice of Christ. God alone has the right to say what atonement for sin shall be and sinful man must accept God's just terms or forever remain defiled.

    a. The spotless offering: vs. 2 with I Peter 1:18,19
      —Slain: vs. 3 with Acts 2:23; I Corinthians 15:3
      —Blood applied: vss. 4,5 with Hebrews 9:11-13
    b. Cleansing provided: vss. 9-20 with Hebrews 9:22; I John 1:7,9
      —For the unclean: vs. 11 with Romans 5:6-11
      —Must be appropriated: vss. 17-20 with John 1:12; 5:24

5. Death of Aaron: 20:23-29.[2]
    a. He knew it beforehand: vss. 23,24 with Matthew 20:28; 16:21
    b. It was sudden. Aaron went up to Mt. Hor for the purpose of dying. No time of sickness is hinted at. It would seem as if he had been cut off suddenly. See Daniel 9:26 and Mark 15:43-45.
    c. It was because of sin: vs. 24 with Isaiah 53:5,6; I Peter 2:24
    d. He murmured not in prospect of it. It is most significant that through all this trying time Aaron's voice is never heard. Like the great Antitype, "He opened not His mouth" (Isaiah 53:7; Hebrews 12:2; Matthew 26:39).
    e. He was stripped: vs. 28 with Matthew 27:35
    f. Two were with him in his death: vss. 25,28 with Matthew 27:44
    g. He died on a mount: vss. 25,28 with Luke 23:33
    h. His work was continued after he was gone: vs. 28 with Matthew 28:19,20; Acts 1:8; II Corinthians 5:20

6. The Brazen Serpent: 21:1-9 with John 3:14-18.[3] The brazen serpent is the only shadow of the Cross pointed out by our Lord. Israel had sinned and in consequence God sent fiery serpents among them, which bit many and caused death. When they cried to God, He instructed Moses to make a serpent of brass, put it upon a pole so that all might see it, and then when a serpent-bitten Israelite looked upon that brazen serpent, he lived. In the midst of vast hoards of human sinners, sin-bitten and dying, there rises a lonely Cross. It was our Lord who said that just as the uplifted serpent was the only means of deliverence then, so the uplifted Son of Man is the only means of deliverance now. From this experience we learn:

    a. The need of salvation: vs. 6 with Romans 3:23; 6:23a
    b. The method of salvation: vs. 8 with Galatians 4:3,4. Salvation is of the Lord. By a serpent they had been bitten and by a symbol in the form of a serpent they must be healed. Through man came death and by Man also came the justification of life (Romans 3:24).
    c. The condition of salvation: vs. 8 with John 12:32; Ephesians 2:8,9
      —They were not told to look at their wounds to be saved
      —They were not told to look at Moses to be saved
      —They were not told to shake off the serpents to be saved
      —They were not told to keep the law to be saved
      —They were not told to help one another to be saved
      —They were not told to go through a ritual to be saved
      —They were told to *look* to the brass serpent to be saved. See Isaiah 45:22
    d. The extent of salvation—*everyone* that looketh: vs. 8 with John 3:16
    e. The effects of salvation—instantaneous life: vs. 9 with John 5:24; II Corinthians 5:17

7. The Cities of Refuge: 35:6; Joshua 20 with Hebrews 6:18-20. See MAP #4.
    a. Six cities were appointed among those of the Levites to be a shelter or refuge from judgment. So is our refuge from sin appointed: John 1:29; 14:6
    b. They were so situated to be easily accessible from all parts of the land. Christ is within easy reach of all: Luke 19:10; Romans 10:8

c. The way to them was prepared—signposts pointed the way. The Holy Spirit has been sent to testify of Christ, using the preaching of the Word, tracts, hymns, and the witness of faithful Christians: John 16:7-14

d. The manslayer must be inside the city gate to be safe. One cannot be *almost* saved. We must be *in* Christ: II Corinthians 5:17

e. Refuge was provided for only *one* kind of offender. So is our salvation in Christ—it is for the sinner *only:* Luke 18:9-14

f. The manslayer had to believe and appropriate this provision to escape punishment. So must we: John 1:12; Acts 16:31; Romans 10:9,10

The names of these cities are also significant, in that each relates directly to the Person of Christ.

a. Kedesh means *holy*: Joshua 20:7 with Mark 1:24

b. Shechem, a *shoulder*: Joshua 20:7 with Isaiah 9:6; Luke 15:5

c. Hebron, *fellowship*: Joshua 20:7 with I John 1:7; I Corinthians 1:9

d. Bezer, a *fortification*: Joshua 20:8 with Nahum 1:7; John 16:33

e. Ramoth, high, or *exalted*: Joshua 20:8 with Philippians 2:9

f. Golan, joy, or *exultation*: Joshua 20:8 with John 15:11

1. The Cloud by Day and the Pillar of Fire by Night: 9:15-23. See CLOUD in Index.

2. Israel burned—punishment for complaining about circumstances of their own doings: 11:1-3

3. Quails sent—to make Israel sick for desiring the fleshly things of Egypt: 11:4-6, 18-20 with Psalm 106:14,15

4. Plague sent—to teach Israel that manna, a type of Christ, was sufficient for their need: 11:6,31-34. See MANNA in Index.

5. Miriam's leprosy—for criticizing God's servant, and her healing in answer to prayer: 12:1-15

6. Earth swallowed up Korah and his followers—for rebellion against God's authority through Moses: 16:30-35

7. Plague sent (14,700 died)—to rebuke Israel for condoning Korah's sin: 16;41-50.

8. Aaron's rod buds, blossoms, and yields almonds—to convince Israel of his authority: 17:1-8

9. Water from the twice-smitten rock—to show Israel God's grace in spite of Moses' disobedience: 20:7-11. See ROCK in Index.

10. Fiery serpents—sent to rebuke Israel (again) for murmuring: 21:5-7

11. The brazen serpent—to "heal those bitten by the serpents" with a look of faith: 21:8,9. See SERPENT in Index.

12. Balaam's ass speaking—to rebuke a disobedient prophet: 22:21-31

1. When the spies returned to Kadesh-barnea from Canaan, they said "the people be strong . . . , and the cities are walled . . ." (13:28). Archaeological discoveries at numerous sites in Palestine give evidence that the spies actually saw mighty walled, well-fortified cities in the land. See SIGHT and WALLS in Index.

2. Moses sought permission to go through the land of Edom, but was denied this request. Moving southward, he tried to go up through the

land by way of the "route of the spies," but King Arad fought against him. No matter where Moses sought to go throughout Seir to Moab, he was rebuffed. Discoveries have revealed the ruins of many well-fortified cities in the valley adjacent to the mountains of Seir, indicating a

Fortified Canaanite City

dense population and powerful people in the time of Israel's wandering. It was because of these well-fortified positions that Moses had to lead the children of Israel ". . . by way of the Red Sea [Gulf of Aqaba] to compass the land of Edom" (20:14-22; 21:1-4). It is no wonder that "the people was much discouraged because of the way." However, it was the way they had chosen. What a "long way around" when God's way is rejected! See MAP, p. 100.

LIGHT FROM BIBLICAL CUSTOMS

4 1. A Covenant of Salt: 18:19. The act of eating salt has always been regarded as a token of fidelity or friendship. Each member of the party making this covenant would wet his finger with his tongue, dip it in salt, and then eat it. The covenant was binding —never to be forgotten nor renounced. Such was the Davidic covenant. "Ought ye not to know that the Lord . . . gave the kingdom of Israel to David forever, even to him and to his sons by a covenant of salt (II Chronicles 13:5). Today, we affix our signatures to an agreement that's binding. See SALT in Index.

2. "Moab is My washpot" (Psalm 60:8). After Israel's refusal to enter the Promised Land from Kadesh-barnea and their encompassing the land of Edom, they settled in Shittim (Moab), committed adultery, and joined themselves to the gods of the Moabites (25;1-3). Because of the dirt and filth of Moab's godlessness, God called her His "washpot." In the East clean water is not poured into the washpot or basin first, and then hands or feet washed. Water is poured on the hands or feet to wash, and the dirty water goes immediately into the washpot. Because of Moab's part in causing Israel to sin, she became God's "washpot" or depository of sin's judgment and consequence—doomed to the most abject and degrading servitude.

Numbers in the New Testament:
1. First-born son sanctified or called holy: 8:16,17 with Luke 2:22,23
2. Bone not broken of the Passover offering: 9:12 with John 19:36

3. Cloud in the wilderness: 9:17-19 with I Corinthians 10:1
4. Israel lusting: 11:4 with I Corinthians 10:6
5. Moses, a faithful servant: 12:7 with Hebrews 3:2
6. The disobedient judged: 14:16,29; 26:65a with I Corinthians 10:5; Hebrews 3:17
7. Murmuring of Israel: 14:27 with I Corinthians 10:10
8. Rebellion of Korah: 16 with Jude 11c
9. Budding of Aaron's Rod: 17:8 with Hebrews 9:4
10. Offering slain without the camp: 19:3 with Hebrews 13:11
11. Water from the rock: 20:8 with I Corinthians 10:4
12. Death by fiery serpents: 21:5,6 with I Corinthians 10:9
13. Brazen serpent: 21:9 with John 3:14
14. Doctrine of Balaam: 22—24 with II Peter 2:25; Jude 11b; Revelation 2:14
15. Balaam's ass: 22:23 with II Peter 2:16
16. Sin of fornication: 25:1,9 with I Corinthians 10:8. A contradition has been imagined here. First Corinthians 10:8 lists 23,000—the total number of deaths in *one day*. Numbers 25:9 lists 24,000—the *total* number of deaths in the plague
17. Many die in the wilderness: 26:65 with I Corinthians 10:5
18. Work on the Sabbath day: 28:9,10 with Matthew 12:5
19. Companion references:
God's knowledge of His own: 16:5 with II Timothy 2:19

1. From 6:24-26 we get a "benediction that can go all the world over, and can give all the time without being impoverished. Every heart may utter it; it is the speech of God; every letter may conclude with it; every day may begin with it; every night may be sanctified by it. Here is the blessing of all heaven's glad morning upon our poor lives. It is the Lord Himself who brings this bar of music from heaven's infinite anthems."[5]

2. The Cloud by day and the Pillar of fire by night: 9:15-23. There are times when God would have us be on the move. There are also times when we should be still before God and wait upon Him. When the cloud moved, Israel moved. When it stood still, they abode in their tents. The *steps* of a good man are ordered by the Lord (Psalm 37:23). So are his *stops* (Psalm 27:14). See CLOUD BY DAY in Index.

"Someone has said that if the Israelites had all the education, experts, committees, boards, etc., to lead them that we have in our churches today, they would have been so far ahead of the cloud by day and the pillar of fire by night that they would have been just as much in the dark as we are!"[6]

3. Sight and Faith—the difference between the ten spies who doubted and Joshua and Caleb who believed: 13,14.

    a. *The Ten*: We be not able to go up: 13:31
      Joshua and Caleb: For we are well able: 13;30
    b. *The Ten*: For they are stronger than we: 13:31
      Joshua and Caleb: Their defense is departed from them: 14:9
    c. *The Ten*: Brought up an evil report: 13:32
      Joshua and Caleb: It is exceeding good land: 14:9
    d. *The Ten*: A land that eateth up inhabitants: 13:32
      Joshua and Caleb: They are bread for us: 14:9
    e. *The Ten*: We are grasshoppers in their sight: 13:33
      Joshua and Caleb: And the Lord is with us; fear them not: 14:9

It would appear that after Israel's wilderness experience, due to the spies' report, that the majority is not always right.

4. Forty years' wandering. It took the spies forty days to search out the land: 13:25. Because of the failure of Israel to go on into the Land which God promised them, she was punished by having to spend a year for each day the spies spent in the land: 14:33,34. Not only do men reap what they sow, they reap more than they sow (Galatians 6:7). See DAVID'S DOWNFALL in Index.

5. Israel took active steps to return to Egypt (14:1-4), but Moses prayed in their behalf and God overruled (14:11-20). "The effectual fervent prayer of a righteous man availeth much" (James 5:16b). See PRAYER in Index.

Had God not answered this prayer—

—Who would have led them back to Egypt?

—Who would have fed them?

—Who would have given them water to drink?

—Who would have clothed them?

—Who would have sheltered them from the noon-day heat and the cold, chilling nights of the desert?

—Who would have parted the waters of the Red Sea to get back into Egypt?

—Who would have been their spokesman if they desired to leave again?

6. God did not remove the fiery serpents for Israel, but He did provide a remedy in the midst of them: 21:8. We live among that old serpent the devil daily, but we, like some of the Israelites, look to God's remedy, Christ, for deliverance. We also live in the midst of trials and tribulation, but God's remedy of His Son has overcome for us: John 16:33; 17:15.

7. When the males twenty years and upward were counted in Sinai, there were 603,550 (ch. 1). After Israel reached Moab, the number had decreased to 601,730 (26:1-51). Such is the case when God's way is rejected—there is no growth nor increase in the things of the Lord, whether it be with individuals or churches (congregations). See MALES in Index.

Picturing in our minds the long wanderings of the children of Israel in the wilderness for forty years, and seeing what could have been theirs in a matter of days from Kadesh-barnea if they by faith had followed the hand of Jehovah, it is no wonder that our *Spiritual Thought* for Numbers is "get somewhere by the grace of God." They could have gotten somewhere by the grace of God in a very short time. The place of God's choice for them after the Red Sea was the Promised Land via Kadesh-barnea. Instead of getting somewhere by the grace of God they went nowhere by their own choosing. However, notice the apt devotion of a man in Numbers by the name of Caleb, who did get somewhere by the grace of God.

HE HATH FOLLOWED ME FULLY—14:24[7]

"This was God's testimony of the consistency of Caleb. May we obtain an equally good report. To follow the Lord fully is to follow Him with all the heart, to follow Him at all hazards, and to follow Him all our days. Except our hearts are engaged in obeying God's will, and participating in Christ's example; except we are willing to risk everything in God's service, and for Christ's honor; except we persevere in following the Lord below until He calls us up above, we cannot be said to follow Him fully. There must be no reserve, no halfheartedness, no cowardice, no seeking to please men at God's expense, or we do not follow the Lord fully. Beloved, this is the only truly happy life. This is the only truly useful life. This is the only way to secure a blessed death and a glorious resurrection of the just. If we follow the Lord fully, some will mock us, some will condemn us, but conscience will approve, saints will admire, and the Lord Jesus will commend. Let us therefore make it our business to imitate the conduct of Caleb, and so shall we inherit a blessing like unto his—a glorious mansion in our Promised Land."

PRAYER THOUGHT: "I feel constrained, dear Lord, to pray for my pastor, who, standing in Christ's stead and facing all the problems of his congregation, needs my loyalty to him and the cooperation I can give in the ministry of the church. In Thy dear name. Amen."[8]

Numbers 16:3; Hebrews 13:17

Deuteronomy—The Book of Preparation for Possession

Name: Its name means "Second Law." Not that it contains new laws, but that the laws given at Sinai are here reviewed and commented upon. Here again we have an occurrence of the *Law of Recurrence.* See RECURRENCE in Index.

Contents: The Law formerly delivered is now reviewed before a new generation, and more largely explained—to which are added instructions and conditions of blessings in Canaan. Besides, Moses is now about to leave them, and having a hearty desire for their welfare, spends the little time he had to be with them by impressing upon them the laws of God, which were to be their rule of obedience and on which their civil happiness depended. Experiences of the old generation are reviewed and warnings against disobedience to God in Canaan, with the consequences, are spelled out (see WARNINGS to Israel in Index). This Book has 34 chapters, 958 verses, and 28,461 words.

The Necessity for the Book:[1]

1. A *new generation* had grown up which had not heard the original promulgation of the law given at Sinai.

2. A *new country* devoted to idolatrous worship of the most seductive kind was about to be entered. See BAAL in Index.

3. *New duties* were soon to be taken up by them. They had been leading a nomadic life; now they were to settle in cities and villages and till the land. The people must be shown the need of conforming to their lives and conduct these new relations and conforming their lives and conduct to God's laws.

Character: Historical and Law: Luke 24:44.

Subject: Review of God's and Israel's ways in the wilderness, precepts to guide Israel in the land, and prophecy concerning Israel's future.

Purpose: To teach us, in view of the trial of our faith, our unfaithfulness and God's never failing faithfulness, and to give us principles for guidance in the present and hope for the future.

Outline:

    I. Moses' First Address: 1—4
        A. God's guidance from Horeb to Kadesh: 1
        B. God's guidance from Kadesh to Jordan: 2,3
        C. Exhortations to obedience with a warning: 4
    II. Moses' Second Address: 5—26
        A. The Sinaitic Law: 5—11
        B. Special Laws: 12—26

III. Moses' Third Address: 27—30
   A. Instructions for setting up the Law in the land: 27
   B. An exposition of the blessing and curses: 28
   C. A renewed declaration of the Covenant: 29,30
IV. Moses' Last Words: 31—34
   A. His final charge: 31
   B. His farewell song: 32
   C. His last blessing: 33
   D. His lonely death: 34

Scope: A period of about 40 years.

Writer: Moses. See AUTHOR, p. 104.

To Whom Written: Primarily to the new generation which had been born after leaving Sinai.

When and Where Written: The last writings of Moses, in the plains of Moab.

Key Chapter: 29. The Palestinian Covenant. See COVENANTS in Index.

Key Verse: 6:5. "Love the Lord Thy God with all thine heart."

Key Words:
   1. Obedience: 10:12,13
   2. Remember:
      a. The works of God and the giving of the Law: 4:9,10
      b. The Covenant of the Lord: 4:23
      c. Their bondage in Egypt: 5:15; 15:15
      d. God's judgment upon Pharaoh and Egypt: 7:18
      e. God's guidance and provisions: 8:2-6
      f. Their rebellion against God: 9:7
      g. Their deliverance from Egypt: 16:3
      h. The divine judgments: 24:9
      i. The power of the enemy: 25:17
      j. The days of old: 32:7

Key Phrase: Observe and do: 12:1. See also 29:29; Joshua 1:7,8; II Peter 1:4-10.

Key Thought: The review of the Law: 4:1.

Spiritual Thought: Stop and think.

Christ Is Seen As: Prophet: 18:15-19 with Acts 3:22,23; 7:37.

Names and Titles of God: See NAME in Dictionary.
   1. God of gods: 10:17
   2. Lord of lords: 10:17
   3. Rock: 32:4,18,31
   4. Most High: 32:8
   5. Eternal God: 33:27

1. Selection of a king: 17:14-20. Though not a "direct" prophecy, it does convey to Israel in the wilderness God's foreknowledge—that He knew what she would do *after* settlement in the land. Several commandments are given, and it is interesting to see the outcome.

   a. Selecting a king among her own brethren: vs. 15 with I Samuel 8:1—10:1. In Israel's rejection of a Theocratic form of government for a monarchy, she was actually rejecting God (I Samuel 10:18,19). Israel later admitted this was a sin on her part but it was too late then. However, God promised to continue His blessings if Israel continued to fear Him (I Samuel 12:19-25 with Galatians 6:7,8)

Stated: ca. 1,450 B.C. *Fulfilled:* ca. 1,095 B.C.

b. King not to multiply unto himself horses from Egypt: vs. 16 with I Kings 4:16; 10:28,29
c. King not to multiply unto himself wives: vs. 17a with I Kings 11:1-8. See SOLOMON'S WIVES in Index.
d. King not to multiply unto himself silver and gold: vs. 17b with II Chronicles 9:13-28
e. King to make a copy of these laws as a reminder to keep them: vss. 18-20. Had this been done, Solomon, no doubt, would not have turned out to be a most "foolish" wise king.

Stated: ca. 1,450 B.C. *Fulfilled:* ca. 1,015-1,000 B.C.

2. Christ, a prophet like unto Moses: 18:15 with Acts 3:20-23
Stated: ca. 1,450 B.C. *Fulfilled:* In Christ's day.

3. Israel to serve other gods: 28:36; 31:20. Israel's history from her settlement in the Land to the end of her captivity is one great fulfillment of this prophecy: Judges 3:5-7; I Kings 11:1-8,33; 16:28-33; II Kings 21:1-9; II Chronicles 36:11-21

Stated: ca. 1,450 B.C. *Fulfilled:* ca. 1,420-500 B.C.

4. Israel's name to become a "by word" among all nations: 28:37. After her failure to follow God (I Samuel 10:17-19), her rejection of Christ as Messiah (John 1:11; Matthew 27:20-25), and her dispersion after Jerusalem's destruction in A.D. 70, this has been true the world over

Stated: ca. 1,450 B.C. *Fulfilled:* ca. 1,400 B.C. to present.

5. Israel's Captivity: 28:47-52 with II Kings 17:6-28 (Northern Kingdom) and II Kings 25:21; II Chronicles 36:17-21 (Southern Kingdom)

Types of Christ:

1. Moses. Probably more than any other Old Testament saint, Moses is an "all-round" type of Christ, from his humble birth, throughout his earthly ministry, and to his reappearance after death.

— Birth and infancy—under Gentile domain: Exodus 2:1-10 with Matthew 2:1,2; Luke 2:1,2

— Edicts issued at birth for destruction of all male children: Exodus 1:22 with Matthew 2:16
— Had peculiar beds—basket in the bulrushes with a manger in a stable: Exodus 2:3 with Luke 2:7
— Both miraculously saved from death: Exodus 2:3 with Matthew 2:13
— Reared by daughters of kingly family: Exodus 2:5-8 with Luke 1:30-33
— Raised in houses of men not their fathers: Exodus 2:9,10 with Matthew 1:18:25; Acts 7:20,21
— Divinely chosen deliverers: Exodus 3:7-10 with John 1:29; 3:16
— Left high exalted position to suffer with and for Israel: Exodus 2:11-15; Hebrews 11:23-29 with Philippians 2:5-8
— Contended with masters of evil: Exodus 17:11 with Matthew 4:1
— Alone with God forty days and nights: Exodus 24:18 with Matthew 4:2
— Rejected by brethren at first advent: Exodus 2:11-14 with John 1:11

— Discredited by members of family: Numbers 12:1 with John 7:5
— Endured murmurings: Exodus 15:24 with Matthew 7:2
— Almost stoned: Exodus 17:4 with John 8:59
— Both established the Law: Exodus 34:27-32 with Matthew 5:17,18
— Had direct contact with God: Exodus 33:11 with John 12:28,29
— Radiated God's glory: Exodus 34:29,35 with Matthew 17:1,2
— Intercessor: 32:30-35 with John 17:9-15; Hebrews 7:25
— Advocate: 17:1-7; 32:11-14 with I John 2:1
— Prophet: 18:15-19 with Acts 3:22,23; Hebrews 3:1-6
— Spoke God's Word: vs. 18 with John 12:50; 14:10; 17:14
— Spoke in God's name: vs. 19 with John 8:42; 17:4,6,26
— Seas obeyed them: Exodus 14:21 with Matthew 8:26
— Fed multitudes: Exodus 16:17 with Matthew 14:15-21
— Voluntarily offered their lives: Exodus 32:31,32 with John 10:17,18
— Provided deliverance by shedding blood: Exodus 12:1-13 with Hebrews 9:11-15
— Led people out of bondage: Exodus 14:26-31 with John 8:36; Galatians 4:4,5
— Completed God's work: Exodus 40:33 with John 17:4; 19:30
— Opened new dispensation: Moses—the Law: Exodus 20:1-17 with Christ—Grace and Truth: John 1:17
— Established memorials: Exodus 12:14 with Luke 22:19
— Rejected by brethren, received Gentile bride: Exodus 2:13-15,21 with John 1:12; Ephesians 3:6.
— Faithful servant: Numbers 12:7 with Hebrews 3:1-5; John 8:29
— Reappeared after death: Matthew 17:3 with Acts 1:3
— Appeared second time and is received by his brethren: Exodus 4:29-31 with Revelation 1:7

2. The Rock: 32. Moses gives us a picture of two rocks: vss. 3,4,31a.
   a. One belongs to the redeemed of the Lord; the other to the heathen
   b. One represents the one and only true God; the other false gods
   c. One is symbolic of the solid foundation of those who have turned to Him who is the Way; the other a false foundation of men who have turned to their own way

   —Our Rock gives doctrine (counsel): vss. 1,2 with John 7:17. Their rock makes them void of counsel.
   —Our Rock is without iniquity: vs. 4 with Hebrews 4:15. Their rock brings corruption: vss. 5,19,20
   —Our Rock gives life (begets): vs. 18a with John 10:10. Their rock brings judgment: vss. 35,43
   —Our Rock saves and supplies every need: vss. 13-15 with Luke 19:10; Philippians 4:19. Their rock makes desolate: vss. 24,25
   —Our Rock's portion is His people: vs. 9 with I Peter 2:9,10. The portion of the wicked't rock is the devil (demons): vs. 17

Types of the Believer's Experiences:

Israel's wandering in the wilderness is, in a sense, a type of the believer in the world, but not of it. Our citizenship is in heaven, and as pilgrims and strangers here, we have a life—

1. Under God's guidance: 8:2a with John 16:13; Romans 8:14
2. Of humbleness before God: 8:2b with I Peter 5:5,6
3. Upheld by God: 8:3a with Philippians 1:6; 4:19
4. Insufficient apart from God: 8:3b with Job 23:12; Matthew 4:4
5. Of anticipation in God: 8:7-10 with Philippians 3:12-14; Colossians 3:1-4; I John 3:1-3
6. Of gratitude to God: 8:10 with I Corinthians 15:57; II Corinthians 9:15; I Thessalonians 5:18
7. Strengthened by God: 8:18 with Luke 24:49; Acts 1:8

1. In this Book of "review," Moses mentions the signs and great miracles which God had performed, and reminded Israel of His goodness in leading them through the wilderness, making every provision for them—food (manna), water, clothing and shoes that couldn't wear out (29:3,5; Exodus 16:33; Numbers 20:8-11). No wonder so many of the women died in the wilderness—it killed them to have to wear the same old dress for forty years!!

2. The lonely and strange death and burial of Moses: 34:5,6. In perfect health, Moses went "up" to die (vss. 1,7). One translation says he "died by the kiss of God. God kissed Moses good night and put him to sleep. What a lovely way to go."[2] No one knows where God buried him but Michael the archangel did contend with Satan for his body (Jude 9).

1. Solomon's Copper Mines. God told Moses that Canaan was a land out of whose hills Israel could dig brass (copper): 8:7-9. First Kings 7:45,46 mentions copper vessels made for Solomon's Temple. If mines from which Solomon got copper ever existed, they had all but disappeared from the memory of man. After searching for more than twenty years, archaeologist Nelson Glueck, in 1944, found a site which was traditionally called "Copper Ruin." Excavating, he found furnaces black with heaps of copper slag which proved to be a once great copper smelter. Other similar sites were excavated. Pottery in all was from Solomon's time. Nearby was discovered a copper mine. From

Rosetta Stone

this same region today, copper is still being mined.

2. Ras Shamra Tablets. See Index.

3. Rosetta Stone. This stone is about 2 ½ feet wide and about 4 feet high. It was discovered in 1799 by one of Napoleon's soldiers in northern Egypt. Containing three languages, the bottom lines were in Greek, the middle lines were in Egyptian Demotic (a script form of hieroglyphics), and the top lines were made up of hieroglyphic symbols. Scholars could easily read the Greek lines. They found some similarity of words in the Demotic, and soon learned that the Greek and Demotic contained the same message. Some hieroglyphics were in the Demotic, and when these were related to the hieroglyphics in the third line, it wasn't long until the third section was deciphered. This section also contained the same message as the other two. Thus, the hieroglyphical code was broken, and scholars today have no problem reading these ancient messages.

4. Behistun Rock, in ancient Persia, is a huge rock mountain on which King Darius, about 390 feet up from its base, carved a record of his deeds and exploits, along with images of himself, his officers, and some prisoners of war. (Darius was the king who confirmed the decree of Cyrus: Ezra 4:23,24; 5:1—6:12.) He, too, left the same message in three different languages—ancient cuneiform, Elamite (a script form of cuneiform), and Persian. Scholars used the same method as was done with the Rosetta Stone, and were able to decipher the cuneiform. With the discovery at Behistun Rock and of the Rosetta Stone, scholars can now make known the happenings of those ancient days. These discoveries enable archaeologists to pinpoint dates, places, people, and events.

5. Tel el-Amarna Tablets. See Index.

6. Code of Hammurabi. See Index.

7. Baal Worship. See Index.

LIGHT FROM BIBLICAL CUSTOMS

3 1. "Thou waterest the land with thy foot": 11:10. In the East water was often available only at one point. Small gullies or trenches were made throughout these areas and filled with water from the main source. When a particular spot needed to be irrigated, a man would walk along the trench and knock down the existing rills with his foot. The water would then spread throughout the arid soil, hence the expression, "watering the land with thy foot."

2. "Plucking Corn" while traveling: 23:24,25. There were no such things as "Fast Food" outlets in olden days such as we have today. If a traveler was near a field around lunch time, the law stated that he could eat of the fruit of the field till he had his fill, and then must be on the move. He could not stuff his pockets with corn or grapes, etc., for an afternoon snack or in the event he might not be near a field around supper time. Ofttimes a farmer would have a "watchtower" in his field to make sure travelers obeyed this law. It was this law which gave the disciples of Christ the right to "pluck ears of corn and eat" (Matthew 12:1). See COTTAGE in Index.

3. Astrology/Divination: 17:1-5; 18:9-14. That astrology and many forms of divination were practiced by heathen nations centuries before Christ is seen in the commandments given by God to Israel forbidding them to practice such "abominations." *Astronomy* is the science which treats with the heavenly bodies—their motions, magnitudes, distances, etc. But *Astrology* is the study of the supposed influence these heavenly bodies have on and in human affairs. It also includes the art of fortune telling (divination), which in essence embraces mediums, familiar spirits, wizardry, witchcraft, a charmer, conversing with the dead (necro-

Field Watch Tower

mancy), signs of the Zodiac, etc. King Saul's consulting with the witch at Endor is a good example of this practice in ancient times (I Samuel 28:7; see SAUL in Index).

Since this custom of astrology/divination was common among the heathens, God restricted Israel from such practices, thus implying that these forms of worship were of the devil. Not only did God oppose astrology, but He condemned astrologers as well (Leviticus 19:26; Deuteronomy 18:9-14; Isaiah 44:24,25; 47:13,14). Astrology, or "star worship," was a part of idol worship (II Kings 17:16,17; 23:4: Job 31:26-28). Star worship is further seen in idolatry when Amos linked the offering of humans as sacrifices to the god Molech, with CHUIN, which is the planet Saturn. When Stephen was berating the religious leaders of his day, he referred to Israel's sin of idolatry in the wilderness, mentioning "Rephan," which is Saturn or Chiun (Acts 7:41-43). When Nebuchadnezzar of Babylon came up to besiege Jerusalem, he used divination (3 forms) to determine the best approach to attack this city (Ezekiel 21:18-24). The heavenly bodies have been given by God to give light and guidance. Man's custom is to take that which is good and turn it into evil. See ASTROLOGY (Purpose of Heavenly Bodies) in Index. God gave continual warning against the evils of astrology, which embraces the following:

a. False prophets: Deuteronomy 13:1-5; 18:20-22; Jeremiah 27:8-10
b. Necromancer (medium): Deuteronomy 18:11. One who tries to communicate with the spirits of the dead—spiritism. One of the principle aims of the necromancer is to discover the future by communicating with the dead, who are no longer bound by mortal limitations and who can foresee events
c. Witchcraft: Exodus 22:18; Deuteronomy 18:1-12; Nahum 3:4-7. Witchcraft has to do with having a conference with the devil to consult him or to do some diabolic act. See WITCH of Endor in Index.
d. Soothsayers: Micah 5:12; Joshua 13:22; Isaiah 2:6. A soothsayer is one who claims to have supernatural power to foretell events
e. Wizards: Leviticus 19:31; 20:6,27. A conjurer who uses sleight-of-hand with black magic (I Samuel 28:9). "Black magic" applies to all diabolical operations
f. Diviner: divination: Deuteronomy 18:14; II Kings 17:17,18; Jeremiah 14—16. A diviner is one who claims the ability to tell the future based on dreams and their interpretations of them and their astrological calculations
g. Enchantments: Leviticus 19:26; Deuteronomy 18:10; Isaiah 47:9,12,13. A charmer, one who by magic predicts the future

h. Augury: Deuteronomy 18:10 ASV. A practice of foretelling by signs (stars) or omens (phenomenon or incident regarding a prophetic sign), fortune telling

i. Sorcery: Isaiah 47:9,12,13; 57:3; Malachi 3:5. One bound to Satan in return for knowledge and skill in magic

The whole gamut of astrology—a study of worship of the heavenly bodies—and which is so commonplace in our society today, is an abomination to the Lord. The child of God must so familiarize himself with the Word of God so as not to be deceived by it (Revelation 18:23). The Christian must be aware that Satan can give power to work signs and wonders (II Thessalonians 2:9-12), and that such who practice this art are in the same category with the abominable, murderers, whoremongers, idolators, and liars (Revelation 21:8). It should be noted that astrology also leads to a cult of "prophets" and that those who claim to have ESP (extrasensory perception) are seldom over 50% correct, which is contrary to a "true" prophet of God, who is correct in each prediction (Deuteronomy 13:1-5; 18:20-22).

4. "Thou shalt not plow with an ox and an ass together": 22:10. For eating purposes the ox was considered clean (sanitary). But the ass was considered to be unclean. The yoking of these two animals together for work was forbidden. The ox is meek, patient, slow, but very strong and very willing. The donkey is just the opposite—stubborn, unpredictable and obstinate, typical of stupidity. You can imagine how much plowing a farmer would get done in a day with such a team. This principle applies to us as God's children (II Corinthians 6:14-18). Pictured is a typical scene in the Holy Land today—an ox and an ass plowing.

Plowing with Ox and Ass

5. "Thou shalt not muzzle the mouth of an ox that treadeth out the corn": 25:4. When God made His covenant with Noah, animals were included as well as humans (Genesis 6:17-22). When the Ten Commandments were given, God, in the fourth, desired His people to be just as humanitarian to animals as they were to others and themselves (Exodus 20:8-11). God's people were to show love to and respect for their "beasts of burden." Even while working—treading out grain—they were not to be muzzled so they could eat when they became hungry. Back in Old Testament days the "laborer was worthy of his hire." Paul used the oxen to illustrate that those who "work" at preaching the gospel shall live by the gospel, just as the ox who worked at treading out the grain shall live by the grain (I Corinthians 9:9-14).

God's loving care and concern for fowls is shown in the command that a mother bird was not to become prey: 22:6. This would tend to preserve wildlife—something man of late recognizes. God's love is also seen in Luke 12:6 regarding sparrows.

6. "Thou shalt not have in thy bag divers (different) weights (stones), a great and a small . . but thou shalt have a perfect and just weight (stones)": 25:13,15. Money was originally paid out in weight. Abraham, in the purchasing of the cave of Machpelah, paid out "four hundred

Muzzling an Ox

Ancient Landmark

shekels of silver, current money with the merchants'' (Genesis 23:16). Dishonesty was practiced by using a lighter stone to balance, or heavier, whichever was to his advantage. God had previously commanded Israel not to steal (Exodus 20:15), and the use of such "just weights" (or properly balanced stones) was for their own protection.

7. "Thou shalt not remove thy neighbor's landmark": 27:17. Evidence of a man's property was the use of a pile of stones at the boundary lines. We can understand how easily such boundary stones could be changed or moved by a jealous or dishonest neighbor. Since there were no drawings or any government surveyors to which appeal could be made in a dispute, landmarks were stones balanced one on top of the other, standing about two feet high.

8. "He shall dwell between his shoulders": 33:12. This expression refers to a mother, who, carrying her child strapped on her back between her shoulders, works with ease in the field. The baby is so covered that he is protected from the blazing sun. The mother does this since there is no one to take care of the baby but herself. "The beloved of the Lord shall dwell safely by him; and the Lord shall cover him all the day long, and he shall dwell between his shoulders." How wonderful of our Lord to keep us bound to Himself—one with Him, protected, co-laborers together with Him!

1. God is said to have "divided (the stars) unto all nations under the whole heaven": 4:19. This is exactly what science tells us today—that each nation sees its own portion of the stars. The "Southern Cross" is never seen in the North. Canada does not have the same stars as Central America. Our only explanation to such a verse is that Moses knew the earth was a sphere. This is one of the things the Egyptians knew when they built the great pyramid with perfect orientation. Moses was schooled in all the wisdom (sciences) of the Egyptians (Acts 7:22).

2. Photosynthesis. "Precious things by the sun" (33:13,14). Here is a scientific fact made by God ca. 1500 B.C., and only discovered by man in the early 1800s A.D. It was demonstrated in 1804 that the carbon of plants came from carbon dioxide, a result of the sun's activity. A scientist in 1844 discovered that the metabolic energy of plants came from the energy of the sun by means of photosynthesis. Today, it is a scientific fact that the light of the sun influences production of plant life. "Precious things" do come by the sun. And, of course, we attribute this all to God who, we believe, created the sun (Psalm 104:14).

Deuteronomy in the New Testament:
1. Christ's Temptation (see TEMPTATION in Index):
    a. To turn stones into bread: 8:3. His reply: Matthew 4:4
    b. To cast self down from pinnacle of Temple: 6:16. His reply: Matthew 4:5-7
    c. To worship Satan: 6:13. His reply: Matthew 4:8-10
2. Two witnesses needed to establish facts: 17:6; 19:15 with Matthew 18:16
3. Levites have no inheritance—live by their work: 18:1,2 with I Corinthians 9:13,14
4. Moses, a Prophet like unto Christ: 18:15,18 with Acts 3:22,23; 7:37
5. Bill of divorcement: 24:1 with Matthew 5:31; 19:7
6. Not muzzle an ox: 25:4 with I Corinthians 9:9
7. Cursed (or judged) for not keeping all the Law: 27:26 with Galatians 3:10
8. Word of God nigh (near): 30:12-14 with Romans 10:6-9
9. Vengeance belongs to the Lord: 32:35,36 with Romans 12:19; Hebrews 10:30
10. Companion references:
    a. Chosen, peculiar people: 7:6; 14:2 with I Peter 2:9
    b. No respect of persons with God: 10:17b with Romans 2:11; Ephesians 6:9b

1. The Lord does not give us everything at once. It is in accordance with our readiness that He gives: 2:31 with Ephesians 3:20

2. Prayer (see PRAYER in Index). God does not always answer prayer according to our petition—
    a. Moses: 3:23-27
    b. Elijah: I Kings 19:4-8
    c. Jonah: 4
    d. Paul: II Corinthians 12:7-10

3. The greatest doctrinal statement in the Old Testament: 6:4,5

4. The riches of divine supplies and the danger of forgetfulness and idolatry: 8. In the chapter we notice the purpose of Israel's wandering in the wilderness (vss. 2-6). It did not take God forty years to get Israel out of Egypt—it took God forty years to get Egypt out of Israel! See FORTY YEARS in Index.

5. Three times over Israel was reminded that God's wondrous dealings with them were "not for their righteousness," but because of Him: 9:4-6

6. Divine Instruction: 10:12,13

    a. Teach me Thy commandments, statutes and judgments: Psalms 119:12,108

    b. Teach me to do Thy will: Psalms 143:10

    c. Teach me to walk in Thy path and to know Thy way: Psalm 25:4; 27:11; 32:8; I Samuel 12:23b; I Kings 8:36

    d. Teach me to pray (not "how to" but "to"): Luke 11:1

    e. Teach me to hold my tongue: Job 6:24

    f. Teach me to number my days: Psalm 90:12

    g. Teach me knowledge: Psalm 119:66

    h. Teach me the difference between holy and profane, between unclean and clean: Ezekiel 44:23

    i. Teach me what to say: Job 37:19

    j. Teach me to teach others about Christ and to remain true to the Truth: I Corinthians 2:4,5; 14:19; II Timothy 4:1-11

7. The women not to dress like a man nor a man like a woman: 22:5. Judging by today's standards, this law is obsolete. Just because grace abounds is no license for one to live in disgrace.

8. The blessings of obedience and the curse of sin: 28

9. The plight of the backslider: 28:65,66. See BACKSLIDER in Index.

10. When God leads, He supplies the shoe leather: 29:5

11. God's Grace and Goodness to Israel: 33:29

    a. Saved: 29a

    b. Shielded: 29b

    c. Sustained: 29c

    d. Strengthened: 29d

A BIT OF HEAVENLY MANNA

Often the children of Israel would take their eyes off the Lord. When they did, they saw the imperfections of Moses. When about to leave this old sin-cursed world, Moses reminded them that the work done by him in their wilderness journey was not his, but God's. He was anxious for the Israelites to know that upon entering the Promised Land, God's work is perfect.

HIS WORK IS PERFECT—32:4[4]

"An infinite perfect mind will produce a perfect work. Every work of God is wrought by a perfect plan, by a perfect agency with the most suitable instruments, and with infallible success. Failure belongs to man, not to God. The work of creation is complete. The work of providence is perfect as far as it is finished, and so is the work of grace. Jesus has perfectly fulfilled the law, answered all the claims of divine justice, frustrated the designs of his foes, and provided the certain salvation of all His people. When the work of salvation is finished, it will be the most magnificent work which even God ever wrought. It will be a mirror to reflect and reveal all the glorious attributes, perfections, purposes, and thoughts of the Most High. Blessed be the Lord Jesus for His perfect work! In this we are justified, in this we are able to approach the throne of God with boldness, in this we can meet death without fear, and in this we shall be acquitted from the penalty of sin. It is our bridal robe, our title to the heavenly mansions, and the ground of our hope.''

PRAYER THOUGHT: "O God, help me to see that in all the choices I make I am either for or against Thee. May I not be tolerant of wrong and intolerant of right, but with courage may I face error for what it is and make the only choice that would glorify Thee. In Thy dear Son's name I pray. Amen."[5]

Deuteronomy 30:19

Israel—From Egypt To Canaan

Israel's settlement in Egypt was in fulfillment of prophecy (Genesis 15:13,14). The circumstances leading up to this prophecy being fulfilled, made by God to Abraham almost 200 years before the first of his seed went down into Egypt, are these: Joseph, who was hated by his brethren, was sold by them at Dothan to merchantmen and taken to Egypt. He was then sold by them to Potiphar, an officer of Pharaoh's guard (Genesis 37:13-36). In time to come, Joseph was exalted and made second only to Pharaoh—the "Secretary to the Department of Agriculture" as a result of his interpretation of Pharaoh's dream (Genesis 41:38-40). Afterward, a famine covered the whole earth and all countries came to Joseph's storehouses to buy corn. When Joseph's father heard there was plenty of food in Egypt, he sent his sons down to purchase some (Genesis 41:56—42:3). Joseph recognized his brothers, kept Simeon, and told his brothers to return to their land and bring the youngest back with them. Having done this, Joseph revealed himself to his brothers saying, "God sent me before you to preserve you a posterity in the earth, and to save your lives by a great deliverance" (Genesis 45:5-11).

According to the above statement by Joseph, it was not God's "permissive" will that placed Israel in Egypt, but His *direct* will. "If Israel were to be the people through whom Messiah was to come, they would have to survive a seven-year famine in which there would be no planting and harvest. God, who foresaw this famine in all the lands, engineered circumstances in such a way that His man was in a land of plenty to save His people from annihilation by starvation."[6] Joseph's family then settled in Egypt with him. Before dying, Joseph's father, Jacob, called unto his sons, who were to become the twelve tribes of Israel, and blessed them (Genesis 43:1—49:33).

Years after Joseph's death, there arose a king who knew him not. Because of Israel's numerical strength in Egypt by this time, Pharaoh placed them in bondage and set taskmasters over them. For fear Israel would increase more, all newborn males were to be killed (Exodus 1:6-22). Thus the prophecy to Abraham was fulfilled—the children of Israel sojourning in Egypt, and later their bondage (Genesis 15:13; Exodus 12:40). In fulfillment of the latter part of the prophecy to Abraham (Genesis 15:14), we see the judgments in Exodus 7:20—12:30 (see PLAGUES in Index). The Israelites left Egypt with great substance (Exodus 12:35).

We now notice the journeyings of Israel from her bondage in Egypt to her settlement in the Land of her fathers—Abraham, Isaac, and Jacob. Points 1—26, under the leadership of Moses: Exodus 12:29—Deuteronomy 34:12. Points 27—34, under the leadership of Joshua: Joshua 1—11.

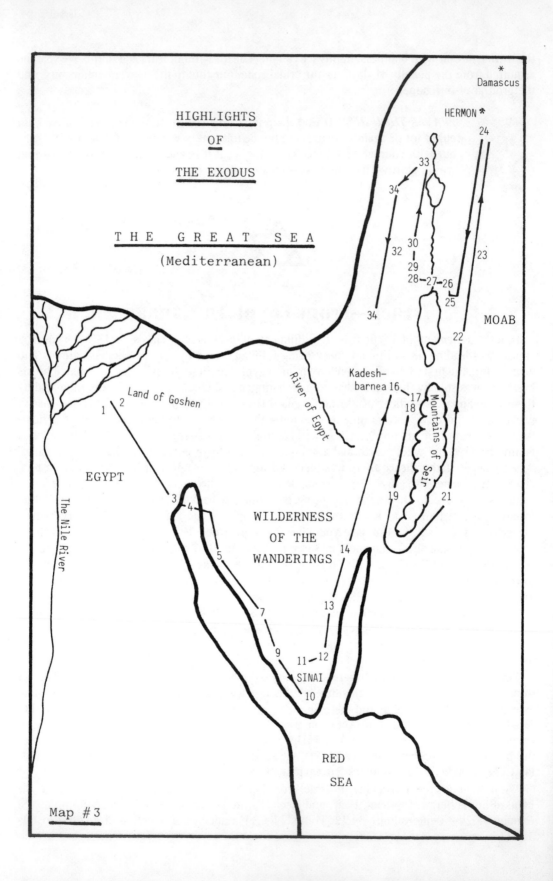

Israel in Egypt:

1. Rameses to Succoth: Exodus 12:33-37

2. Succoth to Etham, in the edge of the wilderness: Exodus 13:20-22. It was here the cloud by day and the pillar of fire by night first began to guide the Israelites. See CLOUD by Day in Index.

3. Etham to Pi-hahiroth, between Migdol and the sea, over against Baal-zephon to encamp by the Red Sea: Exodus 14:2

4. The crossing of the Red Sea: Pharaoh's army in pursuit, and judgment upon his army: Exodus 14:8-31

Israel in the Wilderness:

5. Through the Red Sea to Marah, in the wilderness of Shur: Exodus 15:22-25

6. From Marah to Elim (called the "wells of Moses"): Exodus 15:27

7. From Elim to the wilderness of Sin, between Elim and Sinai: Exodus 16:1. It was in this wilderness that God first fed the children of Israel with manna, and continued to do so until they came to the borders of the land of Canaan (Exodus 16:1-35). See MANNA in Index.

8. Out of the wilderness of Sin they encamped in Dophkah, and from there to Alush: Numbers 33:12,13

9. From Alush to Riphidim, where water came forth from the rock in Horeb. This place was called Massah: Exodus 17:1-7. See ROCK, HOREB, in Index.

10. From Rephidim, in the wilderness of Sin (or the foot of mount Sinai), to the desert of Sinai: Exodus 19:1,2. While Moses was upon the mount receiving the Law, Aaron and the children of Israel were in the valley worshiping the golden calf (Exodus 19:3—32:35). "While the cat's away, the mice will play." It was here that Moses broke the two tablets of stone while in a fit of anger with Israel.

Golden Calf

11. Leaving mount Sinai they went to Horeb, where the Tabernacle was set up for the first time: Exodus 33:1-17. From Sinai and Horeb through Paran (or the wilderness of Zin): Numbers 10:12.

12. Next in the wilderness is Taberah, where the fire of the Lord consumed part of the children of Israel because of their complaint against the Lord: Numbers 11:1-3. See MISCHIEF in Index.

13. From Taberah to Kibroth-hattaavah, where Israel murmured for flesh: the flock of quails and the plague sent. Also the council of 70 elders chosen: Numbers 11:4-35

14. To Hazeroth. Here the sedition of Aaron and Miriam, and leprosy on the latter: Numbers 11:35—12:15

15. From Hazeroth, back into the wilderness of Paran to Rithmah. After much wandering there, they finally pitched in the wilderness of Zin, which is Kadesh: Numbers 33:18-36

16. For the full account of Israel at Kadesh-barnea, see Numbers 13:1—20:21. It was here that the 12 spies were sent into Canaan (Numbers 13:1-24). Returning with their report (Numbers 13:25—14:24), the testimony of ten overshadowed the report of Caleb and Joshua. Because of unbelief, the 40 years' wandering was declared (38 in addition to the 2 years already spent since leaving Egypt: Numbers 14:30-34). See WILDERNESS in Index

17. At Kadesh Miriam died, and was buried there: Numbers 20:1. Here a thirsty people received water from the rock of Meribah: Numbers 20:2-13 (see ROCK in Index). Moses asked permission of the king of Edom to pass through his country, but was refused, even though he promised not to disturb their land (Numbers 20:14-21)

18. The whole congregation of Israel journeyed from Kadesh and came to mount Hor. It was here that Aaron died: Numbers 20:22-29. See AARON in Index

19. Because of the refusal of the king of Edom to let Israel pass through his country, "they journeyed from Mount Hor by way of the Red Sea, to compass the land of Edom: And the soul of the people was much discouraged because of the way": Numbers 21:4. See ARCHAEOLOGY, #2, in Numbers

20. Then they pitched in Zalmonah. Departing there, to Punon: Numbers 33:41,42

21. From Punon they pitched in Oboth: Numbers 33:43. It was between Punon and Oboth, no doubt, that the judgment of the fiery serpents fell upon the Israelites for their speaking against the Lord: Numbers 21:5-10. See SERPENT in Index

22. From Oboth to Ije-abarim, in the wilderness of Moab; from there to the valley of Zarid, and from there to the other side of the river Arnon in Moab: Numbers 21:11-13. Then to Dibon-gad: Numbers 33:45

23. Going north from the other side of the river Arnon, Moses sought permission to pass through the land of the Amorites. Failing to get permission, the Amorites and the children of Israel fought at Jahaz. In winning this battle, Israel possessed King Sihon's land from Arnon to Jabbok, even to the border of Ammon: Numbers 21:21-24. In taking possession of this territory, Israel dwelt in Heshbon, and in all the villages of the Amorites: Numbers 21:25-31

24. Then Israel turned and went up by way of Bashan, from Jaazer, to battle King Og's army at Edrei: Numbers 21:32-35; Deuteronomy 1:4. The two victories, one with King Sihon of the Amorites, and the other with King Og of Bashan, gave Israel possession of the whole country east of the River Jordan, from the River Arnon to Mount Hermon: Numbers 21:21-25; Deuteronomy 3:8

25. Having settled briefly in the mountains of Abarim, before Nebo, Israel departed and settled on the plains of Moab on the east side of Jordan opposite Jericho, in Abel-shittim: Numbers 33:47-49; 22:1; 25:1

From Numbers 22:1 to 32:42 we have the alliance of the Moabites, Ammonites, and Midianites, under Balak, against Israel; Balaam's fruitless attempt to curse Israel; fornication of Israel, and their defection to worship of Baal; 24,000 slain by a plague; zeal of Phinehas; defeat of Midian; and the slaying of Balaam. See MOAB in Index.

26. On the plains of Moab, there is a review of the Israelite army, 601,730 males above 20 years old: Numbers 26:1-51 (see MALES in Index). Moses then gave the conditions of blessings in the land they are about to possess on the other side of Jordan; the Palestinian convenant is set forth; last words to the priests, Levites, and Joshua, with a warning to Joshua of the apostasy of Israel once they enter the Promised Land; a repetition and confirmation of the law

by Moses to the new generation of Israelites; the song of Moses; the blessing of the tribes; Moses' view of Canaan from Pisgah just before his death: Deuteronomy 28:1—34:12. See MOSES, Death of, in Index.

It is estimated that the number of Israelites who left Egypt was between two and three million. Although all of the original ones who left Egypt died in the wilderness except Caleb and Joshua and those who were under twenty years of age when they left Egypt (Numbers 14:23,29,30), God wonderfully preserved and supplied the needs of all the Israelites, both the old and new generations, in their journey to Canaan. He supplied manna, flesh, a cloud by day and a pillar of fire by night, and water. "In the wilderness, where thou hast seen that the Lord thy God bare thee, as a man doth bare his son..., these forty years the Lord thy God hath been with thee; thou hast lacked nothing. Your clothes are not waxen old upon you, and thy shoe is not waxen old upon thy foot" (Deuteronomy 1:31; 2:7; 29:5).

In connection with the warnings Moses gave Israel just before he died, it is well to note that these warnings were actually prophecies. God predicted that Israel would fall into sin, break His covenant, worship other gods, etc. (Deuteronomy 31:16-21). The children of Israel had not been in the land long before they failed to drive out the surrounding nations. The book of Judges records Israel's failure to obey the Lord and her consequent fulfillment of the prophecies given through Moses. They refused a Theocratic form of government for a Monarchy (I Samuel 8), and at the death of the third king (Solomon), the kingdom was divided (I Kings 11,12). All the kings of the kingdom of Israel were evil. Only eight of the kings of the kingdom of Judah were good (see KINGS in Index). The Israelites apostatized to such a degree, even after repeated warnings from many of the prophets, that there was no longer a remedy for her, and the very words—"so that they will say in that day, are not these evils come upon us, because our God is not among us?"—were literally fulfilled when the Babylonians captured them (Deuteronomy 31:17b with II Chronicles 36:11-21; Ezekiel 6:9).

27. After the death of Moses, Joshua took over the leadership of Israel and led them across Jordan: Joshua 1:1—4:18. (Points 27—34 under Joshua's leadership.)

All the children of Israel did not cross Jordan. The possession of the tribes of the Reubenites, the Gadites, and half the tribe of Manasseh was on the east side of Jordan. Their wives and little ones were to remain in the land given them by Moses. The men of these tribes were instructed to go over with the rest of the children of Israel to help in battle, and then after Israel had possessed the land they were to return to their families (Numbers 32:1-33; Joshua 1:12-15). The rest of the Israelites crossed Jordan, and about 40,000 men prepared for war (Joshua 4:1,13).

Israel in Canaan

28. The encampment of Gilgal: Joshua 4:19—5:19. See point b, p. 118, and GILGAL in Index.

29. The fall of Jericho; the march on Ai; Achan's sin; victory at Ai: Joshua 6:1—8:29. See FAILURE in Index.

30. The whole congregation of Israel, half on mount Ebal and half on mount Gerizim, swear to the Covenant in the presence of the Ark. The Law written on twelve stones on Ebal; the cursings read from the same mountain, and the blessings given from mount Gerizim: Joshua 8:30-35.

31. Return to Gilgal, the treaty with the Gibeonites, and their punishment: Joshua 9. See CARRIERS in Index.

32. March to the relief of Gibeon; at Beth-horon, the defeat of Adoni-zedek and four other kings. The conquest of southern Canaan: Joshua 10. See LONG DAY in Index.

33. Final conquest of Canaan, the defeat of the northern Canaanite confederacy at Merom: Joshua 11:1-22.

34. Settlement of the Twelve Tribes in their posessions, the setting up of the tabernacle at

Shiloh, and the Land divided: Joshua 11:23; 13:1—21:45. See SPIRITUAL THOUGHT of Joshua.

Author of the Pentateuch

Who wrote the first five Books of the Bible (called the "Pentateuch")? Since Israel's leaders knew that God spoke through Moses and gave him His Word for His people, they were very careful to preserve and protect his writings. Ancient Jewish records tell us that he was the author of the Pentateuch, and there has never been any question among the most ancient Jews that he wrote it. In the last century many scholars have imagined that the Pentateuch was put together from a variety of sources with several authors. One popular theory suggests four distinct sources—"J" narrative in which God is called Jahweh, "E" narrative in which Elohim is used for God, "P" or priestly writings which contain ritual codes and genealogies, and "D" or Deuteronomical set of laws. Recently (1981—*Newsweek* magazine) experts in Israel fed the Book of Genesis into a computer and found it was probaby written by *one* author. It found the two accounts of creation (Genesis 1 and 2) linguistically identical.

Evangelical Bible scholars believe that Moses did not depend upon oral traditions of the tales of ancient times for the origin of his writings, nor do they believe that the Pentateuch is the work of several authors. Genesis, for example, is not the word of a copyist. Here we find statements of fact, new statements not found in other records. Scientific facts are found in this book which have been proved by modern discovery. While he may have been assisted by oral traditions regarding the nation of Israel and God's covenant with Abraham, the details leave no doubt that God alone, by inspiration, supplied the information we have. Had Genesis not been the inspired Word we would expect to find therein all the unscientific trash and "tall tales" found in secular history which relate to many events recorded in this book, such as creation, sin, the ark and the flood, the tower of Babel, etc., etc. His other four books—Exodus, Leviticus, Numbers, Deuteronomy—plainly state that what he had to say came from God. Concerning their inspiration, there can be no doubt or question.

While the style of writing differs in each book, this is quite understandable in view of the purpose of each book. And, for example, when Moses spoke of conditions in Canaan under the sway of Baalism (see Leviticus 18; BAAL in Index) we must conclude—since he had not been there, and since archaeology has gone a long way to confirm such conditions—that he wrote under inspiration. Why not—he *was* a prophet (Deuteronomy 18:15-19).

There are those who say Moses did not write the Pentateuch. Held to be a collection of myth, fable, folklore, and conflicting oral traditions, the critics of the Bible say these books were written many centuries *after* Moses. Others say that Moses was not scholastically qualifed to write laws and history such as is found in the books attributed to him. Still others say his laws were too advanced for his day—that if such laws did exist then—he copied them from the sources other than Divine revelation. What sayeth evidence?

1. Whether he kept a diary from his boyhood in Egypt to his last days in the wilderness and finally compiled these records, or wrote only as God spoke, there is too much internal evidence of Divine inspiration to think otherwise. The Pentateuch claims for itself that Moses *is* the author, at least in part. See Exodus 17:14; 34:27; Leviticus 1:1,2; Numbers 1:1; 33:2; Deuteronomy 31:9,19,24-26. Such evidence refutes any claim to a date later than Moses' day.

2. Moses was *well* qualified to write. As the "adopted" son of an Egyptian princess, he acquired a princely education, and he was schooled in all the wisdom of the Egyptians (Acts 7:20-23), who were unsurpassed in those days in civilization by any people in the world. This would certainly fit him for any position in the government—even the throne (had he chosen to have been called "the son of Pharaoh's daughter"). Living in Pharaoh's palace for forty years, he became familiar with court life, with the military, with their sciences, literature, and arts, and with the grandeur and pomp of their religion.

Writing had advanced to such a degree in his day that he could have had a choice of at least three styles—early Hebrew, ancient Egyptian hieroglyphics, and Akkadian cuneiform. The discovery of the *Ras Shamra Tablets* (see Index) in northern Syria in 1929 shows that alphabetic writing was common 500 years before Moses' time. The *Rosetta Stone,* discovered by one of Napoleon's soldiers in 1799 in northern Egypt, provided the key to deciphering the ancient hieroglyphics which go back long before Moses (see Index). The *Tel el-Amarna Tablets* (see Index) discovered in 1886 north of Luxor, Egypt, reveal the Akkadian cuneiform language which belonged to the period of Israel's entrance into Canaan. Assyrian (Mesopotamian) cuneiform pre-dates Moses by many centuries. See BEHISTUN ROCK in Index.

3. The discovery of the *Code of Hammurabi* in 1901 in ancient Persia revealed a series of several moral laws and customs of the patriarchal times. This "Code" was written about three centuries before Moses' day. When the critics learned that such laws pre-dated Moses, they then said that Moses copied these and other laws. For some time they appeared to be successful, but after a comparison of Moses' and Hammurabi's laws, it was found that Hammurabi, under the approval of his sun-god Shamash, permitted immorality, as well as other sins, to be practiced. The Mosaic Law, far superior to Hammurabi's, condemns the practice of sin, thus showing that the Hebrew laws dealing with morality and holiness were not derived from other sources as the critic would have us believe. We would expect to find, if the Pentateuch were not inspired, an admixture of Mesopotamian and Egyptian "religions" with God's laws.

Code of Hammurabi

4. There has been some question concerning Deuteronomy as to whether Moses wrote the first five verses of chapter 1 and the record of his death. This brief introduction to Deuteronomy hardly poses a problem. If Moses didn't it is quite possible that his able assistant, Joshua, did. And as to the record of his death (34:1-6), he could have easily done this as a "prophet." If he didn't, here again his successor, Joshua, equally inspired, could have recorded the closing words of this fifth book of Moses.

Archaeology has given us excellent external evidence in supporting the believer's view that Moses wrote the Pentateuch. The most important internal evidence we have is that which Christ Himself gives. In connection with His earthly ministry, all four gospel accounts contain quotations from the first five books of the Bible. Some examples are:

    a. To Moses in general: Luke 24:25-27,44; John 5:46,47; 7:19
    b. Creation of man: Matthew 19:4 with Genesis 1:27; 2:21,22
    c. Marriage: Matthew 19:5,6 with Genesis 2:23,24
    d. Manna: John 6:49,58 with Exodus 16:35
    e. The first five Commandments: Luke 18:20 with Exodus 20:1-12
    f. Cleansing a leper: Matthew 8:1-4 with Leviticus 14:4-32
    g. Adultery: John 8:5 with Leviticus 20:10
    h. Brazen serpent: John 3:14 with Numbers 21:9
    i. The priests and the Sabbath: Matthew 12:4,5 with Numbers 28:9,10
    j. Christ's temptation: Matthew 4:3-10 with Deuteronomy 6:13,16; 8:3
    k. Divorce: Mark 10:2-9 with Deuteronomy 24:1-4
    l. Remarriage of a widow: Luke 20:27-38 with Deuteronomy 25:5,6

Additional internal evidence is that which the apostles and disciples gave when they referred to the Pentateuch, thereby showing their acceptance of Moses' writings as inspired Scriptures. Some examples are—

    a. Concerning Christ's coming and ministry: John 1:45; Acts 26:22,23; 28:23 with Deuteronomy 18:15
    b. Concerning Moses' customs: Acts 6:14
    c. Stephen's references to Moses' history: Acts 7:1-44
    d. Law of Moses read and preached: Acts 13:39; 15:21; II Corinthians 3:15
    e. Circumcision: Acts 15:1,5 with Leviticus 12:3
    f. Muzzling an ox: I Corinthians 9:9 with Deuteronomy 25:4
    g. Faithfulness of Moses: Hebrews 3:2 with Numbers 12:7
    h. Aaronic priesthood: Hebrews 5:4 with Exodus 28:1; Numbers 16:40
    i. Priesthood of Melchizedek: Hebrews 5:6 with Genesis 14:18
    j. Despising Moses' law: Hebrews 10:28

Baal Worship[*7]

The Israelites, after Moses' death, were on the threshold of experiencing the fulfillment of God's promises to their forefathers by being led into a new country—Canaan—by their new leader, Joshua (Joshua 1:1,2). This new country was devoted to idolatrous worship of the most seductive kind. Moses had painted a factual picture of Canaan's awful sins in Leviticus 18. The condition of the land in which Israel was to dwell can best be described by the following evidence from the pick and spade of the archaeologist.

A French archaeologist, professor C. F. A. Schaeffer, in 1929-1937, unearthed the ancient religious city of Ugarit in northern Syria, known today as Ras Shamra. Many artifacts were found, which enable us to have a background knowledge of many of the Canaanite customs of Old Testament days. Most important to us was the discovery of some amazing and exciting religious texts which were found in the Royal Library, located between the temples of Dagon and Baal. The texts were called the "Ras Shamra" tablets and when the scholars deciphered

*For detailed study of Baal Worship, see author's book, "BAAL WORSHIP"

them, the material unfolded the historical account of Baal worship which set forth the mythological stories, sacrificial rituals, and religious practices of the ancient Canaanite people. Copper and bronze images of the god Baal, and inscribed objects found in and near his temple, indicate this shrine to have been built around 1900 B.C., during the time of Abraham and Lot.

The "Ras Shamra" tablets, written in cuneiform on clay, reveal the Canaanite pantheon, whose head was El. The writings indicate he was the "supreme court" in the disputes of other

Father-god "El"

gods. In late years, he yielded routine procedure to lesser gods who were more popular. The wife of El was named Athirat, which in Hebrew is Asherah, and is translated "grove" in such passages as II Kings 13:6 and 21:7. The plural of Asherah, "Asherim," which is found several times in our Bible as "groves," refers to sex-cult objects in Baal worship (II Kings 17:10; 23:14).

El and Athirat bore seventy children. Both Ugarit mythology and the Old Testament declare that Baal became the most popular god. Although El was recognized as "father-god" of all the lesser gods of the nations and the city-states in and around what is commonly called Canaan, Baal became the reigning ruler or lord of all these gods, dominating the pantheon.

A violent battle broke out between Baal, god of Storm, and Yam, god of the Sea, to determine who should be lord of the land. Baal's victory gave him the lordship over the earth, confining Yam to his proper sphere, the sea.

A victory feast followed Baal's conquest of Yam, which signalized his prowess in battle, and Baal was crowned god of War. As god of War, he was supposed to assure victory for his followers over their enemies. Baal was a fierce god (of Storm) who could hurl bolts of fire from heaven to rout the enemy, or to consume anything that might cause them to suffer defeat.

When Baal defeated Yam and became god of Earth, he also became god of Fertility, who provided rain for growth, thus sustaining life. As life-giver, he encountered Mot, the god of Barrenness or Death. In the struggle which ensued, Baal was slain. With his death all rain ceased, the streams dried up, and the death-power of Mot encroached itself upon all lands.

El, the father-god, was mortified at Baal's death. He, along with Anat, Baal's sister, performed mourning rites. He gashed his face, chest, and arms, until his blood flowed freely. It is

Baal

clear from the Ugarit texts that Baal was dead and the loss of his life-sustaining powers endangered his people, lands, and livestock.

Anat began a journey over hills and mountains in search for her brother's body. In her travels, she met Mot, who had slain Baal. They fought, and Anat killed him. In some mysterious way she found the body of Baal and restored him to life. With his return, rains descended, streams began to flow and his life-power revived again the parched earth. El is pictured as jubilant, and the worshipers of Baal, who had believed their god was asleep or on a journey—even in death—joined in all the festivities. In the celebration of Baal's "resurrection," he became the god of all Nature—the god of Rain, Storm, Seasons, Harvest, and Drought. In Canaan there is a dry season and a rainy season. During the dry season Baal was supposedly asleep or on a long journey; in the rainy and harvest seasons he was back on the "job." He was a "seasonal" god.

The sunshine, or lack of it, was associated closely with these agricultural Canaanites, so they worshiped the sun, moon, and stars. Baal, already the god of the Earth and sustainer of all life, became the ruler of Heaven—the ruler of both heaven and earth. His subjects not only worshiped the heavenly bodies because of help derived from them, but for fear of their power also. The sun, blazing in the heat of the day, could cause a sunstroke, resulting in premature death. Its brightness would often weaken the eyes. Superstitious beliefs prevailed regarding the moon. They thought a full moon could cause spoilage of meat, temporary or permanent blindness, temporary insanity, distortion of features such as the mouth drawn to one side and even death to newly born animals. Extreme coldness in the desert regions was attributed to the moon. Since the sun did smite them by day, superstition caused these people to say that the moon could smite them by night. Altars which were erected give every indication that special offerings were made to these heavenly bodies on certain feast days.

Sun-god Altar

In the worshiping of Baal, the Canaanites erected huge temples, usually on the highest hill or mountain in or near their city. Altars were set up inside the temples, and sacrifices were offered to Baal at these high places. When a small village could not afford a temple, a small altar about four feet high was erected on the hillside nearby. In the beginning of Baal worship, the offerings consisted of the first fruits of their harvest and the sacrificing of animals similar to Cain's and Abel's (Genesis 4:3,4). Many temples, like one discovered and still standing at Samaria, had no roof, so that as sacrifices were made, the worshipers could look to the heavens (sun, moon, and stars), and pay homage to these heavenly bodies. Large images of Baal were set up in the temples and smaller ones were displayed in their homes.

Baal always expected the best of the animals and of the first fruits *from* those who sacrificed to him, and he coveted the best houses and lands and animals *for* his followers. If "non-believers" possessed property superior to the worshipers of Baal, it was justifiable for them to covet anything the other man had, and to kill, if necessary, to get it. This is what Anat did on one occasion. She had a man murdered to rob him of his bow. It was not unusual for them to rob and murder for trivial things.

When men or nations "invent" their own god or gods, it is quite natural they create their gods as sinners so that they may practice evil under their patronage and approval. The people of Canaan, whose hearts were deprived like all sinners, saw no wrong in making Baal the god of Sex. We learn from these Ugarit texts that El and Baal represented sex in the most sensual aspect of lust. The three goddesses of the Ugarit pantheon were Anat and Athirat (Asherah), Baal's sister and mother, and Astarte. Astarte was the Ashtareth of the Old Testament. They were the patronesses of sex and war. Anat became Baal's mistress and these two "models" performed sex acts together, giving license for nude priests and priestesses to take part openly in these same acts. These priestesses became "sacred" prostitutes. Their performances permitted Baal's subjects to imitate this "divine" pattern.

The hillsides near towns were dotted with "groves," or "Asherim," which were hand-carved sex-cult objects—tree stumps on each side of an altar—one conspicuously displaying the privates of a man and the other exhibiting in like manner the sex organs of a woman. As the religious leaders of Baalism publicly practiced these immoral sex acts, the people of Canaan gave vent to their own lustful passions and adultery became the norm—daughter with father, mother with son, brother with sister, and in-laws with each other.

Not satisfied with "so-called" normal sex acts, the women, with degrading passions, exchanged the natural use of sex for an unnatural one. Men left the natural desire for women and burned in their lust for men—men yielding to shameful sex acts with men, and women doing the same together. The awful unnatural sex act of sodomy—homosexuality—became a "ritual" among the Canaanites. A classic Old Testament illustration of this sin is found in Genesis 19:1-8 where Lot, in the city of Sodom, sought to appease the men of that city by letting them have his daughters to do as they desired, instead of letting them have his male visitors that they "may know them." Even during the period of Abraham and Lot this sex-sin of sodomy was common, and this, mind you, was normal to the Canaanites long before Israel was led into the same land by Joshua!

Images of four-footed beasts were set up in some villages and were kissed and adored by Baal's subjects. One scene in Ugarit poems shows Baal copulating with a heifer. A part of the cult ritual was bestiality. The picture is that of the Ugarit goddess of Fertility. On each side is a ram, which represents the male element of this cult.

It appears evident from the pick and spade of the archaeologist that human sacrifices were made to Baal and to some of the lesser gods. Athtar, a god who attempted to occupy Baal's throne while Baal was away on a journey or asleep in the nether world, was designated in the Baal Epic as "Athtar, the terrible." He reappears later as Chemosh, the national god of Moab. Athtar appears also as Molech, the god to whom Israel was forbidden to offer her sons and daughters as sacrifices (Leviticus 18:21). The sacrificing of children was done sometimes by a priest who would carve the child with a sharp knife, placing the parts of the body on an altar with a fire underneath, and offering this to Baal as a burnt-offering.

Another method of human sacrifice was that of the fires of Molech, a god-name which meant "king," just as Baal meant "lord." This idol was of brass, having the face of an ox, and heated red-hot. Infants were placed in the outstretched arms of Molech, while the priests would beat drums to drown the noise of crying mothers, lest fathers be moved by compassion to stop the rites. Some children were forced to pass through long rows of idols of Molech, in which fires were heated to such a degree they died in the flames. When Manasseh seduced Israel to do more

Goddess of Fertility

evil than the Canaanites round about them, he made his sons to pass through the fires of Molech (II Kings 21:1-9).

Very often an infant, having on a ceremonial dress and a bracelet on either the wrist or the ankle, would be placed in the footing of some important building, or a city wall. Pictured is a skeleton of a child offered in such a manner, with burial juglets at the mouth, hands and feet, each one having been filled with grain for food in reincarnation.

Human Sacrifice to Baal

Discovery of this skeleton was made by Dr. Joseph Free, excavating at the Old Testament site of Dothan. It was found beneath a wall foundation. The offering of human beings was to the honor of their deities, imagining that the consecrating of their children to these gods in such sacrifices would procure good fortune for them and for the rest of their children. When Jericho was rebuilt by a man named Heil (which rebuilding had been denounced by God), he fulfilled God's Word in the offering of two of his sons as sacrifices in the wall and gate foundations of that city (Joshua 6:26 with I Kings 16:34).

High Place at Petra

Demon worship was associated with the gods of the heathen. Baal was often designated "Zebul"—meaning Prince. Baal-zebub, god of the Ekronites (II Kings 1:2), is a derivative of the name "Baal-zebul." In demon worship, "Princely Baal" was the name for Satan, "Prince of the Demons." During Christ's time, the Pharisees referred to the devil as "Beelzebub, prince of the devils" (Matthew 12:22-27), which is a corruption of "Princely Baal."

The serpent is a symbol of the devil (Genesis 3:1-15 and Revelation 20:2 refer to Satan as a "serpent"), so it is not surprising to find the Canaanites using snakes in their worship to Baal. Near Dagon's temple, archaeologists found an image which depicted a snake priestess with a large snake coiled about her hips and breast. She was holding the neck of the serpent in her hands. The snake was a choice object of worship for the subjects of Baal. Among objects which have been found at other excavations was a design of two "sacred prostitute" dancers, with the headdress of a snake, and a serpent carved out of stone. A large number of silver snakes, resembling those the worshipers offered as sacrifices, were found near one of the sanctuaries at Ras Shamra.

Excavated at Ras Shamra also was a structure which served as a library and school. Many written objects were found in the library part of the building—even a dictionary which defined words used in relation to Baal worship. The school was the "seminary," and was located near the temple of Baal, so that priests and students could have easy access to the worshiping of Baal with their studies.

The evidence unearthed at Ugarit and other related sites in Palestine gives us insight as to the worship of Baal in Old Testament days. It indicates that the Canaanites were fully dedicated to their gods, and would do *anything* to appease them. It might be difficult for us to comprehend what has been presented thus far, but an unfolding of God's instructions to His people—and their *reactions* to these commandments and the ways of the Canaanites—will help us to better understand why God demands obedience and loyalty from those who name His holy name. Not only will we be able to better understand why God demands obedience, but new light illuminating many portions which heretofore may have been obscure, confusing, or even doubtful. Just as a little test, let's see if Paul's account of early man (Romans 1:20-32) doesn't take on new meaning now that we have a better knowledge of the ancient Canaanites as they practiced Baal worship. In effect Paul said—

"The invisible things of God from the creation of the world are clearly seen, being understood by what was made, even His eternal power and Godhead, so that man is without excuse. When they knew God, they glorified Him not as God, neither were thankful, becoming vain in their imaginations and their foolish heart was darkened. They changed the glory of God into an image made like to corruptible man, and to birds, and four-footed beasts, and creeping things. Wherefore God gave them up to uncleanness through the lusts of their own hearts, to dishonor their own bodies with each other. They changed the truth of God into a lie, and served and worshiped the creature more than they did their Creator. Because of this, God gave them up unto vile affections. The women changed the natural use of sex into that which is against nature, and the men burned in their lust toward each other, men with men working that which is shameful. As they were given over to a reprobate mind, they were contaminated with ungodliness, being filled with unrighteousness, fornication, covetousness, maliciousness, envy, murder, malignity, and deceit. They were haters of God, proud, inventors of evil things, disobedient to parents, backbiters, unmerciful, and without natural affection. They knew of God's judgment, but had pleasure in their sins."

It is evident that the Creator had been denied by the Canaanites, and the practice of vulgar, immoral sins had become the norm. Their sins were deliberate, not accidental. They were not victims of circumstances, nor were they ignorant, primitive people. (One group of them, the Phoenicians, gave to the world pure alphabetism. We today are indebted to them for their fixed order of letters, from which our English ABC's are derived.) But they hated a knowledge of truth and devised their own ways. Abraham had been among them centuries before, had established altars to God, and had worshiped Him in Faith. The right of these people to occupy Canaan had been forfeited by their contempt of right, and their wickedness had put them outside the pale of humanity. *Their whole land was defiled* (Leviticus 18:25). Such a people Israel faced upon entrance into the Promised Land. How true is God's Word: "Righteousness exalteth a nation, but sin is a reproach to any people" (Proverbs 14:34). "The wicked shall be turned into hell, and all the nations that forget God" (Psalm 9:17).

Warnings to Israel

It is no wonder Israel was warned of these conditions, and was given certain instructions what to do about it, and why. They were warned not to do after the doings of the Canaanites—commit adultery, sodomy, unnatural sex acts with beasts, erect sex-cult objects (groves), to let their children pass through the fire of Molech (human sacrifice), to worship the heavenly bodies, to let their daughters become prostitute priestesses or their sons become sodomites, nor to do *any* of their abominations (Leviticus 18:3-27; Deuteronomy 16:21,22; 17:1-5; 23:17).

Such warnings were given in view of existing conditions in Canaan. Both the righteousness and love of God demanded judgment upon these people, for His people, through whom the Redeemer of lost mankind was to come, would not be safe otherwise. So Israel was instructed to smite them and utterly destroy them. No mercy was to be shown, no covenant was to be made with them, no marriages with the inhabitants. Israel was to destroy their idols and altars—to detest and utterly abhor such things. The Canaanites were descendants of the man Canaan, who was under a curse because of an immoral sin (Genesis 9:20-27).

The modernist of our day labels the God of the Old Testament a "dirty bully" because in His command to "utterly destroy them," this would include women and children (Deuteronomy 7:1,3,5,26; 32:25; Joshua 6:21). This was not hatred or murder on God's part—it was moral surgery, for God knew what would happen if Israel failed to obey these commands. So then,

Israel must "utterly destroy them . . . as the Lord thy God hath commanded thee: *that they teach you not to do after all their abominations,* which they have done unto their gods; so ye should sin against the Lord your God" (Deuteronomy 20:16-18). With the discovery of the Ras Shamra tablets and other evidence which revealed the gross immorality of the Canaanites, archaeologists have been amazed that the worshipers of Baal were not destroyed sooner. (It should be pointed out in defense of God's love that He did spare many in the land "which were not of the cities of these nations" (Deuteronomy 20:10-15).

Conduct for Israel among the inhabitants of Canaan was to be in harmony with God's *whole* Law. If Israel were to have right living, it would certainly consist of their conforming to *His* divine pattern, giving her acceptance before her God. It would also give them a good standing and respect before others. The concept Israel was to get of God through His Word left no room for them to think that their god would conduct Himself in the manner of heathen gods, nor would it leave any room for them to live like those who worshiped false gods. God gave Israel His commandments that they might reverence Him, and as a guide to live godly and morally in the midst of ungodliness and immorality.

Once before, the wickedness of man had incurred the wrath of God, and the human race was destroyed in the flood (with the exception of Noah and his family). A promise was made by God not to so destroy every living thing again (Genesis 8:21). But since the imagination of man's heart continued to be evil, and since gross wickedness abounded among the Canaanites, Abraham was chosen by God to be the father of a "special people" unto Himself—to be holy and peculiar above all the nations that are upon the earth (Deuteronomy 7:6-11; 14:2). This the Israelites would be if they would glorify their God and walk in the light of His Word, for He is *the* "God of gods and the Lord of lords" (Deuteronomy 10:17).

Thus Israel was chosen, not to be God's "pet," but to be His godly "pattern" in the "midst of a crooked and perverse generation" (Philippians 2:15). She was to let her light shine, manifesting a fruitful life that would glorify *her* God in the presence of *their* gods.

The Old Testament
DIVISION II
Historical Books

Subject: God's acts or dealings with Israel to cause them to possess their inheritance of the Promised Land: Genesis 13:15; Exodus 6:6-8; Joshua 1:1-9; 3:17; 11:23.

Purpose: To illustrate typically God's dealings with us to cause us to enjoy our place and blessings in the heavenlies in Christ Jesus: Ephesians 1:3.

                Joshua
                    Judges
                        Ruth
                            I Samuel
                                II Samuel
                                    I Kings
                                        II Kings
                                            I Chronicles
                                                II Chronicles
                                                    Ezra
                                                        Nehemiah
                                                            Esther

Israel's recorded Old Testament history ends with the return of the remnant from Babylonian captivity as recorded in Ezra and Nehemiah, and with the Jews who chose to remain in Mesopotamia, as recorded by Esther. All the prophets except five prophesied *before* captivity; Ezekiel and Daniel *during* captivity; Haggai, Zechariah, and Malachi *after* the remnant returned from captivity. See POST-CAPTIVITY BOOKS before Ezra.

Joshua—The Book of Conquest and Settlement

Name: Joshua's original name was "Oshea" (Numbers 13:8), a word meaning "salvation." He was also called "Jehoshua" and "Hoshea" (Numbers 13:16; Deuteronomy 32:44). "Joshua" (Numbers 14:6) means "Jehovah saves" or "Jehovah is salvation." The Greek equivalent of "Joshua" is "Jesus" and twice in the King James Version he is referred to by this name (Acts 7:45; Hebrews 4:8).

Contents: Leadership and the government of Israel rested upon Joshua after the death of Moses. The settlement of the Nation under him, the conquests, the division of the land of Canaan to the children of Israel, all show the faithful hand of the Lord in delivering His people from a land not theirs to a land of milk and honey, promised them centuries before. All of this was given in spite of their murmurings, ingratitude, and unbelief in the wilderness. The book of Joshua was to Israel what the book of Ephesians is to the Christian. Canaan is *not* a type of heaven, but a place of victorious living over the power of the enemy. This book has 24 chapters, 658 verses, and 18,858 words. See points 27-34, p. 103. Also MAP at end of Joshua.

Character: Historical.

Subject: Israel's entrance into (1—5), conquest of (6—12), and division of the land of Canaan for their inheritance (13—24).

Purpose: To teach us how Jesus, our Joshua, would lead us into the place of blessing, give us victory over the enemy, and cause us to enjoy our blessings in the heavenlies in Christ.

Outline:

    I. Entering the Land: 1:1—5:12. See MAP, p. 100
        A. Preparation of the People: 1:1—3:13
        B. Passage of the People: 3:14—4:24
        C. Purification of the People: 5:1-12
    II. Conquering the Land: 5:13—12:24
        A. The Central Campaign: 5:13—9:27
        B. The Southern Campaign: 10
        C. The Northern Campaign: 11,12
    III. Possessing the Land: 13—24
        A. The Borders of the Tribes: 13:19
        B. The Cities of Refuge: 20
        C. The Cities of the Levites: 21
        D. Last Acts and Words of Joshua: 22-24

Scope: The events recorded in Joshua cover a period of about twenty-five years. The era of the conquest is thought to be approximately seven years. The clue to this figure is Caleb's age. At Kadesh-barnea, he is forty years old. At the end of the settlement he is eighty-five. This gives forty-five years from Kadesh to the settlement. We already have thirty-eight years as the period of wandering. Thus seven years is the period of the conquest.

Writer: Joshua: 24:26.

When and Where Written: Possibly 1425 to 1420 B.C., somewhere in Canaan.

Key Chapter: 1. God commissions Joshua.

Key Verses: 21:44,45.

Key Word: Possess.

Key Phrase: God's faithfulness: 1:3; 21:45.

Key Thought: Settlement of the Nation: 1:2-6. Thus far Israel has been in three different lands:
    1. In Egypt, the place of bondage: Genesis 46:1—Exodus 14:31
    2. In the wilderness, the place of training: Exodus 15:1—Joshua 3:17
    3. In Canaan, the place of rest: Joshua 4:1—11:23

Later, Babylon, in Mesopotamia, was to become the place of her captivity and repentance: II Chronicles 36:17; Ezra 3:1; Nehemiah 1:5-11.

Spiritual Thought: Take the Land—"Possess your possessions." That Israel *did* possess her possessions (the Land) is found in the following:
    1. God's Promise to give the Land:
        a. To Abraham: Genesis 15:7,18; 17:8
        b. To Isaac: Genesis 24:7; 26:4
        c. To Jacob: Genesis 28:13; 35:12
        d. To Moses: Exodus 6:8; 12:25; Deuteronomy 4:21,22
    2. God's promise for Israel to inhabit and possess the *same* Land:
        a. To Moses: Leviticus 20:24; Numbers 35:34
        b. To Joshua: 1:1-4
    3. God's promise to go before them and fight for them in the Land:
        a. To Moses: Deuteronomy 1:30; 3:22; 9:3; 31:3
        b. To Joshua: 1:5
    4. God's Faithfulness to His Promises—
        a. He never forsook them: 1:2-6

     b. He fought for them: 10:42

     c. He gave them *ALL* the land promised: 11:23; 21:43-45; Nehemiah 9:23-25. That Israel *"rested"* in the Land indicates possession.

The statement has often been made that Israel *did not* possess all the land. The original promise to Abraham included the land from the "river of Egypt to the river Euphrates" (Genesis 15:18). The "river of Egypt" is the dividing line between Canaan and Egypt. It is not really a river, but a "wady"—a stream in its valley—of the desert at the border of Egypt. When the land was divided, the children of Judah received their portion "unto the river of Egypt" (15:4,47). Joshua said God "gave unto Israel *all* the land which He swore to give unto their fathers; and they *possessed* it and dwelt therein. . . . There failed *not ought* of any good thing which the Lord had spoken to the house of Israel; *all came to pass*" (21:43-45 with 1:3-5). If ever a portion of Scripture settled this question, this portion does. *All* certainly does not mean *part.* It is a historical fact that the boundaries of Israel were extended during the reigns of David and Solomon to their fullest. David's dominion was established by the river Euphrates (I Chronicles 18:3). Solomon's was to the border of Egypt. Should someone say this does not mean "the river of Egypt," we need only to refer to his feast celebration "unto the river of Egypt" (II Chronicles 7:8). Solomon testified at the dedication of the Temple that "there hath not failed one word of all His good promise," which the Lord had promised to Israel concerning the land (I Kings 8:56). Nehemiah also said that God gave them the land promised to their fathers (Nehemiah 9:21-25). It appears from Scripture that Israel *did* possess *all* the Land (see MAP p. 152).

    5. Continued possession of the Land was conditioned on obedience to God. The principle announced all throughout God's dealings with Israel in this matter was: "Obey Me and I will bless you; disobey Me and you will be taken out of the Land" (Leviticus 26:27-35; Deuteronomy 4:1,2,23-26). That Israel *failed* to "drive out" all the inhabitants of the Land as God had commanded, did not effectively occupy it, and lost it when taken into captivity, is in no sense a failure of the Divine Promise (Nehemiah 9:26-31).

Christ Is Seen As: Captain of the Lord's host: 5:14.

Names and Titles of God. See NAMES in Dictionary.

    1. The living God: 3:10

    2. The Lord God of gods: 22:22

Types of Christ:

    1. Joshua, whose name means "savior." Moses, who represented the Law, could only take Israel to the threshhold of the Promised Land. It took Joshua—"savior"—to take over and carry through to the inheritance. The Law (Moses) was the schoolmaster that led to Christ (Joshua): John 1:17; Galatians 3:24,25.

    2. Rahab's scarlet thread—a type of Christ's blood which brings about deliverance from judgment and safety from death: 2:12-21; 6:22-25 with Exodus 12:13; Ephesians 1:7; Hebrews 9:19-22.

    3. The Two Memorials: 4.

        a. In the midst of the river Jordan, on the very spot where the Ark of the Covenant rested, a stone memorial was erected; vs. 9. Jesus Christ, the Ark of the Covenant, went down into the Jordan of death. As this first memorial was overwhelmed by the waters of Jordan returning to its place (vs. 18), so Christ in the Jordan of death was overwhelmed by the judgment of my sin (John 12:31-33)

      b. Another memorial was erected in the lodging place of Gilgal: vs. 19,20. Here they stood on resurrection territory. This memorial speaks of rest and victory; the one in Jordan spoke of deliverance. These stones, taken out of Jordan (vs. 3), became a memorial of life and blessing and possession. Typically, it speaks to us—
      —Of the rest of salvation *in* Christ: Matthew 11:28
      —Of victory *by* Christ's resurrection: Romans 6:5,11,14,18
      —Of blessings *through* Christ: Ephesians 1:3
      —Of rest "found" in service *for* Christ: Matthew 11:29,30

  4. Cities of Refuge: 20. See CITIES in Index.

Types of the Believer's Experiences:

  1. Crossing Jordan: 3. The river Jordan, between the wilderness and Canaan, stands for our death with Christ, or separation from self to a life of victory (Romans 6:11).

  2. Entering Canaan: 3:17—4:1. The land of Canaan stands for victory, death to self daily, and the presenting of our bodies as living sacrifices unto the Lord. Canaan is not, nor can be, a type of heaven, as some would have us believe. Battles had to be fought there; giants stood in their way; defeat loomed on occasions. There are no battles to be fought, no enemies to conquer, no defeats to suffer, in heaven.

The crossing of the Red Sea and the river Jordan should be accomplished in one act, spiritually, but with most Christians there is a wilderness experience. It is only when we are living in Canaan and enjoying the milk and honey of that victorious land that we are filled with God's Spirit unto all pleasing. Galatians 2:20 is our *Canaan* verse. Our *test* verse for this experience: "For they themselves show us what manner of entering we had unto you, and how ye turned from idols [Red Sea] to serve the living and true God [across Jordan]" (I Thessalonians 1:9). God brought us *out* that He might bring us *in* (Deuteronomy 6:23).

  3. Gilgal: 5:1-12. By following the will of God, Israel entered into the "rest" of God. Many could not enter in because of unbelief (Hebrews 3:18,19). Gilgal was the first lodging place after they crossed Jordan. Gilgal means a "place of rolling" (vs. 9). All their past sins were rolled away, and they stood, in Canaan, on resurrection territory. The first day in the land of victory was one of great rejoicing. Gilgal is to us:
      a. A place of deliverance from judgment (Jordan): John 5:24; Romans 8:1
      b. A place where the past is blotted out: Psalm 103:12; I John 1:7
      c. A place of freedom: John 8:32,36
      d. A place of rest: Matthew 11:28,29
      e. A place of joy—symbolic of the joy which came the day we tasted of the fruits of salvation: Psalm 34:8
      f. A place of blessing: vss. 11,12 with Ephesians 1:3
      g. A place of victory over sin: Titus 2:11,12
      h. A place for challenge: Philippians 3:13,14

  4. The Canaanites—a type of our spiritual enemies: Ephesians 6:12-18

  5. Overcoming Jericho, or the Victory of Faith: 6 with I John 5:4
      a. The *act* of faith—compassing the city: vs. 3 with Hebrews 11:30
      b. The *use* or means of faith—blowing the trumpets: vs. 4 with our witness: Luke 8:39
      c. The *substance* of faith—carrying the Ark: vs. 6 with Romans 13:14
      d. The *anticipation* or hope of faith—shouting of the people: vs. 20a with Hebrews 11:6. It is interesting to note that the "people shouted" when the priests blew the trumpets. We cannot leave *all* the work up to the ministers. They do the work of the *minister;* the people do the work of the *ministry* (Ephesians 4:11-16). *Both* must do the work to win victories.
      e. The *reality* or demonstration of faith—the wall fell flat: vs. 20b with Mark 11:22-24

  6. Rahab's Deliverance: 6:1-25. Her plight in Jericho is a picture of the sinner's state and deliverance.

a. Straightly shut up (bound by sin): vs. 1 with Romans 3:23: 6:23a
b. Under God's curse or wrath: vs. 17a with John 3:36b
c. Judged and condemned: vs. 21 with John 3:18b
d. She believed in God: 2:9-11 with John 6:29
e. She accepted God's message: 2:12-18 with Romans 10:17
f. She obeyed the word: 2:21 with John 5:24; Romans 6:17
g. She and her family saved from wrath: 6:22-25 with Acts 16:31; I Thessalonians 5:9
h. Her testimony lasted and counted for God: Hebrews 11:31

7. Failure and Victory at Ai: 7:1—8:29. The failure at Ai signifies the power of secret sin, which robs us of fellowship. To lose fellowship with Christ is to lose all power of testimony for Him. Not only is this truth brought out by Achan's individual sin, but the truth of the oneness of God's people suffering as a result of an individual sin. The whole camp suffered defeat at Ai—"Israel hath sinned" (vs. 11). Sin is *individual* in its act, but *collective* in its results. The whole cause of Christ is injured by the sin of one believer, whether the sin of omission or commission. (A little boy was asked the difference between these two sins. He replied: "Sins of commission are sins we committed that we shouldn't have. Sins of omission are sins we should have committed but didn't!")

Sin is sin with God. Adam did not commit a little sin, or a big sin—he committed *sin*. The one act was a *full-grown* sin. The act was an individual one, but, oh, its collective results on the human race! The temptation came by the only method the devil has (see TEMPTATION in Index). Achan's sin followed this same pattern: "When I *saw* among the spoils . . . , then I *coveted* [desired] them, and *took* them . . . " (vs. 21). The power of Achan's secret sin is shown in the shameful defeat of Israel at Ai. It should be a reminder to us as the cause of many of our failures. Note Israel's defeat and victory:

a. Secret sin: vss. 1,21
b. God left out of plans: vs. 2. Note Joshua's dependence upon God for strategy in defeating Jericho (6:2-5).
c. Over-confidence: vs. 3 with I Corinthians 10:12
d. Sin hinders victory: vss. 4,5
e. Sin brings shame and humiliation: vss. 5-9
f. Sin hinders prayer: vs. 10. There is a time to pray, but not until confession of sin is made: Psalm 66:18

Pool at Gibeon

g. Fellowship restored when sin is judged and confessed: vss. 10-26 with Psalm 51:1-13; I John 1:7-9

h. God is glorified when sin is confessed and forsaken. Achan's confession proves this: vss. 19-23. We do not glorify God in our sinning. How do we glorify Him in confession? First, we acknowledge that He, and He alone, can forgive sin, and second, we plead the only source for forgiveness, the blood of Jesus Christ. This is what glorifies Him. When we confess, and forsake (Proverbs 28:13), He is faithful and just to forgive—not faithful to us—but faithful unto Himself and to the shed blood of His Son. For *this* reason He forgives (Ephesians 1:7; I John 1:9) when we confess and forsake our sins (Proverbs 28:13; Ephesians 1:7; I John 1:9)

i. Restored fellowship brought victory: 8:1-29 with II Corinthians 2:14

8. The warfare of Israel in Canaan—a type of the fight of faith: I Timothy 6:12; II Timothy 2:3; I John 5:4.

9. Israel's rest after conquest (11:23)—a type of rest found: Matthew 11:29.

10. The Canaanites partly subdued—a type of the believer's besetting sins: Hebrews 12:1.

1. The Jordan River divided—for God to lead Israel into the Promised Land: 3:14-17. Also to show the Canaanites that their god, Baal, supposedly the god of Nature, was powerless in the presence of Israel's God, who *is* the God of Nature (Job 37:5-14). See BAAL in Index.

2. The appearance of an angel—to assure Joshua of victory at Jericho: 5:13-15.

3. The falling of Jericho's walls—to show Israel that God will fight her battles as promised, and that His methods of victory are foolish to natural reasoning: 6:1-20 with Deuteronomy 1:30; Isaiah 55:8,9; I Corinthians 1:27-29.

4. The strategy in defeating Ai—to show the need to rely upon God for instructions: 8:1-8.

5. The storm of hailstones—to assist Israel in battle: 10:11; also to show the Canaanites that Baal, their god of Storm, not only could not control storms, but was helpless to protect his subjects from death by a storm. See BAAL, god of Storm, in Index.

6. The sun and moon stayed, prolonging time to give Israel victory in the valley of Ajalon—to show that there is always a need to depend upon God for help, and that the effectual fervent prayer of a righteous man availeth much: 10:11-14 with Jeremiah 33:3; James 5:16b; also to show the worshipers of Baal that their god of the sun, moon, and stars had absolutely no control over the God who made them. See BAAL, Sun Worship, and LONG DAY in Index.

1. Fall of Jericho: 6. Ruins of this city were excavated in the late 1930s by Dr. John Garstang. Evidence showed that the walls did indeed "fall down flat" (vs. 20) in such a manner as to permit the invaders (Israel) to have large openings through the wall into the city. Critics of the Bible have raised objections to this story of the Bible. One such was Kathleen Kenyon, who later admitted, while digging at Jericho, that a level dated around 1440 B.C. is the probable one of Israel's destruction.

a. They argued that "engines of war" (Ezekiel 26:9) would have forced city walls *inward,* while the Bible says they *fell flat.* Garstang's findings proved them wrong. See ENGINES in Index.

b. They argued that materials used in ancient buildings, such as mud bricks and stone, could not burn, while the Bible said the city was destroyed by fire (vs. 24a). Ash layers found by

Garstang proved the Word of God correct. Other materials were used in construction which could burn. Even in our day modern "fireproof" buildings have burned!

c. They also argued that "if" the wall did fall, Rahab's house would have crumbled, and Scripture indicates that hers did not. In the first place it wasn't necessary for *all* Jericho's wall to have fallen for Israel in invade and conquer. Garstang found that this city was bounded by an *outer* and *inner* wall, with portions of the inner wall still standing. He also discovered that houses were built on top of the inner wall, which could easily explain why Rahab and her family were safe in her house on the city wall (2:15; 6:22-25).

2. Human Sacrifice: 6:26 with I Kings 16:34. See BAAL, Human Sacrifice, in Index.

3. City of Gibeon: 9:1-21. The men of Gibeon were punished for deceiving Joshua. Their punishment—they became "hewers" of wood, and "carriers" of water (vs. 21). This punishment is significant in view of discoveries at Gibeon, which revealed that it had one of the most extensive water systems in ancient Palestine. Tunnels were hewn out of solid rock 389 feet long, with more than 172 steps for "water carriers" to have easy access to the pools or cisterns. This discovery also confirmed Jeremiah's statement—"by the great waters that are in Gibeon" (41:11,12). See CARRIERS in Index.

4. The Hornets: 24:12. One reason why Israel met with such success in gaining a foothold in the Promised Land was God's having "sent the hornet" before them (Exodus 23:28; Deuteronomy 7:20). While Israel was in her last years of Egyptian bondage, Thutmose III and his successor waged a number of military invasions in Canaan, overcoming their defenses and conquering the inhabitants. Archaeologists have found that Thutmose III had as his personal badge, "The Hornet," which, no doubt, referred to his "hornet army"—the "hornets" which God had sent to soften the Canaanites for Israel's invasion.

5. The Tel el-Amarna Tablets. These tablets, discovered near Luxor, Egypt, in 1886, shed light on Israel's conquests in Canaan. Many of these tablets were written by Canaanite and Syrian kings to Egypt's Pharaohs for help against those who were invading the land. One invading group, east of Jordan, according to these records, was called "Habiri," known as the Israelites, or Hebrews. Such tablets confirm Israel's entrance into Canaan.

6. The Merneptah Tablet. This Pharaoh ruled in Egypt about 1224 to 1214 B.C., and was forced to defend his empire against invaders from the North. In his record of his campaign in Canaan, he mentions Israel. This monument provides the first mention of Israel in Egyptian records, and is evidence that Israel was in Palestine by 1220 B.C. The word "Israel" is designated "a people," and suggests they were not yet known as a settled political unit or "nation," such as they were when Saul was enthroned as king.

LIGHT FROM BIBLICAL
CUSTOMS

1. Rahab, the Harlot: 2:1. To the western mind the word "harlot" means only one thing—an immoral woman. The question is often raised: "Did trusted spies completely ignore responsibilities and seek to satisfy their own lust and passion in the home of such a person?" Scriptural evidence would hardly lend support. It is quite possible Rahab was a widow who had taken a job as a desk clerk in a lodging house on the city wall. Travelers would frequent such a place rather than spend the night deep inside the city. To get such a job—meeting the public—Rahab would have to remove her veil. This would put her in a position of shame since women of ill-repute would dare permit men to see their faces. It was probably for this reason that she was classified as a "harlot."

Whatever the reasoning behind the spies' strategy, it was "public" knowledge that they were in the city. Even the king of Jericho knew about their presence (2:1,1). It hardly seems likely that being in the public eye they would have gone to Rahab's house for immoral purposes. While we cannot condone Rahab's lying (2:3-6), it would appear that a "harlot" would

Merneptah Tablet

be glad to cooperate with a king. It would be bad for business to fall out with those in authority. In addition to Rahab's seeking to protect the men of God, she believed in the God of Israel and confessed Him. It hardly seems likely that a "harlot" would talk about the things of the Lord and confess Him to men who had sought to buy her services (2:9-11). She was also willing to identify herself and her family with God's people rather than with the Jerichoites. This most certainly would not be in keeping with a "citizen" of such a low profession. If she were a keeper in a lodge she would have information from the conversations of traveling guests and connections with prominent citizens of Jericho that would be vital to the spies. And probably for this reason the spies headed for such a place, and met Rahab.

2. Carriers of Water: 9:21. The custom of carrying water in the Holy Land is ancient. However, it was and is the woman's job to go to the well or spring with a pitcher and carry water to their home. When the Gibeonites deceived Joshua (9:3-27), he judged them and made them servants to chop wood and carry water. This punishment may seem mild to us, but how humiliating it was to a man—carrying water in public—a woman's job! This helps us to better understand how easy it was for the disciples to identify the man carrying the waterpot when Jesus sought an upper room to eat the Passover. It was not a question of seeking one man out of many carrying a waterpot—this man would stick out above all others, in that he alone would be carrying one (Mark 14:12-16). A man may carry a waterskin, but seldom does one carry a waterpot.

Joshua's Long Day: 10:12-14. It is interesting to note that parallel accounts in the records of other nations show that the incident of "Joshua's Long Day" is not an isolated one. There is indisputable evidence from the modern science of ethnology that such an event occurred as Joshua records. In ancient Chinese writings there is a legend of a long day. The Incas of Peru and the Aztecs of Mexico have a like record. There is a Babylonian and a Persian legend of a day that was miraculously extended. Herodotus, an ancient historian, recounts that while in Egypt, priests showed him their temple

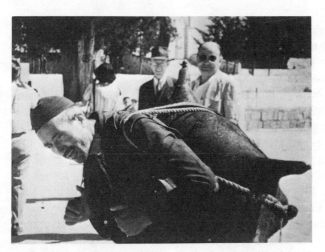

Man Carrying Water Skin

Woman Carrying Water Pot

records, and that he read of a day which was twice the natural length of any day that had ever been recorded.

Yet, "Joshua's Long Day" has been pointed out by the critics of the Word as a *myth* and as being *scientific trash*. Joshua said, "Sun, stand thou still upon Gibeon . . . and the sun stood still" (10:12-14). Since it is a scientific fact that the sun does not revolve around the earth, critics in glee point this out as but *another* mistake in the Bible. It hasn't been too many years that science has known that the spinning of the earth is the result of the gravitational pull of the sun. To stop the earth from turning on its axis, it would be necessary to stop the "pull" of the sun. A reduction in the gravitational pull of the sun would result in the slowing down of the rotation of the earth, and a prolonging of the day, or time.

Did Joshua have this scientific data in his day? Was he so ignorant of the solar system that he thought the sun moved from East to West, and that for time to be prolonged the sun must stand still? By modern standards, he was a primitive man, in a primitive culture, with primitive misconceptions. He probably knew very little about the planet on which he lived, its chemical compounds, or its shape. He knew even less about the solar system. As far as Joshua was concerned, so reason the modern scholars, practically everyone believed the earth was flat, and for this reason the sun rose in the east and hours later sank in the west. Did Joshua know that the earth upon which he stood was a sphere about 8,000 miles in diameter? He had no idea that there were close to 200 million square miles of surface area, 71 percent of which was water. He was unaware that the earth was spinning on its axis in a cycle every twenty-four hours (23 hours, 56 minutes and 4.09 seconds to be exact). And he didn't even know that the earth was traveling through space about 18 ½ miles per second. Did he know that the sun he was commanding to stand still was 93,000,000 miles away, or that at its core it was over 30,000,000 degrees Fahrenheit, or that it was over 100 times bigger than the earth? Did he know that the earth made a complete orbit around the sun yearly?

We might say, "how little Joshua knew." But he knew his God! He knew that God had promised to go before His people and fight their battles to give them victory (Joshua 10:8). And in this battle he saw victory in his grasp, but time was running out. If he didn't conquer the enemy before dark, they would regroup and attack Israel the next day. Knowing his God, his God's power, and his God's promise, he called out to God for help, and in the presence of all Israel, he commanded the "sun to stand still." But the sun was already standing still, Joshua. It is the earth that moves, not the sun. Why didn't Joshua cry out, "Earth, quit moving," or "Earth, slow down your spinning on your axis to prolong time."

Joshua had no idea that his command slowed down 6.6 sextrillion tons of spinning gravel and water to give Israel victory over her enemies. But did Joshua know something that God had revealed to him? Over 3,000 years ago he said something that would have met the approval of today's scientific establishment. His command in the Hebrew language was not "Sun, stand thou still," but "Sun, cease acting," or "Sun, stop working." It was then that the gravitational pull of the sun affected the earth. It was then that the earth began to slow down and the day was lengthened.

An astronomer, who was a professor at Yale, made a startling discovery. He found that the "earth was twenty-four hours out of schedule. Another professor at Yale, Dr. Totten, suggested the astronomer read the Bible, starting at the beginning and going as far as necessary, to see if the Bible could account for the missing time. When he came to the account of the long day of Joshua, the astronomer rechecked the figures and found that at the time of Joshua there were only twenty-three hours and twenty minutes lost. His skepticism justified, he decided that the Bible was not the Word of God, because here was a mistake by forty minutes.

Professor Totten showed him that the Bible account does not say twenty-four hours, but rather 'about the space of a whole day.' On reading farther the astronomer found that God, through the prophet Isaiah and in answer to Hezekiah's prayer, promised to add fifteen years to his life (II Kings 20:1-11; Isaiah 38:1-21). To confirm this promise, the shadow on the sundial was turned back ten degrees. Ten degrees on a sundial is forty minutes on the face of a clock. When he found his day of missing time accounted for in the Bible, the astronomer bowed his head in worship of its Author, saying, "Lord, I believe!"

"Search the heavens, for that truth is there. As long as the stars shall shine, as long as the earth shall spin, as long as time shall last, the long day of Joshua will be attested as a scientific fact. Search the heavens indeed, but search the written Word as well. The heavens only testify to those who have seen first the testimony of the Word. For though the words and the works of God agree, the Word is high above the works, and when the works [heaven and earth] shall melt and pass away, the Word shall forever endure."[2]

Joshua in the New Testament:

1. Joshua is referred to as "Jesus—Jehovah Savior" by Stephen: 1:1 with Acts 7:45
2. God's presence guaranteed: 1:5 with Hebrews 13:5b
3. Rahab: 2:1-16 with James 2:25
4. Crossing Jordan with the Ark and Tabernacle: 3:13-17 with Acts 7:44,45
5. Fall of Jericho: 6:20 with Hebrews 11:30
6. Rahab delivered: 6:23 with Hebrews 11:31
7. Inheritance divided by lot: 14:1,2 with Acts 13:19
8. Burial of Joseph: 24:32 with Hebrews 11:22. See Genesis 50:24,25

1. Conditions for Success: 1:1-16.
    a. Fulfill the purpose of God—*arise* and *go:* vs. 2. God may bury His workman, but He never buries His work. We must "get out of" the wilderness before we can "get into" the place of blessing (Deuteronomy 6:23; Amos 2:10)

    b. Exercise faith in the promises of God: vs. 3. Faith without works is dead (James 2:26
    c. Be assured of the presence of God: vss. 5,9b
       The Father will not forsake us (Hebrews 13:5b), the Son is with us alway (Matthew 28:20; Colossians 1:27), and the Spirit is sent to abide with us forever (John 14:16). The believer *is* the possessor of the Triune God
    d. Faithfulness to God's leading—*observe and do*: vs. 7. This results in being led in right paths for His name's sake (Psalm 23:3)
    e. Meditate in the Word of God—*observe and do*: vs. 8. This, and this alone, assures one of God's approval (Psalm 1:2; II Timothy 2:15)
    f. Apply the Word of God in daily living: vs. 8b. "Observe and do"—"doers as well as hearers" (Colossians 3:16; James 1:22)
    g. Be strong and courageous; be not afraid, neither be thou dismayed: vs. 9. God is still upon the throne. We must rise above our circumstances (Psalm 118:6; II Corinthians 12:9; Philippians 4:13)
    h. Yieldedness to the will of God: vs. 16 with Colossians 3:1-3; I Thessalonians 4:3a,7; 5:18
2. Captain of the Lord's Hosts: 5:14 with Hebrews 2:10.
    a. His soldiers: II Timothy 2:3
    b. His enemies: Ephesians 6:12
    c. Armor: Ephesians 6:10-18
    d. Battle: James 4:7; I Timothy 6:11,12
    e. Victory: Romans 8:37; I Corinthians 15:57; I John 5:4,5
3. Prayer before repentance avails nothing: 7:10 with Proverbs 28:13; Psalm 66:18. See FAILURE in Index.
4. Caleb, who followed the Lord wholly: 14:6-15.
    a. He was honest: vs. 7. He spoke as it was in his heart
    b. He was charitable: vs. 8a. Even though he disagreed with the spies whose report caused Israel to turn back into the wilderness, he called them "my brethren "
    c. He was yielded: vs. 8b. "I wholly followed the Lord my God." This expression is used four other times of Caleb (vss. 9 and 14; Numbers 32:12; Deuteronomy 1:36)
    d. He trusted God's Word: vs. 9. Faith is now turned into sight
    e. He claimed his inheritance: vs. 12. "Now therefore give me this mountain whereof the Lord spake in that day" (Numbers 14:24)
5. Caleb's Testimony: 14:10-13.
    a. As to God's faithfulness: vs. 10 with Philippians 1:6; I Peter 1:5; Jude 24
    b. As to God's goodness: vs. 11 with III John 2
    c. As to God's power: vs. 12 with I Corinthians 15:57
It is not surprising to find that after such a testimony as this that Caleb received Joshua's blessing and God's inheritance: vs. 13 with II Timothy 4:8.
6. Cities of Refuge: Joshua 20. Six cities were appointed among those of the Levites to be a shelter or refuge from judgment. So is our refuge from sin appointed. See CITIES in Index.
7. Joshua had been in bondage with the Israelites for forty years, had wandered another

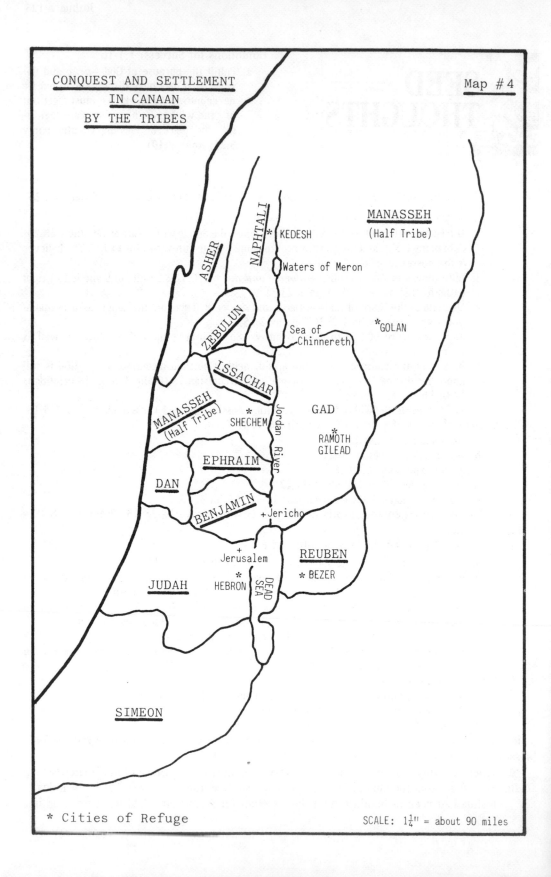

CONQUEST AND SETTLEMENT
IN CANAAN
BY THE TRIBES

Map # 4

MANASSEH
(Half Tribe)

NAPHTALI
* KEDESH

ASHER

Waters of Meron

ZEBULUN

Sea of
Chinnereth

*GOLAN

ISSACHAR

MANASSEH
(Half Tribe)

*
SHECHEM

GAD

Jordan River

*
RAMOTH
GILEAD

EPHRAIM

DAN

BENJAMIN

+Jericho

REUBEN

+
Jerusalem

* BEZER

JUDAH

*
HEBRON

DEAD SEA

SIMEON

* Cities of Refuge

SCALE: 1¼" = about 90 miles

forty years in the wilderness, fought for seven years in the settlement of the land, and had twenty-three years' rest till his death. His dying testimony was that "not one good thing had failed which the Lord your God spake": 23:14.

8. Christian Obligations: 24:14-24
   a. Fear the Lord: vs. 14a
   b. Separation unto the Lord: vs. 14b
   c. Choose the Lord over all: vs. 15
   d. Confess the Lord: vss. 16-18a
   e. Serve the Lord: vss. 18b,21
   f. Witness for the Lord: vs. 22
   g. Make vows to the Lord *(and keep them)*: vs. 24

9. Obedience: 24:13-15. What is it to obey?
   a. Sometimes do something we don't want to. If we don't, we are the losers. See "Rich Young Ruler" (Matthew 19:16-22 and Index).
   b. Must obey though we might want to do something else first. See Luke 9:59-61.
   c. Must obey although it might contradict common sense. Note Israel's march around the walls of Jericho (Joshua 6).
   d. Must obey even though we think we know better how to do the Lord's work. See King Saul (I Samuel 15).

The Key Phrase of this Book is *"God's Faithfulness."* God had promised Israel He would take them into the Land and give them possession of a territory that "flowed with milk and honey." He was faithful to His promise, and the record states that the Lord "gave unto Israel *all* the land which He swore to give to their fathers; and they possessed it; and dwelt therein" (24:43). When Joshua was dying, he reminded the Israelites that "not one thing had failed . . . which the Lord your God [spoke]—all [came] to pass" (23:14). God had fulfilled His Word.

I WILL NOT LEAVE THEE, NOR FORSAKE THEE—1:5[4]

"Earthly friends may fail us; and if we trust them, they will fail us when we need them most. But he that putteth his trust in the Lord shall be safe. God promised Joshua that He would not fail him, and He never did. He tried him. He allowed others to try him. He made him pray. He allowed him to fear. He never failed him in any struggle, but gave him occasion and grace to appeal to Israel and say, 'Ye know in all your hearts, and in all your souls, that not one thing hath failed of all the good things which the Lord your God spake concerning you; all are come to pass unto you, and not one thing hath failed thereof.' What God said to Joshua, He now says to us. He will not fail us, therefore let us trust Him implicitly. He will not forsake us, therefore let us boldly say, 'I will not fear what man can do unto me.' Since God will not fail, and since He will not forsake us, let us claim this promise as Joshua did, and rejoice in this wonderful Name."

 PRAYER THOUGHT: "Dear Lord, it matters not how deeply entrenched the wrong, how hard the battle, how long the day. Just give me the courage to stay on course and stand up to my responsibilities. In Jesus' name I pray. Amen."[5]
Joshua 1:5-7

Judges—The Book of Declension and Apostasy

Name: The book is named after the thirteen Judges, twelve of whom were raised up of God and one was a usurper. The word means "Rulers," from the verb "to put right and then to rule." The origin and description of the name is given in 2:17-19. The Judges are called "saviors" in 3:9 RV, and the word "deliverer" is constantly translated "save" in the margin.

Connection with Preceding Book: Judges is a continuation of the life of Israel after the death of Joshua and the elders after Joshua.

Contents: It gives an account of the lives, actions, and office of the Judges. God was still King in Israel, the government was a Theocracy, and the Judges were His deputies. Their office was not continual and, as they were extraordinary persons, they were only raised up on extraordinary occasions to be instruments in the hands of God in (1) delivering the people out of the hands of their enemies when oppressed, distressed, or carried captive by them; (2) protecting them in the enjoyment of their country, rights, and liberties; (3) leading out their armies against their enemies when needful; and (4) settling differences, judging lawsuits, and administering justice. It contains an account of all the Judges except the last two, Eli and Samuel, who are mentioned in I Samuel. This book begins with compromise and ends in anarchy and confusion. It is a record of Israel's forsaking God (2:13) and of His forsaking her because of disobedience (2:23). Judges has 21 chapters, 618 verses, and 18,976 words.

Israel's apostasy occurred seven times as recorded in this book. God used the surrounding nations to oppress His people and bring them to their knees. When the people called upon God for deliverance, He sent a deliverer (judge) who liberated them. The six servitudes, seven apostasies, and the delivering judges are seen in the following:

OPPRESSION	DELIVERING JUDGE
1. Mesopotamia, under Chushanrishathaim, for 8 years: 3:8	1. Othniel: 3:5-11. Peace for 40 years
2. Moab, under King Eglon (with the Ammonites and Amalekites), for 18 years: 3:14	2. Ehud: 3:15-30. Peace for 80 years
3. Canaanites, under King Jabin of Hazor, for 20 years: 4:3	3. Shamgar: 3:31
	4. Deborah, a prophetess, and Barak: 4:1—5:31. Peace for 40 years
4. Midian, for 7 years: 6:1	5. Gideon: 6;1—8:32. Peace for 40 years
5. Apostasy under Abimelech: 8:33—9:57	Abimelech, the usurper: Peace for 3 years
	6. Tola: 10:1,2. Peace for 23 years
	7. Jair: 10:3-5. Peace for 22 years
6. Ammonites, for 18 years: 10:8	8. Jephthah: 10:6—12:7. Peace for 6 years
	9. Ibzan: 12:8-10. Peace for 7 years
	10. Elon: 12:11,12. Peace for 10 years
	11. Abdon: 12:13-15. Peace for 8 years
7. Philistines, for 40 years: 13:1	12. Samson: 13:1—16:31. Peace for 20 years

Character: Historical.

Subject: Israel's failure to drive out the inhabitants of the Land as God had commanded, and His grace in raising up Judges to save them from their enemies, who became thorns in their sides (Numbers 33:51-56).

Purpose: To reveal to us the cause of the failure to enjoy our blessings, and God's grace in restoring and renewing fellowship.

Outline:

I. Commencing Failure: 1:1—2:13
   A. Compromise with sin: 1:1-36
   B. Condemnation for sin: 2:1-5
   C. Continuation in sin: 2:6-13
II. Combating Failure: 2:14—16:31
   A. Introduction: 2:14—3:4
      1. God's punishment: 2:14-16
      2. God's pity: 2:16
      3. Israel's perversity: 2:17-19
      4. Israel's proving: 2:20—3:4
   B. The Seven Apostasies: 3:15—16:31. Note the steps in Israel's trouble: 3:5-8. They—
      1. Failed to drive out the idolaters
      2. Dwelt among them
      3. Intermarried with them
      4. Served other gods
      5. Forgot their own God
      6. Were sold by God to their enemies
III. Continuing Failure: 17—21
   A. Failure of the Individual: 17:1-5
   B. Failure of the Priesthood: 17:7-13
   C. Failure of the two Tribes: 18:1—20:14
      1. Dan: 18:1-31
      2. Benjamin: 19:1—20:14
   D. Failure of the twelve Tribes: 20:15—21:25

Scope: It contains a history of more than 350 years.

Writer: Probably Samuel.

When and Where Written: Probably in the early years of Samuel's ministry, somewhere in Palestine.

Key Chapter: 2. Beginning of Israel's apostasy.

Key Verse: 21:25. See also 17:6.

Chariot of Iron

Key Word: Delivered, found 28 times.

Key Phrase: "Neither did." In 1:27, 29, 30, 31 and 33 we see incomplete victory because Israel's leaders "neither did" drive out of Canaan her enemies.

Key Thought: Conflicts of a Nation.

Spiritual Thought: Watch the borders (discipline): Isaiah 56:10,11; Ezekiel 3:17-21; I Thessalonians 5:4-8.

Christ Is Seen As:
1. Our Deliverer: 3:9.
2. The angel of the Lord: 6:12.

Names and Titles of God: Jehovah-Shalom, "the Lord our Peace" or "the Lord send peace": 6:24. See NAMES OF GOD in Dictionary.

Of Christ: our Judge: 3:9. As a judge brought Israel back into fellowship with her God, so our Judge (Advocate) brings each of us back into fellowship as we return to Him, confess our sins, and plead His blood for forgiveness, and determine to walk in the light as He is in the light (I John 1:7,9; 2:1).

Types of the Believer's Experiences: Jephthah, saved to serve: 11.[1] The story of Jephthah is the story of every converted sinner—a lifting up "from the dunghill, and a setting among the princes" (Psalm 113:7,8).

1. He was born in sin—son of a harlot: vs. 1. "A mighty man of valor," but a child of iniquity. By birth he was disqualified from entering the congregation of the Lord (Deuteronomy 23:2 with Psalm 51:5; John 3:3,5,7)

2. He was disinherited: vs. 2. By *one man's* disobedience we were made sinners (Romans 5:19a). Adam's sin drove him out of his inheritance and all his posterity have been born *outside* (in *his* likeness—Genesis 5:3). "The unrighteous shall not inherit the kingdom of God" (I Corinthians 6:9). If we would have an inheritance among them that are sanctified, it must be by faith in Jesus Christ (Acts 26:18b)

3. He associated with the vain: vs. 3 with Romans 3:12

4. He received an important invitation: vss. 5,6 with Matthew 11:28; John 6:37

5. He confessed before the Lord: vs. 11 with Romans 10:9,10,13

6. He was endued with power: vs. 29 with Luke 24:49; Acts 1:8

7. He gained the victory: vs. 32 with John 16:33; I John 5:4

1. Fire out of the rock to consume flesh and unleavened bread—to assure Gideon that he had found grace in God's sight: 6:17-23

2. Gideon's fleece—to assure Gideon that God would give him victory: 6:36

3. Selection of men for war by Gideon—to show God's power in the faithful few: 7:1-8. See GIDEON in Index.

4. Their implements of war (pitchers and torches)—to show them that God's strength is made perfect in their weakness: 7:16-21; II Corinthians 12:9

5. Jephthah's rash vow—to show that we should pray and think before speaking: 11:29-40. Jephthah promised the Lord that if he were victorious in battle he would sacrifice whatsoever came out of his house to meet him after the battle. His own daughter first greeted

him. It is unlikely that he offered her as a burnt offering sacrifice, even though the Canaanites round about did offer human beings as sacrifices. It is more likely that he bound her to virginity (spinsterhood). No greater disgrace could come to an Israelitish girl (vs. 36-40).

6. Water from a jawbone—to revive Samson: 15:19.

7. The strength of Samson—to show God's power in one who kept his vow: 14—16 (16:17 with Numbers 6:2,5). See SAMSON in Index.

 a. Lion slain: 14:5,6
 b. Foxes and firebrands: 15:4,5
 c. 1,000 Philistines slain: 15:14-16
 d. City gates carried away: 16:3
 e. Dagon's house pulled down—to show that even in failure one can come back to the Lord and have power restored: 16:22,26,30

8. Gibeah's wickedness—to show how low in sin men will go when God is left out of their lives: 19:1—20:48.

1. Iron in Palestine: 1:19; 4:3. Excavations have revealed many iron relics of ancient Philistia. Iron had its place in international commerce about the period of Moses. By the time of Saul's day (ca. 1,025 B.C.), the Philistines were skilled blacksmiths and controlled the industry in Palestine (I Samuel 13:19-23). Blacksmiths were so valuable they were listed among those taken prisoner (II Kings 24:14). It was "chariots of iron" that caused the tribe of Judah to lose faith and suffer defeat. See IRON in Index.

2. Secret passage into the city: 1:21-25. A fort believed to have been built by King Uzziah, who reigned in the days of Elijah, was recently discovered (the author has been through the one which was tunneled at Ibleam: Judah 1:27). A secret passage in the wall revealed one of the building tricks involved when Old Testament characters bypassed the gates of fortified cities to go in or out secretly. This fort had casement walls—actually two walls with a passage separating them by a few yards. The outer wall was built with oblong stones about three feet long and a foot square. An opening was left to place a slab of stone, three feet by one foot, which could be slipped out, revealing steps which led into the passage and on into the city. A stranger on the outside would not know which one of the many wall-stones was the slab which concealed the secret entrance. A reference in Judges tells of spies from Israel's army at Bethel seeking the secret passageway. They asked a man outside the city wall, "Pray, show us the way into the city, and we will deal kindly with thee" (1:21-25). The man did, and the army sneaked into Bethel. A secret passage offered an escape for King Zedekiah and his army when Nebuchadnezzar broke into the city of Jerusalem—"the king . . . fled by night by the way of the gate [opening] between two walls" (II Kings 25:4).

3. Samson's Death: 16:23-31. The plan of the Philistine temple with its two pillars destroyed by Samson has been illustrated by a recent discovery of a Philistine temple on the outskirts of Tel Aviv.

4. The Period of the Judges. This period of Israel's history was chaotic, one in which every man did that which was right in his own eyes (17:6; 21:25). Throughout the land, archaeological evidence of random destructions correlates with this record of God's Word (19-21).

Judges in the New Testament:

 1. Judges (or deliverers) given: 2:16 with Acts 13:20
 2. The relapse of Israel into idolatry in Judges can be compared with the backsliding of those in the

churches of Galatia into ceremonialism and mixing law with grace
3. Actions of the Judges generally: Hebrews 11:32,40

1. Israel's failure to drive out the Canaanites. Israel had been chosen to be God's peculiar people before godless nations. She was commanded to utterly destroy these nations, lest she learn to commit their sins (Deuteronomy 7:1,2; 20:17,18). Upon entering the Land, she received her inheritance under Joshua, but the first step in her failure to drive out the inhabitants of the land came under Joshua himself.

a. He made a league (covenant) with some of the citizens after God had commanded them not to: Joshua 9:14,15,20 with Deuteronomy 7:2
b. Having "settled" in the Land, they lacked faith in God to fight their battles and to drive out the inhabitants: 1:19. They trusted Him to break down the walls of Jericho, but their hearts melted when they *saw* the chariots of iron, thus walking by sight and not by faith. Israel had been promised a land of plenty in its many valleys, but now the enemy was in the valley and Israel had to content herself with the hillsides (Judges 1:34 with Deuteronomy 8:7). David later drove the Canaanites from the valleys (I Chronicles 12:15). See SIGHT and FAITH in Index.
c. In her failure to "utterly destroy" them as commanded, Israel became greedy and taxed the Canaanites: 1:28 with I Timothy 6:10. Israel had forgotten her own Egyptian bondage and put these people into a form of slavery, or put a yoke upon these people
d. Israel fell in love with the Canaanites and became unequally yoked together in marriage: 3:5,6 with Deuteronomy 7:3; II Corinthians 6:14
e. They compromised their convictions and served other gods: 3:7 with Deuteronomy 7:5,25; II Corinthians 6:14-17. They *served* Baalim (2:11), *forsook* the Lord (2:12), and *forgot* the Lord their God (3:7)

Instead of keeping His commandments and walking in His ways so that other nations would know that Israel was called by His name, Israel is now on the road to becoming the "tail" of nations instead of the "head" (Deuteronomy 28:9,10,13).

2. What a case of *parental* delinquency, which, or course, always leads to *juvenile* delinquency: 2:1-13. See SOLOMON'S Folly in Index.

3. Some Weak Things Made Strong. See I Corinthians 1:27
    a. The left hand: 3:21
    b. An ox-goad: 3:31
    c. A woman: 4:14
    d. A nail: 4:21
    e. A barley-cake: 7:13
    f. Pitcher and trumpet: 7:20
    g. Piece of millstone: 9:53
    h. Jawbone of an ass: 15:16

4. Gideon, A Man of Valor: 6:12
    a. Great humility: 6:15
    b. Deliberate: 6:17
    c. Devoted to God: 6:24
    d. Obedient to God: 6:27
    e. Empowered for service: 6:34
    f. On speaking terms with God: 6:36; 7:9
    g. Wise: 7:16-18
    h. Diplomatic: 8:1-3

    i. Loyal to God: 8:23

 5. Gideon's 32,000 Volunteers, or Many Called but Few Chosen: 7:1-8 with Matthew 22:14

    a. Gideon's call to arms: 6:34,35

    b. 22,000 *self-approved*, fearful, and scared men disqualified: 7:2,3 with II Timothy 2:3.

    c. 9,700 *self-interested* were disqualifed. In their eagerness to quench their thirst, they lapped water with their tongues as a dog laps. No possible chance to keep an eye on the enemy this way: 7:4-6 with I Peter 5:8

    d. 300 *self-alerted* men qualified by bowing their knees and lapping water, putting their hand to their mouth. This gave them a ready eye open to see the enemy: 7:6 with Matthew 26:41. Bowing the knee is symbolic of prayer—crying to God, depending on Him in every circumstance. Soldiers of the Lord do their best when they "cry unto the Lord in battle" (I Chronicles 5:20). Without Him we can do nothing. With Him we can do all things (John 15:5 with Philippians 4:13)

 6. Samson's "Ups and Downs"—

    a. Separated by a Nazarite vow (13:5), yet sought out an evil companion (14:1-4 with II Corinthians 6:14)

    b. Spiritual at times (13:25), yet filled with natural lust (16:1-4)

    c. Strong physically (14:5,6; 15:14,15; 16:3,9,17), yet weak in the time of temptation (16:15-17)

    d. Mature and fearless in battle (15:11-14), yet juvenile in his pranks.

In his weakness he got a haircut in the Devil's Barber Shop and lost his power with God and his influence with others. The Philistines made him *blind*, put him in a *bind*, and made him *grind*. Because he was in a bad place for a bad purpose, he came to a bad end (16:17-21). Though he repented and regained his strength, he died with the Philistines (16:22-31).

Samson's Grindstone

 7. "Every man did that which was right in his own eyes": 17:6; 21:25. Human nature being what it is, we should not be surprised that Judges records seven times that Israel did evil in the sight of the Lord (3:7; 3:12; 4:1; 6:1; 8:33-35; 10:6; and 13:1). Each time she did that which was right in her own eyes, she sinned and went into apostasy. Naturally, when one does that which right in his own eyes, he does not do that which is right in the eyes of the Lord (I Kings 11:33). Just as her forefathers had walked around in circles in the wilderness because of disobedience at Kadesh-barnea, so in the Land, because of disobedience, Israel is still going around in circles. In the Land she—

a. Served God
b. Did evil
c. Forsook God
d. Did "right" in her own eyes
e. Was taken prisoner
f. Was in servitude
g. Turned and cried to God
h. Repented
i. Had judges or deliverers raised up
j. Went back to serving God
k. Did evil, etc., etc., etc., . . .

What applies to a heathen nation also applies to God's—"Righteousness exalteth a nation, but sin is a reproach to any people" (Proverbs 14:34).

8. The children of Israel, as recorded in:

JOSHUA	JUDGES
a. Were victorious	a. Lived in defeat
b. Were at rest and liberty	b. Were in bondage
c. Believed God	c. Exhibited unbelief
d. Advanced	d. Slipped
e. Were heavenly-minded	e. Were earthly-minded
f. Were true to God	f. Turned to the god Baal
g. Enjoyed God's blessings	g. Experienced grief
h. Were empowered by God	h. Weakened by the flesh
i. Had oneness with God	i. Were at enmity with God
j. Would not tolerate sin	j. Condoned sin

A BIT OF **HEAVENLY MANNA**

"When the children of Israel cried unto the Lord, the Lord raised up a deliverer . . . who delivered them" (3:9). The word deliverer means "savior." In thinking along the line of being delivered the Psalmist recognized the necessity of being delivered from the one thing that binds the soul, viz., sin, or transgressions.

DELIVER ME FROM ALL MY TRANSGRESSIONS—Psalm 39:8[2]

"Nothing is so difficult to get rid of as sin. None but God can remove it. Committed in one moment, its effects may remain throughout all eternity. It affects God and man, and therefore deliverance from it is the greatest blessing. But before deliverance, there must be conviction, contrition, faith, and prayer. We must come to realize that it is an evil and bitter thing. We must be truly sorry for our sin. We must cry unto God in earnest prayer. We must believe God's Word, and believe in the Lord Jesus Christ. If God delivers us, He will do it gratuitously, for He saves by grace. He will do it effectually, for 'as far as the east is from the west, so far will He remove our transgressions from us.' He will do it eternally, for 'Israel shall be saved in the Lord, with an everlasting salvation.' My friend, is sin a burden to you? Are you weary of it? Do you long to get rid of it? Carry it to God's throne, confess it there, plead the blood of Jesus to have it removed, and deliverance will come."

PRAYER THOUGHT: "O Lord, as I attend the School of God this day, may I learn the first lesson—not to do that which is right in my own eyes, but to permit Christ to have the pre-eminence in all things in my life so that I may do that which is right in Thine own eyes. In Christ's dear name I pray. Amen."[3]

Judges 17:6b; I Kings 11:33b; Colossians 1:18

Ruth—The Book of Disloyalty, Loyalty, and Royalty

Name: The book takes its name from the chief character of its narrative. Two books of the Bible bear the names of women: Ruth and Esther.

Connection with Preceding Book: The book of Ruth singles out a family that lived during the period of Judges: 1:1.

Contents: "A man of Bethlehem, named Elimelech, with his wife Naomi and his two sons Mahlon and Chilion, left his own country in the time of a famine and went to sojourn in the land of Moab. There he died; and Naomi married her two sons to two Moabitish women: Mahlon married Ruth, who is the chief subject of this book; and Chilion married one named Orpah. In about ten years both these brethren died. Naomi, accompanied by her two daughters-in-law, set out to return to the land of Judah, she having heard that plenty was again restored to her country. On the way she besought her daughters to return to their own country and kindred. Orpah returned but Ruth insisted on accompanying her mother-in-law. They arrived in Bethlehem about the time of harvest and Ruth went to the fields to glean for their support. The ground on which she was providentially employed belonged to Boaz, one of the relatives of Elimelech, her father-in-law. When Boaz found out who she was, he ordered her to be kindly treated and appointed her both meat and drink with his own servants. Finding that she was by marriage his kinswoman, he purposed to take her to wife, if a nearer kinsman who was then living should refuse. He refused to take Ruth and surrendered his right to her, according to the custom of those times, at the Bethlehem gate before the elders of the city. Boaz took this Gentile to wife, by whom she had Obed, who was the father of Jesse, the father of David. Ruth is mentioned by name in the genealogy of Christ (Matthew 1:5)."[1]

The book reveals that in the midst of abounding apostasy and fearful licentiousness, as revealed in Judges 18—20, there were those who still remained loyal to Jehovah and lived in purity and simplicity of life before God, as Boaz. It also makes known how God can take up the most unlikely, and the carrying out of His plan through Ruth's son in keeping alive His promise to Abraham, which was made about a thousand years earlier. Abraham had been called by God to found a Nation for the purpose of one day bringing Messiah to Jew and Gentile alike. Recorded in the book of Ruth is the founding of the *Family* within that Nation through whom this Savior would come. Ruth was the great-grandmother of King David. From this book on, throughout the entire Old Testament, David's family is predominant.

This book is a love story without using the word "love." It is evidently an appendix to the book of Judges, and contains a perfect history of itself. Ruth contains 4 chapters, 85 verses, and 2,578 words.

Character: Historical.

Subject: God's sovereign grace in engineering circumstances and bringing together those who would be a part of the lineage through whom Messiah would come.

Purpose: To teach us that Salvation is of the Jew, but not for the Jew alone: 1:16; John 4:22.

Outline:

    I. Departure and Discipline: 1
       A. Disobedience and Death: 1:1-5
       B. Despair and Determination: 1:6-18
       C. Distrust and Discontent: 1:19-22
    II. Gleaning and Grace: 2
       A. Goodness and Gathering: 2:1-3
       B. Generosity and Guidance: 2:4-17

Scope: The events recorded in Ruth cover a period of over 12 years.

Writer: Probably Samuel.

When and Where Written: About 1300 B.C., in the days when the Judges ruled (1:1), somewhere in Palestine.

Key Chapter: 1. Ruth's decision.

Key Verse: 4:14.

Key Word: Kinsman: 2:1.

Key Phrase: Near of kin: 2:20b.

Key Thought: Individual experience in the time of apostasy: 1:16.

Spiritual Thought: Gather the grain—reap the harvest: Psalm 126:6.

Christ Is Seen As: Our Kinsman-redeemer: 2:1.

Names and Titles of God: Almighty: 1:20. See NAMES in Dictionary.

Types of Christ: This Book wonderfully portrays the Lord Jesus Christ as our Kinsman-redeemer. What Boaz was to Ruth, Christ is to all who draw near unto God through the blood of Christ.

1. The Character of the Kinsman-redeemer must—
  a. Be blood related
  b. Have the ability to pay
  c. Be willing to redeem

2. The Kinsman-redeemer must—
  a. Redeem the property
  b. Redeem the person put to slavery
  c. Execute vengeance on the oppressor

Such was not only Boaz for Ruth, but Christ Jesus is all this for those who are alienated from the life of God, aliens from the commonwealth of Israel, strangers from the covenants of promise who have no hope, and are without God in the world (Ephesians 2:11-13).

3. Boaz is further seen as a type of Christ as:
  a. Lord of the harvest
  b. Giver of rest
  c. Supplier of needs
  d. The bridegroom

Types of the Believer's Experiences: Ruth, as a sinner, having great faith in her kinsman-redeemer—[2]

1. She cast herself at his feet: 3:4-6
2. She claimed him as her redeemer: 3:9
3. She received his promise: 3:10-13

4. She accepted him, and he her: 4:13a
5. She bore fruit: 4:13b with John 15:4,5

LIGHT FROM
BIBLICAL
CUSTOMS

³ 1. Ruth clave unto Naomi: 1:14. A most exacting Bible custom is that of family ties and family religion. To break with family and religion and tradition was an unheard-of event. Ruth had made up her mind to go with Naomi back to Bethlehem from Moab, and in so doing, turned her back on family, custom, and religion. One of the most touching scenes in all the Bible is found in this book of Ruth (1:12-17). A more perfect surrender was never made to anyone as Ruth made to Naomi. The Targum, according to Eastern custom, gives the following interpretation of these verses:

"And Ruth said, 'Entreat me not to leave thee, for I desire to become a proselyte.' And Naomi said, 'We are commanded to keep the Sabbath and other holy days, and on it not to travel more than two thousand cubits.' And Ruth said, 'Whither thou goest, I will go.' And Naomi said, 'We are commanded not to lodge with the Gentiles.' Ruth answered, 'Where thou lodgest, I will lodge.' And Naomi said, 'We are commanded to observe the one hundred and thirteen precepts.' Ruth answered, 'What thy people observe, that will I observe, as if they had been my people of old.' And Naomi said, 'We are commanded not to worship with any strange worship or strange gods.' Ruth answered, 'Thy God shall be my God.' Naomi said, 'It is our custom, if at all possible, to be buried in our own country.' Ruth answered, 'Where thou diest, I will die.' Naomi said, 'We have a family place for burial.' Ruth answered, 'And there I will be buried also.'"

2. Skirt spread over thine handmaid: 3:9. There was nothing immoral about Ruth's uncovering the feet of Boaz and lying crosswise and covering herself with his cloak or skirt. In this act, according to Eastern custom, she was only asking for the right to his protection. Later, Boaz spread his garment over her, which symbolized his willingness to be her kinsman-redeemer: 3:7-14. This ancient custom is referred to in Ezekiel 16:8 concerning God's acceptance of Israel.

3. Ruth's veil: 3:15. In the West a veil is a small piece of netting or gauze-like material, but not so in the East. Ruth's veil was a lightweight mantle or shawl, which was sufficiently large enough to carry bundles. Many are six feet long and four feet wide. While a part of it was used to thinly veil her face, the rest of it was so arranged to cover her neck and shoulders. It is understandable how Boaz could get so much grain in her veil. This ancient Bible custom is still a part of life today for women of poor families who "glean" in the fields after harvest just like Ruth did. See VEIL in Index.

4. Kinsman-redeemer plucked off his shoe: 4:7. After Naomi's and Ruth's return to Bethlehem from Moab, it was determined that Boaz was a close relative who could buy Naomi's husband's property. Ruth as an eligible widow in the family, was included in the bargain so that children would be raised up to preserve the name of the dead. When Boaz learned of a closer kin to Naomi than himself, he gathered a company of witnesses at the city gate to force this relative to purchase all Naomi's property—plus Ruth. When the near-kin learned that Ruth was a part of the deal, he forfeited his "right" to the property and gave it to Boaz. He then took off his shoe and gave it to Boaz in the presence of the elders (4:1-17).

A "bill of sale" was given when something tangible was sold, such as oxen, houses, land, etc. But when an intangible was transferred, such as a "right," as in the case here, a shoe was given in the presence of witnesses, which signified the transaction of it from the nearest of kin to the next nearest of kin. Boaz now had the right not only to buy all that belonged to Elimelech, Chilion, and Mahlon, but claim also to Ruth's hand in marriage. He became her "kinsman-redeemer." This right brought Ruth, a Moabitess, into God's royal family. She became David's great-grandmother, and through him came David's greater Son, the Lord Jesus Christ (4:17; Matthew 1:1-6). When Boaz became "kinsman-redeemer" for Ruth, he bought her with a price, and she was no longer her own. Boaz became a type of Christ, who, in His death, purchased the right to redeem us. We, too, have been bought with a price, and are no longer our own (I Corinthians 6:19,20).

Ruth in the New Testament:
1. Christ's genealogy with Ruth and Boaz: 4:13-22 with Matthew 1:3-6; Luke 3:31,32.
2. Companion references:
   —Perpetuating seed: 4:5,6 with Matthew 22:24

1. In the New Testament we have the record of the prodigal *son* who went into a far country, was stripped of all he had, but returned, was welcomed by his relatives and friends, and received his father's best (Luke 15:11-24). Chapter one of Ruth is a story of a prodigal *family* which had the same experience.

Elimelech and his family lived in Bethlehem, which means "house of bread." This was God's *"there"* for this family—the place of God's choosing for this family. "House of bread" is equivalent to Philippians 4:19—"My God shall supply all your need . . ." Every child of God has a *"there"* (see THERE, Elisha's, in Index). Elimelech and his family left their *"there"* to *"sojour"* (just visit) in Moab, a land called "God's Washpot," which was "off-limits" to a true Israelite because of the awful sins of this land and their idolatry (Psalm 60:8; see WASHPOT in Index). Once in Moab, Elimelech *continued* there (put down his roots), and then the family *dwelt* there for ten years. Outside the place of God's *"there,"* notice what Naomi lost—
   a. She lost her husband: vs. 3
   b. She lost her sons: vs. 5
   c. She lost her witness: vs. 8, 15. See FAMILY GODS in Index.
   d. She lost God's favor: vs. 13b
   e. She lost her beauty: vs. 19b with Job 16:8
   f. She lost her joy: vs. 20
   g. She lost God's fulness: vs. 21a
   h. She suffered God's punishment: vs. 21b
   i. But, she returned to regain God's best: vs. 22
2. Ruth's Threefold Experience.
   a. Decision—Thy God my God: 1:16
   b. Service—gleaned in the fields: 2:3
   c. Reward—Boaz took her ("accepted in the beloved"): 4:13

As Ruth rejoiced in her redemption through Boaz, so we too rejoice because "we have redemption through His blood, the forgiveness of [our] sins according to the riches of His grace" (Ephesians 1:7). Being redeemed, we are now accepted in the beloved, chosen by Him to live a life holy and without blame before Him in love (Ephesians 1:4,6).

JESUS, OUR REDEEMER[4]
"Our state by nature was so fearful that no one but Jesus could redeem us; for an infinite

ransom was required; and it was not only necessary that a ransom price should be paid to satisfy divine justice, but omnipotent power must be exerted to rescue us from the dominion of Satan and sin. The blood of Jesus is the price of our redemption, and the Spirit of God is the Agent by whom our deliverance is effected as the Word of God is proclaimed. There is no other way to be redeemed. We are redeemed unto God, and from all iniquity; so that we shall, by and by, be entirely devoted to God, and be free from all sin. The redemption that is in Christ Jesus is effectual and all His redeemed ones shall celebrate the wonders of His redeeming love forever. This many of them are doing now, as we read, 'And they sung a new song saying, Thou art worthy to take the book and to open the seals thereof: for Thou wast slain, and hast redeemed us to God by Thy blood, out of every kindred, and tongue, and people, and nation; and hast made us unto our God kings and priests, and we shall reign on the earth.' Beloved, while we are still strangers here with our citizenship in heaven with Christ, let us as the redeemed of the Lord say so, with rejoicing that we, too, shall soon be redeemed from the very presence of sin, forever with Him.''

PRAYER THOUGHT: "Give me grace, dear Father, to desire Thee with my whole heart; so that desiring I may seek and find Thee, and so finding Thee I may love Thee, and in loving Thee I may hate the things which Thou dost hate and love the things which Thou dost love. In Thy Son's dear name I pray. Amen.''[5]

Ruth 1:15-17; Psalm 63:1-5

The United Kingdom of Israel

After the death of Joshua, the failure of the children of Israel to follow the Lord wholly gave occasion for the Judges to deliver them from the hands of their oppressors. After the period of the Judges, Eli and Samuel were raised up as leaders of Israel (I Samuel 1—7). It was under Samuel's leadership that Israel, growing tired of a Theocratic form of government, requested a Monarchy. They demanded a king "that we also may be like all the nations" (I Samuel 8). In spite of Samuel's plea to the contrary, God granted their request.

1. The first king—*Saul* (I Samuel 15:1). He reigned for forty years (Acts 13:21), and is known as "the king who lost his crown." In I Samuel we note his:

    a. Fine personal appearance: 9:2; 10:24
    b. Humility: 10:22
    c. Self-control: 10:27; 11:13
    d. Self-will: 13:12,13
    e. Disobedience: 15:11-23
    f. Jealousy and hatred: 18:8; 19:1
    g. Superstition: 28:7
    h. Suicide: 31:4

2. The second king—*David* (I Samuel 16:1-13; II Samuel 2:3,4; 8:15). He reigned for forty years (II Samuel 5:3-5), and is known as "Israel's versatile king."

    a. A man after God's own heart: Psalm 89:20; Acts 13:22
    b. Courageous: I Samuel 17:34-36
    c. A champion: I Samuel 17:40
    d. A great soldier: II Samuel 5;7
    e. Led by passion: II Samuel 5:13; 11:1-27

    f. Listening to Satan: I Chronicles 21:1-7
    g. Repenting, confessing, and returning to the Lord: I Chronicles 21:8; II Samuel 12:1-23; Psalm 51

   3. The third king—*Solomon* (I Kings 1:39,40; 2:1-12; 4:1). He reigned in Jerusalem for forty years (I Chronicles 9:30), and is known as "the king of wisdom and folly." His wisdom came as a result of his desire to be a good king (I Kings 3:5-28). His folly—and downfall—came as a result of his desire for "strange women," who turned him from the true and living God to "strange gods" (I Kings 11:1-25). See WISDOM in Index.

   The period of the United Kingdom of Israel was 120 years. Israel's declension in regard to other nations is seen:

    a. In her being *afraid* of other nations at Kadesh-barnea: Numbers 13:31
    b. In her *mixing* with other nations in Canaan: Judges 1:1—3:7
    c. In her *imitating* other nations after her settlement in Canaan: I Samuel 8:5,19,20

First Samuel—The Book of the People's King

Name: The word "Samuel" means "heard of God." The books of Samuel form but one in the Hebrew canon. They contain a history of his life and times. From the Latin vulgate, these books are also called "The First and Second books of Kings," and consequently the two following are "The Third and Fourth books of Kings."

Connection with Preceding Book: First Samuel is a continuation of the life of Israel as she "did that which was right in her own eyes" (Judges 21:25).

Contents: This book is a history with a personal attraction of biography added. It contains—

   1. The birth of Samuel and his education under Eli, the succession of Samuel in the government of Eli and the resignation of it to Saul when he was chosen king. Samuel is seen as a patriot and judge, with a lowly and consecrated heart, obediently serving God.

   2. Saul's anointing as king and the administration of his office, both before and after his death. Saul is seen as the people's king—a selfish, wayward, jealous king—faulty and unfaithful in his allegiance to God.

   3. An account of David, who is seen as God's king—a man after God's own heart, a man of prayer and praise who was tested, disciplined, persecuted, and finally crowned monarch of all Israel.

   Samuel, the book, is a transition book, and Samuel, the prophet, is a transition man. Herein we see Israel passing from the government of God to a self-determined and self-demanded government. From the rule of God, the Invisible King—which made them unlike other nations, they turn to the rule of a man, a visible king—which made them like other nations. From a Theocracy they passed to a Monarchy. Samuel sees the commencement of a line of kings which had varied influences for good and evil in Israel; and is himself the commencement of a line of prophets which for centuries corrected and constrained the lives of kings, priests, and the people (Acts 3:24). Moses was the transition leader from Egypt to Canaan; Samuel was the transition leader from the Theocratic government to a Monarchy—a task which was second only to that of Moses and carried out in the same humble and courageous spirit. First Samuel has 31 chapters, 810 verses, and 25,061 words.

Character: Historical.

Subject: God's dealings with Israel through Samuel as prophet, priest, and judge, and through Saul and David as kings, to bless and to make Israel a blessing (Genesis 22:17).

Purpose: To show how God would bring us into the enjoyment of our blessing in Him, through Christ as Prophet, Priest, and King.

Outline:

    I. Judicature of Eli: 1—4
        A. Birth of Samuel: 1,2
        B. The call of Samuel: 3
        C. The death of Eli: 4
    II. Judicature of Samuel, The Prophet-Judge: 5—12
        A. The Ark: 5,6
        B. Reformation and Worship: 7
        C. Saul Anointed: 8—11
        D. Samuel's Resignation of Supreme Judicial Power: 12
    III. The History of Saul, the man-made King: 13—31
        A. His sin against Israel: 13—15
        B. His sin against David: 16—27
        C. His sin against himself: 28—31
            1. The witch of Endor: 28
            2. The Philistines and David: 29
            3. The Amalekites and David: 30
            4. The Suicide of Saul: 31

Scope: The events cover a period of approximately 115 years, from the birth of Samuel, the last of the Judges, to the death of Saul, the first king of Israel.

Writer: Probably Samuel through chapter 24; the rest might have been written by Nathan and Gad (I Chronicles 29:29).

When and Where Written: Probably around 1070 B.C., somewhere in Palestine.

Goliath's Helmet

Key Chapter: 8. Israel demands a king.

Key Verse: 10:25. See also 8:7-18.

Key Words: King and Kingdom. Note also the word "prayed" in 1:10-27; 7:5; 8:6; 12:19-23.

Key Phrase: Speak, Lord, for thy servant heareth: 3:9.

Key Thought: The Organization of the Kingdom: 10:25.

Spiritual Thought:
1. The Lord killeth, and maketh alive: 2:6 with Romans 6:11
2. He bringeth low, and lifteth up: 2:7 with Luke 14:11
3. Keep the lamp of God burning brightly: 3:3 with Matthew 5:14-16

Christ Is Seen As: The Seed of David. Romans 1:3,4.

Names and Titles of God: Lord of Hosts: 1:3,1. This name implies One who has never known defeat, a name used when a crisis arises. See NAME in Dictionary.

David, as a type of Christ. There was a time when David, though "a man after God's own heart" (Acts 13:22), was rejected and despised as a servant of the people, the same as was Christ: 22:23 with Acts 10:38; John 1:11. As Christ was betrayed by Judas, so David was betrayed by his own son, Absalom, when he sought to usurp the throne, and as Judas went out and hanged himself, so was Absalom hanged: II Samuel 15—18; Matthew 26:47-50; 27:5.

Types of Believer's Experiences:
1. With David implies suffering: "he that seeketh my life seeketh thy life": 22:23a. To identify one's self with the rejected Christ means suffering: John 17:14; II Timothy 3:12; I Peter 2:21; 4:12-14.
2. With David implies safety: "but with me thou shalt be in safeguard": 22:23b. Our safety is in Christ alone: John 10:27-29; Colossians 3:3b. With Christ we are safe from—
   a. The sentence of death: II Corinthians 1:9,10a
   b. Wrath to come: Romans 5:9
   c. The curse of the Law: Galatians 3:13
   d. The power of sin: Romans 6:6,7,22; II Corinthians 1:10b
   e. The fear of men: Psalm 118:6; II Timothy 1:7; I John 4:18
   f. The cares of life: Matthew 6:25-34; John 15:7; Philippians 4:19
   g. The dread of death: I Corinthians 15:55-57

1. Dagon falling twice before the Ark and emerods on the Philistines—to show the heaviness of God's hand in judgment when things sacred are brought to man's level: 5:1-12.

2. The men of Beth-shemesh smitten for looking into the Ark—to punish "outsiders" for desecrating the Ark: 6:19 with Numbers 4:15,16. See ARK, p. 62.

3. A thunderstorm causing panic in the Philistine's army—to give Israel victory in answer to Samuel's prayer: 7:9-13.

4. Thunder and rain in harvest time—to punish Israel for her wickedness in asking for a king: 12:16-19.

5. David using a small sling to slay the giant Goliath—to show that God uses weak things to confound the mighty: 17:37-49 with I Corinthians 1:27. When the children of Israel saw Goliath, they said he was too big to defeat. When David saw Goliath, he said he was too big to miss!

After Saul's death, the Philistines stripped him of his armor, and placed it in the house of Ashtoreth, the fertility goddess. They cut off his head and placed it in the temple of Dagon (31:6-10; I Chronicles 10:1-10). The Old Testament site of Bethsan has been excavated and the house of Ashtoreth and the temple of Dagon were discovered, believed to be the ones where Saul's armor and his head were placed. Since Ashtoreth was a Canaanite goddess and Dagon was a Philistine god, these portions of Scripture have been questioned. Excavations at Bethshan revealed two such temples—side by side, just as the Bible indicated. Pagans are never limited to just one god.

1. The weaning of Samuel: 1:24. Hannah took Samuel to the Lord's house in Shiloh when she had him weaned—as a young child—not as a babe. In the Near East, children, especially boys, are not weaned until they are three or four and often seven years old. She was not taking a small baby to old Eli to care for, but a boy of several years to be trained for the Lord (1:24-28; 3:1-21).

2. To *ear* the ground: 8:12. When Samuel outlined the duties of those conscripted for the king's service, one was "earing the ground, to reap his harvest." The plowshare was shaped like an "ear," and this expression had reference to farmers tilling the soil.

I Samuel in the New Testament:

1. David, a man after God's own heart: 13:14 with Acts 13:21,22
2. Obedience is better than sacrifice: 15:22 with Mark 12:23
3. Man looketh on the outward appearance: 16:7 with II Corinthians 10:7
4. David eating consecrated bread: 21:1-6 with Matthew 12:3,4
5. Companion references:
    a. Hannah's prayer with Mary's rejoicing: 2:1 with Luke 1:46
    b. Priests (ministers) and filthy lucre: 8:3 with I Timothy 3:3

1. Hannah, a Woman of Grace: 1:1—2:11
    a. Problems plagued her: 1:1-14
        —Divisions in her home: vss. 1-7
        —Misunderstood by her husband: vs. 8
        —She was bitter: vs. 10
        —Misunderstood by her pastor: vss. 9-14
    b. Prayer was offered for help: 1:9-19
    c. Her prayers were answered: 1:19-23
    d. She presented her all to God: 1:24-28 with Mark 12:41-44
    e. She praised God: 2:1-10
        —She emphasized God's Person: vss. 1-3
        —She emphasized God's Program: vss. 4-8
        —She emphasized God's Purpose: vss. 9,10

2. Prayer Dominated Samuel's Life. See PRAYER in Index.
   a. Born in answer to prayer: 1:10-28
   b. His name means "asked of God": 1:20
   c. His prayer brings deliverance at Mispah: 7:2-13
   d. His prayer when Israel asks for a king: 8:6,21
   e. His unceasing prayer for his people: 12:23

3. Parental delinquency always leads to juvenile delinquency. Eli's sin consisted in his negligence to reprimand his sons for profaning themselves and God's work: 2:17; 3:13,14. See FOLLY in Index.

4. It is possible for little children to be spoken to and called by God: 3:1-10 with Matthew 18:1-5; 19:13,14. Many missionaries today testify that they gave their hearts to Christ at an early age and *knew* then they were called of God to become missionaries. When a tender heart is open to the things of God, He will fill it with His call. When children accept Christ as Savior, not only is a soul saved, but a life as well.

5. Israel's trust in a sacred object (the Ark) brought about her defeat with the Philistines: 4:3-10 with Exodus 20:3-5. "There is a way that seemeth right unto man, but the end thereof are the ways of death" (Proverbs 14:12).

6. When Israel demanded a king, Samuel knew it was wrong for them to dethrone God, and pleaded with them to continue under a Theocratic form of government. The people insisted that their demands be met, only to learn later that old Samuel was right in his desire to retain God's rulership. Though Israel confessed she had sinned in asking for a king, she had to reap what she had sown: 8:1-20; 12:19 with Galatians 6:7. Israel also learned that when she got *her* way, she got leanness of soul (Psalm 106:15).

7. Saul's self-will and stubbornness: 15:19-23. This sin is:
   a. Forbidden by God: II Chronicles 30:8; Psalm 95:8
   b. Unbelief: II Kings 17:14
   c. Pride: Nehemiah 9:16,29
   d. An evil heart: Jeremiah 7:24
   e. Refusing to hearken to God: Proverbs 1:24
   f. Refusing to listen to God's messengers: Jeremiah 44:16
   g. Refusing to walk in God's ways: Nehemiah 9:17
   h. Rebelling against God: Psalm 78:8
   i. Resisting the Spirit: Acts 7:51
   j. Following an evil heart: Jeremiah 7:24 with Jeremiah 23:12
   k. Hardening the heart: II Chronicles 36:13

Saul simply said, "I have sinned": 15:30. David said, "I have sinned *against the Lord*" (II Samuel 12:13). When Saul disobeyed the Lord in his failure to destroy the Amalekites, he blamed the people, saying as much, "Don't let the people know my heart is unclean." David said, "Create in me a clean heart" (Psalm 51:10). David was restored to a life of blessing and service (Psalm 32; II Samuel 12:26-31). Saul was eventually slain by one whom he should have destroyed, an Amalekite (I Samuel 15:1-3,18,19 with II Samuel 1:5-10). If we don't master sin, sin will master us.

8. Saul and the "witch at Endor": 28:7-25. In our day when so much emphasis is placed upon "extrasensory perception," it is well to see what God has to say about fortune telling, witchcraft, spiritism, astrology, etc. Such things are an abomination, and are condemned by Him (Leviticus 20:6; Deuteronomy 18:9-12. "Necromancer," in vs. 11, is one who falsely claims to talk with the dead). That Saul went to one was sinful, to say the least. While Samuel's spirit was brought back from the intermediate state, we note this was accomplished by God, not by the medium. The medium's astonishment and fright indicates this. It was not a medium communicating with the spirit of the dead, but God Himself actually calling back Samuel in

spirit to pronounce judgment upon Saul (vss. 15-19). In Saul's tragic experience, God unmasks the fraud of such practices. Since Christ has the keys of Hell and of death (Revelation 1:18), it hardly seems likely that anyone but God can speak to the spirit of the dead. See ASTROLOGY in Index.

This Book cannot be discussed thoroughly unless Samuel's mother (Hannah) is mentioned. The first two chapters reveal the kind of woman she was, not only to her boy, Samuel, but to her God as well. Briefly, we see her petitioning God for a child, the bitterness of her soul, her prayer and her weeping. Even old spiritual Eli didn't understand the pouring out of her soul before the Lord. God heard her prayer, saw her weeping, honored her vow, and when her time was come, she bore a son and called him Samuel. In this experience, she became keenly aware of God's hand and His providence and His dealings with her. In the realization that she had been exalted before the Lord, she also recognized the need to be brought low, hence she cried—

THE LORD BRINGETH LOW, AND LIFTETH UP—2:7[2]

"God does this in temporal things when it is for our good. He strips us and lays us bare, or He prospers us in all we do. But in a spiritual point of view, He does so in the experience of all His children. He strips them of pride, lays them in the dust, and brings them to self-despair. While He is doing so, they often doubt, fear, and despond; they are ready to give up all hope, and conclude that the hand of the Lord is gone out against them. But we must feel that we are lost before we shall seek the Savior. We must be stripped before we shall gratefully receive and thankfully wear the robe of the Redeemer's righteousness. When He has brought us low, He will lift us up. When He has stripped us, He will clothe us. He will send us the Spirit of adoption, robe us in the garments of salvation, assure us of an inheritance incorruptible, undefiled, that fadeth not away. The lower we sink in self-despair, the higher we rise in the enjoyment of God's free grace. Lie low if you would rise high."

PRAYER THOUGHT: "Help me, Lord, to give myself to the essential and to recognize the trivial when I see it. Give me the courage to say 'no' to everything that makes it difficult to say 'yes' to Thee. In Jesus' dear name I pray. Amen."[3]

I Samuel 15:21,22

Second Samuel—The Book of God's King

Name: See NAME in I Samuel.

Contents: Second Samuel is a continuation of I Samuel. Herein is an account of the happy commencement of David's reign, his unhappy fall and miserable consequences, and his restoration to Divine favor, the re-establishment of his kingdom, and events in the latter part of his kingdom. This book has 24 chapters, 695 verses, and 20,612 words.

Character: Historical.

Subject: God's blessings upon Israel through the reign of David.

Purpose: To reveal typically the blessing and rule of Christ over us, and eventually over Israel and the nations.

Outline:

   I. The triumphs of David: 1—10
- A. Lamentations over Saul: 1
- B. Revolt of Abner: 2
- C. Return and Death of Abner: 3
- D. Death of Ish-bosheth: 4
- E. Victories over Enemies: 5—10

   II. The Troubles of David: 11—19
- A. The cause of David's troubles: 11,12
- B. The results of David's troubles: 13—19
  1. Domestic troubles: 13
  2. Public troubles: 14—17
  3. Death of Absalom: 18,19

   III. The Throne of David Restored: 20—24
- A. His return to Jerusalem: 20
- B. The punishment of Saul's sins: 21
- C. His psalm of thanksgiving: 22
- D. His last words: 23
- E. His second great offense against God: 24

Scope: It contains a history of about forty years, from the death of Saul to near the close of David's reign.

Writer: Probably compiled by Ezra or Jeremiah.

Key Chapter: 5. David becomes king over Israel.

Key Verse: 5:12.

Key Word: King.

Key Phrase: Before the Lord: 6:17.

Key Thought: The reign of David.

Spiritual Thought: Call David—God's anointed.

Christ Is Seen As: David's Lord: 7:4-17.

Covenants in Second Samuel. The Davidic or Kingdom Covenant: 7:4-17; II Chronicles 17:4-15. See COVENANTS in Index.

Names and Titles of God. See NAMES in Dictionary.
1. Rock: 22:2,32,47
2. Fortress: 22:2
3. Deliverer: 22:2
4. Shield: 22:3
5. Horn of my Salvation: 22:3
6. High Tower: 22:3,51
7. Refuge: 22:3
8. Savior: 22:3
9. Jehovah, my Stay (Companion): 22:19
10. My Lamp: 22:29
11. The Light of the Morning: 23:4
12. The Tender Grass: 23:4

The Kingdom of Christ: 7:12,13 with Luke 1:31-33; John 18:36.

Stated: ca. 1,000 B.C. *Fulfilled:* Spiritual—Christ's earthly ministry. Natural—yet future.

Types of Christ:

1. David's reign and throne a type of Christ's earthly ministry: 8:15 with Luke 4:17-19; Acts 2:29-31; 10:38

2. Solomon's kingdom: 7:12,13 with Luke 1:31-33

Types of Believer's Experiences: David and Mephibosheth, a type of Salvation by Grace: 9[1].

1. Mephibosheth's condition, or the sinner's need
   a. Fearful, hidden from the king: vss. 1-3
   b. Destitute, "in the house of Machir in Lo-debar"; vs. 4. Machir means "sold," and Lo-debar means "without pasture." How true of the sinner—sold in sin, dwelling in a dry land: Psalm 68:6
   c. Helpless, lame on both feet: vs. 3. We cannot come to God on our own; He must seek us: Luke 10:10

2. David's purpose, or the love of God. He wished to show kindness to the house of Saul (his enemy) for Jonathan's sake. What an illustration of God's showing kindness and mercy to us (His enemy) for Christ's sake: II Corinthians 5:19. This love was—
   a. Spontaneous—the voluntary impulse of a kind and merciful heart: vs.1
   b. Gracious—it sought out the undeserving: vss. 1,3
   c. Self-sacrificing—"I have given all that pertained to Saul": vs. 9

3. Mephibosheth's faith, or salvation enjoyed:
   a. He believed the message and answered David's call: vs. 6
   b. He humbled himself: vss. 6,8
   —Fell on his face
   —Did reverence
   —Confessed himself to be as a "dead dog"
   c. He was accepted: vs. 7
   d. He was adopted: vs. 11
   e. He was made an heir: vs. 7. David said, "I will restore thee all the land of Saul thy father."

Thus we see Mephibosheth lifted from poverty to plenty through the grace of the king—a type of God's grace for us through faith, which lifted us out of the "miry clay" to make us "sons of God," "accepted in the beloved," given the "Spirit of adoption," and made "heirs of God and joint-heirs with Christ" (Ephesians 2:8,9; Psalm 40:2; John 1:12; Ephesians 1:3;

1. Uzzah struck dead—to punish presumption: 6:7 with Numbers 4:15,16

2. David given a choice of punishment for sin—to reveal the grace of God even in chastisement: 24:10-15

The Jebusite "gutter" or watercourse: 5:8. Jerusalem depended upon the Spring of Gihon and other wells located outside its walls for water. In times of siege, city gates were closed, and many times its inhabitants surrendered due to lack of water and food. Long before David's time the Jebusites had hacked a tunnel through solid rock from Gihon and had sunk a shaft from above to connect the city with the water channel. Scripture hints that David's general, Joab, captured Jerusalem through this shaft. After its capture, David made Jerusalem his capital. This shaft can be seen today as one walks through Hezekiah's conduit (see CONDUIT in Index). Also, excavations in Jerusalem from the early 1960s uncovered a corner of the Jebusite wall.

[2] David danced before the Lord: 6:14-16. At the head of a great procession there was seen a half-naked clown dancing, making gestures usual for such occasions. This act was done in honor of the person or thing to whom the process was made, and was the function of a slave only. When David and the Israelites brought up the ark with shouting and trumpets, David "danced with all his might" before the Lord. He took the place of a slave at the head of the procession to honor the Lord. This embarrassed his wife, Michal, so that she despised him. But his was an act of humility before the Lord.

Scientifically Speaking: Channels of the Sea: 22:16. See OCEANS in Index.

Second Samuel in the New Testament:

1. The Davidic Covenant: 7:8-17 with Luke 1:31-33. See COVENANTS in Index.
2. Concerning David's death: 7:12 with Acts 13:36
3. Solomon's birth: 12:24 with Matthew 1:6
4. Companion references:
   —Rewarded according to works: 3:39 with II Timothy 4:14

1. There was great mourning after the deaths of Jonathan and Saul: 1:2. We often mourn over a body from which the soul has departed, but how many of us shed a tear over a soul that is lost? See SOUL-WINNING in Index.

2. David's Downfall—His Sins, His Sins found out, His Confession, Reaping, Forgiveness, and Restoration. See SIN in Index.

    a. His Great Sin: 11
      —Shirked his responsibility: vs. 1
      —Despised God and His Commandments: 12:9,10
      —Failed to "watch and pray"; tempted while at ease: vs.2
      —Desired another's wife: vs. 3 with Exodus 20:17
      —Committed adultery with her: vs. 4 with Exodus 20:14
      —Got her husband, Uriah, drunk: vss. 12,13 with Habakkuk 2:15
      —Plotted Uriah's death: vss. 5-25 with Exodus 20:13
      —Brazenly lived the life of a hypocrite, covering his sins
      —Displeased the Lord in all he did: vs. 27b
    b. His Repentance: 12:1-13 with Psalm 51
      —Rebuked by Nathan: vss. 1-4
      —David's anger due to hypocrisy: vss. 5,6
      —His sin found out: vs. 7 with Numbers 32:23b

—His sins are the result of despising God and His commandments, and begins to see sin as God sees it: vss. 9,10

—Consequences of his sins foretold: vss. 8-12

—David's confession: vs. 13 with Psalm 51:1-3

—He acknowledged his transgressions—that which he had done willfully and deliberately: Psalm 51:1

—He acknowledged his iniquity—his crookedness—the fact that he was a sinner by nature: Psalm 51:2a,3a,5

—He acknowledged his sin—his failure to measure up to God's expectation of him: Psalm 51:2b,3b, with Romans 3:23

—He asks for a cleansing: Psalm 51:2,7. See HYSSOP in Index.

  c. His Reaping or Consequences of his sins: 12:14 with Galatians 6:7

Howbeit, David—

—Just as you sinned in secret, the consequences of your sins will be made public: 12:12

—Just as you committed adultery with Bathsheba, so will other men do to your wives: 12:11

—Just as you saw to it that Uriah died, your son by Bathsheba will die: 12:14

—Just as you wanted and took Bathsheba, so your son, Amnon, will want, and get, his sister and your daughter, Tamar: 13:1-14

—Just as you had Uriah slain, so your son, Absalom, killed Amnon for his dastardly deed: 13:14-30

—Just as you shirked your duty and responsibility as king (11:1), now Absalom seeks to usurp your throne: 15:1-37

—Just as you got Joab to send Uriah into the thick of battle to be killed, now Joab kills Absalom: 18:9-15

—Just as you sowed seeds of discord in your own household in all your actions, now Sheba revolts and bloody battles are fought among your own people against you: 20:1-22

—Just as you turned against Me and despised Me and My commandments, your testimony has caused My enemies to blaspheme My name: 12:14

—Just as you took the sword to cover your sins, "the sword shall not depart from your house:" 12:10

  d. His Joy in being Forgiven: Psalm 32. "Blessings" belong only to the one whose *transgression* is forgiven, whose *sin* is covered, and to whom the Lord does not impute *iniquity*: vss. 1,5. David "shouts for joy" because he *is* forgiven: vs. 11

  e. His Restoration to Service. He had sent Joab to do his job (11:1). Now, Joab, according to custom in letting the king lead his troops victoriously into a conquered city, calls upon David to assume his responsibility. David does, and to him goes the spoils of victory: 12:26-31

"In the dreadful fall of David we see the power of human corruption, even in holy men of God, unless kept by His almighty hand, and the sovereign efficacy of divine grace in His renewal and restoration."[3] We need not stumble at the lives of some of the Bible characters. The Word of God teaches us that salvation is for the sinner, not for the righteous (Matthew 9:13).

3. Lessons to be Learned from David's Downfall

  a. Shirking one's responsibility leads to idleness: 11:1

  b. Idleness leads to temptation: 11:2

  c. Temptation leads to sin: 11:3,4

  d. No matter how large or small we might think sin to be, all sin is full-grown and is displeasing to the Lord: 11:27

  e. One sin leads to another: 11:5-25

  f. It is better to confess sin immediately instead of conniving to cover it up: Proverbs 28:13

  g. If we don't master sin, it will master us. Saul should have killed all the Amalekites; in the end an Amalekite finalized him (I Samuel 15 with II Samuel 1:1-16).

h. Any sin committed willfully and deliberately is tantamount to not only despising God's commandments, but despising God Himself: 12:9,10

i. Be sure *your* sin will find *you* out: 12:1-9 with Numbers 32:23b

j. Before we condemn others, judge ourselves: 12:5-7; Matthew 7:1-5

k. Sin has its consequences: 12:8-12

l. We reap what we sow: Galatians 6:7

m. We reap more than we sow

n. Sin is contagious—it affects others

o. Sin causes us to be a stumbling block to others: 12:14

p. When confessing sin, plead for mercy: Psalm 51:1. Mercy is God's withholding from us what we rightly deserve. Grace is His giving to us what we do not deserve

q. Lay yourselves before the Lord, acknowledge your sin, spell it out: Psalm 51:3. God never forgives sin on the basis of *"If"* I have sinned

r. No matter how or when we sin, God is present to see it all: Psalm 51:4

s. All sin breaks the heart of God: Psalm 51:4

t. Sin makes us deaf to the "still small voice of God": Psalm 51:8

u. Sin stains the heart: Psalm 51:2,10

v. Sin causes us to lose the joy of God's salvation: Psalm 51:12

w. Only when we confess our sin can we witness effectively: Psalm 51:13

x. Only in restoration can we really praise the Lord: Psalm 51:14,15. Confession brings forgiveness, forgivenesss brings joy and blessing: Psalm 32

y. Only in restoration can we begin to do good, obediently serving the Lord: Psalm 51:18,19 with II Samuel 12:26-31. See POEM, God's Job, in Index.

z. Even though God forgives and blots out our transgressions, never to be remembered against us anymore (see DELIVERANCE in Index), our sin is "ever before us" (Psalm 51:3b). Who can forget putting his finger on a hot stove, though they never do it again?

—David never walked on the palace roof again without a penitent reflection of his unhappy walk when he first saw Bathsheba

—David never sent his servant on an errand but what he thought of sending his servant to fetch Bathsheba

—David never laid down to sleep without a sorrowful thought of a bed which he had once defiled with another man's wife

—David never sat down to eat without thinking of his plan to get Uriah drunk and shift the blame of the child on him

—David never sat down to write a letter but what he thought of the letter he wrote to Joab sentencing Uriah to death

—David never shirked his responsibility again without thoughts of his temptation and sin against the Lord

—David never went into battle again without wondering which arrow had his name on it—dying in battle just like Uriah had. See TEAR BOTTLES in Index.

4. Reasons for Backsliding. See I John 2:15-17; BACKSLIDING in Index.

a. David backslid because of the *flesh*: 11:1-4

b. Demas backslid because of the *world*: I Timothy 4:10

c. Peter backslid because of the *devil*: Matthew 16:23

5. Giving Thanks unto God: 22:50 with Psalm 136:1-3; Colossians 3:17

a. In our approach to Him: Psalm 95:2

b. At the remembrance of His holiness: Psalm 30:4

c. For the gift of Christ: II Corinthians 9:15

d. For His goodness and mercy: Psalm 136:1

e. For deliverance from sin: Romans 7:22-25

f. For supplying our need: Romans 14:6,7; I Timothy 4:3,4

g. For all things: II Corinthians 9:11; Ephesians 5:20

h. In everything: I Thessalonians 5:18

i. Continually: Hebrews 13:15,16

j. For victory over death and the grave: I Corinthians 15:57

A BIT OF
HEAVENLY
MANNA

In this Book we have the account of David's great sin of adultery and murder (ch. 11). For just about a year this sin remained within the secret chambers of his heart. Then the Lord sent his best friend, Nathan, to make known that hidden and unconfessed sin was keeping the king in the backslidden condition. Surely if David was to be used of the Lord to help others come to know Him, he must be right with the Lord himself, and so he acknowledges his sin (12:13). His detailed confession is found in Psalm 51. Here he realized his utter helplessness to cleanse himself from his sin, to get back the joy of God's salvation and His peace, or even to teach transgressors God's way. In desperation he cried out to his only source of help—"Have mercy upon me, O God" (Psalm 51:1).

WASH ME THOROUGHLY FROM MINE INIQUITY—Psalm 51:2[4]

"Sin is spiritual filthiness. It defiles the conscience, corrupts the imagination, depraves the heart, perverts the will, pollutes the breath, sets the tongue on fire of hell, stains the life, and renders the man totally and eternally unfit for heaven. It is God's work to cleanse the sinner. No one else can. The sinner cannot cleanse himself; he is without the means, the will, or the power. But God in His mercy does, and He does it by His Son, atoning; by His Spirit, renewing; by His providence, working, and by His Truth, purifying. He saves us by the washing of regeneration and renewing of the Holy Spirit. The passage contains the believer's prayer—'Wash me thoroughly.' It is 'mine iniquity'—'my sin.' Wash me, for I have discovered my filthiness; I loath myself on account of it; and I long to be delivered from it. Wash me thoroughly, take out every stain, erase every impression, make me whiter than snow. Sin always pollutes us. A believer cannot rest in pollution. A backslider must be cleansed before he is restored. God will have us smart for sin before He cleanses us from it."

PRAYER THOUGHT: "O God, keep reminding me that if I regard iniquity in my heart and will not listen to Thee, that Thou wilt not hear my prayers, nor wilt Thou bless unless I confess my sins and forsake them. In Christ's dear name I pray. Amen."[5]

Psalm 66:18 with Proverbs 28:13

The Divided Kingdoms of Israel and Judah

During Solomon's reign, a young man named Jeroboam came to prominence, who later was to become the king of the Northern Tribes after the division. This was predicted by the prophet Ahijah, who tore Jeroboam's coat into twelve pieces, symbolizing the rending of the United Kingdom at the time of Solomon's death. Jeroboam was told that he would rule over ten tribes. When Solomon learned of this, he sought to kill Jeroboam, who escaped the king's wrath by fleeing to Egypt (I Kings 11:26-40).

After the death of Solomon, the people went to Shechem to make Solomon's son, Rehoboam, their king, and they sent for Jeroboam to return from Egypt. Jeroboam and all Israel requested relief from the heavy burdens laid on them by Solomon. Rehoboam required three days to con-

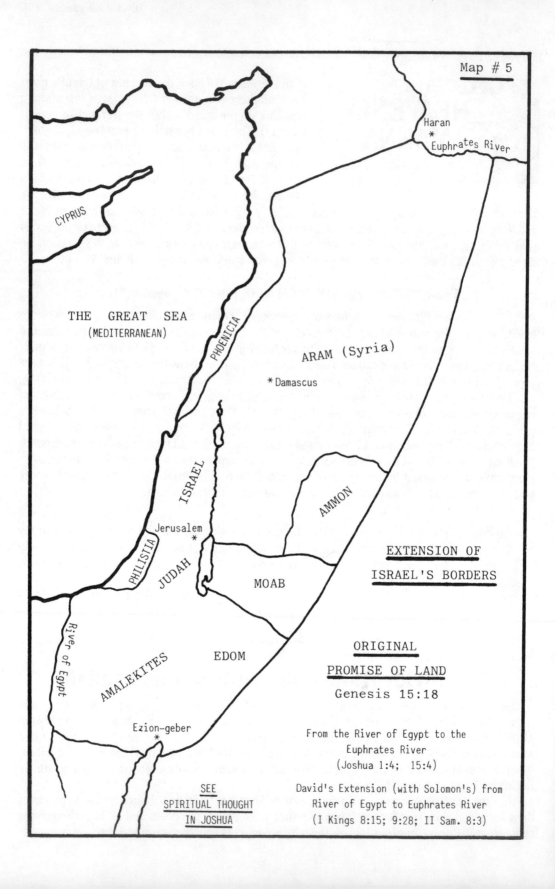

Map # 5

Haran
* Euphrates River

CYPRUS

THE GREAT SEA
(MEDITERRANEAN)

PHOENICIA

ARAM (Syria)

*Damascus

ISRAEL

Jerusalem
*

PHILISTIA

JUDAH

AMMON

MOAB

EXTENSION OF
ISRAEL'S BORDERS

River of Egypt

AMALEKITES

EDOM

ORIGINAL

PROMISE OF LAND

Genesis 15:18

Ezion-geber
*

From the River of Egypt to the
Euphrates River
(Joshua 1:4; 15:4)

SEE
SPIRITUAL THOUGHT
IN JOSHUA

David's Extension (with Solomon's) from
River of Egypt to Euphrates River
(I Kings 8:15; 9:28; II Sam. 8:3)

sider their petition. Rejecting the counsel of the elders who served his father, he followed that of the young men, and returned a provoking answer to the people. The people renounced the family of David, stoned Adoram to death, who came to receive their tribute, and made Jeroboam king. Only two tribes remained with Rehoboam—Judah and Benjamin. Rehoboam went to Jerusalem and assembled 180,000 fighting men of these tribes, with the avowed purpose of forcing the men of Israel to his allegiance. He was forbidden by the prophet Shemaiah, who, speaking in the name of the Lord, said, "this thing [division] is from Me" (I Kings 12:24). The Ten Tribes which followed Jeroboam were called the Northern Kingdom of Israel, while the two Tribes which stayed with Rehoboam were called the Southern Kingdom of Judah.

This division brought Judah under the watchful eye of the Lord, so that, in spite of sin, corruption, idolatry, being scattered, and without a king for years, Judah's people would not be "lost" and the Word of God would be fulfilled in the coming of Christ—"The Scepter shall not depart from Judah, nor a lawgiver from between His feet, until Shiloh [Christ] come" (Genesis 49:10).

Thus we see a division in the Twelve Tribes of Israel, ten cleaving to Jeroboam, and the other two to Rehoboam. Jeroboam headed the Northern Kingdom of Israel, while Rehoboam headed the Southern Kingdom of Judah. "Calf Worship" became the religion of the newly formed Northern Kingdom (I Kings 12:25-33). The calf became the symbol of Israel's independence of Judah and the house of David. Baal worship was also mixed with calf worship. Calf worship was so rooted in the hearts of the people that it was not swept away until after their captivity. It is stated of each of the nineteen Northern kings that they "did that which was evil in the sight of the Lord." Not a single one ever attempted to bring the people back to a singular worship of God. See references with DYNASTIES of the Northern Kingdom in Index.

For the first three years of Rehoboam's reign, Judah walked in the way of David and Solomon, making their sacrifices unto the Lord (II Chronicles 11:16,17). After that, Baal worship was adopted. Out of the nineteen kings and one queen of the Southern Kingdom, eight of them "did that which was right in the sight of the Lord," that the people might come back to the Lord. They were:

1. Asa: I Kings 15:11
2. Jehosaphat: I Kings 22:43
3. Joash: II Kings 12:2
4. Amaziah: II Kings 14:3
5. Uzziah: II Kings 15:3
6. Jotham: II Kings 15:34
7. Hezekiah: II Kings 18:3
8. Josiah: II Kings 22:2

In spite of the great reformations under these kings, and the warnings of the prophets, Judah sank even lower than the Canaanites in gross sin, till there was no remedy (II Kings 21:9; II Chronicles 36:14-17). Captivity in Babylon finally cured Judah of her idolatry.

In the Southern Kingdom there was only one dynasty—that of David, except when Athaliah, the daughter of Omri, broke into David's line by marriage and reigned as queen for six years (I Chronicles 22:2,10-12). In the Northern Kingdom there were nine dynasties:

1. Jeroboam: I Kings 12:20; 13:33,34
    a. Nadab: I Kings 14:20; 15:25,26
2. Baasha: I Kings 15:33,34
    a. Elah: I Kings 16:8-10
3. Zimri: I Kings 16:10-20
4. Omri: I Kings 16:21-26
    a. Ahab (the worst of Israel's kings); I Kings 16:28-33
    b. Ahaziah: I Kings 22:40,51-53

      c. Jehoram: II Kings 3:1-3
   5. Jehu: II Kings 9:11-13. A spark of revival broke out under Jehu when he exterminated Baal worship, but he continued in the sin of calf worship (I Kings 10:19-29)
      a. Jehoahaz: II Kings 13:1,2
      b. Joash (or Jehoash): II Kings 13:9-11
      c. Jeroboam II: II Kings 14:23,24
      d. Zechariah: II Kings 15:8,9
   6. Shallum: II Kings 15:13-15
   7. Menahem: II Kings 15:17,18
      a. Pekahiah: II Kings 15:22-24
   8. Pekah: II Kings 15:27,28
   9. Hoshea: II Kings 17:1,2

For a list of the kings of both Kingdoms, see KINGS in Index.

Capitals of the Two Kingdoms:

The Southern Kingdom had two capitals: Hebron—II Samuel 2:1-11; 5:5 and Jerusalem—I Kings 11:32; 14:21.

The Northern Kingdom apparently had three capitals:
   1. Shechem: I Kings 12:25
   2. Tirzah: I Kings 16:23
   3. Samaria: I Kings 16:24,29; II Kings 18:9-12

The great period from the death of Solomon to the captivity of Judah is recorded for us from three distinct points of view:
   1. From the *Royal* viewpoint: Books of Kings
   2. From the *Religious* viewpoint: Books of Chronicles
   3. From the *Prophetic* viewpoint: Books of the Prophets

The SPIRITUAL THOUGHT for *both* First and Second Kings together is taken from I Corinthians 10:12: *"Take heed lest ye fall."*

First Kings—The Book of the Division of the Kingdom

Name: Originally, I and II Kings formed only one book. They were afterward divided into two books, hence the names I and II Kings.

Contents: "The book carries on the history of the Jewish nation, shows the state of apostasy of the spiritual seed within the nation in these times, and God's providential care of them amidst all the changes and vicissitudes in the state; and, above all, it transmits to us the true genealogy of the Messiah, which serves to confirm Matthew's account."[1] First Kings has 22 chapters, 816 verses, and 24,524 words.

Character: Historical.

Subject: God's dealings with Israel through Solomon and the kings of the divided kingdoms until the time of Elijah the prophet.

Purpose: To show the cause of the establishment and decline of the kingdom and to teach us that our Solomon (Christ) will lead every believer in the full enjoyment of his blessings if unhindered by a divided heart.

Outline:

Scope: It contains a history of about 120 years, from the close of David's reign to the death of King Jehoshaphat of Judah.

Writer: First Kings contains an abstract of the history, compiled from much more copious records (11:41; 14:29; 15:31; 22:39,45). It is uncertain by whom this compilation was made—probably Ezra or Jeremiah.

When and Where Written: While the first Temple was still standing, somewhere in Palestine (probably Jerusalem).

Key Chapter: 22. Ecumenicity—Ahab and Jehoshaphat. See ECUMENICITY in Index.

Key Verse: 11:13.

Key Word: Royalty.

Key Phrase: David his father: 2:12.

Key Thought: The glory and division of the Kingdom.

Spiritual Thought: Set the King on his throne.

Christ Is Seen As: King of kings and Lord of lords.

1. Josiah of Judah to break down Jeroboam's altar: 13:2 with II Kings 23:15-18

Stated: 930 B.C. *Fulfilled:* ca. 630 B.C.

2. Northern Kingdom's captivity: 14:15,16 (13:33,34) with II Kings 18:9-12. See CAPTIVITY in Index.

Stated: ca. 910 B.C. *Fulfilled:* 722 B.C.

3. Elija predicted no rain for three-and-a-half years: 17:1 with James 5:17 and II Kings 18:42-45

4. Elijah pronounced Ahab's doom: 21:19-24 with 22:34-39

5. Elijah pronounced Jezebel's doom: 21:23 with II Kings 9:30-37

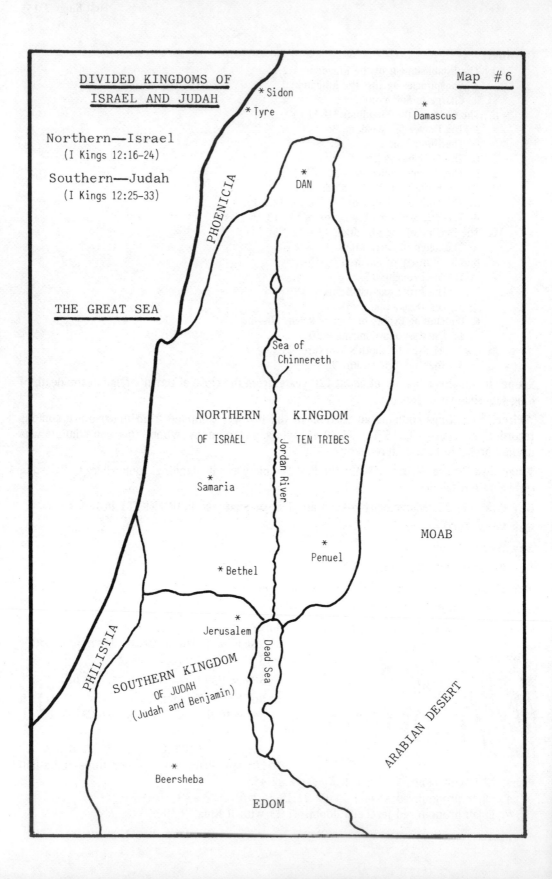

DIVIDED KINGDOMS OF
ISRAEL AND JUDAH

Map # 6

Northern—Israel
(I Kings 12:16-24)

Southern—Judah
(I Kings 12:25-33)

THE GREAT SEA

PHOENICIA

* Sidon
* Tyre

* Damascus

* DAN

Sea of
Chinnereth

NORTHERN   KINGDOM
OF ISRAEL   TEN TRIBES

Jordan River

* Samaria

MOAB

* Penuel

* Bethel

* Jerusalem

PHILISTIA

Dead Sea

SOUTHERN KINGDOM
OF JUDAH
(Judah and Benjamin)

ARABIAN DESERT

* Beersheba

EDOM

1. Solomon's wisdom. Note the incident in 3:16-28 with two women who claimed the same child. See also 4:29-34, which shows him to be an author of proverbs, a song writer and poet, a horticulturist, botanist, zoologist, ornithologist, entomologist, and ichthyologist. See the Book of Proverbs for such wisdom. But Christ is greater than Solomon in that He *is* the wisdom of God (Luke 11:31; I Corinthians 1:30).

2. Solomon's Temple, the place of God's dwelling (which replaced the Tabernacle: Exodus 25:8), is a type of Christ's body (John 2:19-22), and of the body of the believer, which is now God's temple (I Corinthians 3:16,17; 6:19,20)

3. Solomon's Glory
    a. In his Temple: 6:1-38. See TEMPLE SITE in Index. Was proposed by his father David (II Samuel 7), and much of the material for it was gathered by him (I Chronicles 22). Precious metal made up much of the material—108,000 talents of gold, 10,000 drams of gold, and 1,017,000 talents of silver (I Chronicles 22:14; 29:4,7). This is equivalent to about $5,000,000,000. A talent of gold was worth about $28,000, one talent of silver about $1,940, and one dram of gold about $5.00

$$
\begin{array}{lr}
108{,}000 \text{ talents of gold} = & \$3{,}024{,}000{,}000 \\
10{,}000 \text{ drams of gold} = & 50{,}000 \\
1{,}017{,}000 \text{ talents of silver} = & \underline{1{,}972{,}980{,}000} \\
& \$4{,}997{,}030{,}000
\end{array}
$$

This vast store of precious metal—plus copper and iron without weight, and precious stones (I Chronicles 22:3; 29:7,8)—was placed at Solomon's disposal for the Temple (7:51; II Chronicles 5:1). Someone has suggested that with today's inflationary prices (1980), it would cost close to two hundred and forty billion dollars to duplicate Solomon's Temple! Here is a breakdown:
    $58,867,372,400 for gold, silver, and copper (brass)
    200,000,000 for jewels
    80,000,000 for robes
    50,000,000 for musical instruments
    7,500,000,000 for food for laborers
    100,000,000,000 for structure material, trimming, tapestry, etc.
    75,000,000,000 for labor

    b. In his palace: 7:1-12 with John 14:1-3
    c. In his kingdom: 2:12 with Colossians 1:13; II Peter 1:11
    d. In his wisdom: 3:12; 4:29-34 with I Corinthians 1:30

In considering the glory of this king, Christ took the lily of the field and said, "even Solomon in all his glory was not arrayed like one of these" (Matthew 6:29). Though Solomon as a king wore elegant robes of purple and white, and although he had great splendor in his court, all this could not compare in glory to what God had done to a wild flower of the field. Christ used simple truths such as this to teach us "that no flesh should glory in His presence" (I Corinthians 1:29).

Types of the Believer's Experiences:
1. The Queen of Sheba, a type of a sinner being saved: 10:1-13 [2]
    a. She heard the fame of Solomon: vs. 1. This fame was "concerning the name of the Lord." "Faith cometh by hearing and hearing by the Word [of God]" (Romans 10:17)
    b. She came and enquired of him. "She came to prove him with hard questions": vs. 1. Having heard, she did not make light of it like those who were invited to the marriage

> feast (Matthew 22:5), nor postpone it like Felix (Acts 24:25)
> c. She communed with him and the king hid nothing from her: vss. 2,3
> d. She was humbled: vss. 4,5
> e. She confessed: vss. 6,7 with Luke 18:13
> f. Solomon fulfilled her desire: vs. 13 with John 6:37; Romans 6:23b
> g. She testified and praised: vss. 8,9 with Psalm 107:2
> h. She gave the king gold: vs. 10 with Romans 12:1,2

The testimony of Christ as to the queen of Sheba's being an historical figure and her visit with Solomon is found in Matthew 12:42.

Type of the Church: Just as David, the father, proposed the Temple, gathered much of the material for it and gave it to his son, Solomon, to build (II Samuel 7; I Corinthians 22), so God the Father draws the material for the Church, presents it to His Son, Christ, who builds the Church upon the Solid Rock with living stones fitly framed together (John 6:37,44; Matthew 16:18; Ephesians 2:20-22). See TEMPLE in Index.

1. Solomon's request for wisdom that he might be a king worthy of God's choosing: 3:5-15. What would *you* have asked for?

2. Solomon's wisdom tested two women, both claiming the same child—to reveal his wisdom was truly of God and to put the deceiving woman to shame: 3:16-28

3. Jeroboam's hand withered, destruction of the altar at Bethel, and Jeroboam's hand restored—to punish defiance of God's messenger: 13:4-13

4. Drought in the land—to show God's displeasure of idolatry: 17:1 with James 5:17

5. The ravens sent to feed Elijah—to test Elijah's faith and to supply his need: 17:2-6 with Philippians 4:19

6. The widow's meal and oil supplied—to see the hand of God in providing food in the time of famine, revealing the reward that comes when we "give a cup of cold water in Christ's name:" 17:10-16 with Matthew 10:42

7. The raising of the widow's son at Zarephath—to show the widow that Elijah was indeed the man of God: 17:17-24

8. Sacrifice consumed by fire from heaven—to attest Deity and Divine authority: 18:38. See also Leviticus 9:24; Judges 6:21; 13:19,20; II Chronicles 7:1

9. Rain ends a drought—to show the power of prayer: 18:41-45 with James 5:18.

10. Elijah fed by an angel—to encourage a discouraged servant of God: 19:1-8

11. City wall falls upon 27,000 Syrian troops—to reveal that the God of Israel is God of both the hills and valleys: 20:28-30

1. Solomon's Quarries: 5:18; 6:7. Ancient subterranean quarries have been found beneath the city of Jerusalem. When discovered, they were full of limestone chips, indicating that the stones were fitted (cut) and shaped at the quarries, made ready so that there was "neither hammer nor axe nor any tool of iron heard in the house [Temple] while it was in building."

Solomon's Quarries

Gezer Calendar

2. Solomon's Copper Mines: 7:45,46; 9:26. See MINES in Index.

3. Solomon's Stables: 9:15-19 with 4:26. The city of Megiddo was one of Solomon's cities, constructed in all probability for his cavalry. It is estimated that the extensive stables at this city could have held up to 500 of his 40,000 horses and about 150 chariots. Many "hitching posts" were discovered at this ancient site.

4. The Gezer Calendar: 9:17. Gezer was another of Solomon's cities. Found here was an inscribed "calendar," which gave instructions for agricultural activities of the twelve months. As the earliest known Hebrew inscription, it is of interest in that it provides a relatively fixed date to help in the study of the development of the Hebrew language. Furthermore, modern Jews in Israel figured that if the region around Gezer could grow the things listed on the calendar in Solomon's day, so could they. Flax, an item mentioned, is growing in abundance in Israel today.

5. Ophir gold: 9:26-28. Solomon multiplied unto himself much gold and silver (II Chronicles 9:13-28). He accumulated such an abundance of gold that his ivory throne was overlaid with gold; his footstool was gold; all the drinking vessels and the vessels of his house were pure gold (none were of silver). In addition to the shields of gold which David had captured in a Syrian campaign (I Chronicles 18:3,7), Solomon made 300 shields of gold for his soldiers, each weighing about three pounds, and worth, by today's (1980) gold standard, $19,200 (or a total of $5,760,000 for Solomon's 300). Solomon even built a seaport on the Red Sea (Gulf of Aqaba), and a navy to import these metals, much of which came from Ophir. An inscribed stamp at ancient Bethel gives archaeological evidence, not only of Ophir having an abundance of gold, but that extensive trade was carried on between Israel and Sheba. This supports the visit by the Queen of Sheba to see King Solomon (10:1-13). The queen gave him many ex-expensive gifts, including 120 talents of gold (worth about $58,750,000). According to I Kings 10:14-16, Solomon had 666 talents of gold come to him in one year, plus what he received from other sources. The 666 talents alone would be worth over $325,000.000 today!

The "gold of Ophir" is mentioned in other passages of Scripture (I Chronicles 29:4; II Chronicles 9:10; Job 22:24; 28:16; Psalm 45:9; Isaiah 13:12). However, the Bible does not "pinpoint" its location. Perhaps its location was so well known that no description was thought necessary, or, perhaps, Ophir did not refer to a specific single location but to a mining region.

Ophir Ostracon

In 1977, the U.S. Geological Survey announced that they *may* have found the mines of Ophir at Mahd adh Dhahab, an ancient mine in Saudi Arabia between Mecca and Medina. The *New York Times* quoted one of the geologists exploring the area saying, "Our investigations have now confirmed that the old mine could have been as rich as described in Biblical accounts and is a logical candidate to be the lost Ophir . . . 'King Solomon's lost mines' are no longer lost."

An inscribed piece of pottery mentions Ophir gold. This, along with an inscribed stamp found at ancient Bethel, gives archaeological evidence, not only of Ophir having an abundance of gold, but that extensive trade was carried on between Israel and Sheba. This supports the Queen or Sheba's visit to see King Solomon (I Kings 10:1-13).

6. Ahab's Ivory Palace: 22:39. See IVORY in Index.

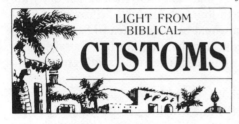

LIGHT FROM BIBLICAL CUSTOMS

3

1. Slept with his fathers: 2:10. Upon the death of the king, he was buried in the "king's tomb," along with others who had died before, hence the expression that "he slept with his fathers." There are thirty-nine ancient rock-hewn vaults in a single tomb in the city of Jerusalem today which convey to us what the "Tombs of the Kings" might have looked like. The entrance is sealed with a rolling stone.

2. Solomon's many wives: 11:1-3. Evidently Solomon failed to heed God's command regarding the king "multiplying unto himself wives" (See ISRAEL, Selection of a king, in Index). Because of eagerness to please unbelievers at the expense of displeasing the Lord, he soon found himself following an international custom practiced by heathen nations—that of "swapping" (or exchanging) daughters and/or wives as a means of State prestige, and to keep peace among themselves. Often a king of a weaker nation would give one of his wives or daughters as a "peace offering" to the king of a stronger nation, so that the stronger nation would not put the weaker one in bondage or servitude. Because of Solomon's fame, he wound up with no less than 700 wives and princesses, and 300 concubines. Pictured is a Hittite king (of a weaker nation—left) presenting his "peace offering" daughter to a Pharaoh of Egypt.

"Peace Offering" Daughter

3. Come home with me, and eat bread: 13:15. This is not a casual, polite invitation, hoping, of course, that the visitor or sojourner will refuse. Easterners *mean* it. The traveler knows this, and upon arrival in a village, even unannounced, someone will invite him to "come home with me, and eat bread." This invitation involves provision of food, shelter, and protection from the weather and possible enemies, as well as enjoying the favor of the family gods. The "welcome mat" stays out for three days and four hours (the length of time it is believed the host's food sustains his body). The guest is "adopted" as one of the group, and is considered the "guest of God." This custom is practiced by all in the East, because the host never knows when he himself will have to ask for similar shelter.

4. A lamp in Jerusalem: 15:4. An Eastern home is never dark unless the inhabitants are dead or the house is deserted. The burning of a lamp at night is symbolic of the continuance of a family. "The light of the wicked shall be put out, . . . and his candle shall be put out with him" (Job 18:5,6). "The light of the righteous rejoiceth [burneth brightly]" (Proverbs 13:9). God had promised David that his throne and kingdom would be perpetuated (II Samuel 7:16). The sins of King Abijam cast a dark shadow over the kingdom, but God, for David's sake, gave "him a lamp in Jerusalem," a promise that the family would continue until David's greater son, Christ, should come.

5. Astrology/Divination: 17:16; 23:4. See ASTROLOGY in Index.

6. Elisha plowing with twelve yoke of oxen: 19:19. One is apt to get the impression that Elisha had a team of twelve oxen. Verse 19 says that he was with the twelfth oxen, which simply means that eleven other men with oxen were plowing ahead of him. Palestinian farmers delight in working in companies; in part for protection but mainly for their love to "rest and gossip."

7. Naboth's vineyard: 21:1-16.[4] It was the right of every Israelite to be a free man and to hold on to his ancestral land (Leviticus 25:23; Numbers 36:7). Naboth owned a piece of property near King Ahab's house, which was desired by the king. Naboth refused the king's offer to purchase it or "swap" for a better vineyard. Ahab, as king, could have demanded it of his subject, but he knew it would be theft. Because Naboth refused to grant the king his wish, Ahab went home, threw himself on his bed, and refused to eat his supper! When his wife, Jezebel, heard of the incident, she was puzzled, but not for long. The standards, by which she, as a king's daughter, had been raised in heathen Phoenicia, permitted her to make a different approach than Ahab. She was a "normal" person who never did anything worse than her gods— Baal and Anat (See BAAL, Anat, in Index). From her covetous heart she had false charges brought against Naboth, hiring lying witnesses to testify against him, and deceivingly wrote letters to the elders of Naboth's city, giving them instructions to slay him so that Ahab could "inherit" the vineyard. The letters were sealed with Ahab's seal, thus making her murder plans "official." See SEAL (Jotham's) in Index.

First Kings in the New Testament:
1. The death of David: 2:10 with Acts 2:29; 13:36
2. Solomon's porch: 7:6 with Acts 3:11
3. All have sinned: 8:46a with John 8:7; Romans 3:23; I John 1:8-10
4. The queen of Sheba: 10:1 with Matthew 12:42
5. The famine and the widow of Zarephath: 17:1-16 with Luke 4:25,26
6. Elijah's effectual prayer: 18:42 with James 5:17,18
7. The 7,000 who bowed not to Baal: 19:10-18 with Romans 11:2-4
8. Companion references:
   a. Withered hand restored: 13:6 with Mark 3:1-5
   b. Child raised from the dead: 17:22: II Kings 4:35 with Hebrews 11:35
   c. Blaspheming God: 21:10 with Acts 6:11-13; 7:58,59

SEED THOUGHTS

1. Solomon's and Christ's Kingdoms
   a. Extent: 4:20, 21 with Psalm 71:8,19
   b. Peace: 4:24,25; 5:4 with Psalm 72:7
   c. Rule: 4:29-31 with Psalm 72:11-16
   d. Justice: 10:8,9 with Psalm 72:1-4,12-14
   e. Prosperity: 10:13,27 with Psalm 72:10,16
2. The Wisdom and Folly of Solomon
   a. His *Wisdom* is seen in his:
      —Asking for an understanding heart to judge Israel: 3:9
      —Judicial insight: 3:16-28
      —Surpassing other wise men: 4:29-31
      —Uttering proverbs and discourses: 4:32-34
      —Erection of the Temple: 5,6
      —His prayer of dedication: 8:22-53
   b. His own wisdom did not teach him self-control. His *folly* is shown in his:
      —Luxurious living: 4:22,23; 10:21
      —Marrying heathen women: 11:1,2; Nehemiah 13:23-26
      —Excessive sensuality: 11:3
      —Sanctioning idolatry: 11:4-10
      —Doing right in own eyes: 11:33. See point #7, p. 133.
      —Oppressing the people: 12:4
3. Solomon's Idolatry: 11:1-13,33
   a. Its Cause: vss. 4,33
      —External cause: vs. 4—his many wives. Accumulation of these wives was a violation of the Word of God (Deuteronomy 17:17). See WIVES in Index.
      —Internal cause: vs. 4b—his heart turned from God
      —While young, he loved the Lord: 3:3
      —In adulthood, still observed the Law with respect to worship: 9:25; II Chronicles 8:12,13
      —At close of reign, his heart not right with the Lord: 11:4b
   b. Its Course: vss. 5-8
      —It affected his spiritual life and walk: vss. 5,6
      —It affected his work: vss. 7,8. In later life, Solomon concluded that all was "vanity" (Ecclesiastes 2:1-26).
   c. Its Cost: vss. 9-13
      —Lost his personal testimony: vss. 9,10
      —Lost God's pleasure: vs. 9
      —Lost the full kingdom through his son: vss. 11-13

Solomon seemed to be an instructor rather than an example. He points the way to wisdom, but in the latter part of his life he "did not practice what he preached." Rehoboam, his son who followed him on the throne, did not heed Solomon's counsels, but like a "chip off the old block" became a foolish and wicked ruler (14:21-24; II Chronicles 12).

4. Elijah's place for God's blessings: 17:2-6. The word "there" (vs. 4) is mighty important in the matter of being in God's will. In no other place than the brook Cherith would God feed Elihah—*there*. When the brook dried up, there was a widow *there* in Zarephath who would feed him (17:9). In no other place would he be fed than in his *there*. When God commanded Jacob to go back to Bethel, the place for his blessing was *there* at Bethel where he was to dwell (Genesis 35:1). Christ's last instructions to all His disciples were to go back to Jerusalem and tarry until they were endued with power from on high. They had to be *there* in Jerusalem to

receive the promise of the Father (Luke 24:49; Acts 1:4,12—2:4). If we are to be blessed with every spiritual blessing in heavenly places in Christ experientially, we must be *there*—abiding in Him and His Word abiding in us (John 15:4-7; Ephesians 1:3). See THERE in Index.

5. The widow of Zarephath put to use her meal and oil according to the word of the man of God, and "the barrel of meal wasted not, neither did the cruse of oil fail" (17:16). Someone has said of Christianity that the more we *export,* the more we have in our hearts and lives.

6. Elijah's Revival: 18. Under King Ahab and Queen Jezebel, God was dethroned and Baalism was enthroned (see BAAL WORSHIP in Index). Due to sin, rain had ceased in the Land and Israel was faced with a famine. In this old-time, Holy Ghost, heaven-born, hell-shaking, death-killing revival, old Elijah—

    a. Faced conditions:
        —Famine in the land: vs. 2. Two kinds of famine are mentioned in Scripture:
        (a) Physical, and (b) of hearing of the Word of God (Amos 8:11). Both stand for judgment, and Samaria had both. Note the—
        —Wickedness of King Ahab: 16:30; 18:17,18
        —Corruption in religion: 16:31-33; 18:19
        —Confused people: 18:21. Note—
            —Baal's prophets knew whose side they were on: vs. 19
            —Elijah knew whose side he was on: vss. 36,37
            —The Israelites were fence stragglers; compromisers, and were "halting between two opinions"

Baal, the so-called "god of all Nature," was supposed to do for Israel what God could not do. Since Baal had failed miserably to send rain to quench a parched land, Elijah called for a "contest" between the true and living God of Israel and the god Baal. Elijah's great advantage over the prophets of Baal was that he *knew* this living God. His next advantage was that he *knew* what the Baalites believed, and he used his knowledge of their religion as a weapon to bring about their defeat: 18:23-28. This "contest" was to decide whose "god" was the true God.

    b. Elijah knew his God had caused the rain to cease: 17:1. This proved Baal's helplessness as the "god of Rain" (see BAAL, Rain, in Index).
    c. Elijah made a bold offer when he said that "the God who answereth by fire, let him be God" (vs. 24). Baal was supposed to have power whereby he would hurl bolts of fire from heaven to bring victory for his subjects. And what a victory this would be for Baal if he could prove himself by following Elijah's suggestions! See BAAL, god of War and Fire, in Index.
    d. When Baal had been previously "slain" by another god, his followers supposed him to be on a journey to help subjects elsewhere, or asleep in the nether world. When his prophets could not call down fire from heaven, Elijah mockingly laughed and said, "Cry aloud: for he is a god; either he is talking, or he is pursuing, or he is on a journey, or peradventure he sleepeth, and must be awakened" (vs. 27). See BAAL, Anat, in Index.
    e. When the prophets of Baal failed to vindicate their god, they "cut themselves *after the manner* with knives and lancets, till the blood gushed out upon them" (vs. 28). See BAAL, El, in Index.
    f. Elijah then called upon the only God to answer prayer and prove Himself: 18:36,37. His effectual, fervent prayer resulted in—
        —God vindicating His name: vss. 38,39
        —The fire of God falling: vs. 38
        —Conviction and confession: vs. 39
        —Judgment upon the unbelievers: vs. 40
        —Rain returning after three-and-one-half years: vss. 41-45 with James 5:17,18. When we break up the fallow ground in true repentance and return to the Lord, He then sends the rain (Hosiah 10:12). With rain—
        —The dust is settled. Doubt and confusion flee

—The grass begins to grow. We bear abundant fruit

—The water supply is increased. We grow in grace

—Prosperity is on the scene. Our need is supplied

There was *one* true man of God (Elijah) who stood up to 850 false prophets of Baal (18:19). However, "one and God make a majority." "If God be for us, who can be against us" (Romans 8:31). While there were 7,000 who had not bowed their knees to Baal (19:18), they could not be found when needed—when they could have been most encouraging to Elijah. There are a great many today who name the name of the Lord, who wouldn't indulge in gross sin, but, like the 7,000, they are not good for much when it takes the Lord to find them!

7. Ecumenicity—Ahab (evil) and Jehoshaphat (good): 22:1-36 [5]

    a. It was a union of believers and nonbelievers: vss. 2-4a

    b. It involved a false sense of oneness: vs. 4b

    c. It followed the advice of a false prophet: vss. 5,6

    d. It attempted to muzzle the true servant of God: vs. 13

    e. It involved the rejection of God's Word: vss. 17,18

    f. It involved persecution of God's man: vss. 24,27

    g. It ended in disaster for both parties: vss. 34-36

    h. It shows that light and darkness will not mix—that a believer should not be unequally yoked with an unbeliever: II Corinthians 6:14-18

A BIT OF HEAVENLY MANNA

"Set the king on his throne" is this Book's Spiritual Thought. Immediately we ask: "Where is the king's throne?" The answer at present is—"on the right hand of the Majesty on high." But the believer has a sure hope of the throne being elsewhere at a future date and the blessed privilege of reigning with the King of kings and Lord of lords while seated on His throne. So blessed is the truth that Jesus is coming again that every blood-bought child of God ought to be "looking for the blessed hope, and the glorious appearing of the great God and our Savior Jesus Christ." When He comes to set up His kingdom of righteousness we shall see our King of kings and Lord of lords in all His glory.

ON HIS HEAD WILL BE MANY CROWNS—Revelation 19:12[6]

"Jesus passed through many trials, engaged in many conflicts; therefore He gained many triumphs, and now wears many crowns. He wears a crown of victory, for every foe is, or will be, overthrown. He wears the crown of sovereignty, for He is king of kings and Lord of lords. He wears the crown of creation, for all things were made by Him, and for Him. He wears the crown of providence, for He sustains, supplies, and rules all that He has made. He wears the crown of grace, for He redeemed His people by His blood, He conquers them by His Spirit, molds them by His Truth, and will bring them all to His kingdom. He wears the crown of glory, for every one of His glorified people owe their honor, happiness, and blessedness to Him. He is crowned by His Father with a splendid diadem, and every knee must bow to Him. Every one of His people crown Him, and cast their crowns at His feet as unworthy to wear them in His presence. His crown is the brightest that wisdom ever devised, mercy jeweled, or power brightened. O to gaze upon His glory, and to see His once thorn-pierced brow with many crowns."

PRAYER THOUGHT: "Dear Father, because Thou hast worked a work of grace in my heart, enable me to have a smiling face, a flashing eye and a ringing testimony that will convince others that Christianity 'works' in the lives of those who walk in Thy statutes and keep Thy commandments. Help me to let others know that Thy Son did not die in vain. In His name I pray. Amen.''[7]

I Kings 8:61; I Timothy 1:16

Second Kings—The Book of the Captivities

Name: See NAME and WRITER in I Kings.

Contents: Second Kings is a continuation of I Kings. It records the decline and fall of both Israel and Judah under her several kings. To this period belongs the ascent of prophecy. The main topics contained herein are: (1) the translation of Elijah; (2) the ministry of Elisha, his successor; and (3) the passing of both Israel (18:9-12) and Judah (25:21) into captivity. This Book has 22 chapters, 719 verses, and 23,532 words.

Character: Historical.

Subject: The completion of the apostasy of the kingdoms of Israel and Judah, and the judgment of both.

Purpose: To warn us of the cause, method, and result of apostasy and to encourage us to look to the Holy Spirit to guide us and keep us in the truth of God's Word.

Outline:

    I. Closing Ministry and Translation of Elijah: 1,2
    II. Ministry of Elisha: 3—8
    III. Kings of Israel (Northern Kingdom): 9—15. See KINGS in Index.
    IV. The Captivity of Israel: 16:1—18:12
    V. Kings of Judah (Southern Kingdom): 18:23. See KINGS in Index.
        A. Hezekiah: 18—20
          1. Revival: 18
          2. Defeat of Assyria: 19
          3. Death of Hezekiah: 20
        B. Manasseh: 21
          1. Worst of Judah's kings: vss. 1-9,16. He seduced Judah to do *more* evil than the worshipers of Baal. See BAAL in Index.
          2. His exile predicted: vss. 10-15. See MANASSEH, p. 175.
          3. His repentance: II Chronicles 33:11-20
        C. Josiah: 22,23
          1. Bible reading instituted: 22
          2. Idolatry destroyed: 23
    VI. The Captivity of Judah: 24,25
        A. Jehoiakim—the first exile: 24
        B. Zedekiah—Jerusalem destroyed: 25

Scope: Second Kings covers a period of about 300 years, from the death of Ahab (853 B.C.) to the end of Jehoiachin's days (ca. 555 B.C.).

Key Chapter: 2. Elijah's translation and Elisha's power.

Key Verse: 10:10.

Key Word: Evil.

Key Phrase: According to the Word of the Lord: 1:17.

Key Thought: History of the Divided Kingdom.

Spiritual Thought: Pray for a double portion of the Spirit: 2:9.

Christ Is Seen As: King of kings and Lord of lords.

1. Death of King Ahaziah: 1:2-17

2. Isaiah's prophecy of Babylonian captivity of the Southern Kingdom of Judah as a result of Hezekiah's foolishness in showing strangers from Babylon the priceless treasures of his palace: 20:16-18; II Chronicles 36

Stated: ca. 690 B.C. *Fulfilled:* 586 B.C.

Types of Christ: Elisha, in following Elijah.

1. In his footsteps: vss. 2,6 with I Peter 2:1-15.

2. In his victory: vs. 8 with Galatians 2:20; I Corinthians 15:57; I John 5:4,5

3. In seeking his power: vs. 9 with Acts 1:8,12; 2:1-4. Every Christian has a common portion of the Holy Spirit (Romans 8:9; I Corinthians 3:16,17), but few seem to have the fullness of the Spirit (Ephesians 5:18b).

4. In seeking his glory: vss. 11,12 with Romans 6:5,11; II Peter 1:16,17

5. In receiving his mantle: vs. 13 with John 14:16,17

6. In receiving his victory: vs. 14 with Ephesians 3:20

7. In his likeness: vs. 15 with Romans 8:28,29; Acts 4:13

Types of the Believer's Experiences:

1. The translation of Elijah: 2:1-11. In preparation for Elisha to take over the ministry of Elijah, they made a journey from Gilgal via Bethel and Jericho to the Jordan River.

    a. Gilgal, a new start—a public confession: vs. 1. See GILGAL in Index.

    b. Bethel, the "place" of blessing—the place of God's choosing, the center of His will: vs. 2. Genesis 28:10-22; 35:1-15. Bethel means "house of God"—church-going (Hebrews 10:25). See THERE in Index.

    c. Jericho: vs. 4b. It was at Jericho that Israel exhibited her faith and God manifested His power (Joshua 6). The sons of the prophets had a "school of theology" at Jericho. Whenever one has Bible study, he has faith, and when he has faith, he has a manifestation of God's power (Romans 10:17; Hebrews 11:6)

    d. Jordan River—death to self but alive unto God—consecration: vs. 6 with Romans 6:11

If we go with the Lord through these stages, we go out into the world on resurrection territory with His power, with a "double portion of His Spirit," to glorify Him, and with the hope of our being raptured or translated (I Thessalonians 4:16-18; I John 3:1-3).

2. The Borrowed Axe, or losing one's power in service: 6:1-7. The truth presented in this portion of Scripture is this: a need for God's servants to get busy for the Lord, and to show us that it is possible for one to lose his power for the Lord, even while working for Him.

    a. All in the group were working together: vs. 2

    b. While working the axe-head fell off: vs. 5. This individual was not lazy or idle. He had a mind to work but no mind to watch the slowly slipping axe-head. We are to "watch and pray" (Matthew 26:41)

    c. He lost that which was not his: vs. 5. All the believer's power for service is borrowed, and he is accountable to God for its use

d. He was made helpless by his loss. God will judge His people when He sees that their power is gone (Deuteronomy 32:36)

e. He was painfully conscious of his loss—"Alas, master!" vs. 5. To whom else could he go? When the prodigal son realized he was stripped of everything, he went to the only one who could give him what he had lost. If only God's people today were painfully conscious of their loss or lack of power, and would return to their Master, the Lord

f. It was miraculously restored: vss. 6,7. See AXE-HEAD in Index.
  —He got it where he lost it. Jacob had his power restored when he went back to Bethel (Genesis 35:1-15). It was when the prodigal son went back home that he had his son-rights restored (Luke 15:2-24)
  —He got it back the only way possible—by obeying his master and reaching out for it

MIRACLES
OR
UNUSUAL EVENTS

1. Ahaziah's men consumed by fire—to rebuke Ahaziah's defiance of God's prophet: 1:9-12

2. The Jordan River divided—to permit passage of Elijah and Elisha in walking in obedience to the Lord and to encourage Elisha: 2:8,14

3. Chariot of fire taking Elijah to heaven—to show God's special regard for him: 2:11

4. Waters of Jericho made fit to drink—in answer to prayer: 2:19-22

5. Mocking children (young men) torn by bears—to rebuke their impudence: 2:24. See BALD-HEAD in Index.

6. Water provided for a large army—to show God's goodness: 3:16-20

7. Moabites mistake reflection of the red sunset on water for blood—to melt their hearts before the Israelites: 3:21-24

8. The widow's oil multiplied—to help her pay her debts: 4:1-7

9. The gift of the son to the Shunammite woman—to increase her faith and to assure her that Elisha was God's prophet: 4:14-17

10. The widow's son raised from the dead—as a reward for her regard for God's servant: 4:32-36

11. Poisonous pottage cured—to show God's power in supplying food for the sons of the prophets: 4:40,41

12. One hundred men fed with twenty loaves—to reveal God's goodness in supplying a need: 4:42-44

13. Naaman's leprosy healed—to show the wisdom of his faith: 5:10-14

14. Gehazi made leprous—as a punishment for selfishness: 5:24-27

15. Axe-head made to float (swim)—to teach the importance of keeping one's mind on his business: 6:6

16. Elisha's servant made to see the Lord's army—to strengthen his faith in God's power over the enemy: 6:13-17

17. Syrian band smitten with blindness and sight restored—to show the enemy the power of God's prophet: 6:18-20

18. Sore famine after Samaria was besieged (some mothers ate their own children!)—to show the awfulness of falling into the hands of the enemy: 6:24-29

19. The Syrian army put to flight—to deliver Samaria: 7:6,7

20. The preservation of the last member of the "seed royal"—to show God's hand in keeping Messiah's family line open: 11:1-3

21. Dead man revived by contact with Elisha's bones—to show God's power even through death: 13:20,21

22. Sennacherib's army destroyed—to deliver Jerusalem in answer to Hezekiah's prayer: 19:35

23. Hezekiah healed and his life prolonged fifteen years—to answer prayer and to show that God is the giver of life: 20:1-7

24. The sun made to go back—as proof of the prophet's word: 20:8-11. See LONG DAY in Index.

1. The Moabite Stone: 3:4,5. After Samaria became the capital of the Northern Kingdom, King Omri made Mesha, king of Moab, pay tribute to him. Part of the tribute was sheep's wool. According to the critics of God's Word, Mesha was a fictitious character, and Moab was too barren to graze sheep. In 1886 in Diban (of Moab), a stone was found which gave evidence from secular history that the Bible account was in fact correct. The inscription was on a block of stone four feet high, about two feet wide and about a foot thick. Part of the record says: "I, Mesha, king of Moab, made this monument to Chemosh [god of Moab] to commemorate my deliverance from Israel. . . . Omri, king of Israel, oppressed Moab, and his son [Ahab] after him. I warred against their cities, devoted the spoil to Chemosh, and in Beth-diblathaim sheep raisers I placed."

Moabite Stone

King Jehu and Shalmaneser

High Place of Amaziah—Petra

2. Jehu's tribute to Shalmaneser III. Archaeological discoveries ofttimes give additional information on Old Testament activities not found in the Bible. An inscribed object of Shalmaneser's, called the "Black Obelisk," was found in the ruins of his palace at Calah (Nimrud). It pictures officials of five different nations paying tribute to this monarch of Assyria, one of whom is Israel's King Jehu (9,10). The inscription reads in part: "Tribute of Jehu, son [or descendent] of Omri, gold, silver, golden goblets and pitchers, golden vases and vessels, scepters from the hand of the king, javelins I received from him." The obelisk, six feet high, bears the only contemporary likeness that has ever been found of any of Israel's kings. The picture shows King Jehu in a bowed position before Shalmaneser. Jehu's officers are behind him with tribute money.

3. This high place in the mountains of Seir is probably the site from which King Amaziah had 10,000 Edomites slain by forcing them to march over the cliff and fall to their deaths (14:1-7). Petra was known as "Selah" then, the land of the Edomites. See EDOM'S Pride in Index. Archaeological evidence found on top shows ruins of houses and buildings which existed during and prior to this time of Amaziah.

4. Tiglath-pileser: 15:19,20; I Chronicles 5:29. God stirred this pagan king's heart to come up against His people. In his palace archaeologists found his royal annals, in which he made a number of references to Old Testament characters, naming Azariah of Judah and Menahem of Samaria who paid him tribute. He said he replaced Pekah with Hoshea on the throne of Israel during his campaign in Palestine in 732 B.C. Menahem had to pay 50 shekels of silver as tribute for each man. Why 50 shekels? Discovered in the Assyrian city of Nimrud were clay tablets which reveal that this was the current price of an able-bodied slave at that time. Tiglath-pileser was also known as "Pul." He is pictured, p. 179.

5. King Jotham's Seal: 15:32-38. The official "seal" of this king was found when the Red Sea port city of Ezion-geber was excavated. It is the only seal yet discovered of Judah's kings. His seal, along with the discovery of one "Shema, servant of Jeroboam," bears the figure of a lion, the symbol of Judah. Christ is referred to as the "Lion of the tribe of Judah" (Revelation 5:5). The seal of Eliakim, steward of Jerhoiachin, has been found, along with the seal of Gedaliah, ruler of those who remained in the land after the Babylonian captivity (25:22-26). Seals are also known as "signets." See LACHISH and SEAL in Index.

6. Assyrian Pass. North of Beirut, Lebanon, at a place called "Dog River," which river empties into the Mediterranean Sea, is an ancient pass over which the Assyrian armies marched as they crossed the Lebanon mountains to besiege Samaria. At the top of this pass are carved the monuments of two of Assyria's kings, Shalmanesser and Esarhaddon (17:3; 18:9; 19:37). Records beside the monuments list their exploits. This discovery assures the believer that the critic's claim to their being fictitious characters is false.

7. The lions at Samaria: 17:24-30. After the Northern Kingdom was taken into captivity, the King of Assyria repeopled the land with those from Babylon, Cuthah, and from Ava, et. Ancient records show that Assyrian and Chaldean kings, along with the people of Cuthah (which was a province of Babylon), worshiped "Nergal," the god of pestilence and disease. This god was symbolized as a devouring lion. Because these people did not fear the Lord God of Israel, He sent lions among them, which slew some of them. It is interesting to see here the true God in control of the beast which symbolized the god of the new inhabitants of God's land.

8. Hezekiah's tribute to Sennacherib: 18:13-16. When Sennacherib invaded the Southern Kingdom, he conquered many cities, one of which was Lachish. Hezekiah was forced to send tribute by his officers. An inscription found in Sennacherib's palace states that Hezekiah paid him 30 talents of gold and 800 silver talents. This record contradicted the account in the Bible, which states that Hezekiah paid 300 talents of silver and 30 talents of gold. Of course the critics of the Bible had a field day—until another record was unearthed which listed Assyrian weights

King Jotham's Seal

Tribute to Sennacherib

and measurements. It was learned that it took 800 Assyrian talents of silver to equal 300 Hebrew talents of silver. Archaeology thus confirmed another passage of Scripture.

9. Sometimes names mentioned in the Bible are meaningless to us. Such names as Tartan, Rabsaris, and Rabshakeh are totally foreign to us. Some discoveries in ancient Assyrian cities reveal these to be offficial titles: Tartan is Commander in Chief; Rabsaris is Chief Eunuch; and Rabshakeh is Chief of the Princes. Such discoveries show that the Bible authors were in direct contact with these Assyrian people, for the Assyrians disappeared as a people in 605 B.C., never to be known again.

10. The Sennacherib prism. This prism (clay inscription) lists the deeds and exploits of this

Assyrian king. He recalls his besieging Jerusalem, and says of King Hezekiah: " As for Hezekiah, the Jew, who did not submit to my yoke, forty-six of his strong walled cities . . . I besieged and took. . . . himself [Hezekiah] like a caged bird I shut up in his city Jerusalem and earthworks I threw against him; the one coming out of the city [Hezekiah's messenger] I turned back to his own misery." No actual claim is made to his capturing Jerusalem itself, implying that he withdrew without successfully defeating Hezekiah. This certainly lends support to the Bible claim that God did deliver the royal city of Jerusalem in answer to prayer (chs. 18, 19). While Sennacherib was careful to give details of his battles and victories, such as the siege of Jerusalem, and receiving tribute after defeating Lachish, he was even more careful to "leave out" anything that might spell "defeat." Ancient monarchs seldom, if ever, recorded their defeats.

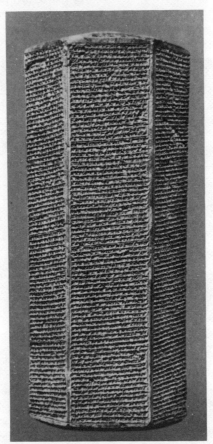

Sennacherib's Prism

11. Hezekiah's conduit: 20:20. One of the greatest engineering feats ever accomplished in Old Testament days was the conduit Hezekiah's men dug beneath the city of Jerusalem from the Spring of Gihon to the Pool of Siloam. Jerusalem depended upon this spring and other wells outside the city wall for their water supply. When cities were besieged, city gates were closed, and many times surrender resulted because of lack of food and water. Hezekiah hit upon the idea that if a tunnel could be dug beneath the city from the Spring of Gihon, he could build a pool inside the city and have water anytime. The diagram shows how he did it. After drawing his plans, he put a group of pickmen (or stone cutters) at the spring, another group where he was going to locate the Pool of Siloam, and said (in effect), "Start digging, and you will meet at the spot marked X."

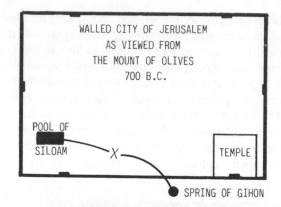

Hezekiah's Conduit Plans

Spring of Gihon

An inscription found at the Siloam end of the tunnel reads as follows: "This is the story [history] of the excavation. While workmen still lifting up their axe [pick], each toward his neighbors, and while three cubits [4 ½ '] remain [to cut through], each heard voices calling one to another. On the day the workmen struck, axe against axe, to meet his neighbors, waters flowed from the [Gihon] Spring to the [Siloam] Pool a thousand and two hundred cubits

Where Pickmen Met

[1800′]; and a hundred cubits [150′] the height over the heads of the workmen.'' Entering the conduit at the Spring of Gihon, one notices the pick marks are in the direction he is moving. At the "spot marked X," it can be seen where the two groups of pickmen met, and from there on out toward the Pool of Siloam, the pick marks are in the opposite direction. The tunnel is about two feet wide and a little over six feet high. Shown is where the pickmen met.

12. Manasseh's captivity by Eserhaddon: 21:1-16. Manasseh became the worst of all the kings of both kingdoms. It was during his reign that the "captains of the host of the king of Assyria" put him in chains and carried him to Babylon (II Chronicles 33:9-11). It is implied that Sennacherib's son, Esarhaddon, was the king who captured Manasseh (19:37). Eserhaddon's own record makes certain he *was* the king. He mentions Manasseh as follows: "I summoned the kings of the Hittite-land [Syria] and [those] across the sea, . . . Ba'lu, king of Tyre, Manasseh, king of Judah, Kaushgabri, king of Edom,ʹ . . . I gave them orders." Critics of the Bible questioned Babylon as the site of Manasseh's captivity because Sennacherib had utterly destroyed this city during his reign. But archaeological records show Esarhaddon rebuilt it.

13. Important texts of the seventh and sixth centuries, B.C., called the "Chaldean Chronicles" were published by D. J. Wiseman in 1956. They provided an explanation for an account by Daniel (1:1) in which he mentions the first of Nebuchadnezzar's attacks on Jerusalem. These Chronicles also reveal a hitherto unknown victory of the Egyptians over the Babylonians in 601 B.C., which may explain why Judah refused to pay tribute to Babylon (II Kings 24:1),

and turned to Egypt in spite of Jeremiah's warning.

14. Secret wall passage: 25:4. See SECRET in Index.

15. King Zedekiah blinded: 25:7. Babylonian and Assyrian torture of their prisoners was most brutal. These heathen kings were murderous tyrants, and punishment inflicted was atrocious. Some were skinned alive, patches of skin flayed from their bodies until they died, and some would have a long pole jammed into their stomachs, some lifted aloft on a high pole and squirmed in agony until they died, some had their ears sliced off, tongues yanked out by the roots, hands and legs and sex organs cut off. Pregnant women had their stomachs ripped open with a sword. King Sargon delighted in having captured prisoners (including women and children) led in review before him on his palace porch while his soldiers cut off their heads, had the heads counted by scribes as they were piled in a heap, and then hung on tree limbs in his garden. One king said: ''Their cities I destroyed and turned them into heaps; the young men and maidens I burned them with fire.''

Impaling Prisoners

Decapitating Prisoners

Counting Heads

Blinding a Prisoner, Hooks in Jaws, Bound Feet

When prisoners were captured, their ankles were bound with ropes or chains, forcing them to take short steps. A hook, tied to a leash, was put in their jaw or tongue. In a forced march to the land of the conqueror, prisoners had to keep pace. If they could not, a yank of the leash would often tear out the tongue by its roots, or rip their jaws. Such is mentioned in connection with Manasseh's capture (II Chronicles 33:11 RSV). After the forced march ended in captivity, a dignitary such as King Zedekiah was forced to kneel in the presence of the victorious monarch. With a hook in his jaw, tongue, or nose, he was commanded to look up at his conqueror. If he failed to look up, a yank was given on the leash, forcing the defeated king to look up, and at that moment a sharp spear literally "poked" out the eyes of the prisoner. This is what King Nebuchadnezzar did to Zedekiah (II Kings 25:6,7). God had prophesied that "hooks" would be a form of punishment for Israel in captivity (19:28; Isaiah 37:29; Ezekiel 29:4; Amos 4:2). The picture shows Sargon blinding a prisoner. Notice hooks in their jaws and tongues, with feet bound.

16. Babylonian Chronicle and King Jehoiachin: 25:27-30. The "Babylonian Chronicle" for 605-594 B.C. is a clay tablet which describes the battle of Charchemish (II Chronicles 35:20) and also mentions the coronation of Nebuchadnezzar, the removal of Jehoiachin and others to Babylonian exile, and lists their rations. It states that Zedekiah was enthroned in King Jehoiachin's place (24:17), and gives March 16, 579 B.C. as the date for Jerusalem's capture in Nebuchadnezzar's first siege.

Babylonian Chronicle

LIGHT FROM BIBLICAL CUSTOMS

[1] 1. **Go up, thou bald head: 2:23,24.** It is not a serious offense to tease a Westerner about being bald-headed. But when one reads the account of Elisha being called one, and the judgment which befell those who labeled him as one, the question is asked: "Why is such punishment meted out to these 'little children'?"

First, Elisha was on his way to Bethel (house of God), which was the place of worship. Second, to call one "bald-headed" in the East is the same as saying that "he is empty-headed," "he has no brains," or "he is stupid." It is the same as calling one a "fool" (Matthew 5:22). These people were as much as saying Elisha was a fool for going up to Bethel to worship God. Third, the "little children" were not what the expression implies, any more than John's expression, "my little children," means youngsters (I John 2:1) The term "little children" usually refers to those younger than the speaker. These "children" were full grown men (young, but full grown). In the East children would not be permitted to roam the forests from the protective care of their parents, nor was one taught to show contempt or disrespect for their elders. They were taught to "honor" their parents and all elders. Punishment ensued when such rebellion was evident.

The men (not little children) who mocked Elisha knew better, and it was for the reason of their training to respect the man of God that old Elisha "cursed [reprimanded] them in the name of the Lord." With this curse, two she-bears came forth out of the woods and "tare forty-two of the children." "Tare" means "to scare." We would probably say: "they were torn up," or "scared to death."

2. Slingers: 3:25. "Slingers" were soldiers whose ammunition was sling stones, weighing about three-quarters of a pound each and two inches in diameter (not to be confused with the "smooth" stones David picked up at the brook to fight against Goliath). Spears were carried by "spearmen" (Psalm 68:30), and "archers" or "bowmen" used bows and arrows (Genesis 49:23; Jeremiah 4:29). See PICTURES, p. 303.

3. Salute no man: 4:29. "Saluting" in the Near East is an act of courtesy. It involves more than a casual "howdy do" and a handshake. It involves falling on one's neck and kissing both cheeks (like the prodigal son's father), extending greetings of peace and friendship and esteem, of enquiring of one's family, which includes wife, each child, sons-in-law and daughters-in-law, grandparents, and uncles and aunts. It is a very time consuming event. With the immediate need for Elisha to know if the widow's son were dead, it is no wonder he told his servant to "salute no man," nor answer if any man saluted him. Because of the urgency to quickly get out Christ's message, He instructed the seventy to "salute no man by the way" (Luke 10:4).

4. A lord (officer) on whose hand (arm) the king leaned: 7:2. Safety belts in our automobiles are not new—chariots were equipped with them centuries ago! The king's chariot was occupied by three men: the driver of the horses, the king himself, and a third man—the "strap-hanger"—an officer whose duty it was to protect the life of the king. Stationed directly back of the king, he held on to a strap. Should the horses suddenly bolt or start up too rapidly and throw the king backward, his "leaning on the hand (or arm) of this officer" would keep him from being thrown out and trampled by oncoming horses and chariots.

"Strap-Hanger"

5. Beds and bedchambers: 11:2. In the East a bed is not a piece of furniture, but a mat. Whole families sleep on their individual mats in a single room. In the morning they are rolled up and stored in the "bedchamber." It was among such "beds" that the surviving member of the royal family, Joash, was hidden from wicked Queen Athaliah. Many times people would carry their "bed" with them from place to place. The man whom Christ healed was told to "arise, take up thy bed, and go into thine house" (Matthew 9:6). When Jacob took "stones for pillows" to lay down in that place to sleep, he simply arranged stones from the rocky soil so that he could spread out his "bed" (mat) and sleep (Genesis 28:11). When Haman fell upon the "bed" where Esther was, he simply "sat" on the same mat with Esther (Esther 7:8). It was upon "beds" such as this that the "saints" had a singspiration (Psalm 149:5). The man who said, "trouble me not; . . . my children are with me in bed; I cannot rise and give thee bread," refused to disturb the sleeping family on their "beds" in the room with him. To have answered the door he would have had to wake some and make them move (Luke 11:7).

The floating (or swimming) axe-head: 6:6. Webster defines a miracle as "an act or happening attributed to a supernatural power." Someone else has said it is "an act of the infinite within the sphere of His laws—natural to Him—but supernatural to the finite." Critics of the Bible who do not accept miracles, do, of course, ridicule the floating of an iron axe-head. Yet man himself can make an iron ship weighing tens of thousands of tons to float. A sewing needle, if balanced properly by anyone, will float on top of water in a glass. What is so unusual about God making a two-pound axe-head float?

Second Kings in the New Testament:
1. Fire from heaven: 1:10-12 with Luke 9:54
2. Cleansing of Naaman: 5:14 with Luke 4:27
3. Companion references:
   a. Not saluting others: 4:29 with Luke 10:4
   b. Restoring life: 4:34 with Acts 20:10
   c. Feeding bread to many: 4:42 with Luke 9:12-16
   d. Kindness toward enemies: 6:22 with Luke 6:27,28; Romans 12:20

1. The Prophet Elijah and John the Baptist—
   a. Their looks: 1:3,8 with Matthew 3:1-4
   b. Their preaching: I Kings 18:17-22 with Matthew 3:7-12
   c. Their work—one and the same: Malachi 4:5,6 with Matthew 11:10,11,14. See also Malachi 3:1 with Luke 1:13,17,76,77. John's work was concluded when he was beheaded. Elijah was translated and will complete the work: Matthew 17:10; Revelation 11:3-12

2. Naaman the Leper: 5:1-15
   a. Brought the *wrong* price for his healing: vs. 5. The gifts of God cannot be bought: Acts 8:17-24. I Peter 1:18,19
   b. Went to the *wrong* person: vss. 3,4,6. The Pharisees had Abraham: John 8:33,39. Christ *is* the right person: John 14:6
   c. Went to the *wrong* place—the door: vs. 9. He was *almost* there, but not altogether: Acts 26:27-29

    d. Had the *wrong* perception: vs. 11. God's invitation is to "come," not "I *thought* he would come to me." See Isaiah 55:1,8,9

    e. Had the *wrong* potion—not rivers of Damascus, but the Jordan River: vss. 10,12

    f. Had the *wrong* pose—he went away in a rage: vs. 12b

    g. But he finally followed the *right* prescription: vss. 14,15

In contrast, notice the Rich Young Ruler: Luke 18:18-23

    a. He went to the *right* person: vs. 18

    b. He went in the *right* spirit—kneeling: Mark 10:17

    c. He asked the *right* question: vs. 18

    d. He got the *right* answer: vs. 22

    e. But he did the *wrong* thing: vs. 23 with Mark 10:22

3. The Brazen Serpent: 18:4. This serpent had been used by God to bring healing to the Israelites (see SERPENT in Index). It has now become an object of worship in connection with Israel's worship of Baal. Just as the Canaanites worshiped snakes, so Israel is now burning incense to this object. With the great revival under King Hezekiah, it was utterly destroyed. See Exodus 20:3-5.

4. Hezekiah's Faithfulness Rewarded: 18:1-7

    a. He did right in the sight of the Lord: vs. 3

    b. He took a stand against sin: vs. 4

    c. He persevered in the way of the Lord: vs. 6a

    d. He kept God's commandments: vs. 6b

    e. He was rewarded with—

    —God's presence: vs. 7a

    —Prosperity: vs. 7b

    —The greatest testimony of all kings: vs. 5

5. Hezekiah's Prolonged Life and Manasseh's Wickedness: 20:1-11 and 21:1-9,16. Hezekiah was twenty-five years old when he began to reign, and he reigned for twenty-nine years (18:1,2). At the age of thirty-nine he was told by Isaiah that he was going to die. As a result of his prayer, God extended his life fifteen years. It was during these last fifteen years of his life that his son Manasseh was born. At the death of his father, Manasseh began to reign at the age of twelve. His was the most wicked reign of all the southern kings. Though he later repented of his sins and sought to clean up the land (II Chronicles 33:11-16), Judah never fully recovered from his wickedness. No one will ever know what would have happened if Hitler had won World War II. Neither will one ever know what Judah would have done if Hezekiah had not lived an extra fifteen years, in which time Manasseh was born. We need to make sure we pray *in* the will of God (I John 5:14 with Psalm 106:15).

6. Hezekiah's Folly: 20:12-18. Prosperity often brings a Christian to shame. In spite of all that God did for Solomon, love for riches turned the king's heart from serving the Lord. Hezekiah had just experienced a wonderful miracle in having his life prolonged. But when God tested him by permitting heathen Babylonians to visit Jerusalem (II Chronicles 32:31), Hezekiah showed them all *his* wealth, but uttered not a word of testimony concerning the true God or of His goodness. Just as Shishak of Egypt "took all" from Rehoboam when he failed to follow the Lord (II Chronicles 12:1,9), so Isaiah prophesied that "nothing shall be left" when the Babylonians conquer Jerusalem and take the Israelites captive (vss. 17,18).

7. First and II Kings Contrasted:

I KINGS BEGINS WITH	II KINGS ENDS WITH
a. Victories by King David	a. Defeat by Nebuchadnezzar
b. Solomon's glory	b. Jehoiachin's shame
c. Obedience	c. Disobedience
d. Temple built	d. Temple destroyed

e. Backsliding begun
f. Kings forsaking God
g. God's patience manifested

e. Failure consummated
f. God forsaking kings
g. No remedy against captivity

A BIT OF HEAVENLY MANNA

In the "Purpose" of this Book we are encouraged to look to the Holy Spirit to guide us and keep us in the Truth. This can be done only as we, with old Elisha, pray for a double portion of God's Holy Spirit. Before Elijah departed from this earth, he sensed the need of power in the life of Elisha. So he, in the language of today, said, "What will you have, Elisha, before I go home to be with the Lord?" He stood in need of and asked for the very same thing Christ knew His followers would need when He was caught up to be with the Lord of hosts after His resurrection, namely, the Holy Spirit and the power of the Spirit (Luke 24:46-49). Elisha wanted and needed this double portion. So did Peter, James, and John and all the rest of the 120 in the upper room. They received the Spirit and His power. And with this thought in mind, may we ask for this need, and rely upon the Holy Spirit to guide us into all Truth and keep it in us (John 16:13; 14:26).

UPHOLD ME WITH THY FREE SPIRIT—Psalm 51:12[2]

"The Holy Spirit always works freely, and leads the soul into freedom. As Jesus did all this without us, The Holy Spirit does all within us. We need His constant presence, power, and grace. Except He uphold us, we shall certainly fall. David had fallen. He deeply felt his weakness, and therefore prayed to be upheld by God's free Spirit. Let this be our daily prayer. It will never be unsuitable. We should have failed Him before this, if God had not kept us; and we may fall any day, except we are upheld by His invisible arm. This day Satan may lay some snare before us, this day our evil hearts may deceive us, this day the world may lay some unexpected bait for us; and if so, unless the Holy Spirit opens our eyes, gives us fresh supplies of grace, or holds us back by an ivisible power, we shall disgrace our profession, dishonor God, and wound our consciences. Remember Christians, we are deeply indebted to the Holy Spirit for our preservation. Realize today *your* obligation and dependence, and while you do so, seek the constant teaching, guiding, and keeping of the blessed Comforter."

PRAYER THOUGHT: "Dear Lord, I ask Thee to endow me with vigor of body, alertness of mind, and strength of Thy Spirit to give Thee the loyal obedience that Thou dost demand of me. In the name of the One Who always pleased Thee. Amen."[3]

II Kings 5:14; Colossians 1:11,12

First Chronicles—The Book of David's Reign

Name: The word "chronicle" means a historical record chronologically arranged. The events of the children of Israel recorded in the Chronicles are in order.

Contents: "The Chronicles give a larger account of the kingdom of Judah and the kings thereof, than what is given in the preceding books; and particularly, they ascertain the genealogy of Christ that it might be clear and plain of what tribe and family Messiah would come, that He descended from the tribe of Judah, and from the kings of the house of David.''[1] First and II Kings give a parallel account of the two kingdoms and the Chronicles confine themselves mainly to the Southern Kingdom. The Chronicles serve as a good commentary of much that is recorded in the books of Samuel and Kings. There is much recorded in the Chronicles which is omitted in the other historical books—another instance in which the *Law of Recurrence* appears (see LAW in Index).

First and II Kings record God's dealings with Israel from the *throne;* the two Chronicles from the *sanctuary.*

BOOKS OF SAMUEL AND KINGS	BOOKS OF THE CHRONICLES
Royal	Religious
Kingly	Priestly
Throne	Temple
Political	Ecclesiastical
Human standpoint	Divine standpoint
As man ruled history	As God overruled history

First and II Chronicles have been called the "Acts" of the Old Testament. The first book has 29 chapters, 941 verses, and 20,369 words.

Character: Historical.

Subject: God's mercy and grace toward men as His co-rulers, from Adam to David's enthronement, and the preparation of the Temple and Temple worship.

Purpose: To refresh the minds of the new generation returning from Babylonian captivity of the genealogy of David and his greater Son, the promised King, and to foreshadow the preparation of the Temple in the making—a building "fitly framed together" for a habitation of God (Ephesians 2:19-22).

Outline:[2]
- I. Genealogical Tablets: 1—10
    - A. Primeval Period—Adam to Abraham: 1:1-27
    - B. Patriarchal Period—Abraham to Jacob: 1:27—2:2
    - C. Israelitish Period—Jacob to Saul: 2:3—10:14
- II. History of David's Reign: 11—29
    - A. Prominent Events in David's Life: 11—22
    - B. Divisions of the People (six): 23—27
    - C. David's Farewell Addresses (three): 28,29

Scope: Events in this book cover a period of about forty years.

Writer: Ezra is the likely author or compiler of this book. Information is drawn from many sources: the chronicles of David (27:24); Samuel the seer, Nathan the prophet, Gad the seer (29:29); the prophecy of Ahijah, visions of Iddo the seer (II Chronicles 9:29); the story of the book of Israel's kings (II Chronicles 20:34); and the book of the kings of Judah (II Chronicles 32:32).

When Written: Probably during or shortly after the captivity.

Key Chapter: 1. David becomes king.

Key Verse: 15:2. From this verse it would seem the motto of David was: "Doing a right thing in a right way.''

Key Word: Reigned.

Key Phrase: Build thee an house: 29:16.

Key Thought: Reign with David. Link with our reign: Revelation 1:5,6; 5:10.

Spiritual Thought: Keep the Royal line.

Christ Is Seen As: King of kings and Lord of lords.

Names and Titles of God: Our Father: 29:10. See NAME in Dictionary.

First Chronicles in the New Testament:
1. Christ's genealogy: 2:4-6; 3:10-16 with Matthew 1:3,7-12
2. David's throne: 17:14 with Luke 1:33
3. Aaronic priesthood: 23:13 with Hebrews 5:4
4. Companion references:
   a. Giving willingly: 29:9 with II Corinthians 9:7
   b. God's excellency: 29:11 with Romans 11:36; I Timothy 1:17; Revelation 4:11; 5:13

1. Temples of God. While the "God that made the world and all things therein . . . dwelleth not in temples made with hands" (Acts 17:24), yet it pleased Him to reveal His glory and honor His name through temples which were made with hands. Note the following:

    a. The Tabernacle (tent) was God's dwelling-place in the wilderness and in Canaan for about 400 years: Exodus 25:8—40:38; Joshua 18:1

b. Solomon's Temple in all its splendor, yet plundered five years after his death and was later used to worship Baal: II Chronicles 5:1; 12:2,9; 3:1-9. See TEMPLE in Index. Pictured is the Temple site as seen today

c. Synagogues. These had their beginnings in homes when Israel was in captivity, and were used for local meetings of worship

d. Zerubbabel's Temple, built after Israel's return from captivity.

e. Herod's Temple, which replaced Zerubbabel's, and was the Temple of Christ's day. It was destroyed by Titus in A.D. 70

Temple Site

    f. Christ's body—a body prepared by God that Christ might "tabernacle" among us: John 1:14; 2:19-21; Hebrews 10:5

    g. The Church—collectively—God's dwelling place, made up of living stones fitly framed together: Ephesians 2:19-22; I Peter 2:5. Just as the stones for Solomon's Temple were cut and fitted for the Temple first, and then brought to the Temple area and placed together in the construction of this building, so the individual is saved and made fit by Christ's finished work at Calvary. He is then placed in the body of Christ by the Spirit (I Corinthians 12:13).

    h. The believer's body: I Corinthians 3:16,17 (see BODY in Index). In Solomon's Temple the gates were to be opened every morning for the service of God (9:23,27). In the believer's body, which is *now* the Temple of God, there are four "gates" which are to remain open for the service of God:

    —Mouth: Psalm 51:15; 119:131; Isaiah 50:4a
    —Ears: Isaiah 50:4b,5
    —Eyes: Psalm 119:18
    —Heart: Acts 16:14

    i. The heavenly tabernacle. The Old Testament tabernacle was a type or pattern of a more perfect tabernacle or temple: Hebrews 9:11,24; Revelation 11:19. John interprets the heavenly temple to be God the Father and Christ His Son: Revelation 21:22

  2. The "Musts" of Thanksgiving: 16:1-36. David's "psalm of thanksgiving" came after the Ark of God had found its rightful place (see "Key Verse"). Thankfulness is sure to come from us when God has His rightful place in our lives. For thankfulness:

    a. We must give to God—
    —Our song: vs. 9a
    —Our talk: vs. 9b with Malachi 3:16,17
    —Glory due His name: vs. 29

    b. We must seek the Lord—
    —For strength: vs. 11a
    —For continued fellowship: vs. 11b

    c. We must remember the Lord—
    —His works: vs. 12a
    —His wonders: vs. 12b
    —His judgments: vs. 12c
    —His covenant (faithfulness): vs. 15

    d. We must witness for the Lord—
    —In showing forth His salvation: vs. 23
    —In declaring His glory among the heathen: vs. 24

    e. RESULT: We *do* give thanks: vs. 8,34 with I Thessalonians 5:18

  3. David's Sin in Numbering the People: 21:1-17. It is not explained just how the numbering of the people by David became a sin. Perhaps Satan's temptation was due to David's pride, or self-centeredness in his refusal to heed his captain's warning (vs. 4). One thing stands out in this sin, even though David repented and offered sacrifices; a person cannot sin without the sin affecting others (vss. 7,14,17). Adam's sin not only affected himself, but the whole human race as well. Achan's sin brought judgment upon all Israel (Joshua 7:1-25), as did Rehoboam's (II Chronicles 12:1-10) and Hezekiah's (II Kings 20:12-19).

First Chronicles records the providence of God in delivering Israel from bondage to the reign of King David. The book also records the story of the preparation of the Temple and its worship. Through hardships, trials, wars, conquests, ups and downs, God had brought them to a permanent place of worship and is now using David in one of his final addresses to point out the goodness of the Lord to

Israel. Solomon, who is about to sit upon the throne, hears David say to the whole congregation—

NOW BLESS THE LORD YOUR GOD—29:20[3]

"Nothing is more reasonable than to bless the Lord your God, yet few things are more neglected by us. Our God daily loadeth us with His benefits, but how seldom do we honestly, heartily, and gratefully bless His name? Our lives should be vocal with His praise. Even self-interest ought to lead us to praise God, for He has said, 'He that offereth praise glorifieth Me; and to him that ordereth his conversation aright, will I show the salvation of God.' The grateful shall see God's plan, understand the Savior's work, and enjoy the Lord's delivering mercy in every time of need. A grateful man may have everything from God. Now, then, let us bless the Lord our God; for His mercies are so numerous, His favors are so great, our privileges so valuable, our prospects so bright, and our obligations so numerous. Every sin has been pardoned, every blessing promised, every real evil prevented, and heaven is at the end of our course! O let us bless the Lord *now*. If we fail to praise Him, we may expect the very stones to cry out (Luke 19:37-40)."

PRAYER THOUGHT: "O Lord, help me to see that victory in life's conflicts is impossible without prayer—that good soldiers of the Lord do their best when they 'cry unto God in battle.' May I constantly use the *whole* armor of God in resisting the devil. In the name of our victorious Savior I pray. Amen."[4]

I Chronicles 5:20

Second Chronicles—The Book of Israel's Final Apostasy

Name: See NAME in I Chronicles.

Connection with Preceding Book: This book is a sequel to I Chronicles and a supplement to I and II Kings (see CONTENTS in I Chronicles).

Contents: This book opens with the ascension of Solomon to David's throne and his ascension to glory and wisdom. The only mention in this book to the Northern Kingdom is the division of the United Kingdom and its first king, Jeroboam (ch. 11 with I Kings 12:16-24). The rest contains a narrative of the kings of the Southern Kingdom of Judah who reigned in succession, until Babylonian captivity, and concludes with an intimation of Cyrus' degree for the restoration of the Jews and the rebuilding of the Temple. This book has 36 chapters, 822 verses, and 26,074 words.

Character: Historical.

Subject: God's gracious and righteous dealings with the rule of David's house from the building of the Temple by Solomon until it was destroyed by Nebuchadnezzar.

Purpose: To teach us that our Lord and Savior is just as loving and faithful and merciful in chastising His children as He is in blessing them (Hebrews 12:6-13; Psalm 119:75; Ephesians 1:3). In this we see that His love makes holiness merciful, and His holiness makes His love unchangeable.

Outline:

    I. The Reign of Solomon: 1—9
        A. The Worship of Solomon: 1

Scope: Second Chronicles covers a period of about 450 years.

Writer: See WRITER in I Chronicles.

Key Chapter: 7. Promises and conditions for Divine blessings.

Key Verses: 15:2; 20:20.

Key Word: Established.

Key Phrase: "Prepareth his heart to seek God:" 30:18b,19.

Key Thought: History of the Southern Kingdom of Judah.

Spiritual Thought: Honor the king.

Christ Is Seen As: King of kings and Lord of lords.

Names and Titles of God: Captain: 13:12. See NAME in Dictionary.

Names and Titles of the Holy Spirit: The Spirit of the Lord: 20:14. See NAME in Dictionary.

Prophecies: Before Elijah's translation, he prophesied that King Jehoram, Jehoshaphat's son, would die because of disobedience: 21:12-20.

Miracles or Unusual Events: King Uzziah smitten with leprosy—to show God's displeasure for his usurping the priest's function: 26:16-21.

1. Shishak, king of Egypt: 12:1-9. After the kingdom was divided into the Northern Kingdom of Israel and the Southern Kingdom of Judah, Judah, under Rehoboam, was the weaker with just two Tribes. Shishak, king of Egypt, knew of this weakness and sent his troops to "sniff" at Judah's borders. Having taken several of her cities, he plundered Jerusalem and took away the treasures of the Temple and the king's palace.

Upon his victorious return to Egypt from Jerusalem, Shishak (or Sheshonk I) erected a temple to his god Amon (Amun). Inscribed on a wall of this temple is a list of walled cities of Judah which he captured, with images of Israelite prisoners taken back to Egypt with him to become slaves. His gold-masked mummy was found in 1939 in a sarcophagus (burial vault) of silver encased in solid gold. This could have been made from some of the gold and silver he took from Jerusalem (vs. 9).

Shishak's invasion actually took place as a result of Rehoboam's having forsaken the Lord (vss. 1,2,5b). What a tragedy that Israel's sins have been on Shishak's "billboard" for the world to see all these centuries (since about 926 B.C.). Sin does *not* pay (Numbers 32:23; Galatians 6;7).

2. Engines of war: 26:15 with Ezekiel 26:9. See ENGINES in Index.

3. Lachish: 32:9. This city has had quite a stormy history. It was captured by Joshua when Israel possessed Canaan (Joshua 10:32). King Sennacherib of Assyria conquered it and made its officers pay tribute to him, as is revealed by a carving on his palace wall (II Kings 18:13-16). In excavations at Lachish, eighteen "Lachish letters" were found. These letters were messages written on pieces of pottery (or potsherds), and contain information of political and military

Shishak's Record

situations prior to the destruction of Jerusalem by Nebuchadnezzar. One letter refers to a messenger making a trip to Egypt for help. In a besieged city an unsuspecting citizen could smuggle out a message written on a piece of pottery. One letter was written by a royal officer, with a warning from a prophet (possibly Jeremiah). A seal was found: "To Gedaliah who is over the house" (probably Judah's last governor—Jeremiah 40:5). See SEAL in Index.

4. Manasseh's captivity by Esarhaddon: 33:9-11. See MANASSEH in Index.

5. Charchemish: 35:20; Jeremiah 46:2. This ancient Hittite city was important commercially and militarily. For years it paid tribute to Assyria. When it was conquered by Sargon ca. 717 B.C., the Hittite Empire fell (Isaiah 10:9). Because of its strategic location, the nation which controlled it had easy access to other countries. In a decisive battle in 605 B.C., Nebuchadnezzar of Babylon defeated Pharaoh Necho of Egypt, thus enabling Nebuchadnezzar to march against Jerusalem without fear of other nations. See CHRONICLE in Index, in which this battle is mentioned.

6. Nebuchadnezzar: 36:7,13,17. This was the man whom God brought against His people for having sinned (36:14-16). Many archaeological finds give evidence of this king's deeds and exploits. The Babylonian Chronicle (see Index) mentions his coronation. A cameo gives us this image of his face. Ruins of his palace and the hanging gardens have been unearthed at Babylon.

Nebuchadnezzar

LIGHT FROM
BIBLICAL
CUSTOMS

1. Covenant of Salt: 13:5. See SALT in Index.

2. Shields of gold and shields of brass (copper) 12:9,10; I Chronicles 18:7. Part of Shishak's bounty when he conquered Jerusalem were Solomon's shields of gold. One method of warfare in ancient days was for soldiers using such shields to position themselves on the battlefield so that the sun was between them and the enemy. When the enemy approached close enough, the gold shields were so moved by the arms of the soldiers as to reflect the light of the sun, casting a blinding beam of light in the eyes of the enemy. As the enemy would throw up their arms to cover their faces, and at the same time dropping their shields and spears, the soldiers with the gold shields would capture them with a minimum of effort. These shields of gold could stand for a testimony that shines and glows for the glory of the Lord. As our lives reflect the light of His countenance, we not only resist the devil that he flee from us, but we show Christ to others. Solomon had made 300 of these shields (I Kings 10:17), and each weighed 3 pounds. By today's standard (1982), each would be worth $19,200, or a total of $5,760,000!

When Rehoboam lost these shields of gold, he quickly substituted shields of brass (vs. 10). He tried to have something in "appearance" that would pass (from a distance) as gold, but there is *no* substitute for the real thing. We either have a testimony that shines and glows and glitters for the glory of God or we don't. A "shield of brass" stands for hypocrisy.

3. A great burning: 16:14. When King Asa died, his bed was filled with sweet odors and different kinds of spices, "and they made a very great burning for him." The burning of aromatic wood and spices (anise, cinnamon, etc.) denoted honor, while the lack of burning denoted a lack of respect and honor, such as in the case of disobedient Jehoram, who was not buried with the kings (21:18,19). In the case of several dignitaries, ordinary burial was denied, such as Jezebel, who was eaten by dogs (II Kings 9;10); Uzziah, who was buried in a field (26:23); and Jehoiakin, who was buried with the burial of an ass (Jeremiah 22:18,19).

Second Chronicles in the New Testament:

1. Veil of the Temple: 3:14 with Matthew 27:51
2. God no respector of persons: 19:7 with Romans 2:11
3. Slaying of Zachariah: 24:20-22 with Luke 11:49-51
4. Touching God's anointed: 36:15,16 with Matthew 23:34
5. Companion references:
   a. Humbling one's self: 12:6 with James 4:10
   b. Wars and rumors of wars: 15:5,6 with Matthew 24:6,7

c. Burial: 16:14 with John 19:39,40
d. Scattering the sheep: 18:16 with Matthew 9:36
e. Kindness toward enemies: 28:15 with Luke 6:27,28; Romans 12:20

1. Greatest Prescription for Revival: 7:14,15
   a. Humility: Matthew 18:4; James 4:10; I Peter 5:5
   b. Prayer: Luke 18:1; I Thessalonians 5:17
   c. Seeking God: Hosea 10:12; Acts 17:27; Isaiah 55:6
   d. Forsaking sin: Acts 8:22; Proverbs 28:13

When we are revived, we are then in a position not only to pray, but for God to hear and answer our prayers: vs. 15 with Psalm 66:18. See PRAYER in Index.

2. He Took All: 12:1-10. When one strengthens himself, forsakes the Law of the Lord, and walks in the energy of the flesh as did Rehoboam (vs. 1), the enemy (Shishak—Satan; vs. 2) will come in and strip us of everything—*"he took all"* (vs. 9). See LOSSES of a Christian in Sermon Index.

3. Asa's Prayer: 14:11. See PRAYER in Index.
   a. It was *sincere*—he cried
   b. It was *direct*—unto the Lord
   c. It was *to the point*—help us
   d. It was in *faith believing*—we rest in Thee
   e. It was *answered*: vss. 12-15

4. The Battle is God's—Lessons from Jehoshaphat: 20:1-30 (vs. 15b)
   a. He feared the enemy: vss. 1-3a (this is natural for all of us)
   b. He sought the Lord: vs. 3b (so do we when trouble comes)
   c. He proclaimed a fast: vs. 3c (we discuss our problems over a meal)
   d. **He led in prayer: vss. 4-12 (we "might" do this in an "all-day" prayer service that starts** at 11:00 a.m. and concludes at noon)
   e. He confessed his weakness and admitted his inability to cope with the situation: vs. 12a (unusual for one to do today)
   f. He looked to the Lord: vs. 12b (we do too, unless committees work it out for us)
   g. He was encouraged by God: vss. 14,15a (just like the Lord to do something like this!)
   h. He was informed that the battle was not his, but God's: vss. 15b,17b (praise the Lord! yet "can't we help a little, Lord?")
   i. He was instructed when to stand still and when to move: vs. 17a (if it's God's battle, we must obey orders, or else)
   j. He worshiped the Lord: vs. 18 (the reasonable thing to do)
   k. He praised the Lord: vss. 19-21 (and why not "praise God from whom all blessings flow"?)
   l. He believed God for victory before going out to meet the enemy: vs. 20 (good for Jehoshaphat—the victory that overcometh is our faith: I John 5:4)
   m. The enemy defeated themselves: vss. 22-24 (which goes to show that when the battle is God's, the enemy *is* a defeated foe)
   n. God's victory brings the spoils (blessings) of victory: vss. 25,30 (man could never know the blessing of salvation until Christ defeated the devil at Calvary. See vs. 17)
   o. God was thanked and blessed for victory: vss. 26-29 (which is the least anyone can do. "In everything give thanks": I Thessalonians 5:18)

5. Apostasy under Ahaz: 28:21-25. Ahaz made an alliance with the king of Assyria. Having compromised with this heathen nation, he soon worshiped their gods. His apostasy resulted in his:

a. Cutting in pieces the vessels of the house of the Lord—a picture of those who "cut up" the Word of God to suit themselves, and who so divide their allegiances that God gets only a portion of their lives, if any at all: vs. 24a with II Timothy 3:16,17; I Corinthians 6:19,20; Romans 12:1

b. Shutting up the doors of the house of the Lord—a picture of those whose lives become stumbling blocks, "shutting up" the way for the lost to come to Christ: vs. 24b with Hebrews 10:25

c. Putting out the lamps—a picture of our lights not shining to glorify our Father in heaven—our testimony gone: 29:7 with Matthew 5:16

d. Not burning incense—a picture of a prayerless life: 29:7 with I Timothy 2:1-3

e. Leading Israel in a general departing from the Lord—a picture of a falling away in these last days: 29:6 with II Timothy 3:1-7

6. Revival under Hezekiah: 29:1-11. When Hezekiah became king, he recognized the low spiritual state of the people:

a. He immediately did that which was right in the sight of the Lord—a picture of *personal* consecration: vs. 2; Proverbs 28:13

b. He opened the doors of the house of the Lord: vs. 3

c. He cleaned up the filthiness in the holy places: vs. 5

d. He made a covenant with the Lord: vs. 10

e. He recognized his responsibilities: vs. 11

The revival under Hezekiah came about by his being obedient to God's Word—which gives the greatest prescription for revival: 7:14.

7. Revival under Josiah: 34:1—35:11. After the death of Hezekiah, his son Manasseh reigned and made Judah to do worse than the Canaanites in the land (33:1-9). It fell to Josiah's lot to "clean up" Manasseh's sin.

a. The Lord was sought: vs. 3a

b. The land was purged from idolatry: vss. 3b-7

c. The ways of David were followed: vs. 2

d. The house of God was repaired: vs. 8b

e. The book (Word of God) was found: vs. 14

f. The book was read (honored): vss. 18:30

g. Josiah made a convenant: vss. 31,32

h. Judah served the Lord: vs. 33

i. The Passover was kept: 35:1-11

8. Speaking of *revival,* maybe the church could have a real old-fashioned one today—[2]

a. If all the sleeping folk would wake up,

b. And all the lukewarm folk would fire up,

c. And all the dishonest folk would confess up,

d. And all the disgruntled folk would sweeten up,

e. And all the discouraged folk would cheer up

f. And all the depressed folk would look up,

g. And all the estranged folk would make up,

h. And all the gossipers would shut up,

i. And all the dry bones would shake up,

j. And all the true soldiers would stand up,

k. And all the tightwads would pay up,

l. And all the church members would pray up—

m. Then your church would have a revival!

9. In this book we note that prevailing prayer brought about success and victory— a. In preserving Judah after the kingdom was divided: 11:16,17

b. In giving Judah victory over Israel: 13:12-16

c. In giving Asa victory over Zerah: 14:11,12
d. In the reform in the land under Asa: 15:12
e. In helping Jehoshaphat not to live like Israel: 17:3,4
f. In giving Judah victory over Moab: 20:4
g. In giving Uzziah prosperity: 26:5
h. In giving cleansing for the people: 30:18-20
i. In giving Hezekiah prosperity: 31:31
j. In defeating the Assyrians: 32:20-22
k. In Josiah's cleansing the land: 34:1-7

One of the "Key Verses" (15:2) in this Book seems to be the condition of God's presence, even for the believer today. The lack of a feeling of God's presence does not necessarily mean that one does not have salvation, but when the presence of God is not full because of sin, then like David, having lost the joy of God's salvation, we are of all creatures most miserable. Sin and the presence of God will not mix. So then, for God to be for us, and for God to be with us, we need to stay in fellowship with Him.

BEHOLD, GOD HIMSELF IS WITH US—13:12[3]

"So said Abijah of Judah, when he and his army went out to war against Jeroboam, and in the strength of this they conquered. Christians, the Lord will not only give His angels charge over us to keep us in all our ways, but He Himself is with us. Never lose sight of this precious truth, for it is at once most holy and comforting. If God Himself is with us, then every sin is committed in His presence, and under His eye. How this aggravates the guilt of all our sins. We think, we speak, we act just as though God were at an infinite distance from us, and that He pays little or no regard to what we say or do. Instead of this, no one is so near to us as God; no one is so attentive to us as He. If God Himself is with us, how unwise, how inconsistent are our fears! If God Himself is with us, will He allow us to want, or permit us to be injured? Can any enemy be too subtle, or too powerful for Him? Impossible! Behold, then, God Himself is with us! He will certainly be with us this day, in every place, during every moment. He will hear every word we speak, witness every sin we commit, and listen to every prayer we utter."

PRAYER THOUGHT: "Dear Father, help me not to give myself to lesser loyalties and spend more time and energies in secondary things, but to yield to the highest and best things of Thee. In Christ's name I pray. Amen."[4]

II Chronicles 20:10b

Reigns and Dates of the Kings

There are several problems in the chronology of the kings of Israel—both of the Northern and Southern Kingdoms.

1. The main one to be wrestled with is the method used in reckoning the date of the ascension of the king to the throne. One was the Accession or Post-dating method. This dictated

recording the reign on the first day of the following year. The other was the Non-accession or Ante-accession method. The king using the latter method recorded the date of his reign on the day of his accession. Evidence by Dr. Edwin R. Thiele seems to indicate that the scribes of Israel used the non-accession system from 931 B.C. to about 796/5 B.C., and the accession method from that date to the last king—Hoshea, 732 B.C. The scribes of Judah used the accession method from 931 B.C. to about 848 B.C., the non-accession system till about 796 B.C., and then the accession system to the last king—Zedekiah, 597 B.C.

2. The Jews employed two years in their calendar—the religious and civil. The kings of Israel began their reignal years in the spring with Nisan, while the kings of Judah began theirs in the fall with Tishri. The second problem arises in trying to determine which year the king used for dating his reign. Thiele has adopted the system of giving both years, i.e., 931/30.

3. Finally, the most elusive problem is that there were several co-regencies among the kings. This must be determined by a process of elimination. Since Hezekiah was given an additional fifteen years to live, it is only logical to assume that he began to train his son, Manasseh, for the throne. The period of training was included in his total reign of fifty-five years.

The Assyrians had an interesting way of computing dates called the "eponymic cycle." On the first day of each year, a man was appointed to an office and the year was named after him. A fairly complete list has been found engraved on a wall. Elsewhere, in the city of Khorshabad, a more complete list has been found which was copied from the engraved list. To further supplement this, Ptolemy, an Alexandrian astrologer, developed a canon of kings based upon the movement of the heavens. It is from this that we are able to arrive at an absolute date, compare that with the few dates given in the Assyrian king list, and come up with a very definite date with which to work. Thus when Tiglath-pileser says that he came up against a coalition of kings, including Ahab of Israel, in 853 B.C., we are able to give that as the last year of Ahab's reign.

Kings and Prophets of Israel—Northern Kingdom

KINGS	PROPHETS
1. Jeroboam I: I Kings 12:16—14:20; II Chronicles 10:12—13:22 Date: 931-910 22 years Bad; Stricken by God	Ahijah: I Kings12:15
2. Nadab: I Kings 14:20; 15:25-28 Date: 910-909 2 years Bad; Murdered by Baasha	
3. Baasha: I Kings 15:27—16:6; II Chronicles 16:1-6 Date: 909-886 24 years Bad; Died	Jehu: I Kings 16:1,7
4. Elah: I Kings 16:6-10 Date: 886-885 2 years Bad; Murdered by Zimri	
5. Zimri: I Kings 16:8-20 Date: 885 7 days Bad; Suicide	
6. Omri: I Kings 16:15-28 Date: 885-874 12 years Bad; Died	

7. Ahab: I Kings 16:28—22:40;
   II Chronicles 18:1-34
   Date: 874-853   22 years
   Bad; Wounded in battle

   Elijah: I Kings 17:1
   Micaiah: I Kings 22:6-28
   Elijah: II Kings 1:3

8. Ahaziah: I Kings 22:40;
   II Chronicles 20:35-37
   Date: 853-852   2 years
   Bad; Fell through lattice

   Elijah: II Kings 1:3

9. Jehoram/Joram: II Kings 1:17;
   3:1—9:25; II Chronicles 22:5-7
   Date: 852-841   12 years
   Bad; Murdered by Jehu

   Elisha: II Kings 8:4

10. Jehu: II Kings 9:11—10:36;
    II Chronicles 22:7-12
    Date: 841-814   28 years
    Bad; Died

    Elisha: II Kings 9:1-3

11. Jehoahaz: I Kings 10:35; 13:1-9
    Date: 814-798   17 years
    Bad; Died

12. Jehoash/Joash: II Kings 13:9—14:16
    II Chronicles 25:17-24
    Date: 798-782   16 years
    Bad; Died

    Elisha: II Kings 13:14

13. Jeroboam II: II Kings 14:16
    Date: 782-753   41 years
    Bad; Died

    Hosea: 1:1
    Amos: 1:1

14. Zachariah: II Kings 14:29—15:12
    Date: 753-752   6 months
    Bad; Murdered by Shallum

15. Shallum: II Kings 15:10-15
    Date: 752   1 month
    Bad; Murdered by Menahem

16. Menehem: II Kings 15:14--22
    First deportation to Assyria: II Kings
    15:19,20; II Chronicles 5:25,26
    Date: 752-742   10 years
    Bad; Died

17. Pekahiah: II Kings 15:22-26
    Date: 742-740   2 years
    Bad; Murdered by Pekah

    Micah, his prophecy concerning Samaria

18. Pekah: II Kings 15:25-31
    Second deportation to Assyria: II Kings
    15:17-30; II Chronicles 5:25,26
    Date: 740-732   20 years. He dated

    Micah

his reign from Menahem in 752
Bad; Murdered by Hoshea

19. Hoshea: II Kings 15:30: 17:1-23   Micah
    Final deportation to Assyria: Hosea
    II Kings 17:1-23
    Date: 732-722   9 years
    Bad; Deposed to Assyria

The approximate date of the Northern Kingdom of Israel is from Jeroboam, 931 B.C., to Hoshea, 722 B.C. It lasted 209 years. Shalmanesser, king of Assyria, finally overthrew Israel. Hoshea's reign ends with these words: "So Israel was carried away out of their own land to Assyria" (II Kings 17:23).

Israel's Captivity

Because of the sin of Israel against the God of their fathers, the Lord stirred up the spirit of Tiglath-pileser (Pul), king of Assyria, to come up against His people. Menahem, king of Israel, paid tribute to him (II Kings 15:19). Later, Tiglath carried away captive the Reubenites, Gadites, and the half tribe of Manasseh to the cities of Mesopotamia (I Chronicles 5:25,26). Later, under the reign of Pekah, Israel again was taken by Tiglath, and he captured the cities of Naphtali and carried off the inhabitants to Assyria (II Kings 15:27-29). Records from Assyria state that Tiglath replaced Pekah with Hoshea. Under Hoshea, the last king of Israel, King Shalmaneser of Assyria (who succeeded Tiglath) came over against Samaria and forced Hoshea to become his servant and pay tribute to him. Hoshea conspired against Shalmaneser because of heavy taxes, and appealed to King So of Egypt for help. Shalmaneser then marched through the land of Israel and besieged Samaria for three years (II Kings 17:1-5). According to this portion of Scripture Shalmaneser started the final siege of Samaria, but Assyrian records indicate that Shalmaneser died and Sargon actually captured the city. Scripture does not list the conquering king—just "they took it" (II Kings 18:9,10).

When Sargon defeated Samaria, he carried into captivity 27,290 people (based on a tablet found in his palace ruins). That he left many Israelites in the land is evident (see SARGON in Index). Those deported were taken to Media and Mesopotamia. He then repeopled Samaria with Assyrians and returned an Israelite priest from captivity to teach these people about the true and living God (II Kings 17:24-28). By introducing foreigners into Samaria, the Assyrians and remaining Israelites intermarried. This resulted in a new and heterogeneous people who occupied the former territory of the ten tribes. This new race of people was called "Samaritans." A Samaritan is of Jewish and Assyrian descent. This new race followed the teachings of Moses, and when Zerubbabel led back his band of exiles from Babylonia to Jerusalem, the Samaritans asked permission to help build the temple, on the ground that they worshiped the God of Israel ever since the time of Eserhaddon (Ezra 4:1,2). They were still worshiping the God of Jacob in the time of Christ (John 4:5,7,19,20). Many Samaritans were won to Christianity through the witness of the woman at the well and the preaching of Philip (John 4:39; Acts 8:8,25). Today, in the City of Nablus, there are several hundred Samaritans still living. They have an ancient scroll of the Pentateuch, which they claim was written by Aaron's grandson, and they still offer the Passover lamb on Mount Gerazim. See SAMARITANS in Index.

Those of the ten tribes of the kingdom of Israel taken into Assyria as captives have become scattered. God had warned Israel that if she did not obey Him, He would scatter them among the nations (Deuteronomy 28:63-67). "If ye walk contrary unto Me, and will not hearken unto Me, . . . I will make you few in number" (Leviticus 26:21,22). "The people shall dwell alone, and shall not be reckoned among the nations" (Numbers 23:9). God further warned that

Sargon's Captivity Count

disobedience would cause Him to scatter them unto a nation, "and thou shalt become a. . . by-word among all nations, whither the Lord shall lead thee" (Deuteronomy 28:36,37). For disobeying, God predicted He would smite Israel as a reed is shaken in the water, and root up Israel out of the good land, which He gave to their fathers, and scatter them . . . because they had made groves, provoking the Lord to anger (I Kings 14:15). See GROVES in Index.

Taken into captivity into Assyria, God fulfilled His Word, and during Isaiah's time, they were called a "scattered and peeled" nation and people (Isaiah 18:2,7). The term "the lost tribes of Israel" is not a scriptural one. It has been imported into the question by those who claim to have discovered their identity. The scriptural expression for Israel's being taken into captivity due to disobedience is "scattered" and the Word of God assures us that "He who scattered Israel will gather him" (Jeremiah 31:10). See ISRAEL REGATHERED in Index.

Kings and Prophets of Judah—Southern Kingdom

Seeming discrepancies in some dates (marked with an *asterisk**) are a result of overlapping co-regencies.

KINGS	PROPHETS
1. Rehoboam: I Kings 11:43—14:31; II Chronicles 10:1—12:16 Date: 931-913 17 years Bad; Died	Shemaiah: I Kings 12:22 Iddo: II Chronicles 12:15

Samaritan Scroll

2. Abijam/Abijah: I Kings 14:31—15:8;
   II Chronicles 13:1-22
   Date: 913-911   3 years
   Bad; Died

3. Asa: I Kings 15:8-24;   Azariah: II Chronicles 15:1,2
   II Chronicles 14:1—16:14   Hanani: II Chronicles 16:7
   Date: 911-870   41 years
   Good; Died

4. Jehoshaphat: I Kings 22:41-50;   Jahaziel: II Chronicles 20:14,15
   II Chronicles 17:1—20:37   Jehu: II Chronicles 19:1,2
   Date: 873-848*   25 years   Eliezer: II Chronicles 21:37
   Good; Died

5. Jehoram/Joram: II Kings 8:16-24;   Elijah: II Chronicles 21:12

II Chronicles 21:1-20
Date: 853-841*   8 years
Bad; Stricken by God

6. Ahaziah: II Kings 8:24—9:29   Jehu: II Chronicles 22:7,8
   II Chronicles 22:1-9
   Date: 841   1 year
   Bad; Murdered by Jehu

7. Athaliah (queen): II Kings 11:1-20;
   II Chronicles 22:10—23:15
   Date: 841-835   6 years
   Bad; Murdered by Army

8. Joash/Jehoash: II Kings 11:1—12:21;   Jehoiada: II Kings 12:2
   II Chronicles 22:10—24:27   Joel
   Date: 835-796   40 years   Zechariah: II Chronicles 24:20-23
   Good; Murdered by servants

9. Amaziah: II Kings 14:1-20;   Unnamed man of God: II Chronicles
   II Chronicles 25:1-28   25:7-9,15,16
   Date: 796-767   29 years
   Good; Murdered

10. Uzziah/Azariah: II Kings 15:1-7   Zechariah: II Chronicles 26:5
    II Chronicles 26:1-23   Amos: 1:1
    Date: 791-740*   52 years   Isaiah: 1:1; II Chronicles 26:22
    Good; Stricken by God   Hosea: 1:1

11. Jotham: II Kings 15:32-38;   Isaiah: 1:1
    II Chronicles 27:1-9   Micah: 1:1
    Date: 750-736*   16 years   Hosea: 1:1
    Good; Died

12. Ahaz: II Kings 16:1-20   Obed: II Chronicles 28:9
    II Chronicles 28:1-27   Isaiah: 1:1; 7:3
    Date: 736-716*   16 years   Micah: 1:1
    Bad; Died

13. Hezekiah: II Kings 18:1—20:21;   Nahum
    II Chronicles 29:1—32:33   Isaiah: 1:1; II Kings 20:16,17
    Date: 716-687   29 years   Micah: 1:1; Jeremiah 26:18
    Good; Died   Hosea: 1:1

14. Manasseh: II Kings 21:1-18   Unnamed prophets: II Kings 21:10;
    II Chronicles 33:1-20   II Chronicles 33:19b
    Date: 696-642*   55 years
    Bad/Good; Died

15. Amon: II Kings 21:19-26
    II Chronicles 33:21-25
    Date: 642-640   2 years

16. Josiah: II Kings 22:1—23:30   Huldah: II Chronicles 34:22

II Chronicles 34:1—35:27
Date: 640-608   31 years
Good; Wounded in battle

Zephaniah: 1:1
Jeremiah: 1:1; I Chronicles 35:25

17. Jehoahaz/Shallum: II Kings
23:30-33; II Chronicles 36:1-4
Date: 608   3 months
Bad; Disposed to Egypt

18. Jehoiakim: II Kings 23:34—24:5;
II Chronicles 36:5-7. First
deportation to Babylon; Daniel captive:
II Chronicles 36:6,7; Daniel 1:1-6
Date: 608-597   11 years
Bad; Died in siege?

Urijah: Jeremiah 26:20-23
Jeremiah: 1:3

19. Jehoiachin/Coniah/Jeconiah: II Kings
24:1-16; II Chronicles 36:8-10. Second
deportation to Babylon; Ezekiel
captive: II Kings 24:11-16;
Ezekiel 1:1,2
Date: 597   3 months
Bad; Deposed to Babylon

20. Zedekiah/Mattaniah: II Kings
24:17—25:21; II Chronicles 36:10-18.
Final overthrow of Jerusalem and
Judah carried captive to Babylon:
II Chronicles 36:11-21
Date: 597-586   11 years

Jeremiah: 1:3; II Chronicles 36:12

The approximate date of the Southern Kingdom of Judah is from Rehoboam, 931 B.C., to Zedekiah, 586 B.C. It lasted 345 years. Nebuchadnezzar, king of Babylon, in his third and final siege of Jerusalem, overthrew the city and brought an end to the kingdom of Judah. Zedekiah's reign ends with these words: "So Judah was carried away out of their land [to Babylon]" (II Kings 25:21).

Judah's Captivity

Soon after Jehoiakim began to reign, Nebuchadnezzar came up to Jerusalem and made him his servant. When Jehoiakim rebelled after serving Nebuchadnezzar three years, the Lord sent bands of Chaldeans, Syrians, Moabites, and Ammonites against him. This judgment came upon Jehoiakim for the innocent blood he shed. Nebuchadnezzar bound him in fetters (chains) and carried him and part of the vessels of the Temple to Babylon (II Kings 24:1-5); II Chronicles 36:5-7). Daniel was in this first deportation (Daniel 1:1-6).

The second deportation took place under the reign of Jehoiachin, when Nebuchadnezzar came back and besieged Jerusalem, this time destroying the vessels of the Temple which remained. Jehoiachin, all the princes, all the mighty men of valor, even 10,000 captives, and all the craftsmen and smiths, were taken to Babylon. Only the poorest of the people remained in the land (II Kings 24:8-16). Ezekiel was in this second deportation. He and Daniel were prophets of the Exile.

The third and final deportation took place under Zedekiah, when Nebuchadnezzar came against Judah again, this time putting a blockade around Jerusalem. Because of lack of water and food, the city was broken up, and, as the inhabitants tried to flee the city, they were captured. Jerusalem was destroyed by fire, and the walls were broken down. No compassion was shown to the people. All were taken captive except the poor of the land, who were left to till the soil (II Kings 25:1-21; II Chronicles 36:11-21). Pictured are captives leaving Jerusalem for Babylon, and the ruins of "Processional Street," over which Ezekiel, Daniel, and the children of Israel marched as they entered Babylon through the Ishtar gate.

Captives to Assyria

"Processional" Street

Judah's captivity was foretold by Moses (Deuteronomy 28:36,47-52). God warned through Moses that His people, if they disobeyed Him, would be scattered unto a nation. Judah's captivity was also predicted 150 years before its fulfillment by Isaiah (6:11,12), and Babylon as the place of captivity was foretold by Micah (4:9,10) and Isaiah (39:6). Jeremiah announced it should continue for seventy years (25:1,11,12). It was effected in 586 B.C. by Nebuchadnezzar, who was God's tool for judgment against His own people (Jeremiah 52:27-30; II Chronicles 36:17).

Reasons for Captivity

Scripture gives us at least four reasons for Judah's captivity for seventy years:

1. Failure to keep the Sabbatical year, resulting in captivity (Leviticus 25:1-7; 26:27,33-35). Jeremiah said that captivity was to "fulfill the word of the Lord" (II Chronicles 36:20,21). It would seem that from about the time of the end of the period of the Judges to the destruction of the Temple—about 490 years—the Sabbatical year had not been kept. By dividing the seventh Sabbatical year into 490 we get 70, the number of years Israel should dwell in captivity, "until the land enjoyed her sabbaths."

2. Idolatry. After Israel entered the land of "milk and honey," she soon waxed fat, and, as predicted by Moses, turned to other gods and served them. In their failure to drive out the inhabitants of the land, they compromised their beliefs, mingled with and married the heathen Canaanites, embraced their gods, and served Baal and made groves (Deuteronomy 31:20; Judges 3:5-7; 8:33; 10:6; I Kings 11:33). Sex was idolized, and groves—the symbol of sex and fertility—were erected throughout the land and *in* the house of God (I Kings 14:24; II Kings 21:7; 23:6,7). Incense was burned to the brazen serpent which Moses made in the wilderness, and they offered their children to Baal and demons as human sacrifices (II Kings 18:4; Jeremiah 19:4,5; Psalm 106:37,38). Israel *wanted* idol worship and she got it—not only in her own land —but for seventy years more in captivity among the Babylonian idolaters (Deuteronomy 28:36).

It was in Babylonian captivity that Judah learned to loathe idols which she had loved and served. Since captivity the Jews have never been guilty of the sin of idolatry. Though a remnant returned from captivity, and God preserved the lineage of Christ through Judah, their house is still swept and garnished and clean of the evil spirit of idolatry, but empty of Messiah, the One who came to redeem the "whole house of Israel."

3. Ungratefulness. God had been faithful in bringing Israel into the land, but she soon ignored His claims upon her. Deliberately embracing idolatry, she just as deliberately "dethroned" God and enthroned man "that we also may be like all the nations" (I Samuel 8:19,20). Not only did she become *like* the other nations, but, as her idolatry deepened, Manasseh "seduced them to do *more* evil than the nations" round about which Israel failed to drive out of the land (II Kings 21:1-9). She became the most ungrateful, the most unstable, the most fickle, and perhaps the most sinful nation that ever existed. This statement is made in view of her calling above all other nations, the light which God had given to her of Himself through His Word, and the way He sought her best interests through His prophets (Deuteronomy 7:6-11; 14:2; Romans 3:2; II Chronicles 36:14-16). Isaiah accused her of being more stupid than dumb animals, and labeled her as "rulers of Sodom—people of Gomorrah" (1:2,3,10). Isaiah also said that had it not been for a "faithful remnant" among the people, God would have done to them what He did to Sodom and Gomorrah (1:9).

Israel made the Temple an object of false security, the Law a mockery of justice, turned separation into a curse, made circumcision a fetish, used the Holy Land for unholy practices, exalted her past, sinned in the present, and ignored future judgment leveled at her through the prophets.

4. Touching God's anointed. God had warned, "Touch not mine anointed, and do My prophets no harm" (I Chronicles 16:22). To touch God's anointed is to touch God. To fight against or murmur against God's servant is to murmur against and fight God (Exodus 16:8). Israel had done this for many generations, and God's patience and longsuffering had finally come to an end. It is no wonder that "the wrath of God arose against His people, till there was no remedy" (II Chronicles 36:15,16). God had prophesied captivity if His people disobeyed, and there was no remedy now for changing His Word. God says what He means and He means what He says.

Those taken into Babylonian captivity were servants of this nation for seventy years, until the reign of the king of Persia (II Chronicles 36:20,21). While in captivity they were given many privileges such as building and occupying their own homes, keeping servants and engaging in business (Jeremiah 29:5-7; Ezra 2:65). In the place of captivity because of disobedience, Israel had lost her song of joy (Psalm 137:1-4). However, they did have one song—a song of bitterness—that of their own disobedience and ungratefulness (Deuteronomy 31:21). After captivity, they were able to sing again (Psalm 126:1,2).

As for the people who remained in the land of Judah after the fall of Jerusalem, including Jeremiah (Jeremiah 40:1-6), they were in subjection to Babylon. Gedaliah was made their governor. These people wanted to flee to Egypt for fear of the Chaldeans, but Jeremiah preached against it. They rebelled, slew Gedaliah, kidnapped Jeremiah, and fled to Egypt (I Kings 25:22-26; Jeremiah 42:15—43:7).

Post-Captivity Books

A study of Daniel and Nehemiah will help us to understand the remaining days of Judah in captivity. In Daniel 5 we read of Darius, the Median, taking over the kingdom of Babylon from Belshazzar. Under Darius, Daniel was made the first president of this new kingdom (Daniel 6:1-3). It was while Darius was reigning that Daniel understood by the books that the captivity was to last seventy years, and, as the time was drawing to a close, began to petition God for the restoration of divine favor to His people (Daniel 9:1-19).

Later, Cyrus, king of Persia, having conquered all the kingdoms of the earth, did a strange thing for a conquered people. Having become acquainted with Daniel, no doubt, because of his high position under Darius, he was shown the places in Isaiah where he was mentioned by name, and his exploits and conquests foretold (Isaiah 44:28; 45:1). Finding himself thus distinguished by the God of the Jews, he was anxious to give Him proofs of his gratitude in return. He made a decree in favor of the Jews, restored their sacred vessels which Nebuchadnezzar had taken from the Temple, gave them liberty to return to their own land, and encouraged them to rebuild the Temple of Jehovah (Ezra 1:1-4). In all probability the actual return to Jerusalem got underway a year or two after the decree of Cyrus.

Judah's captivity took place in three stages (see CAPTIVITY in Index). After Cyrus issued his decree (ca. 536 B.C.—Ezra 1:1-4), the deportation took place in three stages. Note the sequence—

1. 49,897 returned under Zerubbabel, ca. 534 B.C. (Ezra 2:1,2,64,65)
2. Ezra and a later generation returned ca. 457 B.C. (Ezra 7:6-8)
3. Nehemiah returned ca. 445 B.C. (Nehemiah 1:5-11; 13:6,7)

For the chronological sequence, read the post-captivity books as follows:

a. First Return under Zerubbabel: Ezra 2:1,2

　　　—Ezra: 1-4
　　　—Haggai
　　　—Zechariah
　　　　—Ezra 5:1
　　　—Esther
　　　　—Ezra 5,6
　b. Second Return under Ezra: Ezra 7:1; 8:1
　　　Third Return under Nehemiah: Nehemiah 1:5-11; 13:6,7
　　　—Ezra 7-10
　　　—Nehemiah
　　　—Malachi

Old Testament history, as such, ends with the historical books of Ezra, Nehemiah, and Esther, and the prophetical books of Haggai, Zechariah, and Malachi. (Malachi was probably contemporary with Nehemiah in the latter part of Nehemiah's days.) Many Jews preferred to remain in Babylon and the East. Esther records their history. The period of time covered by these historical and prophetical books is approximately 138 years.

"In this and the subsequent history the Jews no longer appear as an independent, prosperous nation, governed by kings of their own race. A small remnant returned from captivity by the favor of Persian kings, and were under their protection and dominion. Struggling, often feebly, with many difficulties and enemies, they were enabled to re-establish the worship of God in the Temple at Jerusalem; to which they outwardly adhered till the coming of Christ; being effectively cured of idolatry, though in other respects exceedingly prone to disobedience.

"During the captivity, nothing is recorded of their history, except what may be collected from the prophecies of Ezekiel and Daniel; and exceedingly little is contained in the Scripture of their condition after their return till the birth of Christ, compared with the regular history given of the Nation from the days of Abraham to captivity. In Ezra and Nehemiah we have the record of the rebuilding of the Temple and Jerusalem. In Haggai the remnant was rebuked for the building of their own houses at the expense of delaying completion of the Temple. Zechariah issued a call to repentance for continued disobedience, with visions of Messiah's first and second coming. Malachi—ca. 450-400 B.C.—took the priests to task for their corruption, rebuked divorce, and accused Israel of robbing God of His tithe. Esther gives to us some insight of the life of the Jews who chose to remain in Persia.

"The old dispensation was about to expire [see SILENCE in Index] and make way for Christianity; the spirit of prophecy was about to be withdrawn for a season; and the people had so often and so flagrantly violated their national covenant, that they were not honored and noticed as they had been in former ages."[1] Only one king of the Davidic family has been crowned since Judah's captivity in 586 B.C., and *He* was crowned with thorns.

The Tribes Regathered

In Ezra (2:1-65) we have the return of those of the two tribes of Judah and Benjamin who were in Babylon in captivity. While the genealogical record of these tribes was closely kept because of Messiah's lineage, we must reckon that in the regathering at Jerusalem after the land enjoyed her Sabbaths that there were those of the other ten tribes.

1. After Jeroboam's rebellion and the repudiation of the house of David (I Kings 12:16-21; II Chronicles 10:15,16), there were those within the Northern Kingdom who later made an allegiance with the house of David (the Southern Kingdom of Judah) and worshiped the Lord at Jerusalem: II Chronicles 19:4; 30:1,10-26; 34:33; 35:17,18.

2. After the Northern Kingdom fell, all were not taken captive. No doubt some of those left in the land after Assyria captured Samaria drifted down to the Southern Kingdom and were among those taken captive to Babylon (II Chronicles 31:6). In Ezra's list of those returning are

men from cities of the Northern Kingdom—e.g., men of Bethel and Ai (2:28), and some of the tribe of Levi (2:40). There were some who could not even show their lineage (2:59).

3. Those returning from captivity now make up "Israel" as a whole—the nation of Israel—not simply two tribes or the Kingdom of Judah (Ezra 2:2,70)

4. That the New Testament recognizes those of *all* twelve tribes as still in existence—and not just two tribes—is seen in the following portions:

    a. The "house of Israel" included all: Matthew 10:5,6

    b. The land of the tribes of Zebulon and Naphtali were still recognized: Matthew 4:13-15

    c. Anna, a prophetess, of the tribe of Asher: Luke 2:36

    d. Joses, of the tribe of Levi: Acts 4:36

    e. Paul, of the tribe of Benjamin: Philippians 3:5

    f. Christ, of the tribe of Judah: Revelation 5:5

    g. All the twelve tribes attested to: Acts 26:7

    h. All the tribes written to: James 1:1

Those who assert that there are "Ten Lost Tribes" which are known only to God and will be found only by Him—yea, are already discovered to be the Anglo-Saxon people—have not "compared Scripture with Scripture" to find that its record includes some from *all* tribes *during* and *after* captivity.

The return of the remnant from Babylon was the *second* "Exodus" of Israel (Ezra 1:2,64,65; Nehemiah 2:5-11). It came almost 1,000 years after their first "Exodus" from Egypt, and was in fulfillment of prophecy (Jeremiah 25:11 with 29:10-14).

Stated: ca. 604 B.C. *Fulfilled:* ca. 537-445 B.C.

Israel's *first* Exodus was also in fulfillment of prophecy: Genesis 15:13,14 with Exodus 12:29—15:22; through the wilderness to Joshua 3:1—4:24.

Stated: ca. 2,000 B.C. *Fulfulled:* ca. 1,440 B.C.

Israel's *third* and final Exodus, in fulfillment of God's Word, is having a partial fulfillment today:

Stated: Deuteronomy 28:64-67, ca. 1,450 B.C., Ezekiel 37:21-28, ca 560 B.C. *Fulfilled:* since 1947 A.D.

Ezra—The Book of the Returning Remnant

Name: This book, in the Latin and Arabic versions, is called the "First Book of Ezra," Nehemiah being recognized as the "Second Book of Ezra." The Jews counted both Ezra and Nehemiah as one book. In the Syriac version it is called the "Writing or Book of Ezra, the Prophet," and in the Arabic version it is referred to as the "First Book of Ezra, the Priest, skillful in the Law."

Contents: "Ezra gives the fulfillment of prophecies concerning the return of the Jews from captivity; rebuilding of the Temple; an account of the state of the spiritual seed within the nation in those times, the troubles and difficulties with which they met, and what care was taken to keep the tribes and families distinct that it might be known from whom the Messiah came."[1]

The sixth chapter of Ezra ends with the completion of the restoration Temple. Chapter seven begins with the events in the life of Ezra about sixty years later. This is probably due to the fact that Ezra's purpose was to deal with the restoring of the Temple, its religious institutions, and the religious life of Israel. To better understand events as they occurred with the Jews, read the book of Esther between chapters six and seven of Ezra. Ezra has 10 chapters, 280 verses, and 7,441 words.

Character: Historical.

Subject: The restoration of the Temple and Temple worship.

Purpose: To teach us God's method of restoring His people to the place of fellowship and blessing (I John 1:7,9).

Outline:[2]

I. Return under Zerubbabel: 1—6
   A. Restoration of the Jews: 1,2
   B. Opposition to the Work: 3,4
   C. Dedication of the Temple: 5,6
II. Return under Ezra: 7—10
   A. Proclamation of Artaxerxes: 7
   B. Liberation of the Jews: 8
   C. Intercession of Ezra: 9
   D. Reformation of the People: 10

Scope: Ezra contains a history of approximately 75 years.

Writer: It is generally accepted by Jews and Christians that Ezra was the author of the book which bears his name. He was a descendant of Hilkiah, the high priest (7:1), who found a copy of the Law during the reign of Josiah (II Chronicles 34:14). As a priest, Ezra was not able to serve during the captivity, but gave his time to a study of the Word of God—"a ready scribe in the Law of Moses" (7:6). He was a great revivalist and reformer, as seen from the reading of the Word of God by him (Nehemiah 8). He was also the writer of the Chronicles and of Psalm 119, which exalts the Word itself. He organized the synagogue, was the founder of the order of Scribes, helped settle the canon of Scripture, and arranged the Psalms.

To Whom Written: To the returning remnant as a record of their identity.

When and Where Written: It is possible that Ezra recorded the first part of this book in Babylon (ca. 460-457 B.C.), and finished the rest after his return to Jerusalem.

Key Chapter: 6. Dedication of the Temple.

Key Verse: 1:5. See also Psalm 127:1.

Decree of Cyrus

Key Word: Build.

Key Phrase: The Word of the Lord: 1:1.

Key Thought: Return from captivity and rebuild the Temple.

Spiritual Thought: Repair God's house. First the Temple is built; afterward, in Nehemiah, the walls of the city are rebuilt. The *inner* is repaired before the *outer.* Cleanse the heart (inner) first and all else (outer) will be clean.

Christ Is Seen As: Lord of heaven and earth.

King Cyrus of Christ. God's choice of Cyrus to liberate His people from Babylonian captivity gives us a picture of Christ as our Liberator from spiritual bondage.

1. Both are referred to as God's anointed (Cyrus, the Gentile; Christ, the Jew): Isaiah 45:1 with Luke 4:18; Acts 10:38

2. Both are God's shepherd: Isaiah 44:28 with John 10:11

3. Both are conquerers of Israel's enemies: Isaiah 45:1 with Revelation 19:11-20

4. Both are restorers of the holy city—Jerusalem: Isaiah 44:28 with Zechariah 14:9-11

5. Both glorify the name of the one true God: Ezra 1:2 with John 17:4

1. The decree which Cyrus issued setting Israel free has been found, and is now in the British Museum in London. It lists his genealogy and tells how the great city of Babylon surrendered to him without resistance (which confirms Daniel's account). King Darius, who acted as vice-regent for Cyrus, took Babylon in the name of Cyrus, "king of the host, the great king." Cyrus later entered Babylon, presented himself in the role of the "liberator of the people," and permitted the liberated captives to return to their original cities and practice their religion according to their own beliefs. The Bible account (as in Ezra 1:1-4) has the Jewish point of view, since the reactions of the other liberated captives were not important to the Biblical account. While the decree included all captives, including all Jews, not all Jews returned to Jerusalem.

2. Behistun Rock of King Darius: 4:23,24; 5:1—6:12. See BEHISTUN in Index.

LIGHT FROM BIBLICAL CUSTOMS

3 The Laws of the Medes and Persians (Daniel 6:8). Their laws were never altered. Regardless of events which transpired before or after issuance, or personalities involved, once issued, they were binding and could *never* be changed. When God prophesied that Cyrus would permit Israel to return to Jerusalem after their captivity, He knew that Cyrus' decree could not be altered, thereby assuring Israel of her return to the land of God's choosing. When adversaries sought to hinder the building of the Temple, and succeeded in stopping the work temporarily, King Darius confirmed the decree of Cyrus and work was resumed til the Temple was completed and dedicated (4:1—6:18). Regardless of the personal feelings Darius had for Daniel, the law (decree) of the Medes and Persians could not be altered, and Daniel was cast into the lion's den (Daniel 6:1-24).

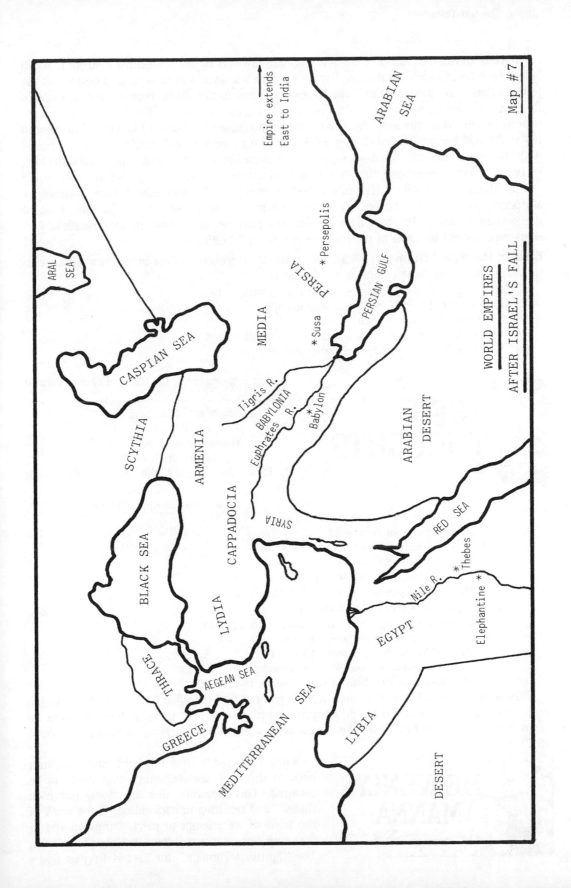

WORLD EMPIRES
AFTER ISRAEL'S FALL

Map #7

There is an instance, however, when a Persian law was turned against the instigator. When Mordecai refused to bow to Haman, Haman's wrath was such that he sought to destroy all the Jews in Persia. He persuaded the king to issue a decree to this effect. Haman wrote the law in the name of the king and sealed it with the king's ring (Esther 3:6-13). Esther then made an appeal to her husband, the king, for her people, explaining what Haman had done. The king in his wrath had Haman hanged (Esther 7). But the king's decree, written by Haman and sealed with the king's ring, still stood—it could not be altered or reversed. Esther persuaded the king to issue a decree permitting the Jews to defend themselves against any and all who would assault them as a result of Haman's decree (Esther 8:5-17). This new decree, dictated by Mordecai, written by the scribes, signed in the king's name and sealed with his ring, enabled the Jews to be spared. It turned Haman's decree on his own head, and upon thousands of Persians who sought the lives of the Jews (Esther 9:1-17,24,25).

Ezra in the New Testament: There are no direct references of Ezra in the New Testament. However, there are some companion references:

1. Doing God's good pleasure: 1:5 with Philippians 2:13
2. All things for good: 8:22 with Romans 8:28
3. Magnitude of sin: 9:6 with Revelation 18:5
4. Greater judgment if sin is continued: 9:14 with John 5:14
5. Guilty before God: 9:15 with Romans 3:19

1. The Importance of the Word of God in Ezra. It is referred to as:
   a. The Word of the Lord: 1:1; 9:4
   b. The Law of Moses: 3:2; 6:18; 7:6
   c. Commandments: 6:14; 10:3,5
   d. The Law of the Lord: 7:10,14

2. Ezra—the Priest, the Scribe (Nehemiah 12:26).
   a. He was trustworthy: 7:11-28
   b. He was a man of prayer: 8:21; 10:1
   c. He was a man of faith: 8:22
   d. He was a man of self-denial: 10:6
   e. He was a reformer: 10:2-5
   f. He was a student of the Word: 7:10a
   g. He was an expositor of the Word: 7:10b; Nehemiah 8:1-8

3. Ezra's Spiritual Secret of Success: 7:10
   a. His heart was prepared by the Word: Psalm 119:130
   b. He sought (studied) the Word: II Timothy 2:15
   c. He lived by the Word: Psalm 119:11,133
   d. He taught (preached) the Word: II Timothy 4:2
   e. The Word produced faith in God: Romans 10:17

This is demonstrated in Ezra's implicit faith and trust when called upon to lead the people and carry great treasures through dangerous places on their journey from Babylon to Jerusalem. He refused help from the king's armies and relied solely upon God's protection (8:21-32).

When we wander from the Lord, and then start back to Him, we discover much that needs to be repaired. This repairing, due to "doing our own thing," and resulting in backsliding, is the work of the Lord. If we attempt to patch things up and to cover up our own ways, then the labor is in vain. The "Spiritual Thought" for Ezra is "repair God's house. "Those who did the repairing were "all them whose spirit God had raised to go up to build the house of the Lord." "Except the Lord build the house, they labor in vain that build it" (Psalm 127:1). Let us realize our helplessness apart from the working of God and see that if anything is to be accomplished, it will be accomplished because of—

GOD WHO WORKETH IN YOU—Philippians 2:13[4]

"This is for our encouragement, and on the ground of it we are exhorted to work with fear and trembling. That God dwells in His people is a glorious fact, but it is also a great mystery. And He dwells in us for our good as well as for His own glory. He helps our infirmities. He subdues our corruptions. He quickens our graces. He enables us to keep His precepts and observe His laws. We must work by the precept, which is our rule, and expect Him to put forth His power and enable us, which is our privilege. Beloved, what an unspeakable blessing is this, to have God working in us both to will and to do of His own good pleasure! Well may He require us to suffer great things and to do great things, and well may we say: 'I can do all things through Christ who strengthens me.' Let us realize this fact today, and let us beseech the Lord to put forth His power in us more manifestly, and so bring every thought into subjection to Christ Jesus. What cannot the man do who has omnipotence working for him? What can we do without the putting forth of divine power in us? Jesus said that without Him we could do nothing."

PRAYER THOUGHT: "Help me, dear Lord, to study to show myself approved unto Thee, a workman who needs not to be ashamed, one who rightly divides Thy Word of Truth, and shares its blessings with others who desperately need a touch from Thee. In Thy precious name I pray. Amen."[5]

Second Timothy 2:15

Nehemiah—The Book of Consolidation and Conclusion

Name: Nehemiah means "comforted of God." Nehemiah was a layman and a businessman, while Ezra was a priest and a scribe. Though Nehemiah had an important office in the king's court—"for I was the king's cupbearer"—his heart was with God and His people in Jerusalem (1:11b; 2:5).

Contents: This book shows the fulfillment of the prophecy of Zechariah, and especially of Daniel concerning the building of the wall of Jerusalem in troublesome times (Daniel 9:25). Emphasis is upon the rebuilding of the Temple in Ezra, and in Nehemiah, emphasis is upon the rebuilding of the walls of the city of Jerusalem after the Temple is built. In Ezra, we note the religious aspect of the return; in Nehemiah there is the political aspect of the return. This book shows what enemies Israel had and what opposition they met, and is a classic example of what must be expected when any work of God is started. Nehemiah has 13 chapters, 406 verses, and 10,483 words.

Character: Historial and autobiographical.

Subject: Third return from captivity and the restoration of the walls and the government of Jerusalem.

Purpose: To teach us how God would restore for His Church the faith that protects and gives victory over the enemy, and what can be accomplished if we have a mind to work—"that we be no more a reproach" (2:17).

Outline:[1]
- I. The Construction of the Walls: 1—7
  - A. Preparation for the Work: 1,2
  - B. Distribution of the Work: 3
  - C. Opposition to the Work: 4:1—6:14
  - D. Completion of the Work: 6:15—7:3
  - E. Registration of the People: 7:4-73
- II. The Consecration of the People: 8—10
  - A. Revival of the Book of the Law: 8
  - B. Public Confession of the People: 9
  - C. Signatories and Terms of the Convenant: 10
- III. Confirmation of the Convenant: 11-13
  - A. Collection of Important Lists: 11:1—12:26
  - B. Dedication of the City Wall: 12:27—13:3
  - C. Correction of Prevailing Abuses: 13:4-31

Scope: Nehemiah contains a history of from twelve to fifteen years.

Writer: Nehemiah.

When and Where Written: About 435 B.C., in Jerusalem. This is the last of the historical books of the Old Testament. As far as time is concerned, the Old Testament goes no farther than the book of Nehemiah.

Key Chapter: 1. Nehemiah's prayer concerning Israel.

Key Verses: 1:8,9.

Key Words:
1. Prayer: 1:4.
2. Work: 6:3.

Key Phrase: Arise and build: 2:20.

Key Thought: Rebuilding the walls of Jerusalem.

Spiritual Thoughts:
1. Rebuild God's city.
2. The people had a mind to work: 4:6. Though the enemy opposed and sought to hinder and create fear in the hearts of the remnant. Nehemiah led them to "walk in the fear of the Lord" (5:9). With a willingness to work, and a determination to set the things of God in order, they overcame and finished the work at hand—*th the shame of their enemies* (6:15,16).

Christ Is Seen As: Lord of heaven and earth.

Names and Titles of God: The God of heaven: 2:4. See NAMES in Dictionary.

Nehemiah, a type of Christ. This Book portrays Nehemiah as God's servant, the same as Mark does the Lord Jesus Christ.
1. Both fasted and prayed: 1:4 with Mark 1:35
2. Both called others to God's work: 2:17,18; 6:15 with Mark 3:13-19
3. Both met opposition: chapters 4,5 with Mark 1:12; 12:3,10
4. Both were exemplary: 5:9,14 with Mark 9:7
5. Both ministered to the people: 5:19 with Mark 10:45
6. Both taught the Word of God: 8:1-3 with Matthew 5:17-45
7. Both cleansed the Temple: 13:7-9 with Mark 11:15-17
8. Both reprimanded hypocrites: 13:15-22 with Matthew 23:13-36

Types of the Believer's Experiences:
1. The Restoration of the Walls
   a. The broken down walls (1:3) may typify the spiritual condition of one who is backslidden, with all barriers broken down and stripped of the armor of God, with which one resists the wiles of the devil (Ephesians 6:11)
   b. The preliminary season of fasting, praying, and repentance (1:4-11) may typify the procedure of a backslider returning to the Lord for forgiveness and the restoration of the joy of God's salvation (I John 1:9; Proverbs 28:13; Psalm 51:1-12)
   c. Nehemiah's sacrifice of a good position (2:4-6) may typify one who, having returned to the Lord, presents his body as a living sacrifice to the Lord for His work, and who no longer is conformed to the world (Romans 12:1,2)
   d. The night inspection of the city by Nehemiah (2:15,16) speaks of surveying the work to be done for the Lord while the enemy sleeps. This is staying one step ahead of those who would discourage us in the things of the Lord
   e. Nehemiah seeking cooperation of the people in rebuilding the walls (2:17,18) may typify the need for all to recognize the fact that we are "laborers together with God" and that we have but one foundation upon which to build (I Corinthians 3:9,11)
   f. The enrolling of the people to rebuild the wall (chapter 3) may typify the need for organization in the things of the Lord, that "all things may be done decently and in order" so that the building may be fitly framed together (I Corinthians 14:40; Ephesians 2:21)
   g. The opposition that Sanballet and Tobiah gave to Nehemiah and the people of God may typify the devil's active opposition to anything that is of God (I Peter 5:8). Note the enemy's form of opposition:
      —Concern: 2:10
      —Laughter: 2:19a
      —Hatred: 2:19b
      —Accusation: 2:19c
      —Wrath: 4:1a
      —Mocking: 4:1b, 3
      —Conspiracy: 4:8
      —Subtlety: 6:1, 2, 10
      —Effort to create fear: 6:19
   h. The completion of the wall (6:15) may typify the victory that comes when we submit ourselves to God and resist the devil that he might flee from us. We *are* more than conquerors through Him who loves us (4:9; James 4:7; Romans 8:37)
   i. Nehemiah's prayer life in the rebuilding of the city wall reveals the need to depend upon God from start to finish in everything we attempt for Him
      —He began his work in prayer: 1:4
      —He continued his work in prayer: 4:9
      —He did not cease to pray at the end of his work: 13:31b
2. The Gates of the Wall: chapter 3. See GATES in Index.
   a. The sheep gate (vs. 1) speaks to us of Christ as the Lamb of God—the cross (Isaiah 53:7; John 1:29)
   b. The fish gate (vs. 3) speaks to us of our need to immediately become "fishers of men" (Matthew 4:19; Proverbs 11:30; Daniel 12:3)
   c. The old gate (vs. 6) speaks to us of the old paths and the good ways wherein we should walk and find rest to our souls (Jeremiah 6:16; Matthew 11:29)
   d. The valley gate (vs. 13) speaks to us of humility—a willingness to take a lowly place in Christ's service (Luke 14:11; Philippians 2:3, 4; I Peter 5:5,6)
   e. The dung gate (vs. 14), through which the filth of the city was carried, speaks to us of the need to keep ourselves cleansed from all filthiness of the flesh and spirit (II Corinthians 7:1; I Thessalonians 4:4,7; Isaiah 52:11)

    f. The gate of the fountain (vs. 15) speaks to us of our being filled with the Holy Spirit (John 7:38,39; Ephesians 5:18b)

    g. The water gate (vs. 26) speaks to us of our constant need of the "water" of the Word (Ephesians 5:26; John 15:3; II Timothy 2:15). When Ezra read from the "book of the law" to the people, they gathered before "the water gate" (8:1-9)

    h. The horse gate (vs. 28). The horse is a symbol of war, and this gate speaks to us of our need to be good soldiers of Christ and to fight the good of faith (II Timothy 2:3; 4:7; Ephesians 6:11-18).

    i. The east gate (vs. 29) speaks to us of Christ's return—as the bright and morning star, the Sun of righteousness with healing in His wings—for His own (John 14:1-3; Revelation 22:12,16; Malachi 4:2)

    j. The gate Miphkad (vs. 31). This gate means "assignment" or "appointment in a designated spot." It could have been the gate where the elders of the city sat in judgment upon matters. It speaks to us of two assignments or appointments for the believer—one at the judgment seat of Christ (II Corinthians 5:10) and the other to reign with Him upon the earth (Revelation 5:10)

It is interesting to note in repairing the gate Miphkad and the section of the wall to the corner that we come back to the sheep gate. Since the sheep gate stands for the Cross, God does not want us to ever forget that we were once purged from our old sins—sinners saved by grace: II Peter 1:9.

Israeli archaeologists (1970) have uncovered remains of the "broad wall" mentioned by Nehemiah (3:8; 12:38). The biblical reference occurs in connection with a description of the restoration of Jerusalem's fortification after the return of the Jews from Babylonian captivity. An eighty-foot stretch of wall approximately twenty-three feet thick has been found on bedrock about 900 feet west of the Temple area. A wall twenty-three feet thick was unusual in the Israelite period and would have been described as a "broad wall." After Nebuchadnezzar leveled their city over seventy years before, Nehemiah wanted to make sure that the wall would hold should Jerusalem be besieged again.

The king's cupbearer: 1:1. A palace official who served beverages at the king's table was called a "cupbearer." They were chosen for this position because they were men of trust and confidence. Cupbearers were also mentioned in Pharaoh's and Solomon's courts (Genesis 40:1-11; I Kings 10:5).

Nehemiah in the New Testament: There are no direct references of Nehemiah in the New Testament. However, there are some companion references:

1. The sheep gate: 3:1 with John 5:2
2. God's just and good laws: 9:13 with Romans 7:12
3. The cloud in the wilderness: 9:19 with I Corinthians 10:1
4. Living by the law: 9:29 with Galatians 3:12

1. Some Lessons from Nehemiah

    —Being in the company of unbelievers can be a blessing if God places us there: 1:1

    —Great movements for God often originate with one person: 1:2-4

    —The reproach of God's people should be ours: 1:3,4; Hebrews 11:24-27

    —Prayer is a sure refuge in trial: 1:4

King's Cupbearer

— If God were no more mindful of His promises than we are of His precepts, we would
    have to say, "woe is me, for I am undone:" 1:5
— Confession of sin is sure to bring God's mercy: 1:6-11
— The best way to reach men is through God: 1:11b
— Favor with men is compatible when it springs from the favor of God: 1:11b—2:4
— One can "pray without ceasing" even when in conversation with others: 2:4,5
— People can be encouraged to work for the Lord if asked: 2:17,18
— Some will serve the Lord if given the opportunity: 2:18b; chapter 3
— If God is served, the devil will oppose: 2:19,20; 4:1-9
— Christians *can* stand up against opposition: 4:14-23
— Self-pity is a deterrent to Christian progress: 5:1-5
— Unselfishness is a characteristic of a true Christian: 5:14-19
— If God be for us, who can be against us: 6:15,16; Romans 8:31
— When God works, even the enemy sits up and takes notice: 6:16
— God's victory is cause for rejoicing and singing: 7:67
— We can show our appreciation to God by our gifts: 7:68-72
— It pays to honor God's Word: 8:1-8
— God should always be blessed and worshiped in humility: 8:6
— Our strength is in the joy of the Lord and His Word: 8:10b,12
— Obedience to God's Word leads to repentance: 9:1-3
— A ringing testimony is the result of obedience: 9:4-6
— Dedication and sacrifice to God with gladness pleases Him: 12:27-43
— Hearing and heeding the Word of God results in separation: 13:1-3
— God will remember us for our faithfulness: 13:14,22b,31b

2. There are twenty-two different words and phrases in this Book which are used some
forty-three times, referring to the Word of God. How many can you find?

    3. Nehemiah's Spiritual Success.

        a. Obedience to the Word of God

        b. A deep prayer life

        c. Unceasing service in the face of opposition

    4. Nehemiah's Prayer[3]

a. It was earnest—accompanied by mourning and fasting, and which continued day and night: 1:4
b. It was hopeful—looking to God's faithfulness and mercy: 1:5,6a
c. It was humble—accompanied by confession of sin: 1:6b-8
d. It was believing—claiming God's promise to the repentant and obedient: 1:9
e. It was practical and unselfish—a particular object in view for his nation and countrymen, benefiting himself only remotely: 1:10,11
f. It was stimulating—inspiring Nehemiah to take steps toward answering his own prayer: 2:4b,5
g. It was successful—"and the king granted me": 2:8b
h. It was God-glorifying—"according to the good hand of my God upon me": 2:8c

Nehemiah had to start rebuilding Jerusalem from "scratch." The city was in total ruin, stones had to be cleared to start new foundations, and people were weary from their many days' journey back from captivity. When one considers the solemnity of the task assigned Nehemiah in recruiting the remnant to rebuild the city walls, and the city itself in face of ridicule and much opposition, it is no wonder he asks—

OUGHT YE NOT TO WALK IN THE FEAR OF YOUR GOD—5:9[4]

"The fear of God is our great preservative, therefore the Lord says, 'I will put my fear in their hearts and they shall not depart from Me.' To fear God is an imperative duty; it is at the same time a favor conferred upon us and the proof of true wisdom. We should fear to offend God in any place, by any action, at any time. Our one ruling desire should be to please Him in all things. If His wrath is so dreadful, if the effects of His displeasure are so painful, if His life is so sweet, if His presence is so delightful as His Word and experience declare them to be, 'Ought ye not to walk in the fear of our God?' Surely we should. But alas! we lose sight of what should ever be uppermost in our minds, and therefore we become careless, trifling, worldly, lukewarm, ill-tempered, and anything but what Christians ought to be! May the Lord deeply convince us of our sin, humble us before His throne, break us down in true repentance, and produce in us a permanent fear of Him."

PRAYER THOUGHT: "Be with me in my place of service, dear Father, so that small things become great and great things become possible. In the great name of our wonderful Co-laborer. Amen."[5]

Nehemiah 4:19-23; I Corinthians 3:9

Esther—The Book of Divine Providence

Name: Esther's Hebrew name was "Hadassah," derived from the myrtle tree, which means beauty. Her Persian name was "Ishtar" or "Venus," meaning beautiful. Her name in the Greek is "Star," meaning bright.

Connection with Preceding Book: Esther is an account of the Jews who chose to remain in Persia after Cyrus gave them their freedom to return to Jerusalem (Ezra 1:1-4). It should be read between chapters six and seven of Ezra, linking the events in Esther not only with the book of Ezra but also the book of Nehemiah.

Contents: This book is the "Romans 8:28" of the Old Testament. Although the name of God is not mentioned, herein we find the singular providence of God in taking care of His people in adversity, in humbling the proud, in exalting the lowly, and in saving those who pray to Him and trust in Him. Esther has 10 chapters, 167 verses, and 5,637 words.

This is the second book in the Old Testament named for a woman. *Ruth* is the story of a Gentile who married a Jew; *Esther* is the story of a Jew who married a Gentile. The events in the book are exciting:

1. Vashti, the queen, was displaced
2. Esther, the orphan, was crowned
3. Mordecai, the detested, was respected
4. Haman, the villain, was executed
5. The Jews, sentenced to die, won their freedom

Haman sought to destroy all Jews because of his hatred for Mordecai, and had a decree issued to this effect (see LAW in Index). This was but another attempt on the part of Satan to destroy the people of God. When the Jews learned of his plot, they fasted and prayed. Through Esther's intercession, the Jews fought for their lives and were spared. As a result of their victory, the "Feast of Purim" was established to commemorate their preservation. The feast lasted two days and was celebrated yearly. It is still observed till this day. See PURIM in Index.

Character: Historical and autobiographical

Subject: God's unseen hand in delivering the Jews

Purpose: To teach us that nothing "just happens" in the life of the believer—

1. *All* things are for your sake: II Corinthians 4:15a
2. *All* things are of God: II Corinthians 5:18a
3. *All* things work together for our good: Romans 8:28

Outline:[1]

   I. The Danger of the Scattered Jews: 1—5
     A. Dethronement of Vashti: 1
     B. Distinction of Esther: 2
     C. Decree of Haman: 3
     D. Distress of Mordecai: 4
     E. Disposition of the King: 5
   II. The Deliverance of the Scattered Jews: 6—10
     A. Exaltation of Mordecai: 6:1-13
     B. Execution of Haman: 6:14—7:10
     C. Eradication (rooting out) of the Foe: 8:1—9:16
     D. Establishment of Purim: 9:17-32
     E. Emminence of Mordecai: 10

Scope: A history of approximately twelve years.

Writer: Probably Mordecai: 9:20,29.

When and Where Written: About 450 B.C. in Susa (Shushan), Persia.

Key Chapter: 6. Mordecai exalted.

Key Verse: 4:14.

Key Word: Deliverance.

Key Phrase: "For such a time as this": 4:14. Have you ever thought that God saved you and desires your service "for such a time as this"? "Only one life t'will soon be past, only what's done for Christ will last."

Key Thought: Escape of the Jews from extermination (in Persia).

Spiritual Thought: Only trust Him.

Christ Is Seen As:
1. Our Mordecai—deliverer.
2. Our Esther—advocate.

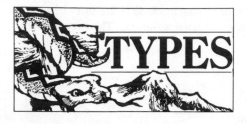

Types of Christ: Mordecai.

1. In adopting Esther, an orphan, he shows his mercy: 2:7. Although we were "orphans," in the world without hope and afar from God, Christ shows His mercy in receiving us into the family of God by faith: John 1:12; Ephesians 2:8,9,12,13

2. As Mordecai was faithful to the king, so Christ was faithful to His Father: 2:21-23 with Luke 2:49; John 8:29; Hebrews 10:7

3. He was consistent: 3:2-4. Christ, knowing His mission, steadfastly set His face as a flint toward Jerusalem for the purpose of dying (Isaiah 50:7; Luke 9:51; 19:10; I Timothy 1:15).

4. As Mordecai was despised, so was Christ: 3:5 with Isaiah 53:3; John 15:25.

5. As Mordecai was tested, so was Christ: 4:1 with Matthew 4:1-11; Luke 22:42

6. As Mordecai finally received a place of honor, so did Christ in His resurrection: 6:1-3; 8:7,8 with Ephesians 1:20-23; Hebrews 1:3.

Remains of Esther's palace in Shushan (Susa) Persia, have been found. From wall foundations, rooms, records, etc., archaeologists have been able to make a model of the palace itself. The throne room had thirty-six fluted columns, and it can be pin-pointed where Mordecai worried Haman in the "king's gate;" where Esther appeared in the "inner court of the king's house" without being bidden; where Haman came in the "outward court of the king's house" to ask that Mordecai be hanged; and where the king went in the "palace garden" to cool off his anger (5:1; 6:4; 7:7). The discovery of this palace shows that the setting of the book of Esther truly depicts Persian life and customs of her day.

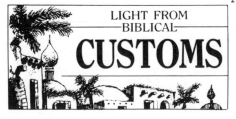

[2] 1. Put on sackcloth: 4:1. Sackcloth, often mentioned in the Bible, was a heavy, coarse, dark cloth made from goats' hair. It was a sign of mourning and was worn next to the skin. Mordecai tore his clothes, put on sackcloth, and cried with a loud and bitter cry (4:1). At the funeral of Abner, David instructed the people to rend their clothes, put on sackcloth, and mourn (II Samuel 3:31). Putting off sackcloth was an occasion for mirth and gladness (Psalm 30:11,12).

2. The half of the kingdom: 5:3. This expression was a common one of Near East kings, made especially when they were pleased by the one making a request. With Esther's exaltation as queen, her husband, the king, had already shown his pleasure toward her. He made a feast and called it "Esther's feast." He released taxes in his provinces and gave gifts so that Esther's people would share his favors. With her request concerning the sparing of her people, the king said, "It shall be even given thee to the half of the kingdom." Such an answer protected the king from losing all, but was binding even though the request might have been rash or foolish.

John the Baptist lost his life because of such a request and such an oath (Mark 6:20-28).

3. The Laws of the Medes and Persians. See LAW in Index.

4. Haman upon Esther's bed: 7:8. Many have supposed this to mean that these two were in bed together, but a background knowledge of this incident seems to prove otherwise. First, see BEDS in Index. Haman was simply on a "part" of the "mat" in Esther's presence, begging for his life. When the king returned and saw Haman there, he exclaimed, "Will he force the queen also before me in this house?" This had no reference to rape or adultery. The king was mindful of the law Haman had written that all Jews—including Esther—were to be exterminated. His remark reflects his personal concern for and protective care of his wife.

Esther in the New Testament: There is no mention of this Book in the New Testament, but there is a companion reference to that of the Jews being troublemakers: 3:8 with Acts 16:20.

SEED THOUGHTS

1. Esther, the Woman: 2:1-9.
   a. Her self-denial—heroism: 4:16
   b. Her tact: 5:8
   c. Her courage: 7:6
   d. Her patriotism: 8:3-6

2. Haman's Anger, which resulted in his downfall: 3:5-10; 7:9,10.

   a. Anger is connected with—
      —Pride: 3:2,5 with Proverbs 21:24
      —Cruelty: 3:6 with Genesis 49:7
      —Clamor and evil speaking: 3:8 with Ephesians 4:31
      —Strife and contention: 3:9 with Proverbs 21:19
   b. Anger is—
      —Evidence of fleshly desires: Galatians 5:19,20
      —A characteristic of fools: Proverbs 12:16
      —Forbidden by God: Matthew 5:22; Romans 12:19
   c. Admonition concerning anger—
      —Make no friendship with the angry: Proverbs 22:24
      —Do not provoke others to anger: Ephesians 6:4
      —Eliminate words that stir up anger: Proverbs 15:1
      —Be swift to hear but slow to wrath: James 1:19

3. The Sleepless King: 6:1. The king asked for the records of the chronicles to be read to him when he could not sleep. Have you ever wondered just why you have from time to time a restless night? Maybe God wants to speak to you out of His chronicles (Word). Try reading it sometime when you cannot sleep. Maybe He wants you to listen to His still small voice and pray for what He mentioned in His Word, or to bring to mind some sin that has gone unconfessed, or maybe some selfish ambition that He wants you to confess or place on the altar. A sleepless night could be for this purpose. We ought to be like Samuel of old: "Speak, Lord, for thy servant heareth" (I Samuel 3:1-10). Whatever you do, don't count sheep—just talk to the Shepherd and let the Shepherd talk to you.

A BIT OF HEAVENLY MANNA

The "Spiritual Thought" for the "Romans 8:28" of the Old Testament (Book of Esther) is a phrase that is familiar to every evangelical child of God—"only trust Him." Maybe you were led to make a decision to accept Christ as your own personal Savior while this invitational hymn, "Only Trust Him," was being sung. Certainly by experience we have learned that the safest policy for the believer is to trust Him and Him only. And if our trust is in Him, with the Psalmist we say "The

Lord is on my side; I will not fear, what can man do unto me?'' (118:6). And again, as the Psalmist said:

OF WHOM SHALL I BE AFRAID?—Psalm 27:1[3]

"If you are in Christ, if you are following that which is good, if you are living and walking by faith, if you are aiming at God's glory in all you do, then you need not be afraid of anyone. For in Christ you are safe from danger; while you follow that which is good, nothing can harm you; living and walking by faith, you will overcome every difficulty and conquer every foe; and while aiming at His glory, He will support you, supply your every need, and will defend you. David could say, 'The Lord is my light and my salvation; the Lord is the strength of my life,' and therefore he fearlessly asks, 'Of whom shall I be afraid?' The guilty may fear, but you are pardoned. The friendless may fear, but God is your Friend. The defenseless may fear, but the Lord is your defense, and the Holy One of Israel is your King. The idle may fear, but you are employed in the Lord's service, and He is your Co-laborer. Whom should you fear? Satan? Jesus has defeated him and overcome the world. Death? It has been conquered; its sting is removed and soon it will be swallowed up in victory. What shall I fear? *Nothing!* For God *is* my refuge and my strength.''

PRAYER THOUGHT: "Because Thou art my Light and my Salvation, O God, I will not fear. And because Thou art the strength of my life, neither will I be afraid. Even though a host should encamp against me, help me to have confidence in Thee and Thy Word. In Jesus' name I ask this of Thee. Amen.''[4]

Esther 3:5,6; Psalm 27:1-3

Books of the Old Testament
DIVISION III
Poetical Books

Subject: Experiences of God's people in Old Testament times as He sought to reveal Himself to and through them: Job 42:5,6,10; Psalm 11:4,5; 23.

Purpose: To reveal to us the experiences of Christ and our experiences in and through Him. Romans 6:5,6,11; 13:14; Colossians 1:6; John 15:7; Galatians 6:14.

Job

Psalms

Proverbs

Ecclesiastes

Song of Solomon

The preceding Books of the Bible (Genesis through Esther) contain many spiritual truths, but are historical in character. Except for some small portions, they were written in prose. These five Books of Division III were written in Hebrew metre. They are more entirely of a religious character, and they are of great importance to us for the special instructions which they convey.

The Book of *Job* has been particularly distinguished as *doctrinal.*

The Book of *Psalms* distinguishes itself as *devotional* and *prophetical.*

The Book of *Proverbs* is *practical.*

The Book of *Ecclesiastes* is *penitential.*

The *Song of Solomon* is *experiential.*

Job—The Book of Suffering and Patience

Name: Job means "hated" or "persecuted." In the Vulgate it is called the "Book of Job"; in the Arabic, it is called the "Writing or Book of Job, the Just." Some believe Job to be the "Jobad" of I Chronicles 1:44, a great-grandson of Esau. This would make Job a contemporary of Moses. Many commentators place Job during or before the time of Abraham, considering him a link between Noah and Abraham. Because Job makes no mention of the Law, any of the old patriarchs, or the Tabernacle, and, because of his great age (which was common in this era), they reckon that he did live ca. 2200-2100 B.C., long before Abraham's day. That he was an historical person, Ezekiel (14:14,20) and James (5:11) confirm. If this latter view is correct, Job, written by himself and perfected in the form we now have by Moses, is the most ancient writing in the Bible.

Contents: This book derives its name from the person whose history it records. It contains an account of the single piety, riches, afflictions, and restoration of this extraordinary character who lived in Uz, in the Arabian desert. Emphasis is mainly upon Job's trials and sufferings. This book may be considered either as:[1]

    1. A history of the life of Job, in which an account is given:

        a. Of his in his prosperity

        b. Of his afflictions and how they came upon him

        c. Of a visit paid by his friends

        d. Of the discourses that passed between him and them

e. And of his restoration to greater affluence than before

2. A drama or dialogue consisting of divers parts, in which various speakers introduce themselves: God, Satan, Job, Job's servants, Job's wife, Job's three friends (Eliphas, Bildad, and Zophar, and Elihu.

3. A dispute, in which:

   a. Job's three friends are the opponents
   b. Job himself is the respondent
   c. Elihu is the moderator
   d. And God is the Umpire, who settled and determined the point in question

The desperate struggle between Job and his adversary (Satan) is allowed to take place in the open that we might learn the secret of resistance. Satan is the "accuser of the brethren" (Revelation 12:9,10), and in this book we get an insight of Satan doing his best to crush and overthrow and bring low this "perfect man" who has been encased in "an hedge" (1:6-22; 2:1-10). He seeks to set God and Job at variance (1:11). Although the special providence of God and God's environments were all a man could desire, this did not permit an escape for Job from the powerful temptations of the devil. Job himself could only offer feeble resistance. Even the environments of Christ did not save Him from satanic assaults. Nor was Peter, in the presence of Christ, spared the onslaughts of Satan. Job was a very wealthy man, but riches are not everything that a man needs if he is to stand firm against all the wiles of the devil. He *needs* the Lord. He needs to humble himself before the Lord first that he might resist the devil (James 4:7).

Job's adversary was a *person,* not an influence. Personal pronouns are used of Satan which unmistakenly reveal personality (1:6-12; 2:1-7; 16:6,9). He is referred to at least 18 times in three verses. See SATAN in Index. Notice the manner of the adversary's working: 1:12 with John 3:19,20. This working—

   1. Separates from the best company: 16:7
   2. Disfigures the face: 16:8a
   3. Brings leanness into the life: 16:8b
   4. Takes advantage of the helpless: 16:9.
   5. Breaks asunder and shakes to pieces: 16:12
   6. Has many helpers: 16:13
   7. Uses powerful tactics: 16:14

Job, having been brought low by Satan, sat among the ashes, scraping his boils with a potsherd. Satan had thought Job served God for wealth. Job's wife thought loss of wealth meant loss of everything, and told him to "curse God and die" (2:9). His three friends: Eliphaz, Bildad, and Zophar, sat before him in silence for seven days and seven nights, smitten dumb by the catastrophe which had befallen their friend. Each sought to advance their theory as to the "why" of Job's sufferings. Eliphaz, who thought himself to be a theologian and a pragmatist, relied upon experience and argued that "if you sin, you suffer"; that only the wicked suffer because God is righteous, and that He punishes the wicked and blesses the good. Bildad was more of an historian and a legalist, and relied on tradition. He argued that "Job must be sinning, and that the sinner suffers." He reasoned that God is a stern Judge, an immovable lawgiver. Zophar came right out and said that sin was the cause of Job's suffering. He was a moralist, a dogmatist, a blunt spokesman who relied on assumption, and said "You are sinning and the wicked are short-lived." He thought God to be unbending and merciless. Job gave a rebuttal for each, but accused God wrongly. Elihu, a young man, was more of a theologian, an intellectual. His voice was that of logic, and he thought of God as a disciplinarian and teacher. He took Job to task for unjustly accusing God and suggested that Job, with patience, humble himself and submit to God's will.

Why had Job suffered so? God gave the correct answer. By asking Job a number of questions about the natural world, He revealed man's lack of knowledge in this sphere (chs. 38—41). Job soon saw that he understood less about God's ways in the life of man. When he saw his own littleness and God's greatness, he was brought to see himself and know himself as God saw and knew him. Upon his repentance and prayer for his friends who had wronged him, God gave Job twice as much as he had before (42:1-10). Evidently he was not supposed to know the full answer as to why God's people suffer, but to learn of:

1. The Divine Being, and the perfections of His nature, His wisdom, power and justice, His goodness and sovereignty
2. The works of creation and providence
3. Original sin, and the corruption of mankind
4. Redemption by Christ (19:25), and good works to be done by men who believe
5. The resurrection of the dead, and eternal life

"The design of this book is not only in general to assert and explain the doctrine of Providence; but in particular to show that, though good men are afflicted, yet sooner or later they are delivered out of their afflictions; and that it becomes them to bear them patiently, and not murmur at them; nor complain of God on account of them, whose ways and works are unsearchable, and who gives no account of His matters to men, but is sovereign, wise, and just in all He does; and whatsoever is done by Him issues in the good of His people, as well as in His own glory, as the events show."[2] Job contains 42 chapters, 1,070 verses, and 10,102 words.

"Job was a moral philosopher, and he belonged to the old-fashioned school. It is quite evident his back had never brushed the walls of a modern college or theological seminary. He had more boils than degrees. To him Satan was no myth of tail and hooves; he was the same 'angel of light' that is revealed in the New Testament, and his ministers of righteousness (so-called) were quite adept at giving added light on revelation or subtracting from the things which God had spoken. Job had no apish theories that man was a monkey with his tail rubbed off. He said nothing about how man wiggled out of protoplasm, nor by what law of nature he finally developed two ears on his head instead of a dozen on the bottom of his feet. He advanced no weighty opinion concerning the age he left the quadruped school and entered that of the bipeds. We doubt whether his day saw either zoological gardens or lunatic asylums.

"Yes, Job was old-fashioned. He actually believed in the God of Revelation, knew that his Redeemer lived, and in the latter day He would stand upon the earth, and that in his flesh he would see God. He did not try to make a god to suit himself, nor give a distorted picture to suit the modern concept of men.

"What Job asked throughout this book and the answers he got are worthy of the mettle of theological professors and liberal teachers who think man has been having a Rip Van Winkle nap and at this time is rubbing his eyes and awakening from his sleep of centuries. They say man is beginning to think for himself, bursting off the eggshell of religious dogma and superstition, and that he is quite capable of making his own religion, creating his own destiny, and carving out a Savior to suit himself. To them we would like to recommend that they take a postgraduate course in Job's school of experience, lest 'their wisdom shall die with them' (12:2b)."[3] An example of Job's wisdom is seen in SCIENTIFICALLY SPEAKING in this chapter.

Character: A poem showing the philosophical breadth and intellectual culture of the patriarchal age.

Subject: The trial of Job's patience and the ways of the Lord with His suffering children: James 5:11.

Purpose:
1. To reveal that the righteous, as well as the wicked, suffer: Romans 8:18; II Corinthians 12:9,10
2. To show that nothing "just happens" in the life of a believer: II Corinthians 5:18a; 4:15a; Romans 8:28
3. To show that man's ways are not God's: Isaiah 55:8,9

4. To reveal Job to himself: 40:4
5. To teach repentance: 42:5,6; II Corinthians 7:10
6. To show that Satan's attacks come only as God permits
7. To show how to refute the slander of Satan
8. To show that Satan is powerful, but God is all-powerful
9. To show how tribulation worketh patience, which is the purpose of God in the trial of our faith: Romans 5:3; Proverbs 17:3; I Peter 1:7; Matthew 5:10
10. To show that God alone can comfort and deliver in our sufferings and persecutions: John 16:33; II Corinthians 1:3,4; I Peter 5:10
11. To show that God's grace is sufficient under any circumstance: II Corinthians 12:9
12. To show that God can be praised in the midst of trials: 1:20-22; 2:9,10; Acts 16:23-25; I Peter 4:12;14

Outline:
    I. The Charge of Satan: 1,2
   II. The Controversy with Three Friends: 3:31
      A. The first cycle: 4—14
      B. The second cycle: 15—21
      C. The third cycle: 22—31
  III. The Contention of Elihu: 32—37
  IV. The Climax by Jehovah: 38—41
   V. The Confession of Job: 42:1-6
  VI. The Conclusion: 42:7-17

Scope: The period of time covered by the experience of Job is uncertain.

Writer and When Written: Elihu, Job, or possibly Moses. See Job's NAME.

Key Chapter: 38. Job's consciousness of God.

Key Verses: 23:10 with 13:15.

Key Word: Tried.

Key Phrase: Blessed by the name of the Lord: 1:21.

Key Thought: Testing—the death of self: Philippians 4:13,19. Includes suffering.

Spiritual Thought: Let God have His way with us, or "Let go and let God."

Christ Is Seen As:
1. Our Hedge: 1:10 with Colossians 3:3; John 10:27-29.
2. Our Daysman: 9:33 with I John 2:1; Revelation 12:9,10. See DAYSMAN on next page.

Names and Titles of the Holy Spirit: Inspiration of the Almighty: 32:8. See NAMES in Dictionary.

Job, a type of Christ [4]
1. In his affliction and suffering
2. In his patience under affliction and trials and his deliverance out of them
3. In his exaltation to a high pitch of happiness and prosperity
4. In his intercession for his friends

[5]

1. A Daysman: 8:33. "An ancient custom among Arabians when they enter into covenants or any agreements with each other is that another man [daysman] stands in the midst of them both, and with a sharp stone, cuts the inside of the hands of the covenanters near the larger fingers, and then takes a piece out of each of their garments and

anoints with the blood seven stones that lie between them. While this is being done, the man [daysman] calls upon deity. When this is finished the covenant-maker [daysman] goes with his friends to a host and the friends reckon it a righteous thing to keep the covenant."[6] A "daysman" also served as an arbitrator or umpire who, by consent of both parties, judged between them as he heard their arguments. Sometimes both were wrong; other times one was guilty and the other innocent. The "daysman's" job was to bring the two to a peaceful settlement. It was, no doubt, to such a custom that Job alluded when he was having his differences with his three friends.

This is a beautiful picture of Christ, our Daysman, who has come between us and God to settle our differences that we might be reconciled to God (I Timothy 2:5; I John 2:1; II Corinthians 5:18).

2. An iron pen and lead: 19:23-26. According to some authorities Job referred to a process of writing which has but recently been brought to light. At the ruins of Assur, archaeologists found what seemed to be thin lead scrolls. On the face of these were symbols or words inscribed with a metal stylus or pen—written with an iron pen on lead. It appears that important documents or statements were so preserved, as well as some on stone or clay. Job wanted his testimony to last, hence his cry, "O that my words were written . . . that they were graven with an iron and lead."

3. Idol worship—throwing kisses at heavenly bodies: 31:26-28. See ASTROLOGY in Index.

4. Drinking up scorning like water: 34:7. This expression is common among Arabs. They associate expressions of eating and drinking with everyday incidents. If, for example, they are caught in a shower, they speak of it as "drinking a great rain." If caught in a wind storm, during a dry season, they refer to it as "eating a strong wind." They "drink up scorning like water." Even in our day, we use an expression such as "drinking" in a sermon or "drinking" in a conversation, etc.

5. Repenting in dust and ashes: 42:6. This expression is often used in the Old Testament. It denotes humility, repentance, and death to self. In Job's case, it had been revealed to him his true condition before God. Upon seeing himself as God saw him, he could no longer face the Lord, his friends, or even himself. Ofttimes one would put on sackcloth and fall prostrate on the ground in dust. He was then covered with ashes. Sackcloth symbolizes death, and dust and ashes symbolize burial. Job had come to the end of himself. He realized that no good thing dwelled in him, so by his repentance (turning from his old self to God), he died to self in sackcloth, dust, and ashes. Blessings followed which indicated he was "raised to walk in newness of life," with far more than he had before (42:1-13).

SCIENTIFICALLY SPEAKING

It is amazing the number of accurate scientific statements Job made as well as the number of accurate scientific questions he raised. If nothing else, they confirm the fact that although the Bible isn't a "scientific textbook," yet when it does make a scientific statement, mark it down—it is accurate (another good reason for believing in the Divine inspiration of the Bible).

1. His bones are anointed with marrow: 21:24. See BLOOD in Index.

2. Height of the stars: 22:12. See STARS in Index.

3. The moon, it shineth not: 25:5. Early "scientists" thought the moon was a great luminous body like the sun. It was a great scientific discovery when it was found that it did not shine of itself, but only reflected the light of the sun. Yet God stated this *fact* centuries before Christ.

4. The north over the empty place: 26:7a. After Lord Rosse invented his great telescope, so

Earth from the Moon

powerful that newspaper print could be read twenty miles away, it was discovered that in the northern part of the heavens there was a great empty space without a single, solitary star. In all other parts there were millions, but *none* in the northern space. The great 200-inch telescope also confirms this.

5. The earth hanging in space: 26:7b. Copernicus, in A.D. 1543, made the bold statement that the earth is round and hangs in space. Discoveries by Copernicus, plus those of Sir Isaac Newton, form the basis of our modern concepts of planetary motion—their gravitational attraction. Yet Job had been told in his day (ca. 2250 B.C.) "that He [God] . . . hangeth the earth upon nothing." Solomon had said 1000 B.C. that God "set a compass [circle] upon the face of the earth" (Proverbs 8:27). Isaiah, over 2700 years ago, said that it was God "that sitteth upon the *circle* of the earth" (40:22). For the believer, it is good to know that our God "upholds all things by the Word of His power" (Hebrews 1:3b). It was thrilling when the American astronauts (Dec. 1968) circled the moon and took pictures of the "round earth hanging upon nothing in space." See EARTH in Index.

6. Rain—water in the clouds: 26:8. This verse mentions the fact that water is bound up in a thick cloud—yet the cloud does not fall (cloud balancing) or "break" beneath its weight. The weight of the water vapor (minute droplets) may be a tremendous amount and when these

vapor droplets become too large to "float" with the cloud, they fall as rain (Job 36:27). As Solomon put it: "If the clouds be full of rain, they empty themselves upon the earth" (Ecclesiastes 11:3). And Job (36:28) also makes another scientific statement that when the clouds do drop rain: it "distills" or "drips"—not splashes—but drips upon man abundantly. Science confirms that when water is sprayed into a charged area, drops are formed from the vapor. In like manner, lightning provides the necessary electric charge to make vapor droplets unite, and, as the Psalmist said, "He maketh lightnings for the rain" (135:7; Jeremiah 10:13). See OCEAN in Index.

7. The vulture's eye: 28:7. It was once thought that scavenger fowls such as the vulture found their food by means of a keen sense of smell. Experiments by ornithologists have shown that they have little, if any, sense of smell. Rather, it has been discovered that they have a remarkable vision—that the shape of the cornea varies while the bird is descending, enabling it to keep a perfect focus.

8. Weight for the winds: 28:25a. No scientist before Galileo (A.D. 1630) was aware that air had weight (pressure). Today it is common knowledge that automobile tires carry so much "air weight" or "pounds of air" and that trains and trucks use "air" for brakes.

9. He weigheth the waters by measure: 28:25b. Implied in this expression is "density," indicating weight or mass/volume—closeness of parts. "The density of water serves as a standard of comparison for specific gravity calculations in chemistry. Specific gravity is the comparison of the weight of a material or object with the weight of an equal volume of water."[7] Since ice has less density than water, it is lighter and will float, resulting in preserving life in streams and lakes. Job made this statement of "weighing" the waters by measure thousands of years before chemistry was born to discover it.

10. Clouds:

    a. Spreading the clouds: 36:29. Weather reports today are a part of everyday life. Science has so perfected this study that predictions can be given well in advance. Satellites can view one-half of the world at a glance and transmit pictures. Infrared photography enables weathermen to "see" during the night, and a twenty-four hour watch is kept on the spreading of clouds to interpret high and low pressure areas. When vapors from the earth ascend, they cool and condense to form clouds, temperatures, tornadoes, etc. Job's question was very scientific when he asked: "Can any [but God] understand the spreading of the clouds?"

    b. Balancing of the clouds: 37:16. A twentieth century discovery now enables the scientist to know that clouds are balanced in the air by two forces—gravity, which pushes down, and rising warm air, which forces upward. This perfect balance keeps both moisture and dust-filled clouds aloft. Job's question about "cloud-balancing" is accurate

    c. Numbering the clouds: 38:37. Some have questioned this statement as being nonscientific. The Hebrew text has no thought of numbering each cloud (an impossibility for man but not for God who has numbered the hairs on our head: Matthew 10:30). The thought is taking into account the "cloud coverage"—not counting each cloud, but a recording of cloud coverage—especially the number of storm clouds covering an area (or in our scientific age, covering the earth). Job was correct, scientifically

11. Ocean boundaries: 38:8-11. Science knows that the gravitational pull of the moon governs the oceanic tides, permitting oceans to "come in" just so far. If our earth were smooth, water would cover it to a depth of 12,000 feet. There are "mountains" in the oceans (another modern discovery) which, in the valleys (recesses and trenches) store vast amounts of water. Some of our highest mountains could be swallowed up in these ocean valleys. This scientific knowledge was given by the Psalmist centuries ago (33:7). This all has to do with keeping the oceans within their bounds, as mentioned by Job. "Channels" of the sea are mentioned in II Samuel 22:16. A sea channel is a valley in the ocean floor. In the discovery of these vast ocean depths, it has been revealed that sea life is found at all depths, something that had previously been denied. When the Psalmist mentioned "deep calleth unto deep at the noise of

thy waterspouts," he could well have had reference to sea life "talking" due to this roaring (42:7). We now know that sea life can communicate with each other. See OCEAN CURRENTS in Index.

12. Earth revolving around the sun: 38:12-14. About A.D. 1500, Copernicus discovered this startling fact—that the earth revolved around the sun instead of the sun revolving around the earth. Job had said more than 3000 years before that "it"—the dayspring or sun—takes hold of the ends of the earth, and that "it"—the earth, not the sun—is turned as clay to the seal. See LONG DAY in Index.

13. Springs in the ocean: 38:16a. It has been estimated by science that there are great submarine springs at the bottom of the oceans which empty into the seas. Genesis 7:11 mentions "fountains [springs] of the great deep [oceans]."

14. Ocean depths: 38:16b. It has only been in recent years that science has developed techniques whereby they might "walk," or get to the bottom or to great depths of the seas.

15. The way where light dwelleth: 38:19. The Scripture does not say *place,* but *way.* Place would have been scientifically wrong, as light travels at the rate of 186,000 miles per second, and so could not dwell in any one "place." How scientifically accurate is the Word of God when it does mention such matters!

16. The treasures of the snow and hail: 38:22,23. Snow has been scientifically proven a "must" for our survival. Some of its "treasures" include a top-coat to keep the earth from freezing; protection of winter seeds; a purifying, cleansing agent for the soil; supplying streams and reservoirs with an abundance of water as it melts. Isaiah mentions its scientific value—the snow coming down from heaven, and returneth not hither, but watereth the earth, and making it bring forth and bud, that it may give seed to the sower, and bread to the eater (Isaiah 55:10). Snow and hail have revealed their worth in times of battle. Napoleon and Hitler were stopped "cold" because of Russia's snow. The Israelites were assisted in battle with hail stones, which killed more of the enemy than were slain with the sword (Joshua 10:11). After several experiments in trying to make the high explosive TNT safe for shipment during World War I, it was discovered that the treasures of snow water, which is absolutely pure, made it possible for every particle of impure matter to be removed from this explosive.

17. The sun and the wind: 38:24. Science has established that the sun is the earth's source of energy. The Psalmist hints at this (19:4b-6). Job lets us know that the sun is the source of our wind systems—an established scientific fact. "By what way is the light parted [energy of the sun distributed] which scattereth the east wind upon the earth."

18. Lightning: 38:25. Job correctly (scientifically) describes the way in which lightning travels. The word "way" means "path," and it is now known that lightning travels along a charged path a few inches wide, sometimes as hot as 35,000-45,000 degrees centigrade!

19. Canst thou bind Pleiades or loose Orion?: 38:31. Stars, often spoken of as "fixed" because their patterns, or constellations, appear to have remained unchanged. However, the exact measurements of today's astronomers reveal a slight change in positions as compared with the earliest observation records of man. It has been discovered that the two stars at the opposite end of the Great Dipper are *moving* in one direction while the rest of the group are moving in the opposite direction. The Pleiades and Orion are *true* star groups. All the stars of these groups are bound—that is, they move together, not in various directions like the stars of the Great Dipper. Science, centuries after Job's question, has confirmed God's "binding" of these stars. See STARS in Index.

20. The Zodiac: 38:32a. "Mazzaroth" in Hebrew is "constellation." Each of the twelve constellations of the Zodiac make their appearance for about a month at a time—brought forth in their seasons, as Job states. He was a student of *astronomy,* not astrology.

21. Canst thou guide Arcturus with his sons? 38:32b. Halley, in 1718, found that Arcturus had unmistakably shifted its position since days of Ptolomy (2nd Cen., A.D.). Our largest

telescopes have revealed that Arcturus is moving at such speed that it is regarded as a runaway star. Who could guide such a star, which is 14,000 times the volume of our sun and has 90 times its light? What does "with the sons" mean? Astronomers know that this star, like our sun, is surrounded by satellites, or planets, appropriately called "sons." Once again science has confirmed a biblical statement, uttered many centuries before Christ.

Points 19-21 show that stars have names, and this is in keeping with Psalm 147:4—"He calleth them by name."

22. Ordinances of heaven: 38:33. Job is asked if he knew the "ordinances of heaven." This expression has to do with the physical laws which control all our billions of heavenly or solar bodies. Nothing is as exact as their "fixed" motion. Mariners through the ages have depended on these "ordinances of heaven" for safe passage, but it wasn't until the modern telescope that man knew of their scientific accuracy. No wonder the Psalmist said: "When I consider Thy heavens, and the work of Thy fingers, the moon and the stars which Thou hast ordained [fixed]" and exclaimed "The heavens declare the glory of God . . ." (8:3; 19:1a). Jeremiah assures us that these ordinances are obeying their laws—the stars and sun shining—the moon going through its phases—that God's covenant is just as sure (31:35,36). God put them in the firmament of the heaven as signs (Genesis 1:14-18).

23. Messages by lightnings: 38:35. Paul prayed that the Word might have free course (run) and be glorified (II Thessalonians 3:1; see also Psalm 147:15). Paul's thought, no doubt, was that prayer would cause the message to "take wings" and reach a great many within a short time. Today, thanks to radio, wireless, telephone, television, etc., someone has suggested that these scientific discoveries make it possible for the message of His Word (as well as other messages) to be "sent by lightnings (electricity)."

24. The ostrich: 39:13-18,29. A scientific study of the life history, mating habits, nesting behavior, and care of the young of the ostrich proves the Bible account in every detail. Her eggs *are* left on the earth, and are often broken by wild beasts. The mother is more than cruel to her young. Lacking wisdom as the Scripture says, they often reveal their stupidity, such as eating prickly pears until the fruit spines stick through their necks and kill them. At times they can outrun a rider on his horse. They also have keen eyesight. See OSTRICH in Index.

Job in the New Testament:

1. Job's patience: 1:21; 2:9,10 with James 5:10,11
2. The wise frustrated: 5:12,13 with I Corinthians 3:19
3. Despise not chastening: 5:17 with Hebrews 12:5
4. Companion references:
   a. The devil on earth: 1:7 with I Peter 5:8; Revelation 12:9,10
   b. Entrance into and exit from this world: 1:21 with I Timothy 6:7
   c. Angel's folly: 4:18b with II Peter 2:4
   d. God's deliverance: 5:19 with I Corinthians 10:13
   e. Life from God: 12:10 with Acts 17:28
   f. Assurance for the future: 19:25 with II Timothy 1:12
   g. A new body in the resurrection: 19:26,27 with Philippians 3:20,21; I John 3:2
   h. Self-centeredness: 22:6,7 with Matthew 25:42-45
   i. The hypocrite's loss: 27:8 with Matthew 16:26

SEED THOUGHTS

1. In the first chapter of Job he is called "perfect" (1:1). In the last chapter he "abhors" himself (42:6). The more one grows in grace the more he realizes he is only a "sinner saved by grace." Such was Paul, considering himself to be the "chiefest of sinners" and the "least of the apostles" (I Timothy 1:15; I Corinthians 15:9).

2. Job's adversary was powerful, even destroy-

ing his possessions, but Satan is utterly powerless to touch a child of God, or anything he has, without God's permission (1:12; 2:6). Satan may be our "drill sergeant," but Christ is the "Captain" of our salvation (Joshua 5:15).

3. Precious Trials: 23:10 with I Peter 1:7 [8]
   a. Trial is a Divine process:
      —God's will appoints it
      —God's love effects it
      —God's presence comforts in it
   b. Trial is a useful process:
      —It is a token of value
      —It is a test for genuineness
      —It is a medium for purification
      —It is a preparation for service

4. Job's Discourse on Wisdom. Read chapter 28.

5. A Spiritual Diet: 23:12—"I have esteemed the words of His mouth more than my necessary food." Just as food is necessary to the physical body, so the Word of God is essential or necessary food for the soul. Nutritionists tell us that four essential foods for the body are: milk, bread, meat, and honey (100% natural). So it is for the believer—
   a. The "milk" of the Word: I Peter 2:2
   b. The "bread" of the Word: Matthew 4:4
   c. The "meat" of the Word: Hebrews 5:12-14
   d. The "honey" of the Word: Psalm 119:103

Jeremiah was so well versed in the Scriptures that when he became discouraged to the point of quitting, he said: "I will not make mention of Him, nor speak anymore in His name. But His Word was in my heart like a burning fire shut up in my bones, and I was weary with forebearing, and I could not quit" (20:7-9). Job's value of God's Word was above necessary food to sustain the body (23:12). If a man on the verge of starvation were to sit down to a table with food before him and declined to eat until he had arrived at a scientific solution of the process of germination, fermentation, calorification, degulition, digestion, and physical assimilation, what would you think of him? A fool? Sure! If you waited for an understanding of all this, you wouldn't be here reading this book now. Don't quibble about the things of the Bible you don't understand. Partake of the Bread of Life, and you will live.

A BIT OF HEAVENLY MANNA

It would do well for us to consider Job's confession (42:1-6). We cannot overlook the fact that even though Job was one of the best men that ever lived, he was good enough to be lost. Much of the book itself deals with his afflictions and the conversations between his three friends. But underneath it all, we must see that Job was self-righteous. When God got through with this good, self-righteous man, the least he could do and did do was to repent in dust and ashes. When we see ourselves as God sees us, even dust and ashes seem high for us to repent in. But if God is to exalt us, we must humble ourselves, and with Job exclaim

BEHOLD, I AM VILE—40:4[9]

"Job did not always think so; he did not always feel thus. While at a distance from God, he could boast, argue, and contend with God; but when brought into the presence of God's holiness, the contrast was so striking that he sank down in astonishment, clothed with shame, and filled with self-loathing. The manifestation of God's glory to a sinner always produces the same effect. Isaiah felt as Job did and exclaimed, 'I am undone, for mine eyes have seen the King the Lord of hosts.' Pride and self-righteousness can never live in God's presence. The nearer to God, the more we discover our depravity, the more we loathe ourselves, and the more precious does the Person and work of Jesus become. Proud sinners have never been brought into God's presence. Conceited professors, if they follow God at all, do so at a great distance. O for a clear, correct, and humbling view of self; that God may be glorified in us, and Jesus be precious to us! It is only as we see our own vileness, that we shall value our Savior's righteousness; and only as we feel our own weakness, that we shall prize and pray for the Spirit's power.''

PRAYER THOUGHT: ''If things seemingly go wrong today, dear Lord, help me not to sulk as a child or to be stubborn in any of my ways, but to be Christlike even if my loved ones misunderstand or friends disagree. In the name of the One who overcame all moods, even Christ, Thy Son. Amen.''[10]

Job 1:21,22; I Corinthians 13:11; Hebrews 4:15

WRITERS OF THE PSALMS

Writer	Date—B.C.	Psalm	Occasion
Moses	ca. 1460	90	God's providential care
David	ca. 1030-1020	8, 19, 23	Experiences as a shepherd
David	ca. 1020-1011	7, 17, 22 31, 35, 52, 54, 56-59, 64, 69, 109, 140-142	Persecuted by Saul: I Samual 18:7—31:13
David	ca. 1011-971	9, 11, 12, 14, 15, 16, 18, 20, 21, 24-29, 32, 34, 36-41, 53, 60-62, 65, 66, 68, 86, 103, 108, 110, 122, 124, 131, 133, 139, 144, 145	Experiences during his reign
David	ca. 1000	51	His sin with Bathsheba: II Samuel 11:1—12:13
David	ca. 990	3-6, 13, 55, 63, 70, 143	During Absalom's rebellion: II Samuel 15:1—18:18
David		72, 101, 138	For Solomon's reign
Asaph	ca. 980-940	50, 73-83	Service and praise to God
Solomon	ca. 965	127	Temple preparation
Ethan	ca. 970	89	God's fidelity
Sons of Korah	ca. 970-586	42-49, 84, 85, 87, 88	Service and praise to God
Anonymous	ca. 1000-500	1, 2, 10, 30, 33, 67, 71, 91-100, 102, 104-107, 111-121, 123, 125, 126, 128-130, 132, 134-137, 146-150	Various experiences and praise to God

Psalms—The Book of Devotion and Praise

Name: The Hebrew word for Psalms means "praise" or "hymns." The Greek word means Psalms. This book was the national hymn book for the Israelites. It has been called the "heart of the Bible." Luther called it "The Little Bible." Jerome called it "The Bible within the Bible."

Contents: "The subject matter of this book is exceeding great and excellent. Many of the Psalms respect the person, offices, and grace of Christ; His sufferings and death, resurrection, ascension, and session at the right hand of God; and so are exceedingly suitable to the gospel dispensation."[1]

The Psalms reveal the most varied feelings and experiences of God's people found anywhere in the Bible: adoration, penitence, prayers for deliverance, devotion to God's Word, joy, faith, grace, hope, love, and witnessing. Many contrast the righteous and the wicked. Some reveal the moral and personal attributes of God, such as holiness, righteousness, justice, mercy, truth, goodness, omniscience, omnipresence, omnipotence, and immutability.

Psalm 119 is the longest chapter in the Bible. Psalm 117 is the shortest, and the middle chapter in the Bible. Psalm 118:8 is the middle verse in the Bible—"It is better to trust in the Lord than to put confidence in man." The word "Selah" occurs 71 times in the Psalms. Various definitions have been given for this expression. It is thought by some to have meant an orchestral interlude. There are 150 Psalms, 2,461 verses, and 43,743 words.

Subject Classification

1. Instructive
   a. On the perfection of God's law: 119
   b. On the blessing of piety and the misery of vice: 1, 7, 10, 12, 14, 15, 17, 25, 36, 37, 52, 53, 58, 73, 84, 92, 112, 125, 127, 128, 133
   c. On the vanity of human life: 39, 49, 90
   d. On the duty of rulers: 82
2. Devotional—Prayer
   a. Penitence: 6, 32, 38, 51, 130, 143
   b. Resignation: 3, 26, 27, 31, 54, 56, 57, 61, 62, 71, 86, 123, 131
   c. Contrition: 13, 77, 88
   d. In severe trouble: 4, 5, 11, 28, 41, 55, 59, 64, 70, 109, 120, 140, 141, 142
   e. In affliction: 44, 60, 74, 79, 80, 83, 94, 102, 129, 137
   f. When deprived of public worship: 42, 43, 63
   g. Intercession: 67, 122
3. Praise
   a. For God's providential care: 34, 35, 87, 91, 100, 107, 117, 121, 145, 146
   b. Of God's attributes: 19, 29, 33, 47, 50, 76, 93, 95, 96, 99, 104, 111, 113-115, 134, 139, 147, 148, 150
4. Thanksgiving
   a. For individual mercies: 9, 30, 75, 103, 108, 116, 138, 144
   b. For general or national mercies: 46, 48, 65, 66, 68, 81, 85, 98, 124, 126, 135, 136, 140
5. Historical: 78, 105, 106
6. Prophetical—Messianic. Messianic Psalms have to do with the coming Messiah. While locally voicing the cry of David under varying circumstances, they give a complete and perfect illustration of David's Greater Son, the Lord Jesus Christ. There is probably a more complete picture of Christ in the Psalms than we find in the Gospel accounts. In the Gospels we find that He went out to pray; in the Psalms we have His prayer. The Gospels tell of His crucifixion; Psalms gives us insight to His heart while being crucified. The Gospels tell us that He went back

to be with His Father in heaven; Psalms show us Christ seated in the heavens with His Father. The Messianic Psalms portray Christ in four general characters: (1) as the suffering Messiah; (2) as the reigning King; (3) as the Son of Man—the Son of David; and (4) as the Son of God—very God.

1. The King rejected, established, and reigning: 2
2. The Son of Man: 8
3. The resurrection of the King: 16
4. Christ's experience in death, resurrection, and glory: 18
5. Christ and His salvation: 20
6. Christ's kingly glory: 21
7. The crucifixion of the Good Shepherd: 22
8. The Good Shepherd's care for His sheep: 23
9. The Chief Shepherd as King of glory: 24
10. The obedient Christ: 40
11. The King's eternal throne: 45
12. The suffering of Christ: 69
13. The eternal, universal reign of the King: 72
14. Confirmation of the endless Davidic dynasty: 89
15. The reigning King: 97
16. Christ's righteous rule: 101
17. The eternal Priest: 11
18. The exaltation of the rejectd Stone: 118
19. The eternal Inheritor of David's throne: 132

Character: Poetical.

Subject: The experiences of God's people.

Purpose: To reveal to us the experience of Christ as the blessed Man, born under the Law, and our spiritual experience in Him.

Outline:[2] Psalms consists of 150 poems set to music for worship. It is subdivided into five books, following the lines of the Pentateuch. Each section closes with a doxology. These doxologies serve, not only to divide the Psalter, but to indicate that these separate poems, the production of different persons, and belonging to different periods, were collected gradually, and the completion of these separate collections was marked by a doxology.

Division I. The *Genesis* section—concerning man: 1—41
  A. Man's blessedness: 1
  B. Man as fallen: 2—8
  C. Man's enmity culminating in the Antichrist: 9—15
  D. Man's recovery through Christ: 16—41

Division II. The *Exodus* section—concerning Israel as a nation: 42—72
  A. Israel's ruin: 42—49
  B. Israel's Redeemer: 50—60
  C. Israel's redemption: 61—72

Division III. The *Leviticus* section—concerning the Sanctuary: 73—89. The Sanctuary is referred to in nearly every chapter, and is viewed from its ruin to its establishment in fullness and blessing.
  A. The Sanctuary in relation to man: 73—83
  B. The Sanctuary in relation to Jehovah: 84—89

Division IV. The *Numbers* section—concerning Israel and other nations: 90—106.
  Prologue: The Rest—lost and needed: 90

A. The rest for the earth desired: 91—104
B. The rest for the earth anticipated: 100—105
C. The rest for the earth celebrated: 100—105
    Epilogue: The Rest—how lost and valued: 106

Division V. The *Deuteronomy* section—concerning God and His Word: 107—150.
A. Experiences: 107—118
B. Exposition: 119
C. Expectation: 120—150

Scope: From Moses, ca. 1475 B.C., to the days after Israel's return from captivity, ca. 530 B.C.

Writers: The Psalms are not arranged in chronological order. Example: In David's experience with Bathsheba, Psalm 32 follows Psalm 51. See CHART, p. 229.
1. Moses, the Law Giver: 1. (He may have written Psalms 90-100.)
2. David, the shepherd, soldier, and king, at least 73 and a prayer for Solomon
3. Asaph, choir director in the time of David and Solomon (I Chronicles 16:4,5; II Chronicles 5:12):12
4. Solomon, the foolish wise king: 1
5. Ethan, a wise man of Solomon's day (I Kings 4:31): 1
6. Sons of Korah, doorkeepers and musicians of the tabernacle and Temple (*Korahites, Korhites,* I Chronicles 9:19; II Chronicles 20:19): 12
7. The remaining Psalms are anonymous. It is thought that David might have written some of these

Key Chapter: 119. The Word of God.

Key Verses: 29:2; 95:1.

Key Word: Praise, used over 150 times.

Key Phrase: Praise the Lord: 7:17.

Key Thought: The life of God.

Spiritual Thought: The saint on his knees: 34:6. The phrase "I cried" is found 18 times in the Psalms. In Job man is taught to know himself; in Psalms he is taught to know the Lord.

Christ Is Seen As: As a whole throughout the Psalms He is seen as "Our All in all" (Colossians 1:17-19; 3:11b). He is also seen as:
1. *Priest,* offering Himself as a spotless sacrifice, but ever living through the resurrection to make intercession for us. As Priest we have pardon from sin and acceptance by God (Hebrews 10:12,14)
2. *Prophet,* proclaiming the name of Jehovah as Father—revealing the will of God to us (Acts 3:22; Matthew 17:5)
3. *King,* triumphant over death, fulfilling the Davidic covenant and restoring man's dominion over creation. As King, we have deliverance from our enemy—Satan (Ephesians 1:22,23; Romans 8:37)
4. The Son: 2:12
5. The Blessed: 72:17
6. The Son of Man: 80:17
7. My First Born: 89:27
8. The Lord: 110:1
9. The Headstone of the corner: 118:22

Names and Titles of God: See NAMES in Dictionary.
1. My Shield: 3:3a; 59:11
2. My Glory: 3:3b
3. The Lifter-up of my head: 3:3c
4. My Rock: 18:2a; 31:3a; 62:2a

5. My Fortress: 18:2b; 31:3b
6. My Deliverer: 18:2c; 144:2
7. My God: 18:2d
8. My Strength: 18:2e; 81:1
9. My Buckler: 18:2f
10. The Horn of my salvation: 18:2g
11. My High Tower: 18:2h
12. My Shepherd: 23:1
13. The King of Glory: 24:8,10; 47:7
14. My Light: 27:1a
15. My Salvation: 27:1b; 62:6
16. My Strong Rock: 31:2a
17. An House of defense: 31:2b; 59:17; 62:2b
18. Lord God of Truth: 31:5
19. My Helper: 54:4
20. God of Hosts: 59:5
21. The Rock that is Higher than I: 61:2
22. The God of Israel: 68:8
23. The Holy One of Israel: 71:22
24. The God of Jacob: 75:9
25. The High God: 78:35,56; 91:1
26. The Shepherd of Israel: 80:1
27. Jehovah: 83:18
28. Father: 89:26
29. My Refuge: 91:2
30. A Great God: 95:3
31. God, the enduring, changeless One: 102:24-27
32. Holy and Reverend: 111:9
33. The Lord: 118:27
34. Thy Keeper: 121:5a
35. Thy Shade: 121:5b
36. Lord God of gods: 136.2
37. Lord of lords: 136:3
38. God the Lord: 140:7
39. My Goodness: 144:2
40. Excellent: 148:13
41. Beautician: 149:4

1. Adoration by the Magi: 72:10,11,15 with Matthew 2:1-12
2. Human generation: 132:11 with Acts 13:22,23
3. Divine and spiritual graces: 45:6,7 with Matthew 3:16; John 3:34; Acts 10:38; Hebrews 1:8,9; Revelation 19:1-3
4. Preacher: 2:7 with Luke 1:32; John 18:37
5. Teacher: 78:2 with Matthew 13:34,35
6. Purification of the Temple: 69:9 with John 2:13-17
7. Opposition from rulers: 2:1,2 with Luke 23:11,12
8. Rejection by the Jews: 69:8 with John 1:11; Luke 23:18
9. The Rejected Stone: 118:22 with Matthew 21:41-46
10. Pleased not Himself: 69:9 with Romans 15:3
11. Betrayed by a friend: 41:9 with John 13:18-27
12. False accusations: 35:11; 109:2 with Matthew 26:59,60

13. Silence under accusation: 38:13 with Mark 15:3
14. Mocked and persecuted: 35:15,16 with Matthew 20:19; 27:26
15. Insulted: 22:6,7 with Matthew 27:41-44
16. Hated without a cause: 35:19; 109:3-5 with John 15:25
17. Crucifixion: 22:13-15 with Matthew 27:26
18. King: 2:6 with Matthew 21:5; John 12:12-15; 18:37
19. Reproach: 69:20 with Matthew 27:29
20. Stared upon: 22:17 with Matthew 27:36
21. Friends stand afar off: 38:11 with Luke 23:49
22. Casting off His robe: 22:18 with Matthew 27:35
23. Prayer for His enemies: 109:4 with Luke 23:34
24. Gall and vinegar given: 69:21 with Matthew 27:34
25. Pierced: 22:16 with John 19:34
26. Bones not broken: 34:20 with John 19:33,36
27. Forsaken by God: 22:1 with Matthew 27:46
28. Dying: 31:5 with Luke 23:46
29. Death in the prime of life: 89:45
30. Buried, but not left in the grave: 16:10 with Acts 2:27-31
31. Resurrection: 16:10; 30:3 with Luke 24:6,7
32. Lead captivity captive: 68:18a with Ephesians 4:8a. See CAPTIVITY Captive in Index.
33. To impart gifts: 68:18 with Ephesians 4:8b
34. Ascension and exaltation: 16:11; 110:1 with Acts 1:9; Hebrews 1:3; Ephesians 1:20-23. Prophecies listed in points 1—34 were—

> *Stated:* ca. 1000-970 B.C. *Fulfilled:* Earthly ministry of Christ

35. Head of the Church: 118:22 with Matthew 21:42; Ephesians 1:22
36. Priest like Melchizedec: 110:4 with Hebrews 5:5,6; 6:20

> *Stated:* ca. 1000-970 B.C. *Fulfilled:* After resurrection and continuing today

37. Shall overcome all enemies: 110:1 with I Corinthians 15:25,54-57

> *Stated:* ca. 1000-970 B.C. *Fulfilled:* Yet future

Type of Christ: Melchizedek, the priest: 110:4 with Hebrews 6:20; 7:1-25

"Truth shall spring out of the earth . . ." 85:11. While some would say we are "taking the text out of the context," one thought from this statement could be the "truth" of many archaeological discoveries which have come to light from the earth—dug-up evidence from many buried Bible cities which confirm many passages of the Scriptures. For illustrations, see ARCHAEOLOGY Index.

[3] 1. "In the name of our God we will set up our banners" 20:5. It is not unusual for people in the Near East to hold a grudge against a murderer and his family, even for many generations. The children and grandchildren of a murdered man feel obligated to "avenge" the descendents of the murderer for generations. If any of the children of both parties meet, the victim's child will seek to take the life of the other. He may succeed, or the intended victim may flee to a City of Refuge (see CITIES in Index). Or, he may throw up his arms, and, in the name of a respected citizen, beg for mercy and

pardon. If this is granted, the pardoned one then goes to the home of the man whose good name he relied upon for deliverance.

Afterwards, he will gather a group of men, and they will go throughout the whole village proclaiming the good news of deliverance. Some of the men will carry a banner, or canopy, over his head and he literally shouts as he invites the whole town to "come and see the man by whose name I am set free from the penalty of death." We deserve death ourselves but when we cried out for deliverance in Christ's good name, He gave us pardon for our souls and we were delivered. It is up to us to tell the whole world this good news, to rejoice in His salvation, to praise Him for fulfilling our petitions, and in the name of our God set up our banner (canopy) for all to "come and see the Man [Christ] by whose good name we are alive, the Man by whom we have this so great salvation."

2. The Testimony of a Sheep[4]: Psalm 23. This Psalm, commonly referred to as "The Shepherd's Psalm," is *not* the Shepherd's Psalm. Although the shepherd is being praised, not once does he speak. A sheep does all the talking—giving a word of testimony as to the goodness of his shepherd, hence the expression, "the Lord is my Shepherd." This Psalm is in fact "The Testimony of a Sheep." Shown is the regalia of a Palestinian shepherd: the robe, cloak, staff, rod, oil cruse, flute, knife, and kafeiah (head-dress).

   a. He maketh me to lie down in green pastures: vss. 2,3a. A sheep is an animal that chews the cud (eats so much, regurgitates, then chews it again). Lest the shepherd permit the sheep to roam and eat at will, knowing that on their own they will eat too much and get indigestion, he often separates them in a pasture, tapping each with his staff and calling each by name as he taps. This tap with the staff is a signal of authority and the sheep lie down in response. They can eat only just the grass around them, avoiding being stuffed or

Shepherd's Outfit

getting indigestion due to their nature of eating. While lying down, they also rest. After a good meal, they are led to a small stream or overflowing spring and drink from still waters. Now that their appetites have been satisfied and their thirst quenched, their whole being has been strengthened and refreshed—"he restoreth my soul" (or my whole being). How wonderful of our Shepherd to lead us into the "green pastures and still waters" of His Word—giving us only enough at each feeding for our strength to be renewed and for growth so that we do not get spiritual indigestion or are carried about with every wind of doctrine (Ephesians 4:14,15). O to accept the authority of the staff of His Word and have His best!

b. He leadeth me: vs. 3b. In traveling from pasture to pasture, shepherds must lead their flocks over the barren, sun-baked desert (wilderness). To avoid cracks in the soil lest a sheep get a foot caught and break a leg, or to lead where the wool is not caught and snagged in the thorny brush, the shepherd leads them in a "right" path, away from such pitfalls. This he does "for his name's sake." His desire is to present his flock to the wool buyers at the marketplace "without spot and without blemish." If the shepherd has so cared for his flock—maintained his reputation—the buyers do not even have to look at his flock; they go by the shepherd's name and give him top price. This is why our Shepherd leads us in a "path of righteousness for His name's sake"—it is His reputation that is at stake. The world judges Him by us. O the need to "hear His voice and follow Him!"

c. Valley of the shadow of death: vs. 4a. Ofttimes the flock must cross a high mountain to get to another pasture. For centuries rock-hewn paths about two feet wide have been the only means of getting to the other side. As the shepherd slowly leads his flock upward, a height of 750 to 1000 feet above the valley might be reached. They are always in view of the "valley of the shadow of death." One slip of a foot and a sheep could plunge into the "valley of death." The shepherd talks continuously, assuring the sheep that he is with them—"for thou art with me." We might find many dangers in our Christian pathway, but our Shepherd "is with us always."

d. Thy rod and thy staff: vs. 4b. About halfway up the dangerous path, the shepherd will stop and make his way back to the end of the line to see that all is well. As he does this, he taps each sheep with his staff, calling each by name. This tap of the staff denotes a personal relationship between shepherd and sheep. What a comforting thought that our Shepherd knows us by name—assured by the staff of His Word of our personal relationship with Him. If a sheep falls over the side of the path and is caught by brush, the staff is used to rescue it—another comforting thought. If snakes come out of the rocks or wild beasts lurk nearby, the rod is used for protection—"thy rod and thy staff they comfort me." What a source of comfort to know that we have the staff and rod of His Word to resist our enemy that he might flee from us. Sometimes the staff is used to catch an unruly sheep as it tries to run from its shepherd, and the shepherd will use it as a "rod" to correct or discipline. While in disobedience we do not appreciate the staff of God's Word correcting us, what a comfort to know that our Shepherd cares and will bring us back unto Himself, even though He has to chasten us (Hebrews 12:6; II Timothy 3:16,17).

e. A table—mine enemies: vs. 5a. There are times when a wounded sheep must have special attention, and must be protected from his enemies. Ironically, the enemies in this case are not snakes or wild beasts, but members of his own flock. If left alone, the other sheep, smelling blood and sensing trouble because of the wounded sheep being motionless, will come over to it, eat all the grass around it, and will push and butt this afflicted brother. In a sense the "well" sheep become the "enemy" of a sick sheep. (This is true in the chicken family—a "sick chick" will be pecked to death by the well chickens.) The shepherd marks off an area about 20 x 15 feet for this sheep, placing his rod at one end, his staff at the other, takes off his cloak and places it on one side, and he himself lies down. This marked-off area constitutes the "table" prepared in the presence of his "enemies." Not a single sheep of the flock will dare cross over the rod or staff or cloak or shepherd to eat one blade of grass in this "table."

Diagram of Sheep's Table

Too often Christians become the "enemy" of a fallen brother, becoming critical, condemning, and sometimes even ostracizing the "wounded" member of the flock. Many times the Lord—our Shepherd—comes to our rescue, preparing a table in the presence of these enemies. How much more wonderful it would be if we would just show some brotherly love and bear one another's burdens.

    f. Thou anointest my head with oil: vs. 5b. This is done many times because the oil has a cooling, soothing effect upon the sheep when they are in the blazing sun. A wounded, cut, and bleeding sheep is also "anointed" with oil for healing—the oil poured upon the cuts and bruises. Anointing with oil also denotes a personal relationship—a touch—a reward—which shows joy and satisfaction on the part of the shepherd for his sheep. We often do this when we reward a dog with a biscuit. How often our personal Shepherd seeks to "reward" us with His "oil of gladness" (45:7).

    g. My cup runneth over: vs. 5c. The "cup" is a hollowed-out block of stone about 30 inches long, 18 inches wide, and 18 inches high. Cups are located by the many wells and springs scattered through the Judean wilderness. The shepherd scoops up water, pouring it into the cup. Because the cup has been in the blazing sun, he keeps pouring water in, overflowing, until the cup is cooled. He then calls his sheep to drink, never stopping his pouring. He makes sure the water stays cool, and sees to it that the sheep have more than enough. Even if the sheep back away to rest for a moment before drinking more, the good shepherd keeps the cup "running over" to make sure his sheep have fresh, running water—"my cup runneth over." How wonderful of our Shepherd to give us new mercies every morning and benefits every day (Lamentations 3:23; Psalm 68:19).

    h. The house of my shepherd: vs. 6. As the sheep concludes its testimony, the expression "goodness and mercy shall follow me all the days of my life" is but a summary of "I shall not want." Just as the shepherd has cared for the sheep in the past—and is now doing—there is confidence that as long as the sheep lives nothing but the shepherd's goodness and mercy will follow. This is a reminder of our Shepherd—"Jesus Christ, the same, yesterday, today, and forever" (Hebrews 13:8).

But how can a sheep testify—"And I shall dwell in the house of my shepherd forever?" Does a sheep live forever? No. But "forever" to a sheep is as long as it lives. Does a sheep live in its shepherd's house? Yes, just like many of our pets do. When Nathan reprimanded David for his sin, he gave a parable about a poor man who had nothing, "save one little ewe lamb, which he had bought and nourished up: and it grew up together with him, and with his children; it did eat of his own meat, and drank of his own cup, and lay in his bosom, and was unto him as a daughter" (II Samuel 12:1-3). It is nothing for a Palestinian shepherd to take an orphaned lamb or purchase one and "raise" it up together with his family. It becomes unto him "as a daughter." What oneness there is between the shepherd and his pet sheep! It will

Cup of the 23rd Psalm

have the run of the house and everywhere the shepherd goes, the lamb is sure to follow.

Has not our Shepherd "bought" His sheep? Has not our Shepherd nourished us up in the "green pastures" of the "rod and staff" of His Word? Do we not eat of His meat and "sup" with Him as He sups with us? Do we not "lay on His bosom," listening as He speaks peace to our hearts? Has not our Shepherd made us—not *as* a son or a daughter—but "sons and daughters" by our having received Him as our own personal Savior? Is there not the oneness between our Shepherd and His flock—our being made "one" with Him—an heir of God and a joint-heir with Jesus Christ? Has He not given to us a promise that His sheep will "dwell in the house of their Shepherd for ever and ever"? He certainly has! Even now He is preparing a place for us (John 14:2). In the meantime, "goodness and mercy" are following us every day (68:19; Lamentations 3:23).

3. Iniquities as an heavy burden: 38:4. A most common sight in the Holy Land is the enormous load carried on the backs of porters and the poor who eke out a living. Once balanced on the back, it is held by a rope fastened around the head. They are actually "bent" beneath the weight. Arriving at his destinaion, he needs help to get the load lifted off. David's sin was as a heavy burden, and he needed help for relief. Only God could give it, just as Christ alone gives us our rest today from our burdens of iniquity (38:22; Matthew 11:28). See BURDENS in Index.

4. Purge me with hyssop: 51:7. Hyssop was a little shrub—used as a spice and for its medicinal oil. It is an effectual purge, which denotes internal cleansing. Although hyssop was used for external purification (Leviticus 14:1-7; Numbers 19:1-19), David had in mind the cleansing of his sin. In the purification of the leper and the offering of the red heifer as mentioned in the above references, hyssop was dipped in blood and water was applied. "The blood of Jesus Christ, God's son, cleanseth us from all sin" (I John 1:7). Water is a symbol of the

Word (Ephesians 5:26). "Now ye are clean through the Word" (John 15:3). David knew this, hence his cry, "Purge me with hyssop, and I shall be clean; wash me, and I shall be whiter than snow" (Isaiah 1:18). See LEPER in Index.

5. My tears into Thy bottle: 56:8. An ancient custom during the time of heartache and sorrow was for people to hold their "tear bottles" beneath their eyes to catch their tears of grief. These bottles were sealed and put in a conspicuous place in the home. At death, these bottles were buried with the owner as their most sacred possession. Made of thin glass, they varied in size, from three to six inches tall. When David said "my sin is ever before me" (51:3), he could quite possibly have had in mind his tears of repentance in his tear bottles. His sin of adultery and murder was heavy upon his heart (II Samuel 12:1-14). Luke 7:38 mentions a woman who washed the feet of Jesus with her tears. Is it possible that she brought her bottled tears of remorse for her sins to the feet of Jesus? With her tears representing a life of sin, she bathed the feet of Jesus, and found forgiveness and peace. It was a disgrace for anyone to break their sacred tear bottles, or to empty them and not have them intact for burial. This woman did not care for custom, so long as she found God's grace.

Tear Bottles

6. Moab is My Washpot: 60:8a. See MOAB in Index.

7. Over Edom will I cast out my shoe: 60:8b. Shoes in the Near East are considered unclean. They were never spoken of with respect. They were made and worn only to protect the feet from stones and dirt over which the person had to walk. It was customary for the servant to remove the shoes of his master. John didn't even consider himself worthy to unloose the shoes of Christ (Mark 1:7). Shoes were never worn in the house or in a sacred meeting place. Moses and Joshua both had to take off theirs when they stood on holy ground (Exodus 3:5; Joshua 5:15). All entering a home would remove their shoes and place them at the threshold. They would not dare bring "dirt" inside. Because of Edom's wickedness, David made Edom the threshold to the Promised Land and cast out his shoe over the Edomites. To cast the shoe meant to degrade one to the limit. The poor of Amos' day were regarded as dirt. They were sold by the oppressors for a "pair of shoes" (Amos 2:6).

8. Ye have lien among the pots: 68:13. A better translation of this expression is: "Though

ye have been lying in the midst of the sheepfolds, ye shall be as the wings of a dove covered with silver, and her feathers with yellow gold.'' Destitute men in the East, having no home and out of touch with family, roam over the countryside. Like men in America who frequent Rescue Missions, the Easterners will seek permission to sleep in a sheepfold and enjoy the warmth of the sheep. They have no other place to go. We, too, like sheep who have gone astray, have no dwelling place. We drift about carelessly, and at best can make our home with others of the sheepfold. But in turning to Christ, we are lifted out of such to soar in the heavenlies as doves with silver and gold feathers—having been made rich in the peace and blessings of God.

9. Captivity captive: 68:18. This is an Old Testament expression which means to ''lead captive him who held you captive.'' When Israel sinned against the Lord and were taken captive by the Canaanites, God raised up Deborah to deliver them. In her song of deliverance there is mention of her leading ''thy captivity captive'' (Judges 4:1-5; 5:12). In reference to Israel's repossession of their land, it is said ''they shall take them captive whose captives they were'' (Isaiah 14:1,2). The Psalmist uttered this prophetic cry in relation to Christ's victory over the one who had captured the souls of men, namely, the devil. In Christ's death, burial, and resurrection, He judged Satan, spoiled principalities, and came forth from the grave with the keys of hell and of death, giving freedom to those who through fear of death were all their lifetime subject to bondage (John 12:31; Colossians 2:15; Revelation 1:18; Hebrews 2:14b,15). ''He that leadeth [others] into captivity shall [himself] go into captivity'' (Revelation 13:10). The victor (Christ) now leads captivity (Satan) captive (Ephesians 4:8). See CAPTIVITY in Index.

10. The righteous shall flourish like the palm tree: 92:12. The palm tree of the Scriptures had a straight trunk, and grew to a height of 75 to 90 feet. One had no variance or crookedness in its trunk to the leaves, and gave off its fruit the year round. The early part of the year it yielded milk from its fruit, and the rest of the year the fruit itself was eaten. The roots of a palm tree were so steadfast that the tree withstood all storms. It might bend when the wind howled, but would always straighten out after a storm. It needed no cultivation whatsoever; it just thrived on the soil and moisture from its roots. Its purpose was to produce fruit, to supply the needs of others. How true of the true believer—a straight, towering, fruitful, unwavering life and testimony for Christ! As we are nourished by the ''soil'' of Christ's life, rooted in His Word, we, as His ''righteous, flourish like the palm tree.''

11. Oil to make his face to shine: 104:15. Oil was used primarily for anointing for consecration and for joy. Directions for making this oil are found in Exodus 30:22-25. Guests arriving for a social occasion were anointed on their faces (foreheads). It was a sign of satisfaction, which brought joy to the host and a smile to the guest. The entire Psalm (104) is one of joyous praise for God's goodness and kindness and benevolence. These attributes of God were an anointing of joy to the Psalmist—oil to make his face to shine—to beam the joy of God's salvation outwardly. The Psalmist was truly ''anointed with the oil of gladness'' (45:7).

12. Enemies thy footstool: 110:1. An ancient custom was for a conquering monarch to have the images of defeated kings carved on his footstool. Then, seated upon his throne, he would put his feet on the stool, signifying the trampling underfoot of his enemies. The prophetic statement, ''until I make thine enemies thy footstool,'' was used by Paul (Ephesians 1:20-22) with reference to Christ's final triumph over Satan—making him His footstool, putting him under His feet.

13. I am become like a bottle in the smoke: 119:83. ''Bottles'' in Palestine are made of goatskins. When the animal is killed, the head and feet are cut off. Then the carcass is drawn out of the skin by turning the skin inside out. After the skin is tanned, the openings are sewed together with the exception of where one foot was, and then filled with water or wine. After a period of time, the smoke of fires in an Arabian tent dry and blacken these bottles. In such con-

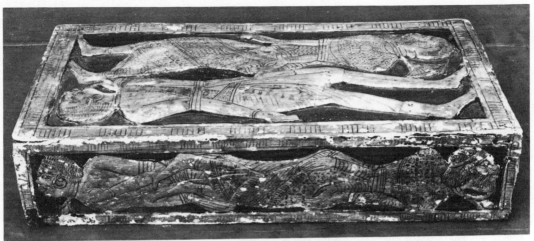

Enemies Carved on Footstool

dition—ugly and dirty—they do not look very presentable for pouring out a drink. The Psalmist was in a mood of despondency and discouragement (vss. 81-88), and sees himself "like a bottle in the smoke." In such a condition he was not only defeated, but in no position for others to gaze upon him and have "poured" out from his life a testimony of God's goodness. His only answer to his getting back into a place of blessing was to "get out into the open" and be quickened by God's lovingkindness and grace.

14. The hand of her mistress: 123:2. Servants are summoned, not by calling, but by clapping the hands. Commands are given by gesture, not by word of mouth. It was imperative that the servant watch closely, lest she fail to observe the command and do her job. "As the eyes of servants look unto their masters, and the eyes of a maiden unto the hand of her mistress; so our eyes wait upon the Lord our God."

15. Thy children like olive plants round about thy table: 128:3. An olive tree will produce for about fifty years, and then stops. Little olive plants grow up all around it, helping to hold it up and produce more fruit. In bloom it looks like a white-headed elderly person, with young trees beneath and around it. This is a picture of Eastern children who support their parents in old age—"like olive plants about the table [house]."

16. Saints . . . sing aloud upon their beds: 149:5. For the believer there are "songs in the night" (Job 35:10). This almost sounds like a "singspiration" in bed. For a better understanding, see BEDS in Index.

1. Deep calleth unto deep: 42:7. See OCEAN BOUNDARIES in Index.

2. Ocean currents: 107:25. Due to a reading of this portion of Scripture (and its context) M. F. Maurey in 1860 concluded that the ocean had a circulating system. Modern scientific technology still holds to his conclusions. Currents are due to paths of the sea (Psalm 8:8), and the cycles of rivers flowing into the oceans and vapor ascending into the clouds, which in turn send the water back to the earth in the form of rain (Ecclesiastes 1:7). "If the clouds be full of rain, they empty themselves upon the earth" (Ecclesiastes 11:3a). Amos confirms this truth of science: "He [the Lord] calleth for the waters of the sea, and poureth them out upon the face of the earth"

(9:6b). Science refers to this process as the "water cycle," which was not generally accepted until around 1600. Wind and water movements have created paths for ships to follow.

3. Lightnings for the rain: 135:7. See RAIN in Index.

4. Embryonic development: 139:13-16. "For Thou hast possessed my reins [inward parts]: Thou hast covered me in my mother's womb. I will praise Thee; for I am fearfully and wonderfully made . . . My substance was not hidden from Thee, when I was made in secret, and curiously [intricately] wrought in the lowest part of the earth. Thine eyes did see my substance, yet being unperfect [unformed]; and in Thy book all my members were written, which in continuance were fashioned, when as yet there was none of them." There is absolutely nothing in this portion of God's Word that would contradict modern medical science. This science confirms that in embryonic development there *is* life, otherwise how could there be development and growth of bones. How do the late twentieth-century abortionists answer this?

Psalms in the New Testament:
1. The heathen rage: 2:1,2 with Acts 4:25,26
2. Christ begotten: 2:7 with Hebrews 1:5; 5:5
3. Out of the mouths of babes: 8:2 with Matthew 21:16
4. The Son of Man: 8:4,5 with Hebrews 2:6,7
5. All things under His feet: 8:6 with Hebrews 2:8
6. None doeth good: 14:1-3 with Romans 3:12
7. Holy One not see corruption: 16:10 with Acts 13:35
8. Sing unto God's name: 18:49 with Romans 15:9
9. The word heard: 19:4 with Romans 10:18
10. Christ forsaken by God: 22:1 with Matthew 27:46
11. Christ despised: 22:6-25 with Matthew 27:39-44
12. Christ's expiration: 31:5 with Luke 23:46
13. Sins forgiven: 32:1 with Romans 4:6-8
14. Hated without a cause: 35:19; 109:3-5 with John 15:25
15. Christ's sacrifice accepted: 40:6-8 with Hebrews 10:5-9
16. Judas' betrayal: 41:9 with John 13:18
17. The Christian's persecution: 44:22 with Romans 8:36
18. God's eternal throne: 45:6 with Hebrews 1:8
19. Captivity captive: 68:18 with Ephesians 4:7,8
20. Zeal for Thine house: 69:9 with John 2:17
21. Vinegar for Christ's thirst: 69:21 with John 19:29,30
22. Israel blinded: 69:22,23 with Romans 11:9,10
23. Speaking in parables: 78:2 with Matthew 13:35
24. Protection by angels: 91:11,12 with Matthew 4:6
25. Israel's temptation: 95:7-11 with Hebrews 3:7-11; 4:7
26. Judas' place filled: 109:8 with Acts 1:15-20
27. Deity of Christ and His victory over His enemies: 110:1 with Acts 2:34,35; Hebrews 1:3,13; 10:12,13
28. Order of Melchizedek: 110:4 with Hebrews 5:6
29. Praising the Lord: 117:1 with Romans 15:11
30. Christ the Stone: 118:22 with Matthew 21:42; Acts 4:11; Ephesians 2:20
31. Blessed is He that cometh: 118:26 with Matthew 21:9
32. Companion references:
    a. Believer with Christ's likeness: 17:15 with I John 3:1,2
    b. Sin not imputed: 32:1 with James 2:23
    c. God is for me: 56:9 with Romans 8:31
    d. David's desire to build the Temple: 132:5 with Acts 7:45,46
    e. God perfecting His work: 138:8 with Philippians 1:6

SEED THOUGHTS

1. The Man Blessed by God is—
   a. Separated from the world: 1:1 with 2:15-17; II Corinthians 6:14-18
   b. Saturated with the Word: 1:2 with Jeremiah 15:16
   c. Secured by the Lord: 1:3a with Psalm 40:2
   d. Situated by water—fruitful: 1:3b with John 15:5
   e. Successful in labor: 1:3c with I Corinthians 3:9; 15:58
   f. Safe in his walk: 1:6a with Psalm 48:14
   g. Satisfied in forgiveness: Psalm 32:1
   h. Steadfast in trust: Psalm 34:8
   i. Staunch in discipline: Psalm 94:12
   j. Shining in his obedience: Psalm 112:1

2. The Wicked Man—Like Chaff Driven Away: 1:4,5. See CHAFF in Index.

3. Looking Unto God: 5:3[5]
   a. If you want to be distressed, *Look Within*
   b. If you want to be defeated, *Look Back*
   c. If you want to be distracted, *Look Around*
   d. If you want to be dismayed, *Look Ahead*
   e. If you want to be disappointed, *Look to Man*
   f. If you want to be delivered, *Look to Christ*
   g. If you want to be delighted, *Look Up*

4. The "Tree" of the Fool: 14:1
   a. Root—no God
   b. Branches—corrupt
   c. Fruit—evil works
   —No fear of God: 36:1
   —Flatters himself: 36:2
   —Filthy conversation: 36:3a
   —Lacks wisdom: 36:3b
   —Is immoral: 36:4a
   —Practices sin: 36:4b
   —Loves evil: 36:4c

5. Pleasures for Evermore: 16:11.[6] The Christian's pleasures are:
   a. A *Life* that can never be forfeited
   b. A *Relation* that can never be abolished
   c. A *Righteousness* that can never be tarnished
   d. An *Acceptance* that can never be questioned
   e. A *Standing* that can never be disputed
   f. A *Justification* that can never be reversed
   g. A *Seal* that can never be broken
   h. An *Inheritance* that can never be alienated
   i. A *Wealth* that can never be depleted
   j. A *Possession* that can never be measured
   k. A *Salvation* that can never be annulled
   l. A *Forgiveness* that can never be rescinded
   m. A *Grace* that can never be arrested
   n. A *Strength* that can never be weakened or exhausted
   o. An *Assurance* that can never be disappointed
   p. An *Attraction* that can never be superseded

q. A *Comfort* that can never be lessened
r. A *Service* that will always be rewarded
s. An *Intercessor* Who can never be disqualified
t. A *Hope* that can never fade away
u. A *Glory* that will outshine the stars forever

6. Purpose of God's Word: 19:7,8
    a. To convert
    b. To make wise
    c. To cause rejoicing
    d. To enlighten

7. The Language of Prayer:[7] 19:14. Good taste is sometimes offended at the tone and terms of familiarity used in addressing Deity in public prayer. Many times the wording or terms lack sacredness, as though one is seeking to put God on man's level. It is no "sin" to address the Lord in tones which denote personal relationship, like a child to his earthly father, but too often this is done at the expense of not considering the attributes of a holy and righteous God and the respect and reverence due Him. Genuineness of the soul and prayer from the heart outweigh style and language, but the Psalmist reminds us of a dignity in prayer: "Let the words of my mouth and the meditation of my heart be acceptable in Thy sight" (19:14).

While the King James Version of the Bible is archaic to many in our day, it does have a dignity about it which "modern" versions do not—a dignity about it when finite addresses Infinite. One of the commendable things the translators of this version did was to put man on his "level" and God on His "level." Man is referred to as "you" when God speaks to him, or when man speaks to man, but never once when man speaks to God. Someone has counted the number of times when God or men refer to men, and the "you" count is over 2,000 times. But when man addresses God, he shows reverence by using "Thou" and "Thee" more than 2,800 times. What a contrast! "You" is not found once in the dedicatory prayer of the Temple, but God's majesty is recognized by Solomon with the use of the term "Thy" over sixty times (II Chronicles 6). Jesus referred to man as "you" or "ye," but not once to His Father. The Lord's prayer in John 17 uses "Thine" and "Thou" over forty times.

It would do the believer good to remember who God *is* and to give the respect due Him. In a world ladened with irreverence, devotion and meditation will go a long way in bringing us back to the place where He has the preeminence in our thoughts and in our vocabulary as we address Him.

8. Names of God in Psalm Twenty-Three. See NAMES in Dictionary.
    a. Jehovah-raah: the Lord—my Shepherd: vs. 1a
    b. **Jehovah-jireh (Genesis 22:14): the Lord will provide—I shall not want vs. 1b**
    c. Jehovah-Shalom (Judges 6:24): the Lord send peace (quietness and rest)—He maketh me to lie down in green pastures: vs. 2a
    d. Jehovah-nakah (Isaiah 58:11): the Lord will guide thee—He leadeth me beside the still waters: vs. 2b
    e. Jehovah-rophe (Exodus 15:26): the Lord that healeth—He restoreth my soul: vs. 3a
    f. Jehovah-tsidkenu (Jeremiah 23:6): the Lord our righteousness—He leadeth me in paths of righteousness for His name's sake: vs. 3b
    g. Jehovah-shammah (Ezekiel 48:35): the Lord is there—Yea though I walk through the valley of the shadow of death, I will fear no evil, for Thou art [there] with me: vs. 4a
    h. Divine Father (II Corinthians 1:3): the God of all comfort—Thy rod and Thy staff they comfort me: vs. 4b
    i. Jehovah-sabaoth (Isaiah 1:9): the Lord of hosts (housekeeper)—Thou preparest a table before me: vs. 5a
    j. The Lord (Leviticus 10:7): the anointing One—Thou anointest my head with oil: vs. 5b
    k. Jehovah, the Lord (Jeremiah 31:12,14): the satisfying One—my cup runneth over: vs. 5c

      l. Jehovah-gemulah (Jeremiah 51:56): the Lord of recompense—goodness and mercy shall follow me: vs. 6a

      m. El Olam (Genesis 21:33): The everlasting God—and I shall dwell in the house of the Lord forever: vs. 6b

9. The Silence of God: 28:1. Sometimes "silence" speaks louder than words and it is only then that we "hear" God's still, small voice

      a. Sometimes He is silent because He has spoken and we did not heed: Proverbs 1:24-28

      b. Sometimes He is silent to test faith: Matthew 15:23

      c. Sometimes He is silent to confound the mighty: Luke 23:9

      d. Sometimes there is rest (silent satisfaction) to show His love to us: Zephaniah 3:17

10. Tasting the Lord: 34:8. His goodness will provide:

      a. Light for darkness

      b. Forgiveness for guilt

      c. Life for death

      d. Righteousness for unrighteousness

      e. Liberty for bondage

      f. Standing for shame

      g. Oneness for alienation

      h. Bread for hunger

      i. Water for thirst

      j. Satisfaction for seasonal pleasures of sin

      k. Hope for despair

      l. Peace for tribulation

      m. Joy for sorrow

      n. Love for hate

      o. Saints for worldly friends

      p. Armor for the devil's attacks

      q. Heaven for hell

      r. A body like Christ's for a vile body

11. A Happy Deliverance: 40:1-3

      a. Condition of the sinner—in the pit, in miry clay: vs. 2b

      b. Plea of the sinner—his cry unto God: vs. 1

      c. Power of the Savior—He brought me up: vs. 2a

      d. Security of the saved—feet on the rock: vs. 2c

      e. Walk of the saved—his goings established: vs. 2d

      f. Testimony of the saved—a new song: vs. 3a

      g. Influence of the saved—many . . . shall trust: vs. 3b

12. David's confession of his Sin with Bathsheba: 51 with II Samuel 11:1—12:9. See David's DOWNFALL in Index.

13. Sin and Its Punishment: 51. See SIN in Index.

      a. It defiles us: vss. 2-7

      b. It haunts us: vs. 3

      c. It makes us sad: vs. 8

      d. It brings condemnation: vs. 9

      e. It drives us from God: vs. 11

      f. It grieves the Holy Spirit: vs. 11

      g. It robs of joy: vs. 12

      h. It destroys our testimony: vss. 13-15

      i. It puts a stumbling block in the way of others: vs. 14

      j. It closes our lips: vs. 15

      k. It brings punishment: II Samuel 12:15-23. See REAPING In Index.

14. Waiting upon God: 62:1-8

    a. For His salvation: vs. 1

    b. For a foundation—He is my rock: vs. 2a

    c. For fortification—He is my defense: vs. 2b

    d. As my expectation—for every need: vs. 5

    e. For deliverance from temptation—He is my refuge: vs. 8

15. Setting our Love upon God: 91:14-16. If we do, God will:

    a. Deliver us: 14a

    b. Set us on high: 14b

    c. Answer our prayer: 15a

    d. Be with us in trouble: 15b

    e. Honor us: 15c

    f. Satisfy us: 16a

    g. Show us His salvation: 16b

16. Conditions to Answered Prayer: 91:15. See PRAYER in Index.

    a. Clean heart: 66:18; Proverbs 28:13

    b. Faithful heart: James 1:6

    c. Broken and humble heart: 51:17

    d. Undivided heart: Jeremiah 29:13

    e. Obedient heart: I John 3:22

    f. Forgiving heart: Mark 11:25,26; Acts 7:60

    g. Abiding heart: John 15:7

    h. Spirit taught heart: Romans 8:26,27; Ephesians 6:18

    i. Seeking heart, for God's glory: John 14:13

17. The Righteous like a Cedar in Lebanon: 92:12-14. The cedar tree is mentioned 75 times in the Bible. Those in Lebanon were the most prominent. The wood, bark, cones, and even the leaves were saturated with resin. The inside or heart had a reddish cedar color and the exterior was whitish. King Solomon used these cedars in many of his buildings, especially in the Temple (I Kings 6:15). Scripture refers to them as "high and lifted up" (Isaiah 2:13). They suggest to us, symbolically, of grandeur, beauty, power, and majesty. There are several lessons we can learn from this tree:

    a. The heart is reddish color, speaking of a heart that has been cleansed by the blood of Christ

    b. The exterior whitish, speaking to us of a life holy and and without blame

    c. The wood, bark, etc.,—the whole of the tree, filled with resin or the sap of life, symbolic of our whole bodies being a living sacrifice, filled with the Spirit of life

    d. It is tall, stately, and very beautiful to behold, symbolic of one's stand for the Lord, manifesting and magnifying His beauty

18. Psalm 101 is an old-fashioned, centuries-old challenge to godly living for all believers *today*

19. The Sinner and the Saint contrasted: 107

SINNER	SAINT
a. Wanderer, no way: vss. 4a,40b	a. Led forth: vs. 7a
b. No city to inhabit: vs. 4b	b. City of habitation: vs. 7b
c. Hungry, thirsty, faint: vs. 5	c. Satisfied and filled: vs.9
d. Sits in darkness: vs. 10a	d. Sees the light: vs. 14a
e. Bound: vs. 10b	e. Bands broken: vss. 14b; 16
f. Afflicted: vs. 17	f. Healed: vs. 20
g. Abhors fruit: vs. 18a	g. Yields fruit: vs. 37
h. Near death: vs. 18b	h. Delivered: vs. 19
i. On stormy sea: vs. 25	i. Calm and still: vs. 29
j. Tossed aimlessly: vs. 27	j. Brought to desired haven: vs.30

20. The "Word of God" Psalm is 119. An interesting study is to underline words which refer to the Word—such as statutes, precepts, law, etc. See how many times *you* can find the Psalmist referring to the Scriptures. A study of the Word gives us:

    a. *Light*—let us hide it in our hearts: vss. 130,99,100,11
    b. *Sight*—let us meditate on it all day: vss. 105,97
    c. *Might*—let us walk circumspectly: vss. 116,117,133
    d. *Delight*—let us be nourished by it: vss. 24,103
    e. *Fight*—let us stick to the Word: 23,31a,98
    f. *Flight*—let us run the way of God: 32,35,101
    g. *Height*—let us lift up His commandments: 48
    h. *Night*—let us remember His name and Word: 55,62,148
    i. *Right*—let us turn from vanity: 36,37,75a
    j. *Fright*—let us tremble for fear of His judgment: 39,120

21. Testimony of a Fruitful Saint in Apostasy: 121.[8] It is quite possible the public worshiping of Baal by Israel prompted one of the faithful remnant to pen the words found in this Psalm. With Baalism in all its ugly setting as a background (see BAAL in Index), we find the author asking a question, rather than making a statement, that he looks to the "hills" or high places for any help.

    a. "Shall I lift up mine eyes unto the hills?"—121:1a. Altars on high places to worship God were not evil in themselves (Genesis 12:7,8; Judges 6:25,26), but the high places had become identified with idolatrous and sinful practices. It appears that all the Canaanites and most of the Israelites were looking to the hills for help—the high places where sacrifices were made to Baal, and where sex acts were performed at the sex cult objects (groves). The Psalmist as much as said, "Everybody else is doing it. Shall I do it too?" "Is this where I am to get help in times of distress?" His answer is an emphatic NO—*not* from Baal! Since Baal is not able to help, the Psalmist asks another question: "From whence cometh my help?"—vs. 1b. The answer—

    b. "My help cometh from the Lord, who made heaven and earth": vs. 2. Baal was supposedly the "lord" of the earth and "ruler" of the heavens, but not for the remnant of Israel! Knowing WHO made and ruled the heaven and earth, the faithful received their help from *this* God and this God *alone*. The word "help" could be rendered "salvation." When Jeremiah pleaded for Israel to return to God he said: "Truly in vain is salvation [help] hoped for from the hills or from the tumult on these mountains" (Jeremiah 3:23)

    c. "He [God] will not suffer thy foot to be moved": vs. 3a. Baal permitted the feet of his followers to slip deeper and deeper into sin by setting the example himself. The sliding of one's foot was common to those in climbing hills, and here we find this expression used to illustrate the great danger of slipping into wicked ways when Baal was worshiped on the mountains. But the God of this remnant had made provision for them *not* to slip into sin—for their feet *not* to be moved off the sure path of their God. "He will keep the feet of His saints" (I Samuel 2:9a)

    d. "He that keepeth thee will not slumber. Behold, He that keepeth Israel shall neither slumber nor sleep:" vss. 3b,4. While Baal would often sleep or take a leave of absence on journeys, the living God of Israel never slumbered nor slept. He is not a seasonal Deity who would leave or neglect His people nor is He a God who is here today and gone tomorrow. On a twenty-four hour basis He kept His own in the hollow of His hand, and in loving kindness He dedicated Himself to their preservation and care

    e. "The Lord is thy keeper, the Lord is thy shade upon the right hand": vs. 5. While Israel was in battle, their God was the God of war—not Baal. God had promised to fight their battles for them, and He did. When they trusted Him for victory, He became their "shade" upon their right side. While holding in the left hand a shield—providing protection there—God was their stronghold, giving shadow (shade) and protection for their right side, thus becoming to them their victory and power. They were abiding under the shadow of the Almighty (91:1). To be under a shadow implies a nearness to the object that casts the shadow. God was this near to His faithful—an "ever present help in the time of trouble"—a God who guarded and kept His very own!

    f. "The sun shall not smite thee by day, nor the moon by night": vs. 6. Baal's worshipers feared the powers of the sun by day and the moon by night. But Israel's remnant trusted the God who made the sun and moon and believed Him to protect them from sunstroke and what the Canaanites supersititiously thought the moon could do to them. Whatever dangers lurked about night or day, God was conscious of it all, for light and darkness are both alike to Him, and nothing will escape His eye. He cannot fail, and the Psalmist paid homage to the God who protected day and night. Those of the remnant were not afraid of the terror of night, of the dangers in the day, the pestilence in darkness nor for any destruction at noonday (91:5,6)

    g. "The Lord shall preserve thee from all evil and He shall preserve thy soul [life], thy going out and thy coming in from this time forth—even for evermore": vss. 7,8. It was impossible for Baal's worshipers to be kept from evil, nor could he help them to live in harmony with right. He could not assure them of anything better for the future. Though his way "seemed" right, it was "the way of death." The steps of God's remnant were "ordered" by Him, and their going out to serve the Lord was directed in the beginning of their life, and shielded by God's presence until the end of life's journey. The Lord was never weary in the exercise of His care for His followers. He was never unacquainted with their condition or lot, never indifferent to it, ever watchful of dangers unseen, never slumbering nor sleeping in the performance of his duty to those who were obedient to Him

The faithful remnant had all this—including the assurance of their soul's keeping, even for evermore. What a testimony in such days of apostasy! How blessed was the life that bypassed Baal, and trusted God for His salvation and blessings.

22. Bearing Precious Seed: 126:6. See SOUL-WINNING in Index. The results of soul-winning are—

    a. Great joy in the heart
    b. Boldness not to be ashamed
    c. Cleansing effect in our personal life
    d. Discernment of people
    e. Spiritual growth
    f. Lifelong friends
    g. Personal experience with the Holy Spirit
    h. Builds up church attendance
    i. Puts some life and power in testimony
    j. Gives zeal in service
    k. Keeps us on fire for God
    l. Gives a greater passion for the lost
    m. Keeps us from forgetting we were once purged from our old sins
    n. Teaches responsibility
    o. Enables us to redeem the time
    p. Enables us to look for opportunities
    q. Teaches us that *now* is the day of salvation—that God has only two seasons for witnessing—"in and out"
    r. Reminder that a soul-winner is only a sinner saved by grace
    s. Gives us a deeper appreciation of Christ's finished work
    t. Causes rejoicing in heaven

23. Some of God's Provisions in Psalms

    a. Salvation: 27:1
    b. Forgiveness: 32:1,2
    c. Establishment: 40:2a

d. Protection: 47:9b; 91:11
e. Victory: 68:17
f. Supplies: 65:9. In 68:19 the expression "daily loadeth us with [His] benefits" is "daily beareth our burdens" in the original. Take your pick (or both), for when He bears our burdens, He loads us with benefits!
g. Fruit: 104:16
h. Harvest: 126:6
i. Goodness and mercy till we die, then with Him: 23:6

Inexhaustible are words to describe God's Son, the Lord Jesus Christ. Artists have sought to portray Him on canvas, poets have penned lovely words about Him, theologians of renown have exalted Him above all others. "Whom say the people that I am?" asked Christ (Luke 9:18; see CHRIST, Whom, in Index). In the Book of Psalms He is seen as our All in all."

> *He's my meat and my drink,*
> *My life and my strength and my store*
> *My Shepherd, my trust and my Friend,*
> *My Saviour from sin and from thrall;*
> *My hope from beginning to end,*
> *My portion, my Lord and my all!*[9]

With Christ being the preeminent one, our "All in all," it is no wonder the Psalmist exclaimed—

LORD, WHO IS LIKE UNTO THEE—35:10[10]

"The ways of God are wonderful, they strike us with surprise. His condescension is so great, His mercy is so free, His power is so vast, and His righteousness so glorious, that when we see them displayed in His dealings with us, or with those about us, we are led to exclaim, 'Lord, who is like unto Thee?' Jehovah has no equal. He is infinitely superior to all others. His ways are as much above our ways as the heavens are above the earth. He doeth wondrous things. Let us then look at Him through the whole of our lives. Let us expect Him to work wondrously. He says, 'Call upon Me, and I will show thee great and mighty things that thou knowest not.' When we can expect from no other, we may expect from our God. When no one else can help us, He can deliver us with ease. His Word is given, His mind is unchangeable, His ways are at times mysterious, but mercy and truth always go before His face. Our God is incomparable! And this is true of His mercy, pity, power, compassion, forebearance, holiness, and love."

 PRAYER THOUGHT: "So often, dear Lord, I pray for that which is already mine, on the shelf and unused; for things that can never be mine, for things that I can do myself. There are times I don't even pray at all and then try to 'earn' what could be mine just for the asking. Help me, I pray, to ask just for what Thou dost know is best for me and what I need more than anything else. In Jesus' dear name I ask this of Thee."[11]

Psalm 138:3,8

Proverbs—Laws of Heaven for Life Upon Earth

Name: The word "proverb" comes from a Hebrew word meaning "to rule or to govern." Thus Proverbs are sayings designed to rule or govern our conduct, and may be called "Heaven's rules for men on earth."

Contents: "This book is part of the wisdom literature of the Hebrews. It is not simply a collection of witty and wise sayings, but there is in it a distinct philosophy of life. The fundamental idea is that the world is morally governed.

"There are two great problems considered: the moral government of the world and the duty of man in such a world. The book contrasts the fear of Jehovah and the folly of self-will. The former is declared to be the foundation for prosperity—'the fear of the Lord is the beginning of wisdom' (9:10a); the latter is denounced as the cause of suffering and death.

"We are not generally to expect any connection, either of sense or sentences, in this book of Proverbs. Other parts of the Bible are like a rich mine where the precious ore runs along in a continuous vein, but Proverbs is like a heap of pearls, which, though they are loose and unstrung, are not the less excellent and valuable."[1]

There is a proverb for every situation, for every person—no matter what he or she is or was. Some subjects specially discussed are:

1. Anger: 14:17,29; 15:18; 16:32; 19:11
2. Correction of children: 13:24; 19:18; 22:6,15; 23:13,14
3. Fear of God: 1:7; 3:7; 9:10; 10:27; 14:26,27; 15:16,33; 16:6; 19:23; 23:17; 24:21
4. Fools: 10:18,21,23; 12:15,16; 14:9,16; 15:2; 17:10,12,24; 20:3; 23:9; 27:22; 28:26; 29:11
5. Friendship: 17:17; 18:24; 19:4; 27:10,17
6. Indolence: 6:6-11; 10:4,5; 12:27; 13:4; 15:19; 18:9; 19:15,24; 20:4,13; 22:13; 24:30-34; 26:13-16
7. Pride: 6:7; 11:2; 13:10; 15:25; 16:18,19; 18:12; 21:4; 29:23; 30:13
8. Strife: 3:30; 10:12; 15:18; 16:28; 17:1,14,19; 18:6,19; 20:3; 22:10; 25:8; 30:33
9. Temperance: 20:1; 21:17; 23:1-3,20; 23:29-35; 25:16; 31:4-7
10. The tongue: 4:24; 10:11-32; 12:6,18,22; 13:3; 20:19; 21:23; 26:28; 30:32
11. Wealth: 10:2,15; 11:4,28; 13:7,11; 15:6; 16:8; 18:11; 19:4; 27:24; 28:6,22

"The wisdom of this book is not human sagacity, cleverness, or ability, but the application to the smallest details of human life the wisdom which built the heavens and the earth and maintains them. This is grace indeed that God should place His wisdom at the disposition of man to order his happiness and for his walk in a safe road in the midst of confusion, evil, and danger. Such wisdom demands obedience, makes understanding clear, the heart clean, the conscience pure, and the will firm."[2]

There are 31 chapters, 915 verses, and 15,043 words in the book of Proverbs.

Character: Poetry.

Subject: The wisdom gained from experience, the result of God's dealings.

Purpose: To teach us the fear of the Lord and to give us wisdom for our daily walk and service: 1:7; 16:6.

Outline:

I. General rules for Guidance: 1—9
Wisdom and Folly contrasted
II. Wise and Foolish Sons: 10—24
The two are contrasted and compared.
III. God-given Wisdom for Conduct: 25—29
IV. Summary of Things Learned by Experience: 30

Writers: Their origin may be set forth as follows:[3]

1. *Scattered Proverbs.* These were proverbs collected under the guidance of God, that had come into being at various times during Israel's history and were probably compiled by King David and used by him either directly, or indirectly through a tutor, in the education of his son.

2. *Solomon's Proverbs.* Solomon spoke 3,000 proverbs (I Kings 4:32). The wisdom thus to speak was a direct gift from God (I Kings 3:5-12; 4:29-31). His proverbs fall into two groups: (1) Those which Solomon himself edited include chapters 1 through 24 (Ecclesiastes 12:9). (2) Those edited by the Scribes of Hezekiah's time and contained in chapters 25 to 29.

3. *Sundry Proverbs.* Proverbs spoken by Agur and King Lemuel. Lemuel's proverbs had been passed on to him by his mother. Whether she was the writer or merely the repeater of them we do not know.

The three groups of proverbs were probably brought together in their present form by Ezra.

Key Chapter: 8. Value of wisdom.

Key Verses: 4:23; 8:13a; 9:10a.

Key Word: Wisdom, mentioned 104 times. See I Corinthians 2:13.

Key Phrase: The fear of the Lord: 9:10.

Key Thought: The School of God.

Spiritual Thought: The saint on his feet. The "Spiritual Thought" for Psalms is "the saint on his knees." He that would be wise, let him read Proverbs. He that would be holy, let him read the Psalms.

PSALMS	PROVERBS
Devotion	Duty
Knees	Feet, walk
Prayer and praise	Practice

Christ Is Seen As:
1. The Wisdom of God: 8:12,22 with I Corinthians 1:30; Colossians 2:3
2. A Friend who sticks closer than a brother: 18:24

LIGHT FROM BIBLICAL CUSTOMS

[4] 1. A contentious woman: 27:15,16. Solomon likens the continual downpour of a very rainy day to a contentious woman—a woman who can no more be hid than the wind. In the Holy Land during rainy seasons flat-top houses are thoroughly soaked, causing leaks throughout all the rooms. The continual dripping is nervewracking—day and night. Often when arguments erupt between women of the East, they last for hours, continuously, disturbing the neighbors night and day. To quiet one is like trying to catch the wind and hide it. When the "contentious" woman becomes exhausted, her ceaseless chatter dies down, and soon the argument is over.

Trying to hide and quiet a contentious woman is linked to "the ointment of his right hand, which betrayeth itself." Near East perfumes are rather powerful, and their odors scent the very streets where the people walk. The right hand, which they say belongs to God, is anointed, and is used for making gestures and salutations. The hand cannot be hidden in the bosom—the ointment will betray itself, like a contentious woman who cannot be hid.

2. Who can find a virtuous woman: 31:10-31. A Near East woman has never had the standing of Western women. In fact, many are married while girls, sold by their fathers, without

regard to the affections of her heart. Husbands keep them in ignorance, never showing affection nor trust. To find a virtuous woman is a prize—a jewel. She is trusted by her husband, and will do him good all the days of her life.

Scientifically Speaking: The earth a compass: 8:27. See EARTH in Index.

Proverbs in the New Testament:
1. Chastisement: 3:11,12 with Hebrews 12:5,6; Revelation 3:19
2. Grace to the lowly: 3:34 with James 4:6; I Peter 5:5
3. Loving your enemies: 25:21,22 with Romans 12:19,20
4. Dogs: 26:11 with II Peter 2:22
5. Comparative references:
    a. Evil feet: 1:16 with Romans 3:15
    b. Self-esteem: 3:7 with Romans 12:16
    c. Love covers sin: 10:12 with I Peter 4:8
    d. Soul-winning: 11:30 with I Corinthians 9:19; James 5:20
    e. Good for evil: 17:13; 20:22 with Romans 12:17; I Peter 3:9
    f. Sparing words: 17:27 with James 1:19
    g. Power of the tongue: 18:21 with Matthew 12:37
    h. Pity upon the poor: 19:17 with Matthew 25:42-46
    i. Sin a reality: 20:9 with I John 1:8
    j. Disrespect for parents: 20:20 with Matthew 15:4
    k. Training children: 22:6 with Ephesians 6:4; II Timothy 3:15
    l. Have not respect of persons: 24:23b with James 2:1
    m. Lowliness: 25:6,7 with Luke 14:8-10
    n. Uncertainty of tomorrow: 27:1 with James 4:13-15
    o. Knowing truth: 28:5b with John 7:17; I Corinthians 2:15; I John 2:20-27
    p. Supplying the need: 30:8 with Matthew 6:11

1. Each proverb is a "Seed Thought" in itself
2. Go to the ant, thou sluggard: 6:6-8. Communities of ants are made up of winged males, females winged till after pairing, and wingless neuters (workers), showing remarkable intelligence. No insect is more laborous and none is more fondly attached to or more careful of their young. It is a remarkable creature for foresight and economy. This little creature is a "miracle" to observe, and can teach a lazy, as well as an industrious person, many lessons.
    a. Not all who serve God have to be big and great
    b. They are industrious
    c. They persevere
    d. They work together
    e. They are not selfish
    f. They observe law and order
3. Incentives for Soul-winning: 11:30. See SOUL-WINNING in Index.
    a. Our prayer: Matthew 9:38
    b. Our obligation: Romans 1:14
    c. Our motive: II Corinthians 5:14
    d. Our example: Matthew 4:19; Luke 2:49; John 4:6-39
    e. Our power: Acts 1:8
    f. Our helper: Philippians 4:13
    g. Our message: Romans 1:16; I Corinthians 15:3,4

h. Our theme: John 3:16
i. Our tool: II Timothy 4:2
j. Our time: Romans 1:15; II Corinthians 6:2
k. Our field: Mark 5:19,20
l. Our reward: I Thessalonians 2:19,20

4. The Way of the Transgressor is Hard: 13:15. It is hard because he is:
   a. Fighting against God
   b. Fighting against Christ and the Cross
   c. Fighting against the Holy Spirit
   d. Fighting against the Bible
   e. Fighting against the church
   f. Fighting against believers—the salt of the earth
   g. Fighting against hymns
   h. Fighting against prayer

Paul said it was "hard for him to kick against the pricks" (Acts 9:5. See KICKING in Index). The sinner is fighting a losing battle. He is haunted by a guilty conscience, lives in defeat, and has only one prospect—hell.

5. Train up a Child: 22:6. One has never improved on God's method of training children. Worldly philosophy, embraced by many parents today, says—"We will not influence our children by making choices and decisions in matters of religion." *Why Not?*
   a. The ads will
   b. The press will
   c. Radio and TV will
   d. The movies will
   e. The neighbors will
   f. School teachers will
   g. Politicians will, and
   h. The forces of evil will [5]

We will use our influence over our vegetable and flower gardens, over our lawns, and over our pets. Yet parents ignore their children. Luther Burbank, the famous botanist, once said: "If parents paid no more attention to the plants around them than they do their children, we would be living in a jungle today."

"Foolishness is bound in the heart of a child; but the rod of correction shall drive it far from him" (22:15). Dwight L. Moody said: "Better the child cry than the father sigh."

6. In Psalm 119:31 we are "stuck" to the Word. In Proverbs 18:24 we have a Friend (Christ, the Living Word), who "sticketh" closer than a brother. With this combination —our abiding in Christ and His Words abiding is us—we shall ask what we will, and it shall be done unto us (John 15:7).

A BIT OF
HEAVENLY MANNA

If ever a Christian ought to walk with God, it is today. Few have experienced this walk, but for those of us who have and are walking with God, it is a worthy walk unto all pleasing, fruitful in every good work, and increasing in the knowledge of God (Colossians 1:10). Proverbs will give us wisdom for our daily walk and service. Without this wisdom, without this understanding of the precepts of God that cause us to walk upright, we will "turn everyone to his own way." If we are to be led in "paths of righteousness for His name's sake," we must walk with Him.

ENOCH WALKED WITH GOD—Genesis 5:22[6]

"Sinners walk *from* God; they go in a contrary direction; they are opposed to His requirements; they refuse to listen to His call. But believers walk *with* God. In conversion they turn to God; in justification they are accepted before God; in sanctification they are conformed to the will of God; and then they walk with God. His precepts are their rule, His ways are their delight, His glory is their aim, and fellowship with Him is their source of satisfaction. They communicate with God, place their confidence in God, expect every blessing from God, and strive to be conformed to God's character. They walk with Him in filial love, as their Father; in holy communion as their Friend; and in grateful obedience as to their covenant God. They walk with God in faith, believing His promises. They walk with God in hope, expecting His communications. They walk with God in grace, enjoying His gracious presence and blessings. To walk with God is their honor, the proof of their reconciliation, and the evidence of their adoption. *Walking* with God on earth, they shall *rest* with God in heaven."

PRAYER THOUGHT: "Help me to see, dear Father, that there is no risk in committing my life completely to Thee, but that it is an investment that pays sure dividends. Help me to 'cash' in on this investment daily. In the name of the One who invested His all for me at Calvary. Amen."[7]

Proverbs 10:22

Ecclesiastes—Ancient Wisdom for Modern Man

Name: The word "Ecclesiastes" means preacher. "Koheleth" is the Hebrew name for this book and means "an assembler or convener." This is what Solomon was: he gathered the people together and then preached to them this sermon describing his backsliding.

Contents: "The very scope and design of this book is to expose the vanity of all worldly enjoyments; to show that man's happiness does not lie in natural wisdom and knowledge; nor in worldly wealth; nor in civil honor, power and authority; nor in the mere externals of religion, but in the single God and the worship of Him.

"Ecclesiastes is a divine commentary on the words of Christ: 'Whosoever drinketh of this water shall thirst again" (John 4:13). It is well that this book is followed by the Song of Solomon for the one is the compliment of the other. In Ecclesiastes we learn that without Christ we cannot be satisfied even if we possess the whole world, the heart is too large for the object. In the Song of Solomon we learn that if we turn from the world and set our affections on Christ, we cannot fathom the infinite preciousness of His love. The Object is too large for the heart."[1] Ecclesiastes contains 12 chapters, 222 verses, and 5,584 words.

Character: Poetic philosophy.

Subject: The experience of a man who tried everything under the sun to satisfy his heart and found that it was all vanity and vexation of spirit.

Purpose: To spare us the bitterness of learning through experience that nothing under the sun really satisfies the human heart apart from God. We are shown our purpose in being in the world (12:13).

Outline:[2]

    I. Introduction: 1:1

II. The Argument: 1:2—12:7
   A. Stated: 1:2-11. There is everywhere wearisome monotony and all labor is profitless.
   B. Proven: 1:12—9:16
      1. From the king's experience: 1:12—2:26
         a. Pursuit after *Knowledge* vain: 1:12-15
         b. Pursuit after *Wisdom* vain: 1:16-18
         c. Pursuit after *Pleasure* vain: 2:1-3
         d. Pursuit after *Riches* vain: 2:4-26
      2. From the king's observation: 3:1—9:16
         a. The *World* testifies to the vanity of things: 3
         b. The *Society* testifies to the vanity of things: 4
         c. The *Individual* testifies to the vanity of things: 5,6
         d. The *Whole Human System* testfies to the vanity of things: 7:1—9:16
   C. Applied: 9:17—12:7
   D. Conclusion: 12:8-14

Writer: Solomon: 1:1,12,16; 12:9. "Ecclesiastes is the dramatic autobiography of his life and experience when he got away from God and tried various methods of happiness. He reveals this one truth: 'If a man thinketh he stand, take heed lest he fall' (I Corinthians 10:12). The Song of Solomon was written in the glory of his first love, Proverbs at the height of his glory and wisdom, and Ecclesiastes, probably late in old age, as a seal and testimony of genuine repentance. See Psalm 89:30-33."[3]

To Whom Written: His subjects in particular and man in general.

Key Chapter: 12. A call to remember God.

Key Verses: 1:2,3. The *only* sure thing the natural man can look forward to is death and his giving an account to God (12:7,14).

Key Word: Vanity, found 37 times.

Key Phrases:
   1. Under the sun ("apart from God"): 29 times
   2. Under the heaven: 3 times
   3. Upon the earth: 7 times
   4. Vanity of vanities: 3 times
   5. Vexation of spirit: 7 times
   6. I communed with my own heart: 7 times

Key Thought: The vanity of earthly life: I John 2:15-17.

Spiritual Thought: Happiness and hopefulness are impossible apart from God.

Christ Is Seen As:
   1. The poor wise Man: 9:14-16 with II Corinthians 8:9; I Corinthians 1:30.
   2. The Creator: 12:1 with John 1:1-3.

ARCHAEOLOGY

I made me pools of water: 2:6. These pools, built by Solomon, served as reservoirs, and conduits (pipelines) carried the water to Jerusalem. Today, with cemented walls, they are still in use. In 1948 construction workers built a new road from Jerusalem to Bethlehem and unearthed two conduits, one about a foot over the other. The lower conduit turned out to be one of Solomon's day, and the upper one had been built by the Romans about 900 years later. Had the Romans gone about a foot deeper, they could have utilized Solomon's conduit.

Solomon's Pool

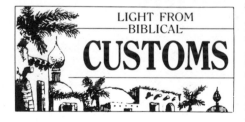

[4] 1. A good name is better than precious ointment: 7:1. Eastern perfumes and ointments are extremely costly, and are kept in expensive vases and jars of alabaster stone or costly metal. It is the pride of a Palestinian to own or use such perfumes on his person. But a man whose character was such that he maintained a good reputation, his name was more precious, and his life was the envy of all his neighbors. "A good name is rather to be chosen than great riches" (also Proverbs 22:1a).

2. The silver cord be loosed: 12:6. The twelfth chapter of this book describes for us old age and an Eastern funeral. Verses 3 through 7 give us this description:

"In the day when the keepers of the house shall tremble." The nervous system (keepers) causes the elderly to become shaky.

"The strong men shall bow themselves." Old age has caused the aged to become somewhat stoop-shouldered.

"The grinders cease because they are few." The "grinders" are teeth, mostly, if not all gone.

"Those that look out of windows be darkened." The "windows" are the eyes that have become dim—vision is somewhat blurred.

"The doors shall be shut in the street." The ears are heavy and outside street noises hardly bother them anymore.

"When the sound of grinding is low." The elderly do not eat as much now, and the grinding of grain for meals doesn't take as long as it used to.

"He shall rise up at the voice of the bird." It doesn't take as much sleep now as before, and

Conduits from Solomons Pools

they are up with the birds.

"All the daughters of music shall be brought low." The merrymaking of the young has become a burden, and all effort is made to "shut them out."

"They shall be afraid of that which is high, and fears shall be in their way." Anything is avoided that might cause a fall.

"The almond tree shall flourish." The almond tree in bloom looks like a gray-headed person in old age.

"The grasshopper shall be a burden." Plagues of locusts ruin crops, stripping them of savings. In old age there is no work, very little income, which is a burden to them.

"Desire shall fail." Barrenness is a mark of old age.

"Because man goeth to his long home and the mourners go about in the streets." The "grave" is his long home, and mourners wail in his home as well as in the funeral procession. "Mourners" usually include all the townspeople, since a funeral is a big event to the Easterners.

"The silver cord be loosed." The only woman who accompanies the body to the grave is the wife. She goes to the open casket and loosens the silver cord around her neck which she received as a bride, and places it in the grave with her husband's body.

"The golden bowl be broken." The eldest son is of great importance in this event. He carries a clay bowl overlaid with gold on the outside and filled with live coals. At the head of the grave the bowl is broken by this son to symbolize the release of the spirit from the deceased.

"The pitcher be broken at the fountain, or the wheel be broken at the cistern." Immediately after the deceased is buried, the men bearing the coffin go to the fountain or cistern nearby and wash themselves. The pitchers used for pouring water on them are then broken so that any contamination with the deceased will not be spread. The women wash at home, having burned the clothes of the dead. The broken pitcher or cistern wheel also symbolizes cessation of life and usefulness.

"Then shall the dust return to the earth as it was; and the spirit shall return unto God who gave it."

1. Wind circuits: 1:6[5] Not until Galileo's time (A.D. 1630) did man discover that the winds had regular circuits. Our wind systems are due to the earth's rotation and the sun's radiation on various surfaces of the earth. Added to Galileo's discovery, it was found in the mid-1800s that the circulating winds of the northern hemisphere deflect to the right and those of the southern hemisphere deflect to the left, which shows a pole to equator circulation. How "wise" Solomon was when he mentioned this great scientific fact ca. 935 B.C. See SUN in Index.

2. Rivers: 1:7. Solomon also mentioned that rain clouds are composed of evaporated water, water that before had fallen from the clouds to the earth and had been taken back to the clouds again—"Unto the place from whence the rivers come [precipitation from the clouds], thither they return again [by evaporation to form new clouds]." See OCEAN CURRENTS in Index.

3. Bones do grow in the womb: 1:5. See EMBRYONIC in Index.

4. Man as dust: 12:7. See DUST in Index.

Ecclesiastes in the New Testament: There are no direct references of this Book in the New Testament. The companion references are:

1. All is vanity: 1:2 with Romans 8:20
2. Judgment for all: 3:17 with II Corinthians 5:10; II Thessalonians 1:6-9
3. Uncertainty of life: 6:12 with James 4:16
4. All have sinned: 7:20 with Romans 3:10-12,23
5. Death and judgment: 12:7,14 with Hebrews 9:27; Romans 2:6

1. Vanity of Vanities: 1:2[6]
   a. Man at his best state is vanity: Psalm 39:5
   b. Man's own righteousness is vanity: Isaiah 57:12; 64:6
   c. Vanity consists of:
     —Worldly pleasures: 2:1
     —Worldly wisdom: I Corinthians 3:19,20
     —Worldly anxiety: Psalm 127:2
     —Worldly labor: 4:4
     —Worldly possessions: 2:4-11
     —Heaping up riches: 4:8
     —The love of riches: 5:10
     —Foolish questions: Titus 3:9
     —Ungodly conduct: II Peter 2:18
     —Mere external religion: II Timothy 3:2-5; Hebrews 13:9; James 2:14
   d. The wicked:
     —Love vanity: Psalm 4:2
     —Devise iniquity (vanity): Psalm 36:4
     —Walk in vanity: Ephesians 4:17
     —Reap vanity: Jeremiah 12:13
     —Count God's services as vanity: Job 21:7,13-15
     —Are characterized by vanity: Job 11:11
   e. Christians:
     —Hate the thoughts of vanity: Psalm 119:113
     —Pray to be kept from vanity: Proverbs 30:8
     —Avoid vanity: Psalm 24:4,5
     —Avoid those given to vanity: Psalm 26:4

2. Remembering God in Youth: 12:1,2. It is an established fact that the vast majority of those saved were converted while young. A simple test is to take an average congregation, ask how many were saved before they were twenty years old, then 30, 40, 50, and 60. It is amazing how few were saved after twenty. In the flower of Solomon's youth, he remembered God. When the cares of life and the love of luxury weighed him down in later life, he saw that a shadow had darkened the most precious things of life. So he advised young people to remember the following things before they become darkened in their lives—

    a. The sun—a type of Christ: vs. 2a. Cling to Christ and all will not be vanity: Colossians 1:27; 3:11b

    b. The light—a type of the Word of God: vs. 2b. Forsake not the Law, and God will keep you in the old paths: Jeremiah 6:16

    c. The moon—type of the Church: 2c. Children brought up in Sunday school and church are seldom brought up in court: Hebrews 10:25.

    d. The stars—a type of individual believers: 2d. Seek companions whose lights shine, and be thou an example to all believers: Psalm 119:63; Proverbs 13:20; I Timothy 4:12

    e. Conclusion: vss. 13,14

A BIT OF **HEAVENLY MANNA**

It seems a shame that Solomon, with all the wisdom he had, would dare look for happiness anywhere else other than in the Lord. But Solomon seemed to run true to nature. Instead of his being content with milk and honey, he looked for more outside God's pasture. If you have ever seen cattle graze, you notice at least one cow with its head stuck through the barbed-wire fence, eating the outside grass. When the cow decides it's time to go back to the barn, some fence mark is usually left on its neck. So it is with the believer who tries to incorporate any and everything not listed in the category of God's vineyard. We cannot do the things of the world and be found in fellowship with the Lord. Solomon learned this lesson by bitter experience. It will do us well to profit by his mistake. Human nature says, "Love the world and the things of the world." But for the believer—

YE CANNOT DO THE THINGS THAT YE WOULD—Galatians 5:17[7]

"Humbling consideration this! But depravity has weakened, as well as perverted all our powers. Once we had no will to do good; now we have the will but often lack or want for power. The flesh lusts, and strives against the Spirit; Satan assists the flesh in the conflict, therefore we are often foiled and fail to accomplish our object. We would abstain from all sin but we cannot. We would bring every sinner we know to Jesus, but we cannot. We would repent daily, always believe, and invariably love, but we cannot. This is our infirmity, but as it was produced by sin, it ought to be our grief. It is a mercy to have the will for if we have the will now, we shall have the power by and by. Our weakness ought not to discourge us nor ought we ever to plead our feebleness as an excuse for the neglect of or failure in duty. But we ought to cleave the more closely to Jesus, pray the more earnestly for the power of the Holy Spirit, mourn more over our shortcomings before God, and long for the time when we shall be able to willingly do everything which God requires of us, and be content where he puts us in His will."

PRAYER THOUGHT: "O God, whatever my hands find to do today, may I do it with all my might, and may they be used especially to help someone lift their burden. In the name of the One whose hands were pierced for me. Amen."[8]

Ecclesiastes 9:10; Colossians 3:17

Song of Solomon—The Book of Heavenly Love

Name: This book is called Canticles or Song of Songs, i.e., most beautiful of songs. It is a love song exhibiting also the fondness of nature, springtime, flocks, and vineyards.

Contents: Since the writer does not state his purpose, this book has been difficult to interpret. In fact, there are several interpretations or views:

1. Allegorical view, which says: "The whole is figurative and allegorical, expressing in a variety of lively metaphors the union on the one hand between Israel and Jehovah, and on the other hand, in the light of the New Testament, between our blessed Lord Jesus Christ and the Church."[1]

2. Literal view, which says that the book presents actual history and nothing more.

3. Dramatic view, which presents the book as "the story of a simple country maiden who is taken from her home and her shepherd-lover of the hills to be one of the numerous wives of King Solomon. The Shulamite maiden resists every effort of Solomon to win her away from the one who has plighted her troth and whose praises she sings. She is taken away to the court but amid all its glory and glamor she remains faithful to her shepherd-lover of the hills. Finally, when love has withstood every conceivable test, she is permitted to return to her lover and to her simple country home. Thus by her faithfulness, she rebukes polygamy of an oriental court, resists the empty pomp and pageantry of the world and proves the truth of Paul's wonderful classic on love—that 'love never fails' (I Corinthians 13)."[2]

4. Literary view, which says that this book is simply a collection of love songs.

5. Liturgical view, which says that this book is nothing more than borrowed pagan liturgy linked to fertility or sex cults. The fact that this book is an accepted part of the Canon, that the ancient Jews have always included it as inspired, would rule out the Liturgical interpretation.

6. Didactic-moral view, which says that this Song represents the purity of true love—the sacredness of the love and marriage relationship ordained by God between husband and wife.

7. The late Dr. Harry A. Ironside, in his book *The Song of Solomon,* gives this brief analysis: "A girl of a poor family worked in a vineyard, which belonged to Solomon (8:11). He, as a young shepherd, met this girl, and they fell in love. The shepherd-lover had to go away, with the promise of his return. She became despondent over her long wait, but remained faithful to her lover. While working in the field one day, word was brought to her that king Solomon, who was in her village, wanted to see her. Amazed, she immediately recognized him as her shepherd-lover. They go together to his palace in Jerusalem, and it is here that most of the story takes place."

It may be remarked that no unregenerate, sensual person can understand this book: none but the heavenly-minded men, who can truly say of Christ, "This is my beloved, and this is my friend." Song of Solomon contains 8 chapters, 117 verses, and 2,661 words.

Character: A dramatic poem.

Subject: View No. 1—the union or oneness between God and His people.

Purpose: View No. 1—to show us the importance of our being faithful to the "Lover" of our souls.

Subject: View No. 2—Solomon's experience in trying to win the affection of a peasant girl betrothed to her shepherd-lover of the hills, and his failure.

Purpose: View No. 2—to teach us how the world seeks to draw away the redeemed from Christ, their Shepherd-lover of the heavenly hills, and how His love always "never fails."

Subject: View No. 3—the sacredness of love and sex as ordained by God for married couples

Purpose: View No. 3—to show that continuing love in marriage is God's method of perpetuating a happy home.

Subject: View No. 4—the faithfulness of a maiden while separated from her lover.

Purpose: View No. 4—to show us the importance of "occupying" till our Shepherd-lover returns for His bride.

Outline: This book does not easily yield to an outline. It is suggested that the reader form his own, based on which view or interpretation is acceptable to him.

Writer: Solomon: 1:1. Solomon is responsible for Proverbs—his book on *Wisdom,* for Ecclesiastes—his book on *Folly,* and for Song of Solomon—his book on *love.* He was a master on these three subjects (I Kings 4:32, 33, 11:1,2).

Key Chapter: 1. Communion of bride and bridegroom.

Key Verse: 6:3.

Key Word: Beloved, found 23 times. See I John 3:1,2.

Key Phrase: My beloved is mine, and I am his: 2:16.

Key Thought: The fullness of Christ.

Spiritual Thought: Love Him with all your heart.

Christ Is Seen As:
1. The Rose of Sharon: 2:1a
2. The Lily of the Valleys: 2:1b
3. The Chiefest among ten thousand—the heavenly Bridegroom: 5:10
4. The altogether lovely One: 5:16

The Song of Solomon gives us a picture of the Church, and the relationship between the believer and the Bridegroom. Previously stated, Dr. Ironside's view seems to bring this this out.

1. The Bridegroom:
   a. His love covers all defects of the bride: 4:7; 7:10
   b. He rejoices over her: Isaiah 62:5
   c. He gave His life for her: Ephesians 5:25
   d. He will come to claim her as His own: I Thessalonians 4:16,17
   e. He will present her to His Father a glorious bride: Ephesians 5:27

2. The Bride—
   a. Feels her unworthiness: 1:5
   b. Loves the Bridegroom because He first loved her: 2:16 with I John 4:19
   c. Is purified and dressed in a robe of righteousness: Revelation 19:8
   d. Wears the jewels of divine grace: Isaiah 61:10
   e. Looks for His appearing: Hebrews 9:28
   f. Invites others to the wedding: Revelation 22:17

Song of Solomon in the New Testament: There are no direct references of this book in the New Testament. The following are companion references.
1. Drawn by God: 1:4a with John 6:44
2. Running the race: 1:4b with I Corinthians 9:24-26a; Philippians 3:12-14
3. The believer spotless: 4:7 with Ephesians 5:27
4. Vineyard let out to keepers: 8:11 with Matthew 21:33-43

1. The Song of Solomon is scented with the fragrance of flowers, blossoms, and spices. Flowers are illustrative of the Christian life. See FLOWERS in Index.

    a. Scented flowers—a fragrant, attractive life: 1:12; 4:13,14 with II Corinthians 2:15a

    b. Living flowers—abundant life in the soul: Matthew 6:28,29 with John 10:10b

    c. Blossoming flowers—a testifying life: Isaiah 35:1,2 with Psalm 107:2

    d. Trusting flowers—a mature life: Luke 12:27 with Proverbs 3:5,6

    e. A growing flower—a life without sham: Hosea 14:5 with II Peter 3:18

    f. Flowers of brevity—serving while living: Job 14:2 with II Timothy 4:6,7

    g. Resurrection flowers: 2:11,12 with Philippians 3:21; I John 3:1,2

2. Little Foxes that Spoil the Vines: 2:15 (see FRUIT OF SPIRIT in Index). D. L. Moody has linked this verse with the "fruit of the spirit" (Galatians 5:22,23) and shows how the little foxes of—

    a. Selfishness spoil love

    b. Discontent spoil joy

    c. Anxious thoughts spoil peace

    d. Impatience spoil longsuffering

    e. Bitter words spoil gentleness

    f. Indolence spoil goodness

    g. Doubt spoil faith

    h. Pride spoil meekness

    i. Worldly pleasure spoil temperance

    j. Disobedience spoil fellowship with God

    k. Misplaced activity spoil service

    l. Envy spoil Christian unity

    m. Imagination spoil worship and devotion

Lovers always call one another sweet names. Sometimes those names are not understood except by those involved. The general public will say they are silly names, but the lovers know their meaning, silly or not! These names are for the person or persons loved, not for every Tom, Dick, and Harry. Even our heavenly Father has names for His loved ones. They will sound silly to the world, but to us who are the redeemed of the Lord, we anxiously await the time we stand before the Lord and hear the Lover of our souls call us by a name that only we will understand (Revelation 2:17). As we read this Song of Solomon, we cannot help but notice the love and devotion the bride has for her shepherd-lover. And such name calling by the bride! Each name is worthy of His being.

THY NAME IS AS OINTMENT POURED OUT—1:3[3]

"The name of Jesus is incomparably sweet and precious. There is no name in heaven like His, it is above every name. It perfumes heaven above and the Church below. Its fragrance is unequalled. We are never weary of it and we never shall be. It comprises all we need; it contains all we desire. Having Christ we have all things. He is Christ, or God anointed; consecrated to be a Priest perpetually; sanctified to be God's Prophet and Apostle; qualified to be God's King to reign over and on His holy hill Zion. He is Jesus, God's Savior, by whom God saves sinners, millions of sinners, the vilest sinners. He is Lord—all power in heaven and earth is given to Him. He is supreme, or head over all. He is the Lord Jesus Christ. He is all that God can give, all that we can require or enjoy. When the Holy Spirit opens up the meaning of His precious name and gives us to realize our interest in it, it appears divinely sweet and glorious. Precious name! May I know it more fully, enjoy it more powerfully, publish it more effectually, and praise it more frequently. Name of Jesus, be Thou my Solace, my Subject, my Song.''

 PRAYER THOUGHT: ''Just as bees gather their pollen in the midst of the flowers' fragrance, may I gather from Christ, dear Father, all that is necessary to attract others to Him who is the 'Rose of Sharon' and the 'Lily of the Valley.' In His name, Amen.''[4]

Song of Solomon 2:1; I Timothy 1:16

Books of the Old Testament
DIVISION IV
Prophetical Books

Subject: God's counsels concerning Israel, the Nations, and His Son, Jesus Christ: Daniel 9:20-27.

Purpose: To give us a "light in a dark place": II Peter 1:19.

Major Prophets

Isaiah

Jeremiah and his Lamentations

Ezekiel

Daniel

Minor Prophets

Hosea

Joel

Amos

Obediah

Jonah

Micah

Nahum

Habakkuk

Zephaniah

Haggai

Zechariah

Malachi

The reader should keep in mind that all the prophets except five prophesied *before* Israel's captivity in Babylon; Ezekiel and Daniel *during* captivity; Haggai, Zechariah, and Malachi *after* captivity. See KINGS in Index.

Prophets and Prophecy

The prophets, whose writings make up this fourth section of the Bible, were *true* prophets who spoke (and wrote) as they were moved by the Holy Spirit. None of the writings of false prophets are in the Canon of Scripture—only those whose writings are of a "more sure word of prophecy" (II Peter 1:19-21).

Prophecy, simply defined, is speaking forth the revealed Word of God, whether the message pertains to the present or to the future. It is "the revelation of the will of God by a man or woman who is God's chosen spokesman. That man or woman is a prophet of God who stands first before God to discern His will, and then stands before men to declare that divine will."[1]

Thus, while false prophets usually "seek" to receive messages of a prophetic nature (through a study of the heavens, potions, dreams, etc.), true biblical prophecy is not inherently sought after. Rather, God seeks out His man, fills him with the spirit of prophecy, and reveals His message through him.

Moses gave the test of a true prophet (Deuteronomy 18:20-22). This alone qualifies a man for the office of a prophet. There are times, however, when we might "limit" this calling to those of our own little group. Joshua was concerned about Eldad and Medad prophesying. But Moses assured him that others besides the seventy elders could prophesy (Numbers 11:26-29). This account is similar to the jealousy of the disciples when one outside their "circle" was casting out demons (Luke 9:49,50). Just as Jesus said, "He that is not against us is for us," so Moses replied to Joshua, "Would to God that all the Lord's people were prophets and that the Lord would put His Spirit upon them!" We are to "try the spirits." If one speaks "not according to [the] Word, there is no light in them" (I John 4:1; Isaiah 8:20).

Old Testament prophets were passionate nationalists, telling forth (preaching) and forth-telling (prophesying) their message to the people of Israel. They rebuked sin in field and palace, before priest and king, pulling no punches nor showing favor with anyone. Priests and kings had stooped so low in sin that there were no spiritual leaders among the people. Prophets filled this gap for God, but due to their message of truth and prediction, they were mocked as God's messengers, their messages were despised, and they were misused—(were told to leave town, beaten, imprisoned, sawn asunder, etc.—II Chronicles 36:14-16; Amos 7:12,13; Jeremiah 20:1-3; 37:11-15; Hebrews 11:37).

Prophecy is God's way of writing history in advance. For those who accept the Bible as the revealed Word of God, there is no question regarding prophecy. Fulfilled prophecies is one of the infallible proofs of the inspiration of Scripture. It assures the believer that unfulfilled proph-ecy *will,* in God's time, be fulfilled.

While some prophetical books are designated *Major* and *Minor,* one is no less important than the other. Major and Minor have to do with size—not the content of the book. There are five main themes of Bible prophecy, which concern:

1. Israel
2. Christ—the Messiah
3. Gentile nations
4. The Church
5. Last things

Chronological Order of the Prophets

	Prophet	Approx. Date of Prophecy	To Whom	Theme
1.	Joel	835-796 B.C.	South. Kingdom	The day of the Lord
2.	Jonah	784-722 B.C.	Nineveh	God's concern for Gentiles
3.	Amos	764-755 B.C.	North. Kingdom	Judgment and sin's consequence
4.	Hosea	755-714 B.C.	North. Kingdom	God's enduring love in spite of sin
5.	Isaiah	745-680 B.C.	South. Kingdom	Glorious future for God's remnant
6.	Micah	740-698 B.C.	South. and North. Kingdom	Present sins and future hopes
7.	Nahum	648-620 B.C.	Nineveh	Judgment and Nineveh's fall
8.	Zephaniah	634-625 B.C.	South. Kingdom	Jerusalem's sin and doom
9.	Jeremiah	626-580 B.C.	South. Kingdom	Lamenting Jerusalem's destruction
10.	Habakkuk	625-610 B.C.	South. Kingdom	A call to faith
11.	Daniel	605-530 B.C.	Remnant	World kingdoms; God's future kingdom
12.	Ezekiel	592-570 B.C.	Remnant	Israel's judgment and glory
13.	Obediah	586 B.C. (?)	Edom	Edom's doom
14.	Haggai	520 B.C.	Remnant	Put God's work first—rebuild the Temple
15.	Zechariah	520-518 B.C.	Remnant	Present needs and future glory
16.	Malachi	450-400 B.C.	Remnant	A rebuke for selfishness

Isaiah—The Evangelical Prophet

Name: Isaiah means "the salvation of Jehovah."

Writer: Isaiah: 1:1. See 6:1 with John 12:41; 53:1 with John 12:38. Because there are two sections in his book, critics have said there were two different Isaiahs. Their chief arguments center on the style in the second section, which is vastly different from that in the first, and certain prophecies relating to the Babylonian captivity and the naming of Cyrus as Israel's liberator over 100 years before he was born. Isaiah prophesied for approximately 65 years, and it is understandable that in his late years his style would change, especially since this section has to do with future events. Anyone who accepts the Bible as inspired of God has no difficulty in matters of prophesy. Isaiah was well qualified, as God's prophet, to predict Israel's captor and liberator.

New Testament evidence supports the believer's acceptance of just *one* Isaiah. He is quoted over 300 times in the New Testament—more than from all other Old Testament prophecies combined. In each instance, whether referred to by Christ or other writers, he is called "Isaiah," or "Isaiah the prophet"—*singular.* Never is there inference in the New Testament that there was more than one Isaiah. Interesting, too, that many of Isaiah's statements in the New Testament are from the *second* section of his book! See SCROLLS in Index.

Period of His Prophecy: 1:1. "In the days of Uzziah, Jotham, Ahaz, and Hezekiah, kings of Juday." This period was ca. 745-680 B.C., approximately 25 years before the Assyrian captivity of the Northern Kingdom to about 40 years after it. Isaiah was contemporary with Hosea, Micah, and Nahum. He was the *fifth* prophet.

People of His Prophesy: His ministry was confined almost exclusively to the Southern Kingdom of Judah.

Contents: Isaiah's message, which contains some things historical, but is chiefly prophetical, is threefold:
1. Indictment against Israel for her sinful condition and the need for repentance
2. Impending Babylonian captivity
3. God's redemption through the coming, suffering Messiah, and the glory to be revealed through Him in His future kingdom on earth

"This book has the same number of chapters that the Bible has books—66. The Bible has two main divisions—Isaiah has two main divisions. The first division of Isaiah includes chapters 1—39; the first division of the Bible, the Old Testament, contains 39 books. The second division of Isaiah contains 27 chapters (40—66). The second division of the Bible, the New Testament, contains 27 books.

"The 'Old Testament' section of Isaiah begins where the first book of the Bible begins, viz., with the heavens and the earth (1:2 with Genesis 1:1). The 39th or last book of the Old Testament (Malachi) ends with a malediction and a prediction of judgment. So does the first section of Isaiah (39:6 with Malachi 4:1). The 'New Testament' section of Isaiah (chs. 40-66) begins where the 40th book of the Bible (Matthew) begins. Isaiah (40:3) *predicts* the ministry of John the Baptist, and in the 40th book of the Bible we have the *performance* of John's ministry (Matthew 3:1-3). The last chapter of Isaiah ends just where the last book of the Bible ends—with a new heaven and a new earth (66:22 with Revelation 21:1)."[1] In the 66 chapters of Isaiah there are 1,292 verses and 37,044 words.

Character: Mainly prophetical.

Subject: God's message of salvation for Israel and the nations through the Holy One of Israel.

Purpose: To reveal God's way of salvation for us through Jesus Christ, the Messiah, and the kingdom of Christ, over which we are to be co-rulers with Him.

Outline:[2]

    I. Division I—*Prophetic:* 1—35.
        A. Prophecies Concerning Judah and Israel: 1—12
            1. God's Indictment and Prediction of Judgment: 1—5
            2. Isaiah's Call and Commission: 6
            3. Promised Restoration and Thanksgiving: 7—12
        B. Predictions against Foreign Nations: 13:23
        C. Announcements of Judgments and Deliverances: 24—35
            1. Picture of universal judgment: 24
            2. Book of songs—four: 25—27
            3. Book of woes—six: 28—33
            4. Future of Nations and Israel contrasted: 34,35
    II. Division II—*Historic:* 36—39
        Key Note: Confiscation   *Outlook:* Assyrian and Babylonian
        A. Events in the Life of Hezekiah: II Kings 18—20; II Chronicles 29—32
            1. Looking backward—Assyrian: 36,37
            2. Looking forward—Babylonian: 38,39
    III. Division III—*Messianic:* 40—66
        Key Note: Consolation   *Outlook:* Babylonian
        A. The Deliverance: 40—48
            1. God and the gods
            2. Israel and the heathen compared
        B. The Deliverer—the suffering and glory of Jehovah's Servant: 49—57
        C. The Delivered—the faithful and unfaithful compared, and their end: 58—66

Key Chapter: 53. The suffering Savior.

Key Verse: 53:5.

Key Word: Salvation, found 28 times.

Key Phrase: The Holy One of Israel: 1:4.

Key Thought: Consolation and salvation.

Spiritual Thought: He (Messiah) *is* coming.

Christ Is Seen As: In no other book in all the Old Testament is Christ revealed in such fullness, in so many different offices, with such glory and beauty as He is in the prophecy of Isaiah. He is portrayed as to His mission of the first advent, what He is to the believer, and as to His second coming.

    1. *As to His mission: first Advent—*
        —Branch of the Lord: 4:2
        —Immanuel—God with us: 7:14; 9:6; 40:3
        —Illuminator: 9:2
        —Branch of David: 11:1
        —A tried Stone: 28:16
        —The Glory of the Lord: 40:5
        —God's Elect: 42:1
        —God's wise, righteous Servant: 42:1; 52:13; 53:11
        —Light of the Gentiles to liberate: 42:6,7
        —The Arm of the Lord: 53:1
        —A tender Plant: 53:2
        —A Root out of dry ground: 53:2
        —The uncomely Savior: 53:2
        —The despised and rejected Messiah: 53:3
        —The Man of sorrows: 53:3
        —The divine substitute: 53:5

   —The Sin-bearer: 53:6
   —The silent Sufferer: 53:7
   —The cut-off Branch: 53:8
   —The stricken Shepherd: 53:8
   —The Offering for my sin: 53:10
   —The satisfied Redeemer: 53:11
   —A Witness to the People: 55:4
   —The Holy One of Israel: 55:5

2. *What He is to the believer—*
   —A Sanctuary: 8:14
   —Wonderful: 9:6
   —Our Counselor: 9:6
   —Our mighty God: 9:6
   —Our everlasting Father: 9:6
   —Our Strength: 12:2
   —Our Song: 12:2
   —Our Salvation: 12:2
   —A Nail in a sure place: 22:23
   —A glorious Throne to His Father's house: 22:23
   —Strength to the poor and needy: 25:4
   —Our Covert (Refuge) from the tempest: 25:4; 32:2
   —Shadow of a great rock in a weary land: 25:4; 32:2
   —Precious Cornerstone: 28:16
   —Our sure Foundation: 28:16
   —Our hiding Place: 32:2
   —Rivers of water in a dry place: 32:2
   —Our Judge: 33:22
   —Our Law-giver: 33:22
   —Our Shepherd: 40:11
   —A polished Shaft: 49:2
   —Our grief and sorrow Bearer: 53:4
   —Our righteous Mediator: 53:11
   —Our conquering Hero: 53:12
   —Our interceding Priest: 53:12
   —Our Witness: 55:4
   —Our Leader and Commander: 55:4
   —Our Redeemer: 59:20
   —The everlasting Light: 60:20
    —of Israel: 10:17; but also a Stone of stumbling: 8:14
    —of the Gentiles: 42:6
   —The Angel of His presence: 63:9

3. *His second Advent—*
   —The Prince of peace: 9:6
   —An Ensign of the people: 11:10
   —A Crown of glory: 28:5
   —A Diadem of beauty: 28:5
   —The righteous King: 32:1; 33:17,22
   —The Silencer of kings: 52:15

Names and Titles of God. See NAMES in Dictionary.
  1. The Holy One of Israel: 1:4; 47:4b
  2. The Lord of hosts: 6:3; 47:4a; 54:5
  3. Jehovah: everlasting strength—Rock of Ages: 26:4
  4. Maker: 54:5

5. Savior and Redeemer: 54:5; 60:16
6. The God of the whole earth: 54:5
7. The mighty One. of Jacob: 60:16
8. Our Father: 64:8
9. Our Potter: 64:8

Names and Titles of the Holy Spirit. See NAMES in Dictionary.

1. The Spirit of judgment: 4:4
2. The Spirit of burning: 4:4
3. The Spirit of the Lord (God): 11:2; 61:1
4. The Spirit of wisdom and understanding: 11:2
5. The Spirit of counsel and might: 11:2
6. The Spirit of knowledge: 11:2
7. The Spirit of the fear of the Lord: 11:2
8. His Holy Spirit: 63:10

1. Messianic. "In our study of Isaiah, very particular attention is drawn to the prophecies of Christ. He prophesies of His virgin birth, His twofold nature, His many names—human and Divine, His mission to the Gentiles as well as to the Jews, His humiliation and His glory. If these things were spoken before they came to pass they must be Divine in their origin. If they meet and find fulfillment in Jesus of Nazareth and in Him only, He must be the Son of God and Redeemer of the world."[3]

a. Divinity: 9:6; 25:9 with John 10:30
b. First advent: 9:6; 28:16 with Matthew 1:21-23; Luke 2:7
c. Virgin birth and human generation: 7:14; 11:1 with Matthew 1; Luke 1:26-38; 2:1-20
d. Adoration by Magi: 60:3,6 with Matthew 2:1,2,11,12
e. Forerunner: 40:3 with Matthew 3:1-3
f. Ministry in Galilee: 9:1,2 with Matthew 4:13-16
g. Rejection by Jews: 8:14 with Matthew 12; John 1:11
h. Acceptance by Gentiles: 49:6 with Matthew 13; John 1:12,13
i. Method of Teaching: 6:9 with Matthew 13:10,13,14
j. Mission and Miracles: 61:1,2a with Luke 4:17-19
k. Patience and Silence under Accusation: 53:7,9 with Matthew 27:12
l. Mocked, insulted, buffeted, spit upon, scourged: 50:6; 52:14 with Matthew 26:67; 27:30,31; Mark 14:65; Luke 22:63-65; John 19:3
m. Vicarious suffering: 53:4 with Matthew 8:14-17; Luke 24:20,26; Hebrews 2:9
n. Death with transgressors: 53:12 with Matthew 27:38; Mark 15:27,28
o. Burial with the rich: 53:9 with Matthew 27:57-60
p. Sin offering: 53:10 with John 1:29; Hebrews 9:26; I Corinthians 5:7b

   Stated: ca. 700 B.C. *Fulfilled:* Birth, life, death of Christ

2. Historical—
a. Judah's deliverance from Syria and Israel: 7:4-7,16
b. Assyria to capture Syria and Israel: 8:4; 17:1-14
c. Judah invaded by Assyria: 8:7,8
d. Defeat of the Philistines: 14:28-32
e. Destruction of Moab: 15,16
f. Assyria conquering Egypt and Ethiopia: 20:4
g. Plundering of Arabia: 21:13-17
h. Subjection of Tyre: 23:1-12
i. Deliverance of Jerusalem from Assyria: 36

j. Hezekiah's life extended 15 years: 38:5

Stated: ca. 680 B.C. *Fulfilled:* In Isaiah's lifetime

k. Babylonian captivity: 39:5-7. Judah's captivity was foretold by Moses (Deuteronomy 28:36,47-52—*Stated* ca. 1450 B.C.). Isaiah repeats the prophecy, naming the place of captivity as Babylon (so does Micah: 4:9,10). Jeremiah informs us that these predictions were fulfilled when Nebuchadnezzar conquered Jerusalem (Jeremiah 52:27-30)

Stated: ca. 736 B.C. *Fulfilled:* 586 B.C.

l. Cyrus, called by name to be Israel's liberator from Babylonian captivity: 44:28; 45:1,2

Stated: ca. 700 B.C. *Fulfilled:* ca. 530 B.C.

m. Babylon's defeat by the Medes: 13:1-9,17

Stated: ca. 700 B.C. *Fulfulled:* 528 B.C.

n. Cyrus to let Israel return and rebuild Jerusalem and the Temple: 44:28; 45:13

Stated: ca. 700 B.C. *Fulfilled:* 528 B.C.

o. Final destruction of Babylon: 13:17-22. The ancient historian, Herodotus, said that Babylon's wall was 60 miles in length, 15 miles on each side, 300 feet high, and almost 80 feet thick. Over 250 pillars (monuments) had been erected to her war lords, from 50 to 250 feet high. In the city's center were 150 pillars, 88 feet high and 19 feet in diameter, supporting a chapel of solid marble. It contained an image of the god "Bel," 40 feet high and overlaid with solid gold. Isaiah described this city as "the glory of kingdoms, the beauty of the Chaldees' excellency . . . the lady of kingdoms" (13:19; 47:5). Nebuchadnezzar boasted to Daniel, saying, "this great Babylon" (Daniel 4:30). Yet Isaiah prophesied that Babylon would be brought to dust. How unthinkable for such a mighty city as Babylon. After the Medes and Persians occupied this city, they held it until conquered by Alexander the Great. He found it too costly to rebuild after he destroyed it in 330 B.C., and from then on until ca. 10 B.C. it deteriorated to exactly what Isaiah predicted. Pictured are Babylon's ruins as they are seen today

Stated: ca. 700 B.C. *Fulfilled:* ca. 125—10 B.C.

p. Tyre's captivity and restoration: 23:13-18. See TYRE in Index.

Stated: ca. 700 B.C. *Fulfilled:* ca. 650 B.C.

Babylon's Ruins

q. As birds flying: 31:5[4] "When Gen. Allenby came to capture Jerusalem during the First World War, he thought he would have to fire upon the sacred city. Knowing that great destruction would follow, he went to God in prayer and besought the Lord to so overrule that Jerusalem would be taken without great damage. He then felt led to send a large number of airplanes to fly over the city, hoping thus to arouse within the Turks a sense of awe. God used this very act to induce the Turks to surrender the city without a single gun being fired." "As birds flying, so will the Lord of hosts defend Jerusalem; defending also He will deliver it; and passing over it He will preserve it." The only damage inflicted was a hole in the wall which the Kaiser of Germany had made for his triumphal entry—through which Allenby made his triumphal entry

Stated: ca. 700 B.C. *Fulfilled:* A.D. 1917

Allenby's Entrance, Jerusalem

r. Doom of Idumaea: 34:6,12. This was "Edom" or the land of the Edomites. Obediah (vss. 10-14), and Ezekiel (25:12-14) both prophesied regarding Edom, and gave us the cause for God's judgment upon the Edomites (their ill treatment of Jerusalem and many survivors after Nebuchadnezzar's victory of Judah). During the Maccabaean period the Idumaeans were defeated in 126 B.C. This is recorded in First Maccabees 5:1-5. John Hyrcanue, another Maccabaean hero, overran all of the Edomite territory, and after Titus destroyed Jerusalem in A.D. 70, the Edomites disappeared.

Stated: ca. 700 B.C. *Fulfilled:* ca. 120 B.C.-A.D. 70

s. The desert shall blossom as the rose: 35:1; 51:3. Since Israel became established as a nation in 1948, the Negev desert, which was written off as uninhabitable on three occasions by the British, has begun to become like Eden. Water has been piped in from the Jordan River, artificial lakes made to catch rain water, irrigation ditches built to permit the flow of water, and today, the land that had become a barren, parched desert through centuries of neglect is now "white unto harvest," blossoming with the increase of her yields. Ezekiel had prophesied that God would "multiply the fruit of the tree, and the increase of the field" (36:30), and Amos had said that "the days come when the plowman shall overtake the reaper, and the treader of grapes him that soweth seed" (9:13). These *are* the days that the desert is "blossoming as the rose." See WELLS in Index.

Stated: ca. 725 B.C. *Fulfilled:* A.D. 1950-

t. They shall repair the ruined cities: 61:4. As a result of the new Israelites in the land today, and their converting the desert into fertile fields, new cities are springing up throughout the area from Beer-sheba to the Gulf of Aqaba on the Red Sea. New industries, business centers, and pleasure resorts have literally fulfilled Isaiah's prophecy—"they shall build the old wastes, they shall raise up the former desolations, they shall repair the waste cities, the desolations [devastations] of many generations."

Stated: ca. 725 B.C. *Fulfilled:* A.D. 1950-

3. Millennial and future—
   a. Judgment "in that day"—the day of the Lord; Isaiah uses the expression "in that day" over 40 times: 2:1-12; 4:1; 24:21
   b. Israel restored to the land: 11:10-12; 14:1,2; 27:12,13; 35:10; 49:8-13
   c. Restoration of Palestine: 30:23-26; 49:19; 65:21-25
   d. Blessings for restored Israel: 12; 32:15-20; 33:24; 46:13; 59:20,21; 61:3—62:12; 65:18
   e. Blessing for all Nations: 2:24; 27:2-6; 60:3-5; 65:25
   f. Victory over death: 65:17; 66:22 with I Corinthians 15:54-57
   g. New Jerusalem, new heaven, new earth: 65:17-66:24
   h. Separation of the saved and lost: 66:22-24

Stated: ca. 745-680 B.C. *Fulfilled:* Yet future

4. Egypt's Glorious Future: 19:18-25. God predicts a bright future for Egypt with Israel even calling Egypt "My people" (vs. 25). Egypt at one time was the most idolatrous nation that ever existed. She had kept Israel in bondage for over 400 years, and had been an enemy of Israel for centuries. The following might serve as clues as to why God, in the future, would favor this land:
   a. When Abraham faced famine and possible death in Canaan by famine, he went into Egypt and found shelter, food, and care until the time of danger was past (Genesis 12:10—13:2). Even though he had sinned with Sara, he came out of Egypt with more than when he entered
   b. Joseph, in the providence of God, though sold into slavery and taken to Egypt, was promoted to be second in command to Pharaoh, and became what we would call today the "Secretary of the Department of Agriculture," especially during the worldwide famine of his day (Genesis 37:2—41:44)
   c. When Jacob and his descendants faced famine, he sent his sons down into Egypt for grain, where upon they met Joseph. Eventually, all of Jacob's family (70 souls) went down to live in Egypt with Pharaoh's blessings under Joseph (see Genesis 41:45—47:27). According to Genesis 45:5-11, it was not God's "permissive will" that put Israel in Egypt, but God's "direct" will. If Israel were to be the people through whom Messiah (Christ) was to come, they would have to survive a seven-year famine in which there would be no rain, no planting, and no harvest. God, who foresaw this famine in all the lands, engineered circumstances in such a way to have His man in a land of plenty so that His own people would be saved from annihilation by starvation. Egypt became that place for God's people
   d. In connection with all of Jacob's family moving to Egypt at this time, God was getting a handful of His people out of a land (Canaan) that was polluted with a disgusting, vulgar, sexual, sensual, immoral religion. Israel, much too small at this time to take possession of the Land, would be easily corrupted by the influence and environment of these worshipers of Baal (see BAAL WORSHIP in Index). They would need more favorable circumstances so they could grow into a Nation strong enough to capture the Land. Time and opportunity must be provided for numerical superiority. Egypt was the *one* Nation able to provide these circumstances. Her civilization was the highest at this time. Intermarriage was impossible because of Egyptian regulations among foreigners. The original seventy Israelites grew into a Nation of several million, and it was during the period of early growth, years before a Pharaoh arose who knew not Joseph, that they were probably instructed in Egyptian schools, learning new trades and sciences. This training, which was

given by Egypt to God's chosen people, was important preparation for a future life of discipline, not only in Egyptian bondage and life in their wilderness wandering, but of their entrance into and possession of Canaan under Joshua

e. When Pharaoh issued the decree that all newborn males should be slaughtered (Exodus 1:15-17), it was Pharaoh's daughter who took Moses to the palace, nourished him, and later made him heir to Egypt's throne, a position he did not attain only because of his deliberate choice (Hebrews 11:24-27). Had Moses made the decision to be called the ''son of Pharaoh's daughter'' he would have become an Egyptian god, for all of Pharaoh's sons were deity, and would have become a brilliant military leader, a multimillionaire and later ascend the throne. But he chose to be numbered among God's people and have the riches of Christ. Although God's people were in bondage and slavery at this time, when Pharaoh did let God's people go, probably because of guilt for their treatment against the Hebrews, the Egyptians heaped upon them many riches (gifts—Exodus 12:31-36)

f. About 300 B.C., Ptolemy of Egypt won a great victory over Seleucus for possession of the land of Israel. One result of this union between Egypt and Israel was that the seaport of Alexandria was opened up to Jewish merchants. Greek had become the language of civilization and commerce, so the Jews, skilled in Greek and woefully lacking in Hebrew, demanded that their sacred Scriptures be translated into Greek. This task was accomplished and the new translation was called the ''Septuagint,'' completed in about 245 B.C. Because it was in the Greek, it was studied by Greek-speaking people. Thus, it was in Egypt that the Hebrew Scriptures (for the first time) were made available to the whole world for them to read and understand

g. King Herod decreed that all males two years and under should be slaughtered. This would have included the child Jesus, so Egypt became shelter for Him, the cradle for the ''Lord of glory,'' until the time of danger was past (Matthew 2:13-21)

h. The fact that God would remember Egypt favorably in the future is a wonderful illustration of the great truth that God does not forget. He has never forgotten the sanctuary that Egypt gave to Abraham, the exaltation Egypt gave to Joseph and Moses, the home Egypt gave to the tiny nation of Israel until she became numerous, the city (Alexandria) Egypt gave for the Hebrew Bible to be made available to the world, and the cradle Egypt provided for the Savior of the world

1. Defeat of Sennacherib—to show that prayer is a mighty weapon: 36:1—37:38

2. Hezekiah healed and his life prolonged fifteen years—to answer prayer and to show that God is the giver of life: 38:1-21; II Kings 20:1-11. See LONG DAY in Index. Also to show that sometimes in making a selfish request, we ask amiss, and bring leanness to our souls. It was during this extra fifteen-year extended life period that Hezekiah's son, Manasseh, was born. He turned out to be the most wicked of all of Israel's Southern kings. Then, too, Hezekiah had a wonderful opportunity to witness to God's goodness after his healing, but failed before heathen dignitaries (II Kings 20:12—21:9 with Psalm 106:15).

1. Recent excavations beneath the present Temple site reveal a secret tunnel dug under the so-called stables of Solomon which lead to the treasure house of the Temple, where valuables were stored. Also uncovered were the royal tombs where the monarchs of Israel were buried. Their graves had been cleared and moved to the slope of the Mount of Olives. King Uzziah's tombstone (Isaiah 6:1), with

inscription, has been found. It reads: "Hither were brought the bones of Uzziah King of Judah. Do not Open." For Uzziah's fort, see SECRET in Index.

King Uzziah's Tombstone

2. King Sargon of Assyria: 20:1. Isaiah's mention of Sargon was the only record of this king for centuries, and was ridiculed as false by critics of the Word since there was no evidence from secular history that he ever existed. Was Isaiah correct? Did Sargon actually exist, or was he simply a fictitious character? In unearthing a palace at Khorsabad in ancient Mesopotamia, bricks of the palace were found to be inscribed. The inscription read: "I Sargon have built this palace to the praise of mine own name." Many statues and records were discovered, one of which confirms Isaiah's statement: "Ashdod's king, Azuri, plotted to avoid paying me tribute. In anger I marched against Ashdod with my captain, conquering." Within recent years the "Ashdod Excavation Project" found an inscription of Sargon's at Ashdod which actually confirmed his conquest there. Another monument states that Shalmeneser died and that he, Sargon, succeeded him in taking Samaria. He even mentioned the number of Israelites he deported when the Northern Kingdom fell—27,290. He then rebuilt Samaria and settled his own people in the area (see SARGON in Index). Isaiah *was* correct.

3. Sennacherib's Prism. See PRISM in Index.

4. The Dead Sea Scrolls. Among the biblical scrolls found by a Bedouin boy in a cave near the Dead Sea in 1947 was a complete prophecy of Isaiah, closely written on parchment. The total length is almost 24 feet. It contains 17 sheets, approximately 10 by 15 inches, which were sewed together. They were hidden in A.D. 69 by a sect of Jews called the Essenes, who feared

for their lives under Vespasian's destruction of Jews.

Prior to this discovery, the oldest known manuscript of the Hebrew Old Testament was dated A.D. 826. We now have portions that date back to between 200-150 B.C. Bible critics were amazed to learn that these biblical scrolls read just like our King James Version, varying slightly, if any at all, in spelling or in copying from one scroll to another. No truth of the Christian faith in these scrolls differs from what we find in our translation today. Christ read from an Isaiah scroll (Luke 4:16-21), and read what we read in our own Bibles. When we quote the Word of God we quote the same truths Christ did when He referred to the Scriptures. What difference we find in the scrolls is minute. Our version (KJV) says "waters of Dimon" and the Isaiah scroll says "waters of Dibon" (15:9). The King James Version says "crooked places straight" and the Isaiah scroll says "hills straight" (45:2). The scroll says "rain down righteousness," and our version says "pour down righteousness" (45:8). Agreement between the "Isaiah" scroll, the Hebrew Text of A.D. 826, and the King James Version shows the care with which the scribes diligently copied Bible manuscripts. There is absolutely nothing in the Isaiah scroll that would lend support to the theory (as the critics claim) that there were *two* different "Isaiahs" as authors of this prophecy. "Isaiah" *is* still the *same* book as it was when it came from the pen of this *same* prophet over 2,700 years ago.

For almost 2,000 years the silence of those who hid the scrolls verified the truth that all flesh is as grass, and that the glory of man fades away. But out of those caves near the Dead Sea has come further evidence and demonstration of the fact that although the grass withers and men die, the Word of God abides forever! (I Peter 1:24,25).

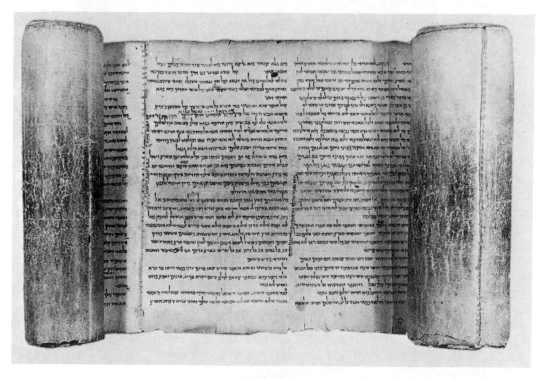

Isaiah Scroll

LIGHT FROM BIBLICAL CUSTOMS

5. 1. The ox knows his owner and the ass his master's crib: 1:3. An ancient Eastern custom is for boys of a village to gather the animals owned by families and take them to pasture and water. At eventime they are brought back to the edge of town. The boys scurry to their own homes, leaving the animals on their own. Each animal makes its way to the proper stall, crib, or fold—each to its own place. knows his owner and the ass his master's crib, but Israel does not know [Me], My people does not consider [Me].'' What an indictment against Israel. She had turned her back on God, and God is saying that dumb animals have more sense than His own people!

2. A cottage in a vineyard, as a lodge in a garden: 1:8. The cottage and lodge were not buildings in the sense that we know these structures. They were flimsy shelters simply to keep the blazing sun off the farmer who watched there daily to keep away would-be robbers from invading his field (see PLUCKING CORN in Index). After the harvest is past, they are left standing, presenting a picture of ruin. Because Israel had grossly sinned, this is the picture God painted of His disobedient people.

Cottage (Booth)

3. Tinkling ornaments on their feet and legs: 3:16-24. The women of Israel had long since forsaken the Lord, and jewelry around their feet and legs was a form of fashion, pride, and vanity. The daughters of Zion were selfishly adorning themselves with beauty aids, etc., and God's judgment was to silence the tinkling ornaments, turn the sweet smell of perfumes into a stink, cause their well-set hair to fall out, and bring ugliness instead of beauty, that they might see their sin as God saw it.

4. Veil—the government upon his shoulder: 9:6. A wedding ceremony is a gala occasion in the Eastern countries. Even in all of the merriment, the bride's face must always be covered with a veil. At the proper moment when the bride and groom are joined together, the groom removes the veil from the bride's face and throws it over his shoulder. This signifies the taking of all responsibility upon himself—the government of his bride and household resting upon his shoulder. How wonderful of our Bridegroom to remove the veil of sin from us, and in our acceptance of Him and His acceptance of us, taking upon Himself the responsibility of the household of faith—governing us according to His will.

5. The key will I lay on his shoulder: 22:22. House locks and keys in the Orient are very large, and when an owner left home to venture into the city, the key, which has a handkerchief tied to it, is flung over the shoulder. The key symbolizes ownership responsibility and identity. This is what David passed on to Eliakim when he laid upon his shoulder "the key of the house of David." This is also implied when Christ gave Peter the keys of the kingdom—identity with Christ and the responsibility of preaching the gospel (Matthew 16:19).

6. Bread corn is bruised: 28:28. The expression "bread corn" has reference to the grain which is crushed (bruised) for bread flour. Without this crushing there would be no bread. This principle is true for fruit bearing in the life of the believer. So often we need to be bruised (or made to suffer) before we can come forth as gold (Job 23:10). Suffering is one of God's methods of drawing His own closer to Himself and fitting them for His service (II Corinthians 12:7-10; James 1:12).

7. A sherd to take fire or to take water: 30:14. A sherd is simply a piece of broken pottery. This verse probably has reference to a large piece, which is from the curved part of the vessel. Such a piece was often used to carry coals of fire to one whose fire had gone out, or used as a dipper for drinking. Sherds (or potsherds) remind us of man's being at enmity with God, without strength, and constantly at strife with his fellowman (Psalm 22:15; Isaiah 45:9). Every broken piece of pottery will be a reminder of a sinner's heart—broken and completely beyond human repair, forgotten like a broken vessel (Psalm 31:12; Proverbs 26:23).

8. Hooks in the jaws and nose: 30:28; 37:29. See ZEDEKIAH in Index.

9. Double for all her sins: 40:2. This verse presents a problem to our Western minds. If war is over and sin has been pardoned, why *double* for her sins? In one breath God forgives, in the next He apparently metes out twice the punishment. What then is the meaning?

When domestic or business problems are settled in the East, the elders at the city gate sit as a jury (Deuteronomy 16:18). Suppose a debtor is unable to pay off his debt. All records have been produced to show the amount of indebtednesss. They are in view of the public, embarrassing the debtor beyond measure. They are kept public until the debt is paid. Usually a kinsman (like Boaz) will come to his rescue, satisfying the creditors in the presence of the elders. The moderator of the elders will then take the sheets upon which the debts are listed and folds them double, tacking it on the back of the gate. Everyone who passes by now sees nothing—the debt has been wiped out. Isaiah saw prophetically in this passage that Christ would settle "double" for our debt of sin. We could by no means "pay off," and as our Kinsman-redeemer He settled the bill. Our list of sins has been folded—doubled—and nailed to His cross, and all who pass by now see a new creature in Him. The old has passed away, behold, all things are new (II Corinthians 5:17).

10. Lambs carried in his bosom: 40:11. A shepherd often takes a weary lamb into his arms, and then, with his large robe, places the lamb in its fold and carries it "in his bosom." His hands are then free to perform many other duties. The lamb rests securely as a result of the shepherd's personal care and concern. As Christ is in the bosom of the Father—possessing the closest intimacy with His Father—so we, as His sheep, are in His bosom, nestled securely in Him.

11. A bruised reed shall he not break, and the smoking flax shall he not quench: 42:3. A shepherd's reed pipe (flute) is a precious, handmade instrument, used to "pipe" music while leading and resting his flock. It is easily broken, and if crushed by a foot, the music is stilled. A new one could be easily made, but the shepherd so values this instrument that he spends hours, if necessary, repairing it until he can play it again. "A bruised reed shall he not break." The picture is twofold: (1) that of a sinner who is bruised and broken by sin, and of no value to anyone except God, whose love picks him up and restores broken life; and (2) that of a believer, who seemingly is crushed beneath the weight of burdens, but is assured by God that He will lift the burden (I Corinthians 10:13; I Peter 5:7).

The same is true of the "smoking flax," the wick in a lamp whose oil supply is so low that the flame has gone out, but is still smoking. The wick is trimmed and a fresh supply of oil is added. God does not throw us out when we fail to burn brightly, but His Word does clean us up and His Spirit does refresh us that we might once again have a glowing, burning testimony.

12. I will pour water on him that is thirsty: 44:3. What a strange thing to do when one is thirsty—pour water *on* him! When we are thirsty the last thing we would want someone to do is pour water *on* us. But to those in the East, this Scripture is not perplexing. An Easterner, in drinking water, never touches the water pot or jar to his lips. He simply throws back his head, holds the vessel high above him, and *pours* a stream of water down into his mouth. The water is swallowed as it is poured in. "I will pour water on him" is but their way of giving a drink of water to the thirsty. As the Holy Spirit is poured out upon us, He fills within, just as water poured out upon the thirsty fills them within. With the Holy Spirit upon us, filling us within, Christ said that out of our innermost being would flow rivers of living water—life giving water that would quench the spiritual thirst of those in need.

Pouring Water "On" Him

13. Diviners: 44:24,25; 47:13,14. See ASTROLOGY in Index.

14. Take the millstone, and grind meal: uncover thy locks, make bare the leg, and uncover the thigh: 47:2. See WOMEN in Index.

15. I have graven thee upon the palms of my hands: 49:15,16. In the East it is a custom for a mother, whose son is away from home, to have something tatooed in the palm of her hand as a reminder of the son she longs to see. The way Palestinian women use their hands in work and while talking, this mark is a constant reminder of this loved one. "Can a woman forget her sucking child, that she should not have compassion upon the son of her womb?" Those whose hands have been marked with tattooing do not, as will not God forget those who are "graven upon the palms" of His hands.

16. Walk in the light of your fire: 50:11. Eastern farmers usually get up before dawn, and the first thing they do is build a fire to warm themselves. When the time comes for them to go out into the fields, they put the end of a heavy rope into the fire. Once it begins to burn, they take it out, and as they walk, they blow on the burning end. This shoots out sparks ahead of them to light their path, so as not to step on a poisonous snake or scorpion or stumble over rocks with their bar feet. They walk in the light of their fire, in the sparks they have kindled. With the fire that has been kindled in our souls by the Word of God, we are to take the individual verses (sparks) to light our path so that we might walk out of the danger of sin and harm (Psalm 119:11,105).

17. The Lord hath made bare His holy arm: 52:10. It is interesting to see women of the East as they take their long sleeves, tie the ends in a knot, and throw them over their shoulders.

This leaves the arms bare to do their work unhindered. Men also, especially in battle, will do the same thing, so that their arms will be free to fight. The Western counterpart to this expression is "let's roll up our sleeves and go to work." This is exactly what God did when He wrought salvation in our behalf—He "made bare His holy arm" that we might see that salvation is His work, not ours.

18. Come buy without money and without price: 55:1. The cry of one who sells milk, water, etc., is: "Ho, everyone that thirsteth, come, buy water. . . ." and then the price is mentioned. Many cannot buy because they are destitute. Sometimes, however, the cry is, "Come, buy . . . without money, without price." Why the switch? How can one "buy" without money or price? In our culture, when one has a birthday, we buy them presents. In the East, the one celebrating his birthday will buy something for others. Often he will go to the seller of water and milk, give him a sum of money, and instruct him to give free drinks to those who pass by who cannot afford one. Hence the cry: "Come, buy, without money and without price." The one celebrating his birthday does this to make others happy, to show his appreciation to God for His goodness to him.

With this in mind, Isaiah is showing that we are destitute, and cannot "buy" God's water of life—salvation. Christ, in celebration of His virgin birth, shows His appreciation to His Father by paying the price of our "so great salvation." It is then offered to all who pass by: "Ho everyone that thirsteth, come, buy . . . without money and without price."

1. Great height or distance to the stars: 14:13. In this verse Satan said that he would ascend to heaven "above the stars." Job also mentioned the "height of the stars, how high they are!" (22:22). Inference here is that it must be a very great distance to the stars. It hasn't been too long since the astronomers found this to be true. It was not known until 1838 when distance of stars was first computed by the parallax method by Bessel. These distances are not know to be more than 100,000 times the distance of our solar system. See STARS in Index.

2. Hezekiah's prolonged life: 38:1-21. See JOSHUA'S LONG DAY in Index.

3. Substances measured and weighed: 40:12. It hasn't been too many years since our chemists discovered that all substances to combine chemically must be weighed or measured. This is called "isostatic balance," or equilibrium. For instance, table salt is designated "NaCl" (Na for sodium, and Cl for chlorine gas). The atomic weight for chlorine gas is 35.5. This means that in 58.5 pounds of salt we have 23 pounds of sodium and 35.5 pounds of chlorine gas. *Only* in these proportions will sodium and chlorine gas combine. Again, take water. We term it "H_2O," and that means two parts of hydrogen to one part of oxygen. The combining weight of hydrogen is 2; the combining weight of oxygen is 16. To form 18 pounds of water God must carefully measure out two pounds of hydrogen and 16 pounds of oxygen. Water can be formed only by mixing these two gasses together in these exact proportions. The ingredients of each substance can only be combined as they are measured or weighted out in certain exact proportions. Isaiah expressed this great scientific truth ca. 700 B.C. when he wrote: "Who hath measured the waters in the hollow of His hand, and meted out heaven with the span, and comprehended the dust of the earth in a measure, and weighed the mountain in scales, and the hills in a balance?" This simply means that God weighed and measured the ingredients of every substance He created.

4. The circle of the earth (or more literally—"the roundness of the earth"): 40:22. Isaiah wrote this statement ca. 700 B.C., yet it was only when Magellan's expedition sailed around the world (A.D. 1475) that it was generally believed that the earth was round. While it is true that

Isaiah (11:12) mentioned the "four corners of the earth," it is simply a metaphor, referring to four directions, the extreme limits of land. The Hebrew word for "corners" is translated "borders" (Numbers 15:38); "four corners" (Ezekiel 7:2; Isaiah 11:12); "ends" (Job 37:3; 38:13); and in Greek—"divisions, angles" (Revelation 7:1), such as a map is divided into quadrants which is shown by the four directions. Isaiah did not mean that the earth was flat with four corners any more than modern speakers and writers mean the earth is flat when they speak of the "four corners of the earth" or the "ends of the earth." They are, along with Isaiah, referring to the farthest extent of habitation on the earth. See EARTH in Index.

5. Hidden Treasure—"I will give thee the treasures of darkness and hidden riches in secret places:" 45:3. Most of us have very little appreciation for the darkness. We seem to take things in stride much better in daylight than in darkness. Yet most of earth's valued treasures are found only in dark, secret places—in deep mines which give us our most priceless minerals—gold, silver, diamonds, other precious stones, and even fuel (coal and oil). Then, too, how much more beautiful are the heavens, the moon and the stars—the works of God's fingers, when we see them on a dark, dark night (Psalm 8:3).

6. Watering the earth: 55:10. It was believed for centuries that as rain descended, its waters ran off into streams, rivers, lakes, and finally into the ocean. It is now known that part seeps into the ground, thus making the surface moist for plant life. This is called "ground water." See RAIN in Index. And, of course, as the rains do fall upon the earth, plant life is nourished then as well as with "ground water," keeping them nourished (Isaiah 44:14b). See PHOTOSYN-THESIS in Index.

Isaiah in the New Testament: Every writer in the New Testament except James and Jude quotes from Isaiah 52:1—53:12. Direct or indirect quotations from this Book are found over 300 times in the New Testament. No attempt is made to list all, but just some of the more important ones—

1. Israel's remnant: 1:9 with Romans 9:29
2. God's glory revealed: 6:1 with John 12:41
3. Blinded eyes: 6:9,10 with John 12:39,40
4. Virgin birth: 7:14 with Matthew 1:21
5. Christ, a stumbling stone: 8:14 with I Peter 2:8
6. God's children: 8:18 with Hebrews 2:13
7. Ministry of Christ: 9:1,2 with Matthew 4:12-16
8. Christ's kingdom: 9:7 with Luke 1:32,33
9. Salvation for Gentiles: 11:10 with Romans 15:12
10. Judgment in the heavens: 13:10 with Matthew 24:29
11. Babylon's judgment: 21:9 with Revelation 18:2
12. Victory over death: 25:8a with I Corinthians 15:54
13. Tears wiped away: 25:8b with Revelation 21:4
14. The foundation stone: 28:16 with Romans 9:33; I Peter 2:4
15. Lip service: 29:13 with Matthew 15:8,9
16. Miracles of Christ: 35:5,6 with Matthew 11:5; 15:30
17. John the Baptist: 40:3 with Matthew 3:3
18. Frailty of life: 40:6 with James 1:10; I Peter 1:24
19. Christ, the Shepherd: 40:11 with John 10:11
20. Christ, the Servant: 42:1-4 with Matthew 12:18-21
21. Outpouring of the Spirit: 44:3b with John 7:38,39; Acts 2:14-18
22. Every knee bow to God: 45:23 with Romans 14:11
23. Light for Gentiles: 49:6 with Acts 13:47
24. Preaching the Word: 52:7 with Romans 10:15
25. God's report: 53:1 with John 12:38
26. Christ despised and rejected: 53:3a with Matthew 27:30,31; John 1:11

27. Healing by His stripes: 53:5 with Matthew 8:17
28. Christ bore our sins: 53:5,12c with I Peter 2:24
29. Opened not His mouth: 53:7 with Matthew 27:11-14
30. Taken from judgment: 53:8a with Matthew 27:11-26
31. Grave with the rich: 53:9 with Matthew 27:57-60
32. Christ made sin for us: 53:10 with II Corinthians 5:21
33. Justification by Christ's righteousness: 53:11 with Romans 5:18
34. Death of Christ: 53:12a with Romans 3:25; I Corinthians 15:3,4
35. Numbered with transgressors: 53:12b with Mark 15:28
36. Christ's intercession: 53:12c with Luke 23:34; Hebrews 7:25
37. Gentile conversion: 54:1; 65:1 with Romans 10:20; Galatians 4:27
38. Taught of God: 54:13 with John 6:45
39. Christ, the Deliverer: 59:20 with Romans 11:26
40. Christ's earthly ministry: 61:1,2 with Luke 4:17-20
41. Companion references:
    a. Parable of the vineyard: 5:1,2 with Matthew 21:33-43
    b. Christ, the seed of David: 11:1 with Romans 1:3
    c. Opening doors: 22:22 with Revelation 3:7
    d. God, the Potter: 45:9 with Romans 9:20,21
    e. Righteousness imputed: 45:24 with II Corinthians 5:21
    f. Earth's destruction: 51:6 with II Peter 3:10-13
    g. Selfishness: 58:7 with Matthew 25:34-40
    h. Eternal torment: 66:24 with Mark 9:43-48
    i. New heaven and new earth: 66:22-24 with Revelation 21:1

1. Picture of Sinners; What the Wicked are Like. See WICKED and UNGODLY in Index.

    a. In rebellion against God: 1:2b
    b. Do not know God: 1:3b
    c. Do not consider God: 1:3c
    d. People laden with iniquity: 1:4a
    e. A seed of evil doers: 1:4b
    f. Children that are corrupters: 1:4c
    g. Have forsaken God: 1:4d
    h. Have provoked God: 1:4e
    i. Have gone away backward: 1:4f
    j. Whole head is sick and the heart faint: 1:5
    k. No soundness from sole of foot to top of head: 1:6a
    l. Full of wounds, bruises, and putrifying sores: 1:6b
    m. Like the people of Sodom and Gomorrah: 1:10 with Genesis 18:20—19:26
    n. Their "religion" became iniquity: 1:11-13
    o. Like a long man in a short bed: insufficient covering: 28:20
    p. Have gone astray: 53:6
    q. Like the troubled sea—no rest nor peace: 57:20,21
    r. Righteousnesses as filthy rags: 64:6
    s. Heart deceitful and desperately wicked: Jeremiah 17:9. A heart of this nature is described by Paul as "vain in imaginations, foolish and darkened" (Romans 1:21). Paul describes the sins of such a deceitful and wicked heart in Romans 1:28-32; 3:10-23; Galatians 5:19-21; and II Timothy 3:2-5.

What the Wicked are Like:
    a. The troubled sea: 57:20,21
    b. A briar: Micah 7:4
    c. Heath (shrub) in the desert: Jeremiah 17:6

    d. The chaff: Psalm 1:4

    e. A wheel: Psalm 83:13a

    f. Stubble: Psalm 83:13b

    g. Birds caught in a snare: Ecclesiastes 9:12

    h. Fishes taken in a net: Ecclesiastes 9:12

    i. A deaf adder: Psalm 58:4

    j. A ravening lion: Psalm 17:12

    k. Sheep laid in a grave: Psalm 49:14

2. Remedy for Sin: 1:16-20. See SIN in Index.

    a. Wash you, make you clean: vs. 16a

    b. Put away evil: vs. 16b

    c. Cease to do evil: vs. 16c

    d. Learn to do well: vs. 17a

    e. Seek judgment: vs. 17b

    f. Relieve the oppressed: vs. 17c

    g. Judge the fatherless: vs. 17d

    h. Plead for the widow: vs. 17e

    i. Reason with the Lord: vs. 18. Also 55:1-3

    j. Be willing and obedient to do these things: vs. 19

    k. Judgment if God's remedy is not accepted: vs.20

3. God's Mercy Revealed: 1:18

    a. He will forgive—*come now*

    b. He will forgive all—*let us*

    c. He condescends to reason—*let us reason together*

    d. He forgives and transforms—*shall be as white as snow*

    e. He does it on such easy terms—*just come and reason*

4. Isaiah's Need for Soul-winning: 6:5-8. See SOUL-WINNING in Index.

    a. Saw himself as God saw him: vs. 5a

    b. Saw his own need: vs. 7

    c. Saw condition and needs of others: vs. 5b

    d. Was given a call to reach others: vs. 8a

    e. Willingly responded to this call: vs. 8b. God's method of reaching others is the yieldedness of a *man* who knows what he is—a sinner saved by grace—and will dare step out before others to stand in Christ's stead (II Corinthians 5:20).

    f. Isaiah's message: 55:6,7

    g. His invitation: 55:1

5. "Salvation" in Isaiah

    a. Wells of salvation—to satisfy us: 12:3

    b. Joy of salvation—to keep us rejoicing: 25:9

    c. Walls of salvation—to protect us: 26:1

    d. Everlasting salvation—to secure us: 45:17

    e. Day of salvation—a present possession: 49:8

    f. Arm of salvation—to lift us when we slip: 59:16

    g. Helmet of salvation—to endure hardness as a good soldier: 59:17

    h. Garments of salvation—to give us standing and position: 61:10

    i. Light of salvation—to guide: 62:1

6. The "I Wills" of Satan: 14:12-17 with I Timothy 3:6. Originally, Satan was "Lucifer, son of the morning" (meaning "day star, brightness; to make a show; boastful"). This led to "pride," and pride led to his downfall. Notice:

    a. "I will" ascend into heaven: vs. 13a, implying that God's domain was much higher than his. Heaven is usually divided into three parts: (1) heaven of clouds: (2) of stars, which was probably Lucifer's domain; and (3) third heaven, place of God's abode and throne (II

Corinthians 12:1-3; Psalm 11:4)

b. "I will" exalt my throne above the stars of God: vs. 13b. "My throne" implies he had authority, possibly over the angelic hosts. "Exalt" meaning he was going to place his **throne alongside God's**

c. "I will" sit also upon the mount of the congregation: 13c. "Mount" is the holy mount of God, His seat of authority (Ezekiel 28:14)

d. "I will" ascend above the heights of the clouds: 14a. The implication here is, "I will ascend above God Himself."

e. "I will" **be like the Most High: 14b. This is the epitome of blasphemy—"I will enthrone myself as god." "The Most High" One is Supreme.** Satan sought to dethrone God and enthrone himself as god. And his "pride" led to his downfall (vss. 15-17). This is what John meant when he said "the devil sinneth from the beginning" (I John 3:8). This is the "creature" turning from the "Creator" to worship self, and it ties in with Paul's statement of "not retaining a knowledge of God in the mind, but worshiping and serving the creature more than the Creator" (Romans 1:25, 28a). See SATAN in Index.

7. Christ—the Living Refuge: 32:2

    a. He is a hiding place—from the storms and temptations of Life: John 16:33; I Corinthians 10:13. Our life is hid with Him: Colossians 3:3b

    b. He satisfies—as rivers of water in a dry place: Psalm 107:9; John 15:11

    c. He shelters—as a shadow in a weary land: Matthew 11:28-30

8. Unto Me—

    a. Look unto Me—for salvation: 45:22

    b. Come unto Me—for rest: Matthew 11:28

    c. Learn of Me—for Truth: Matthew 11:29

    d. Follow Me—to win others to Christ: Matthew 4:19

    e. Watch with Me—to escape temptation: Matthew 26:38,41

    f. Abide in Me—to bear fruit and for answered prayer: John 15:4,7

    g. Lovest thou Me?—to test for devotion: John 21:15

9. He was wounded for our transgressions: 53:5. See WOUNDS in Index.

10. Guidance: 58:11

    a. How?

      —By His voice: John 10:27

      —With His eye: Psalm 32:8

      —With His counsel: Psalm 73:24

      —By His presence: John 10:4

    b. Where?

      —Into paths of peace: Luke 1:79

      —Into all Truth: John 16:13

    c. How Long?

      —Continually: Isaiah 58:11

      —Unto death: Psalm 48:14

    d. The Condition?

      —Acknowledge Him in all thy ways: Proverbs 3:5,6

      —Commit thy way unto Him: Psalm 37:5

11. A New Name: 62:2. See NAMES in Index.

    a. Believers—because of faith: Acts 5:14; I Timothy 4:12

    b. Sons—because of trust: John 1:12,13

    c. Children—because of the Spirit's witness: Romans 8:16

    d. Friends—because of obedience: John 15:14

    e. Disciples—because of following Christ: Luke 14:26,27

    f. Brethren—because of devotion to each other: I John 3:14; I Peter 1:22

    g. Christians—because of Christlikeness: Acts 11:26

    h. Saints—because of holiness: I Corinthians 1:2

12. Lovingkindnesses of the Lord: 63:7
   a. Are through Christ: Ephesians 2:7; Titus 3:4-6
   b. Provide mercy: Psalm 51:1
   c. Extend mercy: Isaiah 54:8
   d. Are prayed for: Psalm 89:49; 143:8
   e. Are the result of worship: Psalm 48:9
   f. Are understood by obedience: Psalm 107:43
   g. Quicken us: Psalm 119:88
   h. Draw us to Him: Jeremiah 31:3
   i. Give us an audience before Him: Psalm 119:149
   j. Given for being kind: II Samuel 2:5,6
   k. Engage us to Him: Hosea 2:19
   l. Preserve us: Psalm 40:11
   m. Are sent in affliction: Psalm 42:7,8
   n. Comfort us: Psalm 119:76
   o. Are present with us: Psalm 26:3
   p. Continue upon His own: Psalm 36:10
   q. Are marvelous: Psalm 17:7
   r. Are lasting: Psalm 89:33; Isaiah 54:10
   s. Crown us: Psalm 103:4
   t. Are worthy of praise: Psalm 92:1,2; 138:2
   u. Are to be proclaimed to others: Psalm 40:10

A BIT OF HEAVENLY MANNA

Although Isaiah was called upon by God to charge Israel with her sinfulness, he also was charged with a message of hope for such sinful people. The "Key Word" in this Book is "salvation," and it is mentioned at least 28 times. God needs only to say a thing once, but to repeat it so much is to reveal the depth of His great love for the unlovely. Isaiah did not hesitate to declare his message of judgment and grace. However, he emphasized grace, and declared—

BEHOLD, GOD IS MY SALVATION—12:2[6]

"This fact is so glorious, so stupendous, that we may well be called upon to behold and admire it. God was angry with us, and justly. He threatened us, and righteously. We deserved nothing at His hands but punishment, and on the principles of the Law we could expect nothing but wrath. But, behold, God is our salvation! This flows purely from His love. It is the effect of His free, sovereign, and distinguishing grace. To save us, he entered into covenant. To save us, He sent His Son to make an atonement. To save us, He sent His Holy Spirit into our hearts. To save us, He was determined, and in saving us He rejoices. Our salvation is a gift conferred, a work wrought, a change effected. No one could accomplish our salvation but God, and He has done it. Our God is our Savior. He will save us; He will rest in His love. Do we know God in this glorious character? Have we felt our need of an almighty Savior? Have we thrown ourselves into the open arms of Jesus? Has He spoken peace to our hearts by His blood? Has He shed abroad His love within us? Let nothing satisfy us but the inward witness of the Holy Spirit that God *is* our salvation."

PRAYER THOUGHT: "As I go through this day, O God, May I place myself at Thy disposal and be just an 'errand boy' for my Savior. May I, with Isaiah of old, say, "Here am I Lord, send me.' In My Savior's wonderful name I pray. Amen."[7]

Isaiah 6:8

Jeremiah—The Book of Horror and Hope

Name: Jeremiah, the writer of this book (1:1-3), means "one whom Jehovah appoints or launches forth." He has been called the Weeping Prophet, the Prophet of the Broken Heart, and the Prophet of the Minor Strains. He is the solemn seer of the sixteen prophets. His sobs and lamentations have been broadcast through the centuries. He was the Job among the prophets yet to his lasting glory he reminded the world of Christ (Matthew 16:14). He could weep but was not weak. He was sensitive but not strengthless. He was compassionate but would not compromise. He was a little child before God but a lion-hearted champion of righteousness before men. Jeremiah was the only man in the Bible who was told not to marry (16:2). His work was twofold in its character: both constructive and destructive. As a result of his bold preaching—

1. He was rejected: 11:18-21
2. His brethren dealt treacherously with him: 12:2-6
3. He contended with false prophets face to face: 14:13-16; 28:10-17
4. He suffered persecution: 15:10-18
5. He was smitten and placed in stocks: 20:1,2
6. His life was threatened: 26:8; 36:26
7. He was imprisoned, charged with treason: 32:2,3; 37:11-15
8. Some of his prophecies were burned: 36:22-25
9. He was placed in a cistern to die: 38:6
10. He was bound in chains: 40:1

Judging from the treatment he received in preaching the message of God, it is doubtful that he had a single convert (11:18-23). He found the message so heavy that it broke his own heart (9:1). He tried to resign, but God's Word was in his heart "as a burning fire shut up in my bones . . . , and I could not . . ." (20:9).

After Nebuchadnezzar captured Jerusalem, he was offered a position if he would go to Babylon. He felt he should remain with the remnant not taken into captivity (40:1-6). For fear of the Chaldeans, the remnant wanted to go to Egypt. Jeremiah preached against this move, but the remnant left Canaan for Egypt, taking Jeremiah captive with them (42:15—43:7). Tradition tells us that the people rebelled against God's Word and stoned Jeremiah to death. Compare Jeremiah with Paul. See PAUL, Cost, in Index.

Period of His Prophecy: 1:2,3. From the reformation under Josiah (II Chronicles 34:3) until the subjugation unto Babylon (52:12: II Kings 25:3,4). This period was ca. 626-580 B.C. Jeremiah was contemporary with Ezekiel, Daniel, Habakkuk, Zephaniah, Nahum, and Obediah. He was the *ninth* prophet.

While some of Jeremiah's messages are dated, they are not arranged in chronological order:

1. During Josiah's reigh: 1:2; 3:6
2. During Jehoiakim's reign: 22:18; 25:1; 35:1; 36:1; 45:2
3. During Zedekiah's reigh: 21:1; 24:1,8; 27:3,12; 28:1; 29:3; 32:1; 34:2; 37:1; 38:5; 39:1; 49:34; 51:59
4. During his stay in Egypt: 43:7,8; 44:1

People of His Prophesy: His ministry was confined to the Southern Kingdom of Judah.

Contents: "There are many interesting things to note about the book of Jeremiah. It is a book of interrogation: there are more questions in Jeremiah perhaps than in Job. It is a book of restoration which is set forth fully in chapters 30—33. It is a book of lamentations; a book of persecutions. It is a book of symbolics: the picture of the potter (18:1-6); the girdle (13:1-11); bottles (13:12-15); etc. In Jeremiah there are 151 clearly marked prophecies commencing with the prophetic formula, 'The word of the Lord came.'

"This prophecy contains several descriptions delivered to the people of the Jews; charging them with the many sins of which they were guilty; exhorting them to repentance; threatening them with the destruction of their city and temple with captivity in Babylon; and comforting the saints not only with the promise of deliverance for them but of spiritual redemption by the Messiah. It also has in it several predictions of judgment upon other nations; and gives a particular account of the destruction of Jerusalem and of the carrying of the Jews into Babylon, which he lived to see as a fulfillment of his own prophecies."[1] He referred to Babylon 164 times—more than in the rest of the Bible put together. This book contains 52 chapters, 1,364 verses, and 42,659 words.

Character: Combination of history, biography, and prophecy.

Subject: God's message concerning the sins of Judah in general and Jerusalem in particular, the inevitable judgment that came as a result of their sins, and future restoration of the Jews through the Righteous Branch in the millennium.

Purpose: To teach us how sin, unconfessed and unjudged, will bring full judgment from God in order that His people may be restored. Judgment always precedes blessing.

Outline:[2]
    I.   The Call of Jeremiah: 1
    II. Rebukes, Warnings, Promises to the Jews: 2—20
    III. Denunciation of Rulers, False Shepherds, and prophets: 21—23
    IV. Predictions of Divine Judgments, the Overthrow of Jerusalem; Seventy Weeks Captivity: 24—29
    V. Promises of Restorations of the Jews: 30—33
    VI. Prophecies Occasioned by the Sins of Jehoiakim and Zedekiah: 34—39
    VII. Wretched Condition of Remnant left in Judah, and Prophecies Uttered to Them: 40—44
    VIII. Consolation to Baruch: 45
    IX. Prophecies concerning Hostile Nations: 46—51

Key Chapter: 2. Plea for Israel to return to God.

Key Verse: 2:19.

Key Words:
    1. Backsliding, found 13 times.
    2. Return, found 47 times.

Key Phrase: Go and cry: 2:2

Key Thought: Denunciation and wickedness.

Spiritual Thoughts:
    1. Get ready with cleansing: 13:27.
    2. If a man thinketh he stand, take heed lest he fall: I Corinthians 10:12.

Christ Is Seen As:
    1. Balm of Gilead: 8:22
    2. Hope of Israel: 14:8
    3. Our Potter: 18:6
    4. A Righteous Branch: 23:5a
    5. A King: 23:5b
    6. David their King: 30:9
    7. Our Resting-place: 50:6·

Covenants in Jeremiah—a New Covenant: 31:31-33. See COVENANT in Index.

Names and Titles of God: Jehovah-Tsidkenu, the Lord our Righteousness: 23:6; 33:16. See NAME in Dictionary.

This Book is filled with prophecy relating to God's judgment upon Israel and her Babylonian captivity, which was fulfilled in Jeremiah's days: 25:1-14. Second Chronicles 36:14-21 sums up the reasons for her captivity, with emphasis upon its duration; namely, seventy years. This seventy-year period is based upon Israel's failure to keep the "Sabbatical Year"—tilling the soil for six years, and then letting the land rest during the seventh (Leviticus 25:1-7; 26:27-35). See CAPTIVITY, Reasons for, in Index.

1. Israel's 70-year captivity: 25:11 with II Chronicles 36:17-21

   Stated: ca. 610 B.C. *Fulfilled:* ca. 604-586 to 534-445 B.C.

2. Babylon's fall: 25:12-14

   Stated: ca. 610 B.C. *Fulfilled:* ca. 536 B.C.

3. Israel regathered after Babylonian Captivity: 29:10-14. See Israel REGATHERED in Index.

   Stated: ca. 590 B.C. *Fulfilled:* ca. 534-445 B.C.

4. A New Jerusalem for Israel: 31:35-40

   Stated: ca. 600 B.C. *Fulfilled:* Yet future

5. Messianic Prophecies:
   a. Human generation: 23:5; 33:15 with Acts 13:22; Romans 1:3
   b. Divinity: 23:6 with I Corinthians 1:30
   c. Massacre of innocents: 31:15 with Matthew 2:16-18
   d. Nativity, from virgin: 31:22 with Luke 1:26-38

   Stated: ca. 600 B.C. *Fulfilled:* Birth and life of Christ

Archaeological Tidbits: Great Waters of Gibeon: 41:11,12. See GIBEON in Index.

Potter's House and Wheel

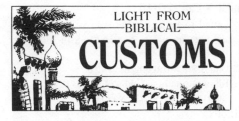

LIGHT FROM BIBLICAL CUSTOMS

³ The Potter's House: 18:1—19:13. Jeremiah gives a good illustration of the potter's skill. In turning the potter's wheel, a vessel might be marred, but a good potter doesn't give up; he works until he makes an excellent vessel. The picture shows a potter at his wheel. The interpretation of Jeremiah's illustration of the potter concerns God's complete control over the clay—over individuals, nations, and especially His own people, Israel. It is also a good spiritual application as noted by the hymn writer, Adelaide A. Pollard:

> Have Thine own way, Lord, Have Thine own way!
> Thou art the Potter, I am the clay;
> Mould me and make me after Thy will,
> While I am waiting, yielded and still.

For other illustrations about the potter and his vessels, see POTTER in Index.

SCIENTIFICALLY SPEAKING

1. Signs of heaven: 10:2. See ASTROLOGY in Index.

2. Ordinances of heaven: 31:35,36; 33:25. See ORDINANCES of Heaven in Index.

3. Rain: 10:13; 51:16. See RAIN in Index.

4. Numberless stars: 33:22. "Hipparchus, who lived a few hundred years after Jeremiah (ca. 150 B.C.), said there were exactly 1,026 stars in the universe. Ptolemy, the Roman scientist who lived in the time of Christ, said there were 1,056. It was not until Galileo's telescope that man began to realize the heavens contained a vast number of stars."[4] It is estimated that there are about 10 billion galaxies within range of the 200-inch telescope today. Einstein figured that total space is at least 100,000 times greater than observable space. With this deduction, there could be at least 100 septillion stars in space (however many that is!). Actually, it is 1,000,000,000,000,000,000,000,000,000 (one with 27 zeros). When Jeremiah said "the hosts of heaven cannot be numbered," he meant it! To count the stars would be like trying to count all the grains of sand on all the shores of the earth (Genesis 15:5). If everyone in the world were to count the stars, each person could count more than 50 billion of them without the same star being counted twice! And just think, the God who made them all, knows each by name! (Psalm 147:4). See STARS in Index.

Jeremiah in the New Testament:

1. The Temple a house of prayer: 7:11 with Matthew 21:13
2. Glorying in the Lord: 9:24 with I Corinthians 1:31
3. Herod's prediction: 31:15 with Matthew 2:16-18
4. God's New Covenant: 31:31-34 with Hebrews 8:8-10; 10:16,17. See COVENANTS in Index.
5. Companion references:
   a. Eternal water: 2:13 with John 4:14
   b. Israel fruitless: 2:21 with Matthew 21:33-41
   c. Prophets persecuted: 2:30 with Acts 7:51,52
   d. Rest in Christ: 6:16 with Matthew 11:29,30
   e. God, the Potter: 18:6 with Romans 9:20,21
   f. Christ's humanity: 23:5; 33:15 with Acts 13:22; Romans 1:3
   g. Christ, our Righteousness: 23:6 with I Corinthians 1:30
   h. Nativity, from virgin: 31:22 with Luke 1:26-38

SEED THOUGHTS

1. Jeremiah's Call: 1:1-10.
   a. Called to be a prophet: vs. 5
   b. His excuse: vs. 6. See EXCUSE in Index.
   c. His commission: vs. 7
   d. God's encouragement: vs. 8
   e. His equipment—God's Word: vs. 9
   f. Nature of his work: vs. 10
2. The Sinner's Two Evils: 2:13. See SINNER in Index.
   a. Desertion—they have forsaken and forgotten God: 2:13a,32
      —Result of man's first sin: Genesis 3:9
      —Result of Israel's backsliding: Deuteronomy 31:20
      —Result of Jonah's disobedience: Jonah 1:2,3
      Desertion is unnatural: 2:11. Even animals know their owners: Isaiah 1:3
   b. Worthless works—hewed cisterns that hold no water: 2:13b
      —Leads to slavery: 2:14. The prodigal son "hired himself" to another: Luke 15:15
      —No possible hope of cleansing sin: 2:22. It is not by "works of righteousness" that we
        are saved: 2:23; Titus 3:5
      —The way of transgressors is hard: Proverbs 13:15b
         —Tower of Babel: Genesis 11:1-9
         —Israel's captivity: Psalm 137:1-4
         —Man's house built upon sand: Matthew 7:26,27
         —Rich farmer's barns: Luke 12:16-20
   c. Sinner's state is appalling
      —Ways are clean in own eyes: Proverbs 16:2
      —Claims innocency: 2:35
      —Is spoiled: 2:14c
      —Has dirty garments: 2:34
      —Guilty of spiritual adultery: 3:9
   d. Sinner's condition is not hopeless: 3:13a; 6:16a; 7:23; 29:13
3. Causes for Backsliding: 8:5-9
   a. Holding fast to deceit: vs. 5b; II Thessalonians 2:11,12
   b. Speaking not aright: vs. 6a; I Timothy 4:2
   c. Not repenting: vs. 6b
   d. Going one's own way: vs. 6c
   e. Ignorant of the times: vs. 7a
   f. Ignoring the judgments of the Lord: vs. 7b
   g. Having vain confidence: vss. 8,9
   h. Being ashamed of the Lord: vs. 9a
   i. Rejecting the Word of the Lord: vs. 9b
4. Procrastination: 8:20
   a. Today is the day of salvation: II Corinthians 6:2
   b. The present is the best time to remember God: Ecclesiastes 12:1
   c. There is no assurance for tomorrow: Proverbs 27:1; James 4:14
   d. Tomorrow is too late: Hebrews 9:27
5. A Spiritual Diet: 15:16. See DIET in Index.
6. Remedies for a Deceitful, Wicked Heart: 17:9
   a. Psalm 34:1 for a bad temper
   b. Psalm 35:28 for evil speaking
   c. Psalm 70:4 for being melancholy
   d. Psalm 71:8 for scandal
   e. Psalm 71:15 for self-righteousness
   f. Psalm 71:24 for fear
   g. Psalm 44:8 for boasting

h. Proverbs 23:17 for envy

i. Psalm 119:97 for evil thoughts

j. Matthew 26:41; I Corinthians 10:13 for temptations

k. II Corinthians 10:5 for imaginations

l. Psalm 37:1-11 for fretting

m. Proverbs 3:5,6 for doubt

7. An Object Lesson—the Potter's Vessel: 18:1-6

    a. The clay is the "house of Israel," vs. 6, dug out of Egypt and brought into Canaan. The Potter (God) seeks to fashion a people like unto Himself—new creatures in Christ Jesus: Deuteronomy 14:2; Romans 8:29; II Corinthians 5:17.

    b. The wheels, vs. 3, are the promises, purposes, and providences of God, all working **together to mold and shape us for His glory and good pleasure: Romans 8:28; Ephesians 1:9-12**

    c. The vessel—our lives in His hands: Romans 12:1,2; I Corinthians 6:19,10; II Corinthians 4:7; II Timothy 2:2

8. Warning to False Pastors: 23:1-4

    a. Satan does call men to preach: II Corinthians 11:13-15

    b. His ministers are in the majority:

      —Moses' warning against them: Deuteronomy 13:1-5; 18:20-22

      —One Elijah to 850 false prophets: I Kings 18:17-19

      —Christ against the Pharisees: Matthew 23:1-36

      —Paul in perils among false brethren: II Corinthians 11:26

      —Titus warned about vain talkers and deceivers: 1:7,10

      Peter warns about false teachers: II Peter 2:1

      —**John mentions false prophets and the spirit of Antichrist: I John 4:1-3**

      —Paul constantly warns about false prophets in our day: II Timothy 3:1-13

      —Note the *few* Bible-believing, gospel-preaching, soul-saving, missionary-minded, fundamental churches in our day as compared to the vast multitude of liberal and modernistic ones in our midst

    c. Their message: II Corinthians 11:4. See MODERNISM in Index.

      —Another gospel (good works, church membership, ordinances, humanism, enthroning science, etc.—Galatians 1:8,9; Matthew 7:21-23; Titus 3:5)

      —Another spirit (new morals, liberalism, lawlessness, etc., "turning the grace of God into lasciviousness [license to sin]"—Jude 4)

      —Another Jesus (not virgin born, not omnipotent, not raised from the grave, not coming back, etc.)

It is interesting to note that the devil and his demons know who Christ is—they believe and tremble (Matthew 8:28,29; James 2:19). Yet, they will call preachers to deny what they believe! See HOMILETICS in Index.

    d. Warnings:

      —To false pastors: II Peter 2

      —To God's pastors: Galatians 1:8-10; I Corinthians 9:16. May God's Word burn in our bones as a fire (Jeremiah 20:9)

9. The Sinner's Plight and the Believer's Position: 30:11-22

    a. The sinner's plight. See SIN in Index.

      —Incurable: vs. 12a

      —Wounded: vs. 12b

      —Lonely: vs. 13a

      —Sick and helpless: vs. 13b

      —Bereft: vs. 14a

      —Wounded; God's wrath upon him: vs. 14b; John 3:36

      —Cannot control increase of sin: vss. 14c,15c

      —Miserable: vs. 15a

    —Sorrow incurable: vs. 15b

    —An outcast: vs. 17c

  b. The believer's position. See CHART in Index.

    —Healthy: vs. 17a with II John 2

    —Healed: vs. 17b with Isaiah 53:5

    —Emanicpated: vs. 18 with John 8:32,36

    —Thankful: vs. 19a with I Thessalonians 5:18

    —Fruitful: vs. 19b with John 15:4,5

    —Glorified: vs. 19c with Romans 8:30

    —Established: vs. 20a with Psalm 40:2

    —Protected: vs. 20b with Romans 8:31

    —One with God: vs. 22 with John 10:27-30; 17:20,21

10. God's New Covenant: 31:1-34. See COVENANTS in Index.

  a. Has a future fulfillment: vs. 1

  b. Rests upon God's changeless love; vss. 2,3

  c. Will give Israel true spiritual perception: vss. 29,30

  d. Will involve a new promise: vss. 31,32

  e. Will feature Israel's regeneration: vss. 33,34

11. The "I Wills" of God: 32:37-41. See "I WILLS" in Index.

  a. I will gather them out—*Deliverance:* vs. 37a with Ephesians 2:5,6

  b. I will bring them back—*Security:* vs. 37b with Romans 8:38,39

  c. I will be their God—*Assurance:* vs. 38b with I John 3:1,2

  d. I will give them one heart—*Identity:* vs. 39 with Philippians 1:21a

  e. I will make an everlasting covenant with them—*Contentment:* vs. 40a with Philippians 4:10-19

  f. I will put my fear in their hearts—*Devotion:* vs. 40b with Ephesians 3:14; Colossians 3:1,2

  g. I will rejoice over them—*Praise:* vs. 41a with Philippians 4:4

  h. I will plant them—*Stability:* vs. 41b with I Corinthians 16:13

12. Call unto me: 33:3

  a. Nothing is too hard for God: 32:17

  b. With God nothing is impossible: Luke 1:37

  c. Every good gift comes from God: James 1:17

  d. Call while He is near: Isaiah 55:6b

  e. Effectual praying avails much: James 5:16b

  f. We have not if we ask not: James 4:2b

  Warning—Do not ask amiss: James 4:3

    —Do not regard iniquity in the heart: Psalm 66:18

13. A Retrospect—Judah's Captivity: 52. This portion of the prophet's writings shows that man cannot play with sin and get by with it. Two verses bear out the consequence of sin as found in this chapter: (1) "Be sure your sin will find you out" (Numbers 32:23), and (2) "Be not deceived, God is not mocked, for whatsoever a man soweth, that shall he also reap" (Galatians 6:7).

A BIT OF HEAVENLY MANNA

I wonder how the reader stands with the Lord. I trust you are listed with the minority of believers who are pressing toward the mark for the prize of the high calling of God in Christ Jesus. If so, God's blessings rest upon you. If not, if you are numbered among the majority of believers who are carnal, then you are of all people most miserable. You are backslidden. You do not have the joy of God's salvation. Your conscience condemns you. God's peace is no longer a present possession with you. Unconfessed and unjudged sin in your life has brought the chastening of the Lord upon you, and—

THY BACKSLIDING SHALL REPROVE THEE—2:19[5]

"God sometimes punishes one sin by allowing us to fall into another. Every sin brings its own punishment, and we can sometimes read the sin in the punishment. Our backslidings reprove us, they become our preachers, and they solemnly address us. They point backward to the past, to the days of our first love when our evidences were bright, our joys strong, our hopes lively, our faith vigorous, and our prospects intense. These are placed in contrast with our gloomy doubts, harassing fears, worldly frames, painful suspicions, and dreary forebodings. As these are placed in contrast, a soul-searching voice cries, 'Know and see that it is an evil thing and bitter, that thou hast forsaken the Lord thy God.' Beloved, what is our experience this moment. Is it that of the child who walks and converses with his beloved Father in Peace? Or, is it that of the ungrateful, disobedient prodigal, who has slighted a Father's love, shunned a Father's presence, and who is fearing a Father's frown? If we have backslidden, let us return, saith the Lord, 'for I am merciful, and I will not keep anger forever' (3:12)."

PRAYER THOUGHT: "Father, I ask of Thee to reveal to me once again how personal Thou art and how practical are Thy ways. May I this day not make the things of the Lord difficult and hard by detouring off Thy old paths. In Jesus' name I pray. Amen."[6]

Jeremiah 6:16

Lamentations—The Book of Tears

Name: Lamentations might be rendered "dirge." Jeremiah in his prophecy used the word in 7:29; 9:10,20.

Contents: "These pathetic compositions deplore the fulfillment of the prophecies already uttered by Jeremiah. The leading object was to teach the suffering Jew neither to despise the chastening of the Lord nor to faint when rebuked of Him, but to turn to God with deep repentance, to confess their sins and humbly look to Him alone for pardon and deliverance. The prophet portrays some comfortable hope that God would be merciful to them and restore them again to their former privileges.

"Only great love is capable of great sorrow. Song of Solomon gives us an example of perfect love; Lamentations gives an example of perfect sorrow. Jeremiah's vision of Jerusalem wasted and Babylon exalted should be compared with John's vision of Babylon destroyed and the new Jerusalem revealed in triumph and heavenly beauty (Revelation 18:19)."[1] Lamentations has 5 chapters, 154 verses, and 3,415 words.

Character: Personal testimony of the weeping prophet.

Subject: Jehovah's love and sorrow for the people of Israel, whom He is chastening. This sorrow is wrought by the Spirit in the heart of Jeremiah.

Purpose: To teach us how to have fellowship with Him in His sufferings (Romans 8:18; Philippians 3:10).

Outline:

     I. Ruin and Misery in Jerusalem: 1
    II. Cause of Jerusalem's Overthrow: 2
   III. Jeremiah's Grief over Jerusalem's Affliction: 3
  IV. Israel's Former Glory Contrasted with Present Misery: 4
   V. Appeal to God and Prayer for Mercy: 5

Writer: Jeremiah. See NAME in Jeremiah.

When and Where Written: This book was probably written during the three-month interval between the capture of Jerusalem in 586 B.C. and Jeremiah's kidnapped journey to Egypt.

Key Chapter: 3. Jeremiah sharing Israel's affliction.

Key Verse: 1:1.

Key Word: Tears.

Key Phrase: Mourning and lamentations: 2:5.

Key Thought: Affliction, found 9 times.

Spiritual Thoughts:

    1. Repent . . . that your sins may be blotted out, when the times of refreshing shall come from the presence of the Lord: 3:25; Acts 3:19
    2. The Lord's mercies, compassions, and faithfulness: 3:22,23
    3. The Lord will not cast off forever: 3:31

Christ Is Seen As:

    1. My Portion: 3:24.
    2. The Smitten One: 3:30.

Winepress

LIGHT FROM BIBLICAL CUSTOMS

² The Lord hath trodden as in a winepress: 1:15. The winepress was a home necessity in the days of old. The picture shows a small press about five feet long, two feet wide and ten inches deep. Ripe grapes were crushed by one or more persons treading them. As the juice flowed into the opening (arrow), it was scooped up and bottled in jars or wineskins. In larger vats or winepresses, the treaders would hold on to overhead ropes to prevent their slipping. Jeremiah used a winepress to illustrate how God in judgment will crush and tread upon Israel for her sins.

Lamentations in the New Testament: There are no direct references of this Book in the New Testament, but there are two companion references:

1. World's opinion of God's people: 3:45 with I Corinthians 4:13
2. Murdering God's prophets: 4:13 with Matthew 23:31-35

SEED THOUGHTS

1. New Mercies every Morning: 3:22,23
   a. Every good and perfect gift is from God: James 1:17
   b. Joy in the morning: Psalm 30:5b
   c. Songs in the morning: Psalm 59:16
   d. Directions in the morning: Psalm 143:8
   e. Daily benefits: Psalm 68:19
   f. Every spiritual blessing—*now:* Ephesians 1:3
   g. I shall not want—goodness and mercy follow me *all* of the time: Psalm 23
   h. No good thing will the Lord withhold from those who walk uprightly before Him: Psalm 84:11
   i. O taste and see that the Lord is good: Psalm 34:8
2. Advice to Backsliders: 3:40
   a. Respond to the invitation—let us
   b. Examine self—search and try our ways
   c. Repent—turn . . . turn to the Lord
3. Thou hast Redeemed my Life: 3:58
   a. From the curse of the law: Galatians 3:10
   b. By the blood of Jesus: I Peter 1:18,19
   c. To serve Him: Titus 2:14
   d. To look for His return: Hebrews 9:28

A BIT OF HEAVENLY MANNA

The goodness of God is one of His attributes that ought to humble every person, whether sinner or saint. Paul tells us that "the goodness of God leads to repentance" (Romans 2:4b). All through the sin and misery and woe of Israel, which afflicted God's prophet, Jeremiah could still look up and thank God for His goodness and faithfulness. Though we may wander and turn our backs on the Lord, "He will never leave us nor forsake us" (Joshua 1:5). The goodness of God sometimes includes grief and affliction. Though God may permit grief, He does not afflict willingly; He will have compassion according to the multitude of His tender mercies (Psalm 51:1).

YET HE WILL HAVE COMPASSION—3:31-33a[3]

"Are you sorely tried? Are you writing bitter things against yourself? Is the hand of God gone out against you? Does He hold back the face of His throne and hang a cloud upon it? Does He break you with breach upon breach? Are you ready to say, 'All these things are against me?' Then cheer up, the storm will soon pass, the dark clouds are floating into the distance, the sun will soon burst forth, even now faith may see the bow in the cloud, for 'though He cause grief, yet will He have compassion according to the multitude of His mercies.' Even now He pities you with a father's pity. He waits for the fittest time to manifest Himself to you again. Infinite compassion reigns in His heart even while frowns may seem to cover His face and the rod is seen in His hand. Keep fast hold of His precious promise. Wait in hourly expectation at His gracious throne. Come to the determination of afflicted Job, 'though He slay me, yet will I trust in Him.' But He will not slay you; He will try you, purify you, fit you for service, and prepare you for heaven—all the while having compassion on you!"

PRAYER THOUGHT: "Dear heavenly Father, as I take inventory of the many blessings which Thou hast been pleased to bestow upon me, I thank Thee for new mercies every morning, especially mercies sent this morning for my day's tasks. Help me to appreciate Thy goodness always. In Thy dear name I pray. Amen."[4]

Lamentations 3:22,23

Ezekiel—The Book of Glory Lost and Regained

Name: Ezekiel, the writer of this book (1:1-3), means "God strengthens me": (2:5; 3:7,8). He was the son of a priest—a parabolic prophet, and actor prophet. His ministry was calculated to impress children, yet this book is one of the most difficult ones of the Bible to understand. He was addressed by God as "son of man" (2:1). This expression was used of him 90 times; it was used of Christ 80 times. This expression was used to show him his own weakness and his need to depend upon God for strength and success. He was a powerful preacher. His favorite expression was "the hand of the Lord was upon me," showing how strongly he felt the need to go forth and preach God's message. Isaiah was the statesman prophet of faith, Jeremiah the martyr prophet of love, and Ezekiel the exile prophet of hope. Isaiah's prophecies exalt the Son; Jeremiah, the Father; and Ezekiel, the Holy Spirit. He was married, and his wife died in captivity (24:15-18). During captivity he resided northeast of Babylon at Tel-abib with other captives by the river Chebar, a canal branching off from the Euphrates. He lived about 40 miles from Fara, the traditional home of Noah. He also lived about 100 miles from the site of the Garden of Eden, which could explain his use of Noah's name and the Garden of Eden (14:14,20; 28:13; 31:8,9,16,18; 36:35).

Period of His Prophecy: Ezekiel's prophetic utterances commenced seven years before the destruction of Jerusalem and concluded about fifteen years after its destruction, yet it should be distinctly noted that during his whole ministry Ezekiel was an exile in Babylon. It covers a period of about 22 years (592-570 B.C.). He was contemporary with Jeremiah, Daniel, probably Habakkuk and Obadiah (?), and was the *twelfth* prophet.

His visions are mainly given in chronological sequence: 1:2; 8:1; 20:1; 24:1; 26:1; 29:1,17; 30:20; 31:1; 32:1,17; 33:21; 40:1.

People of His Prophecy: His ministry was confined to those of the Southern Kingdom of Judah during the early years of captivity. They were mainly the older group, still hardened by their rebellion against God and the prophets.

Contents:[1] Ezekiel's predictions before the destruction of Jerusalem have for their chief object a call to repentance for those living in careless security; to warn them against indulging in the hope that by the help of Egypt the Babylonian yoke would be shaken off; to assure them that the destruction of their city and temple was inevitable, and thus he pronounces the doom and vindicates the justice of God in punishing the people for their sins. He made it clear that to return to Jerusalem they must first of all return to the Lord (1—24).

His predictions after the destruction of Jerusalem have for their chief object his care to console the exiled Jews by promises of future deliverances and restoration to their own land and an abundance of comfortable promies concerning the Messiah and of the blessings of grace by Him. The book shows the withdrawal of the Lord from Israel and declares the reason why, and the return of the Lord to Israel and reveals the method how (25—48). His prophecy abounds in:

1. Symbolic action: 4,5
2. Open prophecies: 6,7,30
3. Visions: 8—11
4. Similitudes: 12:15
5. Parables:17
6. Proverbs: 18
7. Allegories: 23,24

Much of his prophecy was in signs and acted out by him. This action was intended to attract the attention of the rebellious exiles. The *accounts* in the following references *explain* to Israel what these signs and actions meant:

1. At times he was speechless and used sign language: 3:26,27; 24:27; 33:22. He gave ten messages in the sign language of the dumb in the first 24 chapters.
2. The sign of the tile: 4:1-4
3. For a whole year he had to lie, first on one side and then on the other: 4:4-9
4. Had to eat loathsome food: 4:9-17
5. The sign of the razor and fire: 5;1-11
6. Had to pack his baggage and move: 12:1-16
7. His sighing: 21:1-7
8. Had to clap his hands: 21:14-17
9. The sign of the pot: 24:1-14
10. Could not mourn his wife's death: 24:15-27

The **Contents** can be summed up in three outstanding events:

1. The departure of the glory of the Lord from the Temple: 10:16-18; 11:23
2. The fall of Jerusalem: 33:21
3. The return of the Shekinah glory prophesied: 44:4

Ezekiel has 48 chapters, 1,273 verses, and 39,407 words.

Character: Highly figurative prophecy.

Subject: The vision of the glory of the Lord departing from the Temple at the time of captivity and the return of His "Shekinah Glory" to His house in the millennium.

Purpose: To encourage and strengthen our hearts in the time of sorrow and trial by the revelation of the glory that is yet to be ours with Him in His kingdom.

Outline:

I. Ezekiel's Call: 1—3:15

   II. Carrying out his Commission: 3:16—7:27
  III. Rejection of the People: 8—11
     A. Idolatrous worship: 8:5-18
     B. God's glory departs from the Temple: 10:18
  IV. Their Sins Rebuked: 12—19
   V. Nature of Judgment and their Guilt: 20—24
  VI. Judgment upon Seven Heathen Nations: 25—32
 VII. Destruction of Jerusalem: 33:21
VIII. Prophecies after Destruction—Israel's Future: 33—48
     A. New life to be bestowed: 33—39
     B. New order to be established: 40—48
     C. God's glory returns: 44:4

Key Chapter: 37. The "Dry Bone" chapter. See JEWISH in Index.

Key Verse: 1:1.

Key Word: Vision. See Proverbs 29:18a.

Key Phrase: "And ye shall know that I am the Lord": 6:7. This phrase occurs over 60 times.

Key Thought: The glory of the Lord: 1:28; 10:4,18; 43:2.

Spiritual Thought: I will restore the sanctuary.

Christ Is Seen As:
   1. A tender Twig: 17:22 with Isaiah 53:2
   2. Shepherd: 34:23a; 37:24
   3. David: 34:23b; 37;24
   4. Plant of Renown: 34:29

Names and Titles of God: Jehovah-shammah—Jehovah is there, ever present: 48:35. See NAMES in Dictionary.

1. Edom: 25:12-14. See IDUMAEA in Index.

2. Tyre: 26:3-14,19. Isaiah had prophesied Tyre's capture and restoration (23:13-18), but Ezekiel prophesied its doom. The city has long since been forgotten because its king spoke out against Jerusalem. At one time—even in Ezekiel's day—it was a mighty city, so strong that Sennacherib of Assyria failed to conquer it after a thirteen-year war. It was stormed by another mighty conqueror, Nebuchadnezzar, and he failed. Yet God prophesied that Tyre's walls would be broken, her pleasant houses destroyed, and the stones of the city would be in the midst of the water. Alexander the Great set the stage for fulfilling God's Word in destroying the city. Noting that the citizens of Tyre had relocated their city on an island just off shore to escape further besieging and possible capture, he built a causeway to the island from the main shore and conquered it. Reduced to an insignificant city, it was visited by Christ and Paul (Matthew 15:21; Acts 21:3-7). It was destroyed in the thirteenth century by Moslems who took it from the Crusaders, and has never been rebuilt since. Today, all archaeologists can find of Tyre are stones along the shore and parts of the causeway at low tide, which the fisherman use to dry their nets. How true the Word of God, even in such small details as fishermen drying their nets (vs. 14).

Stated: ca. 590 B.C. *Fulfilled:* ca. 332 B.C.—A.D. 1,200

3. Sidon: 28:21-23. This was a neighboring city of Tyre. Ezekiel prophesied (ca. 590 B.C.) that pestilence and flood and violence would befall Sidon, and this has been its history down

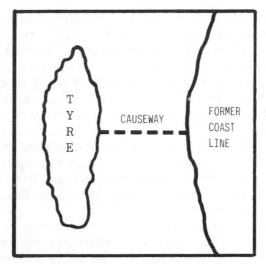

Alexander's Causeway

Tyre's Shore Stones

through the centuries, having been bombarded as late as 1840 by British and Turk soldiers. It still exists till this day. Ezekiel did not prophesy its doom like he did that of Tyre.

4. "Dry Bones"—Israel's Future Restoration: 37. In this vision of Ezekiel (ca. 590 B.C.) we have the valley of dry bones—Israel in her "cutoff" state. Having rejected Messiah, blindness in part has happened to them, and God is now calling out from among the Gentiles a people for His name (Romans 11:25; Acts 15:14-17). The fullness of the Gentiles is fast coming to a close with the establishment of a Jewish nation (1948) and great numbers are returning to their ancient homeland today. Israel is going back in unbelief—"flesh upon the bones, but no breath in them" (vss. 1-8). When the Lord returns in glory they will "look upon Him whom they have pierced" (Revelation 1:7), and will accept Christ as their Messiah. With the acceptance of Christ, God will put His Spirit in them and they shall live (vs. 14). Since 1948, there has been partial fulfillment of point 5.

5. Israel's homeland to be like Eden: 36:34,35. See DESERT in Index.

6. Prophecy against Gog—the Future Battle: 38,39. In this prophecy of Ezekiel (ca. 590 B.C.) we have what some believe to be the next to last greatest battle on earth. This battle is not the "Gog and Magog" of the book of Revelation. Ezekiel's prophecy has to do with the Jews and countries from the north (possibly Russia), but the "Gog and Magog" battle of Revelation (20:7-9) has to do with the saints of God in the last ditch battle against Satan and his allies. There is no question about this battle being in the future. When we list the nations that go against Israel in this battle (38:2-6), we find that history records no battle with these nations against Israel. The record demands that when this battle takes place Israel must be back in her own land. It is quite possible that the names listed in 38:2,3 make up Russia and the Balkans of the north and the nations of vs. 5 will come over and up against Israel with those of the north to try to wipe out God's people. The battle is seen from start to finish:

a. The war forecast; allies named: 38:1-6
b. The invasion planned: 38:7-10
c. The motive stated: 38:11-13. When we consider the worth of the chemicals in the Dead Sea and the oil of the surrounding Arabic nations, it is no wonder that the nations of the "north" keep their eyes on this part of the world. Even now, Russia's interest is such that aid is sent and given to some of these countries to be used against Israel. It is evident that Russia wants to take a spoil and a prey (vs. 12).
d. The invasion attempted: 38:14-17
e. The Divine opposition: 38:18—39:1
f. The defeat of the invaders: 39:2-8
   —Five out of six die: vs. 2. In the Gog and Magog of the Revelation *all* of God's enemies are destroyed (20:7-10)
   —Weapons useless: vs. 3. "The weirdest and most conclusive evidence that we are faced with in a foretelling of events yet to occur is the startling statement that this raiding army is armed only with wooden weapons! This conclusion is inescapable when we ponder the strange circumstances which are given as a result of the debacle of the assailing horde. The children of Israel gather their weapons of war, and burn them for fuel. The supply is sufficient to last for seven years, in and during which the Jews cut no timber nor split any wood for their stoves and fireplaces. Verses 9 and 10 seem to admit no other interpretation than this.
   "The question frequently and naturally arises, 'Why should nations in the future give up guns, tanks, airplanes, cannons, and weapons of steel for a reversion to implements of wood?' At first sight this looks like a real difficulty, but we gather some light on the question in the birth of new nuclear weapons, which are capable of destroying cities and killing millions with one blast. Other new and potent scientific weapons can render modern weapons useless. Powerful nations know that they dare not strike with such weapons lest the enemy nations 'push a button' and fire destructive missiles which in minutes will rain destruction upon people thousands of miles away. Warring nations in a future battle will have to turn to weapons of wood, or rubber! Of what use would it be to give a man a gun, when a power plant 50 miles away can turn it red hot in his hands. Men in metal tanks would burn to a cinder. Cannons would be red hot, and powder would explode the second it touched the chamber or breech, making loading impossible. The imagination of man literally staggers at the thought of all the consequences which may eventually result from new scientific weapons, but one thing appears certain—it spells the ultimate doom of metal weapons of warfare. It is also easy to understand why John, in the Revelation, makes so much mention of horses in this period. Cavalry plays an important role in war when mechanized implements fail."[2]
   —God triumphant in battle: vss. 4-8. It is interesting to note that God "brings" these invaders out from their own countries to Palestine against Israel (38:3-6). In considering Russia, she has never known defeat on her own soil. Both Napoleon and Hitler failed in

their attempt to defeat the Russians. But God "puts hooks in their jaws" and leads them out to a place of defeat.

    g. The "mopping up" period: 39:9-16. It will take seven years to clean up the debris and bury the dead

    h. Final grace of God on the land and people—the conversion of restored Israel: 39:17-29

    7. The Sealed Gate: 44:1-3. The gate which opened into the Temple area was called the "Golden Gate" or the gate "Beautiful" (Acts 3:2). After Jerusalem was destroyed in A.D. 70 by Titus, the present wall was not rebuilt until about A.D. 1500, at which time the gate at this site was sealed. However, upon the return of Christ in glory to this earth as "Prince of Peace," this gate will be opened, as predicted by Ezekiel.

Sealed Gate

Archeological Tidbits: City of Tyre. See TYRE in Index.

LIGHT FROM
BIBLICAL
CUSTOMS

³   1. A watchman to give warning: 3:17-21; 33:7-11. Cities of long ago were built upon hills. A high tower was built upon the city wall, and in the tower was a watchman who could see the approach of an enemy. His job was to warn the people, who, in turn, closed the city gates and prepared for battle. The position of the city on a hill, with the valley between them and the outlying mountains, served as a natural fortification. Because of such security, Israel had settled in ease and was "trusting in the mountains of Samaria" rather than in her God (Amos 6:1).

    Ezekiel's spiritual application is that the Christian is a "watchman" to warn sinners of impending doom unless they repent and get right with God. Christ gave further application to a "city set on a hill" (Matthew 5:14). It cannot be hid, and how true of our lives, which, having been set before the public by God, must reveal the life of Christ if our warning as a watchman is to become effective. And what protection we have—"God is our stronghold tower . . . and He knoweth them that trust in Him" (Nahum 1:7).

City Set on a Hill

2. A writer's inkhorn by his side: 9:2. In olden days only a few could write. A scribe was ever handy in a village, and often one accompanied men of importance on a mission. An animal's horn, filled with an ink made from lampblack (or soot), and mixed with water and gum, was strapped to the scribe's side much like a pistol holster. Fastened to the horn were wooden or bone pens. He was ready at a moment's notice to take dictation.

3. Thou wast not salted at all, nor swaddled at all: 16:4. Omission of this custom was an unheard of thing in the East. Only an unwanted or neglected baby would be treated thus. Newborn babies were rubbed with salt, their arms and legs tightly bound, and were kept swaddled (or wrapped) many days. Mothers believed this would keep them strong, keep away infection, and make them pure. This is what Mary did to the babe Jesus. "She brought forth her firstborn son and wrapped him in swaddling clothes, and laid him in a manger [feeding trough for animals]." See MANGER in Index.

4. I will spread my skirt over me: 16:8. See SKIRT in Index.

5. Divination: 21:21-24. See ASTROLOGY in Index.

6. Engines of war: 26:9 with II Chronicles 26:16. This instrument of war was the forerunner of our modern-day tank—a crudely built, box-type "engine" on wheels which hurled large stones to batter down city walls, or was filled with bowmen who shot arrows at soldiers on city walls or in wall towers. The walls of unearthed Assyrian palaces show carvings of such "engines." See picture of wall towers, p. 85.

Other weapons of war in olden days consisted of slingstones, spears, bows and arrows. A slingstone weighed about three-quarters of a pound and was two inches in diameter. They were used by "slingers" (II Kings 3:25). Spears were used by "spearmen" (Psalm 68:30), and "archers" or "bowmen" used bows and arrows (Genesis 49:23; Jeremiah 4:29).

Ezekiel in the New Testament:
1. Christ, the Shepherd: 34:23 with John 10:11.
2. Companion references. In the book of Revelation there are several allusions and parallel passages which show that John was familiar with Ezekiel:
    a. Ezekiel's beast: 1:5,10 with Revelation 4:5,7
    b. Mark on foreheads: 9:4 with Revelation 13:16

Engine of War

Sling Stones

Slingers and Bowmen

SEED
THOUGHTS

1. When God Saves: 16:6-14.
  a. He makes alive—Live: vs. 6
  b. He cleanses—washes us thoroughly: vs. 9a
  c. He clothes—covers our nakedness: vs. 8a,11
  d. He claims—thou becamest mine: vs. 8b
  e. He anoints—with fine oil: vs. 9b
  f. He crowns—a jewel on thy forehead: vs.12
  g. He uses in service—the renown went among the heathen: vs. 14

2. Israel's Threefold Sin: 16:49
  a. Pride—which leads to rebellion against God; *ends in a fall*
  b. Fullness of bread—self-satisfaction; *lack of spiritual values*
  c. Abundance of idleness—the devil's workshop; *anything goes*

3. The Individual's Responsibility: 18:20-32. The writer of Judges states: ". . . and there arose another generation after them, which knew not the Lord" (2:10). Each individual is responsible for himself or herself. Spiritual life and health are not inherited. God knows no such thing as His own "grandchildren"—we are either sons and daughters by spiritual birth, or we are not His. Notice:
  a. The individual that sinneth shall die: vs. 20a
  b. No man can bear another's sins: vs. 20b
  c. If the individual repents, he shall live: vs. 21
  d. He shall be forgiven: vs. 22
  e. He shall be saved: vs. 27
  f. God has no pleasure in the death of the wicked: vs. 23
  g. No man can redeem another: Psalm 49:7
  h. *Ye* must be born again: John 3:3,5,7; Acts 16;31

4. A Man in the Gap: 22:30. Just as Christ is the mediator between man and God (I Timothy 2:5), so redeemed man is the "gap" between the lost and Christ. With Christ in heaven and the Holy Spirit in the believer, the believer is the only person on earth to represent God before others. This is *our* responsibility—*our* calling as "ambassadors of Christ" (II Corinthians 5:20). But, alas, too few respond to their calling. With the Psalmist the world cries, "I looked on my right hand, and beheld, but there was no man that would know me: refuge failed me; no man cared for my soul" (142:4). With Ezekiel we *must* be the man in the "gap." See WATCH-MAN in Index. As a watchman, we will—
  a. *Obey* like Abraham: Genesis 12:1-4
  b. *Trust* like Isaac: Genesis 22:6-14
  c. *Serve* like Isaiah: Isaiah 6:8
  d. *Stand* like Elijah: I Kings 18:17-22
  e. *Be bold* like Peter and John: Acts 4:13
  f. *Walk* like Enoch: Genesis 5:22
  g. *Flee* temptation like Joseph: Genesis 39:12
  h. *Work* like Noah: Genesis 6:13-22
  i. *Testify* like Paul: Acts 26:1-29
  j. *Be convincing* like Elisha: II Kings 6:15-17
  k. *Suffer* like Moses: Hebrews 11:23-25
  l. *Be yielded* like Stephen: Acts 7:55-60

5. Hearers but Not Doers: 33:31,32; James 1:22. "They hear Thy Words, but they will not do them." This results in:
  a. Giving lip service: 33:31a; Matthew 15:8
  b. Heart goeth after covetousness: 33:31b
  c. Light turned into darkness: Matthew 6:23

     d. Blinded eyes: Matthew 13:13a

     e. Deaf ears: Matthew 13:13b

     f. Understanding dulled: Matthew 13:14,15; Ephesians 4:18

     g. Perversion of the will: John 5:40

     h. Hating God's men: II Chronicles 36:15,16; Matthew 23:34

     i. A conscience seared as with a hot iron: I Timothy 4:2

     j. Being past feeling: Ephesians 4:19

     k. Being sealed with a strong delusion: John 12:39,40; II Thessalonians 2:10-12

     l. Deception: Matthew 7:21-23

     m. Death: John 8:24

   The Remedy: Joshua 1:7; Psalm 119:133.

6. The "I Wills" of Ezekiel: 34:11-31. See "I WILLS" in Index.

     a. I will search and seek them: vss. 11,16a

     b. I will deliver them: vs. 12

     c. I will bring them out: vs. 13a. "Brought us *out* from thence [Egypt], that He might bring us *in* [to the Promised Land]": Deuteronomy 6:23

     d. I will gather them unto Myself (bring in): vs. 13b

     e. I will feed them: vs. 14

     f. I will cause them to lie down (rest): vs. 15b

     g. I will bind up the broken: vs. 16b

     h. I will strengthen the sick: vs. 16c

     i. I will take care of the enemy: vs. 16d

     j. I will judge My sheeps' differences: vss. 17-22

     k. I will watch over them: vs. 23

     l. I will be their God: vs. 24

     m. I will bless them: vss. 25a,26b

     n. I will cause them to dwell in safety: vs. 25b

     o. I will make them a blessing: vs. 26

     p. I will abundantly satisfy them: vss. 29-31

7. Changing a Heart: 36:25-32

     a. The condition—a stony heart: vs. 26

      —Hard, unyielding

      —Cold, past feeling

      —Dead in trespasses and in sin

     b. The change—a new heart: vs. 26

      —A living heart—dead to sin but alive to God

      —A receptive heart—to be Christlike

      —A hungry heart—to be filled with things spiritual

     c. The evidence of a new heart:

      —Possession of the Spirit: vs. 27a

      —Walking in His statues: vs. 27b

      —Resting in His promises: vss. 29-32

8. Waters to Swim In: 47:1-12. This mystical river is like God's salvation for the sinner and his growth in grace and knowledge of his Lord and Savior Jesus Christ. The river came out and down from the house (Temple) at the side of the altar, just like Christ came down from His Father to be placed on the altar (Cross). The purpose of this river was to—

     a. Heal: vs. 8

     b. Revive: vs. 9

     c. Bring forth fruit: vs. 12

"Waters to swim in" is a picture of the believer's growth. God's river of healing and blessing *is* to be entered—

     a. Ankle deep: vs. 3. This represents a definite act of stepping into the current of God's divine will

    b. Knee deep: vs. 3. This represents prayer life

    c. Loin deep: vs. 4b. This represents study of the Word of God—"loins girt about with truth" (Ephesians 6:14)

    d. Swimming: vs. 5. The Christian is now fully supported by the water, having "put off the old man, putting on Christ Jesus, and making not provision for the flesh" (Romans 13:14). The closer one stays to the shore, the more of self is seen. The farther one goes into the river, the less is seen of self and the more is seen of God's river of salvation. "I must decrease, He must increase."

One would think that Israel, with all her glory and pomp, and because of her favor with God, would have remained true and loyal to their God Jehovah. His glory had been manifested time and time again. Abraham's seed was to be blessed forever. To them had been entrusted the sacred oracles of God (Romans 3:2). Salvation is of them (John 4:22). And yet, with all the personal glory of God round about them, Ezekiel testifies to their rejection by God because of idolatrous worship. But someday Israel will look upon Him whom they have pierced and then God's promise of His returned glory will be fulfilled. For New Testament believers, God's glory will be manifested before it will be to the Jew. When the clouds are rolled back and the Lord Himself descends from heaven with a shout, with the trump of God, we shall be caught up in the clouds to meet the Lord in the air (I Thessalonians 4:16,17). When He appears, we shall be like Him; for we shall see Him as He is (I John 3:2). Not only will His glory be revealed then, but it will be revealed in us (II Thessalonians 1:10). But there is a *present* glory of God for His children.

THE GLORY OF THE LORD CAME—43:4[4]

"The essential glory of God's nature cannot be seen by us. Our powers and faculties are not able to bear it, but the glory of His perfections, as they shine forth in His works, and especially in our salvation, may be seen. Jesus is the brightness of His glory, and the express image of His person. He is the image of the invisible God. He is the mirror in which the glory of God is seen. If God, therefore, answers this prayer to show us His glory in our experience, He will shine into our hearts, and give us the light of the knowledge of His glory, in the face of Jesus Christ. All the glory of God is in Christ; if therefore the eyes of our mind are opened, if the Holy Spirit reveals Jesus to us, we shall see the Lord's glory. This sight will humble us in the dust before Him, overwhelm us with shame on account of our sins, inspire us with confidence to trust in His Word, and draw out our warmest love and most solemn reverence toward Him. The more we see of God's glory, the more we shall hate sin, be weaned from the world, pant after holiness, delight in worship, and pactice His precepts. Lord, manifest Thyself to me in Jesus."

PRAYER THOUGHT: "Today, dear Savior, it is possible that my path may cross someone who needs Thee. Give me discernment to know who, wisdom to know what to say, and genuine compassion to win that soul to Thee. In Thy dear name I pray. Amen."[5]

Ezekiel 3:17-19

Daniel—The Book of Loyalty and Light

Name: Daniel means "God is my judge." He is the political prophet, the seer of world government, the father of Gentile history. He is the prophet of dreams and visions—he sets dates and events in advance. He is the prophet of the "times of the Gentiles."

Writer: The book itself recognizes Daniel as its author: 7:1,28; 8:2; 9:2; 10:1,2; 12:4. Christ accepted his writings (Matthew 24:15). Critics assert his writings belong to the period of the Maccabeans (168-164 B.C.) because of the accuracy of events described (see MACCABEANS in Index). Ezekiel's prophecy has been generally accepted as of his day (592-570 B.C.), and his reference to Daniel (28:3), who was his contemporary, should be sufficient evidence that his writings belonged to *that* day (of Daniel—605-530 B.C.).

The first part of Daniel is written in Aramaic, the language of the Gentiles of that day (2:4—7:28). The latter part is written in Hebrew. In the former Daniel is spoken of in the third person; in the latter he is spoken of in the first person.

Period of His Prophecy: Daniel was in the first group of captives taken to Babylon—"in the third year of the reign of Jehoiakin, king of Judah": 1:1-6. His period of prophecy was ca. 605-530 B.C., from King Nebuchadnezzar of Babylon to Kings Cyrus and Darius of the Medes and Persians (see NEBUCHADNEZZAR, CYRUS, and DARIUS in Index). Daniel was a contemporary of Ezekiel and Nehemiah, and of Joshua and Zerubbabel of the remnant. He was the *eleventh* prophet.

People of His Prophecy: The Southern Kingdom of Judah, during their Babylonian captivity.

Contents: The book is partly historical (1—6), relating facts in which Daniel was personally concerned; and partly prophetical (7—12), of things relating to:

1. His time to the period of Messiah's first coming. This is borne out in Daniel's interpretation of Nebuchadnezzar's dream—the great image which represented four great Gentile world powers (2:1-45):
   a. Babylonian—head of gold, a lion: vss. 37,38; 7:4
   b. Medo-Persian—breast and arms of silver, a bear: 7:5
   c. Grecian—belly and thighs of brass, a leopard: vs. 39; 7:6
   d. Roman—legs of iron, a beast with 10 horns: vs. 40; 7:7

2. Christ's earthly ministry (9:20-26a), the setting up of Christ's spiritual kingdom (2:44,45; John 18:36), and the destruction of Jerusalem by Titus in A.D. 70 (9:27; 11:31; 12:11; Matthew 24:15; Luke 21:20-24)

3. The fall of the Roman Empire—the ten toes of iron and clay—Gentile nations to the end of the "times of the Gentiles": 2:41-43; Luke 21:24b

In Daniel the sovereignty of God is seen over the affairs of men of all ages. The pagan king's confessions of this fact is seen in 2:47; 4:37; and 6:26. Daniel has 12 chapters, 357 verses, and 11,606 words.

Character: Prophetical.

Subject: History and prophecy concerning Gentile world rule from Nebuchadnezzar until the Antichrist, and the sovereignty of God over all kingdoms: 2:20,21.

Purpose: To reveal to us Christ as the One in whose image we are to be conformed, the One in whose kingdom we shall shine as the brightness of the firmament: 12:3.

Outline:
    I. Historical: 1—6
      A. Heathen Customs Judged: 1
      B. Heathen Philosophy Judged: 2
      C. Heathen Pride Judged: 3,4

Key Chapter: 2. Nebuchadnezzar's dream and its interpretation.

Key Verses: 2:44; 7:14.

Key Word: Kingdom, found 57 times.

Key Phrase: In the latter days: 2:28.

Key Thought: The most High ruleth in the kingdom of men: 4:25; Romans 13:1. Throughout this book the "God of heaven" (2:44) often revealed Himself as the "God of gods" (2:47), able to do the impossible, such as—

    1. Daniel's interpretation of the king's forgotten dream when his gods failed his own wise men: 2.

    2. Deliverance of the three Hebrew children from the fiery furnace when the gods of the image failed to destroy them: 3.

    3. The gods of Nebuchadnezzar failing to help him when this proud king was forced by God to eat grass like an animal: 4:28-33

    4. Deliverance of Daniel by God's angel from the lion's den when man's law failed: ch. 6

Spiritual Thought: He will bring in the kingdom.

Christ Is Seen As:

    1. The Stone: 2:35,45

      a. To Israel—a stone of stumbling: Romans 9:31-33

      b. To Gentiles—the smiting stone: 2:35,45

      c. To the Church—the head of the corner: I Peter 2:6,7

    2. A great Mountain: 2:35

    3. Son of God: 3:25

    4. Ancient of days: 7:9

    5. Son of man: 7:13

    6. Lord of His kingdom: 7:14

    7. Prince of princes: 8:25

    8. The most Holy: 9:24

    9. Messiah: 9:25

Names and Titles of God. See NAMES in Dictionary.

    1. God of heaven: 2:44

    2. God of gods: 2:47; 11:36

    3. Lord of kings: 2:47

    4. Revealer of secrets: 2:47

    5. Most High God: 3:26; 4:25

    6. The Deliverer: 3:29

    7. King of heaven: 4:37

    8. The living God: 6:20

    9. Lord God: 9:3

    10. Great and dreadful God: 9:4

11. Covenant-keeping God: 9:4
12. God of his Fathers: 11:37

1. Times of the Gentiles—
   a. Babylonian: 2:37,38; ca. 605-539 B.C.
   b. Persian: 7:5; 8:20; ca. 539-331 B.C.

Daniel gave a remarkable prediction about four kings, the last one of the richest of them all, and that his kingdom would fall (11:2,4). Cambyses, Smerdis, and Darius were the first three kings, then the richest of all—Xerxes. Herodotus tells us he stirred up his people against Greece, invaded that country with two-and-a-half-million men, but was utterly defeated by Salamis in 480 B.C., thus fulfilling this prediction by Daniel.

   c. Grecian: 2:39; 8:21; ca. 331-63 B.C. Daniel predicted that Alexander's great kingdom would be divided into four parts (8:22). It was so divided after his death, the four parts becoming Macedonia, Thrace, Egypt, and Syria.
   d. Roman: 2:40; 7:7; ca. 63 B.C.—A.D. 476
   e. "Ten toes of iron"—other nations and world powers after Rome: 2:41-43; ca. A.D. 476—"until the times of the Gentiles be fulfilled" (Luke 21:24b; Romans 11:25)

2. Maccabean Period.[1] Syria's success is foretold under a certain fierce king who would obtain the kingdom by flattery (8:22-25). This was true of Antiochus Epiphanes (176 B.C.). After his brother died, his infant nephew was to have taken the throne. Antiochus mingled so freely with the people, was so kind and genial, and flattered them so wisely, they at last made him king. Note some of Daniel's predictions regarding this cruel monarch:

   a. Daniel said he would break the prince of the covenant, meaning the high priest (11:22). He did when he put Onias III out of office, and another in
   b. Daniel 8:11 predicted that Antiochus would destroy the holy people (the Jews), pollute their sanctuary, and take away their daily sacrifices (8:11). He did these very things, for history records that he captured Jerusalem and killed 40,000 Jews. He then slew a sow in the Holy of Holies, and sprinkled its blood over the altars and all the sacred vessels. He then forbade the Jews to sacrifice to Jehovah under penalty of death
   c. Daniel also predicted that by peace this cruel king would destroy many Jews (8:25). He did this when he sent his general, Apollonius, with 22,000 men to Jerusalem on a mission of peace. These soldiers went in and out among the Jewish people, and were so kind and affable, that they disarmed all suspicion. Then on the Sabbath, when the Jews were worshiping in their Temple, the order was given to slaughter them, and thousands perished. Thus by "peace" Antiochus did destroy many Jews
   d. Daniel predicted further that this cruel king, Antiochus, "shall also stand up against the prince . . . but he shall be broken without hand" (8:25). This simply means that he would stand up against God Himself and be slain without the help of any human being. When Antiochus Epiphanes heard that the Jews, under the Maccabeans, had cast out of their temple the image of Jupiter Olympus, which he himself had placed therein, he was so enraged that he at once raised an army to exterminate the whole Jewish race; but before he could set forth he was seized with a dreadful pain in his intestines and soon died in awful agony, slain by God, without human help

3. Messianic—
   a. Time of advent: 9:24-26 with Luke 2:1,2; Galatians 4:4. Daniel gives a wonderful prediction regarding the time element of Christ's first coming—"from the going forth of the commandment to restore and to build Jerusalem unto the Messiah, the Prince, shall be seven weeks, and three score and two weeks" (9:25,26). A "week" in the Hebrew is seven years—69 × 7 = 483 years. Daniel's prophetic date began when Artaxerxes issued his order, on March 14, 445 B.C., to restore and rebuild Jerusalem. It was fulfilled

when Messiah—the Lord Jesus Christ—was cut off (slain) at Calvary 483 years later.
This prophecy of Daniel is the most damaging evidence to the blinded Jew of today who says that the Messiah's coming to "make an end of sins" is yet future.

    b. Ministry of Christ: 9:24 with Matthew 20:28; Hebrews 1:1,2; Acts 10:38. Of His ministry Daniel said that "Messiah shall be cut off" (John 1:11; Matthew 12)

    c. Vicarious suffering: 9:26a

    d. His dominion universal and everlasting: 7:14 with Luke 1:32,33; Philippians 2:9-11

  4. The Tribulation Period: 9:27. "Seventy weeks" were determined upon Israel (9:24). The first sixty-nine have been fulfilled, which culminated in the crucifixion of Christ. What about the last—or seventieth week? Several interpretations are given regarding this week, the most popular being the "pretribulation, premillennial"view. It is set forth as follows:

The "tribulation period" is a seven-year period of awful tribulation which takes place on the earth after the rapture of the Church, and relates especially to the Jews who have gone back to their own land in unbelief. A covenant will be made with the Jews for Temple worship and their sacrifices but in the midst of the seventieth week, or this seven-year period, the prince (Antichrist) shall break the covenant, causing the sacrifice and oblation to cease, and for the overspreading of abominations he shall make it desolate. This is the "abomination of desolation spoken of by Daniel the prophet" (vs. 27; Matthew 24:15). It is also known as—

    a. The "great tribulation": Matthew 24:21

    b. A "time of trouble": Daniel 12:1

    c. The "time of Jacob's trouble": Jeremiah 30:7

    d. The "day of the Lord's wrath": Zephaniah 1:18

    e. A "time of great tribulation": Revelation 7:14

A description of this tribulation period—the "time of Jacob's trouble"—is found in Revelation 6:15-17; 11:1-14; 12:6-17. After this "day of wrath," Satan, who had empowered the Antichrist in this last week of Daniel's prophecy, is cast down out of the heavenlies and is bound during the millennium, or Christ's reign upon the earth.

1. Daniel's interpretation of Nebuchadnezzar's forgotten dream—to reveal that Daniel's God is Omniscient: 2:1-47.

2. Shadrach, Meshach, and Abed-nego saved in the fiery furnace—to attest to God's power and providence: 3:19-28.

3. Nebuchadnezzar eating like the beasts of the field—to humble a proud king and reveal that Israel's God is Lord over all kingdoms: 4:24-28; 2:21.

  4. The "handwriting on the wall" during Belshazzar's great feast—to show that all men are accountable to God and will be judged by Him for their sins: ch. 5.

  5. Daniel saved from the lion's den—to reward God's servant for his faithfulness: ch. 6. Darius is the Persian king who had Daniel put in the lion's den.

1. Daniel's interpretation of Nebuchadnezzar's dream: 2. When Nebuchadnezzar dreamed dreams and commanded his magicians and astrologers to give their interpretations, they failed miserably. Daniel correctly interpreted them, and was promoted. A very interesting discovery in Babylon has revealed the ruins of a college, a library and curricula, for native princes to be trained especially for interpretations of

of dreams and visions. One record stipulated two regulations:

King Darius

     a. Impiety to any gods—cast alive into a fiery furnace
     b. Untoward act relative to a king—cast alive into the den of lions

  2. Nebuchadnezzar's "image of gold" and the fiery furnace: ch. 3. Nebuchadnezzar's pride is seen in his "image of gold" and the command for all people to worship it. It was ninety feet high and nine feet wide. Discovered records show that it was Nebuchadnezzar's custom, not only in Babylon but in Ur of the Chaldees, to make public the worshiping of huge images. The three Hebrew boys refused to bow to this image and were cast alive into a blazing fiery furnace. God's deliverance of these boys resulted in Nebuchadnezzar's recognition of Israel's God. Excavators at Babylon found this furnace, with an inscription: "This is the place of burning where men who blaspheme the gods of Chaldea die by fire."

  3. Belshazzar and Nabonidus: ch. 5. Daniel's interpretation of the "handwriting on the wall" foresaw Belshazzar's doom, and the Bible mentions him as the last king of Babylon, killed when the Medes and Persians conquered Babylon. A clay tablet reveals that *Nabonidus* was the last king of Babylon, and that he was allowed by the Persians to live out his life in retirement. With this discovery, critics were quick to condemn Daniel's account. But a search among hundreds of clay tablets which recorded the reign of Nabonidus showed that he had a son by the name of Belshazzar who was "regent" in his stead. This was common practice in those days—to appoint a son to reign in his father's place. While Nabonidus was in one of his palaces remote from Babylon, Belshazzar was king when Babylon fell. We can understand better Belshazzar's saying that if Daniel could interpret his dream he would make him the "*third ruler in the kingdom*" (vs. 16). He could not have made him the first—that was Nabonidus' position. Belshazzar was *second,* so Daniel was offered the position next to the *reigning* monarch. This shows that Daniel's historical record *is* accurate.

  4. The lion's den: ch. 6. Because of Daniel's faithfulness to his God, others in the Persian kingdom sought to bring him into disrepute with King Darius. Daniel defied the king's decree and was cast into the lion's den. Discovery has been made in Babylon of such a place, with this inscription: "The place of execution where men who angered the king die, torn by wild beasts."

  5. Laws of the Medes and Persians: 6:7-17. See LAW in Index.

  6. In 612 B.C. the Assyrians were overturned by a coalition of the Medes and the Neo-

Site of Lion's Den

Babylonians (or Chaldeans). The second Neo-Babylonian king was Nebuchadnezzar, who carried off Daniel in 605 and who destroyed the Temple in 586. The book of Daniel has been dated by critics to the second century B.C. for a number of reasons including the presence of Greek words. But the abundant evidence of the presence of Greeks in the Near East, including Greek mercenary soldiers fighting both for and against Nebuchadnezzar, demonstrates the weakness of such an argument.

Daniel in the New Testament:

1. Eternal kingdom: 2:44 with I Corinthians 15:24
2. Reconciliation for iniquity: 9:24 with II Corinthians 5:21; Hebrews 9:12
3. Christ "cut off"—His rejection and suffering: 9:26a with Matthew 27:22-35
4. Abomination of desolation: 9:27 with Matthew 24:15
5. Companion references:
   a. Daniel unharmed in lion's den: 6:23 with Hebrews 11:33
   b. Names written in book: 12:1 with Luke 10:20b; Revelation 13:8
   c. Eternal punishment: 12:2 with Matthew 25:46; John 5:28,29
   d. Reward for soul-winning: 12:3 with I Thessalonians 2:19,20

It can be said that Daniel is the introduction to New Testament prophecy. Such themes as the manifestation of the man of sin, the great tribulation, the return of the Lord, the two resurrections, and the judgments are found in both Daniel and the New Testament. Daniel's language is adopted in the Revelation by John, which is the counterpart of his book in the New Testament.

SEED THOUGHTS

1. Man *versus* God—
   a. Contest No. One—the palace diet: 1:3-21. King's meat and wine *versus* God's health food
   Result: Temperance wins, Daniel's plan accepted: vss. 15-21
   b. Contest No. Two—interpreting the king's dream: ch. 2. The king's magicians *versus* God's wise man
   Result: God's wisdom wins—Daniel promoted: vss. 46-49

c. Contest No. Three—the image of gold: 3:1—4:3. Obedience to the king *versus* Faithfulness to God.
   Result: Faithfulness to God wins—God exalted: 3:26—4:3
d. Contest No. Four—Nebuchadnezzar's pride: ch. 4. A mighty king *versus* a sovereign God.
   Result: Humility wins—God honored: vss. 34-37
e. Contest No. Five—Belshazzar's feast: ch. 5. Worldly pleasure *versus* God's standard.
   Result: Truth wins—Belshazzar judged: vss. 28-31
f. Contest No. Six—the plot against Daniel: ch. 6. Man's law and the lions *versus* God's providence
   Result: Providence wins—God is feared: vss. 23:28

2. Daniel's servitude before royalty resembled that of Joseph; he was promoted to the highest office in the realm next to the king (2:48), and he maintained a consistent testimony for his God in the midst of a heathen court (6:10). Daniel was:

a. Attractive: 1:4-9
b. Temperate: 1:8
c. Courteous: 1:8-12
d. Studious: 1:17-19; 9:2
e. Courageous: 2:13-16; 6:7-11
f. Humble: 2:30; 9:7-20
g. Honored: 2:48; 6:23; 12:13
h. Faithful: 6:4
i. Prayerful: 6:10; 9:3,4

3. Godly Youth *versus* Paganism: ch. 3.[2] The testimony of these three Hebrew boys seemed to be, "Let no man despise thy youth, but be thou an example . . ." (I Timothy 4:12). And an example they were!

a. Image set up (vs. 1) just like the world is setting up images for our youth today. Made of the best—gold to attract—just like idols today, attractive and sexy. Commercial ads never show the finished product
b. Invitation simple—come to the dedication of the image (vss. 2,3). Youth today receive invitations to and for innocent looking things
c. Majority responded, just like the world today responds to and indulges in fashionable idolatry
d. Invitation became a "demand" for all to worship image (vss. 4-6). When there is response to an "innocent" invitation one soon becomes involved in its demands
e. Demands become commands (vs. 6)—a bowing to the "accepted" thing
f. The world picks on those who refuse to go along with the crowd (vss. 8-12). It angers them (vs. 13). Often parents get angry with children who confess faith in Christ
g. World never lets up—Shadrach, Meshach, and Abed-nego given another chance (vss. 14,15)
h. A stand for God is taken—trusting in God for deliverance (vss. 16,17). They could have argued among themselves:
   —Everybody is doing it
   —Nobody will see us in the crowd
   —Only asking us to do it this once
   —Why not compromise—not bow down all the way
   —Our parents will never know
i. Didn't say that, but did say "our God is able . . . we will *not* serve thy gods" (vss. 17,18)
j. Nebuchadnezzar full of fury at their stand (vs. 19). Natural reaction of the world. Believer not called upon to be popular. World hated Christ; will hate His own (John 17:14)
k. World seeks to crush those who live godly (vss. 20-23)
l. God is ever present in any circumstance or trial when He is honored (vss. 24,25; I Corinthians 10:13)
m. A true stand for God results in:

—God being recognized as true and living God (vs. 25)
—God's power made available
—Recognition that godly have something the world doesn't
—That others may mock us to our faces, but admire us behind our backs
—When circumstances are such that one is helpless, God's strength is made perfect in our weakness
—If God be for us, who can be against us (Romans 8:31)

4. Three Grand Men—Shadrach, Meshach, and Abed-nego[3]
    a. They wouldn't bow: 3:12
    b. The wouldn't budge: 3:16
    c. They wouldn't burn: 3:27

5. Belshazzar's Folly: ch. 5[4].
    The Calloused king—
    a. Irrational behavior: vs. 1
    b. Irreverent frivolity: vss. 2,3
    c. Irresponsible pastime: vs. 4a
    d. Inconsiderate religion: vs. 4b
    The Confounded king—
    a. Unexpected message: vs. 5
    b. Undeniable amazement: vs. 6
    c. Unqualified mystics: vss. 7-9
    d. Uncompromising man of God: vss. 10-16
    The Condemned king—
    a. Unlearned lessons: vss. 17-22
    b. Unrepentant libertine: vs. 23
    c. Unexpected loss: vss. 24-28
    d. Untimely death: vss. 29-31

6. Lessons from Belshazzar:
    a. God speaks when men least expect it: vs. 5
    b. God speaks when men least desire it: vss. 1-4
    c. God speaks without warning: vs. 5
    d. When God speaks, hearts and minds are troubled: vs. 6
    e. Men in sin come short of God's glory: vs. 27
    f. The wages of sin is death: vs.30

7. Daniel, a Man of Prayer: 6:10,11
    a. Habitual—as he did aforetime
    b. Systematic—three times a day
    c. Secret—he went to his chamber (Matthew 6:6)
    d. Earnest—set my face . . . to seek by prayer: 9:3a
    e. Self-denial—with fasting: 9:3b
    f. Humble—with sackcloth and ashes: 9:3c
    g. Reverential—he knelt upon his knees
    h. Made confession—my sins: 9:20
    i. Believing—his windows opened toward Jerusalem
    j. Grateful—gave thanks before His God
    k. Courageous—in spite of the king's decree
    l. God glorifying—for His sake: 9:17-19

8. Someone has said the reason the lions did not eat Daniel was that he had too much *grit* and *backbone:* 6:16-22

9. Different Ways of Expressing Sin: 9:5-15.[5] See SIN in Index.
    a. We have sinned: vss. 5,8,11,15
    b. We have committed iniquity: vs. 5
    c. We have done wickedly: vs. 5

    d. We have rebelled: vss. 5,9

    e. We have not hearkened unto Thy servants: vs. 6

    f. We have transgressed: vs. 7

    g. We have been disobedient: vss. 10,11

    h. We have transgressed: vs. 11

    i. We have neglected to pray: vs. 13

10. The Soul-winner's Promise: 12:3. See SOUL-WINNING in Index.

A BIT OF **HEAVENLY MANNA**

When Daniel was threatened by those who sought his life, he could look up with a smile of real confidence to His God, knowing full well that his life was in His hands. Has this Book taught us this rich spiritual truth? When the world begins to ask questions when they see us in difficulties, we can with calm assurance look up to God with His peace flooding our souls. When the king was forced by an irrevocable decree to thrust him in the lion's den, he knew his God would take care of him. The king, frightened with the knowledge that his own gods were helpless, asked Daniel:

IS THY GOD ABLE TO DELIVER THEE—6:20[6]

"This was the question of a heathen monarch put to a servant of the most High God. He did not seem to question but what He would deliver him if He could. But Daniel's God both *could* and *did!* Beloved, this question may be very often put to us, not only to encourage, but to reprove us. Let our trouble, trial, or difficulty be what it may, the question meets us, 'Is thy God able to deliver thee?' If so, why do you droop, doubt, or despond? Has He promised to deliver us? He has! Then your fears must be sinful, since they indicate unbelief and distrust. Until we come into some trial from which God will not deliver, or into some state to which the promise does not reach, we ought not to fear but rather encourage a cheerful hope. Let us then endeavor, under our sorest trials, to remember this great truth—our God *is* able to deliver us. He has given us His Word that He will. It is impossible for Him to lie or change His mind. He has delivered thousands out of similar difficulties before; therefore, we should trust Him *now* and not be afraid. Beloved, God can deliver. If you seek Him now, He will be found of you."

PRAYER THOUGHT: "Dear Lord, I ask Thee to perform a surgical operation on external events which will confront me this day, and fortify me inwardly that I might meet each circumstance head-on, knowing full well that all things will work together for my good. In the name of the One who survived Calvary's operation I pray. Amen."[7]

Daniel 3:16; Romans 8:28

Hosea—The Backslider's Book

Name: Hosea, the writer of this book (1:1,2), means "salvation." The prophet of domestic distress, he was the "home missionary," while Jonah was the "foreign missionary." Hosea was the Jeremiah of the Northern Kingdom—both alike scolded the divided kingdom for their backsliding. Hosea's experiences were in his home while Jeremiah's were in his nation.

To get Israel to see the error of their ways, God commanded Hosea to take a wife, who became unfaithful to him (1:2,3; 2:5). His children were a great source of trouble—even their names stood for distaste and became symbols of Hosea's messages.

1. Jezreel: 1:4,5. This name represented God's punishment upon Ahab and Jezebel for their sin against Naboth (see NABOTH in Index) and symbolized God's punishment to Israel in Hosea's day

2. Lo-ruhaman: 1:6. This name means "no more mercy," which God would not have on Israel for her sins

3. Lo-ammi: 1:9. His name meant "no more my people." God had to turn from His people, who acted more like the devil's children. (The prefix "Lo" is dropped from Ruhaman and Ammi 2:1, indicating that God would again have mercy on Israel and claim her as His own.)

Each experience Hosea had in his home pictured Israel's experience in spiritual adultery. He and his wife portrayed God as the husband (2:20; Isaiah 54;5) and Israel as the unchaste wife (2:2). He illustrated God's great love for His backslidden people. His circumstances enabled him to speak with "authority" when he reprimanded Israel for her sins.

Period of His Prophecy: 1:1. "In the days of Uzziah, Jotham, Ahaz, and Hezekiah, kings of Judah, and in the days of Jeroboam II . . . king of Israel." This period was ca. 755—714 B.C. He was contemporary with Amos of the Northern Kingdom, and Isaiah and Micah of the Southern Kingdom, and lived to see the fulfillment of his prophecy in the capture of Israel by Assyria. He was the *fourth* prophet.

People of His Prophecy: His ministry was to the Northern Kingdom of Israel, with occasional references to the Southern Kingdom.

Contents: "Hosea chiefly prophesied against the ten tribes of Israel, reproved them for their sins, exhorted them to repentance, threatened them with destruction in case of impenitence, and comforted the truly godly with the promise of the Messiah and of the happy state of the spiritual seed in the latter days. Israel is spoken of as Jehovah's adulterous wife, which any of God's children will become if they fall into sin. Israel's spiritual adultery was the sin of idolatry, which began with the Northern Kingdom's first king, Jeroboam I (I Kings 12:25-33; 14:1-16), and which produced all kinds of vice in the land":[1]

1. Immorality of the kings: II Kings 14:23,24
2. Feasts and Sabbaths became days when mirth ceased: 2:11
3. A rejection of knowledge: 4:6a
4. God's law forgotten: 4:6b
5. Living in spiritual adultery: 4:12
6. People instead of priests offered sacrifices: 4:13
7. Sacrifices offered in the wrong place: 4:13
8. Priests became corrupted:
   a. Became a snare to the people: 5:1
   b. Aided and abetted murder: 6:9
   c. Rejoiced in idolatry—calf worship: 10:5
9. Forgot God—looked to Egypt and Assyria for help: 7:11

In his denunciation of Israel's sins, Hosea's illustrations are taken from rural and domestic pursuits; e.g., snaring of birds, sowing, reaping, threshing, and baking bread. His book has 14 chapters, 197 verses, and 5,175 words.

Character: Prophetical.

Subject: The apostasy and restoration of Israel.

Purpose: To teach us the unchangeableness of God's counsels concerning Israel.

Outline:[2]

    I. Personal—the Faithless Wife and the Faithful Husband: 1—3
        A. The Children, or Signs: 1:2—2:1
        B. The Wife, or Backsliding: 2:2-23
        C. The Husband, or Deliverance: ch.3
    II. National—the Faithless People and their Faithful Lord: 4—14
        A. Transgression of Israel is Prominent—Idolatry and Anarchy: 4—8
        B. Visitation upon Israel is Prominent—Egypt and Assyria: 9:1—11:11
        C. Restoration of Israel is Prominent—Retrospect and Prospect: 11:12—14:9

Key Chapter: 3. God's undying love.

Key Verses: 13:9,10.

Key Word: Return, found 15 times.

Key Phrase: Latter days: 3:5.

Key Thought: Backsliding.

Spiritual Thought: Return, O Israel.

Christ Is Seen As:
    1. David: 3:5.
    2. The Lord God of hosts: 12:5.

    1. Israel's Assyrian captivity: 13:16 with II Kings 17:20-23
        Stated: ca. 745 B.C. *Fulfilled:* 722 B.C.
    2. Relating to Christ:
        a. Called out of Egypt: 1:1 with Matthew 2:13-15
            Stated: 725 B.C. *Fulfilled:* Early boyhood

        b. Mercy to Gentiles: 2:3 with John 1:12; Acts 15:14; I Peter 2:9,10
            Stated: ca. 725 B.C. *Fulfilled:* Christ's ministry

        c. Sabbaths to cease: 2:11 with Matthew 28:1. When Christ came forth from the grave the old Jewish Sabbaths came to an end. The word "sabbath" (Matthew 28:1) is plural in the Greek, and in the original it reads thus—"At the end of the sabbaths" or "after the sabbaths." After Christ's resurrection the day of worship for the Christian in this dispensation is the "first day of the week" (Mark 16:9; John 20:19; Acts 20:7; I Corinthians 16:2). The first day is a memorial to the resurrection—Christ's victory over death
            Stated: ca. 725 B.C. *Fulfilled:* Christ's resurrection

        d. Israel without a king: 5:5
            Stated: ca. 725 B.C. *Fulfilled:* before 586 B.C.

Hosea in the New Testament:
    1. People of God: 1:9,10; 2:23 with Romans 9:25,26; I Peter 2:10
    2. Desiring mercy: 6:6 with Matthew 9:13; 12:7
    3. Vain pleading: 10:8 with Luke 23:20; Revelation 6:16
    4. Christ called out of Egypt: 11:1 with Matthew 2:15
    5. Companion references:
        a. Seeking the Lord: 5:6 with John 7:34
        b. Israel, an empty vine: 10:1 with Matthew 21:33-43
        c. Reaping: 10:12,13 with Galatians 6:7
        d. Victory over death: 13:14 with I Corinthians 15:54-56
        e. Lips praising God: 14:2 with Hebrews 13:15

SEED THOUGHTS

1. Spiritual Ignorance: 4:6-10. Israel had been given God's oracles and as a result knew of God's laws and promises (Romans 3:2; 9:4). Yet she had failed to heed the Word, which resulted in a willful ignorance of it—a "famine of the Word" (Amos 8:11,12). To be ignorant of the Word is to be—

    a. Ignorant of Messiah—for He is the Word, the Wisdom of God, God's revealed nowledge: John 1:1; I Corinthians 1:30

    b. Rejected of God—no fellowship with Him, no blessing from Him: vs. 6

    c. Barren—to have the glory and service and testimony turned to shame: vs. 7

    d. Turned from God with a heart set on iniquity: vs. 8

    e. Fruitless—eating, but not having enough, to have a form of godliness but no power of God: vs. 19 with II Timothy 3:5

    f. Judged by God: vs. 9

2. Ephraim—the Symbol of Israel's Sins:
    —Joined to idols: 4:17; 11:2
    —Dealt treacherously against God: 5:7
    —Became desolate: 5:9
    —Broken: 5:11
    —Sick: 5:13
    —Sought unbeliever's help: 5:13; 7:11b
    —Became as dew—down and up—here and there: 6:4
    —Committed whoredom: 6:10; 8:9
    —Iniquitous: 7:1
    —Mixed with the people: 7:8a
    —Half-baked—a cake not turned: 7:8a
    —Strength devoured: 7:9
    —Silly dove without a heart: 7:11a
    —Fled from God: 7:13a
    —Transgressed against God: 7:13b
    —Spoke lies against God: 7:13c; 11:12
    —Hypocritical in prayer: 7:14a
    —Assembled for wordly pleasure: 7:14b
    —Rebelled against God: 7:14c
    —Imagined mischief against God: 7:15
    —Religious—without God: 7:17a
    —Deceitful: 7:16b
    —Cast off God: 8:3
    —Made altars to sin: 8:11
    —In shame—glory gone: 9:10; 10:6
    —Bring children to murder: 9:13
    —Fruitless: 9:16; 10:1
    —As an heifer—unruly: 10:11
    —Ignorant of God's works: 11:3,4
    —Followed own counsel: 11:6
    —Backslidden: 11:7
    —Lived in deceit: 11:12a
    —Provoked God: 12:14
    —Sinned more and more: 13:2
    —Bound in sin: 13:12

3. Rebellion: 7:14.
    a. Forbidden by God: Numbers 14:9

b. Provokes God: Nehemiah 9:26,27a
c. Vexes the Holy Spirit: Isaiah 63:10
d. It is shown by:
—Unbelief: Deuteronomy 9:23
—Revolting against God: Isaiah 1:2,5
—Despising God's law: Nehemiah 9:26a
—Misusing His servants: Nehemiah 9:26b; II Chronicles 36:16
—Distrusting God's power—relying on others: Ezekiel 17:15
—Hypocrisy: Hosea 7:14

4. Israel *versus* God: ch. 11

ISRAEL	GOD
a. Worshiped idols: vs. 2	a. Loved them: vs. 1a
b. Ignored God: vs. 3b	b. Called them: vs. 1b
c. Refused God's Lordship: vs. 5	c. Taught them: vs. 3a
d. Followed own counsel: vs. 6	d. Drew them: vs. 4a
e. Backslid: vs. 7	e. Fed them: vs. 4b
f. Lied about God: vs. 12a	f. Encouraged them: vs. 8
g. Lived in deceit: vs. 12b	g. Assured them: vs. 9

5. Returning to God—Backsliding Healed: ch. 14
a. The Call—our part
—Return: vs. 1
—Pray: vs. 2a
—Praise: vs. 2b
—Confess: vs.3
b. The Promises—God's part
—Will heal: vs. 4a
—Will love: vs. 4b
—Will give peace: vs. 4c
—Will refresh: vs. 5a
—Will cause growth: vs. 5b
—Will cause fruit: vss. 6a,8
—Will beautify: vs. 6b; Psalm 149:4
—Will have fellowship: vs. 7a; Psalm 91:1
—Will revive: vs. 7b
—Will give fragrance: vs. 7c
—Will lead: vs. 9; Psalm 23:3

A BIT OF HEAVENLY MANNA

The father-heart of Hosea was ever pleading with God's wayward people to return, to repent of their backsliding. Invitation after gracious invitation was given, yet when one considers the awfulness of Israel's sins as listed in this Book, we stand amazed at God's gracious call to return. But this is just like His great love, and the invitation to all who have backslidden is a simple one:

COME AND LET US RETURN UNTO THE LORD—6:1[3]

"We have wandered far from Him, in our thoughts, in our desires, and in our pursuits. We have been running after other lovers, and have set up idols in our hearts. Our conduct has been sinful and the effect most injurious to ourselves. Come then, and let us return unto the Lord. He is willing to receive us. He will kindly pardon us. 'If we confess our sins, He is faithful and just to forgive us our sins and to cleanse us from all unrighteousness.' Let us fall at His feet and frankly confess our folly. Let us endeavor to turn our thoughts, desires, and affections back to Him again. Especially, let us seek from Him the Spirit of grace and supplication for without His holy operations there will be no godly sorrow, no hatred for sin, no self-abhorrence, no faith in His promise or restoration of the joys of His salvation. We must return or our sin will be aggravated. We must return or our misery will deepen. Let us then at once, without any delay, return, approach His throne of grace and plead His past mercies, plead His glorious name, and plead the Savior's blood. Our pleading will not be in vain.''

PRAYER THOUGHT: "Dear heavenly Father, because I am a child of the living God, make me ever conscious of Thy loving, watchful care, stronger through conflict, joyous in my thoughts of Thee, and more Christ-like in my companionship and fellowship with Thee. In Thy loving name I pray. Amen."[4]

Hosea 1:10; Philippians 3:10

Joel—The Book of God's Severity and Goodness

Name: Joel, the writer of this prophecy (1:1), means "Jehovah is My God." He is the prophet tion of all real revival, and this he labored to produce. He is the prophet of the Pentateuch, inasmuch as 25 references to the books of Moses are found in his prophecy. He is also known prophet of Pentecost (2:28,29).

Period of His Prophecy: Joel's prophecy is undated, but his period of prophecy is generally accepted ca. 835-796 B.C. The fact that he mentions priests and elders might indicate his ministry was during Joash's minority (II Kings 11:21). Amos, who prophesied after Joel, was acquainted with some of his prophecies (3:16 with Amos 1:2; 3:8).

Some of the Southern Kingdom's early enemies are mentioned—the Philistines and Phoenicians (3:4) and Egypt and Edom (3:19). Much evidence points to his having been the *first* prophet. He would have known Elijah and Elisha in his youth. A. T. Pierson called him "the Pioneer of the Prophets."

People of His Prophecy: His ministry was confined to the Southern Kingdom of Judah.

Contents: There had been a devastating scourge of locusts in the land which had devoured everything and left the people impoverished. This judgment had befallen Judah because of her sins—chastisement by God to cause His people to see their need of turning to Him. This act by God had been prophesied by Moses (Deuteronomy 28:38,39). Not only did Joel use this catastrophe to call Judah to repentance, but used it to picture a greater judgment yet to come— armies that would invade their land if they continued in sin. See LOCUSTS in Index.

Joel saw a bright side—the day in which God's Spirit would be poured out on all flesh, and the day when Israel's enemy nations would be brought to the valley of Jehoshaphat for judgment. Joel used *local* things to teach *last* things. There are 3 chapters, 73 verses, and 2,034 words in his prophecy.

Character: Prophetical.

Subject: Judgment of the day of the Lord with blessings that follow.

Purpose: To teach us that judgment always precedes blessing.

Outline:[1]

   I. Historical—Desolation: 1:1—2:17
      A. The Fact of Desolation: 1
         1. The situation: vss. 2:12—locusts relentless
         2. The exhortation: vss. 13,14—a call to penitence
         3. The supplication: vss. 15—20—a cry in prayer
      B. The Cause of Desolation: 2:1-17
         1. The situation: vss. 1-11—locusts resistless
         2. The exhortation: vss. 12-17a—a call to penitence
         3. The supplication: vs. 17b—a cry in prayer
  II. Prophetical—Deliverance: 2:18—3:21
      A. Promise of Present Blessing: 2:18-27
         1. Restoration of Judah: 2:18,19,28—3:1
         2. Visitation of Enemies: 2:20; 3:2-17
         3. Fertilization of the Land: 2:21-27; 3:18-21

Key Chapter: 2. The day of the Lord.

Key Verses: 2:12-14,32.

Key Word: Repent.

Key Phrase: The day of the Lord: 1:15; 2:1,2,10,11,30,31; 3:14-16.

Key Thought: Turn, ye, even to Me, saith the Lord: 2:12.

Spiritual Thought: Sound the alarm.

Christ Is Seen As:
    1. The Lord your God (margin-teacher of righteousness): 2:23.
    2. The Hope of His people: 3:16.

    1. The Spirit of God to be poured out: 2:28-31 with Acts 2:1-20
    2. Salvation by grace through faith: 2:23 with Acts 2:21; Romans 10:13; Ephesians 2:8,9.

Stated: ca. 825 B.C. *Fulfilled:* Day of Pentecost

    3. Judgment of the Nations: 3:1-17 with Matthew 25:31,32
    4. Israel's blessings after judgement: 3:18-21

Stated: ca. 825 B.C. *Fulfilled:* Yet future

Miracles or Unusual Events: The plagues of locusts—to show Israel that a life of sin will strip and rob one of God's blessings: 1:4.

Archaeological Tidbits: The priest's trumpets: 2:15. See DESTRUCTION of Jerusalem in Index.

Joel in the New Testament:
    1. Outpouring of the Holy Spirit: 2:28,29 with Acts 2:17-21
    2. Calling on the Lord: 2:32 with Romans 10:13
    3. Companion references:
       —Teeth as a lion: 1:6 with Revelation 9:8

—Locust like horses:: 2:4 with Revelation 9:7
—Undefiled Jerusalem: 3:17 with Revelation 21:23-27
—Fountain from God: 3:18 with Revelation 22:1

SEED THOUGHTS

1. The Severity and Goodness of God (Romans 11:22):

    a. Israel impoverished: 1
    —Land desolate: vss. 4,7,10-12,17
    —Drinking abounds: vs. 5
    —Overwhelmed by enemy: vs. 6
    —Like a virgin girded with sackcloth: vs. 8

    —God's offering withheld: vss. 9,13b
    —Ministers untrue: vss. 13,14
    —Joy and gladness gone: vs. 16
    —Animals starving: vs. 18
    —Streams dried up: vs. 20
  b. Judgment impending: 2:1-11
  c. A call to repentance: 2:12-17. See REPENTANCE in Index.
    —Turn to God: vs. 12a
    —Turn with all your heart: vs. 12b
    —Turn with fasting: vs. 12c
    —Turn with weeping and mourning: vs. 12d
    —Rend the heart (broken and contrite): vs. 13a
  d. The goodness of God: 2:18-27
    —Will pity His people: vs. 18
    —Will answer His people: vs. 19a
    —Will supply their need: vs. 19b
    —Will exalt them: vs. 19c
    —Will command the enemy: vs. 20
    —Will remove fear: vs. 21a
    —Will return joy and gladness: vss. 21b,23a; II Chronicles 6:41
    —Will feed their animals: vs. 22a
    —Will produce fruit: vss. 22b,24
    —Will restore the years the locust hath eaten: vs. 25
    —Will satisfy: vs. 26a; Psalm 65:4; Jeremiah 31:14
    —Will remove shame: vs. 26b
    —Will assure Israel of Himself: vs. 27
    —Will preserve us: Psalm 21:3
    —Will follow us all the days of our lives: Psalm 23:6
    —Will keep us alert: Psalm 27:13
    —Will bless when we fear and respect Him: Psalm 31:19; Jeremiah 33:9
    —Will endure continually: Psalm 52:1
    —Will crown our years: Psalm 65:11
    —Will provide for the poor: Psalm 68:10
    —Will produce praise: Psalm 107:8,15,21,31
    —Will provide for spiritual hunger: Psalm 107:9
    —Will enrich: Romans 2:4a
    —Will lead to repentance: Romans 2:4b

In seeing God's goodness in spite of sin, it is no wonder that Joel said that the Lord is gracious and merciful, slow to anger, and of great kindness, and that He will revoke His penalty for sin when one returns to Him (2:13). "Goodness" is what God is to all of His children (Psalm 144:2), and it is what should be fulfilled in the life of every believer (II Thessalonians 1:11). Read also I Samuel 12:24 and Psalm 103:1-18.

A BIT OF

HEAVENLY MANNA

The Book of Joel gives a wonderful promise relative to one's being empowered by the Holy Spirit—"I will pour out My Spirit" (2:28). In the past age He came again and again and filled or clothed His chosen servants for their God-appointed tasks. But at Pentecost He was "poured out." As Jesus poured out Himself for our redemption, so God poured out His Spirit for our guidance and enduement with power for service. The extent of the promise—"upon all flesh." The prerequisite for this "outpouring" of the Spirit upon the individual is: "Whosoever shall call upon the name of the Lord shall be saved" (2:32; Romans 10:13). The Spirit of God indwells each believer at spiritual birth (I Corinthians 3:16,17).

THE PROMISE OF THE HOLY SPIRIT—2:28,29[2]

"Nothing is so necessary for us as the Holy Spirit. If dead, He will quicken us. If dull, He will enliven us. If dark, He will enlighten us. If cold, He will warm us. If ignorant, He will instruct us. If wavering, He will settle us. If in doubt, He will satisfy us. If in perplexity, He will direct us. If our conscience is guilty, He will purge it. If burdens are on our minds, He will remove them. If questions, He will answer them. If problems He will solve them. He will do all that is necessary within us, as Jesus did all that was required without us. This blessed Spirit is promised by the Father to all who ask Him. He was given to Jesus for us, and He is imparted by Jesus to us. The promise of the Holy Spirit is plain; we cannot well misunderstand it. It is positive, and therefore we may plead it with all confidence. It is to all who ask, or who go to Jesus that they might drink. Lord, fulfill this promise to us! Give us the fullness of the Spirit that we may walk in the light, act under His influence. Hear Him as He testified of Christ, obey Him as He guides us into all Truth, and yield to God's will as He reveals it unto us."

PRAYER THOUGHT: "O Lord, while situations need understanding, heartaches need healing, the destitute need hope, and the unrepentant need Thy mercy and kindness and salvation, give me a heart that will work to this end. In Jesus' name. Amen."[3]

Joel 2:12-14

Amos—The Book of the Plumbline

Name: Amos, the writer of this prophecy (1:1), means "burdened" (2:13). He was known as the "farmer prophet"—a layman—working man. "I was no prophet, neither was I a prophet's son; but . . . an herdman, and a gatherer of sycamore fruit" (7:14). Because of his background he was at first rejected as a prophet. He was a citizen of the Southern Kingdom of Judah.

Period of His Prophecy: "In the days of Uzziah king of Judah, and in the days of Jeroboam [II] . . . two years before the earthquake" (1:1). Josephus states this earthquake took place when Uzziah was struck with leprosy. (This earthquake was so severe that it was mentioned 200 years later by Zechariah: 14:5.) Amos prophesied ca. 764-755 B.C. He probably knew Jonah and Elisha as a youth, Isaiah and Micah as an older man, and was a contemporary of Hosea. Amos was the *third* prophet.

People of His Prophecy: Although Amos belonged to the Southern Kingdom, his ministry was chiefly to the Northern Kingdom of Israel.

Contents: Upon the success and victory of Jeroboam II over Syria, the people enjoyed great prosperity. This resulted in wantonness, luxuriousness, and gross sin. Calf worship, which 200 years before had become the kingdom's religion (I Kings 12:25-33), had been "mixed" with Baal worship. Priests were committing shameful acts and the people were living as though God did not exist. Amos was sent to Bethel, the seat of calf worship, to exhort the king and the people to repent of injustice, greed, drunkenness, swearing, adultery, oppression, etc. He threatened them with captivity in case of impenitence, thundering out the judgment of God. He backed up his messages 40 times with the use of the expression, "thus saith the Lord." His preaching brought such conviction the king ordered him out of town. His prophecy at Bethel came about thirty years before the Northern Kingdom fell and was taken captive by the Assyrians. Even though God still raised up prophets to cry unto His people, Israel had by this time, no doubt, reached the point of no return (II Kings 17:18-20).

Although his message was stern, he intoned God's mercy, as seen in his oft-repeated invitation to "seek the Lord." He brought comfort to the truly godly within the kingdom with a promise of the Messiah's coming and kingdom. As a "layman" he illustrated his messages with common figures of speech. Some are listed, shown by his comparing—

1. The load and pressures of his ministry to a cart that is full of grain: 2:13
2. His call from God to be a prophet to the roaring of a lion: 3:8
3. Israel as a sheep—the sinful majority having been devoured by a lion and the remnant as two legs and a piece of ear taken out of the lion's mouth by a shepherd: 3:12
4. Clean teeth to judgment by a famine in the land: 4:6
5. A plumbline of truth to Israel's crooked sins, and the consequence of these sins: 7:7,8
6. A basket of summer fruit to Israel's spoilage: 8:1-3

In the 9 chapters of this book, there are 146 verses and 4,217 words.

Character: Prophetical.

Subject: God's certain judgment upon nations about Israel, and upon Judah and Israel, with exhortations to repent and seek the Lord, and the promise of Israel's restoration.

Purpose: To teach us that the sins that separate us from God must be judged before fellowship can be restored (I John 1:9).

Outline:[1]

I. Amos denounces the sins of nations bordering Israel and Judah: 1:1—2:3
II. Amos describes the state of Israel and Judah and predicts their judgment: 2:4—6:14
III. Amos relates visit to Bethel and sketches impending punishment of Israel, which he predicts to Amaziah: 7:1—9:10
IV. Amos projects thoughts to the fulfillment of Messiah's kingdom when God's people will be forgiven and enjoy His blessings throughout eternity: 9:11-15

Key Chapter: 9. Israel's dispersion and restoration.

Key Verse: 7:8.

Key Word: Plumbline: 7:7, which is a symbol of judgment according to righteousness, to test the uprightness of God's people (II Kings 21:13; Isaiah 28:17).

Key Phrases:

1. Can two walk together except they be agreed? 3:3.
2. For three transgressions . . . and for four: 1:3,6,9,11, etc. This expression was used to show that their cup of iniquity was full and running over

Key Thought: Prepare to meet thy God: 4:12.

Spiritual Thought: Drop (use) the plumbline.

Christ Is Seen As: The God of hosts: 4:13.

Names and Titles of God. See NAMES in Dictionary.
1. The God of hosts: 4:13
2. The Lord: 5:8
3. Lord—Adonai, meaning Master: 9:1

1. Destruction of Samaria: 3:15
   Stated: ca. 760 B.C. *Fulfilled:* 722 B.C.
2. Hooks in jaws: 4:2. See HOOKS in Index.
   Stated: ca. 760 B.C. *Fulfilled:* 722 B.C.
3. Earth darkened at Christ's crucifixion: 8:9
   with Matthew 27:45
   Stated: ca. 755 B.C. *Fulfilled:* At crucifixion
4. Famine of hearing the Word of God: 8:11
   Stated: 755 B.C. *Fulfilled:* After captivity (and today)

There are several characteristics of the man Amos and his ministry which correspond to that of Christ—
1. Lowly origin: 7:14,15 with Luke 2:7,49
2. His preaching. Amos used figures of speech; Christ used parables
3. Dependence upon God and His Word. Amos said, "thus saith the Lord": Christ said, "as it is written "
4. Both had busy schedules: 3:9; 7:15 with John 9:4; Acts 10:38
5. Both took the rich to task: 6:4-6 with Luke 12:15-34
6. Both were charged with treason: 7:10; John 19:12

1. Houses of the rich and the poor: 3:15; 5:11; 6:11. Discoveries at the site of Samaria, denote house construction for the summer and winter use—the rich having had their summer cottages built among the permanent ones. Many foundations gave evidence of houses having been built with hewn stone (houses of the poor were built with field stones), the rich living in great (large) houses and the poor in little houses.

2. Ivory at Samaria: 6:4. Because of Israel's prosperity, ivory, which had been a luxury, was made a "necessity." Much of their furniture, such as beds, were overlaid with ivory carvings—decorations with figures of animals, flowers, and Egyptian gods. A luxury in Solomon's day, he had his throne made of ivory, overlaid with gold (I Kings 10:18). Ahab, a most industrious builder, built a summer palace for himself and Jezebel, and it was known as "Ahab's ivory palace" (I Kings 22:39). This building covered an area between seven and eight acres. Concerning the ivory miniatures, inlays, and friezes found there, an archaeologist said: "These ivories are the most charming example of miniature art ever found on an Israelite site."

3. Wine and ointments (oils): 6:6. In robbing God of His tithe, Israel was spending His money on the fads of her day—ivory, wine, and costly perfumes. Several inscribed potsherds

Samaritan Ivory

tell of payments of taxes to the royal treasury, listing vast amounts of wine and oil. These inscriptions show how such payment provided a supply of oil and wine for those "living at ease in Zion."

1. Edom as a shoe: 1:11; 2:6. See EDOM in Index.
2. He will take you away with hooks: 4:2. See HOOKS in Index.
3. Molech and Chiun: 5:25,26. See ASTROLOGY in Index.
4. City set on a hill: 6:1. See WATCHMAN in Index.

1. The order of some stars: 5:8a. See STARS in Index.
2. Earth rotating on its axis—"Turning the shadow of death [darkness of night] into the morning and maketh the day dark with night." 5:8b
3. "Calleth for the waters of the sea [evaporation], and poureth them out [rain] upon the face of the earth:" 5:8c; 9:6b. See RAIN in Index.

Amos in the New Testament:
1. Sacrifices in the wilderness: 5:25 with Acts 7:42
2. Israel's idolatry: 5:26 with Acts 7:43
3. Tabernacle of David: 9:11 with Acts 15:16,17
4. Companion references:

    a. Eating food offered to idols: 2:8 with I Corinthians 8:13

b. Enlightening His servants: 3:7 with John 15:15

1. Prepare to Meet Thy God: 4:12[3].
   a. There is one God: Isaiah 45:22
   b. We are accountable to Him: Romans 14:11,12
   c. We will stand before Him: Hebrews 9:27
   d. We must prepare to meet Him: John 1:12; Acts 16:30,31

2. At Ease in Zion: 6:1.
   a. What it means to be at ease in Zion
      —Indifferent to the things of the Lord: Hebrews 2:1-4
      —Trusting in false security: 6:1; Psalm 20:7; 118:8
      —Putting away the day of judgment: 6:3; Matthew 24:48-51
      —Worldly-minded: 6:4-6; Romans 12:1,2; I John 2:15-17
   b. What happens to those at ease in Zion?:
      —Go into bankruptcy and captivity: 6:7
      —Go into disfavor with God: 6:8
      —Go into dearth: 8:11,12
      —Go to a premature grave: 6:9 with I Corinthians 5:1-5; I John 5:16b
   c. What should be done about being at ease in Zion:
      —Prepare to meet thy God: 4:12
      —By examining our basket of fruit (condition): 8:2
      —By seeking God: 5:4; Jeremiah 29:13
      —By submitting to God's plumbline (Christ): 7:8

3. The "Woes" of God: 6:1. See WOES in Index.
   a. For being wicked: Job 10:15
   b. For falling (or being) without God: Ecclesiastes 4:10
   c. For calling evil good: Isaiah 5:20
   d. For rebellious children: Isaiah 30:1
   e. For striving or fighting against God: Isaiah 43:9
   f. For false and foolish pastors: Jeremiah 23:1; Ezekiel 13:1
   g. For divising iniquity: Micah 2:1
   h. For being at ease in Zion: Amos 6:1
   i. For giving strong drink to others: Habakkuk 2:15
   j. For hypocrisy: Matthew 23:13
   k. Against riches: Luke 6:24
   l. When men speak well of you: Luke 6:26
   m. For not preaching the gospel: I Corinthians 9:16
   n. For going the way of Cain: Jude 11a

It was bad enough that Israel was in such a backslidden state, but to have remained in that condition and do nothing about it was even worse. Israel *was* at ease in Zion. At ease she was idle, and "an idle mind is the devil's workshop." To be idle is to neglect the things of the Lord, and the writer of Hebrews gives us this warning: "How shall we escape if we neglect so great salvation?" (2:3). God has entrusted us with being His ambassadors, yet the world is crying—"I looked on my right hand, and beheld, but there was no man that would know me: refuge failed me; no man cared for my soul" (Psalm 142:4).

AT EASE IN ZION—6:1[4]

"Man was formed for employment, and he cannot be happy except he work. Idleness always breeds misery and unhappiness. But believers especially should be industrious. They should be diligent in their earthly vocation and every one should be working for God. Why stand ye *idle?* You cannot say that you have nothing to do. There is the Truth; circulate it. There are the ignorant; instruct them. There are the sick; visit them. There are the poor; relieve them. Why stand ye *here* idle? There is so much to be done, and so much wants doing immediately. Look in what direction you will, you will find plenty of work. Why stand ye all *the day* idle? If you rested for awhile, you should work the remainder of your time. Work all the day, for the night cometh when no man worketh, and it will soon be here. Why are *ye* idle? Satan is busy. Erroneous men are busy. Angels are busy. Other believers are busy. Why are *ye* idle? Why *stand* ye idle? As if you were willing to work, or going to work, when you know you do not intend to? Reader, God calls the slothful wicked, and all idlers, especially idlers in the church, will be visited with correction. The idle man with one talent not only lost a reward for not putting his talent to use, but lost his talent as well. *Lord, put me to work, now!"*

PRAYER THOUGHT: "Lord, since I am the only Bible the world will read and the only Christ they will ever see, help me to be so enriched by Thy Word that what others read and see in me will be accepted and applied in their lives. In Jesus' name. Amen."[5]

Amos 8:11; Acts 3:4-6

Obadiah—The Book of Doom for Anti-Semitics

Name: Obadiah, the writer of this book (vs. 1), means "a servant."

Period of His Prophecy: Obadiah is undated, but internal evidence (vss. 11,12) seems to fix its date near the time of the final overthrow of Jerusalem by Nebuchadnezzar—ca. 597 B.C. If this is the date of his prophecy, then he probably knew Habakkuk and Ezekiel, and was contemporary with Jeremiah and Daniel. This would make him the *thirteenth* prophet.

People of His Prophecy: His ministry was largely to the Edomites, with a promise to future hope for Israel.

Contents: Edom, one of Israel's enemies, is the main theme of Obadiah's prophecy. The Edomites were descendents of Essau, and they never forgave Jacob (and his descendents) for cheating their ancestor out of his birthright. Their grudge led to a threefold sin:

1. When the Israelites were approaching Canaan, they sought permission from the king of Edom to pass through his territory, giving assurance that the privilege would not be abused. The king refused their request, and was prepared to fight if the Israelites had persisted in moving forward. Israel then had to turn back to mount Hor and "they journeyed from mount Hor by way of the Red Sea, to compass the land of Edom" (Numbers 20:14-22; 21:4). See MAP, p. 100.

2. In the reign of Ahaz, when Judah was attacked by Pekah and Rezin, the Edomites invaded Judah, and carried off captives (II Chronicles 28:17). There had been other skirmishes between Israel and Edom: II Chronicles 21:8,16,17; 25:11-24.

3. The Edomites rejoiced when Nebuchadnezzar destroyed Jerusalem: II Chronicles 36:17-20 with Psalm 137:7.

Siq-Petra's Entrance

View of Petra

Obadiah predicts judgment upon Edom for her grudge against and treatment of God's people through Jacob's lineage. Obadiah's prophecy was a detailed pronouncement of the general prophecy of God to Abraham, that any nation which cursed His people would be cursed (Genesis 12:3). Edom's behavior and doom is a classic warning against anti-Semitism: vs. 10.

In vss. 17-21 Israel's salvation and final restoration are foretold. This is the shortest book in the Old Testament, with only 1 chapter, 21 verses, and 670 words.

Character: Prophetical.

Subject: God's special care over the Jews, and the certainty of punishment of those who persecute them.

Purpose: To assure us of final victory over our enemies in the heavenlies, and the eternal possession of our blessings in Christ.

Outline:

    I. The Doom of Edom: vss. 1-16
       A. The charge against Edom: vss. 1-9
       B. The crime of Edom: vss. 10-14
       C. The catastrophe to Edom: vss. 15,16
    II. The Deliverance of Israel: vss. 17-21
       A. The triumph of Israel: vss. 17,18
       B. The possession of Israel: vss. 19,20
       C. The establishment of Israel: vs. 21

Key Verse: 1:15.

Key Word: Retribution.

Key Phrase: The house of Jacob shall possess their possessions: vs. 17.

Key Thought: Edom's punishment and Israel's glory.

Spiritual Thought: Possess your possessions.

Christ Is Seen As: The Lord of the kingdom: vs. 21.

1. The thrust of Obadiah's prophecy, stated ca. 597 B.C., is that Edom "shall be forever cut off" (vs. 10). Four years after their shouting with glee that Jerusalem had fallen (Psalm 137:7), they were conquered by the Babylonians in 582 B.C. From this point till their extermination, they never regained their full power. They were subdued by Maccabeans in 126 B.C. Under Roman rule they were under control of the Herods, an Edomite family. Because of the enmity between the Jews and the Edomites, it is easy to understand why the Jews of Christ's day had such a hatred for the Herods, and it could also explain why Herod sought to kill all males two years and under that he might eliminate the One who had been born the "king of the Jews" (Matthew 2:1,2,16). The Edomites were finally "cut off forever" with the destruction of Jerusalem in A.D. 70. See IDUMAEA in Index.

2. Israel's restoration: vss. 17-21. *Stated:* ca. 597 B.C. *Fulfilled:* Yet future.

Edom's pride (vs. 3) was that her habitation in the mountains of Seir was impregnable. She lived by making lightning strikes at caravans passing by or upon cities nearby, and then retiring to her home in the clefts of the rocks. If you picture in your mind a football field completely surrounded by a stadium, and then enlarge the field to about two miles long and a mile wide, completely surrounded by rock mountains, some as high as 3,500 feet, you have a picture of Edom's capital city—Selah (II Kings 14:7). The site today is known as Petra. The only entrance into the city is a narrow gorge called the Siq (pronounced "sick"), and a half dozen men strategically located in this pass could hold off an invading army. In the picture "Petra's Buildings," it is just about a mile from where the picture was taken to the rock mountain. These buildings were not structures; facings of buildings were carved out of the side of the rock mountain, and rooms were hollowed out inside. The highest mountain peak was leveled off as the rock of sacrifice, where Baal was worshiped (see picture, p. 112). See Picture on p. 170 for the site where Amaziah of Judah forced 10,000 Edomites to march over the cliff-side to their deaths (II Chronicles 25:11,12).

Obadiah in the New Testament: There are no direct references to this Book in the New Testament. There are two companion references:
1. Destroying the wisdom of the wise: vs. 8 with I Corinthians 1:19.
2. The kingdoms of Christ: vs. 21 with Revelation 11:15.

1. Edom's sin was pride (vs. 3). See PRIDE in Index. Having stubbornly refused to forgive Jacob and his descendants for taking the birthright from Esau, their hearts were hardened to the point where forgiveness had no meaning. What a different prophecy Obadiah's might have been if Edom had only forgiven the Jews. Edom's *direct* fight against Israel was an *indirect* fight against God. In her arrogance and pride she failed to reckon with God and finally their impregnable fort was brought low by God Himself and they were "cut off forever."

Is it any wonder today that churches are experiencing defeat. Members, filled with pride, in need of nothing (so they think!) like the Laodiceans (Revelation 3:14-18), with grudges and ill-feelings against their fellowman, and no concern for the Jews, are bringing destruction to themselves. O, to heed the Word of God—"He that covereth his sins shall not prosper; but whoso confesseth and forsaketh them shall have mercy" (Proverbs 28:13).

Pride always goes before a fall (destruction—Proverbs 16:18). Luke says the same thing (14:11a). And because of Edom's pride, she was brought low. Far better to be humble that God may exalt us (Luke 14:11b). For those of us who dare to be humble before God, we—

    a. Are regarded by God: Psalm 138:6; Isaiah 66:2
    b. Are heard by God: Psalm 9:12; 10:17
    c. Enjoy the presence of God: Isaiah 57:15
    d. Are delivered by God: Job 22:29
    e. Are lifted up by God: James 4:10
    f. Are exalted by God: Luke 14:11b
    g. Are greatest in Christ's kingdom: Matthew 18:4; 20:26-28
    h. Receive more of His grace: Proverbs 3:34; James 4:6

Humility is necessary to the service of God (Micah 6:8), and saints should put it on (Colossians 3:12), be clothed in it (I Peter 5:5), and walk with it (Ephesians 4:1,2).

    2. Deliverance: vs. 17. God alone is the only One who can deliver anyone from their sins. And what does He do with our sins upon deliverance?

    a. Lays them on Christ: Isaiah 53:6; I Peter 2:24
    b. Washes them away in Christ's blood: Revelation 1:5
    c. Purges them: Hebrews 1:3
    d. Forgives and covers them: Romans 4:7
    e. Subdues them: Micah 7:19a
    f. Casts them into the depths of the sea: Micah 7:19b
    g. Puts them away: Hebrews 9:26
    h. Casts them behind His back: Isaiah 38:17b
    i. Sees to it that they are passed away: Zechariah 3:4
    j. Removes them as far as the east is from the west: Psalm 103:12
    k. Blots them out: Isaiah 43:25a
    l. Forgets them: Isaiah 43:25b; Hebrews 8:12

A BIT OF HEAVENLY MANNA

As the name "Obadiah" signifies a "servant of Jehovah," so we, as new creatures in Christ, are servants of God and His righteousness (Romans 6:18,22). Though redeemed by the precious blood of Christ, made sons of God and partakers of His divine nature—heirs of God and joint-heirs with Christ Jesus, yet we are His servants nonetheless. Paul delighted in being known as a "servant," a "bond slave," and a "prisoner" of Christ. We have been saved to serve, and God is dependent upon His human instruments to accomplish His purpose upon the earth.

A SERVANT OF GOD—James 1:1[1]

"Better to be God's servant than a king's son. The apostles gloried in this character. They all styled themselves God's servants and rejoiced to add that they were servants of Jesus too. If God is our Father, He is also our Master. If we are saved by Jesus, we shall rejoice to serve Him also. If we are God's servants we shall love our Master, prefer His work, consult His will, be jealous of His honor, and seek to enjoy His approbation. If God is our Master He will appoint us to our work, find us supplies, correct our mistakes, always keep us employed, and at last will reward us for our labors. As servants we should be honest and not waste our Master's time or property. We should be industrious, always at work or waiting for orders. We should be attentive, listening to the Master's voice and treasuring up His words. We should be kind, courteous, and obliging to our fellow servants. If Jesus is our Master, we have the best "boss" in the universe, and if we see things rightly, we should conclude that no one has a better place than that of a servant of God and of our Lord Jesus Christ."

 PRAYER THOUGHT: "Dear Lord, grant to me implicit faith in Thy watchcare over me, and whatever Thou dost have for me, may I not be choosy but possess them all in the belief that each is for my best interest. In Christ's name I pray. Amen."[2]

Obadiah 17; Psalm 36:8

Jonah—The Book of God's Mercy

Name: Jonah means "a dove," and he answered his name by flying away as fast as he could. He was the "run-away" prophet who returned, the "missionary" prophet, the "messenger from the sea-monster." Christ recognized him as the "sign" prophet (Matthew 12:39-41). As David was among the kings, so was Jonah among the prophets.

1. They greatly sinned
2. They repented heartily
3. They were never forsaken by God
4. They discovered there is no escape from God

Writer: As always, when a miracle is involved, critics rise to discredit God's Word. The book of Jonah seems to have become the "whipping boy" of biblical criticism because of the "fish story" he told (that is, if he told it!). Critics claim that someone other than Jonah wrote this book. Their argument is that Jonah is not mentioned as the author, and that it was written in the third person. So what! Many authors have written about themselves in the third person. And it has *never* been necessary for an author to state that he wrote a book about himself.

Critics have sought to make this book an allegorical tale, not history *per se.* There are no added moral applications, as would be the case if it were simply allegorical. Jonah, to them, is a ficticious character. Yet Jews of old have accepted it as historical fact. The writer of II Kings recognized him as a person (14:25). Christ Himself accepted the account of Jonah as historical, and referred to him as such (Matthew 12:39,40). He also believed as history Jonah's account of Nineveh (Matthew 12:41; Luke 11:29,30). One can either accept the critic's assertion or take the word of Christ.

Period of His Prophecy: The experience of Jonah happened during the reign of King Jeroboam II of Israel, ca. 784-772 B.C. (II Kings 14:23-25). He was the *second* of the prophets.

Contents: This book tells the story of a man who was called of God to preach but sought to run away from the call. His congregation (Gentiles of Nineveh) were people he, as a Jew, despised. His attempt to run away could be due to the 40-day time limit God put on Nineveh to repent. If Jonah could avoid God for 50 days, then his religious bigotry would triumph and these Gentiles would fail to receive God's warning to repent, thereby suffering God's judgment. This would have pleased Jonah, but God engineered circumstances in such a way through a great fish that Jonah got to Nineveh in plenty of time and Nineveh did repent. How disgusted Jonah must have been when he learned that the 40 days did not begin until he started preaching in Nineveh!

God's mercy overrode His judgment and these Gentiles had one of the mightiest revivals history has known. See REFORM in Index. Jonah's resentment of this great work of God's grace, power, and mercy is seen in his desire to die, but out of this experience Jonah saw how sinful his resentment was—how futile it was to try and keep back God's salvation from the "Whosoever wills."

"Jonah set forth in himself the type of the death and resurrection of Christ. He declares the grace and mercy of God to repenting sinners, and signifies the calling of the Gentiles after the death and resurrection of Christ. Jonah is very profitable in instructing us about the power and goodness of God; the nature of repentance and the effects of it; the imperfection and infirmities of the best of men in this life; and the call and mission of the ministers of the Word, and the necessity of their conformity and attendance to it."[1] Jonah has 4 chapters, 48 verses, and 1,321 words.

Character: Personal history.

Subject: God's dealing with a disobedient prophet, and Nineveh's repentance.

Purpose: To reveal to us typically God's dealing with His Son as a substitute for disobedient ones; and to teach us that God's mercy and faithfulness are extended to each of His servants.

Outline:[2]
  - I. The Prodigal Prophet: 1
  - II. The Praying Prophet: 2
  - III. The Preaching Prophet: 3
  - IV. The Pouting Prophet: 4

Key Chapter: 2, The prayer of Jonah.

Key Verse: 3:2.

Key Word: Preach.

Key Phrase: Arise and go: 1:2.

Key Thoughts:
  1. Then Jonah prayed: 2:1.
  2. Salvation is of the Lord: 2:9.

Spiritual Thought: "Woe is unto me, if I preach not the gospel": I Corinthians 9:16.

Christ Is Seen As: The risen Prophet: Matthew 12:39-41.

Names and Titles of God: The God of heaven: 1:9. See NAMES in Dictionary.

1. Jonah is a type of Christ's death, burial, and resurrection: Matthew 12:38-41

2. Jonah is a type of the believer's ministry in this age—that of witnessing to Gentiles; for God to call out from among them a people for His name: Acts 15:14-18

3. Jonah is a type of Israel, swallowed by the nations of the world but never digested

1. A great wind—to bring about cause for concern in trying to flee from God: 1:4

2. Jonah asleep in the storm—to show how one can become hardened to God's call: 1:5b

3. A prepared fish to swallow Jonah—to serve

God's purpose in rescuing His disobedient servant from sure death: 1;17a.

4. Survival in the fish's stomach three days and three nights—punishment for attempting to escape duty: 1:17b.

5. Jonah's deliverance from the fish—in answer to his repentant prayer: 2:10.

6. The prepared gourd, worm, and the vehement east wind—to teach Jonah humility: 4:1-11.

1. There was a time when critics of the Word did not believe the account of Nineveh's population (more than 120,000), as recorded by Jonah (4:11). No city in that day was that large, they said. Excavations at Nimrud, 20 miles from Nineveh, revealed an inscription of King Ashurnasipal II, whose Assyrian armies first began to come up against Israel. This inscription mentioned a banquet at the dedication of his palace—attended by 70,000. Those in attendance were the "chief" people of Nimrud, which leaves one with the impression that many, many more people inhabited the city.

2. Assyria's Reform. The only record of Nineveh's repentance is what we have from the pen of Jonah. Because of a lack of evidence in secular history, many critics have doubted Jonah's story. This is not an honest criticism. Possibly our own land has been spared catastrophes because of the spiritual impact of such men as Finney, Moody, or Billy Sunday on people. Secular history would never record this. But circumstantial evidence from the pick and spade of the archaeologist shows there was a period of reformation in the period of Jonah's day. Assyrian kings recorded their exploits, never their defeats or humiliations. Adad-nirari was the Assyrian king who repented under Jonah's preaching, and under him and the three kings who followed him, there was a let-up in Assyrian assaults and conquests. It was in this period that Israel had some of her territory recovered (II Kings 14:25). Such reform does indicate that Jonah's message did have some influence upon those at Nineveh.

Biblical Customs: Jonah's booth: 4:5. See COTTAGE in Index.

1. Some object to Jonah's experience because it is said that a whale's throat is too small to swallow a man. Jonah does not call it a "whale" but a "great fish" (1:17). The New Testament translators do refer to this account as a "whale," but the Greek word is "ketos," which means huge fish. It is a known scientific fact that there are some sea monsters capable of swallowing a man. Air chambers are sufficiently large enough to "house" a man. There are records of some men who have had such an experience and survived.

2. Mountains in the sea: 2:6. See OCEAN in Index.

Jonah in the New Testament:
1. Jonah in the fish: 1:17 with Matthew 12:39,40
2. Repentance of Nineveh: 3:5 with Matthew 12:41
3. Companion reference:
   —Sacrifice of thanksgiving: 2:9 with Hebrews 13:15

1. Lessons from Jonah
    a. God's call is man's opportunity
    b. Man's surrender is God's opportunity
    c. There is danger in running away from God
    d. There is no detour in the path of Christian service
    e. Religious bigotry and national pride will keep one from winning souls to Christ
    f. If we do not judge ourselves, God will chasten us.
    g. God does not cast us aside for faithlessness. He called Jonah the second time (3:1)
    h. When we try to run from God or backslide, we have to go back where we got off the track
    i. A run-away preacher may return to the place and path of duty with restored power
    j. If God sends North, East, South, or West, the way God sends is always best
    k. A pouting servant of the Lord is a pitiful sight. A praising servant is a proper sight
    l. Salvation is of the Lord, not of works: 2:9
    m. It is even possible for great cities to repent
    n. God is not willing that any should perish
    o. God does not look for perfection, but for obedience
    p. Though salvation is of the Jew because the sacred oracles of God were committed to them, it is for the Gentile or "whosoevers" as well. God is no tribal deity

2. Disobedience to God: 1:3
    a. Forfeits God's favor: I Samuel 13:14
    b. Deprives of His promised blessings: Jeremiah 18:10
    c. Provokes His anger: Isaiah 3:8
    d. Brings judgment: Deuteronomy 11:28
    e. Shall be punished: Hebrews 2:2

3. A great fish to swallow Jonah: 1:17. A Sunday school girl was ridiculed by the town skeptic regarding her faith in Christ and her belief in the Bible. When asked if she believed the "fish story of Jonah," she answered "Yes." Asked to explain the miracle, she couldn't, but said, "When I get to heaven, I'll ask Jonah all about it." The skeptic asked, "Suppose he's not in heaven?" The little girl said sweetly, "Then you ask him!"

4. "And Jonah was in the belly of the fish three days and three nights": 1:17. Someone has said they have no difficulty in believing that the great fish swallowed Jonah, but they do have difficulty in believing that a fish could keep a backslidden preacher on its stomach for three days and three nights!

5. Salvation vs. Man's Works: 1:1-16. The experience of the mariners of the ship which Jonah boarded gives to us an excellent picture of man's extremity becoming God's opportunity.
    a. They were awakened to and convicted of their danger. "Then the mariners were afraid": 1:4,5a
    b. They suddenly became religious. "And cried every man unto his god": 1:5b
    c. "And cast forth the wares that were in the ship into the sea": 1:5c. This is like "turning over a new leaf," or quitting a few bad habits
    d. They sought human help—and from a backslider at that: 1:6. Human help is needed to tell the story of the gospel, but it's hardly likely that one running *from* God can help those in need of salvation come *to* God.
    e. "Nevertheless the men rowed hard to bring it [the ship] to the land": 1:13a. They did "good works," but man does not reach "the haven of rest" by his good works (Matthew 7:21-23)
    f. "But they could not: for the sea wrought, and was tempestuous against them": 1:13b. God is *against* anyone who "tries" to rescue himself—the same is a "thief and a

robber.'' Man is utterly helpless to save himself

    g. In desperation they got rid of the cause of the storm—Jonah—and the storm subsided: 1:15. When we get rid of sin through Christ, we have peace with God (Romans 5:1).

    h. Surrendered to God: 1:16

      —Feared the Lord exceedingly—believed *Him* to be the only true God, forsaking their own gods

      —Offered a sacrifice unto the Lord—gave themselves to Him (Romans 12:1)

      —Made vows—promised the Lord to serve Him, which should be done by all who trust Him. Vows are made to be kept (Deuteronomy 23:21; Ecclesiastes 5:4)

6. God's job for Jonah. God's first call to Jonah, his experience in the great fish, and the second call from God to Jonah to do a work in Nineveh, could well be illustrated in this poem:

God's Job for Me[3]

The Lord had a job for me,
   But I had so much to do
I said, "You get somebody else
   or wait till I get through."
I don't know how the Lord came out,
   I suppose He must have got along;
But I had a feeling—sneaking like-
   That I'd done God wrong.

One day I needed the Lord,
   Needed Him right away;
But He never answered me at all.
   I could hear Him say,
Way down in my accusing heart—
   "My child, I've got too much to do,
You get somebody else,
   or wait till I get through."

Now, when the Lord has a job for me,
   I never try to shirk;
I drop what I have on hand
   And do the good Lord's work.
My affairs can run along,
   Or wait till I get through,
'Cause nobody else can do the work,
   That God's marked out for me.

7. Salvation is of the Lord: 2:9.

    a. The Word reveals our condition: I Corinthians 1:21; Romans 3:10-23

    b. God the Father draws: John 6:44a

    c. The Spirit convicts of sin: John 16:7-9; Job 32:8

    d. The heart is prepared by the Lord: Proverbs 16:1

    e. Faith is given to believe: Ephesians 2:8,9

    f. We are justified by the faith of Christ: Galatians 2:16

    g. We are then presented to the Son by the Father: John 6:37a

    h. Our security of our salvation is in Christ: John 6:37b

i. Jesus paid it all, all to Him I owe: John 19:30; I Peter 1:18,19

8. Jonah's pouting and discouragement after Nineveh's repentance is a classic example of the devil's work in trying to keep God's saints depressed and defeated: 4:1-9

"The Devil's Best Tool"[4]

It was announced that the devil was going out of business and would offer all his tools for sale to whoever would pay his price. On the night of the sale they were all attractively displayed, and what a bad looking lot they were. There were malice, greed, hatred, envy, jealousy, sensuality, deceit, and all the other implements of evil that hell alone offers. Each was marked with its own price.

Apart from the rest lay a harmless looking wedge-shaped tool, very much worn. This too was priced higher than the rest. Someone asked the devil what it was. "That's *Discouragement*," was his reply. Asked why he had priced it so high above the others, the devil said, "Because, it is more useful to me than any of the others. I can pry open and get inside a man's consciousness with that tool when I could not get near him with any of the others. When once inside I can use him in whatever way suits me best. It is so worn because I use it with nearly everybody. It is most valuable to me because very few people know that it belongs to me." It hardly need be added that the devil's price for "Discouragement" was so high that it was never sold. He still owns it and is still using it.

One of the greatest truths Jonah reveals is that "salvation is of the Lord" (2:9). He got it in the depths of the great fish, and in the depths of the greatest trial that ever came to him. In the hour of our greatest trials, truths are made real to us. This great truth not only reveals that salvation is of the Lord, but all the provisions of salvation are of the Lord. The power to appropriate salvation is of the Lord, the grace to persevere in salvation is of the Lord. Salvation, from start to finish, is of Him, and is revealed to us in His Son, the Lord Jesus Christ. He is the Author and Finisher of our faith in Him (Hebrews 12:2).

THE SAVIOR OF THE WORLD—John 4:42[5]

"Jesus is the Savior of sinners, of sinners of *every* nation, including Nineveh. The Jews, and Jonah, fancied that God's salvation was confined only to them, but, thank God, it is sent to the Gentiles as well. There is *no* difference between the Jew and the Gentile—*all* have sinned and come short of God's glory, *all* need salvation, Jesus is able to save *all*, and *all* are welcome to seek and find salvation in Him. *The Gospel excludes no one.* There is no sinner but what Christ can save. There is no sinner but what He is willing to save, if that sinner is willing to be saved by Him His way. But how does He save? He fulfilled the precepts of the Law in His own life and He paid the penalty in His death. His one sacrifice once for all made an infinite atonement for sin. It met and satisfied all the claims of divine justice. In His life and death He did all that was necessary to procure the pardon, justification, and eternal life of poor sinners. His resurrection and ascension to heaven prove this. He now places to the account of every sinner who believes on Him the merit of what He did and suffered. Thus, 'as by one man's disobedience many were made sinners, so by the righteousness of one shall many be made righteous.' "

PRAYER THOUGHT: "Lord, I now stand at attention before Thee. Speak, Lord, for Thy servant heareth. If my mind or thoughts need to be changed, perform this miracle and not only tell me what to do, what to say, and where to go, but please help me, and show me how to do it, and I will do it for Thee. In Jesus' name. Amen."[6]

Jonah 3:1-3a

Micah—The Book of Doom and Glory

Name: Micah's name is an interrogation; namely, "Who is like Jehovah?" Micah, the writer of this book (1:1), lived up to his name by showing how our God hates sin but loves the sinner (7:18,19). He is the "Commoner" among the prophets, the "Champion" of the people against those who wronged them politically and religiously, the "prophet of the poor" because of his defense of them. He is the "Herald" prophet, having heralded the place of Christ's birth (5:2). He was also the prophet of "practical religion." Isaiah was the "elite" prophet, Micah was the rustic type.

Period of His Prophecy: It was during the days of Jotham, Ahaz, and Hezekiah, kings of Judah (1:1). Micah witnessed both the wickedness of Ahaz and revival under Hezekiah, and lived to see his own prophecy fulfilled against Samaria when the Northern Kingdom fell to the Assyrians in 722 B.C. He prophesied ca. 740-698 B.C., and was contemporary with Hosea and Isaiah. He was the *sixth* prophet.

People of His Prophecy: His ministry was to both Kingdoms—Samaria of the Northern and Jerusalem of the Southern (1:1b).

Contents: "Micah's prophecies concerned both Israel and Judah. He reproved both for their sins, and foretold their individual captivities. He pulled no punches in elucidating their sins:

1. Idolatry: 1:7
2. Immorality: 2:1
3. Covetousness: 2:2a
4. Lawlessness: 2:2b
5. Bloodshed: 3:2,3,10
6. Heeding false prophets: 3:5-7
7. Soothsaying: 5:12
8. Dishonest business practices: 6:10,11
9. Rich oppressing poor: 6:12a
10. Gossiping and deceit: 6:12b
11. Strife and hatred: 7:2
12. Bribery: 7:3
13. Treachery: 7:5,6

"For the comfort of God's people he says many things concerning the Messiah. His incarnation, the place of His birth, which no prophet so clearly points out as he. He also points out the execution of His offices—prophetic, priestly, and kingly; the blessings of grace that came by Him—pardon, forgiveness, etc., and the happiness and glory of Israel in the latter days."[1] Micah's future expectations included:

1. A righteous kingdom: 4:1-8
2. The Messiah as king: 5:2
3. Israel's ministry: 5:7,8

4. Israel's restoration: 7:7-17
5. Israel's triumph over sin: 7:18-20

His prophecies seem to be "mixed-up," sentences incomplete or disconnected. One moment he is talking about present situations, the next about future glory. He repeats himself often but uses different settings when he does, adding details frequently. Micah has 7 chapters, 105 verses, and 3,153 words.

Character: Prophetical.

Subject: The declaration of Israel's sin and God's grace in sending the Savior and King.

Purpose: To reveal to us God's unfathomable love in seeking and saving us when we were dead in trespasses and sins.

Outline:[2]
    I. Proclaiming Future Judgment for Past Sins: 1—3
    II. Prophesying Future Glory because of Past Promises: 4,5
    III. Pleading Present Repentance because of Past Redemption: 6
    IV. Pardoning all Iniquity because of Whom God is and what He does: 7

Key Chapter: 7. Confession and Intercession.

Key Verse: 1:2.

Key Word: Hear.

Key Phrase: The Lord hath a controversy with His people: 6:2.

Key Thoughts: Three thoughts seem to occupy Micah's heart:
    1. The return of the remnant
    2. The restoration of Israel
    3. The reign of the Messiah

Spiritual Thought: Look and live.

Christ Is Seen As:
    1. The Witness against the nations: 1:2,3
    2. The smitten Judge: 5:1
    3. The Ruler in Israel: 5:2

1. Historical—
    a. Captivity of Samaria, the Northern Kingdom of Israel: 1:6-16 with II Kings 17:7-23
       Stated: ca. 740 B.C. *Fulfilled:* 722 B.C.
    b. Captivity of Jerusalem—the Southern Kingdom of Judah: 3:12 with Jeremiah 52:27-30; II Chronicles 36:17-21
       Stated: ca. 740 B.C. *Fulfilled:* 586 B.C.

When Jeremiah was threatened with his life (ca. 590 B.C.) because of his prophecy against the sins of Jerusalem, this prophecy of Micah was cited in defense of his message and his life was spared (Jeremiah 26:16-19).

    c. Babylon is cited as the place of Judah's captivity: 4:10
       Stated: ca. 740 B.C. *Fulfilled:* 586 B.C.

2. Messianic—
    a. Birthplace—Bethlehem: 5:2a. "Note the amazing accuracy and definiteness of this prophecy. Messiah must have a birthplace. Three continents—Europe, Asia, and Africa—were known to the ancient world. Asia was chosen. But Asia has many countries. One of

them is indicated, a little country we call Palestine—the Promised Land. Here were three districts: Judea, Galilee, and Samaria. It is Judah that is the elect and favored one. But here again are many villages. Out of the 'thousands' of obscure villages, Bethlehem is chosen. The prophet puts his finger on 'Bethlehem Ephratah.' Why *this* Bethlehem? Because there were two Bethlehems in the Promised Land—the other being in the northern part in the territory of Zebulun, which is in Galilee (Joshua 19:15). Micah's Bethlehem was in Judah (Ruth 1:1). Bethlehem means 'house of bread,' and how fitting that it was *this* Bethlehem where the 'Bread of Life' was born. Ephratah means 'fruitful,' and how fitting this name—the place where all the fruits of salvation began (Luke 2:1-20). The Omniscient God spoke through Micah.''[3]

   b. Smitten: 5:1 with Matthew 27:30

Stated: ca. 710 B.C. *Fulfilled:* Birth and life of Christ

3. Future, stated ca. 710 B.C.
   a. Christ as king: 5:2b with Matthew 2:2
   b. Israel's glory: 5:7
   c. Israel forgiven: 7:18-20

Micah in the New Testament:
   1. Bethlehem—birthplace of Christ: 5:2 with Matthew 2:6; John 7:42
   2. Household enemies: 7:6 with Matthew 10:35,36
   3. Companion references:
      a. False prophets: 3:5 with Matthew 7:15
      b. Travailing in birth: 4:9,10 with Revelation 12:2
      c. Performing God's oath: 7:20 with Luke 1:72,73

1. The "Golden Rule" of the Old Testament: 6:8.
   a. Do justly
   b. Love mercy
   c. Walk humbly with thy God

2. Sin and Grace: 7:18-20. Micah enumerated and denounced the many sins of Israel, but at the same time emphasized the grace of God. "Where sin abounded, grace did much more abound" (Romans 5:20). All have sinned and come short of the glory of God, but the grace of God that brought salvation has appeared unto all men (Romans 3:23; Titus 2:11).

SIN	*versus*	GRACE
Depletes: Romans 1:21-31		Enriches: I Timothy 6:17
Enslaves: Proverbs 5:21-23		Frees: Romans 6:22
Intoxicates: Revelation 17:2		Sobers: Titus 2:11,12
Blinds: II Corinthians 4:4		Illuminates: John 9:25
Bruises: Isaiah 1:4-6		Heals: Isaiah 53:5
Kills: Romans 6:23a		Makes alive: Ephesians 2:1
Dooms: II Thessalonians 1:7-9		Gives hope: Titus 2:13

Israel's sins brought about a worshiping of other gods. Micah sought to get Israel to see that there was none like God, who could pardon their iniquity and delight in His mercy (7:18). All other gods fail—there is none like our great God and Savior. The devil gets us in a ditch and leaves us there, but God never leaves us nor forsakes us. Though an enemy should encamp against us and seek to destroy us, we can have confidence that God is our Refuge, that in the secret of His tabernacle He shall hide us (Psalm 27:1-5).

GOD IS OUR REFUGE AND STRENGTH—Psalm 46:1[4]

"The present evil world is a wilderness. Here we are exposed to storms and tempests, to dangers and foes. If left to provide for ourselves, we must perish, and our enemies would triumph over us. But the Lord has condescended to become the refuge of His people. To Him we may repair and find safety, receive supplies, and enjoy repose. If He defends us, no one can injure us. If He is our refuge, nothing can overcome us. Every Christian can say, 'The Lord is my Refuge.' Beloved, let us keep this in view that whatever tempests we may have to pass through, whatever foes may assail us, the Lord will protect and defend us. From the wrath of man, from the rage of hell, from the storms of time, He will shelter and screen us. He will not only receive and protect us, but He will strengthen us with His strength when we are weak. If God is our refuge, we are safe. If God is our strength, we overcome the world. Let us therefore fly to Him and trust in His Word."

PRAYER THOUGHT: "Help me, dear Lord, not to forget my benefits as a Christian, but to emphasize all my assets in Christ Jesus. May I ever remember that He is my 'All in all,' and that without Him I can do nothing. In His wonderful, matchless name I pray. Amen."[5]

Micah 7:7,18,19; Psalm 103

Nahum—The Book of Perversity and Penalty

Name: Nahum, the writer of this prophecy (1:1), means "Consoler" or "Comforter." He is the "World's" prophet, inasmuch as Nineveh's judgment is the world's object lesson of the doom of the wicked. He is the prophet of "Wrath," in that he describes God as Vindicator of right, Avenger of wrong, and final Judge of all issues.

Period of His Prophecy: Nahum prophesied the doom of Nineveh, ca. 648-620 B.C., when the city was at its height. His message of doom came more than 100 years after Jonah's message to the same city. This prophecy was written after the Egyptian city of No-Amon (Thebes) fell ca. 660 B.C., for Nahum used its fall to illustrate the fall of Nineveh (3:8-10). It was written before ca. 612 B.C., for this is when Nineveh was sacked and defeated. Nahum was contemporary with Zephaniah, Jeremiah, and Habakkuk, and was the *seventh* prophet.

People of His Prophecy: Nineveh, with a promise of peace to Judah.

Contents: This book concerns itself with Nineveh. Someone has suggested that Nahum is a sequel to Jonah. There had been a turning to God under Jonah's preaching, but Nineveh gradually went back to her ways of sin. God had been patient with the inhabitants (1:3), but in Nahum's day sin was so rampant, hearts were so hardened, and wills so stubborn that God declared them incurable (3:19). Nineveh had become like a lion's den full of prey (2:11,12). Hence Nahum's prophecy of doom—the announcement that not only Nineveh, but all Assyria, would be destroyed.

Assyria had been used as God's rod against His disobedient people (Isaiah 10:5). Having served His purpose, their defeat for their own sins is certain. The "powers that be" were, and still are, ordained of God (Romans 13:1). Russia (Communism) is not on the scene by accident. Though strong and godless nations cause people of smaller nations to live in fear, God is still upon the throne and will take vengeance upon any and all nations that forget Him. Nations, as well as people, reap what they sow. Nineveh and Assyria serve to illustrate God's truth of retribution.

Nahum's prophecy was unusual. His prophecy foretold Nineveh's total destruction. Empires usually fall but cities survive. Nahum predicted "an utter end" for this great city (1:8). Chapter two predicts the capture of the city. Chapter three gives the reason why God was justified in bringing about the city's destruction and describes its burning. In less than 300 years after its destruction by the Medes and Babylonians, Alexander the Great took an expedition over the site, ignorant of the fact that he was walking over the ruins of one of the mightiest empires that ever existed.

This book has 3 chapters, 47 verses, and 1,285 words.

Character: Prophetical.

Subject: The revelation of the majesty of God, and the announcement of the sure and final judgment of bloody Nineveh.

Purpose: To teach us that God is longsuffering and full of mercy but that He is also just and must punish sin: 1:7,8 with Galatians 6:7.

Outline:[1]
    I. The Overthrow of Nineveh Declared: 1
       A. Character and Power of the Lord: 1:1-6
       B. Destruction of Nineveh and Peace of Judah: 1:7-15
    II. The Overthrow of Nineveh Described: 2
       A. Siege and Capture of the City: 2:1-8
       B. Utter Spoiling of the City: 2:9-13
    III. The Overthrow of Nineveh Defended: 3
       A. Because of Nineveh's Sin: 3:1-7
       B. Wealth and Strength could not save Nineveh: 3:8-19

Key Chapter: 3, with Galatians 6:7. Israel's reaping.

Key Verses: 1:2,3,7.

Key Word: Jealous: 1:2.

Key Phrase: An utter end: 1:8,9.

Key Thought: Judgment follows sin.

Spiritual Thought: The severity of God. See SEVERITY in Index.

Christ Is Seen As:
    1. A Stronghold: 1:7.
    2. Bringer of good tidings and peace: 1:15.

1. By applying Nahum 1:2 to the thirty emperors and governors who persecuted the early Christians, history reveals that none came to a peaceful end. As an example, see NERO in Index. "Vengeance is Mine, I will repay, saith the Lord" (Deuteronomy 32:35; Romans 12:19).

2. Nineveh's doom: 1:8.

Stated: ca. 648 B.C. *Fulfilled:* ca. 612 B.C.

3. Christ's earthly message: 1:15 with Luke 4:18,19.
   Stated: ca. 648 B.C. *Fulfilled:* Life of Christ

Nineveh's Fall. Archaeology has teamed up with Nahum's prophecy to corroborate the accuracy of his predictions, even to the minutest details. This great city stood on the left bank of the Tigris River. Its walls were one hundred feet high, which were strengthened by 1,500 towers, wide enough for three chariots to ride abreast, and sixty miles in circumference. The side of the city not protected by the Tigris was surrounded by a moat. The oldest aqueduct in history supplied the city with water, even in times of siege, and the city maintained its own food supply. To the Ninevehites, their city was impregnable. Yet Nahum predicted its destruction as follows:

1. With an overwhelming flood: 1:8
2. While its leaders are drunk they shall be devoured as stubble: 1:10
3. The enemy against them shall be like chariots with flaming torches: 2:3,4
4. In drunkenness they shall seek to prepare their defenses: 2:5
5. The gates of the river shall be opened, and the palace shall be dissolved: 2:6
6. "Nineveh is like a [flooded] pool, whose waters run wild": 2:8
7. By its being leveled it will become "empty, and void, and waste": 2:10; 3:7
8. "I am against you, saith the Lord of hosts, and I will burn her chariots in the smoke": 2:13
9. Fire to destroy her strongholds: 3:13
10. No hope for survival—God will "make an utter end of the place," with "no healing of thy bruises:" 1:8; 3:19

When Nineveh was conquered in ca. 612 B.C. by Cyaxares of the Medes and Nabopolassar of Babylon, the destruction fulfilled Nahum's prophecy to the last detail! They sent a demolition squad to destroy the city's aqueduct, and to divert the Tigris River simultaneously, which flooded Nineveh (1:8; 2:6). The flood waters dissolved the mud-brick foundations of houses and buildings, and the walls crumbled. Evidence also shows that, along with the flood, the city was burned (2:13; 3:13). Those in authority, as drunk as they were (2:5), and seeing their doom, mounted a funeral pyre and died as they were devoured by the flames. No one wept over her funeral, and she was no more heard of (3:7; 2:13). From 612 B.C. till A.D. 1845 it was a forgotten site. Since then, discovered evidence tips the scales in favor of God's Word through Nahum.

The type of chariot that will appear in the day of Christ's preparation (before His earthly reign), is given by Nahum (2:3,4). Some of today's expositors have seen in these verses an allusion to the modern automobile—"raging in the streets, and jostling one against another in the broad ways . . . running like lightnings."

Nahum in the New Testament:
1. Preaching the gospel of peace: 1:15 with Romans 10:15.
2. Companion references.
   —Nations committing whoredom: 3:4 with Revelation 18:2,3

SEED THOUGHTS

Sinning against the Light. Nineveh had "seen the light" under Jonah's preaching. From the darkness of paganism through the preaching of the Word, she had come into the light of God's blessings (Jonah 3). Years later, in Nahum's day, she was like those "that rebel against the light" (Job 24:13). Light then became darkness to them, and how great was that darkness (Matthew 6:23b).

"Light has a sovereignty in it, so that to resist it is to rebel against it. God has given it to be a display of Himself, for God is Light; and He has clothed it with a measure of His majesty and power of judgment."[2] Rebelling against the light results in:

1. Becoming traitors of God
2. Complacency
3. Hypocrisy
4. Darkness
5. Godlessness
6. Leading others into darkness
7. Drunkenness
8. Violence
9. Fighting a loosing battle against God
10. Doom

Light is our best friend, and the wise obey it. To oppose it is useless. Owls may hoot but the moon still shines! Light will lead to more light, producing godliness. Light here will lead to heaven where there is no need for the sun, neither of the moon, to shine on it: for the glory of the Lord will light it, because the Lamb is the Light thereof, and we shall reign for ever and ever with Him (Revelation 21:23; 22:5). Light is illustrative of—

1. God's glory: Psalm 104:2 with I Timothy 6:16
2. God's purity: I John 1:5
3. God's wisdom: Daniel 2:22
4. God's guidance: Psalm 27:1; 36:9
5. God's favor: Psalm 4:6; Isaiah 2:5
6. Christ: John 8:12
7. Christ's glory: Acts 9:3,5; 26:13
8. God's Word: Psalm 119:105,130; II Peter 1:19
9. The gospel: II Corinthians 4:4; I Peter 2:9b
10. Believers: Matthew 5:14; Ephesians 5:8; Philippians 2:15
11. The path of the just: Proverbs 4:18
12. Future glory of the church: Isaiah 60:1-3
13. Future glory of saints: Psalm 97:11; Colossians 1:12

A BIT OF **HEAVENLY MANNA**

So often people think that because one has become a Christian their troubles are over. This is far from the truth. God never promised His children a bed of roses. He never promised us a "utopia" as long as we are in the flesh. Even Jesus was tempted in all points like as we are (yet without sin). As a pilgrim and a stranger down here, this old life offers little compared to the glory that shall be revealed in us when we see Jesus face to face. Although having this glorious hope, we are not immune to trials, temptations, infirmities, and trouble from our adversary the devil. But like the manslayer fleeing to one of the Cities of Refuge, we, too, have—

A STRONGHOLD IN THE DAY OF TROUBLE—1:7[3]

"Man is born to trouble, and his second birth exposes him to trouble as well as the first. There is a furnace for everyone to pass through: a dreary wilderness between our Egypt and our Canaan. Many are the stormy days that we shall see. Troubles will come but every trouble may be turned into a blessing. If rightly applied, it will endear the Savior, wean us from the world, make the Bible more precious, and strengthen our desires for the better things of the Lord. Jesus is a stronghold in the day of trouble. To Him we may repair and find safety. If we enter into Him we shall find and enjoy supplies, which He provides according to His riches. He will protect us from every foe, secure us amidst all the wars, convulsions, and tempests of this present world. The door of this hold is always opened to every sinner that flees to it. Its walls are impregnable and cannot be stormed, and its resources are boundless and cannot be exhausted. 'The name of the Lord is a strong tower, the righteous runneth into it and is safe.'' Beloved, in every trial and trouble let us flee to Jesus. He will receive us, He will soothe our sorrows, and He will effectually prevent our being injured.''

 PRAYER THOUGHT: "Dear Father, make me ever mindful of Thy presence so that should any danger arise, seen or unseen; or should any fear come nigh; or any frustration cause anxiety; or any discouragement cause depression, I might simply rest in Thy peace and security. In the peaceful name of Jesus I pray. Amen."[4]

Nahum 1:7; John 16:33

Habakkuk—The Book of the Mysteries of Providence

Name: Habakkuk, the writer, of this prophecy (1:1), means "Embrace." He was the "Questioning" prophet—the "Job" among the prophets, inasmuch as the problem of both was "Why a just and omnipotent God at times permits the wicked to flourish and the more righteous to suffer affliction." With Job the problem was *personal,* while with Habakkuk it was *national.* Habakkuk was the prophet of "Faith," the grandfather of the Reformation under Martin Luther (2:4 with Acts 13:38,39; Romans 1:17; Galatians 3:11; Hebrews 10:37,38). He was one of the Levitical choristers in the Temple—a "Praying" prophet (3:1,19).

Period of His Prophecy: Habakkuk prophesied just before the Babylonians came against Jerusalem in the first siege (II Chronicles 36:5,6)—when the Babylonians were on the way (1:6), but had not yet arrived (3:16). This was ca. 625-610 B.C. Habakkuk was contemporary with Nahum, Jeremiah, and possibly Zephaniah. He was the *tenth* prophet.

People of His Prophecy: The Southern Kingdom of Judah, with "hints" of woe to the invading Chaldeans.

Contents: "The book is a mixture of the prophet's address to God in the people's name and to the people in God's name. It was the office of the prophets to carry messages both ways. We have in it a lively representation of the intercourse and communion between a gracious God and a gracious soul. The whole refers particularly to the invasion of the land of Judah by the Chaldeans, but it is of general use, especially to help us through that great temptation, with which good men have in all ages been exercised, arising from the power and prosperity of the wicked, and the sufferings of the righteous by it."[1]

Habakkuk was the "doubting Thomas" of the Old Testament. He had a question to ask God about everything. He wanted to know why a just God would use a wicked, sinful nation to punish a less sinful people. Why this injustice? Will God straighten out the mess Judah is in? Will He do anything about the wrongs in the world? (These same questions are being asked today.) He wanted to know the mysteries of Providence, to understand everything. Unlike most Christians, he took his problems to the Lord, and learned through this to trust God in the dark. The book opens in darkness and closes in light—opens with a question mark and closes with an exclamation point. It has 3 chapters, 56 verses, and 1,476 words.

Character: Prophetical.

Subject: God's holiness manifested through His judgments upon Judah by the hands of the Chaldeans.

Purpose: To teach us that God is holy and must always act in righteousness to every man.

Outline:
    I. The first Prayer and Answer: 1:1-11
       A. The indictment against Judah: vss. 1-4
       B. The invasion of the Chaldeans: vss. 5:11
    II. The second Prayer and Answer: 1:12—2:20
       A. The Prayer: 1:12—2:1
          1. The challenge: 1:12-13
          2. The charge: 1:15,16
          3. The conclusion: 1:17—2:1
       B. The Answer: 2:2-20
          1. The principle of righteousness announced to Habakkuk: vss. 2-4
          2. This principle applied to the Chaldeans: vss. 5-20
    III. The third Prayer and Answer: 3
       A. The Cry for Revival: vs. 2
       B. The Vision of Jehovah: vss. 3-15
       C. The Effect upon the Prophet: vss. 16:19

Key Chapter: 3. Habakkuk's faith.

Key Verse: 2:4, ". . . the just shall live by faith."

Key Word: Faith.

Key Phrase: Why dost Thou: 1:3.

Key Thought: Prayer changes things. Or, better yet—"Prayer changes people and people change things."

Spiritual Thought: There's light ahead: 3:4.

Christ Is Seen As:
    1. The Man who justifies by faith: 2:4 with Acts 13:38,39; Galatians 2:16.
    2. The Lord in His holy Temple: 2:20.

Prophecies:
    1. The redemptive work of Christ: 1:5 with Acts 13:41.
    2. The millennnium: 2:14.

ARCHAEOLOGY

Among the scrolls found at the Dead Sea in 1947 was a commentary on the first two chapters of Habakkuk. Very little light has been cast on these chapters, but it does enlighten us as to the thinking of the Essenes on this prophecy during and after the days of Christ.

Habakkuk in the New Testament:
1. Working God's works: 1:5 with Acts 13:41.
2. The just shall live by faith: 2:4 with Acts 13:38,39; Romans 1:17; Galatians 3:11; Hebrews 10:37,38.

1. Faith: 2;4. Although Habakkuk was the "doubting Thomas" of the Old Testament, he, like Thomas, "saw the light" and realized the true meaning of faith. See FAITH in Index.

    a. What is faith?
        —Faith is perceiving as fact what is not revealed to the natural senses, the substance of things hoped for, the evidence of things which are not seen: Hebrews 11:1
    —Believing that we have already received: Mark 11:24
    —Believing God: Romans 4:3; Hebrews 11:6
  b. Results of faith:
    —Access to God: Romans 5:2
    —Justification: Romans 3:28; 5:1; Galatians 2:16
    —Indwelling of Christ: Ephesians 3:17
    —Living: Romans 1:17; Galatians 2:20
    —Walking: II Corinthians 5:7
    —Purified: Acts 15:9
    —Sanctified: Acts 26:18
    —Prayer answered: James 1:6
    —Standing: II Corinthians 1:24
    —Fighting: I Timothy 6:12
    —Boldness: I Timothy 3:13
    —Overcoming: I John 5:4
    —Resists the devil: I Peter 5:9
    —Makes rich: James 2:5
    —Enables us to continue: I Timothy 2:15
    —Keeps: I Peter 1:5
    —Can die in it: Hebrews 11:13
  c. Exercise of faith:
    —Look unto Jesus: Hebrews 12:2
    —Be strong: Romans 4:20
    —Pray for an increase: Luke 17:5
    —Abound: II Corinthians 8:7
    —Contend for it: Jude 3
    —Anything not of faith is sin: Romans 14:23b
2. The Five "Woes" of Habakkuk. See WOES in Index.
  a. Against dishonesty: 2:6
  b. Against covetousness: 2:9
  c. Against bloody building enterprises: 2:12
  d. Against the liquor dispenser: 2:15,16
  e. Against idolatry: 2:18-20
3. Guilty by Association: 2:15. Among those who will not inherit the kingdom of God are drunkards (I Corinthians 6:9,10). Equally guilty before God is one who makes another drink—"woe unto him that giveth his neighbor drink, . . . and makest him drunk also."

Pigs Must Be Careful[2]

One night in late October,
 When I was far from being sober;
I was returning home with my load in manly pride
 When my feet began to stutter,
So I laid down in a gutter,
 And a pig came near and laid down by my side.

A lady passing by was heard to say:
 "You can tell who boozes,
By the company he chooses,"
 And the pig got up and slowly walked away!

4. Alcohol Advertising[3]
   In the Theatre,
     On the Radio,
   Over the Television,
     On the Signboard,
   In Paper and Magazines
     I say what I'm paid to say.

   But in the Laboratory,
     In the wrecked Automobile,
   In the City Jail,
     In the Tavern,
   In the veins of the Drunks,
     I tell the truth.

5. The Song of a Soul Set Free: 3:17-19.

A BIT OF **HEAVENLY MANNA**

Revival is just the life of the Lord Jesus poured into our broken hearts. Jesus is always victorious. Whatever may be our experience of failure or barrenness, He is never defeated. His power is boundless. We, for our part, have only to get in a right relationship with Him to see His power being demonstrated in our hearts and lives and service, and His victorious life will fill us and overflow through us to others. That is revival in essence, yet how few of us know revival. Our wills are not broken; the life is too much "I" and not "Christ." When Habakkuk saw conditions as they were, and realized the people had failed, he prayed for a real revival of the works of the Lord.

O LORD, REVIVE THY WORK!—3:2[4]

"Christianity is the work of the Lord. He begins it, He carries it on, and He completes it in the day of Christ. It is the work of His own hands which He never forsakes, the work which is to reflect the glory of all His divine perfections. But this work often needs reviving. Our graces become weak, our evidences decline, our spirituality decays, and we grow cold, careless, and worldly-minded. Then we have no sweet visits, no tokens for good, no heart-affecting fellowship, no longings for glory. Our affections fix on some earthly object, our conscience becomes numb or accuses us, our understanding is darkened, and we sink into an unhealthy state. Our souls cleave to the dust, and all we can do is cry, 'Quicken me according to Thy Word.' When the Lord comes to revive His work, He often sends some painful cross, brings us down into the dust by some affliction, makes us see our sin and smart for our folly. He convinces us, humbles us, empties us, and makes us feel thoroughly ashamed of our conduct. He then is able to lead us to confession. He produces contrition, speaks pardon, and smiles upon us again. O Lord, revive Thy work in me, *now!*''

PRAYER THOUGHT: "Dear Lord, open to me Thy sacred Truths. Give me a reverent and teachable mind and enable me to believe what I ought so that I might be established in Thy way and prosperous in Thy blessings. Help me, I pray, to be all that Thou hast ordained me to be in Christ. In His precious name I pray. Amen."[5]

Habakkuk 3:19

Zephaniah—The Book of Wonder and Wrath

Name: Zephaniah, the writer of this prophecy (1:1), means "hidden of Jehovah." He was the "judgment" prophet, the prophet of "punishment and promise." He was also the prophet of "Gentile conversion." He indentified himself better than any of the rest of the Minor Prophets. Habakkuk concealed himself in silence, but Zephaniah went to the opposite extreme in telling the world who he was. Habakkuk stood high and looked far; Zaphaniah stooped low and looked close. He was the "Hellfire and Brimstone" preacher of the Old Testament; the great great-grandson of Hizkiah (or King Hezekiah), and was related to King Josiah, in whose reign he prophesied.

Period of His Prophecy: "The word of the Lord came unto Zephaniah . . . in the days of Josiah . . . king of Judah" (1:1). He prophesied ca. 634-625 B.C., and was possibly an important person in the revival in Josiah's day (II Chronicles 34). Contemporary with Nahum and Jeremiah, he was the *eighth* prophet.

People of His Prophecy: The people of his day (Southern Kngdom of Judah), and all nations. It has a universal appeal.

Contents: He foretold the destruction of the Jews by the Chaldeans for their sins. He called them to repentance, but bluntly told of judgment to come if they did not. He also predicted the ruin of many other nations, all of which came to pass. He prophesied the calling of the Gentiles, the conversion of the Jews, and of the comfortable state of the spiritual seed in gospel times, especially in the latter day. He placed much emphasis on the "day of the Lord," a period believed by many to not only include the great tribulation, which precedes the millennium, but the millennium itself. This book has 3 chapters, 53 verses, and 1,617 words.

Character: Prophetical.

Subject: God's great wrath upon the world, and upon Judah in particular, in the "day of the Lord," and His great mercy in hiding the "remnant of Israel," who will seek Him.

Purpose: To show us that our heavenly Father, who saved us from His wrath by placing it upon His Son, will keep us safe from wrath to come.

Outline:
    I. The Retribution upon the Chosen Nation: 1:1—2:3
    II. The Retribution upon Gentile Nations: 2:4-15
    III. The Accusation against Jerusalem: 3:1-7
    IV. The Restoration of the Chosen Nation: 3:8-20

Key Chapter: 3. God's deliverance.

Key Verse: 1:12.

Key Word: Search.

Key Phrase: The day of the Lord: 1:14.

Key Thought: The fire of jealousy: 1:18.

Spiritual Thoughts:
    1. Trust in the name of the Lord: 3:12.
    2. Sing as you go: 3:14.

Christ Is Seen As:
    1. Israel's King: 3:15.
    2. The Lord in Israel's midst: 3:17.

Prophecies:
    1. Universal judgment, which only a remnant escapes: 3:8-13.
    2. The future glory of Israel: 3:14-20.

Zephaniah in the New Testament:
    1. Day of the Lord (God): 1:7 with II Thessalonians 2:2.
    2. Companion references:
        a. Christ's sacrifice: 1:7 with John 1:29
        b. Worship God anywhere: 2:11 with John 4:20-23
        c. The poor chosen: 3:12 with James 2:5

SEED THOUGHTS

1. Call to Repentance: 2:1-3. See REPENTANCE in Index. Repentance includes:
    a. Seeking the Lord: vs. 3a
    b. Seeking righteousness: vs. 3b
    c. Seeking meekness (humility): vs. 3c. See HUMILITY in Index.
    d. Sorrow for sins: II Corinthians 7:9,10
    e. Confession of sins: I John 1:9; Joshua 7:19-21
    f. Forsaking of sinful ways: Isaiah 55:7; Proverbs 28:13
    g. A forgiving spirit: Matthew 18:35
    h. Restitution of all wrongs: Ezekiel 33:15; Luke 19:8
2. God's Blessings: 3:9, 14-17.
    a. What God has done for us—
        —Taken away our judgments: vs. 15a with Isaiah 53:6
        —Cast out the enemy: vs. 15b with Ephesians 1:20-23
        —Made us nigh Him: vs. 15c with Ephesians 2:13-18
        —Removed fear: vs. 16 with I John 4:18
        —Delivered: vs. 17a with II Corinthians 1:9,10
        —Rejoiced over us: vs. 17b with Romans 5:11
        —Rested in His Love: vs. 17c with Hebrews 1:1-3

b. What we should do for Him—
    —Not be ashamed of Him: vs. 9 with Romans 1:15,16
    —Fear not: vs. 16a with Psalm 27:1-5; Hebrews 13:5,6
    —Let not our hands be slack: vs. 16b with I Corinthians 4:2
    —Praise His name: vs. 14 with Psalm 107:15

3. Trust: 3:12b.
    a. Who to trust? vs. 12b with Isaiah 26:4
    b. When to trust: Psalm 62:8
    c. How to trust? Proverbs 3:5
    d. Results of trusting—
        —Salvation: Psalm 37:40
        —Establishment: Psalm 125:1
        —Happiness: Proverbs 16:20
        —Safety: Proverbs 29:25
        —Deliverance: Daniel 3:28
        —Absence of fear: Isaiah 12:2
        —Perfect peace: Isaiah 26:3

4. Songs of the Saints: 3:14,15.
    a. Of redemption: Psalm 40:3
    b. Of deliverance: vs. 15a
    c. Of joy: Job 38:7
    d. Of service: II Chronicles 20:21; Acts 16:25
    e. Of triumph: vs. 15b; Revelation 15:3

A BIT OF HEAVENLY MANNA

Zephaniah reveals that the wrath and love of God are inseparable. You cannot have one without the other any more than you can have a heaven without a hell. Sin brings wrath and judgment. Sin cannot be overlooked; so God judges it. But because He is a God of love as well as a God of wrath, He judged sin in the sacrifice of His Son and extends His love to all who will believe in Him. Those who believe are passed from death unto life, and there is therefore no condemnation to those who are in Christ Jesus. To reject Christ means to die in sin, to die with the judgment and wrath of God abiding in the sinner. To escape God's wrath we need to flee to Christ.

TO WHOM WILL YE FLEE FOR HELP?—Isaiah 10:3[1]

"This is addressed to those who know not God, to those who know not our Lord Jesus Christ. What multitudes there are of such! Let us ask, 'Am I one of them? Have I fled for refuge to lay hold on the hope set before me in the gospel? Is Christ formed in my heart the hope of glory? Is God my Friend, my Father, and my joy?' If not, when trouble comes and overwhelms you, when Satan harasses you, when conscience accuses you, when the world frowns upon you, when sickness seizes you, when death stares you in the face, to whom will you flee for help? Who can support you in trouble? Who can deliver you from God's wrath, or from Satan? Who can calm and pacify a guilty conscience? Who can comfort you when the world frowns? Who can give you patience when suffering from disease? Who can raise you above the fears of death, or entitle you to a glorious immortality? He that cannot do these things for you *now* cannot do them for you *then*. To whom then will you flee? Creatures are vain, they cannot help you. God alone can, and if you will flee to Him *now,* it will be well with your soul, for He invites you and promises to receive you. 'Him that cometh to Me I will in no wise cast out.' When you come He delivers from the wrath that now abides upon you and will deliver you from wrath to come."

PRAYER THOUGHT: "Today, dear heavenly Father, help me in Thy service to be more sensitive to hurting Thy feelings than I am in hurting those of my loved ones and my friends. May I trust all consequences to Thee, and be man enough to 'take' whatever reproach I might suffer for Thy name's sake. Amen."[2]

Zephaniah 3:17; Psalm 118:6

Haggai—The Builder's Book

Name: Haggai, the writer of this prophecy (1:1), means "my feast," or "festival," probably in anticipation of the return from captivity. He was the "businessman" among the prophets. His style is short, curt, plain, and to the point. He was the prophet of "interrogation" (1:4; 2:3,12,13). He was the first of the Post-exile prophets, having returned, no doubt, with Zerubbabel. He is mentioned by Ezra (5:1; 6:14).

Period of His Prophecy: "In the second year of Darius the king [of Persia]." This was in 520 B.C. Haggai was contemporary with Zechariah, and was the *fourteenth* prophet. His ministry lasted four months, in which he delivered four messages, each dated (1:1; 2:1; 2:10; 2:20). This book should be read between chapters four and five of Ezra.

People of His Prophecy: The remnant who had returned to Jerusalem and Judah after Babylonian captivity.

Contents: The prophecy of Haggai is one of a group of three—Haggai, Zechariah, Malachi—that belongs to the period following Israel's captivity in Babylon. See POST-CAPTIVITY BOOKS in Index. These prophecies contain the last words of the Lord to His people Israel, and they bring the volume of the Old Testament Scriptures to an end. A special interest is attached to these three prophecies, because they were addressed to a select company of Israelites, namely, to that small "remnant of the people" (1;12,14), which had returned to the desolate land of Judah, and to the ruined and forsaken city of Jerusalem.

The people whom Haggai addressed were a company very different in character from those addressed by Jeremiah prior to captivity. The latter's message was rejected and derided. It was sent to an apostate generation that was ripe for judgment. It fell on hearts that were hardened and consciences that were seared, and it was without effect except to increase the condemnation of those who heard it. But the message of Haggai, to those after captivity, was heeded and obeyed. It came to a people who, in spite of neglecting for awhile to build God's house at the expense of building theirs, had a heart for the Word of God. His message bore prompt and fruitful results. For the order of Haggai's messages, see PERIOD of Zechariah's prophecy.

Haggai's message is twofold: the need to forget self and rebuild the Temple which Nebuchadnezzar had destroyed, and the glory of the latter Temple. In the two chapters, there are 38 verses and 1,131 words.

Character: Prophetical and Historical.

Subject: God's message of encouragement to the weak remnant that they might build the Temple, the house of the Lord.

Purpose: To encourage us in getting the gospel to the uttermost parts of the earth, and thus help build the spiritual Temple, the church of the living God.

Outline:

    I. A Summons to Build: 1

    A. Purpose of summons: vss. 1,2
    B. Reason for delay: vss. 3-11
    C. Obedience to the summons: vss. 12-15
  II. A Summons to Look: 2:1-9
    A. At the present Temple: vss. 1-3
    B. At the past Covenant: vss. 4,5
    C. At the glory of the latter Temple: vss. 6-9
  III. A Summons to Obey and Live Godly: 2:10-19
    A. Consider personal condition: vss. 10-14
    B. Consider the unfinished Temple: vss. 15-17
    C. Consider the promised blessing: vss. 18,19
  IV. A Summons to Exercise Faith: 2:20-23
    A. Faith in God's omnipotence: vs. 21
    B. Faith in God's justice: vs. 22
    C. Faith in God's security: vs. 23

Key Chapter: 2. Beholding and Behaving.

Key Verse: 1:8.

Key Word: Build.

Key Phrase: Be strong and work: 2:4.

Key Thought: Consider your ways: 1:7.

Spiritual Thought: Put first things first.

Christ Is Seen As: The Desire of all nations: 2:7.

Prophecies:
  1. Christ, the Desire of all nations: 2:7.
  2. The glory of the latter Temple in the millennium: 2:9.

LIGHT FROM BIBLICAL CUSTOMS

[1] "I will make thee as a signet": 2:23. The signet ring was used to stamp documents and articles, thereby making them legal. No document was considered authentic unless it had been stamped by a signet. See NABOTH in Index. The Lord, having chosen Zerubbabel said, "I will make thee as a signet." He stood before the people, having been stamped by God, as God's authority. We, too, have been chosen by God to bear in our body His stamp (the image of His dear Son), and to appear before others in His name with His message of authority (John 15:16; Romans 8:29; II Corinthians 4:9,10). See JOTHAM in Index.

Haggai in the New Testament:
  1. God shaking the heavens: 2:6 with Hebrews 12:26.
  2. Companion references: Lo, I am with You: 1:13 with Matthew 28:20.

SEED THOUGHTS

1. Consider Your Ways: 1:2-14. Though Israel was grateful for God's deliverance from Babylonian captivity and had shown it by beginning to rebuild the Temple (Ezra 1—4), she became lax and put second things first. Her homes and crops became more important than God's house. How easy it is many times to substitute what is good for the best. To bring Israel to see that God's principle is to "seek first . . . God and His righteousness, and all things will be added to you," Haggai asked the peo-

ple to take a good look at themselves—to "consider your ways" (vs. 5). It is necessary often to take a good look at ourselves, to begin to consider God for a change, and when we do, our thoughts turn to Him. But notice what happened when Israel was told to consider her ways—

 a. They said, "The time is not come . . . that the Lord's house should be built" (vs. 2). The time to do God's work is right *now*—which is an ever-present opportunity. "Procrastination is the art of keeping up with yesterday." God's admonition is still to "redeem the time" (Ephesians 5:16)

 b. They dwelt in their own ceiled houses while God's house lay waste (vs. 4). They said, "Lord, Lord," but did not do what He had commanded. See LORD in Index.

I'll Do It . . . But[2]

I'll go where You want me to go, dear Lord,
Real service is what I desire;
I'll say what You want me to say, dear Lord,
But don't ask me to sing in the choir.

I'll say what You want me to say, dear Lord,
I like to see things come to pass;
But don't ask me to teach girls and boys, dear Lord,
I'd rather just stay in my class.

I'll do what You want me to do, dear Lord,
I yearn for Thy Kingdom to thrive;
I'll give you my nickels and dimes, dear Lord,
But please don't ask me to tithe.

I'll go where You want me to go, dear Lord,
I'll say what You want me to say;
I'm busy just now with myself, dear Lord,
But . . . I'll help You some other day.

 c. They sowed much but brought in little harvest (vs. 6a). They had a lot of activity, but were leaning on the arm of the flesh. Putting God first enables Him to "give the increase"

 d. They ate but were not filled (vs. 6b). They had no appetite for spiritual things, consequently they were not filled with the things of God. An appetite for the things of this life—wealth, position, the praise of men, honor—will never satisfy a heart which was made by God for God

 e. They were clothed by still cold (vs. 6c). The "fig leaves of self-righteousness" could not satisfy our first parents, and such garments have never fully clothed their offspring in God's presence. "Put ye on the Lord Jesus Christ, and make not provision for the flesh to fulfill the lusts thereof" (Romans 13:14)

 f. Their wages were put in a bag filled with holes (vs. 6d). "What shall it profit a man if he should gain the whole world and lose his own soul" (Mark 8:36). Man has *nothing* to offer God by the fruit of his own labor (Genesis 4:3,5; Jude 11a)

A consideration of Israel's ways led to—

 a. Obedience to God's Word through Haggai: vs. 12a

 b. Fear before the Lord: vs. 12b

 c. A stirring of their spirits to work: vs. 14

 d. God's blessings on them and His being glorified: vs. 8. See POEM, "A Job," in Index.

2. The Glory of Considering. Haggai used the word "consider" five times (1:5,7; 2:15,18a,b). It is only when we consider things in their proper setting that we have the right perspective of any situation.

 a. What consideration is:

  —Taking stock: 1:5-7; Isaiah 1:2,3

—Heeding good advice: Ecclesiastes 7:13; II Timothy 2:7
—Trust in the Word of God: Psalm 119:95

  b. What we are to consider:

—Jesus Christ—a lesson of purity, faithfulness, and God-likeness: Hebrews 3:1; 12:3
—Ourselves—a lesson of meekness and humility: Galatians 6:1
—Others—a lesson in unselfishness: Hebrews 10:24
—The works of God—a lesson in submission: Job 37:14; Psalm 8:3,4a;
  Ecclesiastes 7:13
—The ant—a lesson of wisdom: Proverbs 6:6-8
—The ravens—a lesson of trust: Luke 12:24
—The lilies—a lesson of receiving: Luke 12:27
—New things in Christ—a lesson in forgetfulness of former things: Isaiah 43:18;
  Philippians 3:13,14
—Meditation—a lesson in prayer: Psalm 5:1-3

3. Working for God: 2:4-9 with I Corinthians 3:9.

  a. Assures us of His presence: vs. 4
  b. Gives confidence in the Spirit's leading: vs. 5a
  c. Eliminates fear: vs. 5b
  d. Floods us with His glory: vs. 7
  e. Brings peace to the soul: vs. 9

4. Glory of God: 2:9. This verse could well be speaking of the former Tabernacle and Temple of Old Testament days versus the latter Temple of today—the body of the born-again believer (I Corinthians 3:16,17). The glory of God in each believer is greater than in those "buildings made with hands," even though God's Shekinah glory dwelt in them (Exodus 25:8; I Kings 8:1-11). *What is glory?* It is the splendor of God Himself, the light of His countenance, the brilliant light emanating from His person (as the glow of light from the sun).

  a. God is glory to His children: Psalm 3:3; Zechariah 2:5
  b. Christ is glory to His followers: Isaiah 60:1; Luke 2:32
  c. The Gospel is glory to His saints and far exceeds the glory of the Law: II Corinthians
    3:9,10
  d. Rejoicing saints are full of glory: I Peter 1:8
  e. Eternal glory

—Is procured by the death of Christ: Hebrews 2:10; I Corinthians 2:8
—Accompanies salvation by Christ: II Timothy 2:10
—Is inherited by His saints: I Samuel 2:8; Proverbs 3:35a
—What saints are called to: II Thessalonians 2:14; I Peter 5:10
—What saints are prepared unto: Romans 9:23
—Present affliction cannot be compared to it: Romans 8:18
—What the saints will be raised in: I Corinthians 15:43; Philippians 3:21

A BIT OF HEAVENLY MANNA

This old world today depicts what men and nations will do when they do not know Jesus Christ. The United Nations does not give place to God, for fear they will hurt someone's faith. When God is left out of the planning of nations, chaos follows. Sooner or later these nations fall. But cheer up ye saints of God, there is coming a time when the "Desire of all nations" shall come, and then, in a glorious millennium, man's desire will be met in Him.

THE DESIRE OF ALL NATIONS SHALL COME—2:7[3]

"There is a desire in every heart for something which it doesn't have, and that something is only to be found in Christ. It is a universal craving after an unknown good. Perhaps there have always been some in all the nations who have been really desiring to know the Lord Jesus. However, wherever He is known He is desired. All nations have desired Him, or will desire Him. He possesses all they need. He alone can make them happy. They want all He has, for less would not meet their case. He came once and laid a solid foundation for hope. He will come again and satisfy the desire of all who love His appearing. He will then be manifestly the desire of all nations, for all kings shall fall down before Him, all nations shall serve Him. 'All the earth shall worship Thee, and shall sing unto Thee; they shall sing to Thy name.' He will come and fill the earth with His knowledge, and perform the ancient prediction, 'The whole earth shall be filled with My glory.' May our desires center in Jesus *now*. May His truth be our treasure, His love our delight, His salvation our theme, His glory our aim, and His presence our heaven.''

 PRAYER THOUGHT: ''Dear Lord, help me to never forget that Thou art present with me no matter where I go, what I do, or what I say. May I 'practice the presence of God,' knowing that Thou wilt never leave me nor forsake me, that Thy Son is with me always, and that the Holy Spirit abides within me forever. In Thy name I pray. Amen.''[4]

Haggai 2:4; Psalm 139:7

Zechariah—The Book of the Future

Name: Zechariah means ''one whom Jehovah remembers.'' He was the ''son of Berechiah,'' which means ''Jehovah blesses,'' and Berechiah was the ''son of Iddo,'' which means ''the appointed time.'' The rich meaning of these names are suggestive of the encouragement God gave to the remnant—God remembered to bless in His appointed time. He is the prophet of ''Last and final things.'' He saw the Royal Root and the sovereign Stem of Jesse (Messiah) in His coming judgment and justice. He was the prophet of ''restoration and glory.''

It has been said that while Haggai was a realist—with his feet on the ground, Zechariah was a visionary—with his head in the clouds. Haggai dealt with the *material*; Zechariah, mainly with the *spiritual*. In addition to his being a prophet, Zechariah was also a priest (Nehemiah 12:16). Josephus and the Jewish Targum state that he was slain in the Temple (sanctuary). This would identify him as the Zechariah mentioned by Christ (Matthew 23:35).

Writer: Zechariah claims for himself authorship of his prophecy (1:1,7; 7:1). As always, critics have questioned his authorship because the latter part of his prophecy deals with the future, because its style differs from the first part of the book. In his assisting Haggai, he was young, and concerned with the realities of the present. In old age, when he wrote the latter part of his prophecy, he was concerned with the glories of the future. Consequently, the book lends to two styles.

Period of His Prophecy: See first paragraph, CONTENTS in Haggai. ''In the eighth month, in the second year of Darius, came the Word of the Lord to Zechariah'' (1:1). He was contemporary with Haggai, prophesying after the Babylonian captivity, 520-518 B.C. He was the *fifteenth* prophet, and the younger of the two. This book should be read between chapters four and five of Ezra. The chronological order of Haggai's and Zechariah's messages is as follows:

1. During Darius' second year of reign:
   a. Haggai's first: 1:1, 6th month, 1st day. Twenty-four days later, work began on the Temple: 1:15
   b. Haggai's second: 2:1, 7th month, 21st day

      c. Zechariah's first: 1:1, 8th month
      d. Haggai's third and fourth: 2:10; 2:20, 9th month, 24th day
      e. Zechariah's second: 1:7, 11th month, 24th day
  2. During Darius' fourth year of reign:
    —Zechariah's third: 7:1, 9th month, 4th day

People of His Prophecy: The remnant in Judah after Babylonian captivity.

Contents: "Zechariah, as a prophet to the remnant, stirred them up to build the Temple. As a priest, he stirred them up to restore the pure worship of sacrifices and feasts to God. He also wrote to encourage their faith and hope in the expectation of the Messiah. The book consists of various visions and prophecies relating to Christ's first coming, the times of the gospel, and the glories of the future kingdom."[1] This is the largest book of the Minor Prophets, containing 14 chapters, 211 verses, and 6,444 words.

Character: Prophetical.

Subject: God's unchangeable purpose in grace toward Jerusalem as His dwelling place in the midst of His people Israel.

Purpose: To encourage our hearts by assuring us of His love and purpose for us in grace, reassuring us that the promises for His heavenly people are unchangeable and must be fulfilled.

Outline:
    I. Introduction. A warning: 1:1-7
   II. Apocalyptic Visions (all in one night): 1:7—6:15
      A. The rider on the red horse: 1:7-17. A picture of Israel's condition today
      B. The four horns: 1:18,19. The four world empires which have scattered Judah, Israel, and Jerusalem
      C. The four carpenters: 1:20,21. Four divine judgments upon those nations
      D. The man with the measuring line: ch. 2. The restoration of the nation Israel, and particularly Jerusalem
      E. Joshua, the high priest: ch. 3. A cleansed people
      F. The golden candlestick and the two olive trees: ch. 4. An ideal picture of Israel to come
      G. The flying roll: 5:1-4. The rebuke of sin by the Word of God: from previous version
      H. The Ephah: 5:5-11. Judgment against wickedness in the land
      I. The four chariots: 6:1-8. Divine judgments upon Gentile nations
  III. Interlude: 7,8
      A. The question of fasting, a religious ritual: 7:1-3
      B. The question answered: 7:4—8:23
        1. When the heart is right, the ritual is right: 7:4-7
        2. When the heart is wrong, so is the ritual: 7:8-14
        3. God's purpose is unchanged by any ritual: ch. 8
  IV. Prophetic Burdens: 9—14
      A. The first burden: 9—11
        1. The King of peace and the invasion of Palestine: ch. 9
        2. The apostasy and restoration of Israel: ch. 10
        3. The rejection of Messiah: ch.11
      B. The second burden: 12—14
        1. The victory of Israel: 12:1—13:6
        2. The victorious King: 13:7—14:21

Key Chapter: 14, The visible return of Christ.

Key Verse: 1:3.

Key Word: Turn.

Key Phrase: I am jealous: 1:14.

Key Thought: God's love and care for His people.

Spiritual Thoughts:
1. The Lord shall yet comfort Zion: 1:17
2. Not by might, nor by power, but by My Spirit: 4:6
3. The eyes of the Lord run to and fro: 4:10
4. Holiness unto the Lord: 14:20

Christ Is Seen As:
1. The Branch—our Servant: 3:8; 6:12 with Mark 10:45
2. Priest and King—our Intercessor and Lord: 6:13 with Hebrews 7:25
3. Just and Lowly—our Salvation: 9:9 with John 14:6
4. The Corner—our Foundation: 10:4a with I Corinthians 3:11
5. The Nail—our Burden-bearer: 10:4b with Matthew 11:28
6. The Battle-bow—our Defense: 10:4c with Romans 8:37
7. The Spirit of Grace—our Gift: 12:10 with Ephesians 2:8,9; II Corinthians 9:15
8. The Fountain—our Cleanser: 13:1 with John 15:3
9. The Shepherd—our Guide: 13:7 with Psalm 23:1,3,4
10. King of all the earth—our Ruler: 14:9 with Romans 14:9
11. The King, the Lord of hosts—our Object of worship: 14:16 with Colossians 1:18

Messianic Prophecies:
1. First Advent, as Servant: 3:8 with Mark 10:45; Philippians 2:7.
2. Speaking peace to Gentiles: 9:10 with John 1:12.
3. Entry into Jerusalem riding upon an ass: 9:9 with Matthew 21:1-9.
4. Betrayed for 30 pieces of silver: 11:12 with Matthew 26:14,15.
5. Deserted by His disciples: 13:7 with Matthew 26:31,56.
6. Hands and feet pierced: 12:10 with John 19:34,37.
7. Potter's field: 11:13 with Matthew 27:6,7.

Stated: 520 B.C. *Fulfilled:* Christ's earthly ministry

8. The battle of Armageddon—yet future: 14:4-21 with Revelation 16:14.

9. Christ's second coming in glory—yet future: 14:4-21 with Revelation 19:11-16; II Thessalonians 1:8-10. This period is called the "Millennium" or the thousand-year reign of Christ upon the earth (Revelation 20:1-6).

Joshua, the high priest, in a backslidden condition and reclaimed by the Lord, is a type of many Christians who lose their first love and forget they were once purged from their old sins: ch. 3 with Revelation 2:4,5; II Peter 1:9.
1. Resisted by the devil, the accuser of the brethren: vs. 1 with Job 1:6; Revelation 12:10
2. Satan rebuked by God: vs. 2 with Matthew 4:1-10
3. Joshua's condition revealed: vs. 3 with Isaiah 64:6; Romans 7:15-24
4. Filthy garments forsaken: vs. 4a with Proverbs 28:13
5. Sin forgiven: vs. 4b with I John 1:9
6. New raiment given: vs. 4c with Romans 13:14; Revelation 19:8

7. Crowned: vs. 5a with Revelation 1:6
8. Fellowship with God: vs. 5b with I Corinthians 3:9; I John 1:7
9. Will love the brethren: vs. 10 with I John 2:10; 3:14
10. Must continue in obedience: vss. 6,7 with Romans 6:16-18; 22

Zechariah in the New Testament:

1. The red horse: 1:8 with Revelation 6:4
2. Speak every man the truth: 8:16 with Ephesians 4:25
3. Christ's triumphal entry into Jerusalem: 9:9 with John 12:12-15
4. Thirty pieces of silver: 11:13 with Matthew 27:3-10
5. Piercing Christ: 12:10 with John 19:34-37
6. Smiting the Shepherd: 13:7 with Matthew 26:31
7. Companion references:
   a. God incarnate: 2:10 with John 1:14; II Corinthians 5:19
   b. Seven eyes of the Lord: 3:9; 4:10 with Revelation 5:6
   c. The four horses: 6:1-8 with Revelation 6:1-8
   d. Christ building God's house: 6:12 with Hebrews 3:1-3
   e. Blood of the covenant: 9:11 with Hebrews 13:20
   f. Judas returns the betrayal money: 11:13 with Matthew 27:3-5
   g. The King: 14:16 with I Timothy 6:15
   h. A hope for the Gentiles: 14:21 with Ephesians 2:11-22

1. Seven Eyes of the Lord: 3:9; 4:10. The seven eyes of the Lord are the seven Spirits of the Lord, each representative of what Christ is to the believer (Revelation 5:6). See EYES in Index.
   a. The Lord: Isaiah 11:2a with Romans 1:3
   b. Wisdom: Isaiah 11:2b with I Corinthians 1:30
   c. Understanding: Isaiah 11:2c with Matthew 11:29; Luke 2:46,47
   d. Counsel: Isaiah 11:2d with Isaiah 9:6
   e. Might: Isaiah 11:2e with Matthew 28:18
   f. Knowledge: Isaiah 11:2f with John 2:25
   g. Fear of the Lord (reverence): Isaiah 11:2g with Colossians 1:18

2. Christ, the Branch: 6:12,13.
   a. He shall grow up: His earthly ministry—*Past*
   b. He shall build His Temple: His body—*Present*
   c. He shall rule: His glorious kingdom—*Future*

3. In our day when emphasis is on the mighty, the popular, the vastness of programs, the personalities, it would do us good to pause and let God remind us how despised (disrespected) small things are (4:10). God's method of accomplishment never was by might, nor by power, but by His Spirit (4:6). The world has always demanded the opposite of God's ways, and this is why the Church is so powerless today. It is competing with the world and not capitulating to God's divine order as is found in these two verses. God *never* does anything man's way so that no flesh may glory in His presence (I Corinthians 1:26-29). His ways are not our ways, neither His thoughts ours (Isaiah 55:8,9).

4. The Revelation of Christ: 14:4-21.
   a. It will be personal: vs. 4 with Acts 1:11; Revelation 1:7
   b. It will be an earth-shaking event: vs. 5a
   c. It will be a return of His raptured saints: vs. 5b
   d. It will be a day of light: vs. 7
   e. It will be to reign upon the earth: vs. 9
   f. It will be a time of safety: vs. 11

g. It will be a time of universal worship: vs. 16
h. It will be a time of obedience and judgment: vss. 17-19
i. It will be a time of holiness: vss. 20,21a
j. It will be a time of victory over the enemy: vs. 21b

Fountains often speak to us of a refreshing life (John 7:38,39), guidance and satisfaction (Isaiah 58:11), a constant supply of grace (Psalm 87:7), spiritual wisdom (Proverbs 18:4), and prosperity (Deuteronomy 33:28). But one of great importance is the fountain which inspired William Cowper to write the grand old Gospel hymn "There is a Fountain Filled with Blood" (13:1).

There is a fountain filled with blood,
Drawn from Immanuel's veins:
And sinners, plunged beneath that flood,
Lose all their guilty stain.
Dear dying Lamb, Thy precious blood
Shall never lose its power,
Till all the ransomed Church of God,
Be saved, to sin no more.

THERE SHALL BE A FOUNTAIN OPENED—13:1[2]

"Blessed be God there has been! A fountain to cleanse from all sin. A fountain open to all sinners. A fountain to which we can repair at all times. Grace opened it and grace keeps it open. The precious blood of Jesus is that fountain. It was shed for sinners. It was shed for sin. Its efficacy is infinite and eternal. It has cleansed the vilest, and it cleanses such still. Its virtue may be proved a thousand times. It not only suits the sinner but the saint as well. It is just what the backslider needs. It is open *now,* it is open for us. Let us go to it, let us step into it. Its virtues far exceed the famed Bethesda. It will heal more perfectly than did Shiloam once. O what a mercy that God should keep this fountain open! What would we do without it? We could have no peace, we could never obtain pardon, our case would be very desperate. But now there is ground for the strongest confidence. We may exercise the liveliest hope. This fountain not only cleanses, it forgives us. It opens heaven to us, it brings down into our possession all the riches of His grace, and promises all the blessings of His glory."

PRAYER THOUGHT: "O God, help me to look away from self and my own desires to the hopes and needs of others, and to use whatever gifts and blessings and privileges I have to brighten the path of all those I contact. In Christ's name I pray. Amen."[3]

Zechariah 8:16; Romans 12:16

Malachi—The Book of Denunciation and Hope

Name: Malachi, the writer of this prophecy (1:1), means "Jehovah's messenger." He is sometimes called the "unknown prophet with an angel's name." He was the last messenger of God till Messiah—the connecting link between Old Testament prophecy and New Testament fulfillment. As Nehemiah was the last of the historical writers, so Malachi was the last of the prophetical writers.

Period of His Prophecy: See first paragraph, CONTENTS in Haggai. Malachi's prophecy came about 75-100 years after Haggai and Zechariah—ca. 540-400 B.C. The second Temple was standing, the altar was in use, and the Jews were under the jurisdiction of the Persians. He prophesied either during the latter part of Nehemiah's governorship or soon following, and his prophecy should be read after the book of Nehemiah. He was the *sixteenth* prophet. The "Four Hundred Silent Years" follow his prophecy, the period between the Testaments in which no voice from God was heard.

People of His Prophecy: The settled remnant in Judah and Jerusalem after their Babylonian captivity, with an appeal to all Christians.

Contents: After Haggai and Zechariah had passed off the scene, the Israelites became complacent, and gross sin ensued. Hypocrisy and irreverance characterized her religious life; the world, the flesh, and the devil characterized her social life. Malachi charged Israel with her sins (unfaithful and deceitful priests, stolen animals for sacrifices, adultery, intermarriage, perjury, witchcraft, dishonesty, oppression, materialism, formalism, and skepticism). Though they had been cured of idolatry in captivity, their foreign wives had introduced it again in the land.

Malachi's book reveals a nation wedded to their sins. The people held God in contempt, and were indignant that He would take them to task for their "sin-drunkenness." Malachi represents God as having a dialogue with the remnant. They ask God eight sarcastic questions, say "Ye say" eleven times, and Malachi replies "Thus saith the Lord" twenty-five times.

In the midst of such apostasy, Malachi predicts certain judgment. He reminds the people that a time of mercy will precede the day of God's wrath in the person of Elijah, who was identified as John the Baptist, the forerunner of Christ (3:1 with Matthew 11:9-14; 17:10-13). Israel is admonished to obey the Mosaic law, and is assured that Messiah will come as prophesied. The "faithful remnant" within the remnant was highly encouraged, not only by the reminder of Messiah's coming, but by the fact that they made up God's jewels and that they were listed in God's book of remembrance. There are 4 chapters, 55 verses, and 1,782 words in the book of Malachi.

"The Old Testament opens with man in the Garden, free from sin and happy in His Creator's love; but it closes with fallen man, miserable and unhappy. It opens with a man in paradise and closes with him under a curse (4:6). In this manner God would remind us that the only safe place is in His will."[1]

Character: Prophetical.

Subject: God's last message to Israel, revealing His love and holiness in judging their sins, and promises to the godly remnant of future blessings in the coming of Messiah.

Purpose: To search and comfort our hearts with the blessed hope of Christ's return.

Outline:[2]

     I. Religious Declension: 1:1—2:9
        A. Expression of Jehovah's love for Israel: 1:1-5
        B. Expostulation with the Priests for their Offenses: 1:6-14
        C. Execration of the Priests for their Indifference: 2:1-9
    II. Social Debasement: 2:10-16

A. Condemnation of the Priests and the People
   1. For alien marriages: vs. 11
   2. For cruel divorces: vss. 1b,16
III. Moral Deflection: 2:17—4:6
   A. The Coming of the Lord for Judgment: 2:17—3:6
   B. The Charge preferred against the People: 3:7-12
   C. The Contrast between the Righteous and the Wicked: 3:13—4:6

Key Chapter: 4. The day of the Lord.

Key Verse: 4:2.

Key Word: Wherein.

Key Phrase: Yet ye say: 2:17; 3:8.

Key Thought: Will ye rob God?

Spiritual Thought: Lo! His messenger. Listen to him (Matthew 17:5).

Christ Is Seen As:
   1. Messenger of the covenant: 3:1
   2. A Refiner and Purifier: 3:3
   3. The Sun of Righteousness: 4:2

1. The coming of John the Baptist to prepare the way for Christ: 3:1a with Mark 1:2
2. Christ's first advent as the Messenger of God's Covenant, the Purifier, and the Purger of sin: 3:1b-3 with Hebrews 1:1-3; Proverbs 16:6
3. The Sun of Righteousness—Christ's return to earth: 4:2
4. Elijah sent before judgment: 4:5. Israel's refusal to heed Malachi's message led to a political priesthood which listened to the "traditions of their fathers" instead of the Word of God. This produced the formal, legalistic Pharisees and skeptical Sadducees of Christ's time, who rejected Elijah (in the person of John the Baptist—3:1a with Matthew 11:9-14), and led to the rejection and crucifixion of Christ

Malachi in the New Testament:
   1. Jacob loved, Esau hated: 1:2,3 with Romans 9:13
   2. Mission of John the Baptist: 3:1a with Mark 1:2
   3. Elijah in Christ's day: 4:5 with Matthew 11:14; 17:10-13
   4. Companion references:
     a. King: 1:14 with I Timothy 6:15
     b. Man and wife as one: 2:14 with Matthew 19:4,5
     c. Tithing: 3:8-10 with Matthew 23:23
     d. Christ's coming: 4:2 with Luke 1:78; Ephesians 5:14; II Peter 1:19

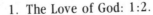

1. The Love of God: 1:2.
   a. Part of His character: I John 4:8a
   b. He manifests it towards:
     —Perishing sinners: John 3:16; Titus 3:3,4
     —His saints: John 17:23; II Thessalonians 2:16
     —The cheerful giver: II Corinthians 9:7
   c. He demands that we love Him: Deuteronomy 11:1; Matthew 22:37

2. The Characteristics of a True Minister: 2:5-7[3].
  a. Fearing God—his state of mind: vs. 5
  b. Proclaiming the truth—his message: vs. 6a
  c. Avoiding iniquity—his purpose: vs. 6b
  d. Walking with God—his habit: vs. 6c
  e. Turning men to God—his work: vs. 6d
  f. Teaching the law of God—his duty: vs. 7a
  g. Acting as God's messenger—his commission: vs. 7b

3. Will a Man Rob God? 3:8.
  a. Of His love: 1:2
  b. Of His honor: 1:6
  c. Of a proper sacrifice: 1:7,8,13,14
  d. Of a pure priesthood: 2:1-8
  e. Of His covenant: 2:10
  f. Of His holiness: 2:11
  g. Of His family blessings: 2:14-16
  h. Of morality: 2:17; 3:15
  i. Of His tithes: 3:8
  j. Of His service: 3:14

4. Tithing, the Fullness of Blessing: 3:10. Tithing was *commenced* by Abraham before the Law, *continued* by Jacob, *confirmed* by Moses, *commanded* by Malachi, and *commended* by Jesus.
  a. Tithing is an act of love. It is one way to manifest loyalty to God
  b. Tithing is God's plan for financing His work. That is why He commands it
  c. Tithing gives us a part in His program. It is an act of worship
  d. Tithing deepens the spiritual life. It gives wisdom in distributing His portion of 10%, as well as the remaining
  e. Tithing unlocks heaven's windows for all who will take God at His Word
  f. Tithing brings real Christian happiness and blessing when we give God what rightfully belongs to Him (Leviticus 27:30)
  g. Tithing teaches us that real giving begins *after* we give our tithe. This enables us to trust God with all we have. The only freedom a New Testament Christian has is to give *more* than the tithe. To give less than a tithe is to say that the Jew gave more by command than the Christian does out of a heart of love, thus making the Old Testament Law more powerful than the Cross. See TITHING in Index

5. A Jew and a Gentile were bosom friends. They decided to take turns going to a Synagogue and a church. The first Saturday the Gentile went with his Jewish friend to hear the Rabbi. During the service, the Jew put a ten-dollar bill in the offering. The Gentile was observing everything, yet put in his usual fifty cents.

The next day, being Sunday, the Jew attended church with his Gentile friend. When the offering was being taken, the Gentile again put in his usual fifty cents. In a few moments the Jew leaned over and whispered to his Gentile friend: "Almost thou persuadest me'to become a Christian."

6. The story is told of a young convert who promised God in the pastor's study that he would give God His tenth the rest of his life, no matter how much he made.

As the years rolled by, the one who had made this vow unto God became successful and wealthy. He began to become concerned about his vow because he was giving large amounts to the church each week and he felt he could no longer afford to tithe. With troubled soul he visited his former pastor, now retired. Explaining the situation to the one who witnessed his vow, he asked the old preacher how he could be released from his vow. It wasn't that he objected giving *some* to the church, but he felt he couldn't afford these large amounts. The old preacher slipped to his knees, asking the businessman to join him, saying, "I don't know how you can be released from your vow, but let us pray that God will reduce your income so you can afford to tithe.''

7. There are three kinds of givers—the flint, the sponge, and the honeycomb:[4]

    a. To get anything out of a *flint,* you must hammer it, and then you get only sparks and chips

    b. To get anything out of a *sponge,* you must squeeze it. The more you squeeze the more you get

    c. But the *honeycomb* just overflows with its own sweetness—a cheerful giver

Seriously, why don't we ''open up.'' If we *subtract* from our pocketbook, we *divide* what we have, but we *add* to God's kingdom many workers, who in turn *multiply* the number of souls won to Christ.

> *What I earned I spent,*
> *What I saved I lost,*
> *What I gave I have.*

A BIT OF
HEAVENLY MANNA

In this day and age when everything is changing, it is good to know that Jesus Christ is the *same* yesterday, today, and forever. Scientific discoveries demand change. Medical discoveries demand change. Forms of government require change. Wars and rumors of war change economics. But one thing is certain, *God changes not!*

I CHANGE NOT—3:6[5]

''No man can use this language but God; for all other persons and all things, change. We are constantly changing either for the better or the worse, but Jesus Christ is the same always (Hebrews 13:8). His nature is unchangeable, His office is permanent. His love is immutable. He is the Rock of Ages, the unchanging Sun of Righteousness. This is our comfort. We have One who always thinks of us, loves us and cares for us without any variation. This is the ground of our confidence. Jesus is always the same. We may expect Him to sympathize with us, confer blessings upon us, and appear to supply and deliver us, for He is One in mind and He has promised to do so. Could Jesus change our confidence we would be destroyed, our hope would dwindle, and our comfort vanish. But He is the same and His years fail not. Let us this day, amidst all the changes we may witness, amidst all the trials we may encounter, rejoice that we have an unchangeable Friend who sticks closer than a brother, and let us endeavor to exercise faith in His Word.''

PRAYER THOUGHT: ''Dear gracious Father, make me aware of the record which Thou art writing of my thoughts, my words, and my deeds. Help me to speak often of Thee so that when that record is opened, I might be numbered among Thy jewels. In Thy name. Amen.''[6]

Malachi 3:16,17

INTRODUCTION TO THE NEW TESTAMENT
The Silence of God—Intertestamental Period

The span between the close of the Old Testament and the opening of the New Testament times is about 400 years. With Nehemiah's historical record and Malachi's prophecy, no voice was heard nor vision seen from heaven until God spoke through an angel to Zacharias, who was to become the father of John the Baptist. This era is called the "Intertestamental Period."

It was at the close of the Old Testament period that the canon of this portion of our Bible was formed. Before Israel's captivity there were only faint traces of the mode of preserving the sacred writings. Moses ordered the "book of the Law" to be put in the "side of the Ark" (Deuteronomy 31:24-26). After the Temple was erected, the Law was kept there (II Kings 22:8). To Moses' writings were subsequently added that of Joshua, and other Annals; and later Proverbs and some prophecies, for Daniel refers to the "Books" (9:2), Zechariah to the "Law and former Prophets" (7:12), and Isaiah to the "Book of the Lord" (29:18; 34:16). Ezra and the "Great Synagogue" most probably determined the canon of the Law in its final shape, and Nehemiah "gathered together the acts of the kings and prophets, and those of David" when "founding a library" for the Second Temple (II Macc. 2:13). This took place ca. 430 B.C.

The first notice of the Old Testament as a collection of sacred writings is in the Prologue to the Greek translation of Ecclesiasticus, ca. 131 B.C., which specifies the "Law and the prophets, and the rest of the books." ("Ecclesiasticus" is not to be confused with the book of Ecclesiastes. This book was written ca. 175 B.C., and is a part of apocryphal literature, known as *Hokmah*, or "Hebrew wisdom literature.") Philo Judaeus (20 B.C.—A.D. 40) refers to the constant use of the "Laws and oracles produced by the prophets, and hymns and other [writings]." Josephus (A.D. 30—100) enumerates twenty-two books as "divine," viz., five of Moses, thirteen of the prophets, and four "hymns and directions of life." He mentions all the books of the Old Testament as canonical, except Job, Proverbs, Ecclesiastes, and the Song of Solomon, to which he does not allude, as none of them furnish any material for his work. He also adds, that, since the death of Artaxerxes (424 B.C.), "no one has dared, up to his day, to add anything to them, to take anything from them, or to make any change in them."

Thus, the Jewish canon was finally settled in the time of Ezra and Nehemiah, and its contents are identical with our own thirty-nine books. They are grouped so as to accord with the twenty-two letters of the Hebrew alphabet—the twelve Minor Prophets counted as one book, Ruth coupled with Judges, Ezra with Nehemiah, Lamentations with Jeremiah, while the two books of Samuel, two of Kings, and two of Chronicles were reckoned as one each. That these did not constitute the entire Hebrew sacred writings is evident from the fact that reference is made in the Old Testament to fifteen other books, while others again are mentioned in the Apocrypha, which were rejected from the Jewish canon. The whole of the books of the Hebrew canon are quoted in the New Testament as "Scripture," except Judges, Ecclesiastes, the Song of Solomon, Ezra, Esther, and Nehemiah. But, in addition, the "prophecy of Enoch" is quoted by Jude (vs. 14). Christ evidently quoted from two unknown sources (Luke 11:49-51; John 7:38), and so, too, James (4:4,5).

As the Old Testament era closed, the Persians, who liberated Israel from Babylonian captivity, were in control of world powers. The Samaritans, a mixed breed of Jews and Assyrians who had come into existence after the fall of the Northern Kingdom of Israel in 722 B.C., had rejected Jerusalem as the seat of worship and erected a temple on Mount Gerazim (ca. 400 B.C.). Those of the remnant of Judah who had intermarried and refused to heed Ezra's and Malachi's pleas to free themselves of these heathen idolaters (Ezra 10:3,19), also refused to return to the pure worship of God and joined in with the Samaritans. A split came between the strict Jews and these "apostates," which resulted in two separate groups—the "Jews" and the "Samaritans." This division was still in existence in Christ's day—"for the Jews have no dealings with the Samaritans" (John 4:9). See SAMARITANS in Index.

In fulfillment of Daniel's prophecy, the Grecians conquered the Persians and became the world ruler. Under Alexander the Great, Grecian culture and language dominated the peoples. When he died, his kingdom was divided among several of his generals. By 168-164 B.C., Antiochus Epiphanes IV, king of Syria, sought to bring the Jews under the sway of Grecian culture and religions. He polluted the Temple in Jerusalem, set up altars and groves, chapels of idols, and sacrificed swine's flesh in the sanctuary. He forbade the Jews to circumcise their children, and added insult to injury by looting the Temple. He vowed to exterminate all Jews. His crimes touched off a rebellion and war under the Maccabeans, who finally liberated Jerusalem and cleansed the Temple.

The Maccabeans, contrary to Levitical law, took to themselves the priesthood. They became more and more engaged in war and politics until the priesthood became corrupted. This paved the way for the rise of many sects which were in existence in Christ's day, one of which was the "Essenes," who hid the famous "Dead Sea Scrolls."* In the meantime, Greece had fallen to the Romans (in 146 B.C.). With the retention of Grecian culture and language, this period became known as "Graeco-Roman." In 63 B.C., Pompey conquered Palestine, and the Jews were under the yoke of the Romans. Rome held sway as a world power until A.D. 476.

Jewish Writings

Many writings came into existence during this period. Some just recently came to light with the discovery of the Dead Sea Scrolls, owned and produced by the sect of the Essenes. These people had settled at the little village of Qumran to avoid persecution of the political priests. The Essenes held themselves to be the "fundamentalists" of their day. Other writings include:

1. *Apochrypha,* a name given to fourteen historical books. These books were never accepted by the Jews as being inspired, and were not in the Hebrew Old Testament canon. Neither were they ever referred to by Christ, nor accepted by any of the New Testament writers and the early church fathers. They were, however, added to the Latin translation in the second century A.D., and included as part of the Scriptures by the Roman Catholics at the Council of Trent in A.D. 1564.

2. The *Targums,* which are renderings of the Old Testament Scriptures in Aramaic when this language became common after Israel's return from captivity in Babylon.

3. The *Talmud,* a compilation of Hebrew civil and ceremonial laws based on the Torah, or Law, of Moses. This writing consisted of the Rabbis' own "interpretation" of these laws, and became known as the "traditions of their fathers" (referred to by Christ in Matthew 15:1-6).

4. The *Septuagint,* a translation of the Hebrew Scriptures into the Greek language. Many Jewish merchants in Alexandria, Egypt (2nd century B.C.), had adopted the Greek language, and requested that their Scriptures be translated into the language they understood. This version not only contributed greatly to a widespread knowledge of the Jewish faith and history where Grecian culture had spread, but was the means of opening to the world at large God's Word in an understandable language.

Another important development in this period was the *Synagogue.* The Synagogue probably had its beginnings in homes of the exiles in Babylon (Ezekiel 8:1; 20:1-3). After the remnant returned from captivity, many Jews were scattered, and could no longer go to Jerusalem for Temple worship. Worship, prayer, instruction in the Scriptures were done in the synagogues in

*See ESSENES in author's book, *A Pictorial Guide to Biblical Archaeology*

practically every town where the Jews lived. They were among the first places where the gospel was proclaimed (Luke 4:15,44; Acts 9:20).

Old and New Testament Groups and Sects

1. The *Samaritans*. See SAMARITANS in Index.
   a. Boasted descent from Jacob: John 4:12
   b. Their true descent: II Kings 17:24; Ezra 4:9,10
   c. Proud and arrogant: Isaiah 9:9
   d. Professed to worship God: Ezra 4:2; John 4:20
   e. Mixed religion with idolatry: I Kings 17:41 with John 4:22
   f. Opposed the Jews after captivity: Nehemiah 4:1-18
   g. Abhorred the Jews: John 4:9; 8:48
   h. More humane than the Jews: Luke 10:33-37
   i. Some expected the Messiah: John 4:25,29
   j. Ready to hear and embrace the gospel: John 4:39-42; Acts 8:4-8
   k. Many churches established in Samaria: Acts 9:31

2. The *Pharisees,* who refused to bow to Antiochus Epiphanes and stood true to the Law, the Prophets, and the Psalms. They were legalistic separatists who, by Christ's time, were mere religionists, relying more upon the traditions of their fathers than they did upon the Scriptures.
   a. A sect of Jews: Acts 15:5
   b. Strictest observers of Mosaic ritual: Acts 26:5
   c. Zealous of the law: Philippians 3:5
   d. Zealous of tradition: Mark 7:3,5-8; Galatians 1:14
   e. Outwardly moral: Luke 18:11; Philippians 3:5,6
   f. Active in proselytizing: Matthew 23:15
   g. Self-righteous: Luke 16:15; 18:9
   h. Fond of public salutations: Matthew 23:7
   i. Fond of distinguished titles: Matthew 23:7-10
   j. Cruel in persecuting: Acts 9:1,2
   k. Made broad their phylacteries: Matthew 23:5
   l. As a body rejected John's baptism: Luke 7:30
   m. Compared to whited sepulchres: Matthew 23:27
   n. Believed in the resurrection: Acts 23:8
   o. Condemned Christ: Matthew 9:11; Luke 7:39; 15:1,2
   p. Tempted Christ: Matthew 16:1
   q. Imputed Christ's miracles to Satan's power: Matthew 9:34; 12:24
   r. Often sought to destroy Christ: Matthew 12:14; John 11:47,53
   s. Sent officers to apprehend Christ: John 7:32,45

3. The *Scribes,* or Lawyers, whose responsibility it was to copy the Scriptures. They often sided with the Pharisees in trying to trap Christ in matters of the Mosaic law. They were more concerned with the "letter" of the law than with its spirit.
   a. Their authority: Judges 5:14
   b. Learned in the Law: Ezra 7:6
   c. Men of great wisdom: I Chronicles 27:32
   d. Were doctors of law: Mark 12:28 with Matthew 22:35
   e. Were interpreters of Scriptures: Matthew 2:4; Mark 12:35
   f. Taught in Moses' seat: Nehemiah 8:2-6
   g. Wore long robes; loved preeminence: Mark 12:38,39
   h. Were frequently Pharisees: Acts 23:9
   i. Tempted Christ: John 18:3
   j. Offended by Christ's teaching: Matthew 21:15; Mark 2:6-17
   k. Their teachings contrasted with Christ's: Matthew 7:29; Mark 1:22

      l. Condemned as hypocrites: Matthew 23:15

      m. Active in procuring Christ's death: Matthew 26:3; Luke 23:10

      n. Persecuted early Christians: Acts 4:5,18,21; 6:12

    4. The *Sadducees,* worldly-minded or rationalistic priests who obeyed the letter of the Law, but conformed to the culture of their day. They hated the Pharisees, but were their allies in opposition to Christ.

      a. A sect of the Jews: Acts 5:17

      b. Denied the resurrection: Matthew 22:23; Luke 20:27 (that's why they were "sad, you see!")

      c. Resurrection caused dispute with Pharisees: Acts 23:6-9

      d. Were refused baptism by John: Matthew 3:7

      e. Tempted Christ: Matthew 16:1

      f. Rebuked and silenced by Christ: Matthew 16:6; 22:34

    5. The *Sanhedrin,* which probably originated in King Jehoshaphat's day (II Chronicles 19:4-11), was a body of seventy elders (judges), presided over by the High Priest. It was the "Supreme Court" in Christ's day, and it judged both civil and religious matters until Jerusalem's fall in A.D. 70. It had the power to pass the death sentence, but not to execute it. This is why they had to appeal to Rome for Christ's crucifixion. Possibly the idea of the number "seventy" could have originated with the seventy elders chosen to stand with Moses (Numbers 11:16,17).

    6. *Political* groups also arose during this period. Two among them were the *Herodians,* who sought to perpetuate the Herods on the throne in Palestine (Mark 3:6), and the *Zealots,* who wanted no foreign power to rule them (Acts 1:13). The Jews hated the Herods because of their relations to the Edomites (descendants of Esau). See IDUMAEA in Index.

    7. *Publicans,* or tax-collectors for the Roman government:

      a. Collected public tax: Luke 5:27

      b. Often guilty of extortion: Luke 3:13; 19:8

      c. Chief publicans were rich: Luke 19:2

      d. Despised by the Jews: Luke 18:11

      e. Classed as infamous characters: Matthew 11:19; 21:23

      f. Often kind and hospitable: Matthew 5:46,47; Luke 5:29

      g. Received John's message and baptism: Matthew 21:32; Luke 3:12

      h. Attended Christ's preaching: Mark 2:15; Luke 15:1

      i. One chosen to be an apostle—Matthew: Matthew 10:3. See NAME in Matthew.

    "Greek learning and culture, Roman law and Roman roads, Jewish monotheism and Jewish synagogues . . . and Jewish apocalyptic and messianic hopes prepared the world for the coming of Christ and Christianity. Divine providence can be traced everywhere in the long interval between the Testaments. The goal was the incarnation and birth of the long awaited Messiah and Savior of the world, prophesied so often in the Old Testament. To this great event all preceding centuries of world history, especially Jewish history, pointed."[1]

    As the 400 silent years came to a close, the "fullness of the time was come, [and] God sent forth His Son, made of a woman, made under the law, to redeem them that were under the law" (Galatians 4:4,5).

Time and Date of Christ's Birth

    Julius Caesar introduced a calendar in 46 B.C. which, while an improvement over the calendars of his day was, nevertheless, off. A civil calendar by A. Exiguus of Rome in the sixth century A.D. was adopted for civil chronology. These two were superseded by the Gregorian calendar in A.D. 1582. Such changes have resulted in errors of time, and it is generally agreed that the birth of Christ, or the beginning of the Christian Era, should be at least four years earlier.

The gospel accounts make it clear that Jesus was born while Herod was still living. According to Josephus, Herod died after an eclipse of the moon, which has been astronomically fixed at March 12,13, 4 B.C., and before the Passover, which fell that year on April 4. His death in 4 B.C. is also affirmed from the beginning of the reigns of his three sons. How old Jesus was when Herod issued the decree for all males two years and under to be slaughtered, no one knows. Herod's timing was such to include a part of a year as one year. It is safe to say that Christ was born the latter part of 5 B.C.

The date accepted by most Christians for Christ's birth is December 25th. This does not mean, however, that Christians the world over are convinced that the Savior was born on this date. The New Testament designates *no* particular day as the date of His birth. There are numerous indications which point to a date *other* than December 25th. We are told, for example, that when Christ was born in Bethlehem, "There was no room in the inn." This could be said only in the seasons of Passover, Pentecost, and Tabernacles, when Jewish pilgrims flocked from all parts of Palestine and lands beyond and took every available accommodation in and near Jerusalem (including Bethlehem—six miles away). These feasts were observed in the spring or autumn, not in the winter.

Weather would be mild at these seasons of feasts, and giving birth to a child in the open or in a stable would not be accompanied with dangers to child and mother as would during the winter months. It is quite conceivable that, if the "blessed event" had happened in the dead of winter, anyone occupying a room would have yielded his room to a woman in such need. Winters then were probably much worse than winters there today (Matthew 24:20). It might be supposed, thinking along these lines, that the Roman government would not have chosen this time of the year for taxation or registration, if such command necessitated long journeys on the part of the people. It would seem that the Nativity took place on a day other than the 25th of mid-winter December. But regardless of the date, it is the Christ of Christmas we celebrate, and not the day.

The Mission of Christ

Jesus Christ was born to die. To say that He came to earth for any other reason is to err. If one will take the time to search the historical records of His life, they will find 55 passages in Matthew, 24 in Mark, 44 in Luke, and 75 in John—all bearing upon the sin problem and the salvation of individuals. Luke, the author of Acts, lists 21 passages along the same line. The student will not find one clear statement suggesting that it was God's program at that time for Christ to overthrow the Roman government and establish the throne of David in Jerusalem. If it had been, then Christ would have been guilty of treason as charged! The New Testament makes it clear with positive statements what His mission was.

1. When Joseph was troubled about Mary being with child, an angel settled his fears, and announced the child's name to be "Jesus, for He shall save His people from their sins" (Matthew 1:21).

2. We are told by an inspired Paul (Galatians 4:4,5) that Christ came at the *exact* appointed time, the "fulness of time" to accomplish *one* thing—namely, the redemption of sinners. This fulfilled the prophecy God made to Satan (Genesis 3:15). Paul also stated that this was what the gospel was all about—the death, burial, and resurrection of Christ *according* to the Scriptures (I Corinthians 15:3,4), and that His death was for the purpose of producing a glorious church (Ephesians 5:25-27). Peter tells us that Christ's death was to bring us nigh to God (I Peter 3:18), and John states that He was "manifested to destroy" or undo what the devil had done (I John 3:8).

3. Simeon, a just, devout man, waiting for the "consolation of Israel" (the coming of Messiah), was assured that he would not see death until he had seen the Lord's Christ. When he

saw Him and took Him in his arms, he said, "Mine eyes have seen the salvation of the Lord, which Thou hast prepared for *all* people" (Luke 2:25-32). Anna, the prophetess, "spake of Him to all that looked for *redemption* in Jerusalem" (Luke 2:36-38). Anyone sufficiently acquainted with the Old Testament Scriptures, as these two were, knew that Messiah's first coming was for redemption and not for physical deliverance. They affirmed their knowledge by recognizing the babe Christ as such.

4. "We see Jesus, who was made a little lower than the angels for the suffering of death" (Hebrews 2:9). "And being found in fashion as a man . . . became obedient unto death, even the death of the cross" (Philippians 2:5-8).

5. At the age of twelve we find Christ "about His father's business" (Luke 2:49). Was not His Father's business the fulfillment of all that had been prophesied relating to His coming—virgin born—and to have laid upon Him the iniquity of us all? This was God's will for Him (Hebrews 10:4-10).

6. At the introduction of His earthly ministry by John the Baptist, He was presented as "the Lamb of God who taketh away the sin of the world" (John 1:29). In the redemptive plan of God, He was the Lamb slain from before the foundation of the world" (Revelation 13:8).

7. When Christ returned from His temptation experience in the wilderness, He taught in the Synagogue. In Nazareth He stood up to read, and from the book of Isaiah He showed them exactly where He stood in their prophecies. He was the *predicted* Messiah to preach the gospel to the poor, to heal the sick and brokenhearted, to preach deliverance of those captive to sin, to preach the acceptable year of the Lord (Luke 4:14-19 with Isaiah 61:1,2a). He stopped at "the acceptable year of the Lord," which is related to His first advent of "grace and truth." He did not finish the second verse—"the day of vengeance of our God," which related to His second coming. There *is* no room here for offering to restore the Davidic kingdom at this time.

8. Christ Himself made clear His mission from the very first when He referred to His body as the Temple of God (John 2:18-22). "As Moses lifted up the serpent in the wilderness, even so must the Son of Man be lifted up" (John 3:14). "I am He [Messiah]" (John 4:25,26). "The Son of Man is come to seek and to save the lost" (Matthew 18:11; Luke 9:10). "The Son of man came not to be ministered unto [as a king], but to minister, and to give His life a ransom for many" (Matthew 20:28). He constantly foretold His death (Matthew 12:40; 16:21; 17:22,23; Mark 8:31; 9:31; Luke 9:22,44; 18:31-33; John 12:23-33).

9. The testimony of Matthew was to prepare the Jewish mind for Messiah. During the "Silence of God" the Jews (Pharisees, Sadducees, etc.) had made the Word of God of no effect through their traditions and commandments of men (Mark 7:3,7,8,13). Matthew quoted 120 references from twenty books of the Old Testament, often using the phrase, "that it might be fulfilled." He does not present a different gospel or a different kingdom, but uses a different emphasis and terminology suitable to the Jews. The "kingdom" parables (ch. 13) and the Sermon on the Mount (chs. 5—7) can only apply to conditions in the present age of grace and could not be applied to the earthly kingdom. One would not pray—"Thy kingdom come"—if it were already here! Matthew's recording of statements bearing on our Lord's earthly mission are clear and direct. He came to—

    a. Save from sin: 1:21
    b. Send the Holy Spirit and fire: 3:11,12
    c. To fulfill the Law: 5:17
    d. To call sinners to repentance: 9:10-13
    e. Not to send peace but a sword: 10:34
    f. To reveal the Father: 11:27
    g. To save the Gentiles: 12:18
    h. To build His Church: 16:18
    i. To seek and save the lost: 18:11

j. To give His life a ransom for many: 20:28

k. Make remission for sins: 26:28

While it is true that the twelve were first sent out by Jesus to the "lost sheep of the house of Israel" and not in the way of the Gentiles, it must be remembered that He came unto His own first, and the message of the twelve was to the "*lost* sheep" (Matthew 10:5-7). "Lost sheep" need only *one* message—the same that both John the Baptist and Christ preached—"Repent, for the kingdom of heaven is at hand" and "the time is fulfilled, and the kingdom of God is at hand: repent ye, and believe the gospel" (Matthew 3:2; Mark 1:14,15). Not only do "lost sheep" need one message, they need one thing—*salvation,* which comes through repentance, belief in, and acceptance of the gospel.

The terms "kingdom of heaven" and "kingdom of God" are used interchangeably by the gospel writers (Matthew 13:3-11 with Luke 8:4-10). While there are those who insist that John the Baptist preached the "gospel of the kingdom" and not the "gospel of grace," Mark tells us that the gospel of Jesus Christ *began* with John's crying in the wilderness (1:1-3). Luke tells us that "beginning with John the kingdom of *God* was preached" (16:16), and John states that "grace and truth" followed the Mosaic dispensation.

True, Matthew *does* term it the "gospel of the kingdom" (4:23). Some tell us that miracles accompanied this gospel and not the "gospel of the grace of God." Paul, by miracles, testified to the "word of His grace," even among Gentiles (Acts 13:7-12; 14:3). Throughout the years of his ministry he "fully preached the gospel" with mighty signs and wonders (Romans 15:18,19). The *same* gospel that was preached to the Jews only was the gospel that was taken to the whole wide world (Acts 10:34-37,42; 13:23-26,46-48).

10. After Lazarus was raised from the dead, the chief priests and Pharisees questioned what they should do with Jesus because of His popularity. One of them, Caiaphas, being the high priest that same year, said, "Ye know nothing at all, nor consider that it is expedient for us, that one man should die for the people, and that the whole nation perish not. And this he spake not of himself: but . . . prophesied that Jesus should die for that nation; and not for that nation only, but that also He should gather together in one the children of God that were scattered abroad" (John 11:47-52).

11. The prophets of old "prophesied of the grace that should come," testifying "beforehand the suffering of Christ, and the glory that should *follow*" (I Peter 1:10,11). This is precisely what Christ told the two on the road to Emmaus who thought His first coming was for an earthly kingdom—"O fools, and slow of heart to believe all that the prophets have spoken: Ought not Christ to have suffered these things, and to enter into His glory?" (Luke 24:13-27).

12. That Christ recognized Himself as King at His *second* coming is seen in His answer to the disciples' question: "What shall be the sign of Thy coming?" (Matthew 24:3). Christ's answer was: "When the Son of Man shall come in glory, and all the holy angels with Him, *then* shall he sit upon the throne of His glory: And before Him shall be gathered all nations . . . Then shall the *King* say unto them . . ." (Matthew 25:31-41).

His first coming was *not* the time, or the conditions, for the establishment of the Davidic throne (Ezekiel 37:21-25; Zechariah 12:1-10). The world stage was strangely set for His first coming. Morally and religiously it was at its lowest ebb. He came "in the fullness of God's time," at a time that would bring Him to the Cross at the Passover of a certain year. Every misunderstanding of Him by the Jews, every plot of the leaders to strike at Him before His hour, brought Him one step closer to that hour. He was rejected of the Jews, not because He sought kingly power over them, but "because He made Himself the Son of God" (John 19:7), and because "He made Himself equal with God" (John 5:18). One of the Savior's last assertions was that had He set out to establish a throne; no power on earth could have prevented it (John 18:36,37). While admitting to Pilate that He was a king, it is plain to see that He was King of a spiritual kingdom—"the kingdom of heaven"—"the kingdom of God," consisting of those who had repented and believed the gospel.

Anyone familiar with Scripture must conclude that Christ's first coming was for Him to be God's salvation for a lost and dying world—that He was born to die. "This is a faithful saying and worthy of all acceptation, that Christ Jesus came into the world to save sinners" (I Timothy 1:15), that "they might have [eternal] life" (John 10:10). To this end He came. He refused to be a "pre-Calvary millennialist" when the people tried to make Him a king (John 6:15), and on schedule He was "delivered by the determinate counsel and foreknowledge of God . . . and by wicked hands [was] crucified and slain" (Acts 2:22). He will come again as King—this time, not to die, but with power and majesty, to reign over the kingdoms of the earth (Matthew 24:30; Hebrews 9:28). He was the Lamb slain from before the foundation of the world (Revelation 13:8) who came to suffer *first,* and *then* to enter into His glory (Luke 24:26). See WHY CHRIST CAME in Index.

Names of Christ

1. *Jesus.* In the gospel records He is called "Jesus," His *personal* name by birth into the world (Matthew 1:21; Luke 1:31). Its basic meaning is "Savior—salvation" (He saves, delivers, makes free, makes safe). It also speaks of reproach, suffering, and shame (Acts 5:40,41). It is the New Testament equivalent of "Joshua" (See NAME in Joshua). This precious name occurs nearly 700 times in the New Testament; over 600 times in the gospels alone. We account for the infrequent use of this peerless name in the Epistles due to the *new* position of Jesus as risen and exalted. "Christ Jesus" or "Jesus Christ" is the name used in the Epistles for this new position of exaltation and glorification. These titles are used upwards of 200 times. "Jesus" alone is used about 40 times in the Epistles.

2. *Christ.* This is the Greek word for the Hebrew "Messiah," meaning "anointed." This title occurs about 50 times in the gospels as compared to about 300 times in the Epistles. "Christ" is an official designation, or title, and is usually written with the article prefixed as *"the Christ."*

When Jesus said to His disciples—"whom say ye that I am?" Peter replied, "Thou art *the Christ,* the Son of *the* living God" (Matthew 16:15,16). See CHRIST in Dictionary of Names.

3. *Jesus Christ.* This double title appears but five or six times in the gospels, but is frequently used by Paul, Peter, and John in their Letters. The lowly humbled Man on the earth, *Jesus,* is now the exalted and glorified Man in the heavens, *Christ.* What He *was* as "Jesus," and what He *is* as "Christ" combined, give the force of this title. The sufferings of earth and the glories of heaven are thus wonderously linked in the divine order of the names "Jesus Christ."

4. *Christ Jesus.* "Jesus Christ" is a title common enough in all the Epistles, but "Christ Jesus" is almost wholly confined to Paul. The Apostles and writers of the New Testament were converted when Jesus was on earth, all but Paul, whose first acquaintance with the Savior was made with Christ in *the glory* (Acts 9:3-6), hence they and he speak of Jesus as they knew Him. In this way we account for the rare occurrence of Paul's favorite title, "Christ Jesus." Peter, John, and others *first* knowing Jesus on earth, speak and write of Him as "Jesus Christ," while Paul, *first* knowing Jesus in glory, uses the expressive title "Christ Jesus." This title is not found in any of the gospel accounts.

5. *Lord Jesus Christ.* This is the full written title of our blessed Savior, connecting His *authority* (Lord) with His *manhood* (Jesus) and *glory* (Christ). Thus His power is indissolubly linked with His humanity and present exaltation (Matthew 28:18).

6. *Son of God.* This grand Divine title is neither official nor is it dispensational, but one of personal and moral glory. John the revealer of Divine mysteries, emphasizes this title. It is upon the glory of Christ's person *(Son of the living God)* that Christ builds His church. Paul,

too, in accord with this double ministry received of the Lord the *gospel and the church* (Colossians 1:23-26), and "straightway preached that Jesus is the Son of God" (Acts 9:20). The Divine glory of that name and person formed the ground of all his gospel preaching and church testimony. The Divine and heavenly glory of the "Son" is needed for church foundation, church blessing, and church glory, and also as a basis, solid and imperishable, on which our individual salvation rests. The Divine glory of the "Son" for the gathering, blessing, character and moral likeness of the family in the Father's house are the happy themes of John, who, himself, reposing on the bosom of his Master, knew something of the intimacies of the heart of God.

7. *Son of Man.* Ezekiel and Daniel, prophets of the captivity, found their sphere of ministry *outside* Israel, used this title, "Son of Man." Christ, who came to His own and was rejected by them, found Himself *outside,* and applies this title "Son of Man" to Himself. By His use of it, He oversteps the narrow and circumscribed limits of Judaism, and instead of a glory filling Immanuel's land merely, the scene widens, for the dominion of the "Son of Man" embraces the heavens and earth, and instead of a glory skirting the coasts of Judea, the *whole* earth becomes lightened with His glory under this name and character. Universal dominion and absolute sovereignty are glories resting upon this exceedingly interesting title, one in which every human being is concerned, for universal judgment and authority to exercise that judgment are referred to the "Son of Man" (John 12:23-48; Acts 17:31). As "Son of Man" He comes in glory to Israel (Matthew 24:30), and to the Gentiles or living nations on the earth whom He gathers before His throne of glory (Matthew 25:31,32); then He will bring in universal blessing and righteous rule (Matthew 13:41-43).

It is interesting to note that while the title "Son of Man" occurs in the gospels about 80 times, it is only directly applied by the Lord to Himself; it is not once (in the gospels) applied by others to Him. It is used by Stephen upon his death (Acts 7:56), and by John in the Revelation (1:3; 14:14). It is possible that occasionally the title stresses Jesus' humility, but the widespread teaching that "Son of Man" expresses His humanity just as "Son of God" expresses His deity, is misleading (see Luke 22:69,70).

8. *Son of David.* This title is found in the synoptical gospels 14 times (8 in Matthew, 3 in Mark, 3 in Luke, and none in John). This title is more confined in its application than the broader and more comprehensive one, "Son of Man." The former has Judea in its range and the Jews as its subjects of blessing; while the latter has earth as its sphere and mankind in general as the subject of its exercise.

God has been pleased to reveal Himself in four general relationships. For additional relationships, see NAMES in Dictionary of Names.

   a. To creation as *God*
   b. To Israel as *Jehovah*
   c. To the patriarchs as *God Almighty*
   d. To Christians as *Father*

There is also a fourfold relationship of the Sonship of Christ:

   a. *Son of God*—title of personal and Divine glory
   b. *Son of the Father*—expressing the ever-abiding relationship of the Son to the Father
   c. *Son of Man*—righteous and gracious ruler over the millennial earth
   d. *Son of David*—the fulfiller of every glorious promise and prediction of His ancient people

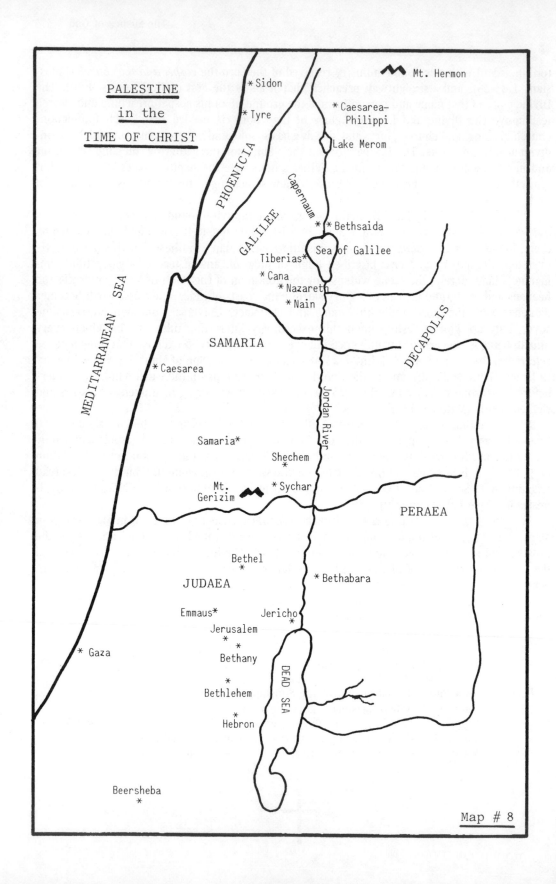

PALESTINE
in the
TIME OF CHRIST

* Sidon

* Tyre

Mt. Hermon

* Caesarea-
  Philippi

Lake Merom

PHOENICIA

Capernaum

GALILEE

* * Bethsaida

Sea of Galilee

Tiberias *

* Cana

* Nazareth

* Nain

MEDITARRANEAN SEA

SAMARIA

* Caesarea

DECAPOLIS

Jordan River

Samaria *

Shechem
*

Mt.
Gerizim

* Sychar

PERAEA

Bethel
*

JUDAEA

* Bethabara

Emmaus *

Jericho
*

Jerusalem
* *

* Gaza

Bethany

DEAD SEA

*

Bethlehem

*

Hebron

Beersheba
*

Map # 8

Part Two

THE NEW TESTAMENT

Subject: Redemption as accomplished through the Person and work of Jesus Christ: Hebrews 9:24-28.

Purpose: To make us wise unto salvation and service, and to reveal to us what God has done *for* us and *with* us in Christ that we might be conformed to the image of His dear Son: II Timothy 3:15; Ephesians 2:8-10; Galatians 3:13; Ephesians 2:5,6; Romans 8:28,29. The Old Testament reveals human need. The New Testament supplies that need.

In the gospel accounts we have revealed Christ's gospel of redemption which is provided through His death, burial, and resurrection. The book of Acts is the promulgation of this gospel to the world. In the Epistles this gospel is exposed in its doctrinal and practical aspects, and in the Revelation of John all of God's redemptive purposes are culminated for all time.

The New Testament has:

27 Books

260 Chapters

7,959 Verses

181,253 Words

838,380 Letters

The Language of the New Testament

It is often argued by critics of the Bible that the New Testament was written in a style which no literary man of that time would have permitted himself to use. Since the New Testament is written in *Koine* Greek (the vernacular), and not in the classical Greek of that day, scholars had a field day ridiculing its authority.

While excavating in ancient Tebtunis (southern Egypt) in 1899, B. P. Grenfell and A. S. Hunt discovered a sacred crocodile cemetery. In disgust, a workman flung a mummified crocodile against a rock. Out popped some papyrus. Other crocodiles were opened, and it was discovered that they had been stuffed with papyri to help hold their shape. All kinds of documents were included in these finds, including ancient classics, royal ordinances, petitions, contracts, accounts, private letters, and for the most part, these papyri were dated to the first and second centuries A.D. Before the papyri were found nobody had ever read a manuscript of a first century scribe that had been written in the language of the common people of Egypt and Palestine. It must be remembered that Greek was the universal language of the Roman empire. Among these papyri were some Bible texts one hundred years earlier than any other manuscripts on the New Testament known at that time.

In making a study of these papyri, it was discovered that they were written in the same exact language of the New Testament. The New Testament books were written in the dialect of the middle class in the vernacular of the home and shop. They were written by both the learned and unlearned to working men in the tongue of the working man—its authors freely using the colloquialisms and even the solecisms of the market places. "It meant that Wycliffe only did for England what Matthew, Mark, etc., etc., did for the Roman world. Christianity from its beginning spoke the tongue of the peasant." It is no wonder then that the "common people heard Him gladly" (Mark 12:37). See ARCHAEOLOGY in Luke.

Books of the New Testament
DIVISION I
The Four Gospels

Subject: The history of the birth, life, ministry, death, resurrection, and ascension of Jesus Christ: Matthew 1:18-25; John 1:4; Luke 19:10; Matthew 20:28; John 19:16-18; Mark 16:6,19.

Purpose: To reveal how God accomplished the work of redemption, and to give us a foundation for the doctrines in the Epistles: Romans 4:25; Galatians 4:4-6.

> Matthew—the *Teachings* of Christ
> Mark—the *Works* of Christ
> Luke—the *Parables* of Christ
> John—the *Conversations* of Christ

Why Four Gospel Accounts[2]

"The question has often been raised as to why we have four gospel accounts instead of one. It is a proper question, for the Spirit of God has done nothing at random in producing the Scriptures, and the answer to our question is to be found therein. In the Tabernacle which Moses set up in the wilderness, and in the Temple which afterwards replaced the Tabernacle, the Holy of Holies where God dwelt was separated from the other parts of the structure by a great veil or curtain. This veil always remained closed, barring the way of approach to God's presence, except on the annual Day of Atonement, when the High Priest entered with blood for his own sins and the sins of the people.

"This veil, according to the testimony of Scripture itself, was a type of Jesus Christ in His manifestation as Son of Man and Son of God, the living Word, who became flesh and dwelt among men. When He was crucified on Calvary, the veil of the Temple was rent in twain from the top to the bottom, thus signifying that by His death the way into God's presence is open to all who come unto God by Him. Under the old covenant it would have been sure death to enter the Holy of Holies, but now it is sure death to remain without (Hebrews 10:19-22).

"All this makes the veil very interesting to us, for it is, in a figure, the person of Christ. The veil was hung upon *four* pillars of shittim wood overlaid with gold. There were *four* sockets of silver for the pillars, and the veil was attached to the pillars by hooks of gold. Upon the veil were embroidered figures of cherubim, and because the veil itself is a type of Christ in the flesh, we assume that the cherubim must have some definite relation to Him. There were also other cherubim with outstretched wings overshadowing the mercy-seat within the Holy of Holies, and it was here, between the cherubim, that God appeared 'in the cloud upon the mercy-seat.' The cherubim appear elsewhere in Scripture, and always in connection with the manifestation of the glory of God. In Ezekiel and Revelation the cherubim are seen as *four* living creatures. John saw them 'in the midst of the throne, and round about the throne.' The first living creature was like a lion, the second like a calf (or ox), the third had a face as a man, and the fourth was like a flying eagle.

"We have here doubtless the answer to our question as to the reason for *four* gospel accounts instead of one, and the key to the interpretation to the four. For just as the *four* living creatures are typical of our Lord Jesus Christ, showing forth the glory of God, so the four gospel accounts are *four* representations of Christ as He lived and walked among men, revealing the glory of His Father. In *Matthew* He is seen in one aspect of His ministry as the 'Lion of the tribe of Judah,' King of the Jews. In *Mark* He is shown as the devoted Servant, toiling as an ox according to the Father's will. In *Luke* He appears as the Son of Man, the representative of lost men, bearing their sins. And *John* describes Him as the Son of God who, like a 'flying eagle,' came down from heaven and returned to heaven the eternal God incarnate.

"We shall expect to find marked differences in the structure and contents of these four books, and yet they have a common testimony, revealing the light of the knowledge of the glory of God in the face of Jesus Christ, even as the four living creatures rested not day and night, saying, 'Holy, Holy, Holy, Lord God Almighty, which was, and is, and is to come' (Revelation 4:8).

"*Four* is the earthly number, as the 'four corners of the earth,' the four winds, the four seasons. It is the number of the world as the place of trial. These four gospel accounts reveal our Lord Jesus under test, and shown to be the true and faithful Witness, the spotless Lamb, who need not die for Himself but for our sins.

"These four gospel accounts are divided into *three* and *one*. Matthew, Mark, and Luke form the synoptic group (synoptic meaning 'to see the whole together, to make a comprehensive view'). These three accounts emphasize Christ's humanity. John stands by itself in that he emphasizes Christ's Deity. The first three are represented by earthly creatures—the lion, the ox, and the man. The last is typified by a bird of the heavens. Taken together, these records show unto us God, manifested in the flesh."

Arrangement of the Gospels

No one is of the opinion that the arrangement of the books of the Bible is inspired, yet it is a historical fact that godly men supervised the arrangement of both the Old and New Testament canon. The New Testament, like the old, is not arranged chronologically. Why then the order as we have it—especially the order of the gospel accounts?

The Jews had been entrusted with the "sacred oracles of God" (Romans 3:2). The coming of Messiah was chiefly a Jewish subject. Since Matthew is filled with Old Testament quotations, it would seem logical to introduce the New Testament with a book that placed such emphasis on the Old Testament Scriptures. It is like opening the New Testament door with an Old Testament key. An Old Testament reader would be in familiar territory in the book of Matthew. The genealogy that Matthew gives shows Christ as the son of David, the son of Abraham, two of the most familiar persons to the Jews. It also contains more of the teachings of Christ than the other gospel accounts, and would enable the reader to become familiar more readily with what Christ had to say about His mission.

Possibly Mark was placed second because he jumps right into Christ's earthly ministry as a Servant, revealing that He had a job to do—a purpose to fulfill—not to be ministered unto, but to minister, and give His life for a ransom for many (10:45).

Luke might be third because his genealogy ends with Mary, the virgin who bore the man-Christ—the Son of Man who came to seek and to save man—to be identified with man.

John could be last because the emphasis is placed on the Deity of Christ—that all the Old Testament prophecies which relate to His coming, to His mission, rest upon the fact that Christ was God.

There is one further item of interest regarding the *Four Gospels*. There are a total of 89 chapters in these accounts. Four deal with the first 30 years of Christ's life, and 85 deal with the last three years. Yet 27 of these chapters deal with the last 8 days of His life. The reader readily observes that the last days of His life are more important than the first 30 years. The emphasis, of course, is on His death, burial, and resurrection, which provided the main theme for the apostles in that book of Acts and the foundation for the doctrines of the church that we have in the Epistles.

Matthew—The Book of Christ, the King

Name: Matthew means "the gift of God." He was a Galillean Jew; also called Levi (Mark 2:14; Luke 5:27-29). He resided at Capernaum where he was a publican or tax-collector, under the Romans. This was an office of bad repute among the Jews, partly because of the covetous exactions of those who were appointed to it, and partly because it was a proof of their being subject to a foreign power. Publicans were of two classes: general receivers of whom Zacchaeus was one (Luke 19:2), and collectors of the ordinary taxes, of whom Matthew was one (Luke 5:27). While engaged in tax collecting, Matthew was called by our Lord (Matthew 9:9). See PUBLICANS in Index.

Matthew was an eyewitness of Christ's earthly ministry, and continued with the rest of the apostles till after the ascension of Christ. Little is known of him after this event. It is related that for eight years he preached the gospel in Judaea, and then went to spread the faith of Christ among the Gentiles, laboring to evangelize Ethiopia, Persia, and Parthia. At length he suffered martyrdom in Ethiopia ca. A.D. 62.

Contents: This book is a divinely inspired account of the birth, life, ministry, death, resurrection, and ascension of Jesus of Nazareth, the Messiah of Jewish prophecy. The Jews in general believed that Christ was to be Messiah, but did not accept Jesus as the Christ. Matthew sought to present Jesus as the Christ. His genealogy is different from Luke's. Matthew gave the kingly line, showing Christ as the son of David. Isaiah asked the question: "Who shall declare His generation?" (53:8). Matthew answered, and proved most conclusively that this virgin-born Jesus had every right to David's throne. See GENEALOGIES in Index.

Sometime after His birth He was recognized as King of the Jews by the wise men. Their coming to Christ is not related to the visit of the shepherds. The shepherds visited Him immediately after His birth—finding "the *babe*" in a manger (Luke 2:11,12). The wise men arrived when Christ was a "young *child*" (2:11). This was, no doubt, before He was two years old, because after their visit an angel led Joseph to take the young child and His mother to Egypt to escape Herod's decree (2:13-16). Herod was of an Edomite family. The Edomites, descendents of Esau, had an unholy hatred for the Jews because they never forgave Jacob and his descendents for receiving the inheritance that Esau was to have received. This could explain why Herod sought to kill all males under two years, which would have included "the king of the Jews," and also why the Jews had such hatred for Herod.

At the outset of His earthly ministry He showed His power to rule in His defeat of Satan in the wilderness, by giving some of His disciples power over diseases and demons, and by His authorative teachings. His "Sermon on the Mount" revealed His kingdom as a spiritual one. He elevated Moses' law to include the spiritual as well as the moral, and condemned Jewish traditions and interpretations. This certainly was not the kind of "kingdom" the Jews had looked for, nor the kind of king they would enthrone. His miracles confirmed His Deity and His truths elevated Him above all other teachers, to the end that the Jews began to openly rebel. He denounced their hypocrisy, foretold His death and resurrection by wicked hands, and predicted Jerusalem's downfall and the destruction of the Temple.

With the betrayal of Christ by Judas, which set the stage for His trial before Pilate and His ultimate death on the Cross, Matthew concludes with an empty tomb—a resurrected Christ—and His commission to preach the gospel to all nations. His Book contains 28 chapters, 1,071 verses, and 23,684 words.

As compared with the other gospel accounts, Matthew alone records:
1. The descent of Christ through Joseph: 1:16
2. The coming of the wise men: 2:1-12

3. The flight into Egypt: 2:13-15
4. Murder of the children: 2:16-18
5. Christ's return to Nazareth: 2:19-23
6. The Pharisees and the Sadducees to see John the Baptist: 3:7
7. Sermon on the Mount: chs. 5—7
8. Two blind men cured: 9:27-31
9. Dumb spirit cast out: 9:32,33
10. Invitation to rest and take Christ's yoke: 11:28-30
11. Sick healed in Jerusalem: 14:14
12. Peter walking on water: 14:28-31
13. Tribute money taken from fish: 17:24-27
14. Denunciation of the Pharisees: ch. 23
15. The betrayal price: 26:15
16. Return of the 30 pieces of silver: 27:3-10
17. Dream of Pilate's wife: 27:19
18. Resurrected saints: 27:52
19. Roman watch at Christ's tomb: 27:64-66
20. Earthquake at Christ's resurrection: 28:2
21. Bribing of soldiers: 28:11-15
22. The "Great Commission": 28:18-20
23. See PARABLES Peculiar to Matthew, p. 387

Character: Historical.

Subject: The teachings (discourses) of Christ.

Purpose: To prove that Jesus is *the* Christ, the son of David, the son of Abraham. The opening verse connects Christ with the two most important Old Testament covenants—the Davidic and Abrahamic.

Outline:
    I. The Infancy of the King: 1,2
    II. The Manifestation of the King: 3,4
    III. The Proclamation of the King: 5—7
    IV. The Authority of the King: 8:1—9:34
    V. The Ministry of the King: 9:35—12:50
    VI. The Mystery Reign of the King: 13:1-50
  VII. The Rejection of the King: 13:53—23:39
 VIII. The Prophecy of the King: 24,25
    IX. The Trial and Death of the King: 26,27
    X. The Resurrection and Commission of the King: 28

Scope: The events recorded by Matthew cover a period of about 34 years.

Writer: The church has always credited this first gospel account to Matthew the publican, one of Christ's twelve apostles. No one has ever proved that he did not write it. Some have asserted that he copied his from Mark, but this is unlikely since Matthew, as a tax collector, was good at keeping detailed accounts of events.

To Whom Written: Very probably Greek-speaking Jews, for he finds it necessary to interpret words like "Emmanual" (1:23), "Golgotha" (27:33), and Christ's prayer on the Cross (27:46). That his gospel account had appeal to Gentiles is found in the account of Gentile wise men making a visit at Christ's birth (2:1-12), the healing of a Gentile (8:5), Gentiles to be included in His kingdom (8:11; 21:43), Christ's coming to call sinners (Jews and Gentiles) to repentance and His invitation for *all* to come to Him for rest (9:10-13; 11:28), Christ's showing judgment to the Gentiles (12:18), and Gentiles (all nations) included in the "Great Commission" (28:18-20).

When and Where Written: Matthew has been assigned various dates. It would be safe to say it was written about A.D. 60. The place of its writing is unknown. Early in the second century, Ignatius of Antioch, referred to Matthew as "the gospel."

Key Chapter: 16, which contains Peter's confession of Christ.

Key Verse: 1:1, "The book of the generation . . ." Only once before does this expression occur: "The book of the generation of [the first] Adam" (Genesis 5:1). Matthew records the generation of the "last Adam," the son of David, the son of Abraham (I Corinthians 15:21,22,45).

Key Words:
1. King (Christ as), which occurs 5 times.
2. Kingdom, which occurs 50 times.

Key Phrase: That it might be fulfilled: 1:22.

Key Thought: Christ's Ministry: 20:28.

Spiritual Thought: Repent.

Christ Is Seen As: King of the Jews: 2:2.

Names and Titles of Christ. See NAME in Dictionary.
1. Jesus Christ: 1:1
2. The Son of David: 1:1; 9:27
3. The Son of Abraham: 1:1
4. Jesus: 1:21
5. Emmanuel: 1:23
6. King of the Jews: 2:2; 27:11,37
7. Governor: 2:6
8. A Nazarene: 2:23; 26:71
9. The Lord: 3:3; 7:21
10. My beloved Son: 3:17; 17:5
11. The Son of God: 4:6; 8:29
12. Master: 8:19; 23:8
13. Son of Man: 8:20
14. Friend of sinners: 11:19
15. The Son: 11:27
16. Lord of the Sabbath: 12:8
17. The Servant of God: 12:18a
18. My Beloved: 12:18b
19. Greater than Jonah: 12:41
20. Greater than Solomon: 12:42
21. Our elder Brother: 12:50
22. The Sower: 13:3,37
23. The Christ, the Son of the living God: 16:16
24. Jesus the Christ: 16:20
25. Good Master: 19:16
26. A Ransom: 20:28
27. King: 21:5; 25:34
28. Prophet of Nazareth: 21:11
29. The Heir: 21:38
30. This Stone: 21:44
31. The Bridegroom: 25:10
32. The risen Lord: 28:6

Names and Titles of God. See NAME in Dictionary.
1. Lord: 2:15,19
2. Lord thy God: 4:7; 22:37

3. Father: 5:16 (used 43 times in Matthew)
4. Our Father: 6:9
5. Heavenly Father: 6:26; 15:13
6. Lord of heaven and earth: 11:25
7. The living God: 16:16
8. Certain Householder: 21:33
9. God of Abraham, Isaac, and Jacob: 22:32a
10. God of the living: 22:32b

Names and Titles of the Holy Spirit: See NAME in Dictionary.

1. Holy Ghost: 1:20; 3:11
2. Spirit of God: 3:16; 12:28
3. The Spirit: 4:1
4. Spirit of your Father: 10:20
5. My Spirit: 12:18

Prophecy Fulfilled in Christ: See p. 471.

1. Destruction of the Temple: 24:1,2 with Mark 13:1,2; Luke 21:5,6,20-24

Stated: A.D. 29 *Fulfilled:* A.D. 70

This prophecy of Christ regarding the destruction of the Temple includes the city of Jerusalem as well (see DESTRUCTION, P. 387). Because of Jewish rebellion against Roman rule, Vespasian and his army had routed the Jews in Jericho and the little village of Qumran in A.D. 68-69. The Essenes, who hid the Dead Sea Scrolls, lived at Qumran. Vespasian became Emperor of Rome and his son, Titus, took his place in Palestine. It was he who fulfilled Christ's prophecy. The city was razed, the Temple destroyed, and Josephus tells us that 600,000 Jews were slaughtered in the city's fall.

The Arch of Titus in Rome, erected in A.D. 82 to commemorate Jerusalem's downfall, shows the Roman soldiers making their triumphal entry into the city on one side, and their carrying the trumpets of the priests, the table of showbread, and the seven-branched candlestick from the Temple on the other side.

Christ predicted in the destruction of the Temple that "there shall not be left here one stone upon another that shall not be thrown down" (24:2). In war, buildings were usually burned or walls would crumble from the force of battering rams. But always some foundation stones were left standing. Was Christ's prophecy literally fulfilled? Yes. In many important buildings, especially temples, the stones were held together with metal bars, usually gold and/or silver. The bars were bent and fitted into grooves and holes. We use mortar today. The soldiers of Titus knew of this method of construction, and they also knew that "to the victor belongs the spoils." To get to this precious metal, which would be money in their pockets, they literally took each stone from off the other, thus fulfilling Christ's prophecy.

"Judaea Capta" coins were minted by the Romans in honor of Jerusalem's downfall and the dispersion of the Jews. Read Deuteronomy 28:63-68.

2. The sign of Christ's coming—wars, rumors of wars, earthquakes, false Christs, the days of Noah, etc.: 24:3-26,37-44. See SIGNS in Index.

Stated: A.D. 29 *Fulfilled:* In the process

3. Great tribulation: 24:27-29
4. Christ's return to earth as King: 24:30,31
5. Judgment of the nations: 25:31-46

Stated: A.D. 29 *Fulfilled:* Yet future

Spoils from Temple

Temple Stone

"Judea Capta" Coin

MIRACLES
OR
UNUSUAL EVENTS

1. Peculiar to Matthew:
    a. Two blind men cured: 9:27-31
    b. Dumb spirit cast out: 9:32,33
    c. Sick healed in Jerusalem: 14:14
    d. Peter walking on water: 14:29
    e. Tribute money provided from a fish: 17:24-27
2. Common to Matthew and Mark:
    a. Healing in Galilee: 9:35; Mark 6:5,6
b. Syrophenician's daughter healed: 15:21-28; Mark 7:24-30
c. Multitudes healed in Galilee: 15:29-31; Mark 7:31-37
d. The 4000 fed: 15:32-39; Mark 8:1-9
e. Fig tree cursed: 21:18-21; Mark 11:13

3. Common to Matthew and Luke:
   a. Centurion's servant healed: 8:5-13; Luke 7:1-10
   b. Blind and dumb demoniac healed: 12:22; Luke 11:14
4. Common to Matthew, Mark, Luke:
   a. Leper cleansed: 8:1-4; Mark 1:40; Luke 5:12-14
   b. Peter's mother-in-law healed: 8:14-17; Mark 1:29-31; Luke 4:38-41
   c. Stilling the waves: 8:23-27; Mark 4:36-41; Luke 8:22-25
   d. Demoniac cured: 8:28-33; Mark 5:1-20; Luke 8:26-40
   e. Palsied man healed: 9:1,2, Mark 2:3; Luke 5:18
   f. Jairus' daughter healed: 9:18-25; Mark 5:23; Luke 8:41
   g. Woman's blood issue healed: 9:20; Mark 5:25; Luke 8:43
   h. Withered hand healed on Sabbath: 12:9-13; Mark 3:1-6; Luke 6:6-11
   i. Transfiguration: 17:1-8; Mark 9:2-9; Luke 9:28-36
   j. Lunatic healed: 17:14-18; Mark 9:14-29; Luke 9:37-43
   k. Blind men cured: 20:29-34; Mark 10:46-52; Luke 18:35-43
5. Common to Matthew, Mark, and John:
   a. Walking on water: 14:22-27; Mark 6:48; John 6:19
6. Common to Matthew, Mark, Luke, and John:
   a. 5000 fed: 14:15; Mark 6:30-44; Luke 9:10-17; John 6:1-14

Other Miracles or Unusual Events:
1. The virgin birth of Christ—to reveal God's supernatural power in His becoming flesh to dwell among us: 1:18-25; John 1:14. See VIRGIN BIRTH in Index.
2. Star leading the wise men to Christ—God's way of bringing those other than Jews to a recognition of His Son: 2:1-12
3. Slaughter of innocent children and the escape of Christ to Egypt—to reveal how the devil, still chafing under God's pronounced defeat (Genesis 3:15), sought to destroy Christ at the outset of His earthly life: 2:13-18
4. The Baptism of Christ—to fulfill righteousness: 3:13-16; Mark 1:9; Luke 3:21,22. See BAPTISM in Index.
5. God's voice from heaven—to reveal God's identity with His Son: 3:16,17; 17:5; Mark 1:10,11; Luke 9:34-36
6. The Transfiguration—to reveal that Christ was God come down from heaven and to give us a picture of Himself in His future glory: 17:1-9; Mark 9:1-9; Luke 9:28-36
7. The appearance of Moses and Elijah on the mount of Transfiguration with Christ—to reveal the truth of eternal life for Old Testament saints, and recognition of others in the hereafter: 17:3; Mark 9:4,5; Luke 9:30,31
8. Darkness at the crucifixion—possibly to hide the ignominious death of Christ from those who gloated over it: 27:45; Mark 15:32,33; Luke 23:44,45
9. Veil of the Temple rent—to signify a new and living way had been opened for believers to have access to God: 27:51a with Hebrews 10:19-22; Mark 15:37,38; Luke 23:45. See VEIL in Index.
10. Earthquake at Christ's death—to reveal man's helplessness over nature, even though they thought they could control their own destiny: 27:51b
11. Resurrection of saints—to show that He who is life (John 14:6) can still give life even in death: 27:52,53
12. The resurrection of Christ—to set God's stamp of approval upon His finished work of redemption: 28:1-6; Mark 16:1-6; Luke 24:1-12; John 20:1-10. See RESURRECTION in Index.
13. Earthquake on resurrection morning—for the angel of the Lord to roll back the sealed stone from the empty tomb: 28:2

Parables of Christ:

1. Peculiar to Matthew:

Lesson

a. The tares: 13:24-30,36-43	Good and evil in life and judgment
b. The hidden treasure: 13:44	Value of the gospel
c. The goodly pearl: 13:45,46	Seeking salvation
d. The draw-net: 13:47-50	Visible church
e. Meats not defiling: 15:10-20	Inward purity
f. Unmerciful servant: 18:23-35	Ingratitude
g. Laborers in the vineyard: 20:1-16	Faithfulness to God's call
h. Two sons: 21:28-32	Insincerity and repentance
i. Marriage feast: 22:2-14	Need of God's righteousness
j. Ten virgins: 25:1-13	Preparation and watchfulness
k. Talents: 25:14-30	Use of advantages
l. Sheep and the goats: 25:31-46	Final separation of good and bad

2. Common to Matthew and Luke:

a. House built on rock and sand: 7:24-27; Luke 6:47-49	Consistent and false profession
b. Leaven: 13:33; Luke 13;20,21	Evil influence
c. Lost sheep: 18:11-14; Luke 15:3-7	Joy over the penitent

3. Common to Matthew, Mark and Luke:

a. New cloth and old garment: 9:16; Mark 2:21; Luke 5:36	New doctrine vs. old prejudices
b. New wine in old bottles: 9:17; Mark 2:22; Luke 5:37-39	Christ's teachings vs. traditions of the Pharisees
c. The sower: 13:3,18; Mark 4:1-20; Luke 8:4-15	Classes of hearers
d. The mustard seed: 13:31,32; Mark 4:30-32; Luke 13:18,19	Spreading the gospel
e. The wicked husbandman: 21:33-45	Christ rejected by the Jews
f. Fig tree: 24:32-34; Mark 13:28,29; Luke 21:29-31	Indication of Christ's Second Coming

1. Destruction of Jerusalem: 24:1,2. *The New York Times Service* reports that in January, 1970, an Israeli archaeologist unearthed the ruins of a building in the Jewish quarter of Jerusalem which was destroyed by the Romans in A.D. 70. It was the first evidence of the dramatic razing of Jerusalem under Titus. The archaeologist, Professor Nahum Avigad, of the Hebrew University, said, "We have never had evidence of the destruction before. Here we see fire for the first time." See DESTRUCTION, p. 383.

In the spring of 1970, archaeologists found a fragment in Jerusalem of the inscribed column a Roman emperor erected to commemorate the conquest of Jerusalem and the destruction of the Jewish Temple a little over 1,900 years ago. Later, in the fall, Israeli archaeologists working at some excavations inside the old city of Jerusalem discovered a parapet stone believed to be a part of the tower of the old Temple. The six-foot wide limestone block bears an inscription in

Hebrew: "To the house of the blowing of the ram's horn." This eight-ton stone is surmised to be a part of a tower above the priest's chambers in the southwest corner of the Temple. It was from this tower, according to Josephus, that priests would blow their trumpets which would herald the beginning and end of the Sabbath, as well as to call Israel for other purposes (Joel 2:25-17).

Prior to the discoveries of Jerusalem's destruction in A.D. 70, there had been found an inscribed monument which mentioned the stationing of the Tenth Roman Legion there by Titus. An inscription of Vespasian and Titus was also discovered. Coins commemorating Jerusalem's fall—the capture of the Jews ("Judea Capta" coin)—have been found (see COIN, p. 385).

Roman Legion Monument

While finding evidence of Jerusalem's destruction in A.D. 70 by Titus, archaeologists, in an area near the southwest corner of the Herodian Temple platform, uncovered magnificent stones, some thirty feet long (Mark 13:1), a wide street, and a plaza with a broad staircase leading up to the Temple area. Up these same steps Jesus walked as He went to the Temple. A most striking discovery was the *Royal Portico* along the entire width of the southern side, on top of the flattened Mount. The main entrance to the Temple and its courts was through two massive gates—the *Double Gate* and the *Triple Gate,* both called the "Huldah Gates" in ancient sources. An eyewitness, Flavius Josephus, wrote during the first century, "This portico was more deserving of mention than any under the sun." When traces of this portico were found, there were four rows of monolithic pillars, 162 of them, each thirty feet high and five feet in diameter, each topped with Corinthian capitals. It was in these porticos that Rabbi Gamaliel taught Paul, and certainly one of the places where Jesus Himself preached.

2. The rite of Crucifixion: 27:33-50. Crucifixion is known to have been practiced by the ancient Phoenicians. In 519 B.C. King Darius I of Persia crucified 3,000 Babylonians. In ca. A.D. 66 the Romans crucified 3,600 Jews, thereby igniting the Jewish revolt, and by the time this revolt was settled, so many Jews had been crucified that the executioners ran out of wood for crosses! Among the countless thousands of Jews crucified over the years, the one who con-

cerns us is Jesus Christ. See CRUCIFIXION in Index.

The generally accepted conception of Christ's crucifixion is what we have accepted from paintings (none of which were done earlier than A.D. 400). In 1970 Israeli archaeologists discovered in a hillside cave near Jerusalem the first remains of a crucified victim—the skeleton, including spike-pierced heel bones, of a man executed about 2,000 years ago. An inscription identified the victim as "Jehohannan Ben" (son of Jehohannan). The remainder of the inscription was too defaced for the scholars to decipher more.

What particularly interested the archaeologists were the marks found on the crucified man's bones. They indicated the crucified position was not the erect, cruciform pose so commonly portrayed by artists. Jehohannan was probably held down by the Romans soldiers while his outstretched arms were fastened to the cross bar. The spikes were not driven in the palms of his hands, but between the ulnar and radial bones just above the wrist. Spike marks on these two sets of bones are clearly discernible just above the wrist. Once the arms were nailed, the legs were pressed together and twisted to one side (something like a knee-bend). A large spike (approx. seven inches long) was driven through his heel bones and into the wood. To keep the victim from sagging, and possibly being torn loose from the cross, a small piece of wood, called a "sedecula," was nailed to the upright post of the cross. This provided a "support shelf" for the crucified man's buttocks.

When Jehohannan was crucified, the spike through his heel bones had struck a knot. It became so tightly imbedded that the executioner was unable to extract it from the cross. An axe was taken and the feet were chopped off above the ankles. Those who buried him placed his body in a 3 by 2 by 2 foot limestone ossuary, along with his amputated, but still pierced feet. The cave in which Jehohannan's ossuary was found came to light as bulldozers were digging foundations for new Israeli apartments. Along with Jehohannan's skeleton were found fourteen similar ossuaries.

Crucifixion, Roman

3. An inscription, called the "Nazareth Decree," or "Tomb Robbers' Inscription" was discovered in Nazareth in 1878. It was a decree one of the Caesars had given, which demanded a trial of anyone who "has in any way extracted the buried or maliciously transferred them to another place . . . or has displaced the sealing or moved other stones." If found guilty, they could be punished by death. This ordinance possibly explained one of the reasons why a watch

was set at Christ's tomb and why it was sealed (27:62-66). Another reason, of course, was the ulterior motive of the Jews—to prove that Christ would not come forth from the grave as He had predicted. They refused to believe that Jesus was God, and that nothing could contain Him.

¹ 1. Mary was espoused to Joseph before they came together: 1:18-25. The Jewish custom of marriage is quite different from ours. Matthew's account of Mary and Joseph and the birth of Christ tells of events *after* Mary and Joseph were married. In the East when a couple is married, they do not immediately consummate their marriage in sexual relationship. The time for this act is usually set by the priest, who chooses a day when a certain star will appear. It is believed that if conception occurs on that day, the child will be of good character.

Joseph was already her husband (vs. 19), but before they came together (in sexual relationship), Mary was already found with child (vs. 18). Under existing Jewish law, Joseph had a legal right to divorce her, and Mary could have been stoned to death (Leviticus 20:10). But Joseph, being a just man and not willing to make a public example of her, thought about putting her away privately (meaning, divorcing her since they were, under law, married). While he thought on these things, he dreamed, and an angel of the Lord straightened him out as to the facts of Mary's pregnancy. It was not until *after* Jesus was born that Joseph *knew* her. Some are shocked to suppose that Mary and Joseph consummated their marriage relationship, but the Scripture says so, and this is in keeping with the sacredness of marriage, as given by God regarding husband and wife to be fruitful and multiply (Genesis 1:27,28; 2:24). According to Mark, this couple had at least four sons and two daughters after the birth of Christ (6:3).

2. Shoes I am not worthy to bear—John's humility: 3:11. See SHOES in Index.

3. City set on a hill: 5:14. See WATCHMAN in Index.

4. Agree with thine adversary quickly: 5:25. There are three types of judges in the East. Elders, who sit at the city gate, are often called upon to settle disputes; "daysmen" to settle personal matters (see DAYSMAN in Index); and "the judge," who was called upon to settle major matters. A judge was usually located quite a distance from a village.

When a dispute arises that necessitates his judgment, the accused and the accuser travel together with their lawyers to see the judge. The journey takes many days. Christ urged two such people to settle their dispute "out of court," to "agree with thine adversary, whiles thou art in the way with him; lest at any time the adversary deliver thee to the judge, and the judge deliver thee to the officer, and thou be cast into prison." If they do agree on the way to court, the two men return home happily, but the lawyers continue on to inform the judge that the matter is settled. Going to court can become a nasty, costly situation, often resulting in imprisonment, and leaving bitter feelings. Paul confirmed Christ's teachings, showing that it is wrong for Christian brothers to go to court before unbelieving judges (I Corinthians 6:1-8).

5. The grass of the field: 6:30. After the rainy season in the Holy Land the hills and valleys are beautiful with a green thorny grass. Then comes the hot season, and the grass is killed by the sun. Women go out into the fields and cut it for fuel. Hence Christ's remark, "The grass of the field, which today is, and tomorrow is cast into the oven." See TREES Walking in Index.

6. Take up thy bed and walk: 9:6. See BEDS in Index.

7. Shake off the dust of your feet: 10:14. Our Western minds have thought this to mean one who angrily points a finger of ridicule and condemnation at the individual who refuses to heed God's message, especially after taking the time and effort to go forth and preach the Word (or witness). The thought is not this at all, but rather to shake off any *natural* feelings of bit-

terness or animosity that might arise in one's heart, and act with godly compassion, revealing peace and joy. After all, the seed of the Word has been planted, and any bitterness might "turn them off" for good. Rather, leave demonstrating the Christian life, to let them know what we said really works. We might have another opportunity someday to witness to them, and it could be ruined if we left them in the wrong spirit.

8. Shout (preach) ye upon the housetops: 10:27. Housetops in the East are conventional gathering places for people—relatives and friends. It is a flat roof, and often became a place for prayer (Acts 10:9). It was an ideal place for one to call to another, to deliver a message, or to gather a crowd to make an announcement. Jesus knew that such a place would be ideal to spread the good news of salvation, hence His words, "Preach ye upon the housetops." See PIC-TURE, point 14.

9. Tares among the wheat: 13:25,30. The tare is a nuisance to the Eastern farmer. It looks like wheat, but it is bitter if mixed with the wheat flour and causes dizziness. To pull it up or separate it from the wheat during growth would be impossible. But at harvest time the tares stand erect while the wheat bends over from the weight of the grain. This enables the farmer to go through his field, cutting first the tares and burning them, and then reaping a harvest of wheat free of tares. This parable is explained in 13:36-43.

10. Millstone hanged about his neck: 18:1-6. One method of capital punishment in the Graeco-Roman world was to tie a millstone around the neck of the condemned and cast him in-to the sea. Jesus, in teaching the importance of an older person setting a good example before children, said that if a proper example were not set, "better for him that a millstone were hanged about his neck, and that he be drowned in the depth of the sea."

Millstones

11. The seat of Moses: 23:2. This was the "teacher's" or chief seat in the synagogue, where the Rabbis taught the people. No doubt Christ taught from such a seat when He spoke in the synagogues, especially after He stood and read from the book of Isaiah (Luke 4:14-28). Christ berated the hypocritical Pharisees for their desire to have the chief seats in the synagogues (23:6). Several seats were on both sides of the "seat of Moses." While all were of importance, the ones on the right and left were next in importance to the chief seat. The mother of James and John, supposing such seats to be in Christ's kingdom, requested of Jesus that her sons "may sit, the one on thy right hand, and the other on the left, in thy kingdom" (20:20,21). Paul also sat in such a seat in the synagogue at Antioch (Acts 13:14,15).

12. Their phylacteries: 23:5. These were passages of Scripture enclosed in a small case, and

Seat of Moses

White Sepulchres

worn on the arm or forehead. This was an Old Testament custom, based upon instructions given by Moses to remind Israel of the importance of the Word of God for their lives and for their children (Exodus 13:9,14-16; Deuteronomy 6:6-8; 11:18,19). The Pharisees had turned this outward sign for inward spiritual growth into a "show," and it had no spiritual meaning or value for them. Their only purpose was to be seen of men and not to glorify God.

13. Ye are like unto whited sepulchres: 23:27,28. On certain occasions the Jewish leaders would go to the cemetery and whitewash tombs, notably those of their fathers, or religious leaders. They prided themselves in keeping these tombs beautifully white. But Jesus saw through this outward show, denounced their hypocrisy, and likened them to such tombs—clean and beautful on the outside, but full of dead men's bones, and of all uncleanness.

14. The housetop and the upper room: 24:17; Mark 14:15. Housetops in the East are conventional gathering places for people (friends and relatives). The house roof is flat, and often an upper room is adjacent to the roof, reached only by an outside stairway. To get into the other rooms of the house, one must come down from the housetop to get inside. These upper rooms often served as guest chambers, and it was in a room such as this that a great feast like the Passover was held, and the Lord's Supper instituted.

15. Two women shall be grinding at the mill: 24:41. Our thoughts of a "mill" usually picture a building with a large water wheel and grinding stones. A mill in the Holy Land is called a "saddle quern." It is about 24" × 18" and is slightly curved. For a meal, two women will

Upper Room (House Top)

Two Women Grinding

gather at a ''mill,'' and one will drop grain on the stone while the other rubs a smaller stone back and forth over the grain. Such a job is done by the women, and never by the men. How embarrassing it must have been for Samson to grind for the Philistines (Judges 16:21). Grinding was a daily routine. Sometimes a ''mill'' consisted of two circular stones, one on top of the other. The top stone had an opening into which grain was poured. Other mills are turned by animals. See SAMSON'S Grindstone in Index.

Not only is grinding grain a daily task for women, but they did it in privacy. It is a time when they remove their veils and "let down their hair." "Take a millstone and grind meal; uncover their locks, make bare the leg, and uncover the thigh" (Isaiah 47:2). Grinding is also a time for joy—it means there is food in the home. Evil is the day when the "sound of the grinding is low" (Ecclesiastes 12:4).

16. Lamps and oil cruses: 25:1-13. The type of lamp to which Christ referred in the parable of the Ten Virgins is a small one that fits in the palm of the hand. An extra supply of oil must be carried in a cruse if the lamp is to burn any length of time. The spiritual application of an extra supply of oil is found in vss. 10,13.

17. Dipping the sop: 26:23. In our scientific age, "dipping the sop" is an unsanitary way of eating. Food is placed in bowls on a long table or mat on the floor, and seated guests constantly dip their hands into these bowls to serve themselves. The food is eaten right out of their hands.

Lamps and Oil Cruse

The Resurrection: 28:1-6. Many years ago a certain scientist said dogmatically: "At death the life of a man is snuffed out like a candle flame." Today, many scientists would ask him to prove this assertion. Of course, he could not prove it. It only represented his opinion.

Dr. W. Von Braun, the eminent director of the Army Ballistic Missile Agency and one of the leading authorities in space exploration, wrote: "In this modern world of ours many people seem to think that Science has somehow made such 'religious ideas' [as mortality] untimely or old-fashioned. I think Science has a real surprise for the skeptics. Science, for instance, tells us that nothing in nature, not even the tiniest particle, can disappear without a trace. Nature does not know extinction. All it knows is transformation! If God applies this fundamental principle to the most minute and insignificant parts of His universe, doesn't it make sense to assume that He applies it also to the masterpiece of His creation, the human soul?" This scientist thinks it makes sense, and flatly states that everything science has taught him strengthens hie belief in the continuity of our spiritual existence after death.

scientists, and summarizes his findings: "The materialistic theory of existence is on the defensive. The spiritual version of reality is not the one supported by the weight of evidence. Our

"Dipping the Sop"

true existence is beyond both space and time, and the event called 'death' in our earthly lives can be but an episode in a far vaster adventure.'' To illustrate, a grain or seed is planted in the earth. It dies, but in death "it bringeth forth much fruit" (John 12:24).

What these men of science have said, the Bible has been saying for ages! Jesus Christ came to bring immortality to light—to show us the way beyond the grave. He *is* risen, and those who have experienced His saving grace shall be raised incorruptible, the same as He (I Corinthians 15:52-57).

The Old Testament in Matthew: In addition to the verses found listed in PROPHECIES fulfilled in Christ (see p. 471), note the following:

1. Man shall not live by bread alone: 4:4 with Deuteronomy 8:3
2. Angels given charge over Him: 4:6 with Psalm 91:11,12
3. Thou shalt not tempt the Lord: 4:7 with Deuteronomy 6:16
4. Worship (fear) the Lord thy God: 4:10 with Deuteronomy 6:13

5. People saw a great light: 4:16 with Isaiah 42:6,7
6. Thou shalt not kill: 5:21 with Exodus 20:13
7. Thou shalt not commit adultery: 5:27 Exodus 20:14
8. Putting away thy wife: 5:31 with Deuteronomy 24:1
9. Thou shalt not forswear: 5:33 with Leviticus 19:12
10. Eye for an eye, tooth for a tooth: 5:38 with Exodus 21:24
11. Love thy neighbor: 5:43; 22:39 with Leviticus 19:18
12. Be ye therefore perfect: 5:48 with Genesis 17:1
13. Lord of the Sabbath: 12:1-8 with I Samuel 21:6; Numbers 28:9,10
14. Christ in earth three days, three nights: 12:40 with Jonah 1:17
15. Honoring parents: 15:4a with Exodus 20:12
16. Cursing parents: 15:4b with Exodus 21:17
17. Branding hypocrites: 15:7-9 with Isaiah 29:13
18. Husband leaving parents: 19:4,5 with Genesis 2:24
19. Purification of the Temple: 21:12-15 with Isaiah 56:7
20. Out of the mouths of babes: 21:16 with Psalm 8:2
21. The God of Abraham: 22:32 with Exodus 3:6
22. Sit thou on My right hand: 22:44 with Psalm 110:1
23. Companion references:
   a. Meek inherit the earth: 5:5 with Psalm 37:11
   b. Summary of the law and prophets: 7:12
   c. Workers of iniquity: 7:23; 25:41 with Psalm 6:8
   d. Show thyself to the priest: 8:4 with Leviticus 14:3
   e. Mercy and not sacrifice: 9:13; 12:7 with Hosea 6:6
   f. Blind receive sight: 11:5 with Isaiah 29:18
   g. Tyre and Sidon: 11:21 with Ezekiel 26:3-14; 28:21-23
   h. Greater than Jonah: 12:38-41 with Jonah 1:17; 3:5-9
   i. Queen of Sheba: 12:42a with I Kings 10:1
   j. Greater than Solomon: 12:42b with II Chronicles 9
   k. Two or three witnesses: 18:16 with Deuteronomy 19:15
   l. Writing of divorcement: 19:7 with Deuteronomy 24:1
   m. Various commandments: 19:18,19 with Exodus 20
   n. Nothing impossible with God: 19:26 with Jeremiah 32:17
   o. Parable of the vineyard: 21:33 with Isaiah 5:1-7
   p. Marriage and the resurrection: 22:23-33 with Deuteronomy 25:5
   q. Greatest commandment: 22:37 with Deuteronomy 6:5
   r. Death of Abel: 23:35 with Genesis 4:8
   s. Death of Zacharias: 23:35 with II Chronicles 24:20,21
   t. House left desolate: 23:38 with Jeremiah 22:5
   u. Abomination of desolation: 24:15 with Daniel 12:11
   v. Sun darkened: 24:29 with Isaiah 13:10
   w. Heaven and earth pass away: 24:35 with Isaiah 51:6
   x. Days of Noah: 24:37-39 with Genesis 6:5-8
   y. Son of Man goeth: 26:24 with Psalm 22
   z. All power given to Christ: 28:18 with Daniel 7:14

SEED THOUGHTS

1. Four women are named in Matthew's genealogy of Jesus, and all of them are connected in some way with shame and heathenism. They are Thamar (Genesis 38), Rahab (Joshua 2:1), Ruth (Ruth 1:4,14-17), and Bathsheba (II Samuel 11:3). Three of them, probably all, were Gentiles (one a Canaanite and one a Moabitess). It is thus shown how truly the Lord Jesus identified Himself with sinners, and how

grace overlapped all bounds (Jeremiah 13:1). See GENEALOGY in Index.

2. Why the Wise Men were Wise: 2:1-12. They—
   a. Followed the light they had: vss. 1,2
   b. Were not discouraged by distance or inconveniences: vs. 2
   c. Sought Christ: vss. 2-8
   d. Followed additional light: vs. 9
   e. Worshiped Him (Christ): vs. 11a
   f. Gave Him gifts: vs. 11b
   g. Obeyed God—put Him first: vs. 12 with Acts 5:29
   h. The Wise Men came to Christ one way, and went back another: vs. 12. When one comes to Christ and accepts Him as Lord and King, he does not go back the old way—back to the old things of the old life. He goes a different way—the *new* way—the highway of holiness, for all things have now become new (II Corinthians 5:17).

3. Christ's Baptism: 3:13-17. Se BAPTISM in Index.

4. Christ's Temptation: 4:1-10. See TEMPTATION in Index.

5. Salt of the Earth: 5:13. Salt is important in connection with maintaining our life and health. In the bloodstream there is always an exact percentage of salt, and any great plus or minus variation of this amount would result in sickness or death. It helps to maintain life in our bodies. Sea water, which is salty, will support much more organic life than fresh water. It preserves as well as hinders spoilage. It flavors our food, making it palatable. The Scriptures refer to it as:
   a. A healing and cleansing aid: II Kings 2:20,21. See SALTED in Index.
   b. A binding covenant: Leviticus 2:13; II Chronicles 13:5. See SALT in Index.
   c. Useful: Mark 9:50a
   d. Evidence of grace in the heart: Mark 9:50b
   e. Peace: Mark 9:50c
   f. Saints—believers: Matthew 5:13a
   g. Wisdom in speech: Colossians 4:6
   h. Soundness: Luke 14:34,35
   i. Satisfaction: Job 6:6
   j. Acceptable sacrifices: Ezekiel 43:21-27
   k. A bond of friendship: Ezra 4:14 (ASV)
   l. An ineffective testimony: Matthew 5:13b
   m. Desolation: Judges 9:45; Zephaniah 2:9
   n. Barrenness and unfruitfulness: Jeremiah 17:6; Ezekiel 47:11

6. Christian Living: 5:13-16
   a. Inward purification—salt of the earth: vs. 13
   b. Outward illumination—light of the world: vss. 14a,15
   c. Forward manifestation—city on a hill: vs. 14b
   d. Upward revelation—glorify your Father in heaven: vs. 16

7. Heavenly Father's Care: 6:25-34[2]

> *Said the Robin to the Sparrow:*
> *"I should really like to know,*
> *Why these anxious human beings*
> *Rush about and worry so?"*

> *Said the Sparrow to the Robin:*
> *"Friend, I think it must be,*
> *That they have no heavenly Father*
> *Such as cares for you and me!"*

8. The "Two's" of Matthew Seven
   a. Two gates—strait and wide: vs. 13

      b. Two ways—broad and narrow: vss. 13,14
      c. Two classes—many and few: vss. 13,14
      d. Two destinations—destruction and life: vss. 13,14
      e. Two trees—good and corrupt: vs. 17
      f. Two fruits—evil and good: vs. 18
      g. Two judgments of evil tree—cut down and cast out: vs. 19
      h. Two house builders—wise and foolish: vss. 24,26
      i. Two foundations—rock and sand: vss. 24,26
      j. Two results—one stood, the other fell: vss. 25,27

9. The Church Zoo: 7:15-20[3]

    —Some folks are like wolves; in sheep's clothing, spreading false doctrines
    —Some are like chameleons, changing colors with the crowd
    —Many are like bugs, who seek darkness because their deeds are evil
    —Some are like buzzards; you don't see them in church unless a member is dead
    —Still others are like snails; no backbone
    —Some are like pigs; greedy to get all for self
    —Others are like roosters; always crowing about something
    —Some are like goats; always butting the other fellow
    —Some are like porcupines; always needling somebody else
    —Some are like frogs; leaping from church to church
    —Some are like gnats; nothing but pests
    —Some are like geese; fair-weather church-goers
    —Some are like bumble bees; they'll sting you every time
    —Some Board members are like lions; always roaring about something
    —Some are like donkeys; just plain stubborn
    —Many are like mules; the extent of their joy is shown by their long faces
    —There are those like owls; always "hooting" about some folks when they're not around
    —Some are like cats and dogs; just can't get along together
    —There are those like hawks; preying on others
    —Some folks are like elephants; a long memory that always remembers the wrong someone did years ago
    —Some are like leopards; with spots in their lives which hinder spiritual growth
    —Some are like monkeys. Watch how they act if you don't believe it
    —Some are like beavers; eager
    —Some are like ants; real workers
    —Some are like canaries; singing along life's way
    —Some are like eagles; soaring above the clouds of circumstances and living in the heavenlies
    —Then there are those who are just like sheep; they follow their Shepherd wherever He leads

10. Miracles Typical of Salvation.
      a. Blindness—condition of a sinner: 9:27-31
      b. Leprosy—guilt: 8:1-4
      c. Palsy—impotence: 8:6-13
      d. Fever—passion: 8:14-17
      e. Demoniacy—slavery to sin: 8:28-33
      f. Blood issue—made whole from sin: 9:20-22
      g. Calming the sea—peace; result of forgiveness: 8:23-27
      h. Peter walking on water—walking by faith: 14:29
      i. Feeding the 4000—supplying our need: 15:32-39
      j. Dumb spirit—witnessing: 9:32,33
      k. Transfiguration—we shall be like Him: 17:1-8

11. The Believer's Cross: 10:38; 16:24. No place in Scripture do we find Christ speaking of "His" cross. Others do, but not He. When He spoke of a cross, it was always in relation to the believer bearing his own. "The everlasting God in His wisdom foresaw from eternity the cross that He now presents to you as a gift from His inmost heart. This cross He now sends you He had considered with His all-knowing eyes, understood with His divine mind, tested with His wise justice, warmed with loving arms, and weighed with His own hands to see that it is not one inch too large nor one ounce too heavy for you. He blessed it with His holy name, anointed it with His grace, perfumed it with His consolation, took one glance at you and your courage, and then sent it to you from heaven, a special greeting from God to you, an alms of the all-merciful love of God."[4] Whatever your cross is, accept it as from the Lord.

12. Christ's Invitation—Salvation and Service: 11:28-30
   a. Something to do: *come* unto Me
   b. Something to leave: *burdens* of sin
   c. Something to receive: *rest* of salvation
   d. Something to take: His *yoke*. The Eastern yoke is made for two necks. Christ shares His work with us (I Corinthians 3:9).
   e. Something to learn: *of Me,* knowing Him and the power of His resurrection (Philippians 3:8-10)
   f. Something to find: *rest* for service; sufficient *grace* for daily living

13. The "Mysteries" of Scripture
   a. The kingdom of God and/or heaven—to understand the truth of God: 13:11; Luke 8:10
   b. Israel's blindness—to call Gentiles in this age. Romans 11:25
   c. The gospel—for the obedience of faith: Romans 16:25,26
   d. God's wisdom—to reveal the deep things of God: I Corinthians 2:7-13
   e. The resurrection—to give assurance of immortality: I Corinthians 15:51-57
   f. God's will—to gather in one all things in Christ: Ephesians 1:9,10
   g. Christ—His Church—that Gentiles should be fellow heirs of the same body (with Jews): Ephesians 3:3-6
   h. Fellowship—in the manifold wisdom of God: Ephesians 3:9,10
   i. The oneness of husband and wife—revealing the oneness of Christ and His Church: Ephesians 5:30-32
   j. The gospel—to make Christ known: Ephesians 6:19,20; Colossians 4:3,4
   k. Christ in us—to give us our hope for glory: Colossians 1:27
   l. God—to comfort and enlighten all saints in Christ: Colossians 2:2
   m. Iniquity—a falling away as Christ's coming draws nigh: II Thessalonians 2:7-12
   n. Faith—to live godly: I Timothy 3:9
   o. Godliness—to reveal the incarnation of Christ: I Timothy 3:16
   p. The seven stars—to reveal church truth: Revelation 1:20
   q. Babylon—to reveal false religions: Revelation 17:5,7
   r. We are stewards of these mysteries: I Corinthians 4:1,2

14. Facts for Soul Winners: 13:36-43.[5] See SOUL-WINNING in Index.
   a. We must ever be found in the presence of Jesus: vs. 36a. Jesus said: "Follow Me, and I will make you fishers of men" (4:19).
   b. We must constantly seek wisdom from Him: vs. 36b
   c. We must work together with Him: vs. 37
   d. We must firmly believe the seed is incorruptible: vs. 37
   e. We must not limit our witnessing to one area: vs. 38a
   f. We must not be confused: vs. 38b
   g. We must not minimize Satan's power: vs. 39a
   h. We must remember there will be a harvest: vs. 39b
   i. We must never forget the wicked are doomed: vss. 40-42

    j. We must labor diligently with goal in view: vs. 43a

    k. We must know that each man is responsible for his own soul: vs. 43b with Psalm 49:7

15. Brothers and Sisters of Christ: 13:55,56. See Index.

16. Lip Service: 15:8. There are—

    a. People who talk about prayer but never pray

    b. People who say tithing is right but never tithe

    c. People who say belonging to a church is necessary, but never go or support its program

    d. People who say the Bible is God's Word to man, but never read it

    e. People who say eternity is more important than time, but live for the present life

    f. People who criticize others for the things they do themselves

    g. People who stay away from church for trivial reasons, and then sing, "Oh how I love Jesus"

    h. People who live for the devil all their lives and expect to die like an angel

17. Whom do Men Say that I Am? 16:13-16. See CHRIST, Whom Say, in Index.

18. What Think Ye of Christ? 22:42[6] "Jesus Christ was born in the meanest of circumstances, but the air above was filled with hallelujahs of a heavenly host. His lodging was a cattle pen, but a star drew distinguished visitors from afar to do Him homage.

"His relatives were inconspicuous and uninfluential. In infancy He startled a king; in boyhood He puzzled the doctors; in manhood He ruled the elements, defying the law of gravitation by walking on water, and then quieting the raging sea. He healed the multitudes without medicine, and He made no charge for His services. He never wrote a book, yet all the libraries of the world could not hold the books that have been written about Him. He never wrote a song, yet He has furnished the theme of more songs than all the songwriters combined. He never founded a college, yet all the schools together cannot boast of as many students as He has. He never practiced medicine, yet He healed more broken hearts than the doctors have broken bodies.

"He never marshalled an army or drafted a soldier or fired a gun, yet no leader ever had more volunteers who have, under His orders, made rebels stack arms or surrender without a shot being fired. He is the Harmonizer of all discords. Great men have come and gone, yet He lives on. Herod could not kill Him, Satan could not seduce Him, even demons obeyed Him. He had no cornfields or fisheries, but He could spread a table for five thousand and have bread and fish to spare. He broke up every funeral He saw!

"He had nothing He could call His own. The foxes have holes and the birds of the air have nests, but the Son of Man had no place to lay His head. He was born in a borrowed stable, rode on a borrowed beast, preached from another's boat, was nailed to another's cross, and was buried in a borrowed tomb. His crucifixion was the crime of crimes, the innocent suffering for the guilty. When He died, few men mourned; but a black crepe was hung over the sun. Though men trembled not for their sins, the earth beneath shook under the load. All nature honored Him, sinners alone rejected Him. He forgave His enemies and loved those who hated His truth. He gave His life that others might live."

19. The "Woes" of Hypocrisy: 23:13-36. See WOES in Index.

    a. The "woe" of selfish denominationalism: vs. 13

    b. The "woe" of "paid" service: vs. 14

    c. The "woe" of proselytizing: vs. 15

    d. The "woe" of spiritual blindness: vss. 16-22

    e. The "woe" of works: vss. 23,24

    f. The "woe" of morality: vss. 25,26

    g. The "woe" of deceit: vss. 27,28

    h. The "woe" of touching God's anointed: vss. 29-36 with I Chronicles 16:22

20. Signs of the Times: 24:3. Through Israel's disobedience to the Word of God, she rejected

her Messiah when He came in the person of Jesus Christ (John 1:11). As a result, she is now blinded in part (Romans 11:25), which is part of God's judgment upon His people (Romans 11:21a). God has now turned to the Gentiles for them to bring fruit unto Him (Matthew 21:33-46; Acts 15:14). Now that Christ has come the first time in fulfillment of His Word to be the Savior of the world—to die for our sins according to the Scriptures (I Corinthians 15:3,4), the church, as His fruit-bearing witness, awaits the fulfillment of prophecy relating to Christ's return.

Just before the Sanhedrin plotted Jesus' death and Judas plotted to betray Him, Jesus gave His Olivet Discourse (Matthew 23—25). His disciples were concerned about the destruction of the Temple, the sign of His return, and the end of the age (23:3). Jesus then began to enumerate some signs of His coming, all of which are increasing in our day, all pointing to the nearness of His soon coming (I Thessalonians 4:16-18). What are some of these signs?

- a. False Christs (Moonies, etc.): vs. 5; Mark 13:22
- b. Wars and rumors of war: vs. 5
- c. Political distress of nations—national independence: vs. 7a
- d. Famines, pestilences, and earthquakes: vs. 7b
- e. False preachers: vs. 11
- f. Christians growing cold and not enduring sound doctrine: vs. 12; II Timothy 4:1-4
- g. Increase in gospel preaching (Radio and T.V.): vs. 14; Mark 13:10
- h. Israel back in her land: vss. 32,33; Ezekiel 37:21; Isaiah 61:4
- i. Noah's Days: vs. 37. There are four characteristics of Noah's day:
  - —Progress of mechanical arts—music: Genesis 4:21 (today, it's "noise")
  - —Increase in population: Genesis 6:1
  - —Undue prominence of women: Genesis 6:2
  - —A breakdown in society: Genesis 6:5,11-13. A population explosion results in (1) sin, (2) rebellion, (3) lawlessness, and (4) dethroning of God (increased atheism and humanism in education).
- j. Economics—buying, selling, planting, building, capital and labor: Luke 17:28; James 5:4
- k. Crime (personal harm): vs. 49a
- l. Increase in eating (Fast Food Chains): vss. 38a,49b
- m. Increase in drinking: vss. 38b,49b
- n. Increase in divorce-broken homes: vs. 38c
- o. Speed (travel): Daniel 12:4a
- p. Increase in knowledge: Daniel 12:4b
- q. Increase in riches: James 5:1-3
- r. Men's hearts failing because of fear: Luke 21:26
- s. Apostasy: II Thessalonians 2:3
- t. Perilous times: II Timothy 3:1-5. Men shall be—
  - —Lovers of selves . . . blasphemers . . . disobedient to parents
  - —Unthankful . . . unholy . . . without natural affection (homosexuals, lesbians: Romans 1:24-27)
  - —Trucebreakers . . . false accusers
  - —Incontinent: unrestrained, without self-control
  - —Despisers of those who are good
  - —Lovers of pleasure more than of God, religious outwardly but having no godly power
  - —Evil men becoming more evil: vs. 13, ungodly, and walking after their own lusts: Jude 14-19

Luke (21:28) says: "When these things begin to come to pass, then look up, and lift up your heads, for your redemption draweth nigh." "Watch therefore, and abide in Him, for ye know not what hour your Lord cometh, and be not ashamed before Him at His coming" (Matthew 24:42; I John 2:28). When the men of Issachar rallied around David, they were "men who had understanding of the times, to know . . . what to do" (I Chronicles 12:32). Do we have understanding of the times in which we live? What would you like to be doing when Christ comes? What would you like to be saying when Christ comes? Where would you like to be when Christ comes? Then *do* it, *say* it, and *be there!*

21. Peter's Downfall: 26:69-75. See DOWNFALL of Peter in Index.
22. Lessons from the Dying Thief: 27:38,44. See THIEF in Index.

For points 23—43, see HIGHLIGHTS of Christ's Life, pp. 452-473.

23. The Passover and the Lord's Supper: 26:17-28
24. Christ in Gethsemane: 26:36-46
25. The Betrayal by Judas: 26:47-50
26. The (mis-) Trial of Jesus: 26:47-68
27. Christ's Innocency Attested: 27:34
28. Christ's Rejection by the Jews: 27:15-25
29. The Crucifixion: 27:26-50
30. The Wounds of Christ: 27:30
31. Superscriptions on the Cross: 27:37
32. Seven Last Sayings of Christ
33. Seven Last Sayings of the Crowd
34. Christ was Forsaken: 27:46
35. Twelve Views of the Cross
36. Veil of the Temple Rent: 27:51
37. Three Days and Three Nights in the Grave
38. He Descended into Hell
39. The Meaning of Christ's Death
40. Christ's Resurrection: 28:1-6
41. Post-Resurrection Appearances
42. Prophecies Fulfilled in Christ
43. Archaeological Evidence of Christ's Life
44. The Great Commission: 28:19,20 with Ezekiel 3:17-21. See SOUL WINNING in Index.
    a. "Go ye." If not *YOU,* who? Those who have believed and know the reviving power of His resurrection: I Peter 1:3
    b. Go where—to whom? If not *HERE,* where? All the world, to every creature
    c. Why go? Because all have sinned, and we who are saved are indebted to them: Romans 1:14; Ezekiel 3:17-21
    d. When to go? If not *NOW,* when? Now is the accepted time; now is the day of salvation: II Corinthians 6:2 with Proverbs 27:1
    e. What to preach? The gospel, how that Christ died for our sins, was buried, and rose again according to the Scriptures: I Corinthians 15:3,4

A BIT OF HEAVENLY MANNA

One of the greatest needs today in Christian circles is a knowledge of Jesus Christ; not simply a knowledge of His saving power, but a knowledge of *Him.* Paul wanted to know the "excellency of the knowledge of Christ Jesus my Lord . . . *to know Him*" (Philippians 3:8-10). He realized the importance of "knowing Him" before he tried to "make Him known." That is why Christ instructed us to "come . . . and learn of Me."

LEARN OF ME—11:29[7]

"Jesus is our greatest Pattern and Example, and every disciple should learn of Him. He goes before us through all the duties and trials of life, and shows us how they should be performed and borne. He teaches us how to bear poverty without complaining, popularity without pride, endure contradiction without resentment, and to bestow favors on the unthankful and unworthy. Go, learn of Jesus to live by faith in the Father's Word, to cultivate fellowship with the Father in private, to do the Father's will in public, to suffer all the Father has appointed thee, and to prefer His will before our own. Go, learn of Him how to sympathize with the poor, to labor for the sick, and to pour benefits and blessings on all. Go, learn of Him to be meek and lowly, patient and forgiving, industrious and devout, and to glorify God in the body and spirit which are His. Learn not of the heathens however virtuous; learn not of the professors however amiable; but learn of Jesus, know Him and the power of His resurrection, for His motives are pure and His conduct perfect.''

PRAYER THOUGHT: ''As I start this day, O Lord, I confess that I have not loved Thee with all my heart and soul, or with all my mind and strength. I have not loved my neighbor as myself. I have no reason for not obeying this commandment, and I ask Thee to help me to obey it. In Jesus' name I pray. Amen.''[8]

Matthew 22:36-40

Mark—The Book of Christ, the Servant

Name: Mark means ''hammer.'' His Hebrew name was John, and his Graeco-Roman name was Marcus (Acts 12:25; I Peter 5:13). He was the son of Mary (Acts 12:12), the sister of Barnabas (Colossians 4:10), dwelling at Jerusalem. He was converted to Christ through Peter, who called him ''my son'' (I Peter 5:13). He is not mentioned in the gospel accounts but is mentioned eight times in the Acts. He has been called Peter's interpreter, and became a companion of Paul on his first missionary journey (Acts 12:25). His leaving Paul on this journey gave rise to the dispute between Paul and Barnabas (Acts 13:13; 15:36-40. See ARCHAEOLOGY in Second Corinthians). Mark later became profitable to both Paul and Peter (II Timothy 4:11; I Peter 5:13).

Mark is said to have been sent by Peter to advance the cause of Christ in Egypt. His ministry was eminently successful in Lybia, Marmorica, and Pentapolis. He returned to Alexandria, where he suffered persecutions from the idolatrous rabble of the great festivals of Serapis, an Egyptian divinity, and died of wounds.

Contents: Mark introduced his gospel account with a statement relating to the Divinity of Christ, and then jumped right in to His earthly ministry. Matthew took his readers back into Jewish prophecies and concentrated on the *teachings* of Jesus, while Mark, mentioning His discourses, emphasized the *works* of Christ. Although Mark emphasized the divine power of Christ, he often alluded to His human feelings:

1. Anger and grief: 3:5
2. Weariness: 4:38
3. Wonder: 6:6
4. Sighs: 7:34; 8:12
5. Affection: 10:21

His account records most of the things recorded in Matthew from John's ministry (ch. 3) to the end, with some few additional particulars in a more concise form. Considering the simplicity and plainness of the writing, and the momentous subjects which he narrates, this gospel account has been called ''the shortest and clearest, the most marvelous, and at the same time the most satisfactory history in the world." This book contains 16 chapters, 678 verses, and 15,171 words.

As compared with the other gospel accounts, Mark alone records:
1. The parable of fasting—to teach us the need to fast and pray: 2:19,20
2. The parable of one soil; the seed growing secretly—to teach us the need to grow in grace: 4:26-29 with II Peter 3:18
3. Cure of the deaf and dumb man: 7:31-37
4. Cure of the blind man at Bethsaida: 8:22-25

Character: Historical.

Subject: The works (miracles) of Jehovah's Servant.

Purpose: To prove that Jesus of Nazareth is the Servant of God, who wholly fulfills the Father's will, and that we should serve as we follow Him.

Outline:[1]
I. The Servant Tested and Triumphant over Satan: 1:1-13
II. The Servant Teaching and Touching the Needs: 1:14—9:1
III. The Servant Transfigured and Treading the Path of the Tomb: 9:2—14:72
IV. The Servant Giving His Life a Ransom for Many: 15
V. The Servant's Ransom Accepted by God: 16

Scope: Mark's history covers a period of about three-and-one-half years.

Writer: Mark has been accepted since ancient times as the author of this gospel account. As early as A.D. 60-150, it was recognized as Mark's work by Papias. There are some who hold that Mark wrote and Peter dictated, since he is Peter's convert.

To Whom Written: Gentile Christians, as evidenced by the frequent use of Latin terms, such as "legion" and "centurion." The Roman division of the night is given instead of the Jewish. He omitted Christ's genealogy, for the Romans did not look for a Messiah. He made no mention of Jewish law, certainly of no interest to Gentiles. He also omitted many Old Testament prophecies, and found it necessary to explain that Jordan is a "river" (1:5), that the Mount of Olives is over against the Temple, and other details which the nation Israel would have understood without explanation.

When and Where Written: Rome, Alexandria, and Antioch each lays claim to the place where this account was written. The date is uncertain; probably A.D. 53 to 60. It was the first gospel account written.

Key Chapter: 10. Christ's purpose of ministry.

Key Verse: 10:45.

Key Word: Straightway, found 42 times. This particular Greek word has been variously translated "anon" (at once), forthwith, immediately, and straightway.

Key Phrase: And straightway He: 1:20.

Key Thought: Behold My Servant: Isaiah 42:1.

Spiritual Thought: His wonderful works prove Him.

Christ Is Seen As: God's righteous Servant: Isaiah 53:11.

Names and Titles of Christ: See NAME in Dictionary.
1. Jesus Christ: 1:1
2. Son of God: 1:1
3. Lord: 1:3; 5:19
4. My beloved Son: 1:11; 9:7
5. Jesus of Nazareth: 1:24a; 16:6

6. Holy One of God: 1:24b
7. Forgiver of sins: 2:5-10
8. Son of Man: 2:10
9. Lord of Sabbath: 2:28
10. Our Brother: 3:35
11. Master: 4:38; 14:14
12. Jesus: 5:7,20
13. Son of the Most High God: 5:7
14. The Carpenter: 6:3
15. The Christ: 8:29
16. Good Master: 10:17
17. A Ransom: 10:45
18. Son of David: 10:47
19. His Well-beloved: 12:6
20. The Heir: 12:7,8
21. The Stone: 12:10
22. Son of the blessed: 14:61
23. King of the Jews: 15:2,18,26
24. King of Israel: 15:32
25. The risen Saviour: 16:6

Names and Titles of God: See NAME in Dictionary.
1. Father: 8:38; 13:32
2. The God of Abraham, Isaac, and Jacob: 12:26
3. God of the living: 12:27
4. Lord: 12:29
5. Abba, Father: 14:36

Names and Titles of the Holy Spirit: See NAME in Dictionary.
1. Holy Ghost: 1:8; 12:36
2. The Spirit: 1:10

Prophecy Fulfilled in Christ: See p. 471.

Prophecy: Destruction of Jerusalem: 13:1-27. See DESTRUCTION in Index.

MIRACLES OR UNUSUAL EVENTS

1. Peculiar to Mark:
   a. Deaf and dumb man cured: 7:31-37
   b. Blind man cured: 8:22-26
2. Common to Mark and Matthew:
   a. Healing in Galilee: 6:5,6; Matthew 9:35
   b. Syrophenician's daughter healed: 7:24-30; Matthew 15:21-28
   c. Multitudes healed in Galilee: 7:31-37; Matthew 15:29-31
   d. The 4,000 fed: 8:1-9
   e. Fig tree cursed: 11:3; Matthew 21:18-21
3. Common to Mark and Luke:
   a. Demoniac in synagogue cured: 1:23; Luke 4:33
   b. Healing of blind Bartimaeus: 10:46-52; Luke 18:35-43
4. Common to Mark, Matthew, and Luke. See p. 386.
5. Common to Mark, Matthew, and John:
   a. Walking on water: 6:48; Matthew 14:22-27; John 6:19
6. Common to all gospel writers:
   a. 5,000 fed: 6:30-44; Matthew 14:15; Luke 9:10-17; John 6:1-14

Other Miracles or Unusual Events: See points 4—9, 12, p. 386.

Parables of Christ:

1. Peculiar to Mark   *Lesson*

   a. Fasting: 2:19,20   Prayer and fasting

   b. Seed growing secretly: 4:26-29   Gradual growth in grace

2. Common to Mark and Luke

   a. The lighted candle: 4:21-23; Luke 8:16; 11:33   Let your light so shine

3. Common to Mark, Matthew, and Luke. See p. 387.

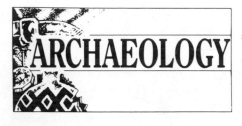

The healing of blind Bartimaeus: 10:46 with Luke 18:35. Mark said Christ healed him when He "went out of Jericho" and Luke said He did it when He "was come nigh unto Jericho." Some have suggested a contradiction here; others that these were two different events. Excavations have brought to light that in the time of Jesus Jericho was a double city—the old Jewish city, and then the newer Roman city. It was while Jesus was leaving one and entering the other that He healed Bartimaeus.

2

1. The latchet of whose shoes I am not worthy to stoop down and unloose—showing John's humility: 1:7. See SHOES in Index.

2. Shod with sandals: 6:9. See SHOD in Index.

3. Men as trees walking: 8:24. When the grassy weeds are full grown, women go out into the fields and gather it, forming huge bundles which they place on their heads and carry back to their homes. It is dried out and used for firewood or fuel. When Jesus healed a blind man in Bethsaida, He asked him what he first saw. Replying, he said: "I see men as trees walking." In the distance he saw a group of women carrying bundles of grassy weeds on their heads, and to him they looked like "walking trees." See GRASS in Index.

Men as Trees Walking

4. Casting away his garment: 10:50. There are two classes of beggars in the East. The true beggar, who is usually poor and/or physically handicapped and in need, and the other class, made up of some who are incurables (lepers, lame, blind, etc.) and have been told by their physicians that their only hope is in God. They are not necessarily poor. There are three places where these beggars go, believing that some day a holy man will pass by and heal them. One is at the Temple gate, where many pass by daily. A lame man was healed there by Peter (Acts 3:1-8). An impotent man was made whole by Christ at the Pool of Bethesda (John 5:2-9). The other place is by the roadside.

Many times a sick "beggar" would wear a robe which designated him as one in need of physical help—not money. The robe might even stand for family prestige and wealth. If wealth, the family might even take this "beggar" to his spot each day and return him home at night. Those who gave alms to this type of beggar did it knowing he would use it to help others. Such was the case of the beggar mentioned in Mark 10:46-52. When Jesus came by and called unto him, he, "casting away his garment, rose and came to Jesus." In the casting away of his garment, he turned his back on his family, houses and lands, fortune, prestige, etc., to come to Jesus. It was an act of humility—renouncing all to follow Jesus. He no longer needed his robe for others to know who he was—he was now identified with the Son of God, following Jesus in the way.

5. Cursing a fig tree: 11:12-14,20,21. One strange thing about an Eastern fig tree is that the fruit appears before the leaves. Anyone seeing a fig tree having leaves would naturally expect to find fruit on it. This is what Jesus and His disciples expected to find. But finding none, Christ cursed (or condemned) the barren tree. This is a picture of a professing Christian giving the appearance of productiveness, but bearing no fruit.

6. Chief seats in the synagogues: 12:38,39. See SEAT in Index.

7. The widow's mites: 12:42. A mite was worth one-eighth of a cent; two equalled a farthing, or one-quarter of a cent. This was an insignificant offering in view of what others were giving, but it was *all* the widow had, which was more in the sight of God than all which cast their money in the treasure. The "widow's mites" are shown below the American half-dollar.

Widow's Mites

8. A man bearing a pitcher of water: 14:13. When Jesus had need of an upper room for the feast of the Passover, He told two of His disciples to follow a "man bearing a pitcher." Westerners ask the question, "*Which* man carrying a pitcher?" In Palestine it is the job of the women to carry water (on the head). A man doing this would be very conspicuous to all passing by. See CARRIERS in Index.

9. Housetop and upper room: 14:15. See HOUSES in Index.
10. Dipping in the dish: 14:20. See DIPPING in Index.

Scientifically Speaking: The resurrection: 16:1-6. See RESURRECTION in Index.

The Old Testament in Mark: In addition to the verses found in PROPHECIES fulfilled in Christ (see p. 471), note the following:

1. Seeing, they perceive not: 4:12 with Isaiah 6:9,10
2. Lip service: 7:6,7 with Isaiah 29:13
3. Honoring parents: 7:10 with Exodus 20:12
4. Dishonoring parents: 7:10 with Exodus 21:17
5. Male and female created: 10:6 with Genesis 1:27
6. The twain shall be one flesh: 10:7,8 with Genesis 2:24
7. God's house a house of prayer: 11:17 with Isaiah 56:7
8. The God of Abraham: 12:26 with Exodus 3:6
9. The Lord God is one Lord: 12:29 with Deuteronomy 6:4
10. Love the Lord: 12:30 with Deuteronomy 6:5
11. Love thy neighbor: 12:31 with Leviticus 19:18
12. The Lord said to my Lord: 12:36 with Psalm 110:1
13. Companion references:
    a. Show thyself to a priest: 1:44 with Leviticus 14:3
    b. David eating showbread: 2:26 with I Samuel 21:6
    c. Elijah must come first: 9:11 with Malachi 4:5
    d. Where the worm dieth not: 9:44 with Isaiah 66:24
    e. Bill of divorcement: 10:4 with Deuteronomy 24:1
    f. Various commandments: 10:19 with Exodus 20
    g. Temple a den of thieves: 11:17 with Jeremiah 7:11
    h. A vineyard: 12:1 with Isaiah 5:1
    i. Husband childless: 12:19 with Deuteronomy 25:5
    j. Love (obedience) more than sacrifice: 12:33 with I Samuel 15:22
    k. Lest ye be deceived: 13:5 with Jeremiah 29:8
    l. Brother shall betray brother: 13:12 with Micah 7:6
    m. Abomination of desolation: 13:14 with Daniel 12:11
    n. Sun shall be darkened: 13:24 with Isaiah 12:10
    o. My words shall not pass away: 13:31 with Isaiah 40:8

SEED THOUGHTS

1. Christ's Baptism: 1:9-11. See BAPTISM in Index.
2. Christ's Temptation: 1:12,13. See TEMPTATION, and SINLESSNESS of Christ, and SATAN in Index.
3. Repentance: 1:15. See REPENTANCE In Index. Repentance simply means a "turn about face," turning with sorrow from a past course of action—hating what we once loved and loving what we once hated (II Corinthians 5:17).
    a. Repentance is a change of mind—[3]
       —Concerning God
       —Concerning the Law
       —Concerning sin
       —Concerning self
       —Concerning Christ
       —Concerning holiness
       —Concerning judgment
    b. Repentance is manifested by its effects—

—Contrition
—Confession
—Self-abhorrence
—Self-abandonment

4. The Faithful Four: 2:1-5[4]
   a. If Christ is in your house, your neighbors will soon know it: vs. 1
   b. Four men thought it worth while to bring one man to Christ: vs. 3
   c. They thought it more important to get this man to Christ than to have an orderly meeting: vs. 4
   d. Christ saw *their* faith and rewarded it: vs. 5

5. A Sick Woman Healed: 5:27-34
   a. She heard of Jesus: vs. 27a
   b. She came to Him: vs. 27b
   c. She touched Him: vs. 27c
   d. She believed Him: vs. 28
   e. She was healed: vs. 29a
   f. She *knew* she was healed: vs. 29b
   g. She confessed: vs. 33
   h. She left in peace: vs. 34

6. Whom Say Ye that I Am? 8:27. See CHRIST, Whom Say, in Index.

7. The Believer's Cross: 8:34; 10:21. See CROSS in Index.

8. Discipleship: 8:34,35. See DISCIPLESHIP in Index.
   a. "Come after Me" for *service:* 1:17
   b. "Deny . . . self" as a *sacrifice:* Romans 12:1
   c. "Take up his cross" to *suffer:* Philippians 3:10

9. The Christian Life: 9:1-9[5]

On the Mountain-Top: vs. 2	*In the Valley:* vs. 9
a. Spiritual	a. Practical
b. Communion	b. Conflict
c. Occupied *with* Jesus	c. Occupied *for* Jesus

10. The Rich Young Ruler: 10:17-22. See NAAMAN in Index.

11. With All Your Heart: 12:30
    a. Love the Lord: 12:30
    b. Trust the Lord: Proverbs 3:5
    c. Seek the Lord: Deuteronomy 4:29
    d. Turn unto the Lord: Deuteronomy 30:10
    e. Obey the Lord: Deuteronomy 30:2
    f. Follow the Lord: I Kings 14:8
    g. Walk before the Lord: I Kings 2:4
    h. Serve the Lord: Deuteronomy 10:12
    i. Praise the Lord: Psalm 86:12

12. The Passover and the Lord's Supper: 14:17-25. See PASSOVER in Index.

13. Peter's Downfall: 14:26-72. See NAME in I Peter.
    a. Self-confidence: vs. 29
    b. Proud boasting: vs. 31
    c. Indifference: sleeps amidst great issues: vs. 37
    d. Impulsively acted in energy of the flesh: vs. 47 with John 18:10
    e. Forsook his Master: vs. 50
    f. Followed afar off: vs. 54a
    g. Sought worldly companions; warms self at the devil's fire: vs. 54b
    h. Open denial of Christ: vss. 68,70
    i. Bolder denial; flesh has full sway: vs. 71

j. Peter called to mind the words of Christ: vs. 30. When the cock crowed, and "when he thought thereon, he wept": vs. 72. Having repented of his sin, he was restored to full fellowship and was used mightily as a servant of the Lord (Acts 2). See I Corinthians 10:12.

14. Cups of the Bible
   a. Of my sins: Mark 14:35,36
   b. Of salvation: Psalm 116:13; Revelation 3:20
   c. Of blessing: I Corinthians 10:16; Psalm 23:5
   d. Of sacrifice: Matthew 20:22-28
   e. Of fellowship: I Corinthians 10:21
   f. Of communion: I Corinthians 10:16; 11:25
   g. Of hypocrisy: I Corinthians 10:21
   h. Of reaping: Lamentations 4:21; Ezekiel 23:33
   i. Of Apostasy: Revelation 17:4
   j. Of divine wrath: Isaiah 51:17
   k. Of divine judgment: Psalm 11:6

15. Lessons from the Dying Thief: 15:27,28. See THIEF in Index. For points 16—35, see HIGHLIGHTS of Christ's Life, pp. 454-473.

16. Christ in Gethsemane: 14:32-42
17. The Betrayal by Judas: 14:43-50
18. The (mis-) Trial of Jesus: 14:53-65; 15:1-15
19. Christ's Innocency Attested
20. Christ's Rejection by the Jews: 15:7-15
21. The Crucifixion: 15:22-25
22. The Wounds of Christ: 15:16-23
23. Superscriptions on the Cross: 15:26
24. Seven Last Sayings of Christ
25. Seven Last Sayings of the Crowd
26. Christ was Forsaken
27. Twelve Views of the Cross
28. Veil of the Temple Rent
29. Three Days and Three Nights in the grave
30. He Descended into Hell
31. The Meaning of Christ's Death
32. Christ's Resurrection
33. Post-Resurrection Appearances
34. Prophecies Fulfilled in Christ
35. Archaeological Evidence of Christ's Life

A BIT OF HEAVENLY MANNA

Nothing is clearer from the New Testament than that the Lord Jesus expects us to take the low position of servants. We are to be bond-servants of One who Himself was (Philippians 2:6,7). This is not just an extra obligation which we may or may not assume as we please. It is the very heart of that new relationship which the disciple must accept if he is to know fellowship with Christ in any degree of holiness in his life. The New Testament word "bond-servant" in the Greek is meant to show that our position is one where we have no rights and no appeals, where we are the absolute property of our Master, to be treated and disposed of just as He wishes. "We preach not ourselves, but Christ Jesus, the Lord, and ourselves you [bond] servants for Jesus' sake" (II Corinthians 4:5). As bond-servants then,

TO EVERY MAN HIS WORK—13:34[6]

"The Lord Jesus, in going home to His Father, assigned every believer his place in the world and in the church. He has appointed to each one his work, for He never intended that a saint should be idle, or live and labor for himself. Jesus *is* our Master. As such He is present with us, has power over us, is generous to us, but is nevertheless jealous of us. We are *His* servants. He engaged us to serve Him. He supports us while employed by Him, directs us in all our efforts to serve Him, and holds us accountable for our time and our talents. There is work for every one of us; for some in the school with the young; for some in the world with the unconverted; and for some in the local church with the saints. He expects that every one of us will be employed. This will prevent many evils which result from idleness. This will secure much good as it will exercise our graces, spread the truth, bring souls to the Savior, and prevent our backsliding. Beloved, that we may work we have talents given to us, opportunities afforded us, motives presented to us, and rewards promised for laboring together with Him."

PRAYER THOUGHT: "O God, deliver me from pride and indifference and all that is false in thought and action, and help me to watch that I might not enter into temptation. In Jesus' name and for His sake I pray. Amen."[7]

Mark 14:38

Luke—The Book of Christ, the Perfect Man

Name: Luke means "luminous"—a light. He was a physician (Colossians 4:14); a man of education and culture. He was with Paul toward the latter part of his life. It is believed he was a Greek and a proselyte. He seems to disappear at the end of his writing in Acts. Two views are held regarding his martyrdom: one, at the hand of Nero, the same emperor responsible for Paul's death (see NERO in Index); and two, he was hanged on an olive tree in Greece by a party of pagans.

Contents: The first four verses of this book addressed to Theophilus (possibly a convert of Luke's), is an introduction to what Luke sets forth in the remainder of his gospel account. His account records most of the things contained in Matthew (see CONTENTS in Matthew), but with some additions prior to Christ's birth. He also sets forth Christ's genealogy (see GENEALOGY in Index). This book contains 24 chapters, 1,151 verses, and 25,944 words. Luke alone records:

1. The birth of John the Baptist: 1:5-25,57-66
2. The angel's visit with Mary: 1:26-38
3. Mary's visit with John's mother, Elizabeth: 1:39-45
4. Mary's song: 1:46-56
5. The Roman census: 2:1-4
6. Christ's birth: 2:4-7
7. The account of the shepherds: 2:8-20
8. The angel's announcement of Christ's birth: 2:9-15a
9. Circumcision of Christ: 2:21-24
10. The account of Simeon and Anna: 2:25-38

11. Christ's childhood days: 2:39,40
12. Christ with the doctors: 2:41-49
13. Draft of fish: 5:1-11
14. Raising the widow's son: 7:11-15
15. Christ rejoicing: 10:21
16. Intimate story of Mary and Martha: 10:38-42
17. Healing a woman with an infirmity: 13:10-17
18. Healing a man with leprosy: 14:1-6
19. Story of the rich man and Lazarus: 16:19-31
20. Ten lepers healed: 17:11-19
21. Days of Lot and his wife: 17:28-32
22. Story of Zacchaeus: 19:1-10
23. Restoring Malchus' right ear: 22:51
24. Prayer on the Cross: 23:34,46
25. Conversion of the penitent thief: 23:39-43
26. Conversation with two on road to Emmaus: 24:13-35
27. At Bethany for His ascension: 24:50,51
28. See PARABLES peculiar to Luke, p. 414

In addition to the above, Luke

1. Emphasizes Christ's prayer life: 3:21; 5:12-16; 6:12; 9:28,29; 11:1-4; 18:1-8; 21:36; 23:34,46
2. Gives special recognition to the poor: 6:20-25; 8:2,3; 12:16-21; 14:12-15; 16:13; 18:25
3. Exalts womanhood: 1:24-58; 2:1-7,36-38,46-52; 7:11-17; 8:1-3,48; 10:38-42; 13:16; 23:28
4. Gives much space to music. Several great songs are listed in the first two chapters, which the church has been singing ever since.

Character: Historical.

Subject: The illustrative truths (parables) of Christ.

Purpose: To prove that Jesus is the Son of Man, the Savior of the world (19:10).

Outline:[1]

I. The Savior Predicted and Provided: 1:1—4:13
II. The Savior Preaching and Practicing the Grace of God: 4:14—9:50
III. The Savior Pressing toward the Performance of His Passion: 9:51—22:71
IV. The Savior Pouring out the Passion of His Heart: 23
V. The Savior's Profession Perfected: 24

Scope: Luke covers a period of about 34 years.

Writer: Luke has been generally accepted as the author of this third Gospel account down through the centuries. Such early church fathers as Justine, Polycarp, Papias, etc., often refer to this account. It is mentioned as Luke's work by the Muratorian Fragment (A.D. 170). See ACCURACY of Luke under ARCHAEOLOGY in Luke and Acts.

To Whom Written: The great hobby of the Greeks was *perfect manhood* and Luke, finding the Perfect Manhood in Jesus, wrote to the Greeks to commend Christ to them as the *perfect ideal Man,* the Savior of sinners. Specifically, however, it was written to one Theophilus (1:1-4), but intended for all believers.

When and Where Written: Sometime between A.D. 63-68, probably at Philippi or Caesarea.

Key Chapter: 15. The "Lost and Found" chapter.

Key Verse: 19:10.

Key Words: Seek and save.

Key Phrase: The Son of Man.

Key Thought: Behold the Man.

Spiritual Thought: He is the Friend of sinners: 19:7.

Christ Is Seen As: The Son of Man: 19:10.

Names and Titles of Christ. See NAME in Dictionary.

1. Jesus: 1:31; 2:21
2. Son of the Highest: 1:32
3. That Holy Thing: 1:35
4. Son of God: 1:35
5. God my Savior: 1:47
6. Horn of Salvation: 1:69
7. The Prophet of the Highest: 1:76
8. Dayspring from on High: 1:78
9. Savior: 2:11a
10. Christ the Lord: 2:11b
11. Consolation of Israel: 2:25
12. The Lord's Christ: 2:26
13. The Salvation of God: 2:30; 3:6
14. A Light to the Gentiles: 2:32a
15. The Glory of Israel: 2:32b
16. A Sign: 2:34; 11:30
17. Redemption: 2:38
18. Lord: 3:4; 24.34
19. My Beloved Son: 3:22; 9:35
20. Physician: 4:23
21. Jesus of Nazareth: 4:34a; 24:19a
22. The Holy One of God: 4:34b
23. Christ: 4:41; 24:26
24. Son of Man: 5:24; 19:10
25. Lord of the Sabbath: 6:5
26. A great Prophet: 7:16
27. Friend of sinners: 7:34
28. Forgiver of sins: 7:48-50
29. Son of God Most High: 8:28
30. The Christ of God: 9:20
31. Master: 9:33,38,49
32. The Son: 10:22
33. Greater than Solomon: 11:31
34. Greater than Jonah: 11:32
35. Good Master: 18:18
36. Son of David: 18:38
37. Guest of sinners: 19:7
38. The King: 19:38
39. The Chosen of God: 23:35
40. King of the Jews: 23:38
41. A Righteous Man: 23:47
42. The risen Son: 24:6,7

Names and Titles of God. See Name in Dictionary.

1. Lord: 1:6; 4:18
2. The Highest: 1:35,76; 6:35
3. Lord God: 1:68
4. Father: 2:49; 6:36

5. God Most High: 8:28
6. Lord of heaven and earth: 10:21
7. Heavenly Father: 11:31

Names and Titles of the Holy Spirit: See NAME in Index.
1. Holy Ghost: 1:35; 12:10
2. The Spirit: 2:27; 4:1
3. Lord of the harvest: 10:2
4. Holy Spirit: 11:13
5. Promise of the Father: 24:49

Prophecy Fulfilled in Christ: See p. 471..

Prophecy: Destruction of Jerusalem: 21:7-36. See DESTRUCTION in Index.

1. Peculiar to Luke:
   a. Draught of fish: 5:1-11
   b. Raising a widow's son: 7:11-15
   c. Healing a woman with an infirmity: 13:10-17
   d. Healing a man with dropsy: 14:1-6
   e. The ten lepers healed: 17:11-19
   f. Restoring right ear of Malchus: 22:51

2. Common to Luke and Matthew:
   a. Centurion's servant healed: 7:1-10; Matthew 8:5-13
   b. Blind and dumb demoniac healed: 11:14; Matthew 12:22

3. Common to Luke and Mark:
   a. Demoniac cured in synagogue: 4:33; Mark 1:23
   b. Healing of blind Bartimaeus: 18:35-43; Mark 10:46-52

4. Common to Luke, Matthew, and Mark. See p. 386.

5. Common to all gospel writers.
   a. 5000 fed: 9:1-17; Matthew 14:15; Mark 6:30-44; John 6:1-14

Other Miracles or Unusual Events:

1. Virgin birth of Christ—to reveal God's supernatural power in His becoming flesh to dwell among us: 2:5-7. See VIRGIN BIRTH in Index.

2. The angel's announcement of Christ's birth—to reveal heaven's joy in this blessed event: 2:9-14

3. Christ passing through the midst of the people—to demonstrate His Deity: 4:30

4. Power given to the Seventy to heal—to confirm the purpose of Christ's coming to deliver the oppressed: 10:1-9

5. See points 4-9,12, p. 386

6. Christ's appearance in the disciples' midst—to assure them of His resurrection: 24:36

Parables of Christ:

1. Peculiar to Luke:	*Lesson*
a. The two debtors: 7:41-43	Gratitude for pardon
b. Good Samaritan: 10:30-37	Compassion to the suffering
c. Importunate neighbor: 11:5-8	Perseverance in prayer
d. The lighted candle: 11:33-36	An open testimony
e. The rich fool: 12:16-21	Worldly-mindedness
f. The wedding feast: 12:35-40	Vigilance—Christ's return
g. Wise steward: 12:42-48	Conscientiousness in trust
h. Barren fig tree: 13:6-9	Unprofitableness under grace
i. Ambitious guest: 14:7-15	Humility

j. The great supper: 14:16-24   God's call to everyone
k. The lost coin: 15:8-10   Joy in penitence
l. The prodigal son: 15:11-32   Fatherly love to penitent son
m. Unjust steward: 16:1-13   Preparation for eternity
n. Unprofitable servant: 17:7-10   God's claim to our service
o. The unjust judge: 18:1-8   The need for persistent faith
p. Pharisee and Publican: 18:9-14   Self-righteousness and humility
q. The ten pounds: 19:11-27   Diligence rewarded; sloth punished

2. Common to Luke and Matthew. See p. 387.
3. Common to Luke, Matthew, and Mark. See p. 387.
4. Common to Luke and Mark:
     a. The lighted candle: 11:33;   Let your light so shine
        Mark 4:21-23

1. Luke's accuracy in the use of the Greek language of his day has been questioned by critics of the Bible. He used many words and expressions not found in manuscripts of the first century, manuscripts which in most cases used classical Greek. Discoveries in some papyri in Egypt revealed a vernacular Greek which was spoken and written by the common people of that day. This is the Greek used in the New Testament, and these discoveries confirm Luke's correct use of the Greek in his gospel account. See Luke's ACCURACY under Archaeology in Acts and LANGUAGE of the New Testament in Index.

2. The census of Caesar Augustus: 2:1-3. Critics of this account state that Luke made five errors in recording this census: (1) that Augustus did not order a census; (2) that Cyrenius was governor of Syria at a later date; (3) that in those days there was no such system of taking a census; (4) that if one had been ordered, it was not necessary for a man to go to his own city; and (5) if the husband went, it was not necessary for any other member of the family to go. William Ramsey discovered a number of inscriptions which confirm the accuracy of Luke's account. Quirinius (or Cyrenius) was twice governor of Syria—the first time when Christ was born, the second time at a later period. Egyptian papyri reveals that a census was taken every fourteen years, indicating a system was used in census taking. The cycle of such enrollments reveals the approximate time of the one recorded by Luke was 6-5 B.C., which is the accepted time of Christ's birth. One document states: "Tiberius Claudius Caesar Augustus Germanicus Emperor," and supports Luke's statement that one had to journey to his homeland *with* his household to settle his taxes.

Here are some exerpts from some ancient documents: "Gaius Vibius, chief perfect of Egypt. Because of the approaching census it is necessary for all those residing for any cause away from their own districts to prepare to return at once to their own governments, in order that they may complete the family administration of enrollment and that the titled lands may retain those belonging to them."

"To Arius, son of Lysimachus . . ." He then lists his parents and their parents who are inhabitants of his village. Then he registers his son: "I register Pakebkis, the son born to me and my wife, Taasies, daughter of . . . and Taopis in the 10th year of Tiberius Claudius Caesar Augustus Germanicus Imperator, and request that the name of my aforesaid son Pakebis be entered on the list." It was such a custom of census taking that necessitated Joseph's taking Mary with him to Bethlehem, where Christ was born in fulfillment of God's Word (Micah 5:2).

3. Destruction of Jerusalem: 21:10-24. See DESTRUCTION in Index.

Manger

² 1. Christ laid in a manger: 2:7. Because there was no room in the Inn for Mary and Joseph, they probably stayed in a cave which provided shelter for animals. After Christ's birth, Mary wrapped Him in swaddling clothes, and placed Him in an animal feeding trough—a manger. It was probably bedded with straw which had been left by the animals. See SALTED in Index.

2. The latchet of whose shoes I am not worthy to unloose—John's humility: 3:16. See SHOES in Index.

3. Wash His feet with tears: 7:37,38. See TEAR BOTTLES in Index.

4. Suffer me first to bury my father . . . let the dead bury the dead: 9:59,60. In the Near East the firstborn son becomes heir of all his father's possessions. It is his duty and responsibility to stay at home and care for his father until death. He then takes care of his father's funeral, and inherits all possessions (houses, lands, livestock, etc.). Even though he may have some other brothers and sisters, they have no part in this custom—they are "dead" to any part of the inheritance; dead to the relationship the firstborn son had with his father. Jesus knew this man who had said he would follow Him might have to stay home for years until his father's death, hence His remark, "let the dead bury the dead [those dead to the firstborn's relationship with his father]," let them bury him, "but go thou [now] and preach . . ."

There is a custom whereby other sons and daughters by physical birth can be brought into the same relationship with the father that the firstborn son has, and that is by *"adoption"*—adopted into that relationship. Should a father decide that he would like for the other children to share equally with the heir, he can go to the city gate, confer with the elders, and upon agreement, they will make a "covenant of salt" and the father "adopts" his other children into the relationship of the heir (see SALT in Index). Each child will then share equally in what the father possesses. God has only one begotten Son, the Lord Jesus Christ, who is heir of all that the Father possesses. But God has other sons and daughters who are His by spiritual birth, and He loves them and wants them to share in His estate. Within the framework of His government, He, having predestined us unto the adoption of children by Christ Jesus, gives us His Spirit of adoption, and makes us an heir of His and a joint-heir with Jesus Christ. All that is His is mine—all that is mine is His (Ephesians 1:5; Romans 8:14-17).

5. Let me first go bid them farewell: 9:61. Family tradition is such in the Holy Land that an individual does not decide for himself what he or she is to do—one's vocation is determined by the father of the household, who in turn influences all his relatives to side with him in his decision. For an individual (such as the one who said he would follow Christ) to go home and say goodby, this would be the end of him. Every relative would persuade him to stay home and fulfill his father's wish. They would have a time of festivities—mirth and song—to kill any desire of leaving. He would then forfeit his own desires, and never would follow Christ. This is one reason why Jacob "stole away unawares" from his uncle Laban. God had said to Jacob to go back to Bethel, the place of God's blessing. Had Jacob tarried to tell all his relatives goodby, or permit Laban to give him a going-away party, he may never have fulfilled God's command (Genesis 31:25-28).

6. Having put his hand to the plow: 9:62. An Eastern plow has only *one* handle, and must of necessity be held tightly to keep the plowshare in the ground. The other hand is used to hold the reins and often a long stick (goad or prick) to prod the animal along. A farmer keeps looking ahead, mainly because of the rocky soil. Should he look back and his plow strike a rock, the furrow would be crooked, or, with such a tight grip on the handle, he would lose his balance and probably be thrown to the ground. He then would become the laughingstock of other farmers and would seriously damage his reputation. Christ emphasized the need to keep looking ahead so that as we "watch and pray" we would not be tripped up by the devil and his tactics. See PLOWING in Index.

Plow, Hand to

7. Salute no man by the way . . . go not from house to house: 10:4,7. See SALUTE in Index.

8. Children in bed with me: 11:7. See BEDS in Index.

9. Sit in the lowest seat: 14:10. Seats in the upper room were so arranged that the upper seats, or the most important ones, were closest to the table, and the lowest seats, or those farthest away, were less important. A good guest would be humble, taking a *low* seat until the host decides where he will be placed. He then may be placed in a seat of higher importance. "Whosoever exalteth himself shall be abased, but whoso humbleth himself shall be exalted" (Luke 14:11).

10. They all with one consent began to make excuses: 14:18. Religion and culture are one and the same in the East. Everything that is done is linked with their religion. Whatever is

bought, whatever is done, God is considered first, and dedication follows. In the parable of the great supper (14:16-27), the invitation to it is declined by three people, each making his own excuse. We Westerners think each excuse is foolish, in view of such an invitation to a great supper. The first, who had bought a piece of ground, said, "I must needs go and see it." We would look at the property *first,* then buy. The second said he had bought five oxen, and "I go to prove them." We examine animals *first,* then buy. The third said, "I have married a wife, and therefore I cannot come." We could think of no better place to take a new bride than to a banquet.

The first man would not accept because of his *religion.* Having bought property, it was the custom in early evening to dedicate the property to God. An altar was built, friends joined him in the dedicatory prayer, and a sacrifice was offered. The second man asked to be excused for the same reason, to dedicate his oxen, but also to put them to work as quickly as possible. His motive was more for the *material* than to honor God, although he had a "form of godliness." The third man was just recently married. Jewish custom forbade a newly married couple to do anything the first year except to stay and feast with their relatives and dedicate their new home (Deuteronomy 20:5; 24:5). To accept an invitation elsewhere would insult their families, and would go contrary to *family custom and tradition.*

The causes which prompted these excuses are the same which keep people from coming to Christ today—from accepting His gracious invitation to have salvation full and free. To be a follower of Christ, one must forsake all—religion, houses, lands, family, friends, traditional custom, even the material. This is the *only* way one can be a disciple (Matthew 19:29).

11. A lost coin: 15:8,9. When an Eastern woman marries, her bridegroom gives her a wedding gift of ten pieces of silver, which she wears on a chain hanging from her curious piece of headdress. She prizes the gift highly and guards it carefully, for the loss of even one coin would be regarded by her husband as a lack of affection and respect for him. He could even accuse his wife of unfaithfulness and seek a divorce. These coins were held sacred and could only be spent in need in widowhood. We can understand the woman's concern and anxiety when she lost a coin, and why there was such rejoicing with her neighbors when she found it. (See coins on woman's headdress in picture, p. 393). Whatever we lose that affects our testimony should be sought until found (or regained), so that we may continue in the joy of God's salvation.

Chaff Blown Away

12. Highest seat in the synagogue: 20:46. See SEAT in Index.

13. The widow's mites: 21:1-4. See MITES in Index.

14. Man carrying water pitcher: 22:10. See PITCHER in Index.

15. Upper room: 22:12. See HOUSES in Index.

16. To sift as wheat: 22:31. A most interesting sight in the Holy Land is to see the men bring in shocks of wheat to the threshing floor. Women gather in a circle, either seated on the floor or on a small stool, and with club-like sticks beat the pile of wheat to separate the kernel from the stalks. After several hours of beating, a couple of men come with wooden pitchforks and scoop up the stalks. In the process of scooping, the kernels remain on the threshing floor and the broken stalks are thrown in the air, causing the wind to drive "the chaff away." The sight is such that one hardly notices the "fruit of the stalk" (grain) on the floor. Jesus told Peter that this is what Satan wanted to do with him—sift as wheat—attract attention to the imperfections in his life, to magnify his faults, while the real fruit of his Christian experience went unnoticed. The "accuser of the brethren" knows that if the world does not see Christ in us, they will not turn to Him. "Chaff driven away" also applies to the unregenerate—those without Christ: Psalm 1:4,5.

1. Circumcision of Christ: 2:21. See CIRCUMCISION in Index.

2. When Christ spoke of His second coming "as the lightning that lighteneth out of one part under heaven, shineth unto the other part under heaven" (17:24). He said: "In that night there shall be two men in bed . . . two women shall be grinding together . . . two men shall be in the field" (17:34-36). This sudden event is described as taking place while it is night in one place, early morning in another, and daylight in the other. Because the earth is a sphere, part of it will be illuminated by the sun and the other half will be in darkness.

3. Christ's resurrection: 24:1-6. See RESURRECTION in Index.

The Old Testament in Luke: In addition to the verses found listed in PROPHECIES Fulfilled in Christ (see p. 471), note the following—

1. To turn the hearts of the fathers: 1:17 with Malachi 4:6
2. Every male that openeth the womb: 2:23 with Exodus 13:2,12
3. A pair of turtledoves: 2:24 with Leviticus 12:8
4. Man shall not live by bread alone: 4:4 with Deuteronomy 8:3
5. Worship the Lord thy God: 4:8 with Deuteronomy 6:13
6. Angels charge over thee: 4:10,11 with Psalm 91:11,12
7. Not tempt the Lord thy God: 4:12 with Deuteronomy 6:16
8. The Spirit . . . upon Me: 4:18 with Isaiah 61:1,2
9. I send my messenger: 7:27 with Malachi 3:1
10. Seeing they might not see: 8:10 with Isaiah 6:9
11. Love the Lord thy God: 10:27 with Deuteronomy 6:5
12. Love thy neighbor: 10:27 with Leviticus 19:18
13. Coming in the name of the Lord: 13:35 with Psalm 118:26
14. Various commandments: 18:20 with Exodus 20:12-16
15. If a man's brother die: 20:28 with Deuteronomy 25:5
16. The Lord said unto my Lord: 20:42,43 with Psalm 110:1
17. Companion references:
    a. David's throne: 1:32 with Psalm 132:11
    b. His kingdom . . . no end: 1:33 with Daniel 4:3
    c. Abraham . . . his seed forever: 1:55 with Genesis 17:19

d. Oath . . . to Abraham: 1:73 with Genesis 12:3
e. Dayspring from on high: 1:78 with Numbers 24:17; Malachi 4:2
f. Light in darkness: 1:79 with Isaiah 9:2
g. Eight days . . . circumcision: 2:21 with Leviticus 12:3
h. Days of her purification: 2:22 with Leviticus 12:2-4
i. The fall and the rising again: 2:34 with Isaiah 8:14
j. Famine in Elijah's day: 4:25,26 with I Kings 17
k. Naaman the leper: 4:27 with II Kings 5
l. Show thyself unto the priest: 5:14 with Leviticus 14:3
m. David . . . take and eat the showbread: 6:4 with I Samuel 21:6
n. This do, and thou shalt live: 10:28 with Leviticus 18:5
o. Depart, ye workers of iniquity: 13:27 with Psalm 6:8
p. House left to you desolate: 13:35 with Jeremiah 22:25,26
q. Thy brother trespass against thee: 17:3 with Leviticus 19:17
r. Days of Noah: 17:26,27 with Genesis 6:1-8
s. Days of Lot in Sodom: 17:28,29 with Genesis 19:1-25
t. Remember Lot's wife: 17:32 with Genesis 19:26
u. Parable of the vineyard: 20:9 with Isaiah 5:1
v. Blessed are the barren: 23:29 with Isaiah 54:1
w. It behooved Christ to suffer: 24:46 with Isaiah 53:5

1. The Annunciation: 1:26-38. Christ was foretold:[3]

a. To Adam—as to becoming a man: Genesis 3:15 with Galatians 4:4,5
b. To Abraham—as to His nation: Genesis 22:18
c. To Jacob—as to His tribe: Genesis 49:10
d. To Isaiah—as to His family: Isaiah 11:1-5
e. To Micah—as to His village of birth: Micah 5:2
f. To Daniel—as to His time: Daniel 9:25
g. To Mary—as to His person: Luke 1:30,32
h. By angels—as to His date: Luke 2:11
i. By a star—as to His birthplace: Matthew 2:9

2. At His birth the night was turned into day (2:8,9). At His death the day was turned into night (23:44).

3. The First Christian Message, to Shepherds: 2:8-20
a. The message proclaimed: vss. 10-12
b. Proclaimed to men of low estate: vs. 8
c. There was fear: vs. 9 with Genesis 3:10
d. They believed: vs. 15
e. Their faith was put into action: vs. 16
f. Faith was confirmed: vs. 17a
g. They testified: vss. 17b,18
h. They were filled with joy and praise: vs. 20.

4. What Shall I Do?
a. Asked under conviction: 3:10,12,14. Answer: *Repent*
b. Asked to test Christ: 10:25-37. Answer: *Obey*
c. Asked to secure self: 12:17-31. Answer: *Seek God first*
d. Asked in trial: 16:3-13. Answer: *Be faithful*
e. Asked in search for security: 18:18. Answer: *Give*
f. Asked by Jesus to heal: 18:41. Answer: *Have faith*

      g. Asked by God for unbelief: 20:13. Answer: *God's Son*

5. Christian Baptism: 3:21,22. See BAPTISM In Index.
6. Christ's Temptation: 4:1-13. See TEMPTATION and Satan in Index.
7. The Christian Life: 4:1-13[4]
    a. A life not of this world—man shall not live by bread alone: vs. 4a
    b. A life of faith—but [live] by the Word of God: vs. 4b
    c. A life of adoration—worship the Lord thy God: vs. 8a
    d. A life of service—Him only shalt thou serve: vs. 8b
    e. A life of humble obedience—thou shalt not tempt the Lord thy God: vs. 12
    f. An overcoming life—the devil departed (for a season): vs. 13
8. Types of Christ's Enemies
    a. Jews—prejudice: 4:28,29; John 12:37
    b. Lawyers—education: 10:25
    c. Evil-minded people—blasphemy: 11:14-23
    d. The sophisticated—trivial matters: 11:37,38
    e. Self-righteous—hypocrisy: 11:39,44
    f. Hypocrites—dishonesty: 11:53,54
    g. The wealthy—self-reliance: 12:16-21
    h. Politicians—prestige: 13:31-33
    i. Religionists—tradition: 14:1-6
    j. Church members—lip service: Matthew 7:21-23
    k. Board members—ulterior motives: Mark 14:3-5
    l. False teachers—two-faced: Matthew 7:15
    m. Unbelievers—indifference: Matthew 27:36
    n. Lazy servants—shirkers: Matthew 25:24,25
    o. Proud—fearful: John 12:42
    p. Betraying friends—deceit: Matthew 26:49,50
    q. Boasters—denyers: Mark 14:29,67,68
    r. Governments—banning truth: John 18:38—19:6
9. Why Call Me Lord, and Do Not Obey: 6:46. See POEM "I'll Do It" in Index.
    a. I am *Master*. Do you *ask* of Me?
    b. I am *Almighty*. Do you *honor* Me?
    c. I am *Righteous*. Do you *fear* Me?
    d. I am *Everlasting*. Do you *seek* Me?
    e. I am *Merciful*. Do you *trust* Me?
    f. I am *Light*. Do you *see* Me?
    g. I am *Love*. Do you *love* Me?
    h. I am the *Way*. Do you *follow* me?
    i. I am *Truth*. Do you *believe* Me?
    j. I am *Life*. Do you *live* for Me?
    k. I am *Rich*. Do you *lack* anything?
    l. I am *Lord*. Do you *worship* Me?
    m. I am *God*. Do you *acknowledge* Me?
10. Seed-time and Harvest: 8:11[5]
    a. The field: Matthew 13:38
    b. The seed: Luke 8:11
    c. The sowing: Ecclesiastes: 11:6
    d. The growth: John 12:24
    e. The fruit: I Corinthians 3:6,7
    f. The harvest: John 4:35
      (1) Sure: Galatians 6:7
      (2) Plenteous: II Corinthians 9:6
      (3) Bountiful: Matthew 9:37

    g. The reaping: Revelation 14:15-18

    h. The reward: Psalm 126:6; Daniel 12:3

  11. **Whom Say the People that I Am?** 9:18.[6] See CHRIST, Whom Say, in Index. To the world in general, Christ has been given a host of titles. To the—

Architect, He is the Chief Cornerstone: I Peter 2:6

Artist, the All-together Lovely One: Song of Solomon 5:16

Astronomer, The Bright and Morning Star and the Sun of Righteousness: Revelation 22:16; Malachi 4:2

Baker, the Bread of Life: John 6:35

Banker, the Supplier of every need: Philippians 4:19; Genesis 22:14

Battalion, the Leader and Commander: Isaiah 55:4

Biologist, the Life: John 14:6

Builder, the Foundation: Isaiah 28:16; I Corinthians 3:11

Carpenter, the Door and the Nail: John 10:7; Isaiah 22:23

Chief, the Chiefest of Ten Thousand: Song of Solomon 5:10

Defendent, the Righteous Judge: II Timothy 4:8

Doctor, The Great Physician: Matthew 8:17; Luke 4:23

Educator, the Teacher: John 3:2

Electrician, the Light of the world: John 8:12

Engineer, the New and Living Way: Hebrews 10:19,20

Executive, the Head of the Church: Ephesians 1:22; Colossians 1:18

Executor, the Heir of all things: Hebrews 1:2

Farmer, the Sower and Lord of the harvest: Matthew 13:37; Luke 10:2

Fireman, the Water of Life: John 4:10,14,15

Fisherman, the Calmer of the seas: Matthew 8:23-27

Florist, The Lily of the Valley; the Rose of Sharon: Song of Solomon 2:1

Geologist, the Tried Stone (Rock of Ages): Isaiah 28:16

Herbalist, a Cluster of Camphire: Song of Solomon 1:14

Historian, Ancient of Days: Daniel 7:9

Horticulturist, the Tender Plant: Isaiah 53:2

Host, the Perfect Guest: Luke 19:5-10

Industrialist, the Faithful Servant: Matthew 20:28

Jeweler, the Precious Stone: I Peter 2:6

Juror, the Faithful and True Witness: Revelation 3:14

King, the Crown and Septre: Isaiah 28:5; Numbers 24:17

Laborer, the Burden-bearer: Matthew 11:28,29; Isaiah 53:4-6

Lawmaker, the Law Giver: Isaiah 33:22

Lawyer, the Advocate-Mediator: I John 2:1; I Timothy 2:5

Machinist, the Polished Shaft: Isaiah 49:2

Merchant, the Pearl of Great Price: Matthew 13:46

Mortician, the Resurrection and the Life: John 11:25

Musician, the Horn of Salvation: Luke 1:69

News Reporter, Good Tidings of great joy: Luke 2:10,11

Nurseryman, the True Vine: John 15:1

Oculist, the Light of the eyes: Proverbs 29:13

Pharmacist, The Balm of Gilead and Ointment: Jeremiah 8:22; Song of Solomon 1:3

Philanthropist, the Unspeakable Gift: II Corinthians 9:15

Philosopher, the Wisdom of God: I Corinthians 1:24,30

Photographer, the Express Image of God: Hebrews 1:3

Policeman, Shiloh (Peacemaker): Genesis 49:10
Printer, the Word: John 1:1; Revelation 19:13
Publisher, the Author: Hebrews 12:2
Rancher, the Owner of cattle on a thousand hills: Psalm 50:10
Refiner, the Purifier: Malachi 3:3; Hebrews 1:3
Royalty, the King of kings: I Timothy 6:15
Sailor, the Desired Haven: Psalm 107:30
Scholar, the Alpha and Omega: Revelation 1:8
Scientist, the Creator of all things: Colossians 1:16
Sculptor, the Living Stone: I Peter 2:4
Sea Captain, Refuge in a storm: Isaiah 25:4
Servant, the Good Master: Matthew 23:8
Shepherd, the Lamb of God: John 1:29
Shipbuilder, the Anchor: Hebrews 6:19
Soldier, the Captain: Joshua 5:15; Hebrews 2:10
Statesman, the Desire of all Nations: Haggai 2:7
Student, the Truth: John 14:6
Teacher, the Example: I Peter 2:21
Theologian, the Author and Finisher of our faith: Hebrews 12:2
Toiler, the Giver of rest: Matthew 11:28
Traveler, the Narrow Way: Matthew 7:14; John 14:6
United Nations, Peace: Ephesians 2:14
Warrior, a Shield: Psalm 3:3
Zoologist, Lion of the Tribe of Judah: Revelation 5:5

And to the *Christian* He is the Son of the living God, the Savior, our Redeemer, and the loving Lord and Master.

12. The Believer's Cross: 9:23; 14:27. See CROSS in Index.

13. Putting God First: 9:59,61. This involves—
    a. Unaltering faith: Hebrews 11:6a
    b. Uncompromising obedience: Hebrews 11:8
    c. Unselfish sacrifices: Romans 12:1,2
    d. Results in:
       —An undeniable gain: Hebrews 11:6b
       —Revealing Christ: I Timothy 1:16

14. Jesus' visit to Martha's house: 10:38-42. This visit of Jesus to the home of His friends brought out the true feelings of those who profess to know Him. One sister, Mary, "sat at Jesus' feet, and heard His word." While the daily routine of home-life was important, to know more of Jesus and His love was more important to this sister, but not to Martha, who no doubt loved Jesus also. Her "house" was her castle; she "was occupied with much serving, . . . and upset about many things." She no doubt welcomed Jesus with her lips, but her heart was not prepared for this visit.

If Jesus Came to Your House[7]

If Jesus came to your house to spend a day or two—
If He came unexpectedly, I wonder what you'd do?
Oh, I know you'd give Him your nicest room—this honored Guest,
  And all the food you'd serve to Him would be the very best;
And you would keep assuring Him you're glad to have Him there,
  That serving Him in your home is joy beyond compare.

But—when you saw Him coming, would you meet Him at the door
   With arms outstretched in welcome to your Heavenly Visitor?
Or would you have to change your clothes before you let Him in?
   Or hide some magazines and put the Bible where they'd been?
Would you turn off the television and hope He hadn't heard?
   And wish you hadn't uttered that loud, hasty word?

Would you hide your worldly music and put some hymn books out?
   Could you let Jesus walk right in, or would you rush about?
And I wonder—if the Saviour spent a day or two with you,
   Would you go right on doing the things you always do?
Would you go right on saying the things you always say?
   Would life for you continue as it does from day to day?

Would your family conversation keep up its usual pace?
   And would you find it hard each meal to say a table grace?
Would you sing the songs you always sing, and read the books you read?
   And let Him know the things on which your mind and spirit feed?
Would you take Jesus with you everywhere you'd planned to go?
   Or would you, maybe, change your plans for just a day or so?

Would you be glad to have Him meet your closest friends?
   Or would you hope they'd stay away till His visit ends?
Would you be glad to have Him stay forever on and on?
   Or would you sigh with great relief when He at last was gone?
It might be interesting to know the things that you would do
   If Jesus Christ in person came to spend some time with you!

15. The Disciple's Prayer: 11:1-4. When we pray, say—
    a. Our Father—as sons
    b. Hallowed by Thy Name—as worshipers
    c. Thy kingdom come—as subjects
    d. Thy will be done—as servants
    e. Give us this day—as recipients
    f. Forgive us our sins—as sinners
    g. Lead us not into temptation—as helpless ones
    h. But deliver us from evil—as conquerors
16. Without Excuse: 14:18 with Romans 1:20. If you are looking for a good excuse, see your pastor. He's probably heard more than anyone else! See EXCUSES in Index.
17. Proof of Discipleship: 14:25-33. See DISCIPLESHIP in Index.
    a. Leaving kindred: vs. 26a
    b. Hating self (loving less than the Lord): vs. 26b
    c. Bearing one's cross: vs. 27a
    d. Following Christ: vs. 27b
    e. Forsaking possessions: vs. 33
    f. Continuing in Christ's Word: John 8:31
    g. Loving one another: John 13:34
    h. Fruitbearing: John 15:8
    i. Enduring hardness: II Timothy 2:3
18. Parables in Luke Fifteen—
    a. The lost sheep—one lost in one hundred: vss. 3-7. *Christ* seeking the lost
    b. The lost coin—one lost in ten: vss. 8-10. The *Holy Spirit* seeking to find the misplaced to put it in its proper place

    c. The lost son—one lost in two: vss. 11-24. The *Father* hurrying to welcome the returning prodigal to restore him to full and wonderful fellowship. He gives—
      —A robe of righteousness
      —A ring of assurance
      —Shoes of peace

19. **Chapters in the Prodigal's Life: 15:11-24**
    a. Chapter One—Sick of Home: Rashness; vs. 12
    b. Chapter Two—Away from Home: Reveling; vs. 13
    c. Chapter Three—Lack of Home: Remote, Reduced, Rank, Ruin; vss. 14-16
    d. Chapter Four—Homesick: Reflection, Regret, Repentance, Resolution; vss. 17-19
    e. Chapter Five—Homeward Bound: Return; vs. 20a
    f. Chapter Six—Back Home: Received, Rewarded, Rejoicing, Renewed; vss. 20b-24

20. **The Prodigal's Father: 15:12-24**
    a. Giving his all: vs. 12
    b. Waiting in love: vs. 20
    c. Restoring in grace: vss. 22-24

21. **Hell: 16:19-31.** Jesus was the greatest "hell-fire and brimstone" preacher that ever lived. He preached more on this subject than He did on heaven (three times more). He taught there was a hell by—
    a. Direct statements: Matthew 10:28; 11:23; 23:33
    b. Powerful allusions: Mark 9:43
    c. Historical reference: Luke 16:19-31

Hell is described in the Bible as—
    a. A flame of fire: Luke 16:24
    b. A furnace of fire: Matthew 13:42
    c. A lake of fire: Revelation 20:15
    d. A place of darkness: Matthew 8:12; II Peter 2:4; Jude 13
    e. A place of sorrows: Psalm 18:5
    f. A place of torment: Luke 16:24
    g. A place of filth: Revelation 21:8
    h. A place where the worm dieth not, where the fire is not quenched. It is everlasting: Matthew 25:41; Mark 9:43; Revelation 14:11

The location of hell. Heaven is "from above." Hell is "from beneath" (Isaiah 14:9). It is "down . . . to the sides of the pit" (Isaiah 14:15). When the sons of Korah questioned the authority of Moses, "the earth opened . . . and swallowed them up, and . . . they . . . went down alive into the pit . . . to the nether parts of the earth" (Numbers 16:32,33; Ezekiel 31:14). "Hell is God's one last act of love to people who will accept nothing else at His hand. He leaves one corner of the universe for which they can call their own, and in which they can continue to live for all eternity as though He did not exist."[8]

The inhabitants of hell are—
    a. The devil and his angels: Matthew 25:41
    b. The wicked: Psalm 9:17a; I Corinthians 6:9,10; Revelation 21:8
    c. All Nations that forget God: Psalm 9:17b
    d. Moral Christ-rejectors: Matthew 7:21-23

What the inhabitants of hell discover—
    a. That hell is a reality
    b. That hell is not soul sleep
    c. That death does not end it all
    d. That punishment is eternal
    e. That there is no mercy there
    f. That there is but one way to stay out—none to get out

Activity of the inhabitants of hell—
    a. Weeping and gnashing of teeth: Matthew 8:12

   b. Crying for relief: Luke 16:24
   c. Remembering the past: Luke 16:25
   d. Looking across a great gulf: Luke 16:26
   e. Praying for the lost on earth: Luke 16:27-31
22. **What's Good about Hell?** 16:19-31
   a. One has good sight: vs. 23
   b. One has good feeling: vs. 23
   c. One has good thirst: vs. 24
   d. One has good memory: vs. 25
   e. One has good concern for others: vs. 26
   f. One says "good bye forever:" vs. 26
23. **Servants for Christ:** 17:7-10. See SERVANTS in Index.
24. **Remember Lot's Wife:** 17:32 with Genesis 19:1-26. See LOT'S WIFE in Index.
   Remember her privileges—
   a. Faithfully instructed
   b. Relative to one of God's chosen—Abraham
   c. Warned of danger
   Remember her fate—
   a. Merited
   b. Sudden
   c. Final
   Practical reflections—
   a. Beware of earthly entanglements
   b. Beware of questioning God's commands
   c. Beware of delays
   d. Beware of disobedience
25. **Men Ought Always to Pray:** 18:1.[9] See PRAYER in Index.
   a. The purpose of prayer is that God might be glorified in the answers
   b. One does not pray to change God's mind or will, but for God to adjust us to His will
   c. It is permissible for one to pray for whatever is permissible to desire
   d. Prayer is not so much the getting of answers as it is getting a hold of the God who answers prayer
   e. Your ability to stay with God in the prayer closet is the measure of your ability to stay with God when outside the prayer closet
   f. An attitude of prayer will create an atmosphere of prayer
   g. Kneeling in prayer will always keep one in good standing with the Lord
   h. Seven days without prayer makes one weak
   i. If you are too busy to pray, then you are too busy
   j. Prayer is weakness leaning on Omnipotence
   k. Prayer is faith laying hold on God's promises
   l. Prayer is the thirsty soul's cry for the Living Water
   m. Prayer is a virtue that prevails against all temptations
   n. Prayer is the Christian's staff by which he is helped along his homeward way
   o. Prayer is the atmosphere in which all Christian virtue grows
   p. Prayer is the believer's outstretched hand and upward vision seeking the fulness of God
   q. Prayer is the child taking hold of God's hand for strength
   r. Prayer is inspiration, accepting the challenge to lay hold on Divine realities
   s. Prayer is the open door by which the individual may pass from struggle to victory
   t. Prayer is God's instrument by which one's tribulations become patience
   u. Prayer is trusting God in the dark
   v. Prayer is a "Golden River" at whose brink some die of thirst, while others kneel and drink
   w. The end of worry is prayer. The end of prayer is peace

26. Lessons from the Pharisee and Publican: 18:9-14

Pharisee: he was a liar: vss. 11,12

a. He was as other men—a sinner: Romans 3:23
b. He was an extortioner: Mark 12:40
c. He was unjust—his attitude proved this
d. He was an adulterer—spiritually
e. He was worse than the Publican—blinded to his own needs
f. He only fasted to boast
g. He didn't tithe all he possessed—he hadn't surrendered his own heart and life to God: Luke 20:25

He was too polished to take a drink from a bottle, but could sip cocktails and keep beer in the refrigerator.

He was too refined to skip the Sunday morning church service, but could spend the rest of the day for self and sports.

He was too cultured to frequent the honky-tonks of his town, but could throw parties in his home that would put Jezebel to shame!

He was too sophisticated to fraternize with those on the other side of the tracks, but could conduct shady business deals.

He was so religious he could "talk" the language, but his dirty jokes would make Satan blush.

He had a zeal of God but not according to the Bible: Romans 10:1-3.

Publican: he was honest: vss. 13,14

a. He knew what he was—a sinner, condemned, lost
b. He knew where he stood with God—at a distance
c. He knew how he felt—guilty and ashamed
d. He knew what he needed—mercy
e. He knew how to get it—confess and call upon God
f. He knew he got it—he went down to his house justified

Pharisee	*Publican*
1. Trusted in self	1. Did what he felt
2. No sense of sin and guilt	2. Meant what he said
3. No sense of need	3. Ask what he needed
4. No humility	4. Went home forgiven
5. Went home with sins	5. Enjoyed what he got

27. Cost of not Becoming a Christian: Luke 18:18-23. We often, like the rich young ruler, try to determine what it will cost us *to* become a Christian. What will it cost *not* to become one?

a. God's saving grace and power. He alone has salvation: Isaiah 45:22
b. Forgiveness of sin and guilt: Jeremiah 2:22 with I John 1:7 and 9
c. Comforting presence of the Holy Spirit: I Corinthians 3:16
d. Assurance of the Word of God: I John 5:13
e. Joy of the Lord: vs. 23 with Psalm 16:11; 43:4
f. Blessed hope of ever seeing Jesus and loved ones in Christ again: I Thessalonians 4:16,17

28. Peter's Downfall: 22:54-62. See DOWNFALL in Index.

29. Lessons from the Dying Thief: 23:39-43

a. He admitted he was a sinner—justly
b. He knew sin must be punished
c. He witnessed to his buddy
d. He called upon the name of the Lord
e. Christ is never too busy to talk to us
f. No sinner is too great to be overlooked
g. He put first things first—*remember me*
h. He believed in Christ's return—"when Thou comest into Thy kingdom"

i. God will receive anyone, anytime, if there is true repentance
j. Today is the day of salvation
k. It takes faith in Christ's death to be saved
l. The dying thief probably exercised the greatest faith ever manifested. To believe in Christ when miracles were performed would have been easy. But when it appeared that Christ was fighting a losing battle, dying as a condemned criminal, dying when all government, religion, people in general, and even the disciples (having fled) were against Him, the thief *did* believe in Him!

For points 30—50, see HIGHLIGHTS of Christ's Life, pp. 452-473.
30. The Passover and the Lord's Supper: 22:14-20
31. Christ in Gethsemane: 22:39-46
32. The Betrayal by Judas: 22:47,48
33. The (mis-) Trial of Christ: 22:66—22:25
34. Christ's Innocency Attested: 23:41
35. Christ's Rejections by the Jews: 23:13-24
36. The Crucifixion: 23:23-46
37. The Wounds of Jesus
38. Superscriptions on the Cross
39. Seven Last Sayings of Christ
40. Seven Last Sayings of the Crowd
41. Christ was Forsaken
42. Twelve Views of the Cross
43. Veil of the Temple Rent: 23:45
44. Three Days and Three Nights in the Grave
45. He Descended into Hell
46. The Meaning of Christ's Death
47. Christ's Resurrection: 24:1-6
48. Post-Resurrection Appearances
49. Prophecy Fulfilled in Christ
50. Archaeological Evidence of Christ's Life

A BIT OF
HEAVENLY MANNA

Luke places much emphasis on humility and exaltation. The publican was brought low in repentance before he was exalted (18:13,14). So was the prodigal son (15:13-24). Just the opposite is true for one who seeks to exalt himself. The Pharisee who boasted of all his good works was abased—he did not go back to his house justified (18:9-12,14). Cross bearing is humiliating, but it exalts one as a disciple of Christ (9:23,24). This is a paradox—the way "up" is "down"—the way to victory is surrender, but it is God's way of true blessing (see PARADOX in Index). We must ever be learning the truth that—

WHOSOEVER EXALTETH HIMSELF SHALL BE ABASED—14:11[10]

"If we would rise high, we must lie low; for before honor is humility. We are all prone to exalt ourselves, and to justify ourselves in doing so. There is very much pride remaining in our hearts, and it often lies concealed under our most humiliating expressions. We need to be stripped daily, to be emptied from vessel to vessel; for if we are not, self-will will soon puff us up. Every Christian should aim to exalt his God, to honor the Lord Jesus, and to leave his own reputation in his Savior's hands. Honor follows the truly humble even like his shadow, but it flies away from the proud like a bird. Pride must be abased. The proud professor must be laid low. Every doctrine of the Gospel, and every precept of God's Law, is opposed to our pride. If therefore we swell with self-conceit, if we make much of ourselves, if we set ourselves up before, or above our fellow man, God will bring us down; for whosoever exalteth himself shall be abased, but he that humbleth himself shall be exalted. May we be daily clothed with humility."

PRAYER THOUGHT: "Though Satan desires to sift me as wheat, remind me, blessed Savior, that Thou art praying for me. Give me the strength I need to answer Thy prayer, that my faith fail not, yea, that I fail Thee not. In Thy dear name I pray. Amen."[11]

Luke 22:31,32

John—The Book of Christ, the Son of God

Name: John or Johanan means "grace, gift, or mercy of the Lord." He is one of the best-known disciples—called "the beloved disciple," or the disciple "whom Jesus loved" (13:23; 19:26; 20:2; 21:7,20). The New Testament mentions Matthew and Mark five times each, Luke three times, and John thirty-five times. Though "Beloved," he was fiery—"the son of thunder" (Mark 3:17). He revealed this characteristic when he wished to destroy the Samaritans with fire (Luke 9:54), and his taking to task one for casting out demons who was not following Jesus (Mark 9:38). John was the son of Zebedee (Matthew 4:21) and Salome (Mark 15:40), who apparently was the sister of Mary, Jesus' mother (19:25). If Mary and Salome were sisters, John and Jesus were first cousins. This would also make him related to John the Baptist (Luke 1:36).

John was a fisherman, in partnership with Simon (Peter) and his father (Matthew 4:21,22; Luke 5:10,11), a man of means who owned his own home and had hired servants (19:27; Mark 1:19,20). He was acquainted with the high priest in Jerusalem (18:15,16) and was a disciple of John the Baptist (1:35,40). He became one of Jesus' first disciples (1:35-37), and remained with Christ until the ascension. John was one of three disciples privileged to be at the raising of Jairus' daughter (Luke 8:51-56), the transfiguration of Christ (Mark 9:2), and when Christ prayed in the garden (Mark 14:32,33). His acquaintance with the high priest at Jerusalem enabled him to gain admission to Christ's trial before Annas and Caiaphas (18:12-16). He was probably the only disciple at the crucifixion (19:26). He outran Peter to reach the empty tomb, and was the first to recognize the risen Savior in Galilee (20:1-4; 21:7).

He was in attendance at the Council at Jerusalem in A.D. 49-50 (Acts 15:4), and later went to Asia Minor, where he was Bishop or pastor of the seven churches, residing mostly at Ephesus. He was banished to the island of Patmos, where he wrote the book of Revelation. Returning to Ephesus, he died ca. A.D. 100. He was the only apostle who did not suffer martyrdom. Next to Paul, he was the leading writer of the New Testament, having written five books—the fourth gospel account, three Epistles, and the Revelation.

Contents: This book is a divinely inspired record of the pre-existence, life, ministry, death, resurrection, and post-resurrection appearances of Christ, the Son of God. The first three gospel accounts are called the "Synoptic" gospels, because they are written according to a similar pattern. John's account is different. Matthew, Mark, and Luke *recorded;* John *inter-*

preted. The Synoptic gospels give attention to the historical—to Christ's ministry in Galilee; John majors on the doctrinal and spiritual aspects of Christ's witness and teachings in Jerusalem and Judea. Over one-half of John's account is devoted to events during "Passion Week," and it is from this fact that we deduce the length of Christ's public ministry—approximately three-and-one-half years.

The prophet Isaiah (9:6) reported the coming of Christ as the "child born" and the "Son given," which sets forth Messiah's humanity and deity. The genealogies of Matthew and Luke reveal the "child born." John reveals to us the "Son given." His record of Christ is filled with symbolism. Christ is the *"Lamb"* to be sacrificed for sin (1:29), *"Water"* to the thirsty (4:14; 7:37), *"Bread"* for the hungry (6:35), *"Light"* for those in darkness (8:12), the *"Door"* to enter into God's presence (10:9), the *"Good Shepherd"* to lead those who have gone astray (10:11), the *"Way"* or Road to travel to glory (14:6), and the *"True Vine"* for spiritual growth (15:1). Each of these supplies God's provision for man's spiritual need. Christ is presented as God's answer to *any* man's need—rich or poor, moral or immoral, religious or unbelieving (e.g., Nicodemus: 3:1-18; the Samaritan women: 4:5-39; the adulterous woman: 8:1-11; and the believing Jews: 11:45).

The selection of miracles in this book was deliberate. They are called "signs," due to the fact that they signified the deity of Christ. In chapter two, John gives three proofs of Christ's deity—

1. His divine *power*—shown by the first of His many miracles: vss. 1-11
2. His divine *authority*—shown by His driving out the money-changers from the Temple: vss. 13-17
3. His divine *knowledge*—as shown by His first prediction of His death and resurrection: vss. 19-22

In stressing Christ's deity, John emphasized His humanity also—"the Word became flesh" and "I came forth from the Father, and am come into the world (1:14; 16:28), and uses the name "Jesus" almost to the exclusion of "Christ." He goes into minute detail regarding events, such as "the next day" (1:29,35,43), and gives specific locations, such as "Bethabara, beyond Jordan" (1:28) and "Cana of Galilee" (2:1).

The book closes with the statement that "there are also many other things which Jesus did, the which, if they should be written every one, I suppose that even the world itself could not contain the books that should be written. Amen." What John did write contains 21 chapters, 879 verses, and 19,099 words.

In addition to the discourses peculiar to John's gospel account, he alone records—

1. His own personal testimony to Christ: 1:1-17
2. The first Passover: 2:13-22
3. The last testimony of John the Baptist: 3:23-26
4. The second Passover: 6:4
5. The anointing of Jesus: 12:1-11
6. Christ's high priestly prayer: 17
7. Meeting His disciples at the sea of Galilee: 21
8. Certain miracles: See p. 434

Character: Historical and Doctrinal.

Subject: The conversations of Jesus.

Purpose: To prove that Jesus is the Christ, the Son of God, and that by believing on Him one might have eternal life through His name (20:31).

Outline:[1]

    I. The Son of God: 1
        A. His eternal Deity: vss. 1,2
        B. His incarnation: vs. 14

      C. His revelation: vs. 29
- II. The Son of Man: 2
  - A. His perfect humanity: vs.2
  - B. His divine authority: vss. 3-5
  - C. His superhuman power: vss. 7-11
- III. The Divine Teacher: 3
  - A. His authority: vs. 2
  - B. His message: vss. 3-21
  - C. His wisdom: vs. 11
- IV. The Soul-winner: 4
  - A. His approach: vss. 4,6
  - B. His method: vss. 7-30
  - C. His zeal: vs. 32
- V. The Great Physician: 5
  - A. His tender compassion: vs.6
  - B. His supernatural power: vs. 8
  - C. His unique claim: vss. 17-27
- VI. The Bread of Life: 6
  - A. His superiority: vs. 15
  - B. His necessity: vs. 34
  - C. His sufficiency: vs. 35
- VII. The Water of Life: 7
  - A. His satisfying quality: vs. 37
  - B. His super-abundant supply: vs. 38
  - C. His method of impartation: vs. 39
- VIII. The Light of the World: 8
  - A. His penetrating power: vs. 7
  - B. His dispelling power: vss. 9-11
  - C. His illuminating power: vs. 12
- IX. The Miracle Worker: 9
  - A. HIs untiring zeal: vss. 4,5
  - B. His supernatural power: vss. 6,7
  - C. His ultimate object: vss. 35-38
- X. The Good Shepherd: 10
  - A. His gracious design: vs. 14
  - B. His personal care: vss. 3,9
  - C. His divine credentials: vss. 14,30
- XI. The Resurrection and the Life: 11
  - A. His superiority to space: vs.21
  - B. His superiority to time: vss. 23,24
  - C. His superiority to circumstances: vss. 39,43,44
- XII. The King of Israel: 12
  - A. His anointing: vss. 12,13
  - B. His presentation: vss. 14,15
  - C. His rejection: vss. 27-33
- XIII. The Humble Servant: 13
  - A. His condescension: vs. 3
  - B. His humility: vss. 4-12
  - C. His superiority: vss. 13-16
- XIV. The Royal Comforter: 14
  - A. His sympathetic nature: vs. 1a
  - B. His absolute trustworthiness: vs. 1b
  - C. His reassuring message: vss. 2,6
- XV. The True Vine: 15

      A. His life-giving power: vs. 4
      B. His life-enabling power: vs. 5
      C. His life-enriching power: vss. 11,16

XVI. The Sender of the Holy Spirit: 16
      A. His concern for their success in soul-winning: vss. 7-11
      B. His concern for their knowledge of truth: vss. 13,14
      C. His concern for their joy and peace in tribulation: vs. 33

XVII. The Great Intercessor: 17
      A. His prayer for Himself: vss. 1-8
      B. His prayer for His eleven disciples: vss. 9-19
      C. His prayer for yet future disciples: vss. 20-26

XVIII. The Model Sufferer: 18
      A. His composure: vss. 2-9
      B. His submissiveness: vss. 10-14
      C. His superiority: vss. 19-23,33-38

XIX. The Uplifted Savior: 19
      A. His sinlessness: vss. 4-12
      B. His supremacy: vss. 13-15,19-22
      C. His humiliation: vss. 1-3,16-18,23-27

XX. The Conqueror of Death: 20
      A. His compassion for the sorrowing: vss. 16-18
      B. His solicitude for the discouraged: vss. 19-23
      C. His patience with the doubting: vss. 24-29

XXI. The Restorer of the Penitent: 21
      A. His never failing interest in the penitent: vss. 4-14
      B. His jealous demand of the penitent child: vss. 15-17
      C. His solemn commission to the restored child: vss. 15-23

Scope: From eternity past to post-resurrection events.

Writer: Such early Church fathers as Theophilus, Bishop of Antioch in A.D. 180, Iraneaus in A.D. 190, a pupil of Polycarp, who in turn was a disciple of John, and Clement of Alexandria in A.D. 200 ascribe this fourth Gospel account to John. See ARCHAEOLOGY in this chapter.

To Whom Written: To all who believe on Christ: 20:31. "It is also possible that John wrote this Gospel account to refute the teachings of Plato. Everywhere in the Greek-speaking world his writings were circulated. He had spoken of the insolubility of many mysteries, but had expressed the hope that someday there would come forth a 'Word' (Logos) from God that would make everything clear. John might even have had this in mind when, as directed by the Holy Spirit, he penned the wonderful sentences with which this Gospel begins. It is as though God was saying: 'The Word has now been spoken. In Christ the mind of God is fully revealed. He who hears Him hears God, for in Him are hid all the treasures of wisdom and knowledge.' "[2]

When and Where Written: Sometime between A.D. 90-100, in Ephesus.

Key Chapter: 1. The presentation of Christ; the Word as flesh.

Key Verse: 20:31.

Key Words:
    1. God as Father, over 100 times
    2. Believe, at least 98 times
    3. Eternal life, 35 times
    4. Witness, 21 times
    5. Love, 20 times

Key Phrase: He that believeth: 3:18,36.

Key Thought: That ye might believe.

Spiritual Thought: He is the only begotten Son of God: 3:16.

Christ Is Seen As: God's only begotten Son: 1:14,18.

Names and Titles of Christ. See NAME in Dictionary.

1. Word: 1:1,14
2. Creator: 1:3,10
3. True Light: 1:7-9
4. Only begotten of the Father: 1:14
5. Jesus Christ: 1:17; 17:3
6. Only begotten Son: 1:18; 3:16,18
7. Prophet: 1:21; 9:17
8. Lamb of God: 1:29,36
9. Son of God: 1:34; 20:31
10. Rabbi (Master): 1:38; 20:16
11. Messiah: 1:41; 4:25,26
12. Jesus of Nazareth: 1:45; 19:19
13. King of Israel: 1:49; 12:13,15
14. Son of Man: 1:51; 3:14
15. His Son: 3:17
16. The Gift of God: 4:10
17. Christ: 4:25; 11:27
18. Savior of the world: 4:42
19. Bread of God: 6:33
20. Bread of life: 6:35,48
21. Living Bread: 6:51
22. Son of the Living God: 6:69
23. Light of the world: 8:12; 9:5
24. I AM: 8:58
25. Jesus: 9:11
26. The Door: 10:7,9
27. The Good Shepherd: 10:11,14
28. Resurrection and the Life: 11:25
29. Master and Lord: 13:13; 20:28
30. The Way, the Truth, the Life: 14:6
31. The True Vine: 15:1,5
32. The Overcomer: 16:33
33. Our Keeper: 17:12
34. King of the Jews: 18:33-39; 19:19
35. The Man: 19:5
36. The risen Lord: 20:2-18
37. God: 20:28

Names and Titles of God. See NAME in Dictionary.

1. Father: 1:18
2. Spirit: 4:24
3. Holy Father: 17:11
4. Righteous Father: 17:25

Names and Titles of the Holy Spirit. See NAME in Dictionary.

1. The Spirit: 1:32; 3:5,6
2. Holy Ghost: 1:33; 14:26
3. Comforter: 14:16; 16:7
4. Spirit of Truth: 14:17; 15:26

Prophecy Fulfilled in Christ: See p. 471.

1. Peculiar to John:
   a. Turning water into wine: 2:1-11. See WINE in Index.
   b. Healing the nobleman's son: 4:46-54
   c. Healing the impotent man at Bethesda: 5:1-9
   d. Healing the man born blind: 9:1-7
   e. Raising of Lazarus: 11:1-44
   f. Draught of fish: 21:3-6
2. Common to all gospel writers: Feeding the 5,000: 6:1-14; Matthew 14:15; Mark 6:30-44; Luke 9:1-17

Other Miracles or Unusual Events:

1. Jesus walking on water—to reveal His deity and to calm the disciples' fear of the storm: 6:16-21
2. Jesus passing through the midst of the Jews—to escape punishment before His hour of crucifixion: 8:57-59
3. Christ's resurrection—to set God's stamp of approval on His redemptive work: 20:1-12
4. Christ's sudden entrance through the closed door—to assure His disciples of HIs resurrection: 20:19

Discourses of Christ: John lists no parables of Christ, but His gospel account does contain some discourses which are peculiar to his Book.
1. The new birth: 3:1-21
2. Everlasting life: 4:5-21
3. Witness of Christ as Life: 5:19-47
4. The Bread of Life: 6:29-59
5. The source of doctrine (or Truth): 7:14-29
6. The Light of the world: 8:12-20
7. Christ, the Object of trust: 8:21-30
8. Liberty or freedom: 8:31-59
9. The Good Shepherd: 10:1-18
10. Christ's Deity and His union with His Father: 10:22-28
11. Christ's death to be for all mankind: 12:20-36
12. Miscellaneous teaching regarding discipleship: 13:31—16:6

These discourses are divided into two groups: (1) the first ten were given to individuals or the public, and present Christ to the world as absolute Truth, and (2) the remainder, given in private to His disciples, present Christ to His followers as eternally sufficient for any and every situation in this life and in the life to come.

John is probably the only New Testament writer after Jerusalem's destruction in A.D. 70, having written five books. Critics have waged a mighty battle against his authority, possibly because of his exaltation of Christ as the Son of God. They have also questioned the dates ascribed to his books, placing them at a much later date. Papyrus fragments, discovered in Egypt, contain John 18:31-33,37,38, and show a style used no later than A.D. 150. Written and used in Egypt, it points to the fact that the original book had been in circulation some time before this copy was made.

The manuscripts discovered at the Dead Sea in 1947 show that John's gospel account reflects the Jewish background of Christ's day, and not the Gnostic background of the latter part of the second century A.D. In 1945 some Gnostic documents were discovered in Egypt, which were dated from the third century A.D., and show that the Gnostics based their material on John's writing rather than John's gospel being based on their texts.

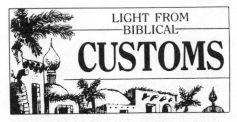
LIGHT FROM BIBLICAL CUSTOMS

3 1. Christ's shoe latchet—John's humility: 1:27. See SHOES in Index.

2. When thou wast under the fig tree, I saw thee: 1:48. The fig tree in the East is considered a sacred tree—a symbol of prosperity. Its shadow is beautiful and restful. Often, when mothers worked in the fields they placed their babies under a fig tree for shade and hopefully prosperity. It is indeed an interesting site to see babies sleeping and small children playing in the shadow of these trees. When Jesus told Nathanael that He saw him under the fig tree, He meant He had known him since he was a little boy. "I saw thee under a fig tree" is a Bible land expression meaning just this. It is no wonder Nathanael exclaimed, "Rabbi, thou art the Son of God."

3. Take up thy bed, and walk: 5:8. See BEDS in Index.

4. Christ wrote on the ground with His finger: 8:6. This has been a common practice of Near East people for centuries. Sketches are often drawn on the ground to describe ideas. When bargaining for animals or other commodities, the Arabs will stoop to do their arithmetic with their fingers in the sand. Often during a hearing at a city gate an elder would scribble something in the sand with his finger—maybe a symbol, a few words—but something to make the others sit up and take notice. Whatever the message Christ wrote for the Pharisees and/or the woman taken in adultery, He followed this practice.

5. A dipped sop: 13:26. See DIPPING in Index.

6. In my father's house are many mansions: 14:1-3. After a newly married couple has finished their year's honeymoon at the homes of their families (Deuteronomy 25:4), the husband will settle with his father to work in the fields and tend the flocks. There are several houses in the family settlement, but the couple will have a piece of land given to them to build their own home. The husband will say to his bride, "In my father's house (settlement) are many dwellings or apartments. I go to prepare a place for you. I will come again and receive you unto myself, that where I am, there ye may be also." Upon completion, he takes his bride to their new home, to their own private quarters, but they still have fellowship and eat with the father and family. How wonderful our position with Christ. We are married to Him, and at present He has gone to prepare a place for us that we might continue forever to have fellowship with Him and His Father.

Scientifically Speaking: The Resurrection: 20:1-12. See RESURRECTION in Index.

The Old Testament in John: In addition to the verses found listed in PROPHECIES fulfilled in Christ (see p. 471), note the following—

1. The zeal of Thine house: 2:17 with Psalm 69:9
2. Bread from heaven: 6:31 with Psalm 78:24
3. Taught of God: 6:45 with Isaiah 54:13
4. I said, ye are gods: 10:34 with Psalm 82:6
5. Who hath believed our report: 12:38 with Isaiah 53:1
6. He hath blinded their eyes: 12:40 with Isaiah 6:9,10
7. He that eateth bread with Me: 13:18 with Psalm 41:9
8. They hated Me without a cause: 15:25 with Psalm 35:19; 69:4
9. Companion references:
   a. One soweth, another reapeth: 4:37 with Micah 6:15

b. If any thirst, come unto Me: 7:37 with Isaiah 55:1
c. Wells of living water: 7:38 with Proverbs 18:4; Isaiah 12:3
d. Of the Spirit they should receive: 7:39 with Isaiah 44:3
e. Bethlehem and David's house: 7:42 with Jeremiah 23:5; Micah 5:2
f. Testimony of two is true: 8:17 with Deuteronomy 19:15
g. Christ abideth forever: 12:34 with Psalm 89:36,37
h. God's command what Christ shall say: 12:49 with Deuteronomy 18:18
i. None lost but the son of perdition: 17:12 with Psalm 109:8

1. Christ Incarnate: 1:14
   The Word became flesh to—
   a. Manifest the will of God: Hebrews 10:7
   b. Confirm prophecy: Luke 24:44,45
   c. Provide for the need of man: John 10:10,11
   The Word dwelt among us to—
   a. Fulfill the law: Matthew 5:17,18
   b. Minister to those in need: Matthew 20:28
   c. Demand the humility of the sinner: Luke 18:13,14

   The Word accomplished His purpose by—
   a. Bringing God's grace: Titus 2:11 with John 1:17b
   b. Revealing Truth: John 8:31,32
   c. Dying for the lost: Romans 5:6,8
2. Christ Became Flesh—His Body the Temple of God: 1:14; 2:19-21; Hebrews 10:5. See TEMPLES in Index.
3. Law and Grace: 1:17. See LAW in Index.
4. Lessons from Andrew: 1:40
   a. He was hungry for the truth: 1:35,36
   b. He forsook all to follow Christ: 1:37; Mark 1:16-18
   c. He sought the deeper things of God: 1:38; Mark 13:3
   d. He brought his brother (Peter) to Christ: 1:40-42
   e. He attended church: Mark 1:29a
   f. He was a family man: Mark 1:29b
   g. He took notice of little things, which resulted in the feeding of 5000: 6:8,9
   h. He was interested in the unsaved: 12:20-22
   i. He was a man of obedience and prayer: Acts 1:4,12-14
5. The Man Nicodemus: 3:1
   a. His *desire for* Christ came about—
      —By Christ's preaching: 3:2a
      —By example: 3:2b
   b. His *defense of* Christ—
      —Was simple: 7:50,51
      —Was bold (his being a Pharisee and a ruler): 3:1; 7:48
   c. His *devotion to* Christ—
      —Was loving and sacrificial: 19:38-42
      —Was lasting—still remembered till this day
6. The New Birth—Regeneration: 3:3-7. See REGENERATION in Index.
7. The Brazen Serpent: 3:14. See SERPENT in Index.
8. The *Necessities* of John
   a. God's—even so *must* the Son . . . be lifted up: 3:14
   b. Man's—ye *must* be born again: 3:3,7

    c. Christ's—He *must* increase: 3:30a

    d. The disciple's—I *must* decrease: 3:30b

    e. The saint's—*must* worship Him in spirit and truth: 4:24

9. The Greatest Statement ever Made: 3:16

    a. *God*—the Greatest Lover

    b. *So loved*—the Greatest Degree

    c. *The world*—The Greatest Company

    d. *That He gave*—the Greatest Act

    e. *His only begotten Son*—the Greatest Gift

    f. *That whosoever*—the Greatest Opportunity

    g. *Believeth*—the Greatest Simplicity

    h. *In Him*—the Greatest Attraction

    i. *Should not perish*—the Greatest Promise

    j. *But*—the Greatest Difference

    k. *Have*—the Greatest Certainty

    l. *Everlasting life*—the Greatest Possession

10. John Three Sixteen

    a. *For God,* the Lord of earth and heaven,

    b. *So loved,* and longed to see forgiven,

    c. *The world,* in sin and pleasure mad,

    d. *That He gave* the greatest gift He had—

    e. *His only Son*—to take our place,

    f. *That whosoever*—oh, what grace!—

    g. *Believeth*—placing simple trust

    h. *In Him,* the Righteous and the Just,

    i. *Should not perish,* lost in sin,

    j. *But have eternal life* in Him.

11. God's Perfect Answer: 3:16

    a. To Atheism, by the affirmation "God"

    b. To Agnosticism, by the statement "God so loved"

    c. To Deism, by the declaration "God gave"

    d. To Pantheism, by proclaiming "God so loved the world"

    e. To Eddyism, by the personal pronoun "God gave *His* Son"

    f. To Unitarianism, by announcing "His *only* Son"

    g. To Skepticism, by broadcasting "shall have"

    h. To Legalism, by specifying "whosoever believeth"

    i. To Naturalism, by predicting "shall never perish"

12. Lessons in Soul-winning: 4:4-34.[4] See SOUL-WINNING in Index.

    a. Must go where the sinner is: vs.4

    b. Must speak to the sinner first: vs. 7: Matthew 5:47

    c. Must remember unsaved are often ignorant: vs. 10: I Corinthians 2:14

    d. Must tell of God's gift: vs. 10; Romans 6:23

    e. Must draw spiritual lessons from common things: vss. 10-12

    f. Must tell something that satisfies: vss. 13,14; Psalm 107:9

    g. Must bring sinner face to face with his sin: vs. 16; Numbers 32:23

    h. Must not be sidetracked; the sinner will try to change the subject: vss. 19-21

    i. Must not let sinner put off decision: vs. 25; II Corinthians 6:2

    j. Must trust God to reveal Christ through the Word: vs. 26; Matthew 16:16,17

    k. Must expect results: vss. 28,29; Matthew 9:29

    l. Must expect converts to go to work for the Lord: vss. 34,35,39

    m. Must make soul-winning our meat and drink: vss. 34,35

13. Worshiping God: 4:23,24[5]

To worship God is to—

    a. Purge the imaginations by the beauty of God
    b. Open the heart to the love of God
    c. Feed the mind with the Word of God
    d. Quicken the conscience by the holiness of God
    e. Devote the will to the purpose of God
    f. Yield to the Spirit and obey the truth of God

14. Search the Scriptures: 5:39

S-tudiously: Psalm 119:12; II Timothy 2:15
E-arnestly: Psalm 119:4
A-nxiously: Psalm 119:9,20
R-egularly: Psalm 1:2; Acts 17:2,11
C-arefully: Psalm 119:30; II Timothy 3:15-17
H-umbly: Psalm 119:36; James 1:22

T-hankfully: Psalm 119:7; Jeremiah 15:16
H-appily: Psalm 19:8; 119:16
E-agerly: Psalm 119:33; I Peter 2:2

S-ystematically: Luke 24:27
C-oncernedly: Psalm 1:1,2; 119:34
R-espectfully: Psalm 19:9; 119:15
I-ntently: Psalm 119:40; Proverbs 2:1-5
P-rayerfully: Psalm 119:18; James 1:5-7
T-rustingly: Psalm 119:43; Acts 24:14
U-nashamedly: Psalm 119:6,35,59
R-etentively: Psalm 119:11; Jeremiah 20:9
E-xpectantly: Joshua 1:8; Isaiah 55:11
S-atisfyingly: Job 23:12; Psalm 119:50

15. The *"If's"* of John: 8:31-54.[6] See "IF'S" in Index.
    a. The "if" of discipleship: vs. 31
    b. The "if" of freedom: vs. 36
    c. The "if" of service: vs. 39
    d. The "if" of sonship: vs. 42
    e. The "if" of responsibility: vs. 46
    f. The "if" of assurance: vs. 51
    g. The "if" of humility: vs. 54

16. The Way of Salvation: 10:9[7]
    a. Is positive—*I am*
    b. Is plain—*the door*
    c. Is imperative—*by Me*
    d. Is optional—*if*
    e. Is impartial—*any man*
    f. Is practical—*enter in*
    g. Is saving—*he shall be saved*
    h. Is certain—*shall be saved*
    i. Is accessible—*shall go in and out*
    j. Is provisional—*and find pasture*

17. Follow Me: 10:27. There are at least eight distinct instances where Christ gives this command:
    a. Call to salvation: 1:43
    b. Call to service: 12:26
    c. Call to concentration: 21:19-22
    d. Call to soul-winning: Matthew 4:19

e. Call to separation: Matthew 8:22

f. Call to self-denial: Matthew 16:24

g. Call to consecration: Matthew 19:21

h. Call to Himself: Matthew 9:9

18. Save Me from *This* Hour: 12:27. See GETHSEMANE in Index.

a. Save Me from the hour of loneliness in the Garden when three of My disciples sleep

b. Save Me from the hour of drinking the bitter dregs of the sin-cup

c. Save Me from the hour of betrayal by one of My friends

d. Save Me from the hour when all of My disciples will forsake Me and flee

e. Save Me from the hour of Peter's denial—from hearing one of My very own curse and swear at the mention of My name

f. Save Me from the hour of My own People rejecting Me in favor of a condemned criminal

g. Save Me from the hour of Pilate's blindness to truth

h. Save Me from the hour of the brutal lash of the scourge

i. Save Me from the hour of those who mimic My kingship by placing upon My brow a crown of thorns, clothe Me with a scarlet robe, and place in My hand a reed

j. Save Me from the hour when I am identified as a criminal between two thieves

k. Save Me from the hour when I must bear in My body the sins of the whole world

l. Save Me from the hour of humiliation when those whom I came to save mock Me

m. Save me from the hour when My own Father will turn His back on Me

n. Save Me from the hour of tasting death for every man, nevertheless, not My will be done, but Thine

19. Passover and the Lord's Supper: 13:1,2. See PASSOVER in Index.

20. A New Commandment of Love: 13:34. All the Ten Commandments are repeated in the New Testament and are to be kept—except the fourth, which is a sign between Israel and God: Exodus 20:8-11 with 31:12-18

a. Supreme love to God can have no other gods: Exodus 20:3 with Mark 12:29,30

b. Love resents every effort to represent its object: Exodus 20:4,5 with I Corinthians 10:14; I John 5:21

c. Love never dishonors God's name: Exodus 20:7 with Matthew 5:33-37; Philippians 2:9-11

d. Love induces us to reverence the Lord's day: Exodus 20:8-11 with Acts 20:7; I Corinthians 16:2

e. Love makes the home happy: Exodus 20:12 with Matthew 15:4a; Ephesians 6:2,3; Colossians 3:20

f. Love cannot hate or kill: Exodus 20:13 with Matthew 5:21,22

g. Love overcomes the lust of the flesh: Exodus 20:14 with Matthew 5:27,28

h. Love will give but never steal: Exodus 20:15 with Romans 13:9

i. Love prevents lying lips, stops the voice of slander: Exodus 20:16 with Romans 13:9

j. Love has no covetous eyes for possessions of others: Exodus 20:17 with Romans 7:7

21. True Discipleship: 13:35. "By this shall all men know that ye are My disciples, *if* ye have love one to another." When we love one another, we—

a. Have the *Badge* of Discipleship. It was "by this" or "in this way" that people who observed the early Christians took knowledge that they had been with Jesus (Acts 4:13).

b. Are in the *Bounds* of Discipleship. Disciples means "learners"—we are "learners" of limitless Truth. A student not only learns lessons from his teacher; he also becomes like him (Luke 6:40).

c. Experience is the *Bond* of Discipleship. "One to another" is a reciprocal pronoun in Greek. We love on a one-to-one basis, showing loving concern and personal care for each other. See DISCIPLESHIP in Index.

22. The Way to Heaven: 14:6

A man may go to heaven—

    a. Without health
    b. Without wealth
    c. Without fame
    d. Without a great name
    e. Without learning
    f. Without works
    g. Without culture
    h. Without beauty
    i. Without friends
    j. Without a thousand other things—
    k. But you cannot go to heaven without Jesus Christ

23. **John Fourteen Six**
    a. Without the WAY you cannot *go*
    b. Without the TRUTH you cannot *know*
    c. Without the LIFE you cannot *grow*

24. **Who Said What: 14:6**
    a. Philosophy says—think your way out
    b. Science says—invent your way out
    c. Legislators say—legislate your way out
    d. Politicians say—spend your way out
    e. Government says—socialize your way out
    f. The Liquor crowd says—drink your way out
    g. The Tobacco crowd says—smoke your way out
    h. Youth says—drug your way out
    i. Psychiatry says—talk your way out
    j. Money says—buy your way out
    k. Fascism says—bluff your way out
    l. Communism says—strike your way out
    m. Demonstrators say—shout your way out
    n. Rioters say—fight and wreck your way out
    o. Industry says—work your way out
    p. Religion says—liturgize and creed your way out
    q. Satan says—there is no way out
    r. Jesus says—I am the WAY out
            —I am the TRUTH to know within
            —I am the LIFE to go out and live

25. **Fruitbearing: 15:1-8**
    a. A time for plowing: Jeremiah 4:3
    b. A time for sowing: Mark 4:3
    c. A time for pruning: John 15:2
    d. A time for reaping: Psalm 126:6

26. **Abiding in Christ: 15:4-7**
    It results in—
    a. Fruit-bearing: vs. 5
    b. Answered prayer: vs.7
    c. Peace: 16:33
    d. New life: II Corinthians 5:17
    e. Good works: Ephesians 2:10
    f. Robe of righteousness: Philippians 3:9

27. **Ministry of the Holy Spirit: 16:7-11**
    a. To testify of Christ: 15:26
    b. To glorify Christ: 16:14

    c. To guide into truth: 16:13

    d. To convict of sin: 16:7-11

    e. To quicken: 6:63

    f. To inhabit the believer: 14:16

    g. To teach us all things: 14:26

    h. To give the downpayment of our inheritance: Ephesians 1:13,14

    i. To impart the love of God: Romans 5:3-5

    j. To search the deep things of God: I Corinthians 2:10

    k. To fill the believer: Ephesians 5:18b

    l. To guide the believer in godliness: Ezekiel 36:27

    m. To communicate comfort to the saints: Acts 9:31

    n. To help our infirmities: Romans 8:26

    o. To intercede for the saints: Romans 8:26,27

    p. To impart hope: Romans 15:13; Galatians 5:5

    q. To give assurance: Romans 8:9,14,16; I John 4:13

    r. To empower Christians for witnessing: Luke 24:46-49; Acts 1:8

    s. To reveal future events: Acts 1:16; 28:25

    t. To edify the Church: Acts 9:31

    u. To call pastors: Acts 20:28

    v. To call missionaries: Acts 13:2

Believers can—

    a. Grieve Him: Ephesians 4:30

    b. Vex (worry, hurt, displease) Him: Isaiah 63:10

    c. Resist Him: Acts 7:51

    d. Lie to Him: Acts 5:3

    e. Tempt Him: Acts 5:9

28. Peter's Downfall: 18:15-18,25-27. See DOWNFALL in Index.

29. Lessons from the Dying Thief: 19:18. See THIEF in Index.
For points 30—49, see HIGHLIGHTS of Christ's Life, pp. 454-473.

30. Christ in Gethsemane: 18:1

31. The Betrayal by Judas: 18:2-5

32. The (mis-) Trial of Jesus: 18:12-14,19-24,28—19:16

33. Christ's Innocency Attested

34. Christ's Rejection by the Jews: 1:11; 19:15

35. The Crucifixion: 19:17,18

36. The Wounds of Christ

37. Superscriptions on the Cross: 19:19-22

38. Seven Last Sayings of Christ

39. Seven Last Sayings of the Crowd

40. Christ was Forsaken

41. Twelve Views of the Cross

42. Veil of the Temple Rent

43. Three Days and Three Nights in the Grave

44. He Descended into Hell

45. The Meaning of Christ's Death

46. Christ's Resurrection: 20:1-12

47. Post-Resurrection Appearances

48. Prophecies Fulfilled in Christ

49. Archaeological Evidence of Christ's Life

If all the books of the Bible were lost except John's Gospel, the believer would have a wealth of truth to feast upon till his dying day. The language is such that this book has been called the "Simple Gospel." Though one will find simple statements such as "ye in Me, and I in you," yet who can fathom the depths of such a truth? If all the verses in the Bible were lost except John 3:16, the sinner would have the Gospel in a nutshell and would be without excuse as to his ignorance of the plan of salvation.

HE GAVE HIS ONLY BEGOTTEN SON—3:16[8]

"For *whom* did He give His Son? For sinners—for sinners such as you and me. For those who had violated His law, despised His mercy, abused His creatures, enthroned His enemy, and worshiped the works of their own hands. For those who did not like to retain a knowledge of God in their hearts and turned to evil, vile practices. What amazing love is this! Love to determined enemies! For *what* did God give His Son? To live as the sinner's representative and to die as the sinner's substitute. In His life He obeyed the law for us; in His death He endures its curse. By living and dying He accomplished all that was necessary for our salvation, and now whosoever believeth in Him shall not perish, but have everlasting life. God cannot do anything greater than He has already done, nor can He give anything greater than He has given. He who gave His Son will surely give us anything we need. He who delivered up His only begotten Son to die for us will surely do anything that we ask consistent with His will. Hence the Apostle reasons—'He spared not His own Son, but delivered Him up for us all.' By so doing, shall He not with Him freely give us all things?"

PRAYER THOUGHT: "Help me, dear Savior, not to say that I believe Thee and then doubt Thy Word; that I trust Thee and then worry and complain; that I love Thee with all my heart and then disobey Thee; or that I have faith in Thee and then try to solve my own problems. May I obediently be Thy friend. In Thy Name I pray. Amen."[9]

John 15:14

Highlights of Christ's Life and Ministry

Genealogies of Christ

The Old Testament (Isaiah 53:8) asks the question: "Who shall declare His generation?" Both Matthew and Luke answer in their gospel accounts (Matthew 1:1-17; Luke 3:23-38). Mark, in presenting Christ as a Servant, does not list Christ's lineage. A servant is known for his service, and does not need a pedigree—just character. John, in presenting Christ as the Son of God, does not list His genealogy either. God is ever-existent, and has none.

"The first verse in Matthew may be termed a superscription for the genealogy which follows—'The book of the generation of Jesus Christ, the son of David, the son of Abraham.' Son of David because a king is promised to rule in righteousness upon the throne of His father David; but in a larger sense, son of Abraham, through whom all the families of the earth are to be blessed and the nations to receive spiritual blessings.

"In the genealogy of Matthew, Christ is shown to be the King legally; in Luke's we have His genealogy as the Son of Man, and as such linked to the whole human race. This is why Luke's genealogy takes Christ's genealogy back to Adam (3:38). The genealogy in Matthew proves that Joseph is a descendant of David through the house of Solomon. The one in Luke proves that Mary, the virgin, is likewise the descendant of David; not through the house of Solomon but through the house of Nathan. The Messiah was to be born of a virgin, one who must be a descendant of David. But a woman has no right to the throne. As the son of the virgin alone He could not have a legal right to the throne. For this reason, to make the One begotten in her of the Holy Ghost, the rightful heir to the throne of David in the eyes of the nation, the virgin had to be the wife of a man who had a perfect, unchallenged right to the throne. He is the legal descendant and heir of David through Joseph, but never Joseph's son."[1]

The Virgin Mary

There is very little in the New Testament about the virgin birth of Christ. Matthew and Luke speak of it; possibly John also, and Paul makes no mention of it at all. To speak of the virgin birth of necessity includes the virgin Mary, and there isn't too much in the Bible about her either. Luke portrays her as humbly obedient when she hears she is to be the one through whom Messiah is to be born, and John pictures her role at the Cross. Luke again speaks of Mary being highly favored, and says, "Blessed art thou among women" (1:26-28). Other women also had this distinction: Sarah with Isaac, becoming the mother of nations (Genesis 17:15,16), and Jael, the woman who smote Sisera with hammer and nail when Israel was oppressed (Judges 5:24-26). It is interesting to note that Luke did not say: "Blessed art thou *above* women." Favored, yes, but blessed above or exalted above, no.

As mentioned, the Bible has little to say about Mary, and much of what it does say is not highly complimentary to her. She cannot seem to comprehend what her son is about and often interferes. Indeed, the blood relationship between Jesus and Mary appears to stand in the way of her faith relationship. When He was missed after the Passover and later found in the Temple, her self-pity was overshadowed by His remark: "Wist ye not that I must be about My Father's business" (Luke 2:49,50). When Jesus performed His first miracle, He used a common form of the day in addressing His mother—"woman," not the tender name of "mother" (John 2:1-5). In fact, He never once called her "mother." On another occasion when a woman said to Jesus (Luke 11:27), "Blessed is the womb that bore thee, and the breasts which nursed thee," He responded, "Blessed rather are those who hear the Word of God, and keep it" (11:28). When His brothers and mother called for Jesus, the multitude outside informed Him that "your mother and brothers are outside asking for you." But He replied, "Who is my mother and My brothers? He who does the will of My Father, the same is My brother, My sister, and mother" (Mark 3:31-35). Even when dying on the cross, He still used the common form for greeting one of the opposite sex "woman." And then He said to John, the disciple whom He loved, "Behold, *thy* mother," as though to put her on a human level with all mothers (John 19:25-27). According to the New Testament accounts, there seems to be a distance between Jesus and His mother that can be bridged only by faith. On each occasion when Jesus and Mary met or spoke to each other, or when others mentioned His mother to Him, Jesus always put her on a level with others, never above.

Possibly the early church had a proper perspective of Mary. They were interested in her not for her own sake but only as a sign, a guarantee of the reality of the Incarnation. She is a signpost pointing to Jesus Christ and to the historical intervention of God in human history. She is a link in a long chain which began with the promise of "the *seed* of a woman," and was fulfilled in the fullness of God's time when He sent forth His Son, who was made of a woman, to redeem those who were sinners (Genesis 3:15; Galatians 4:4,5). It is never the exaltation of the mother, but is of her offspring—the "Seed" or the "Son."

In later developments in the life of the Roman Catholic Church, Mary increasingly became an object of interest and worship. Matthew confirms that the virgin birth fulfilled the prophecy of Isaiah (7:14), and certainly the virgin birth of Christ assures us that Mary gave birth to the Son of God without the aid of a human father. This marvelous act does show that the advent of Jesus was not a human possibility but solely a divine one, but nowhere, as has been mentioned, does the Bible put Mary above others or in a position to be worshiped because of her role in this event.

What are some of the development or theories of the Roman Catholic Church regarding Mary?

1. Jesus, as most Protestants believe, was preserved from the human predicament in which the whole human race finds itself, viz., having original sin, or an Adamic nature (Romans 5:12; Psalm 51:5). Christ is not involved in original sin (or any sin for that matter), because He was conceived, not by an earthly father, but by the Holy Spirit (Matthew 1:21). But what about Mary, reasoned the Catholics? Could she as a sinner produce or re-create a sinless child? Not according to their theology. Is it not fitting for the mother of Jesus also to be preserved from original sin? Would that not contribute to the guarantee that her son could not be involved in hereditary sinfulness? If there is no sinful procreation, and if the mother herself is preserved from original sin, then surely the Savior is free from all taint of sin. The Catholic church does not affirm that Mary was also born of a virgin, but rather that she was sanctified and preserved from sin through an immaculate conception. Although Mary had parents who were sinners by nature, at conception, she was made sinless. According to Catholic theology, this "miracle" gives greater honor to Jesus by saying that He preserved her from sin than by saying He saved her as a sinner through His redemption on the cross. (The Immaculate Conception of the virgin Mary was proclaimed by Pope Pius IX in the year 1854.)

2. Mary was not only a virgin, but a mother also. She merited the choice of God to be the mother of Christ. In accepting the message of the angel (Luke 1:26-38), she gives her assent, and that choice, that assent, that cooperation, is *meritorious*. God respects her and her choice, and deals with her as a responsible *covenant partner*. She becomes the example to the church, and the church is called upon to imitate Mary, her obedience, and selfless love. To them she is the "mother of God," and the "queen of heaven." (Jeremiah refers to the "queen of heaven"—7:18. The "moon" was worshiped as the "queen of heaven" under the title of "Ashtoreth," a pagan goddess, and was associated with "Baal" and "sun" worship.) Mary, as the "mother of God" and "queen of heaven," *deserves* worship. (These terms and worship of Mary were a result of the Council of Ephesus, A.D. 431.)

3. Another tenet of their faith is Mary's cooperation in redemption. As a "covenant partner," she does not stand above or below her son; she stands beside Him, sharing in His sorrows and sufferings as only a mother can suffer when her son is dying. For the good of the church and its redemption, Mary takes the suffering of her son upon herself. She offers Him to God for the sake of the church. And through the sufferings of Mary and her son, the church is born. Jesus came from her womb, but the church comes from her broken heart. She is faithful to the end at the Cross. And from her faithfulness and the faithfulness of Christ, the redemption of the world is effected. As she consented to the Incarnation, so she consents to the Cross, and by her consent and self-sacrifice she cooperated in the work of redemption. As the church comes from Mary, so the church becomes the mother of the faithful. A Christian is born in the womb of the church, nourished by its sacraments. Like Mary, the church stands by the Cross, not the Cross of Calvary, but the Cross over the altar, making a re-representation of the body and blood of Christ for the sins of the people in the bloodless sacrifice of the mass. (Mass as a daily celebration was adopted in 394, and developed gradually as a sacrifice and attendance made obligatory in the eleventh century.)

4. Mary is not only a virgin (later made sinless—the immaculate conception), a mother, a partner in redemption, but Rome has made her an intecessor—a mediator. In the Middle Ages it became difficult for many to believe that Jesus was really a man (with Deity). They thought of Him solely as divine, and that while here on earth, He had been obedient in the power of His divine nature. Since we mortals do not have this advantage, they reasoned, Mary was looked to for compassion. How could Jesus really understand our dilemma when temptations befall us? How can He, solely divine, have compassion? But Mary, on the other hand, is human (though sinless). She enjoyed pleasing God without a divine nature. Therefore, she can have pity on us for our sins and our temptations. She will pray to her Son for us. And her Son cannot really deny His mother's requests. Thus, to get to God, pray to Mary first, and she in turn will influence her Son, who in turn will counsel with the Father.

These positions of the Catholic church—immaculate conception, mother of God, mother of the church, covenant partner in Christ's redemption, salvation in the church because of Mary, and Mary as an intercessor and mediator—are not accepted by most Protestants. We believe Mary was born in sin like any other human. She certainly wouldn't have mentioned God as her Saviour had she been made immaculate (Luke 1:47). She shares absolutely nothing in redemption, for it is the blood of Christ which cleanses from all sin (I John 1:9). Salvation is in a Person, not a thing or a church (Luke 2:22-30). And certainly there is but *one* mediator between God and man, the Man Christ Jesus (I Timothy 2:5). Why would one expect Jesus to listen to Mary now when He didn't listen to her while on earth?

Mary is not only the obedient virgin; she is not only the sorrowing mother—she is also one who does not understand what God's purposes are, who intervenes when she should have kept silent, who pleads the ties of filial affection when she should have been learning faith. And, it is false theology to say that Mary, because she is feminine, adds an element of compassion that is somehow missing in God. On the contrary, there are no bounds to the compassion of God, of which the compassion of Mary is a finite and limited reflection. It is also false to say a child of God does not have God's divine nature to help in temptations and trials, because we do (II Peter 1:4).

One other thing is worthy of note regarding the virgin Mary. The Catholic church teaches that Mary was a perpetual virgin, that the brothers and sisters of Christ were children of Joseph by a former marriage (he being a widower), thus making them half brothers and sisters of Christ. It is true that she knew no man . . . that Christ was virgin born, conceived by the Holy Spirit. But the Bible emphatically teaches that "Joseph knew her not *till* she had brought forth her firstborn son" (Matthew 1:24,25). There is only one interpretation to this statement—she did not know Joseph in the husband-wife relationship *until* Jesus was born. And when she knew Joseph after Christ's birth, they had their own children (Matthew 13:55,56).

It appears that the church at Rome seeks to reward Mary for all the claims of her that they support. Even in 1950, Pope Pius XII issued the dogma of the Assumption of the Virgin Mary—her bodily resurrection into heaven.

There is *no* evidence from the Catholic version of the Scriptures (the Douay version) or even their traditions to support any of these claims or tenets of their faith which have to do with Mary. They are all conclusions of the natural mind to support a system that believes in a person who died for the sins of the world, but had to have support and assistance from His mother. To the Catholics, it is salvation in Christ, *plus*. To the saved Protestant, it is Christ, *period* (John 3:16; 14:6; Acts 4:12; I Timothy 1:15).

If Mary was ever to have been exalted above other women or equated with Christ, the Son of God, a good time to have done it would have been when the Wise Men of the East came to the house where the "holy family" lived in the city of Bethlehem. What a splendid example these men set for us to follow. When they saw the child with Mary, they worshiped *Him,* and gave their gifts to *Him* (Matthew 2:11). Yes, Mary was there, too, but they worshiped *Him,* not her. Another good example to follow is that of Mary's: "Whatsoever *He* saith unto you, do it" (John 2:5).

The Virgin Birth

The references to Christ's virgin birth are to be found in Matthew 1:18-25; Luke 1:26-38; 2:1-20. "The fact is that Jesus Christ is not only firmly imbedded in human history and written upon the pages of Scripture, but is also interwoven in the fabric of all civilization worthy of the name. It would be easier to untwist all the beams of light in the sky and to separate and erase one of the primary colors, than to get the character of Jesus out of the world.

"You may have Confusianism without Confucius; Buddhism without Buddha; Mohammedanism without Mohammed; Mormanism without Joseph Smith, Christian Science without Mary Baker Eddy; Millennial Dawnism without Russell (Jehovah's Witnesses); but you cannot have Christianity without Christ—for, strictly speaking, Christianity is Christ and Christ is Christianity."[2]

To statements such as these there is no denial. It is not a question as to the Person of Christ. Rather, how did He get here? What about His birth? Is it possible for one to be born of a woman without a human father? Even Mary herself raised this question when the angel told her of Messiah's birth. "How can these things be, seeing I know not a man?" The angel answered, "The Holy Spirit shall come upon thee, and the power of the Highest shall overshadow thee: [and] that holy thing which shall be born shall be called the Son of God" (Luke 1:26-35).

This story is in perfect harmony with the whole claim of the natural and supernatural events and circumstances connected with the Advent. It fits beautifully withe the Annunciation, the psalm of Elizabeth, the hymn of Mary, the song of the angels, the visit of the shepherds, the appearance of the wise men from the East and the star that followed them, the adoration of Simeon and Anna in the Temple, Herod's attempt to kill the prophetic Babe, and the flight into Egypt. All this commotion is far more congruous with the virgin birth than with an ordinary birth.

The biological argument supports the truth of the virgin birth. According to biological law, each type of life produces after its own kind. When it is possible for two types to unite in offspring, in the latter the natures of both unite. The virgin birth unites in Christ the divine and the human, the natural and the supernatural. The miraculous conception was true to the law of inheritance from both its natural and supernatural factors. The natures of the two parents, which united by conception in the embryo, determine the nature or natures of that begotten by them. Only that begotten by the divine and the human can be accounted generically divine and human.

"Mary and Joseph had several other children after the birth of Jesus (Matthew 13:55,56). If the virgin birth were not true, James, Joses, Judas, Simon, and their sisters were generically the same in personality as Jesus. It is the combined human and divine parentage of our Lord which forever settles the status of His person. With a human father, He would be generically the same as all of us, and leaving us with no more reason to hold to His personal Deity than to the personal deity of us all."[3]

Note carefully that Luke calls Christ Mary's "firstborn" (2:7). If this had been the only child of Mary, Luke would have had to use the same language God did in reference to His "only" Son. Matthew makes it clear that Joseph knew not Mary until *after* Christ was born (1:25). He also goes to lengths to let us know what the angel said to Joseph about Christ's father (1:20), and Luke is careful to say that "Jesus . . . being *(as we supposed)* the son of Joseph" (3:23).

If Joseph had been the father of Jesus, then it would make it utterly impossible for Christ to have been very God, and to have lived in heaven before He came to this earth, born of a virgin. His previous existence and His deity depend altogether on the virgin birth, and such verses as John 1:1,14; 3:31; and Isaiah 9:6 prove Him to be the Son of God, existing before the virgin birth. If Christ had been born of Joseph, it would have made it impossible for Him to have died for our sins, since He, too, would have inherited a sinful nature. See SINLESSNESS in Index.

Since Joseph was not the father of our Lord Jesus Christ, no human blood (tainted and sinful) flowed through His veins. Conceived by the Holy Ghost, born of a virgin and given life by God the Father, our Lord's blood was "precious . . . without blemish [perfectly pure—faultless] and without spot [righteous, stainless—without physical defects]" (I Peter 1:19). In spite of "human" explanations regarding the virgin birth of Christ, this miracle can never be fully explained this side of glory. It is one of the truths in the Word of God which *must* be accepted by faith. "And without controversy great is the mystery of godliness: God was manifested in the flesh—God was in Christ" (I Timothy 3:16; II Corinthians 5:19).

Baptism of Christ

The question has been raised, and rightly so, "Why did the sinless Savior request baptism of John, and why was He baptized?" (Matthew 3:13-17; Mark 1:9-11; Luke 3:21,22). The Scriptural answer is: "To fulfill all righteousness"—the righteousness required by the law of Moses (Matthew 3:15). The Levitical law required all priests at the age of thirty to be consecrated (Numbers 4:3). Jesus was now thirty years old (Luke 3:23). Consecration involved washing, and then anointing (Exodus 29:4-7). Aaron, as a sinner, in following this pattern, set forth in type the baptism of Christ, who, though sinless, identified Himself with sinners. After His baptism (washing: Matthew 3:16), He was anointed by the Holy Spirit, thus fulfilling the Old Testament Priesthood type for His redemptive work (Matthew 3:16b,17; Acts 4:27; 10:38).

In addition to Christ's fulfilling all righteousness, note the following:

1. He approved John's ministry by submitting Himself to baptism.

2. He identified Himself with John and his call to the Jews by following through with John's message: "Repent, for the kingdom of heaven is at hand" (Matthew 3:2; 4:17).

3. In submitting to John's baptism He not only identified Himself with His own people (the Jews) but with all He had come to redeem. Christ, as the "second Adam," immediately became identified with the fallen descendants of the "first Adam" by submitting to the baptism "unto repentance."

4. God's approving voice (Matthew 3:17) sets the Father's seal to the sinlessness of Christ prior to His public ministry.

5. This is the first exhibition of the Trinity—God the Father who speaks to His Son from

heaven, and the Spirit descending like a dove to rest upon the Son (Matthew 3:16,17).

Temptation and Sinlessness of Christ

1. Temptation: Matthew 4:1-11; Mark 1:12,13; Luke 4:1-13

As soon as Jesus emerged from the waters of Jordan, He went up to the solitary hills of the Judean desert where no human face was to be seen, and where no human voice was to be heard for forty days. Forty is the number for being away from people—alone or alone with God. Israel was forty years in her wilderness wandering; Moses was forty days alone with God on Mt. Sinai; Elijah was forty days wandering in the wilderness while fleeing from Queen Jezebel, and now for forty days Christ is to be all alone, led by the Spirit during which time Satan would culminate this stay with severe temptations for the Son of God to yield and sin.

Let us keep in mind that Jesus Christ was the *God/Man.* We cannot divorce the two, although we do not understand this *Infinite/finite* union. "Great is the mystery of godliness . . . that God was manifested in the flesh [in the person of Christ]" (John 1:1-14; I Timothy 3:16). It is not surprising that Jesus, since he was also *Man,* should have undergone temptation.

1. In the first temptation, Satan strikes at a human weakness—hunger. "If Thou be the Son of God" (probably referring to God's voice at Christ's baptism—Matthew 3:16,17)—"command these stones be made bread." This sounds like a reasonable, human request. Jesus was there in this situation, and as a *Man* replied: "It is written, Man shall not live by bread alone, but by every Word that proceedeth out of the mouth of God" (Matthew 4:3,4 with Deuteronomy 8:3). Here He mastered the flesh.

2. In the second temptation, Satan again strikes at another human weakness—that of one's seeking to become one's own god. "Cast Thyself down" from this pinnacle and "He [God] will give His angels charge over Thee." Satan seeks to get Christ to tempt God, but God cannot be tempted (James 1:13). The enemy here sought to get Christ to question His position in the God-head and act on His own. Jesus replied "Thou shalt not tempt the Lord Thy God" (Matthew 4:5-7 with Deuteronomy 6:16). Here He mastered self.

3. In the third temptation Satan goes from the reasonable to the questionable to the damnable—"fall down and worship me." Satan (once Lucifer) never got over his defeat in trying to dethrone God and exalt himself above God (Isaiah 14:12-17). Now he strikes at Jesus as Man—"worship me." In the first temptation there was a degree of sympathy —"you are hungry . . ." In the second temptation, there is hypocritical respect or admiration. And now in this third temptation, Satan exposes his real self and motive—"worship me." Jesus replied: "It is written, Thou [mankind] shalt worship [fear] the Lord thy God, and Him only shalt thou serve" (Matthew 4:8-10 with Deuteronomy 6:13; 10:20). Here He masters Satan.

In each of these recorded temptations, Jesus set an example for all believers (I John 2:15-17). He used the Scriptures to overcome those temptations and defeat the devil. John tells us that God's Word was written to enable us to overcome temptation and sin not (I John 2:1). The Psalmist stored up God's Word in his heart that he might not sin against the Lord (119:11). If Jesus needed to rely upon the Word of God to rout the enemy, how much more do we need to do the same. Please note that Satan used Scripture to tempt Christ, but he never quoted them verbatim. He twists them to suit himself and his purposes, as we also noted in the case of Eve (Genesis 3:1-7). He questioned God's command (Genesis 2:17 with 3:1); he confused Eve so that she added to Scripture (Genesis 3:3); and then he misquoted God's Word (Genesis 3:4). If Eve had met that old serpent the devil head-on with God's direct command, as did Christ, things would be vastly different today. See TEMPTATION and EVE in Index.

2. Christ's Sinlessness

There are some who have the notion that while Christ was here on earth He could have sinned. If He could not have sinned, then the temptations which came His way were meaningless. A person who cannot sin, it is argued, cannot be tempted to sin, yet the Scriptures say that He was "tempted in all points like as we are, yet without sin" (Hebrews 4:15). Well might a person reason that because an army cannot be defeated, it cannot be attacked! In making a thorough study of the life of Christ and His ministry as found in the gospel accounts, one should first consider what is called in theological circles the "Impeccability of Christ" (or His incapability of sinning).

Living in a world of sin on every hand, it is refreshing to fix our gaze upon One who was immaculately holy and pure, and who passed through this scene unspoiled by its evils. For thirty-three years Christ was in immediate contact with sin, yet He was never, to the slightest degree, contaminated by it. He touched the leper, yet was not defiled, even ceremonially. He ate with sinners, yet He did not indulge in their ways. Just as the rays of the sun shine upon a stagnant pool without being sullied thereby, so Christ was unaffected by the iniquity which surrounded Him.

1. He did no sin: I Peter 2:22
2. In Him was no sin: I John 3:5 (contrast wth vs. 8)
3. He knew no sin: II Corinthians 5:21
4. He was without sin: Hebrews 4:15
5. He was holy, undefiled, separate from sinners: Hebrews 7:26
6. First Corinthians 13 gives us some insight into His character. We can substitute the word "charity" in verses 1-4,8,13 for "love" (which it is in the original Greek). Since "God is love" (I John 4:8) and God and Christ are one (John 17:11), we can use the name "Christ" in place of "charity" (love) as follows: "Christ suffereth long and is kind; Christ envieth not; Christ vaunteth not Himself, is not puffed up. He does not behave Himself unseemly, seeketh not His own, is not easily provoked, thinketh no evil; rejoiceth not in iniquity, but rejoiceth in truth; beareth all things, believeth all things, hopeth all things, endureth all things. Christ never faileth" (vs. 4-8). Such could be said only of One who did no sin, had no sin in Him, knew no sin, was without sin, and was holy, harmless, undefiled, and separate from sinners.

He was not only sinless; he was impeccable—that is, incapable of sinning. The last Adam differed from the first Adam in His impeccability. Adam was sinless (innocent) until he disobeyed God, certainly showing that he was not impeccable. Christ was not only able to overcome temptation; He was unable to be overcome by it. He was the "Almighty" (Revelation 1:8). True, Christ was man, but He was God-man, and as such, absolute Master and Lord of *all* things. Being Master of all things, He had dominion over the winds and waves, disease and death, which clearly demonstrate that it was impossible that anything should master Him.

a. The immutability (unchangeableness) of Christ proves His impeccability, or His incapability of sinning. Jesus Christ is the *same* yesterday, today, and forever (Hebrews 13:8). Because He was not susceptible to any change, it was impossible for the incarnate Son of God to sin. Herein we behold again His uniqueness. Sinless angels sinned and fell. So did sinless man. They were creatures, and creaturehood and mutability are correlated terms. But was not the manhood of Christ created? Yes, but it was never placed on probation—*it never had a separate existence*. From the very first moment of its conception in Mary's womb, the humanity of Christ was taken into union with Deity; and therefore *could not* sin. "That *Holy thing* which shall be born . . ." (Luke 1:35). The "manhood" of Christ was "born a Holy thing." "A body Thou hast prepared for Me" (Hebrews 10:5).

b. The Omnipotence of Christ proves His impeccability. That the Lord Jesus Christ, even during His days of humiliation, was possessed with omnipotence (or *of* omnipotence), is clear from many passages. "What things so ever He (the Father) doeth, *these also* doeth the Son likewise." "For as the Father raiseth up the dead, and quickeneth, even so the Son also quickeneth whom He will" (John 5:19,21). When we say Christ possessed omnipotence during His earthly sojourn, we do not mean that He was so endowed by the Holy Spirit, but that He *was* essentially, personally, omnipotent. To speak of an omnipotent person yielding to sin is a contradiction of terms. All temptation to sin must proceed from a created being—a finite power or being. It is *impossible* for a finite power to overcome omnipotence (or One who is Infinite). Creature tempts, but Creator (God), NEVER, (James 1:13).

c. The constitution of Christ's person proves His impeccability. In Him were united the Divine and human natures. This is altogether incomprehensible to created intelligence. This is why Paul said, "Great is the mystery of godliness [that] God was manifested in the flesh . . ." (I Timothy 3:16). Now "God cannot be tempted with evil" (James 1:13); "It is impossible for God to lie" (Hebrews 6:8). And Christ was "God manifested in the flesh"—"God in Christ"—and "Immanuel—God with us." (I Timothy 3:16; II Corinthians 5:19; Matthew 1:23). Personality centered not in His humanity. Christ was Divine—a Divine person—who had been "made in the likeness of man" (Philippians 2:7). Utterly impossible was it, then, for the God-man to sin. To affirm the contrary is to be guilty of the most awful blasphemy. It is irreverent speculation to discuss what the human nature of Christ *might* have done if it had been alone. It *never* was alone; it *never* had a separate existence. From the first moment of its being it was united with (or to) a Divine Person.

It is objected to the truth of Christ's impeccability that it is inconsistent with His temptability—that is, His temptation was meaningless if He could not have sinned. A person who cannot sin, it is argued, cannot be tempted to sin. Well might a person reason that because an army cannot be defeated, it cannot be attacked. So far as His natural susceptibility to temptation was concerned, both physical and mental, Jesus Christ was open to all forms of human temptation, excepting those that spring out of or from lust, or corruption of the human nature. He possessed a human body prepared by the Holy Spirit, but not a human nature after the first Adam (I John 3:5 with I John 1:8).

Probably there are many reasons why God ordained that His incarnate Son should be tempted by man, the devil, and circumstances. One of these, I am sure, was to show or demonstrate His impeccability. Throw a lighted match into a barrel of gunpowder and there will be an explosion, simply because there is something in gunpowder which is susceptible to fire. Throw a lighted match into a barrel of water, and the match will be quenched, simply because there is something in water which is not susceptible to fire. This is but a crude way to illustrate the difference between Satan's tempting us and his tempting the God-man. In the human nature, which is sinful, there is that which is susceptible to Satan's fiery darts; but the Holy God-man could say, "The Prince of this world cometh and hath nothing in Me" (John 14:30). The Lord Jesus was exposed to far more severe testing and trying than the first Adam was, in order to make manifest His mighty power of resistance. It was to Satan that Jesus said: "Thou shalt not tempt the Lord, thy God" (Matthew 4:7). No other person could ever say that.

If the humanity of Christ was, because of its union to His Divine person, incapable of sinning, then in view of its being Divinely sustained, how could it hunger and thirst, suffer and die? And seeing that it did, then why was it incapable of yielding to temptation? While Christ was commissioned to die (John 10:18), He was not commissioned to sin. The human nature of Christ was permitted to function freely and normally, hence it wearied and wept; but to sin was not a normal act of His humanity since it was a "prepared" body (Hebrews 10:5).

To be the Redeemer of His people, Christ must be "mighty to save, marching in the greatness of His strength" (Isaiah 63:1). He must have to overcome all temptations when they assail His person, in order that He may be able to "succor them that are tempted" (Hebrews 2:18). Here then is one of the solid planks in that platform on which the faith of the Christian rests; because the Lord Jesus Christ *is* Almighty, having absolute power over sin, the feeble and sorely tried saint may turn to Him in implicit confidence, seeking the efficacious aid of the One who was "tempted in all points like as we are"—but not to sin, because His "form of man" was "without sin" (Hebrews 4:15). Only He who triumphed over sin, both in life and death, can save a sinner from his sins.

Once again it bears repeating—Christ had no sin nature, therefore He could not have sinned. His Father was the Holy Spirit—not Joseph. Every human being—with a human mother and a human father—is shapened in iniquity and conceived in sin (Psalm 51:5). But Jesus was conceived by the Holy Spirit (Matthew 1:20). Like produced like—human father/sinner son: Divine Father/Divine Son. "Great is the mystery . . . that Christ was born in the flesh" (I Timothy 3:16).

If Jesus was the Lamb slain from before the foundation of the world—if Calvary was settled then (Revelation 13:8); if Jesus was delivered by the determinate counsel and foreknowledge of God (Acts 2:23); if God was in Christ to reconcile sinners unto Himself (II Corinthians 5:19); if Christ came to seek and to save the lost (Luke 19:10); if He came to give His life a ransom for sinners (Matthew 20:28); if Christ came to save sinners (Matthew 1:21; I Timothy 1:15), how could He have sinned? Could a sinning Savior save a lost sinner? How could anyone preach a positive salvation? How could we preach deliverance to those in sin if we have a Redeemer who could not deliver Himself, who could have sinned? Christ was tempted in all points like as we are—not to see if He could sin, but to show us that He was without sin.

Thank God, we have a Savior who, according to Scripture, (1) did no sin—I Peter 2:22; (2) had no sin in Him—I John 3:5; (3) knew no sin—II Corinthians 5:21; (4) was without sin—Hebrews 4:15; and (5) was holy, harmless, undefiled, separate from sinners—Hebrews 7:26, having a body that was "prepared" a "Holy thing"—Luke 1:35; Hebrews 10:5.

This, then, is the Christ who is presented by the New Testament writers. This is the Christ who—[4]

1. Took upon Himself the likeness of men (Philippians 2:7) that I might be conformed to His image and likeness (Romans 8:29)
2. Became poor that I might become rich in Him (II Corinthians 8:9)
3. Suffered hunger (Matthew 4:2) that I might be fully and forever satisfied (John 6:35)
4. Suffered thirst (John 19:28) that I might have the water of life and never thirst (John 4:14)
5. Became weary (John 4:6) that I might have rest (Matthew 11:28)
6. Was tempted (Matthew 4:1) that I might be delivered in the hour of temptation (Hebrews 4:15)
7. Became a servant (Philippians 2:7) that I might become a son of God (John 1:12)
8. Wept (John 11:35) that God might wipe away all my tears (Revelation 21:4)
9. Was troubled (John 12:27) that I might have a peace that passeth all understanding (Philippians 4:7)
10. Suffered persecution (Luke 4:28,29) that I might be of good cheer (John 16:23)
11. Was exceedingly sorrowful (Matthew 26:38) that I might have joy (John 15:11)
12. Was falsely accused and misrepresented (Luke 23:13,14) that I might have in Him a Friend who understands (Hebrews 4:15,16)
13. Was despised (Isaiah 53:3) that I might be exalted (Revelation 3:21)
14. Became an outcast (Matthew 8:20) that I might be welcomed (Revelation 22:17)
15. Became homeless in His own country (Luke 4:24) that I might have a home in glory with Him (John 14:2,3)
16. Was lonely (John 6:66) that I might never be alone (Matthew 28:20)
17. Was forsaken (Matthew 26:56) that I might never be forsaken (Hebrews 13:5)
18. Was separated from God (Matthew 27:46) that I might never be separated from Him in eternity (I Thessalonians 4:16-18)
19. Suffered the wrath of God (Isaiah 53:3-11) that I might know the love of God (I John 4:10)
20. Endured darkness (Matthew 27:45) that I might be called out of darkness into His marvelous light (John 12:46; I Peter 2:9)
21. Was stripped of His robe (Matthew 27:31,35) that I might wear His robe of righteousness (Philippians 3:9; Revelation 19:7,8)
22. Became a curse (Galatians 3:13) that I might be blessed with every spiritual blessing (Ephesians 1:3)

23. Died (Matthew 27:50) that I might live (John 3:16)
24. Endured the cross (Luke 23:33) that I might wear a crown (I Peter 5:4). See POVERTY in Index.

The Passover and the Lord's Supper

Whether the Passover was a symbol of the Lord's Supper or not, they have much in common in that one followed the other (Matthew 26:17-28; Mark 14:17-25; Luke 22:14-20; John 13:1,2). The Passover looked back to the deliverance from the death angel in Egypt after blood had been sprinkled on the door posts prior to the Exodus. It also looked to the coming Passover, the Lamb of God, the Messiah (I Corinthians 5:7b).

The Lord's Supper looks back to Christ's death—His death for the deliverance of our sins. It also looks forward to His coming—deliverance from the presence of sin itself (Hebrews 9:28). "As oft as ye eat this bread and drink this cup, ye do show the Lord's death [by looking back] till He come [by looking forward]" (I Corinthians 11:26). "The Lord's Supper is a memorial of a departed Friend, a prophecy of a returning Friend, and the assurance of a present Friend."[5]

Three elements were used in the Passover (Exodus 12:5-8)

1. Roast lamb. This could be a type of Christ as real meat for the mature Christian (Hebrews 5:12-14).
2. Unleavened bread. This could be a type of separation from evil.
3. Bitter herbs. This could speak of the bitter agony of death, not only of Christ's but of our death to self.

Two elements are used in the Lord's Supper (Matthew 26:26-28)

1. Bread—a symbol of Christ as the Bread of life; food for our souls
2. The cup, or fruit of the vine (*never* called "wine")—a symbol of the work of Christ; the shedding of His blood for the remission of sin

Notice that the bread comes first. This typifies what Christ *is*. Then the fruit of the vine, or cup, is second. This typifies what Christ has *done*. The bread comes first because those who feast upon Him have a realization of what He has done. Bread is the result of a harvest of wheat. The wheat is crushed, water mixed, and then put into the fire. Our Lord was crushed, blood mixed with His suffering for our iniquities, and then put to the fiery test of death.

In the Passover the roast lamb was to be eaten all night. What was left was to be burnt by fire—the burnt offering. This typifies giving to God the part that belongs to Him. It is here we might find the true meaning of the Lord's Supper—a gathering together of a company of believers to offer up or give back to God praise and thanksgiving. The Lord's Supper is not primarily a place to *get,* but to remember—to *give*; to give glory to God for our entire redemption—of soul, in His death; of body, in His coming again.

Paul gives the prerequisite to one's taking the Lord's Supper: "But let a man examine himself, and so let him eat of that bread, and drink of that cup." It is *a man examining himself.* This excludes all others saying who can and who cannot partake. When one examines the real self, it is an examination of the inner man, not the outward. No man can do this for another—only a man for himself—and he alone knows whether he is eating and drinking worthily or unworthily. If he does not examine and judge himself, God will, not man.

The Lord's Supper is the only meeting for which Christ gave specific instructions (Matthew 25:26-28; I Corinthians 11:23-32). Three times in Scripture we are told, "this do in remembrance of Me." It is not "do this," implying asking, but "this do," making it a command to be observed. Let the reader also observe that it is the *Lord's* table. Paul received instructions regarding the Supper from the *Lord.* It is not *my* table, not *my* supper, not a *denominational church* table or supper, BUT THE LORD'S.

The Passover was held the fourteenth day of the first month. In the Lord's Supper, there is no limit. Apparently the early church held it daily. Later, believers observed it primarily on the first day of the week. *Note this:* We are simply requested to remember *Him*. Remembrance of the One who suffered the agony of the cross that we might enjoy the blessedness of His presence touches a responsive chord in every heart that loves Him. He leaves it to our love for and remembrance of Him as to how often we shall respond to the desire of our heart. To those who know the blessed meaning of this Supper, no other meeting is so precious.

The Passover Today[6]

What about observance of the Passover today? "Originally there were three elements on the Passover Table: the Passover Lamb, the unleavened bread, and bitter herbs (Exodus 12:8). The lamb symbolized *redemption*. Every firstborn in Egypt was under the judgment of God, and wherever the blood was *not* applied, the firstborn died. The unleavened bread symbolized *sanctification*. Leaven in the Bible speaks of evil and error. Having been redeemed in Egypt, they were to put away 'leaven'—their former manner of life, and live a life holy unto the Lord (Leviticus 20:26). During Passover, leaven is scattered throughout the house and then cleanly swept into a dustpan and then burned or thrown out of the house, thus symbolizing the discarding of that which is unholy. The bitter herbs are a reminder that the lot of their forefathers had been harsh as slaves under Pharaoh. Each member of the family partakes of these bitter herbs until tears come to their eyes—thus identifying themselves with their forefathers who were slaves before God redeemed them through His mighty power.

"According to the esteemed rabbi, Hillel, the lamb, the unleavened bread, and the bitter herbs were the only elements on the Passover Table as late as A.D. 10. Additional elements (discussed later) were added after A.D. 70 to radically alter the Passover Table. The crucifixion of Christ about A.D. 30 and the destruction of the Temple by the Romans in A.D. 70 forever altered the Passover. Not only would animal sacrifice be no longer efficacious because of Christ's sacrifice of Himself, but the destruction of the Temple and the cessation of the priesthood has made it impossible to perpetuate the Passover as God instituted it.

"Three choices, then, were left open to the Jewish people: (1) Accept Christ as *the* Passover Lamb; (2) discontinue the Passover observance; or (3) without Divine authorization, alter the Passover observance to meet the contemporary situation. Regrettably, most of the nation followed the latter course, and Judaism, which had its origin in God, became simply the creation of man. In altering the Passover, two elements were added to the Table. They cannot be prophetic—pointing toward Messiah's coming, but rather, they are historic, pointing *backward* to something that has already occurred.

"These two new elements are a roasted egg and wine. The Passover lamb is no longer present, and is replaced by the shankbone of a lamb. The unleavened bread is still on the Table, but arranged differently, and has taken on new meaning. Rabbis suggest that the egg commemorates the sacrifice that in Temple times was offered on each festival, but there is absolutely no justification for this identification. Rather, in many heathen religions the 'pasche' egg was used to symbolize resurrection—life from the dead. From this heathen practice, the egg found its way into the Easter holiday and on into the Jewish Passover Table. It speaks uncompromisingly of the resurrected Passover Lamb.

"Perhaps the most dramatic spectacle on the Jewish Passover Table involves the unleavened bread. Three pieces of matzo are placed one on top of the other, separated by special napkins. The center, or second piece of matzo is broken, wrapped, and hidden away. After drinking the third glass of wine, called the 'cup of blessing,' the children are sent out to locate the hidden piece of matzo. When it is found, a reward is given, there is rejoicing, and everyone at the table *must eat* from that broken piece of matzo. Although this is done, Jewish authorities are hard pressed to explain the significance of this drama.

"The broken piece of matzo is always brought forth after the third glass of wine. The broken piece of matzo takes the place of the Passover lamb. How significant this all is—the three pieces of matzo speak of the triune God, Father, Son, and Holy Spirit. The center piece 'broken' speaks of the broken body of Messiah, "wrapped" because His body was gently wrapped for burial, and partaking of it after the third glass of wine is symbolic of Christ's resurrection on the third day.

"How did so much which points to Christ find its way into the Passover observance? With the destruction of the Temple, cessation of the priesthood, and the Jews being scattered throughout the world, it was no longer possible to observe Passover as they had for more than 1,400 years. Among those scattered Jews were some who had accepted Christ as Messiah—the One alone who had fulfilled Old Testament messianic prophecy. These early Hebrew Christians introduced New Testament truth into the Jewish Passover. After all, had not Jesus introduced the Lord's Table from the Passover? The penetrating words of the Lord during the last Passover could never be erased from their minds and hearts . . . He took bread, blessed it . . . break it and gave to His disciples to eat—symbolic of His body (Matthew 26:26). This is exactly what the Jews do with the broken matzo. These early Hebrew Christians remembered the cup—drink ye all of it (Matthew 26:27,28). Wine on the Passover Table is used as a symbol of blood. It is for this reason that rabbis unknowingly insist there must be wine and that it must be red, which symbolizes blood.

"Four cups of wine are consumed during the Jewish Passover. The fourth cup is the 'cup of anticipation.' Remember Jesus said there was a cup He would not drink then (Matthew 26:29), but would drink it when He comes to establish His kingdom. The fourth cup of today's Passover anticipates that day 'when they look upon Him whom they have pierced' (Zechariah 12:10).

"Israel today celebrates the Passover, but she experiences no redemption. She has on her Passover Table the shankbone of a lamb, but no lamb, no blood. All these centuries of observance without a priesthood—no blood, no lamb, crying for Messiah to come. There is no greater irony and tragedy than this—religious Jews continue to await the coming of Him who has already come. And down through the centuries the words of their Messiah continue to echo—'O Jerusalem, Jerusalem, thou that killest the prophets, and stonest them which are sent unto thee, how often would I have gathered thy children together, even as a hen gathereth her chickens under her wings, and ye would not! Behold, your house is left desolate. For I say unto you, Ye shall not see me henceforth, till ye shall say, Blessed is He that cometh in the name of the Lord' (Matthew 23:37-39)."

Christ in Gethsemane[7]

After Christ predicted Peter's denial of Himself, He took Peter, John, and James to the Garden of Gethsemane for watchfulness and prayer. In the agony of His anticipation of the Cross, Christ prayed concerning this event. His desire was for this cup (crucifixion) to pass from Him. Possibly this request may have arisen because He knew He would soon be utterly forsaken. There may be sterner trials or temptations than this, but surely this one is the worst—to be utterly forsaken (Matthew 26:36-46).

At this point Satan goes all out to bring Christ to defeat. The hellish craft of one who had been thousands of years tempting men would know how to invent all manner of mischief. He would now pour the hottest coals of hell upon the Savior. It was in struggling with this temptation of being forsaken that Christ, in agony of soul, prayed more earnestly. It is always when God's child is in earnest prayer that Satan works his hardest. "See," said Satan to Christ as he hissed it out between his teeth: "see, Thou hast a friend nowhere! Look to heaven, Thy Father hath shut up the bowels of His compassion against Thee. Not an angel in Thy Father's courts will stretch out his hands to help Thee. Look Thou yonder, not one of those spirits who honored Thy birth will interfere to protect Thy life now. All heaven is false to Thee; Thou art left alone. As for the earth, do not all men thirst for Thy blood? Will not the Jews, Thy people, be gratified to see Thy flesh torn with nails, and will not the Romans gloat themselves when Thou, the King of the Jews, are fastened to the cross? Thou hast no friend among the nations; the high and mighty scoff at Thee, and the poor thrust out their tongues in derision. Thou didst not have where to lay Thy head when in Thy best estate; Thou hast no place now where shelter may be given Thee. See the companions with whom Thou hast taken sweet counsel, what are they worth? Son of Mary, see there Thy brother James, see there Thy beloved disciple John, and Thy bold Apostle Peter—they sleep—they sleep! And where are the others who said they would follow Thee? They, too, sleep when Thou art in Thy sufferings! They have forgotten Thee; they will be at their farms and merchandise by morning. Lo! Thou has no friend left in heaven or earth. All hell is against Thee. I have stirred up mine infernal den. I have sent my missives throughout all regions, summoning every prince of darkness to set upon Thee this night, and we will spare no arrows, we will use all our devilish might to overwhelm Thee, Thou solitary One!''

It may be that this was His temptation in the Garden. Three times He sought to have the cup pass. ''Backward and forwards thrice He ran, as if He sought some help from man.'' But in view of His soon being betrayed, being smitten by God and abhorred by men, to be publicly put to shame and forsaken by His Father and disciples, He knew He had come for this hour. And with a determination to do only His Father's will, He overcame the evil one again and said to His sleeping disciples, ''Rise, let us be going; behold, he is at hand that doth betray me.'' See SAVE ME in Index.

Judas, the Betrayer

The account of this dastardly act is recorded in Matthew 26:47-50; Mark 14:43-46; Luke 22:47,48; John 18:1-5.

''Friend, wherefore art thou come? Betrayest the Son of Man with a kiss?'' (Matthew 26:50a with Luke 22:48). We can understand without any difficulty the depravity of Herod, the rancor of the Pharisees, the revengeful anger of Annas and Caiaphas, the cowardly laxity of Pilate, but we have little evidence to understand the abomination of Judas. The four Gospel accounts tell us too little of him and of the reasons which induced him to sell the Messiah. Why did Satan enter him and not one of the others? While we are aware that Jesus knew from the beginning He had chosen His betrayer (John 6:70), that Judas was called the ''son of perdition'' (John 17:12), that Jesus said that it would have been better for him not to have been born (Mark 14:21), and that Judas' betrayal was in fulfillment of prophecy (Psalm 41:9), there are some hints in Scripture that might give an answer as to why it was Judas who committed this dastardly act of betrayal.

One reason was his disillusionment of Jesus—what he thought the purpose of Jesus to be. Judas had probably seen himself as one of the ''inner men'' in an earthly kingdom which he had supposed Jesus had come to establish. In this kingdom Judas would be a key figure, and his people would be delivered from the oppression of Rome. He had gone along with Jesus, hoping that He would revenge the enemy and restore Israel. As time passed, there was the realization that his hopes were false, that he had fallen in with a Messiah of quite another kind. Jesus had talked about His death; there was the threatening hostility of the Jews against Christ, the delay of His victorious manifestation, and he did not see a Kingdom approaching. Mingling with the people to find out the temper of the day, he had perhaps heard a rumor as to the decisions of the meeting of the elders and feared that the Sanhedrin would not be satisfied with one victim alone, but would condemn all those who had long followed Jesus. Overcome by fear, Judas thought he could ward off the danger and save his life by treachery; unbelief and cowardice thus being the ignominious motives of his betrayal.

Being hurt by another can lead to betrayal. Judas had come to this point. He had been stung for his hypocrisy when a woman poured out ointment on the feet of Jesus (John 12:1-8). The reproof for his stinginess and hypocrisy must have exasperated the disciple who perhaps had been reproved for these faults on other occasions. To the rancor of this rebuff was added envy, which always flourishes in vulgar souls. With all his misgivings, we find him ripe for betrayal.

Coupled with disillusionment and fear, there was his love for money, which is the root of all evil (I Timothy 6:10). He had been chosen to be the treasurer, the one who held "the bag" (John 13:29). It is difficult to understand why a treasurer might think this is his money, but then, so do many church treasurers think the same when it comes to spending it for the Lord's work! But money was pleasing to Judas, pleasing in itself, and pleasing in its possibility of power. He spoke of the poor, but he did not think of the poor. He was envious as well as grasping; envious as all misers are. That silent anointing which was the consecration of the King and the Messiah, those honors offered by a beautiful woman to his leader, made him suffer. It produced a jealousy second to none as he thought what might be his but in his opinion was wasted.

Judas is a victim sacrificed to the curse of money. Money carries with it, together with the filth of the hands which have clutched and handled it, a contagious desire of crime. Among the things which men have manufactured, money is perhaps the one which defiles the most. That it soils the souls of men is quite evident. It is desired by all; sought for, stolen, envied, loved more than love and often more than life itself. These ugly pieces of stamped matter, which the assassin gives to the cutthroat, the usurer to the hungry, the enemy to the traitor, the swindler to his partner, the trafficker to barter in religious offices, the lustful to the woman bought and sold, these foul vehicles of evil which persuade the son to kill his father, the wife to betray her husband, the brother to defraud his brother, the wicked poor man to stab the wicked rich man, the servant to cheat his master, the highwayman to take advantage of the traveler—this money, which has been the death of so many bodies, is every day the death of thousands of souls. It is more deadly than all the deadly diseases combined. It is no wonder some have called it "The Devil's Dirt." But this is what Judas wanted, and this is what Judas got to betray the Son of God into cruel hands.

Jesus was not only betrayed, but sold, sold for a price, sold for a small price, bought with coins. He was the object of a bargain, a bargain struck and paid for. Judas, the man of the purse, the cashier, did not present hmself as an accuser, did not offer himself as a cutthroat criminal but as a merchant doing business in blood. This is the same Judas who had been chosen to be among the Twelve to carry the gospel to the world. Three-and-a-half years Christ had kept Judas with Him, had him with Him in all His travels, had eaten, slept, and prayed with him. He had washed and wiped the feet of Judas in the Upper Room. To him, as to the others, Christ gave His body, symbolized by the bread, and He gave His blood symbolized by the cup. But at the table, the die was cast—he already had with him on his person the thirty pieces of silver to betray the One who had so lovingly treated him as one of His own (Matthew 26:15; Zechariah 11:11,12). He had them on his person wrapped so tightly so that they would not clink. But this "friend" of Jesus knew no peace. Possibly he could see beyond the veil of his covetous heart the blessed Messiah, calm, but with the pensive expression of the only One in the room who knew he was a traitor; seeing Him, still at liberty in the company of those who did love Him, still alive, all the blood still in His veins—yet knowing that those bargainers who had paid the price to him refused to wait any longer, that the affair was already arranged for that very night! Judas was the seller, Jesus had been bought.

Judas ate the bread and swallowed the fruit of the vine—partook of that body in which he had trafficked, drank that blood which he was to help shed, but had not the courage to confess his infamy, to throw himself down weeping at the feet of the One who would have wept with him. Then the only Friend remaining to Judas warned: "Verily I say unto you, that one of you shall betray Me . . . that thou doest, do quickly" (John 13:21-27). And Judas did just that. He went out immediately, "and it was night" (John 13:30). One always goes out into darkness when he turns his back on Jesus.

After Communion, the Lord went out to Gethsemane to pray. Judas, knowing where Jesus had gone, led the mob to arrest Him. The pale faces of the disciples, the livid face of Judas seemed to flicker in the red lights of the torches. Christ offered His face, stained with the blood of His agonizing prayer but more luminous than the lights, to the kiss of Judas. "Friend, wherefore art thou come? Betrayest thou the Son of Man with a kiss?" He knew what Judas had come to do, and He knew that this kiss was the first of His tortures and the most unendurable. This kiss was the signal for guards to make their arrest. "Whomsoever I shall kiss, the same is He: take Him and lead Him away safely," the merchant of blood had told the rough crowd who followed him as he came along the road. The spitting, the buffeting, the accusations of the Jewish rabble, the spikes of the Roman soldiers, and the sponge dipped in vinegar, were to be less tolerable than that kiss, the kiss of a mouth which had called Him Friend and Master, which had eaten from His dish and which had drunk from His cup.

The last word of Jesus to Judas was "Friend." In spite of all that Judas had done against Him, in spite of all that Christ had done for Judas, here the two were face to face in this dreadful moment. Yes, in spite of all that Jesus had to say about Judas—"woe to that man by whom the Son of Man is betrayed . . . better for him that he had not been born"—in spite of the fact that the treachery was complete, that Judas had added to his betrayal the outrage of the kiss laid on the face of Him who had commanded love for our enemies, He answered him with sweet and divine words of their habitual friendship—"Friend, wherefore art thou come?"

Peter summed up the real reason for it all—the "why" of one to betray Christ: "Jesus of Nazareth . . . , being delivered by the determinate counsel and foreknowledge of God, ye have taken, and by wicked hands have crucified and slain" (Acts 2:22,23). Judas had fulfilled his mission. He made the choice as was stated by John when the mob came to arrest the Son of Man: "And Judas . . . stood *with* them" (18:5). To stand with the crowd is to betray Christ.

The Two Mothers[8]

Long time ago, so I have been told,
　　Two angels once met on streets paved with gold.
"By the stars in your crown," said the one to the other
　　"I see that on earth, you too, were a mother.

And by the blue-tinted halo you wear
　　You, too, have known sorrow and deepest despair."
"Ah, yes," she replied, "I once had a son,
　　A sweet little lad, full of laughter and fun."

"But tell of your child." "Oh, I knew I was blessed
　　From the moment I first held him close to my breast,
And my heart almost burst with the joy of that day."
　　"Ah, yes," said the other, "I felt the same way."

The former continued: "The first steps he took—
　　So eager and breathless; the sweet startled look
Which came over his face—he trusted me so."
　　"Ah, yes," said the other, "How well do I know."

"But soon he had grown to a tall handsome boy,
So stalwart and kind—and it gave me so much joy
To have him just walk down the street by my side."
"Ah yes," said the other, "I felt the same pride."

"How often I shielded and spared him from pain
and when he for others was so cruelly slain.
When they crucified him—and they spat in his face,
How gladly would I have hung there in his place!"

A moment of silence— "Oh, then you are she—
The mother of Christ"; and she fell on one knee.
But the Blessed one raised her up, drawing her near,
And kissed from the cheek of the woman, a tear.

"Tell me the name of the son you love so,
That I may share with your grief and your woe."
She lifted her eyes, looking straight at the other,
"He was Judas Iscariot; I am his mother."

The (Mis-) Trial of Jesus

The following references serve as a background study for His trial: Matthew 26:57-58; 27:1,2,11-26; Mark 14:53-65; 15:1-15; Luke 22:66—23:25; John 18:12-14,19-24,28—19:16.

Considerable controversy concerning the propriety of the trial of Jesus has existed ever since His crucifixion. Volumes have been searched in an effort to find some legal justification for the verdict rendered, but nowhere is there to be found any logical or legal excuse for the absolute disregard of the then existing Hebrew code, nor the customs usually followed in criminal proceedings before Jewish courts.

Jesus had to undergo *two* trials: one ecclesiastical and the other civil; the first before Caiaphas and the second before Pontius Pilate, the Roman governor. This was necessary at that time because Judaea was under the jurisdiction of Rome and under the administration of a Roman ruler. In matters of religion Rome permitted the Jews to continue their ecclesiastical courts (the Sanhedrin), before which body all religious offenders were prosecuted and by which all punishment was meted out. In the case of Jesus' trial, however, where the only punishment which would satisfy His accusers was death, the ecclesiastical court did not have the power to inflict the desired penalty, thus making it necessary to resort to the civil tribune to procure their object. Knowing full well that Jesus had many followers, the entire plan to capture, try, and convict Him was carefully laid, so that all would be fully completed after sunset and before daybreak. Then only a few persons beside the horde which made up the army of conspirators would know what was taking place and only the actual execution would be left to be done after sunrise.

There were a number of steps which had to be followed in a Hebrew trial, especially if the accused was guilty of a crime worthy of death.

1. A court could not meet for capital punishment during Feast Days (Matthew 26:4,5).
2. When a trial was in order, before anything was done, the morning sacrifice had to be offered first.
3. There had to be the assemblying of *all* the Sanhedrin (Judges)—in their appointed place (the Temple in this case). The Sanhedrin was comprised of seventy men—the highest tribunal of the Jews. There were 23 priests, 23 scribes, 23 elders, and the presiding officer; namely, the High Priest (Numbers 11:16,17).

4. When convened, there was an examination of all witnesses, both in private and in the presence of the accused. No one could speak against the accused until someone spoke in his favor. Testimony was never admitted from women, minors, idiots, slaves, blind men, gamblers, relatives, or Gentiles. *All* evidence had to be heard. The witnesses had to agree on essential details. All evidence had to be established in the mouth of two or three witnesses (Deuteronomy 17:6; 19:15). If not, the testimony was rejected. Each witness was required to give evidence separately *and* in the presence of the accused and corroborated *both* times. The accused could testify on his behalf but was not compelled to do so. He could not be compelled to testify against himself, and a confession alone was not acceptable as a basis of conviction.

5. Afterward, there was a debate and balloting on the innocence or guilt of the accused. If any member of the Sanhedrin had a preconceived idea about the guilt or innocence of the accused, the case was thrown out of court. The youngest voted first, then the next youngest, next junior jurors, and last the seniors. This was done so the youngest would not be influenced by the elders. If the defendant was acquitted, he was freed immediately. If convicted, the court met again the next day, re-discussed all the evidence, and took another vote (the second trial was like an appeal). If a judge voted "not guilty" in the first trial, he could not change to "guilty" in the second trial. But if he had voted "guilty" the first time, he could change to "not guilty" after due consideration of all the evidence. The verdict of the court could not be unanimous. "A simultaneous and unanimous verdict of guilt on the day of this trial had the effect of an acquittal." If found guilty both days, there was no delay in the execution of the person (that is, if the sentence was death). The execution was at sundown, and the guilty was stoned to death (the Jewish method of capital punishment).

What happened in the trial of Jesus? The Sanhedrin certainly had the right, the jurisdiction, to try Jesus because of the charges brought against Him; namely blasphemy. After all, He had claimed to be one with the Father (John 10:30), He had forgiven sin, the prerogative of God alone (Mark 2:7-11), and He had said He was the Christ, *the* Son of the Blessed (Mark 14:61,62).

In the haste of the mob to try and condemn Jesus, almost every rule of the then existing law of Moses and Hebrew custom was violated, which, of course, made His trial illegal.

1. To begin with, the Sanhedrin decreed that Jesus should be killed (Matthew 26:1-5). This was "pre-trial" judgment. "No judge could sit in judgment if he be at enmity with the accused or if he had formed a preconceived idea concerning him."
2. His arrest was effected through the information of a traitor, which violated the code of Leviticus 19:15-18. See Luke 22:1-6,47-53.
3. He was arrested by members of the Sanhedrin (Luke 22:52-54).
4. The arrest was made without the issuance of any legal warrant. It was not the result of a legal mandate from a court whose intention it was to conduct a legal trial.
5. His arrest was at night (Mark 14:17,27,32,43-66).
6. He was taken to the house of Annas, who was not the high priest at that time (John 18:12-14,19-23).
7. This trial was in a house, not in the Temple.
8. All the Sanhedrin were not present in Annas' house.
9. Jesus was struck physically by a member (John 18:22) and spat upon (Matthew 26:67).
10. He was judged and bound over to the high priest (John 18:24).
11. The trial before Caiaphas, the high priest, was before the morning sacrifice.
12. The witnesses could not agree (Mark 14:56).
13. Jesus testified against Himself (Mark 14:56,60-63).
14. The high priest rent his clothes (Matthew 26:65). An ordinary Israelite could tear his garment as a sign of grief, but priests were forbidden because their vestments were made according to specific directions from God and were figurative of his office.
15. The trial before Caiaphas was also in a house, not a Temple (Luke 22:54). Not only should a trial of this nature be held in the Temple, but any sentence of condemnation also had to be pronounced there.

16. Jesus had two trials by the Jews, only hours apart, not on separate days (Matthew 27:1,2; John 18:28a).
17. The high priest could never say the accused was innocent or guilty. Yet Caiaphas did (Matthew 26:65).
18. Jesus was never afforded the opportunity for someone to speak in His favor (remember, all his disciples had forsaken Him; Mark 14:50).
19. He was found guilty upon His uncorroborated testimony.
20. All condemned Him to death (Mark 14:64).

After considerable mockery and efforts to find some accusation of merit against Jesus, the Sanhedrin simmered down to the charge of blasphemy, for which it finally pronounced Jesus guilty, basing its finding on the most flimsy and prejudiced testimony, for the most part given by persons who knew nothing of Jesus' teachings. Having accomplished their objective in sentencing Jesus to death for blasphemy, the Sanhedrin, being powerless under the Roman law to carry out their sentence, next sent Jesus for a civil trial to the Roman governor, who could either affirm or reverse their findings.

Pontius Pilate was the imperial Roman representative at this time. He was not popular with his subjects, having been accused of robbery, maladministration, etc. He feared that their continued complaints would make trouble for him with the emperor. Jesus was the victim of Pilate's fears and thus the last avenue of escape was strewn with obstacles which Pilate had not the courage to surmount.

Some of the things Jesus was charged with were that He was perverting the nation, He forbade to pay the imperial tribute, and that He had set Himself up as a king. The most significant thing about all these charges is that not one covered the charge on which they themselves had condemned Jesus, that of blasphemy. Pilate began questioning Jesus about the charge that He had proclaimed Himself a king. Asked by Pilate, "Art thou the king of the Jews?" Jesus quite fully and convincingly disposed of this charge when He replied: "My kingdom is not of this world. Everyone that is of the truth heareth My voice." Being fully satisfied with the answer of Jesus to the charge, Pilate went out and stated to the accusers: "I find in Him no fault," which was tantamount to a complete acquittal. Legally this should have been the end of the proceedings, and Jesus should have been released from custody at once.

As soon as Pilate announced his finding, the accusers let out an uproar of threats and other charges, among others, "He stirreth up the people, teaching throughout all Jewry, beginning from Galilee to this place." However, this gave Pilate a new thought, through which he might rid himself of responsibility, by sending Jesus to Herod, the ruler of Galilee, who was in Jerusalem for the Passover. So on to Herod's palace they went. The proceedings before Herod, if they are to be termed a trial, were a sad spectacle. Unable to find any guilt in Him, Herod, without any further order of judgment, drove them from his palace. Then back to Pilate with their prisoner they had to go. Quite annoyed, Pilate reluctantly resumed the case. There was nothing for him to do legally except to discharge Jesus. But he thought it would appease the clamor of the persecutors if he would chastise Jesus, and then set Him free; and thus we witness the spectacle of a prisoner, twice declared to be innocent by Pilate, chastised, just to satisfy a desire of some of his subjects. Had the release of Jesus followed, this unwarranted punishment might have been overlooked. Pilate's conscience was quite disturbed because of this predicament, and to add to this, his wife sent word to him that she had had a terrible dream and to have nothing to do with "that just man." Pilate had one more idea. It was customary at Passover time to release a prisoner. For starting an insurrection against the government, one Barabbas was placed in solitary confinement. Pilate asked the people: "Whom shall I release unto you, this man Jesus or Barabbas?" They answered loudly, "Give us Barabbas . . . crucify Jesus."

Earth has no tragedy comparable to this cry. After waiting centuries for Messiah to come, the people to whom He came rejected Him with scoffing and jeers. We cannot evade the fact that

Pilate made a desperate and determined attempt to release Him. Israel informed Pilate they accepted full responsibility for His execution. The elders and leaders of the people acted for the race, and there is no more tragic echo that comes from the place called Golgotha than the voice of Israel, raised in that frightful cry: "Upon our heads and the heads of our children be the blood of this Man forever." There is a striking and unusual significance in that cry. Pilate was a keen student of Jewish customs. No man ever governed for Rome over that turbulent and restless people who was as well versed in Jewish psychology as was Pilate. This great statesman was better fitted to rule Israel than any Gentile who ever attempted the task. He had studied the law of Israel and knew their customs and history—their antiquity.

In spite of this fact, he literally despised them. From his own point of view, he had good reason. Rome never really conquered Israel. While she did establish her yoke over the people and settled her dominion in the land, her position was that of a man sitting on the crest of a volcano. At any time, any moment, any thoughtless Roman soldier might violate some traditional taboo of Israel, and the volcano would erupt. Palestine gave Rome more trouble than any province the great empire possessed. All of this naturally reacted not only upon the spirit of Pilate, but against his record as well. His particular enemy was the high priest. They despised each other with a cordial hatred that brought them into constant friction. Very naturally then, when Pilate saw that the high priest was determined to crucify Christ, the governor made a notable fight to save His life. Three times he had said, "I find no fault in Him," which was tantamount to three acquittals. But this battle of Pilate for the life of Jesus terminated finally in capitulation to the Jews when he called for water and a basin and washed his hands.

What is the significance of this "washing" act? Pilate knew God's law (Deuteronomy 21:1-9). Where there was murder, and no criminal to blame, Israel's elders would gather where the body was, and, confident that there was no guilt upon the village, would wash their hands in token of the innocence of their people. What a stinging rebuke this must have been to the accusers of Christ when Pilate called for water to wash his hands (Matthew 27:24). They understood exactly what Pilate was saying—"This is murder—I am innocent. If you crucify Him, you are acknowledging your own law and are guilty of murder." But they cried, "His blood be on us, and on our children." Every Jew in that throng who joined in that utterance, as well as every Hebrew individual who heard it without protest, was familiar, for instance, with Numbers 35:33. In no uncertain terms, the Lord God Jehovah here states that He will bring retribution upon those who shed innocent blood. They were equally familiar with Moses' law (Deuteronomy 19:10-13) where the God of justice and holiness said, "There is no sanctuary for such as shed innocent blood." They also knew the utterance of God in Joshua 2:19 that the blood of the innocent will surely fall upon the heads of those who slay such. There was not a Jew in that throng but what was familiar with II Samuel 1:16, where it expressly taught that it is death to slay the Lord's anointed (yes, they knew He was the Messiah; John 11:49-52). But with a knowledge of truth, and with an understanding of God's stern and righteous judgment, the willfully lifted their voices in the face of an outraged heaven in that awful cry—"Crucify Him . . . release Barabbas . . . upon our heads be the blood of this Man forever." And God heard! Their wish was granted and Jesus was led away to be crucified.

Thus we see the world's most brutal miscarriage of justice. He went through five trials. One before Annas, one before Caiaphas (both Jewish), one before Pilate, one mockery before Herod, and then back to Pilate. Not only were His trials before the Jews illegal for the reasons already given; they were illegal before Pilate because they were based upon lies. His sentence was also illegal because He had been acquitted three times. We see Jesus apprehended, convicted, and put to death in less than twenty-four hours, in a proceeding fraught with utter disregard for justice and righteousness. This conviction ended the greatest court case in all history. An innocent man was condemned on false charges and illegal trials, and was sentenced to die upon a cross.

Innocency of Christ Attested

1. By Judas—"innocent blood": Matthew 27:3,4
2. By Pilate's wife—"that just Man": Matthew 27:19
3. By Pilate—"this just person": Matthew 27:24
4. By Herod—"nothing worthy of death": Luke 23:15
5. By Pilate—"I find no fault in Him": John 18:38
6. By the thief—"nothing amiss": Luke 23:41
7. By the centurion—"a righteous man": Luke 23:47

Jew's Rejection of Christ

Christ "came unto His own, and His own received Him not" (John 1:11). They chose Barabbas instead, and in their demand to have Jesus crucified they said: "His blood be upon us, and our children" (Matthew 26:15-25; Mark 15:6-14; Luke 23:13-24; John 18:28—19:16). The desire of the Jews to have the blood of Jesus upon them and their children has been literally fulfilled down through the centuries that followed. Because of this, the Jew has known no peace, has had no Temple or sacrifice, had no home until recently, and is being trodden down by the Gentiles until their fulness comes to an end.

However, the rejection and crucifixion of Christ by the Jews did not affect the purpose of the coming of Christ, for He came to give His life a ransom for many (Matthew 20:28). He offers Himself to those who will receive Him, whether Jew or Gentile (John 1:12). Because the Jew could not bring to nought the work of Christ, Christianity took hold of the souls of men. Today His name is the name above every name and His good news of salvation still saves those who believe in Him.

A Modern Jew Looks at Jesus[9]

For more than nineteen centuries the Jews have been living in a world fired by a religion which was cradled by them. After all, Christ was a Jew. His followers were Jews. The New Testament was written by Jews, and Palestine, the land of the Jews, was the place from which sprang the faith of over six hundred million people of today. Dare the Jews assert that 600,000,000 people are demented and that they, the sixteen million Jews, are sane?

Does it not strike the Jew rather strange that the Jew, Jesus of Nazareth, should have superseded the national heroes of every civilized land? Towering above Washington or Abraham Lincoln looms Jesus, the Jew, in the estimation of the people of America. Greater than Shakespeare or Darwin is the significance of Jesus to the people of England. Higher than Zola or Clemenceau rises Jesus in the veneration of the French people.

Destiny wills it that the Jew should live among Christians. Even in Palestine, in the new nation of Israel today, they look to the United States and Britain for help and advice, yet England's priceless cathedrals have immortalized, not her kings and statesmen, but Him who was born "King of the Jews." America has been made great because she was founded on the Bible, and because she has permitted the Christ of the Book to be proclaimed.

Does it mean nothing to the Jews that mankind reveres "flesh of their flesh and bone of their bone?" If Jesus were an American and all the world would do Him homage except America, the Jew would say that America was stupid. What must the world think of the Jew for rejecting their own Messiah?

Christ Condemned to Be Crucified

When Pilate concluded the (mis-) trial of Christ, he "released Barabbas unto them [the Jews]: and when he had scourged Jesus, he delivered Him to be crucified" (Matthew 27:33-50; Mark 15:22-39; Luke 23:33-46; John 19:16-30). "Victims condemned to the cross first underwent the hideous torture of the scourge, and this was immediately inflicted on Jesus. He was now seized by some soldiers nearby, and after being stripped to the waist, was bound in a stooping posture, His hands being tied behind his back, to a post, or a block of wood, near the tribunal. The Jews had a law that no person should be given more than forty stripes save one when flogged, but the Romans had no such law; so they often scourged their victims until they bled to death. Jesus was beaten at the pleasure of the soldiers, with knots of rope, or plaited leathern thongs, armed at the ends with acorn-shaped drops of lead, or small pointed bones. In many cases not only was the back of the person scourged cut open in all directions, but even the eyes, the face, and the breast were torn open, and the teeth not seldom knocked out. Under the fury of the countless stripes, the victims sometimes sank—amid screams, convulsive leaps, and distortions—into a senseless heap; sometimes died on the spot; sometimes were taken away, an unrecognizable mass of bleeding flesh, to find deliverance in death from the inflammation and fever, sickness and shame.''[10] Besides scourging Christ until His back was a bloody mass of pulp—one great bruise—the Roman soldiers plucked out His whiskers by the roots, and spat upon Him (Isaiah 50:6). Eusebius, the early church historian, described a Roman scourging of some martyrs thus: ''All around were horrified to see them so torn with the scourges that their very own veins were laid bare, and the inner muscles and sinews, and even their very bowels, were exposed.''

It was after such that they laid the cross on the back of the One who lived through such an ordeal. ''There never was a moment in all history like this one when the cross laid its awkward might on the shoulders of this Man Christ Jesus. No animate thing, no man or devil, had possessed the body of Christ. Men had sought to stone Him, but He had hidden himself. Men attempted to make Him king, but He avoided them. The devil had tempted Him in the wilderness, yet He victoriously overcame the evil one. With a divine independence the Savior of men walked on earth. Yet He was apprehended in the garden of Gethsemane. The high priests sought to do away with Him. Herod trembled in His silent presence. Pilate hesitated to condemn Him. God's very presence distinguished Him before a bloodthirsty mob. The lashing scourge had just bitten His flesh. The crown of thorns cut deeply into His brow and now the very cross He was to bear to Calvary began to make its mark on His body.

''All else had been a prelude to this moment. For this cruel journey He had been born. At the end of this wearisome trek the reverse would take place. Instead of the cross being on Him, He would be nailed to the cross, there to suffer the awful penalty of sin. From the time the cross was placed on Him until the time He gave up His spirit on the cross and was taken down by Joseph of Arimathaea and Nicodemus, He suffered such as no mortal tongue could describe.

''What a tragic yet fruitful role this cross of the Redeemer was to play. In the cross we see man's unpredictable perverseness. Its weight was made heavy with the iniquities of a world laden with sin. Its course roughness was the leprous crust, the scaly hardness of men's hearts. Its sweating, slippery surface was the clammy coldness of man's sin-stained flesh. Its burden-some hulk was the clumsy effort of men made mad with the impression that they had become gods.

''No wonder then that the cross alone could do what all the terrible brutality of the soldiers had been powerless to accomplish. The scourges did tear Him apart; the thorns did sear with piercing, blinding fire; His body was beaten and bruised with unmerciful savagery. But none of these broke Him down, and sent Him crashing like a mighty tree, as did this unsupportable weight of the cross. Those favorite politicians of Pilate, those sly henchmen of the high priests, and the insane mob, they were all but puny stage hands compared to the Act of the Ages being culminated by God Incarnate. The cross was the collective will of a world gone roaring mad and filled with the poison of sin. It alone could represent the entire essence of a stricken humanity. It alone could beat Him who had chosen to bear the cross without sins upon Him.

Place of the Skull (Calvary)

"But redemption had not yet been purchased. Though the weighty cross had felled its victim, the mob, not knowing the purpose of such an event, for had they known they would not have crucified this One, laid hold upon one Simon, a Cyrenian, and on him they laid the cross, that he might bear it after Jesus (Luke 23:26). The way to the place called 'Skull' is now stretched out before Him. He was to baptize every foot of it with His own precious blood. Eternally it would remain moistened with the blood of this Man of Sorrows.

"Christ had long awaited this hour. It was to be the road which He first would travel so that men might follow after Him, its darkness lighted by the shining of the Light of the world. He would tread the way alone in order to stamp it with the marks of His divine footsteps, making the Way of the Cross the lone avenue to the mount of salvation. All men henceforth must make a trip to Calvary or perish on the broad highway that leads to destruction. The narrow road to eternal life has been blazed at a terrible cost, it has been cleared at a Divine sacrifice by the Lamb of God.

"Christ found His cross a terrible burden, so great that it bore Him down and crushed Him. But it drew out His strength, to preserve it, and to impart it to those who are yet without strength. We also see in His cross-bearing that which has become the insignia of His kingdom on earth and heaven. He transformed it from a symbol of shame to one of glory, from a sign of death to one of immortality. At the crossroads of life it would point to the *Way*; in the midst of uncertainty it would shine with *Truth*; and in the darkness of sorrow and sin and death, the Christ of the cross would illuminate the heart of man and give *Life*."[11] See CRUCIFIXION in Index.

The Wounds of Christ[12]

It is remarkable that in the statement "He was wounded for our transgressions" (Isaiah 53:5), we have the five classifications of wounds as defined by a surgeon—

1. The *contused* wound is a wound produced by a blunt instrument. Such would result from a blow by a rod, as foretold by Micah (5:1). This was fulfill-

when they smote Christ with a reed (rod—Matthew 27:30 with John 18:22, RSV, margin).

2. The *lacerated* wound is a wound produced by a tearing instrument. Christ was lacerated as a result of scourging (Psalm 129:3; Isaiah 50:6; Matthew 27:26; John 19:1). Let us never forget that upon His lacerated back the Cross was laid as He went forth to Calvary.

3. The *penetrating* wound is a deep wound caused by a sharp-pointed instrument. This happened to Jesus when they placed upon His head a crown of thorns (Matthew 27:29; John 19:2), wounds which were deepened by the blow of the rod when they smote Him on the head (Matthew 27:30).

4. The *perforating* wound receives its name from the Latin word meaning "to pierce through." The iron spikes were driven between the bones, separating but not breaking them—"they pierced My hands and My feet" (Psalm 22:16). The New Testament does not mention the actual driving of spikes in His hands and feet, but evidence presented to Thomas is sufficient that it happened in His crucifixion (John 20:24,25,27-29). See CRUCIFIXION in Index.

5. The *incised* wound is a cut produced by a sharp-edged instrument. A spear was thrust into His side, "and forthwith came there out blood and water" (John 19:34). This wound was afflicted by the practiced hand of the Roman soldier to make certain that whatever vestige of life was present would be extinguished, but while it did not cause death in the case of Christ, it was an assurance to all men that death had actually occurred, and it was also a fulfillment of the Scripture which says, "They shall look on Him whom they have pierced." From this wound there came "out blood and water." This wonderful sight awakened surprise and deep interest in John and may surely engage our attention also; namely, the water that flowed from the pericardium and the blood that flowed from the heart. The pericardium is a closed sac encasing the heart and lubricated by a small amount of fluid (about a teaspoonful) to facilitate the motion of the heart. How could John, it may be asked, distinguish such a small quantity of water? To answer this question I quote a significant statement from a standard work—Mallory and Wright's Pathological Technique: "The normal amount (of the pericardial fluid) is about a teaspoonful, but may be increased to 100 c.c. (24 teaspoonfuls) where the death agony is prolonged." Here, then, is confirmation by scientists of the mute testimony borne by "the water" to the intense suffering of our Lord. The last wound offered to the body prepared for Him proclaimed both purification and redemption, for the very spear that pierced His side drew forth His blood to save.

Superscriptions on the Cross

"This is Jesus the King of the Jews" (Matthew 27:37); "The King of the Jews" (Mark 15:26); "This is the King of the Jews" (Luke 23:38); and "Jesus of Nazareth the King of the Jews" (John 19:19-21). No two superscriptions are exactly alike. John gives the reason why: "It was written in Hebrew, and in Greek, and in Latin," the three languages of Christ's day (John 19:20). Matthew wrote especially for the Jews and gave the inscription in Hebrew. Mark gave the inscription in Latin beause he wrote mainly to the Romans. Luke's was in Greek because he wrote mainly to the Greeks, and John's in Latin, giving the full Roman title, "Jesus of Nazareth."

Events at the Crucifixion
Seven Last Sayings of the Lord

1. Arrival at Golgotha: Matthew 27:33
2. Stupefying drink refused: Matthew 27:34
3. Crucified between two thieves: Luke 23:32,33
4. FIRST CRY: "Father, forgive them, for they know not what they do": Luke 23:34a
5. Soldiers part His garments: Luke 23:34b

6. People revile Him: Matthew 27:39,40
7. Priests mock Him: Matthew 27:41-43
8. Rulers deride Him: Luke 23:35
9. Soldiers mock Him: Luke 23:36,37
10. Two thieves rail on Him, but one repents: Matthew 27:44 with Luke 23:39-43
11. SECOND CRY: "Today shalt thou be with Me in paradise": Luke 23:43
12. THIRD CRY: "Woman, behold Thy Son": John 19:26
13. The supernatural darkness: Luke 23:44,45a
14. FOURTH CRY: "My God, My God, why hast Thou forsaken Me?" Mark 15:34
15. FIFTH CRY: "I Thirst": John 19:28
16. SIXTH CRY: "It is finished": John 19:30
17. SEVENTH CRY: "Father, into Thy hands I commend My Spirit": Luke 23:46a
18. Jesus yielded up His spirit: Matthew 27:50b
19. Veil of the Temple rent in twain: Matthew 27:51a
20. The earth quakes: Matthew 27:51b
21. Bodies of many saints resurrected: Matthew 27:52,53
22. Christ's side pierced: John 19:34
23. Christ's body taken from cross: Matthew 27:57-61; John 19:38-42

Seven Last Sayings of the Crowd

1. "Thou that destroyeth the Temple, and buildest it in three days, save Thyself. If Thou be the Son of God, come down from the cross": Matthew 27:40
2. "He saved others, Himself He cannot save. If He be the king of Israel, let Him now come down from the cross, and we will believe Him": Matthew 27:42
3. "He trusted in God, let Him [God] deliver Him now": Matthew 27:43
4. "If Thou be the Christ, save Thyself": Luke 23:39
5. "Remember me when Thou comest into Thy kingdom": Luke 23:42
6. "This Man calleth for Elijah . . . let us see whether Elijah will come to save Him": Matthew 27:46-49
7. "Truly this man was the Son of God": Mark 15:39

Christ Was Forsaken

Loneliness is a tragic thing to experience—a widow has untold hours with seemingly nothing to do—a widower whose children live in faraway places pines his time away—teenagers longing for affection from parents who are too busy to give a little of their time to them. But, if loneliness is a tragic thing, to be "forsaken" is far worse. Forsake means "to leave," "to utterly abandon." Jesus was forsaken to a degree that no other man has ever known. He was utterly forsaken—

1. By the world He created: John 1:10 with 1:3
2. By the Nation from which He sprang. He was from the seed of Abraham, the Tribe of Judah, the family of David. He was a Jew according to the flesh, but when He came to His own people, they received Him not: John 1:11.
3. By His own village, Nazareth, where He spent His childhood. When He preached His first sermon they sought to kill Him, and He never returned to do mighty works there because they did not believe in Him. No prophet is accepted in his own country: Luke 4:16-30.
4. By His own brothers. Yes, He had half brothers and sisters, but they did not believe in Him until after the resurrections: Matthew 13:55,56; John 7:5.
5. By the disciples He trained: Mark 14:50 with Zechariah 13:7—"smite the Shepherd, and the sheep shall be scattered."
6. By His own eternal Father when He hung on the cross: Matthew 27:46 with Romans 8:32 when God "spared Him not."

He was forsaken that you and I, through faith in Him, need never be—"lo, I am with you always," and "I will never leave thee nor forsake thee" (Matthew 28:20; Joshua 1:5).

Twelve Views of the Cross[13]

1. The soldiers saw in Christ a criminal—*with cruelty*
2. The women saw in Christ a benefactor—*with sorrow*
3. The mother of Christ saw in Him a son—*with anguish*
4. The disciples saw in Christ blighted hopes—*with perplexity*
5. The first thief saw in Christ a malefactor—*with hardness*
6. The second thief saw in Christ a King—*with penitence*
7. The centurion saw in Christ divinity—*with conviction*
8. The priests saw in Christ an imposter—*with mockery*
9. The angels saw in Christ love—*with wonder*
10. The devil saw in Christ the seed of the woman—*with dismay*
11. The passers-by saw in Christ nothing—*with indifference*
12. Jehovah saw in Christ obedience—*with affection*

Veil of the Temple Rent

The veil in the Temple was a type of Christ. With His finished work on the cross, this veil, which heretofore had blocked entrance to all into God's presence except the high priest, is now torn—from top to the bottom (Matthew 27:51a; Mark 15:38; Luke 23:45).

1. The torn veil now opened the way of salvation for *all* to come unto God by Christ (Hebrews 10:19-22). Notice the rending was from "the top to the bottom." "Salvation is of the Lord"; (Jonah 2:9). It is "God coming down to man—not man going up to God."
2. The rending of the veil, enabling *any* man to enter into God's presence through Christ, assures us of the truth of the "priesthood of the believer," that all believers are "a kingdom of priests" (Exodus 19:6; Hebrews 10:19,20; I Peter 2:5,9; Revelation 1:6).
3. The rending also signified that the separation between Jews and Gentiles was now abolished (Ephesians 2:13-18). See VEIL of Ark in Index.

Christ in the Grave Three Days and Three Nights

Jesus Himself made the statement that He would be three days and three nights in the heart of the earth (Matthew 12:40). According to tradition and practice the church holds that Christ was crucified on Friday and then raised from the grave early Sunday morning. This would make Him in the grave only two nights. The Jewish sabbath began Friday at sunset and ended at sunset on the sabbath (Saturday). Because of *this* sabbath, the church has supposed our Lord was crucified on Friday. However, we learn from the Old Testament that there were other Jewish sabbaths—sabbaths of feasts and sabbaths of years.

John (19:14) indicates that the Jews, during the week of Christ's crucifixion, were observing a *Passover* sabbath, which, no doubt, fell on Friday of that week. Mark (15:42) tells us that Christ's crucifixion took place on the *day before the sabbath*. This was not Friday—the day before the *weekly* sabbath, but Thursday—the day before the *Passover sabbath*. This would enable Christ to be, as He predicted, in the grave three days and three nights.

He Descended Into Hell[14]

If Jesus paid the penalty for our sins, this would have included not only His tasting death for every man (Hebrews 2:9), for the wages of sin is death, but it would have included His descending into hell, the place where all sinners deserve to go. The Apostles' Creed states it this way: "He descended into hell." Scripture gives us some hints to show that in hell Christ was conscious after His death on the cross and that His performance in hell was an important part of His earthly ministry. Peter, in mentioning the crucified Christ, said: "Whom God raised up, having loosed the pangs of death, because it was not possible that He should be holden of it" (Acts 2:24). Two things are implied in this verse: (1) that death exerted "pangs," and (2) that something called "death" tried so hard to hold Him that God Himself had to intervene. Clearly there was a titanic struggle going on those three days and three nights in the grave.''

During this awful battle, several things took place. There was punishment for our sins. Christ took on Himself the guilt of the human race, including its worst crimes. In God's sight, Christ was "made sin." His whole being reeked with our sin. That sin had to be punished. Punishment for sin required more than physical death. If punishment consisted merely of separating spirit from body, which physical death does, then Christ could have almost instantly revived after three o'clock that awful afternoon and sped back to His Father. Punishment for sin *follows* physical death. Peter said He was "put to death in the flesh, but made alive in the spirit, in which also He went . . . in prison . . . " (I Peter 3:18,19). He carried on activities which show He was alive and fully aware of His mission there. And, as He predicted, He was "three days and three nights in the heart of the earth," not just in the garden tomb (Matthew 12:40).

If punishment for sin is not mere physical death, what is it? Christ received the same type of punishment the rich man in Luke 16 experienced, cut off from God and godly men, abandoned to the torments of hell fire, and gloated over by Satan. It is the horror awaiting every Christ rejecter. When Jesus said in the garden, "If it be possible for this cup to pass . . . " (Mark 14:35,36), it was the prospect of what went beyond his unspeakable death—the spikes, the nakedness, the sun's heat, the flies, the spitting, the jeering, the wracking of His body in hideous pain. It was the horrible, black anguish of the coming guilt of our sins and the fear of His Father's rejection. Surely this was the bitterest drop in the cup. He who had seen from before the foundation of the world what awaited any spirit delivered to "him who has the power of death, that is the devil," knew full well the horror that lurked for Him the moment He passed through "the gates of Hades."

Something of the gloating spirit that animated all Hades as Jesus descended may be guessed at from His parable of the vineyard where wicked servants, having killed a succession of prophets, said to each other, "This is the heir. Come, let us kill Him and take His inheritance" (Matthew 21:38). Surely this is what Satan had in mind. If somehow he could incarcerate Jesus, then the earth's inheritance would be his. Every sinner is Satan's prey; here is Christ—with all our sins, and in Satan's sight the greatest sinner of all, forsaken by God and assigned to "taste of death for every man." Satan determined His punishment would be full measure.

Scripture does not tell us what "the pangs of death" were like, but it does say that God "loosed" them. Hell's handcuffs were snapped on Christ, its gates clanged shut behind Him. For over four thousand years no sinful human soul had ever escaped that prison. The "gulf" was "fixed" too deep and wide for any transition (Luke 16:25,26). Try to imagine what this time in Hell would be like. How like all eternity it would seem! Perhaps in the spiritual realm time loses all meaning, for "one day is with the Lord as a thousand years." What would three days be like?

Here was Christ—all alone. "I looked, and there was none to help, and I wondered that there was none to uphold" (Isaiah 63:5). No angel was there, except hell's angels. For the first time in all eternity the Son of God was alone. Yet not entirely. The Holy Spirit was still with Him. It was "through the eternal Spirit" that He "offered Himself without blemish unto God" (Hebrews 9:14). It was this faithful Companion who plumbed with Christ the depths of Hell. He empowered the Savior's arm for combat, and the outcome is described as follows: "He spoiled [disarmed] principalities and powers. He made a show of them openly, triumphing over them in it" (Colossians 2:14,15). These principalities are infernal, not heavenly. They represent Satan's most potent warriors. Christ took them on in their own den and despoiled them—He stripped them, threw them down, and left them impotent. These evil beings are immobilized, not annihilated. Christ subjected them with His God-given power. "Therefore God exalted Him to the highest place and gave Him the name that is above every name, that at the name of Jesus every knee should bow, in heaven and on earth and under the earth [or of the world below]" (Philippians 2:9,10 with ASV note).

Christ also bruised Satan's head. The promise given in Eden was fulfilled (Genesis 3:15). The "serpent" that bruised Christ's "heel" was crushed by the heel. "To this end was the Son of God manifested that He might destroy the works of the devil" (I John 3:8). Hebrews 2:14 agrees: ". . . that through death He might bring to nought him that had the power of death, that is, the devil." It was the three days and nights of invisible combat in hell that "brought to nought" Satan's power over humanity. Satan must live to witness the absolute triumph of Christ over all creation.

Hell's bars and gates had defied the ages, taking all and releasing none. Job had known their awful impregnability—"I go whence I shall not return, to the land . . . of the shadow of death" (10:21). But now these gates, which Christ declared would be no obstacle to His church, gave way to the One who "broke the gates of brass and cut the bars of iron in sunder" (Psalm 107:16). Christ also seized the keys of death and of hell. "I am He that liveth, and was dead; and, behold I am alive forevermore, Amen; and have the keys of hell and of death" (Revelation 1:18).

Having descended into the lower parts of the earth and becoming the Victor, Christ now begins to make His exit "leading captivity captive" (Ephesians 4:8-11). What does the expression "captivity captive" mean? The key to our understanding this expression is the phrase "wherefore he saith" (vs. 8). Whenever an expression such as this occurs, it has reference to something said in the Old Testament. It is used in connection with an enemy capturing a people. When Jaban, king of Canaan, and Sisera, his captain, oppressed Israel for twenty years, Jaban and Sisera became "captivity" and Israel became "captive." Deborah, as Judge of Israel, led Israel to victory, and Jaban and Sisera—"captivity," were led "captive." The enemy is "captivity." Read Judges 4:1—5:12. When Christ defeated the devil and spoiled principalities, He led "captivity" (the devil) "captive!" He is *now* the Victor—"captivity." See CAPTIVITY in Index.

Some would suggest that Hades (hell-Sheol) was in two compartments—one for those who died in their sins, and the other for the Old Testament saints who had died in faith (Luke 16:22-26). The compartment for saints is sometimes referred to as "Abraham's bosom." When Christ ascended up on high (Ephesians 4:8), the "captivity" He led, so they say, were these Old Testament saints who were then taken to heaven to be with Himself—their faith being rewarded with the same victory that is ours (Hebrews 11:39,40).

The Meaning of Christ's Death[15]

1. Its nature:
   a. It was predetermined: Acts 2:23; I Peter 1:18-20; Revelation 13:8
   b. It was voluntary: John 10:17,18; Galatians 2:20b
   c. It was vicarious: I Peter 3:18; I Corinthians 15:3; Romans 4:25a
   d. It was sacrificial: I Corinthians 5:7b; Isaiah 53:10; Hebrews 9:14,26
   e. It was expiatory: Galatians 3:13
   f. It was propitiatory: I John 2:1,2; 4:10; Romans 3:25
   g. It was redemptive: Galatians 4:4,5; Acts 20:28b
   h. It was substitutionary: I Peter 2:24; II Corinthians 5:21
2. Its scope:
   a. For the whole world: I John 2:2; I Timothy 2:6; John 1:29
   b. For each individual: Hebrews 2:9. One creature cannot, in the government of God, take the place of another. An angel cannot act in the place of man, because man, not angels, sinned, and came short of the glory of God. Consequently, angels do not know the meaning of redemption (I Peter 1:12). One sinner cannot take the place of another sinner, for

both need redemption (Psalm 49:7). If allowed to do so, one perfect creature could only take the place of one sinful creature. For every sinner there would be need of a perfect creature. But Christ, the only begotten of the Father—not a creature—could give universal value to His death for all, and because He was the sinless Son of God, He tasted death for every man. In considering every individual, every class and type of sinner comes under the benefit and potential saving power of the Cross; none is too low, too vile, too unworthy (Romans 5:6-8; I Timothy 1:15; I Peter 3:18).

    c. For the Church and all believers: Ephesians 5:25-27; I Timothy 4:10

3. Its results:

In relation to man in general—

    a. A new probation is secured: Romans 3:25; Acts 17:30,31
    b. Men are drawn to Him: John 12:32,33; Jeremiah 31:3
    c. A new propitiation is provided: I John 2:2; 4:10
    —Sin forgiven: Ephesians 1:7; Romans 4:7
    —Sin removed: Psalm 103:12
    —Sin blotted out: Isaiah 44:22
    —Sin buried: Micah 7:19
    —Sin remembered no more: Hebrews 10:17
    —Righteousness imputed: Romans 3:25; 4:6,8

In relation to the believer—

    a. The distance between God and man is annihilated: Ephesians 2:13
    b. Redemption from the curse of the law is secured: Galatians 3:13
    c. Deliverance from bondage to the law is provided: Colossians 2:14
    d. Ground for justification from guilt is provided: Romans 5:9
    e. Reconciliation with God is provided: Romans 5:10
    f. Forgiveness of sin is secured: Ephesians 1:7
    g. Ground for sonship is furnished: Galatians 4:3-5
    h. Cleansing from all sin is provided: I John 1:7,9
    i. Power of sin is potentially nullified: Romans 6:6-11
    j. Condemnation is forever removed: Romans 8:1-3,33,34
    k. Fear of death removed: Hebrews 2:14,15; I Corinthians 15:20-23,54-57

Christ's Resurrection[16]

The gospel accounts list the following references for Christ's resurrection: Matthew 28:1-6; Mark 16:1-6; Luke 24:1-8; John 20:1-14 with Psalm 16:10; 30:3.

1. Its logic: Paul presents the resurrection of Christ from two standpoints, *negative* and *positive.* He first shows what the result would be "if Christ be not risen" (I Corinthians 15:12-19):
    a. Christ would still be in the grave
    b. Christ would be a liar
    c. His disciples were deceived
    d. Their preaching was vain
    e. Our faith is vain
    f. We are found false witnesses
    g. The Christian Church is a farce
    h. Christian experience is purely imagination
    i. We are still in our sins
    j. We perish like animals
    k. We are of all men most miserable

To present the *positive* side we take the statement, "But now *is* Christ risen from the grave," and just reverse the above points.

2. Its evidences:
    a. The empty tomb: Luke 24:3; John 20:1,2
    b. The recovered grave clothes: John 20:3-8

c. Post-resurrection Appearances—
—To Mary Magdalene, as *Consoler:* John 20:16
—To the disciples, as the *Restorer of joy:* John 20:19,20
—To Peter, as the *Friend who never forsakes:* Luke 24:34
—To the two of Emmaus, as the *sympathetic Instructor:* Luke 24:13-32
—To the disciples in the upper room (Thomas absent), as the *Bestower of peace:* John 20:19-24
—To Thomas (with the disciples), as the *Confirmer of faith:* John 20:26-29
—To the seven who went fishing, as the *Concerned One:* John 21:2-23
—To over 500 at once, as the *Resurrection and the Life:* I Corinthians 15:6
—To James, as the *Assurer of the individual:* I Corinthians 15:7
—To the eleven, as the *Embodiment of headship and authority:* Matthew 28:18-20; and as the *Giver of power:* Luke 24:49; Acts 1:4-9
—To Paul, as *Victor:* Acts 9:3-6; I Corinthians 15:8
—To Stephen, as the *Welcomer to heaven:* Acts 7:55
—To Paul in the Temple, as *Protector and Comforter:* Acts 22:17-21; 23:11
—To John on Patmos, as *Head of the church:* Revelation 1:10-19

Statements in Acts 1:3, 10:41, and 13:31 seem to imply that during the forty days between Christ's resurrection and ascension that Christ made many appearances beside those recorded, and this His post-resurrection ministry may have been greater than we know.

d. Change wrought in the disciples. Note the book of Acts.
e. Change in the day of rest and worship—now also a day of service: Acts 20:7; I Corinthians 16:2

3. Its results:
a. Fulfillment of God's promises: Acts 13:32,33
b. Establishes the Deity of Christ: Romans 1:4
c. Furnishes justification for believers: Romans 4:23-25
d. Gives believers a living hope: I Peter 1:3,4
e. Empowers believers: Ephesians 1:19,20
f. Enables believers to bear fruit: Romans 7:4
g. Assures the believer of his own resurrection: I Corinthians 15:51-57
h. It is God's pledge of future judgment: Acts 17:31

Prophecy Fulfilled in Christ

1. Advent—for Jew and Gentile: Genesis 3:15; Numbers 24:17; Deuteronomy 18:15; Isaiah 9:6; 42:6; Galatians 4:4,5
2. Time of Advent: Daniel 9:24-26a; Malachi 3:1
3. Born of a virgin: Matthew 1:23; Luke 1:26-35; 2:5-7 with Isaiah 7:14
4. Divinity—name Immanuel; God with us: Matthew 1:22,23; Luke 1:31-35 with Isaiah 7:14b
5. Born in Bethlehem: Matthew 2:6 with Micah 5:2. See BETHLEHEM in Index.
6. Adored by great persons: Matthew 2:1-12 with Psalm 72:10
7. Flight into Egypt and return: Matthew 2:13-15 with Hosea 11:1
8. Herod's slaughter of innocents: Matthew 2:16-18 with Jeremiah 31:15
9. Dwelling in Nazareth: Matthew 2:23. It is difficult to ascertain which prophet spoke this. Judges 13:5 gives the characteristics of a Nazarene. This verse in Matthew probably refers to Isaiah 11:1, where Christ is spoken of as "a netzer [or rod] out of the stem of Jesse."
10. Ministry of John the Baptist: Matthew 3:3; Mark 1:2-4; Luke 1:76; 3:2-4 with Isaiah 40:3
11. Anointed by the Spirit: Matthew 3:16; Mark 1:9-11; Luke 3:21,22; John 1:33 with Isaiah 11:1,2
12. Galilee, place of public ministry: Matthew 4:12-17; Mark 1:14,15; Luke 4:14 with Isaiah 9:1,2
13. Taking our infirmities: Matthew 8:16,17 with Isaiah 53:4
14. Working miracles: Matthew 11:4-6; Luke 7:18-23 with Isaiah 35:2b-8

15. Spirit of Elijah in John the Baptist to prepare the way for Christ: Matthew 11:10-14; 17:9-13; Mark 9:11-13; Luke 1:17 with Malachi 4:5
16. Servant for Gentile salvation: Matthew 12:15-18 with Isaiah 42:1
17. Meekness and compassion: Matthew 12:19,20 with Isaiah 42:2,3
18. Speaking in parables: Matthew 13:13,14,34; Mark 4:2; Luke 8:4 with Psalm 78:2; Isaiah 6:9,10
19. Purification of the Temple: Matthew 21:12,13; Mark 11:15-17; Luke 19:45,46; John 2:13-17 with Psalm 69:9
20. Riding into Jerusalem upon an ass: Matthew 21:1-11; Mark 11:1-11; Luke 19:28-38; John 12:12-15; with Psalm 118:26; Zechariah 9:9
21. The rejected Stone: Matthew 21:42; Mark 12:10; Luke 20:17 with Psalm 118:22,23
22. Betrayal by a friend: Matthew 26:47-50; Mark 14:10,43-46; Luke 22:47,48; John 18:2 with Psalm 41:9
23. Sold for thirty pieces of silver: Matthew 26:14-16 with Zechariah 11:13
24. Disciples forsaking Him: Matthew 26:31; Mark 14:27,50 with Zechariah 13:7
25. False witness against Him: Matthew 26:59,60; Mark 14:55,56 with Psalm 35:11
26. Potter's field purchased with betrayal money: Matthew 27:3-10. This allusion is to Jeremiah 18:1-4; 19:1-3, but more directly to Zechariah 11:12,13.
27. Opened not His mouth: Matthew 27:13,14; Mark 15:1-6; Luke 23:8,9 with Psalm 38:13; Isaiah 53:7
28. Dishonored and shamed: Matthew 27:18,29; Mark 15:16-20; John 19:2,3 with Psalm 69:19
29. The Shepherd smitten and visage marred: Matthew 26:31; 27:30; Mark 14:27 with Isaiah 50:6; 52:14; Zechariah 13:7
30. Falling beneath the Cross: Matthew 27:32; Mark 15:21; Luke 23:26 with Psalm 109:24
31. Crucified in prime of life: Psalm 89:45
32. Messiah cut off—hands and feet pierced, wounded for our transgressions: Matthew 27:35a; Mark 15:22-24; Luke 23:33; John 19:16-18 with Psalm 22:16; Daniel 9:24-26a; Isaiah 53:5,6,10; Micah 5:1. Christ was crucified in the customary Roman manner, the hands and feet being pierced by huge spikes which fastened the body to the wooden cross (see John 20:25-27).
33. His death voluntary: John 12:27-33 with Psalm 40:6-8
34. Casting lots for His garments: Matthew 27:35b; Mark 15:24; Luke 23:34; John 19:23,24 with Psalm 22:18. How exact this prophecy! The garments were to be *parted* among them, but the vesture was to be awarded to one by *lots*. These are statements that would appear almost contradictory unless explained by the record of this scene at the cross.
35. Prayer for His enemies: Luke 23:34 with Psalm 109:4; Isaiah 53:12
36. Stared at on the cross: Matthew 27:36; Luke 23:35a,48 with Psalm 22:17
37. Crucified between two thieves: Matthew 27:38; Mark 15:28; Luke 23:32; John 19:18 with Isaiah 53:12
38. Mocked by the crowd: Matthew 27:39-43; Mark 15:29-32; Luke 23:35-38 with Psalm 22:7,8; 109:25
39. Darkness at the crucifixion: Matthew 27:45; Mark 15:33; Luke 23:44,45a with Amos 8:9
40. Forsaken by God: Matthew 27:46; Mark 15:34 with Psalm 22:1
41. Given vinegar to drink: Matthew 27:48; Mark 15:36; Luke 23:36; John 19:28,29 with Psalm 69:21
42. Friends stood afar off: Luke 23:49 with Psalm 38:11
43. Committed Himself to God; His death: Matthew 27:50; Mark 15:37; Luke 23:46; John 19:30 with Psalm 31:5; Isaiah 53:12
44. Not a bone broken: John 19:31-36 with Psalm 34:20
45. Side pierced: John 19:34,37 with Zechariah 12:10
46. His grave with the rich: Matthew 27:57-61; Mark 15:42-47; Luke 23:50-56; John 19:38-42 with Isaiah 53:9
47. In the grave three days and three nights: Matthew 27:57-66; Mark 15:42-47; Luke 23:50-56; John 19:38-42 with Matthew 12:41 and John 2:19. See THREE DAYS in Index.

48. Sabbaths to cease: Matthew 28:1 with Hosea 2:11. See SABBATHS in Index.
49. The resurrection: Matthew 28:1-6; Mark 16:1-6; Luke 24:1-6; John 20:1-12 with Psalm 16:10. See RESURRECTION in Index.

Archaeological Evidence of Christ's Life

The pick and spade of the archaeologists have produced evidence which confirms the reality of Christ as a historical figure. Christ Himself left very little, if any, material evidence of His earthly ministry and life. Critics claim, because of this, plus the fact that the New Testament *alone* contains the record of Christ, that we do not have sufficient evident, especially from secular history, to prove His existence.

The existence of Jesus is recorded by a Jewish historian, Flavius Josephus, who was born in A.D. 37, about four years after the death, burial, and resurrection of Christ. Josephus not only mentioned John the Baptist, a preacher of virtue who baptized his proselytes, and James, the brother of him who is called Jesus, but of Christ Himself in these words: "Now there was about this time Jesus, a wise man, if it be lawful to call him a man; for he was a doer of wonderful works, a teacher of such men as receive the truth with pleasure. He drew over to him both many of the Jews and many of the Gentiles. He was [the] Christ; and when Pilate, at the suggestion of the principal men amongst them, had condemned him to the cross, those who loved him at the first did not forsake him, for he appeared to them alive again the third day, as the divine prophets had foretold these and ten thousand other wonderful things concerning him; and the tribe of Christians so named for him, are not extinct at this day."[17]

The Roman historian, Tacitus, who recorded the persecution of Nero, remarked that the people called "Christian" derived their name "from one Christus, who was executed in the reign of Tiberius by the procurator of Judaea, Pontius Pilate." This record alone establishes two facts—that both Christ and Pilate were historical figures, and that each was recognized by imperial Rome. In seeking to discredit the New Testament record and the existence of Christ, some critics have stated that one called Pontius Pilate never existed. Pliny also wrote about him (see NERO in Index). Excavations at Caesarea have revealed a "Pilate Stone." Previously, coins were found that had been minted in his honor.

Pilate Stone and Coins

Tacitus, elsewhere in his *Histories,* refers to Christianity when alluding to the burning of the Temple of Jerusalem in A.D. 70. Christ, as a historical figure, is also mentioned by other Romans historians—Celsus, Suetonius, Severus, and Lucian the Cynic. In writing to the Emperor Trajan, Pliny the younger mentioned the treatment given Christians by Romans, and testified of their piety and allegiance to their founder, one Christ.

Both the sacred writings of Scripture and secular history confirm His existence. It is indeed difficult for the critic, or anyone else for that matter, to prove the non-existence of Jesus Christ, the Son of God. Have you ever wondered why those who deny the existence of Christ always date their checks and letters after His birth!

Books of the New Testament
DIVISION II
The Acts

Subject: What Jesus continues to do and teach by the Holy Spirit, through believers, since His ascension: John 14:12,16; Acts 1:4,5,8.

Purpose: To give us God's purpose, plan, and power for every believer during this dispensation of grace: Acts 1:8; 4:31; 15:14; 26:16-18.

Christianity: Fraud or Truth

As we approach the book of Acts, we should consider what a prince of lawyers, Simon Greenleaf (1783-1853, one of America's most noted jurists) had to say as he examined the testimony of the men who followed the Lord after His death, as is recorded in the Book of Acts.

"Christianity demands nothing more than is readily conceded to every branch of human science. All have their data and their axioms. Christianity, too, has her first principles, the admission of which is essential to any real progress in knowledge. Christianity, says Bishop Wilson, 'does not profess to convince the headstrong, to bring irresistible evidence to the daring and profane, to vanquish the proud scorner, and afford evidences from which the careless and perverse cannot possibly escape. This might go to destroy man's responsibility. All that Christianity professes is to propose such evidences as may satisfy the meek, the tractable, the candid, the serious inquirer.'

"The great truths which the Apostles declared were that Christ had risen from the dead, and that only through repentance of sin, and faith in Him, could men hope for salvation. This doctrine they asserted with one voice everywhere not only under the greatest discouragements, but in the face of the most appalling terrors that can be presented to the mind of man. Their Master had recently perished as a malefactor by the sentence of the public tribunal. His message sought to overthrow the religions of the whole world. The laws of every country were against the teachings of His disciples. The interests and passion of all the rulers and great men in the world were against them. The fashion of the world was against them. Propagating this new faith, even in the most inoffensive and peaceful manner, they could expect nothing but contempt, opposition, revilings, bitter persecutions, stripes, imprisonments, torments, and cruel deaths.

"Yet this faith they zealously did propagate; and all these miseries they endured undismayed, nay, rejoicing [counting it worthy to suffer shame for His name—Acts 5:41]. As one after another was put to a miserable death, the survivors only prosecuted their work with increased vigor and resolution. They had every possible motive to review carefully the grounds of their faith, and the evidences of the great facts and truths which they asserted; and these motives were pressed upon their attention with the most melancholy and terrific frequency. It was therefore impossible that they could have persisted in affirming the truths they have narrated, had not Jesus actually risen from the dead, and had they not known this fact as certainly as they knew any other fact. If it were morally possible for them to have been deceived in this matter, every human motive operated to lead them to discover and avow their error. To have persisted in so gross a falsehood, after it was known to them, was not only to encounter for life all the evils which man could inflict, but to endure also the pangs of inward and conscious guilt with no hope of future peace, no testimony of a good conscience, no expectation of honor or esteem among men, no hope of happiness in this life or in the world to come.

"Such conduct in the Apostles would moreover have been utterly irreconcilable with the fact that they possessed the ordinary constitution of our common nature. Yet their lives show them to have been men like all others of our race; swayed by the same joys, subdued by the same sorrows, agitated by the same fears, and subject to the same passions, temptations and infirmities, as ourselves. And their writings show them to have been men of vigorous understanding. If then their testimony was not true, there was no possible motive for its fabrication. It would also have been irreconcilable with the fact that they were good men. But it is impossible to read their writings and not feel that we are conversing with men eminently holy and of tender consciences; with men acting under an abiding sense of the presence and omniscience of God, and of their accountability to Him, living in His fear and walking in His ways. It is incredible that bad men should invent falsehoods to promote the God of truth. The supposition is suicidal. If they did believe in a future state of retribution, a heaven and a hell hereafter, they took the most certain course, if false witnesses, to secure the latter for their portion. And if, still being bad men, they did not believe in future punishment, how came they to invent falsehoods, the direct and certain tendency of which was to destroy all their prospects of worldly honor and happiness, and to ensure their misery in this life? From these absurdities there is no escape, other than the perfect conviction and admission that they were good men, testifying to that which they had carefully observed and considered, and well knew to be the truth.

"There are other internal marks of truth in the narratives of the Evangelists. Among these may be mentioned the nakedness of the narratives; the absence of all parade by the writers about their own integrity; of all anxiety to be believed, or to impress others with a good opinion of themselves or their cause; of all marks of wonder, or of desire to excite astonishment at the greatness of the events they recorded, and of all appearance of design to exalt their Master. On the contrary, there is apparently the most perfect indifference on their part, whether or not they are believed; rather, the evident consciousness that they were recording events well known to all, in their own country and times, and undoubtedly to be believed, like any other matter of public history, by readers in all other countries and ages. Their simplicity and artlessness, also, should not pass unnoticed, in readily stating even those things most disparaging to themselves. Their want of faith in their Master, their dullness of apprehension of His teachings, their strifes for preeminence, their inclination to call fire down from heaven upon their enemies, their desertion of their Lord in His hour of extreme peril; these and many other incidents tending directly to their own dishonor are nevertheless set down with all the directness and sincerity of truth as by men writing under the deepest sense of responsibility to God.

"Lastly, consider the great character of a sinless Being; of One supremely wise and supremely good. It exhibits no error, no sinister intention, no imprudence, no ignorance, no evil passion, no impatience; in a word, no fault; but all is perfect uprightness, innocence, wisdom, goodness and truth. The doctrines and precepts of Jesus are in strict accordance with the attributes of God. They are strikingly adapted to the capacity of mankind, and yet are delivered with a simplicity and majesty wholly divine. He spake as never man spake. He spake with authority; yet addressed Himself to the reason and the understanding of men; and He spake with wisdom, which men could neither gainsay nor resist. In His private life He exhibits a character not merely of strict justice but of overflowing benignity. He is temperate with austerity; His meekness and humilty are signal; His patience is invincible; truth and sincerity illustrate His whole conduct; everyone of His virtues is regulated by consummate prudence; and He both wins the love of His friends and extorts the wonder and admiration of His enemies. He is represented in every variety of situation in life, from the height of worldly grandeur, amid the acclamations of an admiring multitude, to the deepest abyss of human degradation and woe, apparently deserted of God and man. Yet everywhere He is the same; displaying a character symmetrical in all its proportions, and encircled with splendor more than human.

"Either the men of Galilee were men of superlative wisdom, or extensive knowledge and experience, and of deeper skill in the arts of deception, than any and all others, before or after them, or they have truly stated the astonishing things which they saw and heard."

Acts—The Book of Christian Action

Name: In the earliest manuscripts this historical narrative has the title of "Acts" or "The Acts," though the title by which we know it, "The Acts of the Apostles," was used in the subscription even in some of these. Strictly speaking, the book is not a record of the acts of the Apostles, but rather of some of the acts of only two of them: Peter (1—12), and Paul (13—26). John is mentioned three times, but only as a co-worker of Peter. James is referred to because of his martyrdom. No other act of the eight Apostles is mentioned. Technically speaking, the book is a continuation of the acts of Jesus Christ by the Holy Spirit through human instruments.

Contents: "Acts is a most excellent and useful work giving in detail the fulfillment of Joel's prophecy—the outpouring of the Holy Spirit upon all flesh; showing the first planting of Christianity and of Christian churches, both among the Jews and Gentiles; the spread and progress of the gospel in several parts of the world; what sufferings some Apostles endured, with what patience and courage they bore them, and what success attended their sufferings. Acts is a standing proof and confirmation of Christianity."[1] Notice:

1. The great prominence given to the sovereignty and work of the Holy Spirit: 1:8; 2:4,38; 5:9,32; 13:2,52; 15:28
2. The church frequently revealed as a growing organism: 2:47; 4:4,13,31-33; 5:14-16, etc.
3. The universal outlook: 39 different cities and 30 different countries, provinces, and islands are referred to, and almost all of them located outside the land of Israel.

In the four gospel accounts we have the life of Jesus recorded as He lived it. In the book of Acts we have an account of the life of Jesus in the lives of His disciples as they were empowered by the Holy Spirit. Because Acts is a continuation of the life and acts of Christ in His servants, it has sometimes been called the "fifth" gospel. In the book of Acts we have the "Great Commission" of Matthew 28:19,20 put into practice. In Acts we have the disciples preaching everywhere, fulfilling Mark 16:19,20. Luke 24:49 is fulfilled in Acts 1:5; 2:1-4. The first time the Law was preached, 3,000 men were killed (Exodus 32:28). The first sermon preached after the outpouring of the Holy Spirit netted 3,000 saved (Acts 2:41). (With the church today "toiling" in her many "programs" instead of seeking power from on high, it takes about 3,000 sermons to get one saved!) Acts 1:10,11 confirms the truth of the second coming of Christ as mentioned in John 21:21-23.

Four words summarize the book of Acts: (1) Power; (2) Preaching; (3) Persecution; and (4) Progress. It has 28 chapters, 1,007 verses, and 24,250 words.

Character: Historical.

Subject and Purpose: See p. 475.

Outline:

   I. The Church at Jerusalem: 1:1—8:4
     A. Five years: Peter prominent
  II. The Church of Palestine and Syria: 8:5—12:25
     A. Fifteen years: Peter prominent with Antioch the center
 III. The Church of the Gentiles: 13:1—28:31
     A. Eighteen years: Paul prominent with Rome the center
       1. Paul's Three Missionary Journeys—
         a. First: 13:1—15:35 (A.D. 45-47)—1,400 miles
         b. Second: 15:36—18:22 (A.D. 51-54)—2,800 miles
         c. Third: 18:33—21:16 (A.D. 54-58)—2,800 miles
       2. Paul's Three Captives—
         a. Jerusalem: 21:17—23:35 (A.D. 58)
         b. Caesarea: 24:1—26:32 (A.D. 58-60)
         c. Rome: 27:1—28:31 (A.D. 61-63)

Scope: Acts covers a period of about thirty-three years (A.D. 30—63).

Writer: Luke: 1:1 with Luke 1:1. See WRITER in Luke.

To Whom Written: Theophilus (1:1), but intended for *all* believers.

When and Where Written: About A.D. 65, probably in Rome or in Achaia.

Key Chapter: 2. The outpouring of the Holy Spirit.

Key Verse: 1:8.

Key Word: Witness.

Key Phrase: The promise of the Father: 1:4 with Luke 24:49.

Key Thoughts:
  1. We ought to obey God rather than man: 5:29
  2. Let the redeemed of the Lord say so: 4:20 with Psalm 107:2

Spiritual Thought: Power . . . upon you: 1:8. See also 5:32; Galatians 3:14; Ephesians 5:18b.

Christ Is Seen As: Our ascended Lord: 1:2,10,11a.

Names and Titles of Christ. See NAME in Dictionary.
  1. Jesus: 1:11; 9:5
  2. Jesus of Nazareth: 2:22a
  3. A Man approved of God: 2:22b
  4. Holy One: 2:27; 13:35
  5. Christ: 2:30; 8:5
  6. Jesus Christ: 2:38; 8:12
  7. His Son: 3:13
  8. The Just One: 3:14b; 22:14
  9. The Prince of life: 3:15
  10. Prophet: 3:22; 7:37
  11. Stone: 4:11
  12. Holy Child Jesus: 4:27,30
  13. The Healer: 4:29,30
  14. Lord Jesus: 4:33; 19:5
  15. Prince: 5:31a
  16. Savior: 5:31b; 13:23
  17. Forgiver of sins: 5:31c; 10:43
  18. Son of Man: 7:56
  19. Son of God: 8:37; 9:20
  20. Lord: 9:5,6
  21. The Very Christ: 9:22
  22. Lord of all: 10:36
  23. God's Anointed: 10:38
  24. Judge of the quick and the dead: 10:42
  25. Lord Jesus Christ: 11:17
  26. God's ordained Man: 17:31
  27. Christ Jesus: 19:4
  28. Purchaser of the Church: 20:28

Names and Titles of God: See NAMES in Dictionary.
  1. Father: 1:7; 2:33
  2. Lord: 2:39; 17:27
  3. God of Abraham . . . and our fathers: 3:13; 22:14
  4. God of glory: 7:2
  5. God of Jacob: 7:46
  6. The Most High: 7:48; 16:17

7. God of Israel: 13:17
8. The living God: 14:15
9. The "Known" God: 17:23,24
10. Lord of heaven and earth: 17:24
11. Judge: 17:31

Names and Titles of the Holy Spirit: See NAME in Dictionary.

1. Holy Ghost: 1:2; 5:3; 28:25
2. Promise of the Father: 1:4 with Luke 24:49
3. Spirit: 2:4; 16:7
4. Spirit of the Lord: 5:9; 8:39

1. The outpouring of the Holy Spirit with accompanying signs—to fulfill God's Word: 2:14 with Joel 2:28-32.

2. The gift of tongues—to enable every man to hear the gospel in his own native tongue: 2:4-11.

3. Death of Ananias and Sapphira for lying and tempting the Holy Spirit—to bring fear upon the church: 5:1-11.

4. Prison opened for the apostles—to release them that they might continue preaching: 5:19,20; to demonstrate the power of prayer: 12:1-11.

5. Stephen's dying vision of Christ—to reveal the preciousness of the death of a saint in the sight of God: 7:55,56 with Psalm 116:15.

6. Christ's appearance to Saul (Paul) on the Damascus road—to show that where sin abounded, grace did much more abound: 9:1-6 with Romans 5:20b.

7. Saul's sight restored—to enable him to "go" and fulfill his commission: 9:15-22.

8. The vision of Cornelius—to reveal to him what he lacked to have perfect peace with God: 10:1-8,30-32.

9. The vision of Peter—to break his stubborn Jewish pride to reach a Gentile for Christ: 10:9-48.

10. Prophecy of Agabus concerning a famine—to encourage fellow-believers to help one another: 11:28.

11. Paul raised up after being stoned and left for dead—to show the Jews that they cannot fight God and succeed: 14:19,20 with 5:34-39.

12. Paul's Macedonian vision—to enable the gospel to come westward: 16:9.

13. The earthquake at Philippi—to bring the Philippian jailer to see his need of salvation: 16:25-31.

14. Sceva's sons put to flight by an evil spirit—to reveal that one must be a believer of Christ to have the Holy Spirit: 19:13-16.

15. Prophecy of Agabus concerning Paul—to warn him not to go up to Jerusalem: 21:10,11.

16. Paul unharmed by viper's bite—to reveal to others that Paul was God's servant: 28:3-5.

17. By Peter—
    a. Lame man cured: 3:7
    b. The sick healed: 5:15,16
    c. Aeneas cured of palsey: 9:33,34
    d. Dorcas restored to life: 9:36-40
18. By Stephen; great miracles: 6:8.
19. By Phillip; various miracles and signs: 8:6,7,13.
20. By Paul and Barnabas; signs and wonders: 14:3.
21. By Paul—
    a. Elymas smitten with blindness: 13:11
    b. Lame man cured: 14:10
    c. Unclean spirit cast out: 16:18

d. Special miracles at Ephesus: 19:11,12
e. Eutychus restored to life: 20:10-12
f. Miracles at Melita: 28:8,9

1. Luke's accuracy of Greek words and expressions (see ARCHAEOLOGY in Luke). Cyprus, annexed by Rome, had four types of Roman government over a period of thirty-five years, each type using different titled Officers. Luke, a brilliant scholar and historian, was well acquainted with such facts, and would hardly use the wrong title. His knowledge also shows that he correctly identified certain geographical areas. He correctly used the title "deputy" (proconsul—13:7), which would have appeared in classical Greek. He knew exactly how the local officers were described: magistrate (praetors—16:20); serjeants (lictors—16:35). He associates particular deities with certain areas: Zeus and Hermes at Lystra (Jupiter and Mercurcius—14:11,12); and Diana at Ephesus (Artemis—19:28). Two inscriptions found at Malta, one written in Greek and the other in Latin, confirm his correct use of the expression "chief man" (28:7). Another inscription in Greek, from the gate of Vardar at Thessalonica, lists six "politarchs," which was the common Greek expression for "rulers of the city" (17:8).

2. Three Thousand Baptized in One Day—Immersed or Sprinkled?: 2:41. It is plain to note that people baptized before Christ's death were immersed—*"in Jordan"*—assumed to be the River Jordan, because when Christ came to Jordan unto John to be baptized of him, Jesus "went up straightway out of the water . . ." (Matthew 3:1-17). To come up *out of the water* implies that one must first be *in* the water. The word "baptize" means to dip, immerse, or wholly overwhelm in water. And since this same method was employed after Christ's resurrection as recorded in Acts 8:35-39 with both Philip and the Eunuch going *down* into the water and both coming *up out of* the water, we can readily assume that no change had taken place in the method of baptism when 3,000 were baptized on the *same* day (Pentecost).

"The lack of sufficient water to baptize by immersion, and the impossibility of immersing 3,000 converts in one day, is an argument centuries old. In 1840, Edward Robinson made a careful study of the water supplies in and around Jerusalem, and in his book, *Biblical Research,* he lists these current water supplies: (1) Pool of Bethesda, which was 360' long by 130' wide, and 75' deep at its maximum; a large pool with five porches, room for multitudes waiting around it (John 5:1-7); (2) Pool of Siloam which was 53' long by 18' wide, and 19' deep at its maximum; built by King Hezekiah (700 B.C.), known as the "lower pool" (Isaiah 22:9). It is an artificial pool (Nehemiah 3:15,16; John 9:7,11). See CONDUIT in Index; (3) the Upper Pool, 316' long by 218' wide, and 18' deep at its maximum, connected to the Spring of Gihon, where Saul was anointed king (I Kings 1:32,39; II Kings 18:17: II Chronicles 32:30); (4) the pool of Hezekiah, 240' long by 144' wide, and partially filled with water [in 1840]; and (5) the Lower Pool or the pool of Gihon, which was 592' long by 260' wide, and 40' deep at its center. They were all constructed with sides which gradually sloped inward and downward, allowing safe and easy descent into the water to any required depth. They were in daily use for purposes of absolution, as was practiced constantly by the Jews. Sources other than Edward Robinson confirm these named pools in and around the city of Jerusalem. It should be noted that Pentecost was in the spring time, after the rainy season, and the pools were filled (Psalm 84:6b).

"Could 3,000 be baptized in one day? Immersionists say yes—that among the 12 apostles, and all 12 were baptizing simultaneously (easily possible), there would have been no problem as to time. Each apostle would have 250 converts to immerse, and if one minute were given to immerse each convert, it would have taken four hours and 10 minutes (longer if there were rest periods, but all within one day). There were both ample supplies of water and time to bap-

Hezekiah's Pool

Altar to "Unknown God"

tize 3,000 people in one day."[2] While it is true there is no such evidence today of the sources of water mentioned (that is, the size of each), the picture of Hezekiah's Pool, taken around 1900, shows that there was an abundant supply of water in it then.

3. Site of Gamaliel's admonition: 5:34-39. See PORTICO in Index.

4. The great dearth: 11:27-30. Agabus predicted a great famine, which resulted in the disciples at Antioch sending help to those in Jerusalem by Paul. Two Roman writers of this period, Cassius and Tacitus, recorded there were bad harvests in this area, and even mentioned prices for food decreed by Cladius.

5. To the Jew first: 13:14,15,42. See JEW in Index.

6. Athens given wholly to idolatry: 17:16. Paul's spirit was stirred when he saw raw paganism in Athens. Images of idols were everywhere, even carved on the stage fronts of amphitheatres. When preaching his famous "Mars' Hill" sermon, he made mention that such idols of stone and wood, "graven by art and man's device," could in no way represent the Godhead. Many of these same idols can be seen among the ancient ruins of Athens today.

7. Altar to an unknown god: 17:23. Paul was very observant. When being taken to Mars' Hill by the Epicureans, he noticed an altar with this inscription: TO THE UNKNOWN GOD. The Greeks were polytheistic; that is, they worshiped multiple gods. In the event they overlooked a god, and lest offending it, such altars were erected. Paul took advantage of this belief, and "Him the true and living God declare I unto you." The inscription on the altar below reads. "Sacred, whether it be to a god or goddess."

8. Mars' Hill: 17:22,31. Mars' Hill is a low, rocky hill near the Acropolis in Athens, and is often referred to as the Areopagus (courthouse). According to legend, this is where the goddess of Wisdom, Athena, presided, acquitting the legendary figure Orestes of blood-guilt in the murder of his mother. It became the site in antiquity where the Athenean court convened. Down through the centuries opinions were heard; decisions were made. Bribes were offered the gods and goddesses, "plea" bargaining was made, and often the guilty were set free at the expense of the innocent. "Unrighteous judgment" was often made here, and what a fitting place for Paul to preach his famous "Mars' Hill Sermon" (Acts 17:15-34), and to conclude with the presentation to repent and face a "Judge" who would judge in righteousness. These philosophers who took Paul to Mars' Hill well understood Paul's pointed implications.

9. Paul's visit to Corinth: 18:1-18. See ARCHAEOLOGY in I Corinthians.

10. Curious (magical) books: 19:19. Many significant articles connected with Paul's visit to Athens have been brought to light by the archaeologist. The magical books which were burned corresponded to many magical text discovered, one volume which may be seen today in the British Museum in London. Some inscriptions have come to light which refer to

Diana of Ephesus

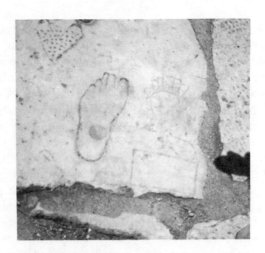

Brothel Footprint

Asiarchs—"chief of Asia" (19:31). He was numbered among Paul's friends in Ephesus. Other inscriptions deal with the town clerk, who was responsible for quieting the silversmiths and the rioters (19:35).

11. Great is Diana of the Ephesians: 19:27,28. Paul's preaching in Ephesus produced a hearing of the Word of the Lord Jesus throughout Asia, which resulted in many converts and a turning from idols to serve God (19:10,17-20). It also resulted in loss of revenue for the idol makers (silversmiths), and led to the uproar which exalted the goddess of Ephesus, Diana (19:23-41). See NAME in Index.

Evidence from Ephesus has produced much information about this religion. Many statues of Diana have been found, one as a multiple-breasted goddess of fertility. Coins, minted in her honor, show her head on the obverse side, and the cult image of this lewd religion on the reverse. Remains of her temple, which was one of the seven wonders of the ancient world, have been unearthed. It was considered so holy that citizens of foreign countries brought gifts to her, and deposited huge sums of money (gold and silver) for safekeeping. One inscription mentions a man who gave twenty-nine gold and silver images to Diana to be used in public processions. A month each year was dedicated to the worship of this goddess, with such cries as, "Great is Diana of the Ephesians." Prostitute priestesses gave their wages for the upkeep of this magnificent temple. Brothels were scattered throughout the city, with footprints carved in stone, to point men to these illicit places. The amphitheatre, in which the riot and uproar was held in her behalf (19:29), has also been unearthed.

12. Decree of Caesar—Emperor Worship. See DEFENSE of Paul in Seed Thoughts of Acts, point 24.

LIGHT FROM BIBLICAL CUSTOMS

3 1. A Sabbath day's journey: 1:12,13. Jesus led His disciples out to Bethany before His ascension (Luke 24:50), and when they returned to the upper room, they traveled "a Sabbath's day's journey." Bethany is on the other side of the Mount of Olives from Jerusalem, a distance of only two or three miles. The Jews were forbidden to do any work on the Sabbath (Exodus 21:10), but they could take a short walk—"a Sabbath day's journey." The inscribed stone denotes the "end of a Sabbath day's journey," the distance Jews were permitted to walk.

2. Kicking against the pricks: 9:5. A farmer, while plowing, would hold on to the plow handle with one hand (see PLOW in Index), and hold the reins and a long pointed stick—a prick—in the other hand. If the animal pulling the plow became unruly, balked, kicked, or stopped plowing, the farmer would "prick" the animal with the pointed stick until it would submit and serve properly. It soon learned that it did not pay to "kick against the pricks." Paul had been fighting God, but the "pricks" of circumstances had so caught up with him that on the road to Damascus, he submitted to Christ. What are some of the "pricks" that Paul kicked against? (a) a guilty conscience because of his persecution against fellow human beings; (b) conviction by the Holy Spirit. Paul knew the Old Testament Scriptures. Although he persecuted the saints and blasphemed the name of God in ignorance, he was still without excuse; (c) possibly the face of Stephen and his dying remarks; and (d) no doubt the prayers of his Christian relatives were catching up with him (Romans 16:7). See WAY in Index.

3. Peter knocked at the door of the gate: 12:11-16. When a guest arrives at a door and knocks, the host from within asks, "Who is there?" The person outside replies, but does not give his name. If the voice is recognized, the door will be opened. If not, the guest remains outside. When Peter was released from prison, he went to the home of John Mark's mother and knocked. A damsel answered, and immediately recognized Peter's voice. Not being the host, she rushed to the others with gladness to announce that it was Peter. Peter continued knocking, announcing it was he, and the door was finally opened.

4. Paul seated, teaching in the Synagogue: 13:14,15. See SEAT in Index.

5. Molech and Rephan (Remphan): 7:43. See ASTROLOGY in Index.

Scientists have discovered how Egyptian craftsmen produced brilliant colors—paintings for their Temple walls and ceilings. We are fortunate if we can find paint produced by today's technologists which lasts more than twenty years on our houses! Yet, Egyptian paint has lasted more than 3,500 years. The blues and reds and yellows of ancient Egypt, whether on stone or metal, have remained vivid. Scientists (1970) of the Egyptian Department of Antiquity, worked over three years and spent more than two million dollars to "break the historic formula." The formula includes one molecule each of copper oxide and four molecules of silicone oxide. The resulting compound is heated to 1,050 degrees centigrade, and then ground and mixed with egg yoke and gum. This compound resists heat as high as 1,700 degrees C. and is insoluble in the most potent acids known to modern science. The ancients obtained the stable color by trapping copper oxide atoms in a ring of hydrogen, produced by the ions of the egg yoke and acid from the gum. Ironically, said one of the scientists, "the ancients got their color by teaming advanced knowledge with primitive logic." How true the Scripture when it speaks of the "wisdom [or sciences] of the Egyptians" in Moses' day (Acts 7:22). See WISDOM in Index.

The Old Testament in Acts:
1. Judas' betrayal: 1:16-19 with Psalm 41:9
2. Replacing Judas: 1:20 with Psalm 109:8
3. Promise of the Spirit: 2:17 with Joel 2:28
4. Christ's death and resurrection: 2:25-27 with Psalm 16:9,10
5. Exaltation of Christ after the resurrection: 2:34,35 with Psalm 110:1
6. Christ, a Prophet like Moses: 3:22 with Deuteronomy 18:15,18,19
7. Abraham's seed blessed: 3:25 with Genesis 22:18
8. The rejected Stone: 4:11 with Psalm 118:22
9. Persecution of the early saints: 4:25,26 with Psalm 2:1,2

"Day's Journey" Boundary Stone

10. Stephen's address before the council: 6:8—7:60. His entire address before the high priests was a review of Old Testament events in the life of Israel from the call of Abraham to the rejection of Christ and the persecution of the Spirit-filled Apostles. Stephen makes at least 53 references to the Old Testament. How many can you find?
11. Christ's sufferings: 8:32,33 with Isaiah 53:7,8
12. God no respecter of persons: 10:34 with Deuteronomy 10:17; Job 34:19
13. Christ begotten in His resurrection: 13:33 with Psalm 2:7
14. Victory in Christ's death: 13:34,35 with Isaiah 55:3; Psalm 16:10
15. Christ's ministry and rejection: 13:41 with Habakkuk 1:5
16. The gospel for the Gentiles: 13:47 with Isaiah 49:6
17. Rebuilding David's tabernacle: 15:16,17 with Amos 9:11,12
18. Speaking evil against those in authority: 23:5 with Exodus 22:28
19. Salvation rejected by the Jews: 28:25-28 with Isaiah 6:9,10

SEED THOUGHTS

1. Why the Apostles were Successful—
   a. Were in fellowship with Christ: 1:4a
   b. Obedient to His commands: 1:12 with 1:4b
   c. Were in one accord with each other: 1:14a
   d. Honored the Scriptures: 1:16a
   e. Prayed: 1:14,24a
   f. Filled with the Spirit: 2:1-4
   g. Continued steadfastly in the Apostles's doctrine: 2:42-47
   h. Lived Christlike: 4:13
   i. Bold in spite of threatenings: 4:29-31

      j. Obeyed God rather than man: 5:29

      k. Counted it worthy to suffer shame for Christ: 5:41

      l. Witnessed daily: 5:42

  2. Ministry of the Holy Spirit: 1:8. See HOLY SPIRIT in Index.

  3. Need for Power to Witness: 1:8 (see SOUL-WINNING in Index). A Christian begins his life by coming under the blood for salvation; but he continues by the blood for daily cleansing and the bread [of the Word] for daily food. But still the Christian life is not complete: there must be the experience of fire—the fire of pentecost—the fire of the Holy Spirit for power in service and testimony. The early Christians in the upper room had come under the blood; they had fed upon the Word of Christ, the bread, some of them for three years. Yet He bade them tarry until they were "fire baptized." The blood makes safe and the bread makes strong but more is needed for witnessing. And it is just here that thousands of believers fall short with a pre-Pentecost experience. They have been taught that a personal knowledge of Christ is all that one needs, which is true as to salvation, but it is overlooked that these Christians knew the Lord yet they must wait for power.

  "It is true that Pentecost, historically, took place once and for all. So did Calvary. But each individual must personally appropriate the blood by faith and so must each believer receive by faith the Spirit for power. The promise of the Spirit is received by faith (Galatians 3:14). It is an experience of spiritual thirst, then coming to Christ, drinking of the Spirit by faith, believing and overflowing (John 7:37-39)."[4]

  4. Where to Witness: 1:8. See SOUL-WINNING in Index.

      a. At home, with loved ones: John 1:40-42

      b. Among friends: John 1:45-49

      c. Among neighbors: John 4:28-30,39

      d. On the highways: Luke 14:23

      e. By the wayside: Acts 8:26-36

      f. To strangers: John 12:20-22

      g. The uttermost parts of the world: Mark 16:15

  If a man cannot be a witnessing Christian where he is, it is quite certain he cannot be a witnessing Christian where he isn't. To win others to Christ there must be the conviction that we have something worth telling, no matter where we are. To God, the "world is the field," and in the place where He puts us, we *are* his witnesses *there*.

  5. Prayer in Acts. See PRAYER in Index.

      a. Prayer of unity: 1:14

      b. Prayer for the will of God: 1:24

      c. Prayer for things in general: 3:1

      d. Prayer in a study of the Word: 6:4

      e. Prayer for new converts: 8:15

      f. Prayer for friends in trouble: 12:5

      g. Prayer for missionaries: 13:2-4

      h. Prayer for the unsaved for Christians to help: 16:9

      i. Prayer when in trials: 16:25

      j. Prayer for church leaders: 21:4,5

  6. The Spirit's Coming: 2:1-4.

      a. Promised (1:4) for power (1:8)

      b. Fulfilled (2:1-3) for witnessing (2:4)

      c. Manifestation (2:41) in service (4:20; 5:29,42)

  7. The Lord Added to the Church *Daily:* 2:47. One is amazed when he reads of the success of the early church, and then compares it with the "paralyzed" church today. What makes the difference between the church then and today? To the early New Testament saints the church was a recruiting station from which men would go out to fight the battles of the Lord. Today it is a convalescent home in which to live idly upon God's pension. What the church needs today is

it is a convalescent home in which to live idly upon God's pension. What the church needs today is:[5]

 —More tithes and fewer drives
 —More action and less faction
 —More workers and fewer shirkers
 —More backers and fewer slackers
 —More of God's plans and less of man's
 —More praying and less playing
 —More divine power and less human "pow-wow"
 —More Good News and less book reviews
 —More burden bearers and fewer tale bearers
 —More praying and less fainting
 —More fighting squads and fewer tight-wads
 —More liberal males and fewer food sales
 —More "tongues of fire" and fewer fiery tongues
 —More zealous effort and less jealous thought
 —More soul service combined with social service
 —More love for the Word and less of the world
 —More seeking for grace and less seeking for place
 —More holiness of life and less bickering and strife
 —More fasting and less feasting
 —More praying and less straying

8. Perfect Soundness: 3:16
 a. Of body: 3:16
 b. Of mind: II Timothy 1:7
 c. Of the Word: II Timothy 1:13
 d. Of doctrine: Titus 2:1
 e. Of faith: Titus 2:2
 f. Of speech: Titus 2:8

9. Times of Refreshing: 3:19. Sin, repentance, and pardon are like the three vernal months of the year—March, April, and May.
 a. *Sin*, like March—blustering, stormy, and full of bold violence: Isaiah 1:2-6; Romans 3:10-18,23
 b. *Repentance*, like April—showery, weeping, sorrowful, and full of tears: II Corinthians 7:10
 c. *Pardon*, like May—springing, singing, flowery (fruitful), full of the joy of forgiveness: Romans 5:1; Ephesians 5:19

10. Jailed for Christ: 4:1-23; 5:17-42; 12:1-17. If you were arrested for being a Christian, could the court produce enough evidence to find you guilty? These New Testament saints may not have had enough influence to keep them out of jail, but they had enough "prayer-power" to get them out!

11. Great Results in Prayer: 4:31-37. See PRAYER in Index.
 a. Place shaken—new awakening of God's presence: vs. 31a
 b. All filled with the Holy Spirit: vs. 31b
 c. Spake with great boldness: vs. 31c
 d. Were of one heart and soul—unity: vs. 32
 e. Great power in witnessing: vs. 33a
 f. Great grace upon them: vs. 33b
 g. None lacked—need fully met: vss. 34-37

12. The "Oughts" of the Christian Life: 5:29.
 a. Of obedience: 5:29
 b. Of sacrifice: I John 3:16

  c. Of service: John 13:14
  d. Of giving: Acts 20:35
  e. Of prayer: Luke 18:1
  f. Of love: I John 4:11
  g. Of forgiving: II Corinthians 2:7 with Ephesians 4:32
  h. Of walk and abounding: I Thessalonians 4:1

13. Gave Themselves to Prayer: 6:4. "What the Church needs today is not more machinery or better, not new organizations or more and novel methods, but men whom the Holy Spirit can use—men of prayer, men mighty in prayer. The Holy Spirit does not flow through methods, but through men. He does not come upon machinery, but on men. He does not anoint plans, but men—men of prayer. Talking to men for God is one thing, but talking to God for men is greater still. He will never talk well and with real success to men for God who has not learned well how to talk to God for men."[6] This lesson the early church knew—they did not ask the Lord to teach them *how* to pray, but "Lord, teach us *to* pray" (Luke 11:1). And pray they did! Acts alone records at least 35 times their praying.

14. Slander against Stephen: 6:11
  Slander is—
  a. An abomination unto the Lord: Proverbs 6:16,19
  b. Whispering: Romans 1:29
  c. Backbiting: Romans 1:30
  d. Tale-bearing: Leviticus 19:16
  e. Bearing false witness: Luke 3:14
  f. Tattling: I Timothy 5:13
  g. Evil speaking: Psalm 109:20
  h. Raising false reports: Exodus 23:1
  i. Judging unlovingly: James 4:11,12
  Effects of slander—
  a. Separates friends: Proverbs 17:9
  b. Produces strife: Proverbs 26:20
  c. Inflicts deadly wounds: Proverbs 26:22
  Christians should—
  a. Keep their tongues from evil: I Peter 3:10
  b. Lay aside evil speaking: Ephesians: 4:31
  c. Return good for slander: Romans 12:21
  d. Rejoice when slandered: Matthew 5:11,12
  e. Not trust those who do slander: Jeremiah 9:4

15. Results of Soul-winning. Acts 7 is a resume of the history of the children of Israel from Abraham to the rejection of Christ and the persecution of the New Testament believers. As far as we know, this sermon by Stephen is the only one he preached, but out of it and his death came Paul, the greatest preacher since Christ. From Andrew's witness came Peter, and from a simple witness by a shoe clerk came the great Dwight L. Moody. Only God knows what will come out of a simple, faithful witness from us, if only He can get us to witness. See SOUL-WINNING in Index.

16. Lessons from the Ethiopian Eunuch: 8:26-39
  a. Sinners are in the desert (of sin): vs. 26
  b. One's position in life does not satisfy: vs. 27a
  c. One's religion does not satisfy: vs. 27b
  d. It takes the Word to reveal one's spiritual need: vss. 28-35
  e. Shows the necessity of preaching the gospel: Romans 10:14,15
  f. Christians must go where the sinner is: vss. 26,29
  g. Salvation is in a Person, not a creed: vs. 37
  h. Salvation is for the individual

i. One can be saved right where he is: vs. 37

j. God uses the foolishness of preaching to save those who believe: I Corinthians 1:21

k. A public confession must be made of Christ: vs. 37 with Matthew 10:32,33

l. Water baptism follows conversion: vss. 36-38

m. There is joy and satisfaction in God's salvation: vs. 39b

n. Each convert must be committed to the Holy Spirit. The Spirit caught Philip away, and the Spirit was left to guide the Eunuch into all truth: vs. 39a with John 16:13. Paul also had to commit the Thessalonians to the Spirit after witnessing to them for three weeks (Acts 17:1,2).

17. Saul's (Paul's) Conversion: 9:1-22

　　a. He was an enemy of Christ: vss. 1,2

　　b. He was convicted by Christ: vss. 3,4

　　c. He was called unto Christ: vs.5

　　d. He surrendered to Christ: vs. 6

　　e. He prayed to Christ: vs. 11

　　f. He witnessed for Christ: vss. 20-22

18. The Way: 9:2. Christ had presented Himself as *the* Way (John 14:6), and this expression of Christ was used by the disciples to make known the Christ of Christianity. Even unbelievers, such as Saul, recognized the followers of Christ as those "that were of the way [of Christ]."

19. Names of God's People: 11:26. See NAMES in Index.

　　Indicating their nature—

　　a. Believers: 5:14

　　b. Christians: 11:26

　　c. Children of God: Romans 8:16

　　d. Children of the kingdom: Matthew 13:38

　　e. Sons of God: I John 3:1,2

　　f. Disciples: John 8:31

　　g. Sheep: John 10:14

　　h. Saints: I Corinthians 1:2; Ephesians 3:18

　　i. The Ransomed of the Lord: Isaiah 35:10

　　j. The Redeemed of the Lord: Isaiah 51:11

　　Indicating their position—

　　a. Witnesses: 1:8

　　b. Ambassadors: II Corinthians 5:20

　　c. Fishers of men: Matthew 4:19

　　d. Servants of Christ: I Corinthians 7:22

　　e. Peculiar: Titus 2:14; I Peter 2:9

　　f. Holy: Isaiah 62:12

　　g. Royal priesthood: I Peter 2:9; Revelation 1:6

　　h. Pillars in God's Temple: Revelation 3:12

　　i. Vessels of honor: II Timothy 2:21

　　Indicating their relationship to Christ—

　　a. Brethren: Hebrews 2:11

　　b. Friends: John 15:15

　　Indicating their relationship to one another (see MEMBERS in Index)—

　　a. Brothers, or brethren: I Corinthians 16:20; I John 2:10

　　b. Fellow-laborers: Philippians 4:3

　　c. Fellow-servants: Colossians 1:7

　　Indicating their Christian heritage—

　　a. Heirs of God: Galatians 4:7

　　b. Joint-heirs with Christ: Romans 8:17

　　c. Heirs of the kingdom: James 2:5

　　d. Heirs of the promise: Hebrews 6:17

e. Heirs of salvation: Hebrews 1:14

20. Praying for "Sent-forth" Missionaries:[7] 13:2,3. Your missionary friends have gone out to invade the territory of the enemy and are immediately subject to spiritual attack under pressure of heathen darkness. Their busy lives place them in constant danger of despair, neglect, and failure. That they may obtain spiritual and physical and mental victory depends largely upon our prayers for their ministry. As Christians we are sinning against the Lord if we do not pray for all Christians (I Samuel 12:23). How much more should we pray for those who have gone to the far-flung battle fields of sin to uphold the blood-stained banner of Christ! As "prayer warriors" we can fight side by side with our missionaries, using the one and only effective weapon agaisnt the invisible foe—*prayer.*

Pray for their Spiritual life that—
a. They might be in constant prayer
b. They might regularly study the Word
c. Their fellowship might be sweet with other believers
d. They might have discernment of spiritual wickedness
e. They might be delivered from fear and despondency and loneliness
f. They might be obedient to the Spirit of God
g. They might live consistent Christian lives
h. They might have God's wisdom for all contacts

Pray for their Physical life that—
a. They might have sufficient and proper food
b. They might properly exercise their bodies
c. They might be delivered from all diseases common to their particular field
d. They might have safety in their travels from tribal opposition, wild animals, jungle insects, etc.
e. They might have sufficient rest

Pray for their Material needs that—
a. They might have sufficient support to do a good job
b. They might have suitable living quarters
c. They might have adequate traveling facilities
d. They might have sufficient native help
e. They might have some helpful reading material
f. What Christians back home send them is not second hand, but first rate (we answer this prayer)
g. They might have periodic correspondence from those back home (we alone answer this prayer)

21. One result of Paul's *first* missionary journey (13,14)—the effect of his preaching Christ in Antioch:

a. Anxiety to hear his message: 13:42
b. Many believed: 13:43
c. A whole city stirred: 13:44
d. Opposition to his preaching: 13:45
e. Gentiles received the gospel with joy: 13:46-48
f. Gospel published throughout the region: 13:49
g. Persecution followed: 13:50 with II Timothy 3:12
h. Victory and joy: 13:51,52

22. The Macedonian Call (16:6-10)—one of the results of Paul's *second* missionary journey (15:36—18:22). Paul's desire was to go through Asia (Minor) and into Bithynia, and on throughout Asia, but was forbidden by the Holy Spirit. Instead, he went to Troas where, in a vision, he heard a man saying, "Come over into Macedonia, and help us." A look at a map of his second missionary journey reveals that had Paul gone into Asia (Minor) and on over into Bithynia, he would have taken the gospel *eastward.* In the grace and providence of God he was

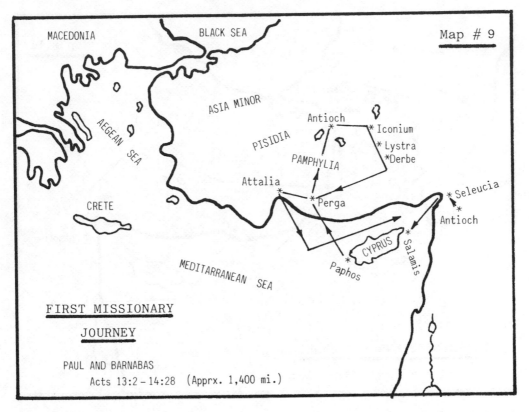

MACEDONIA   BLACK SEA   Map # 9

ASIA MINOR

PISIDIA

Antioch
*Iconium
*Lystra
*Derbe

PAMPHYLIA

AEGEAN SEA

Attalia
*Perga
*Seleucia
*Antioch

CRETE

CYPRUS
Salamis

MEDITARRANEAN SEA

Paphos

FIRST MISSIONARY

JOURNEY

PAUL AND BARNABAS
    Acts 13:2 – 14:28 (Apprx. 1,400 mi.)

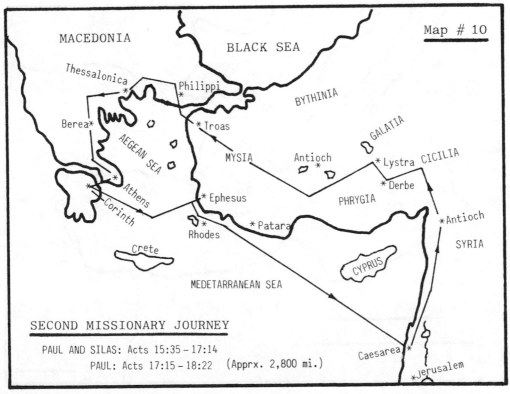

MACEDONIA   BLACK SEA   Map # 10

Thessalonica
*Philippi
BYTHINIA

Berea*
GALATIA
*Troas

AEGEAN SEA

MYSIA   Antioch   *Lystra   CICILIA
*Derbe

*Athens
*Ephesus   PHRYGIA
Corinth
*Antioch
*Patara
*Rhodes   SYRIA

Crete

CYPRUS

MEDETARRANEAN SEA

Caesarea*

SECOND MISSIONARY JOURNEY

PAUL AND SILAS: Acts 15:35 – 17:14
    PAUL: Acts 17:15 – 18:22   (Apprx. 2,800 mi.)

*Jerusalem

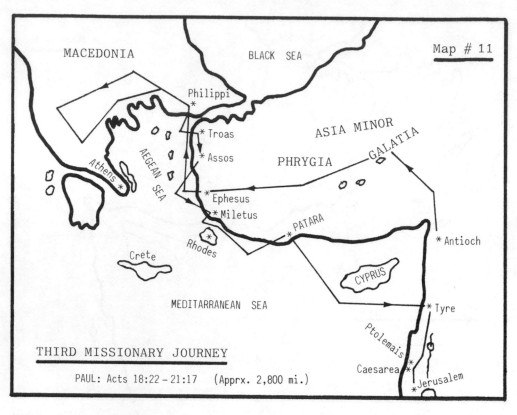

THIRD MISSIONARY JOURNEY

PAUL: Acts 18:22 – 21:17   (Apprx. 2,800 mi.)

Map # 11

MACEDONIA · BLACK SEA · Philippi · Troas · Assos · ASIA MINOR · GALATIA · PHRYGIA · AEGEAN SEA · Athens · Ephesus · Miletus · PATARA · Antioch · Rhodes · Crete · CYPRUS · Tyre · MEDITARRANEAN SEA · Ptolemais · Caesarea · Jerusalem

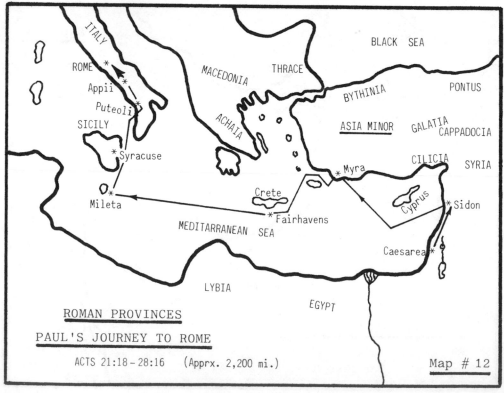

ITALY · BLACK SEA · ROME · MACEDONIA · THRACE · Appii · Puteoli · BYTHINIA · PONTUS · SICILY · ACHAIA · ASIA MINOR · GALATIA · CAPPADOCIA · Syracuse · CILICIA · SYRIA · Myra · Mileta · Crete · Cyprus · Sidon · Fairhavens · MEDITERRANEAN SEA · Caesarea · LYBIA · EGYPT

ROMAN PROVINCES

PAUL'S JOURNEY TO ROME

ACTS 21:18 – 28:16   (Apprx. 2,200 mi.)

Map # 12

called to go *westward*. Lydia became the first European convert at Philippi. As a result, instead of the gospel going eastward (possibly to Persia, India, China, etc.), it came westward—into Greece, Italy, on through Europe, and finally to the shores of America. As people left the Old World because of religious persecution, they came to the New World to worship God according to the dictates of their own conscience. We today are the recipients of Paul's obedience to this Macedonian call. Instead of missionaries coming to us from foreign lands (such as those to whom Paul at first desired to visit), God's grace has priviledged us to know His Son, Jesus Christ, and to take the gospel to others still in heathenism.

23. One result of Paul's *third* missionary journey (18:23—21:16) is his declaration of "all the counsel of God" to the Ephesian elders at Miletus, which included the purchasing of the Church with the blood of Christ: 20:27,28. Some things obtained by Christ's blood are:
   a. Redemption: Colossians 1:13,14; I Peter 1:18,19
   b. Forgiveness: Ephesians 1:7; Matthew 26:28
   c. Justification: Romans 5:9; 3:24; 4:25
   d. Sanctification: Hebrews 13:12; 10:10-14; I John 1:7
   e. Peace: Colossians 1:19,20
   f. Access: Hebrews 10:19,20; Ephesians 2:13
   g. Victory: Revelation 12:11
24. Paul's Defense before Agrippa: 26
   a. He testified of his *conversion:* vss. 1-15
   b. He stated his *call:* vss. 16,17
   c. He announced his *convictions:* vss. 18-23
   d. He manifested the *courage* of his convictions: vs. 19,21-27. Paul's courage and boldness is seen not only in his standing up before Roman nobility and "answering for myself," but in his declaration as a Roman citizen that Jesus Christ was Savior, not Caesar. An interesting archaeological discovery reveals a decree issued by one of the Caesar's that Caesar was "God and Savior." A certificate has been discovered which indicates that Roman citizens had to affirm their allegiance to Caesar as "God and Savior" (Emperor worship). This certificate had to be carried on the person, just like we must have our driver's permit when we drive an automobile. Roman soldiers were at liberty to stop anyone and ask to see their certificate. If it could not be produced, and the early New Testament Christians could not produce any, the individuals were hailed into court and asked questions concerning their religious beliefs. If, for example, any said he was a follower of Christ, opportunity was given twice to deny Christ and embrace "Emperor worship." Christians who refused were slain (crucified, thrown to wild beasts, became lighted torches, etc.).

An ancient bronze plaque states that in A.D. 37 the government of Assos begs the favor of Emperor Caligula, saying that "Every city and every nation is eager to behold the face of God, feeling that the most delightful age for mankind is now begun . . . We swear by the Savior and God, Caesar Augustus, and by our holy local deity, Athena, to be loyal to Gaius Caesar Augustus and all his house, to deem as friends those whom he favors and as enemies those whom he designates; with things to go well with us if we keep our oath, and the opposite if we break it."

The following is a certificate of pagan sacrifice. "To the commissioners of sacrifices from Aurelia Demos, daughter of Helene . . . of the Quarter of the Helleneum. It has ever been my habit to sacrifice to the gods, and now also I have in your presence, in accordance with the command, made sacrifice and libation and tasted the offering, and I beg you to certify my statement. Farewell. I, Aurelia Demos, have presented this declaration. I, Aurelius Irenaeus, wrote for her, as she is illiterate. I, Aurelius Sabinus, prytanis, saw you sacrificing. The first year of the Emperor Caesar Gaius Quintus Trajanus Decius Pius Felix Augustus, Pauni 20."

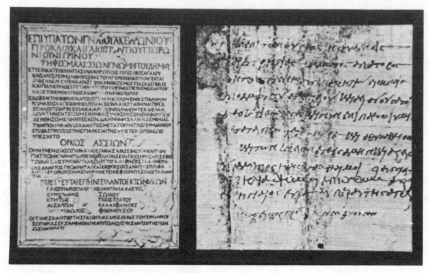

Caesar's Decree

Paul, as a Roman citizen (22:25-28), certainly did not acknowledge Caesar as "God and Savior," let alone possess a certificate so stating. Agrippa and/or Festus could have, at any moment, demanded of "citizen" Paul his certificate. It is quite possible that the Spirit of God had so blinded their minds to this "point of order" because of Paul's happiness (26:2) in answering for himself about his love for and devotion to *his* God and Savior, Jesus Christ, that they completely forgot about it. This leads to our next point—

    e. His defense was *convincing:* vs. 28
    f. He revealed his *compassion* for the lost: vs. 29a
    g. He showed them his *consecration*—"such as I am": vs. 29b

The account of Saul's (Paul's) conversion is given in Acts 9. The rebel went out to fight God and was smitten blind by the light of Christ's glory. The story of his conversion goes back, no doubt, to many of the prayers of some of his relatives who knew the Lord and were very desirous of his salvation (Romans 16:21). Prayers of loved ones contribute to the conversion of any sinner. Saul added fuel to the flame of his conviction as he held the cloaks of those who stoned Stephen. Anyone under conviction becomes all the more enraged as circumstances testify of God's love, and Saul satisfied his anger by going to Damascus to persecute the Church all the more. But on that journey God opened his heart, revealed Christ, poured out His love, and made Paul the "miracle preacher" of the first century.

WHOSE HEART THE LORD OPENED—16:14[8]

"Every heart by nature is closed against God and nothing can open a sinner's heart but invincible power. It takes the same power to open a sinner's heart as it did to create the world or to raise the dead body of Jesus from the grave. Until the heart is opened the Word will not enter, sound conviction will not be felt, and the light of the knowledge of the glory of God in the face of Jesus Christ will not be received. The preacher may preach, judgments may thunder, mercy may call, but until God opens the heart all is in vain. The Lord may work by means; the means generally are His Word and ordinances. Sometimes He throws the heart wide open at once and the change is striking, startling, and apparent to all. Sometimes He opens it by degrees and then the change is gradual and almost imperceptible. But if the heart be at all opened, God opened it, and it is never quite closed again. He openeth and no man shutteth. May the Lord open our hearts, and open them wide, that we may receive Christ, and with Him the whole body of Gospel truth! Lord, not only open our hearts, but enter and fill them with Thy glory.''

 PRAYER THOUGHT: ''Make me, O blessed Savior, strong in heart, full of courage, fearless of danger, and holding pain and tribulation cheap if they lie in the path of service for Thee. In Thy name I pray. Amen.''9

Acts 5:41

Books of the New Testament
DIVISION III
The Epistles

Subject: The doctrine, or teaching concerning what Jesus Christ has done, is doing, and will do for all believers during this age: I Peter 3:18; Hebrews 9:24,28; II Corinthians 1:9,10.

Purpose: To give us the foundation for our faith for salvation, service, suffering, and our hope: Romans 1:16,17; Titus: 2:11-14; II Timothy 2:12; 3:12; I Thessalonians 4:13-18.

Romans	Second Timothy
First Corinthians	Titus
Second Corinthians	Philemon
Galatians	Hebrews
Ephesians	James
Philippians	First Peter
Colossians	Second Peter
First Thessalonians	First John
Second Thessalonians	Second John
First Timothy	Third John

Jude

The Epistles

This third division of the New Testament opens with thirteen of Paul's letters. The gospel accounts give us the *facts* about Christ's earthly life; Paul gives us the *meaning* of it. Nine of his letters—called Church Epistles—were written to seven churches. Three—called Pastoral Epistles (I and II Timothy and Titus)—were written to pastors, and one, Philemon, was written to a personal friend. Five of his thirteen letters—called Prison Epistles (Ephesians, Philippians, Colossians, II Timothy, and Philemon)—were written while imprisoned in Rome.

The Church Epistles are divided into three groups:
1. Romans, with I and II Corinthians and Galatians
2. Ephesians, with Philippians and Colossians
3. I and II Thessalonians

Each group gives us (1) doctrine, (2) reproof, and (3) correction. *Doctrine*—the explanation of established truth; *reproof,* because of departure from moral teaching; and *correction,* because of departure from doctrinal teaching. All give *instruction:* II Timothy 3:16,17.

1. Group One—
   a. Romans: *doctrine*—the mystery of Christ's *Cross*—Justification and Sanctification
   b. Corinthians: *reproof*—failure as to practical sanctification
   c. Galatians: *correction*—denial of justification by faith
2. Group Two—
   a. Ephesians: *doctrine*—the mystery of Christ's *Church*—the Head of His body
   b. Philippians: *reproof*—though there is much praise and joy, there is failure as to complete unity by the members
   c. Colossians: *correction*—denial of the supremacy of the Head
3. Group Three—
   a. Thessalonians: *doctrine*—the mystery of Christ's Coming—in the air to meet His bride; *reproof*—to live unto holiness; *correction*—to be knowledgable concerning those who are asleep, and the apostasy.

These Epistles find us in sin and degradation (Romans 1:10—3:20), and carry us to the heights of glory in Christ (I Thessalonians 4:17,18).

Another item of interest in Paul's Epistles is his prayer life for those to whom he writes (see PRAYER in Index). There are no prayers of his mentioned in I and II Corinthians and Galatians. There were matters in the churches to be straightened out, and Paul gets right down to business with them. He gave instructions to Titus.

a. For the Romans, he prays for *edification:* 1:9-12
b. For the Ephesians he prays for *enlightenment* and *power:* 1:15-19
c. For the Philippians, he prays for *fellowship:* 1:3-5
d. For the Colossians, he prays for a *worthy walk:* 1:9-11
e. For the Thessalonians (I) he prays for *service*—their work of faith and labor of love: 1:2,3; and (II) for *growth in grace:* 1:3,4
f. For Timothy (II), he prays for his *gift to be stirred:* 1:3-6
g. For Philemon, he prays that he might *communicate his faith:* vss. 4-6

For authorship of Hebrews, see WRITER in Hebrews. The probable chronological order and approximate dates of Paul's Epistles are as follows—

First Thessalonians	A.D. 52
Second Thessalonians	A.D. 53
First Corinthians	A.D. 55
Second Corinthians	A.D. 56
Romans	A.D. 57
Galatians	A.D. 58
Philemon	A.D. 61 or 62
Colossians	A.D. 61 or 62
Ephesians	A.D. 61 or 62
Philippians	A.D. 62
First Timothy	A.D. 64 — 66
Titus	A.D. 64 — 66
Second Timothy	A.D. 66 or 67

Excluding Hebrews, James through Third John are called "catholic," in the sense of being circular letters to be read in more than one church. The probable chronological order and approximate dates of these Epistles are as follows:

James	A.D. 45
First Peter	A.D. 65
Second Peter	A.D. 66 or 67
Jude	A.D. 67 or 68
Hebrews	Before A.D. 70
First John	A.D. 85-90
Second John	A.D. 85-90
Third John	A.D. 85-90

The Greek writing (left) is of the first century A.D., and gives us a good idea what an Epistle looked like. The "parchment" (right) gives us an idea what a finished New Testament letter looked like after it had been wrapped, tied, and sealed—ready to give to a messenger to take to the individual or church designated.

As one reads the Epistles, he begins to note that the historical facts of Jesus' earthly life begin to take "doctrinal" form in the life of one who accepts the finished work of Christ in his behalf.

Justification—a change of standing—before God
Regeneration—a change of nature—from God
Repentance—a change of mind—about God
Conversion—a change of life—for God
Adoption—a change of family—in God
Sanctification—a change of service—unto God
Glorification—a change of place—with God

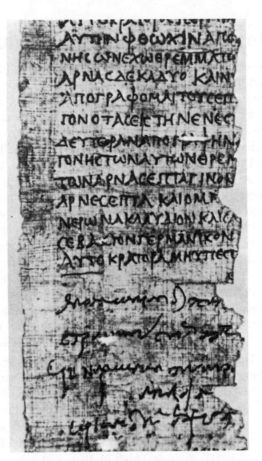

New Testament Script

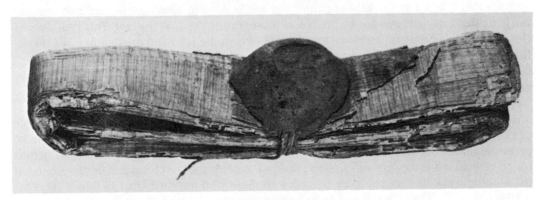

Sealed Parchment

Romans—The Epistle of Faith

Name: This Epistle derives its name from those at Rome, to whom Paul was writing (1:7). He wished to visit Rome on his way to Spain, and this letter was to prepare them for his visit. It was delivered to the saints in Rome by Phoebe, a deaconess of the church at Cenchrea in Corinth (16:1,2). When or by whom the gospel was first preached at Rome cannot be ascertained. Had Peter been the first, it is likely the book of Acts would have given us the account, since Peter was used in the first part of the book to use the "keys of the kingdom." The labors of Paul follow Peter's, and there is no mention of Paul visiting Rome on any of his missionary journeys. It is most likely that no apostle was employed in this important work, but possibly the gospel was first preached in Rome by some of the converts of Peter's preaching on Pentecost, for we find in Jerusalem that day "strangers of Rome, Jews and proselytes" (Acts 2:10). The church of Rome owed its origin, perhaps to the believers who returned from Jerusalem, and to persons converted under Paul's own preaching in other places. This conclusion is strengthened by the long list of salutations to Christian brothers and sisters with whom Paul had previous contact (ch. 16).

In Paul's day, Rome (meaning "strength") was the recognized mistress and metropolis of the world. It was at the height of its greatness, with a population estimated to be near three million, and with unparalleled wealth, luxury, and profligacy. Nero, the sixth of the Caesars, himself the incarnation of whatever was vile, was Emperor. See NERO in Index.

Occasion of Writing: The immediate occasion stems from Paul's knowledge that the Jewish believers were not willing to let the Gentile believers claim equal privileges with them. The argumentation part of this Epistle brings both under sin, short of God's glory, and then, by showing that Abraham's own justification was antecedent to the law and independent of it, proved that any who were justified were justified by faith and that all justified believers were of equal rank in God's favor, whether Jew or Gentile. Paul hoped to reconcile the Jewish converts to the truth that Gentile converts were accepted by God, and that it was done without their being obliged to keep the law of Moses.

Contents:[1] The Apostle sets in clear light the doctrine of justification by faith, showing the Gentiles that it is not by the light of nature and works done in obedience to that, and showing the Jews that salvation was not by the law of Moses or the deeds of the law. This Paul does by clearly portraying the sinful and wretched estate of both the Jews and the Gentiles. His revelation to them is that the righteousness of God is imputed to them by the grace of God through faith in Christ Jesus, Who is God's righteousness. He makes known the effects of salvation by grace through faith; peace and joy in the soul (ch. 5), and holiness in the life and conversation (ch. 6). An account of the justified ones is given, revealing that they are not without sin, illustrated by his own experience and case (ch. 7). "Justification is the standard by which people or things are tested: a level shows that a wall is straight, a plummet that shows the wall to be perpendicular. Doctrinally, it is the act of God whereby He declares ungodly men to be perfect (or righteous) while they are still sinners. God put to death the Lord Jesus and on the ground of His atoning work He declares to be righteous all those who put their trust in Him"[2] (Romans 5:19b; 6:14-22). When I was saved and cleansed, my past was blotted out (Romans 3:25), and God saw me "just-if-I" had never sinned.

In chapter 8 we find the believer possessed with various privileges, such as freedom from condemnation, indwelt by the Spirit of Christ, blessed with adoption, victory in suffering, help in intercession, God as our defense, and a right to the heavenly inheritance. The calling of the Gentiles and of the Jews is outlined in chapters nine through eleven, and the closing chapters exhort all believers to their various duties to God with respect to one another and to the world, to duties of a moral and civil nature, and the use of things indifferent. The Book of Romans has 16 chapters, 433 verses, and 9,447 words.

Character: Doctrinal.

Subject: The gospel as revealing the righteousness of God.

Purpose: To give us the foundation for our faith and to declare to the Church at Rome and to all the world the great fundamental truths of Christianity, especially "justification by faith."

Outline: (Basic).[3]

    I. Righteousness Registered: 1:1-17
   II. Righteousness Required: 1:18—3:20
  III. Righteousness Received: 3:21—5:21
  IV. Righteousness Realized: 6:1—8:39
   V. Righteousness Rejected: 9:1—11:36
  VI. Righteousness Reproduced: 12:1—15:13
 VII. Righteousness Represented: 15:14—16:27

Outline: (General).

    I. Introduction: 1:1-13
   II. Paul's Relation to the Gospel: 1:14-17
  III. The Need for the Gospel: 1:18—3:20
     A. Man is lost: 1:18—3:18
     B. Man cannot save himself: 3:19,20
  IV. The Gospel's Central Theme: 3:21—5:21
     A. The Righteousness of God: 3:21-26
     B. Justification by Faith in Christ: 3:27—5:21
   V. The Power of the Gospel: 6—8
     A. Gives life from death: 6
     B. Delivers from the Law: 7
     C. Gives union with Christ: 8
  VI. Relation of the Gospel to the Jew: 9—11
     A. Israel's Past: 9
       1. Blessed of God: vss. 1-30
       2. Failed God: vss. 31,32a
       3. Rejected His Son: vss. 32b,33
     B. Israel's Present: 10:1—11:25
       1. Lost: 10:1-3
       2. Salvation nigh them: 10:4—11:6
       3. Blinded in part: 11:7-25
     C. Israel's Future: 11:26-36
       1. Restoration—deliverance to come: vs. 26
       2. Sins to be forgiven: vs. 27
       3. Their election: vss. 28-36
 VII. Transforming Power of the Gospel: 12:1—15:13
     A. In the believer's body: 12:1,2
     B. In service: 12:3-8
     C. In relation to others: 12:9—15:13
VIII. Epilogue—Personal Matters: 15:14—16:27

Writer: Paul: 1:1. "Paul was an Israelite of the tribe of Benjamin, and both of his parents were Hebrews. He was a native of Tarsus, in Cilicia, and by birth a free citizen of imperial Rome. Before his call to apostleship, he was known by his Hebrew name Saul; but he used Paul ("little"), his Roman name, among the Gentiles. His parents sent him early to Jerusalem to study the Jewish law under the direction of Gamaliel, the most celebrated doctor of his nation. The improvement of the pupil corresponded with the fame of his master, and all his influence and talents were devoted to preserve the Jewish traditionary corruptions, to destroy the Church of Christ, and to extirpate even the name 'Christian.' But in the midst of his murderous career, while 'breathing out threatenings and slaughter against the disciples of the Lord,' sovereign grace and mercy renewed his heart, and he consecrated all his powers to the service of Christ. Never, perhaps, was any man so entirely devoted to glorify God, and to promote the best interests of mankind; never, probably, did any disciple of the Savior exhibit so eminent an example of Christian virtues and benevolent labors, as this chosen vessel of the Lord. It has been said that the consideration of the conversion and apostleship of Paul alone must leave every infidel without excuse for his rejection of Christianity. After being the instrument of inestimable blessings to the Church of God by his preaching, example, and writings, he sealed the truth of the gospel with his blood, being beheaded at Rome by order of the emperor Nero in A.D. 66 or early 67. The thirteen Epistles of this man of God are of inestimable value to the Church of the Lord Jesus Christ.''[4]

Paul's estimate of himself as a sinner and a saint are summed up in these words:

1. The chiefest of sinners: I Timothy 1:15.

2. The least of the apostles, not deserving to be called an apostle: I Corinthians 15:9. See SEED THOUGHT, point 1, in Job.

When and Where Written: Probably A.D. 57. It was toward the end of his third missionary journey, just before he left Corinth to take an offering to the saints at Jerusalem (15:22-27).

Key Chapter: 3. All under sin.

Key Verses: 1:16,17.

Key Words:
1. Righteousness; used 66 times
2. Faith; 62 times
3. Justification (justify); 17 times
4. Impute; 19 times
5. In Christ; 33 times
6. Law; 78 times
7. Sin; 60 times
8. Flesh; 20 times
9. Death; 42 times

Key Phrase: The righteousness of God: 1:17.

Key Thought: Justification by faith without the deeds of the law: 3:28.

Spiritual Thought: Come to God clothed in His righteousness.

Christ Is Seen As: The Lord our Righteousness: 10:4 with Jeremiah 23:6.

Names and Titles of Christ: See NAME in Dictionary.
1. Jesus Christ: 1:1
2. Son of God: 1:4
3. Lord Jesus Christ: 1:7
4. Christ Jesus: 3:24
5. Our Propitiation: 3:24,25a
6. God's Righteousness: 3:24,25b
7. Our Lord: 4:24; 7:25
8. Our Sin-bearer: 4:25a
9. Our Justifier: 4:25b
10. Christ: 5:6
11. The Gift of eternal life: 6:23b
12. Firstborn among many brethren: 8:29

13. His own Son: 8:32
14. God Blessed forever: 9:5
15. A Stumblingstone and Rock of offense: 9:33
16. End of the Law for Righteousness: 10:4
17. Jesus as Lord: 10:9 (RV)
18. The Lord: 10:13
19. The Deliverer: 11:26
20. Lord of the dead and living: 14:9
21. Minister of the circumcision: 15:8

Names and Titles of God. See NAME in Dictionary.

1. Our Father: 1:7
2. Creator: 1:25
3. One God: 3:30
4. Lord (Jehovah): 4:8
5. Abba, Father: 8:15
6. The living God: 9:26
7. Lord of Sabaoth (of hosts—housekeeper): 9:29
8. Lord over all: 10:12
9. God of peace: 16:20
10. Everlasting God: 16:26
11. God only wise: 16:27

Names and Titles of the Holy Spirit. See NAME in Dictionary.

1. Spirit of holiness: 1:4
2. Holy Ghost: 5:5; 9:1
3. Spirit: 8:1
4. Spirit of life: 8:2
5. Spirit of God: 8:9a,14; 15:19
6. Spirit of Christ: 8:9b

Miracles or Unusual Events: Mighty signs and wonders by Paul—to make the Gentiles obedient (believe): 15:18,19.

1. To the Jew first: 1:16. "Salvation is of [from among] the Jews" because God first entrusted them with His sacred oracles [His Word] that they might reveal Him to other nations (John 4:22; Romans 3:1,2). But God's salvation was not limited to the Jew—Christ is the "Savior of the world," and this includes both Jew and Gentile (John 4:42). The Jew thought he was something special because of his having been chosen by God; so the Gentile was hated and despised (Matthew 15:21-28).

In spite of this hatred, the Jews tried to convert Gentiles to their religion (Judaism). Synagogues were so erected to include a place for the Gentiles to attend. The Jews met in their "inner court" and would have their worship service first. Upon completion of their service, the Rabbi would then go to the "outer court," where the Gentiles had gathered and preach to them. No Gentile was permitted to enter the "inner court" of the Temple or a synagogue with the Jews to hear the reading of the Law under penalty of death. An inscribed stone of Herod's Temple has been found, and it warns Gentiles of the penalty of death if they enter the Jewish sector of the Temple. Because of this, Paul, in his efforts to reach the lost, went to the "Jew first [in the inner court] and also to the Greek [Gentiles—in the outer court]" (Acts 13:14,15,42-49).

Synagogue

Anti-Gentile Inscription

Warning notice from Herod's Temple in Jerusalem: "No stranger [Gentile] is to enter within the balustrade round the Temple and enclosure. Whoever is caught will be responsible to himself for his death, which will ensue."

2. Roman Catacombs. Early New Testament saints sought refuge in these underground burial places (catacombs) to escape persecution from Roman soldiers. Persecution was such that no Christian was safe. "Emperor Worship" was the rule of the day, and all Rome had to submit to Caesar as "god and savior" (see Paul's COURAGE in Index). If Christians were stopped by Roman soldiers and could not produce a certificate so stating they worshiped the Emperor, they were hailed into court. If they confessed Christ as their Savior, they were given opportunity twice to deny faith in Him. If they did not, they were ordered executed (see methods of execution under TACITUS in Index). Later, many Christians were thrown to the wild beasts in the Colosseum. Paul, on one occasion, said he had "been delivered from the mouth of a lion" (II Timothy 4:17).

Catacomb Painting

Christian Symbols

Christians who managed to escape would often flee to a catacomb. Roman soldiers were superstitious, and would never enter a catacomb. Here Christians felt safe. They left paintings and inscriptions, which indicated their faith and trust in Christ as their Savior. The earliest known inscription is dated A.D. 72, and others, from this date through the third century. Many scenes depict deliverance, such as Noah's escape from the flood, Jonah's escape from the great fish, and Daniel's escape from the lion's den. Other paintings reveal flowers and doves, depicting the loveliness of Christ in the midst of Rome's ugliness and God's peace and inner witness of His Holy Spirit in spite of tribulation in the world. There are signs of an anchor, indicating their security in Christ; the Greek letter "X" which symbolized Christ (X in Greek is "Chi"—first letter in the name Christ); and the sign of the fish, denoting their trust in "Jesus Christ, God's Son, Savior." By taking the initial letters of this Greek expression, the word "icthus" is spelled, which means "fish." This sign let all Rome know that not everyone had bowed to "Emperor Worship"—a worshiping of Caesar as "god and savior." There are no signs, left by these early saints, to indicate a belief in purgatory, confessions of sins to a religious leader, a worshiping of Christ earthly mother, Mary, or that Peter himself had anything to do with a Roman church.

LIGHT FROM BIBLICAL CUSTOMS

[5]

1. Adoption: 8:15. See ADOPTION in Index.

2. Vessels of wrath: 9:22. Ofttimes when a potter finished baking pottery, some of the vessels would be cracked. Rather than discard them, he sought to patch the cracks with a fine powder and then baked them again. Sometimes he succeeded, sometimes he didn't. If he did not succeed, the imperfect vessels were discarded. They were called "vessels of wrath" (see POTTER in Index). Paul used this custom to illustrate those who had opportunities to be saved and used of God, but refused. Some people will just not believe, and they seal their own doom (John 3:18,36; 12:37-39).

3. Vessels of mercy: 9:23. A vessel of water was always kept handy in a home so that when a tired traveler passed by or stopped for a night's lodging, he could have a cool drink, and wash his hands and feet. This was considered an act of mercy—hence a "vessel of mercy." Those who know and love and serve Christ are God's "vessels of mercy" unto others.

4. Coals of fire: 12:30. In Bible lands practically everything is carried on the head—water, jars, fruit, fish, vegetables, etc. Cooking is done on small burners (outside the house), and should the fire go out, one will take a brazier to his neighbor and fill it with live coals, carrying it on his head. Such an act stands for warmth and neighborliness. To be kind to our enemy, even forgiving him, is like heaping "coals of fire on his head"—a burning conscience of guilt in the presence of love and forgiveness. This is one of God's methods of convicting those who are hostile to the gospel.

The Old Testament in Romans: There are over 60 references from fourteen Old Testament books in Romans. The one upon which Paul places the most emphasis is—"The just shall live by faith" (Habakkuk 2:4). He makes this truth the theme of Romans. It was the revelation of this truth that enabled Martin Luther to bring the reformation into the open.

1. The just shall live by faith: 1:17 with Habukkuk 2:4
2. God's name blasphemed: 2:24 with Isaiah 52:5
3. Justified in speaking: 3:4 with Psalm 51:4
4. None righteous: 3:10 with Psalm 14:1,3
5. None understands: 3:11 with Psalm 14:2
6. All gone out of the way: 3:12 with Psalm 14:3
7. Throat an open sepulchre: 3:13 with Psalm 5:9; 140:3
8. Mouth full of cursing: 3:14 with Psalm 10:7
9. Feet swift to shed blood: 3:15 with Isaiah 59:7
10. Destruction and misery in their ways: 3:16,17 with Isaiah 59:7,8
11. No fear of God before their eyes: 3:18 with Psalm 36:1
12. Abraham's faith counted righteousness: 4:3 with Genesis 15:6
13. Iniquities forgiven: 4:7,8 with Psalm 32:1,2
14. Abraham the father of many nations: 4:17 with Genesis 17:5
15. Abraham's seed to become many nations: 4:18 with Genesis 15:5
16. Thou shalt not covet: 7:7 with Exodus 20:17
17. For thy sake they are killed all the day: 8:36 with Psalm 44:22
18. In Isaac shall thy seed by called: 9:7 with Genesis 21:12
19. Sarah shall have a son: 9:9 with Genesis 18:10
20. The elder shall serve the younger: 9:12 with Genesis 25:23
21. Jacob have I loved: 9:13 with Malachi 1:2,3
22. God's mercy upon us: 9:15 with Exodus 33:19
23. Pharaoh raised up for God's purpose: 9:17 with Exodus 9:16
24. Gentiles called a people: 9:25 with Hosea 2:23
25. Jews not called a people: 9:26 with Hosea 1:10
26. Only a remnant in Israel saved: 9:27,28 with Isaiah 10:22,23
27. God's provision of a seed: 9:29 with Isaiah 1:9
28. Christ a stumblingstone: 9:33 with Isaiah 28:16a
29. Living by the law: 10:5 with Leviticus 18:5
30. Who shall ascend into heaven: 10:6,7 with Deuteronomy 30:12,13
31. God's word is nigh: 10:8 with Deuteronomy 30:14
32. Belief in Christ eliminates shame: 10:11 with Isaiah 28:16b
33. Call upon the name of the Lord: 10:13 with Joel 2:32
34. The feet of those who preach: 10:15 with Isaiah 52:7
35. Believing the Lord's report: 10:16 with Isaiah 53:1
36. Hearing the gospel: 10:18 with Psalm 19:4
37. Provoked to jealousy: 10:19 with Deuteronomy 32:21
38. God found by those who seek Him: 10:20 with Isaiah 65:1
39. God's outstretched hands: 10:21 with Isaiah 65:2
40. The prophets killed: 11:3 with I Kings 19:10,14
41. God's reserved prophets: 11:4 with I Kings 19:18

42. The spirit of slumber: 11:8 with Isaiah 29:10
43. Israel's conduct a snare: 11:9,10 with Psalm 69:22,23
44. A Deliverer from Zion: 11:26,27 with Isaiah 59:20,21
45. The mind of the Lord: 11:34 with Isaiah 40:13
46. Given to the Lord: 11:35 with Job 41:11
47. Vengeance is the Lord's: 12:19 with Deuteronomy 32:35
48. Feeding our enemies: 12:20 with Proverbs 25:21,22
49. Various Commandments: 13:9 with Exodus 20:13-17; Leviticus 19:18
50. Every knee shall bow to the Lord: 14:11 with Isaiah 45:23
51. Being reproached: 15:3 with Psalm 69:9
52. God's mercy among the Gentiles: 15:9 with Psalm 18:49
53. Gentiles rejoicing with the Jews: 15:10 with Deuteronomy 32:43
54. Gentiles praising the Lord: 15:11 with Psalm 117:1
55. Christ, the root of Jesse: 15:12 with Isaiah 11:1,10
56. Christ preached to the heathen: 15:21 with Isaiah 52:15
57. Companion references:
    a. Render . . . according to their deeds: 2:6 with Psalm 62:12
    b. God no respector of persons: 2:11 with Deuteronomy 10:17
    c. Shall clay speak to the potter: 9:20 with Isaiah 45:9
    d. Potter power over clay: 9:21 with Jeremiah 18:6
    e. Eyes that see not: 11:8 with Isaiah 29:10

1. The gospel in Romans. See GOSPEL in Index.
    a. The gospel: 1:15. This is God's good news to sinful men, relating what God has done for all sinners (I Corinthians 15:3,4) (I Corinthians 15:3,4)
    b. The gospel of God: 1:1; 15:16. This reveals that God is the source of this good news to sinners.
    c. The gospel of Christ: 1:9,16; 15:19,29. This is the good news of what Christ did for sinful man (4:25)
    d. The gospel of Peace: 10:15. This is the result of our accepting and appropriating this good news by faith (5:1; Ephesians 2:13-17)
    e. The gospel of Paul: 16:25. Paul claims it as "my gospel" because it had been entrusted to him by Christ (as to all believers—Galatians 1:6-12)

These five expressions refer to *one* gospel, "the gospel of the grace of God," which results in salvation to everyone who believes—to the Jew first, and also the Greek (Gentile): 1:16; Acts 20:24.

In connection with the gospel, it should be noted that when Jesus preached the "gospel of the kingdom of heaven" (Matthew 4:23), and John preached the "gospel of the kingdom of God" (Mark 1:14,15), they were both preaching the gospel of deliverance from sin—the *only* gospel known to God (Note: Kingdom of God and Kingdom of Heaven are synonymous terms—Matthew 13:11 with Luke 8:10). To get into the Kingdom of God one must be born-again by believing the gospel (John 3:1-16), and to get into the Kingdom of Heaven, one must repent of his sins (Matthew 3:2; Luke 13:3).

2. The Soul-winners Kit: 1:1-16. See SOUL-WINNING in Index.
    a. Separation: vs. 1
    b. Prayer: vs. 9
    c. Desire: vs. 10
    d. Willingness: vs. 11

  e. Expectation: vs. 13

  f. Obligation: vs. 14. We are debtors to every man to give him the gospel in the same manner as we have received it. Should we hear it twice or more when there are those who have never heard it once?

  g. Passion and readiness: vs. 15

  h. Boldness: vs. 16a

  i. Message: vs. 16b

3. Ready: 1:15—

  a. To preach the gospel: 1:15

  b. To give an answer: I Peter 3:15

  c. To produce good works: Titus 3:1

  d. To distribute (cheerful giver): I Timothy 6:18

  e. To be bound for the gospel's sake: Acts 21:13

  f. To be offered (die) for Christ (if necessary): II Timothy 4:6

  g. To meet the Lord: Luke 12:40; II Timothy 4:6,8; I John 2:28

4. The gospel for the Jew: 1:16. That the Christian Church today ignores the Jew in spiritual matters, none can deny. In New Testament days there was surprise if Gentiles were saved. Today, it is news if a Jew comes to know Christ. What has it cost the Church of Jesus Christ to withhold the gospel from the Jews?[6]

  a. The Church has lost her balance. The gospel is for *all*.

  b. The Church has lost the blessing of God. We are not doing a *full* job, consequently we are losing blessings.

  c. The Church has lost spiritual health and vigor. Her weakness is such that very few Gentiles are able to influence Jews.

  d. The Church has lost her doctrinal unity. Never was Truth intended for one class at the exclusion of another.

  e. The Church has lost her zeal. Since the Church's failure to obey the command to "go," the lost are on the "outside" because Christians are on the "inside." Or, in the language of the vernacular, "our get up and go has got up and went."

  f. The Church has lost the respect and friendship of the Jew himself. Jews *do* blame Christians for much of anti-Semitism.

  g. The Church has lost a blessed fellowship:

   —With God the Father, who loves the Jew with an everlasting love: Jeremiah 31:3

   —With the Holy Spirit, who first came upon the Jew

   —With Christ, who came as the seed of David

   —With Christian Jews, because we do not seek them out

   —In intercession, because we do not burden ourselves for them in prayer: I Samuel 12:23a

5. Are the Heathen Lost: 1:18—2:16

  a. They know there is a God: 1:18-21

  b. They know they have sinned against God: 1:22-25

  c. They know they face judgment for their sins: 1:32

  d. They have God's moral law in their hearts: 2:14,15a

  e. They know right from wrong: 2:15b

  f. They are without excuse: 2:1

  g. They will be judged by God: 2;11,12

  h. Because they do not know that Christ died for their sins, it is *our* responsibility to go and tell them: 1:14; 10:13-17

6. All under Sin: 3:9. Paul pictures man as he is—a sinner in the sight of God (1:18—3:18). Our whole being is filled with the fruits of sin (3:9-18), as well as the works of the flesh (Galatians 6:19-21). See SIN in Index.

MAN'S VIEWPOINT OF SIN	GOD'S VIEWPOINT OF SIN
Man calls sin an accident	God calls it an abomination
Man calls sin a blunder	God calls it blindness
Man calls sin a chance	God calls it a choice
Man calls sin a defect	God calls it a disease
Man calls sin an error	God calls it enmity
Man calls sin fascination	God calls it fatality
Man calls sin infirmity	God calls it iniquity
Man calls sin luxury	God calls it leprosy
Man calls sin liberty	God calls it lawlessness
Man calls sin a trifle	God calls it a tragedy
Man calls sin a mistake	God calls it madness
Man calls sin weakness	God calls it willfulness

7. **All Have Sinned and Come Short of the Glory of God: 3:23.** James (2:10) says that if we keep the whole law and offend in one point, we are guilty of breaking all. A look at the Ten Commandments is a good way to test ourselves as to whether we have broken God's laws and sinned against Him.

 a. Love of selfish pleasures more than God breaks the first

 b. Religious adoration for man-made objects breaks the second

 c. Flippant and hypocritical use of God's name breaks the third

 d. Carelessness about the Lord's Day and failure to worship Him in Spirit and Truth breaks the fourth

 e. Disrespect, ingratitude, and disobedience to parents breaks the fifth

 f. Anger, malicious thoughts, and outward hatred breaks the sixth. Remember, if one hates his brother, he is a murderer (I John 3:15)

 g. Lustful thoughts in the heart, unfaithfulness, and free-sex breaks the seventh

 h. Cheating and taking things from others breaks the eighth

 i. Slanderous statements and gossip breaks the ninth

 j. Coveting what another has breaks the tenth. If we covet, we do not love our neighbor as ourselves (Luke 10:27)

8. **Justification: 3:28**

 a. Its Author is God: 3:21,26

 b. Its Source is Grace: 3:24

 c. Its Ground is the Blood of Christ: 3:25

 d. Its Means is Faith: 3:22,28

 e. Its Proof is the Resurrection: 4:25

 f. Its Evidence is Walking after the Spirit: 8:4

 g. Its Fruit is Good Works: James 2:24

 h. Its Assurance is the Knowledge of His Will: Isaiah 53:11; Hebrews 10:4-10

 i. Its Results—

  —Forgiveness: 3:25

  —Reckoned righteousness:4:9

  —Hope: 5:2

  —Love of God: 5:5

  —Saved from wrath: 5:9

  —Reconciled to God: 5:10

9. **The Secret of True Peace: 5:1**[7]

 a. Just to trust Jesus' blood—day by day: 3:25

 b. Just to rest upon His Word—all the way: Psalm 119:42

 c. Just to do the Father's will—with delight: Psalm 40:8

 d. Just to walk in fellowship—in the light: I John 1:7

 e. Just to know the God of peace—ever near: I Corinthians 14:33

 f. Just to live in perfect love—without fear: I John 4:18

g. Just to roll your care on Him—glad release: I Peter 5:7

h. Just to have a Christlike mind—this *is* peace: Philippians 2:5

10. Joys and Blessings of the Spirit
   a. Hope of glory: 5:2
   b. Daily tribulations working patience: 5:3
   c. Love of God: 5:5
   d. Joy: 5:11
   e. Liberty: 8:1
   f. Life: 8:11
   g. Guidance: 8:14
   h. Assurance: 8:16
   i. Adoption—heirship: 8:15,17
   j. Helping our infirmities: 8:26a
   k. Interceding in our behalf: 8:26b,27

11. The "Much Mores" of Romans Five
   a. Much more being justified by His blood: vs. 9
   b. Much more being reconciled: vs.10
   c. Much more grace abounded: vss. 15,20
   d. Much more we shall reign: vs. 17

12. Relationship of the Believer
   To Christ—
   a. Baptized into His death: 6:3,6
   b. Buried with Him: 6:4a
   c. Raised with Him: 6:4b
   d. Newness of life: 6:4c,11b; II Corinthians 5:17
   e. Partakers of Him: 6:5; 8:29; II Peter 1:4
   To Sin—
   a. Dead: 6:11a
   b. Freed from its claims: 6:7,18
   c. Victorious over its power: 6:14; 8:37
   *To Self—*dead: 6:6
   *To the Law—*dead: 7:4; Galatians 4:9
   *To the flesh—*dead: 8:10,11; 13:14; Galatians 5:24
   *To the world—*dead: it to me, I to it: Galatians 6:14
   To the devil and his emissaries—dead, since he has been defeated and principalities and powers have been spoiled: Colossians 1:13; 2:14,15
   > *Please note:* Sin, self, etc., are not dead—*we are.* Our victory lies in the truth that we are *dead* to sin but *alive* to God—more than a conqueror through Christ: 6:11; 8:37
   To God's service—
   a. Yieldedness: 6:13
   b. Obedience: 6:17
   c. Servants: 6:18,22

13. Servants: 6:16

OF SIN	OF CHRIST
Sold: 7:14	Bought: I Corinthians 6:20
Bound: 7:24	Free: 6:22
Led by the devil: II Timothy 2:26	Led by the Spirit: 8:14
Wicked works: Galatians 5:19-21	Fruitful works: 6:22
Darkness: John 3:19	Light: Matthew 5:16
Coward (flee): Proverbs 28:1a	Bold: Proverbs 28:1b
Shall perish: Luke 13:3; Psalm 1:6	Shall never perish: John 10:28

14. Sin and its Results: 6:23a. See SIN in Index.

Sin Defined—

a. Corruption of the mind and flesh: 1:21-32; 8:7
b. Anything not of faith: 14:23
c. Transgression of the law: I John 3:4
d. All unrighteousness: I John 5:17
e. Knowing to, and not doing good: James 4:17
f. Heart impurity: Jeremiah 17:9
g. A high look, a proud heart: Proverbs 21:4
h. Foolish thoughts: Proverbs 24:9
i. Idols that cannot save: Jeremiah 2:28
j. Idols that one cannot dethrone: Ezekiel 23:49
k. Spots that cannot be removed: II Peter 2:13
l. Burdens that man cannot lift: Isaiah 1:4
m. A captivity from which man cannot flee: Isaiah 59:6-8
n. Cords that cannot be broken: Proverbs 5:22
o. A disease that man cannot cure: Isaiah 1:6
p. A bondage that man cannot escape: Isaiah 61:1

Sin's Extent—

a. Passed upon all: 5:12; Galatians 3:22
b. All naturally depraved: Job 14:4; Ephesians 2:2,3
c. Universal: 3:23; Genesis 6:5-12; Galatians 5:17-21

Sin's Manifestation—

a. Disobedience of commandments: Exodus 20:3-17; James 2:10
b. Self-righteousness: Galatians 6:3; Isaiah 5:21
c. Ambition: Mark 9:33-35
d. Pride: Psalm 12:4
e. Criticism: Luke 6:41
f. Malice: Ephesians 4:31
g. Envy: James 3:14
h. Anger: Ephesians 4:26
i. Strife: Galatians 5:15
j. Flattery: Proverbs 29:5
k. Hypocrisy: Titus 1:16
l. Blasphemy: Colossians 3:8

Sin's Work—

a. Robs a man of God's peace: 3:17
b. Robs a man of fellowship with God: Genesis 3:8
c. Robs a man of courage: Proverbs 28:1
d. Robs a man of prosperity: Proverbs 28:13a
e. Robs a man of liberty: Galatians 5:1
f. Robs a man of life: Romans 6:23
g. Robs a man of glory: Romans 3:23
h. Robs a man of heaven: I Corinthians 6:9,10; Revelation 21:27

Sin's Wages—

a. God's wrath: John 3:36; James 4:4
b. Death: 6:21,23a; James 1:15
c. Judgment: Hebrews 9:27
d. Hell—eternal punishment: Luke 16:22-26; Revelation 20:11-15; 21:8

15. Why No Condemnation: 8:1
    a. Sins laid on Christ: Isaiah 53:6
    b. Sins borne by Christ: I Peter 2:24
    c. Sins subdued: Micah 7:19a
    d. Sins purged: Hebrews 1:3

    e. Sins not imputed: II Corinthians 5:19

    f. Sins forgiven: Romans 4:7a; Acts 10:43

    g. Sins covered: Romans 4:7b

    h. Sins removed: Psalm 103:12

    i. Sins passed away: Zechariah 3:4; Hebrews 9:26

    j. Sins blotted out: Isaiah 43:25a

    k. Sins cast behind God's back: Isaiah 38:17

    l. Sins forgotten: Isaiah 43:25b; Jeremiah 31:34

    m. Sins cast into the depths of the sea: Micah 7:19b

16. Great "Powers" in Romans Eight

    a. Grace—*saving:* vs. 1

    b. The Spirit—*guiding:* vs. 14

    c. Faith—*reckoning:* vs. 18

    d. Love—*providing:* vs. 28

    e. Life—*keeping:* vs. 39

17. The Law *versus* Christ: 8:3,4—

WHAT THE LAW COULD NOT DO	CHRIST CAN
—Make us righteous: 10:3	II Corinthians 5:21
—Justify: 3:20	3:24,28; Galatians 2:16
—Make us heirs: 4:14	8:16,17
—Reconcile us to God: 5:10	II Corinthians 5:18
—Free us from death: 5:12	John 5:24; Hebrews 2:14,15
—Deliver corruptible bodies: 7:24	Philippians 3:20,21
—Make God our Father: 8:15	8:15: Galatians 3:26

18. The Believer's Relationship to God

    a. *Children*—in His family: 8:16

    b. *Sons*—of dignity: 8:14

    c. *Brothers*—in companionship: John 20:17

    d. *Saints*—commissioned: I Corinthians 1:2

    e. *Priests*—in intercession: I Peter 2:5

    f. *Kings*—in victory: Revelation 1:6

    g. *Heirs*—joint-heirs with Christ: 8:17

19. Romans 8:28.[8] "All things work together for *our* good." This must be for three reasons—

    a. Because *all* things are under the absolute control of the God of the universe: II Corinthians 5:18a; 4:15a

    b. Because God desires our good and nothing but our good

    c. Because even Satan himself cannot touch a hair of our heads without God's permission and then only for our good

Not all things are good in themselves, nor in their tendencies; but God makes all things *work* together for our good. Nothing enters our life by blind chance, nor are there any accidents in the life of the believer. Everything is being moved by God, with this end in view—*our good.* Everything being subservient to God's eternal purpose works blessings to those marked out for conformity to the image of His dear Son (8:29). All suffering, sorrow, loss, etc., are used by our Father to minister benefits to His elect.

20. If God be for Us: 8:31[9]

    a. When Noah was building the ark he was very much in the minority, but He and God won

    b. When Joseph was sold into Egypt by his brethren, he was a decided minority, but he and God won

    c. When Elijah prayed down fire from heaven and put to shame the prophets of Baal, he was a notable minority, but he and God won

    d. When David, ridiculed by his brethren, went out to meet Goliath, he was a ridiculous minority, but he and God won. Israel said Goliath was too big to defeat. David said Goliath was too big to miss!

    e. When Gideon and his 300 men armed only with pitchers took on the Midianites, they were a weak minority, but they and God won

    f. When Christ died on Calvary, he was a forsaken minority, but He and His Father won

    g. We Christians are in the minority today, but we can and will be victorious, for "if God be for us, who can be against us"

21. To be More than Conquerors: 8:37
    a. Put on the whole armor of God: Ephesians 6:11-18
    b. Resist the devil: James 4:7
    c. Watch and pray: Matthew 26:41
    d. Exercise faith: I John 5:1-5
    e. Put on Christ: Romans 13:14
    f. Walk in the light: I John 1:7
    g. Abide under the shadow of the Almighty: Psalm 91:1-3
    h. Claim God's promise: Philippians 4:13; I Corinthians 10:13

22. Our Reasonable Service—Surrender: 12

Its Nature: Surrendering our bodies and its members: vss. 1,4

    a. *Our Tongues.* They should be—
    —Testifying: Psalm 107:2
    —Kept: Proverbs 21:23
    —Wholesome: Proverbs 15:4
    —Soft: Proverbs 25:15
    —Bridled: James 1:26

    b. *Our Ears.* They should be—
    —Hearing: Proverbs 20:12
    —Inclined: Proverbs 4:20
    —Apt: Proverbs 23:12
    —Attentive: Nehemiah 8:3

    c. *Our Eyes.* They should be—
    —Single: Matthew 6:22
    —Lifted: Psalm 121:1
    —Bountiful: Proverbs 22:9
    —Seeing: Proverbs 20:12

    d. *Our Feet.* They should be—
    —Clean: John 13:5-10
    —Shod: Ephesians 6:15
    —Unmovable: Psalm 121:3
    —Beautiful: Romans 10:15

    e. *Our Hands.* They should be—
    —Clean: Psalm 24:3-5
    —Helpful: Ecclesiastes 9:10
    —Diligent: Proverbs 12:24
    —Wonderful: Acts 5:12

    f. *Our Minds.* They should be—
    —Renewed: Romans 12:2
    —Pure: II Peter 3:1
    —Stayed on God: Isaiah 26:3
    —Humble: Philippians 2:3

Its Demands:

a. A transformed life: vs.2
b. Talents used for His glory: vss. 6-8
c. Pure love: vs. 9
d. Affection for others: vs. 10
e. Diligent in all things: vs. 11
f. Prayer: vs. 12
g. Generosity: vss. 13-15
h. Humility: vs. 16
i. Honesty: vs. 17
j. Peace with our fellowmen: vs. 18
k. Love for our enemies: vss. 19,20
l. Victory: vs. 21

Its Results:

a. God's mercies: vs.1
b. Measure of faith: vs. 3
c. Confidence in the Lord: vs. 19

23. Members One of Another: 12:5. Believers should—

a. Be kindly affectioned one to another: 12:10a; Ephesians 4:32a
b. Prefer one another: 12:10b
c. Be of the same mind one toward another: 12:16
d. Love one another: 13:8; John 13:34,35
e. Edify one another: 14:19; I Thessalonians 5:11
f. Admonish one another: 15:14
g. Care one for another: I Corinthians 12:25
h. Bear one another's burdens: Galatians 6:2
i. Lie not one to another: Colossians 3:9
j. Speak not evil one of another: James 4:11
k. Grudge not one against another: James 5:9
l. Forebear one another in love: Ephesians 4:2
m. Be tenderhearted one to another: Ephesians 4:32b
n. Forgive one another: Ephesians 4:32c; Colossians 3:13
o. Submit one to another: Ephesians 5:21
p. Esteem other better than self: Philippians 2:3
q. Teach one another: Colossians 3:16
r. Comfort one another: I Thessalonians 4:18
s. Exhort one another: Hebrews 3:13
t. Consider one another: Hebrews 10:24
u. Fellowship one with another: Hebrews 10:25a
v. Confess faults one to another: James 5:16a
w. Pray one for another: James 5:16b; I Samuel 12:23
x. Have compassion one for another: I Peter 3:8
y. Use hospitality one to another: I Peter 4:9
z. Minister the same one to another: I Peter 4:10

24. Be Not Wise in Your Own Conceits: 12:16

a. Pride of Race—white/black, Jew/gentile, bond/free (Galatians 3:28)
b. Pride of Lace—Eastertime, Sunday Services, etc. (I Peter 3:3,4)
c. Pride of Face—Beauty aids, etc., etc. (Psalm 149:4)
d. Pride of Pace—Social groups, Business associates, etc. (Revelation 3:14-18)
e. Pride of Grace—Forgotten once purged from old sins, "too" spiritual, etc. (II Peter 1:5-9)

Summary: Luke 14:11; I Corinthians 10:12; James 4:6-8,10

Our position with Christ is one of death, burial, resurrection, ascension, enthronement, and glory. In that I am a partaker of His divine nature, I am a partaker of His life, temptations, sufferings, and victory. However, it is one thing to be something and quite another thing to put into practice what I am. If my earthly father were king of a country, I would be a prince. Do you think I would live like a commoner or put into practice my position as the son of a king? By virtue of my birth into the royal family my position would be that of a son and a prince, and I would be expected to live my position. To live otherwise would disgrace my father and family. In Christ Jesus I am a son of God, an heir of God, and a joint-heir with Christ. I have been made a king and a priest. In fact, I am complete in Christ (Colossians 2:10). Being so, why should I not put into practice my position as a child of the King of kings and the Lord of lords? We are admonished in the Scriptures to practice our position. See POSITION in Index.

PUT YE ON THE LORD JESUS CHRIST—13:14[10]

"To put on Christ there must be faith in Christ, submission to Christ, the profession of Christ, conformity to Christ, a practical imitation of Christ, and an appropriating of Christ in all His offices and characters. What clothing is to the body, Jesus Christ is to the soul—its covering, comfort, and protection. To put on Christ, we must put off everything that is opposed to Christ, even the old man with his deeds. Christ ought to be seen in His people as the clothing is seen on the person. A consistent Christian is Christ made visible. Christ should be so put on as never to be put off. He forms a clothing garment which will never wear out or go out of fashion. Beloved, men must see our Savior as well as hear about Him. Those who put on the Lord Jesus Christ are the ones who exhibit Him. They wear white robes, the evidence of their acquittal at the bar of justice, of their acceptance with God, and of their enjoying the approbation of God. Christ is not only clothing but our defense. Putting on Jesus we put on the whole armor of God. O for wisdom to wear Christ so that God may accept us, angels may admire us, the devil and his demons flee from us, and the whole world be compelled to commend us!"

PRAYER THOUGHT: "Dear heavenly Father, deliver me from harboring any malicious or revengeful thoughts against those who might have wronged me. Help me to find something good in them, and having found it, to think and speak of them with fairness. In Jesus' name I pray. Amen."[11]

Romans 12:20

First Corinthians—The Epistle of Gifts

Name: This Epistle derives its name from those at Corinth, to whom Paul was writing: 1:2. The church here was founded by Paul on his first visit to the city, which lasted about 18 months (Acts 18:1-7). It was a large church (Acts 18:4,8,10), made up chiefly of Gentile believers (12:2), with some Jewish Christians (Acts 18:8). Both were principally of the poorer class (1:26), with some exceptions, as Crispus (1:14; Acts 18:8).

Under the Romans, Corinth was a wealthy seaport city, given to much luxury and immorality and heathenism. It was also noted for such industry as pottery and brass, and was, as most Roman cities were, sports-minded. To "live like a Corinthian" was to live recklessly in sin and debauchery.

Occasion of Writing: While at Ephesus (A.D. 54-57), disturbing reports reached Paul concerning moral laxity among members of the Corinthian Church. Paul wrote them a sharp letter, demanding withdrawal from licentious "brothers." The fact, subject, and spirit of such a letter is alluded to in chapter 5, verse 9, and the passage in his second letter to them (6:14—7:1) may be a fragment of it, because the subject of this passage would fit the description, while it does not fit the present context. Paul's letter to them did not improve conditions in Corinth. Later, three deputies from Corinth arrived in Ephesus (16:17) delivering a letter from the Corinthian church (7:1), asking Paul questions on marriage, meat offered to idols, the use of spiritual gifts, the collection for Jerusalem, etc. In addition, visitors from the house of Chloe (1:11) brought news to Paul about party divisions, carnality and immorality, litigation, marriage and separation, banqueting at the Lord's Supper, and the denial of the resurrection (chs. 1,2,5—7,11,15).

Contents: "The Apostle first rebukes them for their schisms and divisions; suggests that their regard to the wisdom of men and the philosophy of the Gentiles had brought the simplicity of the gospel into contempt with them; blames them for their conduct in the case of the incestuous person; reproves them for going to law with one another before heathen magistrates; strongly inveighs against fornication; answers several questions and resolves several cases concerning marriage; treats on things offered to idols and of the maintenance of ministers; women's position in the church; takes notice of unbecoming conduct at the Lord's table; discourses concerning the nature and use of spiritual gifts and commends love above them all; observes and corrects irregularities in the use of their gifts; proves the doctrine of the resurrection which some denied; exhorts to a collection for the poor saints, and to several other things; and then concludes the epistle with the salutations of others and of himself."[1] First Corinthians has 16 chapters, 437 verses, and 9,489 words.

Character: Church Epistle.

Subject: The vital relation of every member in Christ's body to the Head, and the sad result when members of the body do not care one for the other. See Ephesians 4:16.

Purpose: To teach us how every member is to care for every other member of the body of Christ as Christ, the Head, cares for each and all.

Outline:
  I. Salutation and Introduction: 1:1-9
 II. Divisions in the Corinthian Church: 1:10—4:21
     A. Christ's oneness eliminates division in His body: 1:10-31
     B. The Holy Spirit's preeminence in wisdom: 2
     C. Christian service clarified: 3
     D. Christian conduct urged: 4
III. Moral Disorders in the Corinthian Church: 5—11
     A. Regarding impurity: 5
     B. Regarding lawsuits: 6
     C. Regarding marriage: 7
     D. Regarding Christian liberty: 8:1—11:1
     E. Regarding women's dress: 11:2-16
     F. Regarding the Lord's table: 11:17-34
     G. Regarding spiritual gifts; use and abuse: 12:1—14:40
        1. Diversity of gifts: 12
        2. The greatest gift: 13
        3. Applying the gifts: 14
 IV. The Doctrine of the Resurrection: 15

V. Final Exhortations and Conclusion: 16

Writer: Paul: 1:1,2. See WRITER in Romans.

When and Where Written: A.D. 55, in Ephesus, at the close of Paul's three-year ministry there: 16:5-8; Acts 20:31.

Key Chapters:
1. 13; Love—*the* way of Christian living
2. 15; Resurrection—victory over death

Key Verses: 2:7,8.

Key Word: Wisdom.

Key Phrase: Let all things be done decently and in order: 14:40.

Key Thought: Church order.

Spiritual Thought: Come to Him for all gifts.

Christ Is Seen As: The firstfruits of the dead: 15:20.

Names and Titles of Christ. See NAMES in Dictionary.
1. Jesus Christ: 1:1
2. Christ Jesus: 1:2
3. Our Lord: 1:2; 9:1
4. Christ: 1:6
5. His Son: 1:9
6. Lord Jesus Christ: 1:10
7. A Stumblingblock . . . to Jews: 1:23
8. Foolishness . . . to Gentiles: 1:23
9. The Power of God: 1:24a
10. The Wisdom of God: 1:24b,30a
11. Righteousness: 1:30b
12. Sanctification: 1:30c
13. Redemption: 1:30d
14. The Lord of glory: 2:8
15. The Foundation: 3:11
16. Our Rewarder: 3:12-15 with Revelation 22:12
17. God: 3:23
18. Lord Jesus: 5:5
19. Our Passover: 5:7
20. The Lord: 6:14; 12:3
21. Maker of all things: 8:6
22. Spiritual Rock: 10:4
23. Head of every man: 11:3
24. Jesus: 12:3
25. Firstfruits of them that sleep: 15:20,23
26. The last Adam: 15:45
27. The Lord from heaven: 15:47
28. Our Victor: 15:57

Names and Titles of God. See NAMES in Dictionary.
1. Father: 1:3; 8:6
2. Lord (Jehovah): 1:31; 10:26
3. Judge: 11:32

Names and Titles of the Holy Spirit. See NAMES in Dictionary.
1. His Spirit: 2:10
2. The Spirit: 2:10

3. Spirit of God: 2:11,14
4. Holy Ghost: 2:13; 6:19
5. Spirit of our God: 6:11

Miracles Referred to:
1. Healing: 12:9,28
2. Various miracles: 12:10,28
3. Tongues: 12:10,28
4. Interpretation of tongues: 12:10
5. Paul speaking in tongues: 14:18
6. Appearances of Christ after His resurrection: 15:4-8

1. Paul's visit to Corinth (Acts 18:1-18). Paul had been in Corinth eighteen months when he was hailed into court before Gallio's "bema" (judgment seat or court) to answer charges brought against him by the Jews. An inscription found at Delphi mentions the emperor Claudius and Gallio, proconsul of Achaia, A.D. 51—53. This inscription enables us to date Paul's visit to Corinth. Gallio was the brother of Seneca, who was the tutor of Nero. Paul probably arrived in Corinth about A.D. 50 and left one-and-a-half years after his encounter with Gallio and the Jews. See BEMA in Index.

2. Our Body, the Temple of God: 3:16,17. At the acropolis in Corinth, scoreless numbers of priestesses practiced prostitution in the name of religion. Their bodies were freely given and sold for such immoral purposes. Paul probably had this in mind when he stressed the importance of the believer's body in relation to Christ, and labeled it as God's "temple," in which the Holy Spirit dwelt. He also showed the sacredness of marriage, and the awfulness of one joining his body with that of a harlot (6:15,16).

3. Sports-minded Corinth. Due to emphasis placed on sports in the Roman world, Paul used a runner in a race and a boxer to illustrate the need for a Christian to be in good physical shape for God's service. The athlete will discipline himself and master his body so he can be at the peak of performance for a race. Only one can win the prize, usually a laurel wreath placed on the victor's head. It is likened to a "corruptible crown," one that fades away. But if

Corruptible Crown

believers will so discipline themselves in the race of life, each can win a trophy—an "incorruptible crown" (9:24-26a). See CROWNS in Index.

The boxer will also discipline himself, so that when he faces his opponent in the ring, he will be able to aim every blow well. Should he fail to train properly, he will swing his arms right and left, just "beating the air." He soon becomes an easy target for his opponent—a castaway, or one who is sidelined. Realizing the value of his body as a believer, Paul did not want to be guilty as one who "beateth the air," and soon becoming sidelined in the Lord's service—or a "castaway" (9:26b,27). Here again he desired an incorruptible crown for Christian victory. See CASTAWAY in Index.

"Beating the Air"

4. Wine in New Testament Days. See WINE in Index.

[2] We see through a glass darkly: 13:12. This refers to a copper mirror, finely polished, which gives a good reflection, but *only* a reflection. At the coming of Christ, we shall see Him "face to face." It also refers to our limited knowledge here on earth as finite beings. We know now by "faith," but when we see Christ we shall be as He is—we shall know ourselves then as He knows us now. See LOOKING-GLASSES in Index.

1. Different kinds of flesh: 15:39. Paul here speaks of a "flesh of men," a "flesh of beasts," a "flesh of fish," and "another of birds." At one time this statement was attacked as being scientifically erroneous. It was an accepted theory that all flesh is made up of protoplasm, and therefore, Paul's statement of different kinds of flesh was wrong. Today, scientists are aware of the cytoplasm and the nuclei

of cells by which four kinds of flesh can be distinguished. Paul's statement is perfectly correct, even though he had nothing scientific in mind.

2. Difference in stars: 15:41. Paul in his day was well aware that stars differed greatly one from the other. J. Bayer, in 1603, devised a method or system to indicate their brightness or magnitude. No astronomer today will deny this fact. Stars are now known to differ in size, color, light emitted, density, and heat. Our sun, which is a star, is over 1,000,000 times the size of our earth, yet there are some stars at least a million times as large as our sun, and some smaller than the planet Mercury (see STARS in Index). A certain cult teaches that this "glory" (vs. 41) refers to our position in eternity—possibly a husband in the sphere of the sun, possibly his wife in the sphere of the stars, but separated for eternity—all based upon their works. When Paul spoke of the "glory of the sun, the moon, and the stars," he was referring to how the saints would be in the resurrection—together with Christ—based upon their faithfulness to the Lord (Matthew 25:14-30; I Thessalonians 4:16-18).

The Old Testament in First Corinthians

1. Man's wisdom brought to naught: 1:19 with Isaiah 29:14
2. Glorying in the Lord: 1:31 with Jeremiah 9:24
3. Truth revealed by the Spirit: 2:9,10 with Isaiah 64:4
4. Possessing the mind of Christ: 2:16 with Isaiah 40:13
5. Foolishness of the world's wisdom: 3:19 with Job 5:13
6. God's omniscience: 3:20 with Psalm 94:11
7. The mystical union in marriage: 6:16 with Genesis 2:24
8. God supplieth all needs: 9:9 with Deuteronomy 15:4; Matthew 6:33
9. Profiting by Israel's wilderness experience: 10:7,11 with Exodus 32:6
10. God, the possessor of all things: 10:26 with Psalm 24:1
11. The gift of prophecy: 14:21 with Isaiah 28:11,12
12. The first Adam: 15:45 with Genesis 2:7
13. Death swallowed up in victory: 15:54
14. Companion references:
    a. Christ's reign till enemies subdued: 15:25 with Psalm 110:1
    b. All things under His feet: 15:27 with Psalm 8:6
    c. Reveling, for tomorrow we die: 15:32 with Isaiah 22:13
    d. O death, where is thy sting? 15:55 with Hosea 13:14

1. The "Call" of Every Believer: 1:2-9
    a. Called by the gospel: II Thessalonians 2:14
    b. Called by grace: I Corinthians 1:4
    c. Called with a holy calling: II Timothy 1:9
    d. Called according to His purpose: Romans 8:28,29
    e. Called out of darkness: I Peter 2:9; Colossians 1:13
    f. Called into His marvelous light: I Peter 2:9
    g. Called to be justified: Romans 8:30
    h. Called into grace: Galatians 1:6
    i. Called to be saints: I Corinthians 1:2; Philippians 4:21
    j. Called to be enriched: I Corinthians 1:5; Ephesians 1:13,14; 2:7
    k. Called to be gifted: I Corinthians 1:7; 12:4-11
    l. Called to glorify His name: II Thessalonians 1:11,12
    m. Called to inherit a blessing: I Peter 3:9
    n. Called to be blameless: I Corinthians 1:8; Ephesians 1:4
    o. Called to fellowship: I Corinthians 1:9; I John 1:7

     p. Called to sanctification and holiness: I Corinthians 1:2; I Thessalonians 4:3,7

     q. Called unto liberty: I Corinthians 8:9; Galatians 5:13

     r. Called to walk worthy: Ephesians 4:1; Colossians 2:6

     s. Called to be servants: I Corinthians 7:22,23

     t. Called to peace: I Corinthians 7:15

     u. Called to virtue: II Peter 1:3

     v. Called unto His eternal glory: I Peter 5:10

     w. Called to partake of a heavenly calling: Hebrews 3:1

2. The Message of the Cross: 1:18-31

     a. To those who court their own ruin—*foolishness:* vs. 18a

     b. To those being saved—*God's power:* vs. 18b

     c. To the Jews—*a stumblingblock:* vs. 23a

     d. To the Gentiles—*foolishness:* vs. 23b

     e. To the believer (Jew or Gentile)—*Christ,* power and wisdom: vs. 24

3. God's Tool Chest: 1:27-29

     a. Foolish things—to put the wise to shame

     b. Weak things—to put the strong to shame

     c. Base things—to put the ignoble to shame

     d. Despised things—to put the contemptible to shame

     e. Things which are not—to put the ignorant to shame

4. Christ For Me: 1:30

     a. Wisdom, for the mind

     b. Righteousness, for the heart

     c. Sanctification, for service

     d. Redemption, for victory

5. Man's Nature

     a. *Natural*—an alien in need of salvation: 2:14

     b. *Carnal*—a babe in need of sanctification: 3:1

     c. *Spiritual*—a man in need of activation: 3:14

6. Rewards and Crowns: 3:11-15. The believer does not work to be saved, but works because he is saved. A foundation has been laid for us to build thereupon. Jesus Christ *is* that foundation. We are promised rewards if we build upon the foundation those things which glorify God; loss of reward if we build upon the foundation that which is not honoring to Him. The wise masterbuilder is straight in his doctrine, faithful in his personal soul-winning, and true in his manner of life. This assures him of rewards. To live a loose life, have a reproachful testimony, and act in the energy of the flesh, is to build upon the foundation that which will cause loss of reward. God's faithfulness in rewarding the faithful servant should be incentive enough for each believer to strive for his rewards. Rewards and crowns are to become ours at Christ's judgment seat for—

     a. Service: Ruth 2:12

     b. Enduring persecution: Matthew 5:11,12

     c. Using talents: Matthew 25:19-23

     d. Insignificant deeds: Mark 9:41

     e. Faithfulness—an incorruptible crown: I Corinthians 9:24,25

     f. Enduring trials—crown of life: James 1:12

     g. Preaching the Word—crown of glory: I Peter 5:1-4

     h. Soul-winning—crown of rejoicing: I Thessalonians 2:19,20

     i. Loving Christ's appearing—crown of righteousness: II Timothy 4:8

  Our motive for receiving rewards should not be a selfish one, but that we might have rewards and crowns to lay at the feet of Jesus in appreciation for all He did for us (Revelation 4:10,11). What a tragedy to be in heaven empty-handed! Better to have it said "saved by grace" than "saved yet so as by fire." Better to have our blessed Savior say "well done, thou good and faithful servant," than to have to stand there and see works burned, and suffer loss of reward. The fact that the Lord Himself is our Reward (Genesis 15:1) is incentive enough for any believer to faithfully serve Him, but how wonderful He is to withhold no good thing (reward) from those who walk uprightly (Psalm 84:11). See CROWNS in Index.

7. The Believer's Body. See TEMPLES in Index.
    a. The temple of God: 3:16,17; 6:19
    b. For the Lord: 6:13,15
    c. Must be presented to God: Romans 12:1
    d. The place of God's habitation: II Corinthians 6:16; Ephesians 2:21,22
    e. The place to glorify God: 6:20
    f. The place of holiness: Psalm 93:5; I Thessalonians 4:7
    g. The place of peace: Haggai 2:9; John 16:33; Philippians 4:7
    h. The object to reveal Christ: Romans 8:29; II Corinthians 4:10,11
    i. Its members instruments of righteousness: Romans 6:13
    j. To be made like Christ's: Philippians 3:20,21; I John 3:2

8. What Believers Should Know: 6
    a. That saints shall judge the world: vs. 2
    b. That we shall judge angels: vs. 3
    c. That the unrighteous shall not inherit the kingdom of God: vs. 9
    d. That their bodies are members of Christ: vs. 15
    e. That husband and wife are one: vs. 16
    f. That their bodies are the temple of the Holy Spirit: vs. 19
    g. That they have been bought with a price: vs. 20

9. Ownership—Bought with a Price: 6:20. "A man walked with his companion by a certain house and said it was his. Soon after, another man walked by the same house and remarked to his friends that it was his. A third man approached the same house with a friend and stated it was his. Pulling a key from his pocket, he opened the door and walked in. What is the explanation? The first man erected the house—it was his because he built it. The second man purchased the house—it was his because he bought it. The third man lived in it—it was his because he had his residence there.

"The Lord Jesus claims possession of Christians on all these grounds. We exist because He made us. When we are saved we are His because He bought us with His own blood. When we surrender our wills to His, He dwells in us to the fullest. We should not be satisfied with anything less than being owned in all three ways by the Lord Jesus."[3]

10. Never a Castaway: 9:26,27[4]—
    a. For believing the Bible
    b. For confessing your sin
    c. For having faith in Christ
    d. For living a godly life
    e. For doing your very best
    f. For being faithful
    g. For thinking before acting
    h. For hearing before judging
    i. For being kind to others
    j. For forgiving your enemies
    k. For helping a fallen brother
    l. For being honest in business
    m. For giving God His tithe
    n. For telling the truth
    o. For having true convictions
    p. For being loyal to Christ

11. Examples of Israel's Wilderness Experience: 10:1-15

God's Provision—

a. The protecting cloud: vs. 1a. See CLOUD in Index.

b. Deliverance through the Red Sea: vs. 1b. See DELIVERANCE in Index.

c. Daily manna: vs. 3. See MANNA in Index.

d. Water from the Rock Christ Jesus: vs. 4. See ROCK in Index.

Israel's Failure—

a. Displeased God: vs. 5

b. Lusted after evil things: vs.6

c. Some became idolaters: vs. 7a

d. Became lovers of pleasure: vs. 7b

e. Some became immoral: vs. 8

f. Tempted God: vs. 9

g. Murmured against God: vs. 10

Our Warning—

a. Recorded for our admonition: vs. 11

b. Take heed lest we fall: vs. 12

c. Rely on God's faithfulness: vs. 13

d. Profit by their mistakes: vs. 15. "Learn from the mistakes of others. You can't live long enough to make them all yourself!"

12. The Lord's Supper: 11:23-32. See PASSOVER in Index.

    a. It is an act of *remembrance* . . . "This do in remembrance of Me." This is the only thing that Jesus asked us to do in His memory.

    b. It is an act of *examination* . . . "Let a man examine himself"

    c. It is an act of *testimony* . . . "Ye do show forth the Lord's death"

    d. It is an act of *obedience* . . . "This do" (John 15:14)

    e. It is an act of *thanksgiving* . . . "He gave thanks"

    f. It is an act of *covenant* . . . "This cup is the new covenant in My blood"

    g. It is an act of *expectation* . . . "Till He comes"

13. A Communion Meditation: 11:26

    a. The *Involvement:* "as oft as ye"

    b. The *Ingredients:* "eat this bread and drink this cup"

    c. The *Individual* remembered: "ye do show the Lord's death"

    d. The *Incentive:* "till He come"

14. Wine. It is interesting to note that the word "wine" is *not* used in connection with the Lord's Supper. "Wine" is a generic term, and can either apply to the fresh juice of the fruit or the fermented stage. In the Supper the drink is referred to as the "cup," or "He took the cup" (Matthew 26:27; Mark 14:23; Luke 22:17,20; I Corinthians 11:25-28). It would hardly seem consistent to use the same type of wine in the Memorial Supper that the Bible elsewhere condemns (Proverbs 20:1; 23:29,30).

Did Christ turn water into fermented wine (John 2:1-11)? Was Timothy advised to drink fermented wine (I Timothy 5:23)? When the word "wine" is used in these instances, it could have well been fermented. Certainly, simple grape juice could not have aided Timothy's condition. When fermented wine was used in those days, according to archaeological discoveries, it was always diluted—sometimes as much as twenty parts water to one part of wine, sometimes the ratio was three parts water to one part wine. Drinking wine, unmixed with water, is referred to as "strong drink," or "red wine," and was looked upon as a "Sythian" or a "barbarian" custom.

In several instances in the Old Testament a distinction was made between "wine" and "strong drink." Aaron and his sons were to drink neither (Leviticus 10:8,9). This also applied to the Nazarite vow (Numbers 6:3). When Proverbs 20:1 refers to "wine as a mocker, and strong drink is raging," the advice is to one who is deceived into thinking he can drink it "straight" and not be contaminated thereby. It was when it is not mixed with water that it becomes evil. See Judges 13:4,7,14; I Samuel 1:15; Isaiah 5:11,22; 56:12 and Proverbs 23:31-33. It appears as though God condemns it for any purpose, including social drinking, unless it is for medicinal purposes, such as in the case of Timothy. Notice even then the dose was to be "a little wine," and as was the custom, mixed with water.

15. The Gift of Helps: 12:28. An important gift, so often overlooked or minimized, is that of "helps," helping one another. Andrew helped Peter to see his need of Christ (John 1:40,41). A lad helped to feed over 5,000 (John 6:8-11). Joseph of Arimathaea, with Nicodemus, helped in the burial of Jesus (John 19:38-42). Women helped spread the good news of Jesus' resurrection (Matthew 28:1-10). Deacons were chosen to help widows in their need (Acts 6:1-6). An "unknown" helped Paul escape persecution in Damascus (Acts 9:22-25). Barnabas helped Paul to be recognized by other believers (Acts 9:26,27). Aquila and Priscilla helped Apollos to have a better understanding of the Scriptures (Acts 18:24-26), and Apollos in turn helped other believers (Acts 18:27,28). Paul spoke highly of "helpers" in the gospel, such as Epaphras, for his fervent prayers (Colossians 4:12), Epaphroditus, because of his sacrificial living and giving (Philippians 2:25,30), Onesimus, for his faithfulness (Colossians 4:9), the women at Philippi because of their labors (Philippians 4:3), those at Thessalonica for their evangelical zeal (1:1-10), Onesiphorus, because of his love and friendship (II Timothy 1:16), etc., etc. Many examples are listed in the Old Testament, such as the widow who helped Elijah (I Kings 17:1-16). The word "helps" refers generally to those who in any way render assistance in the church, and may refer to temporal affairs of its members—to care for the poor, the widows, the orphans in distributing alms and love, to the instruction of the ignorant, to be a real "helper" to the pastor, etc. There is no evidence that this gift refers to an office in the church.

How long has it been since *you* went out of your way to help others with an act of love or kindness, or gift, or friendship, or words of encouragement to a lost soul in need of Christ, or by starting a Bible class, or by giving a cup of cold water in Christ's name, or by entertaining missionaries (angels unawares), etc., etc. Our example is Jesus, who "went about doing good," having compassion on the people (Mark 6:34; Acts 10:38).

16. The "Love" Chapter: 13. The word "charity" is rendered "love." In this chapter we find the qualities of love. It is essential, patient, kind, generous, humble, modest, unselfish, mild, pure, holy, longsuffering, believing, hopeful, eternal, and supreme. It is also peaceful and all-sufficient (Romans 13:10), and divine (I John 4:7). Since God is Love (I John 4:8), and Christ and His Father are one (John 10:30), we can use the word "Christ" in the place of "charity" (vss. 1-3). In verses 4-8, notice what Christ (charity) does and does not do:

DOES	DOES NOT
a. Suffers long: vs. 4a	a. Envy: vs. 4c
b. Is kind: vs. 4b	b. Vaunt Himself: vs. 4d
c. Rejoices in truth: vs. 6	c. Puff Himself up: vs. 4e
d. Bears all things: vs. 7a	d. Behave unseemly: vs. 5a
e. Believes all things: vs. 7b	e. Seek His own: vs. 5b
f. Hopes all things: vs. 7c	f. Provoke easily: vs. 5c
g. Endures all things: vs. 7d	g. Think evil: vs. 5d
h. Never fails: vs. 8a	h. Rejoice in iniquity: vs. 6a

Just as Christ and God are one, so are we in Christ Jesus, one with Him and with the Father (John 17:23). With this truth in mind, we can substitute the pronoun "I" for "charity"—

a. I suffer long	a. I do not envy
b. I am kind	b. I do not vaunt myself
c. I rejoice in truth	c. I am not puffed up
d. I bear all things	d. I do not behave unseemly
e. I believe all things	e. I seek not my own
f. I hope all things	f. I am not easily provoked

g. I endure all things   g. I think no evil

h. I never fail   h. I rejoice not in iniquity

This is the believer's *position*. The question is asked: "Does my *practice* come up to my position?" See CHART, p. 579.

17. The Gospel: 15:3,4. See GOSPEL in Index.

    a. Christ died—for our sin and salvation: vs. 3 with Romans 5:6-11. It delivers us from the penalty of sin: II Corinthians 1:10a

    b. Christ buried—to crucify and bury self: vs. 4a with Romans 6:33-36. We are to "reckon" ourselves dead and buried: Romans 6:11

    c. Christ raised—for our justification: vs. 4b with Romans 4:25b. It gives us power over sin: II Corinthians 1:10b

    d. Christ coming again—for our glorification: vss. 23,51-57. This will deliver us from the presence of sin: II Corinthians 1:10c

18. I Am What I Am: 15:10

—Justified: Romans 5:1a

—Declared righteous: Romans 3:25; II Corinthians 5:21

—Sanctified (set apart): Hebrews 10:10; I Corinthians 6:11. See SANCTIFICATION in Index.

—Child of God by spiritual birth: John 1:12,13

—Child of God by adoption: Romans 8:15; Ephesians 1:5. See ADOPTION in Index.

—New creation: II Corinthians 5:17

—Heir of God: Romans 8:17a

—Joint-heir with Christ: Romans 8:17b

—Member of Christ's body: I Corinthians 12:12,13; Ephesians 5:29,30

—Temple of God: I Corinthians 3:16,17; 6:19,20

—Chosen generation: I Peter 2:9a

—Royal priesthood: I Peter 2:9b

—Holy nation: I Peter 2:9c

—Peculiar: I Peter 2:9d

—Crucified with Christ: Romans 6:6; Galatians 2:20

—Dead with Christ: Romans 6:8

—Buried with Christ: Romans 6:4a,5a

—Raised with Him: Colossians 2:12,13; Romans 6:3-5

—Seated in the heavenlies: Ephesians 2:5,6

—Not of this world: John 17:15,16

—In Christ's kingdom: Colossians 1:13

—Delivered from present evil world: Galatians 1:3,4

—Child of light to the lost: Acts 13:47; Ephesians 5:8

—Co-laborer with God: I Corinthians 3:9

—Servant of righteousness: Romans 6:18

—God's workmanship: Ephesians 2:10

—Like Christ: I John 4:17b

—At peace with God: Romans 5:1b

—Ambassador: II Corinthians 5:20; Acts 1:8

—Salt of the earth: Matthew 5:13

—Victorious: I Corinthians 15:57

—Glorified: Romans 8:30

—Complete in Christ: Colossians 2:10

—Heaven bound: I John 3:1,2; John 14:1-3

Has the grace of God, which made us all this, been bestowed upon us in vain? There is only one way to be sure that it has not—"labor more abundantly than they all: yet not I, but the grace of God with me."

19. Christ's Resurrection: 15:12-20. See RESURRECTION in Index.

20. First Natural, Afterward the Spiritual: 15:42-50. The things of the Old Testament, which were written for our learning (Romans 15:4), are considered *natural*—truth to convey to us that which was to follow—the *spiritual.*

    a. Ensamples (types or object lessons): I Corinthians 10:11
    b. Weak and beggarly elements: Galatians 4:9
    c. Imperfect: Hebrews 7:11; 10:1-4
    d. Shadow of heavenly things: Hebrews 8:5
    e. Worldly (earthly): Hebrews 9:1
    f. Figures of the time then present—figures of the true: Hebrews 9:9,24
    g. Carnal ordinances: Hebrews 9:10
    h. Patterns: Hebrews 9:23
    i. Shadow of good things to come: Hebrews 10:1

"First natural, and afterwards that which is spiritual," does not "spiritualize" the things of God to the extent that things spiritual are not *real* or *literal,* for things spiritual are just as real and literal as things which are natural. Notice—

NATURAL	SPIRITUAL
Adam	*Christ*
I Corinthians 15:45a,47a	I Corinthians 15:45b,47b
Romans 5:12,14a	Romans 5:14b
I Corinthians 15:22a	I Corinthians 15:22b
Abraham's Seed	*Believers in Christ*
Genesis 12:3	Galatians 3:16,29
Nation (Jews only)	*Holy Nation* (believers today)
Genesis 12:2; 17:4,5	Romans 4:11,12,16,17
Exodus 19:6	I Peter 2:9
Rest—the Land (home of the	*Rest—heaven* (home of the
natural seed of Abraham)	spiritual seed of Abraham)
Genesis 15:18-21	Hebrews 3:17—4:11
Joshua 21:43,44	Hebrews 11:13-16
Circumcision of the flesh	*Circumcision of the heart*
Genesis 17:10-14	Romans 2:28,29
	Philippians 3:3
	Colossians 2:11
Passover Lamb	*Christ* (the Lamb of God)
Exodus 12:1-28	John 1:29
	I Corinthians 5:7
	Revelation 13:8
Manna	*Christ*
Exodus 16:4,5,15,16	John 6:30-58
Meat (quail)	*Christ*
Exodus 16:8,12,13	I Corinthians 10:3
Water	*Christ*
Exodus 17:6	I Corinthians 10:4;
	John 4:14
The Old Covenant	*The New Covenant*
Exodus 19:3,5,6,8	Jeremiah 31:31-34
	Matthew 26:26-28
	Hebrews 8:6-13; 10:1-18
Tabernacle	*Christ*
Exodus 25:8,9	John 1:14
	Hebrews 8:1-6; 9:11

Priesthood of Aaron	*Priesthood of Believers*
—by natural birth	—by spiritual birth
Exodus 28:1; Leviticus 8,9	I Peter 2:5,9
Sacrifices by the priests	*Sacrifices by believers*
Leviticus 1—7	Romans 12:1; I Peter 2:5
Numbers 6:17	Hebrews 13:15,16
Jerusalem (earthly)	*Jerusalem* (heavenly)
Psalm 122:3,4; 147:12	Hebrews 11:10
Isaiah 4:3; 52:1	Galatians 4:26
	Hebrews 12:22
David's earthly kingdom	*Christ's kingdom not of this*
—monarchy	*world*—theocracy
II Samuel 7:16b	John 18:36,37
	Colossians 1:13
	Romans 14:17
	Hebrews 12:27,28
Solomon's Temple	*Christ's own body, the Church;*
I Kings 5:1—7:51	*—the believer's body*
	John 2:19-21
	Ephesians 2:20-22
	I Corinthians 3:16,17

21. For the Believer at Christ's Coming.
    a. We shall all be changed: 15:51-53
    b. We shall be like Christ: Philippians 3:20,21; I John 3:2
    c. We shall be judged and rewarded: 3:11-15; Revelation 22:12
    d. We shall receive personal knowledge: 13:12
    e. We shall receive victory
       —Over mortality: 15:53
       —Over death: 15:54
       —Over the grave: 15:55
       —Over sin: 15:56,57
    f. We shall ever be with the Lord: I Thessalonians 4:16,17

A BIT OF HEAVENLY MANNA

Paul certainly must have been a psychologist, for throughout his Epistles he appeals to his hearers to consider what they are in Christ Jesus. This, of course, is true Christian psychology, for the Holy Spirit uses Paul to reveal to the believer what he actually is by the grace of God. What better incentive could be used for godly living! What better incentive could be used to lead us to a complete surrender to the One who dwells within us. It may be hard to fathom the truth that every believer is God's temple, but God's Word is true, and we are told—

THE SPIRIT OF GOD DWELLETH IN YOU—3:16[5]

"Dwelleth in whom? In every Christian. For, 'if any man have not the Spirit of Christ, he is none of His.' Wherever the Spirit dwells, He works, and His work is the efficient cause of our sanctification, comfort, and usefulness. He dwells in us as the Spirit of light, quickening and reviving, instructing and illuminating. As the Spirit of liberty, delivering from bondage, dread, and terror. As the Spirit of love, shedding abroad the love of God in our hearts and leading us to love Him and all His people. As the Spirit of power, enabling us to conquer the world, overcome Satan, and crucify the old man with his deeds. As the Spirit of prayer, teaching us to pray, making intercession for us with groanings which cannot be uttered. As the Spirit of peace, applying the atonement, giving us peace with God through the Lord Jesus Christ, and producing in us a peaceable disposition. As the Spirit of Christ, exalting Him in our minds, enthroning Him in our hearts, and glorifying Him in us and by us. Would to God we lived, moved, and spoke under the influence of this truth—'the Spirit of God dwelleth in me!' If we did, it would have a very sanctifying effect upon us, for we could not *go* to some of the places we go, we could not *say* some of the things we say, and we could not *do* some of the things we do. We will often ask ourselves, 'Is this becoming in one who is the residence of the Spirit of God?' 'Ought I, in whom the Spirit dwells, be found here?' O beloved, what an honor God has put upon us by letting His Spirit dwell within.''

PRAYER THOUGHT: "Dear Lord, deliver me from any habits that harm, from an unforgiving spirit that hinders, and from a life that would cause a weaker child of Thine to stumble. Help me not to be a reproach to Thee. In Christ's name I pray. Amen.''[6]

I Corinthians 8:9-13

Second Corinthians—The Book of a Minister's Heart

Name: See NAME in I Corinthians.

Occasion of Writing: At the conclusion of the first Epistle to the Corinthians, the apostle Paul announced his intention of visiting the believers in Corinth as he was passing through Macedonia, which was a definite change in his previous plan of sailing directly from Ephesus to Corinth, and, consequently, meant a more or less extended postponement of this visitation. This caused great dissatisfaction in the Corinthian church. Some said Paul was inconsistent, others that he was afraid to show his face. In fact, the entire church was immersed in a heated debate over the motive and methods of apostolic authority of the great apostle, which, of course, deeply grieved him. Not more than a year separated the writings of his two epistles to the Corinthians.

Contents: ''We might say, without exaggeration, that not only is II Corinthians the most personal of all Paul's Epistles, but it is, indeed, sort of an apology for his apostolic life and ministry. Unjust charges, calumnies, and insinuations had been made against him. For this reason, we find the whole inner life of the apostle revealed before us. Human weakness, spiritual strength, the deepest and tenderest of affection, wounded feeling, sternness, irony, rebuke, impassioned self-vindication, humility, self-respect, zeal for the welfare of the weak and suffering, as well as for the progress of the church of Christ, and for the spiritual advancement of its members, are all displayed by turns in the course of his appeal, and are bound together by the golden cord of an absolute self-renunciation dictated by love to God and man.''[1] Second Corinthians has 13 chapters, 257 verses, and 6,092 words.

Character: Church Epistle.

Subject: Service unto God resulting from union with the Head of the Church and the members of the body of Christ.

Purpose: To show that the Christian is God's ambassador with a spiritual and glorious ministry, finding in Christ consolation in all His suffering and sufficiency for every trial.

Outline:
  I. Salutation and Thanksgiving: 1:1-11
  II. Characteristics of Paul's Ministry: 1:12—7:16
  III. Concerning the Collection for the Poor at Jerusalem: 8,9
  IV. Paul's Defense of His Apostolic Ministry: 10:1—13:10
  V. Conclusion: 13:11—14

Writer: Paul: 1:1,2. See WRITER in Romans.

When and Where Written: A.D. 56, on Paul's third missionary journey, probably from Philippi, after the events of Acts 19:23—20:3.

Key Chapter: 5. Promise of immortality.

Key Verses: 4:5; 5:17.

Key Word: Boast, or glory. Both are translated from the same Greek word.

Key Phrase: The signs of an apostle: 12:12.

Key Thought: Paul's defense of his ministry.

Spiritual Thought: My grace is sufficient for thee: 12:9.

Christ Is Seen As: Our Sufficiency: 3:5.

Names and Titles of Christ. See NAME in Dictionary.
  1. Jesus Christ: 1:1
  2. Lord Jesus Christ: 1:2
  3. Christ: 1:5
  4. Lord Jesus: 1:14
  5. Son of God: 1:19
  6. Lord: 2:12
  7. Image of God: 4:4
  8. Christ Jesus: 4:5
  9. Jesus: 4:5,10
  10. God: 5:19
  11. God's unspeakable Gift: 9:15

Names and Titles of God. See NAME in Dictionary.
  1. Father: 1:2; 11:31
  2. Father of mercies: 1:3a
  3. God of all comfort: 1:3b
  4. True God: 1:18
  5. The living God: 6:16
  6. Lord Almighty: 6:18b

Names and Titles of the Holy Spirit. See NAME in Dictionary.
  1. The Spirit: 1:22; 5:5
  2. Spirit of the living God: 3:3
  3. Lord: 3:17a
  4. Spirit of the Lord: 3:17b
  5. Holy Ghost: 6:6; 13:14

Miracles Referred to:
  1. Deliverance from death and persecution: 11:23-33
  2. Paul caught up into third heaven: 12:1-4
  3. Signs, wonders, and mighty deeds: 12:12

1. The "Bema," or Judgment Seat of Christ: 5:10. See BEMA in Seed Thoughts, point 9.

2. When Paul wrote his second letter to those in Corinth, he stated he was "in perils of robbers" (11:26). He was probably referring to his journey between Perga and Antioch. A number of inscriptions from this area of Paul's day refer to armed policemen and soldiers who patrolled this section and kept peace because of a conflict with robbers. This could explain why John Mark decided to leave Paul and Barnabas when they reached Perga (Acts 13:13; 15:36-40).

The Old Testament in II Corinthians:
1. A veil over Moses' face: 3:13 with Exodus 34:33
2. The spirit of faith: 4:13 with Psalm 116:10
3. Now is the day of salvation: 6:2 with Isaiah 49:8
4. God indwelling the believer: 6:16 with Leviticus 26:11,12
5. Separation from the unclean thing: 6:17 with Isaiah 52:11
6. God a Father: 6:18 with Jeremiah 31:1,9
7. God abundantly supplying our need: 8:15 with Exodus 16:18
8. God's care for the poor: 9:9 with Psalm 112:9
9. Glorying in the Lord: 10:17 with Jeremiah 9:24
10. Truth established by two witnesses: 13:1 with Deuteronomy 17:6

1. Deliverance from Sin: 1:9,10
   a. *Past*—delivered from the penalty of sin
   b. *Present*—doth deliver from the power of sin
   c. *Future*—will yet deliver from the presence of sin
2. The Promises of God: 1:20
   a. Eternal life—
   Promise: I John 2:25; John 10:28
   Condition: John 5:24
   b. Pardon of sin—
   Promise: Hebrews 10:16-18; Isaiah 1:18
   Condition: Isaiah 55:7; I John 1:9; Proverbs 28:13
   c. Peace—
   Promise: John 14:27
   Condition: Romans 5:1
   d. Joy—
   Promise: John 16:20,22
   Condition: I Peter 1:8,9; Romans 15:13
   e. Deliverance from temptation—
   Promise: I Corinthians 10:13
   Condition: Matthew 26:41
   f. Victory over sin—
   Promise: Romans 6:6
   Condition: Romans 6:11
   g. Rest—
   Promise: Hebrews 4:9

        Condition: Matthew 11:28-30
   h. Heaven—
      Promise: John 14:1-3
      Condition: Hebrews 11:1,10,14,16

3. Characteristics of the Ministry
   a. Ministry of responsibility: 2:14—3:5
   b. Ministry of glory: 3:6—4:6
   c. Ministry in earthen vessels: 4:7-18
   d. Ministry of consummation: 5:1-11
   e. Ministry of reconciliation: 5:12-21
   f. Ministry of approval: 6:1-13
   g. Ministry of purity: 6:14—7:1

4. Living Letters: 3:2,3. The Christian is a living epistle, known and read of all men.
   a. As a letter is written on prepared material, so the Christian is God's prepared material upon which He writes His message—conformed to the image of His dear Son (Romans 8:29).
   b. As a letter must be legible to be read, so the Christian must live (show) so others can see and read God's message (Luke 8:39).
   c. As a letter must be free of blots so the reader can get the full import of its message, so the Christian must not be spotted by the flesh if the message of salvation is to be understood (Jude 23).
   d. As the writer of a letter is recognized by the style of handwriting, so the sinner recognizes a Christian by his style of godly living (Titus 2:12).
   e. As a letter bears the expression of the writer, so the Christian must bear about in his body the life of Jesus Christ (II Corinthians 4:10-13).
   f. As a letter bears the signature of the writer, so the Christian puts his name on the line for God—"yet not I, but Christ in me" (I Corinthians 15:10; Galatians 2:20).
   g. As a letter bears the time of writing (date), so the Christian, in season and out of season, sends forth the time of salvation—"now is the day" (II Timothy 4:2; II Corinthians 6:2).
   h. As a letter bears an address, so the Christian reveals a message of direction—the straight and narrow road that leads to life eternal (Matthew 7:14).
   i. As a letter is sealed and bears a proper stamp to assure readiness for delivery, so the Christian, as a debtor to all men, is stamped with the responsibility of readiness to preach the gospel to every creature (Romans 1:14-16).

5. The Believer's Calling and Responsibility:
   a. Epistles of Christ: 3:3
   b. Ambassadors for Christ: 5:20
   c. Servants of the Lord: John 13:16
   d. Cross-bearing disciples: Luke 14:27
   e. Salt of the earth: Matthew 5:13
   f. Light of the world: Matthew 5:14a
   g. City on a hill: Matthew 5:14b
   h. Fruit-bearing branches: John 15:5
   i. Enduring soldiers: II Timothy 2:3
   j. Witnesses of the gospel: Isaiah 43:10; Acts 1:8
   k. Friends of Christ: John 15:14

6. The Law *versus* the Gospel—

LAW		GOSPEL
Old Covenant	3:6	New Covenant
The letter	3:6	The Spirit
Killeth	3:6	Giveth life
Ministration of death	3:7,8	Ministration of life
Written on stone	3:7,7	Written in the heart
Glorious	3:7-11	Glory that excelleth

Condemns	3:9	Makes righteous
Taken away	3:11	Remaineth
Veiled	3:12-16	Plainness
Binds	3:17	Sets free
Fails to transform	3:18	Transforms

7. Servants for Jesus' Sake: 4:5.[2] Nothing is clearer in the New Testament than that Christ expects us to take the low position of servants. In the Old Testament there were two types of servants: (1) hired servants, receiving wages, and having certain rights; and (2) bondservants, or slaves, with no rights, no wages, and no appeal. The New Testament word for the servant of Christ is not "hired servant" but "bondservant," meaning that our position is one where we are the absolute property of our Master, where we have no rights and no appeal, and are to be treated and disposed of just as our Master wishes.

We see more clearly our position when we see the humility of Christ as a servant, without rights, willing to be treated as the will of the Father and the malice of men might decree, only that He might serve men and bring them back to God (Philippians 2:5-8). Our servanthood to Christ is expressed in our servanthood to others—"we preach not ourselves, but Christ Jesus the Lord, and ourselves your [bond] servants [slaves] for Jesus' sake" (4:5). The low position we take toward the Lord Jesus is judged by the low position we take in relation to others. In Luke 17:7-10 there are five marks of a bondservant:

a. He must be willing to have one thing on top of another put upon him, without any consideration being given him: vss. 7,8
b. He must be willing not to be thanked for his service: vs. 9
c. Even though the master may seem selfish and inconsiderate, the servant must not charge him with selfishness: vs. 10a
d. Having done all the other, the servant has no ground for pride or self-congratulation, but must confess that he is an unprofitable servant: vs. 10b
e. He must admit that doing and bearing what he has in the way of meekness and humility, he has not done one bit more than was his duty to do: vs. 10c

This is the way that God's lowly Bondservant first trod for us, and should not we, the bondservants of that Bondservant, tread it still? Does it seem hard and forbidding, this way down? Be assured, it is the only way up! It was the way by which the Lord Jesus reached the Throne, and it is the way by which we too reach the place of spiritual power, authority, and fruitfulness (Luke 14:11; I Peter 5:5,6).

8. The "New" Things of Chapter Five:

a. A new body—a building of God: vs. 1
b. A new likeness—immortality: vss. 2-4
c. A new assurance—the earnest of the Spirit: vs. 5
d. A new hope—absent from the body, present with the Lord: vss. 6,8
e. A new acceptance—walking and working by faith: vss. 7,9
f. A new judgment—Christ's judgment seat, for believers only: vs. 10
g. A new motive—the love of Christ: vs. 14
h. A new life—not for self, but unto the Lord: vs. 15
i. A new creation—in Christ: vs. 17a
j. A new practice—all things new: vs. 17b
k. A new attitude—acceptance of all things as from God: vs. 18
l. A new message—the word of reconciliation: vs. 19
m. A new service—ambassadors for Christ: vs. 20
n. A new standing—the righteousness of God in Christ: vs. 21

9. The "Bema"—Judgment Seat of Christ: 5:10. When Paul was taken to court in Achaia of Corinth before the judgment seat of Gallio to answer charges raised against him by the Jews for preaching Christ (Acts 18:12-16), he had occasion later to remember this experience when he wrote back to those in Corinth. He said in effect: "Not all of us will have to appear before an

Gallio's "Bema"

earthly judge, but we must all appear before Christ's judgment seat so that each of us may receive our rewards, according to what has been done, whether it be good or bad." See REWARDS and BEMA in Index.

10. "New" in Christ Jesus: 5:17
   Transformations in Christ—
   a. A new creation: 5:17 (RV)
   b. A new man: Ephesians 4:24; Colossians 3:9,10
   c. A new birth: John 3:3
   Inheritance in Christ:
   a. A new covenant: Jeremiah 31:31; Hebrews 9:11-15
   b. A new name: Isaiah 62:2; Revelation 2:17
   Possessions in Christ—

    a. A new heart: Ezekiel 36:26
    b. A new spirit: Ezekiel 11:19
    c. A new tongue: Mark 16:17
    d. A new song: Psalm 40:3
    e. A new highway: Hebrews 10:20
    Expectations in Christ—
    a. A new heaven and a new earth: Isaiah 65:17; II Peter 3:13
    b. All things to be made new: Revelation 21:5
    c. A new Jerusalem: Revelation 21:2

11. The "Alls" of the Bible. The expression "all things" occurs at least 221 times in the Scriptures. In relation to believers—
    a. All things are of God—as to their source: 5:18
    b. All things are for our sake—as to their object: 4:15; I Corinthians 3:21-23
    c. All things work together for our good—as to their purpose: Romans 8:28
    d. All things are arranged by Christ, our Head: Ephesians 1:22
    e. They are privileged to know all things: I John 2:20
    f. They have power to do all things: Philippians 4:13
    g. They have faith to believe that all things are possible: Mark 9:23
    h. They give thanks for all things: Ephesians 5:20
    i. They cast all care on the Lord: I Peter 5:7
    j. They are preserved from all evil: Psalm 121:7
    k. They have all their need supplied: Philippians 4:19
    l. They can pray for all things in faith believing: Matthew 21:22
    m. They are more than conquerors through Christ: Romans 8:37
    n. They can prove all things: I Thessalonians 5:21
    o. They praise God for all His works: Psalm 145:10
    p. All things enable them to live prayerfully and godly: I Peter 4:7
    q. They will inherit all things: Revelation 21:7

12. "Now." The Lord puts His special notice on words to show us the importance of the message. The greatest word in the Bible is *God*. The sweetest word is *love*. The tenderest word is *come*. The longest word is *eternity*. The shortest word is *now*.
    a. *Now* is God's time for mercy: Luke 14:17
    b. *Now* is God's time for salvation: 6:2 with II Kings 7:9
    c. *Now* is God's time for acceptance of Christ: 6:2; Hebrews 3:7,8
    d. *Now* is the right time for blessings: Luke 19:42
    e. *Now* is the right time for watchfulness: Romans 13:11
    f. *Now* is the only time for witnessing: II Timothy 4:2

13. The Separated Life: 6:14—7:1
    God commands it—
    a. Be ye separate: vss. 14,17
    b. Live soberly, righteously, and godly: Titus 2:11-15
    c. Abstain from all appearances of evil: I Thessalonians 5:22
    Success depends upon it—
    a. We cannot love God and the world at the same time: I John 2:15
    b. We cannot serve God and mammon and/or man: Matthew 6:24; Romans 6:16
    c. We cannot be temples of God and defile them: I Corinthians 3:16,17
    d. We become stumbling blocks if we are not separated: I Corinthians 8:9-13
    e. We glorify God if we are separated: I Peter 2:12
    The need of separation—
    a. What fellowship has righteousness with unrighteousness: vs. 14a
    b. What communion has light with darkness: vs. 14b
    c. What concord (harmony) has Christ with Belial (Satan): vs. 15a
    d. What part has the believer with the infidel: vs. 15b

e. What agreement has God's temple with idols: vs. 16

The practice of separation—

a. Cleanse ourselves from all filthiness: vs. 17a; 7:1a

b. Perfect holiness in the fear of God: 7:1b; I Thessalonians 4:3,7

Promises to the separated—

a. I will receive you: vs. 17b

b. I will be a Father unto you: vs. 18a

c. Ye shall be My sons and daughters: vs. 18b

14. Godly Sorrow Worketh Repentance: 7:9,10. See REPENTANCE in Index.

Its importance shown in—

a. Message of John: Matthew 3:1,2

b. Message of Christ: Matthew 4:17; Luke 24:47

c. Message of the Twelve: Mark 6:12

d. Message of Peter: Acts 2:38

e. Message of Paul: Acts 26:20

f. The desire of God: II Peter 3:9

g. God's command: Acts 17:30

Its meaning—

a. As touching the emotions:

—Hatred of sin: Psalm 97:10

—Sorrow for sin: vs. 9

b. As touching the will:

—Change of mind or view concerning God's way: Matthew 21:29

—Obedience with respect to God's will: Luke 15:18-20

Its manifestation—

a. In confession of sin:

—To God—inward: Psalm 32:3-5; I John 1:9

—To man—outward: James 5:16; Matthew 5:23,24; Luke 19:8,9

Its results—

a. Joy in heaven: Luke 15:7,10

b. Pardon, forgiveness, and blessings: Isaiah 55:7; Acts 3:19

15. Systematic Giving: 9:7,8

a. Commanded by God—*so* let him give: vs. 7

b. For every man: Deuteronomy 16:17

c. To give tithes and offerings: Malachi 3:8

d. Not grudgingly, or of necessity, but cheerfully: vs. 7

e. For God's blessings: vs. 8; Proverbs 3:9,10; Mark 10:29,30

An old miser was telling a friend he couldn't understand why people complained about his being tight. "I've willed my money to churches and charitable organizations, yet I'm looked down upon." His friend told him a story about a pig and a cow. Said the pig, "When I die, just look at all the bacon, lard, chops, ham, and bristles they'll get." Said the cow, with a look of contentment, "They'll get a lot from me too, when I die, but just look at all the fresh milk and butter I'm giving while I'm living." So, said the friend to Mr. Miser, "Better to do your givin' while you're livin' and then you're 'a knowin' where it's all a'goin'."[3]

16. Satan's Preachers: 11;13,15. See FALSE Preachers in Index. Satan's ministers are responsible for modernism.

What Is Modernism?[4]

"Modernism has no message, for it denies the only hope of the world, a supernatural Bible and a supernatural Christ. It is rooted in evolution and therefore rotten to the source. It denies the depravity of the human heart and the need of a blood-bought redemption. It laughs at a 'slaughterhouse' theology and eliminates the 'blood' songs from our hymnals. It takes the name of our Lord 'Emmanuel' and removes the 'Em' from the beginning and the 'uel' from the ending, leaving only 'man.' It gives to the congregation a set of blocks, and lets the people spell 'God' the best they can. It calls weakness what God calls wickedness, recommends culture instead of Calvary, and polish instead of pardon. It has tried to revise the Bible, streamline the gospel, remodel heaven, explain away the devil, and air-condition hell. It has no 'hallelujah.' It never produced a revival. It never saved a soul. It never convicted a sinner. It never changed a dope fiend into a disciple. It never transformed a criminal into a Christian. It never took away a drunkard's love for booze or loosed a libertine from the shackles of lust. It never converted a church member. It is a form without force, a religion without redemption. It defies the Book, denies the blood and derides the 'Blessed Hope,' and the wrath of God is upon it.''

17. Satan's Homiletics, or ''How to Preach so that No One will be Converted.''[5]
   a. Study to please the people and thus secure an audience and make a reputation for self.
   b. Take popular, passing, and sensational themes to draw the crowds; spice them with jokes and avoid the essential doctrines of salvation.
   c. Denounce sin in the abstract, but pass over lightly the sins that prevail in your congregation.
   d. When asked: ''Is it wrong for me to participate in worldliness (drinking, dope, smoking, etc.),'' answer pleasantly—''Oh, that's a matter of private judgment; it is not for me to say who shall and who shall not.'' Condone free love and insist there is no moral wrong in pre-marital sex relations, thus receiving the esteem of the young people.
   e. Preach on the loveliness of self-righteousness and the glory of heaven, but not on the sinfulness of sin and the terrors of hell.
   f. Reprove the sins of the absent, but make those present pleased with themselves so they will enjoy the sermon and not go away with their feelings hurt, but still comfortable in their sins.
   g. Let your motive be popularity and salary rather than salvation for the lost and the edification of the saints.
   h. Make the impression on worldly church members that God is too good and loving to send anyone to hell—if there is such a place.
   i. Encourage men to live moral lives, and tell them that if they do they need not fear that they will die wrong.
   j. Preach the universal Fatherhood of God and the Brotherhood of man, so that no second birth is really necessary.
   k. Do not rebuke the worldliness of the church and try to make it fundamental and peculiar, but fall in with the ''Amusement Heresy'' and ''Cooking Stove Apostasy.''
   l. Avoid seriousness, alarm, and earnest efforts to pull sinners out of the fire, and the old-fashioned idea that the church is a Rescue Mission.
   m. Join some leading secret society, taking their dreadful oaths, and become all things to all men even in their wicked associations.
   n. Devote much time to humanitarian organizations instead of spending time in prayer.
   o. To make religion attractive, and to make the church progressive and up-to-date, split it into worldly clubs and societies to cultivate worldly sociability, fun, and merchandising. Instead of meeting for prayer, let the congregation ''Sit down to eat and drink and rise up to play.''
   p. If you must mention Christ at all, present Him as a wonderful teacher and example, but never as God's sacrifice for sin—never as the One who died on a cross to save the world.

18. Satan—His Works; His Ministers: 11:13-15. Originally, Satan was ''Lucifer, son of the morning'' (Isaiah 14:12). Pride brought about his downfall, and ever since he, along with his emissaries (fallen angels—demons), has been God's arch enemy (Isaiah 14:12-15; I John 3:8a; I Timothy 3:6; II Peter 2:4; Jude 6). God promised defeat to Satan (at Calvary—Genesis 3:15) and final judgment in the lake of fire (Revelation 20:10). Though Satan is now a defeated foe (and his emissaries have been spoiled—John 16:11; Colossians 2:15), he still is a busy enemy—

     a. Going about seeking whom he may devour: I Peter 5:8

     b. Trying to keep sinners from being saved: Luke 8:11,12

     c. Trying to keep believers from exalting Christ in their lives: II Corinthians 12:7; I Peter 5:8-10

     d. Causing suffering: Acts 10:38; Luke 13:16; Job 2:7

     e. Alluring to evil—
         —With his devices: II Corinthians 2:11
         —With his wiles: Ephesians 6:11,12RV; Ephesians 4:14 (RV)
         —With miraculous power: II Thessalonians 2:9; Matthew 24:24
         —With deception: II Corinthians 11:14; II Thessalonians 2:10
         —With temptation: I Thessalonians 3:5. See also Christ's Temptation: Matthew 4:1-10

     f. Ensnaring men: I Timothy 3:7

     g. Inspiring wicked thoughts and purposes: John 13:2; Acts 5:3

     h. Taking possession of men: John 13:27; Ephesians 4:27 with James 4:7

     i. Blinding the minds of men: II Corinthians 4:4 (RV)

     j. Dissipating the truth: Mark 4:15; Luke 8:12RV; Matthew 13:19

     k. Mixing his children with God's: Matthew 13:25,28,29

     l. Energizing his ministers: II Corinthians 11:13,15; Ephesians 2:2,3

     m. Opposing God's servants by—
         —Hindering them: I Thessalonians 2:18 (RV)
         —Resisting them: Zechariah 3:1
         —Buffeting them: II Corinthians 12:7. This opposition results in good for true believers. It keeps them humble and drives them to prayer that they might rely upon God's grace: II Corinthians 12:8,9.

     n. Testing believers: Luke 22:31. Peter came out of Satan's merciless sieve purer wheat than he ever was before. Satan simply removed the chaff. Peter's denial and Pentecost prove this. See Romans 8:28.

     o. Accusing the brethren: Revelation 12:9,10

     p. Causing death: Hebrews 2:14. Christ wrested the weapon of death from Satan (Revelation 1:18), but we must remember that death is a by-product of sin. Only the sting of death has been removed. When the devil is finally cast into the lake of fire, death will be swallowed up in victory.

All humans, whether sinner or saint, are subject to the influence of the devil and his demons.

     a. The sinner: Matthew 12:43-45
         —disembodied spirit (demon) is restless apart from its "house"—a body of a human or animal: vs. 43; Luke 8:30,33. (What a revolting thought: if the devil cannot get to a man, he will take a pig!)
         —A sinner's body is empty if no demon or demons dwell therein: vs. 44
         —Demons will re-enter an "empty" house (body): vs. 45

Demons can take possession of humans and beasts (Mark 5:8,11-13 RV). When permitted, they are capable of entering into physical bodies and bringing them under evil control (Matthew 8:28; Luke 9:39; Mark 5:4,5—all RV).

         —Jesus recognized demons in human bodies: Matthew 12:27,28 (RV)
         —The Seventy recognized demons: Luke 10:17 (RV)
         —Paul recognized demons: I Corinthians 10:20 (RV)
         —James recognized demons: James 2:19 (RV)

If Paul and James recognized demons years after Christ ascended, and if the world is as bad today as then, if not worse, who are we to deny them? When demons wanted to know if Christ had come to torment them before the time (Matthew 8:29), they had no reference to Calvary, for Calvary did not destroy the devil and demons. They had in mind their final doom in the place prepared for the devil and his angels. They *are* very much here today.

—Demons are personal intelligences: Matthew 8:29,31 (RV)
—Demons are many in number: Mark 5:9 (RV)
—Demons are vicious, vile, degenerate, and debased

The sinner can only clean house by—

—Repenting of sins, exercising godly sorrow: Mark 1:15; Luke 13:3; II Corinthians 7:10
—Trusting in and receiving Christ as Savior: John 1:12; Romans 10:9,10. As his house (body) is made empty of sin and any demons that might have influenced him, Christ can now come in and fill him with Himself and His salvation. This is the sinner's *only* deliverance.

b. The saint: Matthew 16:16,22,23; Luke 22:31,54-61. If Satan could speak through Peter *after* his confession and get him to deny Christ three times, there is no reason why Satan or his demons could not influence other children of God. If the child of God is not subject to Satan's influence, why—

—Put on the whole armor of God? Ephesians 6:11
—Wrestle against wicked spirits? Ephesians 6:12 (RV)
—Take the shield of faith? Ephesians 6:16
—Give no place to the devil? Ephesians 4:27
—Be sober and vigilant? I Peter 5:8
—Be obedient in all things? II Corinthians 2:9-11
—Not be lifted up with pride? I Timothy 3:6
—Submit ourselves to God and resist the devil? James 4:7
—Have a good report? I Timothy 3:7

The Christian should—

—Claim his redemptive rights: Hebrews 2:14; Colossians 2:15; Revelation 12:9-11; I John 3:8; Ephesians 6:16—all RV. Christ's victory is our victory, therefore we are "more than conquerors" (Romans 8:37).
—Lay hold of his full equipment for demon warfare by putting on the *whole* armor of God: Ephesians 6:11-18. The whole armor of God only protects the front of the believer. The back is exposed. The Christian is always to advance, never retreat. If we turn and flee, we have no protection.
—Maintain strict self-control, fully yielded to God: Ephesians 4:27
—Abide under the shadow of the Almighty: Psalm 91:1-3
—Watch and pray: Matthew 26:41
—Exercise faith in Christ: I John 5:1-5
—Claim God's promises: Philippians 4:13,19
—Exercise unceasing vigilance: I Peter 5:8
—Make trustful resistance: James 4:7
—Put on the Lord Jesus Christ, and make not provision for the flesh. This makes us more than conquerors in Christ (Romans 13:14; 8:37). To be "more than a conqueror" means—

—To have a decisive victory
—To have the spoils of victory
—To gain new territory—to live on resurrection territory, to have positive and even greater conquests
—To honor and respect the Captain of our souls. God may let Satan act as our drill sergeant with His army, but the Captain of our salvation ranks above the sergeant!
—To have victory here, with the promise of final triumph and eternal reward

Believers are to take the attitude of confidence toward their adversary, the devil, relying upon God's provision and power through Christ for victory over him. A believer, filled with God's Spirit, living a victorious life over the world, the flesh, and the devil, needs only to rebuke Satan and his emissaries "in the name of Jesus and in the power of His blood." When Peter and John were used of God to heal a man, they were asked this question: "By what power, or by what name have ye done this?'' (Acts 4:7). Peter answered (vs. 10): ''By the name of Jesus Christ of Nazareth, whom ye crucified.'' His crucifixion speaks of the power of His shed blood. Here we have the *''name''* and the *''power.''*

We have seen what the ''god of this age'' and his ministers are doing; what about their future?

    a. They are perpetually cursed: Genesis 3:14,15; II Peter 2:4

    b. They are to energize the Antichrist: II Thessalonians 2:9,10; Revelation 12:17; 13:2,7

    c. They will be cast out of the heavenlies: Revelation 12:9

    d. They will be confined to the bottomless pit: Revelation 20:1-3

    e. They will be loosed for a little season after this 1000-year binding: Revelation 20:3b,7-9. After 1000 years in the bottomless pit, they are still the same. They do not change. Their methods are the same. Their wiles are the same. They still go out to deceive (Revelation 20:7,8).

    f. They will be cast into the lake of fire: Revelation 20:10

19. **Paul's Apostleship: 11:23-28. See Acts 9:15,16**

    His Cost—
    —In labors more abundant
    —In stripes above measure (scourging—195 lashes from Jews alone)
    —In prisons
    —In deaths often
    —Beaten three times with rods
    —Stoned
    —Three times shipwrecked
    —A night and a day in the sea—peril of waters
    —In journeyings often
    —In perils of robbers
    —In perils of Jews
    —In perils of Gentiles
    —In perils of the wilderness
    —In perils among false brethren
    —In weariness and painfulness
    —In watchings often
    —In hunger and thirst
    —In fastings often
    —In cold and nakedness
    —Care of the churches
    —A fool for Christ's sake: I Corinthians 4:10a
    —Despised: I Corinthians 4:10b
    —Buffeted: I Corinthians 4:11
    —No dwelling place: I Corinthians 4:11
    —Reviled: I Corinthians 4:12b
    —Defamed: I Corinthians 4:13a
    —Became offscouring (filth, garbage) of the world
    —Fought with beasts: I Corinthians 15:32
    —A thorn in the flesh: II Corinthians 12:7
    —Finally, his life: II Timothy 4:6-8
    His Attitude—
    —God's grace sufficient: 12:9a
    —Strength made perfect in weakness: 12:9b
    —Gloried in his infirmities: 12:9c
    —Pleasure to be persecuted for Christ's sake: 12:10
    —Not distressed: 4:8a
    —Not in despair: 4:8b

—Not forsaken: 4:9a
—Not destroyed: 4:9b
—Present suffering incomparable to future glory: Romans 8:18
His Purpose—
—To be dead to self: 4:11a
—To bear in his body the marks of Christ: 4:10a; Galatians 6:17
—To manifest Christ in his life: 4:10b,11b
—For death to work in his life for life to work in others: 4:12
—That Christ's power may rest upon him: 12:9d
—To preach nothing save Jesus Christ and Him crucified: I Corinthians 2:2
—To glory only in the cross of Christ: Galatians 6:14

20. God's Method of Making a True Minister: 12:7-9 with Acts 9:6,15,16. When Paul said—"Lord, what wilt thou have me do?"—little did he realize the cost involved, particularly bodily and mental suffering. God must always have a "broken" vessel before one can be shaped and molded into a "vessel of honor."

> *When God wants to drill a man,*
> *And thrill a man,*
> *And skill a man,*
> *When God wants to mold a man*
> *To play the noblest part;*
> *When He yearns with all His heart*
> *To create so great and bold a man*
> *That all the world shall be amazed,*
> *Watch His methods, watch His ways!*
> *How He ruthlessly perfects*
> *Whom He royally elects!*
> *How He hammers him and hurts him,*
> *And with mighty blows shapes him*
> *Through testings and trials which*
> *Only God understands;*
> *While his tortured heart is crying*
> *And he lifts beseeching hands!*
> *How he bends but never breaks*
> *When his good He undertakes;*
> *How He uses whom He chooses,*
> *And with every purpose fuses him;*
> *By every act induces him*
> *To try His splendor out—*
> *God knows what He's about.* [6]

Paul testifies to this method of God's (11:20-30), and, even though he sought "relief," he said he would "glory" in these experiences if this would bring glory to his Savior. He was even willing to become a "fool" for Christ's sake—made the filth of the world, and even offscouring (garbage) of all things (I Corinthians 4:10-13).

21. Paul's Thorn in the Flesh: 12:7. Many explanations have been given as to what Paul's "thorn in the flesh" was. The most commonly accepted one is that of "ophthalmia" (bad eye trouble). Verses used to support this interpretation are references to the Galatians, who would have "plucked out" their eyes and given them to Paul, and to Paul's "large" letter to them (Galatians 4:15; 6:11). There is no doubt Paul could have had eye trouble, and that he wrote

"large" letters to make for easy reading, but a close examination of the verse in question (12:7) simply states that Paul's thorn in the flesh was not his eyes, but the *messenger* of Satan to buffet him. Messenger refers to a "being" or "beings." While no one should question God, it does seem reasonable, however, that He would not have chosen one with red, runny sore eyes to witness before kings and governors, small and great.

Paul frequently used Old Testament expressions to explain his own messages, and a look at some passages reveal that *people,* used by Satan, became to Israel "pricks in [their] eyes, and thorns in [their] sides," "snares and traps, scourges in [their] sides" (Numbers 33:55; Joshua 23:13). Israel's history confirms this truth—that the surrounding nations, who became Israel's enemies, so tortured them that they became "thorns in the flesh." This is what happened to Paul throughout his ministry—Satan's messenger so stirred up opposition against him that no matter where he went, people violently opposed, even seeking to take his life. In circumstances which did not involve people, this messenger buffeted (shipwreck, etc.).

It is quite true that the result of such opposition and persecution was physical, bodily harm (stoning, scourging, etc.), but his "thorn" was not eye trouble—it was "Satan's messenger to buffet him." In his request for the thorn to depart, he was anxious for the Lord to ease up on the effect of this buffeting, which so mightily affected his physical being and hindered his freedom of travel and freedom in preaching the gospel. Because of Paul's deep spiritual perception, he realized this was God's "Romans 8:28" in his life, so he accepted it as from the Lord, and with God's grace, gloried in these "buffeting infirmities."

When Paul became a Christian, he became a chosen vessel unto the Lord to bear His name before Gentiles, kings, and Israel (Acts 9:15). Paul "straightway preached Christ . . . that He is the Son of God" (Acts 9:21,22). Though his hearers were amazed and Paul increased in strength as he proved that the Son of God was very Christ, this very service to the Lord bearing His name made Paul a marked man for suffering, for the Jews took counsel to kill him (Acts 9:23). This was in fulfillment of God's choosing of Paul, that in addition to bearing the name of the Lord, he would suffer great things for His name's sake (Acts 9:15). From this time forth Paul suffered as no other, except Christ Himself. Paul lists his sufferings (11:20-30; 12:7-9; I Corinthians 4:11-13), but in the midst of intense agony due to his "thorn in the flesh," he exclaimed "most gladly will I take pleasure in my infirmities—"

THAT THE POWER OF CHRIST MAY REST UPON ME—12:9[7]

"The Christian's infirmities are many and very painful. They often discourage, deject, and cast them down. They hinder him in every duty, mar his best performances, and give Satan occasion against him. Few have learned the happy art of glorying in their infirmities that the power of Christ may rest upon them; and yet it is our infirmities which render the Savior so necessary for us, and which endear the Savior so much to our hearts. His power is put forth in our weakness, and it is in His strength that we must overcome. We can do nothing without Him, but through Him we can do all things. The power of Jesus resting upon us will shelter us amidst all the storms of life, protect us from all real danger during our journey home, refresh us amidst all the toils of this weary land, give rest in our most weary hours, and keep us safe until we are beyond the reach of our foes. The power of Christ overshadows His people in their seasons of trials, and makes each to know that His grace is sufficient for them."

PRAYER THOUGHT: "Dear Lord, give me enough tears to keep me tender, enough hurts to keep me humane, enough failures to keep my hand in Thy tightly clenched hand, and enough success to make sure that I walk with Thee moment by moment. In Thy name. Amen."[8]

Second Corinthians 1:3-7

Galatians—The Book of Christian Liberty

Name: This Epistle derives its name from the foolish Galatians to whom Paul was writing (1:1,2; 3:1). Paul visited the churches of Galatia on each of his three missionary journeys. He and Timothy both preached the gospel to the Galatians (Acts 16:6). Galatia derived its name from the Gauls. These Gauls were fickle, as revealed by Paul in Acts 13 and 14. One day they wanted to make Paul a god, the next day they wanted to stone him. They were not content with the grace of God, they wanted to confuse grace with works. Paul said they were foolish because they wanted to mingle law with faith as the ground for justification, and because they insisted that a justified believer was made perfect by keeping the law.

Occasion of Writing: "This is clearly indicated in the epistle itself. Judaizing teachers had followed Paul in Galatia, opposing his doctrine respecting the non-use of the ceremonial law by Gentile converts, and also calling in question his apostolic authority (1:1-12). These teachers required that all converts should be circumcised and keep the law (5:2; 6:12). Evidently a strong party had been raised up against Paul personally, as well as against his doctrine. He had already tesified against these in person (1:9; 4:16), and now, because the evil was still increasing, he wrote this letter to expressly and directly controvert it."[1]

Contents: Galatians vindicates the character of the apostle as such; establishes the true doctrine of justification by faith in opposition to the works of the law; exhorts the saints to stand fast in the liberty of Christ and various other duties of Christianity; gives a true description of the false teachers and their views, so believers everywhere might beware of them and their principles.

Galatians is the Christian's "Magna Charta," or Declaration of Independence, from the law principle of salvation and has served to emancipate millions of Christians from the various forms of externalism which from time to time have endangered the freedom and spirituality of the gospel. It was Luther's favorite epistle which provided him much inspiration in his conflict with Romanism. This book has 6 chapters, 149 verses, and 3,098 words.

Character: Doctrinal.

Subject: The gospel as the power of the life of the believer.

Purpose: To show that faith and faith alone is the only grounds for justification and godly living: 2:16,22.

Outline:
    I. Introduction: 1:1-5
   II. Paul's Defense of His Apostolic Authority: 1:6—2:14
      A. A servant of Christ, preaching the true gospel: 1:6-11
      B. Called of God, not conferring with flesh and blood: 1:12-17
      C. Preached the same gospel as other apostles: 1:18—2:10
      D. Rebuked other apostles for not breaking with the law: 2:11-14

Heavy Burdens

III. The Doctrine of Justification by Faith: 2:15—4:31
    A. The doctrine stated: 2:15-21
    B. The Spirit received by faith: 3:1-5
    C. The doctrine illustrated: 3:6—4:31
        1. The Abrahamic Covenant: 3:6—4:18
        2. The Allegory of Ishmael (flesh) and Isaac (spirit): 4:19-31. See ALLEGORY in Index.
IV. Practical Exhortations: 5,6
    A. Liberty *versus* Bondage: 5:1-15
    B. Spirit *versus* Flesh: 5:16—6:10
    C. Cross of Christ *versus* Circumcision: 6:12,13,15
    D. Cross of Christ *versus* the World: 6:14
    E. Peace and Mercy—the result of walking according to this rule: 6:16

Writer: Paul: 1:1. Of all the Epistles that bear his name, no one is more clearly shown to be genuine than this one. The character of its style and manner of its argumentation are so clearly Pauline that the case admits no question. See WRITER in Romans.

When and Where Written: Uncertain. Probably Corinth. Paul's second visit to Galatia was made about 55 A.D., and the Epistle was written between his second and third visit to Galatia.

Key Chapter: 3. Justification by faith.

Key Verse: 2:16.

Key Word: Liberty.

Key Phrase: Stand fast in the liberty: 5:1.

Key Thought: Redeemed from the curse of the law: 3:13.

Spiritual Thought: Come to Christ for liberty and power.

Christ Is Seen As: Our Liberator: 1:4; 5:1.

Names and Title of Christ. See NAME in Dictionary.
    1. Jesus Christ: 1:1; 2:16
    2. Lord Jesus Christ: 1:3; 6:14

3. Our Sin-bearer: 1:4
4. Christ: 1:6
5. Son: 1:16; 4:4
6. Lord: 1:19; 5:10
7. Christ Jesus: 2:4; 3:26
8. Son of God: 2:20
9. Redeemer: 3:13; 4:5
10. A Curse for sinners: 3:13
11. The Seed: 3:19; 4:4 with Genesis 3:15
12. The Justifier: 2:16; 3:24
13. Lord Jesus: 6:17

Names and Titles of God. See NAME in Dictionary.

1. Father: 1:1,3,4
2. Mediator: 3:20
3. Abba, Father: 4:6

Names and Titles of the Holy Spirit. See NAME in Dictionary.

2

Burden bearing: 6:2,5. "Burdens" in the Near East usually refer to heavy burdens carried by individuals to market. Help is needed to have it placed on the back and secure a rope around the head and bundle. Help is also needed to take the "burden" off his back when a rest is needed or when he arrives at his destination. A wayfarer is called to assist—"to bear one another's burdens." For every man to "bear his own burden" (vs.5) seems like a contradiction. Putting the two verses together we find the need to assist one with a *heavy* burden, but to carry our own *light* burdens. See INIQUITIES in Index. The picture shows a man with a heavy burden who needs help to load and unload.

The Old Testament in Galatians:

1. Abraham believed God: 3:6 with Genesis 15:6
2. In Abraham . . . all nations blessed: 3:8 with Genesis 12:1-3
3. Cursed for breaking the law: 3:10 with Deuteronomy 27:26
4. The just shall live by faith: 3:11 with Habakkuk 2:4
5. Living in the law if kept: 3:12 with Leviticus 18:5
6. Christ cursed on the tree: 3:13 with Deuteronomy 21:23
7. Promises to Abraham: 3:16 with Genesis 13:15; 17:7; 25:5,6
8. The two sons of Abraham: 4:22,23 with Genesis 16:15; 21:2,3
9. Rejoice thou barren that hearest not: 4:26-28 with Isaiah 54:1
10. The son of the flesh cast out: 4:30 with Genesis 21:10
11. Love thy neighbor: 5:14 with Leviticus 19:18
12. Companion references:
    —The promised seed: 4:4 with Genesis 3:15

1. Deliverance: 1:4
   a. From this present evil world: vs. 4; We are in the world but not of it.
   b. From persecution: Psalm 7:1
   c. From my enemies: Psalm 27:12
   d. From trouble: Psalm 41:1
   e. From deceitful people: Psalm 43:1
   f. From slipping (stumbling): Psalm 56:13

     g. From workers of iniquity: Psalm 59:2
     h. From temptation: Psalm 91:3; Matthew 6:13
     i. From oppression: Psalm 119:134
     j. From lying: Psalm 120:2
     k. From evil: Matthew 6:13

2. The Contrasts in Galatians

a. In sin	1:4	a. Delivered from sin
b. "Another" Gospel	1:6-9	b. "The" Gospel of Christ
c. Man-pleaser	1:10	c. God-pleaser
d. Man's reasoning	1:11—2:14	d. Christ's revelation
e. Works	2:15-20	e. Faith
f. Law	2:21	f. Grace
g. Flesh	3:1-5	g. Spirit
h. Condemnation	3:6-16	h. Justification
i. In Adam—lost	3:19-22	i. In Christ—saved
j. Hopeless	3:23-29	j. With promise
k. Servants—in bondage	4:1-7	k. Free sons—heirs
l. Old Covenant	4:10-31	l. New Covenant
m. Falling from grace	5:1-16	m. Advancing in grace
n. Living in the flesh	5:17,18	n. Walking in the Spirit
o. Works of the flesh	5:19—6:6	o. Fruit of the Spirit
p. Discouragement	6:7-10	p. Encouragement
q. Glorying in the world	6:14	q. Glorying in the Cross

3. The Spirit in Galatians
    As Related to the Believer—
    a. He is promised: 3:14
    b. He is sent forth: 4:6
    c. He ministers: 3:5
    d. He is received by faith: 3:2
    e. He indwells: 4:6
    f. He begins a work: 3:3
    g. He leads: 5:18,25
    h. He overcomes the flesh: 5:16-18
    i. He bears fruit: 5:22-24
    j. He gives patience: 5:5
    k. He gives assurance: 6:8

4. The "Crucifixion" of Galatians
    a. Christ cruicified: 3:1. Jesus was crucified, not because He was bad, but because He was good and the world was bad. The world will never crucify me if I am bad.
    b. I am crucified with Christ: 2:20
    c. The flesh crucified: 5:24
    d. The world crucified unto me: 6:14
    e. I am crucified unto the world: 6:14

5. Paul's "Crucifixion" Experiences: 2:20
    a. Crucified with Christ—*death:* Romans 6:5a
    b. Nevertheless I live—*resurrection:* Romans 6:5b
    c. Yet not I, but Christ in me—*life:* Colossians 3:4a

6. Crucified with Christ: 2:20. The Christian who declares himself to be crucified has—
    a. No selfish ambition, so has nothing to be jealous about
    b. No reputation, so has nothing to fight about
    c. No possessions, so has nothing to lose or worry about
    d. No rights, so he cannot suffer wrong
    e. Is dead already, so no one can kill him

7. The Law *versus* Grace: 2:21 with John 1:17[3]—

LAW	GRACE
a. Revealed what God demanded of every man—*Do:* Exodus 20:1-17	a. Reveals what God has done for every man—*'Tis done:* I Corinthians 15:3,4
b. Demanded perfect obedience or death: Ezekiel 18:20; James 2:10	b. Gives life that we may obey: John 10:10b; 14:23
c. Commanded us to love God: Matthew 22:37	c. Tells us that God loves us: I John 3:16; 4:8-10,19
d. Commanded us to love neighbor as self: Matthew 22:39	d. Fills us with God's love for our neighbor: II Corinthians 5:14
e. Revealed sin: Romans 3:20	e. Reveals Christ: Hebrews 9:24-28
f. Worked wrath: Romans 4:15	f. Shows mercy: Ephesians 2:4
g. Curse pronounced: Galatians 3:10	g. Blessings announced: Galatians 3:14
h. Brought bondage: Hebrews 2:15; Galatians 4:1-3	h. Sets free: Galatians 5:1; Romans 8:1; John 8:36
i. Exhorted unwilling service of a bondslave: Romans 7:1-3	i. Wins willing service of a free man: Galatians 5:1; I John 4:19
j. Said do and live: Galatians 3:12	j. Says live and do: Romans 8:2-4
k. Shut man out of God's presence: Exodus 19:12,13,23,24	k. Opens the way to come boldly: Hebrews 4:14-16; 10:19,20
l. Made progress impossible: Ezekiel 33:13	l. Makes growth in grace possible: Romans 5:10; II Peter 3:18
m. Made nothing perfect: Hebrews 7:19	m. Makes perfect: Hebrews 10:14; 7:19
n, Could only condemn, not justify: Acts 13:39	n. Justifies freely: Romans 3:24; 5:1; Galatians 2:16
o. Had a shadow of good things to come: Hebrews 10:1	o. Reveals the very image of good things: Hebrews 10:1
p. Is the strength of sin: I Corinthians 15:56	p. Is the power of God: Romans 1:16
q. Demanded holiness: Deuteronomy 6:24,25	q. Produces holiness: Romans 6:14-22
r. Called forth all energy of the flesh: Romans 8:3	r. Puts to death all energy of the flesh: Romans 8:13
s. Punished every transgression and disobedience: Hebrews 2:2	s. Pardons every transgression and disobedience: I John 1:7,9
t. Believers were "children" under age: Galatians 4:1-3	t. Believers are "sons" full of age: Galatians 4:4-7
u. Is done away: II Corinthians 3:11	u. Remaineth: II Corinthians 3:11

8. Abraham and His Seed: 3:16. See NATURAL in Index.
   a. Natural descendants—as dust of the earth: Genesis 13:16
   b. Spiritual descendants—as the stars of heaven: Genesis 22:17 with Galatians 3:26,29

9. The Law was Added: 3:19. It was added or given—
   a. To provide a standard of righteousness. Oral communication had been sufficient with the patriarchs of the Jews, but now that Israel was constituted as a nation, it was necessary to furnish a written and permanent standard of morality to define God's ideal for conduct and character.
   b. To identify and expose sin—that Israel might have in "black and white" what offends God. "By the law is the knowledge of sin" (Romans 3:20).
   c. To reveal man's wickedness (Jeremiah 17:9) and God's holiness.

The law was added to the Abrahamic covenant. It did not displace the faith-basis of this covenant—it was "added till the Seed [Christ] should come." When "the Seed" came, in the fulness of God's time (Galatians 4:4,5), He became the "end of the law to all who believe [in Him]" (Romans 10:4).

10. The Incarnation: 4:4-7
    a. *Who?* God sent forth His Son: vs. 4
    b. *When?* In the fullness of His time: vs. 4
    c. *How?* Made of a woman, made under the law: vs. 4c; Genesis 3:15
    d. *Why?*
      —To redeem those under the curse of the law: vs. 5a
      —That we might receive the adoption of sons: vs. 5b
      —That we might receive God's Spirit and call Him Father: vs. 6
      —That we might be an heir of God through Christ: vs. 7; Romans 8:17

11. The New Covenant *versus* the Old—an Allegory: 4:22-31. This allegory contrasts Sarah's son with Hagar's (Genesis 21:9-21). Sarah represents the New Covenant; Hagar the Old. Sarah is gracious; Hagar is Mosaic and legal. The sons, Isaac and Ishmael, are the two children of these Covenants. Each has his standing before God—Isaac of the Spirit, Ishmael of the flesh.

It should be noted here that Paul is not discussing the eradication of a carnal nature—"casting out the bondwoman and her son"—but the casting out of the law, for the allegory is not of the two natures in the believer—the flesh and Spirit—but two covenants, Law and Grace (vs. 24). The Law gives way to Grace, for if justification comes by the works of the law, then it is no more grace (Romans 11:6). See COVENANTS in Index.

HAGAR—THE OLD COVENANT	SARAH—THE NEW COVENANT
Law	Grace
Mount Sinai	Mount Calvary
Bound	Free
Earthly Jerusalem	Heavenly Jerusalem
Barren	Fruitful
Bondwoman	Freewoman
Flesh	Spirit (promise)
Slave children	Free sons

12. The Cross of Christ an Offense: 5:11
    a. To good works—good works cannot justify: Galatians 2:16
    b. To the mind—the Cross appeals to faith: I Corinthians 1:18-25; 2:14
    c. To the noble—its truth is revealed to babes: I Corinthians 1:26-29; Matthew 21:16; Luke 10:21
    d. To the rich—God chooses the poor and downcast: Matthew 5:3,5; Luke 18:18-27
    e. To self—the Cross calls for complete surrender: Luke 14:26,27

13. Some "Be's and Be Nots" of Scripture: 5:18. See "B" HIVES in Index.
    —Be exceeding glad: Matthew 5:12
    —Be ye therefore perfect: Matthew 5:48
    —Be in a praying spirit: Matthew 7:7,8; Romans 12:12c
    —Be wise as serpents: Matthew 10:16a
    —Be harmless as doves: Matthew 10:16b
    —Be ready to meet Christ: Luke 12:40
    —Be ready to serve: Luke 17:8; Romans 12:11c
    —Be lifting up Christ: John 12:32
    —Be of good cheer: John 16:33
    —Be ready to suffer: Acts 21:13
    —Be strong in the faith: Romans 4:20
    —Be dead to self and sin: Romans 6:11a
    —Be alive unto God: Romans 6:11b
    —Be concerned for the lost: Romans 10:1

—Be ye transformed: Romans 12:2
—Be kindly affectioned: Romans 12:10
—Be fervent in spirit: Romans 12:11b
—Be rejoicing in hope: Romans 12:12a
—Be patient in tribulation: Romans 12:12b
—Be helpful to saints: Romans 12:13a
—Be given to hospitality: Romans 12:13b
—Be of the same mind one toward another: Romans 12:16a
—Be overcomers through Christ: Romans 12:21
—Be afraid of evil: Romans 13:4
—Be found faithful: I Corinthians 4:2
—Be awake: I Corinthians 15:31
—Be ye steadfast, unmoveable: I Corinthians 15:58
—Be ye reconciled to God: II Corinthians 5:20
—Be ye separate: II Corinthians 6:17
—Be of good comfort: II Corinthians 13:11
—Be led by the Spirit: Galatians 5:18
—Be considerate: Galatians 6:1
—Be able to comprehend Christ's love: Ephesians 3:18,19
—Be renewed in the Spirit: Ephesians 4:23
—Be ye kind one to another: Ephesians 4:32a
—Be tenderhearted: Ephesians 4:32b
—Be forgiving: Ephesians 4:32c
—Be followers of God: Ephesians 5:1
—Be understanding of God's will: Ephesians 5:17b
—Be filled with the Spirit: Ephesians 5:18
—Be strong in the Lord: Ephesians 6:10
—Be able to quench Satan's darts: Ephesians 6:16b
—Be confident: Philippians 1:6
—Be sincere: Philippians 1:10
—Be filled with fruits of righteousness: Philippians 1:11
—Be spiritual: Philippians 1:27
—Be of one mind with Christ: Philippians: 2:5
—Be blameless and harmless: Philippians 2:15a
—Be without rebuke: Philippians 2:15b
—Be found in Him (Christ): Philippians 3:9
—Be moderate: Philippians 4:5
—Be anxious about nothing: Philippians 4:6
—Be content: Philippians 4:11,12
—Be knit together in love: Colossians 2:2
—Be truthful: Colossians 3:9
—Be thankful: Colossians 3:15
—Be sweet in speech: Colossians 4:6
—Be energetic: I Thessalonians 4:11
—Let Christ be glorified in us: II Thessalonians 1:12
—Be an example: I Timothy 4:12
—Be a partaker of affliction: II Timothy 1:8b
—Be strong in grace: II Timothy 2:1
—Be gentle: II Timothy 2:24
—Be thoroughly furnished unto good works: II Timothy 3:17
—Be instant in preaching God's Word: II Timothy 4:2
—Be ready to work: Titus 3:1b
—Be assured: Hebrews 13:5b
—Be swift to hear: James 1:19a

—Be slow to speak: James 1:19b
—Be slow to anger: James 1:19c
—Be ye doers of the Word: James 1:22
—Be patient for Christ's return: James 5:7,8
—We shall be like Him: I John 3:2
—Peace and love of God be with you: Romans 15:33; II Corinthians 13:14
—Grace of Christ be with you: II Corinthians 13:14
—Communion of the Spirit be with you: II Corinthians 13:14
Some "Be Nots"—
—Be not seen of men: Matthew 6:1
—Be not as the hypocrites: Matthew 6:8
—Be not judging and grudging: Matthew 7:1; James 5:9
—Be not afraid or troubled: John 6:20; 14:27
—Be not faithless, but believing: John 20:27
—Be not afraid to speak for Christ: Acts 18:9
—Be not conformed to this world: Romans 12:2
—Be not slothful in business: Romans 12:11a
—Be not highminded: Romans 12:16b
—Be not wise in own conceits: Romans 12:16c
—Be not divisive among you: I Corinthians 1:10
—Be not idolatrous: I Corinthians 10:7,14
—Be not partakers of the Devil's table: I Corinthians 10:21
—Be not condemned with the world: I Corinthians 11:32
—Be not unequally yoked with unbelievers: II Corinthians 6:14
—Be not entangled with the Law: Galatians 5:1
—Be not consumed one of another: Galatians 5:15
—Be not deceived: Galatians 6:7
—Be not weary in well doing: Galatians 6:9
—Be not sinful in anger: Ephesians 4:26
—Be not partakers of disobedience: Ephesians 5:6,7
—Be not unwise: Ephesians 5:17a
—Be not ashamed to live for Christ: Philippians 1:20
—Be not moved from hope: Colossians 1:23
—Be not moved by affliction: I Thessalonians 3:3
—Be not ignorant of Christ's return: I Thessalonians 4:13
—Be not shaken in mind: II Thessalonians 2:2
—Be not ashamed to testify: Matthew 10:32; II Timothy 1:8a
—Be not ashamed to work for God: II Timothy 2:15
—Be not unfruitful: Titus 3:14
—Be not slothful in believing His promises: Hebrews 6:12; 11:6
—Be not forgetful to entertain strangers: Hebrews 13:2
—Be not covetous: Hebrews 13:5a
—Be not carried away with strange doctrine: Hebrews 13:9
—Be not troubled if ye suffer: I Peter 3:14

14. Flesh Works and Spirit Fruit: 5:19-26. It is to be noted that the works (*plural*) of the flesh (vss. 19,21) are those things which naturally flow from fallen man. The fruit (*singular*) of the Spirit are those things which flow from the heart of God, and are characteristic of those in Christ who have crucified the works of the flesh and are walking in the Spirit, loving one another (vss. 22-26).

The fruit of the Spirit is love; only *one* fruit—love! The other qualities mentioned are varieties of love.[4] See FOXES, Little, in Index.

a. Joy is love *singing*
b. Peace is love *resting*

    c. Longsuffering is love *enduring*
    d. Gentleness is love's *touch*
    e. Goodness is love's *character*
    f. Faithfulness is love's *habit*
    g. Meekness is love *denying self*
    h. Temperance is love *holding the reigns*

15. A Fourfold Folly: 6:7,8. See REAPING in Index.
    a. The folly of trying to deceive God
    b. The folly of expecting something different from what we sow
    c. The follow of sowing to the flesh and expecting to reap of the Spirit
    d. The folly of expecting less than we sow

16. Faint Not: 6:9 with I Corinthians 15:58
    a. In service: 6:9; II Thessalonians 3:13
    b. In suffering: Ephesians 3:13; I Peter 4:12,13
    c. In growth: II Corinthians 4:16
    d. In witnessing: II Corinthians 4:1
    e. In corrections: Hebrews 12:5
    f. In prayer: Luke 18:1

17. The Christian and the World: 6:14
    a. Delivered from it: 1:4
    b. Crucified to it: 6:14
    c. Dead to its rudiments: Colossians 2:20
    d. Not conformed to it: Romans 12:2
    e. Unknown by it: I John 3:1
    f. Hated by it: John 17:14a
    g. Not of it: John 17:14b
    h. Loves it not: I John 2:15-17
    i. Unspotted by it: James 1:27
    j. Shuns its friendship: James 4:4
    k. A witness in it: John 17:15,18
    l. Victorious over it: I John 4:4; 5:4,5

18. Glorying in the Cross: 6:14
    In it we have the—
    a. Fulfillment of prophecy: Genesis 3:15; Isaiah 53:55; Daniel 9:24-26
    b. God's love exhibited and declared: John 3:16; 15:13; Galatians 2:20b
    c. Removal of that which was against us: Colossians 2:14
    d. Redemption price of all souls: Ephesians 1:7
    e. Foundation of peace established: Colossians 1:20; Ephesians 2:16
    f. Defeat of Satan: Colossians 2:15; Hebrews 2:14; Revelation 1:18
    g. Victory: Romans 8:37; James 4:7

A BIT OF HEAVENLY MANNA

God's time clock runs on schedule and when the fullness of time was come, He sent forth His Son to make redemption possible for sinful men. When a sinful man avails himself of this so great salvation by receiving Christ as his own personal Savior, he then becomes a son of God (John 1:12). Paul puts it this way—because ye are sons, God hath sent forth the Spirit of His Son into your hears, crying,

"ABBA FATHER"—4:6[5]

"God has a family upon this earth. Every believer is a child of God. He knows God, who is his Father. He loves Jesus, who is his elder Brother. He cleaves to the saints, who form the household of God. But many of the Lord's children question their adoption and fear that they are not born again. Let all such ask themselves, 'Am I of the world?' 'Am I what I was once?' 'Can I love sin?' 'Do I despise the Savior?' 'Do I prefer the things of time to the things of eternity?' 'Can I live in sin?' 'Do I set my affection on things below instead of things above?' Thousands do, and if you do not, why is it? There must be a difference. Satan didn't make the difference. I of myself could not have made the difference. But God did, and He did it when we became His child. I now hate sin, despise the world, resist the devil, trust in Jesus, love the saints, prefer things eternal to things material, set my affection on things above where Christ is seated, and keep in tune with God through prayer. Old things have passed away and behold, all things are become new. Being a child of God does not mean we escape temptation but God our Father delivers us from the hour of temptation (I Corinthians 10:13). Our Father supplies all our need (Philippians 4:19). We hallow His name, seek to do His will on earth as it is in heaven, and forgive others as He has forgiven us. Only as we become children of God can we live a life different from the one we lived when in service of the devil.''

PRAYER THOUGHT: "Dear Lord, give me grace to persevere, so that at this day's end I might not leave my work half done. May I not give up when enthusiasm begins to fade, or other interests rise to attract. In Jesus' name I pray. Amen.''[6]

Galatians 6:9

Ephesians—The Epistle of Fullness

Name: The Epistle derives its name from those at Ephesus to whom Paul was writing: 1:1. However, most ancient manuscripts omit "at Ephesus." It appears to be a circular letter "to the saints and to the faithful in Christ Jesus," since its contents have to do with those who make up the body of Christ. Some scholars favor the notion that this was the epistle to the Laodiceans referred to in Colossians 4:16. Paul was in Ephesus on his second missionary journey (Acts 18:19-21) and then for three months on his third missionary journey, when he founded the church at Ephesus (Acts 19:1-8). The city was the capital of the province of Asia, rich in commerce and industry, a port city through which Orient trade passed. It was the chief seat of the worship of Diana (Artemis), where her famous temple was located. It contained the miraculous image of this goddess (Acts 19:27. See DIANA in Index). Ephesus had a famous race track where Paul fought with beasts (I Corinthians 15:32). The church's membership consisted mostly of Gentiles (2:11-19; 3:1), with some Jews among them (Acts 18:19; 19:8). Paul's success was so great in and around Ephesus that heathenism was shaken to its foundation. The riot of Demetrius took place in the amphitheatre (Acts 19; 20:17-38). Labor unions also opposed further spread of the gospel (Acts 19:23-41; I Corinthians 16:8,9), and because of such opposition, Paul left Ephesus. See EPHESUS in Index.

Occasion of Writing: "This epistle does not appear to have been written to meet any specific demand, but rather an expression of the deep love felt by the apostle for his converts and fellow Christians, and his earnest desire not only that they should remain steadfast in the faith, but also attain to all of their heavenly privileges in Christ Jesus. To the Christian at Ephesus dwelling under the shadow of the great temple Diana, daily seeing its outward grandeur, and almost daily hearing of its pompous ritualism, the allusions in this epistle to that mystic building of which Christ was the cornerstone, the apostles the foundation, and himself and his fellow Christians portions of the august superstructure (2:19-22), must have been spoken with a force, an appropriateness, and a reassuring depth of teaching that cannot be overstated.

"We are unable to perceive from the letter itself any special occasion for it on the part of the Ephesians. It appears that Paul simply availed himself of the opportunity offered by the mission of Tychicus and Onesimus to Colosse, to send oral news of himself and to obtain news from them, but also to address them a written discourse, partly on the glory of redemption and of their state as Christians, and partly on the conduct in keeping with it, appropriating to themselves their blessings in heavenly places."[1]

Contents: "It treats of the most sublime doctrines: (1) of grace; (2) of eternal election; (3) of redemption by Christ; (4) of peace and pardon by His blood; (5) of conversion by the power of efficacious grace; and (6) of salvation by the free grace of God in opposition to works. It also very largely treats on the nature and usefulness of the gospel ministry, and of gifts qualifying for it, and of the several duties incumbent upon Christians, for the apostle first begins with the doctrine of the gospel which he distinctly handles and explains, and then proceeds to enforce the duties belonging to men, both as men and Christians."[2] Ephesians has 6 chapters, 155 verses, and 3,039 words.

Character: Church truth.

Subject: Calling, conduct, and conflict of the church.

Purpose: See 1:17-19.

Outline:

    I. Church Doctrine: 1—3
        A. The Church as a Body: 1
            1. Praise for its origin: vss. 1-14
            2. Prayer for its development: vss. 15—23
        B. The Church as a Holy Temple: 2
            1. Raised to be with Christ: vss. 1-9
            2. Created in Christ unto good works: vs. 10
            3. Brought nigh God and have access to Him: vss. 11-18
            4. A holy temple in the Lord: vss. 19-22
        C. The Church as a Mystery: 3
            1. Explained: vss. 1-5
            2. Defined: vss. 6-12
            3. Church prayed for: vss. 13-21
    II. Church Practice
        A. The Church as a New Man: 4
            1. Walking worthy: vss. 1-3
            2. Exercising our gifts: vss. 7-16
            3. Putting on the "new man": vss. 17-32
        B. The Church as a Bride: 5
            1. Followers of God: vss. 1-17
            2. Filled with the Spirit: vss. 18-20
            3. Submitting to the Bridegroom: vss. 21-33
        C. The Church as a Warrior: 6
            1. The warrior's obedience: vss. 1-9
            2. The warrior's strength: vs. 10
            3. The warrior's equipment: vss. 11-18
    III. Conclusion: 6:19-24

Writer: Paul, the prisoner of the Lord: 1:1; 4:1. See WRITER in Romans.

When and Where Written: Probably ca. A.D. 61 or 62, in the Roman prison. This is the first in the order of the Prison Epistles. As a prisoner for two years, Paul enjoyed certain privileges, such as dwelling in his own hired house with a soldier that kept him (Acts 28:16,30), and being visited by many (Acts 28:23). Of such who came to visit him were Epaphroditus from Philippi (Philippians 4:18); Onesimus of Colosse (Colossians 4:7-9; Philemon 1); Tychicus from Ephesus (Ephesians 6:21) who delivered the letter to those at Ephesus and a letter each to Colosse and Philemon at Colosse; Epaphras from Colosse (Colossians 4:12); Mark, Justus, Luke, Demas, and Timothy (Colossians 1:1; 4:10-14). See PRISON, p. 604.

Key Chapter: 1. The believer in Christ.

Key Verse: 1:3.

Key Word: Fullness—
1. Of God: 3:19
2. Of Christ: 4:13
3. Of the Spirit: 5:18

Key Phrase: In Christ—in the heavenlies: 2:6.

Key Thought: Our blessings in Christ in the heavenlies: 1:3.

Spiritual Thought: Come to Him for fullness of life.

Christ Is Seen As: The Head of the Church: 1:22; 5:23.

Names and Titles of Christ. See NAMES in Dictionary.
1. Jesus Christ: 1:1; 3:1
2. Christ Jesus: 1:1; 2:10
3. Lord Jesus Christ: 1:2; 6:24
4. Christ: 1:3
5. Lord Jesus: 1:15
6. Head of the Church: 1:22; 5:23
7. Our Peace: 2:14
8. The Reconciler: 2:16,18
9. Chief cornerstone: 2:20
10. Lord: 2:21; 4:17
11. Son of God: 4:13
12. Jesus: 4:21
13. A sweet-smelling Savor: 5:2
14. Savior of the body: 5:23
15. Lover of the Church: 5:25
16. Sanctifier of the Church: 5:26
17. Lord of the Church: 5:29
18. Master: 6:9

Names and Titles of God. See NAMES in Dictionary.
1. Father: 1:2; 6:23
2. God of our Lord Jesus Christ: 1:17; 3:14
3. Father of glory: 1:17
4. The Forgiver: 4:32

Names and Titles of the Holy Spirit. See NAME in Dictionary.
1. Holy Spirit of promise: 1:13
2. Spirit: 2:18; 5:18
3. Spirit of God: 4:30

LIGHT FROM
BIBLICAL
CUSTOMS

[3] 1. Chosen (vessel) in Him: 1:4. When a visitor plans to leave the Holy Land and wishes to take with him a souvenir, the merchant might suggest a piece of pottery. You ask that he select it for you. He will hand you one of his choosing—one that he will never be ashamed to admit as his. It becomes a ''chosen'' vessel. While it may look like all the other vessels to you, it is *his* chosen one. All mankind may look alike, but only those who know Christ as their Savior are God's *chosen* vessels. See POTTER in Index.

2. Adoption: 1:5. See ADOPTION in Index.

3. Sealed with the Holy Spirit: 1:13,14. In olden days when merchandise was purchased, it was customary to impress one's seal (or engraved symbol) on the items, while the purchaser went elsewhere to transact other business. The symbol protected the goods until they were removed by the buyer. Should any items be stolen, they could be easily identified by the seal. To secure us in Christ Jesus, God has put His ''seal'' on all his purchased possessions, and when He returns for us, we will be identified because of the Holy Spirit, ''the earnest of our inheritance.'' He *is* our seal.

4. All things under His feet: 1:20-22. See FOOTSTOOL in Index.

5. Captivity captive: 4:8. See CAPTIVITY Captive in Index.

6. Feet shod with the preparation of the gospel: 6:15. ''Shod'' means to bind one's feet, with the thought of keeping the shoes on so that at a moment's notice soldiers would be ready to march. A Near Eastern custom is to wear loosely fitted sandals for walking only; and go barefooted in the house. To ''shod'' a horse is to literally nail the shoe to the horse's hoof, actually making the shoe a part of the horse. The gospel is a part of each believer, not something to put on or kick off at will like a sandal. Since we are to witness—to preach the gospel in season and out of season, even on a moment's notice, we must be ready to go (be on the march) and present the gospel. We can never witness to the wrong person. This is why Christ told His disciples, in sending them out to preach, to be ''shod with sandals'' (Mark 6:9). ''Feet shod'' is listed as a part of the whole armor of God, fitted for each believer in Christ for victory.

The Old Testament in Ephesians:
1. Leading captivity captive: 4:8 with Psalm 68:18; Judges 5:12
2. Speak truth with thy neighbor: 4:25 with Zechariah 8:16
3. Sin not: 4:26 with Psalm 4:4
4. Husband and wife one flesh: 5:31 with Genesis 2:24
5. Honoring parents: 6:1-3 with Exodus 20:12
6. Companion references:
   —Helmet of salvation: 6:17 with Isaiah 59:17

SEED
THOUGHTS

1. In Christ: 1:1
   a. Chosen—to live: 1:4
   b. Adopted—to privileges: 1:5. See ADOPTED in Index.
   c. Accepted—to be like Him: 1:6
   d. Sealed—to serve: 1:13
   e. Raised—to walk: 2:6
   f. Seated—to learn: 2:6

2. Spiritual Blessings: 1:3

      a. Loved by Christ: 5:2
      b. Chosen in Him: 1:4
      c. Given the Word of truth: 1:13
      d. Redemption through His blood: 1:7
      e. Saved by grace: 2:8,9
      f. Forgiven by His blood: 1:7
      g. Quickened with Christ: 2:5
      h. Raised with Christ: 2:6
      i. Adopted into God's family: 1:5
      j. Accepted in the beloved: 1:6
      k. Sealed with the Holy Spirit: 1:13
      l. Given peace: 2:14
      m. Made a new man: 4:23,24
      n. Made children of light: 5:8
      o. Seated with Christ: 2:6
      p. No more strangers: 2:19
      q. His workmanship: 2:10
      r. Given boldness: 3:12
      s. Strengthened by His Spirit: 3:16
      t. His power in us: 3:20
      u. A hope: 4:4
      v. Given grace: 4:7
      w. Given God's armor: 6:11-16
      x. Given full-time ministers for our perfection: 4:11-16
      y. An inheritance: 1:11

  3. Chosen in Him: 1:4

      a. Many called but few chosen: Matthew 20:16
      b. Chosen out of this world: John 15:19
      c. Chosen to salvation: II Thessalonians 2:13
      d. Chosen as God's precious ones: I Peter 2:4
      e. Chosen to live holy and without blame: Ephesians 1:4
      f. A chosen, prepared vessel: Acts 9:15; II Timothy 2:21
      g. Chosen to know His will: Acts 22:14
      h. Chosen generation to show forth praise: I Peter 2:9
      i. Chosen to be rich in faith: James 2:5a
      j. Chosen to work for God: Ephesians 2:10
      k. Chosen to confound the noble: I Corinthians 1:26-29
      l. Chosen to witness: Acts 1:8
      m. Chosen to bear fruit: John 15:16
      n. Chosen to be living epistles: II Corinthians 3:2,3
      o. Chosen to be a soldier: II Timothy 2:3
      p. Chosen to be like Christ: Romans 8:29; I John 3:2
      q. Chosen to be heirs of the kingdom: James 2:5b

Moody once said: "Do not stumble at the doctrine of election (or God's choosing). Preach the gospel to *all,* and if you convert anyone who was not 'chosen,' God will forgive you!"

  4. The Believer's Position "According to God": 1:4

      a. Chosen according to His plan: 1:4
      b. Called according to His purpose: Romans 8:28
      c. Redeemed according to His grace: Ephesians 1:7
      d. Saved according to His mercy: Titus 3:5
      e. Adopted according to His will: Ephesians 1:5
      f. Enlightened according to His pleasure: Ephesians 1:9
      g. Given wisdom according to His eternal purpose: Ephesians 1:10,11

> h. Empowered according to God's power: Colossians 1:11
> i. Made a minister according to God's gift: Ephesians 3:7; 4:11,12
> j. Strengthened according to His glory: Ephesians 3:16
> k. Need supplied according to His riches: Philippians 4:19
> l. Our body to be changed according to His ability: Philippians 3:20,21

5. Forgiveness: 1:7. Someone asked Martin Luther: "Do you feel that you have been forgiven?" He replied: "No, but I'm as sure as God's in heaven—for feelings come and go and feelings are deceiving. My whole warrant is God's own word, naught else is worth believing. I *do* have forgiveness of my sins, *according to the riches of His grace.*"

6. Together in Christ: 1:10
   a. Crucified together: Galatians 2:20
   b. Buried together: Romans 6:5a
   c. Quickened together: Ephesians 2:5
   d. Raised up together: Ephesians 2:6a; Romans 6:5b
   e. Seated together: Ephesians 2:6b
   f. Builded together: Ephesians 2:22
   g. Gathered together at His coming: II Thessalonians 2:1

7. Contrast of Sinner and Saint: 2:1-13—

SINNER	SAINT
Born corruptible: Psalm 51:5	Born again incorruptible: I Peter 1:23
Child of wrath: Ephesians 2:3	Child of God: Romans 8:16,17
Dead in sin: Ephesians 2:1b	Alive unto God: Ephesians 2:5
Under sin: Galatians 3:22	Sins removed: Psalm 103:12
Sold for nought: Isaiah 52:3	Bought with a price: I Peter 1:18,19
Blasphemous: Luke 22:65	Fears God: Colossians 3:22
Workers of iniquity: Proverbs 10:29	Performs good works: Ephesians 2:10
Abominable: Revelation 21:8	Blameless and harmless: Philippians 2:15
Entangled: Galatians 5:1	Free: John 8:32,36; Romans 6:22
Cursed: Galatians 3:10	Redeemed from curse: Galatians 3:13
Condemned: John 3:18	No condemnation: John 5:24
Under God's wrath: John 3:36	Saved from wrath: Romans 5:9
Deceitful heart: Jeremiah 17:9	New heart: Ezekiel 36:26,27
Enemy of the Cross: Philippians 3:18	At peace with God: Ephesians 2:13,14
Without Christ: Ephesians 2:12	Christ in us: Colossians 1:27
Unthankful: II Timothy 3:2	Thankful: II Corinthians 9:15
Fulfills lust of the flesh: Ephesians 2:3	Makes no provision for the flesh: Romans 13:14
Prayerless: Job 21:15	Prayerful: Philippians 4:6
Ungodly: Romans 5:6	Godly: Psalm 4:3
Strangers: Ephesians 2:12	Friends: John 15:14
Without promise: Ephesians 2:12	Given promise: II Peter 1:4
Without hope: Ephesians 2:12	With a hope: I Thessalonians 4:13-18
Without God: Ephesians 2:12	God in us: I John 4:15,16
Child of disobedience: Ephesians 2:2	Child of obedience: Romans 6:16,17
Understands not God: I Corinthians 2:14	Understands God: I Corinthians 2:9-12
Far from God: Ephesians 2:13	Made nigh God: Ephesians 2:13
Blind: II Corinthians 4:4	Watchful: Luke 12:37
Without strength: Romans 5:6	Strengthened: Ephesians 3:16
Taught of Satan: II Corinthians 11:13-15	Taught of God: I John 2:27
Led captive by the devil: II Timothy 2:26	Led by the Spirit: Romans 8:14
Walks according to course of this world: Ephesians 2:2	Walks in the light: Ephesians 5:8

No soundness: Isaiah 1:2-6
Destructive: Isaiah 59:7
Ignorant of God: Galatians 4:8
Not known by Jesus: Matthew 7:21-23
Loves pleasure: II Timothy 3:4
Boastful: Psalm 10:3
Awaits judgment: John 12:47,48
On road to destruction: Matthew 7:13
Shall perish: Psalm 1:6b
Go into everlasting fire:
    Matthew 25:41; Revelation 21:8

Sound mind: II Timothy 1:7
Constructive: Titus 2:14
Knowledge of Him: Ephesians 1:17
Known by Jesus: John 10:27
Loves God: I John 4:19
Humble: Psalm 34:2
Awaits rewards: I Corinthians 3:14
On narrow road: Matthew 7:14
Shall never perish: John 10:28
Inherit the kingdom; go into heaven:
    Matthew 25:31,34; John 14:3

8. The Necessity of Faith: 2:8,9. See FAITH in Index.

Without it—
a. No salvation: 2:8,9
b. No justification: Romans 3:28; 5:1
c. No access into grace: Romans 5:2
d. No living: Romans 1:17; Galatians 2:20b
e. No standing: II Corinthians 1:24
f. No walking: II Corinthians 5:7
g. No fighting: I Timothy 6:12
h. No overcoming: I John 5:4
i. No pleasing God: Hebrews 11:6

9. Without Christ: 2:1-3,11,12
a. Dead
b. Worldly walk
c. Child of disobedience
d. Living for self
e. Child of wrath
f. Uncircumcised
g. Christless
h. Friendless
i. Homeless
j. Hopeless
k. Godless
l. Peaceless

With Christ: 2:13-22
a. Made nigh
b. Have peace
c. One with Him
d. New creation (new man)
e. Reconciled to God
f. Have access to God
g. Are fellow citizens
h. In God's household
i. On a solid foundation
j. Are God's holy temple
k. Habitation of God's Spirit
l. God's workmanship (vs. 10)

10. Unsearchable Riches: 3:8
a. Of grace: 1:7; 2:7
b. Of glory: 1:18; 3:16
c. Of mercy: 2:4
d. Of Christ: 3:8
e. Of goodness: Romans 2:4
f. Of God: Romans 11:33

11. Gifts for Perfecting the Saints: 4:11-16
a. Apostles and prophets—to establish for us a foundation and reveal the mystery of the Church, the body of Christ: 2:20-22; 3:5-11
b. Evangelists—to wake up dead men
c. Pastors—to shepherd and feed the flock
d. Teachers—to search out the deep things of God

12. Names and Titles of Ministers: 4:11
a. Ambassadors for Christ: II Corinthians 5:20
b. Angels of the Church: Revelation 1:20
c. Apostles: Luke 6:13; Titus 1:1
d. Bishops: I Timothy 3:1

    e. Elders: I Timothy 5:17

    f. Evangelists: Ephesians 4:11

    g. Fishers of men: Matthew 4:19

    h. Laborers: Matthew 9:38; I Corinthians 6:1

    i. Messengers: II Corinthians 8:23

    j. Ministers: II Corinthians 6:4; Romans 15:16

    k. Overseers: Acts 20:28

    l. Pastors: Jeremiah 3:15; Ephesians 4:11

    m. Preachers: Romans 10:14; I Timothy 2:7

    n. Servants: Titus 1:1; Judges 1

    o. Shepherds: Jeremiah 23:4

    p. Soldiers: Philippians 2:25; II Timothy 2:3

    q. Stars: Revelation 1:20

    r. Stewards: I Corinthians 4:1; I Peter 4:10

    s. Teachers: Isaiah 30:20; Ephesians 4:11

    t. Watchmen: Isaiah 62:6; Ezekiel 33:7

    u. Witnesses: Acts 1:9; 5:32

13. Your Pastor—A Gift of God: 4:11.[4] The position of your pastor is as that of a general at the head of an Army. He has power derived from Headquarters, but he is alone in that he has a responsibility which he cannot share. He stands before you and speaks on behalf of a Power greater than himself. Your church is the joint-creation of you and your pastor. When the congregation cooperates as one body, preaching is a pleasure and preachers get the lift they need from their people. It is when the "soldiers of the Cross" fall in line with their "General" that this task is made easier. Peter was mighty on the day of Pentecost, not because he had a fluent tongue, but because there stood behind him one hundred and nineteen men and women who backed him in prayer and in whose faces there lingered traces of the glory of fire from heaven.

Your pastor is called to the high ministry of giving to his congregation the most valuable truths ever revealed to man. Every Sunday, in about thirty minutes, he tries to present one of those great truths in the form of a sermon. It is the result of many hours of study, prayer, and composition. When he stands in the pulpit to present this meal for his flock, he wonders how much of his time and effort is in vain, especially when many members could avail themselves of what the church offers but have stayed away.

The pastor is aware of the dangers and threats to the spiritual health of his sheep; he understands the working of sin in a man's soul; he has in his "medicine bag" the cure; the preventive, or the aid to real growth in grace, but unless his flock takes advantage of what God offers through him, he is useless. Yet, thank God, to the few he is "pastor," because they use him. He has many things thrust upon him which cause concern. He is subject to constant and merciless criticism. He is never eager to hear all that people say, but in the course of time he catches enough of the tittle-tattle to trouble and depress him.

Believe it or not, preachers are human. They have hands, organs, dimensions, senses, affections, and passions. If you prick them, they bleed; if you appreciate them, they are encouraged. Don't be afraid of spoiling him. For every man hurt by praise, a thousand are starved to death by lack of it. Many a minister has carried a burdened heart through the years of disappointing labor, hungry for a word of thanks which never came, only to find on the eve of his going to another church or to his heavenly reward how wide was the satisfaction and how genuine was the affection for him in the hearts of the people. It is a shameful thing to sit for months or even years under preaching which makes you nobler and happier without letting your pastor know that in one heart at least the seed had fallen on good ground, and is bringing forth many fold.

To do his best, your pastor must live in an atmosphere of good will. While the busybodies are carrying the pastor stories of dissatisfaction, the saints ought to bear him a message of affection, good cheer, and enthusiastic approval. *Your pastor has no pastor.* He is nourished by his environment—the family of Christ who makes up his congregation. He cannot shape himself; he is molded by those of his own church. He is *your* servant for Christ's sake, and he must give an account to God for his success or failure as pastor of your church. He can give an account with a smile if you will do one thing: "Obey them that have the rule over you, and submit yourselves [to their teachings]: for they watch for your souls, as they that must give account, that they may do it with joy, and not with grief" (Hebrews 13:17). If your pastor gives account with joy, that is profitable for *you*. If with grief, then *it will be unprofitable for you*.

14. Calling a pastor. When a church seeks a pastor, they often want one who has—

> The *strength* of an eagle,
> The *grace* of a swan,
> The *gentleness* of a dove,
> The *friendliness* of a cat-bird,
> The *cheerfulness* of a robin,
> The *assurance* of a barnyard fowl,
> The *industry* of a sparrow,
> The *patience* of turkey-buzzards,
> And the *night hours* of an owl.
> And when they catch that bird,
> They expect him to live
> On the food of a canary!

15. The Plight of Your Pastor[5]
   —If he is young, he lacks experience; if his hair is gray, he is too old
   —If he has five or six children, he has too many; if he has none, he is setting a bad example
   —If his wife sings in the choir, she is being forward; if she doesn't, she isn't interested in her husband's work
   —If he speaks from notes, he has canned sermons and is dry; if he is extemporaneous, he is not deep
   —If he spends too much time in the study, he neglects his people; if he visits, he is a gadabout
   —If he is attentive to the poor, he is playing to the grandstand; if to the wealthy, he is trying to be an aristocrat
   —If he suggests improvements for the Church, he is a dictator; if he makes no suggestions, he is a figurehead
   —If he uses too many illustrations, he neglects his Bible; if not enough, he is not clear
   —If he condemns wrong, he is cranky; if he does not, he is a compromiser
   —If he preaches an hour, he is windy; if less, he is lazy
   —If he preaches the Truth, he is offensive; if not, he is a hypocrite
   —If he fails to please everybody, he is hurting the Church; if he does please everybody, he has no convictions
   —If he preaches tithing, he is a money-grabber; if he does not, he is failing to develop his people
   —If he receives a large salary, he is mercenary; if a small salary, it proves he is not worth much
   —If he preaches all the time, the people get tired of hearing one man; if he invites guest preachers, he is shirking responsibility

So what! They say the preacher has an easy time. And I guess he does at that, but he'll have to wait until he gets to heaven to enjoy it.

16. How to Discourage Your Pastor[6]
   a. Don't attend the Sunday evening service or prayer meeting
   b. Go to church when "convenient"
   c. Habitually come late, and always sit just inside the door

    d. Don't give him your attention, but always whisper

    e. Act cold to show your dignity

    f. Never appreciate his efforts

    g. Tell him what wonderful messages you have heard elsewhere

    h. Always have "roast preacher" for Sunday dinner, criticizing him before your children

    i. Don't make him welcome in your home; leave the T.V. full blast, even when he prays (or tries to)

    j. Accuse his wife of running things

    k. Don't pray for him, and never offer to help

    l. Always do the opposite of what he suggests

    m. Get your "gang" together to oppose him in business meetings

    n. Don't take your Sunday guests to hear him

17. How to Get Rid of Your Pastor[7]

    a. Look him straight in the eye when he is preaching and say "amen" once in awhile. He'll preach himself to death in a few weeks!

    b. Pat him on the back and brag on his good points. He'll soon work himself to death!

    c. Start paying him a living wage. Perhaps he's one of those preachers who has gone on starvation wages for so long he'd eat enough to kill him if he ever got the chance!

    d. Rededicate your life to Christ and ask your Pastor for a job (preferably the name of some lost one you could win to Christ). He'll die of heart failure!

    e. Get the church to unite in prayer for the preacher and he'll soon become so effective that some larger church will take him off your hands!

18. A Vacant Pulpit.[8] A church was in need of a pastor. One of the deacons was interested in knowing just what kind of a minister they desired. He wrote the following letter, as if he had received it from an applicant, and read it to the pulpit committee. It read as follows:

    "Gentlemen:

      "Understanding that your pulpit is vacant, I should like to apply for the position. I have many qualifications that I think you would appreciate. I have been blessed to preach with power and have had some success as a writer. Some say that I am good at organizing. I have been a leader in most places I have gone.

      "Some folks, however, have some things against me. I have some things against myself. I am over 50. I have never preached in one place for more than three years at a time. In some places I have had to leave town after my work caused riots and disturbances. I have to admit I have been in jail three or four times. My health isn't good. I have to work at my trade to make ends meet. All my churches have been small, although located in large cities.

      "I haven't gotten along too well with the ministerial associations in the different churches where I have pastored. In fact, some of them have threatened me, taken me to court, and even attacked me physically.

      "I am not too good at keeping records. I have been known to forget whom I have baptized. However, if you can use me, I shall do my best for you, even if I have to work to help with my support."

The deacon, upon reading the letter, asked the committee if they were interested in the applicant. They replied he would never do for their church. They said they were not interested in an unhealthy, contentious, trouble-making, absent-minded jailbird, and that they were insulted that his application had ever been submitted. When they inquired of the deacon the name of the applicant, he replied, *"The Apostle Paul."*

19. Satan's Swindles: 4:27. See SATAN in Index.

    a. Adam gained wisdom but lost fellowship with God: Genesis 3:9,10

    b. Cain gained self-satisfaction but lost the presence of God: Genesis 4:16

   c. Lot gained the fertile plains of Jordan but lost his testimony in Sodom: Genesis 19:14

   d. Esau gained a meal but lost his birthright: Genesis 25:27-34

   e. Moses got water from the rock but forfeited his right to enter the Promised Land: Numbers 20:10-12

   f. Naomi gained fullness in Moab but lost the sweetness of the Lord: Ruth 1:19-21

   g. Samson gained a woman but lost his sight and his power with God: Judges 16:17-21

   h. Old Eli attained a position but lost his sons to the devil: I Samuel 2:11,12

   i. Achan gained the gold of Jericho but lost his family: Joshua 7:21-25

   j. Israel gained a "man" king but lost her real king—God: I Samuel 8:19-22; 10:18,19

   k. Saul gained the spoils of war but lost his throne: I Samuel 15:9,11,23-26

   l. David satisfied his flesh but lost the joy of God's salvation: II Samuel 11:2-5; Psalm 51:12

   m. Solomon gained fame but lost favor with God because of his love for strange women: I Kings 11:1-10

   n. Gehazi gained Naaman's wealth but lost his health: II Kings 5:20-27

   o. Hezekiah gained his health but lost his godly influence before heathen ambassadors: II Kings 20:1-18

   p. Israel gained the "self-life" but lost her testimony as God's nation: II Chronicles 36:14-21

   q. Belshazzar gained the pleasures of sin but lost his kingdom: Daniel 5

   r. The rich man fared sumptuously every day on earth but lost his soul in hell: Luke 16:19-26

   s. Judas gained 30 pieces of silver but lost the best Friend he ever had: Matthew 27:3-5

   t. Barnabas gained his point but lost his place with Paul: Acts 15:36-40

   u. Paul gained an appeal to Caesar but lost his calling to be on the "go" to the Gentiles: Acts 25:10,11; 26:32

   v. Demas gained the world but lost God's blessing in service: II Timothy 4:10

   w. The Ephesians grew in knowledge and abounded in faith but they lost their first love: Revelation 2:1-4

   x. Those at Pergamos and Thyatira gained prestige in their compromise with apostates and the devil but lost the full import of truth: Revelation 2:12-29

   y. The Laodiceans gained worldly goods but lost their spiritual vision: Revelation 3:14-19; Proverbs 29:18

Summary: "What shall it profit a man if he should gain the whole world and lose his own soul?" (Mark 8:36).

  20. Followers of God: 5:1-21

    Walk in love: vss. 1-7

    a. As Christ loved: 2

    b. As becoming the new man: 3:7; Romans 6:4

    c. Worthy of their calling: 4:1

    Walk as children of light: vss. 8-14

    a. Manifesting the fruit of the Spirit: 9; 2:10

    b. Proving what is of the Lord: 10

    c. Having no fellowship with the works of darkness: 11a

    d. Reproving the unfruitful works of darkness: 11b,12

    e. Manifesting all things in the light: 13

    f. Having fellowship with God: I John 1:7

    Walk circumspectly: vss. 15-17

    a. Not as fools: 15a

    b. Not as Gentiles: 4:17

    c. Not after the flesh: Romans 8:1

    d. Not by sight: II Corinthians 5:7

    e. Not in rioting: Romans 13:13

    f. Not in craftiness: II Corinthians 4:2

    g. As wise: 15b

    h. Redeeming the time: 16a

    i. Because the days are evil: 16b

    j. Understanding the will of God: 17

    k. Honestly: I Thessalonians 4:12

    l. In peace: Ephesians 6:15

    m. As Christ walked: I John 2:6

    n. Consistently: Ephesians 4:1

    o. As commanded: Jeremiah 7:23

    p. In old paths: Jeremiah 6:16

Walk in the Spirit: vss. 18-21

    a. Not filled with wine: 18a

    b. Filled with the Spirit: 18b

       —Making melody in the heart: 19

       —Giving thanks unto God: 20

       —In submission: 21

Result:

    a. Shall not faint: Isaiah 40:31

    b. Shall have good things: Psalm 84:11

    c. Shall walk with God in glory: Revelation 3:4

21. Redeeming the Time: 5:16. In this "Brown 'n Serve," "Heat 'n Eat," "Chill 'n Pour" era, we have become second-wise and hour-foolish. We have 604,800 seconds to live each week. Allowing 201,600 for sleep, 144,000 for work, 50,400 for eating, 20,000 for travel, 40,000 for relaxing, and 360 for a church service, this leaves 148,440 for which we must give account. It has been estimated that the average person of seventy has spent 4 years in education, 8 years in amusements, 6 in eating, 11 working, 23 sleeping, 5½ washing and dressing, 6 in walking, 3 in conversation, 3 in reading, and *only six months* in worship. We do not need more time. What we need to do is learn to use more wisely the time we have, and *redeem* it.

22. When One is Filled with the Spirit (5:18), he—

    a. Prays in the Spirit: 6:18; Jude 20b

    b. Speaks in the Spirit: I Corinthians 12:3

    c. Worships in the Spirit: Philippians 3:3

    d. Walks in the Spirit: Galatians 5:25

    e. Loves in the Spirit: Colossians 1:8

23. Hypocritical Singing: 5:19

    a. We sing *"Sweet Hour of Prayer"* and content ourselves with little or no prayer at all

    b. We sing *"O for a Thousand Tongues"* and seldom witness at all about our wonderful Savior

    c. We sing *"Onward Christian Soldiers"* and wait to be drafted into His service

    d. We sing *"There Shall Be Showers of Blessings"* and let one raindrop knock us out for all the Sunday services

    e. We Sing *"Bless Be the Tie that Binds"* and let the smallest thing sever Christian fellowship

    f. We sing *"Serve the Lord with Gladness"* and gripe about all we have to do

    g. We sing *"We're Marching to Zion"* but fail to march to prayer meeting, Sunday school, or church as we ought

    h. We sing *"I Love to Tell the Story"* but never mention it to the lost around us

    i. We sing *"Cast Thy Burdens on the Lord"* and worry ourselves into a nervous breakdown

    j. We sing *"The Whole, Wide World for Jesus"* and never invite our neighbor to church

    k. We sing *"O Day of Rest and Gladness"* and wear ourselves out cutting the grass, playing golf, or picnicking

    l. We sing *"Throw Out the Life Line"* and content ourselves with throwing out a fishing line

    m. We sing *"Leaning on the Everlasting Arms"* and about all the leaning we do is on the back of an easy chair to watch T.V.

Maybe our singing isn't as hypocritical as it sounds, because when we sing *"Take My Life and Let it Be,"* we mean just that—"Take it and let it be." "Let it be, Lord, just let it be!" Or maybe, "I Shall Not be Moved!"

24. The church: 5:23-32. The word "church" comes from the Greek word "ekklesia," which means "assembly." There are at least two views of the word "ekklesia"—

    a. It has direct reference to a local church, thereby intimating that the local church is the one which Jesus is building, while at the same time those who are born again, whether members of a local assembly or not, make up the *potential* members of His body which shall be, the glorious church which He is to present to Himself (Ephesians 5:27). This view holds that the body of Christ or Church is the Church *in prospect,* the Church which shall be, but which does not now actually exist as a body, for it has not yet been assembled. This view does away with a universal or invisible church of God.

    b. The other view sees the body of Christ, His Church existing *now.* According to this view, the Lord for centuries has been and now is calling out people one by one in salvation through the preaching of the Gospel. Every time one is born again, he is "baptized into the one body [or church] by the Spirit" (I Corinthians 12:13). They say if the body does not already exist, how can the Spirit place anyone in it? There never has been a time in which all believers or members of Christ's body have been present together at one time, but this view holds that this does not mean that His Church cannot actually be until all the members are assembled. What about a local church? Is it just a church or body during stated meetings? Do they cease being members of that body or church when not assembled during the week? How absurd, they say, to think that just because the Church of the Lord Jesus Christ has not yet been assembled with all its members present that it is not a church and that born again ones are simply "potential members of a body that shall be, a body which does not now actually exist as a body, for it has not yet been assembled." The Scripture does say that the Gentiles are made "fellow-heirs . . . of the same body" [with the Jews] (Ephesians 3:6). How could Gentiles be made fellow-heirs or members of a body that did not nor does not now exist? Consider Ephesians 1:20-23. Christ, upon being raised from the grave, has been set down at His Father's right hand. His Father *"hath put* all things under His feet, and gave Him to be the Head over all things to the Church, which *is* His body . . ." Notice the language is in the past and present tense—"hath put"; "is."

The church which was a mystery hid in God (Ephesians 3:9), was partially revealed unto the sons of men in other ages. It was not revealed unto them as it was to Paul and the other apostles (Ephesians 3:5). The full revelation of this mystery is that of a "new man," composed of both Jew and Gentile (Ephesians 2:12-16; 3:6). The Gentiles are no more strangers and foreigners, but fellow citizens . . . and of the household of God (Ephesians 2:19).

In order for God to make the church or this "new man," He—

    a. Broke down the middle wall of partition (Ceremonial Law): 2:14
    b. Abolished in His flesh the enmity: 2:15a
    c. Abolished the Law (of Commandments): 2:15b; Colossians 2:14
    d. Made in Himself of Jew and Gentile one new man: 2:15c
    e. Made peace: 2:15d
    f. Reconciled the two unto Himself by the Cross: 2:16
    g. Preached peace: 2:17
    h. Made us nigh God by the blood of Christ: 2:13
    i. Made access to Himself by the Spirit: 2:18

The purpose of this "new man' or the church is—

    a. For all believers to be built on one foundation: 2:20
    b. For all believers to be fitly framed together: 2:21a
    c. For all believers to grow unto a holy temple: 2:21b; I Corinthians 3:16,17
    d. For all believers to be the habitation of God: 2:22
    e. For all believers to boldly make known to principalities and powers (wicked spirits) in heavenly places the manifold wisdom of God: 3:10-12

Relationship of Christ to the church—
    a. That of a Lover: 5:25
    b. That of the Redeemer: 5:23,25
    c. That of the Head: 5:23
    d. That of the Sanctifier: 5:26
    e. That of the Satisfier: 5:29
    f. That of the Bridegroom: 5:27

Relationship of the church to Christ—
    a. That of a wife to her husband:
      —In subjection to Him: 5:24
      —Reverence for Him: 5:32,33
    b. We are members of His body: 5:30

Names and titles of the church—
    a. Assembly of the saints: Psalm 89:7
    b. Body of Christ: 1:22,23; Colossians 1:24
    c. Bride of Christ: Revelation 21:9
    d. Church of the living God: Acts 20:28; I Timothy 3:15
    e. Church of the first-born: Hebrews 12:23
    f. Family in heaven and earth: 3:15
    g. Flock of God: I Peter 5:2
    h. Fold of God: John 10:16
    i. General assembly of the first-born: Hebrews 12:23
    j. Golden candlestick: Revelation 1:20
    k. God's building: I Corinthians 3:9
    l. God's husbandry: I Corinthians 3:9
    m. God's heritage: I Peter 5:3
    n. Habitation of God: 2:22
    o. House of God: I Timothy 3:15; Hebrews 10:21
    p. House of Christ: Hebrews 3:6
    q. Household of God: 2:19
    r. Israel of God: Galatians 6:16
    s. Lamb's wife: Revelation 19:7
    t. Pillar and ground of the truth: I Timothy 3:15
    u. Spiritual house: I Peter 2:5
    v. Temple of the living God: I Corinthians 3:16,17; II Corinthians 6:16
    w. Vineyard: Matthew 21:41

25. What Constitutes a Local New Testament Church?

The word "church" (ekklesia) means a "called out assembly." Stephen used this meaning in reference to Israel (Acts 7:38). It also refers to a "mob" or assembly at Ephesus (Acts 19:32), to a law court (Acts 19:39), and to the "body of Christ—the redeemed ones" (Colossians 1:18). In answer to our question "What constitutes a local New Testament church?" we must reckon with the fact that Paul went about establishing local assemblies or churches. There are the "churches" of God at Corinth, in Galatia, etc., which demonstrate that the "local church" is an entity, and has the function of carrying out the ordained purposes of God on earth. A local New Testament church has—

    a. Christ as its Head: Matthew 16:18; Ephesians 1:22,23; Acts 20:28b; Colossians 1:18
    b. The Holy Spirit as its Guide: John 16:13; Acts 13:2
      —He convicts of sin, or righteousness, of judgment: John 16:7-9
      —He testifies of Christ: John 15:26
      —He is our Teacher: John 14:26; I Corinthians 2:9,10
      —He is our Source of power: Luke 24:49; Acts 1:8
    c. The Word of God as its Authority: II Timothy 3:16,17, Matthew 28:19,20
    d. Born-again pastors as it undershepherds: Ephesians 4:11-16; Acts 20:28; I Peter 5:1-3

They—
—give attendance to prayer and Bible study: Acts 6:4; I Timothy 4:13-16
—Are good examples: I Timothy 3:8
—Feed the flock: Acts 20:28a; II Timothy 4:2-5
—Care for the church of God: II Corinthians 11:28; Hebrews 13:17

e. Born-Again Believers as its members: Acts 2:41,42,47
—Its leaders must be qualified: Philippians 1:1; I Timothy 3:1-12
—Its members must be faithful: I Corinthians 4:2; Hebrews 10:25
—Its members must be prayer warriors: Acts 1:14,24; 3:1; I Timothy 2:1-4
—Its members must support the local work. See TITHING in Index.
—Its members must support missions: Matthew 9:36-38; Acts 13:1-5
—Its members must consider their Undershepherd: Luke 10:7; Philippians 4:15,16; I Corinthians 16:17; Hebrews 13:17
—Its members must be soul-winners. See SOUL-WINNING in Index.

f. An Autonomous Body
—Answerable only to God: Acts 5:29
—Gets direction only from the Holy Spirit: Revelation 2:29. Each of the seven churches mentioned in Revelation (chps. 2,3) had a separate, distinct message from the Holy Spirit. Each church was self-governing, with a democratic form of government. When an immediate need arose, it was settled by the local church or churches (Acts 1:26; 6:1-7; 13:1-5). The outcome of the democratic settlement of the question of circumcision, for example, "pleased the Holy Spirit" (Acts 15:5-7,28 with II Corinthians 3:17).

g. Separation from the State as its Policy: Matthew 22:21; John 18:26; Acts 4:18-20; 5:25-29

h. Summary: Each member must—
—Live blameless—to be presented faultless: Ephesians 1:4; Jude 24
—Occupy till Christ comes again: Luke 19:13
—Build upon the foundation Christ Jesus: I Corinthians 3:11-15
—Anticipate the rapture of the church: I Thessalonians 4:16-18
—Not be ashamed before Him at His appearing: I John 2:28
—Anticipate the moment when they see Christ, and become like Him: I John 3:2; Philippians 3:20,21

26. **What's Right with the Church?** So much criticism has been leveled against the church that one wonders if there is anything *right* about it. YES, there is—

a. Its Foundation is right: I Corinthians 3:11
—Planned by the Father: Ephesians 1:4
—Purchased by the Son: Ephesians: 1:6,7
—Processed by the Spirit: Ephesians: 1:13,14

b. Its Membership is right—God's choice—the elect: Ephesians 1:4,5

c. Its Message is right: I Corinthians 15:3,4; Galatians 6:14
—Whosoever will call: Romans 10:13
—Without works: Ephesians 2:8,9; Titus 3:5

d. Its Mission is right: II Corinthians 5:18-20
—World Evangelism: Acts 1:8

e. Its Hope is right—ultimate triumph: I Corinthians 15:51-57

f. Its Destiny is right: I Thessalonians 4:16-18; Philippians 3:20,21. And being right, the devil cannot destroy it—the gates of hell cannot prevail against it! (Matthew 16:18)

27. **The Christian's Warfare:** 6:11-18. See SATAN in Index.

a. Enemy—wicked spirits: vs. 12 (RV)

b. Uniform—the armor of God: vss. 13-17. A "well-dressed" child of God wears—
—Loins girt about with truth—inner man protected: vs. 14a
—Breastplate of righteousness—keeping heart pure: vs. 14b
—Feet shod with the preparation of the gospel—walking for God: vs. 15. See SHOD in Index.
Shield of faith—to endure temptation: vs. 16
—Helmet of salvation—to keep mind on God: vs. 17a

Armor, Roman Soldiers

    c. Weapon—sword of the Spirit, the Word of God: vs. 17b
    d. Secret weapon—praying in the Spirit: vs. 18
The uniform is defensive. The weapons are offensive. There is *no* defensive or protective armor for the back. The true Christian soldier does not turn and run—this leaves him with no protection against the enemy. There are no deserters, no defectors, and no cowards here (II Timothy 2:3). The picture above was a common sight in Paul's day—that of Roman soldiers, fully armored, ready for battle at a moment's notice.

In our warfare, we need to stand—
    a. In the faith: I Corinthians 16:13
    b. In His grace: Romans 5:2
    c. In the gospel: I Corinthians 15:1
    d. In the freedom of our liberty: Galatians 5:1
    e. In the Lord—the power of His might: Philippians 4:1
    f. In one Spirit and one mind: Philippians 1:27
    g. Not in man's wisdom: I Corinthians 2:5
    h. Against the wiles of the devil: Ephesians 6:11
If we don't stand for something, we are liable to fall for anything.

A BIT OF
HEAVENLY MANNA

The doctrine of election and predestination have been confusing to many of God's dear people (and the sinner, too). However, the truth is simple when we consider God's foreknowledge first. "Known unto God are all His works from the beginning of the world" (Acts 15:18). Because he *knew* who would and who would not accept Christ as their own personal Savior, he "chose"—"elected" "predestinated" those who would to "the adoption of children" and "to live a life holy and without blame before Him in Love" (Ephesians 1:4,5).

HE HATH CHOSEN US IN HIM—1:4[9]

"Chosen in Christ Jesus! This is the first display of Jehovah's grace toward us. All the creatures (before the foundation of the world) lay spread out before His omniscient eye. He saw the whole of them, that they would sin and become sinners. Nothing was concealed from His eye; everything appeared as it afterward existed. With His foreknowledge of what all would do, He chose those who would believe unto eternal life, He chose them to be a special people unto Himself. He chose them in eternity. His choosing them was an act of gracious sovereignty. He chose them in Christ, who was appointed to be their Substitute, their infallible Savior, their Representative, their Surety, and their Head. His choice of them secures to them an interest in the work of Christ, union to the person of Christ, and a share in the glory of Christ. He chose them to the highest honor of sonship and to exalt them to perfect happiness. He chose them 'to be holy and without blame.' Are we chosen in Christ? It is that we might be holy. Are we redeemed by the precious blood of Christ? It is that we should be a holy people unto the Lord. Are we called by the power of the Holy Spirit? It is to holiness on earth, as introductory to happiness in heaven. Every ordinance we observe, every doctrine we believe, every promise we trust, every precept we perform, and every trial we endure, is intended to promote our sanctification—the very purpose of our calling. O wondrous display of infinite grace! Lord, help me to make my calling and election sure."

PRAYER THOUGHT: "Dear heavenly Father, I know it is impossible for me to do everything, but I pray that I might do something this day that will bring lasting glory to the One who chose me unto Himself. In His matchless name I pray. Amen."[10]

Ephesians 6:7,8

Philippians—Paul's Joy Letter

Name: This Epistle derives its name from those at Philippi to whom Paul was writing: 1:1. The city was a Roman colony in Macedonia enjoying Roman citizenship. The founding of this church on Paul's second missionary journey is graphically described in Acts 16:11-40. Lydia, a seller of purple, was Paul's first convert there. Soon after she was joined by the Philippian jailer and his family. Most of the members were Greek and Roman Gentiles. There were comparatively few Jews being in the place, as proved by the absence of a synagogue and any Hebrew names in the list of converts. The church excelled all others in its attachment and generosity to Paul (4:10-18). Two subsequent visits of Paul are recorded in Acts 20:1,2,6.

Occasion of Writing: "The general state of the church may be gathered from several hints in the epistle and elsewhere. They were (1) poor (II Corinthians 8:1,2); (2) in trouble from persecution (1:28-30); (3) in danger of, if not already in, quarrel and dissension (2:1-4); and (4) apparently inclined to spiritual pride and jealousies. Epaphroditus had brought to the apostle a contribution from his beloved Philippians, and on his return the apostle availed himself of the opportunity to forward them this epistle, and thus to pour out to them the fullness of his heart in thanksgiving and prayers and exhortations for their spiritual welfare, and to encourage them to rejoice always in every circumstance.''[1]

Contents: ''An expression of Paul's love and affection to the Philippians and an account of his imprisonment in Rome; how they encouraged and supported him, and by that same token Paul encouraged them in all affliction and persecution they were suffering for the sake of Christ. He excites them to love, to unity, and to peace among themselves. He cautioned each of them against false teachers and Judaizing Christians that were for joining Moses and Christ, law and Gospel, and works and grace, together. In matters of salvation he exhorts to a humble and holy life, with the challenge, 'to me to live is Christ, and to die is gain.' ''[2] Philippians has 4 chapters, 104 verses, and 2,002 words.

Character: Practical Christianity.

Subject: Christ our Life, Example, Goal, and Strength.

Purpose: Written for the joy and progress of our faith (1:25), and to teach the Christian that his experiences are not shaped by outward circumstances but by the life of Christ within.

Outline:
    I. Introduction: 1:1-7
    II. Christ the Believer's Life—rejoicing in suffering: 1:8-30
    III. Christ the Believer's Ideal—rejoicing in lowly service: 2
    IV. Christ the Believer's Object—rejoicing despite imperfection: 3
    V. Christ the Believer's Power—rejoicing in circumstances: 4:1-19
    VI. Conclusion: 4:20-23

Writer: Paul 1:1. See WRITER in Romans.

When and Where Written: See WHEN WRITTEN in Ephesians. A prison Epistle.

Key Chapter: 2. Christ, the believer's Pattern.

Key Verse: 2:5.

Key Word: Joy (rejoice).

Key Phrase: Rejoice in the Lord: 4:4.

Key Thought: Christian experience.

Spiritual Thought: The mind of Christ; esteeming other better than self: 2:3,5.

Christ Is Seen As: Our Strength: 4:13.

Names and Titles of Christ. See NAMES in Dictionary.
    1. Jesus Christ: 1:1
    2. Christ Jesus: 1:1; 3:3
    3. Lord Jesus Christ: 1:2; 4:23
    4. Christ: 1:10
    5. God: 2:6
    6. Servant: 2:7
    7. Son of Man: 2:7
    8. God's highly exalted One: 2:9a
    9. A Name above every name: 2:9b
    10. Jesus: 2:10
    11. Lord: 2:11; 3:8
    12. Lord Jesus: 2:19
    13. Savior: 3:20

Names and Titles of God. See NAMES in Dictionary.
    1. Father: 1:2; 2:11
    2. God of peace: 4:9

3. Supplier of every need: 4:19

Names and Titles of the Holy Spirit. See NAME in Index.

1. Spirit of Jesus Christ: 1:19.
2. The Spirit: 2:1.

The Old Testament in Philippians: There are no direct references in this Book to the Old Testament; only one companion reference: "every knee shall bow": 2:10 with Isaiah 45:23.

1. The Christian's Joy
   a. When to rejoice—always: 4:4
   b. Why rejoice—we are commanded: Psalm 5:11
   c. Where to rejoice—in whatsoever state we find ourselves: 4:10-12
   d. How to rejoice—
      —In prayer: 1:4
      —In preaching Christ: 1:18
      —In faith: 1:25
      —In godly living: 2:1,2
      —In Christ's day: 2:16
      —In sacrifice and service: 2:17,18
      —In Christian fellowship: 2:24-30
      —In the Lord: 3:1; 4:4
      —In worship of God: 3:3
      —In care of the Church: 4:10
      —In whatsoever state: 4:10-12
      —In salvation: Psalm 9:14; 13:5
      —In truth: I Corinthians 13:6
      —When others walk in truth: II John 4
      —In the salvation of souls: Luke 15:6-10,32; I Thessalonians 2:19,20
      —In the hope of God's glory: Romans 5:2
      —That our names are written in heaven: Luke 10:20
      —In the hope of heaven: I Peter 1:3-9
      —When tempted: James 1:2; I Corinthians 10:13
      —When tried: I Peter 4:12-14
      —When sorrowful: II Corinthians 6:10
      —When persecuted: Matthew 5:11,12
      —When suffering for Christ's sake: Acts 5:41; I Peter 4:13

2. The Gospel in Philippians
   a. Fellowship in the Gospel: 1:5
   b. Confirmation of the Gospel: 1:12
   c. Furtherance of the Gospel: 1:12
   d. Defense of the Gospel: 1:17
   e. Living the Gospel: 1:27a
   f. Faith of the Gospel: 1:27b
   g. Service of the Gospel: 2:22
   h. Laboring in the Gospel: 4:3
   i. Spreading the Gospel: 4:15

3. Christ in Philippians
   a. The *Source* of spiritual fruit: 1:11
   b. The *Theme* of preaching: 1:18
   c. The *Motive* of Christian service: 1:20,21a

    d. The *Example* of humility and loyalty: 2:5-8

    e. The *Height* of character: 2:9-11

    f. The *Object* of fellowship: 3:7-14

    g. The *Desire* of heaven and glory: 3:20,21

    h. The *Strength* of the believer: 4:13

    i. The *Channel* of divine supplies for every need: 4:19

4. The Work of the Spirit in Philippians

    a. *Past*—at conversion: 1:6

    b. *Present*—working out our salvation: 2:12,13

    c. *Future*—fashioned like unto His glorious body: 3:21

5. Divine Resources: 1:7

    a. Fullness of grace—our *resource:* 1:7; John 1:14,16

    b. Fullness of faith—our *incentive:* Acts 6:8a; Hebrews 12:2

    c. Fullness of blessing—our *privilege:* Romans 15:29

    d. Fullness of joy—our *portion:* John 15:11; Psalm 16:11

    e. Fullness of Christ—our *maturity:* Ephesians 4:13

    f. Fullness of power—our *strength:* Acts 6:8b

    g. Fullness of God—our *hope:* Ephesians 3:19

6. Christian Living: 1:21

    a. Life *for* Christ: 1:21a; John 15:8,16

    b. Life *from* Christ: John 14:6; 11:25

    c. Life *with* Christ: Galatians 2:20; John 14:19

    d. Life *like* Christ: I John 4:17b; John 17:14; I Peter 2:21-23

7. Our Humility: 2:3,4

It's Not Always Easy[3]

To apologize,
    To begin over,
        To admit error,
            To be unselfish,
                To take advice,
                    To be charitable,
                        To be considerate,
                            To endure success,
                      To keep on trying,
                To avoid mistakes,
            To forgive and forget,
        To make the most of little,
      To maintain a high standard,
    To shoulder a deserved blame,
But it always pays, doesn't it?

8. The Mind of Christ: 2:5-8

    a. Lowly: 2:7; Zechariah 9:9 with Matthew 21:5

    b. Humble: 2:8a; Luke 22:27

    c. Obedient: 2:8b; John 8:29

    d. Compassionate: Luke 7:13

    e. Forgiving: Luke 23:34

    f. Busy: Luke 2:49

    g. Loving: Matthew 18:11-13; Mark 10:21

    h. Sympathetic: Matthew 11:28

    i. Diligent: Mark 1:35a

    j. Prayerful: Mark 1:35b; Luke 22:32

    k. Steadfast: Luke 9:51

    l. Resigned: Matthew 26:39; John 8:50

      m. Trustful: Luke 22:32

      n. Subjective: John 5:30

      o. Gentle: Matthew 19:14; Luke 22:26

      p. Gracious: Luke 22:28

      q. Faithful: Luke 22:29; Hebrews 3:1,2

      r. Spiritual: Luke 4:18

      s. Pure: I John 3:3

      t. Forebearing: Matthew 27:14

      u. Ministering: Matthew 20:28

9. Christ's Mind for the Believer: 2:5

      a. To reverence, confess, live and serve Him: 2:9-16

      b. To learn of Him: I Corinthians 2:16

      c. To suffer for Him: I Peter 4:1

10. Jesus in Poverty: 2:6-8. Though Christ was rich, yet for our sakes He became poor (II Corinthians 8:9). See CHRIST, Who, in Index.

      a. He was born in a *borrowed* stable: Luke 2:7

      b. He was laid in a *borrowed* manger (crib): Luke 2:7,12

      c. He used as His pulpit a *borrowed* boat: Mark 4:1

      d. He fed thousands with a *borrowed* lunch: John 6:9-11

      e. He taught from a *borrowed* book: Luke 4:16,17

      f. He slept in a *borrowed* bed: Luke 9:58

      g. He rode as King on a *borrowed* beast: Matthew 21:2,3

      h. He observed the Last Supper in a *borrowed* room: Matthew 26:18

      i. He was mocked as king in a *borrowed* robe: Matthew 27:27-31

      j. He was buried in a *borrowed* tomb: Matthew 27:59,60

11. Christ's Humility and Exaltation: 2:6-11 with Luke 14:11

      a. From heaven to a stable: vss. 6,7; Luke 2:7,12

      b. From the crib to Calvary: vss. 7,8; Galatians 4:4,5

      —Made Himself of no reputation: 7a

      —Took upon Himself the form of a servant: 7b

      —Was made in the likeness of men: 7c; Hebrews 4:15

      —He humbled Himself: 8a

      —Became obedient unto death: 8b

      c. From the Cross to the grave—

      —Numbered among the transgressors: Isaiah 53:12b; Matthew 27:38

      —Buried in a borrowed grave: John 19:38-42

      d. From the grave to glory: vss. 9-11

      —An exalted name: 9; Acts 4:12

      —Universal Lordship: 10; Hebrews 1:8

      —Universal worship: 11; John 4:23,24

12. Working Out Our Own Salvation: 2:12-16

      a. God works salvation within: vs. 13

      b. We work out what God has worked within: vs. 12; 1:6

      —Without murmuring against God: vs. 14a; 2:2

      —Without disputing with men: vs. 14b

      —Blameless without rebuke: vs. 15a; Ephesians 1:4

      —Shining as lights in the world: 15b; Matthew 5:16

      —Holding forth the Word of Life: 16a; II Timothy 4:2

      —Running not in vain: 16b; I Corinthians 9:24-27

      —Laboring not in vain: 16c; I Corinthians 15:58

13. Holding Forth the Word of Life: 2:16

      a. *Why?* Because we are debtors to all men, and they cannot hear and know of God's grace unless we go and tell them God's message. We can never witness to the wrong person

about Christ: Romans 1:14; 10:13-15
  b. *When?* NOW—ready in season and out of season: Romans 1:15; II Timothy 4:2
  c. *Where?* Anywhere—wherever people are. The world is the field, and the fields are white unto harvest: John 4:35; Matthew 9:37,38; Acts 1:8
  d. *How?* By preaching Christ, which is the power of God unto salvation unto all who believe: II Corinthians 4:5; Romans 1:16; I Corinthians 1:18,21

14. Paul's Formula for Being Christlike: 3:4-14
  Loss: Confidence in the flesh: vss. 4-6
  Gain: The excellency of the knowledge of Christ: vs. 8a
  Forgetting: The past: vss. 4-7,13b
  Knowing:
    —Him: vs. 10a
    —His resurrection power: vs. 10b
    —His sufferings: vs. 10c
  Ignoring: His own works of righteousness: vs. 9a
  Accepting: Christ's righteousness through faith: vs. 9b
  Dying: To self—conformed to His death: vs. 10d; I Corinthians 15:31
  Living: His resurrected life: vs. 11; Romans 6:11
  Deaf: To man's call: vss. 4-6
  Hearing: God's call: vs. 14
    —Holy: II Timothy 1:9
    —Heavenly: Hebrews 3:1
  Leaving: The old life behind: vs. 13a
  Following: The new things of Christ: vs. 12
  Shirking: Pride: vss. 4-7
  Working: Serving Christ wholeheartedly: vss. 12,13
  Neglecting: Self: vs. 8
  Attentiveness: To eternity's values: vs. 14

15. The Believer's Status
  a. Found in Christ—*position:* 3:9
  b. Fellowship with Christ—*passion:* 3:10
  c. Faithful for Christ—*practice:* 3:14
  d. Fruitful through Christ—*privilege:* 3:15-17
  e. Fashioned like Christ—*promise:* 3:21

16. How to Live a Successful Christian Life: 4:4-13
  a. Rejoice always: vs. 4
  b. Forebear others; vs. 5a; 2:3,4
  c. Be ready for Christ's coming: vs. 5b; I John 2:28
  d. Be careful (anxious) for nothing: vs. 6a
  e. Pray about everything: vs. 6b
  f. Be thankful for everything: vs. 6c
  g. Enjoy God's peace: vs. 7
  h. Be truthful: vs. 8a
  i. Be honest: vs. 8b
  j. Be just: vs. 8c
  k. Be pure: vs. 8d
  l. Be lovely: vs. 8e
  m. Have a good report: vs. 8f
  n. Have a deep spiritual life: vs. 8g
  o. Praise God: vs. 8h
  p. Care for others: vs. 10
  q. Be content in any circumstance: vss. 11,12
  r. Think *on* and *do* all these things: vss. 8i,9,13

17. In Everything by Prayer: 4:6. See PRAYER in Index.
18. A Cure for Worry: 4:6,7
    a. *Unloading*—by prayer: vs. 6a
    b. *Committing*—by supplication: vs. 6b
    c. *Praising*—with thanksgiving: vs. 6c
    d. *Leaving*—the burden with God: vs. 6d
    e. *Getting*—God's peace in return: vs. 7

The end of worry is prayer. The end of prayer is peace. With prayer there are—
    a. *No pressures*—I am careful for nothing
    b. *No restrictions*—I am prayerful in everything
    c. *No complaints*—I am thankful in everything

When to Worry[4]

When we see the lilies spinning in distress,
Taking thought to manufacture loveliness;
When we see the birds all building barns for store,
'Twill then be time for us to worry—not before.

19. Think on These Things: 4:8[5]
    a. *Youth*—too happy to think. Plenty of time left yet.
    b. *Manhood*—too busy to think. Seeking more gold.
    c. *Prime of life*—too anxious to think. Worry has taken over.
    d. *Declining years*—too old to think. Life is wasted; heart hardened.
    e. *Dying bed*—too ill to think. Weak now; suffering alone.
    f. *Death*—too late to think. Opportunity to think is now lost. There is no second chance (Hebrews 9:27).
    g. *Eternity*—forever to think. God's mercy is past. In hell all the time to think of opportunities that would have kept you out of such a place (Luke 16:25).
20. Our Every Need Supplied: 4:19; Matthew 6:25-34
    a. When tired: Isaiah 40:29,31
    b. When hungry: Isaiah 40:11; Matthew 5:6
    c. When thirsty: Isaiah 41:18; Matthew 5:6
    d. When fearful: Isaiah 41:10,13
    e. When in trouble: Nahum 1:7; Psalm 46:1; Isaiah 33:2
    f. When tempted: Isaiah 59:19; I Corinthians 10:13
    g. When persecuted: Isaiah 54:17; II Corinthians 12:9a
    h. When weak: II Corinthians 12:9b
    i. When in sorrow: Matthew 5:4
    j. In whatsoever state we are: Philippians 4:10-12,19
21. According to His Riches: 4:19. A tax collector came one day to a poor minister of the gospel to determine the amount of taxes the minister would have to pay. "What property do you possess?" asked the assessor. "I am very wealthy," replied the minister. "List your possessions, please," the assessor instructed.

    "*First,* I have everlasting life (John 3:16).
    Second, I have a mansion in heaven (John 14:2).
    Third, I have peace that passeth understanding (Philippians 4:7).
    Fourth, I have unspeakable joy (I Peter 1:8).
    Fifth, I have divine love that never faileth (I Corinthians 13:8).
    Sixth, I have a faithful, pious wife (Proverbs 31:10).
    Seventh, I have healthy, happy, obedient children (Exodus 20:12).
    Eighth, I have true, loyal friends (Proverbs 18:24).
    Ninth, I have songs in the night (Psalm 42:8).

Tenth, I have a crown of life (James 1:12).

Eleventh, I have a Savior, Jesus Christ, who supplies all my need" (Philippians 4:19).

The tax assessor closed his book and said, "Truly, you are a very rich man, but your property is not subject to taxation."[6]

Throughout this Epistle Paul constantly places emphasis on Christ by using such phrases as "of Jesus Christ," "by Jesus Christ," "with Jesus Christ," "For to me to live," said Paul, *"is Christ."* What a testimony! And he was ever on the alert to be just that. He wanted to know Christ, fellowship with Him, die for Him, be raised with Him, and, in having these holy aspirations, set his affection on things above where Christ is and pressed "toward the mark for the prize of the high calling of God in Christ Jesus."

I PRESS TOWARD THE MARK—3:14[7]

"The believer's mark is perfection, or exact conformity to the Lord Jesus Christ. Oswald Chambers said, 'Perfection means being made one with Jesus so that the disposition that ruled Him will rule us.' In pressing toward this mark, we must first possess Christ, then be like Christ. 'Let this mind be in you, which was also in Christ Jesus.' When we are like Jesus, every foe is overcome, every difficulty is mastered, and the crown is about to be put on our heads. The prize is won and the honor will be worn forever. Exact likeness to Jesus we shall not attain here, but we may be very much more like Him than we are. Our tempers may be more heavenly, our disposition more spiritual, and our conversation more spiritual. We may be weaned from the present world, our motives may be purified, and holiness may become our element and delight. He who hath begun a good work in us can carry it on, and as we are now very unlike what we were, we may yet become more Christ-like than we are at present. But if we would, it must be the mark at which we aim. We must ever keep it in our eye, as the racer did the mark which was to decide the race. This we too often forget and are too well satisfied with present things. O to say with Paul, 'for to me to live is Christ.' "

PRAYER THOUGHT: "O Lord, remove from me this day all pretense and hypocrisy, making me truthful, unselfish, and strong, so that I may not do anything or say anything that I would be ashamed of later. In Christ's name and for His sake I ask this. Amen."[8]

Philippians 1:20

Colossians—Christ Preeminent

Name: This Epistle derives its name from those at Colosse, to whom Paul was writing: 1:1,2. Colosse was a city of Phrygia in Asia, an unimportant place about twelve miles from Laodicea. Epaphras was the pastor. Under his ministry we learn that this insignificant city, due to faithful saints there, had made a name for itself in the faith (1:4-7). We have Paul's own word that he had not visited or preached at Colosse (2:1). When or by whom the gospel was first preached at

Colosse, and a church founded there, is not known. It is possible that Paul's stay in Ephesus (three years) and his preaching in Phrygia inspired its founding through Epaphras (4:12,13).

Occasion of Writing: The visit and report of Epaphras of the church in Colosse to Paul in Rome, and Paul's desire to write to Philemon at Colosse regarding Onesimus, induced him to write this Epistle and send both to their destination through Tychicus (4:7-9). From Epaphras Paul learned of a need to combat false teaching and wrong practices concerning circumcision, mysticism, salvation through asceticism, worship of angels, all of which errors had the tendency to deny the supremacy and universal mediatorship of Christ, hence this letter to those at Colosse "that in all things He [Christ] might have the preeminence" (1:18).[1]

Contents: The apostle writes to commend and confirm them in the faith of the gospel which Epaphras had preached unto them, the same that he himself preached; to warn them of two forms of error—Judaism and mysticism; and to exhort them to true godly living, dead to the rudiments of the world but alive with Christ. This book bears a similar relationship to Ephesians, the same as does Romans to Galatians. Ephesians emphasizes the *oneness* of Christ; Colossians the *completeness* of Christ. The theme of Ephesians is the *church;* of Colossians, the *Head* of the Church. In Philippians Christ *empties* Himself and becomes a Servant. In Colossians He is restored to His rightful position and is the *fullness* of God.

Chapter one emphasizes *doctrine*—Christ's deity, sufficiency, and His preeminence. He is All in all.

Chapter two emphasizes *polemics*—refuting arguments about Christ's fullness and warning his hearers against being led astray by false teachers.

Chapter three devotes itself to *spiritual things*—solid Christian living by individuals, servants and masters, and families.

Chapter four emphasizes *the need to pray* for others, to walk circumspectly, and be ready to give an answer for their hope in Christ.

In the 4 chapters in this book, there are 95 verses and 1,988 words.

Character: Doctrinal.

Subject: The fullness of Christ and our fullness in Him: 1:19; 2:9,10.

Purpose: To give us the object of our faith: 2:2,3.

Outline:
 I. Introduction: 1:1-8
 II. Paul's Intercession for the Colossians: 1:9-14
 III. Christ the Preeminent Lord: 1:15-29
 IV. Christ the Incarnate Lord: 2:1-23
 V. Believer's Union with the Preeminent and Incarnate Lord: 3:1—4:6
 VI. Conclusion: 4:7-18

Writer: Paul: 1:1,2. See WRITER in Romans.

When and Where Written: See WHEN and WHERE WRITTEN in Ephesians. A Prison Epistle.

Key Chapter: 1. The indwelling Christ.

Key Verses: 2:9,10.

Key Word: Fullness.

Key Phrase: With Christ.

Key Thought: Christ preeminent.

Spiritual Thought: Crown Him Lord of all.

Christ Is Seen As: The Fullness of the Godhead: 1:19; 2:9.

Names and Titles of Christ. See NAME in Dictionary.

1. Jesus Christ: 1:1
2. Christ: 1:2
3. Lord Jesus Christ: 1:2
4. Christ Jesus: 1:4
5. Lord: 1:10; 2:6
6. God's dear Son: 1:13
7. Our Redeemer: 1:14
8. Image of God: 1:15
9. Firstborn of every creature: 1:15
10. Creator: 1:16
11. Head of the Church (body): 1:18; 2:19
12. The Beginning: 1:18
13. Firstborn from the dead: 1:18
14. The Preeminent One: 1:18
15. The Fullness of God: 1:19; 2:9
16. Peacemaker: 1:20
17. The Reconciler: 1:21,22
18. Hope of glory: 1:27
19. The Treasure of wisdom and knowledge: 2:3
20. Head of principalities and powers: 2:10
21. Forgiver of sins: 2:13; 3:13
22. The End of the Law: 2:14; Romans 10:4
23. The Spoiler of principalities and powers: 2:15
24. Our Life: 3:4
25. Our All: 3:11
26. Lord Jesus: 3:17
27. Our Rewarder: 3:24a
28. Lord Christ: 3:24b
29. Master: 4:1

Names and Titles of God. See NAME in Dictionary.
1. Father: 1:2; 2:2.
2. Father of our Lord Jesus Christ: 1:3.

Names and Titles of the Holy Spirit: The Spirit: 1:8. See NAME in Dictionary.

1. Walking Worthy of the Lord: 1:10. See FOLLOWERS in Index.
2. The Glory of the Preeminent Christ.
   His pre-Incarnation glory: 1:15-17
   a. The image of God: 1:15a; John 1:1; Hebrews 1:3
   b. The Creator: 1:16,17; John 1:3
   His manifested glory: 1:13,14,27
   a. In His birth: 1:15b
   b. In His work of redemption: 1:13,14
   c. In His resurrection: 1:18b
   d. In His power: 1:17
   e. In the Church: 1:18a
   f. In indwelling the believer: 1:27
      —To fill with the knowledge of His will: 1:9
      —To enable a walk worthy of the Lord: 1:10a
      —To make us fruitful in every good work: 1:10b
      —To increase the knowledge of God: 1:10c
      —To strengthen with all might: 1:11

   —To make us meet for our inheritance: 1:12
   His ascended glory: 3:1-4
   a. At His Father's right hand: 3:1; Hebrews 1:3
   b. In God: 3:3b
   c. Now the believer's life: 3:4
3. It Pleased God: 1:19.
   a. To make all fullness dwell in Christ: 1:19
   b. To anoint His Son: Matthew 3:17
   c. To bruise His own Son: Isaiah 53:10
   d. To spare not His own Son: Romans 8:32
   e. To deliver us: Psalm 40:13
   f. To save those who believe: I Corinthians 1:21
   g. To make us His people: I Samuel 12:22
   h. To make us one in Christ: I Corinthians 12:18-20
   i. To accept from us proper sacrifices: Hebrews 13:16
   j. To reveal His Son in us: Galatians 1:15,16
   k. To give us resurrection bodies: I Corinthians 15:38-44
4. Christ's Reconciling Work: 1:21,22
   a. *Past*—alienated and enemies
   b. *Present*—reconciled in His body
   c. *Future*—holy, unblamable, unreprovable
5. Risen with Christ: 3:1. If we are risen with Christ, we will—
   a. Seek heavenly things: vs. 1
   b. Set our affection on things above: vs. 2
   c. Mortify the flesh: vss. 3-7
   d. Put off worldly lusts and habits: vss. 8,9
   e. Put on the new man—be Christlike: vss. 10-15
   f. Let God's Word rule in our lives: vs. 16
   g. Do all to the glory of God, not to men: vss. 17,23
   h. Be obedient: vs. 22
   i. Continue in prayer: 4:1
   j. Walk in wisdom: 4:5
   k. Have speech seasoned with grace: 4:6a

Key to Chart:

A. The Sinner's Position. Adam was created in God's *image* and *likeness* (Genesis 1:26,27). When Adam sinned, he died spiritually—his spirit became dead to the things of God. As a result, his offspring were born in *his* image and likeness—becoming sinners by nature (Genesis 3:5; Psalm 51:5). Having been made sinners by his disobedience, death passed upon all men (Romans :19a with 5:12; I Corinthians 15:22a). Because all have sinned, we do not understand the things of God—we come short of His glory (Romans 3:23; I Corinthians 2:14). As a sinner, dead, without Christ, God, and hope, we are on the "broad road" leading to destruction (Ephesians 2:1b,12; Matthew 7:13).

B. The wages of our sin is death, and Hell from beneath is moved to meet us at our coming—to meet every Christ-rejecter (Romans 6:23a; John 3:18; Isaiah 14:9; Luke 16:19-31). See SIN and HELL in Index.

C. God, who is rich in mercy and love, made provision for the sinner's salvation (Ephesians 2:4; John 3:16). Since salvation is of the Lord (Jonah 2:9)—
   1. God reveals His plan of salvation through the preaching of His Word: Romans 10:12-17. Herein the Father draws: John 6:44.
   2. The Almighty (Spirit) illuminates our dead spirits: Job 32:8.

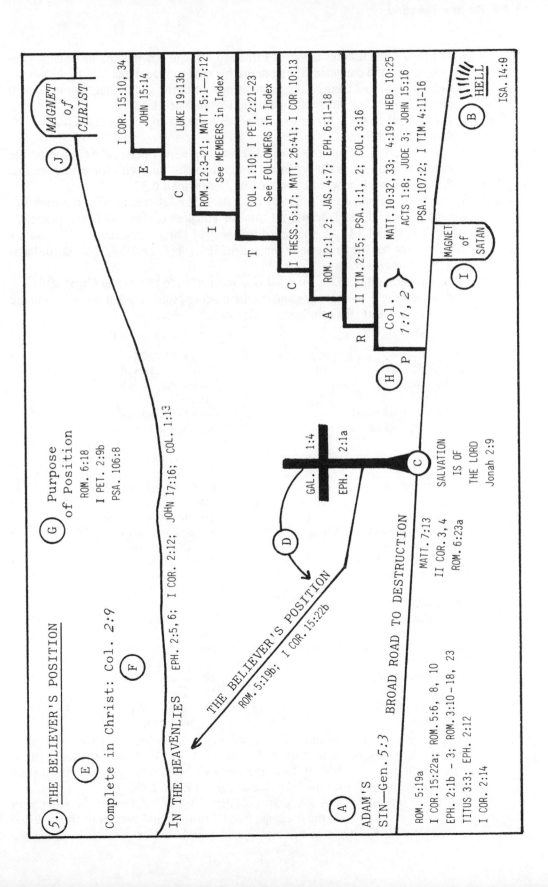

5. THE BELIEVER'S POSITION

(E)

Complete in Christ: Col. 2:9

(F) THE BELIEVER'S POSITION

(G) Purpose of Position
ROM. 6:18
I PET. 2:9b
PSA. 106:8

IN THE HEAVENLIES   EPH. 2:5, 6; I COR. 2:12; JOHN 17:16; COL. 1:13

THE BELIEVER'S POSITION
ROM. 5:19b; I COR. 15:22b

(D)

GAL. 1:4
EPH. 2:1a

(C)

SALVATION
IS OF
THE LORD
Jonah 2:9

(A)
ADAM'S
SIN—Gen. 5:3   BROAD ROAD TO DESTRUCTION

ROM. 5:19a
I COR. 15:22a; ROM. 5:6, 8, 10
EPH. 2:1b - 3; ROM. 3:10-18, 23
TITUS 3:3; EPH. 2:12
I COR. 2:14

MATT. 7:13
II COR. 3, 4
ROM. 6:23a

(J) MAGNET of CHRIST

I COR. 15:10, 34

E   JOHN 15:14

C   LUKE 19:13b

I   ROM. 12:3-21; MATT. 5:1—7:12
     See MEMBERS in Index

T   COL. 1:10; I PET. 2:21-23
     See FOLLOWERS in Index

C   I THESS. 5:17; MATT. 26:41; I COR. 10:13

A   ROM. 12:1, 2; JAS. 4:7; EPH. 6:11-18

R   II TIM. 2:15; PSA. 1:1, 2; COL. 3:16

P   Col. 1:1, 2 }

(H)

MATT. 10:32, 33; 4:19; HEB. 10:25
ACTS 1:8; JUDE 3; JOHN 15:16
PSA. 107:2; I TIM. 4:11-16

(I) MAGNET of SATAN

(B) HELL

ISA. 14:9

3. The Holy Spirit testifies of Christ's finished work of redemption for sinners, convicts of sin, and convinces the sinner of his need to repent and believe the gospel. He also convinces them of the righteousness of Christ and of judgment to come if one fails to accept Christ: John 15:26; 17:7-9; Mark 1:15.

4. The faith of Christ is given to all repentant sinners to be saved: Galatians 2:16; Ephesians 2:8,9.

5. Upon believing in and receiving Christ as one's own personal Savior, God the Father then presents the repentant believer to His Son, with the assurance that those given by Him will be received by Christ: John 6:37.

D. Having been presented to the Son by the Father, the believer is delivered from this present evil world and is translated into the kingdom of God's dear Son (Galatians 1:3,4; Colossians 1:13). He is declared righteous by Christ's obedience to His Father's will, and now has life in the Son (Romans 3:25; 5:19b; Ephesians 2:1a; I Corinthians 15:22b; Colossians 4:4).

E. See I AM, point 18, p. 526, for what God has made the believer in Christ Jesus.

F. "In Christ Jesus," we now *are* and *do* the exact opposite of what we were and did when we were lost: II Corinthians 5:17; Colossians 3:1,2—

LOST—BELOW	SAVED—ABOVE
Are in darkness	Are in the light
Have worldly walk	Have spiritual walk
On the broad road	On the narrow way
Are disobedient	Are obedient
Do not understand God	Do understand God
Are carnally minded	Are spiritually minded
Hate	Love
Are servants of unrighteousness	Are servants of righteousness
Are foolish	Are wise
Have own righteousness	Have God's righteousness
Are blind	Can see
Are not a people	Are the people of God
Are Satan's children	Are God's children
Are enemies of God	Are friends of God
Are alienated from God	Are in Christ
Are afar off from God	Are made nigh God
Are sinners	Are saints
Are ungodly	Are godly
Live in shame	Live in victory
Are in bondage	Are free
Are under God's wrath	Are in God's mercy and love
Are condemned	Are not condemned
Are on sinking sand	Are on the solid Rock
Are dead	Are alive
Have wages of sin	Have gift of eternal life
Are going to hell	Are going to heaven

G. The *purpose* of our position is that we might *do* what we have *become* in Christ—serve righteousness (Romans 5:19b; 6:18). This leads to the *practice* (H) of our position by our "showing forth the praises of Him who called us out of [the] darkness [of our sin] into His marvelous light" (I Peter 2:9b).

H. The *test* of our position is found in Colossians 3:1,2. "*If* ye then be risen with Christ": If so, then seek those things listed "above" and not those things listed "below" (point F). We then begin to put into practice our position by doing the things listed in the "steps" labeled P-R-A-C-T-I-C-E. As we grow in grace and knowledge of our Savior, Jesus Christ, we move upward, farther away from the magnet (power) of Satan (I), and get closer to the magnet of Christ (J). Our old nature is still attracted to the devil. Our new nature (II Peter 1:4) is attracted to Christ (Point J), and the closer we get to Him, the less attracting power Satan has to influence us. Never forget: "Greater is He that is in you than he that is in the world," and "as He is, so are we" (I John 4:4,17b). We overcome as He overcame (see TEMPTATION in Index). In our *practice* we answer His prayers, obey His commands, and labor more abundantly (Luke 22:31,32; John 15:14; I Corinthians 15:10). Let us "awake to righteousness" (I Corinthians 15:34).

6. Life *in* Christ: 3:1-23
   a. Dead to—
   —Self—crucified with Christ: vs. 3a; Romans 6:6; Galatians 2:20a
   —Sin: Romans 6:11a
   —The flesh: Galatians 5:24
   —The rudiments of the world: Galatians 6:14; Colossians 2:20-23
   —The Law: Romans 7:4; Galatians 2:19
   —The devil and principalities and powers: Hebrews 2:14,15; Colossians 2:13-15. It is to be noted that the above mentioned things *are not dead*—they are very much alive, though defeated by Christ. *I am dead* to these things, therefore, they have no dominion over the believer. We have been made alive unto God (Romans 6:11).
   b. Buried with Christ: Romans 6:4,5a
   c. Resurrected to walk in newness of life—risen with Christ: 3:1a; Romans 6:4
   d. Ascended in the heavenlies—elevated in Christ: vss. 1b,2; Ephesians 2:6
   e. Protected life—hid with Christ: vs. 3b
   f. Secured future life—with Christ in glory: vs. 4
   g. Daily life—
   Putting off the old man: vss. 5-9
   —Evil passions of the flesh: 5-7
   —Evil actions of the mind: 8,9
   Putting on the new man: vss. 10-23
   —Bearing fruit of the Spirit: 12
   —Considering one another: 13,14
   —Honoring God: 15-17
   —Faithful in the home: 18-21
   —Serving heartily: 22,23

7. A Test for Glorifying God: 3:17
   a. Will what I am about to say or do or where I am about to go enslave me?
   b. Will such strengthen my faith in Christ and the Word of God?
   c. Will it cause others to get a foggy view of Christ?
   d. Can I really do it for the glory of God?
   e. Can I witness to others while participating?
   f. Will these things keep me away from duty in my own church?

"The rule that governs my life is this: Anything that dims my vision of Christ, or takes away my taste for Bible study, or cramps my prayer life, or makes Christian work difficult, *is wrong for me,* and I must, as a Christian, turn away from it. This simple rule may help you find a safe road for your feet along life's road."[2]

To settle the matter, don't *go* anywhere you wouldn't want to be found when Christ returns, don't *do* anything you wouldn't want to be doing when He comes again, and don't *say* anything you wouldn't want Him to hear when He descends from heaven for His own.

8. Speaking with Grace, Seasoned with Salt: 4:6
   a. Speaking what we know: John 3:11

b. Speaking God's purpose: Titus 2:11-15
c. Speaking boldly: Acts 14:3; Ephesians 6:20
d. Speaking the truth in love: Ephesians 4:15
e. Speaking in psalms, hymns, and spiritual songs: Ephesians 5:19
f. Speaking uprightly: Isaiah 33:15a
g. Speaking in prayer: Daniel 9:21
h. Speaking to warn the wicked and sinning saints: Ezekiel 3:17-21
i. Speaking the wisdom of God: I Corinthians 2:7,13
j. Speaking of His testimonies: Psalm 119:46
k. Speaking of His glory: Psalm 29:9b
l. Speaking of His righteousness and praise: Psalm 35:28
m. Speaking of His glorious honor and works: Psalm 135:5

A BIT OF
HEAVENLY MANNA

One of the comforting truths connected with our position "in Christ" is that our life is hid with Christ in God, and being in Him, no man shall pluck us out of His hand, not even out of the hand of the One who gave us to Christ (Colossians 3:3; John 10:28,29). Because we are "complete in Christ" (Colossians 2:10)—

OUR LIFE IS HID WITH CHRIST IN GOD—3:3[3]

"Our God is our refuge. Christ is in the Father, and the Father is in Christ. Our life is in Christ, and Christ is our life. He represented us. He died for us. He sent His Holy Spirit into our hearts as the Spirit of life. He lives in us from heaven. We are identified with Him, and our interests are identified with His. The union between Christ and us is the closest possible. We are members of His body, of His flesh, and of His bones. We are joined to the Lord by the Spirit, and as such are one spirit with Him. As the husband and wife are no more twain, but one flesh, so Christ and His people are no more two, but one. He is the Head; we are His members. He is the beauty of the Church and in Him dwells all the fullness of the Church. As the Head, He thinks for us, cares for us, provides for us, listens to us, watches over us, sympathizes with us, rules over us, and glories in us. He exercises all the senses for us. He see our foes, dangers, and wants. He hears all that is said against us in all places. He feels the deepest interest in us and He will see to it that all things work together for our good. He takes care of the whole body, even the feeblest member. He clothes all. He feeds all. He adorns all. He preserves all. He represents all. Our heavenly Father looks upon us as the members of His Son, hid with Christ in Himself. He loves us as He loves His Son, and He will place us in His heavenly kingdom with His Son. He has eternally secured us, for it is 'Christ *in us* the hope of glory.' O glorious, soul-supporting truth! May I ever look upon myself as one with Christ, and endeavor to live and walk just as Jesus did. My life is a treasure, and Jesus, to preserve it, hides it with Himself in God."

PRAYER THOUGHT: "Dear Lord, I ask for a sweet disposition to show a world soured by hate and jealousy that my Savior is not a *myth,* but a risen, lovely Savior living in my heart and life. May none ever look at me and say that 'Christ died in vain.' In His precious name I pray. Amen."[4]

Colossians 1:27

First Thessalonians—The Epistle of the Rapture

Name: This Epistle derives its name from those at Thessalonica, to whom Paul was writing: 1:1. Thessalonica (now called Salonica) was a seaport town situated on the Thermaic Gulf, near Mount Olympus, and was the capital of Macedonia. It had a large industrial population, thousands of which were Jews who had a synagogue there. The church was planted by Paul on his second missionary journey in A.D. 52 (Acts 17:1-10), although he was there less than a month. Persecution came about when Paul preached the kingship of Jesus (Acts 17:7), and he was finally driven out of town, going to Berea. The majority of believers were Gentiles (1:9; 2:14), but Jews, proselytes, and 'chief women' are also mentioned (Acts 17:4).[1]

Occasion of Writing: When persecution broke out in Thessalonica, Paul fled to Berea. When persecution befell him there, he fled to Athens, leaving Timothy and Silas behind. When Timothy met Paul in Athens, Paul sent Timothy back to the Thessalonians to comfort them (3:2). Paul was in Corinth (Acts 18:1,5) when Timothy reported (1) that Paul's character and motives had been attacked; and (2) that they were disconcerted by the death of some members, apparently having understood Paul to teach that Christ's return would occur before the death of any. Paul wrote this letter (1) to vindicate his own character (2:3-9); (2) to encourage them to loyalty in spite of persecution (2:13-16); (3) to confirm these young Christians in truth already taught (3:1—4:2); (4) to exhort them to holiness of life (4:3-8); and (5) to comfort them concerning those already asleep in Jesus (4:13—5:11).

Contents: It is significant to note that the first letter Paul wrote to any church was this one to the "Model Church" at Thessalonica. It was pure, upright, and faithful, and Paul had much to praise and nothing to blame. These new converts had a *faith* that worked, a *love* that labored, and *hope* which enabled them to patiently bear afflictions and *wait* for the coming of the Lord Jesus, and a *walk* that revealed they were in the light. The believers at Thessalonica—

1. Received the Word: 1:6b; 2:13
2. Were saved from wrath: 1:10
3. Turned from idols: 1:9a
4. Presented their bodies a living sacrifice: II Corinthians 8:1,5
5. Followed God: 1:6a
6. Served the living and true God: 1:9b
7. Suffered persecution for living godly: 1:6; 3:3,6,7
8. Were joyful in the Spirit: 1:6c
9. Had works of faith and love: 3:6,7
10. Were examples to others: 1:7,8
11. Supported missions: II Corinthians 8:3,4
12. Prayed for missionaries: II Corinthians 8:3,4
13. Were looking for the second coming of Christ: 1:10

Paul's stay in Thessalonica was three short weeks, yet to these raw pagans he unfolded the cardinal doctrines of the Scriptures—

1. Election: 1:4
2. The ministry of the Spirit: 1:5,6; 4:8; 5:19
3. Assurance: 1:5
4. The Trinity: 1:1,5
5. Conversion: 1:9
6. The Second Coming: 1:10
7. The believer's walk: 2:12; 4:1
8. Sanctification: 4:3; 5:23
9. The resurrection: 4:14-17
10. The Day of the Lord: 5:1-3
11. Man's tripartite nature: 5:23

Romans presents God's *way* of salvation—*Justification* (1:16), Ephesians presents God's *purpose* in salvation—*Sanctification* (5:27), and I Thessalonians presents God's *object* of salvation—*Glorification* (4:17). Each chapter to those at Thessalonica speaks of Christ's return—

1. Wait for His Son from heaven: 1:10
2. In Christ's presence at His coming: 2:19
3. At the coming of our Lord: 3:13
4. To meet the Lord in the air: 4:17
5. Unto the coming of the Lord: 5:23

The apostle encourages them under the affliction and suffering; exhorts them to stand fast in the Lord to abide by His truths and ordinances, to live a holy life, and to regard the duties of the faith toward God, one another, and those that were set over them. In this encouragement and exhortation he instructs them concerning the resurrection of the dead and the Second Coming of Christ, which was of deep concern to the church. In the 5 chapters of this book, there are 89 verses and 1,857 words.

Character: Church Epistle.

Subject: The coming of our Lord for His church.

Purpose: To give us hope as to seeing our Savior (1:10); reward us for our service (2:19,20); comfort us in sorrow with the hope of His coming (4:13-18); and to exhort us to readiness for His coming (5:11-27).

Outline:

I. The Model Church—work of faith: 1
II. The Model Servant—labor of love: 2
III. The Model Life—unblameable in holiness: 3
IV. The Model Faith—hope of Christ's return: 4
V. The Model Action—walking in the light: 5

Writer: Paul: 1:1. See WRITER in Romans.

When and Where Written: A.D. 52, in Corinth (Acts 18:1,5; I Thessalonians 3:6). First Thessalonians is the first of the letters written by Paul. It was written before the four gospel accounts. The date of this epistle is important because in the very first verse Paul acknowledges the Deity of Christ with these words, "Lord Jesus Christ." Many critics have held that the Deity of Christ was a later development in order to deify the man Jesus, but Paul in his first letter confirms the belief of the early Christians that Jesus Christ was God the Son.

Key Chapter: 4. The Rapture.

Key Verses: 1:9,10.

Key Word: Coming.

Key Phrase: In Christ—hopeful: 4:13-18.

Key Thought: Waiting for His Son from heaven: 1:10.

Spiritual Thought: He is surely coming again.

Christ Is Seen As: Our *coming* Lord: 1:10; 4:16,17.

Names and Titles of Christ. See NAME in Dictionary.

1. Lord Jesus Christ: 1:1; 5:9
2. Lord: 1:6; 4:16
3. His Son: 1:10a
4. Christ: 2:6; 4:16
5. Jesus: 1:10b; 4:14
6. Christ Jesus: 2:14
7. Lord Jesus: 2:15

Names and Titles of God. See NAME in Dictionary.
1. Father: 1:1; 3:13
2. Living and true God: 1:9
3. God of peace: 5:23

Names and Titles of the Holy Spirit. See NAME in Dictionary.
1. Holy Ghost: 1:5,6
2. His Spirit: 4:8
3. The Spirit: 5:19

Prior to their conversion, those of Thessalonica were idolaters—heathens. In just three short weeks they had received a "seminary course" in doctrine from Paul (Acts 17:1-3). Quite naturally many questions were raised after Paul left—questions which came to mind because of their former pagan beliefs. One concerned what happened to their loved ones after death. Archaeologists have brought to light some interesting inscriptions which give insight into their thinking along this line. One such says: "After death no reviving, after the grave no meeting again." Christian doctrine gives the answer, and probably for this reason Paul placed much emphasis on this truth in his letter to them. How thrilled they must have been when they read this Epistle, especially chapter four, vss. 13-18.

1. The Model Church: 1:1-10. See CONTENTS and OUTLINE.
2. Always: 1:1. Paul's use of the word "always" indicated he knew the secret of an unwearied life, of unfailing strength, and of "sticktuativeness":

   a. *Always* giving thanks: 1:2; Ephesians 5:20
   b. *Always* enjoying peace: II Thessalonians 3:16
   c. *Always* laboring fervently: Colossians 4:12; I Corinthians 15:10
   d. *Always* praying: Colossians 1:3
   e. *Always* rejoicing: Philippians 4:4
   f. *Always* obeying: Philippians 2:12
   g. *Always* being bold: Philippians: 1:20
   h. *Always* triumphing: II Corinthians 2:14
   i. *Always* confident: II Corinthians 5:6
   j. *Always* revealing Christ: II Corinthians 4:10
   k. *Always* abounding in the Lord's work: I Corinthians 15:58
   l. *Always* having all sufficiency: II Corinthians 9:8
   m. *Always* having a good conscience: Acts 24:16

3. The Effect of the Gospel: 1:3,9,10
   a. *Past*—work of faith turning to God from idols, having been delivered from the penalty of sin: 1:3a,9a; II Corinthians 1:10a
   b. *Present*—labor of love serving the living and true God, being delivered from the power of sin: 1:9b; II Corinthians 1:10b

    c. *Future*—waiting for Christ's return, to be delivered from the presence of sin; redemption of the body: 1:10b; II Corinthians 1:10c; Philippians 3:20,21

4. The Soul-winner's Crown: 2:19,20. See CROWN in Index. The Thessalonians became Paul's joy and *crown of rejoicing* because of his having led them to the Lord and because they were a credit to the name of Christ. To win others to Christ there must be the conviction that we have something worth telling, not simply that there is something we ought to tell. As the old country philosopher put it: "You can't tell what you don't know any more than you can come back from somewhere you ain't been." Neither can we tell of Christ unless we know Him and that He is worth telling about.

    Why did Paul witness to the Thessalonicans? See SOUL-WINNING in Index.
    a. He was commanded: Psalm 107:2; Matthew 10:32,33; Romans 10:9,10
    b. Because of what Christ did for him: Psalm 40:1-3; I Peter 3:18
    c. Because he was a pattern to them: I Timothy 1:16
    d. He was indebted to them: Romans 1:14; II Corinthians 4:13; Ephesians 6:20
    e. He was not ashamed: Romans 1:16
    Why did those at Thessalonica need Christ?
    a. They were lost: Luke 19:10
    b. They were perishing: I Corinthians 1:18
    c. They were condemned: John 3:18
    d. They were under God's wrath: John 3:36
    e. They were dead spiritually: Ephesians 2:1b
    f. They were without Christ and God: Ephesians 2:12
    g. They had no hope: Ephesians 2:12
    h. The wages of their sin was death: Romans 6:23a; Ezekiel 18:4
    The result of Paul's witness—
    a. They became a "model" church. See CONTENTS.
    b. They became Paul's "soul-winner's crown": 2:19,20
    c. They became an example for us to follow: 1:3,9,10; II Corinthians 8:5

5. Sanctification: 4:3,7. There is much controversy in Christian circles over the definition of this word—this subject. What does it mean?

    a. Holiness groups state that after one is saved (justified), there is a subsequent, second work of grace (sanctification) which eradicates the carnal nature, baptizing one with the Holy Spirit, and usually enables the individual, now filled with the Holy Spirit, to speak in tongues. They are now sinless, and if anything is done that is wrong, it is a mistake of the head and not the heart. However, such a one can lose both his sanctification and justification, and must be saved all over again.

    b. Conservative groups generally believe sanctification to be a gradual growth in grace and life here on earth until perfection is attained—in heaven.

    c. Some hold that it means "suppression" of the old Adamic nature still within all believers, which "suppression" leads to a victorious life over sin and the devil.

    d. The Bible definition is different from these three, although the end result of Bible sanctification includes total yieldedness, growth in grace and holiness (being filled with the Spirit). Sanctification simply means to "set apart." Apply these four definitions to the following verses and see which is the right one—
    —God sanctified the seventh day: Genesis 2:3
    —Moses to sanctify all firstborn infants: Exodus 13:2a
    —Moses to sanctify all firstborn animals: Exodus 13:2b
    —Moses to sanctify the people: Exodus 19:10
    —Priests to sanctify themselves: Exodus 19:22
    —Moses to sanctify Mount Sinai: Exodus 19:23
    —God sanctified the Tabernacle: Exodus 29:43
    —Moses to sanctify Tabernacle implements: Exodus 40:10,11

—A man to sanctify his house: Leviticus 27:14
—A man to sanctify his field: Leviticus 27:17
—Priests to sanctify the house of God: II Chronicles 29:16,17
—God sanctified in "Gog" before heathens: Ezekiel 38:3,16
—A "fast" is sanctified: Joel 1:14
—Christ sanctified Himself: John 17:19
—Christ sanctified by His Father: John 10:36
—Believers sanctify unbelievers: I Corinthians 7:14
—Believers to sanctify God: I Peter 3:15

These verses tell us that a day, objects, things, animals, people by people, self, Christ, God, and even unbelievers, are sanctified. Definitions "a," "b," and "c" could not possibly apply to this list. Being "set apart" does. For a practical application in the life of the believer, *sanctification is*—

a. Being dead to sin but alive unto God: Romans 6:11
b. Yieldedness: Romans 6:13
c. Dedication: Romans 12:1,2
d. Surrender: Luke 9:23
e. Separation: II Corinthians 6:16,17
f. Abiding in Christ: John 15:7; Philippians 1:21a
g. Serving the Lord: Acts 20:19-24
h. Obedience to Christ's command: Matthew 9:9
i. Fulfilling God's will: II Thessalonians 4:3a
j. See HEAVENLY MANNA in II Thessalonians

We are sanctified (set apart unto godly living)—

a. By God: Jude 1
b. By the offering of Christ: Hebrews 10:10
c. By the blood of Christ: Hebrews 13:12,13
d. By the Holy Spirit: I Corinthians 6:11
e. By faith: Acts 26:18
f. Through truth: John 17:17
g. Being sanctified, we are perfected forever: Hebrews 10:14

6. The Rapture—Christ's Return *for* His own: 4:1-18

The Fact of it Established by—

a. Testimony of the prophets:
—Enoch: Jude 14
—Isaiah: 11:1-9
—Ezekiel: 21:26,27
—Zechariah: 14:3-5
—Malachi: 3:1
b. Testimony of Christ: John 14:13
c. Testimony of angels: Acts 1:10-11
d. Testimony of the Apostles:
—Matthew: 24:37,42,44
—Mark: 13:26
—Luke: 21:27
—John 14:1-3; I John 3:1,2; Revelation 22:12,20
—Paul: I Thessalonians 4:13-18
—James: 5:7
—Peter: I Peter 1:7,13; II Peter 3:3,4

The Character of it—

a. Negatively considered:
—Not death

—Not material progress
—Not an historic event
—Not spiritual—
—As the Holy Spirit of Pentecost
—As in conversion of the sinner
—As in the spread of Christianity
b. Positively considered:
—Personal and bodily: Acts 1:11
—Visible: Hebrews 9:28; I John 3:1,2
—Sudden: Mark 13:36; Revelation 22:7-12,20
—Near: Matthew 24:36-42; James 5:8
—Signs of His coming (see SIGNS in Index)
—In the heavens: Luke 21:25a. It has been necessary in the past sixty years to make new nautical and astronomical almanacs due to sun spots and remarkable changes in the moon. In our scientific age man's exploration into outer space to gather heretofore unknown information, even *on* the moon, could well reveal many new "signs in the heavens."
—Upon the earth: Luke 21:25b,26
—False religions: Matthew 24:5
—Wars and rumors of wars: Matthew 24:6
—Political unrest of nations: Matthew 24:7a
—Famines: Matthew 24:7b
—Pestilences: Matthew 24:7c
—Earthquakes: Matthew 24:7d
—Speed and knowledge: Daniel 12:4
—Physical: Luke 21:26
—Social—capital and labor: James 5:1-8
—Building: Luke 17:28-30
—Immoral: Matthew 24:37-39; II Timothy 3:1-5
—Apostasy: I Timothy 4:1; Jude 3,4; II Thessalonians 2:1-3
—Jewish: Matthew 24:32-34; Ezekiel 37:1-14. Since General Allenby entered Jerusalem December 9, 1917, the "fig tree" (Israel) has been putting forth leaves with amazing rapidity. Jews have been returning to the Holy Land in great numbers. A Hebrew University on Mt. Scopus was opened in 1925. The Sanhedrin has been revived; and the sacred custom of going up to the Passover was observed in the spring of 1922 for the first time in nearly 2,000 years. Since World War II (1945), Jews have been going back "home" by the tens of thousands, and in 1948 they became a full-fledged nation—the first time since her captivity in 586 B.C. Truly this is Israel being resurrected from her graves, having been buried in Gentile nations for centuries, and now going back with "sinews . . . flesh . . .and skin" into the land of Israel. Going back in unbelief, they have no breath in them, but when they look upon Him (when He returns) Whom they have pierced, they will have "breath" in them, with a "new heart . . . and a new Spirit within" (Ezekiel 37:5; 36:26-28).

The Practical Value of it—
a. Hope for the recipients of God's grace: Titus 2:11-13
b. Incentive to holy living:
—Watchfulness: Matthew 24:42-44; Luke 21:34-36
—Sobriety: I Peter 1:13
—Patience: Hebrews 10:36,37
—Mortification of fleshly lusts: Colossians 3:3-5; I John 3:2,3
—Endurance of testing: I Peter 1:6,7
—Abiding fellowship: I John 2:28
—Brotherly love: I Thessalonians 3:12,13

c. Motive to a life of faithful service:
  —Fidelity: Luke 12:42-44; Matthew 25:19-21; Luke 19:13
  —Ministerial constancy: II Timothy 4:1,2; I Peter 5:2-4
  —Soul-winning zeal: I Thessalonians 1:5,6,9,10; 2:19,20
d. Comfort for sorrowing saints: I Thessalonians 4:13-18

The Purpose of it—
a. Resurrection of those asleep in Him: I Thessalonians 4:16
b. Rapture of dead in Christ and living saints: I Thessalonians 4:17
c. Transformation of both: I Corinthians 15:51-53; I John 3:2
d. Judgment and rewards for works: II Corinthians 5:10; I Corinthians 3:12-15
e. Marriage of Christ and the Church: Revelation 19:7-9
f. To be with Him forever: I Thessalonians 4:17; Revelation 22:20

7. **Children of Light: 5:5-23**
  a. Watch: vss. 5,6
  b. Are sober: vs. 8a
  c. Put on the breastplate of faith and love: vs. 8b
  d. Put on the helmet of salvation's hope: vs. 8c
  e. Are not under wrath: vs. 9
  f. Live together with Christ: vs. 10
  g. Comfort themselves together: vs. 11a
  h. Edify one another: vs. 11b
  i. Esteem faithful laborers highly: vss. 12,13a
  j. Are at peace among themselves: vs. 13b
  k. Warn the unruly: vs. 14a
  l. Comfort the feebleminded: vs. 14b
  m. Support the weak: vs. 14c
  n. Are patient toward all men: vs. 14d
  o. Do not render evil for evil: vs. 15a
  p. Follow that which is good: vs. 15b
  q. Rejoice evermore: vs. 16
  r. Pray without ceasing: vs. 17
  s. Give thanks in everything: vs. 18
  t. Do not quench the Spirit: vs. 19
  u. Do not despise prophesyings: vs. 20
  v. Prove all things: vs. 21
  w. Abstain from all appearances of evil: vs. 22
  Summary: God's promise to "children of light": vss. 23,24

8. **God's Will—Giving Thanks: 5:18**
  a. In everything: 5:18
  b. For God's mercy: Psalm 107:1
  c. For His unspeakable Gift: II Corinthians 9:15
  d. For faith of the saints: Romans 1:8
  e. For making us partakers of the inheritance: Colossians 1:12
  f. For spiritual growth: I Thessalonians 1:2,3
  g. For riches in Christian graces: I Corinthians 1:4,5
  h. For unfeigned faith (faith without hypocrisy)—a faith that produces faithfulness: II Timothy 1:3,5
  i. For love unto all saints: Ephesians 1:15,16
  k. For remembrance of the saints: Philippians 1:3
  l. For giving us victory: I Corinthians 15:57
  m. For causing us to triumph in Christ: II Corinthians 2:14
  n. For *all* things—*always:* Ephesians 5:20

To the everlasting glory of the Thessalonians, they "received the Word . . . with joy of the Holy Spirit": (1:6). For this cause Paul thanked God without ceasing, because, when they received the Word of God, they received it not as the word of man,

BUT AS IT IS IN TRUTH, THE WORD OF GOD—2:13[2]

"This is Paul's testimony of the gospel. It is God's truth. It originated in His mind. It was made known by His inspiration. It is published at His command. It is pure like His nature. It is as stable as His throne. It is the rule by which He works. It is the standard by which He judges. It is God's message to you, to me, to all. It is the Word respecting God, setting before us His express image that we may know Him; His exceeding great love that we may believe Him; the way of access to His throne that we may approach Him. As the Word of God, it demands our attention, reverent faith, and obedience. It is solemnly connected with His glory and our destiny. It is to be received into the understanding, the affections, and the heart. As God's Word, we should receive it meekly, believe it wholeheartedly, obey it promptly, and trust it implicitly. The gospel *is* the Truth of God, therefore beware how you trifle with it, neglect it, or disbelieve it. It is the Word of God that will judge you. Have you received it as did those at Thessalonica? Have you received it as the very truth of God? Has it worked effectively in you, producing a radical change? If so, you have received the Word with joy of the Holy Spirit."

 PRAYER THOUGHT: "Help me to see, dear Father, that the 'Blessed Hope' of Thy Son's coming is a perpetual light on my pilgrim pathway that makes the present bearable—that the dark and mysterious *now* will be made plain when the lost chords of life will be found in that moment when I shall see Him and become as He is. In His blessed name I pray. Amen."[3]

I Thessalonians 4:16-18; I John 3:1,2

Second Thessalonians—Christ's Second Coming

Name: See NAME in I Thessalonians.

Occasion of Writing: To clear up their misunderstanding of the term "sudden" in his first letter (5:3), referring to the return of Christ. Some had interpreted it to mean "immediate," and were neglecting their daily work, which led to a disorderly life. This error gained strength by forged letters (2:2; 3:17). Paul wrote this second letter to reassure them of Christ's coming to vindicate their cause (1:5-12); to explain that certain events must first come to pass before Christ's return (2:1-12); and to exhort them to lead a quiet, sober, and industrious life (3:6-15).

Contents: "The apostle comforts and supports the Thessalonians under the afflictions and persecutions they endured for the sake of the gospel; rectifies their mistaken view concerning the coming of the Lord; exhorts them to take notice of disorderly persons, such as were idle and busybodies, and withdraw from them, and remove them from their communion as being not only burdensome to them, but a reproach to their profession."[1] This book has 3 chapters, 47 verses, and 1,042 words.

Character: Church Epistle—Doctrine.

Subject: The coming of Christ to judge those who obey not the gospel: 1:7-9.

Purpose: To warn against false teaching about Christ's coming and to show the relation of the Christian to the day of the Lord.

Outline:
  I. Persecution and the Lord's Coming: 1:1-7
  II. The Impenitent and the Lord's Coming: 1:8-12
  III. The Apostasy and the Lord's Coming: 2:1-12
  IV. Service and the Lord's Coming: 2:13—3:18

Writer: Paul: 1:1. See WRITER in Romans.

When and Where Written: A.D. 53, in Corinth, soon after Paul's first letter to the Thessalonians. It appears that the person who carried the first epistle returned speedily to Corinth and gave Paul a particular account of the state of the Thessalonian church.

Key Chapter: 2. God's day and the man of sin.

Key Verses: 2:13,14.

Key Word: Waiting.

Key Phrase: In Christ—glorified.

Key Thought: The Day of the Lord.

Spiritual Thought: Wait and work till He comes.

Christ Is Seen As: Our *soon* coming Lord.

Names and Titles of Christ. See NAME in Dictionary.
  1. Lord Jesus Christ: 1:1
  2. Lord Jesus: 1:7
  3. Lord: 1:9
  4. Christ: 2:2

Names and Titles of God. See NAME in Dictionary.
  1. Father: 1:1; 2:16.
  2. Lord of Peace: 3:16.

Names and Titles of the Holy Spirit: Spirit: 2:13. See NAME in Dictionary.

The Old Testament in II Thessalonians: The man of sin who shall "exalt himself above God": 2:4 with Daniel 11:36.

1. The Unsaved. See HEATHEN in Index.
  a. Know not God: 1:8a
  b. Obey not the gospel: 1:8b
  c. Receive not the love of the truth: 2:10
  d. Believe not the truth: 2:12
  e. Are guilty before God: Romans 3:10-19
  f. Are without excuse: Romans 1:19,20
  g. Are condemned already: John 3:18
  h. Have God's wrath upon them: John 3:36
  i. The wages of their sin is death: Romans 3:23a
  j. Thank God they can be saved: Romans 10:13; Ephesians 2:8,9

2. Emphasis on Prayer: 1:11; 3:1.[2] See PRAYER in Index. The term "prayer" as used in the largest sense includes all forms of communication with God. It embraces worship, praise, thanksgiving, supplication, and intercession. The definite teaching as found in the Scriptures on the subject of prayer deals principally with the last two aspects—supplication and intercession.

The importance of prayer can be measured only by the prominence given to it in the Scriptures and in the lives of those who have been used of God.

Reason or Necessity for Prayer—
a. It is right: Luke 18:1
b. It is commanded: Colossians 4:2 RV; I Thessalonians 5:17
c. It is sinful to neglect it: I Samuel 12:23
d. Neglect of it grieves God: Isaiah 43:21,22 RV
e. It is the medium through which God bestows blessings: Matthew 7:11
f. It is essential to victory over the forces of evil: Ephesians 6:18
g. Because of the emphasis given to it in the early church: Acts 6:4; 12:5; Romans 1:9; Colossians 1:9

Qualifications for Prayer—
a. Must not regard iniquity in the heart: Psalm 66:18
b. Must not waver: James 1:6
c. Must heed God's Word: Proverbs 28:9
d. Must not ask amiss: James 4:3
e. Must not be proud: Job 35:12,13; James 4:6
f. Must have a forgiving Spirit: Mark 11:25,26; Ephesians 4:32
g. Must hear the cry of the needy: Proverbs 21:13
h. Must have true penitence: Luke 18:13,14
i. Must have faith in Christ: I John 5:13-15; Hebrews 11:6
j. Must be righteous and godly: Psalm 34:15; 32:6
k. Must be obedient: I John 3:22
l. Must be humble: Psalm 10:17; 9:12
m. Must be trustful: Psalm 37:4,5
n. In families, husband must honor wife: I Peter 3:7
o. Must pray in Christ's name: John 14:13; 15:16b

Persons Addressed in Prayer—
a. God: Acts 12:5
b. God the Father: Matthew 6:9; John 17:1
   —Holy Father: John 17:11
   —Righteous Father: John 17:25
c. Jesus Christ: I Corinthians 1:2; Acts 7:59
   —Lord: Romans 10:12,13; II Timothy 2:22
d. The Scriptures intimate that prayer is to be made to the Father in the name of Jesus Christ, the Son, in the power and under the guidance of the Holy Spirit (Ephesians 2:18). The relation of the Holy Spirit to prayer is set forth in such passages as Romans 8:15,16,26,27. There is nothing to forbid prayer to Him. Technically speaking, the Holy Spirit is the Lord of the Harvest. He convicts men of sin, brings them to the place of repentance and acceptance of Christ as their Savior, and baptizes them into the body of Christ (John 16:7-9; Titus 3:5; I Corinthians 12:13). The Lord of the harvest sends forth laborers into the field, and Christ has commanded us to "pray ye therefore the Lord of the harvest, that He will send forth laborers into His harvest" (Matthew 9:38; Acts 13:2-5).

Subjects of Prayer—
a. Ourselves: I Chronicles 4:10; Psalm 106:4,5; II Corinthians 12:7-10
   —As lacking wisdom: James 1:5
   —As in destitute circumstances: Psalm 102:17; 69:33 (RV)
   —As under oppression: Exodus 22:22,23
   —As in affliction: James 5:13a
b. Fellow Christians: I Samuel 12:23
c. Christian workers: Matthew 9:38; Ephesians 6:18-20; Colossians 4:3
d. Young converts: I Thessalonians 3:9,13; John 17:9,20
e. The sick: James 5:14-16

  f. Children: I Chronicles 29:18,19; Ephesians 6:4

  g. Rulers: I Timothy 2:1-3; I Peter 2:17

  h. Israel: Psalm 122:6,7; Romans 10:1

  i. Those who mistrust us: Luke 6:28; Acts 7:59,60

  j. All men: I Timothy 2:1

Method of Prayer—

  a. The time of it:

    —At stated periods: Psalm 55:16,17; Daniel 6:10; Acts 3:1; 10:9,30

    —At meals: I Timothy 4:3-5; Matthew 14:19; Acts 27:35

    —In great extremities: Psalm 50:15; 60:11; 86:7

    —At all seasons: Ephesians 6:18 (RV); I Thessalonians 5:17; Luke 18:1

  b. The place of it:

    —In private: Matthew 6:6; 14:23; 26:36

    —In public: Luke 18:10,13,14; John 11:41; Acts 27:35

    —Everywhere: I Timothy 2:8

  c. The manner of it:

    —Standing: Mark 11:25; Luke 18:13

    —Kneeling: I Kings 8:54; Luke 22:41

    —Prostrate: Matthew 26:39

    —With the heart: Psalm 119:145; Jeremiah 29:12,13; Lamentations 3:41

    —In full assurance of faith: Hebrews 10:22; I John 5:14

    —With the spirit of understanding: I Corinthians 14:15

    —With humility: II Chronicles 7:14; Psalm 10:17

    —With boldness: Hebrews 4:16

    —With earnestness: I Thessalonians 3:10; James 5:16,17

    —With submission to God: Luke 22:41,42

    —With importunity: Genesis 32:26; Luke 11:8,9

    —With thanksgiving: Philippians 4:6,7; I Thessalonians 5:18

The Scriptures sanction no special bodily attitude in prayer; the soul may be in prayer regardless of the posture of the body. We can be in such an attitude of prayer that we create an atmosphere of prayer.

  Results of Prayer—

  a. Great achievements: James 5:16-18

  b. Definite answers: Mark 11:24; John 14:13,14. Someone has said that God always answers prayers. He either says "yes," "no," or "wait awhile."

  c. Accomplishment of a Divine purpose: I John 5:14,15. The aim of prayer is not to overcome God's reluctance but to lay hold of His willingness, i.e., to secure the purpose and provision of His will.

  d. Glorification of God: John 14:13; I John 3:22

The *secret* of prayer is *praying.* The secret is not knowing *how* to pray but simply praying (Luke 11:1). When there is much prayer, there is much power. When there is little prayer, there is little power. And when there is no prayer, there is no power.

  3. Future Events: 1:6-12

    a. Christ's revelation with His angels: vs. 7

    b. Retribution for the ungodly: vs. 8

    c. Glory for His saints: vs. 10

  4. The Man of Sin: 2:1-12

    a. His character—the son of perdition (doom): vs. 3b

    b. Time of his appearing—after apostasy of the church—a falling away: vs. 3a

    c. His mission—to oppose and exalt himself against God: vs. 4

    d. His methods—with the power of Satan, using signs, lying wonders, and deceivableness: vss. 9,10

    e. His temporary assistant—God—who sends a strong delusion on his followers: vss. 9-12

f. His destruction—shall be consumed by the Lord: vs. 8

g. The "delayer" of his appearing—"He"—the Holy Spirit in the church: vs. 7

5. Apostasy—a Sign of Christ's Second Coming: 2:3. The word "apostasy" does not appear in our English Bible. Neither do such words as "rapture" and "Trinity" appear, but the truth of these subjects is found therein. The simplest definition of "apostasy" is "the forsaking of what one has hitherto professed or adhered to." It is deliberate error, false teaching, a heresy, a departure from known truth. It is not due to ignorance, but is a willful act which involves a scornful trampling under foot the Son of God, desecrating His sacrificial blood, and defying the Holy Spirit (Hebrews 10:29). Apostasy is the exact opposite of faith. It is not a single act of sin. It is a state.

Paul emphasized the truth that Christ shall not come until "apostasy" prevails. We are in the days of apostasy *now* and it ought to behoove believers to "earnestly contend for the faith" (Jude 3). Perilous times shall come in these last days. People will not endure sound doctrine. False prophets have arisen, even denying the Lord God that bought them, and they are turning the grace of God into lasciviousness (giving people a license to sin). See II Timothy 3:1-8,13; 4:3,4; II Peter 2; Jude 4-19. "Apostasy" is another way of saying "modernism." See MODERNISM in Index.

6. Wicked Men: 3:2. See WICKED and UNGODLY in Index.

a. Adversaries of the Lord: I Samuel 2:10

b. Children of fools: Job 30:8

c. Children of disobedience and wrath: Ephesians 2:2,3

d. Children in whom there is no faith: Deuteronomy 32:20

e. Children of iniquity: Hosea 10:9

f. Children that are deaf to God's Word: Isaiah 30:9

g. Children of the world: Luke 16:8

h. Corrupters: Isaiah 1:4

i. Enemies of the cross of Christ: Philippians 3:18

j. Enemies of all righteousness: Acts 13:10

k. Evil and adulterous: Matthew 12:39

l. Generation of vipers: Matthew 3:7; 12:34

m. Grievous revolters: Jeremiah 6:28

n. Haters of God: Romans 1:30

o. Inventors of evil things: Romans 1:30

p. Reprobates: II Corinthians 13:5-7

q. Scornful: Psalm 1:1

r. Servants of sin: Romans 6:20; John 8:34

s. Sottish children (foolish; silly): Jeremiah 4:22

t. Stubborn and rebellious: Psalm 78:8

u. Ungodly: Psalm 1:1; Jude 4

v. Perverse and crooked: Deuteronomy 32:5; Matthew 17:17

w. Children of the devil: I John 3:10; Acts 13:10

x. Children of hell: Matthew 23:15

A BIT OF HEAVENLY MANNA

God has two primary wills: one for the sinner to be saved (II Peter 3:9b), and the other for the saved sinner to be sanctified (set apart: I Thessalonians 4:3a). Bible sanctification knows nothing about a carnal nature being eradicated or of anyone being sinless. Bible sanctification pure and simple is separation unto God—set apart by the Holy Spirit unto holiness, set apart by the Father to glorify His

Son (see SANCTIFICATION in Index). When Moses sanctified Mount Sinai he set it apart as the place where God would give the Law. When Christ sanctified Himself He set Himself apart unto the Father to do His will. When we sanctify the Lord God in our hearts we simply set Him apart in our lives that He might have first place therein to rule our lives—to fulfill His will.

THROUGH SANCTIFICATION OF THE SPIRIT—2:13[3]

"The sanctification of the Spirit commences in regeneration, it is carried on through life, and it will be complete in the day of Christ. It consists in making us holy, or inwardly and outwardly conforming us to the likeness of the Lord Jesus Christ. It separates us from the world, sets our hearts against sin, consecrates us to the Lord's service, makes us zealous for His glory, and creates us anew in Christ Jesus. Physically we are the same as before, but morally and spiritually we differ. The more we experience the sanctifying work of the Spirit, the more clearly we shall discover our own sinfulness, the more we shall be tried with our inward corruptions, the more we shall see the need of the Savior's blood, the more we shall bless God for the Redeemer's finished work on Calvary, and the more carefully and cautiously we shall walk in our pilgrimage journey in this ungodly world. Nothing will prove our election by the Father, or our redemption by the Son, but the sanctification of the Holy Spirit."

 PRAYER THOUGHT: "Dear Lord, may I not be content with being 'just average,' but with the absolutes of Christlikeness, laboring more abundantly than all like Paul, and with grit like Daniel to stand against all opposition. In Thy name I pray. Amen."[4]

I Thessalonians 1:11,12

THE PASTORAL EPISTLES
First and Second Timothy, and Titus

Subject: Church order and government.

Purpose: Church discipline.

These Epistles differ in style and language from Paul's other letters. Because of new words found in these letters which are not used elsewhere in the New Testament (82 in I Timothy, 53 in II Timothy, and 33 in Titus), critics have questioned their authorship by Paul. These Epistles contain different subjects than his others—pastoral duties, responsibility, and conduct as contrasted with sin, faith, justification, etc., consequently a difference in vocabulary.

In Paul's Church Epistles and to Philemon his salutation is twofold: "grace and peace." In the "Pastoral Epistles" his salutation is threefold: "grace, mercy, and peace." All believers need grace and peace for their Christian experiences, but a pastor needs the added ingredient—*mercy*—because of his position and his dealings with many Christians from all walks of life. Only a pastor can appreciate this truth. The Lord's servants frequently require something "extra" to heal their bruised spirits and give them the lift they need. *Consider their efforts—*

Have *you* ever tried to preach one hundred and four sermons a year to the same congregation? Have you ever tried to please all the members of your church? Have you ever tried to lead a prayer meeting week after week when one hundred and twenty five of the one hundred and fifty members were absent? Have you ever tried to visit all the newcomers in your community; all the sick at home and in the hospital of your congregation; the lost in your neighborhoods, in about sixty-five homes of the members; and attend all the committee and extra church meetings —all in twelve months. (Pity the pastor who has a much larger church!) Have you ever had to lead when no one would follow? Have you ever tried to get a little man to do a big job, or a big man to do a small job? Have you ever tried to carry the weight of a lost world, plus the weight of your own church and community? Have you ever tried to love when others hate, or praise when others condemn? Have you ever tried to bind up broken hearts or re-establish broken homes? Have you ever tried to sympathize with and help fallen men and women when others seem not to care and even mock? Have you ever tried to smile upon empty collection plates and realize that the world is moving away from God? Have you ever tried to pour out your very own soul to get men to give themselves to Christ and have no response? If not, then you cannot know what it means to be the pastor of a church. It is no wonder that Paul, a pastor himself, offered "mercy" to his fellow-pastors! See PASTOR in Index.

If[1]
(For Preachers)

If you can preach when scowling faces meet your gaze;
If you can smile when frowns are evident apace;
If you can scatter cheer, and sullen gloom supplant;
If you can give the pessimist a different "slant";
If you can still press on when every move is blocked;
If you can tilt your chin when So-and-so has "balked";
If you can take "dictation" from the "powers that be";
If you can rise above the petty things you see;
If you can plan for bigger things and stand alone;
If you can rest your weary head upon a stone;
If you can grip the hand which dealt the cruel blow;
If you can walk "the second mile" and love bestow;

If you can weep with saddened souls who truly weep;
If you can laugh with those whose festive hours keep,
If you can stick, let come what may, to God's own Book;
If you can to its sacred pages ever look;
If you can say, "Thus saith the Lord!" and know it's true;
If you can love the Gentile and the Jew;
If you can preach on Sunday with an empty purse;
If you can make your shabby suit look "none the worse";
If you can drive your ancient car with self-respect;
If you can "let them pass" and keep your head erect;
If you can thrill at being loved for Jesus' sake;
If you can play the hectic game of give and take;
If you can lead the sinner to the cleansing flood;
If you can preach redemption through the precious blood;
If you can build for time and eternity;
If you can say at last, "Thine shall the glory be!"
If you can do all this, O mortal creature,
You are in fact—as well as name—a worthy preacher!

First Timothy—Advice to Ministers

Name: "This Epistle derives its name from the one to whom Paul was writing, 'Timothy, my own son in the faith' (1:1,2). Paul and Barnabas in the course of their first missionary journey among the Gentiles, came to Lystra, a city in Lycaonia (Acts 14:5,6). Here they found a Jewess name Lois, and also her daughter Eunice, both of whom had become converted to the Christian faith. Eunice had married a Gentile, by whom she had Timothy. His father was probably dead at this time; the grandmother, daughter, and son lived together (Acts 16:1-3; II Timothy 1:5). Timothy, it appears, had been brought up in the fear of God (II Timothy 1:5; 3:15), and became a thorough convert to Christianity. A very tender intimacy grew up between him and Paul. Timothy means 'God-honoring.'

"When the apostle came the second time to Lystra from Antioch he found Timothy a member of the church and so highly reputed and warmly commended by his church that Paul took him to be his companion in his travels (Acts 16:1-3). It appears that Timothy, probably because of his Gentile father, had not been circumcised. When Paul was determined to take him he found it necessary to have him circumcised because the Jews would neither have heard him nor Paul had not this been done (Acts 16:3).

"It appears that from the time Timothy first joined Paul as his assistant he never left him except when sent by him on some special errand. By his affection, fidelity, and zeal, he so recommended himself to all the apostles, and acquired such authority over them that Paul inserted his name in the inscription of several of his letters he wrote to the churches (see I Corinthians 16:10). Paul's esteem and affection for Timothy was expressed still more conspicuously by writing to him the [two] excellent letters which bear his name."[1]

Timothy had his weaknesses as well as his strong points. He was weak physically (5:23). At times he was timid (II Timothy 1:6,7), and was encouraged not to be ashamed of his testimony, or of Paul as a prisoner, or of himself as God's workman (II Timothy 1:8; 2:15). Paul used himself as an example of not being ashamed of his own testimony and his being a prisoner (II Timothy 1:12,16). Timothy was exhorted to wage a good warfare by enduring hardness as a good soldier (1:18; II Timothy 2:3,4).

"His strong points seem to have been 'a special call of God for the work of an evangelist, and to this the elders of his church set him apart by the imposition of hands (4:14). In addition to being called to the work of an evangelist certain prophetic declarations were related to him (1:18; 4:14).'[2] He suffered imprisonment (Hebrews 13:23) and according to tradition, died a martyr's death as bishop of Ephesus under Dometian or Nerva.

Occasion of Writing: When Paul and Timothy arrived at Ephesus, heretical teachers, as Paul had predicted, were busily engaged in spreading their errors (Acts 20:29,30; I Timothy 6:3,4). When Paul left the city, he placed Timothy in charge of the church. This young preacher "needed the counsel and guidance and moral support of his older and superior minister. The nature of the false doctrines that had been brought in is somewhat shown in the expression—'oppositions of science falsely so called' (6:20), the beginning of which was already apparent, and this the apostle opposes as wholly incompatible with the gospel. Timothy's early education (4:12) had prepared him in part to become the antagonist of this and other errors; and yet his comparative youth, the short period during which he had been a Christian, and the need to stir up the gift within him, rendered it desirable that he should have in form the explicit instructions of Paul himself, as to both the agreement of his doctrines with those of the apostle, and his authority to direct the administration affairs of the church."[3]

Contents: "Paul teaches Timothy how to behave himself in the house of God, by taking heed to his doctrine and conversation (3:15; 4:12-16); and gives rules relating to the qualifications of bishops and deacons, the care of widows, church censures, and the becoming walk and conversation of all sorts of persons of every office, age, sex, rank, and order."[4] This epistle has 6 chapters, 113 verses, and 2,269 words.

"Whether or not Paul was conscious of the relations that this epistle was to hold in the church through all later times is a question we cannot answer, but whoever believes that the Holy Spirit guided his writing cannot fail to believe that the future wants of the church were cared for, and that herein, more fully than anywhere else, the living church may at all times see a divinely modeled order for church government. Luther has aptly said, 'St. Paul writes this epistle as a model for all bishops, what they shall teach, and how they shall rule the Christian Church in all circumstances, so that they need not guide Christian men by their own human darkness.' "[5]

Character: Pastoral.

Subject: The teaching and conduct which is becoming in the church of God.

Purpose: To give divine caution and guidance to every servant of God in this dispensation.

Outline:
     I. Introduction: 1:1,2
    II. Sound Doctrine in the Church Enjoined: 1:3-20
   III. Intercession by the Church Commanded: 2:1-8
   IV. The Divine Order for Women in the Church: 2:9-15
    V. Qualifications of Bishops and Deacons in the Church: 3:1-13
   VI. The Conduct of a Good Minister of a Church: 3:14—4:16
  VII. The Work of a Good Minister of the Church: 5:1—6:21

Writer: Paul: 1:1,2. See WRITER in Romans.

When and Where Written: Sometime between A.D. 64—67. Whether there were two imprisonments of Paul or not, this letter was probably written in Macedonia (1:3; 3:14), just before his last visit to Jerusalem.

Key Chapter: 1. Legalism and false teaching rebuked.

Key Verses: 3:14,15.

Key Word: Charge.

Key Phrase: In Christ—faithful.

Key Thought: Order in the house of God: 3:15.

Spiritual Thought: Guard the gospel.

Christ Is Seen As: The Mystery of godliness: 3:16.

Names and Titles of Christ. See NAME in Dictionary.
1. Lord Jesus Christ: 1:1; 5:21
2. Our Hope: 1:1
3. Jesus Christ: 1:2a
4. Lord: 1:2a
5. Christ Jesus: 1:12; 6:13
6. The Savior of sinners: 1:15
7. Mediator: 2:5
8. A Ransom: 2:6
9. Christ: 2:7
10. The Mystery of godliness: 3:16
11. The Blessed and only Potentate: 6:15a
12. King of kings: 6:15b
13. Lord of lords: 6:15c

Names and Titles of God. See NAME in Dictionary.
1. Our Savior: 1:1; 4:10
2. Blessed God: 1:11
3. King: 1:17a
4. Wise God: 1:17b
5. The One God: 2:5
6. The living God: 3:15; 4:10
7. The Quickener of all things: 6:13
8. The Giver of all things: 6:17

Names and Titles of the Holy Spirit. The Spirit: 3:16. See NAME in Dictionary.

The Old Testament in I Timothy:
1. A working ox not to be muzzled: 5:18 with Deuteronomy 25:4.
2. Companion references:
   a. Adam's creation: 2:13 with Genesis 2:7,21,22
   b. Adam's sin: 2:14 with Genesis 3:12
   c. We brought nothing into this world: 6:7 with Job 1:21

SEED THOUGHTS

1. Timothy's Stand for the Truth: 1:3—6:20.
   a. By refusing the teaching of good works as gospel truth:1:3-20
   b. By keeping reverence in church services: 2:1-11
   c. By keeping women in their proper place: 2:12-15
   d. By outlining Christian characteristics for the church office: 3:1-16
   e. By emphasizing the danger of false teachers: 4:1-10
   f. By requiring the personal life and habits to be right: 4:11—5:15
   g. By showing no partiality to faithful servants: 5:16-25
   h. By stressing humility in service: 6:1-4
   i. By glorifying eternal things instead of earthly values: 6:5-10

       j. By not believing things contrary to Scripture: 6:20,21a

2. Exhortations to Faith. See FAITH in Index.
   a. To unfeigned faith: 1:5
   b. To hold faith and a good conscience: 1:19
   c. To hold the mystery of faith in a pure conscience: 3:9
   d. To be nourished up in the words of faith: 4:6
   e. To be an example of faith: 4:12
   f. To follow after faith: 6:11
   g. To fight the good fight of faith: 6:12

3. Mercy Obtained: 1:13-17
   a. Mercy needed: vs. 13a
   b. Mercy obtained through Christ: vss. 13b,14
   c. Result of mercy obtained:
      —Abundant grace: vs. 14
      —Gospel committed to our trust: vss. 11,12
      —Longsuffering of Christ revealed: vs. 16a
      —A perfect pattern established: vs. 16b
      —Christ glorified: vs. 17

4. Why Christ Came: 1:15. See CHRIST, Mission of, in Index.
   a. To fulfill prophecy: Matthew 1:22,23
   b. To fulfill the Law: Matthew 5:17
   c. To bear witness of the truth: John 18:37
   d. To call sinners: Luke 5:32
   e. To seek the lost: Luke 19:10
   f. To manifest God's love: John 3:16; I John 4:9
   g. To give His life a ransom: Matthew 20:28; John 10:11
   h. To destroy (undo) the works of the devil: I John 3:8
   i. To die as our sacrifice for sin: John 1:29; I John 4:10
   j. To save sinners: I Timothy 1:15
   k. To redeem those under the Law: Galatians 4:4,5
   l. To give us life: John 10:10a
   m. To give us abundant life: John 10:10b
   n. To bring us to God: I Peter 3:18
   o. To become Lord of our lives: Romans 14:9

5. The Allurements of Pride: 3:6
   Pride is—
   a. A sin: Proverbs: 21:4
   b. Hateful to God: Proverbs 16:5
   c. Forbidden: I Samuel 2:3
   d. Defiling: Mark 7:20,22
   e. Hardening of the mind: Daniel 5:20
   Pride is characteristic of—
   a. The devil: I Timothy 3:6
   b. The world: I John 2:16
   c. False teachers: I Timothy 6:3,4
   d. The wicked: Romans 1:30
   Pride leads men to—
   a. Contempt and rejection of God's Word: Jeremiah 43:2
   b. Wrath: Proverbs 21:24
   c. Contention: Proverbs: 13:10
   d. Self-deception: Jeremiah 49:16
   The proud should be—
   a. Resisted: James 4:6

      b. Subdued: Isaiah 13:11

      c. Abased: Daniel 4:37 with Matthew 23:12

  6. Different Kinds of Consciences: 4:2

      a. Seared by lying and hypocrisy: 4:2

      b. Evil by sin: Hebrews 10:22

      c. Defiled by unbelief: Titus 1:15

      d. Weak by ignorance: I Corinthians 8:10

      e. Convicted by guilt: John 8:9

      f. Cleansed by Christ's blood: Hebrews 9:14

      g. Perfect by Christ's sacrifice: Hebrews 9:9; 10:2

      h. Faithful by obedience: I Peter 2:19

      i. Offenseless by carelessness: Acts 24:16

      j. Good by godliness: Acts 23:1

      k. Pure by fidelity: II Timothy 1:3

      l. Testifying by consecration: II Corinthians 1:12

7. Be Thou an Example: 4:12

'Twas a Sheep, Not a Lamb[6]

It was a sheep, not a lamb that strayed away,
*   In the parable we are told;*
A grown-up sheep that had gone astray . . .
*   From the ninety and nine in the fold.*

Out in the meadows, out in the cold,
*   'Twas a sheep the Good Shepherd sought:*
Back to the flock and into the fold,
*   'Twas a sheep the Good Shepherd brought.*

And why for the sheep should we earnestly long
*   And so earnestly hope and pray?*
Because there is danger, if they go wrong,
*   They will lead the young lambs astray!*

For the lambs follow the sheep, you know,
*   Wherever the sheep may stray;*
If the sheep go wrong, it will not be long
*   Till the lambs are as wrong as they.*

So, with the sheep we earnestly plead,
*   For the sake of the lambs today,*
If the lambs are lost, what a terrible cost
*   Some sheep may have to pay.*

A BIT OF
HEAVENLY MANNA

Ephesus was a mighty, proud city. Her religious life, centered around "Diana the Great," made her a popular city for heathen idolaters. Her hope was built on a lewd, vulgar, immoral religion. But the gospel had changed much of that for man under Paul's preaching (Acts 19), and a strong church had been established. After Paul left Ephasus, evil workers sought to spread false doctrine, and when Paul returned to Ephesus with Timothy, he felt the need to leave Timothy with the Ephesians, in the hope that a pastor on the scene could straighten out the erroneous teachings. A good method of correcting error is to present a hope—a hope based on truth. This Paul did in his letter to Timothy. Christ, not Diana, is the Blessed and only Potentate. Christ, not Diana, is Lord. Christ, not the fables of that day, is Truth. And for a hope to anchor them securely in their faith, Paul said:

THE LORD JESUS CHRIST IS OUR HOPE—1:1[7]

"The apostle sums up the misery of the worldling in these words, 'Having no hope': that is, no well grounded hope. For there is no hope for anyone, sinner or saint, but in Christ. He laid the foundation of it in His meritorious obedience and death. He gave the warrant for it by sending us His everlasting gospel. He produced it by giving us the Holy Spirit. We can have no hope of access to God, or acceptance with God, or any spiritual blessings from God but as we receive Christ, look to His cross, and believe in His glorious gospel. Take away Jesus, and the most virtuous can have no hope; give us Jesus and the vilest transgressor may have hope for the greatest blessing. Let us build on Jesus and on Jesus alone, and we shall find Him to be the foundation which will never give way. Let us live hoping for all necessary good things now and for everlasting glory at the end of our course. Let us do it for the sake of what Jesus did and suffered, and we shall never be disappointed. Beloved, is Jesus your hope? Are you hoping for mercy in His name and heaven through His blood? If so, look up to God and say—

> *Behold, His merit is our plea,*
> *On Him alone our souls depend;*
> *He is our Advocate with Thee,*
> *The helpless sinner's powerful Friend.*"

PRAYER THOUGHT: "In a world where there is so much profession and little love, right words and wrong thoughts, smiling faces and cold, cold hearts, help me, O God, to have such an attitude of love and worship to Thee that I might be a pattern of fidelity, not having my conscience seared as with a hot iron. In Jesus' name. Amen."[8]

I Timothy 4:1,2

Second Timothy—Paul's Final Message

Name: See NAME in I Timothy.

Occasion of Writing: Probably to acquaint Timothy with why Paul failed to return to Ephesus (I Timothy 3:14); to describe his present deplorable condition (1:15; 2:9; 4:10,14,16-18); to urge his visit and to ask other favors (4:9-13).

Contents: "The apostle stirs up Timothy to the faithful and diligent discharge of his duty as a minister of the gospel; to abide constantly by the truths in it, and to inspire him to suffer patiently, cheerfully, and courageously for the sake of it; and to warn him against false teachers and their errors, who were already risen, and would afterward arise and be followed by such who had itching ears, and could not bear sound doctrine; but this should be no discouragement to him in persecution of his work; and lastly, to desire his presence with him at Rome, being now destitute of his several assistants."[1] This letter is also personal; there are references to at least 25 individuals. First Timothy gives specific attention to the duties and responsibilities of a pastor, while II Timothy is concerned with the preacher. This second letter contains 4 chapters, 83 verses, and 1,703 words.

While there is a note of sadness in this letter (he was cold, without his books, and friendless, expecting very soon to be led out to execution—4:6,10,13,16), there is a song of triumph—"The Lord stood with me" (4:17). This Epistle is Paul's "swan song," containing his epitaph (4:6-8). It would seem that Paul was also saying—"Only one life 'twill soon be past, only what's done for Christ will last."

Character: Pastoral.

Subject: The unchangeable authority and power of God's Word in the last days.

Purpose: To show why Scripture has been given to man: 3:16,17.

Outline:
    I. Exhortation and Injunction: 1
   II. Eightfold Aspect of Christians: 2. See TRAITS in Index.
      A. Son—strong: vs. 1
      B. Soldier—fighting: vss. 3,4
      C. Manhood—striving: vs. 5
      D. Husbandman—laboring: vs. 6
      E. Sufferer—victory: vs. 12a
      F. Student—approved: vs. 15
      G. Vessel—separated: vs. 21
      H. Servant—gentle and teaching: vs. 24
  III. Saints Refuge in Perilous Times: 3
  IV. Final Charge and Final Outcome: 4

Writer: Paul: 1:1,2. See WRITER in Romans.

When and Where Written: A.D. 66 or 67, in prison in Rome. The interior of the "cell" in the Mamertine Prison, where Paul wrote to Timothy, displays a plaque in memory of this apostle as he lays hands on a newly won convert. He could be bound, but not the Word of God, which found lodging in the hearts of his hearers (2:9). It was here that he requested his cloak and parchments from Timothy (4:13). See PARCHMENT, p. 499.

Mamertine Prison

Key Chapter: 3. The believer's resource for apostasy.

Key Verse: 2:15.

Key Word: Charge.

Key Phrase: In Christ-exultant.

Key Thought: Responsibility in the house of God.

Spiritual Thought: Guard the witness.

Christ Is Seen As: Our righteous Judge: 4:1.

Names and Titles of Christ. See NAME in Dictionary.
1. Jesus Christ: 1:1
2. Christ Jesus: 1:1; 3:12
3. Lord: 1:2; 4:8
4. Savior: 1:10
5. Seed of David: 2:8
6. Christ: 2:19
7. Lord Jesus Christ: 4:1a
8. Righteous Judge: 4:1b

Names and Titles of God. Father: 1:2. See NAME in Dictionary.

Names and Titles of the Holy Spirit. Holy Ghost: 1:14. See NAME in Dictionary.

Nero, Paul's "unrighteous judge." Because of certain accusations made against Paul by the Jews, Paul appealed to his Roman citizenship, thus assuring him of a hearing before Caesar in Rome (Acts 22:25-30; 25:10-12; 26:32). Archaeology has given much light on the Caesar, Nero, before whom Paul was to have appeared. Nero was born in A.D. 37 of a family of scoundrels. His father, an official of the Roman government, and a cheat and bully with several murders to his credit, died when Nero was three. His mother poisoned his stepfather. She later married Emperor Claudius, who adopted Nero. Persuading the Emperor to designate Nero heir to the throne in place of his own son, Nero's mother murdered Claudius before he could change his mind. At the age of sixteen Nero became Emperor of the Roman empire.

He married his stepfather's thirteen-year-old daughter at the age of fifteen. He had his first wife slain, and he himself killed his second wife. To obtain his third wife, he had her husband killed. To keep Claudius' own son, Britannicus, from any attempt to claim his father's throne, Nero had him poisoned. His greed for publicity in arts, opera, and sports drove him to gory acts of violence. Chariot racing and bloody scenes with wild beasts and gladiators and prisoners became his delight. When Rome burned for a week in July, A.D. 64, it was rumored that he had set fire to the city to make room for a new palace. He made Christians, who refused to bow to "Emperor worship," the scapegoat, charging them with arson and "hatred of the human race."

The Roman historian Tacitus in his Annals (XV, 44), records the persecutions of Christians under Nero in A.D. 64 as follows: "Nero put men in charge who knew how to punish with the most ingenious cruelty and wrought havoc with those the common people hated for their crimes and called 'Christians.' Christ, for whom the name was derived, had been put to death in the region of Tiberius by the procurator Pontius Pilate. The deadly superstition, having been checked for awhile, began to break out again, not only throughout Judea, where this mischief first arose, but also at Rome, where from all sides things scandalous and shameful meet and

Nero

become fashionable. Therefore, at the beginning, some were seized who made confessions; then on their information, a vast multitude was convicted, not so much for arson as of hatred for the human race. And they were not only put to death, but subjected to insults, in that they were either dressed up in the skins of wild animals and perished by the cruel mangling of dogs, or else put on crosses to be set on fire, and, as day declined, to be burned, being used as light by night. Nero had thrown open his gardens for that spectacle, and gave a circus play, mingling with the people dressed in a charioteer's costume or driving in a chariot. From this arose, however, toward men who were, indeed, criminals and deserving extreme penalties, sympathy, on the ground that they were destroyed not for the public good, but to gratify the savage instincts of one man.'' See CATACOMBS in Index.

By the time Nero was 31 years old, the Roman Empire had become so weak that the senate, officers, soldiers, and even the palace guards were defecting. Finally, the senate declared him a public enemy and sentenced him to death by flogging. He escaped this sentence by committing suicide.

This was the ''Caesar'' to whom Paul had appealed. Now in Rome and in prison, Paul wrote to Timothy this last Epistle while awaiting his fate. Doomed to death because of Nero's hatred for Christians, Paul was not crucified as were many other Christians. As a Roman citizen, he was beheaded. His own epitaph is recorded in chapter 4:6-8. One can appreciate Paul's use of the expression, ''the Lord, the righteous Judge'' (vs. 8) in light of this information from archaeology concerning Nero, the ''unrighteous judge.''

The Old Testament in II Timothy: There are no direct quotations of the Old Testament in this Book. The companion references are:

1. The Lord knoweth those that are His: 2:19 with Numbers 16-5.
2. Opposition to Moses: 3:8 with Exodus 7:11.

1. Unfeigned Faith: 1:5. See FAITH in Index.
   a. Is a firm stand for righteousness: Ephesians 6:13-18
   b. Is a victorious life: I John 5:4
   c. Is a heart indwelt by Christ: Ephesians 3:17
   d. Is a growth in spiritual attainments: II Peter 3:18
   e. Is a consistent walk of good report: Hebrews 11:2
   f. Is a life lived to please God: I Thessalonians 4:1
2. God's Salvation: 1:8-10. See SALVATION in Index.
   a. Is according to His power: vs. 8
   b. Is with a holy calling: vs. 9a

    c. Is not according to our works: vs. 9b
    d. Is according to His own purpose and grace; vs. 9c
    e. Is in Christ Jesus: vs. 9d
    f. Is manifested by Christ: vs. 10a
    g. Abolished death: vs. 10b
    h. Gives life and immortality: vs. 10c

3. Certainties of Salvation: 1:12. See SALVATION in Index.
    a. A *Knowledge* of Him (Jesus Christ)—I know whom
    b. A *faith* in Him—I have believed
    c. A *surrender* to Him—I have committed
    d. An *assurance* of Him—I am persuaded
    e. A *confidence* in Him—He is able
    f. A *life* by Him—For to me to live is Christ
    g. An *experience* with Him—I also suffer these things
    h. A *testimony* for Him—I am not ashamed

4. A Fivefold Use of the Word
    a. Hold it: 1:13
    b. Study it: 2:15a
    c. Apply it: 2:15b
    d. Rightly divide it: 2:15c
    e. Preach it: 4:2

5. Characteristics of a Mature Christian: 2:1-25. See OUTLINE.

6. Soldiers of Jesus Christ: 2:3. See WARFARE in Index.
    a. Volunteer: Hebrews 11:25
    b. Are uniformed: Philippians 3:9; Revelation 3:4
    c. Are armed: Ephesians 6:11,18
    d. Are drilled: Ephesians 6:13
    e. Are ready to advance: Exodus 14:15
    f. Endure: II Timothy 2:3
    g. Are victorious: Romans 8:37; II Timothy 4:7
    h. Will have a grand review: Revelation 7:13-15

7. Your Share of Suffering: 2:3-13[2]
    What it may be—
    a. Privation and separation: vss. 4,5
    b. Misunderstanding: vs. 7
    c. Persecution: vss. 9,10
    Why you should accept it—
    a. It is the soldier's part: vs. 3
    b. It is due in loyalty to your enlisting officer: vs. 4
    c. It is necessary discipline: vss. 5,6
    d. It advances the Gospel: vss. 9,10
    e. It is surety of triumph: vss. 11,12

8. The Word of God is not Bound: 2:9.[3] See BIBLE in Index.
    —Generations follow generations . . . yet it lives
    —Nations rise and fall . . . yet it lives
    —Kings, dictators, presidents come and go . . . yet it lives
    —Hated, despised, cursed . . . yet it lives
    —Scoffed at by the scorners . . . yet it lives
    —Its inspiration denied . . . yet it lives.
      Yes, It Lives—
      —as a Light to our path
      —as the Gate to heaven
      —as a Guide for youth

      —as an Inspiration for the matured
      —as a Comfort for the aged
      —as Food for the hungry
      —as Water for the thirsty
      —as Rest for the weary
      —as Hope for the unbeliever
      —as Salvation for the sinner
      —as Grace for the Christian
    —To believe it is to live it
    —To know it is to love it
    —To love it is to accept it
    —To accept it means eternal life

9. Bible Homelitics (Preparing and Preaching a Sermon): 2:15
    a. Call to God for help: Psalm 119:18
    b. Choose a text: Luke 4:17-19
    c. Meditate upon it: Joshua 1:8
    d. Compare Scripture with Scripture: Acts 17:11
    e. Make Christ the center: Luke 24:27; Acts 8:35
    f. Collect illustrations: Matthew 13:34
    g. Condense it: Proverbs 10:19
    h. Continue to pray over it: Romans 12:12 RV
    i. Consecrate it: Psalm 37:5
    j. Preach it: II Timothy 4:2
    k. Challenge with it: Matthew 7:24-29

Testing a Sermon[4]

It's not the:	*It is the:*
Ability	Aim
Beauty	Book
Contention	Cross
Delivery	Decisions
Eloquence	Effect
Fragments	Fruit
Gloominess	Gladness
Hate	Harvest
Imagination	Instruction
Jesting	Justice
Knowledge	Kindness
Language	Love
Method	Message
Noise	New Birth
Offense	Object
Presentation	Power
Quantity	Quality
Reformation	Regeneration
Sleight of mind	Sincerity of heart
Tradition	Truth
Unfamiliarity	Unction
Volume	Vision
Wisdom of man	Word of God
X'cerpts	X'amples

Yap   Yea Lord

Zip   Zeal

10. Study the Word of God: 2:15[5]

> *Study to know the grace our Lord bestowed on thee;*
> *Study to know the love He had for you and me.*
> *Study to lift thy soul above the din of things;*
> *Study to hear His voice which through the ages rings.*
>
> *Study about the price He paid upon the tree;*
> *Study to know His Plan that spans eternity.*
> *Study that thou a workman unashamed may be—*
> *Study to share the Word of Truth entrusted unto thee.*

11. In These Last Days: 3:1. World events are demonstrating the truth of "perilous times" in our day and are confirming the words of Christ—"When I come will I find faith" (Luke 18:8—see SIGNS of Times in Index). The "social gospel," so popular among the liberals, has not produced world conversion nor will it usher in the millennium. While the true gospel is being crowded out to a degree by today's apostasy, Paul encourages us to be faithful to the Word—the fountain source of all truth and blessing (3:15-17; 4:2). Although the visible church has entered into a state of apostasy (falling away), the invisible church is soon to enter into glory, to be presented without spot, without blemish (Ephesians 5:27). Before that day, however, there will be—

    a. General moral and spiritual deterioration: 3:1-7,12,13
    b. Doctrinal apostasy of religious leaders: 4:3,4; II Peter 2:1,2; I Timothy 4:1-3
    c. Rapid increase of science, communication and travel: Daniel 12:4
    d. Anti-supernaturalism among intellectual leaders: 3:5; II Peter 3:3-6
    e. Conflicts between capitalism and labor: James 5:1-8
    f. Preparations for world governments and religions: Revelation 13:7,8
    g. Widespread materialism and secularism: Luke 17:28-30; 18:8
    h. Wars and rumors of wars, famine, earthquakes, disease: Luke 21:10,11

12. All Scripture: 3:16,17

    a. Beautiful in its *language:* Psalm 23
    b. Incorruptible in its *nature:* I Peter 1:23
    c. Loving in its *message:* John 3:16
    d. Enlightening in its *purpose:* Psalm 119:105
    e. Blessed in its *bestowments:* Psalm 32
    f. Effective in its *purpose:* II Timothy 3:16,17
    g. Wonderful in its *accomplishments:* Isaiah 55:11

13. Why Preach the Word: 4:2. See BIBLE, Designed for, and POEM, Preach the Word, in Index

14. Triumphant in Christ: 4:1-8

    a. By preaching the Word: vs. 2
    b. By loving sound doctrine: vs. 3
    c. By watching in all things: vs. 5a
    d. By persevering: vs. 5b
    e. By being evangelistic: vs. 5c
    f. By fully performing all duties: vs. 5d
    g. By being ready to die for your faith in Christ: vs. 6
    h. By fighting a good fight: vs. 7a
    i. By finishing the course: vs. 7b
    j. By keeping the faith: vs. 7c
    k. By being ready to meet Christ: vs. 8

15. A Crown of Righteousness: 4:8. See CROWNS in Index.
16. Luke, a Friend's Friend: 4:11
   a. In effort: Acts 16:10
   b. In testimony: Acts 16:13
   c. In prayer: Acts 16:16
   d. In travel: Acts 16:10-12
   e. In hospitality: Acts 21:8
   f. In tribulation: Acts 27:18
   g. In exile: Acts 28:16
   h. In impending death: II Timothy 4:11

Perilous times seem to be ruling the roost today. In all of man's selfishness, acts of sin, and the ruling of God out of their lives, there is a profession of religion in the air—a "form" of godliness, but a lack of God Himself who gives power for a godly life. But there is also—

TRUE GODLINESS—3:5[6]

"True godliness is the life of God in the soul, in consequence of one's dedication and devotion to God's service and praise. A godly man is a holy man. A godly life is a useful life. When a Christian is clothed in the power of God, he is both beautiful and useful; but having a form without the power is a mere shadow, a deception, a snare. But it is to be feared that many are satisfied with the form; they perform certain duties, avoid outward sins, associate with professors of religion, regularly attend the means of grace, and so doing, they fancy all is right. But this is a fearful delusion. We must be born again. Christ must be formed in us the hope of glory. We must crucify the flesh with its affections and lusts. We must *know* God, feel the power of God, and walk in fellowship with God, or our religion is but a dream, a vain show. Beloved, have you the power of godliness—true godliness? Or are you resting satisfied with the form? Many, through this mistake, fancy they are going to heaven, while they are on the direct road to hell. Search the heart and pray—

> *May truth direct my tongue,*
> *May grace my heart control,*
> *And Jesus be my song*
> *While endless ages roll;*
> *To please Him well my single aim,*
> *And all my trust in His dear name.*"

PRAYER THOUGHT: "O Savior, as Thy redeemed one whom Thou holdest in the hollow of Thy hand, I yield myself to Thee that I might be a vessel of honor, fashioned with Thy form of godliness and Thy true holiness. In Jesus' blessed name I pray. Amen."[7]

Second Timothy 2:21

Titus—Advice to Pastors and Churches

Name: It is believed that Titus, to whom this letter was written (1:1,4), was one of Paul's earliest converts, since he is called Paul's "own son after the common faith" (1:4). He was a talented Greek (Galatians 2:3) whom Paul found very profitable for the ministry, as indicated by mentioning him at least nine times in Second Corinthians (e.g., 2:13; 7:6,13; 8:23). He was a messenger of the church at Corinth (8:16,17); was unselfish and trustworthy (12:18); and journeyed with Barnabas and Paul to Jerusalem (Galatians 2:1). Although active with Paul, Titus is never mentioned in the book of Acts. Titus means "protected."

Titus appears to have been a much stronger man than Timothy, both spiritually and physically, since Paul expressed more concern for Timothy. Timothy's background was Christian, while Titus' was pagan. It takes the grace of God to save all sinners, but one saved *in* sin usually has more zeal than one saved *from* sin. It is not explained in Scripture why Timothy was circumcised and Titus was not (Acts 16:3; Galatians 2:3).

Titus was sent to minister to the Cretians, who were barbarous—"always liars, evil beasts, lazy gluttons" (1:12 RV). Going to a people such as the Cretians, one can appreciate all the more his message that "the grace of God that bringeth salvation hath appeared to *all* men, teaching them to deny ungodliness and worldly lusts, [that] we should live soberly, righteously, and godly in this present world" (2:11,12).

No doubt Paul intended to leave Crete after things were "set in order." Titus is directed to meet Paul at Nicopolis (3:12). The last mention of Titus is that he went from Rome to Dalmatia, probably for the same reason he was sent to Crete, since the Dalmatians were akin to the Cretians (II Timothy 4:10). Ancient tradition affirms that after returning to Crete in old age, he died there and was buried at the age of ninety-four.

Occasion of Writing: There is no record of anyone starting the church on the isle of Crete. There were those from Crete in Jerusalem on the day of Pentecost (Acts 2:5,11), and in all probability a convert under Peter's ministry started a work for the Lord on this island. Word, no doubt, reached Paul of the existing condition of Crete's church, so Titus was sent to set things in order, to ordain elders in every city (1:5), to give instructions in matters of church administration, and to oppose the invasion of mercenary Jewish teachers.

Contents: Paul places before Titus several qualifications of a pastor and instructions to the church in the choice and ordination of pastors. Caution is given regarding the character of the people to whom he ministers. Paul seeks to stir up zeal and diligence in refuting false teachers and dealing with heretics, and gives warnings to avoid foolish questions and contentions and strifes about the law. He shows what kind of doctrine Titus should preach so that all Cretians—including aged men and women, young men and servants—might be godly saints and lawful citizens. In the 3 chapters of Titus, there are 46 verses and 921 words.

Character: Pastoral.

Subject: The good works becoming Christian believers.

Purpose: To teach us that good works are the result and fruit of God's salvation: 3:5; Ephesians 2:8-10.

Outline:[1]
- I. Introduction: 1:1-4
- II. The Rule of the Church: 1:5-16
  - A. The Nature of it: 1:5-9
  - B. The Necessity for it: 1:10-16
- III. The Walk of the Church: 2:1-15
  - A. The Guiding Precepts: 2:1-10
  - B. The Enabling Power: 2:11-15

IV. The State of the Church: 3:1-11
   A. Her Outward Duty: 3:1-7
   B. Her Inward Discipline: 3:8-11
V. Conclusion: 3:12-15

Writer: Paul. 1:1,4. See WRITER in Romans.

When and Where Written: A.D. 64—66, at Ephesus.

Key Chapter: 2. Direction for doctrine and conduct.

Key Verses: 1:5; 3:5.

Key Word: Profitable.

Key Phrase: In Christ—ministering.

Key Thought: Set things in order.

Spiritual Thought: Adorn the doctrine.

Christ Is Seen As: Great God and Savior: 2:10,11; 3:4,6.

Names and Titles of Christ. See NAME in Dictionary.
1. Jesus Christ: 1:1
2. Lord Jesus Christ: 1:4
3. Savior: 1:4; 3:5
4. Great God: 2:13
5. Redeemer: 2:14
6. The Justifier: 3:7

Names and Titles of God. See NAME in Dictionary.
1. Savior: 1:3.
2. Father: 1:4.

Names and Titles of the Holy Spirit: Holy Ghost: 3:5. See NAME in Dictionary.

1. Salvation: 2:11-14. See SALVATION in Index.
   a. *Past*—effected through grace—*hath appeared;* vs. 11 with II Timothy 1:9
   b. *Present*—accepted by faith—for godly living *now:* vss. 12,14 with Ephesians 2:8-10
   c. *Future*—assured by faith—Christ's *second coming:* vs. 13 with John 14:1-3; I John 3:1,2

2. Grace Brings: 2:11
     G-od's
     R-iches
     A-t
     C-hrist's
     E-xpense

Mercy, simply defined, is God's withholding from us what we rightly deserve. Grace is God's giving to us what we do not deserve—*God's Riches At Christ's Expense.*

3. God's Salvation: 2:11-14
   a. Its need—ungodliness and worldy lusts: vs. 12a
   b. Its source—God's grace: vs. 11a
   c. Its scope—to all men: vs. 11b
   d. Its sacrifice—Christ: vs. 14a
   e. Its effect—
      —Redemption: vs. 14b
      —Soberness: vs. 12b

   —Righteousness: vs. 12c
   —Godliness: vs. 12d
   —Purity: vs. 14c
   —Christlikeness: vs. 14d
   —Good works: vs. 14e
  f. Its consummation—Christ's soon return: vs. 13

4. Experiences at Christ's Coming: 2:13
  a. A resurrection: I Thessalonians 4:16; I Corinthians 15:23,51-57
  b. A transfer: I Thessalonians 4:17; Philippians 3:20
  c. A transformation: I John 3:2; Philippians 3:21
  d. A compensation: I Corinthians 3:14; Revelation 22:12
  e. A presentation: Ephesians 5:27; Revelation 19:7-9
  f. A glorification: Romans 8:17,30
  g. A coronation. See REWARDS in Index.
  h. A reunion—and so shall we ever be with the Lord and our saved loved ones and friends: I Thessalonians 4:17
  i. A comfort fulfilled: I Thessalonians 4:18

5. Regeneration (the "New Birth"): 3:5.[2] Access into the family of God is the same as that by which we obtain entrance into the families of men—by generation or birth. A life and nature must be imparted in the one instance as in the other. In the case of the child of God it is an impartation of eternal life and the divine nature. Regeneration, or the new birth, is the door into the kingdom of God, and apart from it, the door must remain inevitably closed, and God and man remain forever separated. Regeneration is *most* important—*it is necessary*. It marks the line of cleavage between eternal life and eternal death, between eternal sonship and eternal alienation.

The New Birth defined—
  a. It is not baptism: Galatians 6:15; I Corinthians 4:15 with 1:4
  b. It is not reformation: 3:7; Matthew 12:43-45
  c. It is not our good works: Isaiah 64:6; Matthew 7:21-23; Titus 3:5
  d. It is a birth from above—a spiritual quickening: Titus 3:3-5
  e. It is the impartation of a new nature: II Peter 1:4
  f. It is a new and divine impulse: I John 3:6-9
  g. It is a spiritual translation: Colossians 1:13
  h. It is a spiritual creation: II Corinthians 5:17; Ephesians 2:10

The Necessity of the New Birth—
  a. Universal—man's sinful condition demands it: Titus 3:3,6; Jeremiah 17:9,10; Romans 3:23
  b. Man's inability to change his sphere of living or impart holiness to himself: Jeremiah 12:23; John 3:3-7
  c. Jesus made it necessary: John 3:3,5,7—"Ye must"
  d. God's holiness demands it: Hebrews 12:14

The Mode of the New Birth—
  a. God's work through the Holy Spirit: John 16:7-9; Titus 3:5
  b. Hearing and believing the gospel: Romans 10:17; James 1:18
  c. Personal acceptance of Christ: John 1:12; Acts 16:31

Result of the New Birth—
  a. Sonship with God: John 1:12,13
  b. Indwelling presence of the Holy Spirit: I Corinthians 3:16,17; 6:19
  c. Godlikeness: Ephesians 4:24
  d. Liberated from the sphere of slavery: Romans 8:2,9
  e. A radical change in life and experience: II Corinthians 5:17; I John 1:5
  f. Righteous living: Titus 2:14; I John 2:29

g. Victory over sin: I John 5:4

h. Love for the brethren: I John 3:14

A BIT OF

HEAVENLY MANNA

So much emphasis is placed on our being justified by faith (and we are), that we sometimes forget we are also justified by God's grace. Man's inability to save himself, to change his deceitful heart, to enter God's kingdom in a natural state, makes the grace of God all the more meaningful when we see how His grace can change all this.

BEING JUSTIFIED BY HIS GRACE—3:7[3]

"The justification of a sinner is a surprising display of the wisdom and grace of God. He is acknowledged to be guilty, and yet proclaimed just. How can this be? He is guilty before God as a creature, because he has broken the law; he is just before God as a Christian because he is united to Christ who obeyed the law for him. One moment he is ungodly and has no defense as to why judgment should not be executed upon him; the next moment by the exercise of faith in Christ he is justified, and has a righteousness which meets all the requirements of the law to plead before God's bar. But, if a sinner is justified, if the ungodly is made righteous, it must be by grace—it is impossible that it should be by works. And if it is of grace, it is of grace from first to last. It was grace that devised the plan in the eternal councils; it was grace that brought the Son of God into our world to work out the righteousness which justifies; it is grace which sends the gospel to reveal this righteousness unto us, and the Holy Spirit to work faith in our hearts to embrace it.

> *Amazing grace, how sweet the sound,*
> *That saved a wretch like me;*
> *I once was lost, but now am found,*
> *Was blind but now I see!"*

PRAYER THOUGHT: "Teach me, dear Lord, that godly living, love, kindness, understanding, and witnessing in the Spirit have won more sinners to a saving knowledge of Christ than zeal, eloquence, or the teachings of 'religious education.' In the saving name of the One who saved me I ask this. Amen."[4]

Titus 2:11-14

Philemon—The Original Emancipation Proclamation

Name: Philemon, to whom this letter was written (vss. 1-13), was a member of the church at Colosse. In fact, the services were held in his home. He was a man of considerable means, a possessor of slaves, and a benevolent believer (vss. 5-7). His name means "affectionate." It is implied he was a convert of Paul's (vs. 19). Apphia was probably his wife; Archippus his son. Descriptive words used of this family denote a godly home (e.g., fellowlaborer; beloved, fellow-soldier, obedience, partner, prayer). Paul never had been to Colosse (Colossians 2:1), but must have met Philemon elsewhere, possibly in Ephesus, which was not too far from Colosse.

Occasion of Writing: A slave of Philemon, Onesimus, had defaulted, run away to Rome, and was converted by Paul, who sends him back to Philemon accompanied by Tychicus. Paul asks the master to receive the slave kindly and to treat him in the future not as a slave but as a brother in Christ.

Contents: The message of this letter is better understood when we consider that over one-third of the Roman Empire was made up of slaves. A slave was the personal property of his owner, was treated worse than an enemy, and subjected to every desire and whim of his master. The picture shows a Roman soldier binding a prisoner to become a slave.

Capturing a Slave

Onesimus, Philemon's slave, found opportunity to escape, probably robbed his master (vs. 18), and went to Rome. He heard Paul preach, was saved (vs. 10), and became a faithful disciple (Colossians 4:9). Paul desired to use him as his own helper, but realized Onesimus had an obligation to his master, Philemon, and felt it his duty to send him back (vss. 13,14). Onesimus knew that to return he would be put to death, as the law required of a runaway slave, so he besought Paul to write to his master in his behalf. Paul does write a letter, first commending Philemon for his stand in the gospel, and then presenting his case in behalf of Onesimus. Though an unprofitable runaway slave, he is now a spiritual son of Paul, a respected brother in Christ, and profitable. Philemon is asked to receive his former slave kindly and to treat him in the future, not as a slave, but as a brother-beloved in the Lord. There are only 25 verses in this short Epistle, and 445 words.

Character: Personal.

Subject: Salvation and restoration of a runaway slave.

Purpose: To picture the gospel.

Outline:

    A. Philemon's love and faith: vss. 4,5
    B. Philemon's works of faith and love: vss. 6,7
III. The Appeal Detailed: vss. 8-16
    A. The ground of it: vss. 8,9
    B. The nature of it: vss. 10-12
    C. The strength of it: vss. 13-16
IV. The Appeal Supported: vss. 17-22
    A. The mutual debt: vss. 17-19
    B. The mutual joy: vss. 20-22
  V. Conclusion: vss. 23-25

Writer: Paul: vss. 1-4. See WRITER. A Prison Epistle.

When and Where Written: See WHEN WRITTEN in Ephesians.

Key Verse: 16.

Key Word: Receive.

Key Phrase: In Christ—a Brotherhood.

Key Thought: Christian servitude.

Spiritual Thought: Be kind to all for Christ's sake.

Christ Is Seen As: The Payer of our sin-debt.

Names and Titles of Christ. See NAME in Dictionary.
    2. Lord Jesus Christ: vs. 3
    3. Lord Jesus: vs. 5
    4. Christ Jesus: vs. 6
    5. Christ: vs. 8
    6. Lord: vs. 20

Names and Titles of God: Father: vs. 3. See NAME in Dictionary.

1. Lessons from this Epistle
    a. This letter shows the great humility of Paul. In his great office as an Apostle he finds time to bring about the reconciliation of a master and a slave. No matter who or what we are, we should never be too busy to help individuals in need, no matter who they are.
    b. It displays the riches of God's grace in the conversion of a vile sinner—the wonderful providence of God in overruling the determination of this slave to be free from slavery to an acceptance of freedom from sin.
    c. It shows that when one becomes a Christian he still has obligations to the law and that restitution, if necessary, must be made. Onesimus *must* return to Philemon. See also Luke 19:6-9 concerning Zaccheus.
    d. It shows the generosity of one Christian (Paul) to pay back what had been taken when the forgiven brother (Onesimus) had nothing—a display of sympathy for the lowly.
    e. It reveals the brotherhood of the saints. There are no social or class distinctions in Christ. This is a practical solution to the age-old problem of capital and labor
    f. As Paul pleaded Onesimus' case before Philemon, so Christ pleaded our case before His Father. As Onesimus now has standing before Philemon, so now we have standing before Christ. As Paul paid the debt of an unworthy slave, so Christ paid the debt for all unworthy sinners.
    g. It shows the need for an older Christian to "stand" for a younger Christian. Just as Barnabas had accepted Paul as a disciple of the Lord and commended him to the Jerusalem

disciples (Acts 9:26,27), so Paul commends Onesimus to Philemon as Christ's servant (see Colossians 4:9).

2. The Man Paul
   a. A prisoner of Jesus Christ: vs. 1
   b. A thankful saint: vs. 4
   c. A laborer for Christ: vs. 1
   d. A soldier of Christ: vs.2
   e. A man of prayer: vs. 4
   f. A soul-winner: vs. 19
   g. A spiritual father: vs. 10

A BIT OF
HEAVENLY MANNA

Although Paul praised Philemon for his depth of spirituality, there was a need to ask for kindness and sympathy in receiving one who had wronged him. It is not always easy to do this, especially if the relationship is "master" and "servant." But for those in Christ, whether "bond or free," there must be an acceptance of each other. Paul's plea was for Philemon to receive Onesimus as:

A BROTHER BELOVED . . . IN THE LORD—vs. 16[1]

"We ought to love one another (I John 4:11). If we are children of the same family, subjects of the same government, travelers on the same road, partakers of the same hope, and are destined to live together forever in the same home, we *ought* to love one another. But God's great love to us is assigned as the principal reason why we should do so. God loves all His children alike. He gave His Son to die for every one of them. He sends His Spirit into all their hearts. He gave His exceeding great and precious promises to the whole of them. He has prepared heaven as the family mansion where they are all to dwell forever. He has laid His command upon them to love one another. Beloved our love should be as extensive as the love of God; it should embrace all that He embraces. We can never justify excluding anyone from our love whom God has included in His. We ought to love every Christian, and to love all believers constantly, tenderly, and as brethren, even as Christ loves us. Let us ask conscience this day—'Do we really and heartily love all that we have reason to believe love the Lord Jesus Christ?' If so, that's good. If not, why not?"

PRAYER THOUGHT: "For this day, dear Lord, I ask Thy Holy Spirit to keep me holy and pure in thought and word, kind one to another, honest in my dealings, and forgiving one another even as Christ has forgiven me, through His dear name I pray. Amen."[2]

Philemon 10-18

Hebrews—The Book of Shadows and Substance

Name: This book derives its name from those to whom it was written—Jewish Christians in general—not those of a local church specifically. That it was written to Jews the whole structure of the Epistle proves. Had it been written to the Gentiles, not one in ten thousand of them could have comprehended the argument because of their unacquaintance with the Jewish system.

Occasion of Writing: Judaism still exerted a powerful influence in the world and these Hebrew Christians had to face many problems:

1. Rabbinical *teachings* were hard to "unlearn"
2. Jewish *tradition,* which had blinded the Jews in Christ's day, was even stronger and harder to overcome
3. The *temple* was still standing in Jerusalem, and the strong fascination of the impressive temple ritualism and sacrifices were carried out daily (8:4; 10:1,11)
4. Family *ties,* very strong among Jews, were hard to break
5. Jewish *tempers* and opposition were difficult to combat
6. The *trend* in the church was more toward Gentiles than Jews, and enmity still existed between Jew and Gentile

The infidel Jews continued to employ their power for the purpose of withdrawing their believing brethren from the Christian faith. To ruinous persecution and incessant threats, they added arguments derived from the acknowledged divinity of the Jewish religion, observing that their law was given by the ministry of angels; that Moses was far superior to Jesus of Nazareth, who was put to death upon the cross; that the public worship of God, instituted by their great legislator and prophet, was truly splendid and worthy of Jehovah while the Christians, on the contrary, had no temple, no priesthood, no altars and no sacrifices, and the early prejudices of those who had embraced the gospel were still strong in favor of these things.

The writer, sensing all this and a discouragement on their part due to persecution, feeling that some were disappointed because their Messianic hopes had not been realized, knowing that some had already succumbed to apostasy, and realizing that there was the constant danger to fall back into Judaism, wrote this Epistle—

1. To stress superiority of Christ over Judaism: 1:1—5:10
2. To check apostasy: 3:6,14
3. To encourage and stimulate faith: 6:1-12
4. To show that the Old Testament system, in spite of all its pomp and glory, was only a shadow: 8;1—9:10
5. To show that Old Testament sacrifices were already abolished by Christ's sacrificial death: 9:11—10:39
6. To urge these believers to live up to their privileges—"go on to perfection": 6:1; 11:1—13:17
7. To show Hebrew Christians that they had to quit being Hebrews. Now that Messiah had come to establish a new covenant, this book was calculated to reconcile the Jew to the destruction of his temple because a more noble temple exists; to reconcile him to the loss of his priesthood because a new priesthood has been established of all believers; a reconciliation to the abolition of sacrifice because the only perfect sacrifice had already been offered once and for all; a reconciliation to the devastation of his country because the believer is assured of a heavenly country; and reconciliation to the extinction of his city because of the heavenly Jerusalem.

Contents: This book sets forth the superior excellency of Christ to angels and men, to Moses, to Joshua, to Aaron and his sons, and of His priesthood and sacrifice to the Levitical priesthood and its sacrifices. It teaches the Hebrews the true knowledge of the mysteries of the law; points out to them the design, use, and the nullifying of its ceremonies; prepares them for what afflictions and persecutions they would be called to endure for Christ; and exhorts them to perseverance and to strengthen themselves against apostasy, as well as instructing them in the various duties of their faith. Hebrews has 13 chapters, 303 verses, and 6,913 words.

Character: Doctrinal.

Uniqueness of Hebrews:

1. This book does not begin as the other Epistles (with an address), although it closes as one (with a benediction and salutation).
2. It is like a miniature Bible in that it begins with God (as in Genesis 1:1), and ends with the heavenly Jerusalem (as in Revelation 21), with Christ from beginning to the end.
3. Hebrews is the commentary of Leviticus, showing Christ is the fulfillment of the ceremonial law—the superiority of Christianity over Judaism. Christ is *better* than anything (types) which pointed to Him.
4. Hebrews is the "faith" book, which shows the fallacy of works to save (declare one righteous) or for one to please God apart from faith (ch. 11, especially vs. 6). The names inscribed in this chapter are there, not because of their fulfillment of the law, but because of their faith. No other book in the Bible defines faith as does this book.

Romans, Galatians, and Hebrews are all three based on the great text of Habakkuk (2:4)—"The just shall live by faith." Romans emphasizes the first two words—"the just," —and answers Job's question, "How then can [an unclean] man be justified with God?" Galatians deals with the next two words—"shall live,"—and shows how faith produces life or evidence (James 2:14-26). Hebrews deals with the last two words—"by faith,"—and exhibits the purpose of faith—that of pleasing God, and illustrates the nature and power of faith from Old Testament characters and events. Romans and Galatians shift from law to grace; Hebrews shifts from shadow to substance.

5. Hebrews is a "tonic" book—a preventative of apostasy.
6. The message of this book, while emphasizing Christ, is also filled with:
   a. Warnings, which have to do with apostasy (2:1; 3:12,13; 4:1,11; 12:1-3,13,15. Notice the word "*lest*" and link with 10:26,27).
   b. Encouragement, by use of the expressions "*let*" or "*let us*" (4:1,11,14,16; 6:1; 10:22-24; 12:1,28; 13:1,5,13,15). These expressions, while commands, denote a fellowship both with God and fellow-believers. "Let *us* go on to perfection" is the key encouragement verse (6:1).
7. "Other epistles state a doctrine and conclude with an application, but Hebrews closes each topic or exposition with an exhortation without reserving it to the end."[1]
8. Other Epistles put emphasis on the content quoted, while Hebrews puts the stress on the one who speaks—God, Christ, and the Holy Spirit.
9. Hebrews is an anonymous Epistle, but it is evident that the writer was well known to those addressed (10:34; 13:18,19). See WRITER.
10. Hebrews is filled with Old Testament quotations, but one does not find the well-known expressions, "It is written," or "that the Scriptures might be fulfilled." It is difficult at times to determine the writer's thoughts and actual Scriptures, so closely are they blended. While the word "Scripture" is not mentioned, the "Word" is referred to only once (4:12). Only one writer of Scripture is mentioned—Moses.

Subject: Christ as *Someone Better Than,* and His work *Something Better Than* anything in Judaism.

Purpose: To draw the Hebrew Christians back from Judaism to Christ and His work, and to draw believers today unto Christ from a life of formality and mere profession.

Outline:[2]

I. Doctrinal Section: 1:1—10:18
   A. Christ is superior to the prophets: 1:1-4
   B. Christ is superior to angels: 1:5—2:18

C. Christ is superior to Moses: 3:1-6
D. Christ is superior to Levitical Priesthood: 4:14—10:18
II. Practical Section: 10:19—13:25
   A. Exhortations to remain loyal to Christ: 10:19-39
   B. Heroes of the faith: 11
     1. Path of faith: vss. 1-6
     2. Patience of faith: vss. 7-22
     3. Power of faith: vss. 23-40
   C. Exhortations to follow these heroes: 12
   D. Sundry exhortations: 13:1-21
   E. Conclusion: 13:22-25

Writer: The writer took pains to conceal his identity, therefore it must be labeled "anonymous." Such men as Luke, Barnabas, Apollos, and Paul have been suggested. Anyone of these *could* have been the author, as well as someone else.

   1. Paul. There is a "streak" of Paul in this Epistle, and this internal evidence has led many to conclude that he was the author. In spite of the fact that there is much difference in style and language not found in Paul's letters, and the fact that Paul's writings were addressed to Gentiles and Hebrews is addressed to Jews, note the following:

     a. Being a Hebrew of the Hebrews (Philippians 3:5), Paul was well qualified to write such a treatise. Since there was such hatred on the part of the Jews toward Paul, this might explain the absence of his name as the author.

     b. Pauline statements in Hebrews—
       —in . . . bonds (10:34)
       —desire to see them later (13:18,19)
       —reference to Timothy (13:23)
       —apostolic benediction (13:20-25)

     c. In Peter's second letter he gives indication that Paul had previously written to Jews (3:15,16).

   2. Apollos. There are those who think he was the author. The book of Hebrews was written in original Greek, the nearest to classical Greek of any New Testament book. There is a polished style which shows an Alexandrian and Philonic influence (20 B.C. to A.D. 55). Paul's educational background in Tarsus provided him with Hebrew in depth, not Greek. Apollos, knowledgable in the Scriptures, was an influential Alexandrian, eloquent, enthusiastic, and a man of courage (Acts 18:24-28). He had a mighty influence on the church at Corinth (I Corinthians 1:11,12; 3:4-6). His humility and modesty are shown in his desire to avoid contention and friction (I Corinthians 16:12). He continued to work with Paul toward Paul's end (Titus 3:13). With his educational and cultural background, coupled with his knowledge of Scriptures as a Jew, he was well qualified to pen such a letter as Hebrews. We can see in Apollos the parallel thoughts of Judaism with Paul as well as the clear-cut differences from Paul.

Where and When Written: Probably A.D. 66, if by Paul, and certainly before A.D. 70, when the temple was destroyed by Titus. Hebrews indicates the temple was still standing (8:4; 10:1). It is not known where this Epistle was written, although the expression "they of Italy salute you" might indicate it was written in that country (possibly in Rome—13:24).

Key Chapters: 9 and 11. Shadows give way to Reality.

Key Verses: 1:3; 11:1,40.

Key Words:
   1. Better, used 13 times, to show the superiority of Christ, the substance, to the shadows of Judaism
   2. Heaven, or heavenly, used 15 times, to show that Christianity is heavenly and spiritual while the ceremonies of Judaism were earthly and physical

3. Once, or once for all, used 9 times, to convey the finality of Christian revelation

Spiritual Thought: He is our Intercessor at God's throne: 1:3; 7:25.

Christ Is Seen As: The Apostle and High Priest of our profession: 3:1.

Names and Titles of Christ. See NAME in Dictionary.

1. His Son: 1:2a,5; 3:6
2. Heir of all things: 1:2b
3. Creator and Preserver of all things: 1:2c,3b,10
4. The Brightness of God's glory: 1:3a
5. The express Image of God: 1:3c
6. Cleanser of sin: 1:3d
7. Firstbegotten: 1:6
8. God: 1:8
9. Lord: 1:10; 7:14
10. Son of man: 2:6
11. Jesus: 2:9; 4:14
12. Captain of salvation: 2:10
13. Our Brother: 2:11
14. Satan's Victor: 2:14
15. Seed of Abraham: 2:16
16. Merciful and Faithful High Priest: 2:17
17. Deliverer of the tempted: 2:18
18. Apostle and High Priest: 3:1
19. Christ Jesus: 3:1
20. Housebuilder: 3:3,4
21. Christ: 3:6,14
22. Better Rest: 4:9
23. Son of God: 4:14; 6:6
24. The sinless High Priest: 4:15
25. Eternal Priest: 5:6
26. Author of eternal salvation: 5:9
27. High Priest after the order of Melchizedek: 5:10
28. The Forerunner: 6:20
29. King of righteousness: 7:2a,3
30. King of peace: 7:2b,3
31. A Surety of a better testament: 7:22
32. Our Intercessor: 7:25
33. Holy, harmless, undefiled High Priest: 7:26
34. A Minister of the sanctuary: 8:2
35. Mediator of a better (new) covenant: 8:6; 9:15; 12:24
36. High Priest of good things to come: 9:11
37. Interceder before God: 9:25
38. Sin Offering: 9:28a
39. Our Salvation: 9:28b
40. Jesus Christ: 10:10
41. The Finisher of sacrifices: 10:12-14
42. The new and living Way: 10:19,20
43. High Priest over the house of God: 10:21
44. Author and Finisher (Perfector) of our faith: 12:2
45. The Same: 13:8
46. Lord Jesus: 13:20
47. Great Shepherd of the sheep: 13:20

Names and Titles of God. See NAME in Dictionary.

1. Majesty on high: 1:3; 8:1
2. Father: 1:5
3. Living God: 9:14
4. Father of spirits: 12:9
5. The Judge: 12:23
6. A consuming Fire: 12:29
7. The Ever-present God: 13:5
8. Our Helper: 13:6
9. God of peace: 13:20

Names and Titles of the Holy Spirit. See NAME in Dictionary.
1. Holy Ghost: 2:4; 3:7
2. Eternal Spirit: 9;14
3. Spirit of grace: 10;29

Biblical Customs: Enemies thy footstool: 1:13. See FOOTSTOOL in Index.

Scientifically Speaking: 4:12 with Job 21:24b. See BLOOD in Index.

The Old Testament in Hebrews:
1. Thou art My Son: 1:5a with Psalm 2:7
2. I will be to Him a Father: 1:5b with II Samuel 7:14a
3. Let all . . . worship Him: 1:6 with Psalm 97:7
4. Who maketh His angels spirits: 1:7 with Psalm 104:4
5. Thy throne . . . is forever: 1:8,9 with Psalm 45:6,7
6. Thou, Lord, in the beginning: 1:10-12 with Psalm 102:25-27
7. Sit on My right hand: 1:13; 10:12,13 with Psalm 110:1
8. What is man: 2:6-8 with Psalm 8:4-6
9. I will declare Thy name: 2:12 with Psalm 22:22
10. I will put my trust in Him: 2:13a with II Samuel 22:3; Isaiah 8:17a (RV)
11. Behold, I and the children: 2:13b with Isaiah 8:18
12. Today if ye hear His voice: 3:7-11 with Psalm 95:7-11
13. As I have sworn in my wrath: 4:3 with Psalm 95:11
14. God rested on the seventh day: 4:4 with Genesis 2:2
15. Thou art my Son: 5:5 with Psalm 2:7
16. A Priest after Melchizedek: 5:6; 7:17 with Psalm 110:4
17. Blessing, I will bless thee: 6:13,14 with Genesis 22:16,17
18. Make all things according to the pattern: 8:15 with Exodus 25:40
19. To make a new covenant: 8:8-12 with Jeremiah 31:31-34
20. The blood of the covenant [testament]: 9:19,20 with Exodus 24:6-8
21. Sacrifice and offering thou wouldest not: 10:5-7 with Psalm 40:6-8
22. My law in their hearts: 10:16,17 with Jeremiah 31:33,34
23. Vengeance belongeth unto the Lord: 10:30 with Deuteronomy 32:35,36
24. The just shall live by faith: 10:38 with Habakkuk 2:4b
25. In Isaac shall thy seed be called: 11:18 with Genesis 21:12
26. Despise not God's chastening: 12:5,6 with Proverbs 3:11,12
27. God to shake the heaven: 12:26 with Haggai 2:6
28. God a consuming fire: 12:29 with Deuteronomy 4:24
29. I will not leave thee nor forsake thee: 13:5 with Deuteronomy 31:6
30. The Lord is my helper: 13:6 with Psalm 118:6
31. Companion references:
    —Ministering angels: 1:14 with Psalm 91:11; Daniel 3:28
    —Faithfulness of Moses: 3:2 with Numbers 12:7
    —God grieved with Israel 40 years: 3:17,18 with Numbers 14:22,29,30
    —Offering of the high priest: 5:12 with Leviticus 9:7-24
    —Melchizedek and Abraham: 7;1,2 with Genesis 14:18

—Sacrifice of priests: 7:27 with Leviticus 14:6-11
—Tabernacle and its furniture: 9:1-6 with Exodus 25:26; 40
—High priest and day of atonement: 9:7 with Exodus 30:10
—People sprinkled with blood: Hebrews 9:19,20 with Exodus 24:8
—Daily offerings: 10:11 with Exodus 29:38
—Despising Moses' law: 10:28 with Deuteronomy 17:2-7
—Creation of the world: 11:3 with Genesis 1
—Abel's sacrifice accepted: 11:4 with Genesis 4:4
—Enoch's translation: 11:5 with Genesis 5:24
—Noah and the ark: 11:7 with Genesis 6:15,16
—Abraham's call: 11:8 with Genesis 12:1
—Abraham's sojourn to Canaan: 11:9 with Genesis 12:5
—Isaac and Jacob in Canaan: 11:9 with Genesis 27:12,14
—Isaac, seed of promise: 11:1 with Genesis 18:11
—Abraham's seed as the stars: 11:12 with Genesis 22:17
—Patriarchs . . . as pilgrims and strangers: 11:13 with Genesis 23:4; 47:9
—Isaac's blessing upon Jacob and Esau: 11:20 with Genesis 27
—Jacob blessing Joseph's sons: 11:21 with Genesis 48:15
—Jacob's dying command: 11:22 with Genesis 50:25
—Moses' parents: 11:23 with Exodus 2:2
—Abraham's offering of Isaac: 11:17-19 with Genesis 22
—Moses returned to his own people: 11:25 with Exodus 2:11
—Moses' flight to the desert: 11:27 with Exodus 2:15
—The passover in Egypt: 11:28 with Exodus 12:21-29
—Israel crossing the Red Sea: 11:29 with Exodus 14
—Jericho's defeat: 11:30 with Joshua 6:12-20
—Sparing of Rahab: 11:31 with Joshua 6:23
—Heroes of the faith: 11:32-40 with Old Testament saints (see Judges; I and II Samuel;
    I Kings 17:23; II Kings 4:34; Daniel 3:27; 6:22)
—Weak hands strengthened: 12:12 with Isaiah 35:3
—Selling of Esau's birthright: 12:16 with Genesis 25:33
—Esau's remorse: 12:17 with Genesis 27:34-38
—Mount Sinai: 12:18,20 with Exodus 19:12,19
—Entertaining angels: 13:2 with Genesis 18:1; 19:1
—Bodies of sacrificed animals burned: 13:11 with Exodus 29:14
—One Shepherd: 13:20 with Ezekiel 34:23

SEED THOUGHTS

1. Better Things in Hebrews—
    a. Better revelation: 1:1-4
    b. Better rest: 4:9
    c. Better things: 6:9; 11:40
    d. Better hope: 7:9
    e. Better testament (covenant): 7:22; 8:6a
    f. Better priesthood: 7:23-28
    g. Better promise: 8:6b
    h. Better sacrifice: 9:23
    i. Better substance (possessions): 10:34; 12:24
    j. Better country: 11:16 (with better rest: 4:9)
    k. Better resurrection: 11:35
2. Eternal Blessings—
    a. Eternal redemption—our deliverance: 9:12
    b. Eternal life—our present possession: John 5:24
    c. Eternal salvation—our transformation: 5:9

    d. Eternal priesthood—our standing: 9:12; 10:19-22

    e. Eternal Son—our Hope: 1:12b; 13:8

    f. Eternal glory—our calling: I Peter 5:10

    g. Eternal Spirit—our Guide: 9:14; John 16:13

    h. Eternal throne—our help: 1:8; 4:16

    i. Eternal sanctification—our walk: 10:14

    j. Eternal consolation—our assurance: II Thessalonians 2:16

    k. Eternal tabernacle—our worshiping place: Matthew 16:18b; Luke 16:9

    l. Eternal judgment—our test: 6:2; I Corinthians 3:13

    m. Eternal weight of glory—our reward: II Corinthians 4:17

    n. Eternal home—our dwelling place: II Corinthians 5:1; John 14:1-3

    o. Eternal inheritance—our prospect: 9:15

    p. Eternal kingdom—our reign: 12:28

    q. Eternal covenant—our pledge: 13:20

3. His Son: 1:2. God's Answer to Man's Need—

    a. Christ is God's answer to man's oldest and greatest *problem*—sin: 2:9

    b. Christ is God's answer to man's oldest and greatest *fear*—death: 2:14,15

    c. Christ is God's answer to man's oldest and greatest *quest*—life: John 14:6

    d. Christ is God's answer to man's oldest and greatest *question*—where do I go from here? John 14:1-3

4. Christ, the Sin Purger: 1:3. Some years ago a Parliament of Religions was held in Chicago, in connection with the 1933 World's Fair. The great ethnic faiths of the world were here represented. One by one the leading men arose and spoke for Buddhism, Confucianism, Hinduism, and Mohammedanism. Then Dr. Joseph Cook, of Boston, who had been chosen to represent Christianity, arose to speak. "Here is Lady Macbeth's hand," he said, "stained with the foul murder of King Duncan. See her as she perambulates through the halls and corridors of her palatial home, stopping to cry, 'Out, damned spot! Out, I say! Will these hands ne'er be clean?' " Then turning to those seated on the platform, he said, "Can any of you who are so anxious to propagate your religious systems offer any cleansing efficacy for the sin and guilt of Lady Macbeth's crime?" An oppressive silence was maintained by them all and well they might, for none of the religions they respresented, nor any other religion on earth, can offer any cleansing efficacy for the guilt of sin. It took the death of Christ, the shedding of His precious blood, to atone for sin, to taste death for every man, and He alone can purge the conscience from dead works to serve the living God.

> *Christ does not save men by His life,*
>   *Though that was holy, sinless, pure;*
> *Nor even by His tender love,*
>   *Though that forever shall endure.*
>
> *He does not save them by His words,*
>   *Though they shall never pass away;*
> *Nor by His vast creative power,*
>   *That holds the elements in sway.*
>
> *He does not save them by His works,*
>   *Though He was ever doing good;*
> *The awful need was greater still,*
>   *It took His death, His cross, His blood.*[3]

5. So Great Salvation: 2:3,4

a. God planned it: Matthew 1:21
b. Christ purchased it: I Peter 1:18,19
c. God's Word describes it: I Corinthians 15:3,4
d. It's just what the sinner needs: I Timothy 1:15
e. Only true faith appropriates it: Ephesians 2:8,9
f. The Holy Spirit presents it: Titus 3:5
g. The devil hates it: II Thessalonians 2:4,9,10
h. The believer possesses it: John 5:24

6. So Great Salvation: 2:3[4]

Longfellow could take a worthless piece of paper, write a poem on it, and make it worth $6,000. *That is genius.*

Rockefeller can sign his name to a piece of paper, and make it worth millions. *That is capital.*

Uncle Sam can take gold or silver, stamp an eagle on it, and make it worth a dollar or more. *That is money.*

A machinist can take material worth $5.00 and make an article worth $50.00. *That is skill.*

An artist can take a piece of fifty-cent canvas and paint a picture on it worth $1,000. *That is art.*

God can take a worthless sinful life, wash it in the blood of Christ, put His Holy Spirit in it, and make it a blessing to all humanity. *That is salvation.*

7. God's "Great" Things: 2:3
    a. Love: Ephesians 2:4
    b. Grace: Acts 4:33
    c. Salvation: Hebrews 2:3
    d. Peace: Psalm 119:165
    e. Joy: Luke 2:10
    f. Power: Acts 4:33
    g. Delight: Song of Solomon 2:3
    h. Promises: II Peter 1:4
    i. Glory to come: Luke 21:27

8. Christ in Hebrews: 2:7,8 with 13:8
    Past—Yesterday—lower than angels for awhile: vs. 2:7a (RV)
    Present—Today—crowned with glory and honor; all things in subjection to Him: vss. 7b,8a
    Future—Forever—all things under His feet: vs. 8b

9. We See Jesus: 2:9,10
    a. In humility (lower than angels)
    b. Suffering death
    c. Crowned with glory and honor
    d. Bringing many sons into glory
    e. Perfected as Savior

10. Grace: 2:9
    a. Atoning grace: 2:9
    b. Saving grace: Ephesians 2:8,9
    c. Access grace: 4:16
    d. Needed grace: 4:16
    e. Establishing grace: 13:9
    f. Abundant grace: 13:25
    g. Working grace: Acts 11:21-23
    h. Strengthening grace: II Corinthians 12:9
    i. Sustaining grace: II Corinthians 9:8

  j. Serving grace: I Corinthians 15:10

  k. Supplying grace: John 1:16

11. Satan and His Works Defeated: 2:14. See SATAN in Index.

12. Partakers of Christ: 3:14. See PARTAKERS in Index.

13. The Sinner's Call: 3:15,16

  a. Hear ye His voice—*privilege:* Matthew 11:28

  b. Harden not your hearts—*warning:* John 5:39,40

  c. As in the provocation—*example:* Numbers 14:1-11

  d. If ye will—*responsibility:* John 3:18,36

  e. While it is today—*opportunity:* Proverbs 27:1; II Corinthians 6:2

14. Let Us: 4:1

  a. Fear: 4:1

  b. Labor: 4:11

  c. Come boldly before the throne: 4:16

  d. Go on: 6:1

  e. Draw near: 10:22

  f. Hold fast: 10:23

  g. Consider one another: 10:24

  h. Lay aside every weight [sin]: 12:1

  i. Run: 12:2

  j. Have grace: 12:28

  k. Have brotherly love: 13:1

  l. Be content: 13:5

  m. Go forth: 13:13

  n. Offer sacrifices of praise: 13:15

15. Eternal Salvation: 5:9. See GOSPEL in Index.

  a. Its Author—Christ—is eternal: Hebrews 13:8

  b. Its message—the gospel—is eternal: Revelation 14;6

  c. Its way—straight and narrow—is eternal: Psalm 139:24; Matthew 7:14

  d. Its Covenant—through Christ's blood—is eternal: Hebrews 13:20

  e. Its gifts to those who obey—

   —Eternal salvation: Isaiah 45:17

   —Eternal life: John 5:24

   —Eternal name: Isaiah 56:5

   —Eternal strength: Isaiah 26:4

   —Eternal love: Jeremiah 31:3

   —Eternal joy: Isaiah 61:7

   —Eternal peace: Isaiah 9:7

   —Eternal light: Isaiah 60:18,19

   —Eternal pleasure: Psalm 16:11

   —Eternal consolation: II Thessalonians 2:16

   —Eternal righteousness: Psalm 119:142

   —Eternal foundation: Proverbs 10:25

   —Eternal assurance: Isaiah 32:17

   —Eternal kingdom: Daniel 4:3; 7:27

16. Jesus, Our Intercessor: 7:25. "If I could hear Christ praying for me in the next room, I would not fear a million enemies. Yet distance makes no difference. He *is* praying for me" (Martin Luther).

17. Christ's Unfinished Ministry: 7:25. Christ's work of redemption is completed—He purged our sins by the sacrifice of Himself—"once for all"—and is now seated on the right hand of God (1:3; 10:10-12). "It [redemption] is finished," was His cry on the cross (John 19:30). Seated at the right hand of the Majesty on high—

a. He is now praying for all who come unto God by Him: 7:25
b. He is now praying for us to receive His mercy and grace to overcome temptation: 4:14-16
c. He is now praying that our faith fail not: Luke 22:31,32
d. He is our Advocate, pleading for us before His Father when we sin and fellowship is broken: I John 2:1
e. He is preparing a place for us—awaiting God's signal to return for His bride: John 14:1-3; I Thessalonians 4:16,17
f. He will judge and reward His children: II Corinthians 5:10; Revelation 22:12; I Corinthians 3:11-15
g. He will be crowned King of kings and Lord of lords to reign upon the earth: Revelation 20:4
h. He is to be the Judge of all unbelievers: John 12:46-48; Acts 17:31

18. God is Able: 7:25
    a. To save: 7:25
    b. To keep our souls: II Timothy 1:12
    c. To more than answer our requests: Ephesians 3:20
    d. To subdue all things: Philippians 3:21
    e. To build us up: Acts 20:32
    f. To make us stand: Romans 14:4
    g. To help in temptation: Hebrews 2:18
    h. To deliver in trouble: Daniel 3:17; 6:20-22
    i. To uphold: Psalm 145:14a
    j. To raise the bowed head: Psalm 145:14b
    k. To give meat (strength): Psalm 145:15
    l. To satisfy: Psalm 145:16
    m. To fulfill desires: Psalm 145:19
    n. To make all grace abound: II Corinthians 9:8
    o. To preserve: Psalm 145:20
    p. To keep us from falling: Jude 24
    q. To keep His promises: Romans 4:21; Philippians 1:6

19. Infinities of Grace: 7:25
    a. Uttermost salvation: 7:25
    b. Unblameable in holiness: I Thessalonians 3:13
    c. All grace abounding: II Corinthians 9:8
    d. Exceeding abundant power: Ephesians 3:20
    e. Unsearchable riches of Christ: Ephesians 3:8
    f. Peace passing understanding: Philippians 4:7
    g. Unspeakable joy: I Peter 1:8
    h. Love passing knowledge: Ephesians 3:18,19
    i. Depths of God's wisdom: Romans 11:33a
    j. Unsearchable judgments: Romans 11:33b
    k. Ways past finding out: Romans 11:33c

20. Church Membership—Attendance and Responsibility: 10:25
    A. "Can I be a Christian without joining the church or attending worship services?" The answer is "Yes, it is possible." It is something like being—
        a. A student who will not go to school
        b. A soldier who will not join the army
        c. A citizen who does not pay taxes or vote
        d. A salesman with no customers
        e. An explorer with no base camp
        f. A seaman on a ship without a crew
        g. A businessman on a deserted island

      h. An author without readers
      i. A tuba player without an orchestra
      j. A parent without a family
      k. A football player without a team
      l. A politician who is a hermit
      m. A scientist who does not share his findings
      n. A bee without a hive
      o. A banker without money
      p. A doctor without patients

B. Reasons for Being Part of a Local Church—

      a. If you love Christ, who loved the church and gave Himself for it, you will want to be active in one: Ephesians 5:25-27
      b. If you want to grow as a Christian, you will participate in the things of the Lord: Psalm 92:13
      c. If you are to be an obedient Christian, you will assemble yourself with other Christians: Hebrews 10:25
      d. If you want the "sweets" of the Christian life, you will be where they are served: Psalm 55:14
      e. If you recognize God's order for the perfecting of the saints, you will be where the pastor preaches: Ephesians 4:11-13
      f. If you are to exercise Christian hospitality, you must be where Christians are: I Corinthians 12:25
      g. If you really intend to serve the Lord, you must be involved in His work, sharing in the responsibility of the church: Ephesians 4:12
      h. If you want to be a happy Christian, you must be were God's gladness is found: Psalm 122:1
      i. If you are going to heaven, you will want to be with as many Christians as possible, and you will find the most of them in church

C. The difference between listening to a radio sermon and hearing one in church is something like talking to your girlfriend on the phone instead of spending the evening with her in person.

D. Some people think they hurt their church when they get made and quit coming, but they are wrong. A tree was never hurt when the dried-up fruit fell off!

E. The extent of some people's religion—they know the name of the church theystay away from!

F. WANTED: Men and women and boys and girls to sit in slightly used church pews every Sunday.

G. To Be or Not to Be Deliquent. A preacher once visited a deliquent church member. He found him seated before a glowing fire. The pastor took the tongs and removed a live coal from the fire and set in on the hearth. Both watched as it turned to a black, charred and useless mass. The member observed the proceedings with interest and finally said. "Reverend, yu need not say a single word. I'll go to church from now on. "Your church is just what *you* make it. You cannot spell church without "U."

H. God never commanded His people to observe His day in spirit, but in body. It is the whole man or woman that must answer to Him for the way they spend the day of worship and rest. Who wants to preach to spirits!

I. Someone has said that the attendance at the Sunday morning worship service shows the popularity of the pastor; the evening service shows the popularity of the church; and the Wednesday evening prayer service shows the popularity of Christ. If this be true, "What think ye of Christ?"

J. Have you voted lately?[5]

Last Sunday I voted to close the church; not intentionally, not maliciously, perhaps, but carelessly, thoughtlessly, indifferently, I voted. I voted to close down its doors that its witness and its testimony might be stopped. I voted to close the open Bible on its pulpit—the Bible that has been given to use by years of struggle and by the blood of many martyrs who died that we might have it read. I voted for our minister to stop preaching the glorious truths of the gospel of Jesus Christ. I voted that the children of the Sunday school no longer be taught the stories of the Bible and no longer lift their tiny voices in singing "Jesus loves me, this I know, for the Bible tells me so." I voted for the voice of the choir and the congregation to be stilled, that they no longer sing in united praise. I voted for every missionary of the church to be called home, every native worker supported by the church to stop preaching, every hospital, every school and dispensary on its foreign missionary fields to be closed. I voted that its colleges close their doors and no longer to retain its youth for Christian service. I voted for every home missionary project to be abandoned, every influence for good and right and for the truth in our community to be curtailed and finally stopped. I voted for the darkness of superstition, the degrading influence of sin, the blight of ignorance and the curse of selfish greed once again to settle their damning load on the shoulders of an already burdened world.

You say: "How did I vote to close the church and all of its activities?" Simply by staying away from the Sunday services, the prayer meeting, by your spending more time for yourself and more money on things that are not bread, cheating the Lord out of His tithe and offerings; by loving the world and its pleasures more than God. Oh, yes, you could have been faithful and gone to church regularly, but 101 excuses got the best of you. So you stayed home and voted to close your church!

K. Importance of Laymen.[6]

> Leave it to the minister,
>   And soon the church will die;
> Leave it to the women folk—
>   And the young will pass it by;
> For the church is all that lifts us
>   From the coarse and selfish mob,
> And the church that is to prosper
>   Needs the Layman on the job.
> It's the church's special function
>   To uphold the finer things,
> To teach the Way of living
>   From which all that's noble springs;
> But the minister can't do it
>   Single-handed and alone,
> For the Layman of the country
>   Are the church's cornerstone.
> When you see a church that's empty,
>   Though its doors are open wide,
> It is not the church that's dying,
>   It's the Laymen who have died;
> For it's not by song or sermon
>   That the church's work is done;
> It's the Laymen of the country
>   Who for God must carry on.

21. Faith Defined: 11:1. There is a difference between biblical faith and positive thinking. Positive thinking seeks knowledge to tap the powers of the mind and to utilize them for confident living. As far as it goes, that may be good. But biblical faith relates to a living God—it

makes promises present and real and unseen things visible. This verse is often referred to as a *definition* of faith. However, it is a *declaration* of its power and action. See SIGHT in Index.

    a. Faith achieves: 11:4-35a
    b. Faith suffers: 11:35b-38
    c. Faith waits on God: James 1:3
    d. Faith rewards: 11:39,40

22. Types of Faith: 11:4-40. See FAITH and SIGHT in Index.

    a. Abel's *justifying* faith—illustrating *worship:* vs. 4
    b. Enoch's *sanctifying* faith—illustrating *walk:* vs. 5
    c. Noah's *separating* faith—illustrating *witness:* vs. 7
    d. Abraham's *obedient* faith—illustrating *trust:* vs. 8
    e. Sarah's *strengthening* faith—illustrating *productiveness:* vs.11
    f. Isaac's *patient* faith—illustrating *overcoming the flesh:* vs. 20
    g. Jacob's *suffering* faith—illustrating overcoming man's will: vs. 21
    h. Joseph's *hopeful* faith—illustrating *waiting:* vs. 22
    i. Moses' *enduring* faith—illustrating *yieldedness:* vss. 23-27
    j. Israel's *victorious* faith—illustrating *joy:* vs. 29
    k. Israel's *walking* faith—illustrating *works:* vs. 30
    l. Rahab's *saving* faith—illustrating *peace:* vs. 31
    m. The saints' *living* faith—illustrating *reward:* vss. 32-40

23. Noah's Faith: 11:7

    a. Beginning of faith—warned of God
    b. Progress of faith—moved with fear
    c. Work of faith—prepared an ark
    d. Reward of faith—saved his house
    e. Result of faith—condemned the world
    f. Inheritance of faith—heir of righteousness

24. Abraham's Faith: 11:8-19

    a. He walked by faith: 11:8; Genesis 12:1-3
    b. He was justified by faith: Genesis 15:6; Romans 4:3
    c. He lived by faith: Romans 4:20,21
    d. He was tried by faith: 11:17
    e. He prospered by faith: 11:9
    f. He was blessed by faith: 11:11,12
    g. He looked and desired by faith: 11:10,16
    h. He died in faith: 11:13

25. Moses' Choice: 11:24-27. See EGYPT'S Wisdom in Index. With "eternity's values in view," he—

    a. Forsook the royalty of Egypt: vs. 24
    b. He forsook the pleasures of Egypt: vs. 25b
    c. Forsook the riches (possessions) of Egypt: vs. 26
    d. Ignored the perils of Egypt: vs. 27
    e. Accepted the reproach of Christ: vs. 25a
    f. Received the riches of Christ: vs. 26

26. The Besetting Sin: 12:1? John Wesley's mother once said to him: "Whatever weakens your reason, impairs the tenderness of your conscience, obscures your sense of God, or takes off the relish of spiritual things, in short, whatever increases the strength and authority of your body over your mind, that thing is sin to you, however innocent it may seem in itself." What is the sin that "so easily besets us?"

    a. The sin for which you do not want to be reproved
    b. The sin you are ready to defend
    c. The sin upon which your thoughts run most

d. The sin for which you find the most excuses

e. The sin that often beclouds your spiritual sky

f. The sin that causes remorse of conscience the most frequently

g. The sin that makes you doubt your present acceptance with God

h. The sin you are most unwilling to acknowledge you possess

i. The sin you are most unwilling to give up

j. The sin you are all the time trying to persuade yourself is an infirmity

k. The sin you always seek to justify

27. The Secret of Victory: 12

a. Lay aside every weight: vs. 1a

b. Run with patience: vs. 1b

c. Look unto Jesus: vs. 2a

d. Despise not correction: vss. 5-11

e. Stand up: vss. 12,13

f. Follow peace: vs. 14

g. Watch to avoid temptation: vs. 15

h. Hear Christ speak: vss. 24,25

i. Serve God acceptably: vs. 28

28. Looking Unto Jesus: 12:2[8]

a. In the Scriptures: John 5:39

b. Revealed by the Holy Spirit: John 15:26

c. Crucified: Romans 4:25a; 5:8,9

d. Risen: Matthew 28:6

e. Glorified: Hebrews 1:3

f. The present One: Colossians 1:18

g. Who gives repentance: Acts 5:31a

h. The forgiver of sins: Acts 5:31b; Ephesians 1:7

i. For grace: II Corinthians 12:9

j. And not to ourselves and others: Luke 14:26,27

k. And not the world: I John 2:15-17

l. And not to Satan: I Peter 5:8,9

m. And not to our creeds: Matthew 7:21-23

n. And not to our works: John 3:3-7; Titus 3:5

o. And not to our brethren: I Corinthians 1:11-13; 3:3-7

p. As our burden-bearer: I Peter 5:7

q. And not the Law: Romans 8:3

r. And not what we are doing for Him: I Corinthians 10:31

s. And not to our spiritual gifts: Romans 12:6-8

t. And not the blessings: I Corinthians 15:58

u. And not the heights of holiness attained: Luke 14:11

v. And not our doubts: Philippians 4:6

w. Who is preparing a place for us: John 14:1-3

x. For His return: I Thessalonians 4:16,17

y. The Author and Finisher of our faith: Hebrews 12:2

29. God's Purpose in Chastening: 12:5-11. See PRECIOUS in Index.

a. For correction (training): 12:9

b. To humble us: Romans 8:18; II Corinthians 4:17; I Peter 4:16; 5:5,6

c. To make us repent: Jeremiah 31:18

d. To lead us to pray: Isaiah 26:16

e. To teach us His Word: Psalm 94:12

f. To keep us from condemnation: I Corinthians 11:32

g. To reveal His love: 12:6

30. The Blood that Speaketh: 12:24. The blood of Abel speaks of retaliation (Genesis 4:10),

but the blood of Christ speaks of "better things," such as—

    a. An eternal purpose: Revelation 13:8
    b. Redemption: Colossians 1:14a
    c. Forgiveness: Colossians 1:14b; Revelation 1:5
    d. Cleansing: I John 1:9
    e. Justification without works: Romans 5:1,9
    f. Nearness to God: Ephesians 2:13
    g. Sanctification: Hebrews 13:12
    h. Boldness (liberty): Hebrews 10:12
    i. Dedication: Hebrews 10:19-25
    j. Peace: Colossians 1:20
    k. Victory: Revelation 12:11
    l. Heaven: Revelation 7:14,15

31. Things Which Cannot Be Shaken: 12:27
    a. The Word of God: Matthew 24:35
    b. The Foundation of God: II Timothy 2:19
    c. The Kingdom of God: Hebrews 12:28
    d. The Hope of the Christian: II Timothy 1:12

32. The Unchanging Christ: 13:8
    a. His Person: 1:3a,8-12
    b. His Position: 1:3b; 10:12b
    c. His Priesthood: 7:24,25
    d. His Procurement: 10;12a,14,19,20
    e. His Presence: 13:5
    f. His Purpose: 10:37

33. Obedience: 13:17
    a. Obedience of hearing: 13:17; Romans 10:17
    b. Obedience of faith: Romans 16:26
    c. Obedience of surrender: Romans 6:13
    d. Obedience of sacrifice: Romans 12:1
    e. Obedience of service: Acts 26:19,20

34. Covenants of God: 13:20. See COVENANTS in Index.
    a. The Eternal Covenant: 13:20. The *redemptive* covenant in eternity past between Father and Son, to effect eternal redemption for fallen man (Revelation 13:8).
    b. The Edenic Covenant: Genesis 1:26-28. The *creative* covenant between man and his Maker, to govern man in his innocent state.
    c. The Adamic Covenant: Genesis 3:14-19. The *discipline* covenant regulating man's life as a sinner, with the promise of a coming Redeemer.
    d. The Noahic Covenant: Genesis 8:20—9:6. The *human government* covenant for man's social life and benefits.
    e. The Abrahamic Covenant: Genesis 12:1-3. The *promise* covenant that through him (in Christ) all the families of the earth would be blessed (Romans 4:16-18; Galatians 3:16).
    f. The Mosaic Covenant: Exodus 20:1—31:18. The *legal* covenant, consisting of God's laws (moral, ceremonial, and social), a conditional covenant of works.
    g. The Palestinian Covenant: Genesis 15:18-21; Deuteronomy 30:1-10. The *land* (territory) covenant for Israel's dwelling place in Canaan.
    h. The Davidic Covenant: II Samuel 7:4-17; I Chronicles 17:4-15. The *kingdom* covenant, outlining David's temporal rule and the eternal rule of the "Greater" David upon the throne of David (Psalm 89:30-37; Acts 2:30-31).
    i. The New Covenant: Jeremiah 31:31-33; Matthew 26:28; Hebrews 8:8-12. The *forgiving* covenant which assures the repentant sinner of forgiveness of sin and a new heart (Ephesians 1:7; II Corinthians 5:17).

One of the paradoxical truths of Scripture is that suffering and trial result in joy. The early Hebrew Christians knew suffering and persecution on every hand—so much the more from their own brethren (kindred). Taking a stand for Christ then was tantamount to signing one's own death warrant. But in and through suffering there was joy unspeakable, a peace that passed all understanding. The joy that came at the end of every trial was but encouragement to face another. To illustrate this truth the writer of Hebrews upheld Jesus as the example of such sufferings and joy.

THE JOY THAT WAS SET BEFORE HIM—12:2[9]

"Jesus could only rejoice in what would gratify His benevolent nature. The object of His joy therefore must be benevolent; and that object was the complete salvation and eternal happiness of His people. To raise millions of fallen souls to the enjoyment of holiness and happiness forever, He was willing to sink in the deep waters and to suffer inconceivable agonies for a time. He kept His eye on the conversion, sanctification, and the glorification of His people, by which His Father would be glorified, and this sustained Him. He is now reaping the fruits of His pains, and waits expecting the time when all for whom He suffered, bled, and died, will be made like Him, stand complete before Him, and enjoy the kingdom with Him for evermore. O how His benevolent heart will be delighted, how His loving heart will overflow with joy when He sees all His people safe in His Father's kingdom! Beloved, if such was the joy of Jesus, what ought to be our joy? Ought it not be to see Him glorified, and to assist in glorifying Him, first on earth and then in heaven."

PRAYER THOUGHT: "I know, Lord, that resistance to Thy will hardens the heart. Help me day by day to keep my heart spiritually flexible, lest it become so hardened that I fail to please Thee. In Jesus' name I pray this. Amen."[10]

Hebrews 3:12,13

James—The Book of Practical Christianity

Name: Several men named James are mentioned in the New Testament and for this reason it has been difficult to ascertain which "James" wrote this Epistle. His introduction simply labels him a "servant of God and the Lord Jesus Christ" (1:1). Two apostles bore this name (Matthew 10:2,3). A half brother of Jesus was also named James (Matthew 13:55). It is *this* James that many accept as this epistle's writer.

This James was not converted during Christ's earthly ministry (John 7:3-10). In all probability he was saved after the resurrection for Christ appeared to him singly (I Corinthians 15:7) and he was numbered among the twelve in the upper room (Acts 1:14). Peter sought him after his release from prison (Acts 12:17). He was the prominent leader in the first church council in Jerusalem (Acts 15:13,23-29; Galatians 1:19; 2:9,12), and Paul learned much from him (Acts 21:18-26). Because of his leadership in the council, he was recognized the "Bishop" of Jerusalem. A strict Jew, he was tolerant to Gentiles, and accepted them as true Christians along with believing Jews, as his letter in Acts (15:13-29) indicates. He was called "James the Just" by Clement of Alexandria and his countrymen because of his "just" dealings with both Jews and Gentiles. James is the Greek equivalent of Jacob—"supplanter."

According to Josephus (Ant. XX, ix), the writer of this epistle was "the brother of Jesus, who was called Christ, whose name was James." The following is an account of James' martyrdom by Josephus and Hegesippus, a Christian Jew (A.D. 160), which account was accepted by Eusebius—"Annanus, the high priest, along with the Scribes and Pharisees, took advantage of the absence of the Roman government and assembled the Sanhedrin, commanding James, 'the brother of Jesus . . .' to proclaim from a Temple balcony that Jesus was not the Messiah, thus restraining the multitudes of people who were believing in Christ. Instead, James cried loudly that Jesus was indeed the Son of God, the Judge of the world. He was then hurled to the ground, stoned, and finally clubbed to death (A.D. 63). A few years after his death Titus destroyed the Temple and Jerusalem, and the Jews were dispersed. Many Jews felt, because of James' influence among the Jews, that had he lived, he might have averted Jerusalem's destruction, and counted it judgment upon them that they had slain him."

Occasion of Writing: James was writing to Christians of Jewish extraction residing outside Palestine in Gentile communities (1:1). Many of these Jewish Christians were probably those who had been saved on the day of Pentecost and had taken back with them to their own countries just the rudiments of Christianity. Because they were babes in Christ, James backed up his practical applications with (O.T.) Scriptures. There was persecution from without and moral defects in their churches (1:2-4). James eliminated doctrine (Christ is mentioned only twice—1:1; 2:1), and got down to the practical side of Christianity—stressing the gospel *of* Christ rather than the gospel *about* Christ. The practicality of James' writing (for both Jew and Gentile) is seen in his "answers" to supposed questions—

QUESTION	ANSWER
What to do when tested?	Count it all joy: 1:2
Why am I tried?	To have patience: 1:3
How can I get wisdom?	Ask God for it: 1:5
How do I ask for it?	In faith, nothing wavering: 1:6
If I endure testings, what then?	Receive a reward: 1:12
Does God tempt?	No: 1:13
How am I tempted?	By lust: 1:14
How can I be victorious?	Receive the Word: 1:21
How can I be blessed?	By obeying the Word: 1:22-25
What is the test of true religion?	Bridle the tongue (ch. 3), consider widows and orphans, and be separated from the world: 1:26,27
What is the test of brotherly love?	Have respect for all: 2:1-13
Is faith alone sufficient?	Without works it is dead: 2:14-26
What is the test of a fruitful life?	Holding the tongue: 3:1-18
Why isn't my prayer heard?	We ask not, or ask amiss: 4:2,3
Can I be a friend of the world?	No: 4:4
How can I receive grace and be lifted (exalted)?	Be humble: 4:6,10
How can I cope with the devil?	Resist him; submit to God: 4:7,8
What is my life?	A vapor: 4:14a
How long will it last?	A little time: 4:14b
Should I make my own plans?	If the Lord wills: 4:15
What about capital and labor?	Labor will have its day: 5:1-6
Is Christ really coming again?	Yes. Be patient: 5:7,8
Shall I hold a grudge?	Better not: 5:9

How can I endure suffering?	With happy patience: 5:10,11
What should I do in afflictions?	Pray: 5:13a
How can I stay happy?	Sing psalms: 5:13b
What if I get sick?	Call the elders and get right with God: 5:14,16a
What does real prayer accomplish?	Much fruit: 5:16b-18
Should I seek to convert others?	YES! 5:19,20

Contents: This Epistle encourages Christians (Jews and Gentiles) to patience under their troubles and persecutions, and to wait and hope for the speedy coming of Christ. It reveals the evil practices of some that boasted of their faith and knowledge, though they lived very hypocritical lives, not "practicing what they preached." The view of James is to show that faith, without the fruitful works of righteousness, is not genuine. He exhorts to duties becoming Christians, and inveighs against a number of vices which were scandalous to them.

Someone has called James the "Proverbs" of the New Testament. "With a single stroke the writer commands a duty, scourges a fault, denounces a wrong, and crowns a virtue with transcendent glory."[1] It is filled with the marks of true religion and false profession. This Epistle, in the mode of its address, is entirely different from all the others, and the general style of it is more like that of a prophet of the Old Testament than that of an apostle of the New. Our blessed Lord is mentioned but twice in the whole letter; it begins without any apostolical salutation and it closes without any such benediction. It may be regarded as a kind of connecting link between Judaism and Christianity, as the ministry of John the Baptist was between the Old and the New Testaments. The elegant and beautiful simplicity of the sacred writers is, however, eminently conspicuous in this Epistle, and it is commended as one of the most finished productions in the New Testament.

James is the first of the seven general Epistles. They are called "catholic" (catholic means "universal") in that they are not addressed to any one particular church, but are to be read by all churches. In the 5 chapters in this Book there are 108 verses and 2,309 words.

Character: Practical. Because James is less theological than any other New Testament book, and because of stress on "works" as proof that one has faith, some have ruled that this Epistle should not be a part of Scripture. Martin Luther, for example, rejected it, calling a strawy or chaffy Epistle.

The seeming opposition of this Epistle of James is his use of the term "justification by works" (2:20-26), and Paul's expression "justification by faith" (Romans 3:28). Paul emphasized the same truth as James—salvation is by faith apart from works, but one works to prove that he does have faith. Evidence of salvation (life in Christ), according to Paul, is a walk of faith, separation, etc. (Ephesians 2:10; Titus 3:8). Or, as James put it, "faith without works [life] is dead" (2:26). There is no conflict between Paul and James. The "works" of James are not the "works" of Paul, nor are they talking about the same faith. For James the "works" of the Christian life are works of mercy, not the "works of the law" of which Paul speaks. Paul is speaking of Christian faith and Jewish works; James speaks of Jewish faith and Christian works. Paul is *doctrinal* while James is *practical.*

Subject: To teach us that saving faith will manifest itself by good works: 2:14.

Outline:
   I. Various Exhortations: 1
  II. Respect of Persons in Assembly: 2:1-13
 III. Works the Proof of Faith: 2:14-26
  IV. The Tongue Unruly: 3:1-12
   V. Heavenly and Devilish Wisdom Contrasted: 3:13-18
  VI. Worldliness Rebuked: 4

VII. Closing Communications: 5

Writer: James: 1:1. See NAME in Dictionary.

When and Where Written: A.D. 45, in Jerusalem. Since there are no references to Gentiles, it has been assumed by some that James wrote this Epistle before the Jerusalem council, in which he made Gentiles equal with Jews in the matter of salvation by faith (Acts 15).

Key Chapter: 2. Test of faith.

Key Verses: 2:20,26.

Key Word: Works.

Key Phrase: Be ye doers of the Word.

Key Thought: The practice of faith.

Spiritual Thought: Prove your faith in your life (Philippians 2:12,13).

Christ Is Seen As: The Lord who draws nigh: 4:6-8.

Names and Titles of Christ: See NAME in Dictionary.
1. Lord Jesus Christ: 1:1
2. Lord: 1:12; 5:8
3. Lord of glory: 2:1

Names and Titles of God. See NAME in Dictionary.
1. Father of lights: 1:17
2. Father: 1:27
3. Lord: 4:10
4. Lord of Sabaoth (of hosts): 5:4

Names and Titles of the Holy Spirit: Spirit: 4:5. See NAME in Dictionary.

Shadow of turning: 1:17. An ancient custom for timekeeping was the "sundial." Common throughout the old biblical world, as well as in China, it is mentioned twice in the Old Testament (II Kings 20:11; Isaiah 38:8). "Shadow of turning" refers to less and less light till there is total darkness. Darkness is a symbol of sin (John 3:19). James, in referring to a "sundial," is stating that with the Lord there is no "shadow of turning"—no less light or darkness—He is unchangeable (I John 1:5b). See LONG DAY in Index.

The Old Testament in James:
1. Love thy neighbor: 2:8 with Leviticus 19:18
2. Do not commit adultery: 2:11a with Exodus 20:14
3. Do not kill: 2:11b with Exodus 20:13
4. Abraham believed God: 2:23a with Genesis 15:6
5. God resisteth the proud: 4:6 with Proverbs 3:34
6. Companion references:
   a. Asking for wisdom: 1:5 with I Kings 3:5-12
   b. As the flowers pass away: 1:10 with Job 14:2
   c. Happiness for enduring temptation: 1:12 with Job 5:17
   d. Abraham, God's friend: 2:23b with II Chronicles 20:7
   e. Rahab and the spies: 2:15 with Joshua 2:1; 6:22,23
   f. The Spirit's ministry: 4:4,5 with Genesis 6:3,5; Nehemiah 9:30
   g. Job's patience: 5:11 with Job 1:21
   h. Elijah's prayer: 5:17 with I Kings 17:1; 18:42

SEED THOUGHTS

1. James and the Word of God
   Its names—
   a. Word of Truth: 1:18
   b. Engrafted Word: 1:21
   c. Perfect Law: 1:25
   Its function—
   a. Convinces and convicts: 2:9; Romans 10:13-17
   b. Begets: 1:18; I Peter 1:23
   c. Implants godliness: 1:21
   d. Activates and energizes: 1:25
   Our responsibility to the Word—
   a. Listen to it: 1:23a
   b. Look into it—examine: 1:25
   c. Receive it: 1:21
   d. Practice it: 1:22

2. God, the Giver: 1:5,17; 3:17
   a. *What?* Every good and perfect gift, particularly wisdom
   b. *To whom?* To those who ask
   c. *How?* Liberally, without grudge, criticism, or scolding
   d. *When?* When we ask
   e. *Where from?* Above, from our heavenly Father
   f. *Why?* To make us—
      —Pure (undefiled)
      —Peaceful (peace-loving)
      —Gentle (courteous)
      —Easy to be entreated (yields to God's reason)
      —Full of mercy (compassion) and good fruits (evidence)
      —Without partiality (considerate of all)
      —Without hypocrisy (fully sincere)

If we lack these things in our lives, we are admonished to ask wisdom of God (1:5).

3. Crown of Life: 1:12. See CROWNS in Index.
4. Hearers but Not Doers: 1:22. See HEARERS in Index.
5. The Blessed Man: 1:25[2]
   a. His foundation—the *Word* of God: II Timothy 3:16,17
   b. His foundation source—the *Love* of God: John 3:16
   c. His fullness expressed—the *Spirit* of God: I Corinthians 3:16
   d. His faith appropriating—the *Work* of God: Acts 3:16
   e. His fruit revealed—the *Peace* of God: II Thessalonians 3:16
   f. His floodtide of joy—the *Grace* of God: Colossians 3:16
   g. His fellowship manifested—the *Remembrance* of God: Malachi 3:16

6. Watch Your Words: 1:26; 3:5-10[3]

> *A careless word may kindle strife;*
> *A cruel word may wreck a life.*
> *A bitter word may hate instill;*
> *A brutal word may smite and kill.*
> *A gracious word may soothe the way;*
> *A joyous word may light the day.*
> *A timely word may lessen stress;*
> *A loving word may heal and bless.*

7. What is Sin? 2:9; 4:17. The Bible gives seven definitions of sin: two each by James, John, and Solomon, and one by Paul.

    a. Having respect of persons—the rich over the poor: 2:9 (vss. 1-9)
    b. Knowing to do right and doing it not: 4:17
    c. Doing things that are doubtful—not of faith: Romans 14:23
    d. Transgression—stepping over or breaking God's law: I John 3:4
    e. All unrighteousness—coming short of God's requirements: I John 5:17
    f. Pride and vanity: Proverbs 21:4
    g. The plans of the foolish—evil thoughts: Proverbs 24:9

Sin *adds* to your troubles, *subtracts* from your energy, *multiplies* your difficulties, and *divides* your interest. Its wages (sum total) is death. See SIN in Index.

8. Faith Without Works: 2:26. We cannot trust God—

    a. For help if we are not making any effort
    b. For strength if we have strength and are not using it
    c. For guidance if we are not following His leading now
    d. For prosperity if we have proved we cannot be trusted with it
    e. For truth when we will not act upon what we already know
    f. For forgiveness if we will not forgive someone else
    g. For mercy if we intend to commit the same sin again
    h. For faith if we neglect His Word

9. The Perfect Man: 3:2

    a. Perfect under discouragements: 1:2-11
    b. Perfect in temptations: 1:12-18
    c. Perfect in hearing and doing: 1:19-27
    d. Perfect in avoiding partiality: 2:1-13
    e. Perfect in works evidencing faith: 2:14-26
    f. Perfect in temperance: 3:2
    g. Perfect in use of the tongue: 3:3-12
    h. Perfect in wisdom: 3:13-18
    i. Perfect in pleasures and desires: 4:1-10
    j. Perfect in judging: 4:11,12
    k. Perfect in submission to God: 4:13-17
    l. Perfect in not loving the world: 5:1-6
    m. Perfect in waiting for Christ's coming: 5:7-11
    n. Perfect in communications: 5:12
    o. Perfect in faith and prayer: 5:13-18
    p. Perfect in witnessing: 5:19,20

10. Why Submit to God? 4:7a

    a. To overcome the lusts of our past life: 4:1-4
    b. To receive God's grace: 4:6
    c. To resist the devil: 4:7b
    d. To be drawn closer to the Lord: 4:8
    e. To be lifted up: 4:10
    f. To be ready when we die: 4:13,14
    g. To know His will daily: 4:15
    h. To do the right thing and sin not: 4:17

11. Resist the devil: 4:7b (see SATAN in Index). Peter tells us the devil, like a roaring lion, goes about, seeking whom he may devour (I Peter 5:8). How then can we win in spiritual warfare with our adversary?

    a. Beware of the nature of his opposition: Ephesians 6:12
    b. Be on guard against the devil's subtle tactics: II Corinthians 11:14
    c. Be alert in handling the sword of the Spirit: Ephesians 6:17
    d. Be equipped with the whole armor of God: Ephesians 6:13. See ARMOR in Index.

e. Be constantly in an attitude of prayer: Ephesians 6:18; Matthew 26:41
f. Be confident about victory—"he will flee from you"
12. Characteristics of Prayer: 5:13-18. See PRAYER in Index.
   a. Individual prayer—let him pray: vs. 13
   b. United prayer—let them pray: vs. 14
   c. Believing prayer—prayer of faith: vs. 15
   d. Intercessory prayer—one for another: vs. 16
   e. Fervent prayer—effectual prayer: vs. 16
   f. Definite prayer—that it might not rain: vs. 17
   g. Effectual prayer—heaven gave rain again: vs. 18

A BIT OF HEAVENLY MANNA

In no other book in the New Testament do we find one's faith "tested" like we do in James. He pulls no punches, names sin for what it is, listing sins of commission and hitting at sins of ommission as well. He spells out what true Christianity is in these words—

PURE RELIGION—1:27[4]

"Religion is devotedness to God, and supposes reconciliation to God, fellowship with God, coming under the yoke of God, and being of one mind and spirit with God. Many profess religion who do not understand its nature, possess its principles, or practice its precepts. They are not enlightened. They are not sincere. They are not devout. Pure religion flows from pure principles, runs in a pure channel, and aims at pure ends. Pure religion is humble, laborious, self-denying. The truly religious man not only embraces the doctrines of the gospel, but practices its truths; not only worships God through his Lord and Savior Jesus Christ, but benefits his fellow men; is not only devout, but devoted. He pities the fatherless, sympathizes with the widow, helping them as God allows, and keeps himself unspotted from the world. If he can dry an orphan's tears, or can minister to a widow's needs, if he can bring a soul to Christ, or in any way promote the holiness and happiness of his fellow man, happy is he. Is this the nature of your religion? If not, it must be spurious. Let us examine ourselves by this test."

PRAYER THOUGHT: "Today, dear Lord, and every day, I need Thy strength to nip temptation in the bud before it blossoms forth as sin in my life. I need Thy help moment by moment to resist the devil. I ask this in the name of the One who overcame temptation for me. Amen."[5]

James 1:13-16

First Peter—The Book of Christian Discipline

Name: Peter, the writer of this Epistle, has a long history. His proper name was Simon, his surname Peter ("rock"—John 1:42; Matthew 16:18), which is Cephas in the Hebrew. He was son of Jonas (or John—Matthew 16:17; John 21:15), a resident of Capernaum, married (Mark 1:21,29,30), a brother of Andrew (John 1:40,41), and was a fisherman by trade with James and John (Matthew 4:18 with Luke 5:10).

He was naturally *impulsive* and *impetuous:* (a) asks to walk on water (Matthew 14:28), (b) sought to bring Christ down to man's level (Matthew 17:4), (c) defended Christ with a sword (John 18:10), (d) asked Christ to wash his hands and head (John 13:9), and (e) ignored the seriousness of the moment by going fishing and jumping into the sea (John 21:3,7). He was *presumptuous:* (a) in rebuking Christ (Matthew 16:22), and (b) in his refusal (at first) to let Christ wash his feet (John 13:8). He was *fainthearted* and *cowardly:* (a) when he started sinking in the water (Matthew 14:30), (b) when he went to sleep in the garden (Matthew 26:40,41), and (c) when he vehemently denied Christ (Matthew 26:69-74). He was also *slow* at times to apprehend truth (Matthew 15:15-20), and was highly self-seeking (Matthew 19:27).

Yet he was self-sacrificing (Mark 1:18), tenderhearted and affectionate (Matthew 26:75; John 21:15-17), quick to confess Christ (Matthew 16:15,16), gifted with spiritual insight (Matthew 16:17; John 6:68,69), and after Pentecost was courageous and immovable (Acts 4:19,20; 5:28,29,40,42). He was one of the three of Christ's "inner circle"—(a) at the Mount of Transfiguration (Matthew 17:1); (b) in the house where Jarius' daughter was raised from the dead (Mark 5:35-42); and (c) in the garden of Gethsemane (Matthew 26:36,37).

He heads the list of apostles in all four gospel accounts, was the first to confess that Jesus was the Christ, the Son of God; the first disciple to enter Christ's empty tomb, even though John outran him; and was the first disciple called by name by Christ after His resurrection (John 20:2-6; Luke 24:12; Mark 16:7). He is referred to 210 times in the New Testament. Paul is referred to 162 times and the combined number of the rest of the apostles is 142.

After Pentecost he is seen as the "dean" of the apostles—the preacher at Pentecost (Acts 2:14-41), the most prominent figure in the first half of the book of Acts, the one who opened the way for Gentiles into the church (Acts 10:1—11:18), and who took a strong stand in defense of salvation by grace through faith in the council at Jerusalem (Acts 15:1-12). He sort of drops out of sight as Paul "took over," and except for his two Epistles, he is only mentioned by Paul in a visit to Antioch—and as the apostle of circumcision because of his interest in his own people (Galatians 2:7-14).

Tradition has it that Peter was martyred in Rome by Nero in A.D. 67, that he was crucified upside down, feeling he was unworthy to die as his Savior had. Christ had foretold of his dying as a martyr (John 21:18,19). There is no historical proof that he met his martyrdom in Rome, however.

Occasion of Writing: Roman persecution had scattered believers everywhere. The church in general was undergoing a "fiery trial," and the devil (through Nero, no doubt—see NERO in Index) was seeking to devour all believers (4:12; 5:8,9). Peter wrote this general Epistle to encourage them in their sufferings, to remind them of important truths such as election by the Father, sanctification by the Spirit, redemption by the blood of Christ (the Trinity), and obedience as proof of their faith (1:2,13,14). He sought to give them hope as strangers on earth, but with an inheritance in heaven. Peter has been called the "apostle of hope," Paul, the "apostle of faith," and John, the "apostle of love."

Peter also probably wrote to show his support of Paul's teaching (II Peter 3:15-18). Many of the believers to whom Peter wrote in Pontus, Galatia, Cappadocia, Asia, and Bythinia (1:1) were members of churches founded by Paul. Some of these members had questioned Paul's apostleship and some, no doubt, had heard of Peter's and Paul's argument on some minor points of law and grace (Galatians 2:7-14). Lest any of the brethren, maligned by Judaizers, felt he might lean toward Judaism, he sought in his letters to show them that the gospel was for Jew and Gentile alike, stressing the chief doctrines emphasized by Paul—

1. Christ's vicarious suffering and death: 2:24
2. Redemption by Christ's blood: 1:18,19
3. The new birth: 1:23
4. The resurrection: 3:21,22
5. Christ's second coming: 1:7,13; 5:4

Contents: "Peter treats of redeeming, regenerating, sanctifying, and persevering grace. He exhorts believers to the exercise of grace, faith, hope, and love, and to the discharge of such duties becoming their several stations, whereby they might evidence to others the truth of grace in themselves, and adorn the doctrine of the grace of God, and recommend it to others. He particularly exhorts them to patiently bear all afflictions and the persecutions and to stand steadfast in the true grace of God."[1] The theme seems to be "victory over suffering in fiery trials with sufficient grace." There are 5 chapters in this book, 105 verses, and 2,482 words.

The letter reflects Peter's life and mind—

Chapter I

1. Verse 3 could reflect the joy that was his when the truth of the resurrection made its impact upon him (Pentecost and after)
2. Verse 7 could reflect his courage when he was beaten for preaching Christ (Acts 5:40)
3. Verse 13 could reflect his brashness at the Lord's supper, when Christ in humility girded Himself with a towel and washed the disciples' feet (John 13:2-9)
4. Verses 18 and 19 could reflect his message to the lame man that the things of God do not come by silver and gold (Acts 3:1-6)
5. Verse 22 could reflect the thought that it is better to obey God rather than man (Acts 5:29)
6. Verses 23 through 25 could reflect the use of Scriptures in his messages in Acts (4:31)

Chapter II

1. Verses 2 and 3 could reflect the admonition to continue in the apostles' doctrine (Acts 2:42)
2. Verses 9 and 10 could reflect his use of the gospel which included Gentiles (Acts 10:1—11:18)
3. Verse 11 could reflect his impulsiveness in cutting off the ear of Malchus (John 18:10)
4. Verses 13 and 14 could reflect his being beaten and imprisoned by those in authority (Acts 5:40; 12:1-4)
5. Verse 15 could reflect the thought of those truly ignorant, having been labeled "ignorant" himself (Acts 4:13)
6. Verse 20 could reflect the thought of Christians rejoicing that they are counted worthy to suffer shame for Christ as he did (Acts 5:40,41)
7. Verse 25 could reflect the experiences he had in following Christ afar off and his restoration (Luke 22:54; Mark 16:7)

Chapter III

1. Verses 1 through 7 could well reflect his own home life and the probability that his wife accompanied him on his "evangelistic" tours (I Corinthians 9:5)
2. Verses 10 and 15 could reflect his denial of Christ and his boldness in confessing Christ after being forgiven (Matthew 26:69-75; Acts 4:18-20; 5:40-42)

Chapter IV

1. Verse 1a could be a reflection on Christ's statement concerning the closing years of his life (John 21:18,19)
2. Verses 17a and 19 could reflect the church's complacency in Jerusalem and the need for persecution to scatter and witness (Acts 8:1-4)

Chapter V

1. Verse 2 could reflect Christ's commission to him (John 21:15-17)
2. Verse 5b could reflect his bold, proud manner on many occasions (e.g., John 13:8a; Matthew 26:33)
3. Verse 8 could reflect Satan's desire to sift him as wheat (Luke 22:31,32)
4. Verse 10 could reflect his own growth in grace and being settled (mature) through years of experience and suffering

Character: General Epistle.

Subject: The pilgrim's pathway of suffering.

Purpose: To encourage us when tried in order that we may be perfect, established, strengthened, and settled: 5:9,10.

Outline:
    I. Introduction: 1:1,2
    II. The Life of Faith: 1:3-25
    III. The Life of Holiness: 2:1—3:9
    IV. The Life of Victory: 3:10—4:19
    V. The Life of Service: 5:1-8a
    VI. The Life of Conflict: 5:8a—11
    VII. The Conclusion: 5:12-14

Writer: Peter: 1:1. See NAME in Dictionary.

When and Where Written: A.D. 65. Babylon is the place mentioned (5:13). Some say that "Babylon" was the symbolic name for Rome. However, I Peter was written long before Rome was referred to as "Babylon." Internal evidence would point to Babylon. The list of countries mentioned in his greeting (1:1) is from east to west, which suggests that Peter was in the east at the writing—mentioning all countries in order of the location to him. Had he written from Rome he no doubt would have listed the countries from west to east. And had it been Rome, he no doubt would have said Rome.

At Pentecost there were men from every nation—including Mesopotamia (Acts 2:5,9). There was at the time of Peter's writing a large colony of Jews in Babylon who not only had undergone persecution by Claudius but were now feeling the sting of Nero's mercilessness. Peter seemed to "put" himself with these sufferers as he wrote.

Tradition has it that Peter lived in Rome twenty-five years before he died—that he was the first Bishop or Pope. Conspicuously absent from Scripture is any mention of his having been in Rome, and there is no substantial evidence from history to support this legend.

Key Chapter: 1. Assurance and promises for believers.

Key Verses: 1:6,7; 4:12,13.

Key Word: Suffer (used 15 times).

Key Phrase: Pilgrims and strangers.

Key Thought: The Christian's hope.

Spiritual Thought: He is Precious: 2:7.

Christ Is Seen As: The suffering Lamb: 1:19; 2:21.

Names and Titles of Christ. See NAME in Dictionary.
    1. Jesus Christ: 1:1
    2. Lord Jesus Christ: 1:3
    3. Christ: 1:11,19
    4. Lamb: 1:19
    5. Living Stone: 2:4
    6. God's Chosen: 2:4
    7. Chief Cornerstone: 2:6
    8. Precious: 2:7a
    9. Head of the Corner: 2:7b
    10. Stone of stumbling: 2:8a
    11. Rock of offense: 2:8b
    12. Example: 2:21
    13. Ideal Sufferer: 2:23
    14. Sin-bearer: 2:24
    15. Shepherd and Bishop of our souls: 2:25
    16. The Just: 3:18

17. Exalted Lord: 3:22
18. Chief Shepherd: 5:4

Names and Titles of God. See NAME in Dictionary.

1. Father: 1:2
2. Lord: 1:25
3. Righteous Judge: 2:23
4. Lord God: 3:15
5. God of all grace: 5:10

Names and Titles of the Holy Spirit. See NAME in Dictionary.

1. Spirit; 1:2; 3:18
2. Spirit of Christ: 1:11
3. Holy Ghost: 1:12
4. Spirit of glory: 4:14
5. Spirit of God: 4:14

The Old Testament in I Peter:

1. Be ye holy: 1:16 with Leviticus 11:44
2. Flesh is as grass: 1:24,25 with Isaiah 40:6-8
3. Chief cornerstone: 2:6 with Isaiah 28:16
4. The stone rejected: 2:7 with Psalm 118:22
5. Rock of offense and stumbling: 2:8 with Isaiah 8:14
6. No sin in Christ: 2:22 with Isaiah 53:9
7. Christ opened not His mouth: 2:23 with Isaiah 53:7
8. Who bore our sins: 2:24 with Isaiah 53:4,5
9. Love life and see good days: 3:10-12 with Psalm 34:12-16
10. Grace to the humble: 5:5 with Proverbs 3:34; Isaiah 57:
11. Companion references:
   a. Old Testament prophets' knowledge of Christ's sufferings: 1:10-12a with Isaiah 53; Daniel 9:24; Haggai 2:7
   b. Tasting the gracious Lord: 2:3 with Psalm 34:8
   c. God's special people: 2:9 with Exodus 19:5,6; Deuteronomy 7:6; 10:15
   d. Times past not a people: 2:10 with Hosea 1:9,10
   e. Fear God, honor the king: 2:17 with Proverbs 24:21
   f. All we like sheep astray: 2:25a with Isaiah 53:6
   g. Abraham called "lord" by Sarah: 3:6 with Genesis 18:12
   h. Noah, his family, and the ark: 3:20 with Genesis 3:7
   i. Love covering faults: 4:8 with Proverbs 10:12
   j. Fiery trials: 4:12 with Isaiah 48:10; Zechariah 13:9
   k. Righteous scarcely saved: 4:18 with Proverbs 11:31
   l. Cast burdens on the Lord: 5:7 with Psalm 55:22

1. Precious Things—
   a. Fiery trials: 1:7. See TRIALS in Index.
   b. Christ's blood: 1:19
   c. The believer: 2:4
   d. Christ as Chief Cornerstone: Isaiah 28:16; I Peter 2:6
   e. Christ Himself: 2:7
   f. Meek and quiet spirit: 3:4 (RV)
   g. Faith: II Peter 1:1
   h. Divine promises: II Peter 1:4
   i. God's thoughts: Psalm 139:17
   j. Unity of the brethren: Psalm 133:1,2
   k. Soul-winning seed: Psalm 126:6

     l. Redemption of souls: Psalm 49:8

    m. Word of God: I Samuel 3:1

     n. Fruits of the sun and earth: Deuteronomy 33:14a,15,16; James 5:7

     o. Things put forth by the moon: Deuteronomy 33:14b. See MOON in Index.

     p. Wisdom: Proverbs 3:13-22

     q. Israel: Isaiah 43:1-4

     r. Good name: Ecclesiastes 7:1

     s. Death of God's saints: Psalm 116:15

     t. Things in heaven: Deuteronomy 33:13. See HEAVEN in Index.

     u. Thoughts of God: Psalm 139:17

     v. Substance of a diligent man: Proverbs 6:26

    w. Life itself: Proverbs 6:26b

2. Peter's "B" Hives. See "B's" in Index.

     a. Grace, peace, mercy and love be multiplied to you: 1:2; Jude 2

     b. Be sober in mind: 1:13

     c. Be holy in character: 1:15,16

     d. Be hungry for God's Word: 2:2,3

     e. Be subject to your master: 2:18

     f. Be pitiful in spirit: 3:8

     g. Be courteous in manner: 3:8

     h. Be followers of good: 3:13

     i. Be ready in testimony: 3:15

     j. Be watchful in prayer: 4:7

     k. Be clothed with humility: 5:5

     l. Be vigilant in watchfulness: 5:8

    m. Be mindful of God's Word: II Peter 3:2

     n. Be godly: II Peter 3:11

     o. Be diligent in service: II Peter 3:14

3. Strangers and Pilgrims on Earth: 1:1

     a. Destination—heaven: 1:4 with Hebrews 11:10,16

     b. Manner of living—obedience: 1:14 with Hebrews 11:8

        —Loves not the world: I John 2:15-17

        —Separated from the world: II Corinthians 6:16-18

        —Loyalty to Christ—overcomes temptation: James 1:12; I John 5:1-4

        —Sets affection on things above: Colossians 3:1,2

     c. Source of encouragement—promises of God: II Peter 1:4 with Hebrews 11:9

     d. Die in faith—hope: 1:9,13 with Hebrews 11:13

4. Results of Christ's Resurrection: 1:3

     a. Fulfillment of God's promises: Acts 13:30-33

     b. Deity of Christ established: Romans 1:3,4

     c. Ground for justification furnished: Romans 4:21-25

     d. Gives believers a living hope: 1:3

     e. Empowers the believer: Ephesians 1:19,20

     f. Enables believers to bear fruit: Romans 7:4

     g. Gives assurance of believer's own resurrection: II Corinthians 4:14

5. Bible Paradoxes: 1:6,7

        —Rejoicing in heaviness: vs. 6

        —Praise in trial: vs. 7

        —Peace amidst tribulation: John 16:33

        —Help through hindrances: John 16:33

        —Blessing those who persecute us: Matthew 5:11; Romans 12:14

        —Unknown but known: II Corinthians 6:9a

        —Dying but living: II Corinthians 6:9b; Galatians 2:20

—Chastened but not killed: II Corinthians 6:9c
—Sorrowful but happy: II Corinthians 6:10a
—Poor but rich: II Corinthians 6:10b
—Having nothing but possessing all things: II Corinthians 6:10c
—Increase through decrease: John 3:30; Matthew 5:39,41
—Profit through loss: Philippians 3:7-9; Matthew 5:46
—Getting through giving: Luke 6:38; Acts 20:35
—Hedged in but not cramped: II Corinthians 4:8a
—Perplexed but not driven to despair: II Corinthians 4:8b
—Persecuted but not deserted: II Corinthians 4:9a
—Knocked down but not knocked out: II Corinthians 4:9b
—Death in us for life in others: II Corinthians 4:10-12
—Heavenly treasure in earthen vessels: II Corinthians 4:7
—Surrender for freedom and victory: Romans 6:16-18
—Strength through weakness: II Corinthians 12:10
—Freedom through slavery: Ephesians 6:20
—Humility through exaltation: Proverbs 18:12; Luke 14:11
—Exaltation through humility: Luke 14:11
—Righteousness for unrighteousness: II Corinthians 5:21
—Rest through labor: Matthew 11:29,30
—Finders weepers, loosers keepers: Matthew 19:39
—Patience through trials: Romans 5:3
—Love through hatred: Luke 14:26
—Brought out to be brought in: Deuteronomy 6:23
—Nakedness for garments: Revelation 3:18
—Foolishness the way to wisdom: I Corinthians 3:18
—Conformable to death to attain a resurrection: Philippians 3:10,11
—Empty but filled: Romans 12:1 with Ephesians 5:18b

6. The Trial of Faith: 1:7. See FAITH in Index.

What tries or tests faith?

a. Pride—of Cain: Genesis 4:3,5
b. Works—by Noah: Genesis 6:13-22
c. Sacrifices—by Abraham: Genesis 22:1-14
d. The flesh—like Joseph's: Genesis 39:7-21
e. Rebellious people—with Moses: Numbers 20:7-12
f. When claiming God's promises—like Joshua; Joshua 1:2,3; 11:23
g. The enemy—against Jehoshaphat: II Chronicles 20:15-26
h. False religions—Baal vs. Elijah: I Kings 16:30—18:46
i. Hypocrites—against Nehemiah: Nehemiah 2:18-20; 4:1; 6:15
j. Hate—like Haman against Mordecai: Esther 3:1-5; 10:1-3
k. Adversity—against Job: Job 1:13—2:10
l. Persecution—against Jeremiah: 1:19; 20:2; 38:6
m. Laws of government—three Hebrew boys: Daniel 3:1-25
n. Evil workers—Daniel: Daniel 6:3-24
o. Prejudice—like Jonah's: 3:10—4:11
p. Love—good Samaritan: Luke 10:30-37
q. Worldly possessions—rich young ruler: Matthew 19:16-22
r. Money—Judas: Matthew 26:14-16
s. Ego—Peter: Matthew 26:33,34,69-75
t. Satan himself—Ananias: Acts 5:3
u. Prestige—Agrippa: Acts 26:28
v. The world—Demas: II Timothy 4:10

Why is faith tested?

To find out if it is pretense or real. Those mentioned who had "precious" faith (II Peter

1:1) when tried in the fires of testing came forth more precious than gold (Job 23:10). "Precious" faith brings forth much more fruit, to the praise and honor and glory of God. It takes a *real* Christian to act like a *real* Christian—to believe what he says he believes.

7. Precious Blood of Christ: 1:18,19
   a. It redeems: 1:18,19
   b. It cleanses: I John 1:9; Revelation 1:5
   c. It forgives: Ephesians 1:7
   d. It brings us nigh God: Ephesians 2:13
   e. It brings peace: Colossians 1:20
   f. It gives us standing: Romans 5:9a
   g. It sanctifies us: Hebrews 13:12,13
   h. It causes growth in life: John 6:53-57
   i. It enables us to overcome on earth: Revelation 12:11
   j. It gives assurance of blessings: Hebrews 9:14,15 with Romans 8:32
   k. It gives boldness before God: Hebrews 10:19
   l. It is the pledge of His return: Luke 22:20 with I Corinthians 11:25,26
   m. It will give boldness in day of judgment: Romans 5:9b

8. The Christian Life Is—
   a. Salvation: 1:18,19
   b. Growth: 2:2
   c. Yieldedness: 2:5
   d. Position: 2:9a. See POSITION in Index.
   e. Testimony: 2:9b
   f. Service: 2:16
   g. Suffering: 4:12,13,19
   h. Conflict: 5:6-9
   i. Maturity: 5:10

9. Love—the Eleventh Commandment: 1:22 with John 13:34
   a. Why love? Because we are commanded—because He first loved us: I John 4:7,19
   b. Love whom? One another: Romans 13:8
   c. How to love?
      —As Christ loved—the same for all
      —With unfeigned love—no pretense
      —With a pure heart—for all, not for some
      —Fervently—not hot one moment and cold the next
   d. What does love do? 4:8,9,11
      —Covers faults: vs. 8 (RV)
      —Forgets as well as forgives
      —Wins the confidence of others
      —Gives without grudging or murmuring: vs. 9
      —Ministers
      —Speaks God's Word: vs. 11a
      —Glorifies God: vs. 11b

10. Things that Continue: 1:25
   a. The Word of God: 1:25
   b. His name: Psalm 72:17-19
   c. His throne: Hebrews 1:8
   d. His priesthood: Hebrews 7:24
   e. His intercession: Hebrews 7:25
   f. His love: John 13:1
   g. His presence: Matthew 28:20
   h. His faithfulness: II Timothy 2:13
   i. His character: Hebrews 13:8

j. His covenant: Hebrews 13:20
k. Our inheritance: I Peter 1:4
l. Our sonship: Galatians 4:7
m. Our life: John 6:51
n. Our consolation: II Thessalonians 2:16
o. Our kingdom: Revelation 22:5
p. Our king: I Timothy 1:17
q. His foundation: II Timothy 2:19
r. Torment in the lake of fire: Luke 16:24
s. Blackness and darkness: Jude 13
t. The wrath of God: John 3:36

11. Christ—the living Stone: 2:4; Isaiah 28:16
a. The *living* Stone—to *save* us: 2:4
b. The *foundation* Stone—to *bear* us: I Corinthians 3:11
c. The *tried* Stone—to *hold* us: I Peter 2:6
d. The *corner* Stone—to *unite* us: Ephesians 2:20
e. The *sure* Stone—to *keep* us: I Peter 2:4
f. The *testing* Stone—to *try* us: I Peter 2:8
g. The *lasting* Stone—to *satisfy* us: I Peter 2:7

12. Salvation: 2:4-10. See SALVATION in Index.
a. Salvation is for Spiritual Union with Christ: vss. 4-8
—As the *living* Stone: vss. 4a,6 with Isaiah 28:16; Ephesians 2:19-22
—As a *precious* Stone to believers: vss. 4b,7
—As a Stone of *stumbling*, a Rock of *offense* to unbelievers: vss. 7b,8 with Psalm 118:22; Isaiah 8:14
b. Salvation is for Spiritual Testimony: vss. 9,10
—To tell others what we *were:* vs. 10a with I Corinthians 6:9-11a
—To tell others what we *now are* in Christ Jesus: vss. 9,10b with II Corinthians 5:17,19,20
—Chosen to be His generation *now:* I Peter 2:9a. "Only one life t'will soon be past, only what's done for Christ will last."
—A royal priesthood, a kingdom of priests to pray one for another: I Peter 2:9b; I Samuel 12:23
—His holy people, called not to uncleanness, but unto holiness: I Peter 2:9c; I Thessalonians 4:3,7
—His peculiar people—His jewel on display to radiate His countenance: I Peter 2:9d; Matthew 5:16

13. Spiritual Sacrifices: 2:5
a. My person: Romans 12:1; II Corinthians 8:1-5
b. My praise: Hebrews 13:15
c. My property (talents): Philippians 4:18

14. God's People: 2:9,10
—Are chosen: vs. 9a; 1:2a
—Are priests: vs. 9b; Revelation 1:6; Samuel 12:23
—Are holy: vs. 9c; 1:15,16
—Are peculiar (trophies of His grace on display): vs. 9d; I Corinthians 6:20
—Are sanctified (set apart): 1:2b. See SANCTIFICATION in Index.
—Are cleansed by His blood: 1:2c,18,19
—Have grace and peace multiplied: 1:2d
—Are begotten (made alive): 1:3a,23
—Are given a living hope: 1:3b
—Are promised an inheritance: 1:4
—Are kept by His power: 1:5

  —Are tried: 1:6,7
  —Are in love with Christ, sight unseen: 1:8a
  —Have unspeakable joy: 1:8b
  —Are obedient: 1:14,22
  —Are hungry for spiritual things: 2:2
  —Offer spiritual sacrifices: 2:5
  —Have good works: 2:12
  —Respect the powers that be: 2:13-15
  —Are free: 2:16a
  —Are God's servants: 2:16b
  —Love their neighbors: 2:17a
  —Love their brethren: 2:17b; 4:8,9
  —Fear God: 2:17c
  —Are subject to their masters: 2:18
  —Often suffer wrongly: 2:19,20
  —Follow Christ: 2:21; 3:13
  —Have family unity: 3:1-7
  —Have compassion: 3:8
  —Do not return evil for evil: 3:9
  —Control their tongues: 3:10
  —Hate evil: 3:11a
  —Seek to follow peace: 3:11b
  —Suffer for righteousness' sake: 3:14
  —Testify of their hope: 3:15
  —Seek God's will: 3:17
  —Become mature through suffering: 4:13-16; 5:10
  —Are humble: 5:6,7
  —Resist the devil: 5:8,9
  —Stand in grace: 5:12
  —Are sure of complete salvation: 1:9,13; Philippians 1:6; 3:20,21

15. A Royal Priesthood: 2:9. This expression means a "royal kingdom of priests" (Revelation 1:6RV). As a kingdom of priests we have the—

  a. *Power* of kings—over sin and Satan
  b. *Riches* of kings—Christ's unsearchable riches
  c. *Apparel* of kings—Christ's robe of righteousness
  d. *Fare* of kings—*all* need supplied
  e. *Retinue* of kings—angels charge over us

16. How to Follow in Christ's Footsteps: 2:21; II Peter 3:18

  B —Believe in Him: John 1:12
  Y —Yield to Him: Romans 12:1

  G —Go to Him in prayer: I John 5:14,15
  R —Read and study His Word: Revelation 1:3; II Timothy 2:15
  O —Obey His commands: John 15:14
  W—Witness by life and testimony: Luke 8:39
  I —Ignore the works of darkness: Ephesians 5:11
  N —Nothing held back: I Thessalonians 5:19
  G —Give talents and tithe: Matthew 25:20; II Corinthians 9:7

  I —Increase in fruit: John 15:8
  N —Neglect not God's gift: I Timothy 4:14; II Timothy 1:6

G —Go to church: Hebrews 10:25
R —Redeem the time: Ephesians 5:16; II Timothy 2:4
A —Abstain from all appearances of evil: I Thessalonians 5:22
C —Conquer Satan and temptation: James 4:7; Matthew 26:41
E —Expect Christ's return: Hebrews 9:28

17. Dead to Sins, Alive unto Righteousness: 2:24. The believer has a twofold death—dead to *sin* (Romans 6:11) and dead to *sins* (I Peter 2:24). See SIN in Index.

Sin is character—*sins* are conduct. Character is what we are; conduct is the manifestation of character. What we are in the heart comes out in actions of daily living. If there is *sin* at the root of character, there are bound to be *sins* in the conduct.

Sin is the center—*sins* the circumference. Just as a wheel has a *hub* with spokes going out to the *rim,* so in my life there is the hub or center which goes out to the rim or circumference. If there is sin at the hub, any spoke on which you go will find sins at the rim. If sin holds sway in the heart (center), there *will* be sins in the life (circumference).

Sin is the producer—*sins* the product. *Sin* is the factory, and the only thing it produces is *sins.* For the believer to reckon with sin, which is very much alive, is for him to reckon himself to be dead indeed to *sin* and to *sins,* but alive unto God, alive unto righteousness. "Let not *sin* therefore reign in your mortal body, that ye should obey it in the lusts [*sins*] thereof" (Romans 6:12).

18. The Suffering Savior: 3:18
    a. Unspeakable suffering—for sin
    b. Unusual substitution—for the unjust
    c. Unmerited salvation—for reconciliation to God

19. A Christian: 4:16. The Jews referred to believers as "Nazarenes" (Acts 24:5). Christ called them His "brethren," "disciples," and "friends" (Matthew 12:48-50; Luke 14:27; John 15:15). The name "Christian" was a nickname give by the citizens of Antioch who were making fun of those whose life was patterned after Christ (Acts 11:26). It was given more out of mockery than respect. In the Latin language, spoken by Romans in New Testament times, *ianos* often joined a slave's name to his master's to show that the slave belonged to his master. Or, a soldier's name was joined to his leader's to show that he would follow his officer's orders. *Christian* meant "a servant belonging to Christ," or "a soldier under Christ's command." Used only three times in the Bible, a Christian is one by—

    a. Choice: Acts 26:28. One does not become a Christian by physical birth, nor by the will of the flesh (mind), nor by the will of man (or a church creed): John 1:13. Decision *for* Christ, not man's character, makes one a Christian. It is a choice—choosing (receiving; believing in) Christ as one's own personal Savior (John 1:12; Acts 16:31).

    b. Change: Acts 11:26. A Christian is a "new creation" in Christ—old things (ways and habits) pass away; the things of God become new (II Corinthians 5:17). "Christian" is Christlikeness.

    c. Challenge: I Peter 4:16
      —To follow Christ: vss. 14,16
      —To endure trials: 4:12-16
      —To bear Christ's reproach: Hebrews 13:12,13
      —To share Christ's suffering: Philippians 3:10
      —To press on: Philippians 3:4
      —To grow in Christ: II Peter 3:18

20. Pastors: 5:1-3. See PASTORS in Index.
21. Crown of Glory: 5:4. See CROWNS in Index.

A BIT OF
HEAVENLY
MANNA

Peter, who had lived on both sides of the fence of pride and humility, was well qualified to tell others how to be humble, and how that through trials, which worked patience and humility, God would exalt His own in due time. It is no wonder that his theme is humility, that one might be exalted.

THAT HE MAY EXALT YOU IN DUE TIME—5:6[2]

"The apostle is exhorting to humility. Nothing is so necessary for us, or more acceptable to God. The humble man is sure to be respected. Saints will love Him and God will do everything for him. Pride is offensive to our fellows and it is detestable in the sight of God. He will hold no fellowship with a proud man. He knoweth the proud afar off and He keeps them at a distance. The Lord's people may be oppressed, and Providence may seem to take part with their oppressors. They may lie long in the dust, and be brought very low. But if they humble themselves under the mighty hand of God, He will exalt them in *due time*. When the trial has accomplished its work, it shall be removed. When the proud spirit is humbled, when the complaining spirit is resigned, when the conceited creature is reduced to its proper level, then the Lord will appear to exalt it. He exalteth by His power, by His grace, and by His providence. He exalteth sometimes in temporals, more frequently in spirituals. He raiseth the spirit above the circumstances, and this is true exaltation."

PRAYER THOUGHT: "Help me, Father, not to contrive my own plans and formulate my own schemes and then have the gall to ask Thee to approve them, but grant that I might seek to do only what I know will meet with Thy approval and be acceptable to Thee. In Thy Son's dear name I pray. Amen."[3]

I Peter 2:5

Second Peter—The Book of Christian Diligence

Name: See NAME in I Peter.

Occasion of Writing: Peter's letters, to strengthen the believer, are twofold: the first to encourage them to keep their *faith* in the midst of suffering—perils from *without;* the second to encourage them to *know* truth in the face of mounting heresies and apostasy—perils from *within.* John mentioned that the spirit of Antichrist was already in the world (I John 4:3), and Peter exhorts in this Epistle to grow in grace as a deterrent to succumbing to this spirit and falling from grace. Having become "partakers of [God's] divine nature" (1:4), Peter urges growth, with a reminder not to forget that they were once purged from their old sins (1:5-10).

Paul's last letter (II Timothy), as well as Peter's, give warnings to believers. Both seem to be saying—"It is not so much how you start in the faith but how you continue." Paul's last letter warns of heresy, coldness, and indifference in the *laity.* Peter warns of heresy in the *pulpit*—false teachers. Both stress the importance of the Word as the solution to events in perilous times (II Timothy 3:16,17; II Peter 1:19-21).

This book is Peter's "swan song." (Paul's was II Timothy—4:6-8). With Paul, he sought to leave a message of guidance for those who would carry on after his death—"he being dead, yet speaketh" (1:13-15).

Contents: II Peter—

1. Places upon saints a concern for a larger increase of grace and spiritual knowledge: 1:1-11
2. Confirms and establishes them in the present truth of the gospel: 1:12-21
3. Warns them against false teachers: ch. 2
4. Stresses the *fact* of Christ's return: 3:1-9. While Peter reminds them of scoffers, heresy, apostasy, his tone is not that of dejection and pessimism, but optimism.
5. Puts them in mind of the awful dissolution of all things: 3:10
6. Shows the need for believers to practice what they preach: 3:11-18

This book has 3 chapters, 61 verses, and 1,559 words.

Character: General Epistle.

Subject: Last things—eternal kingdom, second coming, judgment of the wicked, day of the Lord.

Purpose: To help us grow in grace: 3:18.

Outline:[1]

I. Address: 1:1
II. The Knowledge of God and the Christian's Growth: 1:2-21
   A. Our ample provision: 1:2-4
   B. Our actual progress: 1:5-11
   C. Our abiding pledge: 1:12-21
III. The Knowledge of God and the Christian's Peril: 2:1-22
   A. False teachers—their doctrine defined: 2:1-3a
   B. False teachers—their destruction declared: 2:3b-9
   C. False teachers—their doings described: 2:10-22
IV. The Knowledge of God and the Christian's Hope: 3:1-18a
   A. The advent truth assailed: 3:1-4
   B. The advent truth attested: 3:5-10
   C. The advent truth applied: 3:11-18a
V. Doxology: 3:18b

Writer: Much dispute has arisen over the author of this book. At first the early church fathers did not accept it as Peter's writing, but later it was accepted as genuine. Some attributed it to another "Simon," others believed it to be a forgery, written long after Peter's death.

The style and language of this letter differs from I Peter. The Greek of the first letter is "polished," akin to classical Greek. The second letter is rather crude, more like the dialect of the average citizen. It is quite possible that Silvanus ("Silas," I Peter 5:12) wrote Peter's first letter as Peter dictated, using his own style. Silas was one of Paul's traveling companions (Acts 15:39-41) and had a command of proper Greek terms. It is evident that this second letter was written by Peter himself. When we remember his background—a fisherman and unlearned man (Acts 4:13)—we better understand the style of this book.

Internal evidence points to the same Peter of the first Epistle—the disciple of Christ:

1. An apostle of Jesus Christ: 1:1
2. Words of Christ concerning his death: 1:13,14 with John 21:18,19
3. An eyewitness at the transfiguration: 1:16,17
4. Reference to his first letter: 3:1

When and Where Written: A.D. 66 or 67, probably in Babylon.

Key Chapter: 2. Warning concerning apostate teachers.

Key Verse: 3:2.

Key Word: Knowledge.

Key Phrase: Full knowledge of God: 1:2.

Key Thought: Be mindful: 3:2.

Spiritual Thought: Never stop growing.

Christ Is Seen As: The Lord of Glory: 3:18.

Names and Titles of Christ. Seen NAME in Dictionary.
1. Jesus Christ: 1:1
2. Savior: 1:1
3. Jesus our Lord: 1:2
4. Lord Jesus Christ: 1:8
5. Lord and Savior: 1:11
6. Beloved Son: 1:17
7. The Day Star: 1:19
8. Lord: 2:1

Names and Titles of God. See NAME in Index.
1. Father: 1:17.
2. Lord: 2:11.

Names and Titles of the Holy Spirit: Holy Ghost: 1:21. See NAME in Dictionary.

The Old Testament in II Peter:
1. A dog turned to his own vomit: 2:22 with Proverbs 26:11
2. Companion references:
   a. To the Old Testament in general:1:21 with II Samuel 23:2
   b. False prophets: 2:1 with Jeremiah 23:32
   c. The flood: 2:5 with Genesis 6:1-7,16,23
   d. Destruction of Sodom and Gomorrah: 2:6 with Genesis 19:24,25
   e. Lot's deliverance: 2:7 with Genesis 19:16,22,23
   f. Way of Balaam: 2:15,16 with Numbers 22:5,7,21,23,28
   g. God's promise questioned: 3:4 with Isaiah 5:19
   h. The firmament and the waters: 3:5 with Genesis 1:6-9
   i. The earth flooded: 3:6 with Genesis 7:11-22
   j. A thousand days as one day: 3:8 with Psalm 90:4
   k. God's love for sinners: 3:9 with Ezekiel 33:11
   l. Heavens shall pass away: 3:10 with Psalm 102:25,26
   m. New heaven and new earth: 3:13 with Isaiah 65:17; 66:22

SEED THOUGHTS

1. Great and Precious promises: 1:4. Not only are God's promises "great and precious," they are "yea and amen" in Christ (II Corinthians 1:20). The are sure because—
   a. There is no deceit in God's justice and mercy
   b. There is remembrance in God's grace and goodness
   c. There is no change in His truth
   d. There is compassion in His love
   e. There is effect in His power
2. Partakers: 1:4. See PARTAKERS in Index.
   a. Of Christ: Hebrews 3:14
   b. Of the Holy Spirit: Hebrews 6:4
   c. Of God's divine nature: 1:4
   d. Of holiness: Hebrews 12:10 (RV)
   e. Of a heavenly calling: Hebrews 3:1
   f. Of Christ's suffering: I Peter 4:13

g. Of the afflictions of the gospel: II Timothy 1:8
h. Of chastisement: Hebrews 12:8
i. Of grace: Philippians: 1:7
j. Of consolation: II Corinthians 1:7
k. Of glory: I Peter 5:1
l. Of the inheritance of the saints: Colossians 1:12

3. Scriptural Addition: 1:5-10. The second chapter of this Epistle deals with false prophets and the results of their teachings. They *add* liturgical and ecclesiastical programs, *subtract* God's Word for man's reasoning, *divide* God's people and *multiply* confusion. But the true believer has a solid foundation (faith) upon which to *add*—

a. Virtue—energy and courage: Joshua 1:2-9
b. Knowledge—God's Word: Philippians 2:16; Colossians 3:16
c. Temperance—self-control: Daniel 1:5-21
d. Patience—perseverance: I Peter 4:12,13
e. Godliness—reverence: Proverbs 3:5,6
f. Brotherly kindness—selfless consideration: Romans 12:10
g. Love—demonstrative: Romans 12:13-21

If we do these things we will always remember that we have been forgiven, and will never be barren (unfruitful) or fail the Lord.

4. Spiritual Abundance: 1:11

a. Goodness and truth: Exodus 34:6
b. Grace: II Corinthians 9:8
c. Mercy: I Peter 1:3
d. Hope: Romans 15:13
e. Pardon: Isaiah 55:7
f. An entrance: II Peter 1:11
g. Life: John 10:10
h. Peace: Psalm 37:11
i. God's counsel: Hebrews 6:17
j. Blessings: Psalm 132:15
k. Love: Philippians 1:9
l. Joys: Psalm 36:8
m. Power: Ephesians 3:20
n. Consolation: II Corinthians 1:5
o. Good works: I Corinthians 15:58; II Corinthians 9:8
p. All things: Deuteronomy 28:47
q. Everything (faith and knowledge): II Corinthians 8:7

5. God Spared Not: 2:4-6

a. Angels that sinned: vs. 4
b. The old world: vs. 5
c. Cities of Sodom and Gomorrah: vs. 6
d. The nation Israel: Romans 11:21a
e. Churches: Revelation 2:1-5
f. His own Son: Romans 8:32
g. Take heed lest He spare thee not: Romans 11:21b; Deuteronomy 29:20; Psalm 78:50. God only spares when Christ is received as Savior: John 5:24

6. Jesus is Coming: 3:4,9[2]

If Jesus Should Come Today

If Jesus should come today,
Would He find our hands quite full
With plans so fair,

And Him no share;
What would He as JUDGE *then say?*

If Jesus should come today,
And found that our love is cold,
Faith weak and dim,
No look for Him;
What would He as FRIEND *then say?*

If Jesus should come today,
And found you had never told
About your Friend's
Love without end;
What would He as LORD *then say?*

7. Growth in Grace and Knowledge of Christ: 3:18
   a. Multiplies grace and peace: 1:2
   b. Gives life and godliness: 1:3a
   c. Calls to glory and virtue: 1:3b
   d. Assures of promise: 1:4a
   e. Results in partaking of God's nature: 1:4b
   f. Delivers from worldly lust: 1:4c

A BIT OF HEAVENLY MANNA

So often we are inclined to think that just because God doesn't send judgment the moment we sin, He is either winking at it or will overlook it. He is patient and longsuffering, anxious that we judge ourselves before He has to (I Corinthians 11:31,32). He was patient with Rehoboam after the Law was forsaken, but finally sent in a heathen, godless nation to inflict judgment and punishment (II Chronicles 12:1-9). Israel, as a nation, enjoyed God's favor for a long time before His patience was exhausted (II Chronicles 36:14-17). Scripture is emphatic regarding God's judgment of sin—"be sure *your* sin will find *you* out" (Numbers 32:23). "Be not deceived, God is not mocked; for whatsoever a man soweth, that shall he also reap" (Galatians 6:7). "Take heed lest He spare thee not" (Romans 11:21b).

GOD SPARED NOT—2:4[3]

"God spared not the angels that sinned. Then is it not wonderful that He should spare us? They were more noble in their nature, and more exalted in their station; yet when they sinned God did not spare them, but cast them down to hell. Nor would He have spared us but for the method of His grace, by which His Son became our substitute, took our responsibility, came into the world, and acted as our surity. And when He appeared in this character He was dealt with accordingly—He was not spared Himself, therefore we read, 'He that spared not His own Son, but delivered Him up for us all!' Was not this wonderful! God would not spare His own Son that He might spare us, we who were His enemies, and would have remained so forever if He had not changed our hearts by His grace. Let us this day reflect upon these facts: 'God spared not the angels that sinned'; 'He spared not His own Son,' but He says of us, 'I will spare them as a man that spareth his own son that serveth him.' O mystery of mercy! What depths of love, what heights of grace are here! My soul, adore the Sovereign One and eternally praise the distinguishing grace He manifests in our behalf!"

PRAYER THOUGHT: "As we see so many wonderful and beautiful changes in nature, help me, dear God, to show forth in my life all the wonderful and beautiful changes that Thy divine nature brings about when one is born again. In Jesus' name I pray. Amen."[4]

II Peter 1:3,4

First John—The Epistle of Knowledge and Assurance

Name: See NAME in the Gospel of John.

Occasion of Writing: It would appear that John, in this general Epistle, is considering the body of Christ more as a family than the church. He is the last of the apostles, and sees all believers as children of God—"my little children." He uses the word "Father" 13 times and "little children' 11 times. He sought to emphasize God's *love* for all believers in the midst of the world hate, God's *light* to overshadow heathen darkness, the *joy* of God's salvation in spite of persecution and suffering, and the *life* of God as eternal in view of the insecurity of physical life.

He writes expressly to show Christians what their faith in Christ really means—for a test to find out if they really have eternal life. This Epistle is an interpretation of his gospel account—a sequel. The gospel declares and illustrates the way into eternal life, which comes when one believes in Christ as the Son of God. It was written that one may believe, and believing, have life (John 20:31). This Epistle was written for the test of such an experience. He wrote to combat error. Paul and Peter had been dead for thirty years, and John lived to see corruption, both in doctrine and practice, enter the church. Prevailing philosophers and systems of thought were encroaching upon the minds of some believers, and John refutes such teachings. Gnosticism, in particular, held sway, and was seeking to incorporate Christianity as a part of Greek philosophy and Oriental mysticism—to make it a more natural religion.

Gnostics taught that in human nature there is a principle of dualism—that of spirit and body —two separate entities—each hostile to the other. Sin dwelt in the flesh only, making it totally evil. The body could do as it pleased—living in the lust of the flesh and the pride of life. Spirit was totally good. It could have raptures or visions of God, and as spirit, do good. Accordingly, an individual could live in wickedness in the body, and at the same time be pure and holy in the spirit. Since God was good, He could not have created bodies, which were evil, but spirits only, which were good. Christ, to them, was a man in appearance only—a phantom—which contained His spirit. The deity of Christ was accepted, but His humanity was denied. The word "Gnostic" means "to know," and their philosophy claimed all knowledge.

To combat this false teaching, John wrote to his "little children"—

1. That they cherish the truth that Jesus did come in the flesh (4:1,2). A "phantom" body could not possess blood for sin's atonement—it could not die and be resurrected.
2. That they could not practice sin and at the same time walk in God's truth and light.
3. That they may *know* that they have a superior knowledge of God and His truths. John uses the word "know" (with related words) at least forty times in this Epistle.

Contents: "The apostle seeks to promote brotherly love, and uses the argument that God's love for us, coupled with evidence of our regeneration based upon our obedience to Christ's commands, will achieve it. He seeks to oppose and stop the growth of licentious principles and practices and heretical doctrines.

"The licentious principles and practices he condemned are these: (a) that believers had no sin in them (1:8); (b) that they could love the world, the flesh, and the devil, and still be Christians (2:15), and (c) idolatry (5:21). John insisted on a conscious realization of the new life in Christ. The heresies he sets himself against and refutes are such as regard the doctrines of the Trinity and the Person and office of Christ. There were (a) some who denied a distinction of persons in the Trinity (5:7); (b) others who denied that Jesus was the Messiah (2:2); (c) some who said that Christ had not come in the flesh (4:2,3); (d) others who professed to believe in Jesus Christ but denied His proper deity and asserted He was a mere man (2:22,23); and (e) still others who denied His real humanity and affirmed that he was a mere phantom (1:1,2)[1] First John has 5 chapters, 105 verses, and 2,523 words.

Character: General Epistle.

Subject: The family of God at home.

Purpose: To reveal truth concerning fellowship (1:3), and that we may *know* that we have eternal life (5:11-13).

Outline:[2]

    I. The Believer's Advance in God, who is Light: chs. 1,2
    II. The Believer's Attitude toward God, who is Love: chs. 3,4
    III. The Christian's Affinity with God, who is Life: ch.5

Writer: Among most believers, it has been generally accepted that the apostle John is the author of the three Epistles which bear his name, although his name is not attached to any of them. It is apparent that whoever wrote the second letter also wrote the third. The first Epistle, placed alongside his gospel account, shows a similarity of words and expressions, and should leave not doubt as to the author. See WRITER in gospel of John.

EPISTLE		GOSPEL
1:1	The Word	1:1
1:2	Christ manifested	1:14
1:4	Full joy	15:11
1:5	Light	1:7-9
2:5	Keeping God's Word	14:23
2:6,28	Abiding in Christ	15:4,7
2:8a	New Commandment	13:34a
2:8b	Light in darkness	1:5
2:10	No stumbling in light	11:10
2:13	Knowing God	17:3
3:1	Sons of God	1:12
3:2	Seeing Christ	17:24
3:8	Satan's works	8:44
3:11	Love one another	13:34b
3:13	World hatred	17:14
4:9	Only begotten Son sent	3:16
4:12	God not seen	1:18
5:1	Born of God	1:13
5:12	Hath the Son	3:36
5:13	These things written	20:31
5:14	Ask anything	14:13,14
5:20	The true God	17:2,3

"In his gospel, John does not content himself with simply affirming or denying a thing, but to strengthen his affirmation, he denies the contrary. In like manner, to strengthen his denial of a thing, he affirms its opposite (John 1:20; 3:36; 5:22). The same manner of expressing things strongly is found in this Epistle (2:4,27; 4:2,3). To express things emphatically, John frequently uses the demonstrative pronoun "this." See John 1:19; 3:19; 6:29,40,50; 17:3. See also First John 1:5; 2:25; 3:23; 5:3,4,6,14. Such is the internal evidence on which Christians, from the beginning, have received this First Epistle of John as really written by him, and of Divine authority, although his name is not mentioned in the inscription or in any part of the letter."[3]

Johannine authorship is attested to by his three disciples—Polycarp, Papias, and Ignatus. These men were bishops of churches in Smyrna, Hierapolis, and Antioch. Other early fathers—Clement of Alexandria, Tertullian, and Cyprian also confirmed its authorship. So does the Maratorian fragment (see ARCHAEOLOGY in gospel of John).

When and Where Written: A.D. 85-90, probably in Ephesus, where he was bishop of the church there after the death of Timothy.

Key Chapter: 5. Faith for overcoming.

Key Verse: 5:13.

Key Word: Fellowship.

Key Phrase: "If we say."

Key Thought: Stand in the truth.

Spiritual Thought: He is the Life.

Christ Is Seen As: The Son of God.

Names and Titles of Christ. See NAME in Dictionary.
1. Word of Life: 1:1; 5:7
2. Eternal Life: 1:2; 5:20
3. Son: 1:3; 2:22
4. Jesus Christ: 1:3; 4:2
5. Advocate: 2:1
6. The Righteous: 2:1
7. Propitiation for sin: 2:2; 4:10
8. Jesus: 2:22
9. Christ: 2:22; 5:1
10. Son of God: 3:8
11. Only begotten Son: 4:9
12. Savior: 4:14
13. True God: 5:20

Names and Titles of God. See NAME in Dictionary.
1. Father: 1:2; 5:7
2. Light: 1:5
3. Love: 4:8,16

Names and Titles of the Holy Spirit. See NAME in Dictionary.
1. Holy One: 2:20
2. The Spirit: 3:24
3. Spirit of God: 4:2
4. Holy Ghost: 5:7

The Old Testament in First John: There are no direct references of the Old Testament in this Book, but there are some companion references:
1. Sin cannot be denied: 1:8 with I Kings 8:46; Ecclesiastes 7:20
2. Forgiveness and pardon: 1:9 with Isaiah 55:7
3. Christ's finished work: 3:5 with Isaiah 53
4. Cain's murder of Abel: 3:12 with Genesis 4:8

1. Why John Wrote
    a. That we might have *salvation:* John 20:31
    b. That we might have *satisfaction:* 1:4
    c. That we might have *sactification:* 2:1
    d. That we might have *safety:* 2:26 (RV); 5:18
    e. That we might have *security:* 5:13

2. Evidences of Spiritual Life in First John.
    —Life of personal relationship with Christ: 1:1,2
    —Life of fellowship: 1:3
    —Life of joy: 1:4
    —Life of light: 1:7
    —Life of forgiveness: 1:9; 2:12
    —Life of honesty: 1:8,10
    —Life of holiness: 2:1
    —Life of obedience: 2:3; 5:2,3
    —Life of abiding: 2:6
    —Life of love: 2:10a; 3:14; 4:7
    —Life of example: 2:10b
    —Life of victory: 2:14; 5:4,5
    —Life of separation: 2:15,17
    —Life of perseverence: 2:19,24
    —Life of knowledge and understanding: 2:20; 5:20
    —Life of safety: 2:26 (RV); 5:18
    —Life of anointing: 2:27
    —Life of expectancy: 2:28
    —Life of godliness: 2:29; 3:3
    —Life of relationship: 3:1
    —Life of anticipation: 3:2
    —Life of hope: 3:3a
    —Life of consideration: 3:10
    —Life of sacrifice: 3:16
    —Life of action: 3:18
    —Life of good conscience: 3:21a
    —Life of confidence: 3:21b
    —Life of prayer: 3:22; 5:14,15
    —Life of confession: 4:2,15
    —Life of Christ in us: 4:4
    —Life of truth: 4:6,20
    —Life of boldness: 4:17a
    —Life of participation: 4:17b
    —Life of peace: 4:18
    —Life of faith: 5:4
    —Life of assurance: 5:13
    —Life of help: 5:16
    —Life of reverence: 5:21

3. Triumphant Experiences in First John.
    a. Triumphant joy: 1:4
    b. Triumphant life: 2:1
    c. Triumphant hope: 2:28; 3:3,8
    d. Triumphant love: 4:18
    e. Triumphant faith: 5:1-5

       f. Triumphant truth: 5:11-13
       g. Triumphant prayer: 5:14,15
       h. Triumphant knowledge: 5:20
       i. Triumphant loyalty: 5:21

4. The Spirit in First John
       a. To testify of Christ: 4:2
       b. To bear witness of truth: 5:6,8
       c. To indwell the believer: 3:24
       d. To confirm God's presence in us: 4:13
       e. To anoint (empower) us: 2:20a
       f. To teach us: 2:20b
       g. To guide us into truth: 4:6

5. The "Ifs" of John. See "IF'S" in Index.
       a. Concerning disobedience: 1:6
       b. Concerning fellowship: 1:7
       c. Concerning deception: 1:8
       d. Concerning confession and forgiveness: 1:9
       e. Concerning denial of sin: 1:10
       f. Concerning guilt: 2:1
       g. Concerning obedience: 2:3
       h. Concerning love for the Father: 2:15
       i. Concerning consistency: 2:19
       j. Concerning perseverance: 2:24
       k. Concerning godly living: 2:29
       l. Concerning the world's opinion: 3:13
       m. Concerning confidence: 3:20,21
       n. Concerning brotherly love: 4:11
       o. Concerning God's love for us: 4:12
       p. Concerning hate: 4:20
       q. Concerning God's witness: 5:9
       r. Concerning prayer: 5:14,15
       s. Concerning a brother who sins: 5:16
       t. Concerning false teachers: II John 10
       u. Concerning hospitality: III John 6
       v. Concerning disciplining a brother: III John 9-11

6. The "Knows" of John. Knowing God—
       a. We will keep His commandments: 2:3,4
       b. We will perfect His love: 2:5
       c. We will be conscious of the times: 2:18
       d. We will have His anointing: 2:20
       e. We will know the truth: 2:21
       f. We will practice righteousness; not sin: 2:29; 5:18a
       g. We will become like Christ: 3:2
       h. We will have assurance of sins removed: 3:5
       i. We will love the brethren: 3:14
       j. We will be of the truth: 3:19
       k. We will abide in Christ: 3:24a
       l. We will have Christ and the Spirit in us: 3:24b; 4:13
       m. We will confess Jesus Christ: 4:2
       n. We will hear God's message: 4:6
       o. We will love God: 5:2
       p. We will have eternal life: 5:13
       q. We will have prayers heard and answered: 5:13-15
       r. We will be victorious over Satan: 5:18b

     s. We will be of Him: 5:19
     t. We will have understanding of Him: 5:20
     u. We will be assured God's record is true: III John 12

7. **Fellowship (walking) with God: 1:3**

Conditions of fellowship—
     a. Called: I Corinthians 1:9
     b. Acquaintance: Job 22:21
     c. Agreement: Amos 3:3
     d. United: Matthew 11:28-30

How to have fellowship—
     a. By faith—in God's will: II Corinthians 5:7
     b. By listening to God—to hear His directions: Isaiah 30:21
     c. By going God's way—to reveal trust: Jeremiah 7:23
     d. In the light—to acknowledge Him: I John 1:7
     e. In newness of life—to reveal salvation: Romans 6:4
     f. In the Spirit—to overcome the flesh: Galatians 5:16
     g. In love—to reveal God: Ephesians 5:1,2
     h. Circumspectly—to avoid pitfalls: Ephesians 5:15,16
     i. Worthily—to please God: Ephesians 4:1
     j. In truth—to confirm faith: III John 4

Results of fellowship—
     a. Before God—a walk of perfection: Genesis 17:1
     b. After God—a walk of obedience: Deuteronomy 13:4
     c. With God—a walk of friendship: Genesis 5:22

8. **To Sin or Not to Sin: 1:8—2:1,6**
     a. To say that I cannot sin is to deceive myself: 1:8
     b. To say that I do not sin is to deceive others: 1:8
     c. To say that I have not sinned is to make God a liar: 1:10
     d. To say that I must sin is to deny the Gospel: Romans 6:18
     e. To say that I must not sin is to confirm the Gospel: Colossians 2:6; 3:17
     f. To say that I need not sin is to state my privilege: Ephesians 1:4; I Peter 1:15
     g. To say that I do not have to sin is to trust God's Word: 2:1 with Psalm 119:11
     h. To say by the grace of God I will not sin is to live the Gospel: 2:6

9. **None Occasion of Stumbling: 2:10. See EXAMPLE in Index.**

10. **Worldliness: 2:15-17. See TEMPTATION in Index.**
     a. Lust of the flesh—to *experience* something
     b. Lust of the eye—to *have* something
     c. Pride of life—a desire to *be* something

11. **What Manner of Love: 3:1**
     a. Personal: 3:1
     b. Everlasting: Jeremiah 31:3
     c. Universal: John 3:16
     d. Encompassing: Song of Solomon 2:4
     e. Measureless: Ephesians 3:17-19
     f. Restraining: I John 2:15-17
     g. Constraining: II Corinthians 5:14,15

12. **Sonship: 3:2[4]**
     a. A wonderful privilege—"sons of God"
     b. A comforting negative—"not yet appear what we shall be"
     c. A blessed certainty—"we know . . . we shall be like Him"
     d. A glorious hope—"we shall see Him as He is"

13. **Views of Christ's Return: 3:3**

a. View of John—*purity:* 3:3
b. View of Paul—*rapture:* I Thessalonians 4:16,17
c. View of Peter—*majesty:* II Peter 1:16
d. View of James—*justice:* James 5:1-7
e. View of Jude—*judgment:* Jude 14,15
f. View of Hebrews—*consummation:* Hebrews 9:28

14. Sin: 3:4. See SIN in Index.

    a. Its character—
      —Pollution: Isaiah 1:2-7
      —Bondage: Romans 5:21; 6:17
      —Rebellion: Ephesians 2:2
    b. Its course: broad way to destruction: Matthew 7:13
    c. Its consequence: death: Romans 6:23
    d. Its cure: Christ: Romans 5:8-11

15. Satan and His Works Defeated: 3:8. See SATAN in Index.

    a. Sin is defeated by atonement: Hebrews 1:3
    b. Guilt is defeated by justification: Hebrews 2:9
    c. Defilement is defeated by sanctification: Hebrews 2:11
    d. Satan is defeated by Incarnation: Hebrews 2:14
    e. Fear is defeated by resurrection: Hebrews 2:15
    f. Alienation is defeated by reconciliation: Hebrews 2:17
    g. Temptation is defeated by succor: Hebrews 2:18
    h. Doubt is defeated by faith: Hebrews 11:1,6

16. Why Christ was Manifested: 3:8. See CHRIST, Mission of, in Index.

    a. To defeat the devil: 3:8
    b. To annul sin: Romans 6:11
    c. To bring about redemption: Titus 2:14
    d. To lead to righteousness: II Corinthians 5:21
    e. To impart the Spirit: Galatians 3:13,14
    f. To provide a new deliverance: Galatians 1:4
    g. To pave a new way: Hebrews 10:19,20
    h. To secure a new access: Hebrews 4:16; I Peter 3:18
    i. To lay the basis for a new fellowship: I Thessalonians 5:10
    j. To win a new family: I Peter 2:9,10
    k. To give us a new example: I Peter 2:21
    l. To displace self: II Corinthians 5:14,15
    m. To cause a new death: I Peter 2:24
    n. To involve a new life: Galatians 2:20
    o. To promote humility: Philippians 2:5-8
    p. To beget love: I John 3:16
    q. To be the harbinger of hope: I Thessalonians 4:16
    r. To make a new home: John 14:1-3

17. God's Love for the Believer.

    a. Love's *direction*—toward us: 4:9
    b. Love's *intention*—to us: 4:16
    c. Love's *habitation*—in us: 2:15; 4:12
    d. Love's *work*—with us: 4:17 (*margin*)

18. The Victory that Overcometh: 5:1-5

    a. The *Object* to be overcome—evil: Romans 12:21
    b. The *Means* with which to overcome—
      —Our faith: 5:4
      —Christ's blood: Revelation 12:11a

—Our testimony: Revelation 12:11b

c. The *Example* of overcoming—Christ: John 16:22

d. The *Rewards* for the overcomer—

—Eat of the tree of life: Revelation 2:7

—Shall not be hurt: Revelation 2:11

—Receive a new name: Revelation 2:17

—Given power: Revelation 2:26

—Assurance of life hereafter: Revelation 3:5

—Made a pillar in God's temple: Revelation 3:12

—Shall sit with Christ on His throne: Revelation 3:21

—Crowns. See CROWNS in Index.

19. Christian Traits: 5:2. See TRAITS in Index.

a. We are *sons* to love: 5:2; Colossians 1:4

b. We are *servants* to obey: Romans 6:22; II Timothy 2:24

c. We are *soldiers* to fight: I Timothy 6:12; II Timothy 2:3

d. We are *stewards* to occupy: Luke 19:13; Titus 1:7-9

e. We are *soul-winners* to witness: Matthew 4:19; Acts 1:8

f. We are *saints* to please God: I Corinthians 1:2; I John 3:22

20. Things Satan Cannot stand: 5:4. See SATAN in Index.

a. A saved person—he overcomes: vs. 4a

b. Our faith—it overcomes: vs. 4b

c. Strong believers—they overcome: 2:14

d. Christ's blood—it gives power to overcome: Revelation 12:11a

e. One's testimony—it overcomes: Revelation 12:11b

f. Christ's resurrection—it spells defeat for him: Revelation 1:18; Hebrews 2:14; Colossians 2:14,15

21. Keep Yourselves from Idols: 5:21

Idolaters—

a. Stray from God: Ezekiel 44:10

b. Forget God: Deuteronomy 8:19

c. Are vain in their imaginations: Romans 1:21-23

d. Are carried away with their idols: I Corinthians 12:2

e. Pollute the name of God: Ezekiel 20:13

f. Are estranged from God: Ezekiel 14:5

g. Hate God: II Chronicles 19:2

h. Have fellowship with devils (demons): I Corinthians 10:20

Idols—

a. Of images: Acts 17:29

b. Of self: Mark 8:34-38

c. Of family: Luke 14:26

d. Of man: Galatians 1:10

e. Of money: Matthew 6:24

f. Of worldliness: I John 2:15-17

g. Of religion: Romans 10:1-3; Philippians 3:4-6

How to keep self from idols—

a. Trust God: I Kings 19:18 with Romans 11:4

b. Obey His Commands: Exodus 20:3-5

c. Keep self from them: I John 5:21 with 2:17

d. Flee all kinds: I Corinthians 10:14

e. Testify against them: Acts 14:15

f. Do not condone them: Deuteronomy 7:26

g. Destroy them: Deuteronomy 7:5; II Kings 23:3-7

Too often we think of idols as something the heathens worship—stone, wood, or metal graven by art and man's device (Acts 17:29). Yet, civilized Christians can have idols. It could be your home, family, wealth, automobile, bowling ball, the world, the lust of the flesh, the lust of the eye, the pride of life, your television set, or anything that for a moment would take your eyes off your heavenly father.

John would have us know the seriousness of having anything between our soul and our Savior, hence his plea:

KEEP YOURSELVES FROM IDOLS—5:21[5]

"What did idols ever do for you? What can they do but disappoint, vex, bewilder, and bring us under God's chastening rod? And yet our hearts are naturally set upon idolatry. If God gives us a special mercy, we are apt to place it on our 'mountain tops or hills.' In order to deliver us from our own ways, which are idolatrous, He often has to bereave us. Whatever has the heart is an idol. This God claims. If, therefore, we bestow it upon self, we surely will smart for it. One clause in His covenant is: 'From all your idols I will cleanse you.' This promise shall be sacredly kept. God will sicken us with idolatry, and like Ephriam we shall turn our back upon it, and turning to God with all our heart shall say, 'What have I to do any more with idols?' (Hosea 14:8). Our God is a jealous God, and He will not give His glory to another, nor will He allow us to do it. Israel made an idol out of the brazen serpent, and drank its bitter dregs (II Kings 18:4). Jeremiah asked Israel to get their 'gods' to help them, but their gods failed (Jeremiah 22:27,28). O that the Lord would wean us from all our idols, and cleanse the temple of our hearts of every image of jealousy, and consecrate it entirely to Himself for His worship and praise."

PRAYER THOUGHT: "Knowing that today may be the day of my Savior's return, may I not go anywhere that I should not, say anything that I should not, nor do anything that I should not. Help me, O Lord, to constantly abide in Christ so that I may not be ashamed before Him at His coming. In my Savior's name. Amen."[6]

I John 2:28

Second John—The Epistle of Love and Truth

Name: See NAME in Gospel of John.

Occasion of Writing: To warn against the corrupting influences of false teachers denying the reality of Christ's humanity and to encourage Christians to "love in the truth."

Contents: The apostle John exhorts and encourages the lady to whom he writes to continue in the truth and faith of the gospel in love to God and His people, and to avoid false teachers and their doctrines. Second John has only 1 chapter with 13 verses and 303 words.

Character: Family Epistle.

Subject: The Truth as it is in Christ.

Purpose: That we might abide in the Truth and that the Truth may abide in us.

Outline:

    I. Introduction: vss. 1-3
    II. The Path of the Believer: vss. 4-6
    III. The Peril of the Believer: vss. 7-11
    IV. Conclusion: vss. 12,13

Writer: John, the "elder": vs. 1. See WRITER in I John.

When and Where Written: A.D. 85-90, probably in Ephesus.

Key Verse: 6.

Key Word: Love.

Key Phrase: Abide in the doctrine.

Key Thought: Walk in the Truth.

Spiritual Thought: Preserve the Truth.

Christ Is Seen As: The Truth; the True doctrine: vs. 9 with John 14:6.

Names and Titles of Christ. See NAME in Dictionary.

    1. Lord Jesus Christ: vs.3
    2. Son of the Father: vs. 3
    3. Jesus Christ: vs. 7
    4. The Son: vs. 9
    5. Christ: vs. 9

Names and Titles of God: Father: vss. 3,9. See NAME in Dictionary.

1. The Abiding Word of Truth: vs. 2
    a. Was from the beginning: John 1:1
    b. True from the beginning: Psalm 119:160
    c. Forever settled in heaven: Psalm 119:89,152
    d. Pure (no impurities): Psalm 119:140
    e. Faithful to His saints: Psalm 119:138
    f. A heritage for His children: Psalm 119:111
    g. Greater than His eternal name: Psalm 138:2; 135:13
    h. Will abide forever: Matthew 24:35. See BIBLE in Index.

2. Grace, Mercy, and Peace: vs. 3

MERCY	GRACE
Pardons: I Timothy 1:13	Justifies: Romans 3:24
Removes the guilt and penalty: Proverbs 28:13	Imputes righteousness: Romans 4:4,5
Saves from Peril: Psalm 6:4	Imparts a new nature: Ephesians 2:8-10
Rescues: Luke 10:33,37	Transforms: Titus 2:11,12

PEACE gives us standing with God that we might experience His peace which passes all understanding: Romans 5:1; Philippians 4:7.

3. A Successful Christian—
    a. *Walks* in truth: vs. 4
    b. *Loves* the truth: vs. 6
    c. *Abides* in truth: vs. 9
    d. *Welcomes* no untruth: vss. 9-11
        RESULT: Gives *joy* among believers: vs. 12

4. Walking in Truth: vs. 4—
  a. Expresses life: vs. 2
  b. Encourages believers: vs. 4
  c. Elects to obey: vs. 6
  d. Endears the heritage: vs. 8
  e. Exalts Christ's doctrine: vs. 9
  f. Ejects error: vs. 10

A BIT OF
HEAVENLY MANNA

John's exhibition of "full joy" (I John 1:4) is seen in his rejoicing over believers who walk in truth. When the Lord saves a poor, wretched sinner, He establishes him, and puts a song, or carol, in his heart (Psalm 40:1-3). The ungodly man has no song or joy, but the believer has the very joy of the Son of God, and can live a life filled with joy (John 15:11).

Seeing "joy" being demonstrated in the life of one believer can bring "joy" to others. Hence John's word to the elect lady—

REJOICE GREATLY—vs. 4[1]

"The Lord loves to see His people happy, and therefore He has made full provision for them in His Holy Word. He bids them cast all their cares upon Him, to expect every necessary good thing from Him, and to rejoice always in Him. When John wrote to those in his day he told them that God is love, that Christ was their propitiation and advocate, that they were *now* the sons of God, that God had given unto them eternal life and had admitted them into union with Himself, and that to walk in truth produces joy. To the elect lady he desires her to have full joy. Beloved, all our sorrows spring from our sins but our joys are the gifts of free grace. There is enough in ourselves to make us miserable, but there is enough in Jesus to fill us with joy under the most miserable circumstances. Let us endeavor to live out of self and live upon Christ, to make use of Him for our present happiness as well as our everlasting bliss in glory. Let us bear in mind today that God's Word is to make us happy and that every doctrine, promise, and precept, rightly understood, is calculated to do so. O Lord, Thy saints are a happy people. May I, too, share in their happiness, and greatly rejoice together."

PRAYER THOUGHT: "Dear Lord, let Thy Word break my heart today to let in whatever light is needed to live with boldness and walk in truth, so that others cannot question the reality of Christ living in one who has trusted in Thee. In Thy precious name. Amen."[2]

II John 4; Acts 4:13

Third John—The Epistle of Christian Hospitality

Name: See NAME in gospel of John.

Occasion of Writing: A warning against schism. An ambitious "church boss" named Diotrephes refused to recognize John's authority by treating people sent by him with harshness. He warns Gaius against this tyrannous man.

Contents: This letter was written to Gaius. Three people in the New Testament bear this name:

Gaius of Corinth (I Corinthians 1:14); Gaius of Macedonia (Acts 19:29); and Gaius of Debre (Acts 20:4). The Gaius to whom John wrote could have been any one of these. Whoever he was, he evidently was one of John's converts, for he is referred to as "beloved" four times.

John commends Gaius for hospitality and charity, complains of Diotrephes as proud and overbearing in the church, and particularly recommends Demetrius. He encourages "partnership" in truth. Third John has only 1 chapter, 14 verses, and 299 words.

Character: Personal Epistle.

Subject: Humility—a characteristic becoming an elder or pastor in a church.

Purpose: To teach us God's place for us as witnesses of the truth and to warn against self-exaltation and self-assumption in the ministry.

Outline:

    I. Introduction: vss. 1-4
   II. Confirmation of Gaius: vss. 5-8
  III. Condemnation of Diotrephes: vss. 9-11
  IV. Commendation of Demetrius: vs. 12
   V. Conclusion: vss. 13,14

Writer: John, the elder: vs. 1. See WRITER in Index.

When and Where Written: A.D. 85-90, probably in Ephesus.

Key Verses: 4,8.

Key Word: Truth.

Key Phrase: Follow . . . that which is good: vs. 11.

Key Thought: Spread the Truth.

Spiritual Thought: He is the Way.

Christ Is Seen As: A Worthy Name; vs. 7.

SEED THOUGHTS

1. Truth—
   a. Is a basis for love: vs. 1
   b. Is a motive for consideration: vs. 2
   c. Is an indwelling reality for guidance: vs. 3
   d. Is a source for joy: vs. 4
   e. Is an encouragement for faithfulness: vss. 5,6
   f. Is an incentive for service: vs. 7
   g. Is a guide for togetherness: vs. 8
   h. Is a discerner for schism: vss. 9,10
   i. Is a tool for good: vs. 11
   j. Is a testimony for godly living: vs. 12
   k. Is a bond for fellowship: vss. 13,14

2. Spreading the Truth—
   a. By the life: vss. 1,2
   b. By testimony: vs. 3
   c. By faith hospitality: vss. 5,6
   d. By sacrificial service: vs. 7
   e. By unity: vs. 8
   f. By rebuking hypocrisy: vss. 9,10
   g. By doing good: vs. 11
   h. By correspondence: vs. 13a
   i. By personal contact: vs. 14a

A BIT OF

HEAVENLY MANNA

Many folks seek to do good that they might merit God's favor, or to enhance themselves before others, or to assure themselves of heaven. Such "goodness" is in vain, and the one who acts in this manner is deceiving no one but himself. However, there is a goodness which is acceptable to God, and John's third Epistle reveals the manner in which it can be acceptable to God. It is through Truth and Truth alone.

HE THAT DOETH GOOD IS OF GOD—vs. 11[1]

"If we do good to our fellow men with a view to glorify God, and out of love to the Lord Jesus Christ, it is the effect of the indwelling and the sanctifying work of the Holy Spirit. Everything is as the principle from which it proceeds; if therefore our works proceed from selfishness, or pride or vainglory, they are not good however excellent they may appear before men. Everything partakes from the nature of the motive by which it is influenced. If our motive is not pure, whatever we do is not good. That which is really good springs from a good motive, flows from a good principle, runs in a good channel, is directed by a good rule, and aims at a good end. Now, if we thus do good, we are of God. We are His new creation. We are partakers of His divine nature. The Holy Spirit dwells within us. But if we are not doing good, whatever profession we make, we are not of God. He will not own us now, nor will He acknowledge us at the last. 'He that doeth righteousness, is righteous, even as He is righteous.' Lord, teach us to do good to Thy glory."

PRAYER THOUGHT: "O Lord, help me to enter into the mind of everyone who talks to me this day that I might enter into their feelings and have an understanding heart toward each of their problems. In the Name of the One who bore all my griefs and sorrows, and made my burdens light. Amen."[2]

III John 2

Jude—The Epistle to Remedy Apostasy

Name: This Epistle was written by Jude (1:1), a brother of James, probably Christ's half brother (Matthew 13:55; Mark 6:3). Some scholars are of the opinion that the writer of this letter was the apostle Judas (Matthew 10:2,3), called Lebbaeus or Thaddaeus (Luke 6:16; Acts 1:13). If the writer was the Lord's half brother, he was not a believer in Christ until after His resurrection (John 7:5; Acts 1:14). The early church fathers did not at first accept this epistle as part of the Scriptures, but the Muratorian Canon, dating A.D. 200, included it with the other books of the Bible, indicating it had already been accepted as divinely inspired. Jude means "Judah—praise."

Occasion of Writing: While it is apparent that Jude started to write about the salvation which meets the common need of man, it was urgently pressed upon him by the Holy Spirit to warn believers about the gross abuses of Christian liberty which were committed by the ungodly men (vs. 4). He is writing about the peril of apostasy, and gives advice as to how one might combat it—contending for the faith by enriching faith (Romans 10:17), praying, loving, looking, and serving (3,20-23). Peter's antidote for apostasy was growth in grace and knowledge of Christ (II Peter 3:18), and Paul's was sound doctrine (I Timothy 4:16; II Timothy 4:2,3). See APOSTASY in Index.

Contents: Jude describes false teachers who deny the Lord and give license to sin (vs. 4). He points out their principles and practices—and gives Old Testament illustrations of sins leading to apostasy—

1. Israel—unbelief: vs. 5
2. Angels—rebellion: vs.6
3. Sodom and Gomorrah—immorality and perversion: vs. 7
4. Cain—self-will: vs. 11a
5. Balaam—covetousness; mercenary: vs. 11b
6. Korah—rejection of God's authority: vs. 11c

Jude sums up the awfulness of their sins in vss. 12 and 16, and concludes that "these be they who separate themselves, sensual, having not the Spirit" (vs. 19). Believers are exhorted to recognize their calling—that of continuing in and contending for the faith. He gives an abridgment of the cardinal doctrines of Christianity—

1. The Triune God: vss. 1,20
2. The historicity of the Old Testament: vss. 5-11
3. Existence of angels: vs. 6
4. Satan's existence and power: vs. 9
5. Judgment and retribution: vss. 6,7,13,15
6. Christ's second coming: vss. 14,15
7. Christ's Deity: vs. 25

This book has only 1 chapter with 25 verses and 613 words.

Character: General Epistle.

Subject: The faith that saves in the evil days of apostasy.

Purpose: To keep us from falling and to present us faultless before His presence: vs. 24.

Outline:

I. Introduction: vss. 1-4
II. An Exposition of the Danger: vss. 5-16
III. An Exhortation to the Duty: vss. 17-23
IV. Conclusion: vss. 24,25

Writer: Jude: vs. 1. See NAME in Dictionary.

When and Where Written: A.D. 67,68, probably in Jerusalem.

Key Verse: 24.

Key Word: Kept.

Key Phrase: Earnestly contend.

Key Thought: Present faultless.

Spiritual Thought: He is able.

Christ Is Seen As: The only wise God: vs. 25.

Names and Titles of Christ. See NAME in Dictionary.

1. Jesus Christ: vs. 1
2. Lord Jesus Christ: vs. 4
3. Lord: vs. 14
4. Wise God: vs. 25a
5. Savior: vs. 25b

Names and Titles of God. See NAME in Dictionary.

1. Father: vs. 1

2. Lord God: vs. 4
3. The Lord: vs. 5

Names and Titles of the Holy Spirit. See NAME in Dictionary.

1. The Spirit: vs. 19.
2. Holy Ghost: vs. 20b.

Comets: vs. 13. When Jude refers to "wandering stars," he is not necessarily making a scientific statement. He is comparing these stars, or comets, to false prophets or apostate teachers. Comets shine for only a short time. As one moves toward the sun, gases are vaporized, which leave a "long-haired" trail. As it "wanders," moving away from the sun, the gases freeze and the bright trail disappears as the comet moves into darkness of space. Just as the comet shines forth brightly for a short time as it faces the light (sun), so a false prophet appears as an "angel of light." As the comet turns away and goes into outer darkness, a false prophet goes out from us to show that he was not of us (I John 2:19). A "false" prophet is no more a "true" prophet than a comet is a "true" star.

The Old Testament in Jude:
1. Satan rebuked: vs. 9 with Zechariah 3:2.
2. Companion references:
   a. Israel's exodus from Egypt: vs. 5 with Exodus 12:41
   b. Israel's unbelief in the wilderness: vs. 5b with Numbers 14:22-29; 26:64,65; Hebrews 3:7-19
   c. Sodom and Gomorrah destroyed: vs. 7 with Genesis 19:24; Deuteronomy 29:23
   d. Moses' body: vs. 9 with Deuteronomy 34:5,6
   e. Cain's sacrifice: vs. 11a with Genesis 4:5
   f. Balaam's error: vs. 11b with Numbers 22:7-21
   g. Korah's rebellion: vs. 11c with Numbers 16:1-3
   h. Enoch: vs. 14 with Genesis 5:18

1. Jude, the Salesman: vs. 1
   a. He introduces himself: vs. 1a
   b. He states his calling: vs. 1b
   c. He points to the One he serves: vs. 1c
   d. He focuses attention on his products: vss. 1d,2
   e. He gives a challenge: vs. 3
   f. He makes an offer: vs. 24
   g. He concludes his presentation: vs. 25
2. The Believer's Calling: vs. 1
   a. *What?* Contend for the faith: vs. 3
   b. *Why?* Apostasy: vss. 4-19
   c. *How?*
      —Build up in the faith: vs. 20a with Romans 10:17
      —Pray in the Holy Spirit: vs. 20b with I Thessalonians 5:17
      —Keep self in the love of God: vs. 21a with Romans 12:9a
      —Look for Christ's return: vs. 21b with Luke 19:13
      —Have compassion for the lost: vss. 22,23a; Matthew 9:36-38
      —Be separate: vs. 23b with II Corinthians 6:14-18
      —Rely on Christ: vs. 24a
3. The Common Salvation: vs. 3. See SALVATION in Index.
   a. It comes from a common source—God

    b. It is presented by a common method—preaching

    c. It is offered in a common way—by invitation

    d. It is given to meet a common need—man's sin

    e. It supplies a common need—salvation

4. The "Upward" Christian

    a. Stand up (contend): vs. 3

    b. Built up: vs. 20a

    c. Prayed up: vs. 20b

    d. Kept up: vs. 21a

    e. Loved up: vs. 21b

    f. Looked up: vs. 21c

    g. Stirred up: vs. 22a

    h. Filled up (compassion): vs. 22b

    i. Lifted up (pulling): vs. 23a

    j. Cleaned up (hating): vs. 23b

    k. Held up (kept): vs. 24a

    l. Taken up (presented): vs. 24b

5. The Apostate: vs. 12

    a. Like clouds without water—drifters: vs. 12

    b. Like trees without fruit—barren: vs. 12

    c. Like wells without water—lifeless: II Peter 2:17

    d. Like lamps without oil—darkness: Matthew 25:3

6. The Witness of Enoch: vs. 14

    a. His testimony *for* God: vs. 14

    b. His faith *in* God: Hebrews 11:5

    c. His walk *with* God: Genesis 5:24a

    d. His reward *from* God: Genesis 5:24b

7. The Ungodly: vs. 18. See WICKED in Index.

    a. Their *creed*—no God: Psalm 53:1a

    b. Their *character*—corrupt: Psalm 53:1b

    c. Their *acts*—abominable iniquity: Psalm 53:1c

    d. Their *hopelessness*—none doeth good: Psalm 53:1d,3

    e. Their *ignorance*—no knowledge: Psalm 53:4a

    f. Their *treatment of the godly*—use for their gain: Psalm 53:4b

    g. Their *disrespect for God*—do not call upon Him: Psalm 53:4c

    h. Their *condition*—no peace: Isaiah 57:20,21

    i. Their *distress*—in great fear: Psalm 53:5a

    j. Their *plight*—put to shame: Psalm 53:5b

    k. Their *doom*—they shall perish: Psalm 1:3-6

8. Garments: vs. 23

    Worn by the sinner—

    a. Spotted: vs. 23

    b. Motheaten: James 5:2

    c. Self-righteous: Revelation 3:17

    d. Stolen: Joshua 7:21

    e. Deceptive: Joshua 9:3-5

    f. Grave: John 11:44

    Worn by the Christian—

    a. Salvation: Isaiah 61:10a

    b. White: Revelation 7:14

    c. Undefiled: Revelation 3:4; 16:15

    d. Righteousness: Isaiah 61:10b

    e. Consecrated: Exodus 29:21; Matthew 21:8

f. Humility: I Peter 5:5
g. Beautiful: Isaiah 42:1
h. Christ: Romans 13:14
i. Armor: Ephesians 6:11. See ARMOR in Index.

A BIT OF
HEAVENLY
MANNA

How easy it is to shirk responsibility, to remain silent when we should witness, to talk to others when we should talk to God, to attend to trivial matters when we should be giving heed to the essential. The devil never takes a holiday, therefore it is necessary that we ever be on guard, taking heed to ourselves (I Timothy 4:16) and buying up every opportunity to contend for the faith once delivered unto the saints. If we do, our blessed Savior is then—

ABLE TO KEEP US—vs. 24[1]

"The Lord's people are taught by the Holy Spirit to pray for what they need; and they find, in pursuing God's Word, that He has promised just what they pray for. Every believer prays to be kept. This is one of his daily prayers. He feels that he needs keeping. He is weak, his foes are strong. He is inexperienced, his dangers are numerous and great. He cannot proceed safely, or comfortably, or honorably, but he is kept. He desires to be kept from sin that he may not dishonor God. From self, that he may not injure those about him. From Satan, that he may not be overcome by him. From the world, that he may not be ensnared and entangled by it. None can keep him but the Lord. No one else has the power, the patience, the wisdom, or the love that is necessary. To God therefore he cries; before the throne of grace he often appears; fervently he prays to be kept near God, in holy fellowship active for God in his day and generation; and aiming at the glory of God as the grand end of his existence. Beloved, we shall need keeping today. Satan is now studying us. Our own hearts are false and fickle. But our own God, praises be to Him, is able to keep us from falling."

PRAYER THOUGHT: "Dear Lord, while there are so many on the road to destruction, and while there are so many more false preachers than those true to the Word, help me as one of Thy children to earnestly contend for the faith daily, and to remember that I can never talk to the wrong person about their soul's need. In Christ's lovely name I pray. Amen."[2]

Jude 3; Acts 1:8

Books of the New Testament
DIVISION IV
The Revelation

Subject: Prophecy concerning the judgments of Jesus Christ, the God-appointed Judge: Revelation 1:1-3; John 5:22,27.

Purpose: To make known to us what shall be the end or consummation of all of God's redemptive purposes: Numbers 23:19; Isaiah 55:11; Titus 1:2; Revelation 22:3-5.

Revelation—The Book of Final Consummation

Name: The book is "the revelation of Jesus Christ" (1:1), hence the title, "The Revelation." Its Greek title, "Apocalypse," signifies literally a *revelation* of what was concealed or hidden. This revelation was given by God to Jesus Christ. Christ gave it to His angel. This angel showed it to John, and John sent it to the churches. Thus we find it came from God to Christ, from Christ to the angel, from the angel to John, and from John to us (or the churches). It is properly, therefore, the "Revelation of Jesus Christ by God." "Apocalypse of John" was a title used to set his apart from other apocalypses. The epithet, "St. John the Divine," was added to the book's title in the fourth century.

Occasion of Writing: As with all apocalyptic books, Revelation was occasioned by oppression of the people of God by outside enemies and by disloyalty and worldliness on the part of lukewarm Christians. Its message was intended for the church in general (22:16).

It appears, too, that this last book of the Bible was given to summarize Old and New Testament truth and fulfill all unfilled prophecy. Revelation completes the cycle of truth begun in Genesis.

1. Christ, the Bible's central theme: Genesis 3:15; Revelation 1:1,13-18
2. The church: Matthew 16:18; Revelation 2,3
3. The tribulation: Deuteronomy 4:29,30; Revelation 6:1—19:21
4. Satan and his works: Isaiah 14:12-14; Ezekiel 28:11-18; Revelation 12:3-17
5. The Antichrist: Ezekiel 28:1-10; II Thessalonians 2:7-10; Revelation 13:1-10
6. Israel's blessing: Jeremiah 31:31-33; Revelation 7
7. Times of the Gentiles: Daniel 2; Luke 21-24; Revelation 6:1—19:16
8. Judgment of the nations: Joel 3:1-16; Revelation 16:13-16
9. Second advent of Christ in glory: Zechariah 14:1-14; Revelation 19:11-16
10. Judgment of the wicked: Psalm 9:17; Revelation 20:11-15
11. New heaven and new earth: Isaiah 65:17; 66:22; Revelation 21,22
12. Paradise lost; paradise regained: Genesis 3; Revelation 21,22

These last words from God in Revelation assure the believer of the final triumph of good over evil.

Contents: Revelation is a commentary on what John saw, what things of his day were, and what the future held (1:19)—

1. A vision of Christ: 1:1-18
2. Judgment of the church: 2:1—3:22
3. The tribulation—apostate Israel and the nations: 4:1—19:21
4. The millennium: 20:1-6
5. God's final victory and Satan's doom: 20:7-15
6. New heaven, new earth, and new Jerusalem: 21,22

There are many comparisons and contrasts between the first and last books of the Bible—

GENESIS	REVELATION
Creation of the sun	No need of the sun
Satan victorious	Satan's doom
Sin's entrance	Sin banished
Defeat	Victory
Running from God	Invited back
Curse pronounced	No more curse
Tears and sorrow	No more tears
Garden cursed	City glorified
Tree of life forbidden	Tree of life eaten
Paradise lost	Paradise regained
Death	No more death

The main thrust of the Old Testament is the announcement of the coming Redeemer. The gospel accounts of the New Testament unveil His First Advent, and the last Book unveils the Second Advent. Daniel, who outlived his contemporaries, wrote in exile the events of Revelation, but was told to "shut up the words and seal the book to the end time" before he could describe them (Daniel 12:4). John, who also outlived his contemporaries, witnessed the opening of the book (Revelation 5:1-9), and wrote (in exile) the last prophecies.

There are at least four schools of interpretation of Revelation:

1. The *preterists,* who hold that this book was meant mainly for the people of John's day and had its fulfillment then.
2. The *historicists,* who believe that Revelation takes the whole period of history from John's day to the present time.
3. The *spiritualists,* who claim that the symbols portray spiritual realities.
4. The *futurists,* who believe that the bulk of the book has to do with the future.

One may be safe in accepting a twofold meaning to much that is found in Revelation. For example, what applied to the churches in John's time is applicable to the church in general today, as well as to the individual believer. A safe position as to the interpretation of Revelation may be the blending of a little of the historical theory with much of the futurist's view. Whatever view one takes, the book of Revelation is the unveiling of Jesus Christ, not the unveiling of the Antichrist. While the beasts and the dragon and the woes and the devil are all there, they are seen only in the light that shines when Christ is unveiled.

The language of Revelation is Greek, but it is filled with Old Testament idioms. It is the only book in the Bible that promises a blessing if read and kept (studied and practiced: 1:3). It has 22 chapters, 404 verses, and 12,000 words.

Character: Prophecy.

Subject and Purpose: See p. 673.

Outline:

    I. Prologue: 1:1:8
    II. A Vision of Grace: 1:9—3:22
       A. The Sovereign Christ: 1:9-20
       B. The Seven Churches: 2,3
    III. A Vision of Government: 4:1—19:10
       A. The Platform and Process of Judgment: 4:1—11:19

Writer: John (1:1,9,10). See NAME in gospel of John. Liberals and critics of the Bible, who grab at any straw in the wind to condemn God's Word, have questioned the authorship of Revelation by the Apostle John for several reasons—

1. John's name is listed five times in Revelation (1:1,4,9; 21:2; 22:8), while neither his gospel account nor his Epistles bear his name. The critics attribute this book to "another" John. John's name is attached to this prophecy, the same as Old Testament prophets listed their names, in all probability as a guarantee of its authenticity. Early church fathers, such as Clement of Alexandria, Irenaeus, and Eusebius, state that it was *John the Apostle* who was banished to the isle of Patmos (1:9).

2. The vocabulary and style of Revelation differ from John's other writings, so the author of Revelation must be a different John. As in all apocalyptic writings, there is much imagery or symbolism. Yet one can find many similarities in all of John's writings—

REVELATION		GOSPEL AND EPISTLES
1:1	Signify	John 12:33; 21:19
1:5; 7:14	Christ's blood	I John 1:7
1:7	Whom they pierced	John 19:37
2:10	Faithless; faithful	John 20:27
2:17	Manna; bread	John 6:32
3:4	Walk	John 6:66; II John 4
3:10	Hour	John 12:27
3:21	My Father	John 17:1
4:1	Show	John 16:13
7:10	Lamb	John 1:29
12:9	Satan cast out	John 12:31
19:13	Word of God	John 1:1
21:6	Water of Life	John 4:14

3. There is an objection because the language of Revelation contains expressions characteristic of Hebrew. Revelation is filled with direct and indirect quotations from the Old Testament, and the author relies heavily on the idioms of Daniel and Ezekiel. Consequently, this book, while written in Greek, has much that differs from other New Testament books.

4. Late critics contend that Revelation was written at a much later date than that ascribed to it (ca. A.D. 95). Some have said it was written late in the second century, while others say it was written as late as A.D. 395. Still others say it was written by a church father named John Chrysostom (ca. A.D. 395). Archaeologists in Egypt have found a copy of the book of Revelation which dates from the middle of the fourth century—some 35 to 50 years before the above date. This discovery proves that Revelation had been in circulation long before Chrysostom's time.

Other archaeological findings show that Clement of Alexandria (A.D. 200), Irenaeus (A.D. 180), Martyr (A.D. 135) quote from Revelation and list the apostle John as the author. These men must have had copies of the original text years *after* John received it from the Lord. The Maratorian Fragment (A.D. 170) includes John's Revelation as part of the New Testament canon.

When and Where Written: A.D. 95. The Roman emperor Domitian (A.D. 81-96), toward the end of his reign, banished John to the isle of Patmos, where this book was written (1:9).

Key Chapter: 19. Christ's coming in glory.

Key Verse: 1:19.

Key Word: Overcometh: 2:7,11,17,26; 3:5,12,21.

Key Phrase: He that hath an ear let him hear: 2:7.

Key Thought: The Revelation of Jesus Christ: 1:1.

Spiritual Thought: Read the Word of God: 1:3.

Christ Is Seen As: The living, victorious Savior: 1:18.

Names and Titles of Christ. See NAME in Index.

1. Jesus Christ: 1:1
2. Faithful and True Witness: 1:5; 3:14
3. First Begotten of the dead: 1:5
4. Prince or Ruler of the kings of the earth: 1:5
5. Our sin Cleanser: 1:5
6. Alpha and Omega: 1:8; 21:6
7. Lord: 1:8; 11:8
8. The Almighty: 1:8
9. Son of Man: 1:13
10. First and Last: 1:17; 2:8
11. The living Christ: 1:18
12. Son of God: 2:18
13. Holy and True One: 3:7
14. Amen: 3:14
15. The Beginning of the creation: 3:14
16. Creator: 4:11
17. Lion of the Tribe of Judah: 5:5
18. Root and Offspring of David: 5:5
19. Lamb: 5:6 (mentioned 30 times)
20. Eternal reigning Christ: 11:15
21. Man Child: 12:5a
22. Ruler of nations: 12:5b
23. Christ: 12:10
24. Jesus: 14:12
25. Lord of lords: 17:14; 19:16
26. King of kings: 17:14; 19:16
27. Spirit of prophecy: 19:10
28. The Word of God: 19:13
29. Light of New Jerusalem: 21:23
30. The Rewarder: 22:12
31. Bright and Morning Star: 22:16
32. Water of Life: 22:17
33. Our soon coming Savior: 22:20
34. Lord Jesus: 22:20
35. Lord Jesus Christ: 22:21

Names and Titles of God. See NAME in Index.

1. Father: 1:6; 14:1
2. Lord God Almighty: 4:8; 16:14
3. Living God: 7:2
4. God of heaven: 11:13
5. Lord: 11:15; 18:8
6. King of saints: 15:3

Names and Titles of the Holy Spirit: Spirit: 1:10; 14:13. See NAMES in Dictionary.

1. Authorship of Revelation. See point 4 under WRITER.

2. The Seven Churches. Archaeologists have unearthed much of importance to give a background knowledge of events and customs of these ancient cities in Asia Minor (presently Turkey). See CHURCHES in Index.

a. Ephesus: 2:1-7. When Paul visited Ephesus (ca. A.D. 55), it was a thriving, progressive city. Forty years later when John wrote this message, the inhabitants were resting on past laurels. They had lost their zeal. The saints in Ephesus had once been energetic. They were still sound in doctrine but had left (lost) their first love (vs. 4). John used this condition of the city to drive home his spiritual application. See NAME in Ephesians and Index.

b. Smyrna: 2:8-11. According to mythology, Amazon Smyrna, the foundress of Smyrna, wore a high crown on her head. Ancient writers referred to this city as the "crown of Smyrna." In John's day, the followers of the goddess Cybele wore a laurel wreath (crown), and were faithful to Rome and its paganism. Followers of Christ were severely persecuted because they did not wear such a crown, and John's word of admonition, "Be thou faithful unto death, and I will give thee a crown of life" (vs. 10), was meaningful to them. Polycarp, a disciple of John, was martyred in Smyrna in A.D. 155. Faithful to the end, he died saying: "Eighty and six years I have served Him, and He has done me no wrong. How can I speak evil of my King who saved me!" See SMYRNA in Index.

c. Pergamos (Pergamum): 2:12-17. The city was a religious "seat" for several cults, notably "Emperor worship" (see Index). "Asklepios," the god of healing, was also honored (some scholars are of the opinion Luke took his medical training in this city). This god's symbol was a serpent, which in turn was a symbol of "that old serpent the devil." The temple of Zeus in Pergamos housed the room "where Satan's seat is" (vs. 13). In such atmosphere, John encouraged Christians to remain true to Christ, to reveal in their lives what "true" religion was all about. See PERGAMOS in Index.

d. Thyatira: 2:18-29. The incarnated son of Zeus, Apollos, the sun God, was the chief deity and guardian of this city. In all his brightness, he was no comparison to Christ, the "incarnate Son of God, who hath eyes like a flame, and feet like fine copper" (vs. 18). John's message to believers in Thyatira was to keep their eyes on the One who kept His eyes on them.

e. Sardis: 3:1-6. This city, supposedly impregnable, had failed to watch, and was defeated by the Persians in 564 B.C. This incident had lived with the inhabitants. When John wrote to believers there, he instructed them not to neglect the Lord but to watch, lest the Lord come and overtake them like a thief (vs. 3).

f. Philadelphia: 3:7-13. This city was the doorway into Phrygia through which Grecian culture was to advance eastward. John used the expression "open door" (vs. 8) for the Philadelphia saints to advance the gospel to those in the "synagogue of Satan" (Zeus' temple—vs. 9).

g. Laodicea: 3:14-21. This city was one of the richest cities of its day. Financial aid was rejected when Rome sought to help after a devastating earthquake. The Laodiceans were noted for their glossy black cloth, a salve to cure weak eyes, and a medical center. The Laodicean Christians had succumbed to the ways of the day and were guilty of material compromise. In a lukewarm state, they knew the meaning of "nakedness," "white raiment," and "eye salve." They understood they were in spiritual poverty, that their money could not buy what their hearts needed (vs. 18).

LIGHT FROM BIBLICAL CUSTOMS

1 A White stone: 2:17. White in the East is a symbol of forgiveness. If a man molests a girl, her tribe can demand the death penalty. If sufficient payment is made, the guilty one is set free. Afterwards, he lives in a white tent, with a large white stone at its entrance. The white speaks to all that he has been forgiven, and he cannot be touched or harmed for the price of his forgiveness has been paid by another, and he is free of guilt. The "white stone" given to the overcomer signifies full pardon. A new name written in the stone signifies the old past will never be brought up again.

The Old Testament in Revelation: The whole of this book is a reflex of the prophetic visions of the Old Testament. It contains pictures of that heavenly form of worship in the Tabernacle divinely manifested to Moses and fulfilled in the atonement of Jesus Christ. Revelation repeats the mysterious predictions uttered by Isaiah, Ezekiel, and Daniel, portraying the philosophy of history, the recurrence of its cycles, and the supremacy over all other powers of the kingdom of God. It is, therefore, full of references and allusions to the writings of Moses and the other prophets too numerous to be tabulated and often allusive rather than literal. Revelation exceeds all other New Testament books with Old Testament references. The gospel accounts have over 100 different references, Hebrews has approximately 100, and Revelation has almost 300. Some examples are—

1. Seven Spirits: 1:4 with Isaiah 11:2
2. Looking at the pierced Christ: 1:7 with Zechariah 12:10
3. Almighty Christ: 1:8 with Isaiah 9:6
4. Candlesticks: 1:12,20 with Zechariah 4:2
5. Description of Christ: 1:14,15 with Daniel 7:9
6. Falling in God's presence: 1:17 wih Ezekiel 1:28; Daniel 10:8
7. Tree of life: 2:7 with Genesis 2:9
8. The First and Last: 2:8 with Isaiah 44:6
9. Doctrine of Balaam: 2:14 with Numbers 24:12-14; 25:1
10. Searching the heart: 2:23 with Jeremiah 17:10
11. Rod of iron: 2:27a; 12:5 with Psalm 2:9a
12. Broken vessels: 2:27b with Isaiah 30:14; Psalm 2:9b
13. Keys of David: 3:7 with Isaiah 22:22
14. God's chastening: 3:19 with Proverbs 3:12
15. God's throne: 4:2,3 with Ezekiel 1:26-28
16. Four beasts: 4:6 with Ezekiel 1:5
17. Song of the seraphims: 4:8 with Isaiah 6:2
18. Root of David: 5:5 with Isaiah 11:1,10
19. Ministering angels: 5:11 with Daniel 7:9,10
20. The colored horses: 6:2-8; with Zechariah 6:2-8
21. Heaven rolled as a scroll: 6:14 with Isaiah 34:4
22. Hiding in the rocks: 6:15,16 with Isaiah 2:19; Hosea 10:8
23. The four winds: 7:1 with Daniel 7:2
24. Mark upon their foreheads: 7:3 with Ezekiel 9:4
25. Tears wiped away: 7:17; 21:4 with Isaiah 25:8
26. Hand lifted up to heaven: 10:5 with Daniel 12:7
27. Eating the book: 10:9 with Ezekiel 3:1-3
28. The measuring reed: 11:1 with Ezekiel 40
29. Olive tree and candlesticks: 11:4 with Zechariah 4:2,3
30. The dead come alive: 11:11 with Ezekiel 37:5-14
31. Michael: 12:7 with Daniel 12:1
32. Beasts from the sea: 13:1 with Daniel 7:3

33. Captivity captive: 13:10a with Judges 5:12; Psalm 68:18
34. Capital punishment: 13:10b with Genesis 9:6
35. No guile: 14:5 with Psalm 32:2
36. Babylon is fallen: 14:8 with Isaiah 21:9
37. The wine of God: 14:10 with Psalm 75:8; Jeremiah 25:15
38. Smoke of their torment: 14:11 with Isaiah 34:10
39. Son of man; 14:14 with Daniel 7:13
40. Winepress of blood: 14:20 with Isaiah 63:3
41. The cloud of glory: 15:8 with Exodus 40:34
42. Drunken nations: 17:2 with Jeremiah 51:7
43. Ten horns: 17:12 with Daniel 7:20
44. Babylon's inhabitants: 18:2 with Isaiah 13:19-22
45. Babylon's reward: 18:6 with Psalm 137:8
46. Babylon's pleasures: 18:7 with Isaiah 47:7,8
47. Babylon's permanent doom: 18:21 with Jeremiah 51:64
48. Voices silenced: 18:23 with Jeremiah 25:10
49. Treading the winepress: 19:15 with Isaiah 63:2,3
50. Fiery doom: 19:20 with Daniel 7:11
51. Gog and Magog: 20:8 with Ezekiel 38:2
52. Judgment books opened: 20:11,12 with Daniel 7:9,10
53. New heaven and new earth: 21:1 with Isaiah 65:17; 66:22
54. Glory of God's light: 21:23; 22:5 with Isaiah 60:19
55. No night in heaven: 21:25; 22:5 with Isaiah 60:20
56. No defilement in heaven: 21:27 with Isaiah 35:8
57. God's river: 22:1 with Ezekiel 47:1-12
58. God invitation: 22:17 with Isaiah 55:5

SEED THOUGHTS

1. The "Sevens" of Revelation. See SEVENS in Index.

   a. Seven Churches in Asia: 1:4,11
   b. Seven Spirits: 1:4. See SPIRITS in Index.
   c. Seven Golden Candlesticks (Churches): 1:12,20
   d. Seven Stars (angels—messengers): 1:16,20
   e. Seven Church Letters: 2:1—3:22. See CHURCHES in Index.
   f. Seven Lamps (Spirits): 4:5
   g. Seven Seals: 5:1; 6:1—8:1
     —White horse—conquer: 6:1,2
     —Red horse—war: 6:3,4
     —Black horse—famine: 6:5,6
     —Pale horse—death: 6:7,8
     —Martyred souls: 6:9-11
     —Anarchy: 6:12-17
     —Seven trumpets: 8:1,2
   h. Seven Horns (Spirits): 5:6
   i. Seven Eyes (Spirits): 5:6. See EYES in Index.
   j. Seven Trumpets: 8:2—11:9
     —Hail, fire, and blood on earth: 8:7
     —Burning mountain cast into the sea: 8:8,9
     —Falling, burning star to the earth: 8:10,11
     —Sun, moon, and stars darkened: 8:12,13
     —Plague of locusts: 9:1-12

      —Slaughtering of 200,000,000 horsemen: 9:13-21
      —World kingdoms becoming Christ's kingdom: 11:15-19
  k. Seven Thunders: 10:3,4
  l. Seven Thousand Slain: 11:13
  m. Seven Heads: 12:3
  n. Seven Crowns: 12:3
  o. Seven Angels: 15:1
  p. Seven Plagues (vials) of God's wrath: 15:1—16:21
      —Bodily affliction: 16:1,2
      —Death in the sea: 16:3
      —Water of the earth becomes blood: 16:4-7
      —Sun's heat scorches men: 16:12
      —Earth's darkness and pain: 16:10,11
      —Euphrates river dried up: 16:12
      —Destruction of Babylon: 16:17-21
  q. Seven Mountains (heads): 17:9
  r. Seven Kings: 17:10
  s. Seven "Beatitudes"
      —Blessed are those who read this prophecy: 1:3
      —Blessed are those who die in the Lord: 14:13
      —Blessed are those who watch for Christ's coming: 16:15
      —Blessed are those invited to the marriage supper: 19:9
      —Blessed are those in the first resurrection: 20:6
      —Blessed are those who keep the words of this book: 22:7
      —Blessed are those who wash their robes: 22:14 (margin)
  t. Seven Personages
      —The woman—Israel: 12:1,2
      —Great red dragon—Satan: 12:3,4,9
      —The man child—Christ: 12:5,6
      —Michael, the archangel: 12:7
      —Israel's remnant: 12:17
      —The beast out of the sea: 13:1-8
      —The beast out of the earth: 13:11-18
  u. Seven Judgments
      —Religious Babylon: 17
      —Political Babylon: 18
      —The Beast and the False Prophet: 19:20
      —Godless nations: 19:21
      —Gog and Magog: 20:7-9
      —Satan: 20:10
      —The wicked dead: 20:11-15
  v. Seven "New" Things
      —Heavens: 21:1
      —Earth: 21:
      —City: 21:9-23
      —Beginning of nations: 21:24-27
      —River: 22:1
      —Tree: 22:2
      —Throne: 22:3-5

2. The Churches of Revelation
  a. The Lord's Commendation—
    Ephesus—*sound doctrinally:* 2:1-3,6
    Smyrna—*faithfulness:* 2:8,9
    Pergamos—*faithfulness:* 2:12,13

                Thyatira—*faithfulness:* 2:18,19
                Sardis—*faithful few:* 3:1a,4
                Philadelphia—*faithfulness:* 3:7,8,10a
                Laodicea—*none*

    b. The Lord's Charge—
                Ephesus—*Left first love:* 2:4
                Smyrna—*none*
                Pergamos—*compromise:* 2:14,15
                Thyatira—*false teachers:* 2:20
                Sardis—*hypocrisy:* 3:1b,2b
                Philadelphia—*none*
                Laodicea—*lukewarm:* 3:15

    c. The Lord's Counsel—
                Ephesus—*remember and repent:* 2:5a
                Smyrna—*continue in faithfulness:* 2:10
                Pergamos—*repent:* 2:16a
                Thyatira—*hold fast:* 2:25
                Sardis—*be watchful and repent:* 3:2a,3
                Philadelphia—*hold fast:* 3:10,11
                Laodicea—*repent and get right with God:* 3:17-19

    d. The Lord's Judgment—
                Ephesus—*testimony lost:* 2:5b
                Smyrna—*none*
                Pergamos—*opposed by God:* 2:16
                Thyatira—*burdens:* 2:24
                Sardis—*His sudden appearance:* 3:3
                Philadelphia—*none*
                Laodicea—*chastisement:* 3:19

    e. The Lord's Reward—
                Ephesus—*spiritual fruit:* 2:7
                Smyrna—*crown of life:* 2:10b,11
                Pergamos—*spiritual food and acceptance:* 2:17
                Thyatira—*power:* 2:26-29
                Sardis—*robe of righteousness:* 3:5
                Philadelphia—*tower of strength:* 3:12
                Laodicea—*position:* 3:21

3. What a Christian can Lose—
    a. First love (spirit of evangelism): 2:4
    b. Joy of God's salvation: Psalm 51:12
    c. Fellowship with God: I John 1:7; 2:1
    d. Fellowship with believers: Hebrews 10:25
    e. Vision: Matthew 13:13a; Proverbs 29:18a
    f. Hearing: Matthew 13:13b
    g. Power: Deuteronomy 32:36; Judges 16:20,21
    h. Influence: Genesis 19:14
    i. Life (premature death): I John 5:16; I Corinthians 5:1-5; 11:29,30
    j. Rewards: I Corinthians 3:14,15

4. A Command of Christ: 2:5
    a. Remember
    b. Repent
    c. Return
    d. Rededicate

5. Overcomers: 2:7,11,17,26; 3:5,12,21. See VICTORY in Index.

6. Be Thou Faithful: 2:10. See FAITH, Types of, in Index.
7. The Voices of Jesus: 3:20.
   a. As Savior—*come* unto Me: Matthew 11:28
   b. As Shepherd—*follow* Me: John 10:27
   c. As Instructor—*learn* of Me: Matthew 11:29
   d. As Friend—*sup* with Him: Revelation 3:20
   e. As Physician—*made whole*: John 5:6
   f. As Master—*occupy* till I come: Luke 19:13
8. The Opening of Heaven: 4:1
   a. For judgment: Genesis 7:11
   b. For blessing: Malachi 3:10
   c. For Christ's introduction: Luke 2:9,10,15a
   d. For the Holy Spirit: Matthew 3:16
   e. For a sight of Jesus: Acts 7:56
   f. For a revelation of the future: Revelation 4:1
   g. For a look at the conquering Savior: Revelation 19:11
9. The Rainbows of Scripture: 4:1-3. See RAINBOW in Index.
   In Genesis: 9:9-17
   Purpose: a covenant of promise: vss. 9,16
   Location: in the cloud to the earth: vs. 14
   When: after judgment: vss. 11,15
   Color: as seen today
   Shape: arch (semi-circle)
   In Ezekiel: 1:26-28
   Purpose: reveal the glory of God
   Location: above the firmament
   When: during God's anger against Israel
   Color: amber to fiery red
   Shape: arch
   In Revelation: 4:1-3
   Purpose: reveal the majesty of God
   Location: in heaven at God's throne
   When: just before judgment (tribulation)
   Color: emerald (green)
   Shape: circle (round about the throne)

On earth the rainbow is only a half circle, denoting incompleteness and imperfection. It is a fleeting sign, denoting changes. It is like life on this earth (Ecclesiastes 1:2). The rainbow in heaven is a circle, denoting completeness, perfection, and performance.

10. The Songs of Creation: 4:8-11
    a. The Holiness of God: vs. 8
    b. The Sovereignty of God: vs. 8
    c. The Eternity of God: vs. 9
    d. The Worthiness of God: vs. 10
    e. The Mightiness of God: vs. 11
11. Seven Eyes: 5:6. See EYES in Index.
    a. Of God—beholding evil and good: Proverbs 15:3
    b. Of Christ—seeing our need: Matthew 9:36
    c. Of the Spirit—guiding us into truth: John 16:13,14
    d. Of Satan—hindering Christ's mission; blinding sinners to their need; trapping their souls: Matthew 4:8; II Corinthians 4:4; Psalm 91:3
    e. Of man in general—critical and indifferent to Christ: Matthew 27:36; Mark 3:2
    f. Of the Christian—
       Now—looking unto Jesus for daily help: Hebrews 12:2

—Looking to win others to Him: John 4:35; Matthew 4:19
—Looking for Christ to come again: Titus 2:13
Dying—observing a welcome: Acts 7:56
Hereafter—seeing Christ as He is: I John 3:2

    g. Of the sinner—
       Now—able to see the Lamb of God: John 1:29
       Dying—observing a welcome: Isaiah 14:9
       Hereafter—in hell, seeing the great gulf: Luke 16:23-26

12. Of the Twelve Tribes mentioned which make up the 144,000 sealed Israelites (Revelation 7:4-8), the Tribe of Dan is not mentioned. See DAN in Index.

13. Products of the Everlasting Gospel: 14:6. See SALVATION, Eternal, in Index.

14. Why Satan is Loosed after the Millennium: 20:7[2]

    a. To show that peace and security will not save the souls of men
    b. To show that living in a righteous environment will not save
    c. To show that good government will not change the hearts of men
    d. To show that man is not naturally good
    e. To show that man does not naturally seek after God
    f. To show that Satan does not change. After 1,000 years in the bottomless pit he is still the same old devil. His methods are the same. His devices are the same. His wiles are the same. He still goes on to deceive (Revelation 20:7,8).
    g. To show that the only possible hope for anyone in any dispensation is the saving and keeping power of Christ. Even the millennium is no substitute for the blood. After the Kingdom Age the hearts of men will still be inclined toward evil, still inclined toward the devil. What is said of Jesus in Hebrews 13:8 can be said of the devil since he sinned from the beginning—"Satan, the same yesterday, today, and forever" till his doom. See SATAN in Index.

15. The Judgments of God: Revelation 20:11

    a. The scriptural fact of them: Psalm 96:13; 17:31; Hebrews 9:27
    b. The Judges—
       —God: Romans 14:12; Acts 10:42
       —Jesus Christ: Romans 2:16; 14:10
       —The Word: John 12:47,48
       —Saints as associates: Psalm 149:9; I Corinthians 6:2,3
    c. The Order of them—
       —Of the cross: John 12:31
         —Defeat of Satan and his emissaries: Hebrews 2:14; Colossians 2:15
         —Atonement for sin: John 1:29; Romans 8:3 (RV); I Peter 2:24
       —Of the believer's self-life: I Corinthians 11:31,32
       —Of the believer's works:
         —The time of it—at Christ's return: I Corinthians 4:5
         —The basis of it—works: II Corinthians 5:10; I Corinthians 3:11-13
         —The results of it—rewards or loss: I Corinthians 3:14,15; Revelation 22:12; II John 8.
       See CROWNS IN Index.
       —Of the nations: Joel 3:11-16; Matthew 25:31-45
       —Of Israel: Psalm 50:1-7; Ezekiel 20:33-44
       —Of fallen angels: I Corinthians 6:3; II Peter 2:4; Jude 6
       —Of the Great White Throne: Revelation 20:11-15
         —(a) The time of it—after the millennium: Revelation 20:5
         —(b) The basis of it—rejection of Christ and His words: John 12:47,48; Revelation 20:12
       —The results of it—eternal punishment: Revelation 20:14,15

16. Heaven: 21:1[3]
    a. The Scriptural fact of it: Psalm 80:14; Isaiah 66:1; Matthew 5:12; Colossians 1:5

      b. The Character of it—a place: John 14:1-3; Hebrews 11:10,16; I Peter 1:3,4
         —A place of beauty and splendor: 21:9-21
         —A place of bliss: 21:2
         —A place of joy and gladness: 21:4
         —A place of satisfaction: 21:6,7
         —A place of light and glory: 21:23
         —A place of holiness: II Peter 3:13
      c. The Inhabitants of it:
         —The Bride and the Lamb: 21:9,10,22,23
         —Angelic beings: Isaiah 6:1,2 (RV): II Thessalonians 1:7; Revelation 3:5
      d. The Occupation of it:
         —Rest: 14:13
         —Worship: 5:14
         —Service: 7:15; 22:3
      e. Its duration—eternal: Psalm 23:6; II Corinthians 5:1

Just before going home to be with the Lord, Dr. Harry Rimmer painted this beautiful picture of heaven: "I am interested in that land because I have a clear title to a bit of property there. I did not buy it. It was given to me 'without money and without price.' But the Donor purchased it for me at a tremendous price—a tremendous sacrifice. I am not holding it for speculation, since the title is non-transferrable. It is not a vacant lot.

"Ever since I was saved, I have been sending up material out of which the Master Architect and Builder of our vast universe has been building a home for me, a home which will never be remodeled nor repaired because it will suit me perfectly, and will never, never grow old. Termites can never undermine its foundation, for it rests upon the 'Rock of Ages.' Fire cannot destroy it. Floods cannot wash it away. No locks nor bolts will ever be placed on its doors for no vicious person can ever enter that Land where my dwelling stands—now nearer completion than when I first believed. When I go to meet my Savior—absent from the body, present with the Lord, it will be ready for me to enter in and abide in peace eternally, without any fear of ever being ejected!

"There is a valley of deep shadows between the place where I now live and the place to which I shall journey—maybe sooner than I think. I cannot reach my home in that City of God without passing through this dark valley of shadows (unless I am raptured first); but I am not afraid, because the best Friend I ever had went through this same valley long, long ago, alone, and drove away all its gloom. He has stuck with me through thick and thin since first we became acquainted, and I have His promise in printed form that He will never leave me nor forsake me—that He will be with me always—never to be left alone. He will be with me as I walk through this valley of the shadow of death, and I shall not lose my way because He is with me.

"I have no assurance I will be here another day—that I will hear another sermon on 'heaven.' My ticket to heaven has no date marked for the journey, no return coupon, and no permit for any baggage. Yes, I am all ready to die. And I shall look forward to meeting all my loved ones in Christ over there some day. For those of you who might not be saved and are not prepared to die and meet the Lord, please talk to the pastor after my funeral and find out how, through the Lord Jesus Christ, you can meet me over there in heaven."

  17. The Coming of Christ: 22:7
      a. Affirmation: 22:6
      b. Imminence: 22:7a,12a,20a
      c. Responsibility to His coming—
         —Acceptance of Him: 22:17
         —Obedience to Him: 22:7

—Worshiping Him: 22:9
—Working for Him: 22:12b
—Watching for Him: 22:16
—Praying: 22:20b

d. Result—
—Reigning with Christ as overcomers: 3:21
—Reigning with Christ on earth, 1,000 years: 5:10; 20:6

18. The First and the Last

a. The first book of the Bible places man in a garden: Genesis 2:8. The last book places man in a city—New Jerusalem: Revelation 21:10,23-27.

b. The first book of the Bible records man losing paradise: Genesis 3. The last book records man regaining paradise: Revelation 21,22

c. The first book of the Bible ends with death and a coffin: Genesis 50:56. The last book ends with resurrection and life: Revelation 20:5b; 22:14.

d. The last book of the Old Testament ends with a curse: Malachi 4:6. The first book of the New Testament begins with a promised Savior: Matthew 1:18-25, and the last book of the New Testament ends with a blessing: Revelation 22:21.

The last words of Jesus Christ to His own were not those of the "Great Commission" (Matthew 28:18-20). They are found in the last book of the Bible in the form of warnings, admonitions, and encouragements. One warning in particular is to "remember." How easy it is for us to forget. Peter reminded us not to forget that we had once been purged from our old sins (II Peter 1:9). The church at Ephesus had forgotten—they had become cold to the need of reaching others for Christ (Revelation 2:4). They remembered themselves, their reputation, their faith, their works, their patience, their fundamentals, their stamina. But they forgot others; their need was not considered. What a tragedy in the life of any believer who is so self-centered. What an awful indictment from the lips of our Savior—

THOU HAST LEFT THY FIRST LOVE—2:4,5[4]

"This is a very solemn charge. Let us ask: 'Is it brought against *us?*' Our first love was Jesus. When we felt our lost condition, when we saw the danger to which we were exposed, we were directed to Him; He received us graciously. He pardoned our sins, He introduced us to His Father, and we enjoyed peace. This filled us with love; we admired His dealings, we adored His person, we espoused His cause, we united with His people, we fearlessly professed His name, and consecrated ourselves to His service. Our love to Jesus at first was warm and strong. We thought nothing too hard to undertake for Him, we considered nothing too valuable to surrender to Him, we felt we could suffer in His cause and die for His name, if required. But we have declined since then, and, if Jesus is still the object of our love, we do not love Him as we once did. He deserves our love more now than ever. He asks our love, for He prizes it. But, alas! the world has such power over us, temporal things so powerfully affect us, that we sometimes question if we love Him at all. What He asked of Peter He asks of us too—'lovest thou Me?' O to obey His admonition—'Remember therefore from whence thou art fallen, and repent, and do [again thy] first works.' "

PRAYER THOUGHT: "Grant, O Savior, that I might remember that I am praying to the Conquerer of death, and to think and act in such a way as to reveal a living Christ to all who have concluded that God is dead. In Thy name I pray. Amen."[5]

Revelation 1:18

Summary and Appendix
Character, Influence, and Claims of Christianity[1]

The Holy Scriptures, as we have seen, are the living oracles of God. They are addressed to perishing sinners, designed to make men wise unto salvation, and for the man of God to be mature, thoroughly furnished unto good works—all by and through faith in Jesus Christ.

In every point of view in which we can contemplate Christianity, it exhibits to us the perfection of heavenly wisdom, and is incomparably superior to all the systems which have ever been presented to mankind under the name of religion. Yea, it is the *only* one that can bring fallen man back into a right relation with God.

Its institutes have been written by holy men of God—prophets, apostles, and evangelists. They have been confirmed by an innumerable multitude of pious believers, in the character of confessors and martyrs for their truth, divinity, and saving efficacy. Their transforming influence on those who receive the love of the truth still corresponds with their ancient claims and demonstrates that they came from God.

The Bible alone has clearly revealed the self-existence, the universal providence, and the infinite perfections of the one only living and eternal God. It has both published and illustrated His holy law as the immutable rule of moral duty for all His intelligent creation. As it reveals to fallen man his true condition—a miserable mortal, a guilty transgressor against his Maker—it exhibits to his terrified mind, and brings to his awakened conscience, the rich provisions of mercy and full forgiveness and free justification through the substitution of an almighty Surety. As it reveals the understanding of man being darkened, and his heart corrupted, it sends him an omnipotent Sanctifier, whose influence illuminates and purifies the soul by regeneration and sanctification. Christianity thus destroys the deeply-rooted enmity of the heart, and brings the alienated rebel to God as his heavenly Father, to receive the unspeakable blessings of adoption into the family of God and to enjoy the sweet assurances of His promises now and of immortality in the life everlasting. It announces a future judgment in which all men shall be righteously rewarded as to their belief in or rejection of the Lord Jesus Christ and their works.

This system of sovereign mercy implants the principles and enforces the practice of every virtue which can exalt, adorn, and improve the human character. Even its partial reception has annihilated the cruel barbarities and degrading customs inseparable from former ages. Christianity is the angel of celestial mercy to the sons of wretchedness, affliction, and woe, and where superstition has been mingled with it. "To the influence of Christianity are to be attributed those asylums for the relief of the miserable, which humanity has consecrated as monuments of beneficence." Constantine was the first who built hospitals for the reception of the sick and wounded in the different provinces of the Roman Empire.

Christianity alone has elevated woman to her just equality with man. It alone has sanctified the sexual relationship between husband and wife; it alone has inculcated the duty and exemplified the expression of domestic harmony, and of parental and filial affection. It alone enforces mutual forgiveness, confidence, and brotherly love, irrespective of clime, age, and nation. Christianity binds all classes together in universal sympathy, under a sense of our common necessities, as equal creatures of the same almighty Creator; and, those being Christians, as members of the body of Christ, and fellow-heirs of the grace of life.

Christianity has given to us our inestimable days of our Lord, thus sanctifying a seventh portion of our week for the benign purposes of rest, instruction, and devotion. It prescribes our meetings on the Lord's day, for cherishing fraternal affection, for increasing rational piety, and mutually to encourage our sublimest anticipations of a glorious immortality at the termination of our earthly sorrows.

The sacred exercises of the Christian Sabbath promote the purest, the most enlarged philanthropy. They have been the means of constraining the disciples of Christ to care for the souls of others. The immortal welfare of their neighbors, of their fellow-countrymen, and of the whole earth's population, has engaged their benevolent solicitude. Among the degraded heathen they support many hundreds of apostolical missionaries; to learn their languages, to translate for them the sacred Scriptures, to preach among them the unsearchable riches of Christ, to instruct their children in heavenly wisdom, to show forth to guilty nations the unspeakable blessings of redeeming grace by the only Mediator between God and sinners, which will lead them to the possession of life everlasting.

Such is the noble spirit, and such the imperishable fruits of Christianity, as contained in the Holy Bible. Its language still addresses equally every child of man—the monarch and the peasant, the rich and the poor, the learned and the illiterate, the master and the servant, the parent and the child—all alike are invited and commanded to return to the Lord our God by repentance and faith, in humble sincerity. To believe with the heart the record which God has given of His Son Jesus Christ is to possess eternal life; to reject and disbelieve the gospel is to make God a liar, and how shall there be escape if this great salvation is neglected?

Weights and Measures

It is difficult in some instances to ascertain the exact figure since some terms listed in the Scriptures are Egyptian, Assyrian, Grecian, Roman, and Hebrew. Measurements *then* and *now* may differ. The present equivalent is approximate.

1. Measures of length:
   a. Finger—digit: Jeremiah 52:21 . . . . ¾ in.
   b. Handbreadth—4 fingers; palm: Exodus 25:25 . . . . 3 in.
   c. Span—3 handbreadths: Exodus 28:16 . . . . 9 in.
   d. Gomed—short cubit: Judges 3:16 . . . . 1 ft.
   e. Cubit—2 spans: Genesis 6:15; Matthew 6:27 . . . . 18 in.
   f. Fathom—an armstretch: Acts 27:28 . . . . 6 ft.
   g. Reed: Ezekiel 40:5 . . . . 9 ft., 3 in.
   h. Line—80 cubits: Ezekiel 40:3 . . . . 120 ft.
   i. Furlong—400 cubits; *Stadium:* Luke 24:13 . . . . 600 ft.
   j. Sabbath day's journey: Acts 1:12 . . . . ⅔ mi.
   k. Mile—Roman: Matthew 5:41 . . . . 4,880 ft.
   l. Day's journey: I Kings 19:4; Luke 2:44 . . . . 20-24 mi.

2. Weights:
   a. Gereh: Exodus 30:13 . . . . 9 grains
   b. Bekah—10 gerahs: Exodus 38:26 . . . . 2 oz.
   c. Shekel—2 bekahs: Exodus 38:26 . . . . 4 oz.
   d. Pound—Roman *litra:* John 12:3; 19:39 . . . . 12 oz.
   e. Maneh—50 shekels: Ezekiel 45:12 . . . . 1 ¼ lbs.
   f. Talent—60 manehs: Exodus 25:39 . . . . 75 lbs.

3. Dry Measure:
   a. Cab: II Kings 6:25 . . . . 3 pts.
   b. Omer—a sheaf; ¹⁄₁₀th part of Ephah: Exodus 16:36 . . . . 1 ½ qts.

c. Measure—*seah:* Matthew 13:33; Revelation 6:6 . . . . .2 qts.
d. Ephah—a basket; bath: Exodus 16:36 . . . . .1 bu.
e. Deals—ephahs: Leviticus 14:10 . . . . near bu.
f. Homer—a donkey load: Leviticus 27:16 . . . . .10 bu.

4. Liquid Measure:
a. Log: Leviticus 14:10 . . . . ¾ pt.
b. Pot—*sextarius:* Mark 7:4 . . . . .1 ½ pts.
c. Cab—4 logs: II Kings 6:25 . . . . .3 pts.
d. Hin—pot; 3 cabs: Exodus 30:24 . . . . .4 qts., 1 pt.
e. Bath—6 hins: I Kings 7:26 . . . . .7 gals.
f. Firkins: John 2:6 . . . . .10 gals.
g. Homer—10 baths: Isaiah 5:10 . . . . .70 gals.

MONEY

1. Hebrew:
a. Gerah: Exodus 30:13 . . . . .3¢
b. Bekah—half shekel: Exodus 38:26 . . . . .30¢
c. Shekel—20 gerahs: Exodus 30:13 . . . . .60¢
d. Dram—gold: I Chronicles 29:7 . . . . .5.00
e. Pound—*mina* (12 ½ oz.)—silver: Luke 19:13 . . . . .20.00—40.00
f. Pound—*mina* (12 ½ oz.)—gold: Luke 19:13 . . . . 300.00—600.00
g. *Mina*—silver: 50 silver shekels: Genesis 23:15 . . . . .30.00
h. *Mina*—gold; 50 gold shekels 480.00
i. Talent—silver: II Kings 18:14 . . . . .1,940.00
j. Talent—gold; 3000 shekels: II Chronicles 36:3 . . . . .28,000.00

2. Greek:
a. Mite—*lepton;* copper: Luke 21:2 . . . . .⅛¢
b. Piece of silver—*drachma:* Luke 15:8 . . . . .16¢
c. Half shekel—*didrachma:* silver. Tax for one: Matthew 17:24 . . . . .32¢
d. Piece of money—*stater;* gold alloy and silver. Tax for two:
     Matthew 17:27 . . . . .64¢

3. Roman:
a. Farthing—*quadran;* copper: Matthew 5:26 . . . . ¼ ¢
b. Farthing—*quadrante;* copper: Matthew 10:29 . . . . .1¢
c. Penny—*denarius;* copper or silver: Matthew 22:19 . . . . .16¢
d. Talent—*attic*: Matthew 25:15 . . . .$960.00 to

Naaman's offering to Elisha amounted to a little over $75,000 (II Kings 5:5). The debtor was forgiven 10,000 talents (Matthew 18:24). If silver, $19,400,000. If gold, $280,000,000. Yet this forgiven debtor refused to forgive his fellowservant 100 pence, or $16.00 (Matthew 18:27-30). Joseph was sold by his brethren for 20 pieces of silver, about $12.00 (Genesis 37:28). Judas sold Christ for 30 pieces of silver, about $18.00, the price of a slave (Matthew 26:15). For the value of Solomon's temple, see TEMPLE in Index.

HEBREW FESTIVALS (FEASTS) AND SEASONS

Sabbath Day. The Sabbath was the first and most important of the sacred festivals. The seventh day signified rest, because in it God had rested from all His works of creation. From the beginning it had been set apart for religious services; and by a special injunction it was afterwards observed by the Hebrews as a holy day. They were commanded to sanctify it for special purposes—in honor of God as their creator, and likewise as a memorial of their redemption from slavery in Egypt (Exodus 20:8-11; Deuteronomy 5:12-15).

Daily Sacrifice. The sacrifices of the Hebrews were exceedingly numerous: bullocks, sheep, goats, pigeons, and turtledoves were used by appointment of God for this purpose. These sacrifices were of two general kinds: (1) such as were offered in the way of atonement for sin (Leviticus 4:1-3; Numbers 28:3-8), and (2) such as were designed to express gratitude to God for His mercies and blessings (Leviticus 3).

The daily sacrifice was remarkable: it was a lamb without blemish, offered to God by fire as an atonement for sin—one in the morning throughout the year for the sins of the nation committed through the night, and another in the evening for sins committed during the day. Before the act of sacrificing, the animal had the sins of the whole nation confessed over it by the officiating priest, and the guilt was ceremonially transferred to the animal by the representatives of the people laying their hands upon its head. It was then slain and offered as a burnt offering for them. Meanwhile the congregation worshiped in the court and the priests burnt incense on the golden altars, making supplication for the people. On the Sabbath the sacrifice was doubled—two lambs being offered at each service (Numbers 28:9,10).

The Day of Atonement. This was distinguished with the most solemn annual sacrifice—observed on the 10th day of Ethanim (or Tishri). The priest offered a bullock as an atonement for the sins of himself and his family. Two goats were offered as an atonement for the nation. After the sins of the nation had been confessed over their heads by the high priest, one was slain and offered by fire after the manner of the daily sacrifice and the other (scape goat) was taken, bearing the sins of the people, into the wilderness to be seen no more (Leviticus 16).

Feasts of Trumpets, or New Moons. Sacrifices were appointed for this feast, and the rejoicings were attended with the sounding of silver trumpets by the priests. It was held the first day of Ethanim, which began the civil year of the Jews. The trumpets and horns were blown from morning till evening (Numbers 10:10; 28:11-15; 29:1,7). After captivity, the Jews observed this day by public reading of the law and with great rejoicing. This feast would correspond to our New Year's day.

The Passover, or the *Feast of Unleavened Bread.* This was the first of the annual Jewish festivals, beginning on the 14th day of Abib (or Nisan). This was their first month of the sacred year. It was instituted to commemorate the wonderful preservation of their deliverance from Egyptian slavery (Genesis 15:13,14; Exodus 12). The Passover was typical of Christ (I Corinthians 5:7).

The Feast of Unleavened Bread began the day after Passover—the 15th, and lasted seven days (Leviticus 23:8), during which time God was honored with the firstfruits of the harvests (Leviticus 23:9-14).

Pentecost. Pentecost is a Greek word, signifying the fiftieth. This festival was so called because it was celebrated the 50th day after the second day of Passover—the 6th day of Sivan. It marked the completion of the wheat harvest (Deuteronomy 16:9-12). It also commemorated the giving of the law at Sinai, fifty days after Israel's deliverance from Egypt. The "Feast of Weeks," the "Feast of Harvests," and the "Day of Firstfruits" are other names given to this feast. The public sacrifices were seven animals of that year. A calf and two rams were also offerred for a burnt offering, as well as two lambs for a peace offering and a goat for a sin-offering. Two wave loaves of fine flour from the wheat harvest were presented as the first-fruits to God, with much thanksgiving and rejoicing (Leviticus 23:15-22).

Tabernacles. This feast was the last of the sacred festivals and was held at the close of the whole harvest and vintage to acknowledge the bounty of God in crowning the whole year with His blessings. It began on the 15th day of Ethanim, five days after the Day of Atonement (Leviticus 23:34-43; Deuteronomy 16:13-15). This was the first month of the civil year. It was designed to commemorate the goodness of God in protecting the Israelites in the wilderness. During this feast the people dwelt in tents or booths formed from the boughs of trees to remind them of their forefathers' sojourn in the desert.

On three annual occasions—*Feast of Unleavened Bread, Feast of Weeks* (Pentecost), and the *Feast of Tabernacles*—all Jewish males were to present themselves before the Lord. These appearances were known as "pilgrim festivals," at which time special sacrifices were offered (Deuteronomy 16:16,17 with Numbers 28,29).

Feast of Purim. This feast was kept on the 14th and 15th days of Adar to commemorate the deliverance of Jews still in exile in Persia from their wholesale massacre planned by Haman (Esther 9:20-32). On the 13th, a fast was kept. At the conclusion of an evening service, which climaxed the fast, the reading of the book of Esther was begun. "When the name of Haman was reached, the congregation cried out, 'Let his name be blotted out,' or 'The name of the wicked shall rot,' while the youthful worshipers spring rattles. The names of Haman's sons were all read in one breath to indicate that they were hanged simultaneously. Next morning the people repaired again to the synogogue to finish the formal exercises of the festival. The rest of the day was devoted to mirth and rejoicing before the Lord, and the wealthy giving gifts to the poor."

Feast of Lights, or the *Feast of Dedication* (John 10:22). This feast, known today as *Hanukkah,* is observed for eight days, beginning the 25th day of Chislev (Kislev—December). It was instituted by Judas Maccabeus in 164 B.C. as a result of his having cleansed the temple which had been defiled by Antiochus Epiphanes.

The Sabbatical Year, or the Year of Release. As the sabbath day signified that the people were the Lord's, for which reason they abstained from their own work to do the work of the Lord, so the Sabbatical Year was intended to remind them that both they and their land belonged to God. The observation of this festival consisted principally of two things: (1) in not tilling the ground or pruning the vine, in which the land was said to keep a sabbath (Leviticus 25:6), and (2) in discharging all debtors and releasing all debts, for which it was called the "Lord's Release" (Deuteronomy 15:2-9). To remove all the fears of the timid, God promised to command His blessing upon the sixth year, that the land should bring forth the fruit of three years (Leviticus 25:20-22). Religious instruction was to be particularly communicated to the servants and to the poor in this year of release that the knowledge and fear of God might be preserved among the people (Deuteronomy 31:10-13).

The Jubilee, or Grand Sabbatical Year. This Jubilee year was appointed to be held every fiftieth year, at the end of seven Sabbatical years. This was a year of general release, not only of all debts, but of all slaves and prisoners, and of all lands and possessions, whether they had been sold or mortgaged. This time was wisely announced—in the evening after the solemn services of the Day of Atonement. The rich and the injured would be better prepared to remit the debts of their brethren when they themselves had been forgiven by God, and when their peace was made with Him by the sacrifices of atonement. Such was a time to proclaim liberty and rejoicing throughout the land.

The design of this institution was both political and typical. The Jubilee was political, intended to prevent the oppression of the poor as well as their being liable to perpetual slavery. The rich were prevented from getting the whole of property in their hands, and a kind of equality was maintained in all their families. The distinction of tribes was preserved, in respect both of their estates and families, and it was thus correctly ascertained from what tribe and family the Messiah descended.

The Jubilee had a typical design, to which the prophet Isaiah refers in predicting the character and office of Messiah (61:1,2; Luke 4:17-21). The various terms which the prophet employs alluded to the blessings of the Jubilee, but their full sense refers to the richer blessings of the gospel, which proclaims spiritual release from the bondage of sin and Satan, liberty of returning to our heavenly inheritance by Christ Jesus, and the privilege of being enriched with the treasures of His grace on earth, preparatory to the enjoyment of the celestial glory.

HEBREW CALENDAR

TIME

Time is the measurement of the continuance of anything (Judges 18:31). It is computed by—

1. Years: Genesis 15:13; II Samuel 21:1. Years—appointed by the sun and moon and used to compute time (Genesis 1:14; 5:3). The term "years" is illustrative of:
   a. Old age: Genesis 25:8; Luke 1:7
   b. The gospel dispensation: Isaiah 61:2; Luke 4:19
   c. Redemption by Christ: Isaiah 63:4
   d. Blessings: Psalm 77:10
   e. Judgment: Jeremiah 23:12; Isaiah 34:8

The Jews had a "sacred" year and a "civil" year. The *sacred* year was reckoned from the moon after the vernal equinox (when the sun crosses the equator in the spring, one of the two times in the year when days and nights are equal). The *civil* year began in our September (the less productive period of the year). The year was divided into—
   a. Twelve months: I Kings 7:4; I Chronicles 27:1-15
   b. Four seasons: Genesis 1:14. See AGRICULTURE in Index.
   c. Weeks: Daniel 9:27; Luke 18:12
   d. Days: Genesis 25:7; Esther 9:27

2. Months: Numbers 10:10; Job 3:6. Twelve lunar months equal one year. The *lunar* (sacred) year totaled a fraction over 354 days. To make it correspond to the *solar* (civil) year, a thirteenth month was added every three years. The months would have 29 and 30 days alternately.

3. Weeks: Daniel 10:2; Luke 18:12. Seven days has been called a *week*. It was the origin of computing time (Genesis 2:2). A space of seven years is sometimes called a "week" (Genesis 29:27,28; Daniel 9:24,26,27). The "Feast of Pentecost" is called a "Feast of Weeks"—after seven weeks that included seven sabbaths (Exodus 34:22; Acts 2:1).

4. Days: Genesis 8:3; Job 1:4. Day time was from sunrise to sunset (Judges 9:33; Psalm 113:3) Night time was from sunset to sunrise (Genesis 28:11; Mark 1:32). A full day was from sunset one evening to sunset the next (Leviticus 23:32). The "evening and the morning were the first day" (Genesis 1:5; 8:22). A day is illustrative of—
   a. Salvation: II Corinthians 6:2
   b. Redemption: Ephesians 4:30
   c. Visitation: Jeremiah 27:22; I Peter 2:12
   d. God's power: Psalm 110:3
   e. Spiritual light: I Thessalonians 5:5,8; II Peter 1:19
   f. The path of the just: Proverbs 4:18
   g. Judgment: I Corinthians 3:13

The ancient night was divided into—
   a. First watch till midnight: Lamentations 2:19
   b. Middle watch till 3 a.m.: Judges 7:19
   c. Morning watch till 6 a.m.: Exodus 14:24

HEBREW CALENDAR

NAME	MONTH	YEAR SACRED	YEAR CIVIL	FESTIVAL	PRODUCT
ABID—NISAN Exod. 12:2, 18 Esther 3:7	MAR / APR	1	7	14th—PASSOVER: Exod. 12:18, 19 15th—UNLEAVENED BREAD: Lev. 23:6 16th—FIRST-FRUITS: Lev. 23:10 – 14	BARLEY HARVEST FIG BLOSSOMS
ZIV—IYYAR I Kings 6:1	APR / MAY	2	8	14th—PASSOVER FOR THOSE WHO COULD NOT KEEP IT IN ABIB: Num. 9:10, 11	BARLEY HARVEST
SIVAN: Esth. 8:9	MAY / JUNE	3	9	6th—PENTECOST OR FIRST-FRUITS: Lev. 23:15 – 21 Deut. 16:9, 10	WHEAT HARVEST
TAMMUZ	JUNE / JULY	4	10		EARLY VINTAGE
AB	JULY / AUG	5	11		RIPE FIGS
ELUL: Neh. 6:15	AUG / SEPT	6	12		GENERAL VINTAGE
ETHANIM OR TISHRI I Kings 8:2	SEPT / OCT	7	1	1st—FEASTS OF TRUMPETS: Num. 29:1 10th—DAY OF ATONEMENT: Lev. 23:27 15th—FEAST OF TABERNACLE: Lev. 23:34 FIRST-FRUITS OF WINE AND CORN: Deut. 16:13 22nd—SOLEMN ASSEMBLY Deut. 23:34 – 36	PLOWING AND SOWING
BUL OR HESHVAN I Kings 6:38	OCT / NOV	8	2		LATER GRAPES
CHISLEU: Zech. 7:1	NOV / DEC	9	3	25th—FEAST OF TEMPLE DEDICATION John 10:22	SNOW
TEBETH: Esth. 2:16	DEC / JAN	10	4		GREEN GRASS
SEBAT: Zech. 1:7	JAN / FEB	11	5		WINTER FIG
ADAR: Esth. 3:7	FEB / MAR	12	6	14th, 15th—FEAST OF PURIM: Esth. 9:20	ALMOND BLOSSOMS GENERAL HARVEST

SECOND ADAR—INTERCALARY MONTH

The ancient day was divided into morning, noon, and evening: Psalm 55:17.

    a. Morning till noon: I Kings 18:26; Nehemiah 8:3

    b. Noon—heat of day—till about 2 p.m.: Genesis 18:1; I Samuel 11:9

    c. Evening—cool of day—till after sunset: Genesis 3:8. Some have supposed ''cool of day'' was daybreak and right after.

After Israel's exile, the use of hours became common. Day was sunrise to sunset, and was divided into 12 hours (John 11:9).

Day

    a. Third hour—6 to 9 a.m.: Acts 2:15

    b. Sixth hour—9 to 12 noon: John 4:6

    c. Ninth hour—12 to 3 p.m.: Acts 3:1

    d. Twelfth hour—3 to 6 p.m.

Night was from sunset to sunrise. The Romans divided night into four watches—

Night

    a. First watch—evening; 6 to 9 p.m.: Mark 13:35

    b. Second watch—midnight; 9 till midnight: Luke 12:38a

    c. Third watch—cock crowing; 12 midnight till 3 a.m.: Luke 12:38b

    d. Fourth watch—morning; 3 till 6 a.m.: Matthew 14:25

5. Hours: Daniel 5:5; John 11:9

    Illustrative of:

    a. Christ's appointment at the cross: John 12:27

    b. Christ's appointed return: Matthew 24:42,44

    c. Prayer: Acts 3:1

6. Moments: Exodus 33:5; Luke 4:5

    Illustrative of:

    a. The believer's body change at the Rapture: I Corinthians 15:51-53. Philippians 3:20,21; I John 3:2

    b. Brevity of God's anger: Psalm 30:5

    c. Trials: Job 7:18; II Corinthians 4:17

    d. God's judgment: Numbers 16:21,45; Psalm 73:19

    e. Brevity of the wicked's victory: Job 20:5a

    f. Brevity of the hypocrite's joy: Job 20:5b

    g. Brevity of the wealthy: Job 21:13

    h. Quickness of death: Job 34:20

ASTRONOMY

1. Sun: Genesis 1:14,16

    a. To rule the day: Psalm 136:8

    b. Divides seasons: Genesis 1:14

    c. Has its own glory: I Corinthians 15:41

    d. Diffuses light and heat: Psalm 19:6; Ecclesiastes 11:7

    e. Produces fruit: Deuteronomy 33:14

    f. Frequently destructive: II Kings 4:18-20; Psalm 121:6

        Illustrative of:

        —God's favor: Psalm 84:11

        —Christ's coming: Malachi 4:2

        —Christ's glory: Matthew 17:2

        —Future glory of the saints: Matthew 13:43

        —Praise: Psalm 148:3

        —A bridegroom: Psalm 194b,5a

        —A strong man: Psalm 19:5b

        —Power for saints: Judges 5:31

—Supreme rulers: Genesis 37:9; Isaiah 13:10
—Clearness—Christ's purity: Song of Solomon 6:10
—Judgment and calamities: Ezekiel 32:7,8; Amos 8:9-14

2. Moon: Psalm 8:3
   a. To rule the night: Psalm 136:9
   b. The lesser light: Genesis 1:16; Job 31:26
   c. Has its own glory: I Corinthians 15:41
   d. Divides day from night: Genesis 1:14; Jeremiah 31:35
   e. Signs for seasons: Genesis 1:14; Psalm 104:19
   f. Influences vegetation: Deuteronomy 33:14
   g. No light of its own: Job 25:5
   h. Gravitation pull (tides) alluded to: Job 26:10; 38:8,10,11
   i. Lunacy attributed to its influence: Psalm 121:6 with Matthew 4:24
   Illustrative of:
   —Christ's glory in the Bride: Isaiah 60:20; Revelation 21:23
   —Church's light, reflecting the Son's light: Song of Solomon 6:10
   —Church in subjection to Christ: Revelation 12:1
   —Changeableness of kingdoms: Revelation 12:1-5
   —Judgment and calamities: Jeremiah 8:2; Joel 2:10; Matthew 24:29

3. Stars: Psalm 8:3; Deuteronomy 17:3. See STARS in Index.
   a. To rule the night: Psalm 136:9
   b. Infinite in number: Genesis 15:5
   c. Appointed to give light: Jeremiah 31:35
   d. Named: Psalm 147:6; Job 9:9; 38:32
   e. Revolve in fixed orbits: Judges 5:20
   f. Appear of different magnitudes: I Corinthians 15:41
   g. Appear after sunset: Nehemiah 4:21 with Job 3:9
   h. Navigation by them alluded to: Acts 27:20
   Illustrative of:
   —Christ: Numbers 24:17; Revelation 22:16
   —Angels: Job 38:7
   —God's power: Psalm 8:3; Isaiah 40:26
   —Praise: Psalm 148:3
   —Ministers: Revelation 1:16,20; 2:1
   —Reward: Revelation 2:26-28
   —Glory given to saints: Daniel 12:3
   —Judgment and calamities: Jeremiah 8:2; Joel 2:10
   —Judgment—for pride: Obediah 4
   —Apostate teachers: Jude 13

WEATHER

1. Clouds: I Kings 18:44; Matthew 24:30
   a. Established: Proverbs 8:28
   b. Balanced in the air: Job 37:15
   c. Spread out: Psalm 147:8; Job 26:9
   d. Scattered: Job 37:11; Hosea 13:3
   e. Disposed of: Job 37:15
   f. Waters above the firmament: Genesis 1:7
   g. Supply rain: Judges 5:4; Psalm 104:13,14
   h. Supply dew: Proverbs 3:20; Isaiah 18:4
   i. Moderate heat: Isaiah 25:5
   j. Numberless: Job 38:37

Illustrative of:
—Christ's finished work of redemption: Acts 1:9
—Glory of Christ: Matthew 17:5; Revelation 10:1
—Protection: Isaiah 4:5
—Presence of God: Leviticus 16:2
—God's power: Isaiah 19:1
—Glory of God: Exodus 16:10; 40:34
—Unsearchableness of God: II Samuel 22:12; Psalm 97:2
—Guidance: Exodus 13:21; Numbers 9:17:25
—Light: Psalm 78:14; 105:39
—Defense: Exodus 14:19; Psalm 105:39
—Forgiveness: Isaiah 44:22
—Multitudes of persons: Isaiah 60:8
—Wise rulers: II Samuel 23:3,4; Proverbs 16:15
—Hostile armies: Jeremiah 4:13; Ezekiel 38:9,16
—God's judgment: Lamentations 2:1; Ezekiel 30:3
—Fleeting goodness of hypocrisy: Hosea 6:4; 13:3
—False teachers: II Peter 2:17; Jude 12
—The fraudulent: Proverbs 25:14

2. The wind: Ecclesiastes 1:6; Matthew 11:7
   a. North: Proverbs: 25:23
   b. South: Job 37:17
   c. East: Job 27:21
   d. West: Exodus 10:19
   e. Euroclydon: Acts 27:14
   f. Whirlwind: Job 37:9
   g. Drying: Genesis 8:1; Isaiah 11:15
   h. Restrains: Job 28:25; Psalm 107:29
   i. Raises: Psalm 107:25
   j. Changes: Psalm 78:26
   k. Assuages: Matthew 8:26; 14:32
   l. From unknown source: John 3:8
   m. When violent called—
      —Storm: Job 21:18; Psalm 55:8; Ezekiel 13:11,13
      —Tempest: Job 9:17; 27:20
      —Great and strong: I Kings 19:11
      —Mighty: Acts 2:2
      —Fierce: James 3:4
      —Rough: Isaiah 27:8
   Illustrative of:
   —Operation of the Holy Spirit: John 3:8 with Ezekiel 37:9
   —Purity: Job 37:21
   —The life of man: Job 7:7
   —The speeches of the desperate: Job 6:26
   —Terrors which pursue the soul: Job 30:15
   —Molten images: Isaiah 41:29
   —Iniquity and destruction: Isaiah 64:6
   —False doctrines: Ephesians 4:14
   —The wicked: Job 21:18; Psalm 1:4
   —Judgments of God: Isaiah 27:8; Jeremiah 4:11,12
   —Sowing a course of sin: Hosea 8:7
   —Vain hopes: Hosea 12:1
   —Disappointment of expectations: Isaiah 26:18
3 Rain: Deuteronomy 11:11. See RAIN in Index.

    a. Refreshed the earth: Psalm 68:9; 72:6
    b. Makes fruitful the earth: Hebrews 6:7
    c. Replenishes springs and fountains: Psalm 104:8-13
    d. Often accompanied with thunder and lightning: Psalm 135:7
    e. Often accompanied with storm and tempest: Matthew 7:25,27
    f. Often destructive: Ezekiel 13:13-15
    g. Occasioned by condensation of clouds: Job 36:27,28; Ecclesiastes 11:3
      Illustrative of:
      —Greatness and goodness: Job 36:26,27; Acts 14:17
      —Mercy: Matthew 5:45
      —Encouragement to fear God: Jeremiah 5:24
      —Prompts praise to God: Psalm 147:7,8
      —A promise to the obedient: Leviticus 26:4; Deuteronomy 11:14
      —The Word of God: Isaiah 55:10,11
      —Doctrine: Deuteronomy 32:2
      —Graces of Christ: Psalm 72:6; Hosea 6:3
      —Spritual blessings: Psalm 68:9; 84:6
      —Righteousness: Hosea 10:12
      —God's judgments: Job 20:23; Psalm 11:6
      —Oppression: Proverbs 28:3
4. Snow: Proverbs 25:13. See SNOW in Index.
    a. Winter—the time of snow: II Samuel 23:20
    b. Cold—fear of snow: Proverbs 31:21
    c. Melted by heat: Job 24:19
    d. Treasures—for the earth's good: Job 38:22; Isaiah 55:10
      Illustrative of:
      —God's power: Job 37:5,6
      —The Word of God: Isaiah 55:10,11
      —Purity: Matthew 28:3; Revelation 1:14
      —A cleansed soul: Psalm 51:7; Isaiah 1:18
5. Seasons: Genesis 1:14; 8:22. See AGRICULTURE in Index.
6. Sun. See SUN in Index.

WATER SUPPLIES

1. Water: Genesis 1:2
    a. For man and beast: Isaiah 41:17; I Kings 18:4,5
    b. For vegetation: Genesis 2:5,6; Job 14:9
    c. For culinary purposes: Exodus 12:9
    d. For washing: Genesis 18:4; 24:32
    e. Described as—
      —Fluid: Psalm 78:16; Proverbs 30:4
      —Unstable: Genesis 49:4
      —Penetrating: Psalm 109:18
      —Reflecting images: Proverbs 27:19
      —Cleansing: Ezekiel 36:25; Ephesians 5:26
      —Congealed by cold: Job 38:29; Psalm 147:16,17
      —Refreshing: Job 22:7; Proverbs 25:25
    f. Found in—
      —Rocks: Exodus 17:6
      —Springs: Joshua 15:19
      —Pools: I Kings 22:38; Nehemiah 2:14
      —Ponds: Exodus 7:19; Isaiah 19:10
      —Fountains: I Kings 18:5; II Chronicles 32:3
      —Wells: Genesis 21:19

        —Brooks: II Samuel 17:20; I Kings 18:5
        —Streams: Psalm 78:16; Isaiah 35:6
        —Rivers: Isaiah 8:7; Jeremiah 2:18
        —The seas: Genesis 1:9,10; Isaiah 11:9
        —The clouds: Genesis 1:7; Job 26:8,9

    g. Rises in vapor: Eccesiastes 1:7 with Psalm 104:8
    h. Descends as rain: Deuteronomy 11:11; II Samuel 21:10
    Illustrative of:
        —Voice of Christ: Revelation 1:15
        —Salvation: Isaiah 55:1
        —Gifts and graces of the Spirit: Isaiah 41:17,18; John 7:38,39
        —The Word of God: Ephesians 5:26 with John 15:3
        —The support of God: Isaiah 8:6
        —Counsel in the heart: Proverbs 20:5
        —Wise words: Proverbs 18:4
        —Contentment: Psalm 23:2
        —Healing: II Kings 5:14; John 5:4; 9:7
        —Exaltation: Numbers 24:7
        —Persecutors: Psalm 124:4,5
        —Persecution: Psalm 88:17
        —Hostile armies: Isaiah 8:7; 17:13
        —Severe afllictions: Psalm 66:12; Isaiah 43:2
        —Wrath of God: Hosea 5:10
        —Faintness: Psalm 22:14
        —Wavering disposition: Genesis 49:4
        —Cowardice: Joshua 7:5; Ezekiel 7:17
        —Strife and Contention: Proverbs 17:14
        —Rapid flow—following the line of least resistance; career of the wicked: Job 24:18; Psalm 58:7
        —Different nations: Jeremiah 51:13; Revelation 17:1,15

2. Seas: Genesis 1:10. See OCEANS in Index.
    a. Of immense extent: Job 11:9; Psalm 104:25
    b. Of great depth: Psalm 68:22
    c. Replenished by rivers: Ecclesiastes 1:7; Ezekiel 47:8
    d. Sand its barrier: Jeremiah 5:22; Job 6:3
    e. Inhabited by numerous creatures: Psalm 104:25,26
    f. Raised by the wind: Psalm 107:25,26; Jonah 1:4
    g. Its waves are—
        —Raised: Psalm 93:3; 107:25
        —Tossed to and fro: Jeremiah 5:22
        —Multitudinous: Jeremiah 51:42
        —Tumultuous: Luke 21:25; Jude 13
    h. Habitation of islands: Ezekiel 26:18
    i. Sites of commerce: Genesis 49:13; Ezekiel 27:3
    Illustrative of:
        —Righteousness: Isaiah 48:18
        —Peace: Revelation 4:6; 15:2
        —Knowledge of God: Isaiah 11:9; Habakkuk 2:14
        —God's hiding place for forgiven sin: Micah 7:19
        —Heavy affliction: Isaiah 43:2; Lamentations 2:13
        —The troubled wicked: Isaiah 57:20,21
        —Hostile armies: Isaiah 5:30; Ezekiel 26:3,4
        —Unsteadiness and devastating: James 1:6

3. Rivers: Job 28:10

a. Enclosed with banks: Daniel 12:5
b. Flow through valleys: Psalm 104:8,10
c. Part into many streams: Genesis 2:10; Isaiah 11:15
d. Run into the sea: Ecclesiastes 1:7; Ezekiel 47:8
e. Supplies drinking water: Jeremiah 2:18
f. For commerce: Psalm 46:4; Isaiah 23:3
g. Promote vegetation: Genesis 2:10
h. For bathing: Exodus 2:5
i. Abound with fish: Leviticus 11:9,10
   Illustrative of:
   —Grace in Christ: Isaiah 32:2 with John 1:16
   —Gifts of the Holy Spirit: Psalm 46:4; Isaiah 41:18; 43:19,20
   —Abundance: Job 20:17; 29:6
   —Peace: Isaiah 66:12
   —Overflowing of Divine love and grace: Ezekiel 47
   —Fruitfulness: Psalm 1:3; Jeremiah 17:8
   —The eruption of an invading army: Isaiah 59:19; Jeremiah 46:7,8
   —Heavy affliction: Psalm 69:2; Isaiah 43:2
   —God's judgment: Isaiah 19:1-8; Jeremiah 47:2
   Important rivers—
   —Abana and Pharpar—cleanness: II Kings 5:12
   —Ahava—lacking: Ezra 8:15
   —Arnon—weakness: Deuteronomy 2:36
   —Babylon—captivity; lost joy: Psalm 137:1
   —Chebar—God speaks: Ezekiel 10:15,20
   —Eden—pleasure: Genesis 2:10
   —Egypt—division: Genesis 15:18
   —Ethiopia—woe: Isaiah 18:1
   —Euphrates—stumbling; vengeance: Jeremiah 46:6,10
   —Gihon—gives forth: Genesis 2:13
   —Gozan—captivity: II Kings 17:6
   —Jordan—descender: Numbers 34:12
      Jordan illustrative of:
      —God's promise and presence: Joshua 3:10,11
      —Passage: Joshua 3:12-17; II Kings 2:8
      —Healing: II Kings 5:10,14
      —Approval: Matthew 3:13-17
      —Uncleanness: II Kings 5:10-12
      —Pride: Zechariah 11:3
      —Death: Judges 3:28,29; Jeremiah 12:5
   —Jotbath—refreshing: Deuteronomy 10:7
   —Kanab—straight; erect: Joshua 16:8
   —Pison—dispersive (scatter): Genesis 2:11 with Acts 11:19
4. Brooks:
   a. Canaan abounded in: Deuteronomy 8:7
   b. Afford protection: Isaiah 19:6
   c. Abound with fish: Isaiah 19:8
   Illustrative of:
   —Wisdom: Proverbs 18:4
   —Help in distress: Psalm 110:7
   —Temporal abundance: Job 20:17
   —Deceit: Job 6:15
   Brooks in the Bible—
   —Besor—faint; weakness: I Samuel 30:9,10,21

—Cherith—need supplied: I Kings 17:3-5
—Eschol—fruitfulness: Numbers 13:23,24
—Gaash—agitate: II Samuel 23:30
—Jabbok—prevail for blessing: Genesis 32:22-28
—Kidron—sorrow; judgment: I Kings 15:13
—Kishon—crooked; death: I Kings 18:40
—Willows—judgment: Isaiah 15:7
—Zered—advancing; growth: Deuteronomy 2:13

5. Wells: Deuteronomy 6:11
   a. Supplied by springs and rain: Proverbs 16:22; Psalm 84:6
   b. Surrounded by trees: Genesis 49:22; Exodus 15:27
   c. Near encampments: Genesis 21:30; 26:18
   d. Outside cities: Genesis 24:11; John 4:6,8
   e. In courtyards of houses: II Samuel 17:18
   f. In the desert: II Chronicles 26:10
   g. Frequent cause of strife: Genesis 21:25; 26:21,22
   h. Often stopped up by the enemy: Genesis 26:15,18; II Kings 19:25
   Illustrative of:
   —Salvation: Isaiah 12:3
   —The indwelling Spirit: John 4:14
   —The mouth of the righteous: Proverbs 10:11
   —Wisdom and understanding: Proverbs 16:22; 18:4
   —Enjoyments: Proverbs 5:15
   —Fruitfulness: Genesis 49:22

6. Springs and Fountains: Deuteronomy 8:7; Psalm 74:15; 104:10
   a. Come from the great deep: Genesis 7:11; Job 38:16
   b. In hills and valleys: Deuteronomy 8:7; Psalm 104:10
   c. Refreshment for beasts and fowl: Psalm 104:11,12
   d. Fruitfulness to the earth: I Kings 18:5; Joel 3:18
   Illustrative of:
   —God: Psalm 36:9; Jeremiah 2:13; 17:13
   —Christ's blood: Zechariah 13:1
   —The Holy Spirit: John 7:38,39
   —Constant supplies of grace: Psalm 87:7
   —Eternal life: John 4:14; Revelation 21:6
   —Means of grace: Isaiah 41:18
   —A good wife: Proverbs 5:18
   —Numerous prosperity: Deuteronomy 33:28
   —Spiritual wisdom: Proverbs 16:22; 18:4
   —The law of the wise: Proverbs 13:14
   —Godly fear: Proverbs 14:27
   —Guidance and satisfaction: Isaiah 58:11
   —Israel's wickedness: Jeremiah 6:7
   —Corruption—the natural heart: James 3:11 with Matthew 15:18,19
   —Backsliding: Proverbs 25:26
   —Punishment and judgment (dried up): Psalm 107:33,34

7. Pools and Ponds: Isaiah 19:10; 35:7
   a. Filled by rain: Psalm 84:6
   b. Supplied gardens: Ecclesiastes 2:6
   c. Preserved fish: Isaiah 19:10
   d. Supplied cities with water: II Kings 20:20 (Siloam: John 9:7)
   e. Water of pools brought into cities by conduit or ditch: Isaiah 22:11 with II Kings 20:20. See CONDUIT in Index.

Illustrative of:
—Gifts of the Spirit: Isaiah 35:7; 41:18
—Nineveh—doomed: Nahum 2:8
—Desolation: Isaiah 14:23
Pools in the Bible—
—Bethesda—kindness: John 5:2
—Gibeon—death: II Samuel 2:13
—Hebron—association: II Samuel 4:12
—Samaria—uncleanness: I Kings 22:38
—Siloam—healing: John 9:7
—Upper—faith: Isaiah 7:3-9
—Lower—trouble: Isaiah 22:5-9
—Old—blessings for obedience: Isaiah 22:11

AGRICULTURE—Genesis 3:23

1. Seedtime: Genesis 8:22
   Illustrative of:
   a. The Word of God: Luke 8:11; I Peter 1:23
   b. Preaching the gospel: Matthew 13:3,32; I Corinthians 9:11
   c. Soul-winning: Psalm 126:6
   d. Spiritual life: I John 3:9
   e. Christian liberality: II Corinthians 9:6
   f. Dispersed Israel: Zechariah 10:9
   g. Men's works: Job 4:8; Galatians 6:7,8
   h. Christ's death and its effects: John 12:24
   i. Burial of a body: I Corinthians 15:36-38
2. Plowing: Isaiah 61:5
   Illustrative of:
   a. Effort; service: Genesis 3:17-19; II Timothy 2:6
   b. Repentance and reformation: Jeremiah 4:3; Hosea 10:12
   c. Peace and prosperity: Isaiah 2:4; Micah 4:3
   d. Severe cause of affliction: Hosea 10:11
   e. A course of sin: Job 4:8; Hosea 10:13
   f. Labor of ministers: I Corinthians 9:10
   g. Continual devotedness: Luke 9:62
3. Summer: Psalm 74:17
   Illustrative of:
   a. Wisdom: Proverbs 10:5
   b. Diligence: Proverbs 30:25
   c. Seasons of grace: Jeremiah 8:20
4. Harvest: Mark 4:29; II Samuel 23:13
   Illustrative of:
   a. Supply: Ecclesiastes 5:9
   b. A season of grace: Jeremiah 8:20
   c. God's protection: Isaiah 18:4
   d. Refreshing message: Proverbs 25:13
   e. Judgment and wrath: Jeremiah 51:33; Joel 3:13
5. Reaping: Job 24:6 with Leviticus 23:10
   Illustrative of:
   a. Rejoicing: Psalm 126:5,6
   b. Reward of the righteous: Hosea 10:12
   c. Reward and the wicked: Job 4:8; Proverbs 22:8
   d. Spiritual labors: I Corinthians 9:11

    e. Gathering in of souls: John 4:38
    f. God's judgment: Revelation 14:14-16
    g. Final judgment: Matthew 13:30,39-43
6. Threshing: I Chronicles 21:20
   Illustrative of:
    a. Victory: Isaiah 41:15,16; Micah 4:13
    b. Judgments of God: Isaiah 21:10; Jeremiah 51:33
    c. Imperfection: Luke 22:31
7. Fruit: Genesis 1:29; Ecclesiastes 2:5; Deuteronomy 22:9
   Illustrative of:
    a. Effects of repentance: Matthew 3:8
    b. Works of the Spirit: Galatians 5:22,23; Ephesians 5:9
    c. Doctrines of Christ: Song of Solomon 2:3
    d. Good works: Matthew 7:17,18; Philippians 4:17
    e. Holy conversation: Proverbs 12:14; 18:20
    f. Praise: Hebrews 13:15
    g. Godliness: Proverbs 11:30
    h. Rewards to saints: Isaiah 3:10
    i. Industry: Proverbs 31:16,31
    j. Converts: Psalm 72:16; John 4:36
    k. Evil conduct: Matthew 7:17; 12:33
    l. Rewards to the wicked: Jeremiah 17:9,10
8. Vine—vineyards: Deuteronomy 6:11; 8:8
   Illustrative of:
    a. Christ: John 15:1,2
    b. Israel: Psalm 80:8; Isaiah 5:2,7
    c. Fruitful branches: John 15:5
    d. Professors of religion: John 15:2,6
    e. Growth of saints: Hosea 14:7
    f. Purifying: John 15:2
    g. Works of wickedness: Hosea 10:1
    h. Peace and prosperity: I Kings 4:25; Zechariah 3:10
    i. Joy: Isaiah 24:13,14
9. Winter: Psalm 74:14
   Illustrative of: Spiritual adversity: Song of Solomon 2:11: Matthew 24:20

HORTICULTURE

1. Trees: Genesis 2:9
    a. Various sizes: Ezekiel 17:24
    b. Beautify the earth: Genesis 2:9
    c. Forests: Isaiah 44:14
    d. Some for fuel: Isaiah 44:14-16
    e. Some fruitbearing for man and beast: Genesis 1:29,30
    f. Some for shadow and wood: II Chronicles 2:8,10; Job 40:21
    g. Each kind has its own seed: Genesis 1:11,12
    h. Propagated by fowls carrying seed: Ezekiel 17:3,5
    i. Planted by man: Leviticus 19:23
    j. Each kind known by its fruit: Matthew 12:33
    k. Nourished by the earth, rain, sap: Genesis 1:12; Psalm 104:16; Isaiah 44:14
      Illustrative of:
      —Christ: Romans 11:24; Revelation 22:2,14
      —Wisdom: Proverbs 3:18
      —Christ's innocency: Luke 23:31

—Life of the saints: Psalm 1:1-3
—Conversation of the righteous: Proverbs 11:30; 15:4
—Fruitfulness of the saints: Numbers 24:6
—Fruitfulness: Isaiah 29:17
—Prosperity of the saints: Isaiah 65:22
—Kings: Daniel 4:10-14
—Barrenness: Hosea 9:16; Isaiah 7:2
—Evil fruit: Matthew 7:17-19
—A useless person: Isaiah 56:3
—Judgment: Isaiah 32:16a,19
—Destruction: Isaiah 10:17,18; Jeremiah 21:14
  Some outstanding trees—
  —Cedar: Isaiah 41:19. See CEDAR in Index.
    Illustrative of:
    —Christ's majesty and glory: Song of Solomon 5:15
    —Israel's glory and beauty: Numbers 24:6; Ezekiel 17:22,23
    —Growth of saints: Psalm 92:12
    —Powerful nations: Ezekiel 31:3; Amos 2:9
    —Arrogant rulers: Isaiah 2:13; 10:33,34
  —Fig: Song of Solomon 2:11,13
    Illustrative of:
    —Prosperity of peace: I Kings 4:25; Micah 4:4
    —Good works: Matthew 7:16
    —Sweetness among saints: Judges 9:11
    —Profession of religion: Matthew 21:19; Luke 13:6,7
    —Judgment: Isaiah 34:4; Nahum 3:12
  —Olive: Deuteronomy 6:11
    Illustrative of:
    —God's honor: Judges 9:9
    —Christ: Romans 11:17,24
    —Israel's remnant: Isaiah 24:13; Jeremiah 11:16
    —The righteous: Psalm 52:8
    —Children of godly parents: Psalm 128:3
    —Probably emblems of peace: Genesis 8:11
    —Gentiles: Romans 11:17,24
  —Palm: Exodus 15:27
    Illustrative of:
    —The righteous: Psalm 92:12
    —Fruitfulness: Psalm 92:12,14
    —Emblem of victory: Revelation 7:9
    —Idolatry: Jeremiah 10:5
    —Calamity: Joel 1:12
  —Pomegranate: Numbers 13:23; Deuteronomy 8:8
    Illustrative of:
    —God's favor: Haggai 2:19
    —Saints: Song of Solomon 7:12
    —Christ's beauty: Song of Solomon 6:7
    —Satisfaction: Song of Solomon 8:2
    —Calamity: Joel 1:12
2. Herbs: Genesis 1:11,12
  a. As food: Genesis 1:28,29; 9:3; Proverbs 15:17
  b. Some bitter: Exodus 12:8; Numbers 9:11
  c. Some poisonous: II Kings 4:39,40
    Illustrative of:

—Grace given to saints: Isaiah 18:4
—The wicked: II Kings 19:26; Psalm 37:2
3. Flowers: Psalm 103:15; Song of Solomon 6:2,3. See FLOWERS in Index.
   a. Beautiful: Matthew 6:29
   b. Fragrant: Song of Solomon 5:13
   c. Evanescent: Psalm 103:16; Isaiah 40:8
   Illustrative of:
   —Christ's glory: Matthew 6:28,29 with Matthew 12:42
   —Israel's downfall: Isaiah 28:1
   —Shortness of life: Job 14:2; Psalm 103:15
   —Rich men: James 1:10,11
   —Glory of man: I Peter 1:24
4. Grass: Numbers 22:4; II Samuel 23:4
   Illustrative of:
   —Saints refreshed by grace: Psalm 72:6; Micah 5:7
   —Uncertainty of life: I Peter 1:24
   —Prosperity of the wicked: Psalm 92:7
   —Wickedness: II Kings 19:26; Isaiah 37:27
   —Calamity: Isaiah 15:5,6

THE ANIMAL KINGDOM

1. Beasts: Genesis 2:19; I Kings 4:33
   a. Differ in flesh from birds and fishes: I Corinthians 15:39
   b. Herb for food: Genesis 1:30
   c. Instinctively fear man: Genesis 9:2
   d. By nature wild: Psalm 50:11; Mark 1:13
   e. Many noisome and destructive: Leviticus 26:6; Ezekiel 5:17
   f. Many kinds domestic: Genesis 36:6; 45:17
   g. Possessed of instinct: Isaiah 1:3
   h. Capable of being tamed: James 3:7
   Illustrative of:
   —Wisdom: Job 12:7
   —Kingdoms: Daniel 7:11,17; 8:4
   —Different nationalities: Daniel 4:12,21
   —The wicked: Psalm 49:20; Titus 1:12
   —Ungodly professors: II Peter 2:12; Jude 10
   —Persecutors: I Corinthians 15:32
   —Antichrist: Revelation 13:2; 20:4
   Some Outstanding Animals
   —Sheep: Deuteronomy 14:4
      Illustrative of:
      —Jews: Psalm 74:1; 78:52
      —Christ's own: John 10:7-26; I Peter 5:2
      —Patience: Isaiah 53:7
      —Restored sinners: Luke 15:5,7
      —God's judgment: Psalm 44:11
      —The wicked in their death: Psalm 49:14
      —The unregenerate: Matthew 10:6
      —Separation (from goats): Matthew 25:32,33

      —Ox: Isaiah 1:3
   Illustrative of:
   Ministers: Isaiah 30:24
   —Minister's right to support: I Corinthians 9:9,10
   —The Gospel feast. Matthew 22:4

—Saints under persecution: Jeremiah 11:19
—Heifer: Genesis 15:9
  Illustrative of:
  —A wife: Judges 14:18
  —Backsliding Israel: Hosea 4:6
  —Israel's disobedience: Hosea 10:11
  —Moab in confusion: Isaiah 15:5; Jeremiah 48:34
  —Beauty of Egypt: Jeremiah 46:20
  —Luxury of the Chaldees: Jeremiah 50:11
—Fox: Judges 15:4
  Illustrative of:
  —False prophets: Ezekiel 13:4
  —Cunningness and deceitfulness: Luke 13:32
  —Enemies of Christians: Song of Solomon 2:15
  —Annoyance: Judges 15:4-6
  —Desolation: Lamentations 5:18
—Ass: Genesis 12:16
  Illustrative of:
  —Burden-bearing: Genesis 49:14
  —Humility—carrying Jesus: Matthew 21:7
  —Uncleanness: Leviticus 11:2,3; Deuteronomy 22:10 with II Corinthians 6:17
  —Wildness and stupidity: Job 11:12; Psalm 32:9
—Swine: Leviticus 11:7,8
  Illustrative of:
  —Filthiness: II Peter 2:2
  —The wicked: Matthew 7:6
  —Apostasy: II Peter 2:2
  —Destruction: Psalm 80:13
—Hart (hind; deer): Deuteronomy 12:15; 14:5
  Illustrative of:
  —Voice of God: Psalm 29:9
  —Freedom: Genesis 49:21
  —Kindness and affection: Proverbs 5:19
  —Christ: Song of Solomon 2:9; 8:14
  —Converted sinners: Isaiah 35:6
  —Surefootedness of the saints: Psalm 18:33
  —Longing for God: Psalm 42:1,2
  —Persecution: Lamentations 1:6
—Horse: Genesis 47:14; Ezekiel 27:14
  Illustrative of:
  —Beauty of the Church: Song of Solomon 1:9
  —Strength and conquest: Job 39:19; Revelation 6:2
  —Burden-bearing: Ezra 2:66; Nehemiah 7:68
  —Headstrong disposition: Psalm 32:9; Jeremiah 8:6
  —War and its consequences: Job 39:21; Revelation 6:4-8
—Wolf: Genesis 49:27
  Illustrative of:
  —Destruction: John 10:12
  —The wicked: Matthew 10:16
  —Wicked rulers: Ezekiel 22:27
  —False teachers: Acts 20:29
  —Deception: Matthew 7:15
  —The devil: John 10:12
  —Fierce enemies: Jeremiah 5:6; Luke 10:3

—Peace (in the millennium): Isaiah 11:6; 65:25
—Lion: II Kings 17:25,26
  Illustrative of:
  —Christ: Revelation 5:5
  —Israel: Numbers 24:9
  —The tribe of Judah: Genesis 49:9
  —Strength: Judges 14:18
  —Activity: Deuteronomy 33:22
  —Courage: II Samuel 17:10
  —Protection: Isaiah 31:4
  —Boldness of saints: Proverbs 28:1
  —Majesty: Proverbs 30:30
  —Persecution of saints: II Timothy 4:17
  —Satan: I Peter 5:8
  —Imaginary fears: Proverbs 22:13; 26:13
  —Contentment (in the millennium): Isaiah 11:7

2. Birds: Genesis 2:19; 8:20
  a. Flesh differs from beasts and fishes: I Corinthians 15:39
  b. Propogated by eggs: Deuteronomy 22:6; Jeremiah 17:11
  c. Make, and dwell in nests: Matthew 8:20
  d. Herb for food: Genesis 1:30
  e. Instinctively fear man: Genesis 9:2
  f. Man has power over: Psalm 8:8
  g. Some can be tamed: James 3:7
  h. Some granivorous: Matthew 13:4
  i. Some carnivorous: Genesis 15:11; Deuteronomy 28:26
  j. Hostile to strange kinds: Jeremiah 12:9
  k. Some migratory: Jeremiah 8:7
  l. Furnished with claws: Daniel 4:33
  m. Each has own peculiar note: Psalm 104:12; Ecclesiastes 12:4
  Illustrative of:
  —Wisdom: Job 12:7
  —Sacrifice: Genesis 8:20; Leviticus 1:14
  —Different nationalities: Ezekiel 31:6; Matthew 13:32
  —Unsettled people: Proverbs 27:8; Isaiah 16:2
  —Cruel kings: Isaiah 46:11
  —Hostile nations: Jeremiah 12:9
  —Designs of the wicked: Psalm 124:7; Proverbs 7:23
  —The devil and his spirits: Matthew 13:4,19
  —Death: Ecclesiastes 9:12
  Some Outstanding Birds
  —Dove: Deuteronomy 14:11
  Illustrative of:
  —Christ's meekness: Song of Solomon 5:12
  —The Holy Spirit: Matthew 3:16; John 1:32
  —Harmless: Matthew 10:16
  —Comeliness: Song of Solomon: 2:14
  —Sweetness: Song of Solomon 2:14
  —Life: Genesis 8:8,10,12
  —Peace: Genesis 8:11
  —The harbinger of spring: Song of Solomon: 2:12
  —Converts to the Church: Isaiah 60:8
  —Return of Israel from captivity: Hosea 11:11
  —Mourners: Isaiah 38:14; 59:11

—Eagle: Leviticus 11:13,18; Lamentations 4:19

Illustrative of:

—God's care for His own: Exodus 19:4; Deuteronomy 32:11

—Wisdom and zeal: Ezekiel 1:10; Revelation 4:7

—Protection: Revelation 12:14

—Renewed strength of the saints: Psalm 103:5

—The heavenlies: Isaiah 40:31

—Powerful kings: Ezekiel 17:3; Hosea 8:1

—Swiftness—man's days: Job 9:26

—Swiftness—fleeting riches: Proverbs 23:5

—Swiftness—hostile armies: Deuteronomy 28:49; Jeremiah 4:13

—Height—fatal security of the wicked: Jeremiah 49:16; Obediah 4

—Standard of Rome's armies: Matthew 24:15,28

—Ostrich: Job 39:13. See OSTRICH in Index.

—Void of wisdom: Job 39:17

—Imprudent: Job 39:15

—Cruel to her young: Job 39:16

—Rapid in movement: Job 39:18

   Illustrative of:

   —Unnatural cruelty to Jews: Lamentations 4:3

   —Extreme desolation: Job 30:29 (*margin*)

3. Fish: I Kings 4:33; Job 12:8,9

   a. Flesh different from beasts and fowls: I Corinthians 15:39

   b. Cannot live without water: Isaiah 50:2

   c. Man has dominion over: Psalm 8:8

   Illustrative of:

   —The visible Church: Matthew 13:48

   —Saints (good): Matthew 13:48,49

   —Sinners (bad): Matthew 13:48,49

   —Sufferings for sin: Exodus 7:21; Ezekiel 38:20

   —Those snared by the wicked: Habakkuk 1:14

   —Ignorance of future events: Ecclesiastes 9:12

   —Egypt's population: Ezekiel 29:45

4. Insects: Genesis 1:24,25; Leviticus 11:21-24

   a. Ant: Proverbs 30:25. See ANT in Index.

   Illustrative of:

   —Wisdom: Proverbs 6:6

   —Order: Proverbs 6:7-11

   b. Locusts: Exodus 10:12,13

   Illustrative of:

   —Wisdom and order: Proverbs 30:24,27

   —Horses prepared for battle: Joel 2:4; Revelation 9:7

   —Tossing to and fro: Exodus 10:13,19

   —Punishment for sin: Deuteronomy 28:38,42; Joel 1:4; 2:25

   —Destructive armies: Joel 1:6,7; 2:2-9

   —False teachers and apostasy: Revelation 9:3

   —Ungodly rulers: Nahum 3:17

   —Destruction of God's enemies: Nahum 3:15

   c. Moth: Job 4:19

   Illustrative of:

   —God's judgments: Isaiah 50:9; Hosea 5:12.

   —Suffering judgment: Job 13:28

   —Corruption: Matthew 6:19,20

   —Man's folly in earthly things: Job 27:18

   —Destruction: James 5:12
  d. Scorpion: Deuteronomy 8:15
   Illustrative of:
   —Wicked men: Ezekiel 2:6
   —Chastisement: I Kings 12:11
   —Ministers of antichrist: Revelation 9:3,5,10
   —Defeat: Luke 10:19
 5. Reptiles—serpents: Job 26:13
  a. Produced from eggs: Isaiah 59:5
  b. Creep on their bellies: Genesis 3:14
  c. Food mingled with dust: Micah 7:17
  d. Many kinds poisonous: Deuteronomy 32:24; Psalm 58:4
  e. Some are tame: James 3:7
   Illustrative of:
   —Crookedness: Job 26:13; Isaiah 27:1
   —Subtleness: Genesis 3:1; Matthew 10:16
   —Uncleanness: Matthew 7:10
   —The curse of sin: Genesis 3:14
   —Punishment for sin: Numbers 21:6; I Corinthians 10:9
   —Defeat: Luke 10:19; Revelation 20:2,10
   —The devil: Genesis 3:1 with II Corinthians 11:3; Revelation 12:9
   —Hypocrites: Matthew 23:33
   —Destructive enemies: Isaiah 14:29; Jeremiah 8:17
   —Sharp tongue: Psalm 140:3
   —Drunkenness: Proverbs 23:31,32
   —The tribe of Dan: Genesis 49:17
   —Death and healing: Numbers 21:7-9; John 3:14,15

TOPOGRAPHY

1. Mountains: Genesis 7:19,20; Deuteronomy 11:11. See MOUNTAIN TOP in Index.
  a. Collect vapors from the earth: Psalm 104:6,8
  b. Sources of springs and rivers: Deuteronomy 8:7; Psalm 104:8,10
  c. Many are exceeding high: Psalm 104:18; Isaiah 2:14
  d. Defense to a country: Psalm 125:2
  e. Abound with—
   —Herbs: Proverbs 27:25
   —Minerals: Deuteronomy 8:9; 33:15
   —Stones for buildings: I Kings 5:14,17
   —Forests: II Kings 19:23
   —Game: I Samuel 26:20; I Chronicles 12:8
   —Vineyards: II Chronicles 26:10; Amos 9:13
    Illustrative of:
    —God's righteousness: Psalm 36:6
    —God's glory: Psalm 148:9
    —Stability: Psalm 65:6
    —Strength: Psalm 95:4
    —Pillars of heaven: Job 26:11
    —Fortification: Psalm 125:2; Amos 6:1
    —Refuge: Genesis 14:10; Hebrews 11:38
    —Pasturage: Exodus 3:1; Psalm 147:8
    —Fruit: II Chronicles 26:10; Jeremiah 31:5
    —The Church: Isaiah 2:2; Daniel 2:35,44,45
    —Worship: Genesis 22:2,5; Exodus 3:12
    —Victory: Isaiah 13:2; 30:17

        —Persons in authority: Psalm 72:3; Isaiah 44:23
        —Abundance: Amos 9:13
        —Joy: Isaiah 44:23; 55:12
        —Proud and haughty persons: Isaiah 2:14
        —Judgments: Isaiah 41:15; Jeremiah 51:25
        —Desolations: Isaiah 42:15; Malachi 1:3

2. Valleys: Deuteronomy 11:11
  a. Defined—
      —Plains: Deuteronomy 1:7
      —Vales: Joshua 10:40
      —Dales: Genesis 14:17; II Samuel 18:18
      —Fat valleys when fruitful: Isaiah 28:1,4
      —Rough valleys when barren: Deuteronomy 21:4
  b. Watered by mountain streams; Psalm 104:8,10
  c. Abounds in fountains and springs: Deuteronomy 8:7; Isaiah 41:18
    Illustrative of:
      —Church of Christ: Song of Solomon 6:11
      —Blessings: II Corinthians 20:26
      —Removal of obstacles: Isaiah 40:4; Luke 3:5
      —Victory: Joshua 10:12-14; I Kings 20:23,28
      —Prosperity: Numbers 24:6
      —Disobedience—weeping: Judges 2:1-5; Matthew 26:75
      —Growth—palm trees: Deuteronomy 34:3
      —Refreshings. Joel 3.18
      —Holiness: Psalm 60:6
      —Craftsmanship: I Chronicles 4:14
      —Discouragement: Numbers 32:9
      —Separation or division: I Samuel 13:18
      —Enemies-giants: Joshua 15:8; 18:16
      —War: Genesis 14:8; II Chronicles 35:22
      —Defeat: Hosea 1:5
      —Judgment: Joshua 7:24-26
      —Death: Ezekiel 39:11; II Kings 14:7

3. Deserts (wilderness): Exodus 5:3; Deuteronomy 1:19
  a. Barren: John 6:31
  b. Uninhabitable and lonesome: Matthew 14:15; Jeremiah 2:6
  c. Uncultivated: Numbers 20:5; Jeremiah 2:2
  d. Desolate: Ezekiel 6:14
  e. Dry and without water: Exodus 17:1; Deuteronomy 8:15
  f. Trackless: Job 12:24; Isaiah 43:19,20
  g. Waste and howling: Deuteronomy 32:10
  h. Require guides: Numbers 10:31; Deuteronomy 32:10
  i. Infested by wild beasts and serpents: Deuteronomy 8:15; Isaiah 13:21
    Illustrative of:
      —Barrenness: Psalm 106:9; 107:33,35
      —Those void of blessings: Hosea 2:3
      —The world: Song of Solomon 3:6; 8:5
      —The Gentiles: Isaiah 35:1,6; 41:19
      —Desolation by armies: Jeremiah 12:10-17; 50:12
    Prominent deserts—
      —Arabian, or great desert—defeat of enemies: Exodus 23:31
      —Beth-aven—vanity: Joshua 18:12
      —Beer-sheba—well; refreshment: Genesis 21:14
      —Damascus—obedience: I Kings 19:15

—Edom—hostility: II Kings 3:4-9
—Engedi—place of hiding: I Samuel 24:1
—Gaza—inquiry; strong: Acts 8:26
—Gibeon—civil war: II Samuel 2:24
—Jureal—God's victory: II Chronicles 20:16,17
—Judaea—affliction and hardship: Matthew: 3:1
—Kadesh—sanctuary: Psalm 29:8
—Kedemoth—disappointment: Deuteronomy 2:26-30
—Maon—pursued: I Samuel 23:24,25
—Paran—ornamental: Genesis 21:21
—Red Sea—God's deliverance: Exodus 13:18
—Shur—a wall; defense: Exodus 15:22
—Sin—God's fury: Exodus 16:1; Ezekiel 30:15,16
—Sinai—folly: Exodus 19:1,2 with 32:1-6
—Zin—rebellion; to prick: Numbers 27:14
—Ziph—comforted: I Samuel 23:14-18

4. Caves: Genesis 23:20; Isaiah 2:19
Illustrative of:
—Dwelling places: Genesis 19:3
—Rest: I Samuel 24:3; I Kings 19:9
—Concealment: I Samuel 13:6; 14:1
—Evil companions: Jeremiah 7:11; Matthew 21:13
—No protection from God's judgment: Isaiah 2:19; Revelation 6:15
—Death: Genesis 23:19; John 11:38
Special Caves—
—Adullam—thirst: I Chronicles 11:15-17
—Engedi—place of hiding: I Samuel 24:1-3
—Machpelah—burial: Genesis 23:9
—Makkedah—place of shepherds: Joshua 10:16,17

5. Earthquakes: I Kings 19:11
a. Frequently accompanied by—
—Volcanic eruptions: Psalm 104:32; Nahum 1:5
—Tempestuous sea: II Samuel 22:8,16; Psalm 18:7
—Opening of the earth: Numbers 16:31,32
—Overturning of mountains: Psalm 46:2; Zechariah 14:4
—Rending of rocks: Matthew 27:51
b. Islands and mountains liable to them: Psalm 114:4-7; Revelation 6:14
Illustrative of:
—God's power: Job 9:6; Hebrews 12:26
—God's presence: Psalm 68:7,8; 114:7
—Anger: Psalm 18:7; Isaiah 13:13
—Sign of Christ's coming: Matthew 24:3,7
—God's judgment: Isaiah 24:19,20; 29:6
—Overthrow of kingdoms: Haggai 2:6,22; Revelation 6:12-17

6. Rocks: Job 28:9,10
Illustrative of:
a. God as creator: Deuteronomy 32:18
b. God as strength: Psalm 18:1,2; Isaiah 17:10
c. God as defense: Psalm 31:2,3
d. God as refuge: Psalm 94:22
e. God as salvation: Deuteronomy 32:15; Psalm 89:26; 95:1
f. Christ as refuge: Isaiah 32:2
g. Christ as foundation: I Peter 2:6
h. Christ as source of gifts: I Corinthians 10:4

i. Worship: Judges 6:20,21,26

j. Food: Deuteronomy 32:13; Job 29:6

k. Safety: Psalm 27:5; I Samuel 13:6

l. Shelter: Job 24:8; 30:3,6

m. Defense: Isaiah 33:16

n. Shadow: Isaiah 32:2

o. Foundation of salvation: Matthew 7:24,25

p. Durability: Job 19:24

q. Observation: Exodus 33:21; Numbers 23:9

r. Hardness—rebellion: Jeremiah 5:3

s. Stumbling (to the wicked): Isaiah 8:14; I Peter 2:8

t. Barrenness: Luke 8:6

u. Heathen gods: Deuteronomy 32:31,37; Isaiah 57:5

v. Danger: Acts 27:29

w. Punishment: Joshua 7:24-26; John 8:5

x. Judgment: Ezekiel 26:4,14

y. Death: Isaiah 22:16; Matthew 27:60

Prominent rocks:

—Adullam—Thirst: I Chronicles 11:15-17

—Bozez—shining, and Seneh—thorny: I Samuel 14:4 with John 16:33

—Engedi—place of hiding: I Samuel 24:1,2

—Etam—seeking prey: Judges 15:8

—Horeb—refreshment in drought: Exodus 17:1-6

—Meribah—grace vs. strife: Numbers 20:1-11

—Oreb—swarming; victory: Judges 7:24,25

—Rimmon—upright: Judges 20:45

—Selah—fortress; death: II Chronicles 25:11,12 with II Kings 14:7

—Sela-hammahlekoth—division: I Samuel 23:25,28

7. Minerals. The common minerals mentioned in Scripture are (1) alabaster (Matthew 26:7), (2) Brimstone—sulphur (Genesis 19:24), (3) marble (I Chronicles 29:2), (4) nitre (Proverbs 25:20), (5) salt, and water (see WATER in Index).

a. Salt: Leviticus 2:13. See SALT in Index.

Illustrative of:

—Grace in the heart: Mark 9:50

—Wisdom in speech: Colossians 4:6

—Saints: Matthew 5:13a

—Victory: II Samuel 8:13; II Kings 14:7

—Satisfaction: Job 6:6

—Usefulness: Mark 9:50a

—Peace: Mark 9:50b

—Purification (swaddled): Ezekiel 16:4. See SWADDLED in Index.

—Acceptable sacrifices: Leviticus 2:13; Ezekiel 43:21-27

—Bond of friendship: Ezra 4:14 (ASV)

—Without savor—graceless professors: Matthew 5:13b

—Salted with fire—preparation of the wicked for hell: Mark 9:49

—Desolation: Judges 9:45; Zephaniah 2:9

—Barrenness and unfruitful: Jeremiah 17:6; Ezekiel 47:11

8. Metallurgy: Genesis 4:22

a. Dug out of the earth: Deuteronomy 8:9; Job 28:1,2,6

b. Mixed with dross: Isaiah: 1:25

c. Dross freed by fire: Ezekiel 22:18,20

d. Cast in mold: Judges 17:4; I Kings 7:46; Jeremiah 6:29

—Gold: Job 28:1,6; Psalm 68:13; Isaiah 13:12

Illustrative of:

—Saints after affliction: Job 23:10
—Tried faith: I Peter 1:7
—Doctrines of grace: Revelation 3:18
—True converts: I Corinthians 3:12
—Babylonian empire: Daniel 2:38
—Silver: Job 28:1; Psalm 68:13,14
Illustrative of:
—The words of the Lord: Psalm 12:6
—The tongue of the just: Proverbs 10:20
—Good rulers: Isaiah 1:22,23
—Wisdom: Job 28:15; Proverbs 3:14; 16:16
—True converts: I Corinthians 3:12
—Saints purified in affliction: Psalm 66:10; Zechariah 13:9
—Medo-Persian kingdom: Daniel 2:32,39
—God-rejected men: Jeremiah 6:30
—Copper (brass): Deuteronomy 8:9
Illustrative of:
—Decrees of God: Zechariah 6:1
—Strength and firmness of Christ: Daniel 10:6; Revelation 1:15
—Strength for saints: Jeremiah 15:20; Micah 4:13
—Macedonian empire: Daniel 2:39
—Drought: Deuteronomy 28:23
—Barren earth: Leviticus 26:19
—Obstinate sinners: Isaiah 48;4; Jeremiah 6:28
—Iron: Deuteronomy 8:9; Job 28:2. See IRON in Index.
Illustrative of:
—Strength: Daniel 2:33,40
—Stubbornness: Isaiah 48:4
—Severe affliction: Deuteronomy 4:20; Psalm 107:10
—Hard barren soil: Deuteronomy 28:23
—Severe exercise of power: Psalm 2:9; Revelation 2:27
—Insensibility of conscience: I Timothy 4:2

ARCHITECTURE

1. Cities: Genesis 4:17
   a. Designed for habitations: Psalm 107:7,36
   b. Built to perpetuate a name: Genesis 11:4
   c. Arranged in streets and lanes: Zechariah 8:5; Luke 14:21
   d. Entered through gates: Genesis 34:24; Nehemiah 13:19
   Illustrative of:
   —Christ—Cities of Refuge. See in Index
   —Heavenly inheritance: Hebrews 11:16
   —Saints: Matthew 5:14
   —Visible Church: Song of Solomon 3:2,3; Revelation 11:2
   —Church triumph: Revelation 21:2; 22:19
   —The apostasy: Revelation 16:10; 17:18
   —Riches: Proverbs 10:15
   Important Bible Cities:
   —Anathoth—answer to prayer: Jeremiah 1:1
   —Antioch—honor of Antiochus: Acts 11:26
   —Athens—goddess of wisdom: Acts 17:15
   —Babylon—gate of the gods: II Kings 17:30
   —Beersheba—well of the oath: Genesis 21:14,31
   —Bethany—house of dates: Matthew 21:17

—Bethel—house of God: Genesis 12:8
—Bethlehem—house of bread: Genesis 35:19. See BETHLEHEM in Index.
—Cana—erect (?): John 2:1
—Capernaum—consolation: Matthew 4:13
—Colosse—colossal. See NAME in Colossians.
—Corinth—ornament. See NAME in First Corinthians.
—Damascus—joy, then desolation: Jeremiah 49:23-27
—Dan—judge: Judges 18:30
—Dothan—two wells: Genesis 37:17
—Emmaus—village of grapes: Luke 24:13
—Ephesus—desirable. See NAME in Ephesians.
—Ezion-geber—backbone of a giant: Numbers 33:35
—Gaza—strong; fortified: Amos 1:6. Gaza gave us the word "gauze," from its manufacturing and dying of silks and cottons.
—Gibeon—hill; water. See GIBEON in Index.
—Golan—joy; exultation: Joshua 20:8
—Hebron—alliance; fellowship: Genesis 13:18
—Jericho—fragrance: Deuteronomy 34:3
—Jerusalem—peace (?): Joshua 10:1
   —Ancient Salem: Genesis 14:18; Psalm 76:2
   —Ancient Jebusi, or Jebus: Joshua 18:28; Judges 19:10
   —City of Judah: II Chronicles 25:28
   —Holy City: Nehemiah 11:1; Matthew 4:5
   —City of God: Psalm 46:4; 48:1
   —City of the Great King: Psalm 48:2; Matthew 5:35
   —Zion: Psalm 48:12
   —Faithful city: Isaiah 1:21,26
   —City of righteousness: Isaiah 1:26
   —City of solemnities: Isaiah 33:20
   —City of the Lord: Isaiah 60:14
   —Zion of the holy One of Israel: Isaiah 60:14
   —City not forsaken: Isaiah 62:12
   —Throne of the Lord: Jeremiah 3:17
     Illustrative of:
     —The Church: Galatians 4:25,26; Hebrews 12:22,23
     —The glorified Church: Revelation 3:12; 21:2,10
     —God's protection of His saints: Psalm 125:2
     —Peace: Psalm 122:6,7
—Joppa—beautiful: Jonah 1:3
—Kadesh-barnea—sanctuary: Numbers 32:8
—Kedesh—holy: Joshua 20:7
—Laodicea—judgment. See Index.
—Mizpah—a look-out: Genesis 31:49
—Nain—pasture: Luke 7:11
—Nazareth—branch: Luke 1:26
—Nineveh—dwelling (?): Genesis 10:11
—Pergamos—citadel (?). See Index.
—Philadelphia—brotherly love. See Index.
—Ramoth-gilead—exalted: Deuteronomy 4:43; Joshua 20:8
—Rome—strength. See NAME in Romans.
—Samaria—guard: I Kings 16:24
—Sardis—gem(?). See Index.
—Shechem—shoulder: Joshua 20:7
—Shiloh—rest: Joshua 18:1

—Siloam—sent: Joshua 9:7
—Smyrna—myrrh. See Index.
—Sodom—burning: Genesis 10:19; 19:24
—Sychar—intoxicant: John 4:5
—Tekoa—sound of trumpet: Amos 1:1
—Thessalonica—success; conquest. See NAME in I Thessalonians in Index.
—Thyatira—eager with excitement. See Index.
—Tyre—rock: Joshua 19:29
—Ur of the Chaldees—light. See UR in Index.

2. Walls: Nehemiah 4:6. See SPIES (walls) in Index.
   a. Designed for separation and defense. I Samuel 25:16; Ezekiel 43:8
   b. Were dedicated: Nehemiah 12:27
   c. Surrounded—
      —Cities: Numbers 13:28
      —Temples: I Chronicles 29:4
      —Houses: I Samuel 18:10,11
      —Vineyards: Numbers 22:24
   d. Often very high: Deuteronomy 1:28
   e. Strongly fortified: Isaiah 2:15; 25:12
   f. Houses built on them: Joshua 2:15
   g. Places of public resort: Ii Kings 6:26,30; Psalm 55:10
   h. Kept by watchmen: Isaiah 62:6
   i. Strongly manned in war: II Kings 18:26
   j. Enemies fastened on them as a disgrace: I Samuel 31:10
      Illustrative of:
      —Salvation: Isaiah 26:1; 60:18
      —God's protection: Zechariah 2:5
      —A rich man's trust: Proverbs 18:11
      —Judgment: Psalm 62:3
      —False prophets and teachers: Ezekiel 13:10-15
      —Hypocrisy: Acts 23:3
      —Partition: Ephesians 2:14
      —Escape from trouble: Acts 9:22-25

3. Gates: Isaiah 45:1; 62:10
   a. Chief place of concourse: Proverbs 1:21
   b. Where courts of justice held: Deuteronomy 16:18; II Samuel 15:2
   c. Criminals punished at: Deuteronomy 17:5; Jeremiah 20:2
   d. Place of business: Genesis 23:10,16; Ruth 4:1; II Kings 7:1,18
   e. Proclamations made at: Proverbs 1:21; Jeremiah 17:19
   f. Councils and conferences held at: II Samuel 3:27; II Chronicles 18:9
   g. Chief points of attack in war: Judges 5:8; Isaiah 22:7
   h. Of Jerusalem. See GATES in Index.
      Illustrative of:
      —Christ: John 10:9
      —Entrance to eternal life: Matthew 7:14
      —Heaven's entrance: Genesis 28:12-17; Revelation 21:21
      —Security: Psalm 147:13
      —Praise: Psalm 9:14
      —Satan's power: Matthew 16:18
      —Immediate danger: Job 38:17
      —Entrance to ruin and damnation: Matthew 7:13
      —Death; grave: Psalm 9:13; Isaiah 38:10

4. Towers: Genesis 11:4; Judges 9:51
   a. On city walls: II Chronicles 26:9

b. In forests: II Chronicles 27:4
c. In deserts: II Chronicles 26:10
d. In vineyards: Isaiah 5:2; Matthew 21:33
Illustrative of:
—God's protection: Psalm 18:2; 61:3
—God's name: Proverbs 18:10
—Ministers: Jeremiah 6:27
—Fishers of men: II Kings 9:17; Ezekiel 3:17-21
—Mount Zion: Micah 4:8
—The proud and haughty: Isaiah 2:12,15
5. Complex of houses: Leviticus 25:32; I Chronicles 15:1
Illustrative of:
—The body: Job 4:19; II Chronicles 5:1; II Corinthians 5:1
—Church: Hebrews 3:6
—The saint's inheritance: John 14:1-3
—Rock—hope of the saved: Matthew 7:24,25
—Sand—doom of the ungodly: Matthew 7:26,27
—Prosperity: Isaiah 65:21; Ezekiel 28:26
—Blessings: Deuteronomy 6:10,11
—Calamity: Amos 5:11; Zephaniah 1:13

ENGINEERING

1. Water conduit: II Kings 20:20. See CONDUIT in Index.
2. Highways: Number 20:19; Jeremiah 31:21
Illustrative of:
—Christ: John 14:6
—The way of holiness: Isaiah 35:8
—The way of Israel's remnant: Isaiah 11:16
—The way of spreading the Gospel: Isaiah 40:3; 43:19
—Broad—way to destruction: Matthew 7:13
—Narrow—way to eternal life: Matthew 7:14

MILITARY ARMS

1. Engines of war: II Chronicles 26:15. See ENGINES in Index.
Illustrative of:
—Strength: II Chronicles 26:15
—Destruction: Ezekiel 26:9
2. Armor: I Samuel 16:21; 17:4-7
Illustrative of:
—God's armor for the saints: Romans 13:12. See ARMOR in Index.
3. Sword: Judges 20:15; Psalm 149:6
Illustrative of:
—The Word of God: Ephesians 6:17; Hebrews 4:12
—Word of Christ: Isaiah 49:2; Revelation 1:16
—God's justice: Deuteronomy 32:41
—God's protection: Deuteronomy 33:29
—Obedience—victory: II Corinthians 10:4-6
—Peace and friendship: Jeremiah 47:6
—War and contention: Matthew 10:34; Ezekiel 21:3-5
—Calamities: II Samuel 12:10; Ezekiel 5:2,17
—Mental affliction: Luke 2:35
—The wicked: Psalm 17:13
—Tongue of the wicked: Psalm 57:4; 64:3

—Spirit of the wicked: Psalm 37:14
—End of the wicked: Proverbs 5:4
—False witnesses: Proverbs 25:18
—Judicial authority: Romans 13:4

4. Arrows: Psalm 11:2; Isaiah 7:24
   Illustrative of:
   —Christ: Isaiah 49:2
   —Word of Christ: Psalm 45:5
   —Young children: Psalm 127:4
   —Severe afflictions: Job 6:4; Psalm 38:2
   —Bitter words: Psalm 64:3
   —Slanderous tongues: Jeremiah 9:8
   —False witness: Proverbs 25:18
   —Devices of the wicked: Psalm 11:2
   —Storms: Psalm 77:17,18
   —Paralyzing power: Psalm 76:3; Ezekiel 39:3
   —God's judgement: Deuteronomy 32:23; Ezekiel 5:16

5. Shields: Psalm 115:9; 140:7. See Index.
   Illustrative of:
   —God's protection: Genesis 15:1; Psalm 33:20
   —Favor of God: Psalm 5:12
   —Truth of God: Psalm 91:4
   —God's salvation: II Samuel 22:36; Psalm 18:35
   —Faith: Ephesians 6:16
   —Gold—glowing testimony: II Chronicles 12:9b
   —Brass—hypocrisy: II Chronicles 12:10

6. Spear: Joshua 8:18; II Samuel 23:8,10
   Illustrative of:
   —Bitterness of the wicked: Psalm 57:4
   —Arrogance: Psalm 68:30
   —Pruning-hooks in peace: Isaiah 2:4; Micah 4:3

7. Slingers and stones: II Kings 3:25. See SLINGERS in Index.
   Illustrative of: Discipline and perfection: Judges 20:16; I Chronicles 12:2 with I Corinthians 9:24-27; Philippians 3:12-14

MUSIC

1. Instrumental: I Chronicles 16:4-7; Daniel 6:18. Musical instruments are among the earliest recorded human inventions (Genesis 4:21). In the Scriptures their use seems to be confined to religious worship and social festivities, except that the sound of the trumpet served as a battle-call. The earliest kinds were a tabret, a stringed instrument (incipient harp), cymbals and pipe. From these "germs" all others are developments. Some were made of wood (II Samuel 6:5; I Kings 10:12), brass (I Corinthians 13:1), silver (Numbers 10:2), strings (Psalm 33:2; 150:4), and animal horns (Joshua 6:8). Some were expressly ornamented (Ezekiel 28:13).

   As the Hebrew names were obscure, or unintelligible to the translators of our Bible, one general term expressing a well-known instrument often does duty for several of the same class, while the same Hebrew generic word is sometimes translated by different English specific ones, and in other cases the translation is erroneous. Many are mentioned in the Scriptures: David invented some (I Chronicles 23:5), as well as the children of Israel (Amos 6:5). Possibly some of the invented ones were the Sackbut and Dulcimer (Daniel 3:5), the Viol (Isaiah 14:11), and the Tabret (I Samuel 10:5).
   Important instruments—
   a. Bells: Exodus 28:33-35
   b. Cornet (Sistra or Rattle): II Samuel 6:5

    c. Cymbals: I Corinthians 15:16,19
    d. Flute: Daniel 3:5
    e. Harp: Psalm 137:2
    f. Lyre (harp): Genesis 4:21
    g. Organ (pipes): Genesis 4:21; Job 21:12
    h. Pipes (oboe): I Kings 1:40
    i. Psaltry: Psalm 150:3
    j. Timbrel (Tambourine): Exodus 15:20
    k. Trumpet (Ram's horn): Numbers 10:10; Joshua 6:20
2. Vocal (and instruments): Exodus 15:21; I Samuel 18:6; Acts 16:25
Use and importance in Scripture:
    a. In worship: I Chronicles 16:7-9
    b. At public rejoicings: I Samuel 18:6
    c. At social festivities: II Samuel 19:35
    d. At weddings: Jeremiah 7:34
    e. Accompanied by dancing: II Samuel 6:14-16
    f. Accompanied by clapping hands: Psalm 47:1
    g. Promoted joy: I Chronicles 15:16; Ecclesiastes 2:8,10
    h. Brought blessings: I Samuel 10:5,6; II Kings 3:15
    i. Soothed nerves: I Samuel 16:14-17,23
    j. At sacred processions: II Samuel 6:4,5; I Chronicles 15:27,28
    k. At laying a foundation: Ezra 3:9,10
    l. At consecration of Temple: II Chronicles 5:11-13
    m. At coronation of kings: II Chronicles 23:11,13
    n. At dedication of city walls: Nehemiah 12:27,28
    o. In commemorating great men: II Chronicles 35:25
    p. In regulating army movements: Joshua 6:8; I Corinthians 14:8
    q. Before battles: II Chronicles 20:21
    r. In celebrating victory: Exodus 15:20; I Samuel 18:6,7
    s. When friends part: Genesis 31:27
    t. In funeral ceremonies: Matthew 9:23
Illustrative of:
    —Joy and gladness: Zephaniah 3:17; Ephesians 5:19
    —Praise: I Chronicles 23:5
    —Heavenly bliss: Revelation 5:8,9
    —Ceasing of calamities: Isaiah 24:8,9; Revelation 18:22

PRECIOUS STONES

1. Dug out of the earth: Job 28:5,6
2. Brilliant and glittering: I Chronicles 29:2; Revelation 21:11
3. Often given as presents: I Kings 10:2,10
4. Ornamenting crowns: II Samuel 12:30
5. Set in seals and rings: Song of Solomon 5:14
Illustrative of:
    —Preciousness of Christ: Isaiah 28:16; I Peter 2:6
    —Beauty and stability of the Church: Isaiah 54:11,12
    —Saints: Malachi 3:17; I Corinthians 3:12
    —Glory and stability of heavenly Jerusalem: Revelation 21:11,19
    —Inferiority to wisdom: Job 28:18

Bible Stones

1. *Adamant*—hardness; guard: Ezekiel 3:9; Zechariah 7:12. Used to engrave upon stone. Thought by some to be the diamond.
2. *Agate*—sparkling flame: Exodus 28:19; Isaiah 54:12. White with red or green grain, often

used in windows. Member of the Chalcedony family (see #8). This was the *eighth* stone in the high priest's breastplate.

3. *Amber*—Ezekiel 1:4,27. A fossil resin usually found on seacoasts or in alluvial soil. Bright fire color; shade of yellow.

4. *Amethyst*—dream stone: Exodus 28:19; Revelation 21:20. Purple, transparent quartz. Jews supposed it to bring pleasant dreams; Greeks thought it to be a charm against drunkenness. This was the *ninth* stone in the breastplate.

5. *Bdellium*—Genesis 2:12; Numbers 11:7. Probably associated with gold and the onyx stone. Today it is the gum resin from certain trees.

6. *Beryl*—merchant vessel, full of good things: Daniel 10:6; Revelation 21:20. Aquamarine; used for arrows and cutting, due to its hardness. It was the *tenth* stone in the breastplate.

7. *Carbuncle*—flashing gleam; rainbow: Exodus 28:17; Ezekiel 28:13. Deep red; possibly used for abrasives. This was the *third* stone in the breastplate. (Modern name: Red garnet.)

8. *Chalcedony*—to view; behold: Revelation 21:19 (agate; RV). Transparent; brilliant green.

9. *Chrysolyte*—serviceableness; happiness: Revelation 21:20. Yellow to greenish-yellow.

10. *Chrysoprasus*—same as chalcedony: Revelation 21:20. Apple green.

11. *Coral*—to lift up: Job 28:18; Ezekiel 27:16. A shade of red; used ornamentally, such as beads and necklaces.

12. *Crystal*—innocency; purity: Job 18:17; Revelation 4:6. Transparent; colorless—like ice.

13. *Diamond*—beauty; hardness: Exodus 28:18; Jeremiah 17:1. Prismatic colors. This was the *sixth* stone in the breastplate.

AARON'S BREASTPLATE — EXODUS 39:6-29		
3 CARBUNCLE (7)	2 TOPAZ (24)	1 SARDIUS (22)
6 DIAMOND (13)	5 SAPPHIRE (21)	4 EMERALD (14)
9 AMETHYST (4)	8 AGATE (2)	7 LIGURE (17)
12 JASPER (16)	11 ONYX (18)	10 BERYL (6)

FOUNDATIONS / NEW JERUSALEM: REV. 21:19,20		
1 JASPER (16)	2 SAPPHIRE (21)	3 CHALCEDONY (8)
4 EMERALD (14)	5 SARDONYX (23)	6 SARDIUS (22)
7 CHRYSOLYTE (9)	8 BERLE (6)	9 TOPAZ (24)
10 CHRYSOPRASUS (10)	11 JACINTH (15)	12 AMETHYST (4)

14. *Emerald*—glisten: Ezekiel 27:16; Revelation 4:3. Transparent to translucent green. This was the *fourth* stone in the breastplate.

15. *Jacinth*—to behold: Revelation 9:17; 21:20. Today, it is the transparent red, yellow, orange, or brown form of the mineral zircon.

16. *Jasper*—to polish: Revelation 4:3; 21:11,19. Chief colors are red, yellow, brown, and green, though it comes in many shades. This was the *twelfth* stone in the breastplate.

17. *Ligure*—same as Jacinth: Exodus 28:19 (RSV). This was the *seventh* stone in the breastplate.
18. *Onyx*—a variety of Chalcedony: Exodus 28:20; Job 28:16. A variety of quartz consisting of layers of different colors usually in even places. This was the *eleventh* stone in the breastplate.
19. *Pearl*—rare preciousness: Job 28:18; Matthew 13:45,46.
20. *Ruby*—priceless; in evaluating wisdom and measuring the wealth of a virtuous woman: Job 28:18; Proverbs 3:13-15; 31:10. Red.
21. *Sapphire*—to inscribe; celebrate: Exodus 24:10; Ezekiel 1:26. Blue. Some are colorless, yellow, or pink. This was the *fifth* stone in the breastplate. (Modern name: Lapis lazuli.)
22. *Sardius*—a variety of Chalcedony: Exodus 28:17; Revelation 4:3. It is the Sardine or Carnelian in the R.S.V. Blood-red. This was the *first* stone in the breastplate.
23. *Sardonyx*—or onyx: Revelation 21:20. See no. 18.
24. *Topaz*—a form of quartz or chrysolyte: Job 28:19; Revelation 21:20. Yellow; some colorless, pink, blue, and green varieties. This was the *second* stone in the breastplate.

   The breastplate, with its twelve stones representing the names of the Twelve Tribes of the children of Israel, measured "a span by a span" (about nine inches square; Exodus 28:15-21). See HEAVENLY MANNA in Leviticus.

OATHS

1. Oaths used for:
   a. Confirmation: Genesis 26:28; Hebrews 6:16
   b. Deciding controversies: Exodus 22:11; Numbers 5:19
   c. Pledging allegiance: II Kings 11:4; Ecclesiastes 8:2
   d. Binding of sacred duties: Numbers 30:2; II Chronicles 15:14,15
   e. Binding to performance of acts: Genesis 24:3,4; Joshua 2:12
   f. Judicial form: I Kings 22:16; Matthew 26:63
   g. Showing the immutability of God's counsel: Genesis 22:16; Hebrews 6:17
2. Oaths forbidden:
   a. In the name of idols: Joshua 23:7
   b. In the name of any created thing: Matthew 5:34-36; James 5:12
   c. Falsely taking: Leviticus: 6:3; Jeremiah 5:2; 7:9
   d. In haste: Leviticus 5:4
   Illustrations of rashness—
      —Joshua: Joshua 9:15,16
      —Jephthah: Judges 11:30-36
      —Saul: I Samuel 14:27,44
      —Herod: Matthew 14:7-9
      —Jews seeking to kill Paul: Acts 23:21
3. Expressions used:
   a. By the fear of Isaac: Genesis 31:53
   b. As the Lord liveth: Judges 8:19; Ruth 3:13
   c. The Lord do so to me, and more also: Ruth 1:17
   d. As thy soul liveth: I Samuel 1:26; 25:26
   e. God do so to thee, and more also: I Samuel 3:17
   f. By the Lord: II Samuel 19:7; I Kings 2:42
   g. I call God for a record: II Corinthians 1:23
   h. Before God I lie not: Galatians 1:20
   i. God is witness: I Thessalonians 2:5
   j. I charge you by the Lord: I Thessalonians 5:27
4. Sign of an oath:
   a. Raising of the hand: Genesis 14:22; Daniel 12:7
   b. Placing of hand on other person: Genesis 24:2,9; 47:29
   c. Fear and reverence: Ecclesiastes 9:2

SALUTATIONS

1. Expressions used:
   a. God be gracious unto thee: Genesis 43:19
   b. Peace be with thee: Judges 19:20
   c. The Lord be with you: Ruth 2:4
   d. The Lord bless thee: Ruth 2:4
   e. Blessed be thou of the Lord: I Samuel 15:13
   f. Peace to thee: I Samuel 25:6
   g. Peace to thine house: I Samuel 25:6; Luke 10:5
   h. Peace unto all that thou hast: I Samuel 25:6
   i. Art thou in health? II Samuel 20:9
   j. The blessing of the Lord be upon you: Psalm 129:8
   k. We bless you in the name of the Lord: Psalm 129:8
   l. Hail: Matthew 26:49; Luke 1:28
   m. All hail: Matthew 28:9
2. Accompanied by:
   a. Bowing frequently to the ground: Genesis 18:2; 33:3
   b. Falling on the neck and kissing: Genesis 33:4; Luke 15:20
   c. Laying hold of the beard with the right hand: II Samuel 20:9
   d. Falling prostrate to the ground: Esther 8:3; Luke 8:41
   e. Kissing the dust: Psalm 72:9; Isaiah 49:23
   f. Embracing and kissing the feet: Matthew 28:9; Luke 7:38,45
3. How and by whom given:
   a. By brethren to each other: I Samuel 17:22
   b. By inferiors to superiors: Genesis 47:7
   c. By superiors to inferiors: I Samuel 30:21
   d. By all passers-by: I Samuel 10:3,4; Psalm 129:8
   e. By treachery: II Samuel 20:9; Matthew 26:49
   f. By derision: Matthew 27:29 with Mark 15:18
   g. In conceit: Matthew 5:47
   h. In hypocrisy: Matthew 23:7; Mark 12:38
   i. On entering a house: Judges 18:15; Matthew 10:12
   j. Sent by messengers: I Samuel 25:5,14; II Samuel 8:10
   k. Send through letters: Romans 16:21-23; Colossians 4:18
   l. Sometimes forbidden: II Kings 4:29; Luke 10:24. See SALUTE in Index.
   m. Denied to persons of bad character: II John 10

Dictionary of
Symbolic Language
of the Bible

FIGURES OF SPEECH

1. Metaphor—a figurative expression, founded on some similitude which one object bears to another: e.g., (1) to bridle the tongue (James 1:26); (2) for the sword to devour flesh (Deuteronomy 32:42).
2. Allegory—a continued metaphor, as the discourse of Christ concerning eating His flesh (John 6:35-65).
3. Parable—the representation of some moral or spiritual doctrine under an ingenious similitude: e.g., the Sower (Matthew 13:2-23); (2) the Prodigal Son (Luke 15:11-32); (3) the Ten Virgins (Matthew 25:1-13).
4. Proverb—a concise, sententious saying, founded on a penetrating observation of men and manners. Brevity and elegance are essential to a proverb (see Proverbs 10:15; Luke 4:23).
5. Metonymy—a figure of speech in which one word is put for another: e.g., "They have Moses and the prophets" (Luke 16:29), meaning not their persons, but their writings.
6. Prosopopeia, or Personification, attributes the actions of persons to things: e.g., "Mercy and truth are met together; righteousness and peace have kissed each other" (Psalm 85:10).
7. Synecdoche—puts a part for the whole of anything, or the whole for a part: e.g., (1) "All the world," and "Throughout the world," by which is meant the Roman Empire, or parts of it (Luke 2:1; Acts 24:5); (2) the word "souls" for the whole persons (Acts 27:37).
8. Irony—a figure in which a different thing is intended from that which is spoken. Examples of this kind are not very frequent in the Bible, yet there are a few: e.g., (1) Elijah's address to the priests of Baal concerning the god Baal (I Kings 18:27); (2) the remark of Job to his friends concerning the death of wisdom (Job 12:2).
9. Hyperbole—a representation of anything as being much greater or smaller than it is in reality: e.g., (1) Israel as "grasshoppers" in the presence of the "giants" of Canaan (Numbers 13:33); (2) the city walls of Canaan reaching up to heaven (Deuteronomy 1:28; 9:1).

DICTIONARY OF SYMBOLIC LANGUAGE

Abaddon: Revelation 9:11. Hebrew name for rulers who opposed the early Church: destruction; destroyer

Abomination:
1. Sin, in general: Isaiah 66:3; Ezekiel 16:50,51
2. An idol: II Kings 23:13; Isaiah 44:19
3. Idolatrous rites and ceremonies: Revelation 17:4

Abomination of desolation: Matthew 24:15. Appalling sacrilege; the idolatrous ensigns of the Roman army

Adamant: Ezekiel 3:9; Zechariah 7:12. Hardness of heart toward God

Adder: Psalm 140:3; Proverbs 23:32. Deadly evil

Adulteress, or Harlot: Isaiah 1:21; Revelation 17:5. Apostate church or city

Adultery: Jeremiah 3:8,9; Revelation 2:22. Backsliding; idolatry; apostasy

Air: Ephesians 2:2; Revelation 9;2; 16:17. Moral influences

Almonds: Numbers 17:8. Spirit produced fruit

Anchor: Hebrews 6:19. Confidence and security

Angels:
1. God's ministers of His providence: Ezekiel 10:8; Hebrews 1:4-7
2. Pastors: Revelation 1:20; 2:1,8
3. Angel of the Lord—Jesus Christ: Zechariah 1:11
4. Apostate spirits: Matthew 25:41; Jude 6

Animals: See BEASTS in Index.

Anoint: Leviticus 8:10-12; Acts 10:38. Consecration; appointment; power conferred

Ants. See Index.

Apollyon: Revelation 9:11. Greek name. See **Abaddon**

Ark:
1. Christ: Exodus 25:10-22
2. Seat of divine strength: Psalm 132:8
3. Relationship with God: Revelation 11:19

Arm; Arms:
1. The omnipotence of God: Jeremiah 27:5; 32:17
2. The power and miracles of Christ: Isaiah 53:1; John 12:38
3. God's gracious influences on mankind: Isaiah 51:9; 52:10

Armor: Romans 13:12; Ephesians 6:11. Spiritual graces and stamina

Arrows. See Index.

Ashes:
1. Humiliation; self-judgment: Job 42:6
2. Witness of judgment of sin: Numbers 19:9,10

Ass: See Index.

Babes:
1. Unskilled and foolish princes: Isaiah 3:4
2. Young or feeble Christians: I Corinthians 3:1; Hebrews 5:13

Babylon: Revelation 14:8; 17:1—18:24. Ecclesiastical apostasy

Badger's skins: Exodus 26:14; Ezekiel 16:10. Defiance against evil from without

Balaam: II Peter 2:15; Jude 11. Errors and impurities leading to apostasy

Balance:
1. Man divinely measured: Daniel 5:27
2. Famine: Revelation 6:5,6

Bear: Proverbs 17:12; Daniel 7:5. Powerful and destructive enemy

Beard: II Samuel 10:5; Jeremiah 48:37. Human energy displayed

Beasts. See Index.

Bees:
1. Numerous enemies: Deuteromony 1:44; Psalm 118:12
2. Judgment upon Israel: Isaiah 7:18

Belial: Judges 19:22-25; II Chronicles 13:7; II Corinthians 6:15a. An epithet of Satan—wickedness; baseness; worthlessness

Bells: Exodus 28:33-35. Witness of the Spirit

Belly: John 7:38; Romans 16:18; Revelation 10:9,10. Man's inward condition

Billows: Psalm 42:7; Jonah 2:3. Overwhelming sorrow

Birds. See Index.

Black; blackness: Jeremiah 4:28; 14:2; Joel 2:6. Afflictions; mourning

Blasphemy: Revelation 13:5,6; 17:3. Idolatry

Blindness: Isaiah 29:18; Romans 11:25; Ephesians 4:18. Ignorance of doctrine; without spiritual perception

Blood:
1. Slaughter and mortality: Isaiah 34:3; Ezekiel 32:6; Revelation 14:20
2. Pollutions of human nature: Ezekiel 16:6
3. Atonement by Jesus Christ: Matthew 26:28; Hebrews 13:20
4. Complete apostasy from God and truth: Revelation 16:3

Blue: Leading color in Exodus for Tabernacle. Heavenly character

Body: I Corinthians 12:13,27. Christ's Church (comprised of believers in Him)

Book: Psalm 40:7; Hebrews 10:7. Divine decrees

Book of life: Revelation 3:5; 20:12,15. Heavenly register of God's people

Bosom:
1. Rest: Luke 16:23
2. Deepest affection: Isaiah 40:11; John 13:23
3. Divine communion: John 1:18

Bow:
1. Vigorous health: Job 29:20
2. Evangelical conquest: Revelation 6:2

Bowels: Luke 1:78; Philippians 2:1. Tender sympathy or mercy

Branch: Isaiah 11:1; Jeremiah 23:5; Zechariah 3:8. Christ

Brass (copper). See Index.

Bread: Deuteronomy 8:3; Isaiah 55:2; Matthew 4:4. Divine doctrine; Word of God

Breastplate: Ephesians 6:14; I Thessalonians 5:8. Safeguard for heart and conscience

Breasts: Genesis 49:25. Blessings and fruitfulness

Bride: Revelation 21:9. The Church

Bridegroom: Revelation 21:9. Christ, husband of the Church

Bridle: Psalm 32:9; James 3:2. Moral restraint

Briers: Isaiah 55:13. Persons of pernicious principles

Brimstone:
1. Perpetual desolations: Job 18:15; Isaiah 34:9
2. Emblem of torment: Revelation 14:10
3. Pernicious doctrines: Revelation 9:17

Brooks. See Index.

Buckler: Psalm 18:2,30. Divine protection

Bulls: Psalm 22:12; Jeremiah 50:11. Cruel and powerful enemies

Candlestick. See *Lamp*

Carpenters: Zechariah 1:20,21. Instruments of judgments

Caterpillars: Jeremiah 51:14; Joel 1:4. Devouring enemies

Caves. See Index.

Cedars: Zechariah 11:2. Eminent man. See Index.

Cedars of Lebanon: Isaiah 2:13. Kings; princes of Judah

Cedars, twigs of: Ezekiel 17:3,4. Nobility; military chiefs

Chaff: Psalm 1:4; Matthew 3:12. Worthless, irreligious persons

Chain: Lamentations 3:7. Calamity or affliction

Chariots: Psalm 68:17; Isaiah 66:15. Governmental power and authority of God

Cisterns: Jeremiah 2:13; Isaiah 36:16. Resources

Cities. See Index.

Clay:
1. Sinner's helplessness—no foothold: Psalm 40:2
2. Total depravity: Romans 9:21

Clouds. See Index.

Colors:
1. Varied glories: Genesis 37:3; I Chronicles 29:2
2. Comfort and peace: Isaiah 54:11-14

Concision: Philippians 3:2. Mutilating the body; imposing the Law on Christians

Cords:
1. Divine restraint: Psalm 2:3
2. Compellings of love: Hosea 11:4

Corn, old: Joshua 5:11. Food for heavenly people

Crowns:
1. Delegated authority: Ezekiel 16:12
2. Victorious power: Revelation 9:7; 19:12
3. Kingly dignity: Revelation 4:4-10
4. Rewards. See CROWNS in Index.

Cup. See CUPS in Index.
1. Blessings of providence and grace: Psalm 16:5; 23:5; I Corinthians 10:16
2. Salvation; grace and mercy: Psalm 116:13
3. Communion; Christ's blood: I Corinthians 10:16; 11:25
4. Hypocrisy: I Corinthians 10:21
5. Iniquity: Revelation 17:4
6. Divine judgments: Psalm 11:6
7. Divine wrath: Isaiah 51:7

Darkness:
1. Calamity and misery: Jeremiah 23:12
2. Irreligiousness and worldliness: Romans 13:12,13
3. Of the heavenly bodies—disorders in governments: Isaiah 13:10,11

Darts: Ephesians 6:16. Sharp and sudden temptations

Day:
1. A year: Ezekiel 4:6; Revelation 2:10; 11:9
2. An appointed season: Isaiah 34:8
3. Age of grace: II Corinthians 6:2
4. A state of evangelical knowledge: I Thessalonians 5:5
5. Indefinite period of time with God: II Peter 3:8

Daysman: Job 9:33. Arbiter or referee. See Index.

Death:
1. Natural—separation of spirit from body: Genesis 25:17
2. Moral—insensibility to the evil of sin: Ephesians 2:1b-3; Revelation 3:1
3. Second—eternal banishment from God: Revelation 2:11; 20:14
4. Christian—mortification of sinful affection: Romans 6:8,11
5. Sleep for the believer: I Corinthians 11:30; I Thessalonians 4:14

Desert. See Index.

Dew: Isaiah 26:19. Power of Christ in resurrection

Dogs:
1. An expression of utter contempt: Matthew 15:26
2. Gentiles, as outcasts: Matthew 15:27
3. Idle, luxurious ministers of religion: Isaiah 56:10
4. Cavilling, unprincipled teachers: Philippians 3:2; Revelation 22:15
5. Apostate prophets and teachers: II Peter 2:1,21,22
6. Uncleanness: Proverbs 26:11
7. Persons without conscience or feeling: Psalm 22:16
8. Satan: Psalm 22:10

Door:
1. Commencement of a new government: Revelation 4:1
2. Opening for Gospel presentation: I Corinthians 16:9; Revelation 3:7-9
3. Christ—salvation: John 10:9
4. Communion with Christ: Revelation 3:20

Doves. See Index.

Dragon:
1. Enemy: Ezekiel 29:3
2. Satan actuating his agents: Revelation 12:9
3. Dangers and difficulties: Psalm 91:13

Drunkenness:
1. Emblem of folly: Isaiah 28:1-3; Jeremiah 13:13
2. Insensibility to judgment: Isaiah 29:9; 51:21
3. Carnal excitement: Ephesians 5:18a

Dung: Malachi 2:3; Philippians 3:8. Utter contempt and abhorrance

Dust:
1. Human nature: Genesis 3:19; 18:27
2. Utmost depths of humiliation: Psalm 22:15; Daniel 12:2

Eagle. See Index.

Ears:
1. Attention: Psalm 34:15; Revelation 2:29
2. Devoted obedience: Psalm 40:6

Earthen vessels: II Corinthians 4:7. Bodies of believers

Earthquakes. See Index.

Eating:
1. Appropriating Christ: John 6:51-57
2. Communion and fellowship: Matthew 26:26; I Corinthians 10:16

Egypt:
1. Bondage: Exodus 1:7-14
2. Fleshly world: Numbers 11:5; Romans 13:14
3. Wickedness: Revelation 11:8
4. Mixed multitude: Exodus 12:37,38

Elders, the twenty-four: Revelation 4:10. Rewarded saints

Engines of war. See Index.

Eyes. See Index.
1. Applied to God, denote—
   a. His infinite knowledge: Proverbs 15:3; Psalm 11:4
   b. His watchful providence: Psalm 32:8; 34:15
2. Applied to Christ; His omnipresence: Hebrews 4:13; Revelation 2:18; 5:6

3. Applied to man, denote—
   a. Understanding; eyes of the mind: Psalm 119:18; Ephesians 1:18
   b. A friendly counsellor: Job 29:15
   c. The whole man: Revelation 1:7
   d. Human designs: Deuteronomy 28:54-56
   e. Longing for God: Psalm 123:2

Face:
1. God's presence: Exodus 33:13-23
2. God's favor: Psalm 31:16; Daniel 9:17
3. Intelligence: Ezekiel 1:10; Revelation 4:7
4. Man's profaneness and impenitence: Jeremiah 5:3

Family: Ephesians 3:15. The Church (people) of God

Fat:
1. The most excellent of everything: Psalm 92:14
2. Riches: Jeremiah 5:28
3. Self-satisfaction and apostasy: Deuteronomy 31:20

Feet:
1. Of ministers; beautiful: Romans 10:15
2. Christian's work & witness: Ephesians 6:15
3. Under subjection; victory: Romans 16:20; I Corinthians 15:27,28; Ephesians 1:22

Field: Matthew 13:38. The world; every human being

Fig tree. See Index.

Fire:
1. Judgment: Matthew 25:41
2. Destructive calamity: Ezekiel 22:31
3. Purification: Isaiah 6:6,7; Malachi 3:2
4. Action of the Word of God: Jeremiah 20:8,9; 23:29

Fish. See Index.

Flesh:
1. Riches: Isaiah 17:4
2. Mortal man: Isaiah 40:6
3. Human virtures: Philippians 3:3,4
4. Spiritual immorality: Romans 13:14

Flowers. See Index.

Forehead: Revelation 7:3; 13:16. Public profession of faith

Forest: Ezekiel 20:46; Jeremiah 21:14. Kingdom

Fornication: Ezekiel 16:15; Revelation 2:20,21. Illicit fellowship with the world

Foundation: Isaiah 28:16; II Timothy 2:19. Immovable security

Fountains. See SPRINGS in Index.

Fowls: See BIRDS in Index.

Fox. See Index.

Frankincense: Leviticus 2:1,2; Matthew 2:11. Christ's life; a sweet savor

Fruit. See Index.

Furnace:
1. Deep trial and suffering: Deuteronomy 4:20; Jeremiah 9:7; 11:4
2. Divine judgment: Matthew 13:42,50; Revelation 1:15

Garments. See Index.
1. Purity and joy: Isaiah 52:1; Revelation 3:4,5

2. Effective testimony: Revelation 3:4
3. Carnality: Jude 23b

Gates. See in Index.

Girdle: Exodus 29:9; Psalm 109:19. Readiness for service

Goat: Matthew 25:32,33. Unbelieving nations

Goat's hair: Exodus 25:4. Separation from evil

Gog and Magog: Ezekiel 38:2; Revelation 20:8. Infidel nations; God's enemies

Gold. See Index.

Grapes:

1. Good—blessings: Amos 9:13
2. Wild—sinful tempers and manners; barrenness: Isaiah 5:1-7

Grass. See Index.

Hail:

1. Weapons of God: Joshua 10:11
2. Incursions of violent enemies: Isaiah 28:2; Revelation 8:7
3. Sudden and severe judgment: Isaiah 30:30; Ezekiel 13:13

Hair:

1. Long—a woman's glory: I Corinthians 11:15
2. Short—masculine energy and dignity: Numbers 6:18,19; I Corinthians 11:14

Hand:

1. Right—protection and favor: Psalm 18:35; 73:23
2. Laying on—blessing and authority: Genesis 48:13-22; Numbers 27:18
3. Influence of the Holy Spirit: Ezekiel 8:1
4. Action and service: Psalm 90:17; 123:2
5. Salvation: Isaiah 59:1

Harlot. See *Adulteress.*

Hart. See Index.

Harvest: Jeremiah 8:20. Period of grace. See Index.

Head:

1. Governing principle in man: Isaiah 1:6; Daniel 2:28
2. Chief of a people: Micah 3:1,9,11
3. Christ—of the Church: Ephesians 1:22
4. The metropolis of a country: Isaiah 7:8,9
5. Husband—over wife: Ephesians 5:23

Heart: Proverbs 6:18; Colossians 3:16. Seat of feelings, affections, and understanding

Heavens:

1. Powerful providence of God: Daniel 4:26
2. Authority and light: Matthew 24:29; Revelation 6:13
3. God: Matthew 21:25; Luke 15:18
4. Political or ecclesiastical governments: Isaiah 13:13; Haggai 2:21

Heifer. See Index.

Hell. See Index.

1. General receptacle of departed souls: Isaiah 14:9; Revelation 1:18
2. Place of torment for the unregenerate: Psalm 9:17; Luke 23,24

Helmet: Ephesians 6:17; I Thessalonians 5:8. Protection of the mind

Herbs. See Index.

High Places: II Kings 21:1-9. Idolatrous altars, erected on high hills

Highways. See Index.

Hills:
1. Seat of government: Psalm 2:6; 15:1; 24:3
2. Perpetuity: Deuteronomy 33:15

Hinds: II Samuel 22:34; Proverbs 5:19. Agility; fearlessness; liberty; affection

Honey: Leviticus 2:11. Natural affection, forbidden in sacrifice

Horn:
1. Christ—salvation: Luke 1:69
2. Power: Jeremiah 48:25; Daniel 7:20
3. Protection: Psalm 18:2; Amos 3:14
4. Strength: Revelation 5:1

Horse. See Index.

House. See Index.

Hunger and Thirst:
1. Natural desire for happiness: Proverbs 19:15; Isaiah 55:1
2. Spiritual desires: Amos 8:11; Matthew 5:6

Hyssop: I Kings 4:33; John 19:29. Man in his worst state. See Index.

Idolatry:
1. Covetousness: Colossians 3:5
2. An object excessively beloved: I John 5:21

Image:
1. Idolatry: Exodus 20:4,5
2. Empires: Daniel 2:31,34

Incense: Psalm 141:2; Revelation 5:8. Devotional exercises

Infirmities:
1. Bodily weakness: Isaiah 53:4; Matthew 8:17; II Corinthians 12:7-10
2. Spiritual weakness: Romans 8:26

Insects. See Index.

Iron. See Index.

Jerusalem:
1. Peace and prosperity: Psalm 122:6
2. Rejoicing: Isaiah 65:18
3. Comfort: Isaiah 66:13
4. Freedom: Galatians 4:26
5. Heavenly glory: Hebrews 12:22; Revelation 21:22

Jewels: Isaiah 61:10; Malachi 3:17. Our preciousness to God; marks of divine favor

Jordan River: Descender. See Index.

Keys:
1. Power and authority: Revelation 1:18
2. Commission of the gospel ministry: Matthew 16:19
3. Means of scriptural knowledge: Luke 11:52

Kings: Revelation 1:6; 5:10. Royal dignity of saints

Kiss: Luke 15:20; I Peter 5:14. Holy and divine expression of love

Knee, bowed: Ephesians 3:14; Philippians 2:10. Reverence; subjection

Laborers: Matthew 9:37,38; I Corinthians 3:9. Gospel ministers

Lamb:
1. Gentle, meek, unresisting: Luke 10:3; Acts 8:32

    2. Passover—Christ; sacrifice, Sin-Bearer: Exodus 12:11; John 1:29

    3. In Revelation: strength, glory, worship

Lamp:

    1. A prophetic light: Genesis 15:17,18

    2. Governmental light: I Kings 15:4

    3. A successor: I Kings 15:4; Psalm 132:17

    4. Profession of faith: Matthew 25:3,4

    5. Divine illumination and comfort: II Samuel 22:29

    6. A Christian church: Revelation 1:12,20

Laver: Exodus 30:17-21; Ephesians 5:26. Christ, the *Laver,* the Word of God

Lead: Exodus 15:10; Zechariah 5:7,8. Judgment of evil; wickedness

Leaf:

    1. Hypocrisy: Genesis 3:7; Matthew 21:19

    2. Fruit: Psalm 1:3

    3. Blessing and healing: Revelation 22:2

Leaven: Matthew 16:6; I Corinthians 5:6,8. Moral and doctrinal evil

Legs: Psalm 147:10; Daniel 2:33. Natural strength

Leopard:

    1. A subtle, rapacious enemy: Daniel 7:6

    2. A person of similar disposition: Isaiah 11:6

    3. Antichristian power: Revelation 13:2

Leprosy: Leviticus 13:2. Uncleanness of heart and life; sin. See LEPER in Index.

Life:

    1. Fullness of joy: Psalm 16:11

    2. Christ: John 6:33; 14:6

    3. A state of justification: John 5:24; Colossians 3:3

Light:

    1. Joy, peace, and prosperity: Esther 8:16

    2. Christ: John 8:12

    3. Christians and their testimony: Matthew 5:14a,16

    4. Knowledge: Isaiah 8:20

    5. Holiness: Ephesians 5:8; I John 1:7

Lightning:

    1. Christ's coming: Matthew 24:27

    2. Obedience connected with God's power: Ezekiel 1:13,14, Nahum 2:4

Lily:

    1. Christ: Song of Solomon 2:1,2

    2. Trust: Matthew 6:28

    3. Loveliness; beauty; glory: Matthew 6:29

Linen: Leviticus 16:23; Revelation 19:8. Personal purity; righteousness

Lion. See Index.

Locusts. See Index.

Loins, girt: Ephesians 6:14; I Peter 1:13. Inward strength

Manna: See Index.

    1. Earthly food: Exodus 16:14,15

    2. Spiritual food: Matthew 4:4; John 6:31-35

    3. Deep spiritual truths: Revelation 2:17

Meat:

    1. Christ: John 6:27,55; I Corinthians 10:3,4

    2. Word of God: Hebrews 5:12-14

Metal. See Index.

Minerals. See Index.

Milk: I Corinthians 3:2; I Peter 2:2. Elementary truth of the Word

Mire: Job 30:19; II Peter 2:22. Pollution; moral degradation

Moon. See Index.

Moth. See Index.

Mother:
    1. Good—blessings: Galatians 4:22-31
    2. Bad—religious corruption: Revelation 17:5

Mountains. See Index.

Music. See Index.

Mustard seed: Matthew 13:31; 17:20. Small and insignificant

Mystery: Romans 16:25; I Corinthians 2:7; Colossians 1:26. A thing or doctrine unknown until revealed. See MYSTERIES in Index.

Nail: Ezra 9:8; Zechariah 10:4. Steadfast; firmly established

Naked: II Corinthians 5:3; Revelation 3:17. Destitute of God's righteousness in Christ

Nations: (plural) Gentiles; **nation** (singular): Israel

Net: Psalm 9:15; Proverbs 1:17. Cunning contrivance

Numbers:
    1. **One—**
        a. Unity: John 17:21-23
        b. Supremacy: Ephesians 4:4-6
        c. Sacrifice—Christ's, for sin: Hebrews 9:26,28; 10:10,14
        d. Source of salvation: Isaiah 45:22
        e. Altar; worship: II Chronicles 32:12
        f. Security: Romans 8:31
    2. **Two—**
        a. Redemption: Exodus 26:19; 38:25-27; 30:11-16. See also Numbers 3:44-51. Two silver sockets supported each board of the Tabernacle. The silver came from the "redemption money" given by the children of Israel. Thus, the Tabernacle, which is a type of Christ, rests on "redemption." Also in connection with redemption or forgiveness were *two* turtledoves or *two* young pigeons (Leviticus 5:7,11; Luke 2:24). Blood was sprinkled on *two* door posts (Exodus 12:22), and when Christ died for our sins, He died between *two* thieves (Mark 15:27).
        b. Witness: Mark 6:7; Revelation 11:3
        c. Rapture of the Church—preparation and unpreparedness for Christ's coming: Matthew 24:40,41
    3. **Three—**
        a. Godhead; Trinity: I John 5:7; Matthew 28:19
        b. Blessing: Isaiah 19:24,25; Zechariah 13:9
        c. Strength: Ecclesiastes 4:12
    4. **Four**—earthly; universality: Isaiah 11:12. *Four* kinds of soil (Matthew 13:4), and *four* kinds of flesh (I Corinthians 15:39).
    5. **Five—**
        a. Human responsibility: Numbers 5:7; Matthew 25:2; I Corinthians 14:19
        b. Victory: I Samuel 17:40; Leviticus 26:8; Joshua 10:5,14-27
    6. **Six**—man; one short of seven: Genesis 1:26-31; Revelation 13:18
    7. **Seven**—completion; perfection; rest: Genesis 2:1-3. See SEVENS in Index. NOTE: *Seven* notes of music, *seven* colors in the rainbow, *seven* days in a week, *seven* parables in Matthew

13, *seven* churches in Revelation 2 and 3, and *seven* churches to which Paul wrote.
8. **Eight**—resurrection: Matthew 28:1-6. NOTE: *Eight* people were "resurrected" from the old world of the flood to start a new world—(I Peter 3:20). *Eight* persons in Scripture were raised from the dead (I Kings 17:17-23; II Kings 4:32-37; 13:20,21; Luke 7:12-15; 8:41-56; John 11:41-44; Acts 9:36-41; 20:9-12). Elijah performed *eight* miracles. Elisha, who received a double portion of Elijah's spirit, performed 16.
9. **Nine**—prayer: Acts 3:1; 10:2,3
10. **Ten**—
    a. Responsibility toward God (10 Commandments): Exodus 20:1-17
    b. Expectation; waiting: Matthew 25:1
    c. Testing: Daniel 1:12,18-20
11. **Eleven**—
    a. Incompleteness of administration: Matthew 28:16; Acts 1:15-26
    b. Idolatry and ruin: Judges 3:7 with 17:6
12. **Twelve**—
    a. Administration of Divine government (Israel's tribes): Genesis 49:1-28; Exodus 39:14
    b. Foundation of new Jerusalem: Revelation 21:19,20
    c. Gates—entrance into the new City: Revelation 21:21
    d. Apostles—leadership: Matthew 10:2-4
    e. Abundant blessings: Matthew 14:20
    f. Refreshment and rest: Exodus 15:27
    g. Needs supplied: Revelation 22:12
    h. Protection: Matthew 26:53 with Psalm 91:11
    i. Testimony of God's leading: Joshua 4:20 24
    j. The *twelve* spies—to teach us not to walk by sight: Numbers 13:2,26—14:9,30-34
13. **Thirteen**—usually associated with evil
    a. Rebellion: Genesis 14:4
    b. Selfishness: I Kings 7:1 with 6:37,38
    c. Anti-semitism: Esther 3:12,13
    d. *Thirteen* evil characteristics of man: Mark 7:21-23
14. **Twenty**—when one is out of the place of blessing there is hardship before deliverance: Genesis 31:41-55; Judges 4:3-24; I Samuel 7:2
15. **Twenty-four**—
    a. Doing things decently and in order in God's service: II Chronicles 24:7-19; I Corinthians 14:40
    b. Separation unto God for confession of sin and worship: Nehemiah 9:1-3
    c. Reverence and praise: Revelation 4:10,11
16. **Thirty**—betrayal: Zechariah 11:12; Matthew 26:15
17. **Forty**—trial and probation: Numbers 14:33,34; Deuteronomy 8:2; Matthew 4:2
18. **Fifty**—
    a. Liberty: Leviticus 25:10; II Corinthians 3:17
    b. Rest and abundant satisfaction: Luke 9:14-17
    c. Pentecost—descent of the Holy Spirit fifty days after Christ's resurrection. See PENTECOST in Index.
19. **Seventy**—
    a. Discipleship; service: Numbers 11:24-29; Luke 10:1,2
    b. Bondage; captivity: Leviticus 25:1-6; 26:34,35; II Chronicles 36:21
    c. Times prophecy: Daniel 9:24
    d. Forgiveness: Matthew 18:22
    e. Peace and rest: Exodus 15:27
20. **One Thousand**—
    a. Period of Christ's reign; millennium: Revelation 20:4,5
    b. Limitless time: Psalm 90:4; II Peter 3:8
    c. Limitless number: Daniel 7:10; Revelation 5:11

21. **144,000**—remnant; multitude no man can number: Revelation 7:4,9

Nurse: Numbers 11:12; I Thessalonians 2:7. Affection and tenderness

Oaks: Isaiah 1:30; Amos 2:9. Mighty; prosperity

Oil:
1. Holy Spirit: Psalm 89:20; Matthew 25:1-13
2. Power: Psalm 92:10
3. Cleanliness: Ezekiel 16:9
4. Joy: Isaiah 61:3
5. Gladness: Hebrews 1:9
6. Healing: Luke 10:34; James 5:14

Olive: See Index.
1. Cultivated—the Church: Romans 11:24
2. Wild—sensual man: Romans 11:17

Ostrich: See Index.

Oven: Psalm 21:9; Malachi 4:1. Thorough, severe, unsparing judgment

Owl: Psalm 102:6; Micah 1:8: solitariness; mourning

Ox: See Index.

Palm Tree: John 12:13. Respect; reverence. See Index.

Paradise: Luke 23:43; Revelation 2:7. Heaven, residence of the redeemed

Passover: Exodus 12:1-13; I Corinthians 5:7. Christ, sacrifice for sin. See Index.

Pearl: Matthew 13:46. Church in unity; beauty, costliness

Pharaoh: Exodus 6:1. Satan; bondage

Physician: Matthew 9:12. Christ

Pillar:
1. Chief support of family, city, or state: Galatians 2:9
2. The Church: I Timothy 3:15
3. Monument of grace in God's Temple of glory: Revelation 3:12

Plowing: See Index.

Plumbline: Amos 7:7,8. Exact measurement

Poison: Psalm 140:3; Romans 3:13. Lies; evil principles

Pomegranate Tree: See Index.

Pools: See Index.

Potter: Psalm 2:9; Jeremiah 18:1-10. Sovereignty exercised in grace or in judgment. See Index.

Pounds: Luke 19:11-26. Talents or gifts for public service

Precious Stones: See Index.

Pricks: Numbers 33:35; Acts 9:5. Sharp troubles; opposition. See Index.

Purple: Exodus 25:4; John 19:2. Royalty

Race: I Corinthians 9:24; Hebrews 12:1. Energy in Christian life and service

Rain: Isaiah 44:3. Spiritual influence. See Index.

Ram: Leviticus 8:22. Consecration

Ram's horn: Joshua 6:4,10. Man's weakness consecrated to God's service

Reaping: See Index.

Red: Isaiah 1:18; 63:2; Zechariah 1:8. Sin; judgment; bloodshed

Reed: II Kings 18:21; Matthew 11:7. Inconsistency; weakness

Reins: Psalm 26:2; Jeremiah 20:12. Inward thoughts and feelings

Ring:
1. Honor: Genesis 41:42
2. Royal authority: Esther 3:10
3. Love and friendship: Luke 15:22

Rivers: See Index.

Roast: Exodus 12:8,9; II Chronicles 35:13. Thoroughness of God's judgment

Robe: Luke 15:22. Acceptance

Rocks: See Index.

Rod:
1. Powerful authority: Psalm 2:9; Revelation 19:15
2. Divine faithfulness: Psalm 23:4

Sackcloth: Nehemiah 9:1. Humility. See Index.

Salt: See Index.

Sand: Genesis 22:17; Psalm 139:18. Countless multitudes

Sapphire: Exodus 24:10; Ezekiel 1:26. Glory of God's throne

Scarlet: Revelation 17:3,4. Earthly glory; apostasy

Sceptre: Genesis 49:10; Amos 1:5,8. Authority; power

Scorpion: See Index.

Scourge: Isaiah 28:15,18. Oppression

Seal; sealed: See NABOTH and JOTHAM in Index.
1. Confirmation: II Timothy 2:19
2. Security: Song of Solomon 4:12
3. Secrecy: Isaiah 29:11
4. Restraint: Job 9:7; 37:7
5. Token of special commission: John 6:27
6. Emblem of special interest: Ephesians 1:13; 4:30; Revelation 7:2-4

Seas: See Index.
1. Remote islands and countries of Gentiles: Isaiah 60:5
2. River Euphrates at Babylon: Jeremiah 51:35-37

Seed; seedtime: See Index.

Selah: Psalm 3:8; 9:20; Habakkuk 3:3,9. Possibly to pause; consider

Serpent: See REPTILES in Index.

Sheep: See Index.

Shepherd:
1. Civil and ecclesiastical rulers and guides: Ezekiel 34:2; Nahum 3:18
2. Christ: John 10:11
3. Pastors: Ezekiel 34:2b

Shield. See Index.

Ships: Genesis 49:13; Revelation 8:9. Commerce

Shoulder: Isaiah 22:22; Luke 15:5. Ability; burden-bearing

Silver: See Index.

Sleep:
1. Death of a Christian: I Corinthians 11:30; I Thessalonians 4:14
2. Carnal security: Romans 13:11

Smoke: Isaiah 14:31; Revelation 9:2,3. Blinding and darkening judgment

Snow. See Index.

Sodom and Gomorrah: Isaiah 1:10. Backsliding; an apostate

Sores: Isaiah 1:6; 53:5. Spiritual maladies

Sower: Matthew 13:3,37. A Gospel preacher of the Word

Sparrow: Psalm 84:3; Matthew 10:29,31. God's care in trivial matters

Spear. See Index.

Spices: Exodus 30:23-38; John 19:39,40. Divine and moral graces; love and care

Springs: See Index.

Sprinkle many nations: Isaiah 52:15. Grace to Gentile nations

Spue: Leviticus 18:28; Revelation 3:16. Loathing; utter rejection

Staff:
1. Wilderness journeyings: Psalm 23:4; Mark 6:8
2. Power and judgment: Isaiah 10:5; 14:5

Star: Numbers 24:17. A prince or ruler.

Stone, precious: See Index.

Stone, white: Revelation 2:17. Token of full absolution. See STONES, white, in Index.

Summertime: See Index.

Sun: Psalm 84:11. God's goodness and grace. See Index.

Sun and moon: Joel 2:31; Acts 2:20. States, civil and ecclesiastical

Supper:
1. Grace: Luke 14:16-24
2. Communion: Matthew 26:26-28
3. Worship: Revelation 19:7-10
4. Examination of saints: I Corinthians 11:28,31,32
5. Judgment: Revelation 19:17

Swallow: Proverbs 26:2. Restlessness

Swine. See p. 705

Sword. See Index.

Tabernacle: II Corinthians 5:1; II Peter 1:13,14. The human body

Table: Psalm 23:5; I Corinthians 10:21. Fellowship and communion

Tail: Isaiah 9:14,15. False prophets and false teaching

Talents: Matthew 25:15. Gifts bestowed on man by God

Tares: Matthew 13:38. Wicked infidels; unregenerates

Teeth: Proverbs 30:14; Daniel 7:5,7,19. Cruelty; mischievous power

Tempest: Job 9:17; Psalm 11:6. Afflictions; judgment

Temple: I Corinthians 3:16,17; 6:19,20. The believer's body

Thighs: Genesis 32:25; Psalm 45:3. Strength

Thirst. See *Hunger*

Thorns:
1. Perverse Unbelievers: Ezekiel 2:6
2. Worthlessness: Hebrews 6:8
3. Worldly cares, riches, and pleasures: Luke 8:14
4. Instruments of chastisements: Numbers 33:55; II Corinthians 12:7. See PRICKS in Index.

Threshing. See Index.

Throne:
1. Earthly government or kingdom: Genesis 41:40; II Samuel 7:12,16

2. Spiritual kingdom: Colossians 1:16
3. Christ's resurrection: Acts 2:30,31; Revelation 3:21

Thunders: Revelation 10:4. Prophecies

Tongue:
1. Speech: Proverbs 12:18
2. Remorse and torment: Luke 16:24
3. Mere profession: I John 3:18

Towers. See Index.

Travail:
1. Anguish and misery: Jeremiah 4:31; Mark 13:8
2. Solicitude of Christian ministers: Galatians 4:19

Tree of life: Revelation 2:7; 22:2. Pleasures of immortality

Trees. See Index.

Trumpets. See Horns.

Unicorn: Numbers 23:22. Great strength

Veil:
1. Obscurity of Mosaic dispensation: II Corinthians 3:13-16 with Hebrews 9:8
2. Flesh of Christ: Hebrews 10:20
3. Torn—approach to God: Matthew 27:51; Hebrews 10:19,20

Valleys. See Index.

Vessels, earthen: II Corinthians 4:7. The believer's body

Vine; vineyard. See Index.

Vipers:
1. Poisonous doctrines and ways: Job 20:16
2. Wicked children of wicked parents: Matthew 3:7; 12:34

Virgins: II Corinthians 11:2; Revelation 14:4. Separation from sin; commited to God

Walk:
1. After the flesh; guided by sensual appetites: Romans 8:1
2. After the Spirit; guided by the Word: Romans 8:1; Galatians 5:24-26
3. In secret communion with God: Genesis 5:24; 6:9

Walls. See Index.

Wash; washed; washing:
1. Purification—
   a. Moral: Psalm 26:6; 73:13
   b. Spiritual: Psalm 51:2; John 13:8
2. Pardon and sanctification: I Corinthians 6:11; Revelation 1:5; 7:14

Water. See Index.

Week: Daniel 9:24. Seventy weeks of years—490 years. See WEEKS in Index.

Wells. See Index.

Wheat: Jeremiah 23:28; Matthew 13:24-30. Genuine profession

Wheels: Ezekiel 1:19-21; Daniel 7:9. Course of providential government on earth

Whirlwind: Isaiah 66:15; Zechariah 9:14. Manifestation of Divine power

White: Mark 16:5; Revelation 1:14. Purity

Wilderness:
1. General desolation: Isaiah 27:10; Jeremiah 22:6
2. Trial and testing: Matthew 4:1; I Corinthians 10:5,6
3. Future blessings: Isaiah 41:18

Whoredoms: Ezekiel 16:2,25,26. Religious corruptions; spiritual idolatry

Widow: Isaiah 1:23; 47:8. Desolateness

Wind: See Index.

Winds, the four: Daniel 7:2; Revelation 7:1. General destructions

Wine: See Index.
1. Temporal blessings: Psalm 4:7; Hosea 2:8
2. Gospel provision: Isaiah 25:6; 55:1
3. Divine judgment and wrath: Psalm 75:7,8; Revelation 16:19

Wings:
1. Protection: Psalm 17:8; 36:7; 91:4
2. Blessings: Malachi 4:2

Witnesses: Revelation 11:3-6. Persecuted Churches or believers

Wolf, wolves. See Index.

Women:
1. A state or city: Ezekiel 23:2,3
2. The Church of Christ: Revelation 12:1,2
3. Weakness: Isaiah 19:16
4. The anti-Christian church: Revelation 17:3

Word of God. See Bible in Index.
1. Water: Ephesians 5:26
2. Lamp: Psalm 119:105a
3. Light: Psalm 119:105b
4. Fire: Jeremiah 20:8,9; 23:29a
5. Hammer: Jeremiah 23:29b
6. Sword: Hebrews 4:12
7. Seed: I Peter 1:23; Luke 8:11
8. Spiritual nourishment: Jeremiah 15:16; Job 23:12
   a. Milk: I Peter 2:2
   b. Bread: Matthew 4:4
   c. Meat: Hebrews 5:12-14
   d. Desert—honey: Psalm 19:10; 119:103

Worm:
1. Contemptible: Job 25:6; Psalm 22:6
2. Eternal misery: Mark 11:44,46,48

Yoke:
1. Oppressive servitude: Deuteronomy 28:48
2. Painful religious rites: Acts 15:10; Galatians 5:1
3. Delightful service with Christ: Matthew 11:29,30
4. Moral restraints: Lamentations 3:27

Dictionary of Bible Names, Idols, and Gods

DICTIONARY OF BIBLE NAMES

The Scripture names of both persons and things are generally remarkable for their signification. In several instances names were given immediately by God; in others they were imposed by a spirit of prophecy; and many, both persons and things, received theirs from some particular circumstance in their history.

God called our first parent Adam, which signifies earth, or *red earth,* because from the dust man was created (Genesis 2:7; 5:2). He changed the name of Abram, which signifies *high-father,* to Abraham, which means the *father of a great multitude,* or many nations (Genesis 17:5), and that of his wife, Sarai, *my lady,* to Sarah, *lady or princess of a multitude* (Genesis 17:15,16), and Jacob, *a supplanter,* to *Israel,* a prince with God (Genesis 32:28).

By a prophetic spirit some names were imposed, as Noah, signifying *comfort,* and Jesus, *the Savior.* Many names were given on account of some particular circumstances in their history, as Isaac, meaning *laughter* or gladness (Genesis 17:17; 18:12), Bethel, *the house of God* (Genesis 28:17-19), and Moses, *taken from the water* (Exodus 2:10).

It should be observed that those names which begin or terminate with *EL,* or begin with *JE,* or end with *IAH,* were generally designed to express some relation to God, as Beth*el,* the house of God, Isra*el,* a prince with God, and Jerem*iah,* the exaltation of the Lord.

Aaron: enlightened
Abednego: lofty
Abel: vanity
Abigail: a father's joy
Abijam, or Abijah: Jehovah is father
Abner: light
Abraham: father of multitudes
Abram: high-father
Absalom: father of peace, then shame
Achan: troubler
Adam: red earth
Adonijah: Jehovah is my Lord
Ahab: uncle, mischief
Ahasuerus: mighty man
Ahaz: possessor
Ahaziah: Jehovah sustains
Alexander: defending men
Alphaeus: successor
Amaziah: Jehovah strengthens
Amon: builder
Amos: burden
Ananiah: Jehovah covers; gave
Anna: grace
Andrew: manly
Apollos: orator
Aquila: an eagle
Aristarchus: ruling best
Asa: physician
Asaph: collector
Ashar: happy

Athaliah: God is strong
Augustus: renowned
Azariah: whom Jehovah aids

Baasha: Offensive; wicked
Balaam: destructive
Bar: son of
Barabbas: son, to teach
Barnabas: son of prophecy, consolation
Bartholomew: attendant
Bath-sheba: daughter of the oath
Belshazzer: protect the king
Belteshazzar (Daniel): preserve his life
Benjamin: fortunate
Berachah: blessing
Bernice: bringing victory
Bezaleel: under God's shadow
Bildad: son of contention
Boaz: fleetness

Caiaphas: depression
Cain: possession
Caleb: a dog
Chilion: wasting away
Christ. See NAMES, p. 374. How Christ is
    Seen in each Book; Names and Titles in each
    New Testament Book.
    —Messiah (Hebrew)—anointed: John 1:41
    —Christ (Greek)—anointed: Matthew 16:16
    —Jesus—personal name on earth: Matthew
    1:21

—Jesus Christ—once humbled, now exalted:
I Corinthians 1:1
—Christ Jesus—now exalted, once humbled:
Acts 19:4
—Son of man—seed of woman:
Luke 19:10; Galatians 4:4,5
—Seed of David—Israel's seed: Romans 1:3
—Lamb: John 1:29; Revelation 5:12
—Savior: II Timothy 1:10
—Lord Jesus: I Corinthians 5:5
—Lord Jesus Christ: Acts 11:17
—Lord Christ: Colossians 3:24
—The Lord: Matthew 3:3
—Lord of lords: I Timothy 6:15
—Lord of glory: James 2:1
—God: John 20:28; Romans 9:5
—the Almighty: Revelation 1:8
—Emmanual: Matthew 1:23
—the Word: John 1:1
—I AM: John 8:58
—Son of God—begotten: Ephesians 4:13
—Son of the Highest: Luke 1:32
—Chief Shepherd and Bishop:
I Peter 2:25; 5:4
—Master: Colossians 4:1
—Blessed and only Potentate:
I Timothy 6:15a
—King of kings: I Timothy 6:15
—Wonderful, Counsellor, mighty God,
everlasting Father, Prince of Peace:
Isaiah 9:6

Dan: judge
Daniel: God is my Judge
David: beloved
Deborah: a bee
Dinah: vindicated
Dorcas: gazelle (beauty; fleetness)

Ehud: joined together
Elah: strong oak
Eleazar: God helps
Elephaz: God's strength
Eli: lifting up
Eliakim: established by God
Eliezer: God helps
Elihu: God in him
Elijah: God is Jehovah
Elimelech: God is king
Elisha: my God is salvation
Elizabeth: oath of God
Enoch: dedicated
Epaphroditus: handsome
Erastus: beloved

Esau: hairy
Esther: a star
Etham: strong
Eunice: happily victorious
Euodias: success
Eve: mother of the living
Ezekiel: the strength of God
Ezra: help

Felix: happy
Festus: joyful
Fortunatus: prosperous

Gabriel: man of God
Gad: good fortune
Gaius: gladness
Gamaliel: benefit of God
Gehazi: valley of vision
Gershom: expulsion
Gideon: tree-feller
God—God of gods: Deuteronomy 10:17
—Elohim, glory and power connected with
the God-head and creation:
Genesis 1:1,26
—God of hosts—Creator: Amos 4:13
—Most High, supreme God—the possessor
of heaven and earth:
Genesis 14:18; Deuteronomy 32:8
—God of the whole earth: Isaiah 54:5
—God of heaven—exercising the govern-
ment on earth: Ezra 7:12
—El Olam—everlasting God over ever-
lasting things: Genesis 21:33
—God, the enduring, changeless one:
Psalm 102:24-27
—Eloah—only living and true God;
object of worship and subject of
testimony: Deuteronomy 32:15-17
—Almighty God—omnipotent One:
Genesis 17:1
—Divine sustainer and Father-God to
His children: II Corinthians 6:18
—Divine wrath for sinners:
Revelation 19:15
—God, the Judge of man: Amos 4:12
—Judge of all earth: Genesis 18:25
—I AM THAT I AM (El Shaddai):
Exodus 3:14,15
—Jehovah: Lord—moral relationship
established with His people:
Jeremiah 31:12,14
—adonai—Master: Amos 9:1
—gemulah—Recompense: Jeremiah 51:56
—jirah—Provider: Genesis 22:13,14

—M'kasdesh—Sanctifier: Leviticus 20:7,8
—nakah—Guide: Isaiah 58:11
—nissi—Banner: Exodus 17:15
—raah—Shepherd: Psalm 23:1
—See NAMES, p. 244
—rophe—Healer: Exodus 15:26
—sabaoth—Hosts: Isaiah 1:9
—shalom—Peace: Judges 6:24
—shammah—Omnipresent: Ezekiel 48:35
—my Stay—Companion: II Samuel 22:19
—Rock of Ages (everlasting strength):
Isaiah 26:4
—tsidkenu—Righteousness: Jeremiah
23:6
—Lord God—Master: Genesis 15:2
—Lord God of Truth: Psalm 31:5
—Lord—maker and controller of the
universe: Amos 5:8
—Lord of all the earth—authority over
and proprietorship of all the earth:
Joshua 3:11-13
—Lord of hosts—never defeated; One to
rely upon when crisis arises:
I Samuel 1:3,11
—Lord God—Captain: II Chronicles 13:12
—Lord God—hearer of prayers: Daniel 9:3
—keeper of His word: Daniel 9:4
—Lord—Compassion: Jonah 1:1,2
—Lord of lords: Deuteronomy 10:17
—King of kings, King of glory:
I Timothy 6:16; Psalm 24:8
—Rock—foundation: Deuteronomy 32:4
—Holy One and Shepherd of Israel:
Isaiah 1:4; Psalm 80:1
—Holy and Reverend: Psalm 111:9
—The Highest, Supreme: Luke 1:35
—Saviour; Redeemer: II Samuel 22:3;
Luke 1:47; Isaiah 54:5
—Father—relationship to Israel:
II Chronicles 29:10; Psalm 89:26
—relationship to His Son: John 17:1
—Abba-Father—relationship to believers:
Romans 8:15; Ephesians 1:2

Habakkuk: embrace
Haggai: festive
Ham: warm
Haman: splendid
Hananiah: gracious God
Hannah: gracious
Heman: faithful
Hezekiah: might of Jehovah
Hilkiah: Jehovah's portion
Hiram: nobility

Holy Spirit. See NAMES in Books
—Holy Spirit: Luke 11:13
—Holy Ghost: Matthew 1:20; 3:11
—The Spirit: Matthew 4:1;
I Corinthians 2:10
—His Holy Spirit: Isaiah 63:10
—Spirit of God: Genesis 1:2; Matthew 3:16
—Spirit of the Lord: II Chronicles 20:14
—Spirit of the Lord God: Isaiah 61:1
—Spirit of the living God:
II Corinthians 3:17
—Spirit of His Son: Galatians 4:6
—Spirit of Jesus Christ: Philippians 1:19
—Spirit of Christ: I Peter 1:11
—Spirit of Grace: Hebrews 10:29
—Spirit of Glory: I Peter 4:14
—Eternal Spirit: Hebrews 9:14
—Promise of the Father: Luke 24:49
—Holy Spirit of Promise: Galatians 1:13
—Lord: II Corinthians 3:17
—Lord of the harvest: Luke 10:2
—Holy One: I John 2:20
—Almighty: Job 32:8
Hosea: deliverance (salvation)
Hoshea: delivered

Ichabod: inglorious (God's glory departed)
Isaac: laughter
Isaiah: salvation of Jehovah
Ishmael: God hears
Israel (Jacob): soldier of God; prince
Issachar: to hire

Jabez: causing pain
Jacob: supplanter
Jahaziel: God watches over
Jarius: God enlightens
James (English equiv. of Jacob)
Jason: God is salvation
Jehoahaz: Jehovah holds fast
Jehoash: Jehovah is strong
Jehoiachin, or **Jeconiah:** Jehovah establishes
Jehoiakim: Jehovah will raise
Jehoram, or **Joram:** Jehovah exalted
Jehoshaphat: Jehovah judges
Jehovah. See *God.*
Jehu: Jehovah is he
Jephthah: God opens
Jeremiah: appointed by God
Jeroboam: struggler for the people
Jesse: firm
Jesus. See *Christ.*
Jethro: excellence
Jezebel: chaste

Joab: Jehovah is father
Joash, or Jehoash: Jehovah gathered
Job: persecuted
Joel: Jehovah is might
John: God is gracious
Jonah: dove
Jonathan: God is gracious
Joshua: Saviour; salvation
Josiah: Jehovah heals
Joseph: he shall add
Jotham: Jehovah is perfect
Judah: praise
Judas Iscariot: traitor
Jude: from Judah—praise

Kish: bow
Korah: baldness

Laban: white
Lamech: destroyer
Lazarus: help of God
Leah: weary; to tire
Levi: associated
Lot: covering; vail
Luke: illuminate; light

Malachi: messenger of Jehovah
Manasseh: forgetting
Mara (Naomi): sad, bitter
Mark: large hammer
Martha: lady
Mary: bitterness
Matthew: gift of God
Melchizedek: king of righteousness
Menehem: consoler
Mephibosheth: destroying shame
Meshach (Mishael): borrowed from God
Methuselah: man (adult) of the dart
Micah: who is like Jehovah
Micaiah: like Jehovah
Michal: rivulet
Miriam: bitterness (rebellion)
Mishael (Meshach): who or what God is
Mordecai: consecrated to Merodach; a
    Babylonian and Assyrian god of war—
    "guardian of the people"
Moses: drawn from the water

Naaman: pleasantness
Naboth: fruits
Nadab: liberal
Nahum: comforter
Naomi: pleasant
Naphtali: my wrestling

Nathan: gift
Nathanael: gift of God
Nebuchadnezzar: protect the landmark
Nehemiah: Jehovah comforts
Nicodemus: victor of the people
Noah: rest

Obed: worshiper
Obediah: worshiper of Jehovah
Omri: handful; servant
Onesimus: profitable
Othniel: lion of God

Paul: little
Pekah: open-eyed
Pekahiah: Jehovah opens eyes
Peter: rock
Pharaoh (title): ruler, son of the sun
Phebe: moon
Philemon: affectionate
Philip: lover of horses
Phinehas: serpent's mouth
Pilate: armed with a javelin
Pontius: belonging to the sea
Priscilla: ancient

Rachel: ewe
Rahab: large
Rebekah: a noose
Rehoboam: extension of the people
Reuben: behold a son; unstable
Rhoda: a rose
Ruth: friendship

Salome: perfect; peaceable
Samson: sun-man; strength
Samuel: heard (or asked) of God
Sanballat: perversity; mischief
Sapphira: beautiful
Sarah: princess of many nations
Sarai: my lady
Sargon: God appoints
Saul: asked for
Seth: substitute
Shadrach (Hananiah): reference to god-moon
Shallum: recompense
Silas: of the forest
Simeon: a hearkening
Simon: hearing
Solomon: peaceful
Spirit: See Holy Spirit
Stephen: crown
Syntyche: fortunate

Thaddaeus: praise
Theophilus: loved of God
Thomas: twin
Timothy: honoring God
Titus: protected
Tobiah: God is good
Tychicus: fate

Uriah: God is my light
Uzziah (Azariah): strength of God

Vashti: beautiful

Zabdi: gift of Jehovah
Zachariah; Zacharias: Jehovah remembers
Zebedee: gift of God
Zebulun: habitation
Zechariah: Jehovah remembers
Zedekiah (Mattaniah): righteousness
Zephaniah: Jehovah hides
Zerubbabel: born in Babylon
Zimri: famed in song

IDOLS AND GODS

Adrammelech: II Kings 17:31. Assyrian "sun" deity; king of fire. Humans (children especially) offered to this god. See MOLECH in Index.

Annammelech: II Kings 17:31. Assyrian "moon" deity; queen of fire. Children offered as human sacrifices. See HUMAN Sacrifice in Index.

Ashima: II Kings 17:30. Assyrian deity; a "goat

Ashtoroth (Astarte): I Kings 11:33. Plural of Ashtoreth. Canaanite fertility goddess; sexual love. See QUEEN of Heaven.

Baal: I Kings 18:21. Canaanite deity: Lord or master; sensual. A male deity representing the sun and all nature. There are traces still extant of customs in Ireland, Wales, and parts of Scotland, which evidently show that *Baal* worship was practiced by our ancestors under the ancient Druids. In Perthshire there is a town called Tillie-beltane—*the hill of the fire of Baal*. See BAAL WORSHIP in Index.

Baal-berith: Judges 8:33. Lord of covenants; worship of Baal by the Shechemites.

Baal-peor: Numbers 25:3. Lord of the opening; worship of Baal by the Moabites. It was in Moab that the Israelites were seduced to the filthy form of idolatry.

Baal-zebub: II Kings 1:2. Ekron deity; lord or god of flies, who became the Beelzebub of the New Testament, and who had power of curing certain diseases: Matthew 10:25; 12:24.

B-amah: Ezekiel 20:29. Idolatrous "high place" where idolaters performed their abominable rites: II Kings 21:1-9. See HIGH PLACE in Index.

Bel: Jeremiah 50:2. Babylonian form of Baal.

Brazen Serpent. See Nehashtan.

Chemosh: Numbers 21:29. Moabite deity; subduer. Human sacrifices were made to this god: II Kings 3:27.

Chiun: Amos 5:26. Possibly some idol (form of Egyptian idolatry) worshiped by Israel in the wilderness and still practiced in the days of Amos. A form of "star" worship.

Dagon: I Samuel 5:2. Philistine national deity; part man and part fish.

Diana: Acts 19:24-35. Greek goddess of fertility. See DIANA in Index.

Gad (that troop) and **Meni** (that number): Isaiah 65:11. Possibly representatve of Jupiter and Venus—stars of fortune.

God for forces, or of war: Daniel 11:38. Anti-Christian ruler—probably the Antichrist of the Tribulation Period.

Golden Calf: Exodus 32:1-6; Psalm 106:19,20. Form of Egyptian idolatry embraced by Israel in the wilderness, which not only lowered God's own glory, but changed the glory of the Creator to that of a four-footed beast (Romans 1:23). Centuries later King Jeroboam of the Northern Kingdom of Israel established this form of idolatry (I Kings 12:25-33), no doubt, because of its familiarity to him while he was in Egypt (I Kings 11:40).

Grove (Asherah): Deuteronomy 16:21; Judges 3:7. See GROVES in Index.

High Places. See HIGH PLACE in Index.

Jupiter and Mercurius: Acts 14:11,12. Jupiter to the Greeks was the supreme deity, with absolute control over all gods and creation (Zeus was the Greek name; Jupiter, the Roman name). Mercurius was the god of speech or eloquence—Jupiter's special messenger. Barnabas, probably because of his venerable appearance or supposed likeness to their god, was named "Jupiter" by the Lystrians. Paul, because of his speech, was called "Mercurius."

Meni. See Gad.

Mercurius. See Jupiter.

Merodach: Jeremiah 50:2. Babylonian and Assyrian god of "war," "guardian of the people."

Milcom: I Kings 11:5. An Ammonite idol; same as Molech.

Molech: II Kings 23:10. Moabite god of fire. See MOLECH in Index.

Nebo: Isaiah 46:1. Assyrian and Babylonian god of speech and learning, often incorporated in names of kings. Nebuchadnezzar means "Nebo protect the boundary."

Nehushtan: II Kings 18:4. A word of contempt, meaning "a piece of brass," applied to the brazen serpent (Numbers 21:8). Having preserved this object since their wilderness experience, Israel burnt incense to it in connection with her worship of Baal. See SERPENT in Index.

Nergal: II Kings 17:30. Assyrian deity; a "lion," who supposedly presided over the fortunes of war and hunting. See LIONS in Index.

Nibhaz: II Kings 17:31. Assyrian deity; a "dog."

Nisroch: II Kings 19:37. Assyrian deity; a "great eagle." Sennacherib was worshiping this idol when slain by his two sons (Isaiah 37:37,38).

Queen of heaven: Jeremiah 7:18. The "moon" was worshiped as the "queen of heaven" under the title "Ashtoreth," and was generally associated with "Baal," the sun. In Roman Catholic circles today, Mary, the mother of Jesus, is called "queen of heaven."

Remphan: Acts 7:43. See Chiun.

Rimmon: II Kings 5:18. Syrian deity, representing the sun.

Succoth-benoth: II Kings 17:30. Refers to tents or booths erected by the colonists sent to re-people Samaria after the Northern Kingdom's downfall in honor of the goddess of "uncleanness."

Tammuz: Ezekiel 8:14. Syrian god of fertility, mourned by women due to his long absence when supposedly killed by a wild boar.

Tartak: II Kings 17:31. Assyrian deity; an "ass."

Teraphim: Judges 17:5. Household gods in general as distinguished from national gods (such as *Chemosh* of the Moabites). An idolatrous religion originated by the head of a house, and the idols were handed down from son to grandson, etc. See FAMILY GODS in Index.

Unknown god: Acts 17:23. See Index.

Illustration Credits

Alinari, Fratelli, 384
American Baptist Publications, 189
Am. Bible Soc., 178 (Inscription)
Am. School, Classical Studies, 534
American Numismatic Society, 606
   Coins, 847, 473, 482
Boyd, Bob, 40, 42, 43, 50, 51, 56, 68, 70, 94,
   96, 100, 111, 112, 123 (2), 126, 133, 152,
   161, 170, 174 (2), 175, 184, 197, 207, 235,
   237—239, 272, 279, 294, 299 (2),
   301—303, 375, 385 (2), 389, 391, 392,
   394, 406, 407, 416—418, 464, 473
   (stone), 483, 491 (2), 492 (2), 544, 579,
   604, 693, 718 (2)
British Museum, The, 38, 63, 92, 101, 169,
   170, 172, 173, 178, 179, 200, 205, 213,
   303, 499, 519
Brooklyn Museum, 499
Cairo (Egypt)Museum, 67, 68, 122, 241
Caisse National Monuments, 122
   (Enlarged Inscription)
Cameron, George C., 311
Delachaux & Niestle, 177
Elsevier, B. V., Amsterdam, 277
Felbermeyer, J., 481, 615
Hebrew University, Jerusalem, 109
Israel Antiquities, 160, 392

Israel Information Services, 64, 504
Israel Museum, 176, 275
Istanbul Museum, 159
Musees Nationaux (Louvre), 105, 129, 169,
   196, 567
Matson, 96, 159, 288, 239, 388, 393 (2), 395,
   481
Metropolitan Museum of Art, 45, 67, 520
Miles, George A., 257
Naples Museum, 482
NASA Photograph, 224
Oriental Institute, 85, 108, 141, 161, 172,
   176, 177, 188, 271
Palestine Archaeological Museum, 326
Palestine Exploration Fund, 505
Pfeiffer, Charles F., 107
Pontifical Bible Institute, 39, 41, 200, 256,
   312, 485, 505, 506
Pritchard, James B., 119
Rylands Library, John, 494
Schaeffer, C.F.A., 111
Smithsonian Institute, 172
Trever, John C., 276
Weidner, Ernst (Am. Bible Soc.), 178
Wolfe Worldwide Films, 95

Quotation Credits

The Bible

1. Billy Sunday 2. F. B. Meyer 3. Alan F. Johnson, *Inspiration of the Scriptures: A Look at Inerrancy,* Wheaton College Bulletin "InForum," October 1979 (points 1, 2, 3)* 4. Bancroft's Elemental Theology* 5. New York Christian Herald

Genesis

1. John Gill's Commentary 2. Henry M. Morris, Institute for Creation Research* 3. George Mundell, The Pathway of Faith* 4. P. J. Wiseman, New Discoveries about Genesis 5. Harry Rimmer, Lot's Wife and the Science of Physics, Wm. B. Eerdmans* 6. Clifford Wilson, Secrets of a Forgotten City* 7. Bob Boyd, Light from Biblical Customs* 8. James Smith, Daily Bible Readings, 9. Boyd, Good Morning, Lord*

Exodus

1. John Gill 2. George B. Fletcher* 3. W. W. Rugh 4. Handfuls on Purpose, Eerdmans* 5. Handfuls on Purpose, Eerdmans* 6. Handfuls on Purpose, Eerdmans* 7. The Bible Companion 8. W. F. Albright 9. Joseph P. Free, Archaeology and Bible History, Van Kampen Press* 10. Biblical Customs* 11. James Smith, 12. Good Morning, Lord*

Leviticus

1. George B. Fletcher* 2. M. R. DeHaan, Chemistry of the Blood, Zondervan Publishing House* 3. M. R. DeHaan, Chemistry of the Blood, Zondervan Publishing House* 4. Halley's Bible Handbook Zondervan* 5. James Smith 6. Good Morning, Lord*

Numbers

1. John McNichol 2. Handfuls on Purpose, Eerdmans* 3. Robert L. Moyer, The Saviour and the Shadows* 4. Biblical Customs* 5. Dwight L. Moody, Notes from My Bible, Flemming II. Revell Co.* 6. Boyd, Clip 'n Save* 7. James Smith 8. Good Morning, Lord*

Deuteronomy

1. George B. Fletcher* 2. J. Vernon McGhee, Briefing the Bible, Zondervan* 3. Biblical Customs* 4. James Smith 5. Good Morning, Lord* 6. Boyd, Tells, Tombs and Treasure, Baker Book House* 7. Boyd, Baal Worship in Old Testament Days and Today*

Joshua

1. Biblical Customs* 2. Harry Rimmer, The Harmony and Science of Scripture, Eerdmans*; Stephen A. Bly, excerpts from How Little Did Joshua Know* 3. Handfuls on Purpose, Eerdmans* 4. James Smith 5. Good Morning, Lord*

The asterisk (*) used throughout this Index denotes "Used by Permission"

Judges

1. Handfuls on Purpose, Eerdmans* 2. James Smith 3. Good Morning, Lord*

Ruth

1. Adam Clarke's Commentary 2. Handfuls on Purpose, Eerdmans* 3. Biblical Customs* 4. James Smith 5. Good Morning, Lord*

First Samuel

1. Biblical Customs* 2. James Smith 3. Good Morning, Lord*

Second Samuel

1. Handfuls on Purpose, Eerdmans* 2. Biblical Customs 3. The Bible Companion 4. James Smith 5. Good Morning, Lord*

First Kings

1. John Gill 2. Handfuls on Purpose, Eerdmans* 3. Biblical Customs* 4. Baal Worship* 5. Charles G. Clugh 6. James Smith 7. Good Morning, Lord*

Second Kings

1. Biblical Customs* 2. James Smith 3. Good Morning, Lord*

First Chronicles

1. John Gill 2. George B. Fletcher* 3. James Smith 4. Good Morning, Lord*

Second Chronicles

1. Biblical Customs* 2. Clip 'n Save* 3. James Smith 4. Good Morning, Lord*

Post Captivity Books

1. Thomas Scott

Ezra

1, 2. George B. Fletcher* 3. Biblical Customs* 4. James Smith 5. Good Morning, Lord*

Nehemiah

1. George B. Fletcher* 2. Biblical Customs* 3. James M. Gray 4. James Smith 5. Good Morning, Lord*

Esther

1. George B. Fletcher* 2. Biblical Customs* 4. James Smith 5. Good Morning, Lord*

Job

1. George B. Fletcher* 2, 4, 6. John Gill 3. Author Unknown   5. Biblical Customs* 7. Jean Sloat Morton, Science and the Bible, Moody Press* 8. W. W. Wythe, 188 Heart Searching Sermons, Zondervan* 9. James Smith 10. Good Morning, Lord*

Psalms

1. George B. Fletcher* 2. Bullinger and Sayer 3. Biblical Customs* 5. Boyd, Now Hear This* 6. Clip 'n Save* 7. Frances Little Boyd, Moody Monthly* 8. Ball Worship 9. Author Unknown 10. James Smith 11. Good Morning, Lord*

Proverbs

1. Bishop Hopkins 2. Author Unknown 3. P. G. Parker 4. Biblical Customs* 5. Clip 'n Save* 6. James Smith 7. Good Morning, Lord*

Ecclesiastes

1. John Gill 2, 3. George B. Fletcher* 4. Biblical Customs* 5. T. J. McCrossan, The Bible: Its Christ* 6. Basil W. Miller, Bible Reading for Christian Workers 7. James Smith 8. Good Morning, Lord*

Song of Solomon

1, 2. George B. Fletcher* 3. James Smith 4. Good Morning, Lord*

Prophets and Prophecy

1. Herbert H. Ehrenstein, Fulfilled Prophecy*

Isaiah

1. L. Tucker 2. George B. Fletcher* 3. James M. Gray 4. T. J. McCrossan* 5 Biblical Customs* 6. James Smith 7. Good Morning, Lord*

Jeremiah

1. George B. Fletcher* 2. The New Thompson Chain Reference Bible, B. B. Kirkbride Bible Co., Inc., Indianapolis, IN* 3. Biblical Customs* 4. T. J. McCrossan* 5. James Smith 6. Good Morning, Lord*

Lamentations

1. George B. Fletcher* 2. Biblical Customs* 3. James Smith 4. Good Morning, Lord*

Ezekiel

1. George B. Fletcher* 2. Harry Rimmer, The Shadow of His Coming, Eerdmans* 3. Biblical Customs* 4. James Smith 5. Good Morning, Lord*

Daniel

1. T. J. McCrossan* 2. Peggy Boyd 3. Christian Victory 4. Howard Miller 5. Dwight L. Moody, Notes from My Bible, Revell* 6. James Smith 7. Good Morning, Lord*

Hosea

1, 2. George B. Fletcher* 3. James Smith 4. Good Morning, Lord*

Joel

1. George B. Fletcher* 2. James Smith 3. Good Morning, Lord*

Amos

1. Copied   2. Biblical Customs* 3. Dwight L. Moody, Notes from My Bible, Revell* 4. James Smith 5. Good Morning, Lord*

Obediah

1. James Smith 2. Good Morning, Lord*

Jonah

1. John Gill 2. L. Tucker 3. Paul Dunbar   4. Author Unknown† 5. James Smith 6. Good Morning, Lord*

Micah

1. George B. Fletcher* 2. J. Vernon McGhee, Briefing the Bible, Zondervan* 3. A. T. Pierson 4. James Smith 5. Good Morning, Lord*

Nahum

1. George B. Fletcher* 2. Charles Haddon Spurgeon 3. James Smith 4. Good Morning, Lord*

Habakkuk

1. Matthew Henry 2. Author Unknown   3. Clip 'n Save* 4. James Smith 5. Good Morning, Lord*

Zepheniah

1. James Smith 2. Good Morning, Lord*

Haggai

1. Biblical Customs* 2. Clip 'n Save* 3. James Smith 4. Good Morning, Lord*

Zechariah

1. John Gill 2. James Smith 3. Good Morning, Lord*

Malachi

1. William S. Deal, Baker's Pictorial Introduction to the Bible, Baker* 2. George B. Fletcher* 3. Dwight L. Moody, Notes from My Bible, Revell* 4. Clip 'n Save* 5. James Smith 6. Good Morning, Lord*

New Testament Introduction

1. Unger's Bible Handbook, Moody Press* 2. William Pettingill, Matthew*

Matthew

1. Biblical Customs* 2. Copied   3. Now Hear This* 4. St. Francis DeSales 5. R. C. Steinhart 6. Clip 'n Save* 7. James Smith 8. Good Morning, Lord*

Mark

1. W. W. Rugh 2. Biblical Customs* 3. W. W. Wythe, Pulpit Germs, Judson Press* 4, 5. Dwight L. Moody, Notes from My Bible, Revell* 6. James Smith 7. Good Morning, Lord*

Luke

1. W. W. Rugh 2. Biblical Customs* 3. Dwight L. Moody, Notes from My Bible, Revell* 4. Handfuls on Purpose, Eerdmans* 5. Fred A. Brown 6, 8. Clip 'n Save* 7. Lois Kendall Blanchard, Faith, Prayer and Tract Leage* 9. Now Hear This* 10. James Smith 11. Good Morning, Lord*

John

1. Harold S. Laird, Portraits of Christ, Moody Press* 2. Harry A. Ironside, Addresses on John, Loizeaux* 3. Biblical Customs* 4. Robert L. Layfield 5. Now Hear This* 6. Handfuls on Purpose, Eerdmans* 7. L. J. Derk 8. James Smith 9. Good Morning, Lord*

Highlights in Christ's Life

1, 2, 3. Bancroft* 4. Clip 'n Save* 5. Dwight L. Moody, Notes from My Bible, Revell* 6. Marvin Rosenthal, The Passover Today* 7. George A. Palmer, Christ in Gethsemane* 8. Richard Maxwell, Maxwell-Wirges Pub.* 9. Henry Einspruch 10. Geike's Life of Christ 11. Author Unknown 12. H. A. Cameron, The Wounds of Christ 13. Dwight L. Moody, Notes from My Bible, Revell* 14. Frank S. Murray, He Descended Into Hell, Moody Monthly and The Standart* 15, 16. Bancroft* 17. Josephus, Antiquities, XVIII, iii, 3

Acts

1. John Gill 2. Howard Estep, World Prophetic Ministries* 3. Biblical Customs* 4. Vance Havner, Blood Bread, and Fire, Eerdmans* 5. Clip 'n Save* 6. E. M. Bounds, Power Through Prayer, Nazarene Pub.* 7. Copied 8. James Smith 9. Good Morning, Lord*

Romans

1. John Gill 2. Donald Gray Barnhouse 3. Curvin Stambaugh 4. Bible Companion 5. Biblical Customs* 6. Charles H. Stephens 7. James Shields 8. Authur W. Pink* Clip 'n Save* 10 James Smith 11. Good Morning, Lord*

First Corinthians

1. John Gill 2. Biblical Customs* 3. Church Chimes 4. Now Hear This* 5. James Smith 6. Good Morning, Lord*

Second Corinthians

1. J. J. Lias 2. Roy Hession, The Calvary Road, Christian Literature Crusade, Inc.* 3. Now Hear This* 4. Vance Havner, It Is Time, Revell* 5, 6. Author Unknown 7. James Smith 8. Good Morning, Lord*

Galatians

1. Adam Clark 2. Biblical Customs* 3. W. W. Rugh 4. Now Hear This* 5. James Smith 6. Good Morning, Lord*

Ephesians

1. Adam Clark 2. John Gill 3. Biblical Customs* 4, 5, 6, 8. Copied   7. David C. Boaz   9 James Smith 10. Good Morning, Lord*

Philippians

1. Adam Clark 2. John Gill 3. Now Hear This* 4. Copied   5, 6. Clip 'n Save* 7. James Smith 8. Good Morning, Lord*

Colossians

1. Adam Clark 2. J. Wilbur Chapman 3. James Smith 4. Good Morning, Lord*

First Thessalonians

1. Adam Clark 2. James Smith 3. Good Morning, Lord*

Second Thessalonians

1. John Gill 2. Bancroft* 3. James Smith 4. Good Morning, Lord*

Pastoral Epistles

1. David F. Mygren

First Timothy

1, 2, 3, 5. Adam Clark 4. John Gill 6. Copied   7. James Smith 8. Good Morning, Lord*

Second Timothy

1. John Gill 2. R. Clyde Smith, Moody Monthly 3, 5. Author Unknown   4. Eddie Wagner, Striking Sermon Starters, Zondervan* 6. James Smith 7. Good Morning, Lord*

Titus

1. George B. Fletcher* 2. Bancroft* 3. James Smith 4. Good Morning, Lord*

Philemon

1. James Smith 2. Good Morning, Lord*

Hebrews

1. Clarence H. Benson, A Guide for Bible Study, ETTA* 2. Vollmer 3, 5. Copied   4. Clip 'n Save* 6. Edgar A Guest   7. The Evangelist* 8. Helen Willis   9. James Smith 10. Good Morning, Lord*

James

1. Clarence A. Benson, A Guide for Bible Study, ETTA* 2. Henry Hepburn   3. The Bible Friend 4. James Smith 5. Good Morning, Lord*

First Peter

1. John Gill 2. James Smith 3. Good Morning, Lord*

Second Peter

1. George B. Fletcher* 2. Ernest Sellers 3. James Smith 4. Good Morning, Lord*

First John

1. John Gill 2. George B. Fletcher* 3. Adam Clark 4. The Rod of God 5. John Smith 6. Good Morning, Lord*

Second John

1. James Smith 2. Good Morning, Lord*

Third John

1. James Smith 2. Good Morning, Lord*

Jude

1. James Smith 2. Good Morning, Lord*

Revelation

1. Biblical Customs* 2. B. B. Caldwell 3. Bancroft* 4. James Smith 5. Good Morning, Lord*

Summary

1. The Bible Companion

Bibliography

Allegro, John M., *The People of the Dead Sea Scrolls,* Doubleday & Co., Inc., Garden City, NY

Allen, R. Earl, *Bible Paradoxes,* 1963, Baker Book House, Grand Rapids, MI

Allis, Oswald T., *Prophecy and the Church,* 1945, Presbyterian & Reformed Pub., Philadelphia, PA

Ancient Empires, Vol. I, Newsweek, New York, NY

Ancient Times, Everyday Life in, National Geographic Society, Washington, D.C.

Anderson, Bernhard W., *Understanding the Old Testament,* 1957, Prentice-Hall Inc., Englewood Cliffs, NJ

Archaeological Discoveries in the Holy Land, 1967, The Archaeological Institute of America, Bonanza Publishers, New York, NY

Associates for Biblical Research, Huntingdon Valley, PA

Bancroft, Emery H., Elemental Theology, 1932, Binghamton, NY

Baskin, Wade, *Dictionary of Satanism,* 1972, Crown Pub., New York, NY

Baxter, J. Sidlow, *Explore the Book,* 1967, Zondervan Pub. House, Grand Rapids, MI

Bell, Alvin E., *The Gist of the Bible,* 1926, Geo. H. Doran Co., New York, NY

Benson, Clarence H., *A Guide for Bible Study, Unit III,* 1950, Evangelical Teacher Training Assn., Chicago, IL

Bible and Spade, Word of Truth Publications, Ballston Spa, NY

Bible Companion, The, 1883, Edward C. Miekle Publishers, Philadelphia, PA

Bible Newsletter, Evangelical Ministries, Inc., Philadelphia, PA

Bible Times, Everyday Life in, National Geographic Society, Washington, D.C.

Biblical Archaeologist, Cambridge, MA

Biblical Archaeology Review, Washington, D.C.

Bibliotheca Sacra, Vol. 113, July 1956, Dallas (TX) Theological Seminary

Billheimer, Paul E., *Destined for the Throne,* Christian Literature Crusade, Ft. Washington, PA

Birnbaum, Solomon, *Jewish Contributions to Christmas,* Hermon House, New York, NY

Bounds, E. M., *Power Through Prayer,* Nazarene Publishing House, Kansas City, MO

Boyd, Robert T., *Baal Worship in Old Testament Days and Today,* 1966, 1979, Hagerstown Printing Co., Hagerstown, MD

. . . . . , Biblical Customs, 1970, Vernon Martin Assoc., Lancaster, PA

. . . . . , *Clip 'n Save,* 1961, Vernon Martin Assoc.

. . . . . , *Footsteps in Bible Lands,* 1972, Donald Drake printers, Johnson City, NY

. . . . . , *Good Morning, Lord!,* 1968, Vernon Martin Assoc.

. . . . . , *Now Hear This,* 1966, Vernon Martin Assoc.

. . . . . , *Tells, Tombs and Treasure,* 1969, Baker Book House, Grand Rapids, MI (now *A Pictorial Guide to Biblical Archaeology,* Bonanza, New York; Harvest House Pub., Eugene, OR)

. . . . . , *Testimony of a Sheep,* 1962, Century Press, Scranton, PA

Brooks, Keith L., *The Mission of Jesus Christ,* August 1951, Prophecy Monthly, Los Angeles, CA

. . . . . , *The Summarized Bible,* Bible Institute of Los Angeles, CA

Bryant, T. Alton, *The New Compact Bible Dictionary,* 1967, Zondervan Pub. House, Grand Rapids, MI

Callaway, T. W., *1000 Sermon Outlines,* 1943, Zondervan Pub. House, Grand Rapids, MI

Cameron, H. A., *He Was Wounded,* Faithful Words, St. Louis, MO

Campbell, John L., *The Bible Under Fire,* 1928, Harper & Bros., New York, NY

Christian Herald, Discovery of Ancient Ebla, March 1977

Christianity Today, Washington, D.C.

Clark's Commentary, Abington-Cokesbury Press, New York-Nashville

Coder, Maxwell S., *Our Wonderful Bible,* Moody Press, Chicago, IL

....., and Howe, Geo. F., *Truth Triumphant,* 1965, Moody Press, Chicago, IL

Davis, John D., *A Dictionary of the Bible,* 1942, Baker Book House, Grand Rapids, MI

Deal, William S., *Baker's Pictorial Introduction to the Bible,* 1967, Baker Book House, Grand Rapids, MI

DeHaan, M. R., *The Chemistry of the Blood,* 1943, Zondervan Pub. House, Grand Rapids, MI

....., *The Jew and Palestine in Prophecy,* 1950, Zondervan Pub. House, Grand Rapids, MI

Downie, H. K., *Practical Sermon Outlines,* 1947, Zondervan, Grand Rapids, MI

Edersheim, Alfred, *The Life and Times Jesus the Messiah,* 1971, Wm. B. Eerdsman Pub. Co., Grand Rapids, MI

Ehrenstein, Herbert H., *Fulfilled Prophecy,* 1956, The Evangelical Foundation, Philadelphia, PA

Engstrom, Theo. W. *188 Heart Reaching Sermon Outlines,* 1950, Zondervan

....., *Sermon Outlines and Illustrations,* 1942, Zondervan

Epp, Theo. H., *True Science Agrees with Scripture,* 1953, Good News Broadcasting Assn. Inc., Lincoln, NB

Evans, William, *How to Prepare Sermons,* Moody Press, Chicago, IL

....., *The Book of Books,* 1902, Moody Colportage Assn., Chicago, IL

Everest, F. Alton, *Hidden Treasure,* 1951, Moody Press

Fletcher, George B., *Introductory Bible Study,* 1938

Free, Joseph P., *Archaeology and Bible History,* 1950, Van Kampen, Wheaton, IL

Gasque, W. Ward, *Sir William M. Ramsey,* 1966, Baker Book House Grand Rapids, MI

Gordon, Cyrus, *Adventures in the Near East,* 1957, Phoenix House, Ltd., London, England

....., *Greek and Hebrew Civilizations,* 1965, W. W. Norton & Co., New York, NY

....., *Hammurabi's Code,* 1963, Holt, Rinehart & Winston, Inc., New York, NY

....., *The Ancient Near East,* 1965, W. W. Norton & Co., New York, NY

Gill, John, *Dr. Gill's Commentary of the Bible,* T. Lassetter, Atlanta, GA

Halley, Henry H., *Pocket Bible Handbook,* 1951, Zondervan Pub. House

....., *Handfuls on Purpose,* 1945, Wm. B. Eerdmans, Grand Rapids, MI

Hauser, Ernest O., *Nero: History's Most Spectacular Tyrant,* Dec. 1969, The Readers Digest, Pleasantville, NY

Havner, Vance, *Blood, Bread, and Fire,* 1939, Zondervan Pub. House, Grand Rapids, MI

....., *It Is Time,* Fleming Revell, Westwood, NJ

Henry, Matthew, Commentary

Hession, Roy, *The Calvary Road,* Christian Literature Crusade, Ft. Washington, PA

Hodgkins, Henry E., *Christ in All the Scriptures,* 1936, Pickerings and Inglis, London, England

Horton, T. C., *Wonderful Names of Our Wonderful Lord,* 1928, Los Angeles, CA

International Standard Bible Encyclopaedia, W. B. Eerdmans, Grand Rapids, MI

Ironside, Harry, *Addresses on John,* Loizeaux Bros., Neptune, NJ

....., *Addresses on the Song of Solomon,* Loizeaux

....., *In the Heavenlies,* Loizeaux

....., *Things Seen and Heard in Bible Lands,* Loizeaux

Josephus Flavius, The John C. Winston Co., Philadelphia, PA

Keiper, Ralph L., *The Power of Biblical Thinking,* 1977, Revell, Old Tappan, NJ

Kuiper, H. J., *Sermons on the Ten Commandments,* Zondervan, Grand Rapids, MI

Laird, Harold, *Portraits of Christ in the Gospel of John,* Moody Press, Chicago, IL

Lang, Walter, *Five Minutes with the Bible and Science,* 1972, Baker Book House

LaSor, William S., *Dead Sea Scrolls and the Christian Faith,* 1956, Moody Press

Lee, Robert, *The Outline Bible,* Pickerings and Inglis, London, England

Lindsell, Harold, *The Battle for the Bible,* 1976, Zondervan, Grand Rapids, MI

McComb, John, *Until the Flood,* Loizeaux, Neptune, NJ

McCrossan, *The Bible: Its Christ,* 1929, Seattle, WA

McDowell, Josh, *Evidence that Demands a Verdict,* 1972, Campus Crusade for Christ, Inc.

. . . . . , *More Evidence that Demands a Verdict,* 1975, Campus Crusade

Miller, Basil W., *Bible Reading for Christian Workers,* 1930

Miller, Madeleine S. and J. Lane, *Encyclopedia of Bible Life,* 1944, Harper & Bros., Pub., New York, N.Y.

Moody, Dwight L., *Notes from My Bible,* 1895, Revell, Westwood, NJ

Moorhead, W. G., *Outline Studies in the Old Testament,* 1894, Revell

. . . . . , *Living Messages of the Books of the Bible,* 1912, Revell

Morris, Henry M., *The Bible and Modern Science,* 1951, Moody Press

Morton, Jean Sloat, *Science in the Bible,* 1978, Moody Press

Mundell, George A., *The Pathway of Faith,* Darby, PA

Negenman, Jan H., *New Atlas of the Bible,* 1969, Doubleday & Co., Garden City, NJ

Negev, Abraham, *Archaeology in the Land of the Bible,* 1976, Tel-Aviv, Israel

Newell, Phillip, *The Six Days of Creation,* Moody Press

Owen, G. Frederick, *Jerusalem, 1972,* Baker Book House, Grand Rapids, MI

. . . . . , *Archaeology and the Bible,* 1969, Revell, Westwood, NJ

Papini, Giovanni, *Life of Christ,* 1923, Harcourt, Brace & Co., New York, NY

Parker, Percy G., *Christian Worker's Bible,* Hulbert, Pub. Co., Glasgow, Scotland

Pax, W. E., *In the Footsteps of Jesus,* 1970, C. P. Putnam's Sons, New York, NY

Pettingill, William, *The Gospel of the Kingdom (Matthew)*

Pheiffer, Charles F., *Ancient Israel,* 1965, Baker Book House, Grand Rapids, MI

. . . . . , *Egypt and the Exodus,* 1964, Baker Book House

. . . . . , *Tell el-Amarna Tablets,* 193, Baker Book House

. . . . . , *The Biblical World,* 1966, Baker Book House

. . . . . , *The Dead Sea Scrolls,* 1969, Crown Publishers, New York, NY

. . . . . , and Harrison, Everett F., *The Wycliffe Bible Commentary,* 1962, Moody Press

. . . . . , and Voss, Howard F., *The Wycliffe Historical Geography of Bible Lands,* 1967, Moody Press

. . . . . , *Old Testament History,* 1973, Baker Book House, Grand Rapids, MI

Phillips, John, *Exploring the Scriptures,* 1965, Moody Press, Chicago, IL

Pierson, Arthur T., *Knowing the Scriptures,* 1910, Gospel Publishing House

Pieters, Albertus, *Can We Trust Bible History,* 1954, Wm. B. Eerdmans

. . . . . , *Divine Lord and Saviour,* 1949, Revell

Pillai, K., *Light Through an Eastern Window,* 1959, Madras, India

Pink, Arthur, *Comfort for Christians,* Bible Truth Depot, Swengle, PA

Preacher's Homiletic Commentary, Funk & Wagnalls Co., New York NY

Price, Sellers, and Carlson, *The Monuments and the Old Testament,* 1958, The Judson Press, Philadelphia, PA

Pritchard, James B., *Gibeon, Where the Sun Stood Still,* 1962, Princeton University Press, Princeton, NJ

. . . . . , *The Ancient Near East in Pictures,* 1954, Princeton

Rehwinkle, Alfred M., *The Flood,* 1951, Concordia Pub. House, St. Louis, MO

Rice, Edwin W., *Orientalisms in Bible Lands,* 1910, American Sunday School Union, Philadelphia, PA

Rimmer, Harry, *Crying Stones,* 1941, Wm. B. Eerdmans, Grand Rapids, MI

....., *Dead Men Tell Tales,* 1939, Eerdmans

....., *Lot's Wife and the Science of Physics,* 1947, Eerdmans

....., *Modern Science and the Genesis Record,* 1937, Eerdmans

....., *Palestine—The Coming Storm Center,* 1940, Eerdmans

....., *The Coming War and the Rise of Russia,* 1940, Eerdmans

....., *The Harmony of Science and Scripture,* 1936, Eerdmans

....., *The Shadow of Coming Events,* Eerdmans

....., *The Theory of Evolution and the Facts of Science,* 1935, Eerdmans

....., *The Voice of Israel,* Eerdmans

....., *Voices from the Silent Centuries,* 1935, Eerdmans

Rosenthal, Marvin, *The Lord's Table in Light of the Passover,* 1976, Friends of Israel, W. Collingswood, NJ

Ross, J. J., *Thinging Through the New Testament,* 1921, Revell

Rugh, W. W., *The Tabernacle,* Bible Institute of Pennsylvania, Philadelphia, PA

Ryrie, Charles C., *The Ryrie Study Bible,* 1977, Moody Press, Chicago, IL

Sanford, Don, *Striking Sermon Starters,* 1957, Zondervan, Grand Rapids, MI

Sauer, Erich, *The Dawn of World Redemption,* 1951, Eerdmans, Grand Rapids, MI

....., *The Triumph of the Crucified,* 1951, Eerdmans

Sayer, Jesse, *Alphabetical Studies of Holy Scriptures,* 1930, London, England

Sayles, Harold F., *500 Bible Studies,* 1904, Evangelical Publishers, Chicago, IL

Schilder, Klass, *Christ on Trial,* 1939, Baker Book House, Grand Rapids, MI

Schultz, Samuel J., *The Old Testament Speaks,* 1960, Harper & Row, New York, NY

Schwantes, Seigfreid J., *The Ancient Near East,* 1965, Baker Book House

Scott, Walter, *Handbook to the Bible,* G. Morrish, London, England

Scroggie, W. Graham, *School for Bible Study,* Edinburgh, Scotland

Sellier, Chas. E., Jr., and Dave Balsinger, *In Search for Noah's Ark,* 1976, Sun Classic Books, Los Angeles, CA

Shanks, Hershel, *The City of David,* 1975, BAR Society, Washington, DC

Smith, James, *Daily Bible Readings,* 1894, American Baptist Pub., Philadelphia, PA

Smith, Wilbur M., *The Biblical Doctrine of Heaven,* 1968, Moody Press, Chicago, IL

Soltau, George, *Four Portraits of the Lord Jesus Christ,* C. C. Cook, New York, NY

Spurgeon, Charles Haddon, *Spurgeon's Sermon Notes,* 1884, Revell

....., *The Treasury of the Old Testament,* 1951, Zondervan, Grand Rapids, MI

Stalker, James M., *The Trial and Death of Jesus Christ,* 1894, Zondervan

Stein, Robert H., "Wine Drinking in New Testament Times," June 20, 1975, *Christianity Today,* Washington, DC

Stone, Nathan J., *Names of God,* 1944, Moody Press, Chicago, IL

Tenney, Merril C., *Pictorial Bible Dictionary,* 1968, Zondervan, Grand Rapids, MI

....., *New Testament Survey,* 1971, Wm. B. Eerdmans, Grand Rapids, MI

Thiele, Edwin R., *The Mysterious Numbers of the Hebrew Kings,* 1951, University of Chicago Press, Chicago, IL

Thompson, Frank C., *Chain Reference Bible,* 1934, B. B. Kirkbride Bible Co., Indianapolis, IN

Thompson, J. A., *Archaeology and the Old Testament,* 1959, Eerdmans, Grand Rapids, MI

Topical Text Book, The New, 1935, Revell

Unger, Merrill F., *Famous Archaeological Discoveries,* 1960, Zondervan

....., *The Dead Sea Scrolls,* 1957, Zondervan

....., *Unger's Bible Handbook,* 1966, Moody Press

Vilnay, Zev, *Israel Guide,* 1970, Hamakor Press, Jerusalem, Israel

Vollmer, Philip, *The Writings of the New Testament,* 1924, Revell

Vos, Howard F., *Genesis and Archaeology,* 1963, Moody Press

Weddell, John W., *Your Study Bible,* 1922, Sunday School Times, Philadelphia, PA

Weidner, R. Franklin, *Studies in the Book,* 1890, Revell

Wilson, Clifford A., *Rocks, Relics and Biblical Reliability,* 1977, Zondervan

. . . . ., *Secrets of a Forgotten City (Ebla),* Master Books, San Diego, CA

. . . . ., *Exploring Bible Backgrounds,* 1966, Word of Truth, Victoria, Australia

. . . . ., *Exploring the Old Testament,* 1970, Word of Truth

. . . . ., *In the Beginning God . . . ,* 1970, Word of Truth

. . . . ., *New Light on the Gospels,* 1970, Lakeland, London, England

. . . . ., *New Light on New Testament Letters,* Lakeland

. . . . ., *That Incredible Book . . . the Bible,* 1973, Word of Truth

Wirt, Sherwood Eliot, *Open Your Bible,* 1962, Revell

Wiseman, Peter, *A Survey of the Bible,* 1944, Bible Meditation League, Columbus, OH

Wiseman, P. J., *New Discoveries in Babylon about Genesis,* 1949, Van Kampen Press, Wheaton, IL

Wight, Fred H., *Highlights of Archaeology in Bible Lands,* 1955, Moody Press

Wythe, Wm. W., *Pulpit Germs,* 1950, The Judson Press, Valley Forge, PA

Index

Index of Archaeology

Index of Biblical Customs

Index of Illustrations

Index of Biblical Prophecies

Scientifically Speaking

Seed Thoughts

General Index